MW00666897

# About Pearson

*Pearson is the world's learning company, with presence across 70 countries worldwide. Our unique insights and world-class expertise comes from a long history of working closely with renowned teachers, authors and thought leaders, as a result of which, we have emerged as the preferred choice for millions of teachers and learners across the world.*

*We believe learning opens up opportunities, creates fulfilling careers and hence better lives. We hence collaborate with the best of minds to deliver you class-leading products, spread across the Higher Education and K12 spectrum.*

*Superior learning experience and improved outcomes are at the heart of everything we do. This product is the result of one such effort.*

*Your feedback plays a critical role in the evolution of our products and you can contact us – reachus@pearson.com. We look forward to it.*

# Abnormal Psychology

## In a Changing World

**TENTH EDITION**

**Jeffrey S. Nevid**
*St. John's University*

**Spencer A. Rathus**
*The College of New Jersey*

**Beverly Greene**
*St. John's University*

Pearson

Original edition, entitled *Abnormal Psychology in a Changing World,* 10th Edition, by Nevid, Jeffrey S.; Rathus, Spencer A. and Greene, Beverly Published by Pearson Education, Limited. Copyright © 2018 by Pearson Education, Inc.

Indian Subcontinent Reprint
**Copyright © 2019 Pearson India Education Services Pvt. Ltd**

All rights reserved. This book is sold subject to the condition that it shall not, by way of trade or otherwise, be lent, resold, hired out, or otherwise circulated without the publisher's prior written consent in any form of binding or cover other than that in which it is published and without a similar condition including this condition being imposed on the subsequent purchaser and without limiting the rights under copyright reserved above, no part of this publication may be reproduced, stored in or introduced into a retrieval system, or transmitted in any form or by any means (electronic, mechanical, photocopying, recording or otherwise), without the prior written permission of both the copyright owner and the publisher of this book.
ISBN 978-93-530-6311-5

**First Impression**
***This edition is manufactured in India and is authorized for sale only in India, Bangladesh, Bhutan, Pakistan, Nepal, Sri Lanka and the Maldives. Circulation of this edition outside of these territories is UNAUTHORIZED.***
Published by Pearson India Education Services Pvt. Ltd, CIN: U72200TN2005PTC057128.

Head Office: 15th Floor, Tower-B, World Trade Tower, Plot No. 1, Block-C, Sector 16,
Noida 201 301, Uttar Pradesh, India.
Registered Office: 4th Floor, Software Block, Elnet Software City, TS 140, Block 2 & 9,
Rajiv Gandhi Salai, Taramani, Chennai 600 113, Tamil Nadu, India.
Fax: 080-30461003, Phone: 080-30461060
Website: in.pearson.com; Email: companysecretary.india@pearson.com

*Printed in India at Sai Printo Pack*

# Brief Contents

# Contents

# Preface

Welcome to the tenth edition of *Abnormal Psychology in a Changing World*. In preparing this new edition, we have endeavored to cull the most recent scientific developments that inform and broaden our understanding of abnormal behavior. Our aim in writing this text is to present scientific advances in ways that both stimulate student interest and make complex material accessible and understandable.

We approach the teaching of abnormal psychology with five fundamental goals in mind:

1. To help students distinguish abnormal from normal behavior and acquire a better understanding of abnormal behavior
2. To increase student awareness of and sensitivity to the struggles of people suffering from the challenges we discuss
3. To help students understand the conceptual bases of abnormal behavior patterns
4. To help students understand how our knowledge of abnormal behavior is informed by research developments in the field
5. To help students understand how psychological disorders are classified and treated

**NEW FEATURE: *ABNORMAL PSYCHOLOGY IN THE DIGITAL AGE*** When we began teaching, a *tablet* was something you took if you had a headache, a *text* was a book a professor assigned for class, and a *web* was something that a spider spun. Today, these words have taken on additional meanings, reflecting the many ways in which contemporary life has changed as the result of modern technology. Students today are digital natives who have never known a time without cell phones, laptops, and the Internet. Texting has become the preferred method of communication for many people today, especially college-age students.

Changes in personal technology are among the most important challenges of adjusting to a changing world. In this text, we consider the impact of changing technology on the study of abnormal psychology by examining how advances in electronic communication are applied in assessment and treatment of psychological disorders. We also examine the psychological effects of Internet use and social media on behavior, including concerns about the problem of Internet addiction.

Here are few examples of topics from a new feature called ***Abnormal Psychology in the Digital Age*** that is intended to highlight ways in which personal technology is changing our study of abnormal psychology:

- Smartphones and Social Media as Research Tools
- Tracking Symptoms by Smartphone
- Virtual Therapy: The Next Best Thing to Being There
- Does Facebook Make You Sadder? The Unintended Consequences of Social Comparison
- Internet Addiction
- How Do I Shape Up? Risks of Social Media Comparisons on Body Image
- "Cybersex Addiction"—A New Psychological Disorder?
- Are You a Facebook Extravert? Or a Twitter Narcissist?
- Helping Autistic Children Communicate: We've Got an App for That

## Maintaining Our Focus

*Abnormal Psychology in a Changing World* is a complete learning and teaching package that brings into focus the following major objectives: (1) putting a human face on the study of abnormal psychology; (2) adopting an interactionist or biopsychosocial model of abnormal behavior; (3) exploring the many contributions from neuroscience research to the study of abnormal psychology; (4) maintaining currency with a changing field; (5) examining key issues in a changing world that inform our understanding of abnormal psychology; and (6) adopting a student-centric approach to pedagogy that focuses on helping students succeed in the course.

**FOCUS ON THE HUMAN SIDE OF ABNORMAL PSYCHOLOGY: THE "I" FEATURE** A hallmark of our approach is helping students understand the basic human dimension that underlies the study of abnormal psychology. We study psychological disorders, but we never lose sight of the fact that we're talking about the lives of people affected by these types of problems. We also understand that an undergraduate textbook in abnormal psychology is not a training manual or compendium of psychological disorders, symptoms, and treatments. It is a teaching device to introduce students to the study of abnormal behavior and help them understand the challenges and struggles faced by people with psychological disorders.

We invite students to enter the world of people suffering from many different types of disorders by including many illustrative case examples and video case interviews of real people and by adopting a distinctive pedagogical feature that takes this approach an important step further—the **"I"** feature.

The **"I"** feature brings students directly into the world of people affected by psychological disorders. Here, students will read brief, first-person narratives from people with psychological disorders as they tell their own stories in their own words. Incorporating first-person narratives helps break down barriers between "us" and "them" and encourages students to recognize that mental health problems are a concern to us all. Students will encounter these poignant personal stories at the beginning of every chapter and throughout the text. A sampling of **"I"** features includes the following:

- "Jerry Has a Panic Attack on the Interstate" (Panic Disorder)
- "Jessica's Little Secret" (Bulimia Nervosa)
- "Walking on Eggshells" (Borderline Personality Disorder)
- "I Hear Something You Can't Hear" (Schizophrenia)

**FOCUS ON AN INTERACTIONIST APPROACH** We approach our writing with the belief that a better understanding of abnormal psychology is gained by adopting a biopsychosocial orientation that takes into account the roles of psychological, biological, and sociocultural factors and their interactions in the development of abnormal behavior patterns. We emphasize the value of taking an interactionist approach as a running theme throughout the text. We feature a prominent interactionist model, the diathesis–stress model, to help students better understand the factors contributing to different forms of abnormal behavior.

**FOCUS ON NEUROSCIENCE** We incorporate important advances in neuroscience that inform our understanding of abnormal behavior patterns, building upon the solid foundations of previous editions. Students will read about the search for endophenotypes in schizophrenia, the latest developments in the important emerging field of epigenetics, how brain scans may be used to diagnose psychological disorders and to probe the workings of the meditative brain, the potential use of drugs to enhance the effectiveness of exposure therapy for PTSD, and emerging brain research that focuses on whether disturbing memories linked to PTSD might be erased.

**FOCUS ON KEEPING PACE WITH AN EVER-CHANGING FIELD** The text integrates the latest research findings and scientific developments in the field. In all, we include more than 1,000 references to research developments in the field in just the past few years. We also present these research findings in a way that makes complex material engaging and accessible for students.

**FOCUS ON KEY ISSUES IN OUR CHANGING WORLD** The ***A CLOSER Look*** boxed features provide opportunities for further exploration of selected topics that reflect cutting-edge issues in the field and challenges we face in contemporary society. A number of the ***A CLOSER Look*** features also focus on advances in neuroscience research.

**FOCUS ON STUDENT-CENTRIC PEDAGOGY** We continually examine our pedagogical approach to find even better ways of helping students succeed in this course. To foster deeper understanding, we include many pedagogical aids, including ***TRUTH or FICTION*** chapter openers to capture student attention and interest, ***self-scoring questionnaires*** to encourage active learning through self-examination, ***capsulized summaries*** of disorders that students can use as study charts, and ***chapter summaries*** organized around key learning objectives.

***"TRUTH or FICTION" Chapter Openers*** Each chapter begins with a set of ***TRUTH or FICTION*** questions to whet the student's appetite for the subject matter within the chapter. Some items challenge preconceived ideas and common folklore and debunk myths and misconceptions, whereas others highlight new research developments in the field. Instructors and students have repeatedly reported to us that they find this feature stimulating and challenging.

The ***TRUTH or FICTION*** questions are revisited and answered in the sections of the chapter in which the topics are discussed. Students are thus given feedback concerning the accuracy of their preconceptions in light of the material being addressed.

***Self-Scoring Questionnaires*** These questionnaires on various topics involve students in the discussion at hand and encourage them to evaluate their own attitudes and behavior patterns. In some cases, students may become more aware of troubling concerns, such as states of depression or problems with drug or alcohol use, which they may want to bring to the attention of a helping professional. We have carefully developed and screened the questionnaires to ensure that they provide students with useful information to reflect upon as well as serving as a springboard for class discussion.

***Overview Charts*** These "see-at-a-glance" overview charts provide capsulized summaries of various disorders. We are gratified by the many comments from students and professors regarding the value of these study charts.

***"Summing Up" Chapter Summaries*** Our ***Summing Up*** chapter summaries provide brief answers to the learning objectives posed at the beginning of the chapter. The ***Summing Up*** sections provide students with feedback they can use to compare their answers with those provided in the text.

## The Fully Integrated Textbook

We seek to provide students with a cohesive understanding of abnormal psychology by integrating a number of key features throughout the text.

**INTEGRATING THE *DSM-5*** We integrate the *DSM-5* throughout the text by applying *DSM-5* criteria in both the body of the text and the many accompanying overview charts. We also cover a wide range of newly diagnosed disorders in the *DSM-5*, including hoarding disorder, premenstrual dysphoric disorder, disruptive mood dysregulation disorder, major and mild neurocognitive disorders, somatic symptom disorder, illness anxiety disorder, pyromania, REM sleep behavior disorder, and social (pragmatic) communication disorder.

Although we recognize the importance of the *DSM* system in the classification of psychological or mental disorders, we believe a course in abnormal psychology should not taught as a training course in the *DSM* or as a psychodiagnostic seminar. We also bring to the student's attention the many limitations of the *DSM* system.

**INTEGRATING DIVERSITY** We examine abnormal behavior patterns in relation to factors of diversity such as ethnicity, culture, gender, sexual orientation, and socioeconomic status. We believe students need to understand how issues of diversity affect the conceptualization of abnormal behavior as well as the diagnosis and treatment of psychological disorders. We also believe that coverage of diversity should be fully integrated directly in the text, not separated off in boxed features.

**INTEGRATING THEORETICAL PERSPECTIVES** Students often think that one theoretical perspective must ultimately be right and all the others wrong. Our approach is to dispel this notion by taking into account the different theoretical viewpoints that inform contemporary understandings of abnormal psychology. We also help students integrate these diverse viewpoints in our ***TYING it together*** features. Importantly, we explore potential causal pathways involving interactions of psychological, sociocultural, and biological factors. We hope to impress upon students the importance of taking a broader view of the complex problems we address by considering the influences of multiple factors and their interactions.

**INTEGRATING CRITICAL THINKING** We encourage students to think more deeply about key concepts in abnormal psychology by including two sets of critical thinking items in each chapter. First, the ***@Issue*** feature highlights current controversies in the field and includes several critical thinking questions that challenge students to think further about the issues discussed in the text. Second, the critical thinking activity at the end of each chapter challenges students to think carefully and critically about concepts discussed in the chapter and to reflect on how these concepts relate to their own experiences or experiences of people they know.

The ***@Issue*** critical thinking boxed feature highlights current controversies in the field and poses critical thinking questions students can answer. Students may begin the course with an expectation that our knowledge of abnormal psychology is complete and incontrovertible. They soon learn that while we have learned much about the underpinnings of psychological disorders, much more remains to be learned. They will also learn that there are many current controversies in the field. By spotlighting these controversies, we encourage students to think critically about these important issues and examine different points of view. Examples of ***@Issue*** boxed feature topics include the following:

- Should Therapists Treat Clients Online?
- What Accounts for the Gender Gap in Depression?
- Should We Use Drugs to Treat Drug Abuse?
- Is Mental Illness a Myth?

To integrate writing across the curriculum (WAC) objectives, instructors may wish to assign critical thinking questions in the ***@Issue*** features as well as additional critical thinking questions at the end of each chapter as required or for extra-credit writing assignments.

**INTEGRATING LEARNING OBJECTIVES WITH BLOOM'S TAXONOMY** We introduce learning objectives at the start of each chapter, organized in terms of the IDEA model of course assessment, which comprises four key learning goals in the study of abnormal psychology that spell out the convenient acronym *IDEA*:

- **Identify** parts of the nervous system, major contributors to the study of abnormal psychology, specific disorders within general diagnostic categories, etc.
- **Define** or **Describe** key terms and concepts
- **Evaluate** or **Explain** underlying mechanisms and processes in abnormal behavior
- **Apply** concepts of abnormal behavior to examples in real life

The IDEA model is integrated with the widely used taxonomy of educational objectives developed by renowned educational researcher Benjamin Bloom. Bloom's taxonomy is arranged in increasing levels of cognitive complexity. The lowest levels comprise basic knowledge and understanding, the middle level involves application of knowledge, and the upper levels involve higher-level skills of analysis, synthesis, and evaluation.

The learning objectives identified in IDEA represent three basic levels in Bloom's taxonomy. The **Identify, Describe**, and **Define** learning objectives represent basic levels of cognitive skills in Bloom's taxonomy (i.e., *knowledge* and *comprehension* in the original taxonomy, or *remembering* and *understanding* in the revised taxonomy). The **Apply** learning objective reflects intermediate level skills involved in application of psychological concepts to life examples. The **Evaluate** and **Explain** learning objectives assess more complex, higher-order skills in the hierarchy involving skills relating to analysis, synthesis, and evaluation of psychological knowledge (or *analyzing* and *evaluating* domains as represented in the revised Bloom taxonomy). By building exams around these learning objectives, instructors can assess not just overall student knowledge, but also student acquisition of higher-level skills in Bloom's taxonomy.

## Acknowledgments

With each new edition, we try to capture a moving target, as the literature base that informs our understanding continues to expand. We are deeply indebted to the thousands of talented scholars and investigators whose work has enriched our understanding of abnormal psychology. Thanks to our colleagues who reviewed our manuscript through earlier editions and continue to help us refine and strengthen our presentation of this material:

Laurie Berkshire, *Erie Community College*
Sally Bing, *University of Maryland Eastern Shore*
Tim Boffeli, *Clarke College*
Staci Born, *Johnson State College*
Christiane Brems, *University of Alaska Anchorage*
Wanda Briggs, *Winthrop University*
Joshua Broman-Fulks, *Appalachian State University*
Barbara L. Brown, *Georgia Perimeter College*
Ann Butzin, *Owens State Community College*
Kristen Campbell, *Mississippi State University*
Gerardo Canul, *University of California at Irvine*
Dennis Cash, *Trident Technical College*
Lorry Cology, *Owens Community College*
Michael Connor, *California State University*
Charles Cummings, *Asheville-Buncombe Technical Community College*
Nancy T. Dassoff, *University of Illinois–Chicago*
David Dooley, *University of California at Irvine*
Fred Ernst, *University of Texas - Pan American*
Kristina Faimon, *Southeast Community College–Lincoln Campus*
Jeannine Feldman, *San Diego State University*
Heinz Fischer, *Long Beach City College*
John H. Forthman, *Vermillin Community College*
Pam Gibson, *James Madison University*
Colleen Gift, *Blackhawk Technical College*
Karla J. Gingerich, *Colorado State University*
Bernard Gorman, *Nassau Community College*
Gary Greenberg, *Connecticut College*
Nora Lynn Gussman, *School Forsyth Technical Community College*
John K. Hall, *University of Pittsburgh*
Mo Hannah, *Siena College*
Marc Henley, *Delaware County Community College*
Jennifer Hicks, *Southeastern Oklahoma State University*
Bob Hill, *Appalachian State University*
Jameson Hirsch, *East Tennessee State University*
Kristine Jacquin, *Mississippi State University*
Patricia Johnson, *Craven Community College*
Ruth Ann Johnson, *Augustana College*
Robert Kapche, *California State University at Los Angeles*
Edward Keane, *Housatonic Community College*
Stuart Keeley, *Bowling Green State University*
Cynthia Diane Kreutzer, *Georgia Perimeter College*

Jennifer Langhinrichsen-Rohling, *University of South Alabama*
Marvin Lee, *Tennessee State University*
John Lloyd, *California State University, Fresno*
Janet Logan, *California State University East Bay*
Don Lucas, *Northwest Vista College*
Tom Marsh, *Pitt Community College*
Sara Martino, *Richard Stockton College of New Jersey*
Shay McCordick, *San Diego State University*
Donna Marie McElroy, *Atlantic Cape Community College*
Lillian McMaster, *Hudson County Community College*
Mindy Mechanic, *California State University, Fullerton*
Linda L. Morrison, *University of New England*
Paulina Multhaupt, *Macomb Community College*
C. Michael Nina, *William Paterson University*
Gary Noll, *University of Illinois at Chicago*
Frank O'Neill, *Montgomery County Community College*
Martin M. Oper, *Erie Community College*
Joseph J. Palladino, *University of Southern Indiana*
Carol Pandey, *L. A. Pierce College*
Ramona Parish, *Guilford Technical Community College*
Jackie Robinson, *Florida A&M University*
Esther D. Rosenblum, *University of Vermont*
Sandra Sego, *American International College*
Harold Siegel, *Nassau Community College*
Nancy Simpson, *Trident Technical College*
Ari Solomon, *Williams College*
Robert Sommer, *University of California–Davis*
Linda Sonna, *University of New Mexico, Taos*
Charles Spirrison, *Mississippi State University*
Stephanie Stein, *Central Washington University*
Joanne Hoven Stohs, *California State University–Fullerton*
Larry Stout, *Nicholls State University*
Tamara Sullivan, *SUNY Brockport*
Deborah Thomas, *Washington State Community College*
David Topor, *Harvard University*
Amber Vesotski, *Alpena Community College*
Theresa Wadkins, *University of Nebraska–Kearny*
Naomi Wagner, *San Jose State University*
Sterling Watson, *Chicago State University*
Thomas Weatherly, *Georgia Perimeter College*
Max Zwanziger, *Central Washington University*

We also wish to recognize the exemplary contributions of the many publishing professionals at Pearson who helped guide the development of this edition, especially Amber Chow, Executive Editor, who helped us fine-tune our approach, as well as the superb production and developmental team, especially Ana Piquinela, Melinda Rankin, and Stephanie Laird. It's been a pleasure working with you all.

We especially wish to thank the two people without whose inspiration and support this effort never would have materialized or been completed, Judith Wolf-Nevid and Lois Fichner-Rathus. We invite students and instructors to contact us at the email addresses below with any comments, suggestions, and feedback. We'd love to hear from you.

**J.S.N.**
*New York, New York jeffnevid@gmail.com*

**S.A.R.**
*New York, New York srathus@aol.com*

**B.A.G.**
*Brooklyn, New York*

# About the Authors

**JEFFREY S. NEVID** is Professor of Psychology at St. John's University in New York, where he directs the Doctoral Program in Clinical Psychology, teaches at the undergraduate and graduate levels, and supervises doctoral students in clinical practicum work. He received his Ph.D. in Clinical Psychology from SUNY Albany and was a staff psychologist at Samaritan Hospital in Troy, New York. He was also a National Institute of Mental Health Post-Doctoral Fellow in Mental Health Evaluation Research at Northwestern University. He holds a Diplomate in Clinical Psychology from the American Board of Professional Psychology, is a Fellow of the American Psychological Association and the Academy of Clinical Psychology, and has served on the editorial boards of several journals and as Associate Editor of the *Journal of Consulting and Clinical Psychology*.

Dr. Nevid has amassed more than 200 research publications and professional presentations. His research publications have appeared in such journals as *Journal of Consulting and Clinical Psychology, Health Psychology, Journal of Occupational Medicine, Behavior Therapy, American Journal of Community Psychology, Professional Psychology: Research and Practice, Journal of Clinical Psychology, Journal of Nervous and Mental Disease, Teaching of Psychology, American Journal of Health Promotion, Clinical Psychology and Psychotherapy*, and *Psychology and Psychotherapy: Theory, Research, and Practice*. Dr. Nevid is also author of the book *Choices: Sex in the Age of STDs* and the introductory psychology text, *Psychology: Concepts and Applications*, as well as several other college texts in the fields of psychology and health that he coauthored with Dr. Spencer Rathus. The 9th edition of *Abnormal Psychology in a Changing World* was honored in 2015 by receiving the Best Coverage of Child Maltreatment in Undergraduate Psychology Textbooks award. The award was bestowed by Division 56 (Trauma) of the American Psychological Association in recognition of the textbook's outstanding coverage of traumatic disorders linked to childhood maltreatment. Dr. Nevid is also actively involved in a program of pedagogical research that focuses on helping students become more effective learners.

**SPENCER A. RATHUS** received his Ph.D. from the University at Albany. He is on the faculty of the College of New Jersey. His areas of interest include psychological assessment, cognitive behavior therapy, and deviant behavior. He is the originator of the Rathus Assertiveness Schedule, which has become a Citation Classic. He has authored several college texts, including *PSYCH, HDEV*, and *Childhood and Adolescence: Voyages in Development*. He also coauthored *Making the Most of College* with Lois Fichner-Rathus; *AIDS: What Every Student Needs to Know* with Susan Boughn; *Behavior Therapy, Psychology and the Challenges of Life, Your Health*, and *HLTH* with Jeffrey S. Nevid; and *Human Sexuality in a Changing World* with Jeffrey S. Nevid and Lois Fichner-Rathus. His professional activities include service on the American Psychological Association Task Force on Diversity Issues at the Precollege and Undergraduate Levels of Education in Psychology, and on the Advisory Panel, American Psychological Association, Board of Educational Affairs (BEA) Task Force on Undergraduate Psychology Major Competencies.

**BEVERLY A. GREENE** is Professor of Psychology at St. John's University and a Fellow of seven divisions of the American Psychological Association and the Academy of Clinical Psychology. She holds a Diploma in Clinical Psychology and serves on the editorial boards of numerous scholarly journals. She received her Ph.D. in Clinical Psychology from Adelphi University and was founding coeditor of the *APA Society for the Study of Lesbian, Gay, and Bisexual Issues* series, *Psychological Perspectives on Lesbian, Gay and Bisexual Issues*. Dr. Greene is also coeditor of *The Psychologists Desk Reference; A Minyan of Women: Family Dynamics, Jewish Identity and Psychotherapy Practice*; and *Psychological Health of Women of Color: Intersections, Challenges and Opportunities*. She has more than 100 professional publications, of which 10 have received national awards for distinguished contributions to the psychological literature.

Dr. Greene was the recipient of the APA 2003 Committee on Women in Psychology Distinguished Leadership Award; the 1996 Outstanding Achievement Award from the APA Committee on Lesbian, Gay, and Bisexual Concerns; the 2004 Distinguished Career Contributions to Ethnic Minority Research Award from the APA Society for the Study of Ethnic Minority Issues; the 2000 Heritage Award from the APA Society for the Psychology of Women; the 2004 Award for Distinguished Senior Career Contributions to Ethnic Minority Research (APA Division 45); and the 2005 Stanley Sue Award for Distinguished Professional Contributions to Diversity in Clinical Psychology (APA Division 12). Her coedited book, *Psychotherapy with African American Women: Innovations in Psychodynamic Perspectives and Practice*, was also honored with the Association for Women in Psychology's 2001 Distinguished Publication Award. In 2006, she was the recipient of the Janet Helms Award for Scholarship and Mentoring from the Teacher's College, Columbia University Cross Cultural Roundtable, and the 2006 Florence Halpern Award for Distinguished Professional Contributions to Clinical Psychology (APA Division 12). In 2009, Dr. Greene was honored as the recipient of the APA Award for Distinguished Senior Career Contribution to Psychology in the Public Interest. She has served as an elected representative to the APA Council and member at large of the Women's and Public Interest Caucuses of the Council. Dr. Greene is also the 2012 recipient of the Association for Women in Psychology's Jewish Women's Caucus award for scholarship and the association's 2012 Espin award for scholarship that makes a significant contribution toward the study of the convergence of ethnicity, religion, and sexual orientation. In 2013, she was honored as a Distinguished Elder at the National Multicultural Conference and Summit, and in 2015 she was the recipient of the Henry Tomes Award for Distinguished Senior Career Contributions to the Advancement of Ethnic Minority Psychology.

Chapter 1

# Introduction and Methods of Research

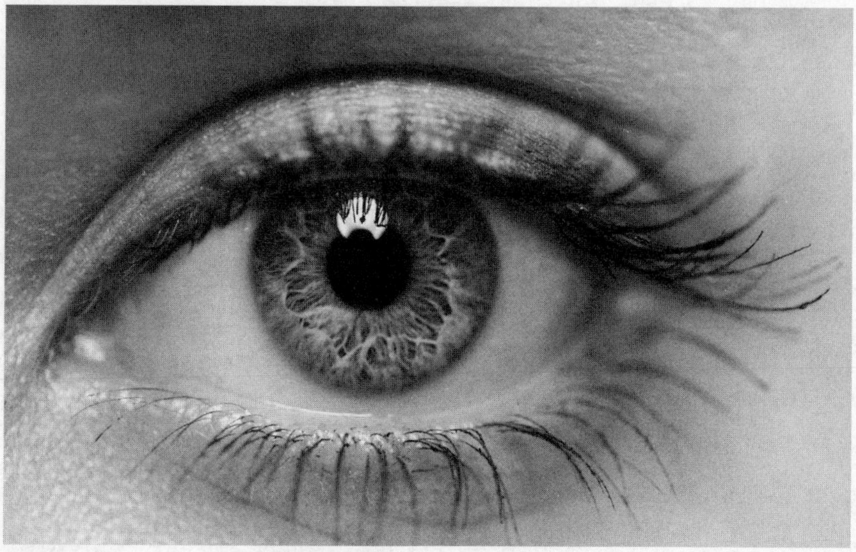

## Learning Objectives

**1.1** **Identify** criteria professionals use to determine whether behavior is abnormal and **apply** these criteria to case examples discussed in the text.

**1.2** **Describe** the current and lifetime prevalence of psychological disorders in the United States and **describe** differences in prevalence as a function of gender and age.

**1.3** **Describe** the cultural bases of abnormal behavior.

**1.4** **Describe** the demonological model of abnormal behavior.

**1.5** **Describe** the origins of the medical model of abnormal behavior.

**1.6** **Describe** the treatment of mental patients during medieval times.

**1.7** **Identify** the leading reformers of the treatment of the mentally ill and **describe** the principle underlying moral therapy and the changes that occurred in the treatment of mental patients during the 19th and early 20th centuries.

**1.8** **Describe** the role of mental hospitals in the mental health system.

**1.9** **Describe** the goals and outcomes of the community mental health movement.

**1.10** **Describe** the medical model of abnormal behavior.

**1.11** **Identify** the major psychological models of abnormal behavior.

**1.12** **Describe** the sociocultural perspective on abnormal behavior.

**1.13** **Describe** the biopsychosocial perspective on abnormal behavior.

**1.14** **Identify** four major objectives of science.

**1.15** **Identify** the four major steps in the scientific method.

**1.16** **Identify** the ethical principles that guide research in psychology.

**1.17** **Explain** the role of the naturalistic method of research and **describe** its key features.

**1.18** **Explain** the role of the correlational method of research and **describe** its key features.

**1.19** **Explain** the role of the experimental method of research and **describe** its key features.

**1.20** **Explain** the role of the epidemiological method of research and **describe** its key features.

**1.21** **Explain** the role of the kinship studies and **describe** their key features.

**1.22** **Explain** the role of the case study and **describe** its limitations.

## TRUTH *or* FICTION

**T☐ F☑** Unusual behavior is abnormal. (p. 5)

**T☐ F☑** About one in 10 American adults suffers from a diagnosable mental or psychological disorder in any given year. (p. 8)

**T☐ F☑** Although effective treatments exist for some psychological disorders, we still lack a means of effectively treating most types of psychological disorders. (p. 9)

**T☑ F☐** Psychological problems like depression may be experienced differently by people in different cultures. (p. 10)

**T☑ F☐** A night's entertainment in London a few hundred years ago might have included gaping at the inmates at the local asylum. (p. 13)

**T☐ F☑** Despite changing attitudes in society toward homosexuality, the psychiatric profession continues to classify homosexuality as a mental disorder. (p. 20)

**T☑ F☐** In a recent experiment, pain patients reported some relief from pain after taking a placebo pill, even though they were told the pill was merely a placebo. (p. 27)

**T☐ F☑** Recent evidence shows there are literally millions of genes in the nucleus of every cell in the body. (p. 30)

**T☑ F☐** Case studies have been conducted on dead people. (p. 31)

## CHAPTER INTRODUCTION: INTRODUCTION AND METHODS OF RESEARCH

### "I" "Pretty Grisly Stuff"

I never thought I'd ever see a psychologist or someone like that, you know. I'm a police photographer and I've shot some pretty grisly stuff, corpses and all. Crime scenes are not like what you see on TV. They're more grisly. I guess you kind of get used to it. It never bothered me, just maybe at first. Before I did this job, I worked on a TV news chopper. We would take shots of fires and rescues, you know. Now I get uptight sitting in the back seat of a car or riding an elevator. I'll avoid taking an elevator unless I really have no other choice. Forget flying anymore. It's not just helicopters. I just won't go in a plane, any kind of plane.

I guess I was younger then and more daring when I was younger. Sometimes, I would hang out of the helicopter to shoot pictures with no fear at all. Now, just thinking about flying makes my heart race. It's not that I'm afraid the plane will crash. That's the funny thing. Not ha-ha funny, but peculiar, you know. I just start trembling when I think of them closing that door, trapping us inside. I can't tell you why.

*From the Author's Files*

*Phil, 42, a police photographer*

### "I" "Cowering Under the Covers"

A 45-year-old woman with bipolar disorder describes what it feels like when she goes into a high: "I no longer feel like an ordinary housewife. Instead I feel organized and accomplished and I begin to feel I am my most creative self. I can write poetry easily. I can compose melodies without effort. I can paint. My mind feels facile and absorbs everything…I see myself as being able to accomplish a great deal for the good of people. I have countless ideas about how the environment problem could inspire a crusade for the health and betterment of everyone…I feel pleasure, a sense of euphoria or elation. I want it to last forever. I don't seem to need much sleep. I've lost weight and feel healthy and I like myself. I've just bought six new dresses, in fact, and they look quite good on me. I feel sexy and men stare at me. Maybe I'll have an affair, or perhaps several."

Feeling exhilarated and in high spirits, she experiences what she describes as *the full joy of living*. But then: "When I go beyond this stage, I become manic [and]…begin to see things in my mind that aren't real." She describes how one night she created an entire movie in her mind that seemed so real it was as though she was watching the movie unfold before her eyes. She was filled with a sense of sheer terror, "as if it were actually happening, when I knew that an assassination scene was about to take place. I cowered under the covers and became a complete shaking wreck…My screams awakened my husband, who tried to reassure me that we were in our bedroom and everything was the same. There was nothing to be afraid of. Nevertheless, I was admitted to the hospital the next day."

**SOURCE:** *Fieve, 1975, pp. 27–28*

"I" **Thomas Hears Voices**

I've been diagnosed as having paranoid schizophrenia. I also suffer from clinical depression. Before I found the correct medications, I was sleeping on the floor, afraid to sleep in my own bed. I was hearing voices that, lately, had turned from being sometimes helpful to being terrorizing. The depression had been responsible for my being irritable and full of dread, especially in the mornings, becoming angry over frustrations at work, and seemingly internalizing other people's problems.

The voices, human sounding, and sounding from a short distance outside my apartment, were slowly turning nearly all bad. I could hear them jeering me, plotting against me, singing songs sometimes that would only make sense later in the day when I would do something wrong at work or at home. I began sleeping on the floor of my living room because I was afraid a presence in the bedroom was torturing good forces around me. If I slept in the bedroom, the nightly torture would cause me to make mistakes during the day. A voice, calling himself Fatty Acid, stopped me from drinking soda. Another voice allowed me only one piece of bread with my meals.

**SOURCE:** *Campbell, 2000, reprinted with permission of the National Institute of Mental Health*

*Thomas, a young man diagnosed with schizophrenia and major depression*

These three people—like many you will meet in this text—struggle with problems that mental health professionals classify as psychological or mental disorders. A **psychological disorder** is a pattern of abnormal behavior associated with states of significant emotional distress, such as anxiety or depression, or with impaired behavior or ability to function, such as difficulty holding a job or distinguishing reality from fantasy. **Abnormal psychology** is the branch of psychology that studies abnormal behavior and ways of helping people who are affected by psychological disorders.

The study of abnormal psychology is illuminated not only by extensive research on the causes and treatments of psychological disorders reported in scientific journals but also by the personal stories of people affected by these problems. In this text, we will learn from these people as they tell their stories in their own words. Through first-person narratives, case examples, and video interviews, researchers enter the world of people struggling with various types of psychological disorders that affect their moods, thinking, and behavior. Some of these stories may remind you of the experiences of people close to you, or perhaps even yourself. We invite you to explore with us the nature and origins of these disorders and ways of helping people who face the many challenges they pose.

Let's pause for a moment to raise an important distinction. Although the terms *psychological disorder* and *mental disorder* are often used interchangeably, we prefer using the term *psychological disorder*, primarily because it puts the study of abnormal behavior squarely within the purview of the field of psychology. Moreover, the term *mental disorder* (also called *mental illness*) is derived from the **medical model** perspective, which views abnormal behaviors as symptoms of an underlying illness or brain disorder (Insel & Cuthbert, 2015). Although the medical model is a major contemporary model for understanding abnormal behavior, we believe we need to take a broader view of abnormal behavior by incorporating psychological and sociocultural perspectives as well.

In this chapter, we first address the difficulties of defining *abnormal behavior*. We see that throughout history, abnormal behavior has been viewed from different perspectives. We chronicle the development of concepts of abnormal behavior and its treatment. We see that in the past, treatment usually referred to what was done *to* rather than *for* people with abnormal behavior. We then describe the ways in which psychologists and other scholars study abnormal behavior today.

# How Do We Define Abnormal Behavior?

We all become anxious or depressed from time to time, but is this abnormal? Anxiety in anticipation of an important job interview or a final examination is perfectly normal. It is appropriate to feel depressed when you have lost someone close to you or when you have failed at a test or on the job. Where is the line between normal and abnormal behavior?

One answer is that emotional states such as anxiety and depression may be considered abnormal when they are not appropriate to the situation. It is normal to feel down when you fail a test, but not when your grades are good or excellent. It is normal to feel anxious before a college admissions interview, but not normal to panic before entering a department store or boarding a crowded elevator.

Abnormality may also be suggested by the magnitude of the problem. Although some anxiety is normal enough before a job interview, feeling that your heart might leap from your chest—and consequently canceling your interview—is not, nor is it normal to feel so anxious in this situation that your clothing becomes soaked with perspiration. **T / F**

## TRUTH *or* FICTION

Unusual behavior is abnormal.

☑ **FALSE** Unusual or statistically deviant behavior is not necessarily abnormal. Exceptional behavior also deviates from the norm.

# Criteria for Determining Abnormality

**1.1 Identify criteria professionals use to determine whether behavior is abnormal and apply these criteria to case examples discussed in the text.**

Mental health professionals apply various criteria when making judgments about whether behavior is abnormal. The most commonly used criteria include the following:

1. *Unusualness.* Behavior that is unusual is often considered abnormal. Only a few of us report seeing or hearing things that are not really there; "seeing things" and "hearing things" are almost always considered abnormal in our culture, but such experiences are sometimes considered normal in certain types of spiritual experiences. Moreover, hearing voices and other forms of hallucinations under some circumstances are not considered unusual in some preliterate societies.

   However, becoming overcome with feelings of panic when entering a department store or when standing in a crowded elevator is uncommon and considered abnormal. Uncommon behavior is not in itself abnormal. Only one person can hold the record for swimming the fastest 100 meters. The record-holding athlete differs from the rest of us but, again, is not considered abnormal. Thus, rarity or statistical deviance is not a sufficient basis for labeling behavior abnormal; nevertheless, it is often one of the yardsticks used to judge abnormality.

2. *Social deviance.* All societies have norms (standards) that define the kinds of behavior that are acceptable in given contexts. Behavior deemed normal in one culture may be viewed as abnormal in another. For example, people in our culture who assume that all male strangers are devious are usually regarded as unduly suspicious or distrustful—but such suspicions were justified among the Mundugumor, a tribe of cannibals studied by anthropologist Margaret Mead (1935). Within that culture, male strangers *were* typically malevolent toward others, and it was normal to feel distrustful of them. Norms, which arise from the practices and beliefs of specific cultures, are relative standards, not universal truths.

   Thus, clinicians need to weigh cultural differences when determining what is normal and abnormal. Moreover, what strikes one generation as abnormal may be considered normal by the next. For example, until the mid-1970s, homosexuality was classified as a mental disorder by the psychiatric profession (see *Thinking Critically: What Is Abnormal Behavior?* on page 20). Today, however, the psychiatric profession no longer considers homosexuality a mental disorder, and many people argue that contemporary societal norms should include homosexuality as a normal variation in behavior.

   When normality is judged on the basis of compliance with social norms, nonconformists may incorrectly be labeled as mentally disturbed. We may come to brand

**WHEN IS ANXIETY ABNORMAL?**
Negative emotions such as anxiety are considered abnormal when they are judged to be excessive or inappropriate to the situation. Anxiety is generally regarded as normal when it is experienced during a job interview, so long as it is not so severe that it prevents the interviewee from performing adequately. Anxiety is deemed to be abnormal if it is experienced whenever one boards an elevator.

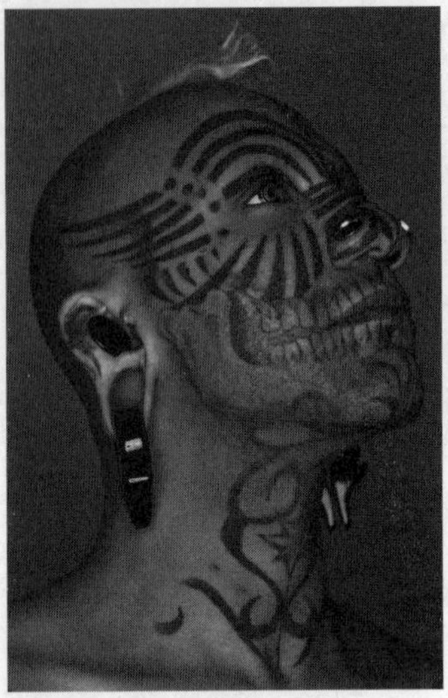

**IS THIS MAN ABNORMAL?**
Judgments of abnormality take into account the social and cultural standards of society. Do you believe this man's body adornment is a sign of abnormality or merely a fashion statement?

behavior that we do not approve of as "sick" rather than accept that the behavior may be normal, even though it offends or puzzles us.

3. *Faulty perceptions or interpretations of reality.* Normally, our sensory systems and cognitive processes permit us to form accurate mental representations of the environment. Seeing things and hearing voices that are not present are considered hallucinations, which in our culture are generally taken as signs of an underlying mental disorder. Similarly, holding unfounded ideas or *delusions*—such as believing that the CIA or the Mafia is out to get you—may be regarded as a sign of mental disturbance—unless, of course, they *are real.* (As former U.S. Secretary of State Henry Kissinger is said to have remarked, "Even paranoid people have enemies.")

   It is normal in the United States to say that one talks to God through prayer. If, however, a person insists on having literally seen God or heard the voice of God—as opposed to, say, being divinely inspired—we may come to regard her or him as mentally disturbed.

4. *Significant personal distress.* States of personal distress caused by troublesome emotions, such as anxiety, fear, or depression, may be abnormal. As we noted earlier, however, anxiety and depression are sometimes appropriate responses to a situation. Real threats and losses do occur in life, and *lack* of an emotional response to them would be regarded as abnormal. Appropriate feelings of distress are not considered abnormal unless the feelings persist long after the source of anguish has been removed (after most people would have adjusted) or if they are so intense that they impair an individual's ability to function.

5. *Maladaptive or self-defeating behavior.* Behavior that leads to unhappiness rather than self-fulfillment can be regarded as abnormal. Behavior that limits one's ability to function in expected roles or to adapt to one's environments may also be considered abnormal. According to these criteria, heavy alcohol consumption that impairs health or social and occupational functioning may be viewed as abnormal. Agoraphobic behavior, characterized by intense fear of venturing into public places, may be considered abnormal; it is both uncommon and maladaptive because it impairs an individual's ability to fulfill work and family responsibilities.

6. *Dangerousness.* Behavior that is dangerous to oneself or other people may be considered abnormal. Here, too, the social context is crucial. In wartime, people who sacrifice their lives or charge the enemy with little apparent concern for their own safety may be characterized as courageous, heroic, and patriotic, but people who threaten or attempt suicide because of the pressures of civilian life are usually considered abnormal.

   Football and hockey players who occasionally get into fistfights or altercations with opposing players may be normal enough. Given the nature of these sports, unaggressive football and hockey players would not last long in college or professional ranks. However, players involved in frequent altercations may be regarded as abnormal. Physically aggressive behavior is most often maladaptive in modern life. Moreover, physical aggression is ineffective as a way of resolving conflicts—although it is by no means uncommon.

Abnormal behavior thus has multiple definitions. Depending on the case, some criteria may be weighted more heavily than others, but in most cases, a combination of these criteria is used to define abnormality.

**THE BIG PICTURE: WHAT DOES IT MEAN TO HAVE A MENTAL DISORDER?**

**APPLYING THE CRITERIA** Let's return to the three cases we introduced at the beginning of the chapter. Consider the criteria we can apply to determine whether the behaviors reported in these vignettes are abnormal. Note that the abnormal behavior patterns in these three cases are unusual in the statistical sense. Most people do not encounter these kinds of problems, although we should add that these problems are far from rare. The problem behaviors also meet other criteria of abnormality, as we shall discuss.

Phil suffered from *claustrophobia*, an excessive fear of enclosed spaces. (This is an example of an anxiety disorder and is discussed more fully in Chapter 5.) His behavior was unusual (relatively few people are so fearful of confinement that they avoid flying in airplanes or riding on elevators) and was associated with significant personal distress. His fear also impaired his ability to carry out his occupational and family responsibilities. However, he was not hampered by faulty perceptions of reality. He recognized that his fears exceeded a realistic appraisal of danger in these situations.

What criterion of abnormality applies in the case of the woman who cowered under the blankets? She was diagnosed with *bipolar disorder* (formerly called manic-depression), a type of mood disorder in which a person experiences extreme mood swings, from the heights of elation and seemingly boundless energy to the depths of depression and despair. (The vignette described the manic phase of the disorder.) Bipolar disorder, which is discussed in Chapter 7, is associated with extreme personal distress and difficulty functioning effectively in normal life. It is also linked to self-defeating and dangerous behavior, such as reckless driving or exorbitant spending during manic phases and attempted suicide during depressive phases. In some cases, like the one presented here, people in manic phases sometimes have faulty perceptions or interpretations of reality, such as hallucinations and delusions.

Thomas suffered from both schizophrenia and depression. It is not unusual for people to have more than one disorder at a time. In the parlance of the psychiatric profession, these clients present with *comorbid* (co-occurring) diagnoses. Comorbidity complicates treatment because clinicians need to design a treatment approach that focuses on treating two or more disorders. Schizophrenia meets a number of criteria of abnormality, including statistical infrequency (it affects about 1% of the general population). The clinical features of schizophrenia include socially deviant or bizarre behavior, disturbed perceptions or interpretations of reality (delusions and hallucinations), maladaptive behavior (difficulty meeting responsibilities of daily life), and personal distress. (See Chapter 11 for more detail on schizophrenia.) Thomas, for example, was plagued by auditory hallucinations (terrorizing voices), which were certainly a source of significant distress. His thinking was also delusional, because he believed that "a presence" in his bedroom was "torturing good forces," surrounding him and causing him to make mistakes during the day. In Thomas's case, schizophrenia was complicated by depression that involved feelings of personal distress (irritability and feelings of dread). Depression is also associated with dampened or downcast mood, maladaptive behavior (difficulty getting to work or school or even getting out of bed in the morning), and potential dangerousness (possible suicidal behavior).

It is one thing to recognize and label behavior as abnormal; it is another to understand and explain it. Philosophers, physicians, natural scientists, and psychologists have used various approaches, or *models*, in the effort to explain abnormal behavior. Some approaches have been based on superstition; others have invoked religious explanations. Some current views are predominantly biological; others are psychological. In considering various historical and contemporary approaches to understanding abnormal behavior, let's first look further at the importance of cultural beliefs in determining which behavior patterns are deemed abnormal.

## Abnormal Psychology—By the Numbers

**1.2 Describe the current and lifetime prevalence of psychological disorders in the United States and describe differences in prevalence as a function of gender and age.**

The problem of abnormal behavior might seem the concern of only a few. After all, relatively few people are ever admitted to a psychiatric hospital. Most people never seek the help of a mental health professional such as a psychologist or psychiatrist. Fewer still ever plead *not*

## TRUTH or FICTION

About one in 10 American adults suffers from a diagnosable mental or psychological disorder in any given year.

☑ **FALSE** It's actually about one in four American adults.

*guilty* to crimes on grounds of insanity. Most of us probably have at least one relative we consider *eccentric*, but how many of us have relatives we consider *crazy*? And yet, the truth is that abnormal behavior affects all of us in one way or another. Let's break down the numbers.

If we limit our discussion to diagnosable mental disorders, nearly one in two of all Americans (46%) are directly affected at some point in their lives (Kessler, Berglund, et al., 2005; see Figure 1.1). About one in four adult Americans (26%) experience a diagnosable psychological disorder in any given year (Kessler, Chiu, et al., 2005). **T / F**

According to the World Health Organization, the United States has the highest rates of diagnosable psychological disorders among 17 countries they surveyed (Kessler et al., 2009). American women are more likely than men to suffer from psychological disorders, especially mood disorders (discussed in Chapter 7; "Women More at Risk," 2012). In addition, twice as many young adults (ages 18–25) are affected by psychological disorders than are people over 50.

If we also include the mental health problems of our family members, friends, and coworkers and take into account those who foot the bill for treatment in the form of taxes and health insurance premiums, as well as lost productivity due to sick days, disability leaves, and impaired job performance inflating product costs, then clearly all of us are affected to one degree or another.

**SURGEON GENERAL'S REPORT ON MENTAL HEALTH** The U.S. Surgeon General issued an important report to the nation at the turn of the new millennium that is still pertinent today. The report focused attention on mental health problems. Here are some of the key conclusions from the report (Satcher, 2000; U.S. Department of Health and Human Services, 1999):

- Mental health reflects the complex interaction of brain functioning and environmental influences.
- Effective treatments exist for most mental disorders, including psychological interventions, such as psychotherapy and counseling and psychopharmacological or

**Figure 1.1** Lifetime and past year prevalences of psychological disorders.

This graph is based on a nationally representative sample of 9,282 English-speaking U.S. residents aged 18 and older. We see percentages of individuals with diagnosable psychological disorders either during the past year or at some point in their lives for several major diagnostic categories. The *mood disorders* category includes major depressive episode and bipolar disorder (discussed in Chapter 7). *Anxiety disorders* include panic disorder, agoraphobia without panic disorder, social phobia, specific phobia, and generalized anxiety disorder (discussed in Chapter 5). *Substance use disorders* involve alcohol or other drugs and are discussed in Chapter 8.

**SOURCE:** Kessler, Chiu, et al., 2005; Kessler, Berglund, et al., 2005.

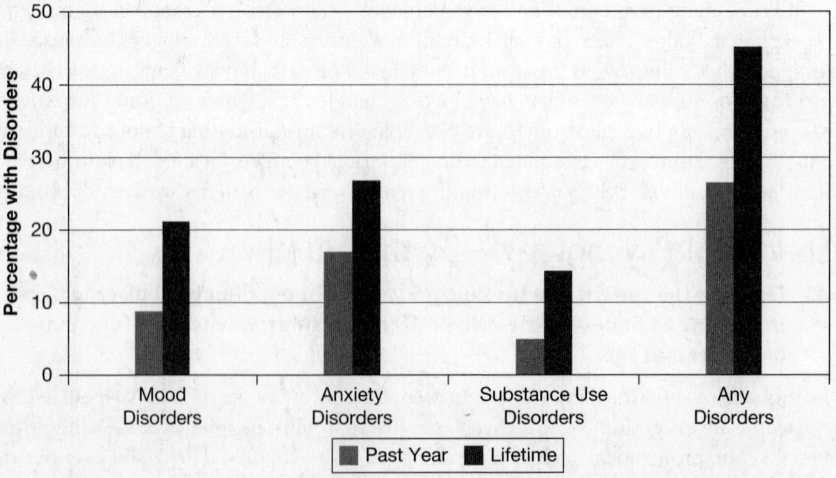

drug therapies. Treatment is often more effective when psychological and psychopharmacological treatments are combined. **T / F**

- Progress in developing effective prevention programs in the mental health field has been slow because we do not know the causes of mental disorders or ways of altering known influences, such as genetic predispositions. Nonetheless, some effective prevention programs have been developed.
- Although 15% of American adults receive some form of help for mental health problems each year, many who need help do not receive it.
- Mental health problems are best understood when we take a broader view and consider the social and cultural contexts in which they occur.
- Mental health services need to be designed and delivered in a manner that takes into account the viewpoints and needs of racial and ethnic minorities.

**TRUTH or FICTION**

Although effective treatments exist for some psychological disorders, we still lack the means of effectively treating most types of psychological disorders.

☑ **FALSE** The good news is that effective treatments exist for most psychological disorders.

The Surgeon General's report provides a backdrop for our study of abnormal psychology. As we shall see throughout the text, we believe that understandings of abnormal behavior are best revealed through a lens that takes into account interactions of biological and environmental factors. We also believe that social and cultural (or *sociocultural*) factors need to be considered in attempts to both understand abnormal behavior and develop effective treatment services.

## Cultural Bases of Abnormal Behavior

**1.3 Describe the cultural bases of abnormal behavior.**

As noted, behavior that is normal in one culture may be deemed abnormal in another. Australian Aborigines believe they can communicate with the spirits of their ancestors and that other people, especially close relatives, share their dreams. These beliefs are considered normal within Aboriginal culture. Were such beliefs to be expressed in our culture, they would likely be deemed delusions, which professionals regard as a common feature of schizophrenia. Thus, the standards we use in making judgments of abnormal behavior must take into account cultural norms.

Kleinman (1987, p. 453) offers an example of "hearing voices" among Native Americans to underscore the ways in which judgments about abnormality are embedded within a cultural context:

> Ten psychiatrists trained in the same assessment technique and diagnostic criteria who are asked to examine 100 American Indians shortly after the latter have experienced the death of a spouse, a parent or a child may determine with close to 100% consistency that those individuals report hearing, in the first month of grieving, the voice of the dead person calling to them as the spirit ascends to the afterworld. [Although such judgments may be consistent across observers,] the determination of whether such reports are a sign of an abnormal mental state is an interpretation based on knowledge of this group's behavioral norms and range of normal experiences of bereavement.

To these Native Americans, bereaved people who report hearing the spirits of the deceased calling to them as they ascend to the afterlife are normal. Behavior that is normative within the cultural setting in which it occurs should not be considered abnormal.

Concepts of health and illness vary across cultures. Traditional Native American cultures distinguish between illnesses that are believed to arise from influences outside the culture, called "White man's sicknesses," such as alcoholism and drug addiction, and those that emanate from a lack of harmony with traditional tribal life and thought, which are called "Indian sicknesses" (Trimble, 1991). Traditional healers, shamans, and medicine men and women are called on to treat Indian sicknesses. When a problem is thought to have its cause outside the community, help is sought from "White man's medicine."

**A TRADITIONAL NATIVE AMERICAN HEALER.** Many traditional Native Americans distinguish between illnesses believed to arise from influences external to their own culture ("White man's sicknesses") and those that emanate from a lack of harmony with traditional tribal life and thought ("Indian sicknesses"). Traditional healers such as the one shown here may be called on to treat Indian sicknesses, whereas "White man's medicine" may be sought to help people deal with problems whose causes are seen as lying outside the community, such as alcoholism and drug addiction.

Abnormal behavior patterns take different forms in different cultures. Westerners experience anxiety, for example, in the form of worrying about paying the mortgage or losing a job. However, "in a number of African cultures, anxiety is expressed as fears of failure in procreation, in dreams and complaints about witchcraft" (Kleinman, 1987), and Australian aborigines can develop intense fears of sorcery, accompanied by the belief that one is in mortal danger from evil spirits (Spencer, 1983). Trancelike states in which young aboriginal women are mute, immobile, and unresponsive are also quite common. If these women do not recover from the trance within hours or, at most, a few days, they may be brought to a sacred site for healing.

The very words that we use to describe psychological disorders—words such as *depression* or *mental health*—have different meanings in other cultures, or no equivalent meaning at all. This doesn't mean that depression doesn't exist in other cultures. Rather, it suggests that we need to learn how people in different cultures experience emotional distress, including states of depression and anxiety, rather than impose our perspectives on their experiences. People in China and other countries in the Far East generally place greater emphasis on the physical or somatic symptoms of depression, such as headaches, fatigue, or weakness, than on feelings of guilt or sadness, compared to people from Western cultures such as our own (Kalibatseva & Leong, 2011; Ryder et al., 2008; Zhou et al., 2011). **T / F**

**TRUTH or FICTION**

Psychological problems like depression may be experienced differently by people in different cultures.

☑ **TRUE** For example, depression is more likely to be associated with the development of physical symptoms among people in East Asian cultures than in Western cultures.

These differences demonstrate how important it is that we determine whether our concepts of abnormal behavior are valid before we apply them to other cultures. Research efforts along these lines have shown that the abnormal behavior pattern associated with our concept of schizophrenia exists in countries as far flung as Colombia, India, China, Denmark, Nigeria, and the former Soviet Union, as well as many others (Jablensky et al., 1992). Furthermore, rates of schizophrenia appear similar among the countries studied. However, differences have been observed in some of the features of schizophrenia across cultures (Myers, 2011).

Views about abnormal behavior vary from society to society. In Western culture, models based on medical disease and psychological factors feature prominently in explaining abnormal behavior. In traditional native cultures, however, models of abnormal behavior often invoke supernatural causes, such as possession by demons or the Devil. For example, in Filipino folk society, psychological problems are often attributed to the influence of "spirits" or the possession of a "weak soul" (Edman & Johnson, 1999).

# Historical Perspectives on Abnormal Behavior

Throughout the history of Western culture, concepts of abnormal behavior have been shaped, to some degree, by the prevailing worldview of a particular era. For hundreds of years, beliefs in supernatural forces, demons, and evil spirits held sway. (As you've just seen, these beliefs still hold true in some societies.) Abnormal behavior was often taken as a sign of possession. In modern times, the predominant—but by no means universal—worldview has shifted toward beliefs in science and reason. In Western culture, abnormal behavior has come to be viewed as the product of physical and psychosocial factors, not demonic possession.

## The Demonological Model

**1.4 Describe the demonological model of abnormal behavior.**

Why would anyone need a hole in the head? Archaeologists have unearthed human skeletons from the Stone Age with egg-sized cavities in the skull. One interpretation of these holes is that our prehistoric ancestors believed abnormal behavior was caused by the inhabitation of evil spirits. These holes might be the result of **trephination**—drilling the skull to provide an outlet for those irascible spirits. Fresh bone growth indicates that some people did survive this "medical procedure."

Just the threat of trephining may have persuaded some people to comply with tribal norms. Because no written accounts of the purpose of trephination exist, other explanations are possible. For instance, perhaps trephination was simply a form of surgery to remove shattered pieces of bone or blood clots that resulted from head injuries (Maher & Maher, 1985).

The notion of supernatural causes of abnormal behavior, or *demonology*, was prominent in Western society until the Age of Enlightenment. The ancients explained nature in terms of the actions of the gods: The Babylonians believed the movements of the stars and the planets expressed the adventures and conflicts of the gods, and the Greeks believed that the gods toyed with humans, that they unleashed havoc on disrespectful or arrogant humans and clouded their minds with madness.

In ancient Greece, people who behaved abnormally were sent to temples dedicated to Aesculapius, the god of healing. The Greeks believed that Aesculapius would visit the afflicted while they slept in the temple and offer them restorative advice through dreams. Rest, a nutritious diet, and exercise were also part of the treatment. Incurables were driven from the temple by stoning.

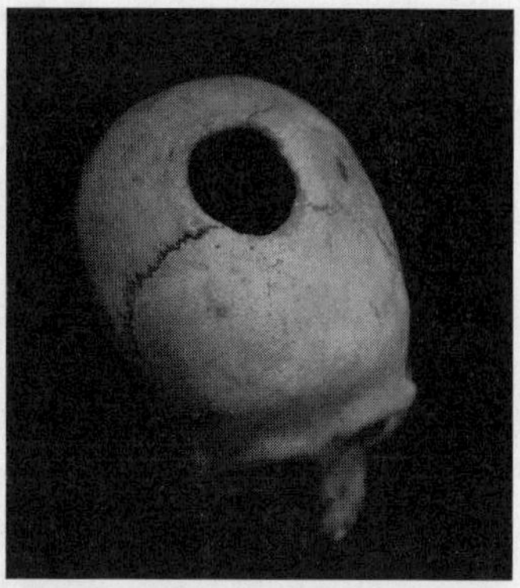

**TREPHINATION.** Trephination refers to a procedure in which a hole is chipped into a person's skull. Some investigators speculate that the practice represented an ancient form of surgery. Perhaps trephination was intended to release the "demons" responsible for abnormal behavior.

**SOURCE:** Photo by Bierwert. American Museum of Natural History Library.

## Origins of the Medical Model: In "Ill Humor"

**1.5 Describe the origins of the medical model of abnormal behavior.**

Not all ancient Greeks believed in the demonological model. The seeds of naturalistic explanations of abnormal behavior were sown by Hippocrates and developed by other physicians in the ancient world, especially Galen.

Hippocrates (ca. 460–377 B.C.E.), the celebrated physician of the Golden Age of Greece, challenged the prevailing beliefs of his time by arguing that illnesses of the body and mind were the result of natural causes, not possession by supernatural spirits. He believed the health of the body and mind depended on the balance of **humors**, or vital fluids, in the body: phlegm, black bile, blood, and yellow bile. An imbalance of humors, he thought, accounted for abnormal behavior. A lethargic or sluggish person was believed to have an excess of phlegm, from which we derive the word *phlegmatic*. An overabundance of black bile was believed to cause depression, or *melancholia*. An excess of blood created a *sanguine* disposition: cheerful, confident, and optimistic. An excess of yellow bile made people *bilious* and *choleric*—quick-tempered.

Though scientists no longer subscribe to Hippocrates's theory of bodily humors, his theory is important because of its break from demonology. It foreshadowed the modern medical model, the view that abnormal behavior results from underlying biological processes. Hippocrates also made other contributions to modern thought and, indeed, to modern medical practice. He classified abnormal behavior patterns into three main categories, which still have equivalents today: *melancholia* to characterize excessive depression, *mania* to refer to exceptional excitement, and *phrenitis* (from the Greek for *inflammation of the brain*) to characterize the bizarre behavior that might today typify schizophrenia. To this day, medical schools honor Hippocrates by having students swear an oath of medical ethics that he originated—the Hippocratic oath.

Galen (ca. 130–200 C.E.), a Greek physician who attended Roman emperor-philosopher Marcus Aurelius, adopted and expanded on the teachings of Hippocrates. Among Galen's contributions was the discovery that arteries carry blood—not air, as had been formerly believed.

## Medieval Times

**1.6 Describe the treatment of mental patients during medieval times.**

The Middle Ages, or medieval times, cover the millennium of European history from about 476 C.E. through 1450 C.E. After the passing of Galen, belief in supernatural causes and especially the doctrine of possession increased in influence and eventually dominated medieval thought. The doctrine of possession held that abnormal behaviors were a sign of

**EXORCISM.** This medieval woodcut illustrates the practice of exorcism, which was used to expel the evil spirits that were believed to have possessed people.

possession by evil spirits or the Devil. This belief was part of the teachings of the Roman Catholic Church, the central institution in Western Europe after the decline of the Roman Empire. Although belief in possession preceded the Church and is found in ancient Egyptian and Greek writings, the Church revitalized it. The Church's treatment of choice for possession was exorcism. Exorcists were employed to persuade evil spirits that the bodies of the "possessed" were no longer habitable. Methods of persuasion included prayer, incantations, waving a cross at the victim, and beating and flogging, even starving, the victim. If the victim continued to display unseemly behavior, there were yet more persuasive remedies, such as the rack, a torture device. No doubt, recipients of these "remedies" desperately wished the Devil would vacate them immediately.

The Renaissance—the great revival of classical learning, art, and literature—began in Italy in the 1400s and spread throughout Europe. Ironically, although the Renaissance is considered the transition from the medieval to the modern world, the fear of witches also reached its height during this period.

**WITCHCRAFT** The late 15th through the late 17th centuries were especially bad times to annoy your neighbors. These were times of massive persecutions, particularly of women, who were accused of witchcraft. Church officials believed that witches made pacts with the Devil, practiced satanic rituals, ate babies, and poisoned crops. In 1484, Pope Innocent VIII decreed that witches be executed. Two Dominican priests compiled a notorious manual for witch-hunting, called the *Malleus Maleficarum* (The Witches' Hammer), to help inquisitors identify suspected witches. Many thousands would be accused of witchcraft and put to death over the next two centuries.

Witch-hunting required innovative "diagnostic" tests. For the water-float test, suspects were dunked in a pool to certify they were not possessed by the Devil. The test was based on the principle of smelting, during which pure metals settle to the bottom and impurities bob up to the surface. Suspects who sank and drowned were ruled pure. Suspects who kept their heads above water were judged to be in league with the Devil. As the saying went, you were "damned if you do and damned if you don't."

**THE WATER-FLOAT TEST.** This so-called test was one way in which medieval authorities sought to detect possession and witchcraft. Managing to float above the waterline was deemed a sign of impurity. In the lower right corner, you can see the bound hands and feet of one poor unfortunate who failed to remain afloat, but whose drowning would have cleared any suspicions of possession.

Modern scholars once believed these so-called witches were actually people with psychological disorders who were persecuted because of their abnormal behavior. Many suspected witches did confess to bizarre behaviors, such as flying or engaging in sexual intercourse with the Devil, which suggests the types of disturbed behavior associated with modern conceptions of schizophrenia. However, these confessions must be discounted because they were extracted under torture by inquisitors who were bent on finding evidence to support accusations of witchcraft (Spanos, 1978). We know today that the threat of torture and other forms of intimidation are sufficient to extract false confessions. Although some who were persecuted as witches probably did show abnormal behavior patterns, most did not (Schoenman, 1984). Rather, it appears that accusations of witchcraft were a convenient means of disposing of social nuisances and political rivals, of seizing property, and of suppressing heresy (Spanos, 1978). In English villages, many of the accused were poor, unmarried elderly women who were forced to beg for food from their neighbors. If misfortune befell the people who declined to give help, the beggar might be accused of having cast a curse on the household. If the woman was generally unpopular, an accusation of witchcraft was likely to follow.

Demons were believed to play roles in both abnormal behavior and witchcraft. However, although some victims of demonic possession were perceived to be afflicted as retribution for their own wrongdoing, others were considered to be innocent victims—possessed by demons through no fault of their own. Witches were believed to have renounced God and voluntarily entered into a pact with the Devil. Witches generally were seen as more deserving of torture and execution (Spanos, 1978).

Historical trends do not follow straight lines. Although the demonological model held sway during the Middle Ages and much of the Renaissance, it did not completely supplant belief in naturalistic causes. In medieval England, for example, demonic possession was only rarely invoked in cases in which a person was held to be insane by legal authorities (Neugebauer, 1979). Most explanations for unusual behavior involved natural causes, such as physical illness or trauma to the brain. In England, in fact, some disturbed people were kept in hospitals until they were restored to sanity (Allderidge, 1979). The Renaissance Belgian physician Johann Weyer (1515–1588) also took up the cause of Hippocrates and Galen by arguing that abnormal behavior and thought patterns were caused by physical problems.

**ASYLUMS** By the late 15th and early 16th centuries, asylums, or madhouses, began to appear throughout Europe. Many were former leprosariums, which were no longer needed because of the decline in leprosy after the late Middle Ages. Asylums often gave refuge to beggars as well as the mentally disturbed, but conditions were appalling. Residents were chained to their beds and left to lie in their own waste or to wander about unassisted. Some asylums became public spectacles. In one asylum in London, St. Mary's of Bethlehem Hospital—from which the word *bedlam* is derived—the public could buy tickets to observe the antics of the inmates, much as we would pay to see a circus sideshow or animals at the zoo. **T / F**

**TRUTH or FICTION**

A night's entertainment in London a few hundred years ago might have included gaping at the inmates at the local asylum.

☑ **TRUE** A night on the town for the gentry of London sometimes included a visit to a local asylum, St. Mary's of Bethlehem Hospital, to gawk at the patients. We derive the word *bedlam* from Bethlehem Hospital.

## The Reform Movement and Moral Therapy

**1.7 Identify the leading reformers of the treatment of the mentally ill and describe the principle underlying moral therapy and the changes that occurred in the treatment of mental patients during the 19th and early 20th centuries.**

Their approach was known as moral treatment

The modern era of treatment begins with the efforts of the Frenchmen Jean-Baptiste Pussin and Philippe Pinel in the late 18th and early 19th centuries. They argued that people who behave abnormally suffer from diseases and should be treated humanely. This view was not popular at the time; mentally disturbed people were regarded as threats to society, not as sick people in need of treatment.

From 1784 to 1802, Pussin, a layman, was placed in charge of a ward for people considered "incurably insane" at La Bicêtre, a large mental hospital in Paris. Although Pinel is often credited with freeing the inmates of La Bicêtre from their chains, Pussin was actually the first official to unchain a group of the "incurably insane." These unfortunates had been considered too dangerous and unpredictable to be left unchained, but Pussin believed that if they were treated with kindness, there would be no need for chains. As he predicted, most of the shut-ins were manageable and calm after their chains were removed. They could walk the hospital grounds and take in fresh air. Pussin also forbade the staff from treating the residents harshly, and he fired employees who ignored his directives.

Pinel (1745–1826) became the medical director for the incurables' ward at La Bicêtre in 1793 and continued the humane treatment Pussin had begun. He stopped harsh practices such as bleeding and purging, and moved patients from darkened dungeons to well-ventilated, sunny rooms. Pinel also spent hours talking to inmates, in the belief that showing understanding and concern would help restore them to normal functioning.

The philosophy of treatment that emerged from these efforts was labeled *moral therapy*. It was based on the belief that providing humane treatment in a relaxed and decent environment could restore functioning. Similar reforms were instituted at about this time in England by William Tuke and later in the United States by Dorothea Dix. Another influential figure was the American physician Benjamin Rush (1745–1813)—also a signatory to the Declaration of Independence and an early leader of the antislavery movement. Rush,

**BEDLAM.** The bizarre antics of the patients at St. Mary's of Bethlehem Hospital in London in the 18th century were a source of entertainment for the well-heeled gentry of the town, such as the two well-dressed women in the middle of the painting.

**THE UNCHAINING OF INMATES AT LA BICÊTRE BY 18TH-CENTURY FRENCH REFORMER PHILIPPE PINEL.** Continuing the work of Jean-Baptiste Pussin, Pinel stopped harsh practices such as bleeding and purging, and moved inmates from darkened dungeons to sunny, airy rooms. Pinel also took the time to converse with inmates, in the belief that understanding and concern would help restore them to normal functioning.

considered the father of American psychiatry, penned the first American textbook on psychiatry in 1812: *Medical Inquiries and Observations Upon the Diseases of the Mind.* He believed that madness is caused by engorgement of the blood vessels of the brain. To relieve pressure, he recommended bloodletting, purging, and ice-cold baths. He advanced humane treatment by encouraging the staff of his Philadelphia Hospital to treat patients with kindness, respect, and understanding. He also favored the therapeutic use of occupational therapy, music, and travel (Farr, 1994). His hospital became the first in the United States to admit patients for psychological disorders.

Dorothea Dix (1802–1887), a Boston schoolteacher, traveled about the country decrying the deplorable conditions in the jails and almshouses where mentally disturbed people were placed. As a result of her efforts, 32 mental hospitals devoted to treating people with psychological disorders were established throughout the United States.

**A STEP BACKWARD** In the latter half of the 19th century, the belief that abnormal behaviors could be successfully treated or cured by moral therapy fell into disfavor. A period of apathy ensued in which patterns of abnormal behavior were deemed incurable (Grob, 1994, 2009). Mental institutions in the United States grew in size but provided little more than custodial care. Conditions deteriorated. Mental hospitals became frightening places. It was not uncommon to find residents "wallowing in their own excrements," in the words of a New York State official of the time (Grob, 1983). Straitjackets, handcuffs, cribs, straps, and other devices were used to restrain excitable or violent patients.

Deplorable hospital conditions remained commonplace through the middle of the 20th century. By the mid-1950s, the population in mental hospitals had risen to half a million. Although some state hospitals provided decent and humane care, many were described as little more than human snake pits. Residents were crowded into wards that lacked even rudimentary sanitation. Mental patients in back wards were essentially *warehoused*—that is, left to live out their lives with little hope or expectation of recovery or a return to the community. Many received little professional care and were abused by poorly trained and supervised staffs. Finally, these appalling conditions led to calls for reforms of the mental health system. These reforms ushered in a movement toward **deinstitutionalization**, a policy of shifting the burden of care from state hospitals to community-based treatment settings, which led to a wholesale exodus from state mental hospitals. The mental hospital population across the United States has plummeted from nearly 600,000 in the 1950s to about 40,000 today ("Rate of Patients," 2012). Some mental hospitals were closed entirely.

Another factor that laid the groundwork for the mass exodus from mental hospitals was the development of a new class of drugs—the *phenothiazines*. This group of antipsychotic drugs, which helped quell the most flagrant behavior patterns associated with schizophrenia, was introduced in the 1950s. Phenothiazines reduced the need for indefinite hospital stays and permitted many people with schizophrenia to be discharged to halfway houses, group homes, and independent living.

**THE MENTAL HOSPITAL.** Under the policy of deinstitutionalization, mental hospitals today provide a range of services, including short-term treatment of people in crisis or in need of a secure treatment setting. They also provide long-term treatment in a structured environment for people who are unable to function in less-restrictive community settings.

## The Role of the Mental Hospital Today

**1.8 Describe the role of mental hospitals in the mental health system.**

Most state hospitals today are better managed and provide more humane care than those of the 19th and early 20th centuries, but here and there, deplorable conditions persist. Today's state hospital is generally more treatment-oriented and focuses on preparing residents to return to community living. State hospitals function as part of an integrated, comprehensive approach to treatment. They provide a structured environment for people who are unable to function in a less-restrictive community setting. When hospitalization has restored patients to a higher level of functioning, the patients are reintegrated in the community and given follow-up care and transitional residences, if needed. If a community-based hospital is not available or if they require more extensive care, patients may be rehospitalized as needed in a state hospital. For younger and less intensely disturbed people, the state hospital stay is typically briefer than it was in the past, lasting only until their conditions allow them to reenter society. Older, chronic patients, however, may be unprepared to handle the most rudimentary tasks of independent life (shopping, cooking, cleaning, and so on)—in part because the state hospital may be the only home such patients have known as adults.

# The Community Mental Health Movement

**1.9 Describe the goals and outcomes of the community mental health movement.**

In 1963, the U.S. Congress established a nationwide system of *community mental health centers* (CMHCs) intended to offer an alternative to long-term custodial care in bleak institutions. CMHCs were charged with providing continuing support and mental health care to former hospital residents released from state mental hospitals. Unfortunately, not enough CMHCs have been established to serve the needs of hundreds of thousands of formerly hospitalized patients and to prevent the need to hospitalize new patients by providing comprehensive, community-based care and structured residential treatment settings, such as halfway houses.

The community mental health movement and the policy of deinstitutionalization were developed in the hope that mental patients could return to their communities and assume more independent and fulfilling lives, but deinstitutionalization has often been criticized for failing to live up to its lofty expectations. The discharge of mental patients from state hospitals left many thousands of marginally functioning people in communities that lacked adequate housing and other forms of support they needed to function. Although the community mental health movement has had some successes, a great many patients with severe and persistent mental health problems fail to receive the range of mental health and social services they need to adjust to life in the community (Lieberman, 2010; Sederer & Sharfstein, 2014). As you shall see, one of the major challenges facing the community mental health system is the problem of psychiatric homelessness.

## DEINSTITUTIONALIZATION AND THE PSYCHIATRIC HOMELESS POPULATION

Many of the homeless wandering city streets and sleeping in bus terminals and train stations are discharged mental patients or persons with disturbed behavior who might well have been hospitalized in earlier times, before deinstitutionalization was in place. Lacking adequate support, they often face more dehumanizing conditions on the street than they did in the hospital. Many compound their problems by turning to illegal street drugs such as crack. Some of the younger psychiatric homeless population might have remained hospitalized in earlier times but are now, in the wake of deinstitutionalization, directed toward community support programs when they are available. The problem of psychiatric homelessness is not limited to the United States. A recent study in Denmark showed that about 60% of the homeless population had diagnosable psychiatric disorders (Nielsen et al., 2011).

An estimated 20% to 30% of the homeless population suffers from severe psychological disorders, such as schizophrenia (Yager, 2015). Many also have neuropsychological impairments, including significant problems with memory, learning, and concentration, which leaves them disadvantaged in seeking and holding a job (Bousman et al., 2011). As many as 50% of the homeless population also suffer from substance abuse problems that largely go untreated (Yager, 2015).

The lack of available housing, transitional care facilities, and effective case management plays an important role in homelessness among people with psychiatric problems (Rosenheck, 2012; Stergiopoulos, Gozdzik, et al., 2015). Some homeless people with severe psychiatric problems are repeatedly hospitalized for brief stays in community-based hospitals during acute episodes. They move back and forth between the hospital and the community as though caught in a revolving door. Frequently, they are released from the hospital with inadequate arrangements for housing and community care. Some are essentially left to fend for themselves. Although many state hospitals closed their doors

**PSYCHIATRIC HOMELESSNESS.** Many homeless people have severe psychological problems but fall through the cracks of the mental health and social service systems.

and others slashed the number of beds, states failed to provide sufficient funds to support services needed in the community to replace the need for long-term hospitalization.

The mental health system alone does not have the resources to resolve the multifaceted problems faced by the psychiatric homeless population. Helping the psychiatric homeless escape from homelessness requires matching services to their needs in an integrated effort involving mental health and alcohol and drug abuse programs; access to decent, affordable housing; and provision of other social services (Stergiopoulos, Gozdzik, et al., 2015). Another difficulty is that homeless people with severe psychological problems typically do not seek out mental health services. Many have become disenfranchised from mental health services because of previous bad hospital stays, during which they were treated poorly or felt disrespected, dehumanized, or simply ignored (Price, 2009). We need intensive outreach and intervention efforts to help homeless people connect with the services they need as well as programs that provide a better quality of care to homeless individuals (Price, 2009; Stergiopoulos, Gozdzik, et al., 2015). All in all, the problems of the psychiatric homeless population remain complex, vexing problems for the mental health system and society at large.

**DEINSTITUTIONALIZATION: A PROMISE AS YET UNFULFILLED** Although the net results of deinstitutionalization may not yet have lived up to expectations, a number of successful community-oriented programs are available. However, they remain underfunded and unable to reach many people needing ongoing community support. If deinstitutionalization is to succeed, patients need continuing care and opportunities for decent housing, gainful employment, and training in social and vocational skills. Most people with severe psychiatric disorders, such as schizophrenia, live in their communities, but only about half of them are currently in treatment (Torrey, 2011).

New, promising services exist to improve community-based care for people with chronic psychological disorders—for example, psychosocial rehabilitation centers, family psychoeducational groups, supportive housing and work programs, and social skills training. Unfortunately, too few of these services exist to meet the needs of many patients who might benefit from them. The community mental health movement must have expanded community support and adequate financial resources if it is to succeed in fulfilling its original promise.

# Contemporary Perspectives on Abnormal Behavior

As noted, beliefs in possession or demonology persisted until the 18th century, when society began to turn toward reason and science to explain natural phenomena and human behavior. The nascent sciences of biology, chemistry, physics, and astronomy promised knowledge derived from scientific methods of observation and experimentation. Scientific observation in turn uncovered the microbial causes of some kinds of diseases and gave rise to preventive measures. Scientific models of abnormal behavior also began to emerge, including models representing biological, psychological, sociocultural, and biopsychosocial perspectives. We briefly discuss each of these models here, particularly in terms of their historical background, which will lead to a fuller discussion in Chapter 2.

## The Biological Perspective

**1.10 Describe the medical model of abnormal behavior.**

Against the backdrop of advances in medical science, the German physician Wilhelm Griesinger (1817–1868) argued that abnormal behavior was rooted in diseases of the brain. Griesinger's views influenced another German physician, Emil Kraepelin (1856–1926), who wrote an influential textbook on psychiatry in 1883 in which he likened mental disorders to physical diseases. Griesinger and Kraepelin paved the way for the modern medical model, which attempts to explain abnormal behavior on the basis of underlying biological defects or abnormalities, not evil spirits. According to the medical model, people behaving abnormally suffer from mental illnesses or disorders that can be classified, like physical illnesses, according to their distinctive causes and symptoms. Adopters of the medical model don't necessarily believe that every mental disorder is a product of defective biology, but they maintain that it is useful to classify patterns of abnormal behavior as disorders that can be identified on the basis of their distinctive features or symptoms.

Kraepelin specified two main groups of mental disorders or diseases: **dementia praecox** (from roots meaning "precocious [premature] insanity"), which we now call *schizophrenia,* and manic–depressive insanity, which we now label *bipolar disorder* (Zivanovic & Nedic, 2012). Kraepelin believed that dementia praecox is caused by a biochemical imbalance, and manic–depressive psychosis by an abnormality in body metabolism. His major contribution was the development of a classification system that forms the cornerstone of current diagnostic systems.

The medical model gained support in the late 19th century with the discovery that an advanced stage of *syphilis*—in which the bacterium that causes the disease directly invades the brain—led to a form of disturbed behavior called **general paresis** (from the Greek *parienai,* meaning "to relax"). General paresis is associated with physical symptoms and psychological impairment, including personality and mood changes, and with progressive deterioration of memory functioning and judgment. With the advent of antibiotics for treating syphilis, the disorder has become extremely uncommon.

General paresis is of interest to scientists mostly for historical reasons. With the discovery of the connection between general paresis and syphilis, scientists became optimistic that other biological causes would soon be discovered for many other types of disturbed behavior. The later discovery of Alzheimer's disease (discussed in Chapter 14), a brain disease that is the major cause of dementia, lent further support to the medical model. However, it is known now that the great majority of psychological disorders involve a complex web of factors scientists are still struggling to understand.

Much of the terminology used in abnormal psychology has been "medicalized." Because of the medical model, we commonly speak of people whose behavior is abnormal as mentally ill and the features of their behavior as *symptoms* of underlying illness. Other commonly used terms spawned by the medical model include **syndromes**, which are clusters of symptoms that may be indicative of a particular disease or condition, as well as *mental health, diagnosis, patient, mental patient, mental hospital, prognosis, treatment, therapy, cure, relapse,* and *remission.*

The medical model is a major advance over demonology. It inspired the idea that abnormal behavior should be treated by learned professionals, not punished. Compassion supplanted hatred, fear, and persecution. However, the medical model has also led to controversy over the extent to which certain behavior patterns should be considered forms of mental illness. We address this topic in *Thinking Critically: What Is Abnormal Behavior?* on page 20.

## The Psychological Perspective

**1.11 Identify the major psychological models of abnormal behavior.**

Even as the medical model was gaining influence in the 19th century, some scientists argued that organic factors alone could not explain the many forms of abnormal behavior. In Paris, a respected neurologist, Jean-Martin Charcot (1825–1893), experimented with hypnosis in treating *hysteria*, a condition characterized by paralysis or numbness that cannot

**CHARCOT'S TEACHING CLINIC.** Parisian neurologist Jean-Martin Charcot presents a female patient who exhibits the highly dramatic behavior associated with hysteria, such as falling faint at a moment's notice. Charcot was an important influence on the young Sigmund Freud.

be explained by any underlying physical cause. Interestingly, cases of hysteria were common in the Victorian period, but are rare today (Spitzer et al., 1989). The thinking at the time was that people with hysteria must have an affliction of the nervous system, which caused their symptoms. Yet Charcot and his associates demonstrated that these symptoms could be removed in hysterical patients or, conversely, induced in normal patients, by means of hypnotic suggestion.

Among those who attended Charcot's demonstrations was a young Austrian physician named Sigmund Freud (1856–1939; Esman, 2011). Freud reasoned that if hysterical symptoms could be made to disappear or appear through hypnosis—the mere "suggestion of ideas"—then they must be psychological, not biological, in origin (Jones, 1953). Freud concluded that whatever psychological factors give rise to hysteria, they must lie outside the range of conscious awareness. This insight underlies the first psychological perspective on abnormal behavior—the **psychodynamic model**. "I received the proudest impression," Freud wrote of his experience with Charcot, "of the possibility that there could be powerful mental processes which nevertheless remained hidden from the consciousness of men" (as cited in Sulloway, 1983, p. 32).

Freud was also influenced by the Viennese physician Joseph Breuer (1842–1925), 14 years his senior. Breuer too had used hypnosis, to treat a 21-year-old woman, Anna O., with hysterical complaints for which there were no apparent medical basis, such as paralysis in her limbs, numbness, and disturbances of vision and hearing (Jones, 1953). Anna O. was Breuer's patient, but Freud studied her case. A "paralyzed" muscle in her neck prevented her from turning her head. Immobilization of the fingers of her left hand made it all but impossible for her to feed herself. Breuer believed there was a strong psychological component to her symptoms. He encouraged her to talk about her symptoms, sometimes under hypnosis. Recalling and talking about events connected with the appearance of the symptoms—especially events that evoked feelings of fear, anxiety, or guilt—provided symptom relief, at least for a time. Anna referred to the treatment as the "talking cure" or, when joking, as "chimney sweeping."

The hysterical symptoms were taken to represent the transformation of these blocked-up emotions, forgotten but not lost, into physical complaints. In Anna's case, the symptoms disappeared once the emotions were brought to the surface and "discharged."

**SIGMUND FREUD AND BERTHA PAPPENHEIM (ANNA O.).** Freud is shown here at around age 30. Pappenheim (1859–1936) is known more widely in the psychological literature as "Anna O." Freud and his colleague Breuer believed that her hysterical symptoms represented the transformation of blocked-up emotions into physical complaints.

Breuer labeled the therapeutic effect *catharsis*, or emotional discharge of feelings (from the Greek word *kathairein*, meaning to clean or to purify).

Freud's theoretical model was the first major psychological model of abnormal behavior. As you'll see in Chapter 2, other psychological perspectives on abnormal behavior based on behavioral, humanistic, and cognitive models soon followed. Each of these perspectives, as well as the contemporary medical model, spawned particular forms of therapy to treat psychological disorders.

## The Sociocultural Perspective

**1.12 Describe the sociocultural perspective on abnormal behavior.**

Mustn't we also consider the broader social context in which behavior occurs to understand the roots of abnormal behavior? Sociocultural theorists believe the causes of abnormal behavior may be found in the failures of society rather than in the person. Accordingly, psychological problems may be rooted in the ills of society, such as unemployment, poverty, family breakdown, injustice, ignorance, and lack of opportunity. Sociocultural factors also focus on relationships between mental health and social factors such as gender, social class, ethnicity, and lifestyle.

Sociocultural theorists also observe that once a person is called "mentally ill," the label is hard to remove. It also distorts other people's responses to the "patient." People classified as mentally ill are stigmatized and marginalized. Job opportunities may disappear, friendships may dissolve, and the "patient" may feel increasingly alienated from society. Sociocultural theorists focus peoples' attention on the social consequences of being labeled as a "mental patient." They argue that society needs to provide access to meaningful societal roles as workers, students, and colleagues to those with long-term mental health problems, rather than shunt them aside.

## The Biopsychosocial Perspective

**1.13 Describe the biopsychosocial perspective on abnormal behavior.**

Aren't patterns of abnormal behavior too complex to be understood from any one model or perspective? Many mental health professionals endorse the view that abnormal behavior is best understood by taking into account multiple causes representing the biological, psychological, and sociocultural domains (Levine & Schmelkin, 2006). The **biopsychosocial model**, or interactionist model, informs this text's approach toward understanding the origins of abnormal behavior. We believe it's essential to consider the interplay of biological, psychological, and sociocultural factors in the development of psychological disorders. Although our understanding of these factors may be incomplete, we must consider all possible pathways and account for multiple factors and how they interact with each other.

Perspectives on psychological disorders provide a framework not only for explanation but also for treatment (see Chapter 2). The perspectives scientists use also lead to the predictions, or *hypotheses*, that guide their research or inquiries into the causes and treatments of abnormal behavior. The medical model, for example, fosters inquiry into genetic and biochemical treatment methods. In the next section, we consider the ways in which psychologists and other mental health professionals study abnormal behavior.

**BASICS: LIVING WITH A DISORDER**

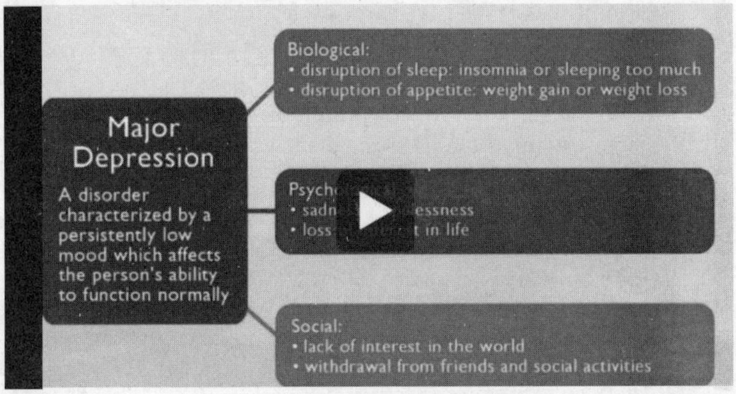

# THINKING CRITICALLY about abnormal psychology

## @ISSUE: WHAT IS ABNORMAL BEHAVIOR?

The question of where to draw the line between normal and abnormal behavior continues to be a subject of debate within the mental health field and broader society. Unlike medical illness, a psychological or mental disorder cannot be identified by a spot on an X-ray or from a blood sample. Classifying these disorders involves clinical judgments, not findings of fact—and as we have noted, these judgments can change over time and can vary from culture to culture. For example, medical professionals once considered masturbation a form of mental illness. Although some people today may object to masturbation on moral grounds, professionals no longer regard it as a mental disturbance.

Consider other behaviors that may blur the boundaries between normal and abnormal: Is body-piercing abnormal, or is it simply a fashion statement? (How much piercing do you consider "normal"?) Might excessive shopping behavior or overuse of the Internet be a form of mental illness? Is bullying a symptom of an underlying disorder, or is it just bad behavior? Mental health professionals base their judgments on the kinds of criteria we outline in this text, but even in professional circles, debate continues about whether some behaviors should be classified as forms of abnormal behavior or mental disorders.

One of the longest of these debates concerns homosexuality. Until 1973, the American Psychiatric Association classified homosexuality as a mental disorder. In that year, the organization voted to drop homosexuality from its listing of classified mental disorders in its diagnostic manual, the *Diagnostic and Statistical Manual of Mental Disorders*, or *DSM* (discussed in Chapter 3). This decision to declassify homosexuality was not unanimous among the nation's psychiatrists, however. Many argued that the decision was motivated more by political reasons than by good science. Some objected to basing such a decision on a vote. After all, would it be reasonable to drop cancer as a recognized medical illness on the basis of a vote? Shouldn't scientific criteria determine these kinds of judgments, rather than a popular vote? **T / F**

### TRUTH or FICTION

Despite changing attitudes in society toward homosexuality, the psychiatric profession continues to classify homosexuality as a mental disorder.

☑ **FALSE** The psychiatric profession dropped homosexuality from its listing of mental disorders in 1973.

What do you think? Is homosexuality a variation in the normal spectrum of sexual orientation, or is it a form of abnormal behavior? What is the basis of your judgment? What criteria did you apply in forming a judgment? What evidence do you have to support your beliefs?

**IS HOMOSEXUALITY A MENTAL DISORDER?** Until 1973, homosexuality was classified as a mental disorder by the American Psychiatric Association. What criteria should be used to form judgments about determining whether particular patterns of behavior comprise a mental or psychological disorder?

Within the *DSM* system, mental disorders are recognized on the basis of behavior patterns associated with emotional distress and/or significant impairment in psychological functioning. Researchers find that people with a gay male or lesbian sexual orientation tend to have a greater frequency of suicide and of states of emotional distress, especially anxiety and depression, than people with a heterosexual orientation (Cochran, Sullivan, & Mays, 2003; King, 2008). However, even if gay males and lesbians are more prone to develop psychological problems, it doesn't necessarily follow that these problems are the result of their sexual orientation.

Gay adolescents in our society come to terms with their sexuality against a backdrop of deep-seated prejudices and resentment toward gays. The process of achieving a sense of self-acceptance against this backdrop of societal intolerance can be so difficult that many gay adolescents seriously consider or attempt suicide. As adults, gay men and lesbians often continue to bear the brunt of prejudice and negative attitudes toward them, including negative reactions from family members that often follow the disclosure of their sexual orientation. The social stress associated with stigma, prejudice, and discrimination that gay people encounter may directly cause mental health problems (Meyer, 2003).

Understood in this context, it is little wonder that many gay males and lesbians develop psychological problems. As a leading authority in the field, psychologist J. Michael Bailey (1999, p. 883) wrote: "Surely, it must be difficult for young people to come to grips with their homosexuality in a world where homosexual people are often scorned, mocked, mourned, and feared."

Should we then accept the claim that societal intolerance is the root cause of psychological problems in people with a homosexual orientation? As critical thinkers, we should recognize that other factors may be involved. Scientists need more evidence before they can arrive at any judgments concerning why gay males and lesbians are more prone to psychological problems, especially suicide.

Imagine a society in which homosexuality was the norm and heterosexual people were shunned, scorned, or ridiculed. Would we find that heterosexual people are more likely to have psychological problems? Would this evidence lead us to assume that heterosexuality is a mental disorder? What do you think?

In thinking critically about the issue, answer the following questions:

- How do you decide when any behavior, such as social drinking or even shopping or Internet use, crosses the line from normal to abnormal?
- Is there a set of criteria you use in all cases? How do your criteria differ from the criteria specified in the text?
- Do you believe that homosexuality is abnormal? Why or why not?

# Research Methods in Abnormal Psychology

Abnormal psychology is a branch of the scientific discipline of psychology. Research in the field is based on the application of the **scientific method**. Before we explore the basic steps in the scientific method, let us consider the four overarching objectives of science: description, explanation, prediction, and control.

## Description, Explanation, Prediction, and Control: The Objectives of Science

**1.14 Identify four major objectives of science.**

To understand abnormal behavior, we must first learn to describe it. Description allows us to recognize abnormal behavior and provides the basis for explaining it. Descriptions should be clear, unbiased, and based on careful observation. In the following vignette, put yourself in the position of a graduate student in psychology who is asked to describe the behavior of a laboratory rat the professor places on the desk.

*Imagine you are a brand-new graduate student in psychology and are sitting in your research methods class on the first day of the term. The professor, a distinguished woman of about 50, enters the class. She is carrying a small wire-mesh cage containing a white rat. The professor removes the rat from the cage and places it on the desk. She asks the class to observe its behavior. As a serious student, you attend closely. The animal moves to the edge of the desk, pauses, peers over the edge, and seems to jiggle its whiskers at the floor below. It maneuvers along the edge of the desk, tracking the perimeter. Now and then the rat pauses and vibrates its whiskers downward in the direction of the floor.*

*The professor picks up the rat and returns it to the cage. She asks the class to describe the animal's behavior.*

*A student responds, "The rat seems to be looking for a way to escape."*

*Another student says, "It is reconnoitering its environment, examining it." "Reconnoitering"? You think. That student has seen too many war movies.*

*The professor writes each response on the blackboard. Another student raises her hand. "The rat is making a visual search of the environment," she says. "Maybe it's looking for food."*

*The professor prompts other students for their descriptions.*

*"It's looking around," says one.*

*"Trying to escape," says another.*

*Your turn arrives. Trying to be scientific, you say, "We can't say what its motivation might be. All we know is that it's scanning its environment."*

*"How so?" the professor asks.*

*"Visually," you reply, confidently.*

*The professor writes the response and then turns to the class, shaking her head. "Each of you observed the rat," she said, "but none of you described its behavior. Instead, you made inferences that the rat was 'looking for a way down' or 'scanning its environment' or 'looking for food,' and the like. These are not unreasonable inferences, but they are inferences, not descriptions. They also happen to be wrong. You see, the rat is blind. It's been blind since birth. It couldn't possibly be looking around, at least not in a visual sense."*

The vignette about the blind rat illustrates that our descriptions of behavior may be influenced by our expectations. Our expectations reflect our preconceptions, or models of behavior, and they may incline us to perceive events—such as the rat's movements and other people's behavior—in certain ways. Describing the rat in the classroom as "scanning" and "looking" for something is an inference, or conclusion, we draw from our observations based on our model of how animals explore their environments. In contrast, description would involve a precise accounting of the animal's movements around the desk, measuring how far in each direction it moves, how long it pauses, how it bobs its head from side to side, and so on.

Nevertheless, inference is important in science. Inference allows us to jump from the particular to the general—to suggest laws and principles of behavior that can be woven into a model or **theory** of behavior. Without a way of organizing our descriptions of phenomena in terms of models and theories, we would be left with a buzzing confusion of unconnected observations.

Theories help scientists explain puzzling data and predict future data. Prediction entails the discovery of factors that anticipate the occurrence of events. Geology, for example, seeks clues in the forces affecting the earth, interpretation of which can forecast natural events such as earthquakes and volcanic eruptions. Scientists who study abnormal behavior seek clues in overt behavior, biological processes, family interactions, and so forth, to predict the development of abnormal behaviors and determine factors that might predict response to various treatments. It is not sufficient that theoretical models help scientists explain or make sense of events or behaviors that have already occurred. Useful models and theories allow them to predict the occurrence of particular behaviors.

The idea of controlling human behavior—especially the behavior of people with serious problems—is controversial. The history of societal response to abnormal behaviors, including abuses such as exorcism and cruel forms of physical restraint, renders the idea particularly distressing. Within science, however, the word *control* does not imply that people are coerced into doing the bidding of others, like puppets dangling on strings. Psychologists, for example, are committed to the dignity of the individual, and the concept of human dignity requires that people be free to make decisions and exercise choices. Within this context, *controlling behavior* means using scientific knowledge to help people shape their own goals and more efficiently use their resources to accomplish them. Today, in the United States, even when helping professionals restrain people who are violently disturbed, the goal is to help them overcome their agitation and regain the ability to exercise meaningful choices in their lives. Ethical standards prohibit the use of injurious techniques in research or practice.

Psychologists and other scientists use the *scientific method* to advance the description, explanation, prediction, and control of abnormal behavior.

## The Scientific Method

### 1.15 Identify the four major steps in the scientific method.

The scientific method tests assumptions and theories about the world through gathering objective evidence. Gathering evidence that is objective requires thoughtful observational and experimental methods. Here, let's focus on the basic steps involved in using the scientific method in experimentation:

1. *Formulating a research question.* Scientists derive research questions from previous observations and current theories. For instance, on the basis of their clinical observations and theoretical understanding of the underlying mechanisms in depression, psychologists may formulate questions about whether certain experimental drugs or particular types of psychotherapy help people overcome depression.

2. *Framing the research question in the form of a hypothesis.* A **hypothesis** is a prediction tested in an experiment. For example, scientists might hypothesize that people who are clinically depressed will show greater improvement on measures of depression if they are given an experimental drug than if they receive an inert placebo (a sugar pill).
3. *Testing the hypothesis.* Scientists test hypotheses through experiments in which variables are controlled and the differences are observed. For instance, they can test the hypothesis about the experimental drug by giving the drug to one group of people with depression and giving another group the placebo. They can then test to see if the people who received the active drug showed greater improvement over a period of time than those who received the placebo.
4. *Drawing conclusions about the hypothesis.* In the final step, scientists draw conclusions from their findings about the accuracy of their hypotheses. Psychologists use statistical methods to determine the likelihood that differences between groups are significant, as opposed to chance fluctuations. Psychologists can be reasonably confident that group differences are significant—that is, not because of chance—when there is a probability of less than 5% that chance alone can explain the differences. When well-designed research findings fail to bear out hypotheses, scientists rethink the theories from which the hypotheses are derived. Research findings often lead to modifications in theory, new hypotheses, and, in turn, subsequent research.

Before we consider the major research methods used by psychologists and others to study abnormal behavior, let's consider some of the principles that guide ethical conduct in research.

## Ethics in Research

**1.16 Identify the ethical principles that guide research in psychology.**

Ethical principles are designed to promote the dignity of the individual, protect human welfare, and preserve scientific integrity (American Psychological Association, 2002). Psychologists are prohibited by the ethical standards of their profession from using methods that cause psychological or physical harm to their research participants or clients. Psychologists also must follow ethical guidelines that protect animals in research.

Institutions such as universities and hospitals have review committees, called *institutional review boards* (IRBs), that review proposed research studies in light of ethical guidelines. Investigators must receive IRB approval before they are permitted to begin their studies. Two of the major principles on which ethical guidelines are based are (a) *informed consent* and (b) *confidentiality*.

The principle of **informed consent** requires that people be free to choose whether they want to participate in research studies. They must be given sufficient information in advance about the study's purposes and methods and its risks and benefits to make an informed decision about their participation. Research participants must be free to withdraw from a study at any time without penalty. In some cases, researchers may withhold certain information until all the data are collected. For instance, participants in placebo-control studies of experimental drugs are told that they may receive an inert placebo rather than the active drug. In studies in which information was withheld or deception was used, participants must be debriefed afterward. That is, they must receive an explanation of the true methods and purposes of the study and why it was necessary to keep them in the dark. After the study is concluded, participants who received the placebo would be given the option of receiving the active treatment, if warranted.

Research participants also have a right to expect that their identities will not be revealed. Investigators are required to protect their **confidentiality** by keeping the records of their participation secure and by not disclosing their identities to others.

We now turn to discussion of the research methods used to investigate abnormal behavior.

**NATURALISTIC OBSERVATION.**
In naturalistic observation, psychologists take their research into the streets, homes, restaurants, schools, and other settings where behavior can be directly observed. For example, psychologists have unobtrusively positioned themselves in school playgrounds to observe how aggressive or socially anxious children interact with peers.

# The Naturalistic Observation Method

**1.17 Explain the role of the naturalistic method of research and describe its key features.**

In the **naturalistic observation method**, the investigator observes behavior in the field, where it happens. Anthropologists have observed behavior patterns in preliterate societies to study human diversity. Sociologists have followed the activities of adolescent gangs in inner cities. Psychologists have spent weeks observing the behavior of homeless people in train stations and bus terminals. They have even observed the eating habits of slender and overweight people in fast-food restaurants, searching for clues to obesity.

Scientists try to ensure that their naturalistic observations are unobtrusive, so as to minimize interference with the behavior they observe. Nevertheless, the presence of the observer may distort the behavior that is observed, and this must be taken into consideration.

Naturalistic observation provides information on how people behave, but it does not reveal why they do so. It may reveal, for example, that men who frequent bars and drink often get into fights, but such observations do not show that alcohol *causes* aggression. As we shall explain, questions of cause and effect are best approached by means of controlled experiments.

# The Correlational Method

**1.18 Explain the role of the correlational method of research and describe its key features.**

One of the primary methods used to study abnormal behavior is the **correlational method**, which involves the use of statistical methods to examine relationships between two or more factors that can vary, called *variables*. For example, in Chapter 7 we will see that there is a statistical relationship, or *correlation*, between the variables of negative thinking and depressive symptoms. The statistical measure used to express the association or correlation between two variables is called the **correlation coefficient**, which can vary along a continuum ranging from −1.00 to +1.00. When higher values in one variable (negative thinking) are associated with higher values in the other variable (depressive symptoms), there is a *positive correlation* between the variables. If higher levels of one variable are associated with lower values of another variable, there is a *negative correlation* between the variables. Positive correlations carry positive signs; negative correlations carry negative signs. The higher the correlation coefficient—meaning the closer it is to either −1.00 or +1.00—the stronger the relationship between the variables.

The correlational method does not involve manipulation of the variables of interest. In the previous example, the experimenter does not manipulate people's depressive symptoms or negative thoughts. Rather, the investigator uses statistical techniques to determine whether these variables tend to be associated with each other. Because the experimenter does not directly manipulate the variables, a correlation between two variables does not prove that they are causally related to each other. It may be the case that two variables are correlated but have no causal connection. For example, children's foot size is correlated with their vocabulary, but growth in foot size does not cause the growth of vocabulary. Depressive symptoms and negative thoughts also are correlated, as we shall see in Chapter 7. Though negative thinking may be a causative factor in depression, it is also possible that the direction of causality works the other way: that depression gives rise to negative thinking. Or perhaps the direction of causality works both ways, with negative thinking contributing to depression and depression in turn influencing negative thinking. Then again, depression and negative thinking may both reflect a common causative factor, such as stress, and not be causally related to each other at all. In sum, we cannot tell from a correlation alone whether or not variables are causally linked. To address questions of cause and effect, investigators use experimental methods in which the experimenter manipulates one or more variables of interest and observes their effects on other variables or outcomes under controlled conditions.

Although the correlational method cannot determine cause-and-effect relationships, it does serve the scientific objective of prediction. When two variables are correlated, scientists can use one to predict the other. Although causal connections are complex and somewhat nebulous, knowledge, for example, of correlations among alcoholism, family history, and attitudes toward drinking helps scientists predict which adolescents are at greater risk of developing problems with alcohol. Knowing which factors predict future problems helps direct preventive efforts toward high-risk groups.

**THE LONGITUDINAL STUDY** The **longitudinal study** is a type of correlational study in which individuals are periodically tested or evaluated over lengthy periods of time, perhaps for decades. By studying people over time, researchers seek to identify factors or events in people's lives that predict the later development of abnormal behavior patterns, such as depression or schizophrenia. Prediction is based on the *correlation* between events or factors that are separated in time. However, this type of research is time-consuming and costly. It requires a commitment that may literally outlive the original investigators. Therefore, long-term longitudinal studies are relatively uncommon. In Chapter 11, we examine one of the best-known longitudinal studies, the Danish high-risk study that tracked a group of children whose mothers had schizophrenia and who were themselves at increased risk of developing the disorder.

## The Experimental Method

**1.19 Explain the role of the experimental method of research and describe its key features.**

The **experimental method** allows scientists to demonstrate causal relationships by manipulating the causal factor and measuring its effects under controlled conditions that minimize the risk of other factors explaining the results.

The term *experiment* can cause some confusion. Broadly speaking, an experiment is a trial or test of a hypothesis. From this vantage point, any method that seeks to test a hypothesis could be considered experimental—including naturalistic observation and correlational studies. However, investigators usually limit the use of the term *experimental method* to refer to studies in which researchers seek to uncover cause-and-effect relationships by directly manipulating possible causal factors.

In experimental research, the factors or variables hypothesized to play a causal role are manipulated or controlled by the investigator. These are called **independent variables**. Factors that are observed in order to determine the effects of manipulating the independent variable are labeled **dependent variables**. Dependent variables are measured, but not manipulated, by the experimenter. Table 1.1 presents examples of independent and dependent variables of interest to investigators of abnormal behavior.

In an experiment, research participants are exposed to an *independent variable*—for example, the type of beverage (alcoholic vs. nonalcoholic) they consume in a laboratory setting. They are then observed or examined to determine whether the independent variable makes a difference in their behavior, or, more precisely, whether the independent variable affects the dependent variable—for example, whether they behave more aggressively if they consume alcohol. Studies need to have a sufficient number of research participants (subjects) to be able to detect statistically meaningful differences between experimental groups.

**Table 1.1** Examples of Independent and Dependent Variables in Experimental Research

| Independent Variables | Dependent Variables |
|---|---|
| Type of treatment: different types of drug treatments or psychological treatments | Behavioral variables: measures of adjustment, activity levels, eating behavior, smoking behavior |
| Treatment factors: brief vs. long-term treatment, inpatient vs. outpatient treatment | Physiological variables: measures of physiological responses such as heart rate, blood pressure, and brain wave activity |
| Experimental manipulations: types of beverage consumed (alcoholic vs. nonalcoholic) | Self-report variables: measures of anxiety, mood, or marital or life satisfaction |

**EXPERIMENTAL AND CONTROL GROUPS** Well-controlled experiments randomly assign research participants to experimental and control groups (Mauri, 2012). The **experimental group** is given the experimental treatment, whereas the **control group** is not. Care is taken to hold other conditions constant for each group. By using **random assignment** and holding other conditions constant, experimenters can be reasonably confident that it was the experimental treatment and not uncontrolled factors, such as room temperature or differences between the types of people in the experimental and control groups, that explains the experimental findings.

Why should experimenters assign research participants to experimental and control groups at random? Consider a study intended to investigate the effects of alcohol on behavior. Let's suppose we allowed research participants to decide for themselves whether they wanted to be in an experimental group in which they were to drink alcohol or in a control group in which they would drink a nonalcoholic beverage. If this were the case, differences between the groups might be due to an underlying **selection factor** (differences in the types of people who would select to be in one group or the other) rather than experimental manipulation.

For example, people who *chose* to consume the alcoholic beverage might differ in their personalities from those who chose the control beverage. They might be more willing to explore or to take risks, for example. Therefore, the experimenter would not know whether the independent variable (type of beverage) or a selection factor (difference in the kinds of people making up the groups) was ultimately responsible for observed differences in behavior. Random assignment controls for selection factors by ensuring that subject characteristics are randomly distributed across both groups. Thus, it is reasonable to assume that differences between groups result from the treatments they receive rather than from differences between the participants who make up the groups. Still, it is possible that apparent treatment effects may stem from a person's expectancies about the treatments they receive rather than from the active components in the treatments themselves. In other words, knowing that you are being given an alcoholic beverage to drink might affect your behavior, quite apart from the alcoholic content of the beverage itself.

**CONTROLLING FOR SUBJECT EXPECTANCIES** To control for subject expectancies, experimenters rely on procedures that render research participants **blind**, or uninformed about the treatments they are receiving. For example, participants in a study designed to test an investigational medication for depression would be kept uninformed about whether they are receiving the actual drug or a **placebo**, an inert drug that physically resembles the active drug. Experimenters use placebos to control for the possibility that treatment effects result from a person's hopeful expectancies rather than from the chemical properties of the drug itself or from the specific techniques used in psychotherapy (Espay et al., 2015; Fox, 2014; Rutherford et al., 2014).

**MAY WE OFFER YOU A PLACEBO?**
Do you think that taking a placebo might help relieve pain, even if pain patients knew they were taking a placebo?

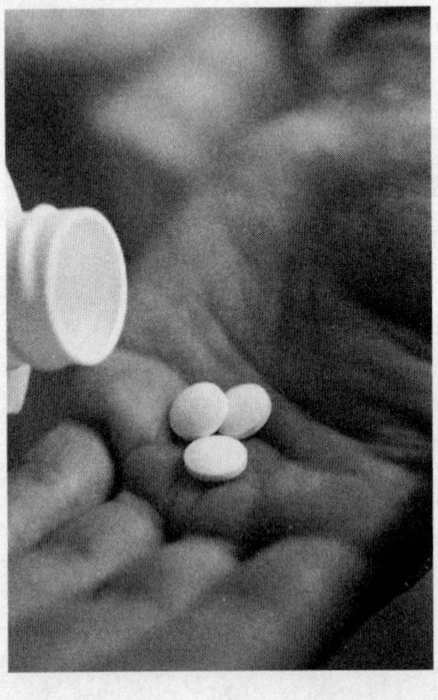

In a *single-blind placebo-control study*, research participants are randomly assigned to treatment conditions in which they receive either an active drug (experimental condition) or an inert placebo (placebo-control condition), but are kept blind about which drug they receive. It is helpful to keep the researchers blind as well as to which substances the research participants receive so as to prevent the researchers' own expectations from affecting the results. In the case of a *double-blind placebo-control design*, neither the researcher nor the subject knows who is receiving the active drug or the placebo.

Double-blind studies control for both subject and experimenter expectancies. However, a major limitation of both single-blind and double-blind studies is that participants and experimenters sometimes can "see through" the blind. Obvious drug-induced effects or telltale side effects can give it away, as can slight differences in the taste or smell between the placebo and the active drug, all of which can make the double-blind seem like a Venetian blind with the slats slightly open. Still, the double-blind placebo control is widely considered the gold standard of experimental designs, especially in drug treatment research.

Placebo effects are generally strongest in studies of pain or negative emotional states, such as anxiety and depression (for example, Meyer et al., 2015; Peciña et al.,

2015), perhaps because these complaints involve subjective experiences that may be influenced more by the power of suggestion than physiological factors measured by objective means, such as blood pressure. In what is surely a most compelling example of the power of suggestion, recent studies showed that pain patients reported reduced levels of pain when they took a placebo, even though they were told they had received a placebo that had no medical value (Kam-Hansen et al., 2014; Schafer, Colloca, & Wager, 2015). Placebos may produce biological effects similar to those of pain medications by blocking pain signals to the brain or leading to the release of endorphins, which are natural chemicals in the brain that have pain-killing effects (Fox, 2014; "Know It's a Placebo?" 2015; Marchant, 2016). **T / F**

## TRUTH *or* FICTION

In a recent experiment, pain patients reported some relief from pain after taking a placebo pill, even though they were told the pill was merely a placebo.

☑ TRUE Placebo effects may occur even when participants are told they are taking a placebo.

Placebo-control groups are also used in psychotherapy research to control for subject expectancies. Assume you were to study the effects of therapy method A on mood. You could randomly assign research participants to either an experimental group in which they receive the new therapy or to a (no-treatment) "waiting list" control group. In such a case, the experimental group might show greater improvement because participation in treatment engendered hopeful expectations, not because of the particular therapy method used. Although a waiting list control group might control for positive effects due simply to the passage of time, it would not account for placebo effects, such as the benefits of therapy resulting from instilling a sense of hope and expectations of success.

To control for placebo effects, experimenters sometimes use an *attention-placebo* control group in which participants are exposed to a believable or credible treatment that contains the nonspecific factors that all therapies share—such as the attention and emotional support of a therapist—but not the specific therapeutic ingredients represented in the active treatment. Attention-placebo treatments commonly substitute general discussions of participants' problems for the specific ingredients of therapy contained in the experimental treatment. Unfortunately, although experimenters may keep attention-placebo study participants blind as to whether they are receiving the experimental treatment, their therapists are generally aware of which treatment is being administered. Therefore, the attention-placebo method may not control for therapists' expectations.

**EXPERIMENTAL VALIDITY** Experimental studies are judged on whether they are valid, or sound. There are many aspects of validity, including *internal validity, external validity*, and *construct validity*. You will see in Chapter 3 that the term *validity* is also applied in the context of tests and measures to refer to the degree to which these instruments measure what they purport to measure.

Experiments have **internal validity** when the observed changes in the dependent variable(s) can be causally related to changes in the independent or treatment variable. Assume that a group of depressed individuals is treated with a new antidepressant medication (the independent variable), and changes in their mood and behavior (the dependent variables) are tracked over time. After several weeks of treatment, the researcher finds that most treated individuals have improved and claims that the new drug is an effective treatment for depression. Not so fast! How does the experimenter know that the independent variable and not some other factor was causally responsible for the improvement? Perhaps the depressed individuals improved naturally as time passed, or perhaps they were exposed to other events responsible for their improvement. Experiments lack internal validity when they fail to control for other factors (called *confounds*, or threats to validity) that might pose rival hypotheses for the results.

Experimenters *randomly assign* research participants to treatment and control groups to control for rival hypotheses (Mitka, 2011). Random assignment helps ensure that individual attributes—intelligence, motivation, age, race, and so on—are randomly distributed across the groups and are not likely to favor one group over the other. Through the random assignment to groups, researchers can be reasonably confident that significant differences between the treatment and control groups reflect the effects of independent (treatment) variables and not confounding selection factors. Well-designed studies include sufficiently large samples of research participants to be able to discern statistically significant differences between experimental and control groups.

**External validity** refers to the generalizability of results of an experimental study to other individuals, settings, and times. In most cases, researchers are interested in generalizing the results of a specific study (e.g., effects of a new antidepressant medication on a sample of people who are depressed) to a larger population (people in general who are depressed). The external validity of a study is strengthened to the degree that the *sample* is representative of the target population. In studying the problems of the urban homeless, it is essential to recruit a representative sample of the homeless population, for example, rather than focusing on a few homeless people who happen to be available. One way of obtaining a representative sample is by means of random sampling. In a *random sample*, every member of the target population has an equal chance of being selected.

Researchers may extend the results of a particular study by means of *replication*, the process of repeating an experiment in other settings or at other times, or with samples drawn from other populations (Brandt et al., 2013; Cesario, 2014; Simons, 2014). A treatment for hyperactivity may be helpful with economically deprived children in an inner-city classroom but not with children in affluent suburbs or rural areas. The external validity of the treatment may be limited if its effects do not generalize to other samples or settings. That does not mean the treatment is less effective, but rather that its range of effectiveness may be limited to certain populations or situations.

**Construct validity** is a conceptually higher level of validity. It is the degree to which treatment effects can be accounted for by the theoretical mechanisms or constructs represented in the independent variables. A drug, for example, may have predictable effects, but perhaps not for the theoretical reasons claimed by the researchers.

Consider a hypothetical experimental study of a new antidepressant medication. The research may have internal validity in the form of solid controls and external validity in the form of generalizability across samples of seriously depressed people. However, it may lack construct validity if the drug does not work for the reasons proposed by the researchers. Perhaps the researchers assumed that the drug would work by raising the levels of certain chemicals in the nervous system, whereas the drug actually works by increasing the sensitivity of receptors for those chemicals. "So what?" we may ask. After all, the drug still works. True enough—in terms of immediate clinical applications. However, a better understanding of why the drug works can advance theoretical knowledge of depression and give rise to the development of yet more effective treatments.

Scientists can never be certain about the construct validity of research. They recognize that their current theories about why their results occurred may eventually be toppled by other theories that better account for the findings.

## The Epidemiological Method

**1.20 Explain the role of the epidemiological method of research and describe its key features.**

The **epidemiological method** examines rates of occurrence of abnormal behavior in various settings or population groups. One type of epidemiological study is the **survey method**, which relies on interviews or questionnaires. Surveys are used to ascertain rates of occurrence of various disorders in the population as a whole and in various subgroups classified according to factors such as race, ethnicity, gender, or social class. Rates of occurrence of a given disorder are expressed in terms of **incidence**, the number of new cases occurring during a specific period of time, and **prevalence**, the overall number of cases of a disorder existing in the population during a given period of time. Prevalence rates, then, include both new and continuing cases.

Epidemiological studies may point to potential causal factors in medical illnesses and psychological disorders, even though they lack the power of experiments. By finding that illnesses or disorders "cluster" in certain groups or locations, researchers can identify distinguishing characteristics that place these groups or regions at higher risk.

Yet such epidemiological studies cannot control for selection factors; that is, they cannot rule out the possibility that other unrecognized factors will play a causal role in putting a certain group at greater risk. Therefore, they must be considered suggestive of possible causal influences that must be tested further in experimental studies.

**SAMPLES AND POPULATIONS** In the best of possible worlds, researchers would conduct surveys in which every member of the population of interest would participate. In that way, they could be sure the survey results accurately represent the population they want to study. In reality, unless the population of interest is rather narrowly defined (say, for example, designating the population of interest as the students living on your dormitory floor), surveying every member of a given population is extremely difficult, if not impossible. Even census takers can't count every head in the general population. Consequently, most surveys are based on a sample, or subset, of the population. Researchers must take steps when constructing a sample to ensure that it *represents* the target population. For example, a researcher who sets out to study smoking rates in a local community by interviewing people drinking coffee in late-night cafés will probably overestimate its true prevalence.

One method of obtaining a representative sample is to use random sampling. A **random sample** is drawn in such a way that each member of the population of interest has an equal probability of selection. Epidemiologists sometimes construct random samples by surveying at random a given number of households within a target community. By repeating this process in a random sample of U.S. communities, the overall sample can approximate the general U.S. population based on even a tiny percentage of the overall population.

Random sampling is often confused with random assignment. *Random sampling* refers to the process of randomly choosing individuals within a target population to participate in a survey or research study. By contrast, *random assignment* refers to the process by which members of a research sample are assigned at random to different experimental conditions or treatments.

## Abnormal Psychology in the Digital Age

### SMARTPHONES AND SOCIAL MEDIA AS RESEARCH TOOLS

Electronic technologies offer opportunities for researchers to collect real-time data from people as they go about their daily lives and cull data collected by online services. Using these technologies, researchers are extending the reach of data collection beyond the confines of the research laboratory or use of traditional survey methods. They employ smartphones to collect data from research participants by texting them or sending them electronic prompts to report about their behaviors, symptoms, moods, and activities at certain times of the day. They also mine data from social networking sites. For example, Cornell University researchers analyzed more than a half billion Twitter messages to see if the emotional tone of words used in tweets (happy vs. sad words) shifted during the course of the day (Weaver, 2012). Indeed, people tended to use happier words in tweets earlier in the day, whereas later in the day, Twitter messages conveyed a gloomier tone. One of the researchers, Michael Macy, summed up by saying, "We found people are happiest around breakfast time in the morning and then it's all downhill from there" (cited in Weaver, 2012). Perhaps one reason for morning glee and afternoon glum is that people may feel chipper when they first awaken from a restful sleep, but their good mood may peter out as they become tired or stressed as the day drags on.

## Kinship Studies

**1.21 Explain the role of kinship studies and describe their key features.**

Kinship studies attempt to disentangle the roles of heredity and environment in determining behavior. Heredity plays a critical role in determining a wide range of traits. The structures we inherit make our behavior possible (humans can walk and run) and at the same time place limits on us (humans cannot fly without artificial equipment). Heredity plays a role in determining not only our physical characteristics (hair color, eye color, height, and the like) but also many of our psychological characteristics. The science of heredity is called *genetics*.

## TRUTH or FICTION

Recent evidence shows there are literally millions of genes in the nucleus of every cell in the body.

☑ **FALSE** Although no one yet knows the precise number, scientists believe there are about 20,000 to 25,000 genes in the nucleus of each body cell, but certainly not millions.

*Genes* are the basic building blocks of heredity. They regulate the development of traits. *Chromosomes*, rod-shaped structures that house our genes, are found in the nuclei of the body's cells. A normal human cell contains 46 chromosomes, organized into 23 pairs. Chromosomes consist of large, complex molecules of *deoxyribonucleic acid* (DNA). Genes occupy various segments along the length of chromosomes. Scientists believe there are about 20,000 to 25,000 genes in the nucleus of a human body cell (Lupski, 2007; Volkow, 2006). **T / F**

The set of traits specified by our genetic code is referred to as our **genotype**. Our appearance and behavior are not determined by our genotype alone. We are also influenced by environmental factors such as nutrition, learning, exercise, accidents and illnesses, and culture. The constellation of observable or expressed traits is called a **phenotype**. Our phenotype represents the interaction of genetic and environmental influences. People who possess genotypes for particular psychological disorders have a *genetic predisposition* that makes them more likely to develop the disorders in response to stressful life events, physical or psychological trauma, or other environmental factors (Kendler, Myers, & Reichborn-Kjennerud, 2011).

The more closely people are related, the more genes they have in common. Children receive half of their genes from each parent. Thus, there is a 50% overlap in genetic heritage between each parent and his or her offspring. Siblings (brothers and sisters) similarly share half their genes in common.

To determine whether abnormal behavior runs in a family, as one would expect if genetics plays a role, researchers locate a person with a particular disorder and then study how the disorder is distributed among the person's family members. The case first diagnosed is referred to as the index case, or **proband**. If the distribution of the disorder among family members of the proband approximates their degree of kinship, there may be a genetic component to the disorder. However, the closer their kinship, the more likely people are to share environmental backgrounds as well. For this reason, twin and adoptee studies are of particular value.

**TWIN STUDIES** Sometimes a fertilized egg cell (or zygote) divides into two cells that separate, and each develops into a separate person. In such cases, there is a 100% overlap in genetic makeup, and the offspring are known as identical twins, or monozygotic (MZ) twins. In some other cases, a woman releases two egg cells, or ova, in the same month, and they are both fertilized. In such cases, the zygotes develop into fraternal twins, or dizygotic (DZ) twins. DZ twins overlap 50% in their genetic heritage, just as other siblings do.

Identical, or MZ, twins are important in the study of the relative influences of heredity and environment because differences between MZ twins are the result of environmental rather than genetic influences. In twin studies, researchers identify individuals with a specific disorder who are members of an MZ or DZ twin pair and then study the other twin in the pairs. A role for genetic factors is suggested when MZ twins (who have 100% genetic overlap) are more likely than DZ twins (who have 50% genetic overlap) to share a disorder in common. The term *concordance rate* refers to the percentage of cases in which both twins have the same trait or disorder. As we shall see, investigators find higher concordance rates for MZ twins than DZ twins for some forms of abnormal behavior, such as schizophrenia and major depression.

Even among MZ twins, environmental influences cannot be ruled out. Parents and teachers, for example, often encourage MZ twins to behave in similar ways. Put another way, if one twin does X, everyone expects the other to do X also. Expectations have a way of influencing behavior and making for self-fulfilling prophecies. Because twins might not be typical of the general population, researchers are cautious when generalizing the results of twin studies to the larger population.

**ADOPTEE STUDIES** **Adoptee studies** provide powerful arguments for or against a role for genetic factors in the appearance of psychological traits and disorders. Assume that children are reared by adoptive parents from a very early age—perhaps from birth. The children share environmental backgrounds with their adoptive parents but not their genetic heritages. Then assume that we compare the traits and behavior patterns of these children with those of their biological parents and their adoptive parents. If the children show a greater similarity to their biological parents than to their adoptive parents on certain traits or disorders, we have strong evidence for genetic factors in these traits and disorders.

The study of MZ twins reared apart can provide even more dramatic testimony to the relative roles of genetics and environment in shaping abnormal behavior. However, this situation is so uncommon that few examples exist in the literature. Although adoptee studies may represent the strongest source of evidence for genetic factors in explaining abnormal behavior patterns, we should recognize that adoptees, like twins, may not be typical of the general population. In later chapters, we explore the role that adoptee and other kinship studies play in ferreting out genetic and environmental influences in many psychological disorders.

**TWIN STUDIES.** Identical twins have 100% of their genes in common, as compared with the 50% overlap among fraternal twins or any two other siblings. Establishing that identical twins are more likely to share a given disorder than are fraternal twins provides strong evidence for a genetic contribution to the disorder.

## Case Studies

**1.22 Explain the role of case studies and describe their limitations.**

Case studies have been important influences in the development of theories and treatment of abnormal behavior. Freud developed his theoretical model primarily on the basis of case studies, such as the case of Anna O. Therapists representing other theoretical viewpoints have also reported cases studies.

**TYPES OF CASE STUDIES** **Case studies** are intensive studies of individuals. Some case studies are based on historical material, involving subjects who have been dead for hundreds of years. Freud, for example, conducted a case study of the Renaissance artist and inventor Leonardo da Vinci. More commonly, case studies reflect an in-depth analysis of an individual's course of treatment. They typically include detailed histories of the subject's background and response to treatment. From a particular client's experience in therapy, the therapist attempts to glean information that may be of help to other therapists treating similar clients. **T / F**

### TRUTH or FICTION

Case studies have been conducted on dead people.

☑ TRUE Case studies have been conducted on people who have been dead for hundreds of years. One example is Freud's study of Leonardo da Vinci. Such studies rely on historical records rather than interviews.

Despite the richness of material that case studies can provide, they are much less rigorous as research designs than experiments. Distortions or gaps in memory are bound to occur when people discuss historical events, especially those of their childhoods. Some people may intentionally color events to make a favorable impression on the interviewer; others aim to shock the interviewer with exaggerated or fabricated recollections. Interviewers themselves may unintentionally guide the people they interview into reporting histories that mirror their theoretical preconceptions.

**SINGLE-CASE EXPERIMENTAL DESIGNS** The lack of control available in the traditional case study method led researchers to develop more sophisticated methods, called **single-case experimental designs** (sometimes called *single-participant research designs*), in which research participants serve as their own controls. One of the most common forms of the single-case experimental design is the A-B-A-B design, or **reversal design** (see Figure 1.2). This method involves repeated measurement of behavior across four successive phases.

The investigator looks for evidence that change in the observed behavior occurred coincident with treatment. If the problem behavior declines whenever treatment is introduced (during the first and second treatment phases) but returns (is "reversed") to baseline levels during the reversal phase, the experimenter can be reasonably confident the treatment had the intended effect.

A reversal design is illustrated by a case study in which Azrin and Peterson (1989) used a controlled blinking treatment to eliminate a severe eye tic—a form of squinting the eyes shut tightly for a fraction of a second—in a 9-year-old girl. The tic occurred

**Figure 1.2** An A-B-A-B reversal design.

1. *Baseline phase (A).* This phase occurs prior to treatment and allows the experimenter to establish a baseline rate for the behavior before treatment begins.
2. *Treatment phase (B).* Target behaviors are measured as the client undergoes treatment.
3. *Second baseline phase (A, again).* Treatment is temporarily withdrawn or suspended. This is the *reversal* in the reversal design, and it is expected that the positive effects of treatment should now be reversed because the treatment has been withdrawn.
4. *Second treatment phase (B, again).* Treatment is reinstated, and the target behaviors are assessed again.

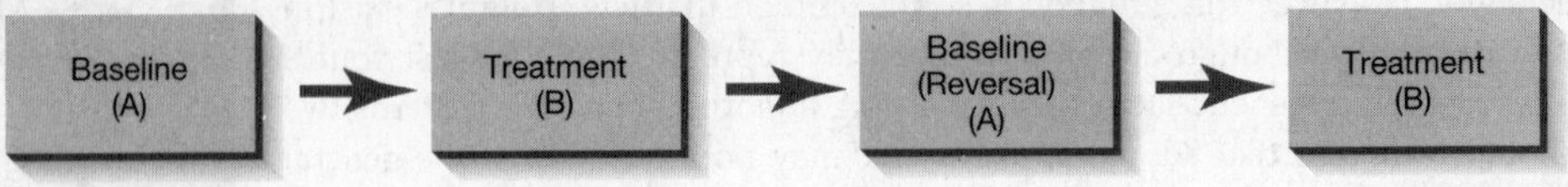


about 20 times a minute when the girl was at home. In the clinic, the rate of eye tics or squinting was measured for 5 minutes during a baseline period (A). Then the girl was prompted to blink her eyes softly every 5 seconds (B). The experimenters reasoned that voluntary "soft" blinking would activate motor (muscle) responses incompatible with those producing the tic, thereby suppressing the tic. As you can see in Figure 1.3, the tic was virtually eliminated in just a few minutes of practicing the incompatible, or competing, response (soft blinking) but returned to near baseline levels during the reversal phase (A), when the competing response was withdrawn. The positive effects were quickly reinstated during the second treatment period (B). The child was also taught to practice the blinking response at home during scheduled 3-minute practice periods and whenever the tic occurred or she felt an urge to squint. The tic was eliminated during the first six weeks of the treatment program and remained absent at a follow-up evaluation two years later.

No matter how well controlled the design or how impressive the results, single-case designs suffer from weak external validity because they cannot show whether a treatment that is effective for one person is effective for others. Replication can help strengthen external validity, but results from controlled experiments on groups of individuals are needed to provide more convincing evidence of treatment effectiveness and generalizability.

**Figure 1.3** Use of an A-B-A-B reversal design in the Azrin and Peterson study.

Notice how the target response, eye tics per minute, decreased when the competing response was introduced in the first B phase. The rate then increased to near baseline levels when the competing response was withdrawn during the second A phase. It decreased again when the competing response was reinstated in the second B phase.

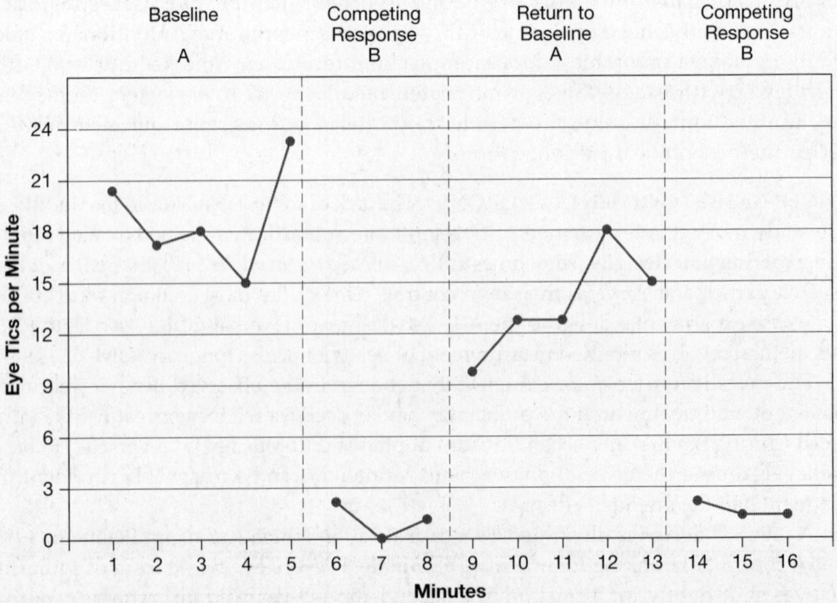

Scientists use different methods to study phenomena of interest to them, but all scientists share a skeptical, hard-nosed way of thinking called **critical thinking**. When thinking critically, scientists adopt a willingness to challenge the conventional wisdom that many take for granted. Scientists maintain open minds and seek *evidence* to support or refute beliefs or claims rather than rely on feelings or gut impressions.

## A CLOSER Look

### THINKING CRITICALLY ABOUT ABNORMAL PSYCHOLOGY

We are exposed to a flood of information about mental health streaming through the popular media—television, radio, and print media (including books, magazines, and newspapers), and increasingly, the Internet. We may hear a news report touting a new drug as a "breakthrough" in the treatment of anxiety, depression, or obesity, only to later learn that the so-called breakthrough doesn't live up to expectations or carries serious side effects. Some reports in the media are accurate and reliable, whereas others are misleading or biased or contain half-truths, exaggerated claims, or unsupported conclusions.

To sort through the welter of confusion, we need to use critical thinking skills, to adopt a questioning attitude toward the information we hear and read. Critical thinkers weigh evidence to see if claims stand up to scrutiny. Becoming a critical thinker means never taking claims at face value. It means looking at both sides of the argument. Most of us take certain "truths" for granted. Critical thinkers, however, evaluate assertions and claims for themselves.

We encourage you to apply critical thinking skills as you study this text. Adopt a skeptical attitude toward information you receive. Carefully examine the definitions of terms. Evaluate the logical bases of arguments. Evaluate claims in the light of available evidence. Here are some key features of critical thinking:

1. *Maintain a skeptical attitude.* Don't take anything at face value, not even claims made by respected scientists or textbook authors. Consider the evidence yourself. Seek additional information. Investigate the credibility of your sources.
2. *Consider the definitions of terms.* Statements may be true or false depending on how the terms they use are defined. Consider the statement, "Stress is bad for you." If we define *stress* in terms of hassles and work or family pressures that stretch our ability to cope to the max, then there is substance to the statement. However, if we define *stress* (see Chapter 4) as conditions that require us to adjust, which may include life events such as a new marriage or the birth of a child, then certain types of stress can be positive, even if they are difficult. Perhaps, as you'll see, we all need some amount of stress to be energized and alert.
3. *Weigh the assumptions or premises on which arguments are based.* Consider a case in which we compare differences in the rates of psychological disorders across racial or ethnic groups in our society. Assuming we find differences, should we conclude that ethnicity or racial identity accounts for these differences? This conclusion might be valid if we can assume that all other factors that distinguish one racial or ethnic group from another are held constant. However, ethnic or racial minorities in the United States and Canada are disproportionately representedv among the poor, and the poor are more apt to develop more severe psychological disorders. Thus, differences we find among racial or ethnic groups may be a function of poverty, not race or ethnicity. These differences also may be due to stereotyping of minorities by clinicians when making diagnostic judgments, rather than due to true differences in underlying rates of the disorder.
4. *Bear in mind that correlation is not causation.* Consider the relationship between depression and stress. Evidence shows a positive correlation between these variables, which means depressed people tend to encounter high levels of stress (e.g., Drieling, van Calker, & Hecht, 2006; Kendler, Kuhn, & Prescott, 2004). But does stress cause depression? Perhaps it does. Or perhaps depression leads to greater stress. After all, depressive symptoms are stressful in themselves and may lead to additional stress as a person finds it increasingly difficult to meet life responsibilities, such as keeping up with work at school or on the job. Perhaps the two variables are not causally linked at all but are linked through a third variable, such as an underlying genetic factor. Is it possible that people inherit clusters of genes that make them more prone to both depression and stress?
5. *Consider the kinds of evidence on which conclusions are based.* Some conclusions, even seemingly "scientific" conclusions, are based on anecdotes and personal endorsements, not sound research. There is much controversy today about so-called recovered memories that are said to suddenly resurface in adulthood, usually during psychotherapy or hypnosis, and usually involving incidents of sexual abuse committed during childhood by the person's parents or family members. Are such recovered memories accurate? (See Chapter 6.)
6. *Do not oversimplify.* Consider the statement, "Alcoholism is inherited." In Chapter 8, we review evidence suggesting that genetic factors may create a predisposition to alcoholism, at least in males. However, the origins of alcoholism, as well as of schizophrenia, depression, and physical health problems such as cancer and heart disease, are complex and reflect the interplay of biological and environmental factors. For instance, people may inherit a predisposition to develop a particular disorder but may be able to avoid developing it if they live in a healthy environment or learn to manage stress effectively.
7. *Do not overgeneralize.* In Chapter 6, we consider evidence showing that a history of severe abuse in childhood figures prominently in the great majority of people who later develop multiple personalities. Does this mean that most abused children go on to develop multiple personalities? Not at all. Actually, very few do.

# Summing Up

## How Do We Define Abnormal Behavior?

### Criteria for Determining Abnormality

**1.1 Identify criteria professionals use to determine whether behavior is abnormal and apply these criteria to case examples discussed in the text.**

A psychological disorder is a pattern of abnormal behavior associated with significant personal distress or impaired functioning or behavior. Psychologists consider behavior abnormal when it meets some combination of the following criteria: when behavior is (a) unusual or statistically infrequent, (b) socially unacceptable or in violation of social norms, (c) fraught with misperceptions or misinterpretations of reality, (d) associated with states of severe personal distress, (e) maladaptive or self-defeating, or (f) dangerous. Psychological disorders are patterns of abnormal behavior associated with states of emotional distress or impaired behavior or ability to function.

The case of Phil illustrated the psychological disorder of claustrophobia, which involves an excessive fear of enclosed spaces. His behavior was abnormal on the basis of the criteria of unusualness, personal distress, and impaired ability to meet occupational and family responsibilities. The woman who cowered under the blankets was diagnosed with bipolar disorder, a psychological disorder characterized by personal distress and difficulty functioning effectively, as well as by possible self-defeating behavior, dangerous behavior (self-harm), and, as in this case, faulty perception or interpretations of reality. Thomas suffered from both schizophrenia and depression. His behavior demonstrated unusualness (deviant or bizarre behavior), disturbed perceptions or interpretations of reality (delusions and hallucinations), maladaptive behavior (difficulty meeting responsibilities of daily life), and personal distress. These disorders may also involve dangerous behavior, as in suicidal behavior.

### Abnormal Psychology—By the Numbers

**1.2 Describe the current and lifetime prevalence of psychological disorders in the United States and describe differences in prevalence as a function of gender and age.**

Nearly half of adult Americans are affected by diagnosable psychological disorders at some point in their lifetimes; about one in four is affected in any given year. Women are more likely to develop psychological disorders, and young adults aged 18 to 25 are about twice as likely to be affected as adults over the age of 50.

### Cultural Bases of Abnormal Behavior

**1.3 Describe the cultural bases of abnormal behavior.**

Behaviors deemed normal in one culture may be considered abnormal in another. Concepts of health and illness are also different in different cultures. Abnormal behavior patterns also take different forms in different cultures, and societal views or models explaining abnormal behavior vary across cultures.

## Historical Perspectives on Abnormal Behavior

### The Demonological Model

**1.4 Describe the demonological model of abnormal behavior.**

The demonological model represents the belief in ancient times that abnormal behavior was the result of evil or demonic spirits or supernatural forces. In medieval times, abnormal behavior was considered a sign of possession by the Devil, and exorcism was intended to rid the possessed of the evil spirits that afflicted them.

### Origins of the Medical Model: In "Ill Humor"

**1.5 Describe the origins of the medical model of abnormal behavior.**

Although demonological explanations of abnormal behavior held sway in early Western culture, some physicians, such as Hippocrates, argued in favor of natural causes. Hippocrates foreshadowed the modern medical model by proposing a system for classifying abnormal behavior patterns and arguing that abnormal behavior results from underlying biological processes.

### Medieval Times

**1.6 Describe the treatment of mental patients during medieval times.**

Asylums, or madhouses, arose throughout Europe in the late 15th and early 16th centuries to house people whose behavior was severely disturbed. Conditions in these asylums were dreadful and the behavior of the residents was sometimes put on display for the amusement of the general public.

### The Reform Movement and Moral Therapy

**1.7 Identify the leading reformers of the treatment of the mentally ill and describe the principle underlying moral therapy and the changes that occurred in the treatment of mental patients during the 19th and early 20th centuries.**

The leading reformers were Frenchmen Jean-Baptiste Pussin and Philippe Pinel in France, William Tuke in England, and

Dorothea Dix in the United States. Proponents of moral therapy believed that mental patients could be restored to functioning if they were treated with dignity and understanding. With the rise of moral therapy in the 19th century, conditions in mental hospitals generally improved. However, the decline of moral therapy in the latter part of the 19th century led to the belief that the "insane" could not be treated successfully. During this period of apathy, mental hospitals deteriorated, offering little more than custodial care. It was not until the middle of the 20th century that public concern about the plight of mental patients lead to the development of community mental health centers as alternatives to long-term hospitalization.

### The Role of the Mental Hospital Today

**1.8 Describe the role of mental hospitals in the mental health system.**

Mental hospitals today provide structured treatment environments for people in acute crisis and for those who are unable to adapt to community living.

### The Community Mental Health Movement

**1.9 Describe the goals and outcomes of the community mental health movement.**

The community mental health movement seeks to provide community-based treatment of people with severe mental health problems. As a result of deinstitutionalization, the population of state mental hospitals has been greatly reduced. However, under the policy of deinstitutionalization, many people with severe and persistent mental health problems have not received the quality of care and range of services they need to adjust to community living. One example of the challenges yet to be met by the community mental health movement is the large number of homeless people with severe psychological problems who are not receiving adequate care in the community.

## Contemporary Perspectives on Abnormal Behavior

### The Biological Perspective

**1.10 Describe the medical model of abnormal behavior.**

The medical model conceptualizes abnormal behavior patterns, like physical diseases, in terms of clusters of symptoms, called syndromes, that have distinctive causes presumed to be biological in nature.

### The Psychological Perspective

**1.11 Identify the major psychological models of abnormal behavior.**

Psychological models focus on the psychological roots of abnormal behavior and derive from psychoanalytic, behavioral, humanistic, and cognitive perspectives.

### The Sociocultural Perspective

**1.12 Describe the sociocultural perspective on abnormal behavior.**

The sociocultural model emphasizes a broader perspective that takes into account social contexts in which abnormal behavior occurs, including factors relating to human diversity, socioeconomic level, and exposure to discrimination and prejudice.

### The Biopsychosocial Perspective

**1.13 Describe the biopsychosocial perspective on abnormal behavior.**

Many theorists today subscribe to a broad-based perspective, called the biopsychosocial model, that posits that multiple causes—representing biological, psychological, and sociocultural domains—interact in the development of abnormal behavior patterns.

## Research Methods in Abnormal Psychology

### Description, Explanation, Prediction, and Control: The Objectives of Science

**1.14 Identify four major objectives of science.**

The scientific approach focuses on four general objectives: description, explanation, prediction, and control.

### The Scientific Method

**1.15 Identify the four major steps in the scientific method.**

There are four steps to the scientific method: (1) formulating a research question, (2) framing the research question in the form of a hypothesis, (3) testing the hypothesis, and (4) drawing conclusions about the correctness of the hypothesis.

### Ethics in Research

**1.16 Identify the ethical principles that guide research in psychology.**

The guiding ethical principles governing research in psychology include (a) informed consent and (b) protecting the confidentiality of records of research participants and not disclosing their identities to others.

### The Naturalistic Observation Method

**1.17 Explain the role of the naturalistic method of research and describe its key features.**

In naturalistic observation, the investigator carefully observes behavior in field settings in order to better understand the occurrence of the behavior in natural settings. Observers need to ensure that they do not affect the behavior they are observing. Although naturalistic observation may provide information about naturally occurring behaviors, it cannot pinpoint cause-and-effect relationships.

## The Correlational Method

**1.18 Explain the role of the correlational method of research and describe its key features.**

The correlational method of research explores relationships between variables in order to predict future occurrences, suggest possible underlying causes of behavior, and understand how variables relate to each other. Investigators use statistical methods to measure the association or strength of relationship between variables. However, correlational research does not demonstrate cause-and-effect relationships because the variables under study are merely observed or measured by experimenters rather than directly manipulated. Longitudinal research is a type of correlational study in which a sample of research participants are repeatedly studied at periodic intervals over long periods of time, sometimes spanning decades.

## The Experimental Method

**1.19 Explain the role of the experimental method of research and describe its key features.**

The experimental method is used to test cause-and-effect relationships by means of manipulating the independent variable under controlled conditions. Investigators use random assignment to determine which research participants receive the experimental treatment and which do not (controls). Investigators may use single-blind and double-blind research designs to control for potential subject and experimenter expectances. Experiments are evaluated in terms of internal, external, and construct validity.

## The Epidemiological Method

**1.20 Explain the role of the epidemiological method of research and describe its key features.**

Epidemiological studies examine the rates of occurrence of abnormal behavior in various population groups or settings in order to better understand how psychological disorders are distributed throughout a population. These studies may point to possible causal relationships, but they lack the power of experimental studies to isolate causal factors.

## Kinship Studies

**1.21 Explain the role of kinship studies and describe their key features.**

Kinship studies, including twin studies and adoptee studies, attempt to differentiate the contributions to abnormal behavior of environmental and genetic factors. However, these types of studies are limited because the findings of studies based on twins and adopted children may not be generalizable to the general population. Similarities among identical twins may also reflect common environmental factors rather than genetic overlap.

## Case Studies

**1.22 Explain the role of case studies and describe their limitations.**

Case studies provide rich material about the personal lives and treatment of individuals with psychological disorders, but they are limited by difficulty obtaining accurate and unbiased client histories, by possible therapist biases, and by the lack of control groups. Single-case experimental designs help researchers overcome some of these limitations.

# Critical Thinking Questions

On the basis of your reading of this chapter, answer the following questions:

- Give an example of a behavior (other than behaviors in the text) that might be deemed normal in one culture but abnormal in another.
- How have beliefs about abnormal behavior changed over time? What changes have occurred in how society treats people whose behavior is deemed abnormal?
- Why should we not assume that because two variables are correlated they are causally linked?
- What are the two major types of placebo-control studies? What are they intended to control? What is the major limitation of these designs?
- How do investigators separate the effects of heredity and environment in the study of abnormal behavior?

## Key Terms

psychological disorder, p. 4
abnormal psychology, p. 4
medical model, p. 4
trephination, p. 10
humors, p. 11
deinstitutionalization, p. 14
dementia praecox, p. 17
general paresis, p. 17
syndromes, p. 17
psychodynamic model, p. 18
biopsychosocial model, p. 19
scientific method, p. 21
theory, p. 22
hypothesis, p. 23
informed consent, p. 23
confidentiality, p. 23
naturalistic observation method, p. 24
correlational method, p. 24
correlation coefficient, p. 24
longitudinal study, p. 25
experimental method, p. 25
independent variables, p. 25
dependent variables, p. 25
experimental group, p. 26
control group, p. 26
random assignment, p. 26
selection factor, p. 26
blind, p. 26
placebo, p. 26
internal validity, p. 27
external validity, p. 28
construct validity, p. 28
epidemiological method, p. 28
survey method, p. 28
incidence, p. 28
prevalence, p. 28
random sample, p. 29
genotype, p. 30
phenotype, p. 30
proband, p. 30
adoptee studies, p. 30
case studies, p. 31
single-case experimental design, p. 31
reversal design, p. 31
critical thinking, p. 33

Chapter 2

# Contemporary Perspectives on Abnormal Behavior and Methods of Treatment

## Learning Objectives

**2.1** **Identify** the major parts of the neuron, the nervous system, and the cerebral cortex, and **describe** their functions.

**2.2** **Evaluate** biological perspectives on abnormal behavior.

**2.3** **Describe** the key features of psychodynamic models of abnormal behavior and **evaluate** their major contributions.

**2.4** **Describe** the key features of learning-based models of abnormal behavior and **evaluate** their major contributions.

**2.5** **Describe** the key features of humanistic models of abnormal behavior and **evaluate** their major contributions.

**2.6** **Describe** the key features of cognitive models of abnormal behavior and **evaluate** their major contributions.

**2.7** **Evaluate** ethnic group differences in rates of psychological disorders.

**2.8** **Evaluate** the sociocultural perspective in our understanding of abnormal behavior.

**2.9** **Describe** the diathesis-stress model of abnormal behavior.

**2.10** **Evaluate** the biopsychosocial perspective on abnormal behavior.

**2.11** **Identify** three of the major types of helping professionals and **describe** their training backgrounds and professional roles.

**2.12** **Describe** the goals and techniques of following forms of psychotherapy: psychodynamic therapy, behavior therapy, person-centered therapy, cognitive therapy, cognitive-behavioral therapy, eclectic therapy, group therapy, family therapy, and couple therapy.

**2.13** **Evaluate** the effectiveness of psychotherapy and the role of nonspecific factors in therapy.

**2.14** **Evaluate** the role of multicultural factors in psychotherapy and barriers to use of mental health services by ethnic minorities.

**2.15** **Identify** the major categories of psychotropic or psychiatric drugs and examples of drugs in each type, and **evaluate** their strengths and weaknesses.

**2.16** **Describe** the use of electroconvulsive therapy and psychosurgery and **evaluate** their effectiveness.

**2.17** **Describe** the use of psychosurgery and **evaluate** its effectiveness.

**2.18** **Evaluate** biomedical treatment approaches.

## TRUTH or FICTION

**T☑ F☐** Anxiety can give you indigestion. (p. 46)

**T☑ F☐** Scientists have not discovered any one gene that causes a psychological disorder. (p. 48)

**T☑ F☐** We one day may be able to silence certain genes or activate others to treat or even prevent psychological disorders. (p. 49)

**T☑ F☐** According to a leading cognitive theorist, people's beliefs about their life experiences cause their emotional problems, not the experiences themselves. (p. 64)

**T☑ F☐** Some psychologists have been trained to prescribe drugs. (p. 71)

**T☑ F☐** In classical psychoanalysis, clients are asked to express whatever thought happens to come to mind, no matter how seemingly trivial or silly. (p. 73)

**T☐ F☑** Psychotherapy is no more effective than simply letting time take its course. (p. 81)

**T☐ F☑** Antidepressants are used only to treat depression. (p. 90)

**T☑ F☐** Sending jolts of electricity into a person's brain can often help relieve severe depression. (p. 91)

**CHAPTER INTRODUCTION: CONTEMPORARY PERSPECTIVES ON ABNORMAL BEHAVIOR AND METHODS OF TREATMENT**

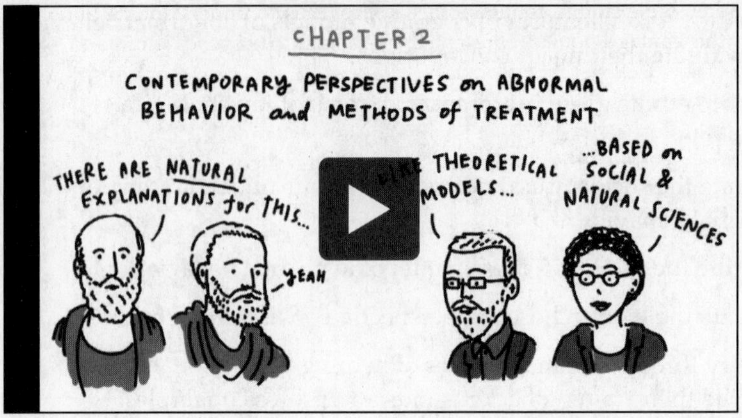


**"I"**

**Jessica's "Little Secret"**

I don't want Ken [her fiancé] to find out. I don't want to bring this into the marriage. I probably should have told him, but I just couldn't do it. Every time I wanted to I just froze up. I guess I figured I'd get over this before the wedding. I have to stop bingeing and throwing up. I just can't stop myself. You know, I want to stop, but I get to thinking about the food I've eaten and it sickens me. I picture myself getting all fat and bloated and I just have to rush to the bathroom and throw it up. I would go on binges, and then throw it all up. It made me feel like I was in control, but really I wasn't.

I have this little ritual when I throw up. I go to the bathroom and run the water in the sink. Nobody ever hears me puking. It's my little secret. I make sure to clean up really well and spray some Lysol before leaving the bathroom. No one suspects I have a problem. Well, that's not quite true. The only one who suspects is my dentist. He said my teeth were beginning to decay from stomach acid. I'm only 20 and I've got rotting teeth. Isn't that awful?

Now I've started throwing up even when I don't binge. Sometimes just eating dinner makes me want to puke. I've just got to get the food out of my body—fast, you know. Right after dinner, I make some excuse about needing to go to the bathroom. It's not every time but at least several times a week. After lunch sometimes, too. I know I need help. It's taken me a long time to come here, but you know I'm getting married in three months and I've got to stop.

*From the Author's Files*

*Jessica, a 20-year-old communications major*

Jessica excuses herself from the dinner table, goes to the bathroom, sticks a finger down her throat to gag, and throws up her dinner. Sometimes she binges first and then forces herself to throw up. In Chapter 1, we described the criteria that mental health professionals generally use to classify behavior patterns as abnormal—and Jessica's behavior clearly meets several of these criteria. Bingeing and throwing up is a source of personal distress and is maladaptive in the sense that it can lead to serious health consequences, such as decaying teeth (see Chapter 9), and social consequences (which is why Jessica kept it a secret and feared it would damage her upcoming marriage). It is also statistically infrequent, although perhaps not as infrequent as you might think. Jessica was diagnosed with *bulimia nervosa*, a type of eating disorder we discuss in Chapter 9.

How can we understand such abnormal behavior? Since earliest times, humans have sought explanations for strange or deviant behavior, often relying on superstitious or supernatural explanations. In the Middle Ages, the predominant view was that severe forms of abnormal behavior that today we might label *schizophrenia* were caused by demons and other supernatural forces, but even in ancient times, there were some thinkers—such as Hippocrates and Galen—who looked for natural explanations of abnormal behavior. Today, of course, superstition and demonology have given way to theoretical models from the natural and social sciences. These approaches have paved the way not only for a scientifically based understanding of abnormal behavior but also for ways of treating people with psychological disorders.

In this chapter, we examine contemporary approaches to understanding abnormal behavior from the vantage points represented by biological, psychological, and sociocultural perspectives. Many scholars today believe that abnormal behavior patterns are complex phenomena that are best understood by taking into account these multiple perspectives. Each perspective provides a window for examining abnormal behavior, but none captures a complete view of the subject. As we shall see later in this chapter, the biological and psychological perspectives on abnormal behavior give rise to specific treatments for these problems.

# The Biological Perspective

The biological perspective, inspired by scientists and physicians since the time of Hippocrates, focuses on the biological underpinnings of abnormal behavior and the use of biologically based approaches, such as drug therapy, to treat psychological disorders. The biological perspective gave rise to the development of the medical model, which remains a powerful force in contemporary understanding of abnormal behavior. The medical model posits that abnormal behaviors represent symptoms of underlying disorders or diseases—called *mental illnesses*—that have biological causes. The medical model is not synonymous with the biological perspective, however. We can speak of biological perspectives without adopting the tenets of the medical model. For example, a behavior pattern such as shyness may have a strong genetic (biological) component but not be considered a "symptom" of any underlying "disorder" or illness.

Our understanding of the biological underpinnings of abnormal behavior has grown in recent years. In Chapter 1, we focused on the methods for studying the role of heredity or genetics. Genetics plays a role in many forms of abnormal behavior, as we shall see throughout the text.

We also know that other biological factors, especially the functioning of the nervous system, are involved in the development of abnormal behavior. To better understand the role of the nervous system in abnormal behavior patterns, we first need to learn how the nervous system is organized and how nerve cells communicate with each other. In Chapter 4, we will examine another body system—the *endocrine system*—and the important roles that it plays in the body's response to stress.

## The Nervous System

**2.1 Identify the major parts of the neuron, the nervous system, and the cerebral cortex, and describe their functions.**

Perhaps if you did not have a nervous system, you would never feel nervous—but neither would you see, hear, or move. However, even calm people have nervous systems. The nervous system is made up of **neurons**, which are nerve cells that transmit signals or "messages" throughout the body. These messages allow us to sense an itch from a bug bite, coordinate our vision and muscles to ice skate, write a research paper, solve a math problem, and, in the case of hallucinations, hear or see things that are not really there.

Every neuron has a cell body that contains the nucleus of the cell and metabolizes oxygen to carry out the work of the cell (see Figure 2.1). Short fibers called **dendrites** project from the cell body to receive messages from adjoining neurons. Each neuron has an **axon** that projects trunklike from the cell body. Axons can extend as long as several feet if they are conveying messages between the toes and the spinal cord. Axons terminate in small branching structures aptly called **terminals**. Some neurons are covered with a **myelin sheath**, an insulating layer that helps speed transmission of neural impulses.

**Figure 2.1** Anatomy of a neuron.

The three basic parts of the neuron are the cell body, the dendrites, and the axon. The axon of this neuron is wrapped in a myelin sheath, which insulates it from the bodily fluids surrounding the neuron and facilitates transmission of neural impulses (messages that travel within the neuron).

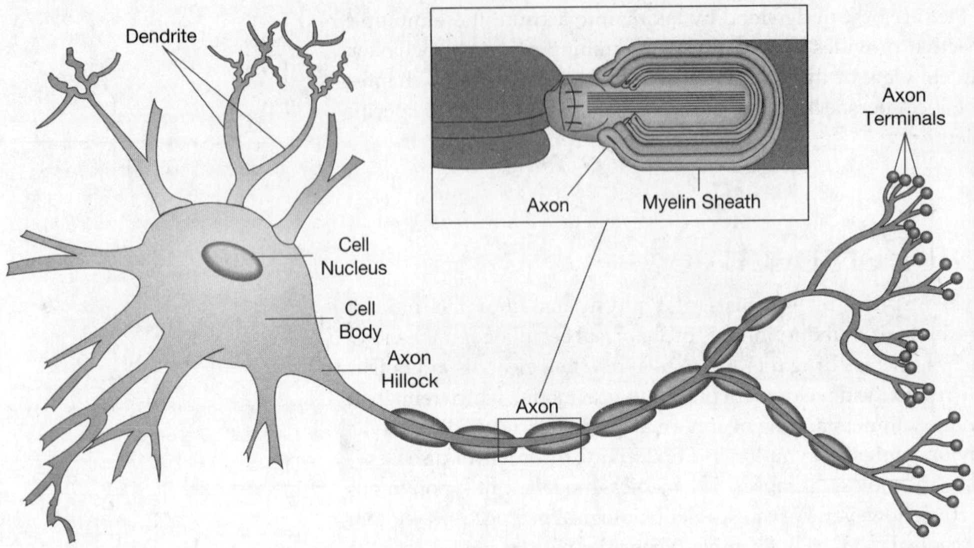


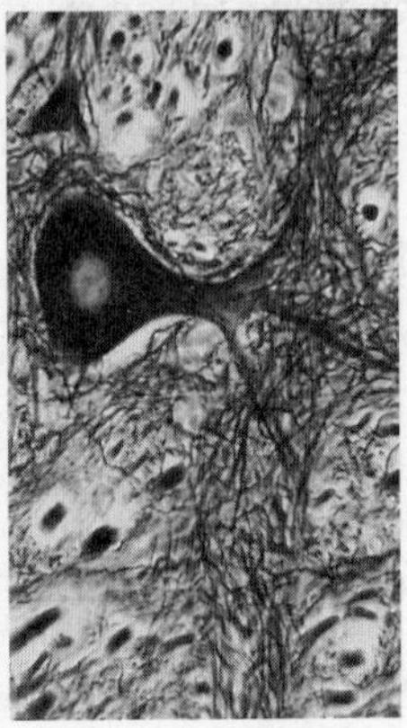

Neurons convey messages from the dendrites or cell body along the axon to the axon terminals. These messages then are conveyed from the terminals to other neurons, muscles, or glands. Neurons transmit messages to other neurons by means of chemical substances called **neurotransmitters**, which induce chemical changes in receiving neurons. These changes cause axons to conduct the messages in electrical form.

The connecting point between neurons is the **synapse**, which is a junction or small gap between a transmitting neuron and a receiving neuron. A message does not jump across the synapse like a spark. Instead, axon terminals release neurotransmitters into the cleft like myriad ships casting off into the sea (Figure 2.2). Each kind of neurotransmitter has a distinctive chemical structure. Each will fit into only one kind of harbor, or **receptor site**, on the receiving neuron. Consider the analogy of a lock and key. Only the right key (neurotransmitter) operates the lock, causing the *post-synaptic* (receiving) neuron to forward the message.

When released, some molecules of a neurotransmitter reach port at receptor sites of other neurons. "Loose" neurotransmitters may be broken down in the synapse by enzymes, or may be reabsorbed by the axon terminal (a process termed *reuptake*), to prevent the receiving cell from continuing to fire.

**CONNECTIONS BETWEEN NEURONS.** This remarkable electron microscope photograph shows connections between neurons. The larger structures are cell bodies of neurons and the stringlike filaments are axons.

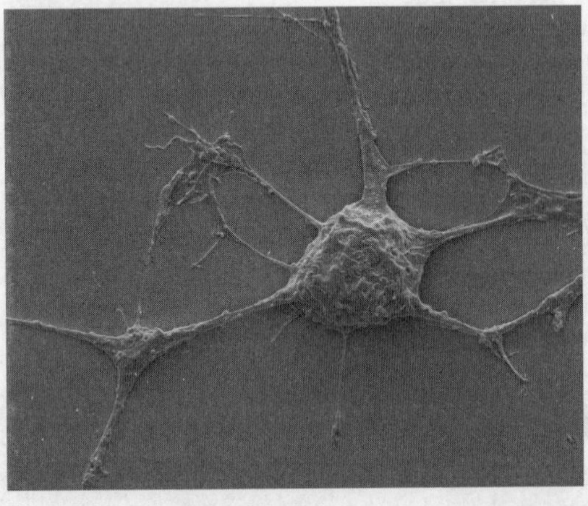

Psychiatric drugs, including drugs used to treat anxiety, depression, and schizophrenia, work by affecting the availability of neurotransmitters in the brain. Consequently, it appears that irregularities in the workings of neurotransmitter systems in the brain play important roles in the development of these abnormal behavior patterns (see Table 2.1).

Depression, for example, is linked to chemical imbalances in the brain involving irregularities in the functioning of several neurotransmitters, especially serotonin (see Chapter 7). Serotonin is a key brain chemical involved in regulating moods, so it is not surprising that it plays a role in depression. Two of the most widely used antidepressant drugs—Prozac and Zoloft—belong to a class of drugs that increase the availability of serotonin in the brain. Serotonin is also linked to anxiety disorders, sleep disorders, and eating disorders.

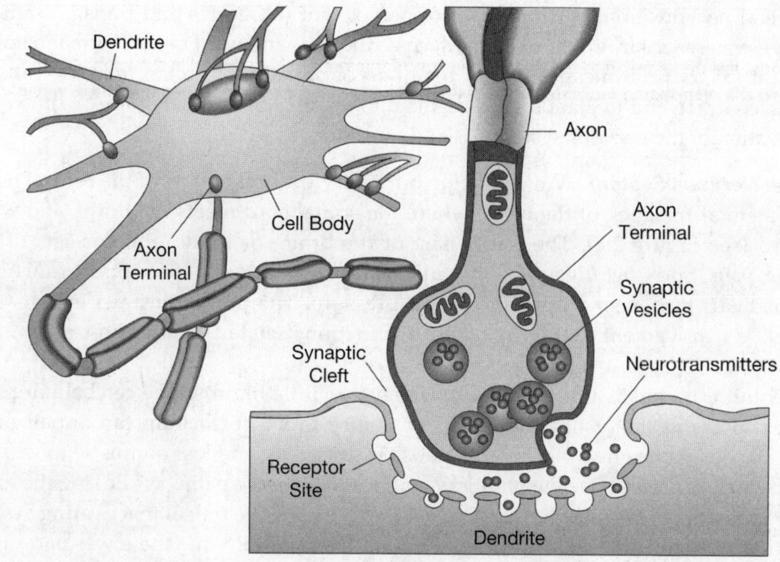


**Figure 2.2** Transmission of neural impulses across the synapse.

Shown here are the structure of the neuron and the mode of transmission of neural impulses between neurons. Neurons transmit messages, or neural impulses, across synapses, which are the tiny gaps between neurons. The "message" is carried by neurotransmitters that are stored in synaptic vesicles at the end of the axon, called an axon terminal, and then released into the synaptic gap or cleft and taken up by receptor sites on dendrites of the receiving neuron. Patterns of firing of many thousands of neurons give rise to psychological events such as thoughts and mental images. Different forms of abnormal behavior are associated with irregularities in the transmission or reception of neural messages.

Alzheimer's disease, a brain disease in which there is a progressive loss of memory and cognitive functioning, is associated with reductions in the levels of the neurotransmitter *acetylcholine* in the brain (see Chapter 14). Irregularities involving the neurotransmitter *dopamine* are implicated in the development of schizophrenia (see Chapter 11). Antipsychotic drugs used to treat schizophrenia apparently work by blocking dopamine receptors in the brain.

Although neurotransmitter systems are implicated in many psychological disorders, the precise causal mechanisms remain to be determined. To learn more about how neurons work, including how they communicate with each other.

HOW THE BRAIN WORKS, PART 1

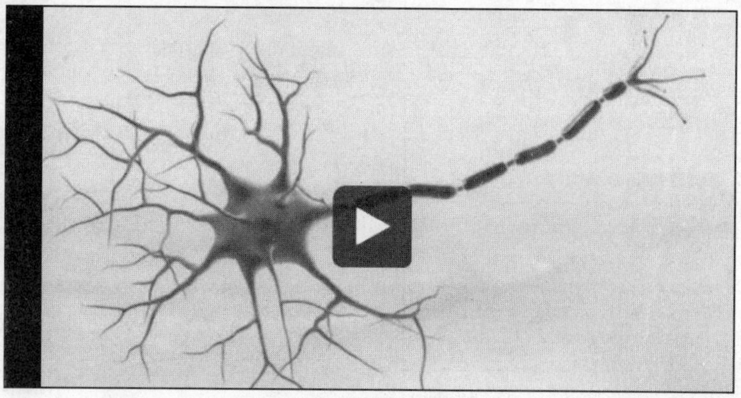

**PARTS OF THE NERVOUS SYSTEM** The nervous system consists of two major parts, the **central nervous system** and the **peripheral nervous system.** The central nervous system consists of the brain and spinal cord, forming the body's master control unit responsible for controlling bodily functions and performing higher mental functions, such as sensation, perception, thinking, and problem solving. The

**Table 2.1** Neurotransmitter Functions and Relationships with Abnormal Behavior Patterns

| Neurotransmitter | Functions | Associations with Abnormal Behavior |
|---|---|---|
| Acetylcholine | Control of muscle contractions and formation of memories | Reduced levels found in patients with Alzheimer's disease (see Chapter 14) |
| Dopamine | Regulation of muscle contractions and mental processes involving learning, memory, and emotions | Irregularities in dopamine transmission in the brain may be involved in the development of schizophrenia (see Chapter 11) |
| Norepinephrine | Mental processes involved in learning and memory | Irregularities linked with mood disorders such as depression (see Chapter 7) |
| Serotonin | Regulation of mood states, satiety, and sleep | Irregularities are implicated in depression and eating disorders (see Chapters 7 and 9) |

peripheral nervous system is made up of nerves that (a) receive and transmit sensory messages (messages from sense organs such as the eyes and ears) to the brain and spinal cord and (b) transmit messages from the brain or spinal cord to the muscles, causing them to contract, and to glands, causing them to secrete hormones. Figure 2.3 shows the organization of the nervous system.

***Central Nervous System*** We will begin our overview of the parts of the central nervous system at the back of the head, where the spinal cord meets the brain, and work forward (see Figure 2.4). The lower part of the brain, or hindbrain, consists of the *medulla, pons,* and *cerebellum*. The **medulla** plays roles in vital life-support functions, such as heart rate, respiration, and blood pressure. The **pons** transmits information about body movement and is involved in functions related to attention, sleep, and respiration.

Behind the pons is the **cerebellum** (Latin for "little brain"). The cerebellum regulates balance and motor (muscle) behavior. Injury to the cerebellum can impair one's ability to coordinate one's movements, causing stumbling and loss of muscle tone.

The *midbrain* lies above the hindbrain and contains nerve pathways linking the hindbrain to the upper region of the brain, called the *forebrain*. The **reticular activating system (RAS)** starts in the hindbrain and rises through the midbrain into the lower part of the forebrain. The RAS is a weblike network of neurons that play important roles in regulating sleep, attention, and states of arousal. Stimulation of the RAS heightens alertness. On the other hand, use of *depressant drugs*, such as alcohol, dampens central nervous system

Figure 2.3 The organization of the nervous system.

**SOURCE:** Adapted from J. S. Nevid (2007). *Psychology: Concepts and applications*, 2nd ed. (p. 56). Boston: Houghton Mifflin Company. Reprinted by permission.

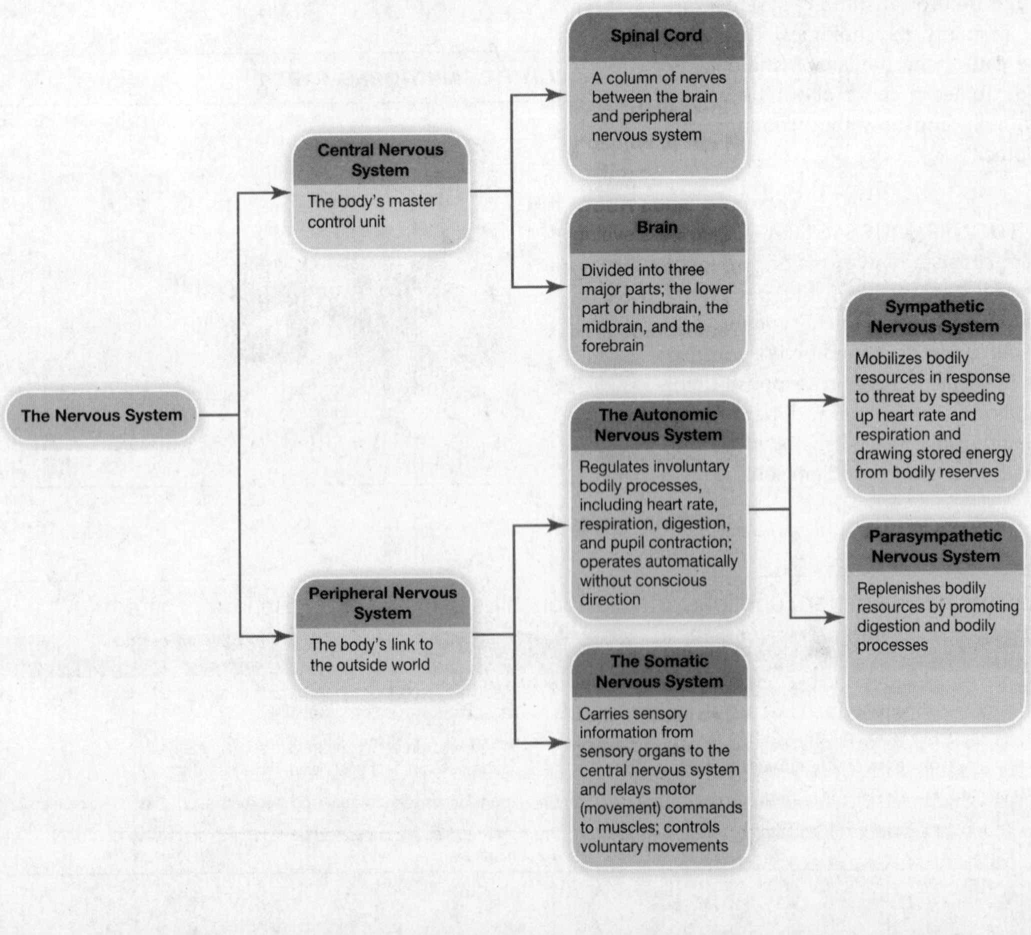

**Figure 2.4** The geography of the brain.

Part A shows parts of the hindbrain, midbrain, and forebrain. Part B shows the four lobes of the cerebral cortex: frontal, parietal, temporal, and occipital. In Part B, the sensory (tactile) and motor areas lie across the central fissure from one another. Researchers are investigating the potential relationships between various patterns of abnormal behavior and abnormalities in the formation or functioning of the structures of the brain.

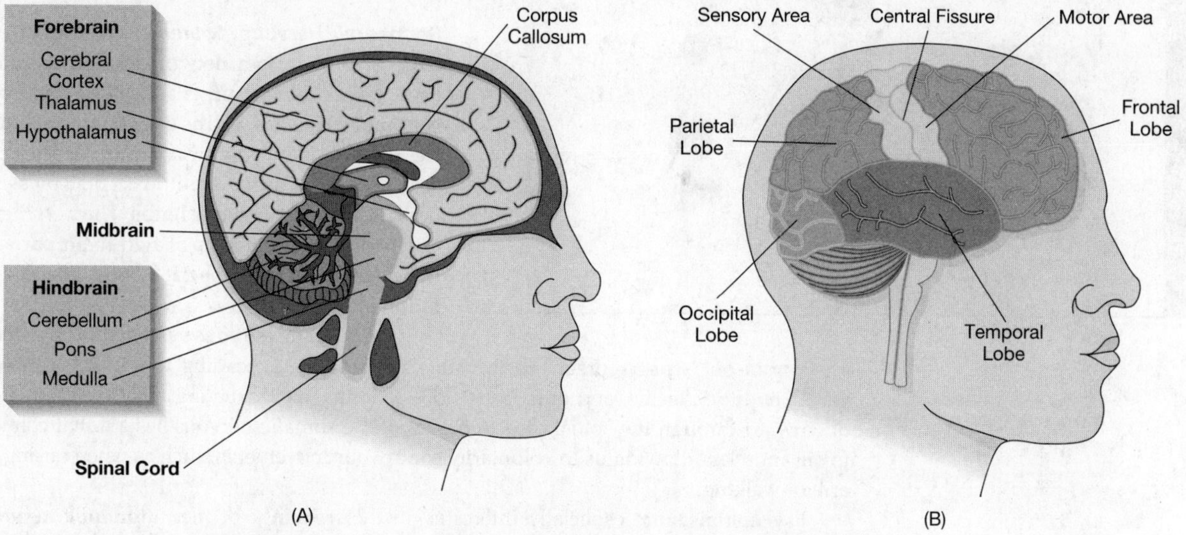


activity, which reduces RAS activity and can induce states of grogginess or even stupor. (Effects of depressants and other drugs are discussed further in Chapter 8.)

The large frontal area of the brain, called the *forebrain*, includes structures such as the thalamus, hypothalamus, basal ganglia, and cerebrum. The **thalamus** relays sensory information (such as tactile and visual stimulation) to the higher regions of the brain. The thalamus, in coordination with the RAS, is also involved in regulating sleep and attention.

The **hypothalamus** (*hypo* means *under*) is a tiny, pea-sized structure located under the thalamus. Despite its small size, the hypothalamus plays a key role in many vital bodily functions, including regulation of body temperature, concentration of fluids in the blood, and reproductive processes, as well as emotional and motivational states. By implanting electrodes in parts of the hypothalamus of animals and observing the effects when a current is switched on, researchers have found that the hypothalamus is involved in a range of motivational drives and behaviors, including hunger, thirst, sex, parenting behaviors, and aggression.

The hypothalamus and parts of the thalamus and other nearby interconnected structures together make up the brain's **limbic system**. The limbic system plays important roles in emotional processing and memory. It also serves important functions for regulating more basic drives involving hunger, thirst, and aggression. The **basal ganglia** lie at the base of the forebrain and are involved in regulating postural movements and coordination.

The **cerebrum** is the brain's crowning glory. It is responsible for higher mental functions, such as thinking and problem solving, and also accounts for the delightfully rounded shape of the human head. The surface of the cerebrum is convoluted with ridges and valleys. This surface area is called the **cerebral cortex**. It is the thinking, planning, and executive center of the brain, as well as the seat of consciousness and the sense of self.

Structural or functional abnormalities of brain structures are involved in various forms of abnormal behavior. For example, investigators have found abnormalities in parts of the cerebral cortex and limbic system in patients with schizophrenia (discussed in Chapter 11). The hypothalamus is implicated in certain types of sleep disorders (see Chapter 9), and deterioration of the basal ganglia is associated with Huntington's disease—a degenerative disease that can lead to disturbances of mood, paranoia, and even dementia (see Chapter 14). These are but a few of the brain–behavior relationships we shall discuss in later sections of this text.

HOW THE BRAIN WORKS, PART 2

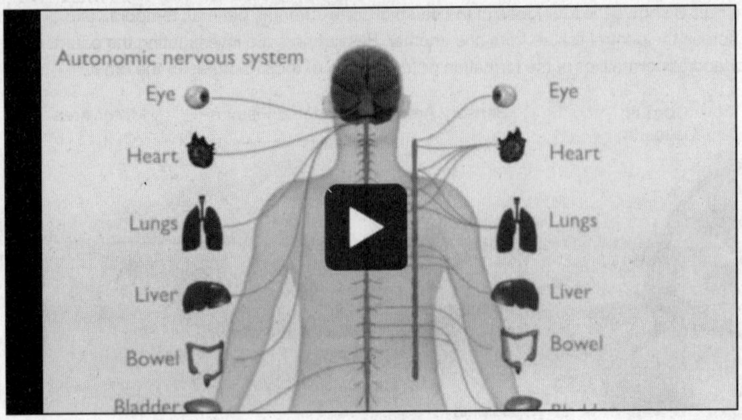


***Peripheral Nervous System*** The peripheral nervous system is a network of neurons connecting the brain to our sense organs—our eyes, ears, and so on—as well as our glands and muscles. These neural pathways allow us to both sense the world around us and act on it by using our muscles to move our limbs. The peripheral nervous system consists of two main parts or divisions, called the *somatic nervous system* and the *autonomic nervous system* (see Figure 2.3).

The **somatic nervous system** transmits messages from our sensory organs to the brain for processing, leading to the experience of visual, auditory, tactile, and other sensations. Commands emanating from the brain pass downward through the spinal cord to nerves of the somatic nervous system that connect to our muscles, allowing us to voluntarily control our movements, such as when raising an arm or walking.

Psychologists are especially interested in the workings of the **autonomic nervous system (ANS)** because of its role in emotional processing. *Autonomic* means *automatic*. The ANS regulates the glands and involuntary processes such as heart rate, breathing, digestion, and dilation of the pupils of the eyes, even when we are sleeping.

The ANS has two branches, the **sympathetic nervous system** and the **parasympathetic nervous system.** These branches have mostly opposing effects. Many organs and glands are served by both branches of the ANS. The sympathetic division is most involved in processes that mobilize the body's resources during physical exertion or responses to stress, such as when drawing energy from stored reserves to prepare a person to deal with imposing threats or dangers (see Chapter 4). When we face a threatening or dangerous situation, the sympathetic branch of the ANS kicks in by accelerating our heart rate and breathing rate, thereby preparing our body to either fight or flee from a threatening stressor. Sympathetic activation in the face of a threatening stimulus is associated with emotional responses such as fear or anxiety. When we relax, the parasympathetic branch decelerates the heart rate. The parasympathetic division is most active during processes that replenish energy reserves, such as digestion. Because the sympathetic branch dominates when we are fearful or anxious, fear or anxiety can lead to indigestion: Activation of the sympathetic nervous system interferes with parasympathetic control of digestive activity. **T / F**

## TRUTH *or* FICTION

Anxiety can give you indigestion.

☑ **TRUE** Anxiety is accompanied by increased arousal of the sympathetic nervous system, which can interfere with parasympathetic control of digestion.

***The Cerebral Cortex*** The parts of the brain responsible for higher mental functions, such as thought and use of language, are the two large masses of the cerebrum called the right and left *cerebral hemispheres*. The outer layer or covering of each hemisphere is called the cerebral cortex. (The word *cortex* literally means *bark* and is so used because the cerebral cortex can be likened to the bark of a tree.) Each hemisphere is divided into four parts, called *lobes*, as shown in Figure 2.4. The *occipital lobe* is primarily involved in processing visual stimuli; the *temporal lobe* is involved in processing sounds or auditory stimuli. The *parietal lobe* is involved in processing sensations of touch, temperature, and pain. The *sensory area* of the parietal lobe receives messages from receptors in the skin all over the body. Neurons in the motor area (also called the *motor cortex*) in the *frontal lobes* control muscle movements, allowing us to walk and move our limbs. The *prefrontal cortex* (the part of the frontal lobe that lies in front of the motor cortex) regulates higher mental functions, such as thinking, problem solving, and use of language.

# Evaluating Biological Perspectives on Abnormal Behavior

## 2.2 Evaluate biological perspectives on abnormal behavior.

**A HUMAN BEING, DECODED.** Here we see a portion of the human genome, the genetic code of a human being. Scientists recognize that genes play an important role in determining predispositions for many psychological traits and disorders. Whether these predispositions are expressed depends on the interactions of genetic and environmental influences.

Biological structures and processes are involved in many patterns of abnormal behavior, as we will see in later chapters. Genetic factors, as well as disturbances in neurotransmitter functioning and underlying brain abnormalities or defects, are implicated in many psychological disorders. For some disorders, such as Alzheimer's disease, biological processes play the direct causative role. (Even then, however, the precise causes remain unknown.) For most disorders, however, we need to examine the interaction of biological and environmental factors.

We each possess a unique genetic code that plays an important role in determining our risks of developing many physical and mental disorders (Hyman, 2011; Kendler et al., 2011). A large body of evidence connects genetic factors to a wide range of psychological disorders, including schizophrenia, bipolar (manic–depressive) disorder, major depression, alcoholism, autism, dementia due to Alzheimer's disease, anxiety disorders, dyslexia, and antisocial personality disorder (e.g., Agerbo et al., 2015; Duffy et al., 2014; Kendler et al., 2011; Psychiatric GWAS Consortium Bipolar Disorder Working Group, 2011; Vacic et al., 2011). The heritable characteristics that increase the risk of psychological disorders include genetic variations (variations in particular genes among people) and genetic mutations (changes in genes from generation to generation).

Scientists are now searching for specific genes involved in psychological disorders such as schizophrenia, mood disorders, and autism (e.g., Boot et al., 2012; Dennis et al., 2012; Sakai et al., 2011). The hope is that in the not-too-distant future, it will be possible to block the actions of defective or harmful genes or enhance the actions of beneficial genes.

Genes play important roles in determining vulnerability or susceptibility to many psychological disorders—but genes don't tell the whole story when it comes to understanding the origins of these disorders. Unlike some physical disorders caused by a single gene, psychological disorders are complex behavioral phenomena that involve multiple genes acting together, along with environmental factors (Nigg, 2013).

Questions about the genetic bases of abnormal behavior touch upon a long-standing debate in psychology, arguably the longest debate—the so-called nature versus nurture debate. The debate has shifted from one pitting nature against nurture to one framed in terms of how much of our behavior is a product of nature (genes) and how much is a product of nurture (environment).

A recent large-scale review of twin studies basically called it even, with genetics and environment each explaining about half of the variation in personality traits and diseases (Polderman et al., 2015). Scientists today are studying complex interactions between genes and environmental factors, such as stress, to better understand the determinants of abnormal behavior patterns (e.g., Eley et al., 2015; van der Meer et al., 2015; Tabak et al., 2016). As the debate over nature and nurture continues to unfold, let us offer a few key points to consider:

1. *Genes do not dictate behavioral outcomes.* Evidence of a genetic contribution in psychological disorders is arguably strongest in the case of schizophrenia. However, as discussed in Chapter 11, even in the case of monozygotic twins who share 100% genetic overlap, when one of the monozygotic twins has schizophrenia, the chance of the other twin having the disorder is slightly less than 50%. In other words, genetics alone does not account for schizophrenia, or any other psychological disorder.
2. *Genetic factors create a predisposition or likelihood—not a certainty—that certain behaviors or disorders will develop.* Genes do not directly cause psychological disorders. Rather, they create predispositions that increase the risk or likelihood of developing particular disorders. Our genes are carried in our chromosomes from the moment of conception and are not affected directly by the environment. However, the effects that genes have on the body and mind may be influenced by environmental factors such as life experiences, family relationships, and life stress (Kendler, 2005; Moffitt, Caspi, & Rutter, 2006).

> **TRUTH or FICTION**
>
> Scientists have not discovered any one gene that causes a psychological disorder.
>
> ☑ TRUE Scientists believe that many genes contribute to the complex behavior patterns associated with psychological disorders, not any one gene.

Even ethnicity and gender may influence how genes operate in the body (Williams et al., 2003).

3. *Multigenic determinism affects psychological disorders.* In disorders in which genetic factors play a role, multiple genes are involved, not individual genes acting alone (Hamilton, 2008; Uhl & Grow, 2004). Scientists have yet to find any psychological disorder that can be explained by defects or variations of a single gene. **T / F**
4. *Genetic factors and environmental influence interact with each other in shaping our personalities and determining our vulnerability to a range of psychological disorders.* The contemporary view of the nature–nurture debate boils down to the understanding of nature and nurture acting together, not nature versus nurture.

One example of the gene–environment interaction occurs when genes increase sensitivity to environmental influences (Dick, 2011). For example, harsh or neglectful parenting may lead to psychological problems, but not all children exposed to a harsh upbringing go on to develop psychological disorders. Some people have genetic tendencies that make them more sensitive to negative effects of these environmental influences (Polanczyk et al., 2009). Complicating the picture further is that environmental influences can also affect the expression of genetic traits, a topic we examine in *A Closer Look: Epigenetics—The Study of How the Environment Affects Genetic Expression.*

## A CLOSER Look

### EPIGENETICS—THE STUDY OF HOW THE ENVIRONMENT AFFECTS GENETIC EXPRESSION

The genetic code imprinted in an organism's DNA provides a set of instructions for building an organism. It determines, for example, that certain cells will differentiate into lungs (for humans) rather than gills (for fish), as well as physical traits such as eye color, height, and hair color and texture. The genetic code also influences the development of behavioral characteristics, including intelligence, personality traits, and tendencies to develop various psychological disorders. Throughout this text, we examine the role of genetics in many of these disorders, from anxiety disorders to mood disorders to schizophrenia, among others. The great majority of psychological disorders, perhaps even all to a certain extent, are influenced by genetic factors. What about the reverse? Can environment influence the workings of our genes? Indeed it can.

The field of **epigenetics** focuses on how environmental factors such as stress influence the expression of genetic characteristics, or genotype, into a set of physical and behavioral traits, or phenotype (Isles, 2015; Pizzimenti & Lattal, 2015). The ability of genes to influence observable traits depends on whether they are actively expressed. Each human cell contains the full complement or set of genes, excepting sperm and ova, which contain half the genetic complement. However, perhaps only about 10% to 20% of genes in a given cell are active (Coila, 2009). Thus, genes that code for eye color are active in the eyes, but not in other parts of the body, such as the liver. Environmental factors affect gene expression by influencing the release of certain bodily chemicals that either turn genes on or turn them off, even though the genetic content (or code) itself remains unchanged. For example, biochemical changes in the brain can affect the functioning of genes linked to the development of depression and schizophrenia (Jaffe et al., 2016; Lockwood, Su, & Youssef, 2015).

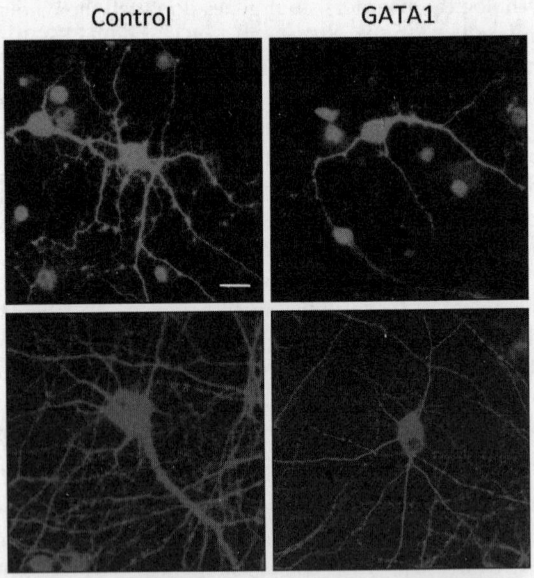


**GENE EXPRESSION IN PSYCHOLOGICAL DISORDERS.** Scientists are studying gene expression in psychological disorders such as depression. Some genes are expressed (turned on and off) differently in the brains of depressed people than in those of other people. Investigators found that turning on a particular gene (Gata1) linked to depression in humans decreased the density of synaptic connections (right) between neurons in the rat brain as compared to controls (left). The density of synaptic connections may play a role in depression in humans. Research along these lines may eventually lead to new targets for treating depression or other psychological disorders.

Let's think about in the following way: Embedded in your computer are codes (software) directing it to perform all of its programs, including web-browsing programs that allow you to surf the net. However, you first need to turn on the power to activate the instructions encoded in the software. Otherwise, the computer is merely a black box that sits there until you flick the power switch. In a similar way, the codes embedded in our genes are a kind of biological software, but whether or not they become expressed or active can be affected by environmental influences that either turn on or turn off these genetic switches (Franklin, Russig, et al., 2011; Murphy et al., 2013). For example, early life experiences, such as stress, diet, sexual or physical abuse, and exposure to toxic chemicals, may determine whether certain genes become switched on or remain dormant later in life. Investigators find that severe abuse in early childhood can alter gene expression, perhaps setting the stage later in life for the development of depression or other emotional disorders (Labonté et al., 2012).

Environmental factors may lead to chemical processes in the body that "tag" or mark certain genes for either activation or suppression but do not change the genetic code or DNA sequence itself. These "tags" may become part of the organism's genetic inheritance that is then passed along to offspring, affecting the workings of genes in future generations (Cloud, 2010; Yehuda et al., 2015). Recently, scientists discovered chemical changes that affect the functioning of DNA in patients with schizophrenia (Melas et al., 2012).

The field of epigenetics is still in its infancy, but scientists hope that by learning more about how environmental factors influence gene expression, we may someday be able to silence certain genes or activate others to treat or even prevent psychological disorders (Dalton, Kolshus, & McLoughlin, 2014; Dempster et al., 2011; Nestler, 2011). **T / F**

**TRUTH or FICTION**

We one day may be able to silence certain genes or activate others to treat or even prevent psychological disorders.

☑ **TRUE** Advances in the field of epigenetics raise hopes that scientists may one day be able to directly control genes involved in mental and physical disorders.

As we continue to learn more about the biological foundations of abnormal behavior patterns, we should recognize that the interface between biology and behavior is a two-way street. Researchers have uncovered links between psychological factors and many physical disorders and conditions (see Chapter 4). Researchers are also investigating whether the combination of psychological and drug treatments for problems such as depression, anxiety disorders, and substance abuse disorders may improve upon the therapeutic benefits of either of the two approaches alone.

# The Psychological Perspective

At about the time that biological models of abnormal behavior were becoming prominent in the late 19th century with the contributions of Kraepelin, Griesinger, and others, another approach to understanding abnormal behavior began to emerge. This approach emphasized the psychological roots of abnormal behavior and was most closely identified with the work of the Austrian physician Sigmund Freud. Over time, other psychological models would emerge from the behaviorist, humanistic, and cognitivist traditions. Let's begin our study of psychological perspectives by examining Freud's contribution and the development of psychodynamic models.

## Psychodynamic Models

**2.3 Describe the key features of psychodynamic models of abnormal behavior and evaluate their major contributions.**

Psychodynamic theory is based on the contributions of Sigmund Freud and his followers. Freud's version of psychodynamic theory, called **psychoanalytic theory**, is based on the belief that the roots of psychological problems involve unconscious motives and conflicts that can be traced back to childhood. Freud put the study of the unconscious mind on the map (Lothane, 2006). To Freud, unconscious motives and conflicts revolve around primitive sexual and aggressive instincts and the need to keep these primitive impulses out of consciousness. Why must the mind keep impulses hidden from conscious awareness? Because,

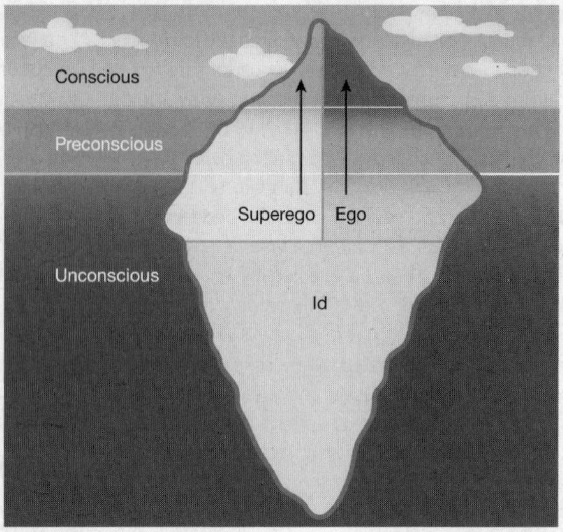


**Figure 2.5** The parts of the mind, according to Freud.

The human mind in classic Freudian theory can be likened to an iceberg; only a small part of it rises to conscious awareness at any moment in time. Although material in the preconscious mind may be brought into consciousness by focusing one's attention on it, the impulses and wishes in the id remain veiled in mystery in the unconscious recesses of the mind. The ego and superego operate at all three levels of consciousness; the workings of the id are mired in the unconscious.

as Freud held, were we to become fully aware of our most basic sexual and aggressive urges—which, according to Freud, include incestuous and violent impulses—our conscious self would be flooded with crippling anxiety. By the Freudian account, abnormal behavior patterns represent "symptoms" of these dynamic struggles taking place within the unconscious mind. The patient is aware of the symptom, but not the unconscious conflict that lies at its root. Let's take a closer look at the key elements in psychoanalytic theory.

**THE STRUCTURE OF THE MIND** We can liken Freud's model of the mind to an iceberg with only the tip visible above the surface of awareness (Figure 2.5). Freud called this region "above the surface," the **conscious** part of the mind. It is the part of the mind that corresponds to our present awareness. The larger part of the mind remains below the surface of consciousness. The regions that lie beneath the surface of awareness were labeled the *preconscious* and the *unconscious*.

In the **preconscious** are memories that are not in awareness but that can be brought into awareness by focusing on them. Your telephone number, for example, remains in the preconscious until you focus on it. The **unconscious**, the largest part of the mind, remains shrouded in mystery. Its contents can be brought to awareness only with great difficulty, if at all. Freud believed the unconscious is the repository of our basic biological impulses or drives, which he called instincts—primarily sexual and aggressive instincts.

**THE STRUCTURE OF PERSONALITY** According to Freud's structural hypothesis, the human personality is divided into three mental entities, or psychic structures: the *id*, *ego*, and *superego*.

The **id** is the original psychic structure, present at birth. It is the repository of our baser drives and instinctual impulses, including hunger, thirst, sex, and aggression. The id, which operates completely in the unconscious, follows the **pleasure principle**: It demands instant gratification of instincts without consideration of social rules or customs or the needs of others.

During the first year of life, a child discovers that every demand is not instantly gratified. He or she must learn to cope with the delay of gratification. The **ego** develops during this first year to organize reasonable ways of coping with frustration. Standing for "reason and good sense" (Freud, 1933/1964, p. 76), the ego seeks to curb the demands of the id and to direct behavior in keeping with social customs and expectations. Gratification can thus be achieved, but not at the expense of social disapproval. Let's say the id floods your consciousness with hunger pangs. Were it to have its way, the id might prompt you to wolf down whatever food is at hand or even to swipe someone else's plate. However, the ego creates the idea of walking to the refrigerator, making a sandwich, and pouring a glass of milk.

The ego is governed by the **reality principle**. It considers what is practical and possible, as well as the urgings of the id. The ego lays the groundwork for developing a conscious sense of ourselves as distinct individuals.

During middle childhood, the **superego** develops from the internalization of the moral standards and values of our parents and other key people in our lives. The superego serves as a conscience, or internal moral guardian, which monitors the ego and passes judgment on right and wrong. When it finds that the ego has failed to adhere to the superego's moral standards, it metes out punishment in the form of guilt and shame. Ego stands between the id and the superego. It endeavors to satisfy the cravings of the id without offending the moral standards of the superego.

**REGRESSION.** Is this a sign of regression? In Freudian theory, the ego may shield itself from anxiety or extreme stress by means of defense mechanisms—including regression, which involves the return of behavior associated with an earlier stage of psychological development.

**DEFENSE MECHANISMS** Although part of the ego rises to consciousness, some of its activity is carried out unconsciously. In the unconscious, the ego serves as a kind of watchdog, or censor, which screens impulses from the id. It uses **defense mechanisms** (psychological defenses) to prevent socially unacceptable impulses from rising into consciousness. If not for these defense mechanisms, the darkest sins of our childhoods, the primitive demands of our ids, and the censures of our superegos might disable us psychologically. *Repression*—or motivated forgetting—by which unacceptable wishes, urges, and impulses are banished to the unconscious, is the most basic of the defense mechanisms (Boag, 2006). Others are described in Table 2.2.

A dynamic unconscious struggle thus takes place between the id and the ego. Biological drives that are striving for expression (the id) are pitted against the ego, which seeks to restrain them or channel them into more acceptable outlets. When these conflicts are not resolved smoothly, they can lead to the development of behavior problems or psychological disorders. Because one cannot view the unconscious mind directly, Freud developed a method of mental detective work called *psychoanalysis*, which is described later in the chapter in the section on psychodynamic therapy.

The use of defense mechanisms to cope with feelings such as anxiety, guilt, and shame is considered normal. These mechanisms enable us to constrain impulses from the id as we go about our daily business. Freud believed that slips of the tongue and ordinary forgetfulness could represent hidden motives that are kept out of consciousness by

## Table 2.2 Types of Defense Mechanisms

| Defense Mechanism | Description | Example |
|---|---|---|
| **Repression** | Banishment of unacceptable urges, wishes, or impulses to the unconscious mind | A man is unaware of having hateful or destructive impulses toward his own father. |
| **Denial** | Refusal to accept the reality of a threatening impulse or unsafe behavior | A person with a heart condition refuses to acknowledge the seriousness of the condition and avoids seeking medical attention or making healthy changes in his lifestyle. |
| **Rationalization** | Self-justifications for unacceptable behavior used as a form of self-deception | A man accused of rape justifies his behavior to himself by thinking that the woman had dressed and acted so provocatively that she was "just asking for it." |
| **Displacement** | Directing one's unacceptable impulses toward threatening objects onto safer or less threatening objects | After a woman is chewed out by her boss at work, she picks a fight with her daughter upon returning home. |
| **Projection** | Attributing one's own impulses or wishes to another person | A hostile and argumentative person perceives others as having difficulty controlling their tempers. |
| **Reaction formation** | Taking the opposite stance to what one truly wishes or believes so as to keep one's genuine impulses repressed | A woman who has difficulty accepting her own sexual impulses mounts a crusade against pornography. |
| **Regression** | Return of behaviors associated with earlier stages of development, generally during times of stress | After his marriage ends, a man becomes completely dependent on his parents. |
| **Sublimation** | Channeling one's own unacceptable impulses into more socially appropriate pursuits or activities | A woman channels her aggressive impulses into her artistic pursuits. |

**DENIAL?** Denial is a defense mechanism in which the ego fends off anxiety by preventing awareness of an underlying threat. Failing to take the warnings of health risks from smoking seriously may be considered a form of denial.

repression. If a friend means to say, "I hear what you're saying," but it comes out as, "I hate what you're saying," perhaps the friend is expressing a repressed hateful impulse. If a lover storms out in anger but forgets his umbrella, perhaps he is unconsciously creating an excuse for returning. Defense mechanisms may also give rise to abnormal behavior, however. The person who regresses to an infantile state under pressures of enormous stress clearly is not acting adaptively to the situation.

**STAGES OF PSYCHOSEXUAL DEVELOPMENT** Freud argued that sexual drives are the dominant factors in the development of personality, even in childhood. Freud believed that a child's basic relationship to the world in the child's first several years of life is organized around the pursuit of sensual or sexual pleasure. In Freud's view, all activities that are physically pleasurable, such as eating or moving one's bowels, are in essence "sexual." (What Freud meant by *sexual* is probably closer in present-day meaning to the word *sensual*.)

The drive for sexual pleasure represents, in Freud's view, the expression of a major life instinct, which he called Eros—the basic drive to preserve and perpetuate life. He called the energy contained in Eros that allows it to fulfill its function *libido*, or sexual energy. Freud believed that libidinal energy is expressed through sexual pleasure in different body parts—called *erogenous zones*—as a child matures. In Freud's view, the stages of human development are psychosexual in nature because they correspond to the transfer of libidinal energy from one erogenous zone to another. Freud proposed the existence of five psychosexual stages of development: oral (first year of life), anal (second year of life), phallic (beginning during the third year of life), latency (from around age 6 to age 12), and genital (beginning in puberty).

In the first year of life, the *oral stage*, infants achieve sexual pleasure by sucking their mothers' breasts and by mouthing anything that happens to be nearby. Oral stimulation, in the form of sucking and biting, is a source of both sexual gratification and nourishment. During the *anal stage* of psychosexual development, the child experiences sexual gratification through contraction and relaxation of the sphincter muscles that control elimination of bodily waste.

The next stage of psychosexual development, the *phallic stage*, generally begins during the third year of life. The major erogenous zone during this stage is the phallic region (the penis in boys, the clitoris in girls). Perhaps the most controversial of Freud's beliefs was his suggestion that phallic-stage children develop unconscious incestuous desires for the parent of the opposite sex and begin to view the parent of the same sex as a rival. Freud dubbed this conflict the *Oedipus complex*, after the legendary Greek king Oedipus, who unwittingly slew his father and married his mother. The female version of the Oedipus complex has been named by some followers (although not by Freud himself) the *Electra complex*. According to Greek legend, Electra avenged the death of her father, King Agamemnon, by slaying her father's murderers—her own mother and her mother's lover. Freud believed that the Oedipus conflict represents a central psychological conflict of early childhood and that failure to successfully resolve the conflict can set the stage for the development of psychological problems in later life.

**THE ORAL STAGE OF PSYCHOSEXUAL DEVELOPMENT?** According to Freud, a child's early encounters with the world are largely experienced through the mouth.

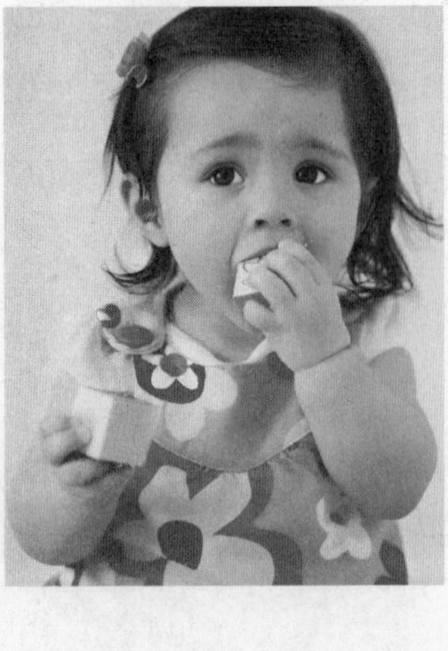

Successful resolution of the Oedipus complex involves a boy repressing his incestuous desires for his mother and identifying with his father. This identification leads to development of the aggressive, independent characteristics associated with the traditional masculine gender role. For a girl, successful resolution involves repression of incestuous desires for her father and identification with her mother, leading to the acquisition of the more passive, dependent characteristics traditionally associated with the feminine gender role.

The Oedipus complex comes to a point of resolution, whether fully resolved or not, by about the age of 5 or 6. From the identification with the parent of the same gender comes the internalization of parental values in the form of the superego. Children then enter the *latency stage* of psychosexual development, a period of late childhood during which sexual impulses remain in a latent state. Interests become directed toward school and play activities.

**AN ORAL FIXATION?** Freud believed that too little or too much gratification at a particular stage of psychosexual development can lead to fixation, resulting in personality traits associated with that stage, such as exaggerated oral traits.

Sexual drives are once again aroused with the *genital stage*, beginning with puberty, which reaches fruition in mature sexuality, marriage, and the bearing of children. The sexual feelings toward the parent of the opposite sex that had remained repressed during the latency period emerge during adolescence but are displaced, or transferred, onto members of the opposite sex. In Freud's view, successful adjustment during the genital stage involves attaining sexual gratification through sexual intercourse with someone of the opposite sex, presumably within the context of marriage.

One of Freud's central beliefs is that a child may encounter conflict during each of the psychosexual stages of development. Conflict in the oral stage, for example, centers on whether or not the infant receives adequate oral gratification. Too much gratification could lead the infant to expect that everything in life is given with little or no effort on his or her part. In contrast, early weaning might lead to frustration. Too little or too much gratification at any stage could lead to **fixation** in that stage, which leads to the development of personality traits characteristic of that stage. Oral fixations could include an exaggerated desire for "oral activities," which could become expressed in later life in smoking, alcohol abuse, overeating, and nail biting. Like the infant who depends on the mother's breast for survival and for gratification of oral pleasure, orally fixated adults may also become clingy and dependent in their interpersonal relationships. In Freud's view, failure to successfully resolve the conflicts of the phallic stage (i.e., the Oedipus complex) can lead to the rejection of the traditional masculine or feminine roles and to homosexuality.

**OTHER PSYCHODYNAMIC THEORISTS** Psychodynamic theory has been shaped over the years by the contributions of psychodynamic theorists who shared certain central tenets in common with Freud—for example, that behavior reflects unconscious motivation, inner conflict, and the operation of defensive responses to anxiety. However, many psychodynamic theorists deviated sharply from Freud's positions on many issues. For example, they tended to place less emphasis than Freud on basic instincts such as sex and aggression, and greater emphasis on conscious choice, self-direction, and creativity.

***Carl Jung*** Swiss psychiatrist Carl Jung (1875–1961) was a member of Freud's inner circle. His break with Freud came when he developed his own psychodynamic theory, which he called *analytical psychology*. Jung believed that an understanding of human behavior must incorporate self-awareness and self-direction as well as impulses of the id and mechanisms of defense. He believed that not only do we have a *personal* unconscious, a repository of repressed memories and impulses, but also that we inherit a collective unconscious. The collective unconscious contains primitive images, or **archetypes**, which reflect the history of our species, including vague, mysterious, mythical images like the all-powerful God; the fertile and nurturing mother; the young hero; the wise old man; the dark, shadowy evil figure; and themes of rebirth or resurrection. Although archetypes remain in the unconscious, in Jung's view, they influence our thoughts, dreams, and emotions and render us responsive to cultural themes in stories and films.

**THE POWER OF ARCHETYPES.** One reason adventure stories such as Harry Potter and the *Star Wars* saga are so compelling may be that they feature archetypes represented in the struggle between good and evil characters.

***Alfred Adler*** Like Jung, Alfred Adler (1870–1937) held a place in Freud's inner circle but broke away as he developed his own beliefs—namely, that people basically are driven by an inferiority complex, not by the sexual instinct, as Freud maintained. For some people, feelings of inferiority are based on physical deficits and the resulting need to compensate for them. But all of us, because of our small size during childhood, encounter feelings of inferiority to some degree. These feelings lead to a powerful drive for superiority, which motivates us to achieve prominence and social dominance. In the healthy personality, however, strivings for dominance are tempered by devotion to helping other people.

Adler, like Jung, believed self-awareness plays a major role in the formation of personality. Adler spoke of a *creative self*, a self-aware aspect of personality that strives to overcome obstacles and develop an individual's potential. With the hypothesis of the creative self, Adler shifted the emphasis of psychodynamic theory from the id to the ego. Because our potentials are uniquely individual, Adler's views have been termed *individual psychology*.

***Karen Horney*** Some psychodynamic theorists, such as Karen Horney (1885–1952; pronounced HORN-eye), stressed the importance of child–parent relationships in the development of emotional problems. Horney maintained that when parents are harsh or uncaring, children come to develop a deep-seated form of anxiety called *basic anxiety*, which she described as a feeling of "being isolated and helpless in a potentially hostile world" (cited in Quinn, 1987, p. 41). Children who harbor deep-seated resentment toward their parents may develop a form of hostility she labeled *basic hostility*. She shared with Freud the view that children repress their hostility toward their parents because of an underlying fear of losing them or of suffering reprisals or punishment. However, repressed hostility generates more anxiety and insecurity. With Horney and other psychodynamic theorists who followed Freud, the emphasis shifted from a focus on sexual and aggressive drives toward a closer examination of social influences on development.

More recent psychodynamic models also place a greater emphasis on the self or the ego and less emphasis on the sexual instinct than Freud's model. Today, most psychoanalysts see people as motivated on two tiers: by the growth-oriented, conscious pursuits of the ego and by the more primitive, conflict-ridden drives of the id. Heinz Hartmann (1894–1970) was one of the originators of **ego psychology**, which posits that the ego has energy and motives of its own. The choices to seek an education, dedicate oneself to art and poetry, and further humanity are not merely defensive forms of sublimation, as Freud had seen them.

***Erik Erikson*** Erik Erikson (1902–1994) was influenced by Freud but became an important theorist in his own right. He focused on psychosocial development in contrast to Freud's emphasis on psychosexual development. Erikson attributed more importance to social relationships and formation of personal identity than to unconscious processes. Whereas Freud's developmental theory ends with the genital stage, Erikson's developmental theory, beginning in early adolescence, posits that our personalities continue to be shaped throughout adulthood as we deal with the psychosocial challenges or crises we face during each period of life. In Erikson's view, for example, the major psychosocial challenge faced by adolescents is development of *ego identity*, a clearly defined sense of who they are and what they believe in.

***Margaret Mahler*** One popular contemporary psychodynamic approach, **object-relations theory**, focuses on how children come to develop symbolic representations of important others in their lives, especially their parents (Blum, 2010). The object-relations theorist

**KAREN HORNEY.**

**ERIK ERIKSON.**

**MARGARET MAHLER.**

Margaret Mahler (1897–1985) saw the process of the child separating from the mother during the first three years of life as crucial to the child's personality development (discussed further in Chapter 12).

According to psychodynamic theory, we introject, or incorporate, parts of parental figures in our lives into our own personalities. For example, you might introject your father's strong sense of responsibility or your mother's eagerness to please others. Introjection is more powerful when we fear losing others because of death or rejection. Thus, we might be particularly apt to incorporate elements of people who *disapprove* of us or who see things differently.

In Mahler's view, these symbolic representations—which are formed from images and memories of others—come to influence our perceptions and behavior. We experience internal conflict as the attitudes of introjected people battle with our own. Some of our perceptions may be distorted or seem unreal to us. Some of our impulses and behavior may seem unlike us, as if they come out of the blue. With such conflict, we may not be able to tell where the influences of other people end and our "real selves" begin. The aim of Mahler's therapeutic approach was to help clients separate their own ideas and feelings from those of the introjected objects so that they could develop as individuals—as their own persons.

**PSYCHODYNAMIC VIEWS ON NORMALITY AND ABNORMALITY** In the Freudian model, mental health is a function of the dynamic balance among the mental structures id, ego, and superego. In mentally healthy people, the ego is strong enough to control the instincts of the id and to withstand the condemnation of the superego. The presence of acceptable outlets for the expression of some primitive impulses, such as the expression of mature sexuality in marriage, decreases the pressures within the id and at the same time lessens the burdens of the ego in repressing the remaining impulses. Being reared by reasonably tolerant parents might prevent the superego from becoming overly harsh and condemnatory.

In people with psychological disorders, the balance among the psychic structures is lopsided. Some unconscious impulses may "leak" into consciousness, producing anxiety or leading to psychological disorders, such as hysteria and phobias. The symptom expresses the conflict among the parts of the personality while it protects the self from recognizing the inner turmoil. A person with a fear of knives, for example, is shielded from becoming aware of her own unconscious aggressive impulses to use a knife to murder someone or attack herself. So long as the symptom is maintained (the person avoids knives), the murderous or suicidal impulses are kept at bay. If the superego becomes overly powerful, it may create excessive feelings of guilt and lead to depression. People who intentionally hurt others without feeling guilty about it are believed to have an underdeveloped superego.

Freud believed that the underlying conflicts that give rise to psychological disorders originate in childhood and are buried in the depths of the unconscious. Through psychoanalysis, he sought to help people uncover underlying conflicts and learn to deal with them. This way, people can free themselves of the need to maintain the overt symptoms.

Perpetual vigilance and defense take their toll, however. The ego can weaken and, in extreme cases, lose the ability to keep a lid on the id. When the urges of the id spill forth, untempered by an ego that is either weakened or underdeveloped, **psychosis** results. Psychosis is characterized in general by bizarre behavior and thoughts and by faulty perceptions of reality, including hallucinations (hearing voices or seeing things that are not present). Speech may become incoherent; there may be bizarre posturing and gestures. Schizophrenia is the major form of psychosis (see Chapter 11).

Freud equated psychological health with the *abilities to love and to work*. The normal person can care deeply for other people, find sexual gratification in an intimate relationship, and engage in productive work. To accomplish these ends, as Freud viewed it, sexual impulses must be expressed in a relationship with a partner of the opposite gender. Other impulses must be channeled (sublimated) into socially productive pursuits, such as work, enjoyment of art or music, or creative expression. Other psychodynamic theorists, such as Jung and Adler, emphasized the need to develop a differentiated self—the unifying force that provides direction to behavior and helps develop a person's potential. Adler also believed that psychological health involves efforts to compensate for feelings of inferiority by striving to excel in one or more arenas of human endeavor. For Mahler, similarly, abnormal behavior derives from failure to develop a distinctive and individual identity.

**EVALUATING PSYCHODYNAMIC MODELS** Psychodynamic theory has pervaded the general culture (Lothane, 2006). Even people who have never read Freud look for symbolic meanings in slips of the tongue and assume that abnormalities can be traced to early childhood. Use of terms such as *ego* and *repression* have become commonplace, although their everyday meanings do not fully overlap with those intended by Freud.

The psychodynamic model led us to recognize that we are not transparent to ourselves (Panek, 2002)—that our behavior may be motivated by hidden drives and impulses of which we are unaware or only dimly aware. Moreover, Freud's beliefs about childhood sexuality were both illuminating and controversial. Before Freud, children were perceived as pure innocents, free of sexual desire. However, Freud recognized that young children—even infants—seek pleasure through stimulation of the oral and anal cavities and the phallic region. Yet his beliefs that primitive drives give rise to incestuous desires, intra-family rivalries, and conflicts remain controversial, even within psychodynamic circles.

Many critics, including even some of Freud's followers, believe he placed too much emphasis on sexual and aggressive impulses and underemphasized social relationships. Critics also have argued that the psychic structures—the id, ego, and superego—may be little more than useful fictions, poetic ways to represent inner conflict. Many critics argue that Freud's hypothetical mental processes are not scientific concepts because they cannot be directly observed or tested. Therapists can speculate, for example, that a client "forgot" about an appointment because "unconsciously" she or he did not want to attend the session. Such unconscious motivation may not be subject to scientific verification, however. On the other hand, psychodynamically oriented researchers have developed scientific approaches to test many of Freud's concepts. They believe that a growing body of evidence supports the existence of unconscious processes that lie outside ordinary awareness, including defense mechanisms such as repression (Cramer, 2000; Westen & Gabbard, 2002).

## Learning-Based Models

**2.4 Describe the key features of learning-based models of abnormal behavior and evaluate their major contributions.**

The psychodynamic models of Freud and his followers were the first major psychological theories of abnormal behavior. Other relevant psychologies also took shape early in the 20th century. The behavioral perspective is associated with the Russian physiologist Ivan Pavlov (1849–1936), the discoverer of the conditioned reflex, and with the American psychologist John B. Watson (1878–1958), the father of **behaviorism**. The behavioral perspective focuses on the role of learning in explaining both normal and abnormal behavior. From a learning perspective, abnormal behavior represents the acquisition, or learning, of inappropriate, maladaptive behaviors.

From the medical and psychodynamic perspectives, respectively, abnormal behavior is *symptomatic* of underlying biological or psychological problems. From the learning perspective, however, the abnormal behavior itself is the problem. In this perspective, abnormal behavior is learned in much the same way as normal behavior. Why do some people behave abnormally? It may be that their learning histories differ from most people's. For example, a person who was harshly punished as a child for masturbating might become anxious about sexuality as an adult. Poor child-rearing practices, such as capricious punishment for misconduct and failure to praise or reward good behavior, might lead to antisocial behavior. Children with abusive or neglectful parents might learn to pay more attention to inner fantasies than to the world outside and have difficulty distinguishing reality from fantasy.

Watson and other behaviorists, such as Harvard University psychologist B. F. Skinner (1904–1990), believed that human behavior is the product of our genetic inheritance

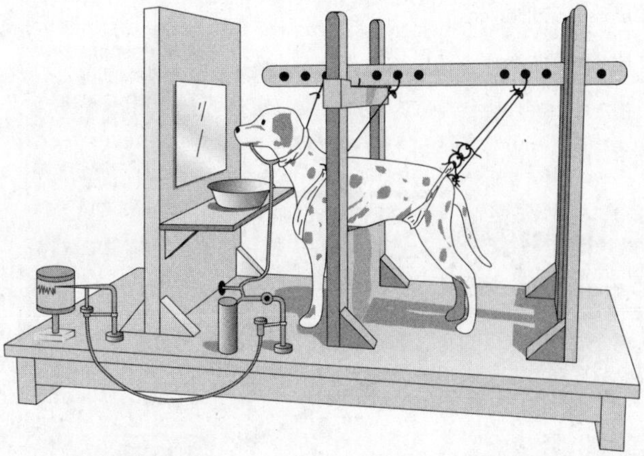

**Figure 2.6 The apparatus used in Ivan Pavlov's experiments on conditioning.**

Pavlov used an apparatus such as this to demonstrate the process of conditioning. To the left is a two-way mirror, behind which a researcher rings a bell. After the bell is rung, meat is placed on the dog's tongue. Following several pairings of the bell and the meat, the dog learns to salivate in response to the bell. The animal's saliva passes through the tube to a vial, where its quantity may be taken as a measure of the strength of the conditioned response.

and environmental or situational influences. Like Freud, Watson and Skinner discarded concepts of personal freedom, choice, and self-direction. But whereas Freud saw us as driven by forces in the unconscious mind, behaviorists see us as products of environmental influences that shape and manipulate our behavior. Behaviorists also believe that we should limit the study of psychology to behavior itself rather than focus on underlying motivations. Therapy, in this view, consists of shaping behavior rather than seeking insight into the workings of the mind. Behaviorists focus on the roles of two forms of learning in shaping both normal and abnormal behavior: classical conditioning and operant conditioning.

**ROLE OF CLASSICAL CONDITIONING** Ivan Pavlov discovered the conditioned reflex (now called a *conditioned response*) quite by accident. In his laboratory, he harnessed dogs to an apparatus like that illustrated in Figure 2.6 to study their salivary response to food. Along the way, he observed that the animals would salivate and secrete gastric juices even before they started to eat. These responses appeared to be elicited by the sound of the food cart as it was wheeled into the room. Pavlov undertook an experiment that showed that animals could learn to salivate in response to other stimuli, such as the sound of a bell, if these stimuli were *associated* with feeding.

Because dogs don't normally salivate to the sound of bells, Pavlov reasoned that they had acquired this response. He called it a **conditioned response** (CR), or conditioned reflex, because it had been paired with what he called an **unconditioned stimulus** (US)—in this case, food—which naturally elicited salivation (see Figure 2.7). The salivation in response to food—an unlearned response—Pavlov called the **unconditioned response** (UR), and the bell—a previously neutral stimulus—he called the **conditioned stimulus** (CS).

Can you recognize examples of **classical conditioning** in your everyday life? Do you flinch in the waiting room at the sound of the dentist's drill? The sound of the drill may be a conditioned stimulus that elicits conditioned responses of fear and muscle tension.

Phobias or excessive fears may be acquired by classical conditioning. For instance, a person may develop a phobia of riding on elevators following a traumatic experience on an elevator. In this example, a previously neutral stimulus (elevator) becomes paired or associated with an aversive stimulus (trauma), which leads to the conditioned response (phobia).

John B. Watson demonstrated how a fear response could be acquired through classical conditioning. Together with his research assistant Rosalie Rayner, who was later to become his wife, Watson classically conditioned an 11-month-old boy, who is well known in the annals of psychology as "Little Albert," to develop a fear response to a white rat (Watson & Rayner, 1920). Prior to conditioning, the boy showed no fear of the rat

**IVAN PAVLOV.** Russian physiologist Ivan Pavlov (center, with the white beard) demonstrates his apparatus for classical conditioning to students. How might the principles of classical conditioning explain the acquisition of excessive irrational fears that psychologists refer to as phobias?

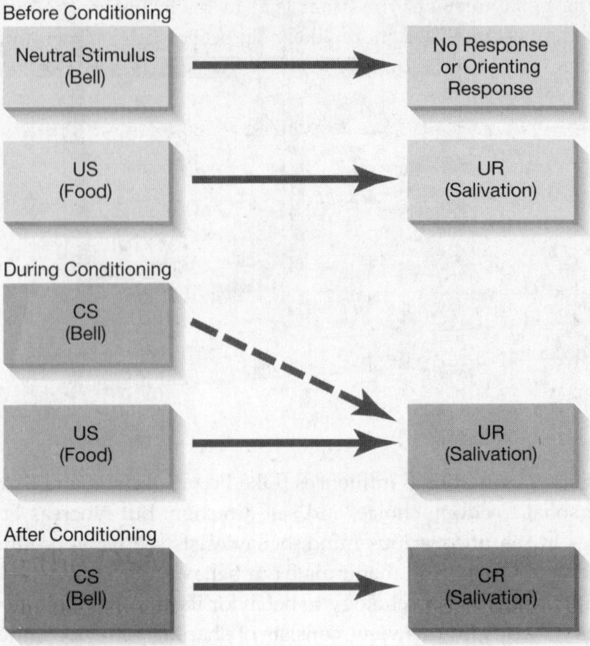


**Figure 2.7** Schematic representation of classical conditioning.

Before conditioning, food (an unconditioned stimulus, or US) placed on a dog's tongue will naturally elicit salivation (an unconditioned response, or UR). The bell, however, is a neutral stimulus that may elicit an orienting response but not salivation. During conditioning, the bell (the conditioned stimulus, or CS) is rung while food (the US) is placed on the dog's tongue. After several conditioning trials have occurred, the bell (the CS) will elicit salivation (the conditioned response, or CR) when it is rung, even though it is not accompanied by food (the US). The dog is said to have been conditioned, or to have learned to display the conditioned response in response to the conditioned stimulus. Learning theorists have suggested that irrational, excessive fears of harmless stimuli may be acquired through principles of classical conditioning.

and actually had reached out to stroke it. Then, as the boy reached for the animal, Watson banged a steel bar with a hammer just behind the boy's head, creating a loud, aversive sound. After repeated pairings of the jarring sound and the presence of the animal, Albert showed a conditioned response, displaying fear of the rat alone.

From the learning perspective, normal behavior involves responding adaptively to stimuli, including conditioned stimuli. After all, if we do not learn to be afraid of putting our hands too close to a hot stove after one or two experiences of being burned or nearly burned, we might repeatedly suffer unnecessary burns. However, acquiring inappropriate and maladaptive fears on the basis of conditioning may cripple our efforts to function in the world. Chapter 5 explains how conditioning may help explain anxiety disorders such as phobias.

**ROLE OF OPERANT CONDITIONING** Classical conditioning can explain the development of simple, reflexive responses, such as salivating to cues associated with food, as well as the emotional response of fear to stimuli that have been paired with painful or aversive experiences. However, classical conditioning does not account for more complex behaviors, such as studying, working, socializing, or preparing meals. The behavioral psychologist B. F. Skinner (1938) called these types of complex behaviors *operant responses* because they operate on the environment to produce effects or consequences. In **operant conditioning**, responses are acquired and strengthened by their consequences.

We acquire responses or skills, such as raising our hand in class, that lead to **reinforcement**. Reinforcers are changes in the environment (stimuli) that increase the frequency

CLASSICAL CONDITIONING: AN INVOLUNTARY RESPONSE

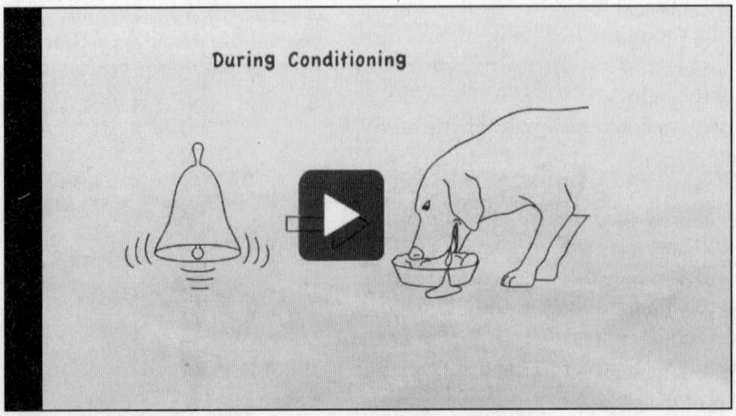

of the preceding behavior. Behaviors that lead to rewarding consequences are strengthened—that is, they are more likely to occur again. Over time, such behaviors become habits (Staddon & Cerutti, 2003). For example, you likely acquired the habit of raising your hand in class on the basis of experiences early in grade school when your teachers responded to you only if you first raised your hand.

B. F. SKINNER.

***Types of Reinforcers*** Skinner identified two types of reinforcers. **Positive reinforcers**, which are commonly called *rewards*, boost the frequency of a behavior when they are introduced or presented. Most of Skinner's work focused on studying operant conditioning in animals, such as pigeons. If a pigeon gets food when it pecks a button, it will continue to peck a button until it has eaten its fill. If we get a friendly response from people when we hold the door open for them, we're more likely to develop the habit of opening the door for others. **Negative reinforcers** increase the frequency of behavior when they are *removed*. If picking up a crying child stops the crying, the behavior (picking up the child) is negatively reinforced (made stronger) because it removes the negative reinforcer (the crying, an aversive stimulus).

Adaptive, normal behavior involves learning responses or skills that lead to reinforcement. We learn behaviors that allow us to obtain positive reinforcers or rewards, such as food, money, and approval, and doing so helps us remove or avoid negative reinforcers, such as pain and disapproval. However, if our early learning environments do not provide opportunities for learning new skills, we might be hampered in our efforts to develop the skills needed to obtain reinforcement. A lack of social skills, for example, may reduce our opportunities for social reinforcement (approval or praise from others), which in turn may lead to depression and social isolation. In Chapter 7, we will examine links between changes in reinforcement levels and the development of depression, and in Chapter 11, we will examine how principles of reinforcement are incorporated in learning-based treatment programs to help people with schizophrenia develop more adaptive social behaviors.

***Punishment vs. Reinforcement*** **Punishment** can be considered the flip side of reinforcement. Punishments are aversive stimuli that *decrease* the frequency of the behavior they follow. Punishment may take many forms, including physical punishment (spanking or use of other painful stimuli), removal of a reinforcing stimulus (turning off the TV), assessment of monetary penalties (parking tickets), taking away privileges ("You're grounded!"), or removal from a reinforcing environment (a time-out).

Before going further, let us review our terms to more clearly distinguish between *negative reinforcement* and *punishment*. The confusion arises because an aversive or painful stimulus can serve as either a negative reinforcer or a punishment, depending on the situation. With punishment, the *introduction* or application of the aversive or painful stimulus weakens the behavior it follows. With negative reinforcement, the removal of the aversive or painful stimulus strengthens the behavior it follows. A baby's crying can be a punishment (if it weakens the preceding behavior, such as turning your attention away from the baby) or a negative reinforcer (if it strengthens the behavior that leads to its removal, such as picking the baby up).

Punishment, especially physical punishment, may not eliminate undesirable behavior, although it may suppress it for a time. The behavior may return when the punishment is withdrawn. Another limitation of punishment is that it does not lead to the development of more desirable alternative behaviors. It may also encourage people to withdraw from learning situations. Punished children may cut classes, drop out of school, or run away. Moreover, punishment may generate anger and hostility rather than constructive learning and may cross the boundary into abuse, especially when it is repetitive and severe. Child abuse figures prominently in many abnormal behavior patterns, including some types of personality disorders (Chapter 12) and dissociative disorders (Chapter 6).

OPERANT CONDITIONING: LEARNING FROM CONSEQUENCES

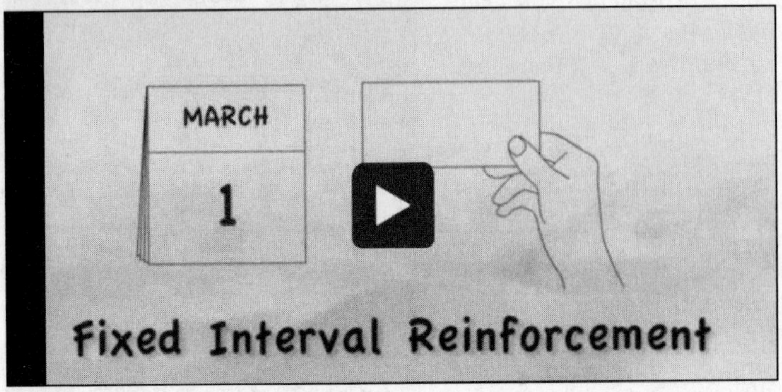


Psychologists recognize that reinforcement is more desirable than punishment. However, rewarding good behavior requires paying attention to it, not just to misbehavior. Some children who develop conduct problems gain attention from others only when they misbehave. Consequently, other people may be inadvertently reinforcing the undesirable behavior of these children. Learning theorists point out that adults need to teach children desirable behavior and regularly reinforce such behavior when they display it.

Let's now consider a contemporary model of learning, called *social-cognitive theory* (formerly called *social-learning theory*), which considers the role of cognitive factors in learning and behavior.

SOCIAL-COGNITIVE THEORY **Social-cognitive theory** represents the contributions of theorists such as Albert Bandura (1925–), Julian B. Rotter (1916–2014), and Walter Mischel (1930–). Social-cognitive theorists expanded traditional learning theory by including roles for thinking, or cognition, and learning by observation, which is also called **modeling** (Bandura, 2004). A phobia of spiders, for example, may be learned by observing the fearful reactions of others in real life, on television, or in the movies.

Social-cognitive theorists believe that people have an impact on their environment, just as their environment has an impact on them (Bandura, 2004). Social-cognitive theorists agree with traditional behaviorists such as Watson and Skinner that theories of human nature should be tied to observable behavior. However, they argue that factors *within* the person, such as **expectancies** and the values placed on particular goals, as well as observational learning, also need to be considered to explain human behavior. For example, we will see in Chapter 8 that people who hold more positive expectancies about the effects of a drug are more likely to use the drug and to use larger quantities of the drug than are people with less positive expectancies.

**OBSERVATIONAL LEARNING.** According to social-cognitive theory, much human behavior is acquired through modeling, or observational learning.

EVALUATING LEARNING MODELS Learning perspectives have spawned a model of therapy called *behavior therapy* (also called *behavior modification*) that involves systematically applying learning principles to help people change their undesirable behavior. Behavior therapy techniques have helped people overcome a wide range of psychological problems, including phobias and other anxiety disorders, sexual dysfunctions, and depression. Moreover, reinforcement-based programs are now widely used to help parents learn better parenting skills and help children learn in the classroom.

Critics contend that behaviorism alone cannot explain the richness of human behavior and that human experience cannot be reduced to observable responses. Many learning theorists too—especially social-cognitive theorists—have been dissatisfied with the strict behavioristic view that environmental influences—rewards and punishments—mechanically control our behavior. Humans experience thoughts and dreams and formulate goals and aspirations; behaviorism does not seem to address much of what it means to be human. Social-cognitive theorists have broadened the scope of traditional behaviorism, but critics claim that social-cognitive theory places too little emphasis on genetic contributions to behavior and doesn't provide a full enough account of subjective experience, such as self-awareness and the flow of consciousness. As we'll see next, subjective experience takes center stage in humanistic models.

## Humanistic Models

**2.5 Describe the key features of humanistic models of abnormal behavior and evaluate their major contributions.**

Humanistic psychology emerged during the mid-20th century and departed from both the psychodynamic and behavioral or learning-based models by emphasizing the personal freedom human beings have in making conscious choices that imbue their lives with a sense of meaning and purpose. American psychologists Carl Rogers (1902–1987) and Abraham Maslow (1908–1970), two principal figures in humanistic psychology, believed that people have an inborn tendency toward **self-actualization**—to strive to become all they are capable of being. Each of us possesses a singular cluster of traits and talents that gives us our own set of feelings and needs and our own perspective on life. By recognizing and accepting our genuine needs and feelings—by being true to ourselves—we live *authentically*, with meaning and purpose. We may not decide to act out every wish and fancy, but awareness of our authentic feelings and subjective experiences can help us make more meaningful choices.

To understand abnormal behavior in the humanist's view, we need to understand the roadblocks that people encounter in striving for self-actualization and authenticity. To accomplish this, psychologists must learn to view the world from clients' own perspectives: Clients' subjective views of their world lead them to interpret and evaluate their experiences in either self-enhancing or self-defeating ways. The humanistic viewpoint involves the attempt to understand the subjective experience of others, the stream of conscious experiences people have of "being in the world."

**SELF-ACTUALIZATION.** Humanistic theorists believe that there exists in each of us a drive toward self-actualization—to become all that we are capable of being. No two people follow quite the same pathway toward self-actualization.

**HUMANISTIC CONCEPTS OF ABNORMAL BEHAVIOR** Rogers held that abnormal behavior results from a distorted concept of the self. Parents can help children develop a positive self-concept by showing them **unconditional positive regard**—that is, by prizing them and showing them that they are worthy of love irrespective of their behavior at any given time. Parents may disapprove of a certain behavior, but they need to convey to their children that the behavior is undesirable, not the child. However, when parents show children **conditional positive regard**—accepting them only when they behave in the way the parents want them to behave—the children may learn to disown all the thoughts, feelings, and behaviors their parents have rejected. Children will learn to develop *conditions of worth*; that is, they will think of themselves as worthwhile only if they behave in certain

**CARL ROGERS (LEFT) AND ABRAHAM MASLOW (RIGHT).** Two of the principal forces in humanistic psychology.

**THE MAKINGS OF UNCONDITIONAL POSITIVE REGARD?** Rogers believed that parents can help their children develop self-esteem and set them on the road toward self-actualization by showing them unconditional positive regard—prizing them on the basis of their inner worth, regardless of their behavior of the moment.

approved ways. For example, children whose parents seem to value them only when they are compliant may deny to themselves that they ever feel angry. Children in some families learn that it is unacceptable to hold their own ideas, lest they depart from their parents' views. Parental disapproval causes them to see themselves as "bad" and their feelings as wrong, selfish, or even evil. To retain their self-esteem, they may have to deny their genuine feelings or disown parts of themselves. The result can be a distorted *self-concept*: The children become strangers to their true selves.

Rogers believed we become anxious when we sense that our feelings and ideas are inconsistent with the distorted concept we have of ourselves that mirrors what others expect us to be—for example, if our parents expect us to be docile and obedient, but we sense ourselves becoming angry or defiant. Because anxiety is unpleasant, we may deny to ourselves that these feelings and ideas even exist, and so the actualization of our authentic self is bridled. We channel our psychological energy not toward growth but toward continued denial and self-defense. Under such conditions, we cannot hope to perceive our genuine values or personal talents. The results are frustration and dissatisfaction, which set the stage for abnormal behavior.

According to the humanists, we cannot fulfill all the wishes of others and remain true to ourselves. However, this does not mean that self-actualization invariably leads to conflict. Rogers believed that people hurt one another or become antisocial in their behavior only when they are frustrated in their endeavors to reach their unique potentials. When parents and others treat children with love and tolerance for their differences, children too grow up to be loving and tolerant—even if some of their values and preferences differ from their parents' choices.

In Rogers's view, the pathway to self-actualization involves a process of self-discovery and self-acceptance, of getting in touch with our true feelings, accepting them as our own, and acting in ways that genuinely reflect them. These are the goals of Rogers's method of psychotherapy, called *client-centered therapy* or *person-centered therapy*.

**EVALUATING HUMANISTIC MODELS** The strength of humanistic models in understanding abnormal behavior lies largely in their focus on conscious experience and their therapy methods that guide people toward self-discovery and self-acceptance. The humanistic movement brought concepts of free choice, inherent goodness, personal responsibility, and authenticity into modern psychology. Ironically, the primary strength of the humanistic approach—its focus on conscious experience—may also be its primary weakness. Conscious experience is private and subjective, which makes it difficult to quantify and study objectively. How can psychologists be certain they accurately perceive the world through the eyes of their clients? Humanists may counter that we should not shrink from the challenge of studying consciousness because to do so would deny an essential aspect of what it means to be human.

Critics also claim that the concept of self-actualization—which is so basic to Maslow and Rogers—cannot be proved or disproved. Like a psychic structure, a self-actualizing force is not directly measurable or observable. It is inferred from its supposed effects. Self-actualization also yields circular explanations for behavior. When someone is observed engaging in striving, what do we learn by attributing striving to a self-actualizing tendency? The source of the tendency remains a mystery. Similarly, when someone is observed *not* to be striving, what do we gain by attributing the lack of endeavor to a blocked or frustrated self-actualizing tendency? We must still determine the source of frustration.

## Cognitive Models

**2.6 Describe the key features of cognitive models of abnormal behavior and evaluate their major contributions.**

The word *cognitive* derives from the Latin *cognitio*, meaning *knowledge*. Cognitive theorists study the cognitions—the thoughts, beliefs, expectations, and attitudes—that accompany and may underlie abnormal behavior. They focus on how reality is colored by our expectations, attitudes, and so forth, and how inaccurate or biased processing of information about the world—and our place within it—can give rise to abnormal behavior. Cognitive theorists believe that our interpretations of the events in our lives—and not the events themselves—determine our emotional states.

**INFORMATION-PROCESSING MODELS** Cognitive psychologists often draw upon concepts in computer science to explain how humans process information and how these processes may break down, leading to problems involving abnormal behavior. In computer terms, information is input into a computer by striking keys on a keyboard (encoded so that it can be accepted by the computer as input) and placed in working memory, where it can be manipulated to solve problems, such as performing statistical or arithmetic operations. Information can also be placed permanently in a storage medium, such as a hard drive or a flash drive, from which it can later be retrieved and output in the form of a printout or a display on a computer screen.

In humans, information about the outside world is *input* through the person's sensory and perceptual processes, *manipulated* (interpreted or processed), *stored* (placed in memory), *retrieved* (accessed from memory), and then *output* in the form of acting upon the information. Psychological disorders may represent disruptions or disturbances in how information is processed. Blocking or distortion of input or faulty storage, retrieval, or manipulation of information can lead to distorted output (e.g., bizarre behavior). People with schizophrenia, for example, may have difficulty accessing and organizing their thoughts, leading to jumbled output in the form of incoherent speech or delusional thinking. They may also have difficulty focusing their attention and filtering out extraneous stimuli, such as distracting noises, which may represent problems in the initial processing of input from their senses.

Manipulation of information may also be distorted by what cognitive therapists call *cognitive distortions*, or errors in thinking. For example, people who are depressed tend to develop an unduly negative view of their personal situations by exaggerating the importance of unfortunate events they experience, such as receiving a poor evaluation at work or being rejected by a dating partner. Cognitive theorists such as Albert Ellis (1913–2007) and Aaron Beck (1921–) have postulated that distorted or irrational thinking patterns can lead to emotional problems and maladaptive behavior.

Social-cognitive theorists, who share many basic ideas with cognitive theorists, focus on the ways in which social information is encoded. For example, aggressive boys and adolescents are likely to incorrectly encode other people's behavior as threatening (see Chapter 13). They assume that other people intend them ill when they do not. Aggressive children and adults may behave in ways that elicit coercive or hostile behavior from others, which serves to confirm their aggressive expectations. Rapists, especially date rapists, may misread a woman's expressed wishes. They may wrongly assume, for example, that the woman who says "no" really means "yes" and is merely playing "hard to get."

**ALBERT ELLIS** Psychologist Albert Ellis (see, e.g., Ellis, 1977, 1993; Ellis & Ellis, 2011), a prominent cognitive theorist, believed that troubling events in themselves do not lead to anxiety, depression, or disturbed behavior. Rather, it is the irrational beliefs people hold about unfortunate experiences that foster negative emotions and maladaptive behavior. Consider someone who loses a job and becomes anxious and despondent about it. It may seem that being fired is the direct cause of the person's misery, but the misery actually stems from the person's beliefs about the loss, not directly from the loss itself.

Ellis used an *ABC approach* to explain the causes of misery. Being fired is an *activating event* (A). The ultimate outcome, or *consequence* (C), is emotional distress. However, the activating event (A) and the consequence (C) are mediated by various *beliefs* (B). Some of these beliefs might include, "that job was the major thing in my life," "what a useless washout I am," "my family will go hungry," "I'll never be able to find another job as good," or "I can't do a thing about it." These exaggerated and irrational beliefs compound depression, nurture helplessness, and distract people from evaluating what to do.

**ALBERT ELLIS.** Cognitive theorist Albert Ellis believed that negative emotions arise from judgments we make about events we experience, not from the events themselves.

The situation can be diagrammed like this:

ACTIVATING EVENT ⟶ BELIEF ⟶ CONSEQUENCES

Ellis pointed out that apprehension about the future and feelings of disappointment are perfectly normal when people face losses. However, the adoption of irrational beliefs leads people to catastrophize their disappointments, leading to profound distress and states of depression. Irrational beliefs—"I must have the love and approval of nearly everyone who is important to me or else I'm a worthless and unlovable person"—impair coping ability. In his later writings, Ellis emphasized the demanding nature of irrational or self-defeating beliefs—tendencies to impose "musts" and "shoulds" on ourselves (Ellis, 1993). Ellis noted that the desire for others' approval is understandable, but it is irrational to assume that one must have it to survive or to feel worthwhile. It would be marvelous to excel in everything we do, but it's absurd to demand it of ourselves or believe that we couldn't stand it if we failed to measure up. Ellis developed a model of therapy called *rational-emotive behavior therapy* to help people dispute these irrational beliefs and substitute more rational ones (discussed later in the chapter). **T / F**

## TRUTH or FICTION

According to a leading cognitive theorist, people's beliefs about their life experiences cause their emotional problems, not the experiences themselves.

☑ **TRUE** Ellis believed that emotional problems are determined by the beliefs people hold about events they experience, not by the events themselves.

Ellis recognized that childhood experiences are involved in the origins of irrational beliefs, but he maintained that it is repetition of these beliefs in the "here and now" that continues to make people miserable. For most people who are anxious and depressed, the key to greater happiness lies not in discovering and liberating deep-seated conflicts, but in recognizing and modifying irrational self-demands.

**AARON BECK** Another prominent cognitive theorist, psychiatrist Aaron Beck, proposed that depression may result from errors in thinking or "cognitive distortions," such as judging oneself entirely on the basis of one's flaws or failures and interpreting events in a negative light (through blue-colored glasses, as it were; Beck et al., 1979). Beck stressed four basic types of cognitive distortions that contribute to emotional distress:

1. *Selective abstraction.* People may *selectively abstract* (focus exclusively on) the parts of their experiences that reveal their flaws and ignore evidence of their competencies. For example, a student may focus entirely on the one mediocre grade received on a math test and ignore all the higher grades.
2. *Overgeneralization.* People may *overgeneralize* from a few isolated experiences. For example, a person may believe he will never marry because he was rejected by a date.
3. *Magnification.* People may blow out of proportion, or *magnify*, the importance of unfortunate events. For example, a student may catastrophize a bad test grade by jumping to the conclusion that she will flunk out of college and her life will be ruined.
4. *Absolutist thinking.* Absolutist thinking is seeing the world in black-and-white terms, rather than in shades of gray. For example, an absolutist thinker may assume that a work evaluation that is less than a total rave is a complete failure.

**AARON BECK.** Aaron Beck, a leading cognitive theorist, focuses on how errors in thinking, or cognitive distortions, set the stage for negative emotional reactions in the face of unfortunate events.

Like Ellis, Beck developed a major model of therapy, called *cognitive therapy*, which focuses on helping individuals with psychological disorders identify and correct faulty ways of thinking (see discussion later in the chapter).

**EVALUATING COGNITIVE MODELS** As we'll see in later chapters, cognitive theorists have had an enormous impact on our understanding of abnormal behavior patterns and development of therapeutic approaches. The overlap between the learning-based and cognitive approaches is best represented by the emergence of *cognitive-behavioral therapy*, a form of therapy that focuses on modifying both self-defeating beliefs and overt behaviors.

One issue concerning cognitive perspectives is their range of applicability. Cognitive therapists have largely focused on emotional disorders relating to anxiety and depression. Until recently, they have had less impact on the development of treatment approaches, or conceptual models, of more severe forms of disturbed behavior, such as schizophrenia. Moreover, in the case of depression, it remains unclear (as we will see in Chapter 7) whether distorted thinking patterns are causes of depression or are themselves effects of depression.

# The Sociocultural Perspective

Does abnormal behavior arise from forces within the person, as the psychodynamic theorists propose, or from learned maladaptive behaviors, as the learning theorists suggest? Or, as the *sociocultural perspective* proposes, does a fuller accounting of abnormal behavior require that we consider the roles of social and cultural factors, including factors relating to ethnicity, gender, and social class? As we noted in Chapter 1, sociocultural theorists seek causes of abnormal behavior in the failures of society rather than in the person. Some of the more radical sociocultural theorists, such as Thomas Szasz, even deny the existence of psychological disorders or mental illness. Szasz (1970, 2011) argues that the word *abnormal* is merely a label society attaches to people whose behavior deviates from accepted social norms. According to Szasz, this label is used to stigmatize social deviants.

Throughout the text, we examine relationships between abnormal behavior patterns and sociocultural factors such as gender, ethnicity, and socioeconomic status. Here, we examine recent research on relationships between ethnicity and mental health.

## Ethnicity and Mental Health

**2.7 Evaluate ethnic group differences in rates of psychological disorders.**

Given the increasing ethnic diversity of the population, researchers have begun to study ethnic group differences in the prevalence of psychological disorders. Knowing that a disorder disproportionately affects one group or another can help planners direct prevention and treatment programs to the groups that are most in need.

We need to take income level or socioeconomic status into account when comparing differences in rates of particular disorders across ethnic groups. Ethnic minority groups tend to be disproportionally represented among lower socioeconomic status levels. In general, as incomes increase, the risk of serious psychological disorders decreases, a trend that points to the effects of financial stress on mental well-being (Weissman et al., 2015). People with household incomes near or below the poverty line stand a higher risk of developing serious psychological disorders, including mood disorders and substance use disorders, than those with higher incomes (Sareen et al., 2011; Weissman et al., 2015).

Exposure to racism and discrimination is also a significant source of stress among ethnic minorities that can take a toll on mental health (Rodriguez-Seijas et al., 2015). For example, evidence links perceived exposure to discrimination to a greater risk of alcohol abuse in Latino women and also a greater risk of drug abuse in Latino men (Verissimo et al., 2014). A recent UCLA study of low-income African Americans and Latinos showed that reported exposure to discrimination was linked to increased risk of suffering psychological distress in the form of depression, anxiety, and posttraumatic stress disorder (PTSD; Liu et al., 2015; Myers et al., 2015). Other factors linked to psychological distress in this population included a history of sexual abuse, exposure to violence in the family or intimate relationships or in the community, and a chronic fear of being hurt or killed.

We also need to account for differences among ethnic subgroups, such as differences among the various subgroups that comprise Hispanic American and Asian American populations. For example, depression is a more prominent problem among Hispanic immigrants to the United States from Central

**COPING WITH DISCRIMINATION.** Exposure to discrimination is a cultural form of stress that can take a toll on the mental health of ethnic minority group members.

**Figure 2.8** Ethnicity and psychological disorders in the United States.

We can see that European Americans (non-Hispanic Whites) tend to have higher prevalence rates of psychological disorders overall than either Hispanic Americans (Latinos) or (non-Hispanic) Black Americans. Although not all of these differences were statistically significant, in none of these comparisons were there significantly higher prevalence rates among Hispanic Americans and Black Americans than among European Americans.

**SOURCE:** Breslau et al., 2005, based on data from the National Comordibity Survey (NCS).

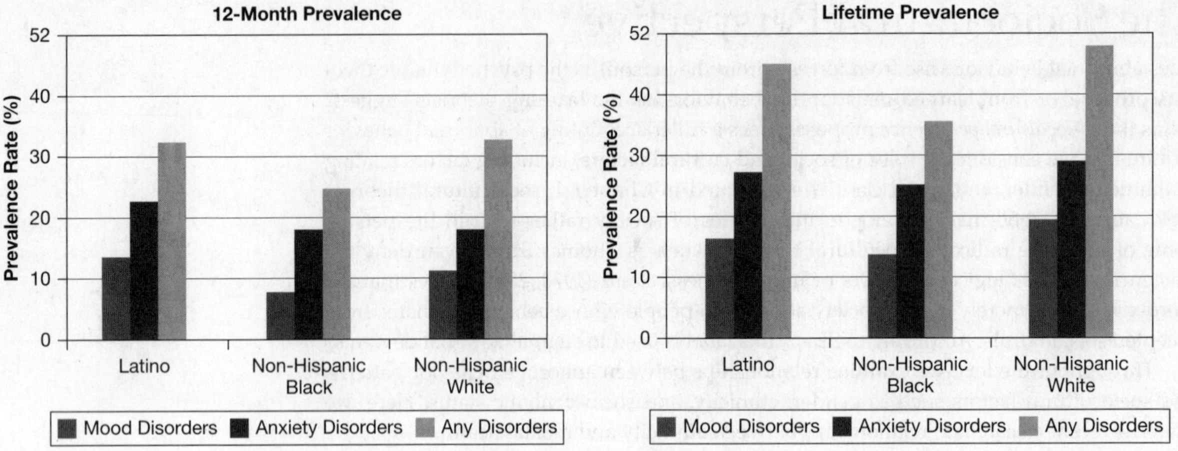


America than from Mexico, even when considering differences in educational backgrounds (Salgado de Snyder, Cervantes, & Padilla, 1990).

Researchers need to be cautious—and to think critically—when interpreting ethnic group differences in rates of diagnoses of psychological disorders. Might these differences reflect ethnic or racial differences, or differences in other factors in which groups may vary, such as socioeconomic level, living conditions, or cultural backgrounds?

An analysis of ethnic group differences in rates of mental disorders revealed an interesting pattern (Breslau et al., 2005). Using data from a nationally representative sample of adult Americans, investigators found that traditionally disadvantaged groups (non-Hispanic Black Americans and Hispanic Americans) had either significantly lower rates of psychological disorders or comparable rates as compared to European Americans (non-Hispanic Whites; see Figure 2.8). However, when the investigators looked at the persistence, or *chronicity*, of psychological disorders, they found that Hispanic Americans and Black Americans tended to experience more persistent mental disorders than European Americans.

What might we make of these findings on persistence of mental disorders? Additional analysis showed that differences in persistence were not a function of socioeconomic level—but might they reflect differences in access to quality care? The question needs to be addressed in further research, but it is conceivable that White European Americans benefit from better access to quality mental health care, which shortens the length of psychological disorders they experience.

**ROOTS OF ABNORMAL BEHAVIOR?** Sociocultural theorists believe that the roots of abnormal behavior are found not in the individual but in the social ills of society, such as poverty, social decay, discrimination based on race and gender, and lack of economic opportunity.

Native Americans are a traditionally disadvantaged minority group with high rates of mental disorders, such as depression and substance use disorders (Gone & Trimble, 2012). They also happen to be among the most impoverished ethnic groups in the United States and Canada. High levels of stress and poverty among Native Americans living on tribal reservations are certainly among the factors contributing to their greater prevalence of depression (Kaufman et al., 2013). The rate of alcohol-related disorders among Native Americans is six times that of other Americans (Rabasca, 2000). The death rate due to suicide among adolescents in the 10- to 14-year-old age range is about four times higher among Native Americans than among other ethnic groups.

Male Native American adolescents and young adults have the highest suicide rates in the nation (USDHHS, 1999).

Asian Americans typically show lower rates of psychological disorders than the general U.S. population (Kim & Lopez, 2014; Ryder et al., 2013; Sue et al., 2012). However, there are exceptions. When you envision stereotypes such as hula dancing, luaus, and wide tropical beaches, you may assume that Native Hawaiians are a carefree people—but reality paints a different picture. One reason for studying the relationship between ethnicity and abnormal behavior is to debunk erroneous stereotypes. Native Hawaiians, like other Native American groups, are economically disadvantaged and suffer a disproportionate share of physical diseases and mental health problems. Native Hawaiians tend to die at a younger age than other residents of Hawaii, largely because they face an increased risk of serious diseases, including hypertension, cancer, and heart disease (Johnson et al., 2004). They also show higher rates of risk factors associated with these life-threatening diseases, such as smoking, alcohol abuse, and obesity. Compared to other Hawaiians, Native Hawaiians also experience higher rates of mental health problems, including higher suicide rates among men, higher rates of alcoholism and drug abuse, and higher rates of antisocial behavior.

The mental health problems, as well as the economic disadvantage, of Native Americans—including Native Hawaiians—may at least partly reflect alienation and disenfranchisement from the land and a way of life that resulted from colonization by European cultures (Rabasca, 2000). Native peoples often attribute mental health problems, especially depression and alcoholism, to the collapse of their traditional culture brought about by colonization. The depression so common among indigenous or native peoples may reflect the loss of a relationship with the world that was based on maintaining harmony with nature.

Whatever the underlying differences in psychopathology among ethnic groups, members of ethnic minority groups tend to underutilize mental health services compared to White European Americans (Lee et al., 2014; USDHHS, 2001). Native Americans, for example, commonly seek help from traditional healers rather than from mental health professionals (Beals et al., 2005). Members of other ethnic minority groups often turn to members of the clergy or to spiritualists. Those who do seek services are more likely to drop out of treatment prematurely. Later in the chapter, we consider barriers that limit the use of mental health services by various ethnic minority groups in American society.

## Evaluating the Sociocultural Perspective

**2.8 Evaluate the sociocultural perspective in our understanding of abnormal behavior.**

Lending support to the link between social class and severe psychological disturbance, a classic research study in New Haven, Connecticut, showed that people from the lower socioeconomic groups were more likely to be institutionalized for psychiatric problems (Hollingshead & Redlich, 1958). More recent research in London, England, showed higher rates of schizophrenia—a severe and persistent type of psychological or mental disorder (see Chapter 11)—in neighborhood communities beset by economic hardship, lower educational levels, high crime rates, overcrowding, and a greater gap between the rich and the poor (Kirkbride et al., 2012).

Two major theoretical viewpoints have been advanced to explain links between SES and severe mental health problems. One viewpoint is the **social causation model**, which holds that people from lower socioeconomic groups are at greater risk of severe behavior problems because living in poverty subjects them to a greater level of social stress than that faced by more well-to-do people (Costello et al., 2003; Wadsworth & Achenbach, 2005). Another view is the **downward drift hypothesis**, which suggests that problem behaviors, such as alcoholism, lead people to drift downward in social status, thereby explaining the link between low socioeconomic status and severe behavior problems.

Sociocultural theorists have focused much-needed attention on the social stressors that can lead to abnormal behavior. Throughout this text, we consider how sociocultural factors relating to gender, race, ethnicity, and lifestyle inform our understanding of abnormal behavior and our response to people deemed mentally ill. Later in this chapter, we consider how issues relating to race, culture, and ethnicity affect the therapeutic process.

# The Biopsychosocial Perspective

Contemporary views of abnormal behavior are informed by several models or perspectives representing biological, psychological, and sociocultural perspectives. The fact that there are different ways of looking at the same phenomenon doesn't mean that one model must be right and the others wrong. No one theoretical perspective accounts for the many complex forms of abnormal behavior we will discuss in this text. Each perspective contributes something to our understanding, but none offers a complete view. Table 2.3 presents an overview of these perspectives.

The final perspective we discuss, the *biopsychosocial perspective*, takes a broader view of abnormal behavior than other models. It examines contributions of multiple factors spanning biological, psychological, and sociocultural domains, as well as their interactions, in the development of psychological disorders. As we'll see in later chapters, most psychological disorders involve multiple causal factors, as well as the interactions among these factors. For some disorders, especially schizophrenia, bipolar disorder, and autism, biological influences appear to be more prominent causal factors. For other disorders, such as anxiety disorders and depression, there appears to be a more intricate interplay of biological, psychological, and environmental causal factors (Weir, 2012b).

Researchers are only beginning to unravel the complex web of factors that underlie many of the disorders we discuss in this text. Even disorders that are primarily biological may be influenced by psychological or environmental factors, or vice versa. For example, some phobias may be learned behaviors that are acquired through experiences in which particular objects became associated with traumatic or painful experiences (see Chapter 5). Yet some people may inherit certain traits that make them susceptible to the development of acquired or conditioned phobias.

**Table 2.3** Perspectives on Abnormal Behavior

| | Model | Focus | Key Questions |
|---|---|---|---|
| **Biological Perspective** | **Medical model** | Biological underpinnings of abnormal behavior | What role is played by neurotransmitters in abnormal behavior? By genetics? By brain abnormalities? |
| **Psychological Perspective** | **Psychodynamic models** | Unconscious conflicts and motives underlying abnormal behavior | How do particular symptoms represent or symbolize unconscious conflicts? What are the childhood roots of a person's problem? |
| | **Learning models** | Learning experiences that shape the development of abnormal behavior | How are abnormal patterns of behavior learned? What role does the environment play in explaining abnormal behavior? |
| | **Humanistic models** | Roadblocks that hinder self-awareness and self-acceptance | How do a person's emotional problems reflect a distorted self-image? What roadblocks did the person encounter in the path toward self-acceptance and self-realization? |
| | **Cognitive models** | Faulty thinking underlying abnormal behavior | What styles of thinking characterize people with particular types of psychological disorders? What role do personal beliefs, thoughts, and ways of interpreting events play in the development of abnormal behavior patterns? |
| **Sociocultural Perspective** | | Social ills, such as poverty, racism, and prolonged unemployment, contributing to the development of abnormal behavior; relationships among abnormal behavior and ethnicity, gender, culture, and socioeconomic level | What relationships exist between social class status and risks of psychological disorders? Are there gender or ethnic group differences in various disorders? How are these explained? What are the effects of stigmatization of people who are labeled mentally ill? |
| **Biopsychosocial Perspective** | | Interactions of biological, psychological, and sociocultural factors in the development of abnormal behavior | How might genetic or other factors predispose individuals to psychological disorders in the face of life stress? How do biological, psychological, and sociocultural factors interact in the development of complex patterns of abnormal behavior? |

**SOURCE:** Adapted from J. S. Nevid (2013). *Psychology: Concepts and applications* (4th ed.). Belmont, CA: Cengage Learning.

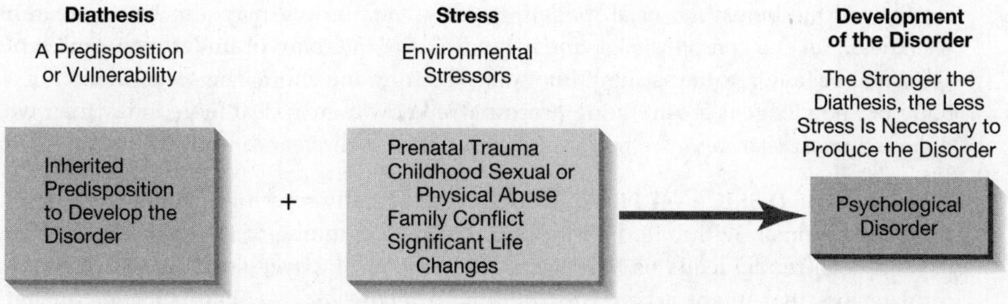


**Figure 2.9** The diathesis-stress model.

Here, we take a closer look at one of the leading examples of a biopsychosocial model, the *diathesis-stress model*, which posits that psychological disorders arise from an interaction of vulnerability factors (primarily biological in nature) and stressful life experiences.

## The Diathesis-Stress Model

**2.9 Describe the diathesis-stress model of abnormal behavior.**

The **diathesis-stress model** was originally developed as a framework for understanding schizophrenia (see Chapter 11). The model holds that certain psychological disorders, such as schizophrenia, arise from a combination or interaction of a **diathesis** (a vulnerability or predisposition to develop the disorder, usually genetic in nature) with stressful life experiences (see Figure 2.9). The diathesis-stress model has also been applied to other psychological disorders, including depression and attention deficit hyperactivity disorder (e.g., Van Meter & Youngstrom, 2015).

Whether a disorder actually develops depends on the nature of the diathesis and the type and severity of stressors the person experiences in life. The life stressors that may contribute to the development of disorders include birth complications, trauma or serious illness in childhood, childhood sexual or physical abuse, prolonged unemployment, loss of loved ones, or significant medical problems (Jablensky et al., 2005).

In some cases, people with a diathesis for a particular disorder, such as schizophrenia, will remain free of the disorder or will develop a milder form of the disorder if the level of stress in their lives remains low or if they develop effective coping responses for handling the stress they encounter. However, the stronger the diathesis, the less stress is generally needed to trigger the disorder. In some cases, the diathesis may be so strong that the disorder develops even under the most benign life circumstances.

A diathesis or predisposition is usually genetic in nature, such as having a particular genetic variant that increases the risk of developing a particular disorder. However, a diathesis may take other forms. A psychological diathesis, such as maladaptive personality traits and negative ways of thinking, may increase vulnerability to psychological disorders in the face of life stress (Morris, Ciesla, & Garber, 2008; Zvolensky et al., 2005). For example, the tendency to blame oneself for negative life events such as a divorce or the loss of a job may put a person at greater risk of developing depression in the face of these stressful events (see Chapter 7; Just, Abramson, & Alloy, 2001).

## Evaluating the Biopsychosocial Perspective

**2.10 Evaluate the biopsychosocial perspective of abnormal behavior.**

The biopsychosocial perspective brings a much needed interactionist focus to the study of abnormal behavior by considering the interplay of biological, psychological, and social factors. The model holds the view that with few exceptions, psychological disorders or other patterns of abnormal behavior are complex phenomena arising from multiple causes. There isn't any one cause that leads to the development of complex patterns of abnormal behaviors, such as schizophrenia or panic disorder. In addition, different people may develop the same disorder because of different sets of causal influences. The strength of the biopsychosocial model—its very complexity—may also be its greatest weakness. Yet the complexity of understanding the interplay of underlying causes of abnormal behavior patterns should not deter us from the effort. The accumulation of a body of knowledge is a continuing process. We know a great deal more today than we did a few short years ago. We will surely know more in the years ahead.

**THE CASE OF JESSICA—A FINAL WORD** Let's briefly return to the case of Jessica, the young woman with bulimia introduced at the beginning of the chapter. The biopsychosocial model leads us to consider the biological, psychological, and sociocultural factors that might account for bulimic behavior. As we shall consider further in Chapter 9, evidence points to biological influences on development of bulimia, such as genetic factors and irregularities in neurotransmitter activity. Evidence also points to contributions of sociocultural factors, such as the social pressures imposed on young women in our society to adhere to unrealistic standards of thinness, as well as psychological influences such as body dissatisfaction, cognitive factors such as thinking in perfectionistic and dichotomous ("black or white") terms, and underlying emotional and interpersonal problems. In all likelihood, multiple factors interact in leading to bulimia and other eating disorders. For example, we might apply the diathesis-stress model to frame a potential causal model of bulimia. From this perspective, we can propose that a genetic predisposition (diathesis) affecting the regulation of neurotransmitters in the brain interacts in some cases with stress in the form of social and family pressures, leading to the development of eating disorders.

We will return to consider these causal influences in Chapter 9. For now, let's simply note that psychological disorders such as bulimia are complex phenomena that are best approached by considering the contributions and interactions of multiple factors.

# Psychological Methods of Treatment

Carla, a 19-year-old college sophomore, had been crying more or less continuously for several days. She felt her life was falling apart, that her college aspirations were in shambles, and that she was a disappointment to her parents. The thought of suicide had crossed her mind. She could not seem to drag herself out of bed in the morning. She had withdrawn from her friends. Her misery had seemed to descend on her from nowhere, although she could pinpoint some pressures in her life: a couple of poor grades, a recent breakup with a boyfriend, some adjustment problems with roommates.

The psychologist who examined her arrived at a diagnosis of major depressive disorder. Had she broken a leg, she would have received a fairly standard course of treatment from a qualified professional. Yet the treatment that Carla or someone else with a psychological disorder receives is likely to vary not only with the type of disorder involved but also with the therapeutic orientation and professional background of the helping professional. A psychiatrist might recommend a course of antidepressant medication, perhaps in combination with some form of psychotherapy. A cognitively oriented psychologist might suggest a program of cognitive therapy to help Carla identify dysfunctional thoughts that may underlie her depression, whereas a psychodynamic therapist might recommend she begin therapy to uncover inner conflicts originating in childhood that may lie at the root of her depression.

In these next sections, we focus on psychological methods of treating psychological disorders. Yet despite the widespread availability of mental health services, there remains a large unmet need, as most people with diagnosed mental disorders remain either untreated or undertreated (Kessler, Demler, et al., 2005; González et al., 2010).

In later chapters, we examine psychological treatments for specific disorders, but here we focus on the treatments themselves. We will see that various psychological perspectives on abnormal behavior have spawned corresponding approaches to treatment. But first, we consider the major types of mental health professionals who treat psychological or mental disorders and the different roles they play.

# Types of Helping Professionals

**2.11 Identify three of the major types of helping professionals and describe their training backgrounds and professional roles.**

Many people are confused about the differences in qualifications and training of the various types of professionals who provide mental health care. It is little wonder people are confused, because there are different types of mental health professionals who represent a wide range of training backgrounds and areas of practice. For example, clinical psychologists and counseling psychologists have completed advanced graduate training in psychology and obtained a license to practice psychology. Psychiatrists are medical doctors who specialize in the diagnosis and treatment of emotional disorders. Three of the major groups of mental health professionals are clinical psychologists, psychiatrists, and clinical social workers. Table 2.4 describes their training backgrounds and areas of practice, as well as those of other professional groups involved in mental health care.

Unfortunately, many states do not limit the use of the titles *therapist* or *psychotherapist* to trained professionals. In such states, anyone can set up shop as a psychotherapist and practice "therapy" without a license. Thus, people seeking help should inquire about the training and licensure of helping professionals. We now consider the major types of psychotherapies and their relationships to the theoretical models from which they are derived. **T / F**

## TRUTH or FICTION

Some psychologists have been trained to prescribe drugs.

☑ TRUE Some psychologists have received specialized training that prepares them to prescribe psychiatric medications.

**Table 2.4** Major Types of Helping Professionals

| Type | Description |
|---|---|
| Clinical psychologists | Have earned a doctoral degree in psychology (a Ph.D. [Doctor of Philosophy]; a Psy.D. [Doctor of Psychology]; or an Ed.D. [Doctor of Education]) from an accredited college or university. Training in clinical psychology typically involves four years of graduate coursework, followed by a year-long internship and completion of a doctoral dissertation. Clinical psychologists specialize in administering psychological tests, diagnosing psychological disorders, and practicing psychotherapy. Until recently, they were not permitted to prescribe psychiatric drugs. However, as of this writing, three states (New Mexico, Louisiana, and Illinois) have enacted laws granting prescription privileges to psychologists who complete specialized training programs (American Psychological Association, 2014; Robiner, Tumlin, & Tompkins, 2013). The granting of prescription privileges to psychologists remains a hotly contested issue between psychologists and psychiatrists and within the field of psychology itself. |
| Counseling psychologists | Also hold doctoral degrees in psychology and have completed graduate training preparing them for careers in college counseling centers and mental health facilities. They typically provide counseling to people with psychological problems falling in a milder range of severity than those treated by clinical psychologists, such as difficulties adjusting to college or uncertainties regarding career choices. |
| Psychiatrists | Have earned a medical degree (M.D.) and completed a residency program in psychiatry. Psychiatrists are physicians who specialize in the diagnosis and treatment of psychological disorders. As licensed physicians, they can prescribe psychiatric drugs and may employ other medical interventions, such as electroconvulsive therapy (ECT). Many also practice psychotherapy based on training they receive during their residency programs or in specialized training institutes. |
| Clinical or psychiatric social workers | Have earned a master's degree in social work (M.S.W.) and use their knowledge of community agencies and organizations to help people with severe mental disorders receive the services they need. For example, they may help people with schizophrenia make a more successful adjustment to the community once they leave the hospital. Many clinical social workers practice psychotherapy or specific forms of therapy, such as marital or family therapy. |
| Psychoanalysts | Typically are either psychiatrists or psychologists who have completed extensive additional training in psychoanalysis. They are required to undergo psychoanalysis themselves as part of their training. |
| Counselors | Have typically earned a master's degree by completing a graduate program in a counseling field. Counselors work in many settings, including private practices, schools, college testing and counseling centers, and hospitals and health clinics. Many specialize in vocational evaluation, marital or family therapy, rehabilitation counseling, or substance abuse counseling. Counselors may focus on providing psychological assistance to people with milder forms of disturbed behavior or those struggling with a chronic or debilitating illness or recovering from a traumatic experience. Some are clergy members who are trained in pastoral counseling programs to help parishioners cope with personal problems. |
| Psychiatric nurses | Typically are registered nurses (R.N.s) who have completed a master's program in psychiatric nursing. They may work in psychiatric facilities or in group medical practices where they treat people suffering from severe psychological disorders. |

**SOURCE:** Adapted from J. S. Nevid (2013). *Psychology: Concepts and applications* (4th ed.). Belmont, CA: Cengage Learning.

## Types of Psychotherapy

**2.12 Describe the goals and techniques of the following forms of psychotherapy: psychodynamic therapy, behavior therapy, person-centered therapy, cognitive therapy, cognitive-behavioral therapy, eclectic therapy, group therapy, family therapy, and couple therapy.**

**Psychotherapy**, commonly referred to as "talk therapy," is a structured form of treatment based on a psychological framework and comprising one or more verbal interchanges between a client and a therapist. Psychotherapy is used to treat psychological disorders, to help clients change maladaptive behaviors or solve problems in living, or to help them develop their unique potentials. Table 2.5 presents an overview of the major types of psychotherapy.

**PSYCHODYNAMIC THERAPY** Sigmund Freud developed the first model of psychotherapy, which he called **psychoanalysis** and used to treat people with psychological disorders. Psychoanalysis was also the first form of **psychodynamic therapy**, a general term referring to forms of psychotherapy based on the Freudian tradition that seeks to help people gain insight into and resolve the dynamic struggles or conflicts between forces within the unconscious mind believed to lie at the root of abnormal behavior. Working through these conflicts, the ego would be freed of the need to maintain defensive behaviors—such as phobias, obsessive–compulsive behaviors, and symptoms of hysteria—that shield it from awareness of inner turmoil.

Freud summed up the goal of psychoanalysis by saying, "Where id was, there shall ego be." This meant in part that psychoanalysis could help shed the light of awareness, represented by the conscious ego, on the inner workings of the id. Through this process, a man might come to realize that unresolved anger toward his dominating or rejecting mother has sabotaged his intimate relationships with women during his adulthood. A woman with a loss of sensation in her hand that cannot be explained medically might come to see that she harbors guilt over urges to masturbate. The loss of sensation might have prevented her from

**Table 2.5** Overview of Major Types of Psychotherapy

| Type of Therapy | Major Figure(s) | Goal | Length of Treatment | Therapist's Approach | Major Techniques |
|---|---|---|---|---|---|
| **Classical psychoanalysis** | Sigmund Freud | Gaining insight and resolving unconscious psychological conflicts | Lengthy, typically lasting several years | Passive, interpretive | Free association, dream analysis, interpretation |
| **Modern psychodynamic approaches** | Various | Focus on developing insight, but with greater emphasis on ego functioning, current interpersonal relationships, and adaptive behavior than traditional psychoanalysis | Briefer than traditional psychoanalysis | More direct probing of client defenses; more back-and-forth discussion | Direct analysis of client's defenses and transference relationships |
| **Behavior therapy** | Various | Directly changing problem behavior through use of learning-based techniques | Relatively brief, typically lasting 10 to 20 sessions | Directive, active problem solving | Systematic desensitization, gradual exposure, modeling, reinforcement techniques |
| **Humanistic, client-centered therapy** | Carl Rogers | Self-acceptance and personal growth | Varies, but briefer than traditional psychoanalysis | Nondirective; allowing client to take the lead, with therapist serving as an empathic listener | Use of reflection; creation of a warm, accepting therapeutic relationship |
| **Ellis's rational emotive behavior therapy** | Albert Ellis | Replacing irrational beliefs with rational alternative beliefs; making adaptive behavioral changes | Relatively brief, typically lasting 10 to 20 sessions | Direct, sometimes confrontational challenging of client's irrational beliefs | Identifying and challenging irrational beliefs; behavioral homework assignments |
| **Beck's cognitive therapy** | Aaron Beck | Identifying and correcting distorted or self-defeating thoughts and beliefs; making adaptive behavioral changes | Relatively brief, typically lasting 10 to 20 sessions | Collaboratively engaging client in process of logically examining thoughts and beliefs and testing them out | Identifying and correcting distorted thoughts; behavioral homework, including reality testing |
| **Cognitive-behavioral therapy** | Various | Use of cognitive and behavioral techniques to change maladaptive behaviors and cognitions | Relatively brief, typically lasting 10 to 20 sessions | Direct, active problem solving | Combination of cognitive and behavioral techniques |

acting on these urges. Through confronting hidden impulses and the conflicts they produce, clients learn to sort out their feelings and find more constructive and socially acceptable ways of handling their impulses and wishes. The ego is then freed to focus on more constructive interests.

The major methods that Freud used to accomplish these goals were free association, dream analysis, and analysis of the transference relationship.

***Free Association*** **Free association** is the process of expressing whatever thoughts come to mind. Free association is believed to gradually break down the defenses that block awareness of unconscious processes. Clients are told not to censor or screen out thoughts, but to let their minds wander "freely" from thought to thought. Although free association may begin with small talk, it may eventually lead to more personally meaningful material.

The ego continues to try to shield the self from awareness of threatening impulses and conflicts. As deeper and more conflicted material is touched upon, the ego may throw up a "mental stop sign" in the form of *resistance*, or unwillingness or inability to recall or discuss disturbing or threatening material. Clients may report that their minds suddenly go blank when they venture into sensitive areas, such as hateful feelings toward family members or sexual yearnings. They may switch topics abruptly or accuse the analyst of trying to pry into material that is too personal or embarrassing to talk about, or they may conveniently "forget" the next appointment after a session in which sensitive material was touched on. Signs of resistance are often suggestive of meaningful material. Now and then, the analyst brings interpretations of this material to the client's attention to help the client gain better insight into deep-seated feelings and conflicts. **T / F**

## TRUTH or FICTION

In classical psychoanalysis, clients are asked to express whatever thought happens to come to mind, no matter how seemingly trivial or silly.

☑ TRUE In classical psychoanalysis, clients are asked to report any thoughts that come to mind. The technique is called *free association*.

***Dream Analysis*** To Freud, dreams represented the "royal road to the unconscious." During sleep, the ego's defenses are lowered, and unacceptable impulses find expression in dreams. Because the defenses are not completely eliminated, the impulses take a disguised or symbolized form. In psychoanalytic theory, dreams have two levels of content:

1. *Manifest content*: the material of the dream the dreamer experiences and reports
2. *Latent content*: the unconscious material the dream symbolizes or represents

A man might dream of flying in an airplane. Flying is the apparent or manifest content of the dream. Freud believed that flying may symbolize erection, so perhaps the latent content of the dream reflects unconscious issues related to fears of impotence. Because such symbols may vary from person to person, analysts ask clients to free associate to the manifest content of the dream to provide clues to the latent content. Although dreams may have a psychological meaning, as Freud believed, researchers lack any independent means of determining what they may truly mean.

**THE THERAPEUTIC RELATIONSHIP.** In the course of successful psychotherapy, a therapeutic relationship is forged between the therapist and client. Therapists use attentive listening to understand as clearly as possible what the client is experiencing and attempting to convey. Skillful therapists are also sensitive to clients' nonverbal cues, such as gestures and posture that may indicate underlying feelings or conflicts.

***Transference*** Freud found that clients responded to him not only as an individual but also in ways that reflected their feelings and attitudes toward other important people in their lives. A young female client might respond to him as a father figure—displacing or transferring onto Freud her feelings toward her own father. A man might also view him as a father figure, responding to him as a rival in a manner that Freud believed might reflect the man's unresolved Oedipus complex.

The process of analyzing and working through the **transference relationship** is considered an essential component of psychoanalysis. Freud believed that the transference relationship provides a vehicle for the reenactment of childhood conflicts with parents. Clients may react to the analyst with the same feelings of anger, love, or jealousy they felt toward their own parents. Freud termed the enactment of these childhood conflicts the *transference neurosis*. This "neurosis" had to be successfully analyzed and worked through for clients to succeed in psychoanalysis.

**WHAT DOES IT MEAN?** Freud believed that dreams represent the "royal road to the unconscious." Dream interpretation was one of the principal techniques Freud used to uncover unconscious material.

Childhood conflicts usually involve unresolved feelings of anger, rejection, or need for love. For example, a client may interpret any slight criticism by the therapist as a devastating blow, transferring feelings of self-loathing that the client had repressed from childhood experiences of parental rejection. Transference may also distort or color the client's relationships with others, such as a spouse or an employer. A client might relate to a spouse as to a parent, perhaps demanding too much or unjustly accusing the spouse of being insensitive or uncaring, or a client who had been mistreated by a past lover might not give new friends or lovers the benefit of a fair chance. The analyst helps the client recognize transference relationships, especially the therapy transference, and work through the residues of childhood feelings and conflicts that lead to self-defeating behavior in the present.

According to Freud, transference is a two-way street. Freud felt he transferred his underlying feelings onto his clients, perhaps viewing a young man as a competitor or a woman as a rejecting love interest. Freud referred to the feelings that he projected onto clients as **countertransference**. Psychoanalysts in training are expected to undergo psychoanalysis themselves to help them uncover motives that might lead to countertransferences in their therapeutic relationships. In their training, psychoanalysts learn to monitor their own reactions in therapy, so as to become better aware of when and how countertransferences intrude on the therapy process.

Although the analysis of transference is a crucial element of psychoanalytic therapy, it generally takes months or years for a transference relationship to develop and be resolved. This is one reason why psychoanalysis is typically a lengthy process.

***Modern Psychodynamic Approaches*** Although some psychoanalysts continue to practice traditional psychoanalysis in much the same manner as Freud did, briefer and less intensive forms of psychodynamic treatment have emerged. They are able to reach clients who are seeking briefer and less costly forms of treatment, perhaps once or twice a week (Grossman, 2003).

Like traditional psychoanalysts, modern psychodynamic therapists explore their clients' psychological defenses and transference relationships—a process described as "peeling an onion" (Gothold, 2009). But unlike traditional psychoanalysis, they focus more on clients' present relationships and less on sexual issues (Knoblauch, 2009). They also place greater emphasis on making adaptive changes in how their clients relate to others. Many contemporary psychodynamic therapists draw more heavily on the ideas of Erik Erikson, Karen Horney, and other theorists than on Freud's ideas. Treatment entails a more open dialogue and direct exploration of the client's defenses and transference relationships than was traditionally the case. The client and therapist generally sit facing each other, and the therapist engages in more frequent verbal give-and-take with the client, as in the following vignette. Note how the therapist uses interpretation to help the client, Mr. Arianes, achieve insight into how his relationship with his wife involves a transference of his childhood relationship with his mother:

***OFFERING AN INTERPRETATION***

MR. ARIANES: I think you've got it there, Doc. We weren't communicating. I wouldn't tell her [his wife] what was wrong or what I wanted from her. Maybe I expected her to understand me without saying anything.

THERAPIST: Like the expectations a child has of its mother.

MR. ARIANES: Not my mother!

THERAPIST: Oh?

MR. ARIANES: No, I always thought she had too many troubles of her [his mother] own to pay attention to mine. I remember once I got hurt on my bike and came to her all bloodied up. When she saw me she got mad and yelled at me for making more trouble for her when she already had her hands full with my father.

THERAPIST: Do you remember how you felt then?

MR. ARIANES: I can't remember, but I know that after that I never brought my troubles to her again.

THERAPIST: How old were you?

MR. ARIANES: Nine. I know that because I got that bike for my ninth birthday. It was a little too big for me still, that's why I got hurt on it.

THERAPIST: Perhaps you carried this attitude into your marriage.

MR. ARIANES: What attitude?

THERAPIST: The feeling that your wife, like your mother, would be unsympathetic to your difficulties. That there was no point in telling her about your experiences because she was too preoccupied or too busy to care.

MR. ARIANES: But she's so different from my mother. I come first with her.

THERAPIST: On one level you know that. On another, deeper level, there may well be the fear that people—or maybe only women, or maybe only women you're close to—are all the same, and you can't take a chance at being rejected again in your need.

MR. ARIANES: Maybe you're right, Doc, but all that was so long ago, and I should be over that by now.

THERAPIST: That's not the way the mind works. If a shock or a disappointment is strong enough, it can permanently freeze our picture of ourselves and our expectations of the world. The rest of us grows up—that is, we let ourselves learn about life from experience and from what we see, hear, or read of the experiences of others, but that one area where we really got hurt stays unchanged. So what I mean when I say you might be carrying that attitude into your relationship with your wife is that when it comes to your hopes of being understood and catered to when you feel hurt or abused by life, you still feel very much like that 9-year-old boy who was rebuffed in his need and gave up hope that anyone would or could respond to him.

—*Offering an Interpretation, from M. F. Basch,* Doing Psychotherapy *(Basic Books, 1980), pp. 29–30. Reprinted by permission of Basic Books, a member of Perseus Books Group.*

Some modern psychodynamic therapists focus more on the role of the ego and less on the role of the id. These therapists, such as Heinz Hartmann, are generally described as *ego analysts.* Other modern psychoanalysts, such as Margaret Mahler, are identified with *object-relations* approaches to psychodynamic therapy. They focus on helping people separate their own ideas and feelings from the elements of significant others they have incorporated or *introjected* onto themselves. Clients can then develop more as individuals—as their own persons, rather than trying to meet the expectations they believe others have of them.

Though psychodynamic therapy is no longer the dominant force in the field it once was, it remains a widely practiced form of therapy. For many years—decades, really—there remained a lack of evidence of its effects based on controlled research trials. However, today there is an accumulating body of evidence supporting the effectiveness of contemporary forms of psychodynamic therapy for treating problems such as anxiety and depression (e.g., Bögels et al., 2014; Driessen et al., 2015; Keefe et al., 2014; Leichsenring & Schauenburg, 2014; Leichsenring et al., 2013, 2014; Levy, Ablon, & Kächele, 2013). Let's now turn to other forms of therapy, beginning with behavior therapy.

**CONTEMPORARY PSYCHODYNAMIC THERAPY.** Modern psychodynamic therapy is generally briefer than traditional Freudian psychoanalysis and involves more direct, face-to-face interactions with clients.

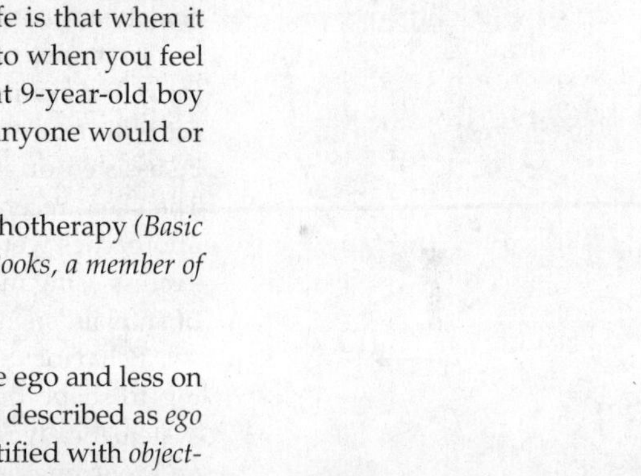

**BEHAVIOR THERAPY** **Behavior therapy** is the systematic application of the principles of learning to the treatment of psychological disorders. Because the focus is on changing behavior—not on personality change or deep probing into the past—behavior therapy is relatively brief, typically lasting from a few weeks to a few months. Behavior therapists, like other therapists, seek to develop warm therapeutic relationships with clients, but they believe the special efficacy of behavior therapy derives from learning-based techniques rather than from the nature of the therapeutic relationship.

Behavior therapy originally gained widespread attention as a means of helping people overcome fears and phobias, problems that had proved resistant to insight-oriented therapies. Among the methods used are systematic desensitization, gradual exposure, and modeling. **Systematic desensitization** involves a therapeutic program of exposure of a client (in imagination or by means of pictures or slides) to progressively more fearful stimuli while he or she remains deeply relaxed. First, the client uses a relaxation technique, such as progressive relaxation (discussed in Chapter 6), to become deeply relaxed. The client is then instructed to imagine (or perhaps view, as through a series of slides) progressively more anxiety-arousing scenes. If fear is evoked, the client again practices a relaxation exercise to restore a relaxed state. The process is repeated until the client can tolerate the scene without anxiety. The client then progresses to the next scene in the *fear-stimulus hierarchy*. The procedure continues until the person can remain relaxed while imagining the most distressing scene in the hierarchy.

In **gradual exposure** (also called *in vivo*, meaning *in life*, exposure), people seeking to overcome phobias put themselves in situations in which they confront fearful stimuli in real-life encounters. As with systematic desensitization, a person moves at his or her own pace through a hierarchy of progressively more anxiety-evoking stimuli. A person with a fear of snakes, for example, might first look at a harmless, caged snake from across the room and then gradually approach and interact with the snake in a step-by-step process, progressing to each new step only when feeling completely calm at the prior step. Gradual exposure is often combined with cognitive techniques that focus on replacing anxiety-arousing, irrational thoughts with calming, rational thoughts.

In **modeling**, individuals learn desired behaviors by observing others performing them. For example, a client may observe and then imitate others who successfully interact with fear-evoking situations or objects. After observing the model, the client may be assisted or guided by the therapist or the model in performing the target behavior. The client receives ample reinforcement from the therapist for each attempt. Modeling approaches were pioneered by Albert Bandura and his colleagues, who had remarkable success using modeling techniques with children to treat various phobias, especially fear of animals, such as snakes and dogs.

Behavior therapists also use reinforcement techniques based on operant conditioning to shape desired behavior. For example, parents and teachers may be trained to systematically reinforce children for appropriate behavior by showing appreciation for it and to extinguish inappropriate behavior by ignoring it. In institutional settings, **token economy** systems seek to increase adaptive behavior by rewarding residents with tokens for performing appropriate behaviors, such as self-grooming and making their beds. The tokens can eventually be exchanged for desired rewards. Token systems also have been used to treat children with conduct disorders.

Other techniques of behavior therapy discussed in later chapters include *aversive conditioning* (used in the treatment of substance abuse problems such as smoking and alcoholism) and *social skills training* (used in the treatment of social anxiety and skills deficits associated with schizophrenia).

**HUMANISTIC THERAPY** Psychodynamic therapists tend to focus on clients' unconscious processes, such as internal conflicts. By contrast, humanistic therapists focus on clients' subjective, conscious experiences. The major form of humanistic therapy is **person-centered therapy** (also called *client-centered therapy*), which was developed by the psychologist Carl Rogers (Rogers, 1951; Raskin, Rogers, & Witty, 2011).

***Person-Centered Therapy*** To Rogers, psychological disorders result largely from roadblocks that other people place in our path toward self-actualization. When others are selective in their approval of our childhood feelings and behaviors, we may disown the criticized parts of ourselves. To earn social approval, we may don social masks or facades. We learn "to be seen and not heard" and may even become deaf to our own inner voices. Over time, we may develop distorted self-concepts that are consistent with others' views of us but are not of our own making and design. As a result, we may become poorly adjusted, unhappy, and confused as to who and what we are.

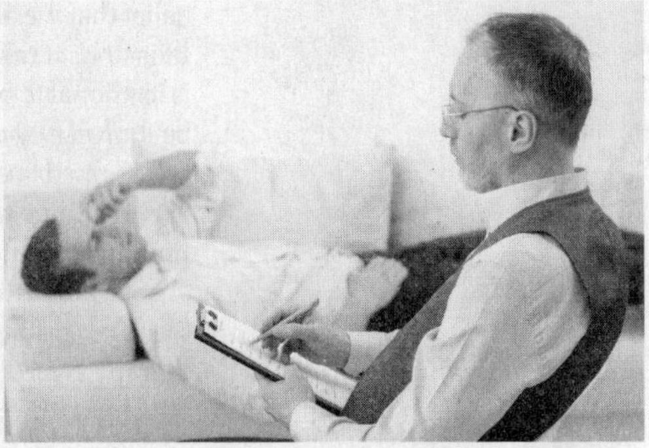

Person-centered therapy creates conditions of warmth and acceptance in the therapeutic relationship that help clients become more and more aware and accepting of their true selves. Rogers did not believe therapists should impose their own goals or values on their clients. His focus in therapy, as the name implies, is on the person.

Person-centered therapy is *nondirective*. The client, not the therapist, takes the lead and directs the course of therapy. The therapist uses *reflection*—the restating or paraphrasing of the client's expressed feelings without interpreting them or passing judgment on them. Reflection communicates to the client that he or she is being heard and encourages the client to explore deeper feelings and parts of the self that had been disowned because of social condemnation.

Rogers stressed the importance of creating a warm, therapeutic relationship that would encourage a client to engage in self-exploration and self-expression. The effective person-centered therapist possesses four basic qualities or attributes: *unconditional positive regard, empathy, genuineness*, and *congruence*. First, the therapist must be able to express unconditional positive regard for clients. In contrast to the conditional approval the client may have received from parents and others in the past, the therapist must be unconditionally accepting of the client as a person, even if the therapist sometimes finds the client's choices or behaviors to be objectionable. Unconditional positive regard provides clients with a sense of security that encourages them to explore their feelings without fear of disapproval. As clients feel accepted or prized for themselves, they are encouraged to accept themselves in turn.

Therapists who display **empathy** are able to accurately reflect or mirror their clients' experiences and feelings. Therapists try to see the world through their clients' eyes or frames of reference. They listen carefully to clients, setting aside their own judgments and interpretations of events. Showing empathy encourages clients to get in touch with feelings of which they may be only dimly aware. **Genuineness** is the ability to be open about one's feelings. Rogers admitted he had negative feelings at times during therapy sessions, typically boredom, but he attempted to express these feelings openly rather than hide them (Bennett, 1985). **Congruence** refers to the coherence or fit among one's thoughts, feelings, and behaviors. The congruent person is one whose behavior, thoughts, and feelings are integrated and consistent. Congruent therapists serve as models of psychological integrity for their clients.

### COGNITIVE THERAPY

> There is nothing either good or bad, but thinking makes it so.
>
> —Shakespeare, *Hamlet*

Shakespeare did not mean to imply that misfortunes or ailments are painless or easy to manage. His point, it seems, was that the ways in which we evaluate upsetting events can heighten or diminish our discomfort and affect our ability to cope. Several hundred years later, cognitive therapists such as Aaron Beck and Albert Ellis adopted this simple but elegant expression as a kind of motto for their approach to therapy.

Cognitive therapists focus on helping clients identify and correct faulty thinking, distorted beliefs, and self-defeating attitudes that create or contribute to emotional problems. They argue that negative emotions such as anxiety and depression are caused by interpretations people place on troubling events, not by the events themselves. Here, we focus on two prominent types of **cognitive therapy**: Albert Ellis's rational emotive behavior therapy and Aaron Beck's cognitive therapy.

***Rational Emotive Behavior Therapy*** Albert Ellis (1993, 2001, 2011) believed that negative emotions such as anxiety and depression are caused by the irrational ways in which we interpret or judge negative events, not by the negative events themselves. Consider the irrational belief that we almost always must have the approval of the people who are important to us. Ellis finds it understandable to want other people's approval and love, but he argues that it is irrational to believe we cannot survive without it. Another irrational belief is that we must be thoroughly competent and achieving in virtually everything we seek to accomplish. We are doomed to eventually fall short of these irrational expectations, and when we do, we may experience negative emotional consequences, such as depression and lowered self-esteem. Emotional difficulties such as anxiety and depression are not directly caused by negative events, but rather by how we distort the meaning of these events by viewing them through the dark-colored glasses of self-defeating beliefs. In Ellis's **rational emotive behavior therapy** (REBT), therapists actively *dispute* clients' irrational beliefs and the premises on which they are based and help clients develop alternative, adaptive beliefs in their place.

Rational emotive behavior therapists help clients substitute more effective interpersonal behavior for self-defeating or maladaptive behavior. Ellis often gave clients specific tasks or homework assignments, such as disagreeing with an overbearing relative or asking someone for a date. He also assisted them in practicing or rehearsing adaptive behaviors.

***Beck's Cognitive Therapy*** Psychiatrist Aaron Beck (e.g., Beck, 2005; Beck & Weishaar, 2011) developed cognitive therapy—which, like REBT, focuses on helping people change faulty or distorted thinking. Cognitive therapy is the fastest growing and most widely researched model of psychotherapy today (Beck & Dozois, 2011).

Cognitive therapists encourage their clients to recognize and change errors in thinking, called *cognitive distortions*—such as tendencies to magnify the importance of negative events and minimize one's personal accomplishments. These self-defeating ways of thinking, Beck argues, underlie negative emotional states such as depression. Like tinted glasses, these distorted or faulty thoughts color a person's perception of life experiences and his or her reactions to the outside world (Smith, 2009). Cognitive therapists ask clients to record their thoughts in response to upsetting events and note connections between their thoughts and their emotional responses. They then help clients dispute distorted thoughts and replace them with rational alternatives.

Cognitive therapists also use behavioral homework assignments, such as encouraging depressed people to fill their free time with structured activities, like gardening or completing work around the house. Another type of homework assignment involves *reality testing*, whereby clients are asked to test their negative beliefs in light of reality. For example, a depressed client who feels unwanted by everyone might be asked to call two or three friends on the phone to gather data about the friends' reactions to the calls. The therapist might then ask the client to report on the assignment: "Did they immediately hang up the phone, or did they seem pleased you called? Did they express any interest at all in talking to you again or getting together sometime? Does the evidence support the conclusion that *no one* has any interest in you?" Such exercises help clients replace distorted beliefs with rational alternatives.

The therapies developed by Beck and Ellis can be classified as forms of cognitive-behavioral therapy, which is the treatment approach we turn to next. We will then consider a growing movement among therapists toward incorporating principles and techniques derived from different schools of therapy. Before reading further, you may wish to review Table 2.5, which summarizes the major approaches to psychotherapy.

**COGNITIVE-BEHAVIORAL THERAPY** Today, most behavior therapists identify with a broader model of behavior therapy called **cognitive-behavioral therapy** (CBT; also called *cognitive behavior therapy*). CBT combines behavioral and cognitive therapeutic techniques to help people make changes in their behavior as well as their underlying thoughts, beliefs, and attitudes. It draws on the assumption that thinking patterns and beliefs affect behavior and that changes in these cognitions can produce desirable behavioral and emotional changes. Cognitive-behavioral therapists focus on helping clients identify and correct the maladaptive beliefs and negative, automatic thoughts that may underlie their emotional problems.

CBT is a merger of sorts, a combining of two therapeutic traditions: behavior therapy and cognitive therapy (Rachman, 2015). Cognitive-behavioral therapists use an assortment of cognitive and behavioral techniques, including behavioral treatments, such as exposure therapy for contronting fearful situations, and cognitive techniques, such as cognitive restructuring (changing maladaptive thinking into more rational, adaptive thinking). CBT has produced impressive results in controlled trials for treating a wide range of emotional disorders, including depression, panic disorder, generalized anxiety disorder, social phobia, posttraumatic stress disorder, agoraphobia, obsessive–compulsive disorder, bulimia, and personality disorders (e.g., DeRubeis et al., 2005; DiMauro et al., 2012; Hofmann et al., 2012; McEvoy et al., 2012; Öst et al., 2015; Resick et al., 2012; Watts et al., 2015). Yet like other forms of treatment, such as drug therapy, CBT is not effective in all cases: Many patients either fail to respond to treatment or continue to show symptoms when evaluated at later points in time (e.g., Durham et al., 2012). This only underscores the need for further efforts to improve current treatment approaches.

**ECLECTIC THERAPY** Each of the major psychological models of abnormal behavior—the psychodynamic, behaviorist, humanistic, and cognitive approaches—has spawned its own approaches to psychotherapy. Although many therapists identify with one or another of these schools of therapy, some others practice **eclectic therapy**, which incorporates principles and techniques from different therapeutic orientations that they believe will produce the greatest benefit in treating a particular client (Norcross & Beutler, 2011). An eclectic or integrative therapist might use behavior therapy techniques to help a client change specific maladaptive behaviors, for example, along with psychodynamic techniques to help the client gain insight into the childhood roots of the problem.

The second largest percentage of clinical psychologists today (22%) identify with an eclectic/integrative theoretical orientation (Norcross & Karpiak, 2012; see Figure 2.10). Therapists who adopt an eclectic approach tend to be older and more experienced (Beitman, Goldfried, & Norcross, 1989). Perhaps they have learned through experience the value of drawing on diverse contributions to the practice of therapy.

There are two general types of eclecticism: technical eclecticism and integrative eclecticism. Therapists who practice *technical eclecticism* draw on techniques from different schools of therapy without necessarily adopting the theoretical positions that spawned those techniques. They assume a pragmatic approach in using techniques from different therapeutic approaches that they believe are most likely to work with a given client.

Therapists who practice *integrative eclecticism* attempt to synthesize and integrate diverse theoretical approaches—to bring together different theoretical concepts and approaches under the roof of one integrated model of therapy. Although various approaches to integrative psychotherapy have been proposed, the field has yet to arrive at a consensus regarding a therapeutic integration of principles and practices. Not all therapists subscribe to the view that therapeutic integration is a desirable or achievable goal. They believe that combining elements of different therapeutic approaches will lead to a hodgepodge of techniques that lack a cohesive conceptual framework. Still, interest in the professional community in therapeutic integration is growing, and we expect to see new models emerging that aim to tie together the contributions of different approaches.

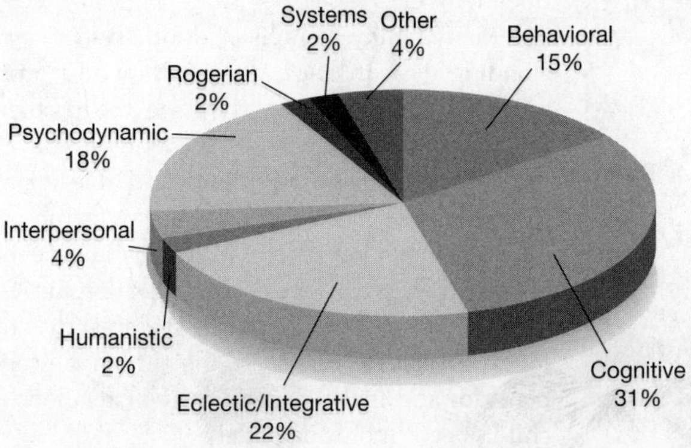


**Figure 2.10** Therapeutic orientations of clinical psychologists.

A recent national survey showed that the cognitive and the eclectic/integrative therapeutic orientations were the most popular among clinical psychologists today. *Source:* Adapted from Norcross & Karpiak (2012).

**GROUP THERAPY.** What are some of the advantages of group therapy over individual therapy? What are some of its disadvantages?

**GROUP, FAMILY, AND COUPLE THERAPY** Some approaches to therapy expand the focus of treatment to include groups of people, families, and couples.

***Group Therapy*** In **group therapy**, a group of clients meets together with a therapist or a pair of therapists. Group therapy has several advantages over individual treatment. For one, group therapy is less costly to individual clients, because several clients are treated at the same time. Many clinicians also believe that group therapy is more effective in treating groups of clients who have similar problems, such as complaints relating to anxiety, depression, lack of social skills, or adjustment to divorce or other life stresses. Clients learn how people with similar problems cope and receive social support from both the group and the therapist. Group therapy also provides members with opportunities to work through their problems in relating to others. For example, the therapist or other group members may point out how a particular member's behavior in a group session mirrors the person's behavior outside the group. Group members may also rehearse social skills with one another in a supportive atmosphere.

Despite these advantages, clients may prefer individual therapy for various reasons. For one, clients might not wish to disclose their problems in a group. Some clients prefer the individual attention of the therapist. Others are too socially inhibited to feel comfortable in a group setting. Because of such concerns, group therapists require that group disclosures be kept confidential, that group members relate to each other supportively and nondestructively, and that group members receive the attention they need.

***Family Therapy*** In **family therapy**, the family, not the individual, is the unit of treatment. Family therapy aims to help troubled families resolve their conflicts and problems so the family functions better as a unit and individual family members are subjected to less stress from family conflicts. In family therapy, family members learn to communicate more effectively and to air their disagreements constructively (Gehar, 2009). Family conflicts often emerge at transitional points in the life cycle, when family patterns are altered by changes in one or more members. Conflicts between parents and children, for example, often emerge when adolescent children seek greater independence or autonomy. Family members with low self-esteem may be unable to tolerate different attitudes or behaviors from other members of the family and may resist their efforts to change or become more independent. Family therapists work with families to resolve these conflicts and help them adjust to life changes.

Family therapists are sensitive to tendencies of families to scapegoat one family member as the source of the problem, or the "identified client." Disturbed families seem to adopt a sort of myth: Change the identified client (the "bad apple") and the "barrel" (or family) will once again become functional. Family therapists encourage families to work together to resolve their disputes and conflicts, instead of scapegoating one member.

**FAMILY THERAPY.** In family therapy, the family, not the individual, is the unit of treatment. Therapists help family members communicate more effectively with one another—for example, by airing disagreements in ways that are not hurtful to individual members. Therapists also try to prevent one member of the family from becoming the scapegoat for the family's problems.

Many family therapists adopt a *systems approach* to understanding the workings of the family and problems that may arise within the family. They see the problem behaviors of individual family members as representing a breakdown in the system of communications and role relationships within the family. For example, a child may feel in competition with other siblings for a parent's attention and develop enuresis, or bed-wetting, as a means of securing attention. Operating from a systems perspective, the family therapist may focus on helping family members understand the hidden messages in the child's behavior and make changes in their relationships to meet the child's needs more adequately.

***Couple Therapy*** **Couple therapy** focuses on resolving conflicts in distressed couples, including married and unmarried couples (Baucom, Atkins, et al., 2015; Baucom, Sheng, et al., 2015; Doss et al., 2015; Christensen et al., 2010). Like family therapy, couple therapy focuses on improving communication and analyzing role relationships. For example, one partner may play a dominant role and resist any request to share power. The couple therapist helps bring these role relationships into the open so that partners can explore alternative ways of relating to one another that can lead to a more satisfying relationship.

# Evaluating the Methods of Psychotherapy

**2.13 Evaluate the effectiveness of psychotherapy and the role of nonspecific factors in therapy.**

What, then, of the effectiveness of psychotherapy? Does psychotherapy work? Are some forms of therapy more effective than others? Are some forms of therapy more effective for some types of clients or for some types of problems than for others?

**USE OF META-ANALYSIS** The notion that psychotherapy is effective receives strong support from the research literature. Reviews of the scientific literature often use a statistical technique called *meta-analysis*, which averages the results of a large number of studies to determine an overall level of effectiveness.

A classic example of a meta-analysis of psychotherapy outcomes involved some 375 controlled studies, each of which compared psychotherapy (of different types, including psychodynamic, behavioral, and humanistic) against control groups (Smith & Glass, 1977). Across these studies, the average client receiving psychotherapy was better off than 75% of clients who remained untreated. A larger analysis of 475 controlled outcome studies showed the average person who received therapy to be better off at the end of treatment than 80% of those who did not (Smith, Glass, & Miller, 1980). **T / F**

**TRUTH or FICTION**

Psychotherapy is no more effective than simply letting time take its course.

☑ **FALSE** There is ample evidence that psychotherapy produces better results than control treatments in which people are placed on waiting lists that allow time to take its course.

Later meta-analyses also showed positive outcomes for particular types of therapy, including cognitive-behavioral therapy and psychodynamic therapy (e.g., Butler et al., 2006; Cuijpers, van Straten, et al., 2010; Okumura & Ichikura, 2014; Shedler, 2010; Tolin, 2010; Town et al., 2012). Psychotherapy proves to be effective not only in the confines of clinical research centers, but also in settings more typical of ordinary clinical practice (Shadish et al., 2000). The greatest gains in psychotherapy typically occur in the first several months of treatment. At least 50% of patients in controlled research studies show clinically significant improvement in about 13 treatment sessions; by 26 sessions, this figure rises to more than 80% (Anderson & Lambert, 2001; Hansen, Lambert, & Forman, 2002; Messer, 2001). Yet we should recognize that many clients drop out prematurely, before therapeutic benefits are achieved.

Evidence supports the effectiveness of psychotherapy, but we lack clarity about why it works—that is, what factors or processes account for therapeutic change. Different forms of therapy produce about the same level (size) of therapeutic change when each is compared to control (untreated) groups or to each other (Clarkin, 2014; Kivlighan et al., 2015; Wampold et al., 2011). This suggests that the effectiveness of different forms of psychotherapy may have more to do with the common features that cut across different types of psychotherapy, called **nonspecific treatment factors**, than with the specific techniques that set them apart.

Nonspecific or common factors in therapy include expectations of improvement and features of the therapist–client relationship, including the following: (1) empathy, support, and attention shown by the therapist; (2) the *therapeutic alliance*, or attachment the client develops toward the therapist and the therapy process; and (3) the *working alliance*, or effective working relationship in which the therapist and client work together identifying and confronting the important problems and concerns the client faces (Crits-Christoph et al., 2011; Norcross & Lambert, 2014; Prochaska & Norcross, 2010). Nonspecific treatment factors appear to have therapeutic benefits in themselves, quite apart from the specific benefits associated with particular forms of therapy (Goldfried, 2012; Marcus et al., 2014; Zilcha-Mano et al., 2014).

Should we conclude that different therapies are about equally effective? Not necessarily. Different therapies may be more or less equivalent in their effects overall, but some may be more effective for some patients or some types of problems. We should also allow that the effectiveness of therapy may have more to do with the effectiveness of the therapist than with a particular form of therapy (Wampold, 2001).

All in all, the question of whether some forms of therapy are more effective than others remains unresolved. Perhaps the time has come for investigators to turn more of their attention to examining the active ingredients that make some therapists more effective than others, such as their interpersonal skills, ability to show empathy, and ability to develop a good therapeutic relationship or alliance with their clients (Laska, Gurman, & Wampold, 2014; Prochaska & Norcross, 2010). Investigators find that a stronger therapeutic alliance, especially when formed early in therapy, is associated with better treatment outcomes (Arnow et al., 2013; Cummings et al., 2013; Lorenzo-Luaces, DeRubeis, & Webb, 2014).

Another question researchers pose is whether specific therapies work as well in the clinic as they do in the research lab. Two types of research studies, *efficacy studies* and *effectiveness studies*, examine these types of effects. Efficacy studies speak to the issue of whether particular treatments work better than control procedures under tightly controlled conditions in a research lab setting—but the fact that a given treatment works well in the research lab does not necessarily mean it also works well in a typical clinic setting. This question is addressed by effectiveness studies that examine the effects of treatment when it is delivered by therapists in real-world practice settings with the kinds of clients they normally see in their practices (Onken et al., 2014; Weisz, Ng, & Bearman, 2014).

**EMPIRICALLY SUPPORTED TREATMENTS** Empirically supported treatments are specific psychological treatments that have been demonstrated to be effective in treating particular types of problem behaviors or disorders on the basis of carefully designed research studies (see the listing in Table 2.6; APA Presidential Task Force on Evidence-Based Practice, 2006; Church et al., 2014; Lohr, 2011). The designation of empirically supported treatments (also called *evidence-based practice*) may change; other treatments may be added to the list as scientific evidence of their efficacy in treating specific types of problems becomes available. We should note, however, that inclusion of a particular treatment in the listing of empirically supported treatments does not mean the treatment is effective in every case.

Let's conclude by noting that it is insufficient to ask which therapy works best. Instead, we must ask: Which therapy works best for which type of problem? Which

**Table 2.6** Examples of Empirically Supported Treatments

| Treatment | Conditions for Which Treatment Is Effective |
|---|---|
| Cognitive therapy | Headache (Chapter 6) |
| | Depression (Chapter 7) |
| Behavior therapy or behavior modification | Depression (Chapter 7) |
| | Persons with developmental disabilities (Chapter 13) |
| | Enuresis (Chapter 13) |
| Cognitive-behavioral therapy | Panic disorder (Chapter 5) |
| | Generalized anxiety disorder (Chapter 5) |
| | Bulimia nervosa (Chapter 9) |
| Exposure treatment | Agoraphobia and specific phobia (Chapter 5) |
| Exposure and response prevention | Obsessive–compulsive disorder (Chapter 5) |
| Interpersonal psychotherapy | Depression (Chapter 7) |
| Parent training programs | Children with oppositional behavior (Chapter 13) |

**Note:** Chapter in text in which treatment is discussed is included in parentheses.

clients are best suited for which type of therapy? What are the advantages and limitations of particular therapies? Although the effort to identify empirically supported treatments moves us in the direction of matching treatments to particular disorders, determining which treatment, practiced by whom, under what conditions is most effective for a given client remains a challenge.

All in all, psychotherapy is a complex process that incorporates common features along with specific techniques that foster adaptive change. Practitioners need to take into account the contributions to therapeutic change of both specific and nonspecific factors, as well as their interactions (Gibbons et al., 2009; Raykos et al., 2014).

## THINKING CRITICALLY about abnormal psychology

### @ISSUE: SHOULD THERAPISTS TREAT CLIENTS ONLINE?

Might better mental health be only a few keystrokes away? You can do almost anything on the Internet these days, from ordering concert tickets to downloading music (legally, of course) or even whole books. You can also receive counseling or therapy services from an online therapist. Online counselors and therapists are using video chat services, such as Skype, as well as email and other electronic and telephonic services to help people cope with emotional problems and relationship issues. As the use of online counseling services increases, so does the controversy.

Many professionals voice concerns about clinical, ethical, and legal issues of online counseling services (e.g., Gabbard, 2012; Harris & Younggren, 2011; Yuen et al., 2012). One problem is that psychologists are licensed in particular states, but Internet communications easily cross state borders (DeAngelis, 2012a). It remains unclear, therefore, whether psychologists or other mental health professionals can legally provide online services to residents of states in which they are not licensed.

Ethical problems and liability issues also arise when psychologists and other helping professionals offer services to clients they never meet in person. Many therapists also express concerns that interacting remotely with a client by computer or by other means, such as by cell phone, would prevent them from evaluating nonverbal cues and gestures that might signal deeper levels of distress than could be communicated by typing words on a keyboard or talking on the telephone (Drum & Littleton, 2014).

Therapists are rightfully concerned about the ethical problems in using technology in therapy—problems such as unauthorized access to client records and dissemination (posting) of client information on social websites (Van Allen & Roberts, 2011). Yet another problem is that online therapists may live at great distances from their clients, so they may not be able to provide the more intensive services clients need during times of emotional crisis. Professionals also express concerns about the potential for unsuspecting clients to be victimized by unqualified practitioners or quacks. There is not yet a system to ensure that only licensed and qualified practitioners offer online therapeutic services.

On the other hand, evidence is accumulating that Internet-based mental health services produce measurable therapeutic benefits in treating a wide range of problems, including anxiety, PTSD, depression, insomnia, obsessive–compulsive disorder, pathological gambling, alcohol abuse, and smoking addiction (e.g., Andersson, Hedman, Ljótsson, et al., 2015; Clark et al., 2014; El Alaoui et al., 2015; Kuester, Niemeyer, & Knaevelsrud, 2016; Mahoney et al.,

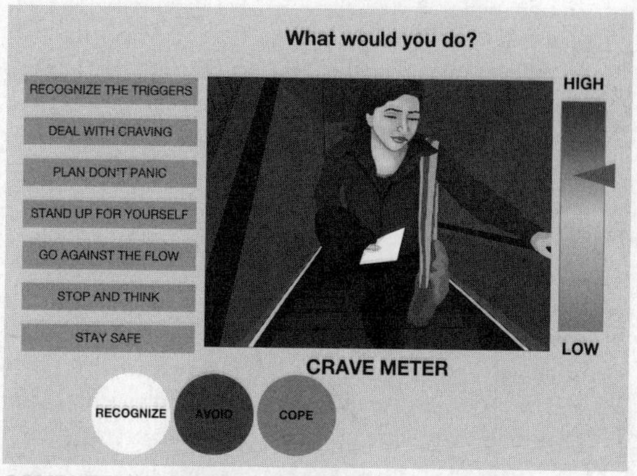


**COMPUTER-ASSISTED THERAPY.** This computerized interactive video is used as part of a cognitive-behavioral treatment program designed to help people with substance abuse problems learn abstinence skills. This scene from a movie shows a woman with a drug abuse problem walking up the stairs to her apartment. She is then confronted with drug-related cues, such as her boyfriend encouraging her to use drugs. At each critical point, the scene stops and the narrator offers some strategies for coping with cravings. When the movie resumes, the woman is shown using some of these coping skills, such as visiting a friend who encourages her to remain abstinent.

**SOURCE:** Adapted from National Institute on Drug Abuse.

2014; Hedman et al., 2014; Lv et al., 2014; Mewton et al., 2014; Pennant et al., 2015; Richards et al., 2015; Silfvernagel et al., 2015; Spence et al., 2014; Wootton et al., 2015). Therapists who adopt these online treatment programs have the responsibility to oversee their quality and implementation. In some cases, therapists provide additional support that supplements online treatment modules via the use of email or periodic telephone contact, in a way similar to that in which a person might access a help line for using a computer software program. Some mental health professionals incorporate computerized therapy tools (computer-assisted therapy) as part of traditional treatment programs rather than as standalone treatments.

One advantage of online treatment is it can reach people who avoid seeking help because of shyness or embarrassment. Online consultation may make some people feel more comfortable about receiving help, making it a first step toward meeting a therapist in person. Online therapy and teleconferencing services may also provide needed services to people who might not otherwise receive help because they lack mobility or live in remote areas (McCord et al., 2011). A recent study showed that online therapy used in the treatment of adolescents with anxiety disorders combined with minimal therapist contact was just as effective as regular, face-to-face sessions with a therapist and had the advantage of reaching families who might have difficulty arranging clinic visits (Spence et al., 2011).

All in all, psychologists are not writing off electronic forms of therapy, but they do remain cautious about its use (Mora, Nevid, & Chaplin, 2008). Psychologists are seeking to put client protections into place for using the Internet and other computerized or electronically delivered psychological services before they are disseminated for widespread use (Hadjistavropoulos et al., 2011). Less controversial is the use of smartphone apps as tools to track symptoms during the flow of daily life.

Smartphone apps are also becoming a part of the therapeutic landscape, either as adjuncts to traditional treatment or as standalone treatments (see Clough & Casey, 2015; Gonzalez & Dulin, 2015). Apps like Beating the Blues and MoodGYM offer help to people combating depression, sometimes with little if any therapist direction (Berger, Boettcher, & Caspar, 2014). In another example, a sample of anxious college students were asked to play a distracting video game on a smartphone just before making a short speech, a task designed to elicit high levels of anxiety (Dennis & O'Toole, 2014). Compared to controls, students who played the video game reported lower levels of anxiety and appeared less nervous. These findings suggest that playing a video game can help divert attention away from an impending threatening stimulus. The public seems eager to use self-help apps, but solid evidence supporting their effectiveness remains lacking (Clough & Casey, 2015; Leigh & Flatt, 2015).

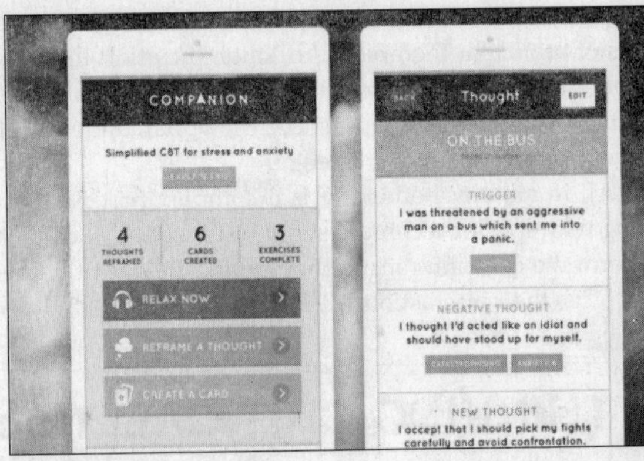


**SMARTPHONE APP.** The Stress & Anxiety Companion is a smartphone app people can use to monitor their thoughts and feelings and that provides suggestions they can use to change negative thoughts and develop relaxation skills and other coping skills. However, questions remain about the effectiveness of self-directed therapy programs and smartphone apps.

**SOURCE:** http://www.designandprosper.com/our-work/stress-anxiety-companion.aspx.

What do you think about the value of online psychological services? In thinking critically about this issue, answer the following questions:

- What ethical and practical problems do therapists who offer online therapy face?
- What are the potential benefits of online therapy? What are the potential risks?
- If you were in need of psychological services, would you seek an Internet-based treatment? Why or why not?

## Multicultural Issues in Psychotherapy

**2.14 Evaluate the role of multicultural factors in psychotherapy and barriers to use of mental health services by ethnic minorities.**

We live in an increasingly diverse, multicultural society in which people bring to therapy not only their personal backgrounds and individual experiences but also their cultural learning, norms, and values. Normal and abnormal behaviors occur in a context of culture and community. Clearly, therapists need to be culturally competent to provide appropriate services to people of varied backgrounds (Stuart, 2004).

Therapists need to be sensitive to cultural differences and how they affect the therapeutic process. Cultural sensitivity involves more than good intentions. Therapists must also have accurate knowledge of cultural factors, as well as ability to use that knowledge effectively in developing culturally sensitive approaches to treatment (e.g., Comas-Diaz, 2011a, 2011b; Inman & DeBoer Kreider, 2014). Moreover, they need to avoid ethnic stereotyping and demonstrate sensitivity to the values, languages, and cultural beliefs of members of racial or ethnic groups different than their own. However, a survey of professional psychologists showed that they applied relatively few of the recommended multicultural psychotherapy competencies in their practices (Hansen et al., 2006).

Just because a given therapy works with one population group does not mean that it will necessarily work with other groups (Windsor, Jemal, & Alessi, 2015). We need to examine the effectiveness of particular therapies with different population or ethnic groups (e.g., Chavira et al., 2014; Kanter et al., 2015). We also need to see whether specific cultural adaptations of culturally specific therapies offer greater benefits than standard treatments.

Along these lines, investigators found that a culturally specific form of behavior therapy for phobias was more effective in treating Asian Americans than a standard behavioral treatment, especially for less well-acculturated clients (Pan, Huey, & Hernandez, 2011). This suggests that therapists using established treatments should consider how they can incorporate culturally specific elements to boost treatment benefits in working with people from different ethnic or racial groups (Burrow-Sanchez & Wrona, 2012; Comas-Diaz, 2011b).

We next touch on factors involved in treating members of the major ethnic minority groups in American society: African Americans, Asian Americans, Hispanic Americans, and Native Americans.

**CULTURAL SENSITIVITY.** Therapists need to be sensitive to cultural differences and how they may affect the therapeutic process. They also need to avoid ethnic stereotyping and to demonstrate sensitivity to the values, languages, and cultural beliefs of members of racial or ethnic groups that are different from their own. Clients who are not fluent in English profit from having therapists who can conduct therapy in the languages their clients speak.

**AFRICAN AMERICANS** The cultural history of African Americans must be understood in the context of persistent racial discrimination and its toxic effects on the psychological adjustment of people of color (Comas-Diaz & Greene, 2013; Greene, 2009; Jackson & Greene, 2000). African Americans have needed to develop coping mechanisms for managing the pervasive racism they encounter in areas such as employment, housing, education, and access to health care. For example, the sensitivity of many African Americans to the potential for maltreatment and exploitation is a survival tool and may take the form of a heightened level of suspiciousness or reserve. Therefore, therapists need to be aware of the tendency of African American clients to minimize their vulnerability by being less self-disclosing, especially in early stages of therapy (Sanchez-Hucles, 2000). Therapists should not confuse such suspiciousness with paranoia.

In addition to the psychological problems African American clients may present, therapists often need to help their clients develop coping mechanisms to deal with racial barriers they encounter in daily life. Contrary to what some believe, the election of an African American president does not alter the day-to-day experiences of prejudice and discrimination that many African Americans across social classes continue to encounter. Therapists also need to be attuned to the tendencies of some African Americans to internalize the negative stereotypes about African Americans that are perpetuated in the dominant culture.

African Americans encounter racism in various forms. There are blatant forms of discrimination in housing and job opportunities, for example, that leave no doubt about what in fact they are; however, some forms are more subtle and harder to identify, such as a suspicious glance by a store security guard. Sue (2010) argues that subtle forms of discrimination can be even more damaging because they leave the victim with a sense of uncertainty about how to respond, if at all.

To be culturally competent, therapists not only must understand the cultural traditions and languages of the groups with which they work, but also recognize their own racial and ethnic attitudes and how these underlying attitudes affect how they practice. Therapists are exposed to the same negative stereotypes about African Americans as other people in society and must recognize how these stereotypes, if left unexamined, can become destructive to the therapeutic relationships they form with African American clients. A core principle in working within a diverse society is the willingness to openly examine one's own racial attitudes and the influences these attitudes may have on the therapeutic process. In addition, Snowden (2012) points out that therapists must be aware of environmental risk factors that affect the mental and physical health of African Americans, such as a lack of access to quality health care.

Therapists must also be aware of the cultural characteristics of African American families, such as strong kinship bonds, often including people who are not biologically related (e.g., a close friend of a parent may have some parenting role and may be addressed as "aunt"); strong religious and spiritual orientation; multigenerational households; adaptability and flexibility of gender roles (African American women have a long history of working outside the home); and distribution of child care responsibilities among different family members (Greene, 1990, 1993a; Jackson & Greene, 2000; USDHHS, 1999).

**ASIAN AMERICANS** Culturally sensitive therapists not only understand the beliefs and values of other cultures but also integrate this knowledge within the therapy process.

Generally speaking, Asian cultures, including Japanese culture, value restraint in talking about oneself and one's feelings. Public expression of emotions is also discouraged in traditional Asian cultures, which may inhibit Asian American clients from revealing their feelings in therapy. In traditional Asian cultures, the failure to keep one's feelings to oneself, especially negative feelings, may be perceived as reflecting poorly on one's upbringing. Asian American clients who appear passive or emotionally restrained when judged by Western standards may be responding in ways that are culturally appropriate and should not be judged as shy, uncooperative, or avoidant by therapists (Hwang, 2006).

Clinicians also note that Asian American clients often express psychological complaints such as anxiety through development of physical symptoms such as tightness in the chest or a racing heart (Hinton et al., 2009). However, the tendency to *somaticize* emotional problems may be explained in part by differences in communication styles (Zane & Sue, 1991). That is, Asian Americans may use more somatic terms to convey emotional distress.

In some cases, the goals of therapy may conflict with the values of a particular culture. The individualism of American society, which is expressed in many forms of psychotherapy that focus on the development of the self, may conflict with the group- and family-centered values of Asian cultures. Therapists working with Asian clients might also emphasize more of a we/us orientation than a me/I orientation to underscore the importance of social connectedness with their Asian American clients (Hayes, Muto, & Masuda, 2011).

Framing the therapy process in culturally appropriate terms may help build bridges—for example, by emphasizing the strong links in Asian cultures among mind, body, and spirit (Hwang, 2006). Therapists may incorporate techniques that reflect East Asian philosophical or cultural traditions, such as *mindfulness meditation*, a widely practiced Buddhist form of meditation (discussed in Chapter 4). They also need to draw upon culturally relevant resources in treatment, such as a strong religious faith tradition, strong extended families, and culturally specific programs in the community (Hays, 2009).

**HISPANIC AMERICANS** Although Hispanic American subcultures differ in various respects, many share certain cultural values and beliefs, such as the importance placed on the family and kinship ties, as well as on respect and dignity (Calzada, Fernandez, & Cortes, 2010). Therapists need to recognize that the traditional Hispanic American value of interdependency within the family may conflict with the values of independence and self-reliance that are stressed in the mainstream U.S. culture (De la Cancela & Guzman, 1991).

Therapists shouldn't assume that outcomes for the same disorders are the same across ethnic groups. A reminder of this lesson comes from a recent study that showed lower rates of recovery for anxiety disorders in Latinos as compared to those found in non-Latino Whites, but similar rates for both groups for recovery from major depression (Bjornsson et al., 2014). Latinos who emigrate to the United States may present with depression, but also with culturally relevant issues, such as problems with immigration and adjusting to a host culture while maintaining identification with their country of origin (Alarcón, Oquendo, & Wainberg, 2014).

Therapists also need to respect differences in values rather than attempt to impose the values of majority cultures. Therapists should also recognize that psychological disorders may manifest differently across ethnic groups. For example, the culture-bound syndrome of *ataques de nervios* (see Chapter 3) affects about 5% of Hispanic children, according to a recent study of children in the Bronx, New York, and San Juan, Puerto Rico (López et al., 2009). Therapists should also be trained to reach beyond the confines of their offices to work within the Hispanic American community itself, in settings that have an impact on the daily lives of Hispanic Americans, such as social clubs, *bodegas* (neighborhood groceries), and neighborhood beauty and barber shops.

**NATIVE AMERICANS** Traditionally underserved groups, including people of color, have the greatest unmet needs for mental health treatment services (Wang et al., 2005). A case in point are Native Americans, who remain underserved, partly as the result of the underfunding of the Indian Health Service that was designated to serve this population (Gone & Trimble, 2012). Also contributing to the disparity in mental health services is the cultural gap between providers and Native American recipients (Duran et al., 2005). Mental health professionals can be successful in helping Native Americans if they work within a context that is relevant and sensitive to Native Americans' customs, culture, and values (Gone & Trimble, 2012). For example, many Native Americans expect that the therapist will do most of the talking and they will play a passive role in treatment. These expectations are in keeping with the traditional healer role in Native American culture, but in conflict with the client-focused approach of many forms of conventional therapy. There may also be differences in gestures, eye contact, facial expression, and other modes of nonverbal expression that can impede effective communication between therapist and client (Renfrey, 1992).

Psychologists recognize the importance of bringing elements of tribal culture into mental health programs for Native Americans (Csordas, Storck, & Strauss, 2008). For example, therapists can use indigenous ceremonies that are part of the client's cultural or religious traditions. Purification and cleansing rites have therapeutic value for many Native American peoples in the United States and elsewhere, as *Santeria* does among the African Cuban community, *umbanda* in the Brazilian community, and *vodou* in the Haitian community (Lefley, 1990). People who believe their problems are caused by failure to placate malevolent spirits or to perform mandatory rituals often seek out cleansing rites.

Respect for cultural differences is a key feature of culturally sensitive therapies. Training in multicultural therapy is becoming more widely integrated into training programs for therapists. Culturally sensitive therapies adopt a respectful attitude that encourages people to tell their own personal stories as well as the story of their culture (Coronado & Peake, 1992).

**BARRIERS TO USE OF MENTAL HEALTH SERVICES BY ETHNIC MINORITIES** People of color in the United States typically have less access to mental health services and receive fewer services for needed mental health care than White Americans (Blumberg, Clarke, & Blackwell, 2015). They also tend to receive lower-quality mental health care than do other Americans (USDHHS, 2001). A major reason for these disparities is that a disproportionate number of minority group members remain uninsured or underinsured, leaving them unable to afford mental health care (Snowden, 2012). It remains to be seen whether increased availability of medical care—including mental health care—under the Affordable Care Act ("Obama Care") will succeed in reducing these disparities.

An importance consequence of these health care disparities is that ethnic minorities shoulder a greater burden of mental health problems that go undiagnosed and untreated (Neighbors et al., 2007). One example of ethnic disparities in health care is the fact that Latino children with autism spectrum disorder tend to be diagnosed at a later age than White, non-Latino children (Zuckerman et al., 2014). Cultural factors are yet another reason for underutilization of mental health services by minority groups. Mental health clinics are not typically the first places where people of color turn for help. They may seek assistance from churches, emergency rooms, friends or family members, or primary care physicians rather than mental health professionals such as psychologists and psychiatrists. Reluctance to seek mental health care reflects, at least in part, a long-standing stigma about mental illness that exists in many minority communities (Vega, Rodriguez, & Ang, 2010).

We can better understand low rates of use of outpatient mental health services by ethnic minorities by examining the barriers to receiving treatment, including the following (based on Cheung, 1991; López et al., 2012; Sanders Thompson, Bazile, & Akbar, 2004; Sue et al., 2012; Venner et al., 2012; and other sources):

1. *Cultural mistrust.* People from minority groups often fail to use mental health services because of a lack of trust. Mistrust may stem from a cultural or personal history of oppression and discrimination, or experiences in which service providers were unresponsive to a person's needs. When ethnic minority clients perceive majority therapists and the institutions in which they work to be cold or impersonal, they are less likely to place their trust in them.
2. *Mental health literacy.* Latinos may not make use of mental health services because they lack knowledge of mental disorders and how to treat them. Increasing public knowledge among Latinos about the features of schizophrenia and depression, for example, may lead to more referrals to mental health professionals for these kinds of problems.

3. *Institutional barriers.* Facilities may be inaccessible to minority group members because they are located at a considerable distance from their homes or because of lack of public transportation. Moreover, minority group members often feel that staff members make them feel stupid for not being familiar with clinic procedures, and their requests for assistance often become tangled in red tape.
4. *Cultural barriers.* Many recent immigrants, especially those from Southeast Asian countries, have had little, if any, previous contact with mental health professionals. They may hold different conceptions of mental health problems or view mental health problems as less severe than physical problems. In some ethnic minority subcultures, the family is expected to take care of members who have psychological problems and may resist use of outside assistance. Other cultural barriers include cultural differences between typically lower socioeconomic strata minority group members and mostly White middle class staff members, and the stigma and shame that is often associated with seeking mental health treatment in ethnic minority communities.
5. *Language barriers.* Differences in language make it difficult for minority group members to describe their problems or obtain needed services. Mental health facilities may lack the resources to hire mental health professionals who are fluent in the languages of minority residents in the communities they serve.
6. *Economic and accessibility barriers.* As mentioned earlier, financial burdens are often a major barrier to use of mental health services by ethnic minorities, many of whom live in economically distressed areas. Moreover, many minority group members live in rural or isolated areas where mental health services may be lacking or inaccessible.

Greater use of mental health services will depend to a large extent on the ability of the mental health system to develop programs that take cultural factors into account and to build staffs comprising culturally sensitive providers, including minority staff members and professionals with competencies in the languages used by community residents (Le Meyer et al., 2009; Sue et al., 2012). Cultural mistrust of the mental health system among minority group members may be grounded in the perception that many mental health professionals are racially biased in how they evaluate and treat members of minority groups.

# Biomedical Therapies

There is a growing emphasis in American psychiatry on the use of biomedical therapies, especially *psychotropic drugs* (also called psychiatric drugs). Today, roughly one in five adult Americans takes psychotropic drugs (Smith, 2012b). Biomedical therapies are generally administered by medical doctors, many of whom have specialized training in psychiatry or **psychopharmacology**. Many family physicians or general practitioners also prescribe psychotherapeutic drugs for their patients.

Biomedical approaches have had dramatic success in treating some forms of abnormal behavior, although they also have their limitations. For one, drugs may have unwelcome or dangerous side effects. Psychosurgery has been all but eliminated as a form of treatment because of serious harmful effects of earlier procedures.

## Drug Therapy

**2.15 Identify the major categories of psychotropic or psychiatric drugs and examples of drugs in each type, and evaluate their strengths and weaknesses.**

Psychotropic or psychiatric drugs used in treating psychological disorders act on neurotransmitter systems in the brain, affecting the delicate balance of chemicals that ferry nerve impulses from neuron to neuron. Psychiatric drugs do not cure mental or psychological disorders, but they can often help control the troubling symptoms or features of these disorders. The major classes of psychiatric drugs are antianxiety drugs, antipsychotic drugs, and antidepressants, as well as lithium and other drugs used to treat mania and mood swings in people with bipolar disorder. The use of other psychotropic drugs, such as stimulants, will be discussed in later chapters.

**ANTIANXIETY DRUGS** **Antianxiety drugs** (also called *anxiolytics*, from the Greek *anxietas*, meaning *anxiety*, and *lysis*, meaning *bringing to an end*) combat anxiety and reduce states of muscle tension. They include mild tranquilizers, such as those of the *benzodiazepine* class of drugs—for example, *diazepam* (Valium) and *alprazolam* (Xanax)—as well as hypnotic sedatives, such as *triazolam* (Halcion).

Antianxiety drugs reduce the level of activity of certain parts of the central nervous system, including the sympathetic nervous system, which slows the respiration rate and heart rate and lessens feelings of anxiety and tension. Side effects of using antianxiety drugs include fatigue, drowsiness, and impaired motor coordination that can impair the ability to function or to operate an automobile. There is also the potential for abuse. One of the most commonly prescribed minor tranquilizers, Valium, has become a major drug of abuse among people who become psychologically and physiologically dependent on it.

When used on a short-term basis, antianxiety drugs can be safe and effective in treating anxiety and insomnia. Yet drugs by themselves do not teach people new skills or more adaptive ways of handling their problems. Instead, people may simply learn to rely on chemical agents to cope with their problems. **Rebound anxiety** is another problem associated with regular use of tranquilizers. Many people who regularly use antianxiety drugs report that anxiety or insomnia returns in a more severe form once they discontinue the drugs.

**ANTIPSYCHOTIC DRUGS** **Antipsychotic drugs**, also called *neuroleptics*, are commonly used to treat the more flagrant features of schizophrenia and other psychotic disorders, such as hallucinations, delusions, and states of confusion. Introduced during the 1950s, many of these drugs, including *chlorpromazine* (Thorazine), *thioridazine* (Mellaril), and *fluphenazine* (Prolixin), belong to the *phenothiazine* class of chemicals. Phenothiazines appear to control psychotic features by blocking the action of the neurotransmitter dopamine at receptor sites in the brain. Although the underlying causes of schizophrenia remain unknown, researchers suspect an irregularity in the dopamine system in the brain may be involved (see Chapter 11). *Clozapine* (Clozaril), a neuroleptic of a different chemical class than the phenothiazines, is effective in treating many people with schizophrenia whose symptoms were unresponsive to other neuroleptics. The use of clozapine must be carefully monitored, however, because of potentially dangerous side effects.

The use of neuroleptics has greatly reduced the need for more restrictive forms of treatment for severely disturbed patients, such as physical restraints and confinement in padded cells, and has lessened the need for long-term hospitalization.

Neuroleptics are not without their problems, including potential side effects such as muscular rigidity and tremors. Although these side effects are generally controllable by use of other drugs, long-term use of antipsychotic drugs (possibly excepting clozapine) can produce a potentially irreversible and disabling motor disorder called *tardive dyskinesia* (see Chapter 11), which is characterized by uncontrollable eye blinking, facial grimaces, lip smacking, and other involuntary movements of the mouth, eyes, and limbs.

**ANTIDEPRESSANTS** Four major classes of **antidepressants** are in use today: *tricyclic antidepressants* (TCAs), *monoamine oxidase* (MAO) *inhibitors*, *selective serotonin-reuptake inhibitors* (SSRIs), and *serotonin-norepinephrine reuptake inhibitors* (SNRIs). Tricyclic antidepressants and MAO inhibitors increase the availability of the neurotransmitters norepinephrine and serotonin in the brain. Some commonly used tricyclics are *imipramine* (Tofranil), *amitriptyline* (Elavil), and *doxepin* (Sinequan). The MAO inhibitors include drugs such as *phenelzine* (Nardil). Tricyclic antidepressants are favored over MAO inhibitors because they cause fewer potentially serious side effects.

*Selective serotonin-reuptake inhibitors* have more specific effects on serotonin levels in the brain. Drugs in this class include *fluoxetine* (Prozac) and *sertraline* (Zoloft). SSRIs increase the availability of serotonin in the brain by interfering with its reuptake (reabsorption) by transmitting neurons. *Serotonin-norepinephrine reuptake inhibitors*, such as *venlafaxine* (Effexor), work specifically on increasing levels of two neurotransmitters linked to mood states—serotonin and norepinephrine—by means of interfering with the reuptake of these chemicals by transmitting neurons.

**TRUTH *or* FICTION**

Antidepressants are used only to treat depression.

☑ **FALSE** Antidepressants have many psychiatric uses, including treatment of many anxiety disorders and bulimia.

Antidepressants have beneficial effects in treating depression and some other psychological disorders as well, including panic disorder, social phobia, obsessive–compulsive disorder (see Chapter 5), and bulimia, the type of eating disorder (see Chapter 9) described earlier in the case of Jessica. As research into the underlying causes of these disorders continues, we may find that irregularities of neurotransmitter functioning in the brain play a key role in their development. **T / F**

**LITHIUM AND ANTICONVULSIVE DRUGS** Lithium carbonate, a salt of the metal lithium in tablet form, helps treat manic symptoms and stabilize mood swings in people with bipolar disorder (formerly *manic depression*; discussed further in Chapter 7). However, people with bipolar disorder may have to continue using lithium indefinitely to control the disorder. Further, because of the potential toxicity associated with lithium, the blood levels of people maintained on the drug must be carefully monitored. Anticonvulsive drugs (e.g., Depakote) used in the treatment of epilepsy also have antimanic and mood-stabilizing effects and are sometimes used in people with bipolar disorder who cannot tolerate lithium (see Chapter 7).

Table 2.7 lists psychotropic drugs according to their drug class and category.

**Table 2.7** Major Psychotropic Drugs

| | Generic Name | Brand Name | Clinical Uses | Possible Side Effects or Complications |
|---|---|---|---|---|
| **Antianxiety Drugs** | Diazepam | Valium | Anxiety, insomnia | Drowsiness, fatigue, impaired coordination, nausea |
| | Chlordiazepoxide | Librium | | |
| | Lorazepam | Ativan | | |
| | Alprazolam | Xanax | | |
| **Antidepressant Drugs** | **Tricyclic Antidepressants (TCAs)** | | | |
| | Imipramine | Tofranil | Depression, bulimia, panic disorder | Changes in blood pressure, heart irregularities, dry mouth, confusion, skin rash |
| | Amitriptyline | Elavil | | |
| | Doxepin | Sinequan | | |
| | **Monoamine Oxidase Inhibitors (MAOIs)** | | | |
| | Phenelzine | Nardil | Depression | Dizziness, headache, sleep disturbance, agitation, anxiety, fatigue |
| | **Selective Serotonin-Reuptake Inhibitors (SSRIs)** | | | |
| | Fluoxetine | Prozac | Depression, bulimia, panic disorder, obsessive–compulsive disorder, posttraumatic stress disorder (Zoloft), social anxiety disorder (Paxil) | Nausea, diarrhea, anxiety, insomnia, sweating, dry mouth, dizziness, drowsiness |
| | Sertraline | Zoloft | | |
| | Paroxetine | Paxil | | |
| | Citalopram | Celexa | | |
| | Escitalopram | Lexapro | | |
| | **Serotonin-Norepinephrine Reuptake Inhibitors (SNRIs)** | | | |
| | Duloxetine | Cymbalta | Depression, generalized anxiety disorder | Nausea, stomachache, loss of appetite, dry mouth, blurred vision, drowsiness, joint or muscle pain, weight gain |
| | Venlafaxine | Effexor | Depression | Nausea, constipation, dry mouth |
| | Desvenlafaxine | Pristiq | Depression | Drowsiness, insomnia, dizziness, anxiety |
| | **Other Antidepressant Drugs** | | | |
| | Bupropion | Wellbutrin | Depression, nicotine dependence | Dry mouth, insomnia, headaches, nausea, constipation, tremors |
| | | Zyban | | |

**Table 2.7 Continued**

| | Generic Name | Brand Name | Clinical Uses | Possible Side Effects or Complications |
|---|---|---|---|---|
| **Antipsychotic Drugs** | **Phenothiazines** | | | |
| | Chlorpromazine | Thorazine | Schizophrenia and other psychotic disorders | Movement disorders (e.g., tardive dyskinesia), drowsiness, restlessness, dry mouth, blurred vision, muscle rigidity |
| | Thioridazine | Mellaril | | |
| | Trifluoperazine | Stelazine | | |
| | Fluphenazine | Prolixin | | |
| | **Atypical Antipsychotics** | | | |
| | Clozapine | Clozaril | Schizophrenia and other psychotic disorders | Potentially lethal blood disorder, seizures, fast heart rate, drowsiness, dizziness, nausea |
| | Risperidone | Risperdal | Schizophrenia and other psychotic disorders | Feeling unable to sit still, constipation, dizziness, drowsiness, weight gain |
| | Olanzapine | Zyprexa | Schizophrenia and other psychotic disorders | Low blood pressure, dizziness, drowsiness, heart palpitations, fatigue, constipation, weight gain |
| | Aripiprazole | Abilify | Schizophrenia, mania, depression when used along with an antidepressant | Headache, nervousness, drowsiness, dizziness, heartburn, constipation, diarrhea, stomach pain, weight gain |
| | **Other Antipsychotic Drugs** | | | |
| | Haloperidol | Haldol | Schizophrenia and other psychotic disorders | Similar to phenothiazines |
| **Antimanic Drugs** | Lithium carbonate | Eskalith | Manic episodes and mood stabilization in bipolar disorder | Tremors, thirst, diarrhea, drowsiness, weakness, lack of coordination |
| | Divalproex sodium | Depakote | Manic episodes and mood stabilization in bipolar disorder | Nausea, vomiting, dizziness, abdominal cramps, sleeplessness |
| **Stimulant Drugs** | Methylphenidate | Ritalin, Concerta | Attention deficit hyperactivity disorder (ADHD) | Nervousness, insomnia, nausea, dizziness, heart palpitations, headache; may temporarily retard growth |
| | Amphetamine with dextroamphetamine | Adderall | | |

**SOURCE:** Adapted from J. S. Nevid (2013). *Psychology: Concepts and applications*, 4th ed., p. 629. Belmont, CA: Cengage Learning. Reprinted by permission.

# Electroconvulsive Therapy

**2.16 Describe the use of electroconvulsive therapy and psychosurgery and evaluate their effectiveness.**

The use of **electroconvulsive therapy (ECT)** seems barbaric and remains controversial. An electric shock is sent through the patient's brain, sufficient to induce convulsions of the type found in people with epilepsy. Although many people with major depression who have failed to respond to antidepressants show significant improvement following ECT (Kellner et al., 2012; Oltedal et al., 2015), it is associated with memory loss for events occurring around the time of treatment and high relapse rates (see Chapter 7). ECT is generally considered a treatment of last resort after less intrusive methods have been tried and failed. **T / F**

> **TRUTH or FICTION**
>
> Sending jolts of electricity into a person's brain can often help relieve severe depression.
>
> ☑ **TRUE** Severely depressed people who have failed to respond to other less intrusive treatments often show rapid improvement from electroconvulsive therapy.

# Psychosurgery

**2.17 Describe the use of psychosurgery and evaluate its effectiveness.**

Psychosurgery is even more controversial than ECT and is rarely practiced today. The most common form of psychosurgery, no longer performed today, was the *prefrontal lobotomy*. This procedure involved surgically severing nerve pathways linking the thalamus to the prefrontal lobes of the brain. The operation was based on the theory that extremely disturbed patients suffer from overexcitation of emotional

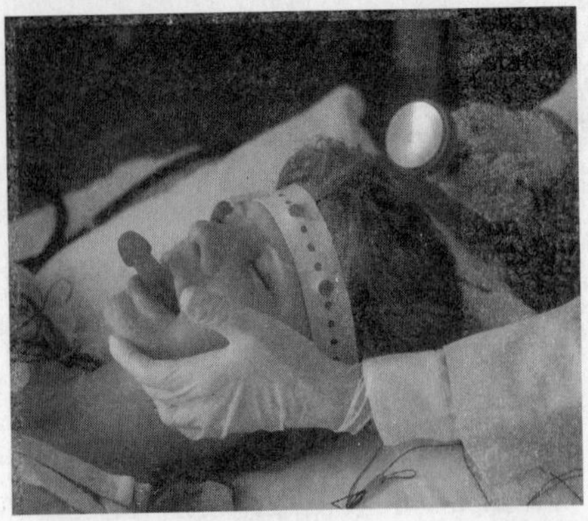

**ELECTROCONVULSIVE THERAPY.** ECT is helpful in many cases of severe or prolonged depression that do not respond to other forms of treatment. Still, it remains a controversial form of treatment.

impulses emanating from lower-brain centers, such as the thalamus and hypothalamus. It was believed that by severing the connections between the thalamus and the higher-brain centers in the frontal lobe of the cerebral cortex, the patient's violent or aggressive tendencies could be controlled. The procedure was abandoned because of lack of evidence of its effectiveness and because it often produced serious complications and even death. The advent in the 1950s of psychiatric drugs that could be used to control violent or disruptive behavior all but eliminated the use of psychosurgery (Hirschfeld, 2011).

More sophisticated psychosurgery techniques have been introduced in recent years. Guided by a better understanding of brain circuitry involved in certain disorders, such as obsessive–compulsive disorder, surgical techniques are now being used to target smaller parts of the brain, producing far less damage than was the case with prefrontal lobotomy. These techniques have been used to treat patients with severe forms of obsessive–compulsive disorder, bipolar disorder, and major depression who have failed to respond to other treatments (Carey, 2009b; Shields et al., 2008; Steele et al., 2008).

Another experimental technique is *deep brain stimulation* (DBS), a surgical procedure in which electrodes are implanted in the brain and used to electrically stimulate deeper brain structures. DBS shows promise in treating cases of severe depression and obsessive–compulsive disorder that have failed to respond to more conservative treatments (Dubovsky, 2015; Grant, 2014; Hamani et al., 2014; Islam et al., 2015; Riva-Possee et al., 2014). However, because the effectiveness of these procedures needs to be more fully investigated and serious complications may occur, these techniques are presently classified as experimental treatments (Berlim et al., 2014; D'Astous et al., 2013).

## Evaluation of Biomedical Approaches

**2.18 Evaluate biomedical treatment approaches.**

There is little doubt that biomedical treatments have helped many people with severe psychological problems. Many thousands of people with schizophrenia who were formerly hospitalized are able to function in the community because of antipsychotic drugs. Antidepressant drugs can help relieve depression in many cases and show therapeutic benefits in treating other disorders, such as panic disorder, obsessive–compulsive disorder, and eating disorders. ECT is helpful in relieving depression in many people who have been unresponsive to other treatments. However, psychiatric drugs and other biomedical treatments such as ECT are not a cure, nor a panacea. There are often troubling side effects of drug treatment and ECT and potential risks for physiological dependence, such as in the case of Valium. Moreover, psychotherapy may be as effective as drug therapy in treating anxiety disorders and depression (see Chapters 5 and 7).

Medical practitioners are sometimes too willing to look for a quick fix by using their prescription pads rather than conducting careful evaluations and helping patients examine their lives or referring them for psychological treatment (Boodman, 2012). We should not expect to solve all of the problems we face in life with a pill (Sroufe, 2012). Physicians often feel pressured, of course, by patients who seek a chemical solution to their life problems.

Researchers are also gathering evidence showing that a combination of psychological and drug treatments for problems such as depression, anxiety disorders, and substance abuse disorders may be more helpful in some cases than either treatment alone (e.g., Cuijpers et al., 2011; Lynch et al., 2011; Oestergaard & Møldrup, 2011; Schneier et al., 2012; Sudak, 2011).

# Summing Up

## The Biological Perspective

### The Nervous System

**2.1 Identify the major parts of the neuron, the nervous system, and the cerebral cortex, and describe their functions.**

The nervous system is composed of neurons, nerve cells that communicate with one another through chemical messengers called neurotransmitters that transmit nerve impulses across the tiny gaps—or synapses—between neurons. The parts of the neuron include the cell body (or soma), which performs the cell's metabolic functions; dendrites, or filaments that receive messages (nerve impulses) from neighboring neurons; axons, which are long cable-like structures that carry nerve impulses across the neuron; terminal buttons, or small branching structures at the tips of axons; and the myelin sheath, the insulating layer in some neurons that speeds transmission of nerve impulses.

The nervous system consists of two major parts, the central nervous system and the peripheral nervous system. The central nervous system consists of the brain and spinal cord and is responsible for controlling bodily functions and performing higher mental functions. The peripheral nervous system consists of two major divisions: the somatic nervous system, which transmits messages between the central nervous system and the sense organs and muscles, and the autonomic nervous system, which controls involuntary bodily processes. The autonomic nervous system has two branches or subdivisions, the sympathetic and the parasympathetic. These two branches have largely opposing effects, with the sympathetic nervous system mobilizing the body's resources needed for physical exertion or responding to stress and the parasympathetic system replenishing bodily resources and taking control during times of relaxation.

The cerebral cortex consists of four parts or lobes: (1) the occipital lobe, involved in processing visual stimuli; (2) the temporal lobe, involved in processing sounds or auditory stimuli; (3) the parietal lobe, responsible for sensations of touch, temperature, and pain; and (4) the frontal lobes, responsible for controlling muscle movement (motor cortex) and higher mental functions (prefrontal cortex).

### Evaluating Biological Perspectives on Abnormal Behavior

**2.2 Evaluate biological perspectives on abnormal behavior.**

Biological factors, such as disturbances in neurotransmitter functioning in the brain, heredity, and underlying brain abnormalities, are implicated in the development of abnormal behavior. However, biology is not destiny, and genes do not dictate behavior outcomes. There is a complex interaction of nature and nurture, of environment and heredity, in the development of abnormal behavior. Genetics creates a predisposition or likelihood—not a certainty—that certain behavior patterns or disorders will develop. Where genetic factors play a role, multiple genes—not any individual gene—are involved.

## The Psychological Perspective

### Psychodynamic Models

**2.3 Describe the key features of psychodynamic models of abnormal behavior and evaluate their major contributions.**

Psychodynamic perspectives reflect the views of Freud and those who follow in this tradition, including Carl Jung, Alfred Adler, Karen Horney, Erik Erikson, and Margaret Mahler, who believed that abnormal behavior stemmed from psychological causes based on underlying psychic forces within the personality. The psychodynamic model led to the development of psychodynamic models of treatment and focused attention on the importance of unconscious processes, but it has been criticized largely on the basis of the degree of importance placed on sexual and aggressive impulses and the difficulty subjecting some of the more abstract concepts to scientific tests.

### Learning-Based Models

**2.4 Describe the key features of learning-based models of abnormal behavior and evaluate their major contributions.**

Learning theorists such as John B. Watson and B. F. Skinner posited that the principles of learning can be used to explain both abnormal and normal behavior. Learning-based theories spawned the development of behavior therapy and a broader conceptual model called social-cognitive theory, but have been criticized for not providing a fuller accounting of the importance of the sense of self and of subjective experiences, as well as the role of genetic factors in explaining abnormal behavior patterns.

### Humanistic Models

**2.5 Describe the key features of humanistic models of abnormal behavior and evaluate their major contributions.**

Humanistic theorists such as Carl Rogers and Abraham Maslow believed it is important to understand the obstacles that people encounter as they strive toward self-actualization and authenticity. Humanistic models increased attention to the importance of conscious, subjective experience, but they have been criticized for the difficulty posed by studying private mental experiences and self-actualization objectively.

### Cognitive Models

**2.6 Describe the key features of cognitive models of abnormal behavior and evaluate their major contributions.**

Cognitive theorists such as Aaron Beck and Albert Ellis focus on the role of distorted and self-defeating thinking in explaining abnormal behavior. Cognitive models spawned cognitive approaches to therapy and led to the emergence of cognitive-behavioral therapy, but CBT has been criticized for being too narrowly focused on emotional disorders and continues to face nagging questions about whether distorted thinking is a cause or merely an effect of depression.

## The Sociocultural Perspective

### Ethnicity and Mental Health

**2.7 Evaluate ethnic group differences in rates of psychological disorders.**

Overall, White Americans of European background (non-Hispanic Whites) tend to have a higher prevalence of psychological disorders than Hispanic Americans (Latinos) or (non-Hispanic Black Americans). Asian Americans tend to have low rates of psychological disorders. Native Americans often have disproportionate rates of depression and alcoholism, in part because of a history of alienation and marginalization from the mainstream culture.

### Evaluating the Sociocultural Perspective

**2.8 Evaluate the sociocultural perspective in our understanding of abnormal behavior.**

The sociocultural perspective is important in broadening our outlook on abnormal behavior by taking into account sociocultural factors relating to the development of psychological disorders, including roles of social class, ethnicity, and exposure to poverty and racism. Sociocultural theorists focus much-needed attention on the role of social stressors in abnormal behavior. Research supports the link between social class and severe psychological disorders.

## The Biopsychosocial Perspective

### The Diathesis-Stress Model

**2.9 Describe the diathesis-stress model of abnormal behavior.**

The diathesis-stress model holds that while a person may have a predisposition, or diathesis, for a particular psychological disorder, whether the disorder actually develops depends on the interaction of the diathesis with stress-inducing life experiences.

### Evaluating the Biopsychosocial Perspective

**2.10 Evaluate the biopsychosocial perspective on abnormal behavior.**

The importance of the biopsychosocial perspective is that it recognizes that abnormal behavior is best understood in terms of the interplay of biological, psychological, and sociocultural factors. Although the biopsychosocial model has emerged as a leading conceptual model, its complexity may also be its greatest weakness.

## Psychological Methods of Treatment

### Types of Helping Professionals

**2.11 Identify three of the major types of helping professionals and describe their training backgrounds and professional roles.**

Clinical psychologists use psychological tests, diagnose mental or psychological disorders, and practice psychotherapy. They complete graduate training in clinical psychology, typically at the doctoral level. Psychiatrists are medical doctors who complete medical residency programs in psychiatry. They can prescribe medication, use other biomedical forms of treatment, and may practice psychotherapy. Clinical or psychiatric social workers are trained in graduate schools of social work or social welfare, generally at the master's level. They help people with severe mental disorders receive the services they need and may practice psychotherapy or marital or family therapy.

### Types of Psychotherapy

**2.12 Describe the goals and techniques of following forms of psychotherapy: psychodynamic therapy, behavior therapy, person-centered therapy, cognitive therapy, cognitive-behavioral therapy, eclectic therapy, group therapy, family therapy, and couple therapy.**

Psychodynamic therapy originated with Freudian psychoanalysis. Psychoanalysts use techniques such as free association and dream analysis to help people gain insight into their unconscious conflicts and work through them in light of their adult personalities. Contemporary psychodynamic therapy is typically briefer and more direct in its approach to exploring the patient's defenses and transference relationships.

Behavior therapy applies the principles of learning to help people make adaptive behavioral changes. Behavior therapy techniques include systematic desensitization, gradual exposure, modeling, operant conditioning approaches, and social skills training. Cognitive-behavioral therapy integrates behavioral and cognitive approaches in treatment.

Humanistic therapy focuses on the client's subjective, conscious experience in the here and now. Rogers's person-centered therapy helps clients increase their awareness and acceptance of inner feelings that had met with social condemnation and been disowned. The effective person-centered therapist possesses the qualities of unconditional positive regard, empathy, genuineness, and congruence.

Cognitive therapy focuses on modifying the maladaptive cognitions believed to underlie emotional problems and self-defeating behavior. Ellis's rational emotive behavior therapy focuses on disputing irrational beliefs that lead to emotional distress and substituting adaptive beliefs and behavior. Beck's cognitive therapy focuses on helping clients identify, challenge, and replace distorted cognitions, such as tendencies to magnify negative events and minimize personal accomplishments. Cognitive-behavioral therapy is a broader form of behavior therapy that integrates cognitive and behavioral techniques in treatment.

There are two general forms of eclectic therapy: *technical eclecticism*, a pragmatic approach that draws on techniques from different schools of therapy without necessarily subscribing to the theoretical positions represented by these schools, and *integrative eclecticism*, a model of therapy that attempts to synthesize and integrate diverse theoretical approaches.

Group therapy provides opportunities for mutual support and shared learning experiences within a group setting to help individuals overcome psychological difficulties and develop more adaptive behaviors. Family therapists work with conflicted families to help them resolve their differences. Family therapists focus on clarifying family communications, resolving role conflicts, guarding against scapegoating individual family members, and helping family members develop greater autonomy. Couple therapists focus on helping couples improve their communications and resolve their differences.

## Evaluating the Methods of Psychotherapy

**2.13 Evaluate the effectiveness of psychotherapy and the role of nonspecific factors in therapy.**

Evidence from meta-analyses of psychotherapy outcome studies that compare psychotherapy with control groups strongly supports the effectiveness of psychotherapy. The question remains, however, whether there are differences in the relative effectiveness of different types of psychotherapy. Empirically supported therapies are those that have demonstrated significant benefits in comparison to control procedures in scientific studies.

Nonspecific factors, including empathy, support, attention from a therapist, and the development of a therapeutic alliance and a working alliance, are common factors shared among different types of therapy. Questions remain about the degree to which therapeutic gains are due to the specific treatments clients receive or to the nonspecific factors that different therapies share in common.

## Multicultural Issues in Psychotherapy

**2.14 Evaluate the role of multicultural factors in psychotherapy and barriers to use of mental health services by ethnic minorities.**

Therapists need to be sensitive to cultural differences and how they affect the therapeutic process. Some forms of therapy may vary in effectiveness when used with members of different cultural groups. Culturally competent therapists both understand and respect cultural differences that may impact the practice of psychotherapy. Factors that limit use of mental health services by ethnic minorities include cultural preferences for other forms of helping, cultural mistrust of the mental health system, cultural and linguistic barriers to mental health treatment, financial barriers, and limited accessibility.

# Biomedical Therapies

## Drug Therapy

**2.15 Identify the major categories of psychotropic or psychiatric drugs and examples of drugs in each type, and evaluate their strengths and weaknesses.**

The three major classes of psychiatric drugs are antianxiety drugs, antidepressants, and antipsychotics. Antianxiety drugs, such as Valium, may relieve short-term anxiety but do not directly help people solve their problems or cope with stress. Antidepressants, such as Prozac and Zoloft, can help relieve depression but are not a cure and also carry risks of side effects. Antianxiety and antidepressant drugs may be no more effective than psychological approaches to treatment. Lithium and anticonvulsive drugs are helpful in many cases in stabilizing mood swings in people with bipolar disorder. Antipsychotic drugs help control flagrant psychotic symptoms, but regular use of these drugs is associated with the risk of serious side effects.

## Electroconvulsive Therapy

**2.16 Describe the use of electroconvulsive therapy and psychosurgery and evaluate their effectiveness.**

ECT involves administration of a series of electric shocks to the brain that can lead to dramatic relief from severe depression, even in people who have failed to respond to other treatments. However, ECT is an invasive treatment associated with high relapse rates and carries a risk of memory loss, especially for events occurring around the time of treatment.

## Psychosurgery

**2.17 Describe the use of psychosurgery and evaluate its effectiveness.**

Psychosurgery involves use of invasive surgical techniques on the brain to control severely disturbed behavior. It has all but disappeared as a form of treatment because of adverse consequences and availability of less intrusive treatments.

## Evaluation of Biomedical Approaches

**2.18 Evaluate biomedical treatment approaches.**

Biomedical therapies in the form of drug therapy or ECT can help relieve troubling symptoms such as anxiety, depression, and mania, help stabilize mood swings in patients with bipolar disorder, and control hallucinations and delusions in patients with schizophrenia, but they are not a cure. Moreover, psychotherapy may be as effective as drug therapy in treating anxiety and depression without the risk of drug side effects and possible physiological dependence. In some cases, a combination of psychological and drug therapy may be more effective than either treatment approach alone.

# Critical Thinking Questions

Based on your reading of this chapter, answer the following questions:

- Give an example or two of your own behavior, or the behavior of others, in which defense mechanisms may have played a role. Which particular defense mechanisms were at play?
- Give an example from your personal experiences in which your thinking reflected one or more of the cognitive distortions identified by Beck: selective abstraction, overgeneralization, magnification, or absolutist thinking. What effects did these thought patterns have on your moods? On your level of motivation? How might you change your thinking about these experiences?
- Why is it necessary to consider multiple perspectives in explaining abnormal behavior?
- How do the different types of mental health professionals differ in their training backgrounds and the roles they perform?
- What type of therapy would you prefer if you were seeking treatment for a psychological disorder? Why?
- Why is it important for therapists to take cultural factors into account when treating members of diverse groups? What cultural factors are important to consider?

# Key Terms

neurons, p. 41
dendrites, p. 41
axon, p. 41
terminals, p. 41
myelin sheath, p. 41
neurotransmitters, p. 42
synapse, p. 42
receptor site, p. 42
central nervous system, p. 43
peripheral nervous system, p. 43
medulla, p. 44
pons, p. 44
cerebellum, p. 44
reticular activating system, p. 44
thalamus, p. 45
hypothalamus, p. 45
limbic system, p. 45
basal ganglia, p. 45
cerebrum, p. 45
cerebral cortex, p. 45
somatic nervous system, p. 46
autonomic nervous system, p. 46
sympathetic nervous system, p. 46
parasympathetic nervous system, p. 46
epigenetics, p. 48
psychoanalytic theory, p. 49
conscious, p. 50
preconscious, p. 50
unconscious, p. 50
id, p. 50
pleasure principle, p. 50
ego, p. 50
reality principle, p. 51
superego, p. 51
defense mechanisms, p. 51
fixation, p. 53
archetypes, p. 53
ego psychology, p. 54
object-relations theory, p. 54
psychosis, p. 55
behaviorism, p. 56
conditioned response, p. 57
unconditioned stimulus, p. 57
unconditioned response, p. 57
conditioned stimulus, p. 57
classical conditioning, p. 57
operant conditioning, p. 58
reinforcement, p. 58
positive reinforcers, p. 59
negative reinforcers, p. 59
punishment, p. 59
social-cognitive theory, p. 60
modeling, p. 60
expectancies, p. 60
self-actualization, p. 61
unconditional positive regard, p. 61
conditional positive regard, p. 61
social causation model, p. 67
downward drift hypothesis, p. 67
diathesis-stress model, p. 69
diathesis, p. 69
psychotherapy, p. 72
psychoanalysis, p. 72
psychodynamic therapy, p. 72
free association, p. 73
transference relationship, p. 73
countertransference, p. 74
behavior therapy, p. 75
systematic desensitization, p. 76
gradual exposure, p. 76
modeling, p. 76
token economy, p. 76
person-centered therapy, p. 76
empathy, p. 77
genuineness, p. 77
congruence, p. 77
cognitive therapy, p. 77
rational emotive behavior therapy, p. 78
cognitive-behavioral therapy, p. 78
eclectic therapy, p. 79
group therapy, p. 80
family therapy, p. 80
couple therapy, p. 81
nonspecific treatment factors, p. 81
psychopharmacology, p. 88
antianxiety drugs, p. 89
rebound anxiety, p. 89
antipsychotic drugs, p. 89
antidepressants, p. 89
electroconvulsive therapy (ECT), p. 91

## Chapter 3

# Classification and Assessment of Abnormal Behavior

## Learning Objectives

**3.1** **Describe** the key features of the *DSM* system of diagnostic classification.

**3.2** **Describe** the concept of culture-bound syndromes and **identify** some examples.

**3.3** **Explain** why the new edition of the *DSM*, the *DSM-5*, is controversial and **evaluate** the strengths and weaknesses of the *DSM* system.

**3.4** **Identify** methods of assessing reliability of tests and measures.

**3.5** **Identify** methods of assessing validity of tests and measures.

**3.6** **Identify** the three major types of clinical interviews.

3.7 **Describe** the two major types of psychological tests—intelligence tests and personality tests—and **identify** examples of each type.

3.8 **Describe** the uses of neuropsychological tests.

3.9 **Identify** methods of behavioral assessment and **describe** the role of a functional analysis.

3.10 **Describe** the role of cognitive assessment and **identify** two examples of cognitive measures.

3.11 **Identify** methods of physiological measurement.

3.12 **Describe** the role of sociocultural aspects of psychological assessment.

## TRUTH *or* FICTION

T☐ F☐ Some men in India have a psychological disorder in which they are troubled by anxiety over losing semen. (p. 104)

T☐ F☐ A psychological test can be highly reliable but also invalid. (p. 110)

T☐ F☐ Although it is not an exact science, the measurement of the bumps on an individual's head can be used to determine his or her personality traits. (p. 111)

T☐ F☐ One of the most widely used personality tests asks people to interpret what they see in a series of inkblots. (p. 118)

T☐ F☐ Testing infants for signs of autistic behaviors: Yes, there's an app for that. (p. 125)

T☐ F☐ Despite advances in technology, physicians today must still perform surgery to study the workings of the brain. (p. 128)

T☐ F☐ Undergoing an MRI scan is like being stuffed into a large magnet. (p. 128)

T☐ F☐ Cocaine cravings in people addicted to cocaine have been linked to parts of the brain that are normally activated during pleasant emotions. (p. 129)

T☐ F☐ Advances in brain scanning allow physicians to diagnose schizophrenia with an MRI scan. (p. 130)

CHAPTER INTRODUCTION: CLASSIFICATION AND ASSESSMENT OF ABNORMAL BEHAVIOR

**"I" "Jerry Has a Panic Attack on the Interstate"**

INTERVIEWER: Can you tell me a bit about what it was that brought you to the clinic?

JERRY: Well...after the first of the year, I started getting these panic attacks. I didn't know what the panic attack was.

INTERVIEWER: Well, what was it that you experienced?

JERRY: Uhm, the heart beating, racing...

INTERVIEWER: Your heart started to race on you.

JERRY: And then uh, I couldn't be in one place, maybe a movie, or a church...things would be closing in on me and I'd have to get up and leave.

INTERVIEWER: The first time that it happened to you, can you remember that?

JERRY: Uhm, yeah I was...

INTERVIEWER: Take me through that, what you experienced.

JERRY: I was driving on an interstate and, oh I might've been on maybe 10 or 15 minutes.

INTERVIEWER: Uh huh.

JERRY: All of a sudden I got this fear. I started to...uh race.

INTERVIEWER: So you noticed you were frightened?

JERRY: Yes.

INTERVIEWER: Your heart was racing and you were perspiring. What else?

JERRY: Perspiring and uh, I was afraid of driving anymore on that interstate for the fear that I would either pull into a car head on, so uhm, I just, I just couldn't function. I just couldn't drive.

INTERVIEWER: What did you do?

JERRY: I pulled, uh well at the nearest exit. I just got off...uh stopped and, I had never experienced anything like that before.

INTERVIEWER: That was just a...

JERRY: Out of the clear blue...

INTERVIEWER: Out of the clear blue? And what'd you think was going on?

JERRY: I had no idea.

JERRY: I thought maybe I was having a heart attack.

INTERVIEWER: You just knew you were...

INTERVIEWER: Okay.

**SOURCE:** Excerpted from *Panic Disorder: The Case of Jerry*, found on the *Videos in Abnormal Psychology.*

Jerry begins to tell his story, guided by the interviewer. Psychologists and other mental health professionals use clinical interviews and a variety of other means to assess abnormal behavior, including psychological testing, behavioral assessment, and physiological monitoring. The clinical interview is an important way of assessing abnormal behavior and arriving at a diagnostic impression—in this case, panic disorder. The clinician matches the presenting problems and associated features with a set of diagnostic criteria to form a diagnostic impression.

The diagnosis of psychological or mental disorders represents a way of classifying patterns of abnormal behavior on the basis of their common features or symptoms. Abnormal behavior has been classified since ancient times. Hippocrates classified abnormal behaviors according to his theory of *humors* (vital bodily fluids). Although his theory proved to be flawed, Hippocrates's classification of some types of mental health problems generally corresponds to diagnostic categories clinicians use today (see Chapter 1). His description of melancholia, for example, is similar to current conceptions of depression. During the Middle Ages, some "authorities" classified abnormal behaviors into two groups: those that resulted from demonic possession and those due to natural causes.

The 19th-century German physician Emil Kraepelin was the first modern theorist to develop a comprehensive model of classification on the basis of distinctive features, or symptoms, associated with abnormal behavior patterns (see Chapter 1). The most commonly used classification system today is largely an outgrowth and extension of Kraepelin's work: the *Diagnostic and Statistical Manual of Mental Disorders* (*DSM*), published by the American Psychiatric Association.

Why is it important to classify abnormal behavior? For one thing, classification is the core of science. Without labeling and organizing patterns of abnormal behavior, researchers could not communicate their findings to one another, and progress toward understanding these disorders would come to a halt. Moreover, important decisions are made on the basis of classification. Certain psychological disorders respond better to one therapy than to another or to one drug than to another. Classification also helps clinicians predict behavior: Schizophrenia, for example, follows a more or less predictable course. Finally, classification helps researchers identify populations with similar patterns of abnormal behavior. By classifying groups of people as depressed, for example, researchers might be able to identify common factors that help explain the origins of depression.

This chapter reviews the classification and assessment of abnormal behavior, beginning with the *DSM*.

# How Are Abnormal Behavior Patterns Classified?

The *DSM* was introduced in 1952. The latest version, published in 2013, is the *DSM-5*. The *DSM* is used widely in the United States; however, the most widely used diagnostic manual worldwide is the World Health Organization's *International Statistical Classification of Diseases and Related Health Problems* (*ICD*), now in a tenth edition (the *ICD-10*). The *ICD*, which comprises a listing of diagnosable mental and physical disorders, is compatible with the *DSM* system, so that *DSM* diagnoses can be coded in the *ICD* system as well. A new edition, the *ICD-11*, is in the works and may be published by the time this text reaches your hands.

The *DSM* has been widely adopted by mental health professionals, which is why we focus on it here. Yet we recognize that many psychologists and other mental health professionals criticize the *DSM* on several grounds, such as relying too strongly on the medical model.

In the *DSM*, abnormal behavior patterns are classified as mental disorders. *Mental disorders* involve emotional distress (typically depression or anxiety), significantly impaired functioning (difficulty meeting responsibilities at work, in the family, or in society at large), or behavior that places people at risk for personal suffering, pain, disability, or death (e.g., suicide attempts, repeated use of harmful drugs).

Note that a behavior pattern that represents an expected or culturally appropriate response to a stressful event, such as signs of bereavement or grief following the death of a loved one, is not considered disordered within the *DSM*, even if behavior is significantly impaired. If a person's behavior remains significantly impaired over an extended period of time, however, a diagnosis of a mental disorder might become appropriate.

## The *DSM* and Models of Abnormal Behavior

**3.1 Describe the key features of the *DSM* system of diagnostic classification.**

The *DSM* system, like the medical model, treats abnormal behaviors as signs or symptoms of underlying disorders or pathologies. However, the *DSM* does not assume that abnormal behaviors necessarily stem from biological causes or defects. It recognizes that the causes of most mental disorders remain unclear: Some disorders may have purely biological causes, whereas others may have psychological causes. Still others—probably most—are best explained within a multifactorial model that takes into account the interaction of biological, psychological, social (socioeconomic, sociocultural, and ethnic), and physical environmental factors.

The *DSM* uses the term *mental disorder* to describe clinical syndromes (clusters of symptoms) involving a significant level of disturbance in a person's cognitive, emotional, or behavioral functioning. In most cases, mental disorders are associated with significant emotional distress or disability (difficulties meeting social, occupational, or other important life functions). For example, in Chapter 7 we discuss

**DETERMINING LEVEL OF CARE.** The assessment of a person's functioning takes into account the individual's ability to manage the responsibilities of daily living. Here, we see a group home for people with intellectual disabilities; the residents assume responsibility for household functions.

the mental disorder called *major depressive disorder*. This disorder is characterized by symptoms and problem behaviors such as significantly downcast mood, loss of interest or pleasure associated with activities of daily life, feelings of worthlessness, difficulties concentrating or thinking clearly, changes in appetite and sleep patterns, and recurring thoughts about death or suicide, among others. This syndrome, then, comprises a composite of symptoms associated with emotional distress (depressed mood), changes in cognitive functioning (difficulties concentrating or thinking clearly, suicidal thoughts) and behavioral changes (loss of interest in daily activities). Not all symptoms need to be present. The manual specifies the minimum number of symptoms needed for particular diagnoses. The examining clinician determines whether the person's symptoms match the *DSM*'s criteria for a particular mental disorder. A diagnosis is given only when the minimum number of symptoms is present to meet the diagnostic criteria for the particular diagnosis.

Although the term "mental disorder" is widely used by medical professionals, psychologists often use the term *psychological disorder* in place of *mental disorder* to represent the fact that these disturbed behavior patterns involve significant impairment of a person's psychological functioning. We adopt the term *psychological disorder* in this text because we believe it is more appropriate to place the study of abnormal behavior squarely within a psychological context. Moreover, the term *psychological* has the advantage of encompassing behavioral patterns as well as strictly "mental" experiences, such as emotions, thoughts, beliefs, and attitudes. The *DSM* classifies disorders people have, not the people themselves. Consequently, clinicians don't classify a person as a *schizophrenic* or a *depressive*. Rather, they refer to *an individual with schizophrenia* or *a person with major depression*. This difference in terminology is not simply a matter of semantics. To label someone a schizophrenic carries the unfortunate and stigmatizing implication that a person's identity is defined by the disorder the person has.

The *DSM* is *descriptive*, not *explanatory*. It describes diagnostic features—or, in medical terms, symptoms—of abnormal behaviors; it does not attempt to explain their origins or adopt any particular theoretical framework, such as psychodynamic or learning theory. Using the *DSM* classification system, the clinician arrives at a diagnosis by matching a client's symptoms and behaviors with the specific criteria that define particular mental disorders. The *DSM-5* is organized into 20 general categories of mental disorders, including anxiety disorders, schizophrenia spectrum and other psychotic disorders, and personality disorders. Table 3.1 lists the 20 diagnostic categories or groupings of disorders in the *DSM-5*, along with examples of disorders in each category and where in the text they are discussed. Table 3.2 presents the *DSM-5* diagnostic criteria for a particular type of anxiety disorder called *generalized anxiety disorder*.

**CATEGORIES VS. DIMENSIONS** The *DSM* is based on a *categorical model of classification*, which means that clinicians needs to make a categorical or *yes–no* type of judgment about whether the disorder is present in a given case. Categorical judgments are commonplace in modern medicine, such as in determining whether or not a person has cancer. A categorical model is often used in classification, such as in the case of making a categorical judgment that a woman is either pregnant or not pregnant.

One limitation of the categorical model is that it does not directly provide a means of evaluating the severity of a disorder. Two people might have the same number of symptoms of a given disorder and both warrant a diagnosis, but differ markedly in the severity of the disorder. To address this limitation, the *DSM-5* expanded upon the categorical model to include a dimensional component for many disorders. This dimensional component gives the evaluator the opportunity to identify "shades of gray." For many disorders, the evaluator is charged not only with determining whether a disorder is present but also with rating the severity of the symptoms of a disorder along a scale ranging from *mild* to *very severe*.

Many critics of the *DSM* system believe the *DSM-5* system should be replaced with a dimensional approach to assessment. We will return to this question when we consider the

**DSM-5.** The *DSM*, now in a fifth edition called the *DSM-5*, is a diagnostic manual for classifying mental disorders. It lists specific criteria clinicians use to diagnose particular disorders.

## Table 3.1 *DSM-5* Categories of Mental Disorders

| Diagnostic Categories (Where Discussed in Text) | Examples of Specific Disorders |
|---|---|
| Neurodevelopmental Disorders (Chapter 13) | Autism spectrum disorder<br>Specific learning disorder<br>Communication disorders |
| Schizophrenia Spectrum and Other Psychotic Disorders (Chapter 11) | Schizophrenia<br>Schizophreniform disorder<br>Schizoaffective disorder<br>Delusional disorder<br>Schizotypal personality disorder (see Chapter 12) |
| Bipolar and Related Disorders (Chapter 7) | Bipolar disorder<br>Cyclothymic disorder |
| Depressive Disorders (Chapter 7) | Major depressive disorder<br>Persistent depressive disorder (dysthymia)<br>Premenstrual dysphoric disorder |
| Anxiety Disorders (Chapter 5) | Panic disorder<br>Phobic disorders<br>Generalized anxiety disorder |
| Obsessive-Compulsive and Related Disorders (Chapter 5) | Obsessive-compulsive disorder<br>Body dysmorphic disorder<br>Hoarding disorder<br>Trichotillomania (Hair-pulling disorder) |
| Trauma- and Stressor-Related Disorders (Chapter 4) | Adjustment disorder<br>Acute stress disorder<br>Posttraumatic stress disorder |
| Dissociative Disorders (Chapter 6) | Dissociative amnesia<br>Depersonalization/derealization disorder<br>Dissociative identity disorder |
| Somatic Symptom and Related Disorders (Chapter 6) | Somatic symptom disorder<br>Illness anxiety disorder<br>Factitious disorder |
| Feeding and Eating Disorders (Chapter 9) | Anorexia nervosa<br>Bulimia nervosa<br>Binge-eating disorder |
| Elimination Disorders (Chapter 13) | Enuresis (bed wetting)<br>Encopresis (soiling) |
| Sleep-Wake Disorders (Chapter 9) | Insomnia disorder<br>Hypersomnolence disorder<br>Narcolepsy<br>Breathing-related sleep disorders<br>Circadian rhythm sleep-wake disorders<br>Nightmare disorder |
| Sexual Dysfunctions (Chapter 10) | Male hypoactive sexual desire disorder<br>Erectile disorder<br>Female sexual interest/arousal disorder<br>Female orgasmic disorder<br>Delayed ejaculation<br>Premature (early) ejaculation |
| Gender Dysphoria (Chapter 10) | Gender dysphoria |
| Disruptive, Impulse-Control, and Conduct Disorders (Chapters 12 and 13) | Conduct disorder<br>Oppositional defiant disorder<br>Intermittent explosive disorder |
| Substance-Related and Addictive Disorders (Chapter 8) | Alcohol use disorder<br>Stimulant use disorder<br>Gambling disorder |
| Neurocognitive Disorders (Chapter 14) | Delirium<br>Mild neurocognitive disorder<br>Major neurocognitive disorder |
| Personality Disorders (Chapter 12) | Paranoid personality disorder<br>Schizoid personality disorder<br>Histrionic personality disorder<br>Antisocial personality disorder<br>Borderline personality disorder<br>Dependent personality disorder<br>Avoidant personality disorder<br>Obsessive-compulsive personality disorder |

Table 3.1 Continued

| Diagnostic Categories (Where Discussed in Text) | Examples of Specific Disorders |
|---|---|
| **Paraphilic Disorders (Chapter 10)** | Exhibitionistic disorder<br>Fetishistic disorder<br>Transvestic disorder<br>Voyeuristic disorder<br>Pedophilic disorder<br>Sexual masochism disorder<br>Sexual sadism disorder |
| **Other Mental Disorders** | Other specified mental disorder |

**SOURCE:** Based on American Psychiatric Association (2013).

## Table 3.2 Criteria for *DSM-5*

### GENERALIZED ANXIETY DISORDER

A. Excessive anxiety and worry (apprehensive expectation), occurring more days than not for at least 6 months, about a number of events or activities (such as work or school performance).

B. The individual finds it difficult to control the worry.

C. The anxiety and worry are associated with three (or more) of the following six symptoms (with at least some symptoms having been present for more days than not for the past 6 months):

**Note:** Only one item is required in children.

1. Restlessness or feeling keyed up or on edge.
2. Being easily fatigued.
3. Difficulty concentrating or mind going blank.
4. Irritability.
5. Muscle tension.
6. Sleep disturbance (difficulty falling or staying asleep, or restless, unsatisfying sleep).

D. The anxiety, worry, or physical symptoms cause clinically significant distress or impairment in social, occupational, or other important areas of functioning.

E. The disturbance is not attributable to the physiological effects of a substance (e.g., a drug of abuse, a medication) or another medical condition (e.g., hyperthyroidism).

F. The disturbance is not better explained by another mental disorder (e.g., anxiety or worry about having panic attacks in panic disorder, negative evaluation in social anxiety disorder [social phobia], contamination or other obsessions in obsessive-compulsive disorder, separation from attachment figures in separation anxiety disorder, reminders of traumatic events in posttraumatic stress disorder, gaining weight in anorexia nervosa, physical complaints in somatic symptom disorder, perceived appearance flaws in body dysmorphic disorder, having a serious illness in illness anxiety disorder, or the content of delusional beliefs in schizophrenia or delusional disorder).

Reprinted with permission from the *Diagnostic and Statistical Manual of Mental Disorders*, Fifth Edition (Copyright 2013). American Psychiatric Association, 2013.

advantages and disadvantages of the *DSM* system. For now, let's note that a dimensional model is predicated on the belief that disturbed behavior patterns such as anxiety, depression, and personality disorders represent extreme or maladaptive variations of emotional states and psychological traits found in the general population.

# Culture-Bound Syndromes

**3.2 Describe the concept of culture-bound syndromes and identify some examples.**

Some patterns of abnormal behavior, called **culture-bound syndromes**, occur in some cultures but are rare or unknown in others.

Culture-bound syndromes may reflect exaggerated forms of common folk superstitions and belief patterns within a particular culture. For example, the psychiatric

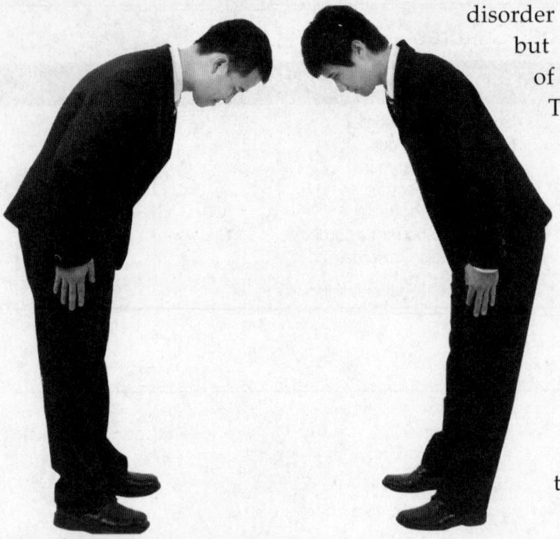

disorder *taijin-kyofu-sho* (TKS) is common among young men in Japan but rare elsewhere. The disorder is characterized by excessive fear of embarrassing or offending other people (Kinoshita et al., 2008). The syndrome is associated with the value placed on not causing others to feel embarrassed or ashamed in traditional Japanese culture. People with TKS may dread blushing in front of others, not because they are afraid of embarrassing themselves but for fear of embarrassing others. People with TKS may also fear mumbling their thoughts aloud, lest they inadvertently offend others.

Culture-bound syndromes in the United States include anorexia nervosa (discussed in Chapter 9) and dissociative identity disorder (formerly called *multiple personality disorder*; discussed in Chapter 6). These abnormal behavior patterns are essentially unknown in less-developed cultures. Table 3.3 lists some other culture-bound syndromes identified in the *DSM*.

**CULTURAL UNDERPINNINGS OF ABNORMAL BEHAVIOR PATTERNS.** Culture-bound syndromes often represent exaggerated forms of cultural beliefs and values. *Taijin-kyofu-sho* is a syndrome characterized by excessive fear that one may embarrass or offend other people. The syndrome primarily affects young Japanese men and appears to be connected with the emphasis in Japanese culture on politeness and avoiding embarrassing other people.

## Evaluating the *DSM* System

**3.3 Explain why the new edition of the *DSM*, the *DSM-5*, is controversial and evaluate the strengths and weaknesses of the *DSM* system.**

To be useful, a diagnostic system must demonstrate **reliability** and **validity**. The *DSM* may be considered reliable, or consistent, if different evaluators using the system are likely to arrive at the same diagnoses when they evaluate the same people. The system may be considered valid if diagnostic judgments correspond with observed behavior. For example, people diagnosed with social phobia should show abnormal levels of anxiety in social situations. Another form of validity is *predictive validity*, or ability to predict the course the disorder is likely to follow or its response to treatment. For example, people diagnosed with bipolar disorder typically respond to the drug lithium (see Chapter 7). Likewise, persons diagnosed with specific phobias (such as fear of heights) tend to be highly responsive to behavioral techniques for reducing fears (see Chapter 5). **T / F**

### TRUTH or FICTION

Some men in India have a psychological disorder in which they are troubled by anxiety over losing semen.

☑ **TRUE** Dhat syndrome is a culture-bound syndrome found in India in which men develop intense fears over loss of semen.

Overall, evidence supports the reliability and validity of many *DSM* categories, including many anxiety disorders and mood disorders, as well as alcohol and drug use disorders (e.g., Grant, Harford, et al., 2006; Hasin et al., 2006). Yet questions about validity persist for some diagnostic categories (e.g., Smith et al., 2011; Widiger & Simonsen, 2005). Many observers also believe the *DSM* needs to become more sensitive to the importance of cultural and ethnic factors in diagnostic assessment (e.g., Alarcón et al., 2009). We should understand that the symptoms or problem behaviors included as diagnostic criteria in the *DSM* were determined by a consensus of mostly U.S.-trained psychiatrists, psychologists, and social workers. Had the American Psychiatric Association asked Asian-trained or Latin American-trained professionals to develop their diagnostic manual, for example, there might have been some different diagnostic criteria or even different diagnostic categories.

In fairness to the *DSM*, however, the more recent editions place greater emphasis than earlier editions on weighing cultural factors when assessing abnormal behavior. The *DSM* system recognizes that clinicians who are unfamiliar with an individual's cultural background may incorrectly classify that individual's behavior as abnormal when in fact it falls within the normal spectrum in that individual's culture. The *DSM* also recognizes that abnormal behaviors may take different forms in different cultures and that some abnormal behavior patterns are culture-specific (see Table 3.3). Although every edition of the *DSM* has had its critics, the *DSM-5*, as we see next, has sparked a firestorm of criticism.

## Table 3.3 Examples of Culture-Bound Syndromes from Other Cultures

| Culture-Bound Syndrome | Description |
|---|---|
| **Amok** | A disorder principally occurring in men in southeastern Asian and Pacific Island cultures, as well as in traditional Puerto Rican and Navajo cultures in the West, it describes a type of dissociative episode (a sudden change in consciousness or self-identity) in which an otherwise normal person suddenly goes berserk and strikes out at others, sometimes killing them. During these episodes, the person may have a sense of acting automatically or robotically. Violence may be directed at people or objects and is often accompanied by perceptions of persecution. A return to the person's usual state of functioning follows the episode. In the West, people use the expression "running amuck" to refer to an episode of losing oneself and running around in a violent frenzy. The word *amuck* is derived from the Malaysian word *amoq*, meaning *engaging furiously in battle*. The word passed into the English language during colonial times when British rulers in Malaysia observed this behavior among the native people. |
| **Ataque de nervios (*attack of nerves*)** | A way of describing states of emotional distress among Latin American and Latin Mediterranean groups, it most commonly involves features such as shouting uncontrollably, fits of crying, trembling, feelings of warmth or heat rising from the chest to the head, and aggressive verbal or physical behavior. These episodes are usually precipitated by a stressful event affecting the family (e.g., receiving news of the death of a family member) and are accompanied by feelings of being out of control. After an attack, a person returns quickly to his or her usual level of functioning, although there may be amnesia for events that occurred during the episode. |
| **Dhat syndrome** | A disorder (described further in Chapter 6) affecting males, found principally in India, that involves intense fear or anxiety over the loss of semen through nocturnal emissions, ejaculations, or excretion with urine (in fact, semen doesn't mix with urine). In Indian culture, there is a popular belief that loss of semen depletes a man of his vital natural energy. |
| **Falling out or blacking out** | Occurring principally among southern U.S. and Caribbean groups, the disorder involves an episode of sudden collapsing or fainting. The attack may occur without warning or be preceded by dizziness or feelings of "swimming" in the head. Although the eyes remain open, an individual reports an inability to see. The person can hear what others are saying and understand what is occurring but feels powerless to move. |
| **Ghost sickness** | A disorder occurring among American Indian groups, it involves a preoccupation with death and with the "spirits" of the deceased. Symptoms include bad dreams, feelings of weakness, loss of appetite, fear, anxiety, and a sense of foreboding. Hallucinations, loss of consciousness, and states of confusion may also be present, among other symptoms. |
| **Koro syndrome** | Found primarily in China and some other south and east Asian countries, the syndrome (discussed further in Chapter 6) refers to an episode of acute anxiety involving the fear that one's genitals (the penis in men and the vulva and nipples in women) are shrinking and retracting into the body and that death may result. |
| **Zar** | A term used in a number of countries in North Africa and the Middle East to describe the experience of spirit possession. Possession by spirits is often used in these cultures to explain dissociative episodes (sudden changes in consciousness or identity) that may be characterized by periods of shouting, banging the head against a wall, laughing, singing, or crying. Affected people may seem apathetic or withdrawn or refuse to eat or carry out their usual responsibilities. |

**SOURCE:** Adapted from the *DSM-5* (American Psychiatric Association, 2013); Dzokoto & Adams (2005); and other sources.

**CHANGES IN THE *DSM-5*** The *DSM* system has been periodically revised ever since it was introduced in 1952. The latest revision, the *DSM-5*, was years in the making and was published in 2013. It represents a major overhaul of the manual. The committees charged with revising the manual comprised experts in their fields. They closely examined the previous edition, the *DSM-IV*, taking a careful look at what parts of the diagnostic system were working well and what parts needed to be revised to improve the manual's clinical utility (how it is used in practice) and to address concerns raised by clinicians and researchers.

Some new disorders have sprung into being with the introduction of the *DSM-5* (see Table 3.4). Some existing disorders were reclassified or consolidated with other disorders under new diagnostic labels. For example, Asperger's disorder and autistic disorder were reclassified under a general category of *autism spectrum disorder* (discussed in Chapter 13). Trichotillomania (hair-pulling disorder) was moved from a category of impulse control disorders to a new category of *Obsessive-Compulsive and Related Disorders* (discussed in Chapter 5). Pathological (compulsive) gambling was moved from the impulse control disorder category to a new category called *Substance Use and Addictive Behaviors* (discussed in Chapter 8). Posttraumatic stress disorder (PTSD) was moved from the category of anxiety disorders to a new category, *Trauma- and Stressor-Related Disorders* (discussed in Chapter 4).

Despite many years of debate, editing, and review, the final version of the *DSM-5* remains steeped in controversy. Controversy has been a constant companion of the *DSM* system, in part because of difficulties involved in forging a consensus. Trying to weave together a consensus by committee reminds many of an old adage: A camel is a horse designed by committee.

**Table 3.4** Examples of New Disorders in the *DSM-5*

| Disorder | Major Feature | Diagnostic Classification | Where Discussed in Text |
|---|---|---|---|
| **Hoarding disorder** | Compulsive need to accumulate things, such as books, clothing, household items, and even junk mail | Obsessive-Compulsive and Related Disorders | Chapter 5 |
| **Disruptive mood dysregulation disorder** | Frequent, excessive temper tantrums in children | Depressive Disorders | Chapter 13 |
| **Mild and major neurocognitive disorders** | Significant declines in mental functioning involving thinking, memory, and attention | Neurocognitive Disorders | Chapter 14 |

One significant change in the *DSM-5* that has been generally well received is a greater emphasis on *dimensional assessment* across most categories of disorders. By conceptualizing disorders more broadly as representing dimensions of dysfunctional behavior rather than simply as "present or absent," diagnostic categories allow clinicians to make judgments about the relative severity of disorders, such as by indicating the frequency of symptoms or the level of suicide risk or anxiety. Still, many psychologists believe that the developers of the *DSM-5* did not go far enough in shifting from a categorical model of assessment to a dimensional model (as discussed further in Chapter 12 with respect to the dimensional model of personality disorders).

**CONTROVERSIES ABOUT THE *DSM-5*** Many controversies about the *DSM-5* remained unsettled at the time of this writing. Here are several of the major points of controversy:

- *Expansion of diagnosable disorders.* One of the most common criticisms concerns the proliferation of new mental disorders—a problem dubbed *diagnostic inflation* (Frances & Widiger, 2012). Ironically, the chairperson of the *DSM-IV* task force, psychiatrist Allen Frances, became one of the leading critics of the *DSM-5*. Frances called the approval of the *DSM-5* a "sad day for psychiatry" (cited in "Critic Calls," 2012). In a scathing criticism, Frances argued that the introduction of new disorders and changes in the definition of existing disorders may medicalize behavioral problems like repeated temper tantrums in children (now classified as a new type of mental disorder called *disruptive mood dysregulation disorder*) and expectable life challenges, such as mild cognitive changes or everyday forgetting in older adults (now classified as a new disorder called *mild neurocognitive disorder*). The result of diagnostic inflation may be to greatly expand the numbers of people labeled as suffering from a mental disorder or mental illness.
- *Changes in classification of mental disorders.* Another frequent criticism is that the *DSM-5* changed the ways in which many disorders are classified. A number of diagnoses were reclassified or folded into broader categories. Some diagnosable disorders under the previous diagnostic manual, such as Asperger's disorder (see Chapter 13), are no longer recognized as distinct diagnoses. Mental health professionals accustomed to using the earlier diagnostic categories have questioned whether many of the changes in classification are justified or whether they will lead to more diagnostic confusion. The debate over classification will likely continue until the next edition of the *DSM* is developed.
- *Changes in diagnostic criteria for particular disorders.* Another criticism is that changes in the clinical definitions or diagnostic criteria for various disorders in the *DSM-5* may change the numbers of cases in which these diagnoses are applied. Critics contend that many of the changes in the diagnostic criteria have not been sufficiently validated. Particular concerns have been raised about the substantial changes made in the set of symptoms or features used to diagnose autism spectrum disorder, which may have profound effects on the numbers of children identified as suffering from autism and related disorders (Smith, Reichow, & Volkmar, 2015).

- *Process of development.* Other criticisms of the *DSM-5* include the contention that the process of development was shrouded in secrecy, that it failed to incorporate input from many leading researchers and scholars in the field, and that changes to the diagnostic manual were not clearly documented on the basis of an adequate body of empirical research.

Why are these changes and controversies important to anyone other than psychologists and psychiatrists? The answer is that the diagnostic manual affects how clinicians identify, conceptualize, classify, and ultimately treat mental or psychological disorders. Changes in diagnostic practices can have far-reaching consequences. For example, Allen Frances argues that bringing behavior problems like recurrent temper tantrums under the umbrella of mental disorders will further increase the "excessive and inappropriate use of [psychiatric] medication in young children" (cited in "Critic Calls," 2012). Under the best of circumstances, however, changes in diagnostic practices lead to improved patient care. Time will tell how successful the *DSM-5* will be and whether it will continue to be the most widely used diagnostic system in the United States or will be replaced by yet another revision—or perhaps with an alternative system, such as the *ICD*.

All in all, the *DSM-5* remains a work in progress, a document that will continue to be argued about and subjected to continuing scrutiny for the foreseeable future.

**ADVANTAGES AND DISADVANTAGES OF THE *DSM* SYSTEM** · The major advantage of the *DSM* may be its designation of specific diagnostic criteria. The *DSM* permits the clinician to readily match a client's complaints and associated features with specific standards to see which diagnosis best fits the symptoms. For example, auditory hallucinations ("hearing voices") and delusions (fixed but false beliefs, such as thinking that other people are devils) are characteristic symptoms of schizophrenia.

Criticisms are also leveled against the *DSM* system. Critics challenge the utility of particular symptoms or features associated with a particular syndrome or of specified diagnostic criteria, such as the requirement that major depression be present for two weeks before a diagnosis is reached. Others challenge the reliance on the medical model. In the *DSM* system, problem behaviors are viewed as symptoms of underlying mental disorders in much the same way that physical symptoms are seen as signs of underlying physical disorders. The very use of the term *diagnosis* presumes the medical model is an appropriate basis for classifying abnormal behaviors—but some clinicians feel that behavior, abnormal or otherwise, is too complex and meaningful to be treated as merely symptomatic. They assert that the medical model focuses too much on what may happen within the individual and not enough on external influences on behavior, such as social factors (socioeconomic, sociocultural, and ethnic) and physical environmental factors.

Another concern is that the medical model focuses on categorizing psychological (or mental) disorders rather than on describing a person's behavioral strengths and weaknesses. Similarly, many investigators question whether the diagnostic model should retain its categorical structure (a disorder is either present or not). As noted earlier, they argue it should be replaced with a full dimensional approach in which abnormal behavior patterns such as anxiety, depression, and personality disorders represent extreme variations that fall along a spectrum of emotional states and psychological traits found in the general population. Another alternative favored by some clinicians is a *mixed model* similar to the *DSM-5* approach that includes elements of both categorical and dimensional classification (e.g., Kraemer, 2015).

Traditionally, clinicians have adopted a categorical approach to diagnosis. They look for patterns of abnormal behaviors that fit particular diagnostic categories. However, a failing of the categorical approach is that it does not account for similar features of disturbed behavior that cut across diagnostic categories. For example, major depression (discussed in Chapter 7) shares features in common with other disorders such as social anxiety disorder, a type of anxiety disorder (see Chapter 5) in which a person avoids social interactions out of an extreme fear of rejection or negative evaluation by others. These shared features or underlying processes may include a tendency to catastrophize or "blow out of proportion" negative events or to heap blame on oneself when disappointments occur. Recently, British researchers reported that unstable moods are common not just in mood disorders as you would expect, but also in a wide range of other psychological disorders, including personality disorders and schizophrenia (Patel et al., 2015).

A new conceptual model, called the **transdiagnostic model**, is now driving research examining interconnections or core features that cut across different diagnostic categories. Research along these lines is underway, as represented by recent research that identified a common neurological substrate in the brain that extended across various diagnostic categories (Goodkind et al., 2015). The hope is that identifying common features across disorders may lead to the development of new treatments for the core processes that underlie these disorders (Clarkin, 2014).

Behaviorally oriented psychologists seek to understand behavior, abnormal or otherwise, by examining the interaction between a person and the environment. The *DSM* aims to determine what "disorders" people "have"—not how well they can function in particular situations. The behavioral model, alternatively, focuses more on behaviors than on underlying processes—more on what people *do* than on what they "are" or "have." Behaviorists and behavior therapists also use the *DSM*, of course, in part because mental health centers and health insurance carriers require the use of a diagnostic code and in part because they want to communicate in a common language with other practitioners. Many behavior therapists view the *DSM* diagnostic code as a convenient means of labeling patterns of abnormal behavior, a shorthand for a more extensive behavioral analysis of the problem.

Critics also complain that the *DSM* system might stigmatize people by labeling them with psychiatric diagnoses. Our society is strongly biased against people who are labeled as mentally ill. They are often shunned by others, even family members, and subjected to discrimination—or **sanism** (Perlin, 2002–2003), the counterpart to other forms of prejudice, such as racism, sexism, and ageism—in housing and employment.

The *DSM* system, despite its critics, has become part and parcel of the everyday practice of most U.S. mental health professionals. It may be the one reference manual found on the bookshelves of nearly all professionals and dog-eared from repeated use. In *Thinking Critically: The DSM—The Bible of Psychiatry—Thomas Widiger*, a prominent investigator in the field shares his views on the *DSM*, or what he refers to as the "bible of psychiatry." Dr. Widiger also discusses the dimensional approach to assessing personality disorders such as antisocial personality disorder. (See Chapter 12 for a description of the features of antisocial personality disorder and other personality disorders.)

Now, let's consider various ways of assessing abnormal behavior. We begin by considering the basic requirements for methods of assessment—that they be reliable and valid.

## THINKING CRITICALLY about abnormal psychology

### @ISSUE: THE *DSM*—THE BIBLE OF PSYCHIATRY—THOMAS WIDIGER

If you are a clinical psychologist, there are probably many reasons to dislike the American Psychiatric Association's *Diagnostic and Statistical Manual of Mental Disorders*. First, it is under the control of a profession with which clinical psychologists are in professional and economic competition. Second, it can be perceived as being used by, or perhaps is in fact used by, insurance companies as a means of limiting coverage of clinical practice. For example, a managed care company might limit the number of sessions they will cover depending on the patient's diagnosis. (They might not even cover the treatment of some disorders.) I am not too sure that these are necessarily valid reasons for disliking the *DSM*, but I do believe they contribute to some of the criticism that it receives. But, third, and most fundamentally important, it doesn't really work that well. A diagnosis of a disorder should lead to the identification of that specific disorder that has a specific pathology that accounts for it and a specific therapy that can be used to cure the patient of that pathology. That hasn't been the case for mental disorders diagnosed by the *DSM* system, not yet at least.

Despite its shortcomings, the *DSM* is a necessary document. Clinicians and researchers need a common language with which to communicate with each other about patterns of psychopathology, and that is the primary function of the *DSM*. Before the *DSM*'s first edition, the clinical practice was awash with a confusing plethora of different names for the same thing and the same name for quite different things. It was, simply put, chaotic.

Many helping professionals are critical of the *DSM* for placing labels on persons. We work with our clients. We don't want to categorize or label them; however, labeling is a necessity. Persons who object to labeling must also use terms (e.g., categories) that describe the problems that clients present. It is not that labeling per se is the problem. It is perhaps in part the negative connotations of receiving a psychiatric diagnosis and the stereotyping of patients diagnosed with various disorders. Each of these concerns will be briefly discussed in turn.

Regrettably, many persons feel shame or embarrassment upon receiving a psychiatric diagnosis or undergoing psychological or psychiatric treatment. In part, the embarrassment or shame reflects the myth that only a small minority of the population experiences psychological problems that warrant a diagnosis of a mental disorder. It's never been clear to me why we believe that we have not suffered, do not suffer, or will not suffer from a mental disorder. All of us have suffered, do suffer, and will suffer from quite a few physical disorders. Why should it be so different for mental disorders? It's not as if any of us are born with perfect genes, or are raised by perfect parents, or go through life untouched by stress, trauma, or psychological problems.

The difficulty with stereotyping is also problematic. People receiving psychiatric diagnoses are lumped into diagnostic categories that seem to treat all members of a particular diagnostic grouping as having the same characteristics. The diagnostic system fails to take individual profiles of psychopathology into account with respect to identifying the distinctive patterns of symptoms and presenting problems that particular individuals present.

Most (if not all) mental disorders appear to result from a complex array of interacting biological vulnerabilities and dispositions with a number of significant environmental and psychosocial factors that often exert their effects over a period of time. The symptoms and pathologies of mental disorders appear to be influenced by a wide range of neurobiological, interpersonal, cognitive, and other factors, leading to the development of particular constellations of symptoms and complaints that characterize an individual's psychopathology profile. This complex web of causal factors and the distinctiveness of individual psychopathology profiles are unlikely to be captured by any single diagnostic category. I prefer the more individualized description of persons provided by dimensional models of classification, for example, the *five-factor model* for the classification of personality disorders.

These five broad domains have been identified as extraversion, agreeableness versus antagonism, conscientiousness, neuroticism or emotional instability, and openness or unconventionality. Each of the five domains can also be differentiated into more specific facets. For example, the domain of agreeableness can be broken down into its underlying components of trust versus mistrust, straightforwardness versus deception, self-sacrifice versus exploitation, compliance versus aggression, modesty versus arrogance, and softheartedness versus callousness.

Most important for clinical psychology, all of the personality disorders are described well in terms of the domains and facets of the five-factor model. For example, antisocial personality disorder includes many of the facets of low conscientiousness (low deliberation, self-discipline, and dutifulness) and high antagonism (callousness, exploitation, and aggression). The glib charm and fearlessness seen in the psychopath are represented by abnormally low levels of the neuroticism facets of self-consciousness, anxiousness, and vulnerability. This approach to describing patients provides a more individualized description of each patient, and it might even help somewhat with the stigmatization of a mental disorder diagnosis. All persons vary in the extent of their neuroticism, in the extent to which they are agreeable versus antagonistic, and in the extent to which they're conscientious. Persons with personality disorders would no longer be said to have disorders that are qualitatively distinct from normal psychological functioning but would instead be seen simply as persons who have relatively extreme and maladaptive variants of the personality traits that are evident within all of us.

In thinking critically about the issue, answer the following questions:

- Do we really need an authoritative diagnostic manual? Why or why not?
- How can we fix the problems of negative, pejorative connotations of diagnoses of mental disorders in our society?

**THOMAS A. WIDIGER.** Dr. Widiger is Professor of psychology at the University of Kentucky. He received his Ph.D. in clinical psychology from Miami University (Ohio) and completed his internship at Cornell University Medical College. He currently serves as Associate Editor of *Journal of Abnormal Psychology* and *Journal of Personality Disorders*, as well as the *Annual Review of Clinical Psychology*. He was a member of the *DSM*-5 Task Force and served as the Research Coordinator for *DSM-IV*.

# Standards of Assessment

Clinicians make important decisions on the basis of classification and assessment. For example, their recommendations for specific treatment techniques vary according to their assessment of the behaviors clients exhibit. Therefore, methods of assessment, like diagnostic categories, must be *reliable* and *valid*.

## Reliability

**3.4 Identify methods of assessing reliability of tests and measures.**

The reliability of a method of assessment, like that of a diagnostic system, is a measurement of its consistency. A gauge of height, for example, would be unreliable if it showed a person to be taller or shorter at every measurement. Also, different people should be able to check the yardstick and agree on the measured height of the subject. A yardstick that shrinks and expands with the slightest change in temperature will be unreliable, as will be one that is difficult to read. A reliable measure of abnormal behavior must yield the same results on different occasions.

An assessment technique has *internal consistency* if the different parts of the test yield consistent results. For example, if responses to the different items on a depression scale are not highly correlated, the items may not be measuring the same characteristic or trait—in this case, depression. On the other hand, some tests are designed to measure a set of different traits or characteristics. For example, a widely used personality test called the Minnesota Multiphasic Personality Inventory (MMPI; now in a revised edition, called the MMPI-2) contains subscales measuring various traits related to abnormal behavior.

An assessment method has *test–retest reliability* if it yields similar results on separate occasions. We would not trust a bathroom scale that yielded different results each time we weighed ourselves—unless we had stuffed or starved ourselves between weighings. The same principle applies to methods of psychological assessment.

Finally, an assessment method that relies on judgments from observers or raters must show *interrater reliability*. That is, raters must show a high level of agreement in their ratings. For example, two teachers may be asked to use a behavioral rating scale to evaluate a child's aggressiveness, hyperactivity, and sociability. The scale would have good interrater reliability if both teachers rated the same child in similar ways.

### TRUTH or FICTION

A psychological test can be highly reliable but also invalid.

☑ TRUE A psychological test can indeed be highly reliable yet also invalid. A test of musical aptitude may have superb reliability but be invalid as a measure of personality or intelligence.

## Validity

**3.5 Identify methods of assessing validity of tests and measures.**

Assessment techniques must also be valid; that is, instruments used in assessment must measure what they intend to measure. Suppose a measure of depression actually turned out to be measuring anxiety. Using such a measure might lead an examiner to an incorrect diagnosis. There are different measures of validity, including *content, criterion,* and *construct validity*. **T / F**

The **content validity** of an assessment technique is the degree to which its content represents the behaviors associated with the trait in question. For example, depression includes features such as sadness and refusal to participate in activities the person once enjoyed. To have content validity, then, techniques that assess depression should include items that address these areas.

**Criterion validity** represents the degree to which the assessment technique correlates with an independent, external criterion (standard) of what the technique is intended to assess. *Predictive validity* is a form of criterion validity. A test or assessment technique shows good predictive validity if it can be used to predict future performance or behavior. For example, a test measuring antisocial behavior would show predictive validity if people scoring high on the measure later showed more evidence of delinquent or criminal behavior than did low scorers.

Another way of measuring criterion validity of a diagnostic test for a particular disorder is to see if it is able to identify people who meet diagnostic criteria for the disorder. Two related concepts are important here: sensitivity and specificity. *Sensitivity* refers to the degree to which a test correctly identifies people who have the disorder the test is intended to detect. Tests that lack sensitivity produce a high number of *false negatives*—individuals identified as not having the disorder who truly do have the disorder. *Specificity* refers to the degree to which the test avoids classifying people as having a particular disorder who truly do not have the disorder. Tests that lack specificity produce a high number of *false positives*—people identified as having the disorder who truly do not have the disorder. By taking into account the sensitivity and specificity of a given test, clinicians can determine the ability of a test to classify individuals correctly.

**Construct validity** is the degree to which a test corresponds to the theoretical model of the underlying construct or trait it purports to measure. Say that we have a test that purports to measure anxiety. Anxiety is not a concrete object or phenomenon; it can't be measured directly, counted, weighed, or touched. Anxiety is a theoretical construct that helps explain phenomena such as a pounding heart or the sudden inability to speak when you are asking someone out on a date. Anxiety may be indirectly measured by such means as self-report (the client rates his or her personal level of anxiety) and physiological techniques (measuring the level of sweat on the palms of the client's hands).

The construct validity of a test of anxiety requires the results of the test to predict other behaviors that would be expected given your theoretical model of anxiety. Say your theoretical model predicts that socially anxious college students will have greater difficulties than calmer students in speaking coherently when asking someone for a date, but not when they are merely rehearsing the invitation in private. When the results of an experimental test of these predictions fit these predicted patterns, we could say the evidence supports the test's construct validity.

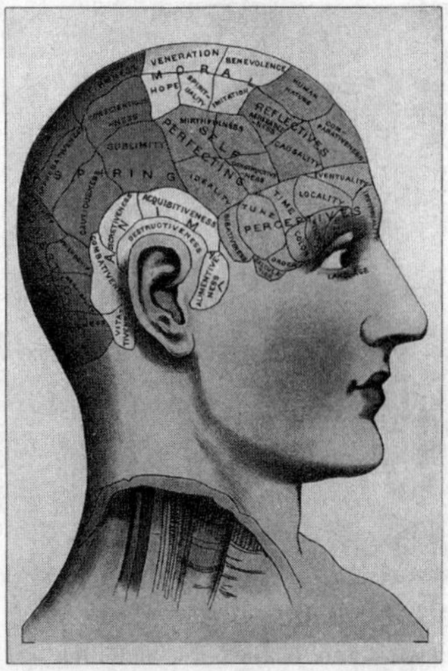

**PHRENOLOGY.** The 19th-century belief in phrenology held that personality and mental faculties were based on the size of certain parts of the brain and could be assessed by measuring the pattern of bumps on a person's head.

A test may be reliable (give you consistent responses) but still not measure what it purports to measure (be invalid). For example, 19th-century phrenologists believed they could gauge people's personalities by measuring the bumps on their heads. Their calipers provided reliable measures of their subjects' bumps and protrusions; the measurements, however, did not provide valid estimates of subjects' psychological traits. The phrenologists were bumping in the dark, so to speak. **T / F**

**TRUTH or FICTION**

Although it is not an exact science, the measurement of the bumps on an individual's head can be used to determine his or her personality traits.

☑ **FALSE** Beliefs in phrenology have long been discredited.

# Methods of Assessment

Clinicians use different methods of assessment to arrive at diagnoses, including interviews, psychological testing, self-report questionnaires, behavioral measures, and physiological measures. The role of assessment, however, goes further than classification. A careful assessment provides a wealth of information about clients' personalities and cognitive functioning. This information helps clinicians acquire a broader understanding of their clients' problems and recommend appropriate forms of treatment. In most cases, the formal assessment involves one or more clinical interviews with the client, leading to a diagnostic impression and a treatment plan. In some cases, more formal psychological testing probes the client's psychological problems and intellectual, personality, and neuropsychological functioning.

## The Clinical Interview

**3.6 Identify the three major types of clinical interviews.**

The *clinical interview* is the most widely used means of assessment. The interview is usually the clinician's first face-to-face contact with a client. Clinicians often begin by asking clients to describe the presenting complaint in their own words, saying something like, "Can you describe to me the problems you've been having lately?" (Therapists learn not to ask, "What brings you here?" to avoid the possibility of receiving such answers as "a car," "a bus," or "my social worker.") The clinician usually will then probe aspects of the presenting complaint, such as behavioral abnormalities and feelings of discomfort, the circumstances surrounding the onset of the problem, history of past episodes, and how the problem affects the client's daily functioning. The clinician may explore possible precipitating events, such as changes in life circumstances, social relationships, employment,

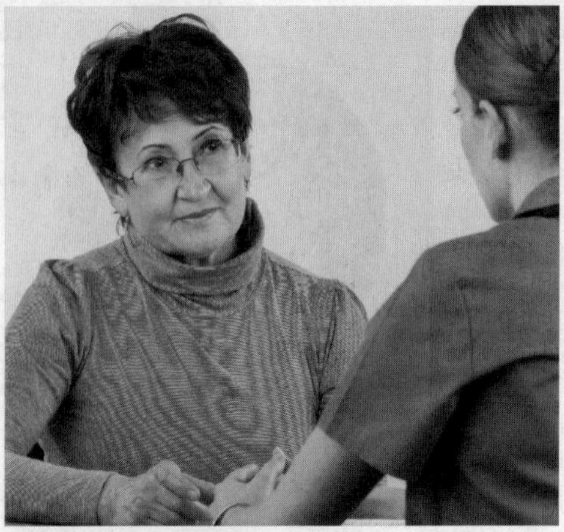

**BUILDING RAPPORT.** By developing rapport and feelings of trust with a client, the skillful interviewer helps put the client at ease and encourages candid communication.

or schooling. The interviewer encourages the client to describe the problem in her or his own words to understand it from the client's viewpoint. For example, the interviewer in the case vignette that opened the chapter asked Jerry to discuss the concerns that prompted him to seek help.

Although the format may vary, most interviews cover these topics:

1. *Identifying data.* This is information regarding the client's sociodemographic characteristics: address and telephone number, marital status, age, gender, racial/ethnic characteristics, religion, employment, family composition, and so on.
2. *Description of the presenting problem(s).* How does the client perceive the problem? What troubling behaviors, thoughts, or feelings are reported? How do they affect the client's functioning? When did they begin?
3. *Psychosocial history.* This is information describing the client's developmental history: educational, social, and occupational history; early family relationships.
4. *Medical/psychiatric history.* Here, the clinician elicits the client's history of medical and psychiatric treatment and hospitalizations: Is the present problem a recurrent episode of a previous problem? If yes, how was the problem handled in the past? Was treatment successful? Why or why not?
5. *Medical problems/medication.* This refers to a description of present medical problems and present treatment, including medication. The clinician is alert to ways in which medical problems may affect the presenting psychological problem. For example, drugs for certain medical conditions can affect people's moods and general levels of arousal.

The interviewer is attentive to the client's nonverbal as well as verbal behavior, forming judgments about the appropriateness of the client's attire and grooming, apparent mood, and ability to focus attention. Clinicians also judge the clarity or soundness of clients' thought and perceptual processes and level of orientation, or awareness of themselves and their surroundings (who they are, where they are, and what the present date is). These clinical judgments form an important part of the initial assessment of the client's mental state.

**INTERVIEW FORMATS** There are three general types of clinical interviews. In an **unstructured interview**, the clinician adopts his or her own style of questioning rather than following a standard format. In a **semistructured interview**, the clinician follows a general outline of questions designed to gather essential information but is free to ask the questions in any particular order and to branch off into other directions to follow up on important information. In a **structured interview**, the interview follows a preset series of questions in a particular order.

The major advantage of the unstructured interview is its spontaneity and conversational style. Because the interviewer is not bound to use any specific set of questions, there is an active give-and-take with the client. The major disadvantage is the lack of standardization. Different interviewers may ask questions in different ways. For example, one interviewer might ask, "How have your moods been lately?" whereas another might pose the question, "Have you had any periods of crying or tearfulness during the past week or two?" The clients' responses may depend to a certain extent on how the questions are worded. Also, the conversational flow of the interview may fail to touch on important clinical information needed to form diagnostic information, such as suicidal tendencies.

A semistructured interview provides more structure and uniformity, but at the expense of some spontaneity. Some clinicians prefer to conduct a semistructured interview in which they follow a general outline of questions but allow themselves the flexibility to depart from the interview protocol when they want to pursue issues that seem important.

Structured interviews (also called *standardized interviews*) provide the highest level of reliability in reaching diagnostic judgments, which is why they are used frequently in research settings. The *Structured Clinical Interview for the DSM* (SCID) includes closed-ended questions to determine the presence of behavior patterns that suggest specific diagnostic categories and open-ended questions that allow clients to elaborate on their problems and feelings. The SCID guides the clinician in testing diagnostic hypotheses as the interview progresses. Evidence supports the reliability of the SCID across various clinical settings (Zanarini et al., 2000).

In the course of the interview, the clinician may also assess the client's cognitive functioning with a **mental status examination**. The specifics of the examination vary, but they typically include features such as the following:

- *Appearance:* appropriateness of the client's attire and grooming
- *Mood:* prevailing emotions displayed during the interview
- *Level of attention:* ability to maintain focus and attend to the interviewer's questions
- *Perceptual and thinking processes:* ability to think clearly and discern reality from fantasy
- *Orientation:* knowing who they are, where they are, and the present date
- *Judgment:* ability to make sound life decisions in daily life

No matter what type of interview is conducted, the interviewer arrives at a diagnostic impression by compiling all the information available: from the interview, from review of the client's background, and from the presenting problems.

**COMPUTERIZED INTERVIEWS** Have you ever taken a test online or administered via a computer? In all likelihood, you have had some experience with computerized assessment, perhaps in an employment screening situation or in an academic course. Computerized assessments are becoming more widely used in clinical settings, although it is unlikely they will replace human interviewers anytime soon.

In a computerized clinical interview, clients respond to questions about their psychological symptoms and related concerns that are posed to them on a computer screen (Trull & Prinstein, 2013). The computer interview may help identify problems that clients may be embarrassed or unwilling to report to a live interviewer (Taylor & Luce, 2003). People may actually reveal more information about themselves to a computer than to a human interviewer. Perhaps people feel less self-conscious if someone isn't looking at them when they are interviewed, or perhaps the computer seems more willing to take the time to note all complaints.

On the other hand, computers lack the human touch that may be helpful in delving into sensitive concerns, such as a person's deepest fears, relationship problems, and sexual matters. A computer also lacks the means of judging the nuances in people's facial expressions that may reveal more about their innermost concerns than their typed or verbal responses. All in all, however, evidence shows that computer programs are as capable as skilled clinicians at obtaining information from clients and reaching an accurate diagnosis (Taylor & Luce, 2003). Computer programs are also less expensive and more time efficient than personal interviews.

Most of the resistance to using computer interviews comes from clinicians rather than clients. Some clinicians believe that personal, eye-to-eye contact is necessary to tease out a client's underlying concerns. Clinicians should also recognize that because computer-administered diagnostic interviews sometimes yield misleading findings, computer assessments should be combined with clinical judgment by a trained clinician (Garb, 2007). Although the computer may never completely replace the human interviewer, a combination of computerized and interviewer-based assessment may strike the best balance of efficiency and sensitivity.

Another change that has sprung into being is the development of online psychological assessment. Some psychologists are now conducting formal psychological assessments via email, videoconferencing, and the Internet (Luxton, Pruitt, & Osenbach, 2014; Shore et al., 2007).

**COMPUTERIZED INTERVIEW.** Would you be more likely to tell your problems to a computer than to a person? Computerized clinical interviews have been used for more than 25 years, and some research suggests that the computer may be more effective than its human counterpart in teasing out problems.

# Psychological Tests

**3.7 Describe the two major types of psychological tests—intelligence tests and personality tests—and identify examples of each type.**

A psychological test is a structured method of assessment used to evaluate reasonably stable traits, such as intelligence and personality. Tests are usually standardized on large numbers of people and provide norms that compare a client's scores with the average. By comparing test results from samples of people who are free of psychological disorders with those of people who have diagnosable psychological disorders, researchers gain some insights into the types of response patterns that are indicative of abnormal behavior. Although researchers tend to think of medical tests as a gold standard of testing, evidence shows that psychological tests are actually on par with many medical tests in their ability to predict criterion variables, such as underlying conditions or future outcomes (Meyer et al., 2001).

Here, we examine two major types of psychological tests: intelligence tests and personality tests.

**INTELLIGENCE TESTS** The assessment of abnormal behavior often includes an evaluation of a client's intelligence. Formal intelligence tests are used to help diagnose intellectual disability (formerly labeled *mental retardation*). They evaluate the intellectual impairment that may be caused by other disorders, such as organic mental disorders caused by damage to the brain. They also provide a profile of the client's intellectual strengths and weaknesses to help develop a treatment plan suited to the client's competencies.

Attempts to define intelligence continue to stir debate in the field. David Wechsler (1975), the originator of the most widely used intelligence tests—the Wechsler scales—defined intelligence as "capacity... to understand the world... and... resourcefulness to cope with its challenges." From his perspective, intelligence has to do with the ways in which people (a) mentally represent the world and (b) adapt to its demands.

The first formal intelligence test was developed by a Frenchman, Alfred Binet (1857–1911). In 1904, Binet was commissioned by school officials in Paris to develop a mental test to identify children who were unable to cope with the demands of regular classroom instruction and who required special classes to meet their needs. Binet and a colleague, Theodore Simon, developed an intelligence test consisting of memory tasks and other short tests of mental abilities that children were likely to encounter in daily life, such as counting. A later version of their test, called the Stanford-Binet Intelligence Scale, is still widely used to measure intelligence in children and young adults.

Intelligence, as given by a person's scores on intelligence tests, is usually expressed in the form of an intelligence quotient, or IQ. An IQ score is typically based on the relative difference (deviation) of a person's score on an intelligence test from the norms for the person's age group. A score of 100 is defined as the mean. People who answer more items correctly than the average obtain IQ scores above 100; those who answer fewer items correctly obtain scores of less than 100.

**Table 3.5** Examples of Items Similar to Those on the Wechsler Adult Intelligence Scale

| | |
|---|---|
| **Comprehension:** Why do people need to obey traffic laws? What does the saying "the early bird catches the worm" mean? | **Picture completion:** Identify the missing part from a picture, such as the picture of the watch in Figure 3.1. |
| **Arithmetic:** John wanted to buy a shirt that cost $31.50, but only had $17. How much more money would he need to buy the shirt? | **Block design:** Using blocks such as those in Figure 3.1, match the design shown. |
| **Similarities:** How are a stapler and a paper clip alike? | **Letter–number sequencing:** Listen to this series of numbers and letters and repeat them back, first saying the numbers from least to most, and then saying the letters in alphabetical order: S-2-C-1. |
| **Digit span:** Forward order: Listen to this series of numbers and repeat them back to me in the same order: 6 4 5 2 7 3. Backward order: Listen to this series of numbers and then repeat them in reverse order: 9 4 2 5 8 7. | |
| **Vocabulary:** What does *capricious* mean? | |

**SOURCE:** Adapted from J. S. Nevid (2013). *Psychology: Concepts and Applications*, 4th ed. (p. 270). Belmont, CA: Wadsworth/Cengage Learning. Reprinted by permission.

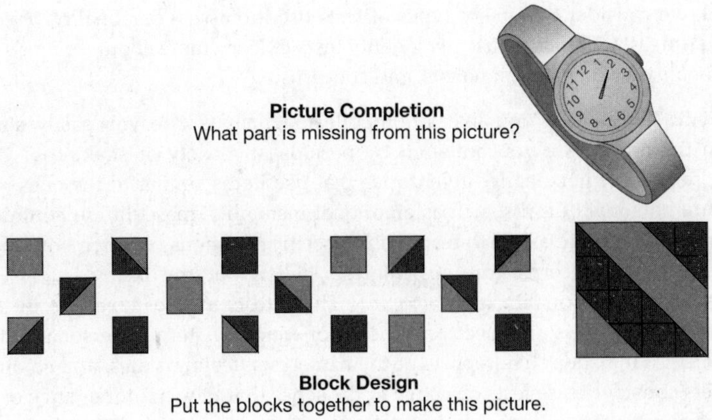


**Figure 3.1** Items similar to those found on two of the perceptual reasoning subtests of the Wechsler Adult Intelligence Scale (WAIS).

The perceptual reasoning subtests measure such skills as nonverbal reasoning ability, spatial perception and problem solving, and ability to perceive visual details.

SOURCE: From the Wechsler Intelligence Scales for Adults and Children. Copyright © 1949, 1955, 1974, 1981, 1991, 1997, 2003, by The Psychological Corporation, a Harcourt Assessment Company. Reproduced by permission. All rights reserved. Wechsler® is a trademark of The Psychological Corporation registered in the United States of America and/or other jurisdictions.

Wechsler's intelligence scales are the most widely used intelligence tests today. Different versions are used for different age groups. The Wechsler scales group questions into subtests or subscales, with each subscale measuring a different intellectual ability. (Table 3.5 shows examples from the adult version of the test.) The Wechsler scales are thus designed to offer insight into a person's relative strengths and weaknesses, not to simply yield an overall score.

The Wechsler scales include subtests of verbal skills, perceptual reasoning, working memory, and processing speed. Scores on these subtests are combined to yield an overall intelligence quotient. (Figure 3.1 shows items similar to those on two of the perceptual reasoning tests on the Wechsler Adult Intelligence Scale [WAIS].)

The Wechsler IQ scores are based on how respondents' answers deviate from those attained by their age-mates. The mean whole test score at any age is defined as 100. Wechsler distributed IQ scores so that 50% of the scores of the population would lie within a "broad average" range of 90 to 110.

Most IQ scores cluster around the mean (see Figure 3.2). Just 5% are above 130 or below 70. Wechsler labeled people who attained scores of 130 or above as *very superior* and those with scores below 70 as *intellectually deficient*.

Clinicians use IQ scales to evaluate a client's intellectual resources and to help diagnose intellectual disability. IQ scores below 70 are one of the criteria used in diagnosing intellectual disability.

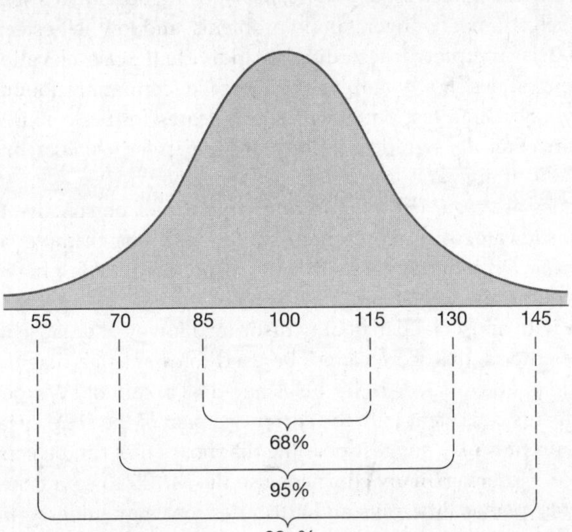


**Figure 3.2** Normal distribution of IQ scores.

The distribution of IQ scores resembles a bell-shaped curve, which is referred to by psychologists as a *normal curve*. Wechsler defined the deviation IQ so that the average (mean) score was 100 and the standard deviation of scores was 15. A standard deviation is a statistical measure of the variability or dispersion of scores around the mean. Here, we see the distribution of scores at one, two, and three standard deviations from the mean. Note that about two-thirds of people score within one standard deviation of the mean (85 to 115).

Next, we consider two major types of tests used to assess personality: *objective tests* and *projective tests*. Clinicians use personality tests to learn more about a client's underlying personality traits, needs, interests, and concerns.

**OBJECTIVE TESTS** Do you like automobile magazines? Are you easily startled by noises in the night? Are you bothered by periods of anxiety or shakiness? **Objective tests** are self-report personality inventories that use items similar to the ones just listed to measure personality traits such as emotional instability, masculinity/femininity, and introversion. People are asked to respond to specific questions or statements about their feelings, thoughts, concerns, attitudes, interests, beliefs, and the like.

What makes personality tests *objective*? These tests are not objective in the sense that a bathroom scale is an objective measure of weight. After all, personality tests rely on subjects' giving subjective reports of their interests, feeling states, and so on. Rather, researchers consider these tests objective in the sense that they limit the range of possible responses and so can be scored objectively. They are considered objective also because they were developed on the basis of empirical evidence supporting their validity. Subjects might be instructed to check adjectives that apply to them, to mark statements as *true* or *false*, to select preferred activities from lists, or to indicate whether items apply to them *always*, *sometimes*, or *never*. For example, a test item may ask you to check either *true* or *false* next to a statement like, "I feel uncomfortable in crowds." Here, we focus on two of the more widely used objective personality tests in clinical settings: the Minnesota Multiphasic Personality Inventory and the Millon Clinical Multiaxial Inventory (MCMI).

***Minnesota Multiphasic Personality Inventory*** The revised version of the MMPI, the MMPI-2, contains more than 567 true–false statements that assess interests, habits, family relationships, physical health complaints, attitudes, beliefs, and behaviors characteristic of psychological disorders. It is widely used both as a test of personality and to assist clinicians in diagnosing abnormal behavior patterns. The MMPI-2 comprises a number of individual scales made up of items that tend to be answered differently by members of carefully selected diagnostic groups, such as patients diagnosed with schizophrenia or depression, than by members of reference groups.

Consider a hypothetical item similar to one you might find on the MMPI-2: "I often read detective novels." If, for example, groups of depressed people tended to answer the item in a direction different than that of nonpatient reference groups, the item would be placed on the depression scale. The items on the MMPI-2 are divided into various clinical scales (see Table 3.6). A score of 65 or higher on a particular scale is considered clinically significant. The MMPI-2 also includes validity scales that assess clients' tendencies to distort test responses in a favorable ("faking good") or unfavorable ("faking bad") direction. Other scales on the tests, called *content scales*, measure an individual's specific complaints and concerns, such as anxiety, anger, family problems, and low self-esteem.

The MMPI-2 is interpreted according to individual scale elevations and interrelationships among scales. For example, a 2–7 profile, commonly found among people seeking therapy, refers to a test pattern in which scores for Scales 2 (*Depression*) and 7 (*Psychasthenia*) are clinically significant. Clinicians may refer to *atlases*, or descriptions, of people who usually attain various profiles.

MMPI-2 scales are regarded as reflecting continua of personality traits associated with the diagnostic categories represented by the test. For example, a high score on Scale 4, *Psychopathic Deviation*, suggests that the respondent holds a higher-than-average number of nonconformist beliefs and may be rebellious, which are characteristics often found in people with antisocial personality disorder. However, because it is not tied specifically to *DSM* criteria, this score cannot be used to establish a diagnosis. The MMPI, which was originally developed in the 1930s and 1940s, cannot be expected to provide diagnostic judgments consistent with the current version of the *DSM* system, the *DSM-5*. Even so, MMPI profiles may suggest possible diagnoses that can be considered in light of other evidence. Moreover, many clinicians use the MMPI to gain general information about respondents' personality traits and attributes that may underlie their psychological problems, rather than to make a diagnosis per se.

**Table 3.6** Clinical Scales of the MMPI-2

| Scale Number | Scale Label | Items Similar to Those Found on MMPI Scale | Sample Traits of High Scorers |
|---|---|---|---|
| 1 | Hypochondriasis | My stomach frequently bothers me. At times, my body seems to ache all over. | Many physical complaints, cynical defeatist attitudes, often perceived as whiny, demanding |
| 2 | Depression | Nothing seems to interest me anymore. My sleep is often disturbed by worrisome thoughts. | Depressed mood, pessimistic, worrisome, despondent, lethargic |
| 3 | Hysteria | I sometimes become flushed for no apparent reason. I tend to take people at their word when they're trying to be nice to me. | Naive, egocentric, little insight into problems, immature, develops physical complaints in response to stress |
| 4 | Psychopathic deviate | My parents often disliked my friends. My behavior sometimes got me into trouble at school. | Difficulties incorporating values of society, rebellious, impulsive, antisocial tendencies, strained family relationships, poor work and school history |
| 5 | Masculinity–femininity | I like reading about electronics. (M) I would like to work in the theater. (F) | Males endorsing feminine attributes: have cultural and artistic interests, effeminate, sensitive, passive; females endorsing male attributes: aggressive, masculine, self-confident, active, assertive, vigorous |
| 6 | Paranoia | I would have been more successful in life, but people didn't give me a fair break. It's not safe to trust anyone these days. | Suspicious, guarded, blames others, resentful, aloof, may have paranoid delusions |
| 7 | Psychasthenia | I'm one of those people who have to have something to worry about. I seem to have more fears than most people I know. | Anxious, fearful, tense, worried, insecure, difficulties concentrating, obsessional, self-doubting |
| 8 | Schizophrenia | Things seem unreal to me at times. I sometimes hear things that other people can't hear. | Confused and illogical thinking; feels alienated and misunderstood; socially isolated or withdrawn; may have blatant psychotic symptoms such as hallucinations or delusional beliefs; may lead detached, schizoid lifestyle |
| 9 | Hypomania | I sometimes take on more tasks than I can possibly do. People have noticed that my speech is sometimes pressured or rushed. | Energetic, possibly manic, impulsive, optimistic, sociable, active, flighty, irritable, may have overly inflated or grandiose self-image or unrealistic plans |
| 10 | Social introversion | I don't like loud parties. I was not very active in school activities. | Shy, inhibited, withdrawn, introverted, lacks self-confidence, reserved, anxious in social situations |

The validity of the MMPI-2 is supported by a large body of research findings (Butcher, 2011; Graham, 2011). The test successfully discriminates between psychiatric patients and controls and between groups of people with different psychological disorders, such as anxiety versus depressive disorders. Moreover, the content scales of the MMPI-2 provide additional information to that provided by the clinical scales, which can help clinicians learn more about a client's specific problems (Graham, 2011).

***The Millon Clinical Multiaxial Inventory*** The MCMI was developed to help clinicians formulate diagnoses, especially for personality disorders (Millon, 1982). The MCMI (now in a third edition, called the MCMI-III) is the only objective personality test that focuses specifically on personality disorders. The MMPI-2, by contrast, focuses on personality traits associated with other clinical disorders, such as mood disorders, anxiety disorders, and schizophrenia. Some clinicians may use both instruments to capture a wider range of personality traits. The MCMI-III also has scales to assess depression and anxiety, but the validity of these scales has been called into question (Saulsmana, 2011).

***Evaluation of Objective Tests*** Objective or self-report tests are relatively easy to administer. Once examiners read the instructions to clients and make sure they can read and understand the items, clients themselves can complete the tests unattended. Because tests permit limited response options, such as requiring a person to mark each item either *true* or *false*, they can be scored with high interrater reliability. These tests often reveal information that might not be gleaned from a clinical interview or by observing the person's behavior. For example, we might learn that a person holds negative views of himself or herself—self-perceptions that might not be directly expressed outwardly in behavior or revealed openly during an interview. All things considered, clinicians might gain more valuable information from self-report tests in some cases and from clinician interviews in others (Cuijpers et al., 2010). Consequently, a combination of assessment methods may be used.

A disadvantage of self-rating tests is that they rely on individuals themselves as the sole source of information. Test responses may therefore reflect underlying response biases, such as tendencies to give socially desirable responses that may not reflect the individual's true feelings. For this reason, self-report inventories, such as the MMPI, contain validity scales to help ferret out response biases. However, built-in validity scales may not be able to detect all sources of bias. Examiners may also look for corroborating information, such as interviewing others who are familiar with the client's behavior.

If a test does nothing more than identify people who are likely to have a particular disorder, its utility is usurped by more economical means of arriving at a diagnosis, such as a structured clinical interview. Clinicians expect more from personality tests than diagnostic classification, and the MMPI has shown its value in providing a wealth of information about underlying personality traits, problem behaviors, interpersonal relationships, and interest patterns. However, psychodynamically oriented critics suggest that self-report instruments tell us little about unconscious processes. The use of self-report tests may also be limited to relatively high-functioning individuals who can read well, respond to verbal material, and focus on a potentially tedious task. Clients who are disorganized, unstable, or confused may not be able to complete the tests.

**PROJECTIVE TESTS** A **projective test**, unlike an objective test, offers no clear, specified response options. Clients are presented with ambiguous stimuli, such as inkblots, and asked to respond to them. The word *projective* is used because these personality tests derive from the psychodynamic belief that people impose, or *project*, their own psychological needs, drives, and motives, much of which lie in the unconscious, onto their interpretations of ambiguous stimuli.

The psychodynamic model holds that potentially disturbing impulses and wishes, often of a sexual or aggressive nature, may be hidden from consciousness by our defense mechanisms. Indirect methods of assessment, such as projective tests, may offer clues to unconscious processes. More behaviorally oriented critics contend, however, that the results of projective tests are based more on clinicians' subjective interpretations of test responses than on empirical evidence.

Many projective tests have been developed, including tests based on how people fill in missing words to complete sentence fragments or how they draw human figures and other objects. The two most prominent projective techniques are the Rorschach Inkblot Test and the Thematic Apperception Test (TAT).

***The Rorschach Inkblot Test*** The Rorschach test was developed by a Swiss psychiatrist, Hermann Rorschach (1884–1922). As a child, Rorschach was intrigued by the game of dripping ink on paper and folding the paper to make symmetrical figures. He noted that people saw different things in the same blot, and he believed their "percepts" reflected their personalities as well as the stimulus cues provided by the blot. Rorschach's fraternity nickname was *Klex*, which means *inkblot* in German. As a psychiatrist, Rorschach experimented with hundreds of blots to identify those that could help in the diagnosis of psychological problems. He finally found a group of 15 blots that seemed to do the job and could be administered in a single session. Ten blots are used today because Rorschach's publisher did not have the funds to reproduce all 15 blots in the first edition of the text on the subject. Rorschach never had the opportunity to learn how popular and influential his inkblot test would become. Sadly, seven months after the publication of the test that bears his name, Rorschach died at age 37 of complications from a ruptured appendix (Exner, 2002).

Five of the inkblots are black and white (see Figure 3.3), and the other five have color. Each inkblot is printed on a separate card, which is handed to subjects in sequence. Subjects are asked to tell the examiner what the blot might be or what it reminds them of. Then, they are asked to explain what features of the blot (its color, form, or texture) they used to form their perceptions. **T / F**

## TRUTH or FICTION

One of the most widely used tests of personality asks people to interpret what they see in a series of inkblots.

☑ **TRUE** The Rorschach is a widely used personality test in which a person's responses to inkblots are interpreted to reveal aspects of his or her personality.

Clinicians who use the Rorschach make interpretations on the basis of the content and the form of the responses. For example, they may infer that people who use the entire blot in their responses show an ability to integrate events in meaningful ways. Those who focus on minor details of the blots may have obsessive–compulsive tendencies, whereas people who respond to the negative (white) spaces may see things in their own idiosyncratic ways, suggesting underlying negativism or stubbornness.

A response consistent with the form or contours of the blot is suggestive of adequate **reality testing**. People who see movement in the blots may be revealing intelligence and creativity. Content analysis may shed light on underlying conflicts. For example, adult clients who see animals but no people may have problems relating to people. Clients who appear confused about whether or not percepts of people are male or female may, according to psychodynamic theory, be in conflict over their own gender identity.

**Figure 3.3** "What does this look like?"

In the Rorschach test, a person is presented with ambiguous stimuli in the form of inkblots and asked to describe what each of the blots looks like. Rorschach assumed that people project aspects of their own personalities into their responses, but controversy whirls around the question of whether the test yields scientifically valid conclusions.

***The Thematic Apperception Test*** The TAT was developed by psychologist Henry Murray at Harvard University in the 1930s. *Apperception* is the mental process of putting new ideas or impressions into a certain context based on past experience or existing ideas. The TAT consists of a series of cards, each depicting an ambiguous scene (see Figure 3.4). It is assumed that clients' responses to the cards will reflect their experiences and outlooks on life—and perhaps shed light on their deep-seated needs and conflicts.

Respondents are asked to describe what is happening in each scene, what led up to it, what the characters are thinking and feeling, and what will happen next. Psychodynamic theorists believe that people will identify with the protagonists in their stories and project underlying psychological needs and conflicts into their responses. More superficially, the stories suggest how respondents might interpret or behave in similar situations in their own lives. TAT results may also be suggestive of clients' attitudes toward others, particularly family members and partners.

***Evaluation of Projective Techniques*** The reliability and validity of projective techniques continue to be a subject of extensive research and debate. One sticking point is that interpretation of a person's responses depends to some degree on the subjective judgment of the examiner. For example, two examiners may interpret the same Rorschach or TAT response differently.

Although more comprehensive scoring systems have improved standardization of scoring the Rorschach, the reliability of the test continues to be debated. Even if a Rorschach response can be scored reliably, the interpretation of the response—what it means—remains an open question (Garb et al., 2005).

Evidence supports some limited uses of the Rorschach in measuring some aspects of psychological functioning, such as impaired thinking and perceptual processing (Mihura et al., 2013, 2015; Wood et al., 2015). However, critics claim that we lack sufficient evidence of validity to support the general use of the Rorschach in clinical settings (see Wood et al., 2010, 2015). All in all, the debate over the clinical use of the Rorschach between supporters and detractors will likely continue with no clear resolution in sight.

**Figure 3.4** "Tell me a story."

In the Thematic Apperception Test, a person is presented with a series of pictures, similar to the one shown here, and asked to tell a story about what is happening in the scene. The person is also asked to describe what events led up to the scene and how the story will turn out. How might the stories you tell reveal underlying aspects of your personality?

The validity of the TAT in eliciting deep-seated material or tapping underlying psychopathology also remains to be demonstrated. A person's responses to the test may say more about the features of the drawings than the person's underlying personality.

Proponents of projective methods point out that allowing subjects freedom of expression through projective testing reduces their tendency to offer socially desirable responses. Psychologist George Stricker (2003, p. 728) appraised the standoff in the field: "The field remains divided between believers and nonbelievers, and each is able to marshal considerable evidence and discount the evidence of their opponents to support their point of view."

# Neuropsychological Assessment

**3.8 Describe the uses of neuropsychological tests.**

**Neuropsychological assessment** involves the use of tests to help determine whether psychological problems reflect underlying neurological impairment or brain damage. When neurological impairment is suspected, a neurological evaluation may be requested from a *neurologist*—a medical doctor who specializes in disorders of the nervous system. A clinical *neuropsychologist* may also be consulted to administer neuropsychological assessment techniques, such as behavioral observation and psychological testing, to reveal signs of possible brain damage. Neuropsychological testing may be used together with brain-imaging techniques such as MRI and CT scanning to shed light on relationships between brain function and underlying abnormalities. The results of neuropsychological testing may not only suggest whether patients suffer from brain damage but also point to the parts of the brain that may be affected.

**THE BENDER VISUAL MOTOR GESTALT TEST** One of the first neuropsychological tests to be developed and still one of the most widely used neuropsychological tests is the Bender-Gestalt II, now in its second edition (Brannigan & Decker, 2006). The Bender consists of geometric figures that illustrate various Gestalt principles of perception. A client is asked to copy geometric designs. Signs of possible brain damage include rotation of the figures, distortions in shape, and incorrect sizing of the figures in relation to one another (see Figure 3.5). The examiner then asks the client to reproduce the designs from memory because neurological damage can impair memory functioning. Although the Bender remains a convenient and economical means of uncovering possible organic impairment, more sophisticated test batteries have been developed for this purpose, including the widely used Halstead-Reitan Neuropsychological Battery.

**THE HALSTEAD-REITAN NEUROPSYCHOLOGICAL BATTERY** Psychologist Ralph Reitan developed a battery by adapting tests used by his mentor, Ward Halstead, an experimental psychologist, to study brain–behavior relationships among organically impaired individuals. The battery contains tests that measure perceptual, intellectual, and motor skills and performance. A battery of tests permits the psychologist to observe patterns of results, and various patterns of performance deficits are suggestive of certain kinds of brain defects, such as those occurring following head trauma (Allen et al., 2011; Holtz, 2011; Reitan & Wolfson, 2012). The Halstead-Reitan test battery comprises a number of subtests, including the following:

1. *The Category Test.* This test measures abstract thinking ability, as indicated by an individual's proficiency at forming principles or categories that relate different stimuli to one another. A series of groups of stimuli that vary in shape, size, location, color, and other characteristics are flashed on a screen. The subject's task is to discern the principle that links them, such as shape or size, and to indicate which stimuli in each grouping represent the correct category by pressing a key. By analyzing the patterns of correct and incorrect choices, the subject normally learns to identify the principles that determine the correct choice. Performance on the test is believed to reflect functioning in the frontal lobes of the cerebral cortex.
2. *The Rhythm Test.* This is a test of concentration and attention. The subject listens to 30 pairs of recorded rhythmic beats and indicates whether the beats in each pair are

**Figure 3.5** The Bender Visual Motor Gestalt Test.

The Bender is intended to assess organic impairment. Part A shows the series of figures respondents are asked to copy. Part B shows the drawings of a person who is known to have brain damage.

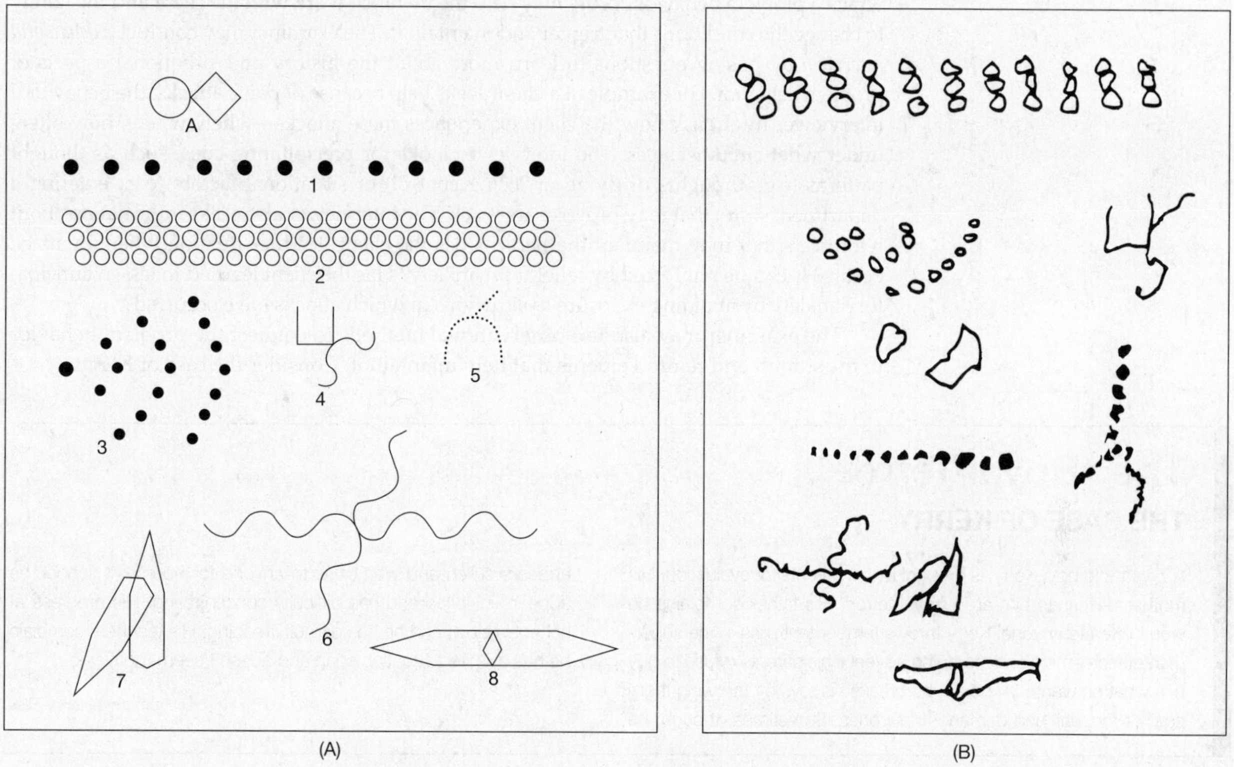


the same or different. Performance deficits are associated with damage to the right temporal lobe of the cerebral cortex.

3. *The Tactual Performance Test.* This test requires the blindfolded subject to fit wooden blocks of different shapes into corresponding depressions on a form board. Afterward, the subject draws the board from memory as a measure of visual memory.

## Behavioral Assessment

**3.9 Identify methods of behavioral assessment and describe the role of a functional analysis.**

Traditional personality tests such as the MMPI, Rorschach, and TAT were designed to measure underlying psychological traits and dispositions. Test responses are interpreted as *signs* of traits and dispositions believed to play important roles in determining people's behavior. For example, certain Rorschach responses are interpreted as revealing underlying traits, such as psychological dependency, that are believed to influence how people relate to others. In contrast, **behavioral assessment** treats test results as *samples* of behavior that occur in specific situations rather than as signs of underlying personality traits. According to the behavioral approach, behavior is primarily determined by environmental or situational factors, such as stimulus cues and reinforcement, not by underlying traits.

Behavioral assessment focuses on clinical or behavioral observation of behavior in a particular setting, such as in the school, hospital, or home situation. It aims to sample an individual's behavior in settings as similar as possible to the real-life situation, thus maximizing the relationship between the testing situation and the criterion. Behavior may be observed and measured in settings such as the home, school, or work environment. The examiner may also try to simulate situations in the clinic or laboratory that serve as analogues of the problems the individual confronts in daily life.

The examiner may conduct a *functional analysis* of the problem behavior—an analysis of the problem behavior in relation to antecedents, or stimulus cues that trigger it, and consequences, or reinforcements that maintain it. Knowledge of the environmental conditions in which a problem behavior occurs may help the therapist work with the client and the family to change the conditions that trigger and maintain it. The examiner may conduct a *behavioral interview* by posing questions to learn more about the history and situational aspects of problem behavior. For example, if a client seeks help because of panic attacks, the behavioral interviewer might ask how the client experiences these attacks—when, where, how often, under what circumstances. The interviewer looks for precipitating cues, such as thought patterns (e.g., thoughts of dying or losing control) or situational factors (e.g., entering a department store) that may provoke an attack. The interviewer also seeks information about reinforcers that may maintain the panic. Does the client flee the situation when an attack occurs? Is escape reinforced by relief from anxiety? Has the client learned to lessen anticipatory anxiety by avoiding exposure to situations in which attacks have occurred?

The examiner may also use observational methods to connect the problem behavior to the stimuli and reinforcements that help maintain it. Consider the case of Kerry.

## The "Royal Terror":

### THE CASE OF KERRY

A 7-year-old boy, Kerry, is brought by his parents for evaluation. His mother describes him as a "royal terror." His father complains he won't listen to anyone. Kerry throws temper tantrums in the supermarket, screaming and stomping his feet if his parents refuse to buy him what he wants. At home, he breaks his toys by throwing them against the wall and demands new ones. Sometimes, though, he appears sullen and won't talk to anyone for hours. At school, he appears inhibited and has difficulty concentrating. His progress at school is slow, and he has difficulty reading. His teachers complain he has a limited attention span and doesn't seem motivated.

*From the Author's Files*

The psychologist may use direct home observation to assess the interactions between Kerry and his parents. Alternatively, the psychologist may observe Kerry and his parents through a one-way mirror in the clinic. Such observations may suggest interactions that explain the child's noncompliance. For example, Kerry's noncompliance may follow parental requests that are vague (e.g., a parent says, "Play nicely now," and Kerry responds by throwing toys) or inconsistent (e.g., a parent says, "Go play with your toys, but don't make a mess," to which Kerry responds by scattering the toys). Observation may suggest ways in which Kerry's parents can improve communication and cue and reinforce desirable behaviors.

*Direct observation*, or behavioral observation, is the hallmark of behavioral assessment. Through direct observation, clinicians can observe and quantify problem behavior. Observations may be videotaped to permit subsequent analysis to identify behavioral patterns. Observers are trained to identify and record targeted patterns of behavior. Behavior coding systems have been developed that enhance the reliability of recording.

There are both advantages and disadvantages to direct observation. One advantage is that direct observation does not rely on the client's self-reports, which may be distorted by efforts to make a favorable or unfavorable impression. In addition to providing accurate measurements of problem behavior, behavioral observation can suggest strategies for intervention. A mother might report that her son is so hyperactive he cannot sit still long enough to complete homework assignments. By using a one-way mirror, the clinician may discover that the boy becomes restless only when he encounters a problem he cannot solve right away. The child may then be helped by being taught ways of coping with frustration and of solving certain kinds of academic problems.

Direct observation also has its drawbacks. One issue is the possible lack of consensus in defining problems in behavioral terms. In coding the child's behavior for hyperactivity, clinicians must agree on which aspects of the child's behavior represent hyperactivity. Another potential problem is a lack of reliability of measurement—that is, inconsistency—across time or between observers. Reliability is reduced when an observer is inconsistent in the coding of specific behaviors or when two or more observers code the same behavior inconsistently.

Observers may also show response biases. An observer who has been sensitized to expect that a child is hyperactive may perceive normal variations in behavior as subtle cues of hyperactivity and erroneously record them as instances of hyperactive behavior. Clinicians can help minimize these biases by keeping observers uninformed or blind about the target subject they are observing.

*Reactivity* is another potential problem. Reactivity refers to the tendency for the behavior being observed to be influenced by the way in which it is measured. For example, people may put their best feet forward when they know they are being observed. Using covert observation techniques, such as hidden cameras or one-way mirrors, may reduce reactivity. Covert observation may not be feasible, however, because of ethical concerns or practical constraints. Another approach is to accustom subjects to observation by watching them a number of times before collecting data. Another potential problem is *observer drift*—the tendency of observers, or groups of raters, to deviate from the coding system in which they were trained as time elapses. One suggestion to help control this problem is to regularly retrain observers to ensure continued compliance with the coding system (Kazdin, 2003). As time elapses, observers may also become fatigued or distracted. It may be helpful to limit the duration of observations and to provide frequent breaks.

Behavioral observation is limited to measuring overt behaviors. Many clinicians also wish to assess subjective or private experiences—for example, feelings of depression and anxiety or distorted thought patterns. Such clinicians may combine direct observation with forms of assessment that permit clients to reveal internal experiences. Staunch behavioral clinicians tend to consider self-reports unreliable and to limit their data collection to direct observation.

In addition to behavioral interviews and direct observation, behavioral assessment may involve the use of other techniques, such as self-monitoring, contrived or analogue measures, and behavioral rating scales.

**SELF-MONITORING** Training clients to record or monitor the problem behavior in their daily lives is another method of relating the problem behavior to the settings in which it occurs. In **self-monitoring**, clients assume the responsibility for assessing the problem behavior in the settings in which it naturally occurs.

Behaviors that can easily be counted, such as food intake, cigarette smoking, nail biting, hair pulling, study periods, or social activities, are well suited for self-monitoring. Self-monitoring can produce highly accurate measurement, because the behavior is recorded as it occurs, not reconstructed from memory.

There are various devices for keeping track of the targeted behavior. A behavioral diary or log is a handy way to record calories ingested or cigarettes smoked. Such logs can be organized in columns and rows to track the frequency of occurrence of the problem behavior and the situations in which it occurs (time, setting, feeling state, etc.). A record of eating may include entries for the type of food eaten, the number of calories, the location in which the eating occurred, the feeling states associated with eating, and the consequences of eating (e.g., how the client felt afterward). In reviewing an eating diary with the clinician, a client can identify problematic eating patterns, such as eating when feeling bored or in response to TV food commercials, and devise better ways of handling these cues.

Behavioral diaries can also help clients increase desirable but low-frequency behaviors, such as assertive behavior and dating behavior. Unassertive clients might track occasions that seem to warrant an assertive response and jot down their actual responses to each occasion. Clients and clinicians then review the log to highlight problematic situations and rehearse assertive responses. A client who is anxious about dating might record social contacts with potential dating partners. To measure the effects of treatment, clinicians may encourage clients to engage in a baseline period of self-monitoring before treatment begins. Today, clinicians are developing smartphone apps to help clients track specific behaviors in their daily lives (Clough & Casey, 2015; see *Abnormal Psychology in the Digital Age: Tracking Symptoms by Smartphone* for more information).

Self-monitoring is not without its disadvantages. Some clients are unreliable and do not keep accurate records. They become forgetful or sloppy, or they under-report undesirable behaviors, such as overeating or smoking, because of embarrassment or fear of criticism. To offset these biases, clinicians may, with client consent, corroborate the accuracy of self-monitoring by gathering information from other parties, such as the clients' spouses. Private behaviors such as eating or smoking alone cannot be corroborated in this way, however. Sometimes, other means of corroboration—such as physiological measures—are available. For example, blood alcohol levels can be used to verify self-reports of alcohol use, or analysis of carbon monoxide levels in clients' breath samples can be used to corroborate reports of abstinence from smoking.

Recording undesirable behaviors may make people more aware of the need to change them. Thus, self-monitoring can be put to therapeutic use if it leads to adaptive behavioral changes, such as focusing attention of people in weight management programs on the calorie contents of foods they consume. However, self-monitoring alone may not be sufficient to produce desired behavioral changes. Motivation to change and skills needed to make behavior changes are also important.

## Abnormal Psychology in the Digital Age

### TRACKING SYMPTOMS BY SMARTPHONE

Therapists are using smartphone apps as therapeutic tools that allow them to go beyond the confines of the consulting room to track the thoughts, behaviors, and symptoms of their clients in their daily lives. Rather than wait for weekly therapy sessions for clients to report on changes in their thoughts, moods, and activities, smartphone apps allow therapists to capture this information on a moment-to-moment basis as clients go about their daily routines (Clough & Casey, 2015; Ehrenreich et al., 2011; Marzano et al., 2015). Some apps prompt users to rate their moods or symptoms at various times during the day. This information can be wirelessly transmitted via a server to their therapists, who keep a running record of their progress and look for patterns in the data to identify situations when symptoms tend to emerge that can be targeted for treatment. One example is *Mobile Therapy*, an app that therapists use to prompt clients to report on their mood levels at specific times during the day by touching icons on a "mood map" on their cell phones (Morris et al., 2010).

Smartphone apps are used not only to collect client data but also to provide help to people struggling with psychological problems, including anxiety and depression (Clough & Casey, 2011; Kazdin & Blasé, 2011). One example is an app that patients in treatment for eating disorders use to report their symptoms by texting their therapists, who then electronically transmit tailored feedback and suggestions (Bauer et al., 2012). Another example is *CareLoop*, a mobile app that depressed patients use to rate and record their moods several times a day, a process that takes about a minute each time (CareLoop, 2015). The data stream is transmitted to therapists, who provide therapeutic interventions when they detect signs of relapse. A texting version of the technology is also available.

In a treatment program for smoking cessation, participants text the word *crave* to their therapists whenever they feel a strong craving for cigarettes, which prompts therapists to reply with suggestions for resisting smoking temptations (Free et al., 2011). *Field Coach* is an app designed to help clients with borderline personality disorder, a type of personality disorder discussed in Chapter 12. This app provides resources such as supportive video and audio messages to help patients cope with difficult situations they face in their daily lives (Dimeff et al., 2011). The future promise of therapy apps as therapeutic tools is limited only by developers' and therapists' imaginations.

At Duke University, researchers have developed an app for screening infants for signs of autistic behaviors (Hashemi et al., 2014). The U.S. government was involved in developing another app called *PTSD Coach*, which is designed to help people with PTSD manage their symptoms and link them to services they may need (Kuehn, 2011d). This app is a supplement to regular treatment by a qualified professional. An interesting application of electronic technology involved a compulsive hoarder whose house was cluttered with mountains of books, magazines, cardboard boxes, and assorted other unneeded items. The client was instructed to send digital pictures of her living space so that her therapist could monitor her progress (Eonta et al., 2011).

Other health care providers are now using text messaging and other electronic means as intervention tools (e.g., O'Leary et al., 2015). With heart disease patients, for example, medical care providers are using a texting program called *TEXT ME* to keep in touch with their patients via text messaging several times a day. This allows them to more closely monitor their patients' symptoms and prompt them to maintain healthy behaviors (Chow et al., 2015). **T / F**

## TRUTH or FICTION

Testing infants for signs of autistic behaviors: Yes, there's an app for that.

☑ TRUE Although it is not used to diagnose autism, Duke researchers have developed an app that is useful for screening infants for signs of autistic behaviors.

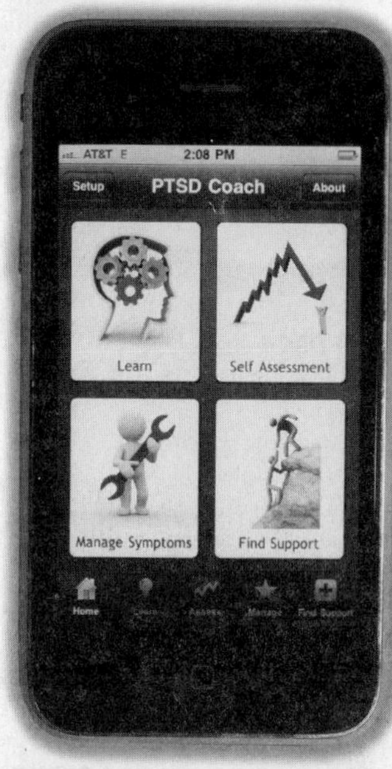


**THE PTSD COACH.** The U.S. government developed an app called PTSD Coach to help PTSD patients manage their symptoms and access services they need.

**SOURCE:** U.S. Department of Veterans Affairs.

**ANALOGUE MEASURES** *Analogue measures* are intended to simulate the setting in which a behavior naturally takes place but are carried out in laboratory or controlled settings. Role-playing exercises are common analogue measures. Suppose a client has difficulty challenging authority figures, such as professors. The clinician might describe a scene to the client as follows: "You've worked very hard on a term paper and received a very poor grade—say, a D or an F. You approach the professor, who asks, 'Is there some problem?' What do you do now?" The client's enactment of the scene may reveal deficits in self-expression that can be addressed in therapy or assertiveness training.

The Behavioral Approach Task, or BAT, is a widely used analogue measure of a phobic person's approach to a feared object, such as a snake (e.g., Ollendick et al., 2011; Vorstenbosch et al., 2011). Approach behavior is broken down into levels of response, such as looking in the direction of the snake from about 20 feet, touching the box holding the snake, and touching the snake. The BAT provides direct measurement of a response to a stimulus in a controlled situation. The subject's approach behavior can be quantified by assigning a score to each level of approach. The BAT is widely used as a measure of treatment effectiveness based on measuring how much more closely the phobic person can approach the feared object during the course of treatment.

**BEHAVIORAL RATING SCALES** A *behavioral rating scale* is a checklist that provides information about the frequency, intensity, and range of problem behaviors. Behavioral rating scales differ from self-report personality inventories in that items assess specific behaviors rather than personality characteristics, interests, or attitudes.

**BEHAVIORAL APPROACH TASK.** One form of behavioral assessment of phobia involves measurement of the degree to which the person can approach or interact with the phobic stimulus. Here, we see a woman with a snake phobia reach out to touch a (harmless) snake. Other people with snake phobia would not be able to touch the snake or even remain in its presence unless it was securely caged.

Behavioral rating scales are often used by parents to assess children's problem behaviors. The Child Behavior Checklist (CBCL; Achenbach & Dumenci, 2001; Ang et al., 2011), for example, asks parents to rate their children on more than 100 specific problem behaviors, including the following:

- ❑ Refuses to eat
- ❑ Is disobedient
- ❑ Hits
- ❑ Is uncooperative
- ❑ Destroys own things

The scale yields an overall problem behavior score and subscale scores on dimensions such as delinquency, aggressiveness, and physical problems. The clinician can compare the child's score on these dimensions with norms based on samples of age-mates.

# Cognitive Assessment

**3.10 Describe the role of cognitive assessment and identify two examples of cognitive measures.**

**Cognitive assessment** involves measurement of *cognitions*—thoughts, beliefs, and attitudes. Cognitive therapists believe that people who hold self-defeating or dysfunctional cognitions are at greater risk of developing emotional problems, such as depression, in the face of stressful or disappointing life experiences. They help clients replace dysfunctional thinking patterns with self-enhancing, rational thought patterns.

Several methods of cognitive assessment have been developed. One of the most straightforward is the thought record or diary. Depressed clients may carry such diaries to record dysfunctional thoughts as they arise. In early work, Aaron Beck (Beck et al., 1979) designed a thought diary, a daily record of dysfunctional thoughts, to help clients identify thought patterns connected with troubling emotional states. Each time a client experiences a negative emotion, such as anger or sadness, the client makes entries to identify

1. the situation in which the emotional state occurred;
2. the automatic or disruptive thoughts that passed through the client's mind;
3. the type or category of disordered thinking that the automatic thought(s) represented (e.g., selective abstraction, overgeneralization, magnification, or absolutist thinking—see Chapter 2);
4. a rational response to the troublesome thought; and
5. the emotional outcome or final emotional response.

A thought diary can become part of a treatment program in which a client learns to replace dysfunctional thoughts with rational, alternative thoughts.

The Automatic Thoughts Questionnaire (ATQ-30-Revised; Hollon & Kendall, 1980) asks people to rate both the frequency of occurrence and the strength of belief associated with 30 automatic negative thoughts. (Automatic thoughts seem just to pop into our minds.) Sample items on the ATQ include the following:

- I don't think I can go on.
- I hate myself.
- I've let people down.

A total score is obtained by summing the frequencies of occurrence of each item. Higher scores are suggestive of depressive thought patterns. Items similar to those found on the ATQ are shown in Table 3.7. The ATQ is widely used to measure changes in cognitions of depressed people undergoing treatment, especially cognitive-behavioral therapy (e.g., Hamilton et al., 2012).

## Table 3.7 Items Similar to Those on the Automatic Thoughts Questionnaire

Negative automatic thoughts such as those shown ahead may pop into a person's head and have a depressing effect on the person's mood and level of motivation. Therapists use questionnaires such as the ATQ to help clients identify their automatic thoughts and replace them with rational alternative thoughts.

| | |
|---|---|
| • I'm a loser. | • I'm incompetent. |
| • I wonder what's the matter with me. | • I wish I were someone else. |
| • I think the worst is about to happen. | • I think I'm going to fail. |
| • What's wrong with me? | • I'm just not as good as other people. |
| • Things always go wrong. | • I'm never going to succeed. |
| • I'm just worthless. | • I'm really disappointed in myself. |

**SOURCE:** Adapted from Hollon & Kendall (1980).

Another cognitive measure, the Dysfunctional Attitudes Scale (DAS) consists of an inventory of a relatively stable set of underlying attitudes or assumptions associated with depression (Weissman & Beck, 1978). Examples include, "I feel like I'm nothing if someone I love doesn't love me back." Subjects use a 7-point scale to rate the degree to which they endorse each belief. The DAS taps underlying assumptions believed to predispose individuals to depression, so it may be useful in detecting vulnerability to depression (Chioqueta & Stiles, 2007; Moore et al., 2014).

Cognitive assessment opens a new domain to the psychologist in understanding how disruptive thoughts are related to abnormal behavior. Only in the past three decades or so have cognitive and cognitive-behavioral therapists begun to explore what B. F. Skinner labeled the *black box*—people's internal states—to learn how thoughts and attitudes influence emotional states and behavior.

The behavioral objection to cognitive techniques is that clinicians have no direct means of verifying clients' subjective experiences, their thoughts and beliefs. These are private experiences that can be reported but not observed and measured directly. However, even though thoughts remain private experiences, reports of cognitions in the form of rating scales or checklists can be quantified and validated by reference to external criteria.

# Physiological Measurement

### 3.11 Identify methods of physiological measurement.

**Physiological assessment** is the study of people's physiological responses. Anxiety, for example, is associated with arousal of the sympathetic division of the autonomic nervous system (see Chapter 2). Anxious people therefore show elevated heart rates and blood pressure, which can be measured directly by means of the pulse and a blood pressure cuff. People also sweat more heavily when they are anxious. When we sweat, our skin becomes wet, increasing its ability to conduct electricity. Sweating can be measured by means of the *electrodermal response* or *galvanic skin response* (GSR). (*Galvanic* is named after the Italian physicist and physician Luigi Galvani, who was a pioneer in research in the study of electricity.) Measures of the GSR assess the amount of electricity that passes through two points on the skin, usually of the hand. Researchers assume the person's anxiety level correlates with the amount of electricity conducted across the skin.

The GSR is just one example of a physiological response measured through probes or sensors connected to the body. Another example is the *electroencephalograph* (EEG), which measures brain waves by attaching electrodes to the scalp (Figure 3.6).

**Figure 3.6** The electroencephalograph.

The EEG can be used to study differences in brain waves between groups of normal people and people with problems such as schizophrenia or organic brain damage.

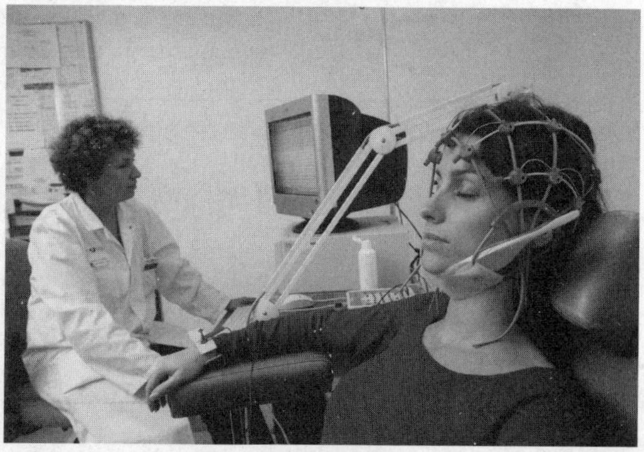

**Figure 3.7** The computed tomography scan.

The CT scan aims a narrow X-ray beam at the head, and the resultant radiation is measured from multiple angles as it passes through. The computer enables researchers to consolidate the measurements into a three-dimensional image of the brain. The CT scan reveals structural abnormalities in the brain that may be implicated in various patterns of abnormal behavior.

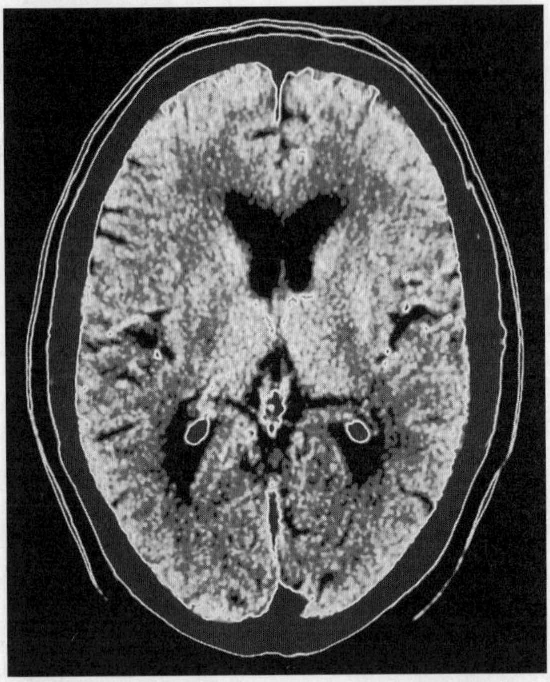

Changes in muscle tension are also often associated with states of anxiety or tension. They can be detected through the *electromyograph* (EMG), which monitors muscle tension through sensors attached to targeted muscle groups. Placement of EMG probes on the forehead can indicate muscle tension associated with tension headaches.

**BRAIN-IMAGING AND RECORDING TECHNIQUES** Advances in medical technology have made it possible to study the workings of the brain without the need for surgery. One of the most common is the EEG, which is a record of the electrical activity of the brain. The EEG detects minute amounts of electrical activity in the brain—or *brain waves*—which are conducted between electrodes placed on the scalp. Certain brain wave patterns are associated with mental states such as relaxation and with the different stages of sleep. The EEG is used to examine brain wave patterns associated with psychological disorders, such as schizophrenia, and with brain damage. The EEG also is used by medical personnel to reveal brain abnormalities such as tumors.

Brain-imaging techniques generate images that reflect the structure and functioning of the brain. In a *computed tomography* (CT) scan, a narrow X-ray beam is aimed at the head (Figure 3.7). The radiation that passes through is measured from multiple angles. The CT scan (also called a CAT scan, for *computerized axial tomography*) reveals abnormalities in brain shape and structure that may be suggestive of lesions, blood clots, or tumors. The computer enables scientists to integrate the measurements into a three-dimensional picture of the brain. Evidence of brain damage that was once detectable only by surgery may now be displayed on a monitor. **T / F**

## TRUTH *or* FICTION

Despite advances in technology, physicians today must still perform surgery to study the workings of the brain.

☑ **FALSE** Advances in brain-imaging techniques make it possible to observe the workings of the brain without invasive surgery.

Another imaging method, the *positron emission tomography* (PET) scan, is used to study the functioning of various parts of the brain (Figure 3.8). In this method, a small amount of a radioactive compound or tracer is mixed with glucose and injected into the bloodstream. When it reaches the brain, patterns of neural activity are revealed by measurement of the *positrons*—positively charged particles—emitted by the tracer. The glucose metabolized by parts of the brain generates a computer image of neural activity. Areas of greater activity metabolize more glucose. The PET scan has been used to learn which parts of the brain are most active (metabolize more glucose) when we are listening to music, solving a math problem, or using language. It also can be used to reveal abnormalities in brain activity in people with schizophrenia (see Chapter 11).

A third imaging technique is *magnetic resonance imaging* (MRI). In MRI, a person is placed in a donut-shaped tunnel that generates a strong magnetic field. The basic idea of the MRI, in the words of its inventor, is to stuff a human being into a large magnet (Weed, 2003). Radio waves of certain frequencies are then directed at the head. As a result, the brain emits signals that can be measured from several angles. As with the CT scan, the signals are integrated into a computer-generated image of the brain, which can reveal brain abnormalities associated with psychological disorders, such as schizophrenia and obsessive–compulsive disorder. **T / F**

## TRUTH *or* FICTION

Undergoing an MRI scan is like being stuffed into a large magnet.

☑ **TRUE** The MRI is like a large magnet that generates a strong magnetic field that can be used to create images of the brain when radio waves are directed toward the head.

**Figure 3.8** The positron emission tomography scan.

These PET scan images suggest differences in the metabolic processes of the brains of people with depression and schizophrenia and controls who are free of psychological disorders.

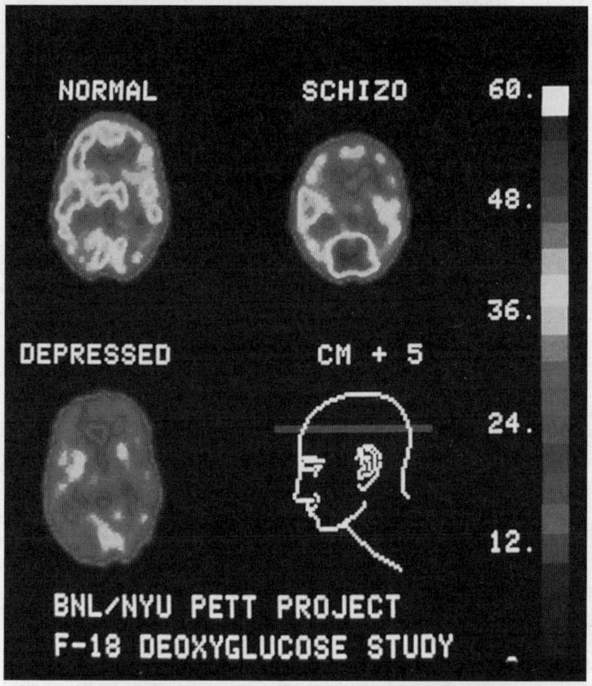


**Figure 3.9** Functional magnetic resonance imaging.

An fMRI is a specialized type of MRI that allows investigators to determine the parts of the brain that are activated during particular tasks. The areas depicted in orange/red are activated during a task in which a person is instructed to indicate whether two words in a word pair match. The large area of orange/red in the left hemisphere (depicted here on the right side) corresponds to a part of the cerebral cortex involved in processing language.

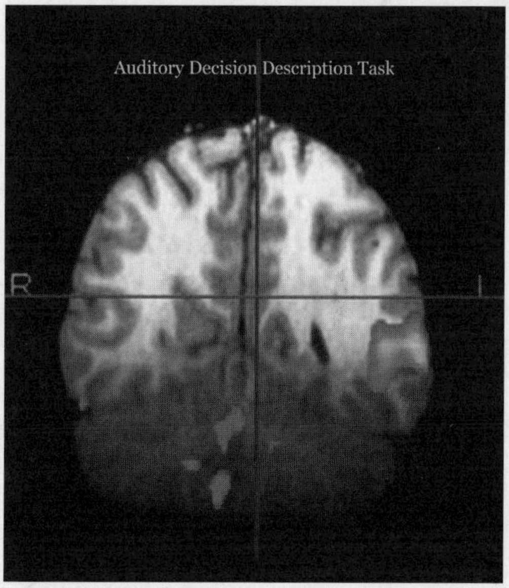


A type of MRI called *functional magnetic resonance imaging* (fMRI) is used to identify parts of the brain that become active when people engage in particular tasks, such as seeing, recalling from memory, or speaking (see Figure 3.9). The fMRI tracks demands for oxygen in different parts of the brain, which reveals their relative level of activity or engagement during particular tasks. In an illustration of an fMRI study, investigators found that when cocaine-addicted subjects experienced cocaine cravings, their brains showed greater activity in areas that become engaged when healthy subjects watch depressing videotapes (Wexler et al., 2001). This suggests that feelings of depression may be involved in triggering drug cravings. **T / F**

## TRUTH *or* FICTION

Cocaine cravings in people addicted to cocaine have been linked to parts of the brain that are normally activated during pleasant emotions.

☑ **FALSE** Just the opposite was the case. Cravings were associated with activation of parts of the brain that normally become active when watching depressing videotapes.

Finally, investigators also use sophisticated EEG recording techniques to provide a picture of the electrical activity of various parts of the brain in people with schizophrenia and other psychological disorders. As you can see in Figure 3.10, multiple electrodes are attached to various areas on the scalp to feed information about a person's brain activity to a computer. The computer analyzes the signals and displays a vivid image of the electrical activity of the working brain. In later chapters, we will see how modern imaging techniques further scientists' understanding of different types of psychological disorders.

Might brain scans be used to diagnose mental disorders? We consider this intriguing question in *A Closer Look: Can Brain Scans See Schizophrenia?*

## A CLOSER Look

### CAN BRAIN SCANS SEE SCHIZOPHRENIA?

The answer: Not yet, but efforts in this direction are well under way (e.g., Bullmore, 2012; Ehlkes, Michie, & Schall, 2012). Scientists hope that brain scans will help clinicians better diagnose and treat psychological disorders such as mood disorders, schizophrenia, and attention-deficit/hyperactivity disorder. Investigators are looking for telltale signs in brain scans of psychiatric patients, in much the same way that physicians today use imaging techniques to reveal the presence of tumors, tissue injuries, and brain damage. **T / F**

### TRUTH *or* FICTION

Advances in brain scanning allow physicians to diagnose schizophrenia with an MRI scan.

☑ **FALSE** Not yet, but perhaps one day we will be able to diagnose psychological disorders by using brain-imaging techniques.

Early enthusiasm in the mental health community that brain scans would herald a new era in the diagnosis of psychological problems proved to be premature. Dr. Steven Hyman, Harvard University professor and former director of the National Institute of Mental Health, explained it this way: "I think that, with some notable exceptions, the community of scientists was excessively optimistic about how quickly imaging would have an impact on psychiatry.... In their enthusiasm, people forgot that the human brain is the most complex object in the history of human inquiry, and it's not at all easy to see what's going wrong" (Carey, 2005).

One of the problems facing investigators is that signs of brain abnormalities in such disorders as schizophrenia are subtle or fall within a normal range of variation in the general population. Some abnormalities also occur in other disorders. However, there is emerging evidence of identifiable brain abnormalities that might be detected by brain scans in the early phases of schizophrenia (Ehlkes, Michie, & Schall, 2012). Investigators now are trying to lock down specific indicators of these brain abnormalities using sophisticated brain-imaging techniques. Looking ahead, it is conceivable that brain scans will someday be used as widely in diagnosing schizophrenia as they are today in diagnosing brain tumors.

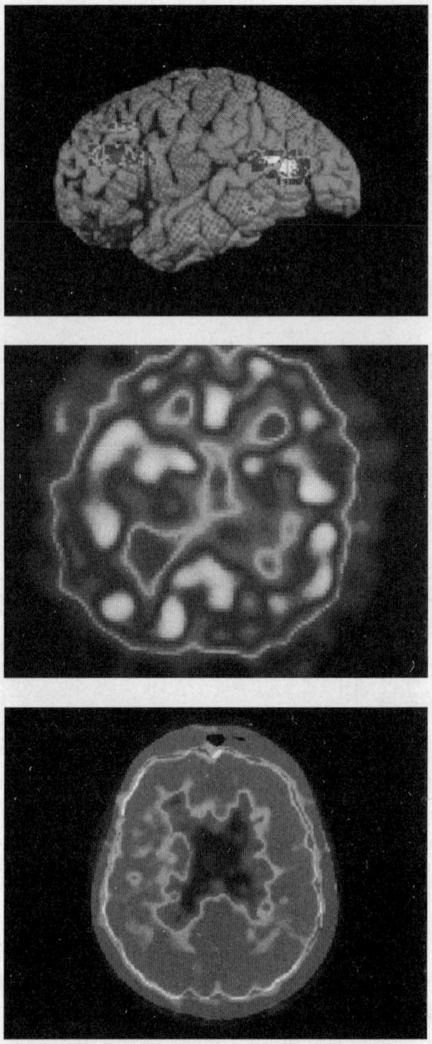

**WHICH OF THESE BRAIN SCANS SHOWS SCHIZOPHRENIA?** We can't yet say, but investigators hope they will someday be able to diagnose mental disorders such as schizophrenia and depression by using brain scans to detect telltale signs of the disorders.

## Sociocultural Factors in Psychological Assessment

**3.12 Describe the role of sociocultural aspects of psychological assessment.**

Researchers and clinicians must keep sociocultural and ethnic factors of clients in mind when assessing personality traits and psychological disorders. For example, in testing people from other cultures, careful translations are essential to capture the meanings of the original items. Clinicians also need to recognize that assessment techniques that may be reliable and valid in one culture may not be in another, even when they are translated accurately (Cheung, Kwong, & Zhang, 2003).

**Figure 3.10** Mapping the electrical activity of the brain.

By placing electrodes on the scalp, researchers can use the EEG to record electrical activity in various regions of the brain.

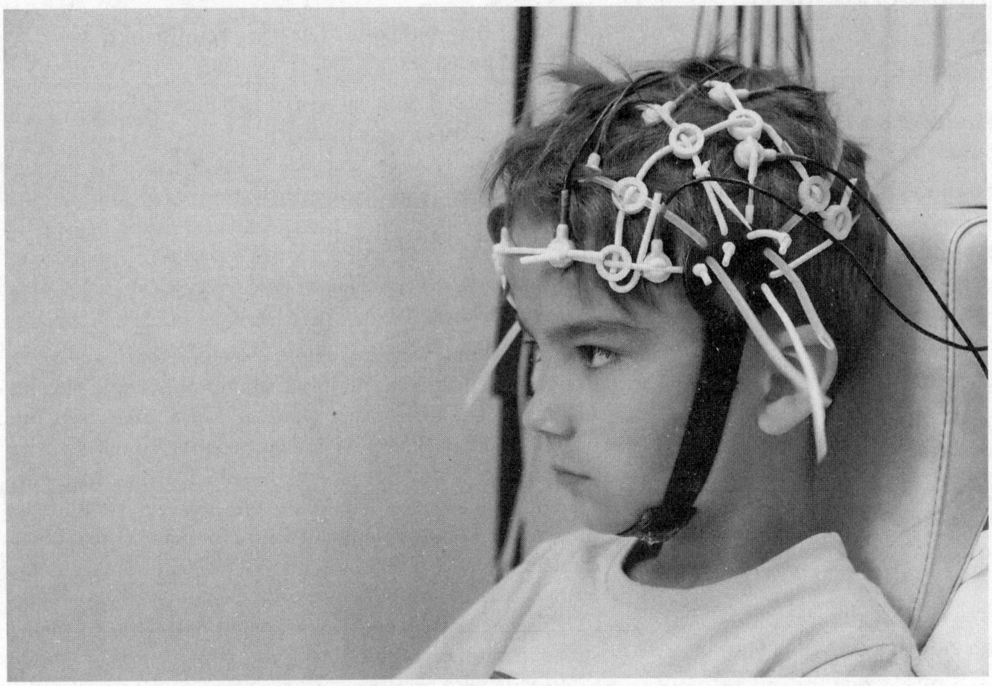

Clinicians need to take sociocultural factors into account so as not to introduce cultural biases in assessment (Braje & Hall, 2015). In other words, examiners need to ensure they are not labeling cultural differences in beliefs or practices as evidence of abnormal or deviant behaviors. Translations of assessment instruments should not only translate words, but also provide instructions that encourage examiners to address the importance of cultural beliefs, norms, and values, so that examiners will consider the client's background when making assessments of abnormal behavior patterns.

Investigators also need to put psychological instruments under a cultural microscope. For example, the Beck Depression Inventory (BDI), an inventory of depressive symptoms used widely in the United States, has good validity when used with ethnic minority groups in the United States and in other cultures in the world in distinguishing between depressed and nondepressed people (Grothe et al., 2005; Yeung et al., 2002). A recent study in China that showed that the MMPI-2 was able to predict the level of adjustment of recruits to army life in the Chinese military (Xiao, Han, & Han, 2011).

Other investigators have found no evidence of clinically significant cultural bias on the MMPI-2 in comparing African American and European American (non-Hispanic White) patients in outpatient and inpatient settings (Arbisi, Ben-Porath, & McNulty, 2002). In other research, investigators found that the MMPI-2 was sensitive to detecting problem behaviors and symptoms in American Indian tribal members (Greene et al., 2003; Robin et al., 2003).

Therapists need to recognize the importance of their clients' language preferences when conducting multicultural assessments. Meanings can get lost in translation—or worse, distorted. For example, Spanish speakers are often judged to be more disturbed when interviewed in English than in Spanish (Fabrega, 1990). Therapists too may fail to appreciate the idioms and subtleties of different languages. We recall, for instance, one clinician—a foreign-born and trained psychiatrist whose native language was not English—reporting that a patient had exhibited the delusional belief that he was outside his body. The clinician based this assessment on the patient's response when asked if he was feeling anxious. "Yes, doc," the patient had replied, "I feel like I'm jumping out of my skin at times."

# Summing Up

## How Are Abnormal Behavior Patterns Classified?

### The *DSM* and Models of Abnormal Behavior

**3.1 Describe the key features of the *DSM* system of diagnostic classification.**

The *DSM*, now in its fifth edition (the *DSM-5*), classifies a wide range of abnormal behavior patterns in terms of categories of mental disorders and identifies specific types of disorders within each category that are diagnosed on the basis of applying specified criteria.

### Culture-Bound Syndromes

**3.2 Describe the concept of culture-bound syndromes and identify some examples.**

Culture-bound syndromes are abnormal behavior patterns found exclusively or predominantly in particular cultures. Examples include the koro syndrome in China and the dhat syndrome in India.

### Evaluating the *DSM* System

**3.3 Explain why the new edition of the *DSM*, the *DSM-5*, is controversial and evaluate the strengths and weaknesses of the *DSM* system.**

Many concerns have been raised about the *DSM-5*, including concerns over the expansion of diagnosable disorders, changes in classification of mental disorders, changes in diagnostic criteria for particular disorders, and lack of research evidence during the process of development.

The major strength of the *DSM* system is the use of specified diagnostic criteria for each disorder. Weaknesses include questions about reliability and validity of some diagnostic categories and, to some critics, adherence to a medical model framework for classifying abnormal behavior patterns. Some investigators favor a dimensional model of classification to replace the categorical model, whereas others prefer a mixed approach that is similar to the current *DSM* system, which combines categorical and dimensional models of classification.

## Standards of Assessment

### Reliability

**3.4 Identify methods of assessing reliability of tests and measures.**

Reliability of assessment techniques is shown in various ways, including internal consistency, test–retest reliability, and interrater reliability.

### Validity

**3.5 Identify methods of assessing validity of tests and measures.**

Validity is based on measures of content validity, criterion validity, and construct validity.

## Methods of Assessment

### The Clinical Interview

**3.6 Identify the three major types of clinical interviews.**

The clinical interview involves the use of a set of questions designed to elicit relevant information from people seeking treatment. The three major types of clinical interviews are unstructured interviews (clinicians use their own style of questioning rather than follow a particular script), semi-structured interviews (clinicians follow a preset outline in directing their questioning but are free to branch off in other directions), and structured interviews (clinicians strictly follow a preset order of questions). Computerized methods of assessing psychological functioning have entered mainstream clinical practice.

### Psychological Tests

**3.7 Describe the two major types of psychological tests—intelligence tests and personality tests—and identify examples of each type.**

Psychological tests are structured methods of assessment used to evaluate reasonably stable traits such as intelligence and personality. Tests of intelligence, such as the Wechsler scales, are used for various purposes in clinical assessment, including determining evidence of intellectual disability or cognitive impairment and assessing cognitive strengths and weaknesses.

Objective personality tests, such as the MMPI, use structured items to measure psychological characteristics or traits, such as anxiety, depression, and masculinity–femininity. These tests are considered objective in the sense that they make use of a limited range of possible responses to items and are based on an empirical, or objective, method of test construction. Objective tests are easy to administer and have high reliability because the limited response options permit objective scoring. However, they may be limited by underlying response biases. Projective personality tests, such as the Rorschach and TAT, require individuals to interpret ambiguous stimuli, based on the belief that a subject's answers shed light on that person's unconscious processes. However, the reliability and validity of projective techniques continue to be debated.

## Neuropsychological Assessment

**3.8 Describe the uses of neuropsychological tests.**

Neuropsychological tests are formally structured tests used to identify possible neurological impairment or brain defects. The Halstead-Reitan Neuropsychological Battery uncovers cognitive skill deficits that are suggestive of underlying brain damage.

## Behavioral Assessment

**3.9 Identify methods of behavioral assessment and describe the role of a functional analysis.**

Methods of behavioral assessment include behavioral interviewing, self-monitoring, use of analogue or contrived measures, direct observation, and behavioral rating scales. The behavioral examiner may conduct a functional analysis, which is used to identify antecedents and consequences of problem behaviors.

## Cognitive Assessment

**3.10 Describe the role of cognitive assessment and identify two examples of cognitive measures.**

Cognitive assessment focuses on the measurement of thoughts, beliefs, and attitudes to help identify distorted thinking patterns. Specific methods of assessment include the use of a thought record or diary and the use of rating scales such as the Automatic Thoughts Questionnaire and the Dysfunctional Attitudes Scale.

## Physiological Measurement

**3.11 Identify methods of physiological measurement.**

Measures of physiological functioning include heart rate, blood pressure, galvanic skin response, muscle tension, and brain wave activity. Brain imaging and recording techniques, such as EEG, CT scans, PET scans, and MRI and fMRI, probe the inner workings and structures of the brain.

## Sociocultural Factors in Psychological Assessment

**3.12 Describe the role of sociocultural aspects of psychological assessment.**

Tests that are reliable and valid in one culture may not be so when used with members of another culture, even when they are translated accurately. Examiners also need to protect against cultural biases when evaluating people from other ethnic or cultural backgrounds. For example, they need to ensure they do not label behaviors as abnormal that are normative within the person's own cultural or ethnic group.

# Critical Thinking Questions

On the basis of your reading of this chapter, answer the following questions:

- Why is it important for clinicians to take cultural factors into account when diagnosing psychological disorders?
- Consider the debate over the use of projective tests. Do you believe that a person's response to inkblots or other unstructured stimuli might reveal aspects of that person's underlying personality? Why or why not?
- Have you ever taken a psychological test, such as an intelligence test or a personality test? What was the experience like? What, if anything, did you learn about yourself from the testing experience?
- Jamie complains of feeling depressed since the death of her brother in a car accident last year. What methods of assessment might a psychologist use to evaluate her mental condition?

# Key Terms

culture-bound syndromes, p. 103
reliability, p. 104
validity, p. 104
transdiagnostic model, p. 108
sanism, p. 108
content validity, p. 110
criterion validity, p. 110
construct validity, p. 111
unstructured interview, p. 112
semistructured interview, p. 112
structured interview, p. 112
mental status examination, p. 113
objective tests, p. 116
projective test, p. 118
reality testing, p. 119
neuropsychological assessment, p. 120
behavioral assessment, p. 121
self-monitoring, p. 123
cognitive assessment, p. 126
physiological assessment, p. 127

## Chapter 4
# Stress-Related Disorders

## Learning Objectives

**4.1** **Evaluate** the effects of stress on health.

**4.2** **Identify** and **describe** the stages of the general adaptation syndrome.

**4.3** **Evaluate** evidence of the relationship between life changes and psychological and physical health.

**4.4** **Evaluate** the role of acculturative stress in psychological adjustment.

**4.5** **Identify** psychological factors that moderate the effects of stress.

**4.6** **Define** the concept of an adjustment disorder and **describe** its key features.

**4.7** **Identify** the specific types of adjustment disorders.

**4.8** **Describe** the key features of acute stress disorder.

**4.9** **Describe** the key features of posttraumatic stress disorder.

**4.10** **Describe** theoretical understandings of PTSD.

**4.11** **Describe** treatment approaches to PTSD.

## TRUTH *or* FICTION

T☐ F☐ As you are reading this page, millions of microscopic warriors in your body are conducting search-and-destroy missions to find and eradicate foreign invaders. (p. 139)

T☐ F☐ Surprisingly, stress makes you more resistant to the common cold. (p. 139)

T☐ F☐ Writing about traumatic experiences may be good for your physical and emotional health. (p. 140)

T☐ F☐ Immigrant groups show better psychological adjustment when they forsake their cultural heritage and adopt the values of a host culture. (p. 146)

T☐ F☐ Optimists may have hopeful expectations, but it's actually the pessimists who have healthier cardiovascular and immunological functioning. (p. 150)

T☐ F☐ If concentrating on your schoolwork has become difficult because of the breakup of a recent romance, you could be experiencing a psychological disorder. (p. 152)

T☐ F☐ Exposure to combat is the most common trauma linked to posttraumatic stress disorder (PTSD). (p. 155)

**CHAPTER INTRODUCTION: STRESS-RELATED DISORDERS**

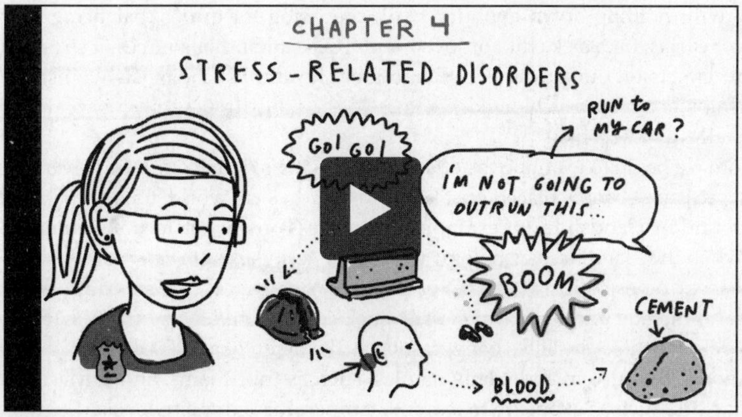


"Is there a problem?" I (J. Nevid) asked as I entered my classroom at St. John's University in Queens, New York, on the morning of September 11, 2001. Many years have passed since that terrible day, but my memory remains vivid. The students were gathered around the window. None replied, but one pointed out the window with a pained expression on her face that I'll never forget. Moments later, I saw for myself the smoke billowing out of one of the towers of the World Trade Center, clearly visible some 15 miles to the west. Then, the second tower suddenly burst into flames. We watched in stunned silence. The unthinkable occurred: Suddenly one tower was gone and then the other. A student who had come into the room asked, "Where are they?" Another answered that they were gone. The first replied, "What do you mean, gone?"

We watched from a distance the horror that we knew was unfolding. But many other New Yorkers experienced the World Trade Center disaster firsthand, including thousands like New York City police officer Terri Tobin who risked their lives to save others. Here, Officer Tobin tells of her experience.

**"I"** **"Go! It's Coming Down"**

Then I saw people running toward me, and they were screaming. "Go! Go! It's coming down!" Just for a second, I looked up and saw it. I thought, *I'm not going to outrun this*. But then I thought, *Maybe I can make it back to my car and jump in the back seat*. Before I could make a move, the force of the explosion literally blew me out of my shoes. It lifted me up and propelled me out, over a concrete barrier, all the way to the other side of the street. I landed face-first on a grassy area outside the Financial Center, and after I landed there, I just got pelted with debris coming out of this big black cloud.

And then I felt it, but what sticks with me is hearing it: The whomp of my helmet when I got hit in the head. The helmet literally went crack, split in half, and fell off my head. I realized then that I'd just taken a real big whack in the head. I felt blood going down the back of my neck, and when I was able to reach around, I felt this chunk of cement sticking out three or four inches from the back of my head. It was completely embedded in my skull.

Then it got pitch black, and I thought, *I must have been knocked unconscious, because it's totally black*. But then I thought, *I wouldn't be thinking about how black it is if I'm unconscious*. And it was really hard to breathe. All I heard were people screaming. Screaming bloody murder. All sorts of cries. At that moment, I thought, *This is it. We're all going to die on the street*.

**SOURCE:** *Hagen & Carouba, 2002*

Exposure to stress, especially traumatic stress like that experienced by many thousands of people on 9/11, can have profound and enduring effects on our mental and physical health. This chapter focuses on the effects of stress on the mind and body, including both stress associated with everyday life experiences and traumatic forms of stress.

Many sources of stress are psychological or situational in nature, such as stress associated with holding down a job (or two), preparing for exams, balancing the family budget, or caring for a sick child or loved one. These and other sources of stress can have profound effects on our physical and emotional health. Psychologists who study interrelationships between psychological factors—including stress—and physical health are called **health psychologists**.

Before we begin to examine the effects of stress, let's define our terms. The term *stress* refers to pressure or force placed on a body. In the physical world, tons of rock that crash to the ground in a landslide, for example, cause stress on impact, forming indentations or craters when they land. In psychology, we use the term **stress** to refer to pressures or demands placed on organisms to adapt or adjust. A **stressor** is a source of stress. Stressors (or stresses) include psychological factors, such as examinations in school and problems in social relationships, and life changes, such as the death of a loved one, divorce, or a job termination. They also include daily hassles, such as traffic jams, and physical environmental factors, such as exposure to extreme temperatures or noise levels. The term *stress* should be distinguished from *distress*, which refers to a state of physical or mental pain or suffering. Some amount of stress is probably healthy for us; it helps keep us active and alert. However, stress that is prolonged or intense can overtax our coping ability and lead to states of emotional distress, such as anxiety or depression, and to physical complaints, such as fatigue and headaches.

Stress is implicated in a wide range of physical and psychological problems. We begin our study of the effects of stress by discussing relationships between stress and health. We then examine stress-related psychological disorders that involve maladaptive reactions to stress.

# Effects of Stress

Psychological sources of stress not only diminish our capacity for adjustment but also may adversely affect our health. Many visits to physicians, perhaps even most, can be traced to stress-related illness. Stress is associated with an increased risk of various types of physical illnesses, ranging from digestive disorders to heart disease (Carlsson et al., 2014; Gianaros & Wager, 2015).

Many Americans feel that the level of stress in their lives is on the rise. According to a recent nationwide study by the American Psychological Association, nearly half of Americans polled reported that their level of stress had increased during the preceding five years; about one in three said they face extreme levels of stress (American Psychological Association, 2007a, 2007b, 2010). Americans recognize that stress is taking its toll. Many say they are experiencing psychological symptoms such as irritability or anger and physical symptoms such as fatigue as a result of stress (see Figure 4.1).

The field of *psychoneuroimmunology* studies relationships between psychological factors, especially stress, and the workings of the immune system (Kiecolt-Glaser, 2009). Here, we examine what scientists have learned about these relationships.

**Figure 4.1 Psychological and physical symptoms resulting from stress.**

Americans report a range of symptoms resulting from stress, including both psychological symptoms—such as irritability, anger, and nervousness—and physical symptoms—such as fatigue, headaches, and upset stomach. How does stress affect you?

**SOURCE OF DATA:** Adapted from American Psychological Association (2010).

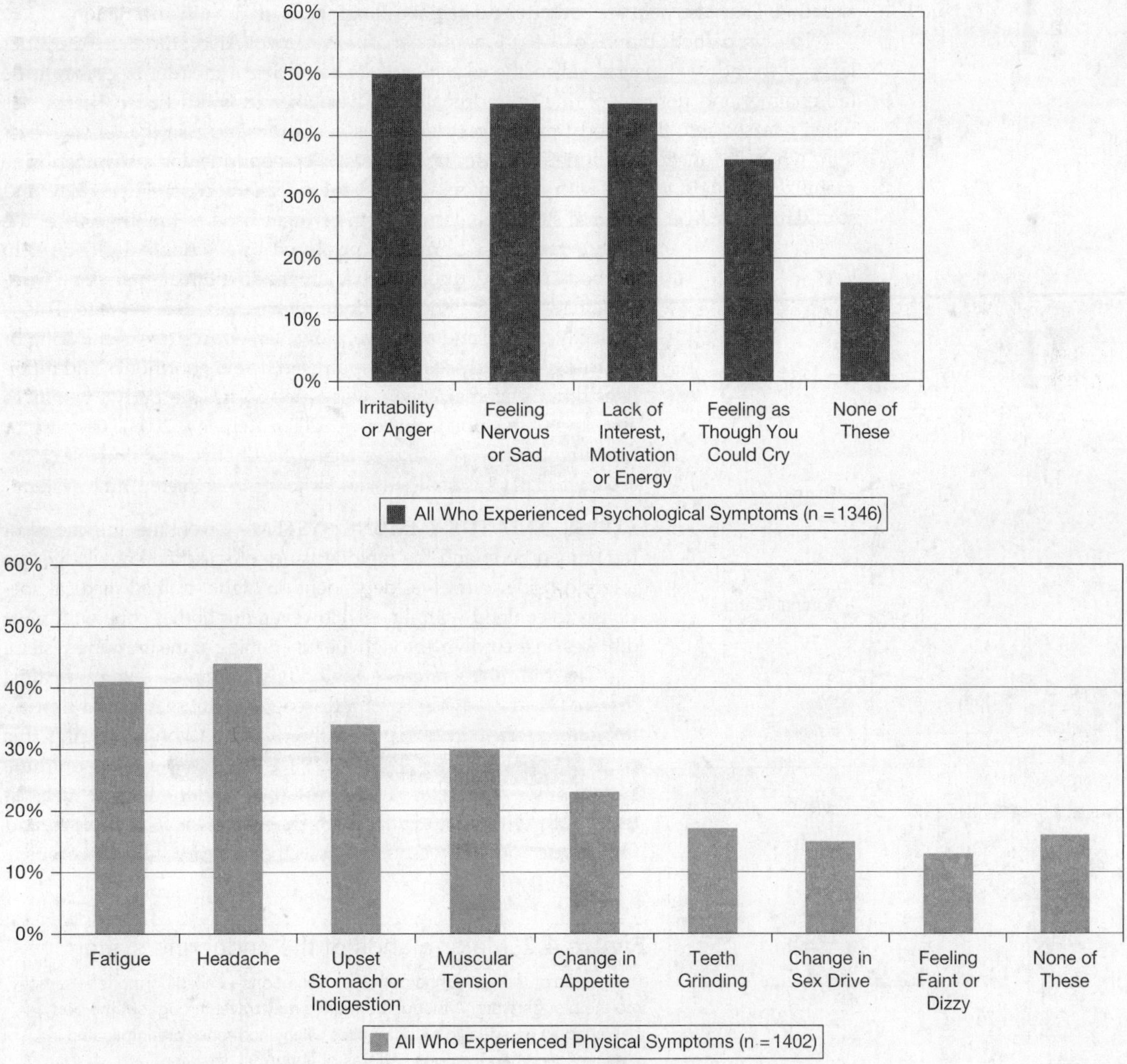

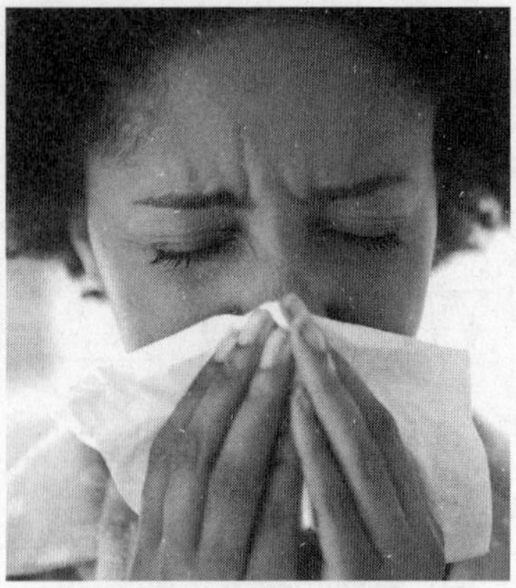

**STRESS AND THE COMMON COLD.** Do you find that you are more likely to develop a cold during stressful times in your life, such as around exams? Investigators have found that people under severe stress are more likely to become sick after exposure to cold viruses.

# Stress and Health

## 4.1 Evaluate the effects of stress on health.

In order to understand the toll that stress can take on the body, we first need to consider how the body reacts when we're under stress.

**STRESS AND THE ENDOCRINE SYSTEM** Stress has a domino effect on the **endocrine system**, the body's system of glands that release secretions called **hormones** directly into the bloodstream. (Other glands, such as the salivary glands that produce saliva, release their secretions into a system of ducts.) Figure 4.2 shows the major endocrine glands, which are distributed throughout the body.

Several endocrine glands are involved in the body's response to stress. First, the hypothalamus, a small structure in the brain, releases a hormone that stimulates the nearby pituitary gland to secrete the *adrenocorticotrophic hormone* (ACTH). ACTH, in turn, stimulates the adrenal glands, which are located above the kidneys. Under the influence of ACTH, the outer layer of the adrenal glands, called the *adrenal cortex*, releases a group of hormones called *cortical steroids* (cortisol and cortisone are examples). Cortical steroids (also called *corticosteroids*) have a number of functions in the body. They boost resistance to stress, foster muscle development, and induce the liver to release sugar, which provides needed bursts of energy for responding to a threatening stressor (e.g., a lurking predator or assailant) or an emergency situation. They also help the body defend against allergic reactions and inflammation.

The sympathetic branch of the autonomic nervous system, or ANS, stimulates the inner layer of the adrenal glands, called the *adrenal medulla*, to release a mixture of epinephrine (adrenaline) and norepinephrine (noradrenaline). These chemicals function as hormones when released into the bloodstream. Norepinephrine is also produced in the nervous system, where it functions as a neurotransmitter. Together, epinephrine and norepinephrine mobilize the body to deal with a threatening stressor by accelerating the heart rate and stimulating the liver to release stored glucose (a form of sugar used as fuel by cells in the body). The stress hormones produced by the adrenal glands help the body prepare to cope with an impending threat or stressor. Once the stressor has passed, the body returns to a normal state. This is perfectly normal and adaptive. However, when stress is enduring or recurring, the body regularly pumps out stress hormones and mobilizes other systems, which over time can tax the body's resources and impair health (Gabb et al., 2006; Kemeny, 2003). Chronic or repetitive stress can damage many bodily systems, including the cardiovascular system (heart and arteries) and the immune system.

**STRESS AND THE IMMUNE SYSTEM** Given the intricacies of the human body and the rapid advance of scientific knowledge, we might consider ourselves dependent on highly trained medical specialists to contend with illness. However, our bodies cope with most diseases on their own, through the functioning of the immune system.

The **immune system** is the body's system of defense against disease. Your body is constantly engaged in search-and-destroy missions against invading microbes, even as you're reading this page. Millions of white blood cells, or *leukocytes*, are the immune system's foot soldiers in this microscopic warfare. Leukocytes systematically envelop and kill pathogens such as bacteria, viruses, and fungi, worn-out body cells, and cells that have become cancerous.

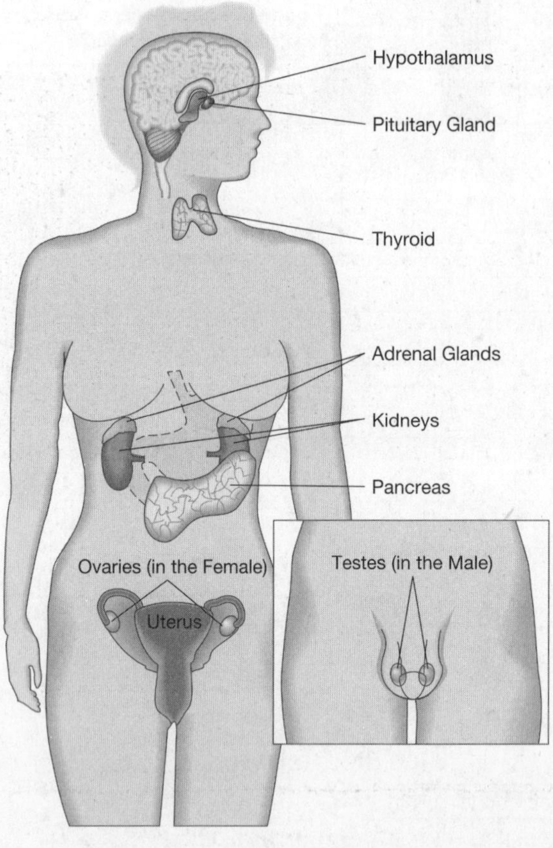


**Figure 4.2** Major glands of the endocrine system.

The glands of the endocrine pour their secretions—called hormones—directly into the bloodstream. Although hormones may travel throughout the body, they act only on specific receptor sites. Many hormones are implicated in stress reactions and various patterns of abnormal behavior.

Leukocytes recognize invading pathogens by their surface fragments, called *antigens*—literally *anti*body *gen*erators. Some leukocytes produce *antibodies*, specialized proteins that lock into position on an antigen, marking it for destruction by specialized "killer" lymphocytes that act like commandos on search-and-destroy missions (Greenwood, 2006; Kay, 2006). **T / F**

Special "memory lymphocytes" (lymphocytes are a type of leukocyte) are held in reserve rather than marking foreign bodies for destruction or going to war against them. They can remain in the bloodstream for years and form the basis for a quick immune response to an invader the second time around (Jiang & Chess, 2006).

Occasional stress may not impair our health, but persistent or prolonged stress can eventually weaken the body's immune system (Fan et al., 2009; Kemeny, 2003). A weakened immune system increases our susceptibility to many illnesses, including the common cold and the flu, and may increase the risk of developing chronic diseases, including cancer.

**TRUTH or FICTION**

As you are reading this page, millions of microscopic warriors in your body are conducting search-and-destroy missions to find and eradicate foreign invaders.

☑ **TRUE** Your immune system is always on guard against invading microbes and continuously dispatches specialized white blood cells to identify and eliminate infectious organisms.

Psychological stressors can dampen the response of the immune system, especially when the stress is intense or prolonged (Segerstrom & Miller, 2004). Even relatively brief periods of stress, such as final exam time, can weaken the immune system, although these effects are more limited than those associated with chronic or prolonged stress. The kinds of life stressors that can take a toll on the immune system, leaving us more vulnerable to disease, include marital conflict, divorce, chronic unemployment, and traumatic stress, such as natural disasters and terrorist attacks (e.g., Kiecolt-Glaser et al., 2002).

Just how does a psychological factor—stress—translate into physical health problems? Scientists believe they have an answer: inflammation (Cohen, Janicki-Deverts, et al., 2012; Gouin et al., 2012). Normally, the immune system regulates the body's inflammatory response to infection or injury. Under stress, the immune system becomes less capable of toning down the inflammatory response, leading to persistent inflammation that may contribute to the development of many physical disorders, including cardiovascular disease, asthma, and arthritis (Cohen, Janicki-Deverts, et al., 2012).

**THE WAR WITHIN.** White blood cells, shown here (colored blue) attacking and engulfing a pathogen, form the major part of the body's system of defense against bacteria, viruses, and other invading organisms.

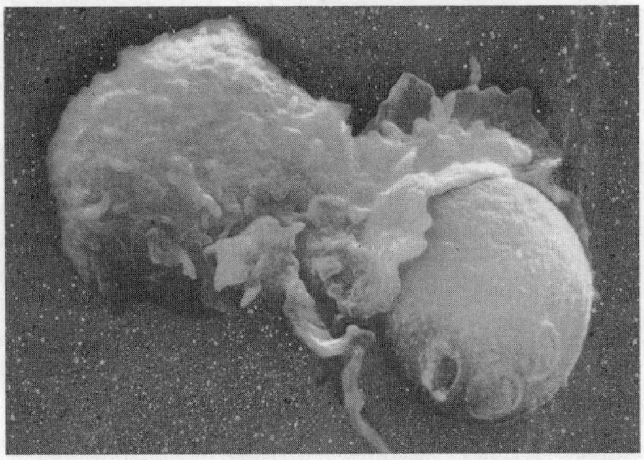

Social support may moderate or buffer the harmful effects of stress on the immune system. Several early studies showed poorer immune system functioning in groups with limited social supports, such as lonely students and medical and dental students with fewer numbers of friends (Glaser et al., 1985; Jemmott et al., 1983; Kiecolt-Glaser et al., 1984). The picture that emerges from this research is that loneliness and social isolation may be damaging to a person's health. More recent evidence shows that lonely and socially isolated people tend to have shorter life spans and more often suffer significant physical health problems, such as serious infections and cardiovascular disease (Holt-Lunstad et al., 2015; White, VanderDrifta, & Heffernan, 2015).

Exposure to stress is linked to greater risk of developing the common cold. However, investigators found that more sociable people tended to have greater resistance to developing the common cold than their less sociable peers after both groups voluntarily received injections of a cold virus (Cohen et al., 2003). This result points to a possible role of socialization or social support in buffering the effects of stress. **T / F**

We should caution that much of the research in psychoneuroimmunology is correlational. Researchers examine immunological functioning in relation to different indices of stress, but do not (nor would they!) directly manipulate stress to observe its effect on subjects' immune systems or general health. Correlational research helps scientists better understand relationships among variables and may point to possible underlying causal factors, but it does not in itself demonstrate causal connections.

**TRUTH or FICTION**

Surprisingly, stress makes you more resistant to the common cold.

☑ **FALSE** Stress increases the risk of developing a cold.

> ## TRUTH or FICTION
>
> Writing about traumatic experiences may be good for your physical and emotional health.
>
> ☑ **TRUE** Talking or writing about your feelings can help enhance both psychological and physical well-being.

**WRITING ABOUT STRESS AND TRAUMA AS A COPING RESPONSE** Expressing emotions in the form of writing about stressful or traumatic events in our lives may have therapeutic benefits. A number of research studies demonstrate that expressive writing reduces stress-related psychological and physical symptoms (e.g., Ironson et al., 2013; Travagin, Margola, & Revenson, 2015; Wisco, Sloan, & Marx, 2013). **T / F**

Scientists don't yet know how expressive writing produces beneficial effects on our health. One possibility is that keeping thoughts and feelings about highly stressful or traumatic events tightly under wraps places a burden on the autonomic nervous system, which in turn may weaken the immune system and increase susceptibility to stress-related disorders. Writing about stress-related thoughts and feelings may lessen their effects on the immune system.

**TERRORISM-RELATED TRAUMA** The 9/11 terrorist attacks on America changed everything. Before 9/11, we may have felt secure in our homes, offices, and other public places from the threat of terrorism. Now, terrorism looms as a constant threat to our safety and sense of security. Still, we endeavor to maintain a sense of normalcy in our lives. We travel and attend public gatherings, although the ever-present security regulations are a constant reminder of the heightened concern about terrorism. Many of us who were directly affected by 9/11 or lost friends or loved ones still may be trying to cope with the emotional consequences of that day. Many survivors, like those of other forms of trauma, such as floods and tornadoes, may experience prolonged, maladaptive stressful reactions, such as posttraumatic stress disorder (PTSD). Evidence from a community-based study in Michigan showed that the number of suicide attempts jumped in the months following the 9/11 attacks (Starkman, 2006).

Although most people exposed to traumatic events do not develop PTSD, many do experience symptoms associated with the disorder, such as difficulties concentrating and high levels of arousal. Since the attacks, many Americans have become sensitized to the emotional consequences of traumatic stress. See *A Closer Look: Coping with Trauma-Related Stress* on page 142 for more information.

People vary in their reactions to traumatic stress. Investigators trying to pinpoint factors that account for resiliency in the face of stress suggest that positive emotions can play an important role. Evidence gathered since 9/11 shows that experiencing positive emotions, such as feelings of gratitude and love, helped buffer the effects of stress (Fredrickson et al., 2003).

## The General Adaptation Syndrome

**4.2 Identify and describe the stages of the general adaptation syndrome.**

Stress researcher Hans Selye (1976) coined the term **general adaptation syndrome (GAS)** to describe a common biological pattern of response to prolonged or excessive stress. Selye pointed out that our bodies respond similarly to many kinds of unpleasant stressors, whether the source of stress is an invasion of microscopic disease organisms, a divorce, or the aftermath of a flood. The GAS model suggests that our bodies under stress are like clocks with alarm systems that do not shut off until their energy is perilously depleted.

The GAS consists of three stages: the alarm reaction, the resistance stage, and the exhaustion stage. Perception of an immediate stressor (e.g., a car that swerves in front of you on the highway) triggers the **alarm reaction**. The alarm reaction mobilizes the body to prepare for challenge or stress. We can think of it as the body's first line of defense against a threatening stressor. The body reacts with a complex, integrated response involving activation of the sympathetic nervous system, which increases bodily arousal and triggers release of stress hormones by the endocrine system.

In 1929, Harvard University physiologist Walter Cannon termed this response pattern the **fight-or-flight reaction**. We noted earlier how the endocrine system responds to stress.

**Table 4.1** Stress-Related Changes in the Body Associated with the Alarm Reaction

| | |
|---|---|
| Corticosteroids are released. | Blood shifts from the internal organs to the skeletal muscles. |
| Epinephrine and norepinephrine are released. | Digestion is inhibited. |
| Heart rate, respiration rate, and blood pressure increase. | Sugar is released by the liver. |
| Muscles tense. | Blood-clotting ability is increased. |

During the alarm reaction, the adrenal glands (controlled by the pituitary gland in the brain) pump out cortical steroids and stress hormones that help mobilize the body's defenses (see Table 4.1).

The fight-or-flight reaction most probably helped our early ancestors cope with the many perils they faced. The reaction may have been provoked by the sight of a predator or by a rustling sound in the undergrowth. However, our ancestors usually did not experience prolonged activation of the alarm reaction. Sensitive alarm reactions increased their chances of survival. Once a threat was eliminated—they either fought off predators or fled quickly—the body reinstated a lower level of arousal; it did not remain for long in a state of heightened arousal after the immediate danger was past. In contrast, people today are continually bombarded with stressors—everything from battling traffic every workday to balancing school and work or rushing from job to job. Consequently, our alarm system is turned on much of the time, which may eventually increase the likelihood of developing stress-related disorders.

IN THE BLEACHERS © 2006 Steve Moore. Reprinted with permission of Universal Press Syndicate. All rights reserved.

When a stressor is persistent, we progress to the **resistance stage**, or adaptation stage, of the GAS. Endocrine and sympathetic nervous system responses (e.g., release of stress hormones) remain at high levels, but not quite as high as during the alarm reaction. During the resistance stage, the body tries to renew spent energy and repair damage. When stressors continue or new ones appear, we may progress to the final stage of the GAS: the **exhaustion stage**. Although there are individual differences in capacity to resist stress, all of us will eventually exhaust our bodily resources. The exhaustion stage is characterized by dominance of the parasympathetic branch of the ANS. Consequently, our heart and respiration rates decelerate. Do we benefit from the respite? Not necessarily. If the source of stress persists, we may develop what Selye termed *diseases of adaptation*. These range from allergic reactions to heart disease—and, at times, even death. The lesson is clear: Chronic stress can weaken the immune system, leaving us more vulnerable to a range of physical health problems (Carlsson et al., 2014; Everson-Rose et al., 2014; McEwen, 2013).

Cortical steroids are perhaps one reason that persistent stress may eventually lead to health problems. Although cortical steroids help the body cope with stress, they also suppress the activity of the immune system. They have negligible effects when they are released only periodically. Continuous secretion, however, weakens the immune system by disrupting the production of antibodies, which can increase vulnerability to colds and other infections over time.

Although Selye's model speaks to the general response pattern of the body under stress, different bodily responses may occur in response to particular kinds of stressors (Denson, Spanovic, & Miller, 2009). For example, exposure to excessive noise may invoke different bodily processes than other sources of stress, as might overcrowding or psychological stressors such as divorce or separation.

FIGHT OR FLIGHT

CHRONIC STRESS EFFECTS

# A CLOSER Look

## COPING WITH TRAUMA-RELATED STRESS

People normally experience psychological distress in the face of trauma. If anything, it would be abnormal to remain blasé at a time of crisis or disaster. The American Psychological Association offers the following suggestions for coping with traumatic experiences.

### How Should I Help Myself and My Family?

There are many steps you can take to help restore emotional well-being and a sense of control following a disaster or other traumatic experience, including the following:

- *Give yourself time to adjust.* Anticipate that this will be a difficult time in your life. Allow yourself to mourn the losses you have experienced. Try to be patient with changes in your emotional state.
- *Ask for support from people who care about you and who will listen and empathize with your situation.* But keep in mind that your typical support system may be weakened if those who are close to you also have experienced or witnessed the trauma.
- *Communicate your experience.* Communicate in whatever ways you feel comfortable with—such as by talking with family or close friends, or keeping a diary.
- *Find out about local support groups that often are available.* Support groups, such as for those who have suffered from natural disasters or other traumatic events, can be especially helpful for people with limited personal support systems.
- *Try to find groups led by appropriately trained and experienced professionals.* Group discussion can help people realize that other individuals in the same circumstances often have similar reactions and emotions.
- *Engage in healthy behaviors to enhance your ability to cope with excessive stress.* Eat well-balanced meals and get plenty of rest. If you experience ongoing difficulties with sleep, you may be able to find some relief through relaxation techniques. Avoid alcohol and drugs.
- *Establish or reestablish routines such as eating meals at regular times and following an exercise program.* Take some time off from the demands of daily life by pursuing hobbies or other enjoyable activities.
- *Avoid major life decisions such as switching careers or jobs if possible.* These activities tend to be highly stressful.

Stress reactions that linger for two or more months and affect an individual's ability to function in everyday life can be a cause for concern. If you or a loved one is experiencing persistent emotional effects of traumatic stress, it may be worthwhile to seek professional mental health assistance. Assistance is available through your college health services (for registered students) or through networks of trained professionals. For more information or a referral, you may contact your local American Red Cross chapter or the American Psychological Association at 202-336-5800.

**SOURCE:** Reprinted from "Managing traumatic stress: Tips for recovering from disasters and other traumatic events," with permission of the American Psychological Association.

# Stress and Life Changes

**4.3 Evaluate evidence of the relationship between life changes and psychological and physical health.**

Researchers have investigated the stress–illness connection by quantifying life stress in terms of life changes (also called *life events*). Life changes are sources of stress because

**FOR BETTER OR FOR WORSE.**
Life changes such as marriage and the death of loved ones are sources of stress that require adjustment. The death of a spouse may be one of the most stressful life changes a person ever faces.

they force us to adjust. They include both positive events, such as getting married, and negative events, such as the death of a loved one. You can gain insight into the level of stressful life changes you may have experienced during the past year by completing the stress inventory ("Going through Changes") on page 144.

People who experience a greater number of life changes are more likely to suffer from psychological and physical health problems than those with fewer life events (Dohrenwend, 2006). Again, however, researchers need to be cautious when interpreting these findings. These reported links are correlational and not experimental. In other words, researchers did not (and would not!) assign subjects to conditions in which they were exposed to either a high or a low level of life changes to see what effects these conditions might have on their health over time. Rather, existing data are based on observations of relationships—say, between life changes on the one hand and physical health problems on the other. Such relationships are open to other interpretations. It could be that physical symptoms are sources of stress in themselves and lead to more life changes. Physical illness may cause disruptions of sleep or financial burdens, and so forth. Hence, in some cases at least, the causal direction may be reversed: Health problems may lead to life changes. Scientists can't yet tease out the possible cause-and-effect relationships.

Although both positive and negative life changes can be stressful, it is reasonable to assume that positive life changes are generally less disruptive than negative life changes. In other words, marriage tends to be less stressful than divorce or separation. Or, to put it another way, a change for the better may be a change, but it is less of a hassle.

## Acculturative Stress: Making It in America

**4.4 Evaluate the role of acculturative stress in psychological adjustment.**

Should Hindu women who immigrate to the United States give up the sari in favor of California casuals? Should Russian immigrants continue to teach their children Russian in the home? Should African American children be acquainted with the music and art of African peoples? Should women from traditional Islamic societies remove the veil and enter the competitive workplace? How do the stresses of acculturation affect the psychological well-being of immigrants and their families?

Sociocultural theorists have alerted us to the importance of accounting for social stressors in explaining abnormal behavior. One of the primary sources of stress imposed on immigrant groups, or on native groups living in the larger mainstream culture, is the need to adapt to a new culture. We can define *acculturation* as the process of adaptation by which immigrants, native groups, and ethnic minority groups adjust to the new culture or majority culture through making behavioral and attitudinal changes. **Acculturative stress** is pressure that results from the demands placed on immigrant, native, and ethnic minority groups to adjust to life in the mainstream culture. Acculturative stress can be a factor among first- and second-generation immigrant groups in emotional problems such as anxiety and depression (Katsiaficas et al., 2013).

Acculturative stress is associated with poorer psychological functioning in immigrant groups (Driscoll & Torres, 2013). There are two general theories of the relationships between acculturation and psychological adjustment. One theory, dubbed the *melting pot theory*, holds that acculturation helps people adjust to living in the host culture. From this perspective, Hispanic Americans, for example, might adjust better

## Questionnaire

### GOING THROUGH CHANGES

How stressful has your life been lately? Life changes or events, such as those listed below, can impose a stressful burden on a person's adjustment. These life events are similar to those reported by samples of college students and are scaled according to the level of stress they impose (Renner & Mackin, 1998). Place a checkmark next to each event you have experienced during the past year. Then, look at the guide at the end of the chapter to interpret your score. (Check all that apply.)

**Low Level of Stress**

✓ ______ Registering for classes
______ Rushing a fraternity or sorority
______ Making new friends
✓ ______ Commuting to work or school
______ Going out on a first date
✓ ______ Beginning a new semester
______ Dating someone steadily
______ Getting sick
______ Maintaining a stable romantic relationship
______ Living away from home for the first time

**Medium Level of Stress**

______ Being in a class you hate
______ Getting involved with drugs
______ Having difficulties with a roommate
______ Cheating on a boyfriend or girlfriend
______ Changing jobs or having hassles at work
______ Missing sleep
______ Having conflicts with parents
______ Moving or adjusting to a new residence
______ Experiencing negative consequences from using alcohol or drugs
______ Having to talk in front of class

**High Level of Stress**

______ Death of a close friend or family member
______ Missing an exam because you overslept
______ Failing a class
______ Terminating a long-standing dating relationship
______ Learning that a boyfriend or girlfriend is cheating on you
______ Having financial problems
______ Dealing with a serious illness of a friend or family member
______ Getting caught cheating
______ Being raped
______ Having someone accuse you of rape

by replacing Spanish with English and adopting the values and customs associated with mainstream American culture. A competing theory, the *bicultural theory*, holds that psychosocial adjustment is marked by identification with both traditional and host cultures. That is, a person's ability to adapt to the ways of the new society combined with a supportive cultural tradition and a sense of ethnic identity may predict good adjustment. From a bicultural perspective, immigrants maintain their ethnic identity and traditional values while learning to adapt to the language and customs of the host culture. Recent evidence with a sample of young Mexican American and Dominican American children showed that having a stronger sense of ethnic identity was associated with better psychological functioning (Serrano-Villar & Calzada, 2016).

**RELATIONSHIPS BETWEEN ACCULTURATION AND PSYCHOLOGICAL ADJUSTMENT** Relationships between acculturation and psychological adjustment are complex. Some research links higher acculturation status to a greater likelihood of developing psychological problems, whereas other research shows the opposite to be the case. First, let's note some findings from research with Hispanic (Latino) Americans that highlight psychological effects associated with acculturation:

**MAINTAINING ETHNIC IDENTITY.** Recent immigrants may be better able to cope with the stress of adjusting to a new culture when they make an effort to adapt while maintaining their ties to their traditional cultures.

- *Increased risk of heavy drinking among women.* Evidence shows that highly acculturated Hispanic American women are more likely than relatively unacculturated Hispanic American women to become heavy drinkers (Caetano, 1987). In Latin American cultures, men tend to drink much more alcohol than women, largely because gender-based cultural prohibitions on drinking constrain alcohol use among women. These constraints appear to have loosened among Hispanic American women who adopt "mainstream" U.S. attitudes and values.
- *Increased risk of smoking and sexual intercourse among adolescents.* In Latino adolescents, higher levels of acculturation are also linked to increased risks of smoking (Ribisl et al., 2000) and engaging in sexual intercourse (Adam et al., 2005; Lee & Hahm, 2010).
- *Increased risk of disturbed eating behaviors.* Highly acculturated Hispanic American high school girls were found more likely than their less acculturated counterparts to show test scores associated with anorexia (an eating disorder characterized by excessive weight loss and fears of becoming fat; see Chapter 8) on an eating attitudes questionnaire (Pumariega, 1986). Acculturation apparently made these girls more vulnerable to the demands of striving toward the contemporary American ideal of the (very!) slender woman. More recently, investigators found that acculturative stress was linked to poorer body image and internalization of the thin ideal among male and female Hispanic undergraduates in West Texas (Menon & Harter, 2012).

A recent large-scale study of nearly 5,000 immigrants from Asia, Africa, Europe, and Latin America showed that rates of diagnosed mood, anxiety, and personality disorders were higher among second-generation immigrants than first-generation immigrants (Salas-Wright, Kagotho, & Vaughn, 2014). We might gather from this and other similar evidence that acculturation has a negative influence on psychological adjustment. One explanation for this negative influence is that erosion of traditional family networks and values in more acculturated immigrant groups may increase susceptibility to psychological disorders in the face of stress (Ortega et al., 2000).

We need to balance this view by taking into account other evidence of psychological benefits of bicultural identification. People with a bicultural identity seek to adjust to the host (American) culture while also maintaining their identity with their traditional culture. In an early study of elderly Mexican Americans, researchers found that subjects who were minimally acculturated showed higher levels of depression than either their highly acculturated or their bicultural counterparts (Zamanian et al., 1992). More recently, a large-scale study of Native American youth in 67 American Indian tribes showed that those who were biculturally competent (i.e., had the ability to adapt to both Indian and White cultures) reported lower levels of hopelessness than did those with competencies in only one culture or neither culture (LaFromboise, Albright, & Harris, 2010).

Why would low acculturation status be linked to increased risk of depression? The answer may be that low acculturation status is often a marker for low socioeconomic status (SES). People who are minimally acculturated often face

**COMING TO AMERICA.** A recent study showed that rates of various psychological disorders were higher among second-generation immigrants than first-generation immigrants. It seems that acculturation may have a negative influence on the psychological adjustment of immigrant groups.

economic hardship and tend to occupy the lower strata of socioeconomic status. Social stress resulting from financial difficulties, lack of proficiency in the host language, and limited economic opportunities add to the stress of adapting to the host culture, all of which may contribute to increased risk of depression and other psychological problems (Ayers et al., 2009; Yeh, 2003). Not surprisingly, one study found that Mexican Americans who were more proficient in English generally had fewer signs of depression and anxiety than did their less English-proficient counterparts (Salgado de Snyder, 1987). Yet socioeconomic status and language proficiency are not the only—nor necessarily the most important—determinants of mental health among immigrant groups. Consider the findings from a northern California sample that showed better mental health profiles among Mexican immigrants than among people of Mexican descent born in the United States, despite the greater socioeconomic disadvantages faced by the immigrant group (Vega et al., 1998). "Americanization" may have damaging effects on the mental health of acculturated minority groups, but such effects may be buffered to a certain extent by retaining cultural traditions. **T / F**

### TRUTH or FICTION

Immigrant groups show better psychological adjustment when they forsake their cultural heritage and adopt the values of the host culture.

☑ **FALSE** Retention of cultural traditions may have a protective or "buffer" effect against the stresses associated with adjusting to a new culture.

In sum, the erosion of traditional family networks and cultural values that may accompany acculturation in immigrant groups may also increase the risk of psychological problems. To a certain extent, the negative effects of acculturation may be offset by more active coping efforts in adjusting to a new culture, as well as by maintaining ties to the traditional culture (Driscoll & Torres, 2013). Evidence shows that a strong sense of ethnic identity and pride is associated with higher self-esteem and better adjustment in ethnic minority children (Oyserman, 2008; Rodriguez et al., 2009; Smith et al., 2009). Also note the results of a study of Asian immigrant adolescents in the United States that showed that feelings of being alienated or caught between two cultures—the United States and the traditional culture—can lead to mental health problems (Yeh, 2003). Some outcomes need careful interpretation. For example, does the finding that highly acculturated Hispanic American women are more likely to drink heavily argue in favor of placing greater social constraints on women? Perhaps a loosening of restraints is a double-edged sword, and all people—male and female, Hispanic and non-Hispanic—encounter adjustment problems when they gain new freedoms.

Finally, we need to consider gender differences in acculturation. In an early study, female immigrants showed higher levels of depression than male immigrants (Salgado de Snyder, Cervantes, & Padilla, 1990). Their higher levels of depression may be linked to the greater level of stress women typically encounter in adjusting to changes in family patterns and personal issues, such as the greater freedom of gender roles for men and women in U.S. society. Because they were reared in cultures in which men are expected to be breadwinners and women homemakers, immigrant women may encounter more family and internal conflict when they enter the workforce, regardless of whether they work because of economic necessity or personal choice. Given these factors, we shouldn't be surprised that wives in more acculturated Mexican American couples tend to report greater marital distress than those in less acculturated couples (Negy & Snyder, 1997). The lead author of this study, psychologist Charles Negy of the University of Central Florida, explores the role of acculturation among Latinos in *A Closer Look: Coming to America.*

## A CLOSER Look

### COMING TO AMERICA: THE CASE OF LATINOS—CHARLES NEGY

As a young man of part Mexican American heritage, I worked in a grocery store in East Los Angeles and was intrigued by the wide range of people of Mexican ancestry I encountered. Many recent immigrants from Mexico seemed eager to practice the little English they knew and were interested in learning more about mainstream American culture. I also knew many immigrants, including many who had lived in California for more than 20 years, who spoke barely any English and hardly ever ventured beyond the local community.

When I entered graduate school, it seemed natural for me to study acculturation among Latino or Hispanic Americans. *Acculturation* refers to adopting the values, attitudes, and behaviors of a host culture. In my early studies, I quickly observed what other researchers had already discovered—namely, that Latinos in the United States varied greatly in their degree of acculturation toward the U.S. culture. In general, the longer they had lived in the United States, the more acculturated they tended to be, and the more acculturated they were, the more they resembled non-Hispanic Whites in their values, attitudes, and customs.

In my early studies (e.g., Negy & Woods, 1992a, 1993), I found that the more acculturated Mexican American college students were, the more similar their scores were to those of non-Hispanic Whites on standardized personality tests. I wasn't surprised to find that those who were more acculturated tended to come from higher socioeconomic backgrounds (Negy & Woods, 1992b). I also found that among lower-income Mexican American adolescents who showed signs of depression, the more acculturated they were, the more likely they were to have experienced thoughts of committing suicide (Rasmussen et al., 1997).

I later began a line of research examining ethnic differences in marital relationships by comparing Mexican American couples with (non-Hispanic) White couples and Mexican couples (Negy & Snyder, 1997; Negy, Snyder, & Diaz-Loving, 2004). As a group, Mexican couples reported more verbal and/or physical aggression in their relationships than did Mexican American couples, who in turn reported more aggression in their relationships than did (non-Hispanic) White couples. I also observed that Mexican American couples had more egalitarian (equal) relationships and higher levels of marital satisfaction than Mexican couples (Negy & Snyder, 2004). I learned from these findings that living in the United States was associated with relationship patterns among Mexican Americans that were closer to the Americanized ideal of mutual respect and shared decision making.

These findings suggested that more highly acculturated Hispanic couples have less conflicted, more egalitarian, and more satisfying marriages. On the other hand, acculturation is linked to some mental health problems, such as increased likelihood of suicidal thinking as a way of dealing with depression. This mixed picture of acculturation among Latinos is consistent with the complex and sometimes conflicting results from studies examining relationships between acculturation and mental health reported in this chapter.

I also observed in my study of Mexican American couples that more highly acculturated women reported less satisfaction with the sexual component of their relationships than did less well-acculturated women. These findings led me to wonder whether American culture imparts greater expectations of female sexual satisfaction in marriages that translate into lower satisfaction when these expectations are not fulfilled.

There are important issues to keep in mind when interpreting these research findings. For starters, the research is correlational in nature. As you may recall about correlational data, we cannot say whether one variable causes another variable. For example, on the basis of the findings from my study of marital couples, I cannot conclude that acculturation is causally related to the development of more egalitarian marriages. It is possible that causation works in the opposite direction—that having an egalitarian marriage influences acculturation. How? We can speculate that Mexican Americans with more egalitarian relationships may be more accepted by mainstream society, and the more interactions they have within the general society, the more opportunities they have to acculturate. Therefore, having egalitarian marriages tends to be associated (correlated) with acculturation, but there is no causal link between the two.

In more recent research, my colleagues and I focused on the role of acculturative stress among Latino immigrants. We found that Latino immigrants reporting the highest levels of acculturative stress tended to be those for whom the experience of living in the United States deviated the most from what they had expected would be the case before they immigrated (Negy, Schwartz, & Reig-Ferrer, 2009). In another sample of Hispanic immigrant women, we found that acculturative stress appeared to both exacerbate previous relationship difficulties among couples and to contribute to stress among married Latinas (Negy et al., 2010).

In 2011, I received a Fulbright Scholarship that allowed me to be a visiting professor at a university in San Salvador, El Salvador, where I also conducted a study on a new construct that intrigued me—*psychological homelessness*. This is a feeling of detachment immigrants may develop toward their country of origin. I had access to Salvadorans who had been deported from the United States and wanted to know if they no longer identified with El Salvador as their country of origin or felt connected or bonded to their fellow Salvadorians (i.e., psychological homelessness). The deportees did indeed tend to struggle to feel "at home" back in El Salvador, and the more acculturated they had become to life in the United States (despite their undocumented status), the more psychological homelessness they reported (Negy et al., 2014).

Learning about the adjustment and acculturation challenges many Latinos face—both here in the United States and in Latin America—as they endeavor to maintain family relations while striving for a better life may help inform the treatment programs and interventions clinicians can offer to Latino individuals and families.

**CHARLES NEGY, PH.D.** Dr. Negy is Associate Professor of Psychology at the University of Central Florida and a Licensed Psychologist in the State of Florida. His research primarily focuses on the psychological well-being of Hispanic Americans and sexual minorities.

# Psychological Factors That Moderate Stress

**4.5 Identify psychological factors that moderate the effects of stress.**

Stress may be a fact of life, but the ways in which we handle stress help determine our ability to cope with it. Individuals react differently to stress depending on psychological factors such as the meaning they ascribe to stressful events. Consider, for example, a major life event—such as pregnancy. Whether it is a positive or negative stressor depends on the couple's desire for a child and their readiness to care for one. We can say the stress of pregnancy is moderated by the perceived value of children in the couple's eyes and their self-efficacy—their confidence in their ability to raise a child. As we see next, psychological factors such as coping styles, self-efficacy expectancies, psychological hardiness, optimism, social support, and ethnic identity may moderate or buffer the effects of stress.

**STYLES OF COPING** What do you do when faced with a serious problem? Do you pretend it does not exist? Like Scarlett O'Hara in the classic film *Gone with the Wind*, do you say to yourself, "I'll think about it tomorrow," and then banish it from your mind? Or do you take charge and confront it squarely?

Pretending that problems do not exist is a form of denial, an example of **emotion-focused coping** (Lazarus & Folkman, 1984). In emotion-focused coping, people take measures that immediately reduce the impact of the stressor, such as denying its existence or withdrawing from the situation. Emotion-focused coping, however, does not eliminate the stressor (a serious illness, for example) or help an individual develop better ways of managing it. In **problem-focused coping**, by contrast, people examine the stressors they face and do what they can to change them or modify their own reactions to render stressors less harmful. These basic styles of coping—emotion-focused and problem-focused—have been applied to ways in which people respond to illness.

Denial of illness can take various forms, including the following:

1. Failing to recognize the seriousness of the illness
2. Minimizing the emotional distress the illness causes
3. Misattributing symptoms to other causes (e.g., assuming the appearance of blood in the stool represents nothing more than a local abrasion)
4. Ignoring threatening information about the illness

Denial can be dangerous to your health, especially if it leads to avoidance of or noncompliance with needed medical treatment. Avoidance is another form of emotion-based coping. Like denial, avoidance may deter people from complying with medical treatments, which can lead to a worsening of their medical conditions. Evidence supports the negative consequences of avoidant coping. In one study, people who had an avoidant style of coping with cancer (e.g., by trying not to think or talk about it) showed greater disease progression when evaluated a year later than did people who more directly confronted the illness (Epping-Jordan, Compas, & Howell, 1994). Other investigators link avoidance to the later development of depression and PTSD among combat veterans (Holahan et al., 2005; Stein et al., 2005).

Another form of emotion-focused coping, the use of wish-fulfillment fantasies, is also linked to poor adjustment in coping with serious illness. Examples of wish-fulfillment fantasies include ruminating about what might have been had the illness not occurred and longing for better times. Wish-fulfillment fantasy offers a patient no means of coping with life's difficulties other than an imaginary escape.

Does this mean that people are invariably better off when they know all the facts concerning their illnesses? Not necessarily. Whether you will be better off knowing all the facts may depend on your preferred style of coping. A mismatch between an individual's style of coping and the amount of information provided may hamper recovery. In an important early study, cardiac patients with a repressive style of coping (relying on denial) who received information about their conditions showed a higher incidence of medical complications than repressors who were largely kept in the dark (Shaw et al., 1985). Sometimes, ignorance helps people manage stress—at least temporarily.

Problem-focused coping involves strategies that address the sources of stress, such as seeking information about the illness through self-study and medical consultation. A person receiving a cancer diagnosis may feel more optimistic or hopeful if he or she receives information from medical providers about the successful outcomes of treatment.

**SELF-EFFICACY EXPECTANCIES** **Self-efficacy expectancies** are the expectations we hold regarding our ability to cope with the challenges we face, to perform certain behaviors skillfully, and to produce positive changes in our lives (Bandura, 1986, 2006). Self-efficacy serves as a buffer to stress (Schönfeld et al., 2016). We are better able to manage stress, including stress of coping with illness, when we feel confident (have higher self-efficacy) in our ability to cope effectively with the challenges we face. A forthcoming exam may be more or less stressful depending on your confidence in your ability to achieve a good grade.

In a classic study, psychologist Albert Bandura and colleagues found that spider-phobic women showed high levels of the stress hormones epinephrine and norepinephrine when they interacted with the phobic object—for example, by allowing a spider to crawl on their laps (Bandura et al., 1985). However, as their confidence or self-efficacy expectancies for coping with these tasks increased, the levels of these stress hormones declined. These hormones make us feel shaky, have "butterflies in the stomach," and feel generally nervous. Because high self-efficacy expectancies appear to be associated with lower secretion of these stress hormones, people who believe they can cope with their problems are less likely to feel nervous.

**PSYCHOLOGICAL HARDINESS** **Psychological hardiness** refers to a cluster of traits that may help people manage stress. Suzanne Kobasa (1979) and her colleagues investigated business executives who resisted illness despite heavy burdens of stress.

Three key traits distinguished the psychologically hardy executives (Kobasa, Maddi, & Kahn, 1982, pp. 169–170):

1. *Commitment.* Rather than feeling alienated from their tasks and situations, hardy executives involved themselves fully. That is, they believed in what they were doing.
2. *Challenge.* Hardy executives believed change was the normal state of things, not sterile sameness or stability for the sake of stability.
3. *Control over their lives.* Hardy executives believed and acted as though they were effectual rather than powerless in controlling the rewards and punishments of life. In terms suggested by social-cognitive theorist Julian Rotter (1966), psychologically hardy individuals have an *internal locus of control.*

**COPING WITH STRESS.** Psychologically hardy people appear to cope more effectively with stress by adopting active, problem-solving approaches and by perceiving themselves as choosing high-stress situations.

Psychologically hardy people appear to cope more effectively with stress by using more active, problem-solving approaches. They are also likely to report fewer physical symptoms and less depression in the face of stress than nonhardy people (Pengilly & Dowd, 2000). Kobasa suggests that hardy people are better able to handle stress because they perceive themselves as *choosing* their stress-creating situations. They perceive the stressors they face as making life more interesting and challenging, not as simply burdening them with additional pressures. A sense of control is a key factor in psychological hardiness.

**OPTIMISM** Seeing the proverbial glass as half-full rather than half-empty is linked to better physical health and emotional well-being (Carver, 2014; Forgeard & Seligman, 2012).

> ### TRUTH or FICTION
>
> Optimists may have hopeful expectations, but it's actually the pessimists who have healthier cardiovascular and immunological functioning.
>
> ☑ **FALSE** Optimism is linked to various indices of mental and physical health, including better cardiovascular and immunological functioning.

For example, evidence shows that more optimistic people tend to have better cardiovascular health and immunological functioning (Hernandez et al., 2015; Jaffe, 2013). Optimists tend to take better care of themselves than pessimists, such as engaging in more physical activity, avoiding harmful substances such as tobacco, and maintaining a healthier body weight. **T / F**

Pain patients who express more pessimistic thoughts during flare-ups tend to report more severe pain and distress than counterparts who have sunnier thoughts (Gil et al., 1990). Examples of these pessimistic thoughts include, "I can no longer do anything," "No one cares about my pain," and "It isn't fair I have to live this way." To date, research shows only correlational links between optimism and health. Perhaps we shall soon discover whether learning to alter attitudes—learning to see the glass as half-full—plays a causal role in maintaining or restoring health. You can evaluate your own level of optimism by completing the questionnaire *Are You an Optimist?*

The study of optimism falls within a broader contemporary movement in psychology called **positive psychology**. The developers of this movement believe that psychology should focus more of its efforts on the positive aspects of the human experience, rather than just the deficit side of the human equation, such as problems of emotional disorders, drug abuse, and violence (Donaldson, Csikszentmihalyi, & Nakamura, 2011; McNulty & Fincham, 2012; Seligman et al., 2005). Proponents of positive psychology do not argue that researchers should turn away from the study of emotional problems, but they believe that more attention is needed on how positive attributes, such as optimism, love, and hope, affect peoples' ability to lead satisfying and fulfilling lives. Another positive aspect of the human experience is the ability to help others in need and to be helped by others in turn, as in the case of social support.

## Questionnaire

### ARE YOU AN OPTIMIST?

Are you someone who looks on the bright side of things? Or do you expect bad things to happen? The following questionnaire may give you insight into whether you are an optimist or a pessimist.

Directions: Indicate whether or not each of the items represents your feelings by writing a number in the blank space according to the following code. Then, turn to the scoring key at the end of the chapter.

5 = strongly agree
4 = agree
3 = neutral
2 = disagree
1 = strongly disagree

1. _______ I believe you're either born lucky or, like me, born unlucky.
2. _______ My attitude is that if something can go wrong, it probably will.
3. _______ I think of myself more as an optimist than a pessimist.
4. _______ I generally expect things will work out in the end.
5. _______ I have these doubts about whether I will eventually succeed.
6. _______ I am hopeful about what the future holds for me.
7. _______ I tend to believe that "every cloud has a silver lining."
8. _______ I think of myself as a realist who thinks the proverbial glass is half-empty rather than half-full.
9. _______ I think the future will be rosy.
10. _______ Things don't generally work out the way I planned.

**ETHNIC PRIDE AS A MODERATOR OF THE EFFECTS OF STRESS.**
Pride in one's racial or ethnic identity may help an individual withstand the stress imposed by racism and intolerance.

**SOCIAL SUPPORT** People with a broad network of social relationships, such as having a spouse, having close family members and friends, and belonging to social organizations, not only show greater resistance to fending off the common cold but also tend to live longer lives than people with narrower social networks (Cohen & Janicki-Deverts, 2009; Cohen et al., 2003). Having a diverse social network may provide a wider range of social support that helps protect the body's immune system by serving as a buffer against stress.

**ETHNIC IDENTITY** African Americans, on average, stand a greater risk than Euro-Americans of suffering chronic health problems, such as obesity, hypertension, heart disease, diabetes, and certain types of cancers (Brown, 2006; Ferdinand & Ferdinand, 2009; Shields, Lerman, & Sullivan, 2005). The particular stressors that African Americans often face, such as racism, poverty, violence, and overcrowded living conditions, may contribute to their heightened risks of serious health-related problems.

Exposure to discrimination is linked to poorer mental and physical health and higher rates of substance abuse among ethnic minorities (Chou, Asnaani, & Hofmann, 2012; Huynh, Devos, & Dunbar, 2012; Stevens-Watkins et al., 2014; Torres & Vallejo, 2015). Studies of Latino and Navajo youth show that negative effects of discrimination may be offset to a certain extent by having strong connections to one's traditional culture and by having parents with strong, culturally based orientations and values (Delgado et al., 2010; Galliher, Jones, & Dahl, 2011).

African Americans often demonstrate a high level of resiliency in coping with stress. Among the factors that help buffer stress among African Americans are strong social networks of family and friends, beliefs in one's ability to handle stress (self-efficacy), coping skills, and ethnic identity. Interestingly, African Americans who reported more active attempts to seek social support were less affected by the effects of perceived racism, a significant life stressor, than were those who were less active in support seeking (Clark, 2006).

Ethnic identity is associated with perceptions of a better quality of life among African Americans (Utsey et al., 2002) and appears to be more strongly related to psychological well-being among African Americans than among White Americans (Gray-Little & Hafdahl, 2000). Acquiring and maintaining pride in their racial identity and cultural heritage may help African Americans and other ethnic minorities withstand stresses imposed by racism. Evidence links stronger racial identity in African Americans to lower levels of depression (Settles et al., 2010). Conversely, African Americans and other ethnic minorities who become alienated from their culture or ethnic identity may be more vulnerable to the effects of stress, which in turn may increase risks of physical and mental health problems.

# Adjustment Disorders

Adjustment disorders are the first psychological disorders we discuss in this book, and they are among the mildest. Adjustment disorders are classified in the *DSM-5* within a category of Trauma- and Stressor-Related Disorders, which also includes traumatic stress disorders, such as acute stress disorder and posttraumatic stress disorder. Let's discuss adjustment disorders.

## What Is an Adjustment Disorder?

**4.6 Define the concept of an adjustment disorder and describe its key features.**

An **adjustment disorder** is a maladaptive reaction to a distressing life event or stressor that develops within 3 months of the onset of the stressor. The stressful event may be either a traumatic experience, such as a natural disaster or a motor vehicle accident with

## TRUTH or FICTION

If concentrating on your schoolwork has become difficult because of the breakup of a recent romance, you could be experiencing a psychological disorder.

☑ **TRUE** If you have trouble concentrating on your schoolwork following the breakup of a romantic relationship, you may have a mild type of psychological disorder called an adjustment disorder.

serious injury, or a nontraumatic life event, such as the breakup of a romantic relationship or starting college. According to the *DSM*, the maladaptive reaction is characterized by significant impairment in a social, occupational, or another important area of functioning, such as academic work, or by marked emotional distress exceeding what would normally be expected in coping with the stressor. Prevalence estimates of the rates of the disorder in the population vary widely. However, the disorder is common among people seeking outpatient mental health care, with estimates indicating that between 5% and 20% of people receiving outpatient mental health services present with a diagnosis of adjustment disorder (American Psychiatric Association, 2013). **T / F**

If your relationship with someone comes to an end (an identified stressor) and your grades are falling off because you are unable to keep your mind on schoolwork, you may fit the bill for an adjustment disorder. If Uncle Harry has been feeling down and pessimistic since his divorce from Aunt Jane, he too may be diagnosed with an adjustment disorder. So too might Cousin Billy if he has been cutting classes and spraying obscene words on the school walls or showing other signs of disturbed conduct.

**DIFFICULTY CONCENTRATING OR ADJUSTMENT DISORDER?** An adjustment disorder is a maladaptive reaction to a stressor that may take the form of impaired functioning at school or at work, such as having difficulty keeping one's mind on one's studies.

## Types of Adjustment Disorders

**4.7 Identify the specific types of adjustment disorders.**

The concept of *adjustment disorder* as a *mental disorder* highlights some of the difficulties in attempting to define what is normal and what is not. When something important goes wrong in life, we should feel bad about it. If there is a crisis in business, if we are victimized by a crime, or if there is a flood or a devastating hurricane, it is understandable that we might become anxious or depressed. There might, in fact, be something more seriously wrong with us if we do not react in a "maladaptive" way, at least temporarily. However, if our emotional reaction exceeds an expected response or our ability to function is impaired (e.g., avoidance of social interactions, difficulty getting out of bed, or falling behind in schoolwork), then a diagnosis of adjustment disorder may be indicated. Thus, if you are having trouble concentrating on your schoolwork following the breakup of a romantic relationship and your grades are slipping, you may have an adjustment disorder. There are several specific types of adjustment disorders that vary in terms of the associated maladaptive reaction (see Table 4.2).

### Table 4.2 Specific Types of Adjustment Disorders

| Disorder | Chief Features |
|---|---|
| Adjustment disorder with depressed mood | Sadness, crying, and feelings of hopelessness. |
| Adjustment disorder with anxiety | Worrying, nervousness, and jitters (or in children, fear of separation from primary attachment figures). |
| Adjustment disorder with mixed anxiety and depressed mood | A combination of anxiety and depression. |
| Adjustment disorder with disturbance of conduct | Violation of the rights of others or violation of social norms appropriate for one's age; sample behaviors include vandalism, truancy, fighting, reckless driving, and defaulting on legal obligations (e.g., stopping alimony payments). |
| Adjustment disorder with mixed disturbance of emotion and conduct | Both emotional disturbance, such as depression or anxiety, and conduct disturbance (as described previously). |
| Adjustment disorder unspecified | A residual category that applies to people not classifiable in one of the other subtypes. |

**SOURCE:** Based on the *DSM-5* (American Psychiatric Association, 2013).

For the diagnosis of an adjustment disorder to apply, the stress-related reaction must not be sufficient to meet the diagnostic criteria for other clinical syndromes, such as traumatic stress disorders (acute stress disorder or posttraumatic stress disorder), or anxiety or mood disorders (see Chapters 5 and 7). The maladaptive reaction may be resolved if the stressor is removed or the individual learns to cope with it. If the adjustment disorder lasts for more than 6 months after the stressor (or its consequences) has been removed, the diagnosis may be changed. Although the *DSM* system distinguishes adjustment disorder from other clinical syndromes, it may be difficult to identify distinguishing features of adjustment disorders that are distinct from other disorders, such as depression (Casey et al., 2006).

# Traumatic Stress Disorders

In adjustment disorders, people may have difficulty adjusting to stressful life events, such as business or marital problems, termination of a romantic relationship, or death of a loved one. However, with traumatic stress disorders, the focus shifts to how people cope with disasters and other traumatic experiences. Exposure to trauma can tax anyone's ability to adjust. For some people, traumatic experiences lead to traumatic stress disorders, which are patterns of abnormal behavior characterized by maladaptive reactions to traumatic stress involving marked personal distress, typically anxiety or depression, or significant impairment of daily functioning. Here, we focus on the two major types of traumatic stress disorders: *acute stress disorder* and *posttraumatic stress disorder*. Table 4.3 provides an overview of these disorders, and Table 4.4 identifies some of their common features.

## Acute Stress Disorder

**4.8 Describe the key features of acute stress disorder.**

In **acute stress disorder**, a person shows a maladaptive pattern of behavior for a period of 3 days to 1 month following exposure to a traumatic event. The traumatic event may involve exposure to either actual or threatened death, a serious accident, or a sexual violation. A person with acute stress disorder may have been directly exposed to the trauma, witnessed other people experiencing the trauma, or learned about a violent or accidental traumatic event experienced by a close friend or family member. First responders who are responsible for collecting human remains or police officers who regularly interview children about the details of child abuse may also develop acute stress disorder.

People with acute stress disorder may feel they are "in a daze" or that the world seems like a dreamlike or unreal place. Acute stress disorder may occur in response to battlefield trauma or exposure to natural or technological disasters. A soldier may have come through a horrific battle not remembering important features of the battle and feeling numb and detached from the environment. People who are injured or who nearly lose their lives in a hurricane may walk around "in a fog" for days or weeks afterward;

**Table 4.3 Overview of Traumatic Stress Disorders**

| Type of Disorder | Lifetime Prevalence in Population (Approx.) | Description | Associated Features |
|---|---|---|---|
| Acute stress disorder | Varies widely with the type of trauma | Acute maladaptive reaction in the days or weeks following a traumatic event | Features similar to those of PTSD, but limited to a period of 1 month following direct exposure to the trauma, witnessing other people exposed to the trauma, or learning about a trauma experienced by a close family member or friend |
| Posttraumatic stress disorder (PTSD) | About 9% | Prolonged maladaptive reaction to a traumatic event | Reexperiencing the traumatic event; avoidance of cues or stimuli associated with the trauma; general or emotional numbing, hyperarousal, emotional distress, and impaired functioning |

SOURCES: American Psychiatric Association, 2013; Conway et al., 2006; Kessler et al., 1995; Ozer & Weiss, 2004.

### Table 4.4 Common Features of Traumatic Stress Disorders

| | |
|---|---|
| **Avoidance behavior** | A person may avoid cues or situations associated with the trauma. A rape survivor may avoid traveling to the part of town where the attack occurred. A combat veteran may avoid reunions with soldiers or watching movies or feature stories about war or combat. |
| **Reexperiencing the trauma** | A person may reexperience the trauma in the form of intrusive memories, recurrent disturbing dreams, or momentary flashbacks of the battlefield or being pursued by an attacker. |
| **Emotional distress, negative thoughts, and impaired functioning** | A person may experience persistent negative thoughts and emotions, feel detached or estranged from others, or have difficulty functioning effectively. |
| **Heightened arousal** | A person may show signs of increased arousal, such as becoming hypervigilant (always on guard); have difficulty sleeping and concentrating; become irritable or have outbursts of anger; or show an exaggerated startle response, such as jumping at any sudden noise. |
| **Emotional numbing** | In PTSD, a person may feel "numb" inside and lose the ability to have loving feelings. |

be bothered by intrusive images, flashbacks, and dreams of the disaster; or relive the experience as though it were happening again.

The symptoms or features of acute stress disorder vary and may include disturbing, intrusive memories or dreams about the trauma; reexperiencing the trauma in the form of flashbacks; feelings of unreality or detachment (dissociation) from one's surroundings or from oneself; avoidance of external reminders of the trauma (such as places or people associated with the trauma); problems sleeping; and development of irritable or aggressive behavior or an exaggerated startle response to sudden noises.

Stronger or more persistent symptoms of dissociation around the time of the trauma are associated with a greater likelihood of later development of PTSD (Cardeña & Carlson, 2011). (Dissociation experiences are discussed further in Chapter 6 in the discussion of dissociative disorders.) Symptoms of acute stress disorder parallel the lingering effects of trauma associated with PTSD, as we'll see next.

## Posttraumatic Stress Disorder

**4.9 Describe the key features of posttraumatic stress disorder.**

Although acute stress disorder is limited to the several weeks following a traumatic event, **posttraumatic stress disorder (PTSD)** is a prolonged maladaptive reaction that lasts longer than 1 month after the traumatic experience. PTSD presents with a similar symptom profile as acute stress disorder, but may persist for months, years, or even decades and may not develop until many months or even years after the traumatic event.

Many people with acute stress disorder, but certainly not all, go on to develop PTSD (Kangas, Henry, & Bryant, 2005). Researchers find both types of traumatic stress disorders in soldiers exposed to combat and among rape survivors, victims of serious motor vehicle and other accidents, and people who have witnessed the destruction of their homes and communities by natural disasters (such as floods, earthquakes, or tornadoes) or technological disasters (such as railroad or airplane crashes). For Margaret, the trauma involved a horrific truck accident.

"I"

### "I Thought the World Was Coming to an End"

Margaret was a 54-year-old woman who lived with her husband, Travis, in a small village in upstate New York. Two winters earlier, in the middle of the night, a fuel truck had skidded down one of the icy inclines that led into the village center. Two blocks away, Margaret was shaken from her bed by the explosion ("I thought the world was coming to an end") when the truck slammed into the general store. The store and the apartments above were immediately engulfed in flames. The fire spread to the church next door. Margaret's first and most enduring visual impression was of shards of red and black that rose into the air in an eerie ballet. On their way down, they bathed the centuries-old tombstones in the church graveyard in hellish light. A dozen people died, mostly those who had lived above and behind the general store. The old caretaker of the church and the truck driver were lost as well.

Margaret shared the village's loss, took in the temporarily homeless, and did her share of what had to be done. Months later, after the general store had been leveled to a memorial park and the church was on the way toward being restored, Margaret started to feel that life was becoming strange, that the world outside was becoming a little unreal. She began to withdraw from her friends, and scenes of the night of the fire would fill her mind. At night she now and then dreamed the scene. Her physician prescribed a sleeping pill, which she discontinued because "I couldn't wake up out of the dream." Her physician turned to Valium, to help her get through the day. The pills helped for a while, but "I quit them because I needed more and more of the things and you can't take drugs forever, can you?"

Over the next year and a half, Margaret tried her best not to think about the disaster, but the intrusive recollections and the dreams came and went, apparently on their own. By the time Margaret sought help, her sleep had been seriously distressed for nearly two months and the recollections were as vivid as ever.

*From the Author's Files.*

Like acute stress disorder, the traumatic event associated with PTSD involves direct exposure to a trauma involving actual or threatened death, serious physical injury, or a sexual violation; witnessing other people experiencing trauma; or learning that a close friend or family member has experienced an accidental or violent traumatic event (death due to natural causes does not apply). In some cases, however, the affected person is exposed to the horrific consequences of traumatic events, such as first responders who collect human remains in the aftermath of an explosion or bombing.

**COUNSELING VETERANS WITH POSTTRAUMATIC STRESS DISORDER.** Storefront counseling centers have been established across the country to provide supportive services to combat veterans suffering from PTSD.

PTSD is found in many cultures. High rates of PTSD are found among earthquake and hurricane survivors in many countries, as well as among civilians who suffered the ravages of war, from the "killing fields" of the 1970s Pol Pot war in Cambodia to the Balkan conflicts of the 1990s to earthquake survivors of the 2010 earthquake in Haiti (Blanc et al., 2015) and to survivors of the wars in Iraq (e.g., Ali et al., 2012; Wagner, Schulz, & Knaevelsrud, 2011). Cultural factors may play a role in determining how people manage and cope with trauma and their vulnerability to traumatic stress reactions and the specific form the disorder might take.

PTSD is closely linked to combat experience (Polusny et al., 2011). Among U.S. soldiers who served in the Vietnam War, the prevalence of PTSD was pegged at about one in five (19%; Dohrenwend et al., 2006). Similarly, about 13% of combat veterans returning from the wars in Iraq and Afghanistan have developed PTSD (Kok et al., 2012). In total, as many as 300,000 American soldiers returning from the war zones in Iraq and Afghanistan show symptoms of posttraumatic stress disorder or depression (Miller, 2011). Veterans with PTSD often have other problem behaviors, including substance abuse, marital problems, poor work histories, and in some cases physical aggression against partners in intimate relationships (Taft et al., 2011).

Although exposure to combat or terrorist attacks may be the types of trauma the public most strongly links to PTSD (Pitman, 2006), the traumatic experiences most commonly associated with PTSD are serious motor vehicle accidents (Blanchard & Hickling, 2004). However, traumas involving terrorist attacks and other violent acts, particularly rape and assault, are more likely to lead to PTSD than other forms of trauma (Norris et al., 2003; North, Oliver, & Pandya, 2012). For example, investigators found that survivors of terrorist acts had double the rate of PTSD as survivors of motor vehicle accidents (Shalev & Freedman, 2005). **T / F**

## TRUTH *or* FICTION

Exposure to combat is the most common trauma linked to posttraumatic stress disorder (PTSD).

☑ **FALSE** Motor vehicle accidents are the most common trauma linked to PTSD.

Traumatic events are actually quite common, as more than two-thirds of people suffer a traumatic experience at some point in their lives (Galea, Nandi, & Vlahov, 2005). However, most people are resilient in the face of traumatic stress and recover without any professional help (Amstadter et al., 2009; Elwood et al., 2009). Fewer than one in 10 go on to develop PTSD (Delahanty, 2011a).

**TRAUMA.** Trauma associated with the development of PTSD may involve combat, acts of terrorism, or violent crimes, including crimes such as mass murders. However, the most frequent source of traumas linked to PTSD is serious motor vehicle accidents.

Investigators have identified certain factors that increase a person's risk of developing PTSD in the face of traumatic stressors (see Table 4.5). Some vulnerability factors relate to the traumatic event itself, such as the degree of exposure to the trauma, whereas others relate to the person or the social environment (Delahanty, 2011b; Gabert-Quillen, Fallon, & Delahanty, 2011; North, Oliver, & Pandya, 2012; Xue et al., 2015). The more direct the exposure to the trauma, the greater the person's likelihood of developing PTSD. Children in the Gulf Coast region of the United States who were more directly exposed to Hurricane Katrina suffered more PTSD symptoms, on average, than did those with less direct exposure (Weems et al., 2007). People who were in the buildings that were struck in the 9/11 terrorist attack were nearly twice as likely to develop PTSD as those who witnessed the attacks but were outside the buildings at the time (Bonanno et al., 2006). Of the more than 3,000 people who evacuated the Twin Towers when they were attacked, nearly all (96%) developed some PTSD symptoms, and about 15% developed diagnosable PTSD 2 to 3 years after the disaster ("More than 3,000," 2011).

Another factor relating to the likelihood of developing PTSD is gender. Although men more often have traumatic experiences, women are more likely to develop PTSD—about twice as likely (Parto, Evans, & Zonderman, 2011; Tolin & Foa, 2006). However, women's greater vulnerability to PTSD may have more to do with their greater incidence of sexual victimization and with their younger ages at the time of trauma than with gender itself (Cortina & Kubiak, 2006; Olff et al., 2007).

**BONNIE: POSTTRAUMATIC STRESS DISORDER**

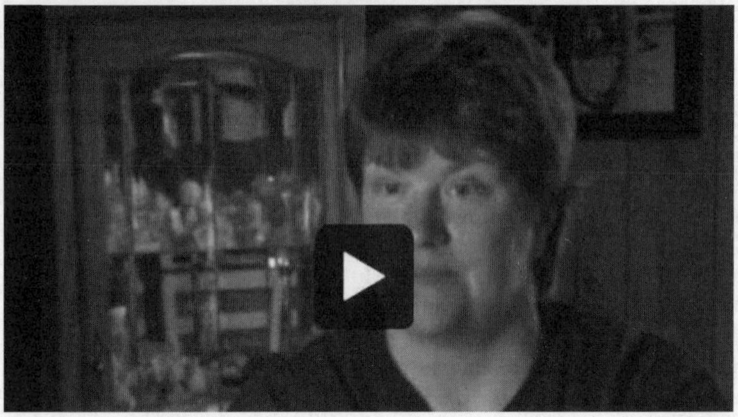

Other vulnerability factors relate to personal and biological factors. Genetic factors involved in regulating the body's response to stress appear to play a part in determining a person's susceptibility to PTSD in the wake of trauma (Afifi et al., 2010; Xie et al., 2009). Recently, investigators reported that the *amygdala*, a small structure in the brain's limbic system that triggers the body's fear response, was smaller in a group of combat veterans with PTSD than in combat veterans without PTSD (Morey et al., 2012). Although more research is needed, these intriguing findings point to a

## Table 4.5 Factors Predictive of PTSD in Trauma Survivors

| Factors Relating to the Event | Factors Relating to the Person or Social Environment |
|---|---|
| Degree of exposure to trauma | History of childhood sexual abuse |
| Severity of the trauma | Genetic predisposition or vulnerability |
| | Lack of social support |
| | Lack of active coping responses in dealing with the traumatic stressor |
| | Feeling shame |
| | Detachment or dissociation shortly following the trauma, or feeling numb |
| | Prior psychiatric history |

**SOURCES:** Afifi et al., 2010; Elwood et al., 2009; Goenjian et al., 2008; Koenen, Stellman, & Stellman, 2003; North, Oliver, & Pandya, 2012; Ozer et al., 2003; Xie et al., 2009.

possible biological factor that may account for why some people develop PTSD in the face of trauma whereas others don't.

Other factors linked to increased vulnerability to PTSD include a history of childhood sexual abuse, lack of social support, and limited coping skills (Lowe, Chan, & Rhodes, 2010; Mehta et al., 2011). Personality factors such as lower levels of self-efficacy and higher levels of hostility are also linked to increased risk of PTSD (Heinrichs et al., 2005). People who experience unusual symptoms during or immediately after the trauma, such as feeling that things are not real or feeling as though one were watching oneself in a movie as the events unfold, stand a greater risk of developing PTSD than do other trauma survivors (Ozer & Weiss, 2004). (As we noted, these unusual reactions are called *dissociative* experiences; see Chapter 6.) On the other hand, finding a sense of purpose or meaning in the traumatic experience—for example, believing that the war one is fighting is just—may bolster one's ability to cope with the stressful circumstances and reduce the risk of PTSD (Sutker et al., 1995).

Although the symptoms of PTSD often diminish within a few months, they may last for years, even decades (Marmar et al., 2015). Most people with PTSD continue to show some symptoms even several years after an initial evaluation (Morina et al., 2014).

## Theoretical Perspectives

**4.10 Describe theoretical understandings of PTSD.**

The major conceptual understanding of PTSD derives from the behavioral or learning perspective. Within a classical conditioning framework, traumatic experiences are unconditioned stimuli that become paired with neutral (conditioned) stimuli such as the sights, sounds, and even smells associated with the trauma—for example, the battlefield or the neighborhood in which a person has been raped or assaulted. Consequently, anxiety becomes a conditioned response that is elicited by exposure to trauma-related stimuli.

Cues that reactivate negative arousal or anxiety are associated with thoughts, memories, or even dream images of the trauma; with hearing someone talking about the trauma; or with visiting the scene of the trauma. Through operant conditioning, a person may learn to avoid any contact with trauma-related stimuli. Avoidance behaviors are operant responses that are negatively reinforced by relief from anxiety. Unfortunately, by avoiding trauma-related cues, a person also avoids opportunities to overcome the underlying fear. Extinction (gradual weakening or elimination) of conditioned anxiety can occur only when a person encounters the conditioned stimuli (the cues associated with the trauma) in the absence of any troubling unconditioned stimuli.

## A CLOSER Look

### CAN DISTURBING MEMORIES BE ERASED?

Might it be possible to erase troubling memories in people with PTSD—or at least to blunt their emotional effects? Although such suggestions may have seemed far-fetched only a few years ago, recent scientific discoveries offer such possibilities.

Researchers are exploring whether certain drugs can block disturbing memories or reduce the anxiety or fear associated with traumatic experiences (Andero et al., 2011). In one study, people with chronic PTSD were asked to recall and describe details of the PTSD-related traumatic event and were then given either a common blood pressure drug, *propranolol*, or a placebo (inactive drug; Brunet et al., 2007). A week later, they were asked to reactivate mental images associated with the traumatic event while the investigators monitored their physiological reactions, including their heart rate and level of muscle tension. Those who had received propranolol showed lower physiological activity compared to those who had received the placebo. It appears the drug may blunt the body's physiological response to traumatic memories. However, more evidence of the effectiveness of propranolol in treating PTSD is needed before it could be recommended for routine use (Steenen et al., 2016).

We also have other evidence that propranolol may reduce acquired fear responses. Investigators in the Netherlands first conditioned a fear response in 60 healthy college students by showing them a picture of a spider while they received a mild electric shock (Kindt, Soeter, & Vervliet, 2009). The students quickly acquired a conditioned fear response to the fearful

**MIGHT SLEEP DEPRIVATION PREVENT TRAUMATIC MEMORIES?** Laboratory research with rats suggests that sleep deprivation may prevent the consolidation of newly formed memories of trauma. If these findings hold up with humans, people who experience trauma may decide to forgo sleep for a day in order to block the formation of disturbing memories.

stimulus (the spider picture) presented without an accompanying shock. The next day, participants received either propranolol or a placebo just before their fear response was reactivated by again viewing the fearful stimulus. The following day, students who had received propranolol showed a weaker fear response while viewing the spider picture than did those who had received the placebo. The experimenters believe the drug interfered with the processing of the fearful memory when it was reactivated, which in turn dulled or erased the behavioral response to the feared stimulus. What's more, when students were then exposed to a second round of conditioning in which the spider picture was again paired with shock, the fear response returned in those who had received the placebo, but not in those given propranolol.

Now to understand these effects, we need to consider how the body responds to stress. When exposed to trauma or to a painful stimulus like electric shock, the body releases the stress hormone adrenaline (also called epinephrine). Adrenaline has many effects on the body, including activating the amygdala, the fear-processing center in the brain. Propranolol blocks adrenaline receptors in the amygdala, which may weaken memories of fearful stimuli.

In people with problems with anxiety or fear, the amygdala appears to be overreactive to cues relating to threat, fear, and rejection. Drugs like propranolol may modulate the brain's response to fearful stimuli, providing a way of lessening or even erasing fear responses and blocking their return. It's conceivable that one day soon, drugs like propranolol may become part of the therapeutic arsenal clinicians use to quell anxiety responses in people with PTSD or other problems with anxiety, such as anxiety disorders. Researchers don't yet know whether such drugs can permanently erase painful memories, or whether they should even try to erase these personal memories. But if these drugs work on networks in the brain that house emotional memories, they may be useful in rendering troubling memories less painful.

Might drugs be used to prevent PTSD symptoms in soldiers who have suffered traumatic injuries in battle? Investigators are exploring whether use of morphine, a powerful opiate drug used to treat pain in wounded soldiers, might also disrupt the process of forming painful memories that can lead to PTSD (Holbrook et al., 2010). Depending on the outcomes of more research, morphine may come to be used by battlefield medics not simply to treat pain in wounded soldiers but also to prevent the later emergence of PTSD symptoms. Other investigators find that in laboratory rats, sleep deprivation disrupts PTSD-like memories associated with trauma (Cohen, Kozlovsky, et al., 2012). It is conceivable that sleep deprivation may have a similar effect on people exposed to trauma.

On a related research front, scientists probing the molecular underpinnings of memory are attempting to isolate and tamp down specific brain circuits associated with particular memories. Recently, investigators reported progress in blocking recall of aversive stimuli in laboratory rats, revealing a potential pathway in the brain that may lead to ways of blocking disturbing memories in people with PTSD (Lauzon et al., 2012). Other investigators were able to erase a particular learned response in a sea snail using a chemical that interfered with biological processes needed to form long-term memories (Cai et al., 2011). The sea snail is used to explore how memory works at the biochemical level. Although it has a much simpler nervous system than more advanced animals, the underlying processes involved in how new memories are laid down in neural circuits in the snail are also involved in memory formation in the brains of mammals, including memories of learned responses.

What scientists learn in the laboratory may lead to breakthrough treatments for PTSD. There may come a day when it becomes possible to identify and effectively control specific brain circuits that house traumatic memories while leaving intact other memories of life experiences.

Scientific advances may someday enable medical care providers to block or dull certain traumatic memories of traumatic survivors. However, having the ability to control memories at the biochemical level raises important moral, legal, and ethical questions for both society and individuals themselves. We raise the following questions for reflection and debate:

- Who should decide whether memory-blocking drugs are used in the immediate aftermath of trauma? The battlefield commander or medic? The health care provider? Or the trauma survivor?
- What if the trauma survivor is rendered unconscious or unable to make this decision? Should the law require a prior medical proxy, or legal agreement stipulating who should make these decisions, and under what conditions?
- Is it right to obliterate a person's memories of a significant life event in the hopes that it may prevent later emotional suffering?
- Would you want to blot out traumatic memories? Or would you rather keep your memories and deal with the emotional consequences that may unfold?

# Treatment Approaches

**4.11 Describe treatment approaches to PTSD.**

Cognitive-behavioral therapy (CBT) has produced impressive results in the treatment of PTSD (e.g., Cloitre, 2014; Cusack et al., 2015; Ehlers et al., 2013, 2014; Haagen et al., 2015; Monson & Shnaider, 2014). The basic component of treatment is repeated exposure to cues and emotions associated with the trauma. A person gradually reexperiences the anxiety associated with the traumatic event in a safe setting, thereby allowing extinction of anxiety to take its course. The patient may be encouraged to repeatedly talk about the traumatic experience, reexperience the emotional aspects of the trauma in imagination, view related slides or films, or visit the scene of the traumatic event. Survivors of serious motor vehicle crashes who have avoided driving since the accident might be instructed to make short driving trips around the neighborhood (Gray & Acierno, 2002). They might also be asked to repeatedly describe the incident and the emotional reactions they experienced. For combat-related PTSD, exposure-based homework assignments might include visiting war memorials or viewing war movies. Evidence shows that supplementing exposure with cognitive restructuring (challenging and replacing distorted thoughts or beliefs with rational alternatives) can enhance treatment gains (Bryant et al., 2003). Exposure therapy is also of benefit in treating people with ASD (Bryant, Jackson, & Ames, 2008).

Therapists may use a more intense form of exposure called *prolonged exposure*, in which a person repeatedly reexperiences the traumatic event in imagination during treatment sessions or directly confronts situations linked to the trauma in real life without seeking to escape from the anxiety (Foa et al., 2013; Mørkved et al., 2014; Perrin, 2013; Schneier et al., 2012). For rape survivors, prolonged exposure may take the form of repeatedly recounting the horrifying ordeal within a supportive therapeutic setting.

Other techniques, such as training in meditation and self-relaxation as well as other stress-management skills, can be brought into play to help people cope with troubling symptoms of PTSD, such as heightened arousal and the desire to run away from trauma-related stimuli. (Two popular forms of meditation, transcendental meditation and mindfulness meditation, are discussed further in Chapter 6.) Anger management training may also be helpful, especially for combat veterans with PTSD with problems relating to anger. Treatment with antidepressant drugs, such as *sertraline* (Zoloft) or *paroxetine* (Paxil), may help reduce the anxiety components of PTSD (Schneier et al., 2012).

*Thinking Critically: Is EMDR a Fad or a Find?* discusses a controversial form of treatment for PTSD: eye movement desensitization and reprocessing. What is EMDR? Does it work? And if it does work, why does it work?

## THINKING CRITICALLY about abnormal psychology

### @ISSUE: IS EMDR A FAD OR A FIND?

A new and controversial technique has emerged in the treatment of PTSD—**eye movement desensitization and reprocessing (EMDR)** treatment (Shapiro, 2001). In EMDR, the client is asked to form a mental picture of an image associated with the trauma while the therapist rapidly moves a finger back and forth in front of the client's eyes for about 20 to 30 seconds. While holding the image in mind, the client is asked to move his or her eyes to follow the therapist's finger. The client then relates to the therapist the images, feelings, bodily sensations, and thoughts that were experienced during the procedure. The procedure is then repeated until the client becomes desensitized to the emotional impact of this disturbing material. Carefully controlled studies demonstrate the therapeutic benefits of using EMDR in treating PTSD (e.g., Chen, Zhang, et al., 2015; Cusack et al., 2015; Oren & Solomon, 2012; van den Berg et al., 2015). However, one recent study showed that exposure therapy is more effective than EMDR in treating veterans with PTSD (Haagen et al., 2015).

The controversy is not so much about whether EMDR works, but *why* it works and whether the key feature of the technique—the eye movements themselves—is a necessary factor in explaining its effects (Karatzias et al., 2011; Lohr, Lilienfeld, & Rosen, 2012; van den Hout et al., 2011). Researchers lack a compelling theoretical model explaining why rapid eye movements would relieve symptoms of PTSD, and this is an important factor in why some clinicians resist using it in practice (Cook, Biyanova, & Coyne, 2009). A related concern is whether the therapeutic effects of EMDR have anything to do with eye movements. Perhaps EMDR is effective because of the role of nonspecific factors it shares with other therapies, such as mobilizing a sense of hope and positive expectancies in clients. Another possibility is that EMDR works because it represents a form of exposure therapy, which is a well-established treatment for PTSD and other anxiety disorders (Taylor et al., 2003). The effective ingredient in EMDR may be repeated exposure to traumatic mental imagery, rather than the rapid eye movements. Although the controversy over EMDR is not yet settled, the technique may turn out to be nothing more than a novel way of conducting exposure-based therapy. Meanwhile, evidence shows that more traditional exposure therapy worked better and faster in reducing avoidance behaviors than did EMDR, at least among people who completed treatment (Taylor et al., 2003).

As the debate over EMDR continues, it is worthwhile to consider the famous dictum known as *Occam's razor*, or the principle of parsimony. In its most widely used form today, the principle holds that the simpler the explanation, the better. In other words, if researchers can explain the effects of EMDR on the basis of exposure, there is no need to posit more complex explanations involving effects of eye movements per se in desensitizing clients to traumatic images.

In thinking critically about the issue, answer the following questions:

- Why is it important to determine why a treatment works and not simply whether it works?
- What types of research studies would be needed to determine whether rapid eye movements are a critical component of the benefits of EMDR?

**EMDR.** A relatively new and controversial treatment for PTSD, EMDR involves the client holding an image of the traumatic experience in mind while moving his or her eyes to follow a sweeping motion of the therapist's finger.

# Summing Up

## Effects of Stress

### Stress and Health

**4.1 Evaluate the effects of stress on health.**

Stress has effects on the body's endocrine and immune systems. Although occasional stress may not impair our health, persistent or prolonged stress can eventually weaken the body's immune system, making us more vulnerable to disease.

### The General Adaptation Syndrome

**4.2 Identify and describe the stages of the general adaptation syndrome.**

The general adaptation syndrome, a term coined by Hans Selye, refers to the body's generalized pattern of response to persistent or enduring stress, which is characterized by three stages: (1) the alarm reaction, in which the body mobilizes its resources to confront a stressor; (2) the resistance stage, in which bodily arousal remains high but the body attempts to adapt to continued stressful demands; and (3) the exhaustion stage, in which bodily resources become dangerously depleted in the face of persistent and intense stress, at which point stress-related disorders, or diseases of adaptation, may develop.

### Stress and Life Changes

**4.3 Evaluate evidence of the relationship between life changes and psychological and physical health.**

Exposure to a high number of significant life changes is linked to increased risk of developing physical health problems. However, because this evidence is correlational, questions of cause and effect remain.

## Acculturative Stress: Making It in America

**4.4 Evaluate the role of acculturative stress in psychological adjustment.**

The pressures of acculturation, or acculturate stress, can affect mental and physical functioning. The relationships between level of acculturation and psychological adjustment are complex, but evidence supports the value of developing a bicultural pattern of acculturation, which involves efforts to adapt to the host culture while maintaining one's traditional ethnic or cultural identity.

## Psychological Factors That Moderate Stress

**4.5 Identify psychological factors that moderate the effects of stress.**

These factors include effective coping styles, self-efficacy expectancies, psychological hardiness, optimism, and social support.

# Adjustment Disorders

## What Is an Adjustment Disorder?

**4.6 Define the concept of an adjustment disorder and describe its key features.**

Adjustment disorders are maladaptive reactions to identified stressors. Adjustment disorders are characterized by emotional reactions that are greater than normally expected given the circumstances or by evidence of significant impairment in functioning. Impairment usually takes the form of problems at work or school or in social relationships or activities.

## Types of Adjustment Disorders

**4.7 Identify the specific types of adjustment disorders.**

The specific types of adjustment disorders are as follows: (1) adjustment disorder with anxiety, (2) adjustment disorder with mixed anxiety and depressed mood, (3) adjustment disorder with disturbance of conduct, (4) adjustment disorder with mixed disturbance of emotion and conduct, and (5) adjustment disorder unspecified.

# Traumatic Stress Disorders

## Acute Stress Disorder

**4.8 Describe the key features of acute stress disorder.**

Two types of traumatic stress disorders are acute stress disorder and posttraumatic stress disorder. Both involve maladaptive reactions to traumatic stressors. The features of acute stress disorder are similar to those of PTSD, but they are limited to the month following exposure to the traumatic event.

## Posttraumatic Stress Disorder

**4.9 Describe the key features of posttraumatic stress disorder.**

Posttraumatic stress disorder persists for months, years, or even decades after the traumatic experience and may not begin until months or years after the event. It is characterized by such features as avoidance behavior, reexperiencing the trauma, emotional distress, negative thoughts, impaired functioning, heightened arousal, and emotional numbing.

## Theoretical Perspectives

**4.10 Describe theoretical understandings of PTSD.**

Learning theory provides a framework for understanding the conditioning of fear to trauma-related stimuli and the role of negative reinforcement in maintaining avoidance behavior. However, other factors come into play in determining vulnerability to PTSD, including degree of exposure to the trauma and personal characteristics, such as a history of childhood sexual abuse and lack of social support.

## Treatment Approaches

**4.11 Describe treatment approaches to PTSD.**

The major treatment approach is cognitive-behavioral therapy, which focuses on repeated exposure to cues associated with the trauma and may be combined with cognitive restructuring and training in stress-management and anger-management techniques. Eye movement desensitization and reprocessing is a relatively new but controversial form of treatment for PTSD.

# Critical Thinking Questions

On the basis of your reading of this chapter, answer the following questions:

- Does evidence presented in the text seem to argue for or against a melting pot model of American culture? What evidence suggests that maintaining a strong ethnic identity may be beneficial?
- Examine your own behavior patterns. Do you believe your behaviors in everyday life enhance or impair your ability to handle stress? What changes can you make in your lifestyle to adopt healthier behaviors?
- Consider the level of stress in your own life. How might stress be affecting your psychological or physical health? In what ways can you reduce the level of stress in your life? What coping strategies can you learn to manage stress more effectively?

# Key Terms

- health psychologist, p. 136
- stress, p. 136
- stressor, p. 136
- endocrine system, p. 138
- hormones, p. 138
- immune system, p. 138
- general adaptation syndrome (GAS), p. 140
- alarm reaction, p. 140
- fight-or-flight reaction, p. 140
- resistance stage, p. 141
- exhaustion stage, p. 141
- acculturative stress, p. 143
- emotion-focused coping, p. 148
- problem-focused coping, p. 148
- self-efficacy expectancies, p. 149
- psychological hardiness, p. 149
- positive psychology, p. 150
- adjustment disorder, p. 151
- acute stress disorder, p. 153
- posttraumatic stress disorder (PTSD), p. 154
- eye movement desensitization and reprocessing (EMDR), p. 159

# Scoring Key for "Going through Changes" Questionnaire

Examining your responses can help you gauge how much life stress you have experienced during the past year. Although everyone experiences some degree of stress, if you checked many of these items—especially those at the higher stress levels—it is likely you have been experiencing a relatively high level of stress during the past year. Bear in mind, however, that the same level of stress may affect different people differently. Your ability to cope with stress depends on many factors, including your coping skills and the level of social support you have available. If you are experiencing a high level of stress, you may wish to examine the sources of stress in your life. Perhaps you can reduce the level of stress you experience or learn more effective ways of handling the sources of stress you can't avoid.

# Scoring Key for "Are You an Optimist?" Questionnaire

To compute your overall score, you first need to reverse your scores on items 1, 2, 5, 8, and 10. This means that a 1 becomes a 5, a 2 becomes a 4, a 3 remains the same, a 4 becomes a 2, and a 5 becomes a 1. Then, total your scores. Total scores can range from 10 (lowest optimism) to 50 (highest optimism). Scores around 30 indicate that you are neither strongly optimistic nor pessimistic. Although we do not have norms for this scale, you may consider scores in the 31 to 39 range as indicating a moderate level of optimism, whereas those in the 21 to 29 range indicate a moderate level of pessimism. Scores of 40 or above suggest higher levels of optimism, whereas those of 20 or below suggest higher levels of pessimism.

1 5
2 3
3 5
4 5
5 5
6 4
7 5
8 4
9 4
10 4

Chapter 5

# Anxiety Disorders and Obsessive-Compulsive and Related Disorders

## Learning Objectives

5.1 **Describe** the prominent physical, behavioral, and cognitive features of anxiety disorders.

5.2 **Evaluate** ethnic differences in rates of anxiety disorders.

5.3 **Describe** the key features of panic attacks.

5.4 **Describe** the leading conceptual model of panic disorder.

5.5 **Evaluate** methods used to treat panic disorder.

5.6 **Describe** the key features and specific types of phobic disorders.

5.7 **Explain** the role of learning, cognitive, and biological factors in the development of phobias.

**5.8** **Evaluate** methods used to treat phobic disorders.

**5.9** **Describe** generalized anxiety disorder and **identify** its key features.

**5.10** **Describe** the theoretical perspective on GAD and **identify** two major ways of treating it.

**5.11** **Describe** the key features of obsessive-compulsive disorder and ways of understanding and treating it.

**5.12** **Describe** the key features of body dysmorphic disorder.

**5.13** **Describe** the key features of hoarding disorder.

## TRUTH *or* FICTION

T☐ F☐ People who experience a panic attack often think they are having a heart attack. (p. 168)

T☐ F☐ Antidepressant drugs are used to treat people who are not depressed but are suffering from anxiety disorders. (p. 173)

T☐ F☐ People with phobias believe their fears to be well founded. (p. 177)

T☐ F☐ Some people are so fearful of leaving their homes that they are unable to venture outside even to mail a letter. (p. 179)

T☐ F☐ We may be genetically predisposed to acquire fears of objects that posed a danger to ancestral humans. (p. 184)

T☐ F☐ If there is a spider in the room, the spider phobic in the group will likely be the first to notice it and point it out. (p. 184)

T☐ F☐ Therapists have used virtual reality to help people overcome phobias. (p. 188)

T☐ F☐ Obsessional thinking helps relieve anxiety. (p. 198)

T☐ F☐ Having skin blemishes leads some people to consider suicide. (p. 200)

**CHAPTER INTRODUCTION: ANXIETY DISORDERS AND OBSESSIVE-COMPULSIVE AND RELATED DISORDERS**

"I"

**"I Felt Like I Was Going to Die Right Then and There"**

I never experienced anything like this before. It happened while I was sitting in the car at a traffic light. I felt my heart beating furiously fast, like it was just going to explode. It just happened, for no reason. I started breathing really fast but couldn't get enough air. It was like I was suffocating and the car was closing in around me. I felt like I was going to die right then and there. I was trembling and sweating heavily. I thought I was having a heart attack. I felt this incredible urge to escape, to just get out of the car and get away. I somehow managed to pull the car over to the side of the road but just sat there waiting for the feelings to pass. I told myself if I was going to die, then I was going to die. I didn't know whether I'd survive long enough to get help. Somehow—I can't say how—it just passed and I sat there a long time, wondering what had just happened to me. Just as suddenly as the panic overcame me, it was gone. My breathing slowed down and my heart stopped thumping in my chest. I was alive. I was not going to die. Not until the next time, anyway.

*"The Case of Michael," from the Author's Files*

What is it like to have a panic attack? People tend to use the word *panic* loosely, as when they say, "I panicked when I couldn't find my keys." Clients in therapy often speak of having panic attacks, although what they describe often falls in a milder spectrum of anxiety reactions. During a true panic attack, like the one Michael describes, the level of anxiety rises to the point of sheer terror. Unless you have suffered one, it is difficult to appreciate just how intense panic attacks can be. People who have panic attacks describe them as the most frightening experiences of their lives. The occurrence of panic attacks is the cardinal feature of a severe type of anxiety disorder called *panic disorder.*

There is much to be anxious about—our health, social relationships, examinations, careers, international relations, and the condition of the environment are but a few sources of possible concern. It is normal, even adaptive, to be somewhat anxious about these aspects of life.

**Anxiety** is a generalized state of apprehension or foreboding. Anxiety is useful: It prompts us to seek regular medical checkups or motivates us to study for tests. Anxiety is a normal response to threats, but it becomes abnormal when it is out of proportion to the reality of a threat or when it seems to simply come out of the blue—that is, when it is not in response to life events.

In Michael's case, panic attacks began spontaneously, without any warning or trigger. This kind of maladaptive anxiety reaction, which can cause significant emotional distress or impair a person's ability to function, is labeled an **anxiety disorder**. Anxiety, the common thread that connects the various types of anxiety disorders, can be experienced in different ways, from the intense fear associated with a panic attack to the generalized sense of foreboding or worry in generalized anxiety disorder. Anxiety disorders are very common, affecting nearly one in five adults in the United States, which works out to more than 40 million people (Torpy, Burke, & Golub, 2011).

# Overview of Anxiety Disorders

Anxiety disorders, along with dissociative disorders and somatic symptom and related disorders (see Chapter 6), were classified as neuroses throughout most of the 19th century. The term *neurosis* derives from roots that mean "an abnormal or diseased condition of the nervous system." The Scottish physician William Cullen coined the term *neurosis* in the 18th century. As the derivation implies, it was assumed that neurosis had biological origins. It was seen as an affliction of the nervous system.

At the beginning of the 20th century, Cullen's organic assumptions were largely replaced by Sigmund Freud's psychodynamic views. Freud maintained that neurotic behavior stems from the threatened emergence of unacceptable, anxiety-evoking ideas into conscious awareness. According to Freud, disorders involving anxiety (as well as the dissociative and somatic symptom disorders discussed in Chapter 6) represent ways in which the ego attempts to defend itself against anxiety. Freud's views on the origins of these problems united them under the general category of *neuroses*. Freud's concepts were so widely accepted in the early 1900s that they formed the basis for the classification systems found in the first two editions of the *Diagnostic and Statistical Manual of Mental Disorders (DSM)*.

## Features of Anxiety Disorders

**5.1 Describe the prominent physical, behavioral, and cognitive features of anxiety disorders.**

Anxiety is characterized by a wide range of symptoms that cut across physical, behavioral, and cognitive domains:

**a)** *Physical features* may include jumpiness, jitteriness, trembling or shaking, tightness in the pit of the stomach or chest, heavy perspiration, sweaty palms, light-headedness or faintness, dryness in the mouth or throat, shortness of breath, heart pounding or racing, cold fingers or limbs, and upset stomach or nausea, among other physical symptoms.

**b)** *Behavioral features* may include avoidance behavior, clinging or dependent behavior, and agitated behavior.

**c)** *Cognitive features* may include worry, a nagging sense of dread or apprehension about the future, preoccupation with or keen awareness of bodily sensations, fear of losing control, thinking the same disturbing thoughts over and over, jumbled or confused thoughts, difficulty concentrating or focusing one's thoughts, and thinking that things are getting out of hand.

Although people with anxiety disorders don't necessarily experience all of these features, it is easy to see why anxiety is so distressing. The *DSM* recognizes the following specific types of anxiety disorders, which we discuss in this chapter: panic disorder, phobic disorders, and generalized anxiety disorder. Certain disorders that were previously classified in the category of anxiety disorders (obsessive-compulsive disorder, acute stress disorder, and posttraumatic stress disorder) are now placed in other diagnostic categories (Stein et al., 2014).

*Obsessive-compulsive disorder* (OCD) is classified in the *DSM-5* within a new diagnostic category called *Obsessive-Compulsive and Related Disorders*, which we discuss later in this chapter. Acute stress disorder and posttraumatic stress disorder, which we discussed in Chapter 4, are classified in another new diagnostic category, *Trauma- and Stressor-Related Disorders*.

Table 5.1 provides an overview of the major types of anxiety disorders. Anxiety disorders are quite common and are not mutually exclusive; people frequently meet diagnostic criteria for more than one of them. Moreover, many people with anxiety disorders also have other types of disorders, especially mood disorders. A recent estimate indicates that nearly 4% of full-time workers in the United States—some 4.3 million people—currently suffer from a definable anxiety disorder or anxiety-related disorder, such as OCD or posttraumatic stress disorder (PTSD; Jacob, 2015).

Since 1980, the *DSM* has not included a category termed *neuroses*. The *DSM* today is based on similarities in observable behavior and distinctive features rather than on causal assumptions, although many clinicians continue to use the terms *neurosis* and *neurotic* in the manner in which Freud described them. Some clinicians use the term *neuroses* to group milder behavioral problems in which people maintain relatively good contact with reality. *Psychoses*, such as schizophrenia, are typified by loss of touch with reality and bizarre behavior, beliefs, and hallucinations. Anxiety is not limited to the diagnostic categories traditionally termed *neuroses*. People with adjustment problems, depression, and psychotic disorders may also encounter problems with anxiety.

We will examine the major types of anxiety disorders in terms of their features or symptoms, their causes, and the ways of treating them, beginning with panic

**Table 5.1** Overview of Major Types of Anxiety Disorders

| Type of Disorder | Approximate Lifetime Prevalence in Population (%) | Description | Associated Features |
|---|---|---|---|
| **Panic Disorder** | 5.1% | Repeated panic attacks (episodes of sheer terror accompanied by strong physiological symptoms, thoughts of imminent danger or impending doom, and an urge to escape) | Fears of recurring attacks may prompt avoidance of situations associated with the attacks or in which help might not be available; attacks begin unexpectedly but may become associated with certain cues or specific situations; may be accompanied by agoraphobia, or general avoidance of public situations |
| **Generalized Anxiety Disorder** | 5.7% | Persistent anxiety that is not limited to particular situations | Excessive worrying; heightened states of bodily arousal, tenseness, being on edge |
| **Specific Phobia** | 12.5% | Excessive fears of particular objects or situations | Avoidance of a phobic stimulus or situation; examples include acrophobia, claustrophobia, and fears of blood, small animals, or insects |
| **Social Anxiety Disorder (Social Phobia)** | 12.1% | Excessive fear of social interactions | Characterized by an underlying fear of rejection, humiliation, or embarrassment in social situations |
| **Agoraphobia** | About 1.4% to 2% | Fear and avoidance of open, public places | May occur secondarily to losses of supportive others to death, separation, or divorce |

SOURCES: Prevalence rates derived from American Psychiatric Association, 2013; Conway et al., 2006; Grant et al., 2005; Grant, Hasin, Stinson, et al., 2006; Kessler, Berglund, et al., 2005; Stein & Sareen, 2015.

disorder—but first, we will consider differences in rates of anxiety disorders among different ethnic groups.

# Ethnic Differences in Anxiety Disorders

**5.2 Evaluate ethnic differences in rates of anxiety disorders.**

Although anxiety disorders have been the subject of extensive study, little attention has been directed toward examining ethnic differences in the prevalence of these disorders. Are anxiety disorders more common in certain racial or ethnic groups? We might think that stressors frequently encountered by African Americans in our society, such as racism and economic hardship, might contribute to a higher rate of anxiety disorders in this population group. On the other hand, an alternative argument is that African Americans, by dint of having to cope with these hardships in early life, develop resiliency in the face of stress that shields them from anxiety disorders. Evidence from large epidemiological surveys lends support to this alternative argument.

A large national survey, the National Comorbidity Survey Replication (NCS-R), showed that African Americans (or non-Hispanic Blacks) and Latinos had lower rates of social anxiety disorder and generalized anxiety disorder than did European Americans (or non-Hispanic Whites; Breslau et al., 2006). We also have evidence from another large national survey that shows higher lifetime rates of panic disorder in European Americans than in Latinos, African Americans, or Asian Americans (Grant et al., 2006b).

We should also recognize that anxiety disorders are hardly unique to our culture. Panic disorder, for example, is known to occur in many countries, perhaps even universally. However, the specific features of panic attacks, such as shortness of breath or fear of dying, may vary from culture to culture. Some culture-bound syndromes have features similar to panic attacks, such as *ataque de nervios* (see Table 3.2 in Chapter 3).

# Panic Disorder

**Panic disorder** is characterized by repeated, unexpected *panic attacks.* These attacks are intense anxiety reactions that are accompanied by physical symptoms such as a pounding heart; rapid respiration, shortness of breath, or difficulty breathing; heavy perspiration; and weakness or dizziness (see Table 5.2).

**Table 5.2 Key Features of Panic Attacks**

Panic attacks are episodes of intense fear or discomfort that develop suddenly and reach a peak within a few minutes. They are characterized by such features as the following:

- Pounding heart, tachycardia (rapid heart rate), or palpitations
- Sweating, trembling, or shaking
- Experience of choking or smothering sensations or shortness of breath
- Fear of either losing control, dying, or going crazy
- Pain or discomfort in the chest
- Tingling or numbing sensations
- Nausea or stomach distress
- Dizziness, light-headedness, faintness, or unsteadiness
- Feelings of being detached from oneself, as if observing oneself from a distance, or sense of unreality or strangeness about one's surroundings
- Hot flashes or chills

## Features of Panic Attacks

**5.3 Describe the key features of panic attacks.**

There is a stronger bodily component to panic attacks than to other forms of anxiety. The attacks are accompanied by feelings of sheer terror and a sense of imminent danger or impending doom and by an urge to escape the situation. They are usually accompanied by thoughts of losing control, "going crazy," or dying.

During panic attacks, people tend to be keenly aware of changes in their heart rates and may think they are having a heart attack, even though there is really nothing wrong with their hearts. However, because symptoms of panic attacks can mimic those of heart attacks or even severe allergic reactions, a thorough medical evaluation should be performed. **T / F**

### TRUTH or FICTION

People who experience a panic attack often think they are having a heart attack.

☑ TRUE People experiencing a panic attack may believe they are having a heart attack, even though their hearts are perfectly healthy.

As in the case of Michael, panic attacks generally begin suddenly and spontaneously, without any warning or clear triggering event. The attack builds to a peak of intensity within 10 to 15 minutes. Attacks usually last for minutes, but can last for hours. They tend to produce a strong urge to escape the situation in which they occur. For a diagnosis of panic disorder to be made, there must be the presence of recurrent panic attacks that begin unexpectedly—attacks that are not triggered by specific objects or situations. These attacks seem to come out of the blue. However, subtle physical symptoms may precede an unexpected panic attack in the hour prior to an attack, even though the person experiencing such symptoms may not be aware of them (Meuret et al., 2011).

The first panic attacks occur spontaneously or unexpectedly, but over time they may become associated with certain situations or cues, such as entering a crowded department store or boarding a train or airplane. A person may associate these situations with panic attacks in the past or may perceive them as difficult to escape from in the event of another attack.

**AGORAPHOBIA.** People with agoraphobia fear venturing into open or crowded places. In extreme cases, they may become literally housebound out of fear of venturing away from the security of their home.

People often describe panic attacks as the worst experiences of their lives. Their coping abilities are overwhelmed. They may feel they must flee. If flight seems useless, they may "freeze." There is a tendency to cling to others for help or support. Some people with panic attacks fear going out alone. Recurring panic attacks may become so difficult to cope with that panic sufferers become suicidal. People with panic disorder may avoid activities related to their attacks, such as exercise or venturing into places where attacks may occur or they fear they may occur, or where they may be cut off from their usual supports. Consequently, panic disorder can lead to **agoraphobia**—an excessive fear of being in public places, where

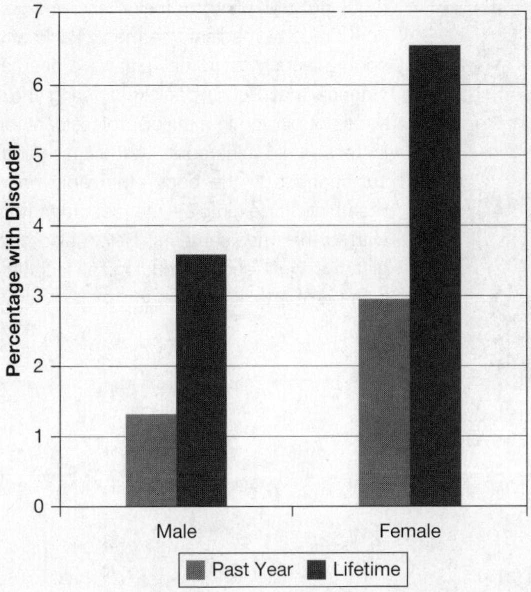


**Figure 5.1** Prevalence of panic disorder by gender.

Panic disorder affects about two times as many women as men.

**SOURCE:** Grant, Hasin, Stinson, et al., 2006.

escape may be difficult or help unavailable (Berle et al., 2008). That said, panic disorder *without* accompanying agoraphobia is much more common than panic disorder *with* agoraphobia (Grant et al., 2006b).

Not all of the features listed in Table 5.2 need to be present during a panic attack, nor are all panic attacks signs of panic disorder; about 10% of otherwise healthy people may experience an isolated attack in a given year (USDHHS, 1999). For a diagnosis of panic disorder to be made, a person must have experienced repeated, unexpected panic attacks, and at least one of the attacks must have been followed by a period of at least one month that included either or both of the following features (based on American Psychiatric Association, 2013):

**a)** Persistent fear of subsequent attacks or of the feared consequences of an attack, such as losing control, having a heart attack, or going crazy

**b)** Significant maladaptive change in behavior, such as limiting activities or refusing to leave the house or venture into public for fear of having another attack

According to a recent national, representative survey, 5.1% of the general U.S. population develops panic disorder at some point in their lives (Grant, Hasin, Stinson, et al., 2006). Panic disorder usually begins between late adolescence and the mid-30s and occurs about twice as often among women as among men (see Figure 5.1). This gender difference fits the general pattern showing that anxiety disorders are more common among women than men (McLean & Anderson, 2009; Seedat et al., 2009).

## Panic on the Golf Course

Athletes are accustomed to playing through aches and pains and even injuries, but this was different. At a professional golf tournament in 2012, rookie golfer Charlie Beljan played through a panic attack that was so severe he feared he was having a heart attack (Crouse & Pennington, 2012). He spent that night in the hospital undergoing medical tests, hooked up to medical equipment while still wearing his golf shoes. Fortunately, the tests revealed no signs of heart problems. All the more surprising, he went on to play another 36 rounds, winning the tournament: his first professional victory. The panic attack on the golf course was not his first; that happened a few months earlier, while he was on an airplane,

**PANIC ON THE LINKS.** Professional golfer Charlie Beljan played through a panic attack during a tournament that he went on to win.

requiring the pilot to make an emergency landing so he could receive medical treatment. Panic attacks typically occur spontaneously, so it may just have been an unfortunate coincidence that Beljan panicked during the tournament, or the stress of playing in a major professional tournament may have increased his vulnerability to the cascading set of neurochemical changes in the body—the rapid heartbeat and difficulty breathing, for example—that accompany panic attacks. Along with further medical tests, Beljan also consulted a psychologist. As we'll see, psychological techniques can help cope with panic attacks.

## Causal Factors

### 5.4 Describe the leading conceptual model of panic disorder.

The prevailing view of panic disorder is that panic attacks involve a combination of cognitive and biological factors, of misattributions (misperceptions of underlying causes of changes in physical sensations) on the one hand and physiological reactions on the other. Figure 5.2 presents a schematic representation of the cognitive-biological model of panic disorder. Like Michael, who feared his physical symptoms were the first signs of a heart attack, panic-prone individuals tend to misattribute minor changes in internal bodily sensations to "underlying dire causes." For example, they may believe that sensations of momentary dizziness, light-headedness, or heart palpitations are signs of an impending heart attack, loss of control, or going crazy.

As shown in Figure 5.2, the perception of bodily sensations as dire threats triggers anxiety, which is accompanied by activation of the sympathetic nervous system. Under control of the sympathetic nervous system, the adrenal glands release the stress hormones epinephrine (adrenaline) and norepinephrine (noradrenaline). These hormones intensify physical sensations by inducing accelerated heart rate, rapid breathing, and sweating. These changes in bodily sensations become misinterpreted in turn as evidence of an impending panic attack or, worse, as a catastrophe in the making ("My God, I'm having a heart attack!"). Catastrophic misattributions of bodily sensations reinforce perceptions of threat, which intensifies anxiety, leading to more anxiety-related bodily symptoms and yet more catastrophic misinterpretations in a vicious cycle that can quickly spiral into a full-fledged panic attack. In summary, the prevailing view of panic disorder reflects a combination of cognitive and biological factors, of misattributions (catastrophic misinterpretations of bodily sensations) on the one hand and physiological reactions and physical sensations on the other (Teachman, Marker, & Clerkin, 2010).

The changes in bodily sensations that trigger a panic attack may result from many factors, such as unrecognized *hyperventilation* (rapid breathing), exertion, changes in temperature, or reactions to certain drugs or medications, or they may be fleeting, normally occurring changes in bodily states that typically go unnoticed. However, panic-prone individuals may misattribute these bodily cues to dire causes, setting in motion a vicious cycle that can bring on a full-fledged attack.

Why are some people more prone to developing panic disorder? Here again, a combination of biological and cognitive factors come into play.

**BIOLOGICAL FACTORS** Evidence indicates that genetic factors contribute to proneness or vulnerability to panic disorder (e.g., Spatola et al., 2011). Genes may create a predisposition or likelihood, but not a certainty, that panic disorder or other psychological disorders will

**Figure 5.2** Cognitive-biological model of panic disorder.

In panic-prone people, perceptions of threat from internal or external cues lead to feelings of worry or fear, which are accompanied by changes in bodily sensations (e.g., heart racing or palpitations). Exaggerated, catastrophic interpretations of these sensations intensify perceptions of threat, resulting in yet more anxiety, more changes in bodily sensations, and so on in a vicious cycle that can culminate in a full-blown panic attack. Anxiety sensitivity increases the likelihood that people will overreact to bodily cues or symptoms of anxiety. Panic attacks may prompt avoidance of situations in which attacks have occurred or in which help might not be available.

**SOURCE:** Adapted from Clark, 1986, and other sources.

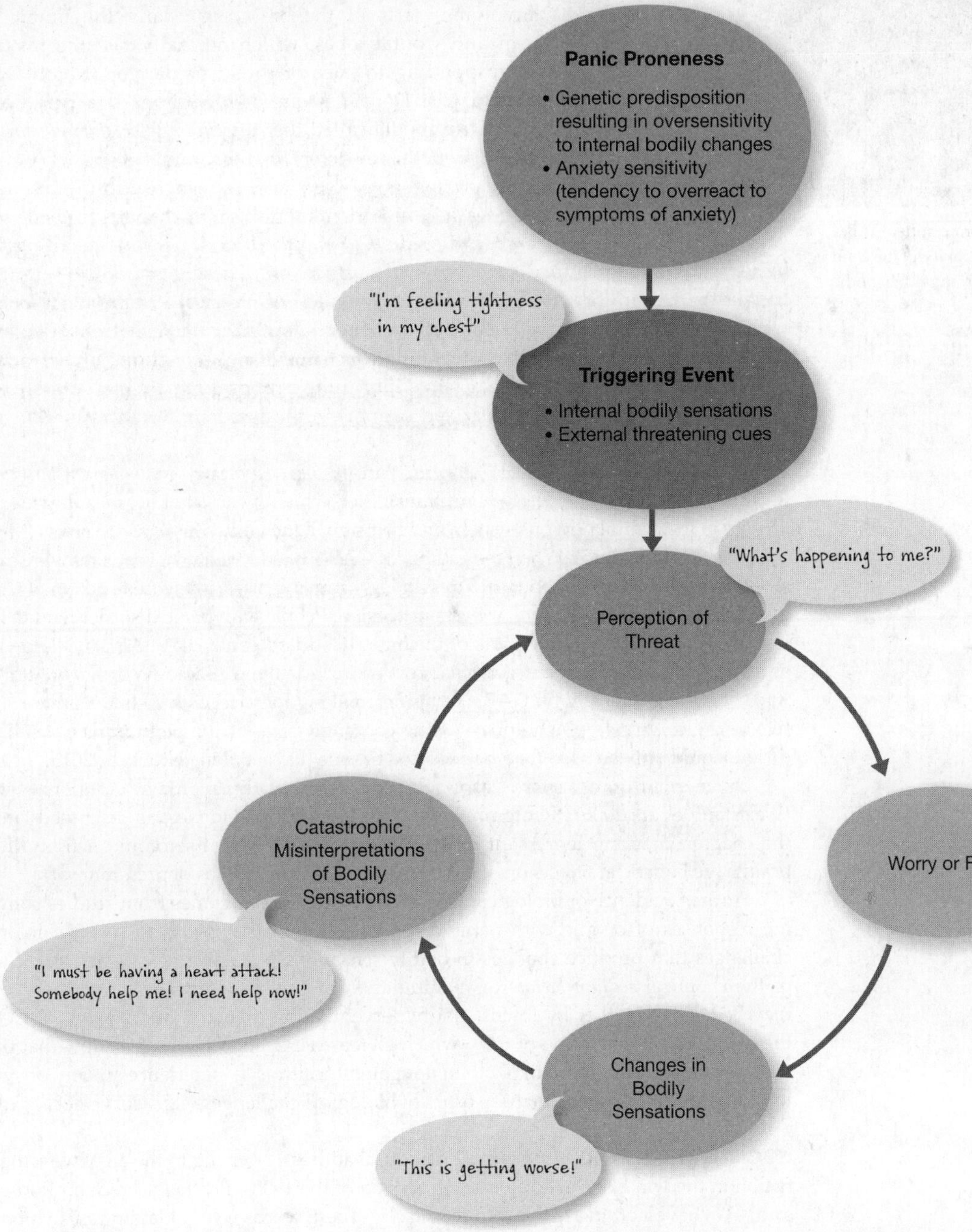

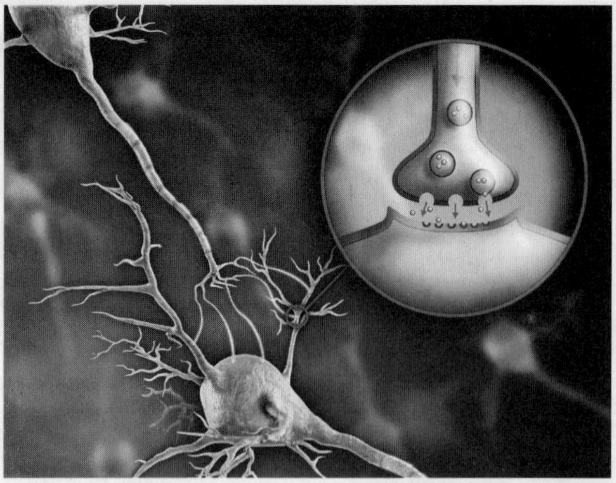

**GABA.** The neurotransmitter GABA helps curb excess activity in the central nervous system, turning down bodily states of arousal. Low levels of GABA activity may play a role in some cases of anxiety disorders.

develop. Other factors play important roles, such as thinking patterns (Casey, Oei, & Newcombe, 2004). For example, people with panic disorder may misinterpret bodily sensations as signs of impending catastrophe. Panic-prone people also tend to be especially sensitive to their own physical sensations, such as heart palpitations.

The biological underpinnings of panic attacks may include an unusually sensitive internal alarm system involving parts of the brain, especially the limbic system and frontal lobes, which normally become involved in responding to cues of threat or danger (Katon, 2006). Psychiatrist Donald Klein (1994) proposed a variation of the alarm model called the *suffocation false alarm theory*. He postulated that a defect in the brain's respiratory alarm system triggers a false alarm in response to minor cues of suffocation. In Klein's model, small changes in the level of carbon dioxide ($CO_2$) in the blood, perhaps resulting from hyperventilation, produce sensations of suffocation. These respiratory sensations trigger the respiratory alarm, leading to a cascade of physical symptoms associated with the classic panic attack: shortness of breath, smothering sensations, dizziness, faintness, increased heart rate or palpitations, trembling, sensations of hot or cold flashes, and feelings of nausea. Klein's intriguing proposal remains to be more fully tested and has received at best mixed support in the research literature to date (e.g., Vickers & McNally, 2005).

Let's also consider the role of neurotransmitters, especially *gamma-aminobutyricacid* (GABA). GABA is an *inhibitory* neurotransmitter, which means that it tones down excess activity in the central nervous system and helps quell the body's response to stress (Müller, Çalışkan, & Stork, 2015). When the activity of GABA is inadequate, neurons may fire excessively, possibly bringing about seizures. In less dramatic cases, inadequate action of GABA may heighten states of anxiety or nervous tension. People with panic disorder tend to have low levels of GABA in some parts of the brain (Goddard et al., 2001). Also, we know that antianxiety drugs called *benzodiazepines*, which include the well-known drugs Valium and Xanax, work specifically on GABA receptors, making these receiving stations more sensitive to the chemical, which enhances the calming effects of the neurotransmitter. These drugs should only be used for a brief period of time (Fava, Balon, & Rickels, 2015).

Other neurotransmitters, especially serotonin, help regulate emotional states (Weisstaub et al., 2006). Serotonin's role is supported by evidence, as discussed later in the chapter, that antidepressant drugs that specifically target serotonin activity in the brain have beneficial effects on some forms of anxiety as well as depression.

Further evidence of biological factors in panic disorder comes from studies comparing responses of people with panic disorder and control subjects to certain biological challenges that produce changes in bodily sensations (e.g., dizziness), such as infusion of the chemical *sodium lactate* or manipulation of $CO_2$ levels in the blood. $CO_2$ levels may be changed either by intentional hyperventilation (which reduces levels of $CO_2$ in the blood) or by inhalation of $CO_2$ (which increases $CO_2$ levels). Studies show that panic disorder patients are more likely than nonpatient controls to experience anxiety or symptoms of panic in response to these types of biological challenges (e.g., Coryell et al., 2006).

**COGNITIVE FACTORS** In his 1932 inaugural address, referring to the anxiety facing the nation in the wake of the economic depression of the 1930s, President Franklin Roosevelt said, "We have nothing to fear but fear itself." These words echo today in research on the role of anxiety sensitivity (AS) in the development of anxiety disorders, including panic disorder, phobic disorders, agoraphobia, and generalized anxiety disorder (e.g., Busscher et al., 2013; Robinson & Freeston, 2014; Sandin, Sánchez-Arribas, Chorot, & Valiente, 2015).

Anxiety sensitivity, or *fear of fear itself*, involves fear of one's emotions and bodily sensations getting out of control. When people with high levels of AS experience bodily signs of anxiety, such as a racing heart or shortness of breath, they perceive these symptoms as signs of dire consequences or even an impending catastrophe, such as a heart attack. These catastrophic thoughts intensify their anxiety reactions, making them vulnerable to a vicious cycle of anxiety building on itself, which can lead to a full-blown panic attack. People with high levels of AS also tend to avoid situations in which they have experienced anxiety in the past, a pattern we often see in people who have panic disorder accompanied by agoraphobia (Wilson & Hayward, 2006).

**FEAR OF FEAR.** In his first presidential inaugural address, Franklin Roosevelt recognized that the greatest fear Americans faced during the Great Depression was fear of fear itself.

Anxiety sensitivity is influenced by genetic factors (Zavos, Gregory, & Eley, 2012). But environmental factors also play a role, including factors relating to ethnicity. A study of high school students showed that Asian and Hispanic students reported higher levels of anxiety sensitivity on average than did Caucasian adolescents (Weems et al., 2002). However, anxiety sensitivity was less strongly connected to panic attacks in the Asian and Hispanic groups than in the Caucasian group. Other investigators have found higher levels of anxiety sensitivity among American Indian and Alaska Native college students than among Caucasian college students (Zvolensky & Eifert, 2001). These findings remind us of the need to consider ethnic differences when exploring the roots of abnormal behavior.

We shouldn't overlook the role that cognitive factors may play in determining oversensitivity of panic-prone people to biological challenges, such as manipulation of $CO_2$ levels in the blood. These challenges produce intense physical sensations that panic-prone people may misinterpret as signs of an impending heart attack or loss of control. Perhaps these misinterpretations—not any underlying biological sensitivities per se—are responsible for inducing the spiraling anxiety that can quickly lead to a panic attack.

The fact that panic attacks often seem to come out of the blue seems to support the belief that the attacks are biologically triggered. However, the cues that set off many panic attacks may be internal, involving changes in bodily sensations, rather than external stimuli. Changes in internal (physical) cues, combined with catastrophic thinking, may lead to a spiraling of anxiety that culminates in a full-blown panic attack.

## Treatment Approaches

**5.5 Evaluate methods used to treat panic disorder.**

The most widely used forms of treatment for panic disorder are drug therapy and cognitive-behavioral therapy (CBT). Drugs commonly used to treat depression, called *antidepressant* drugs, also have *antianxiety* and *antipanic* effects (Baldwin et al., 2014). The term *antidepressants* may be something of a misnomer because these drugs have broader effects than just treating depression. Antidepressants help counter anxiety by normalizing activity of neurotransmitters in the brain. Antidepressants used for treating panic disorder include *paroxetine* (Paxil) and *escitalopram* (Lexapro). However, troublesome side effects may occur, such as sleep problems, drowsiness, nausea, and dry mouth, leading many patients to prematurely stop using the drugs. The high-potency antianxiety drug *alprazolam* (Xanax), a type of benzodiazepine, can also be helpful in treating panic disorder, as well as social anxiety disorder, and generalized anxiety disorder. **T / F**

### TRUTH or FICTION

Antidepressant drugs can be used to treat people who are not depressed but are suffering from anxiety disorders.

☑ **TRUE** Antidepressant drugs also have antianxiety effects and are used to treat anxiety disorders, such as panic disorder and social anxiety disorder, as well as obsessive-compulsive disorder.

A potential problem with drug therapy is that patients may attribute clinical improvement to the drugs and not to their own resources. Also note that psychiatric drugs help control symptoms but do not produce a cure and that relapses

## Table 5.3 Elements of Cognitive-Behavioral Programs for Treatment of Panic Disorder

| | |
|---|---|
| **Self-Monitoring** | Keeping a log of panic attacks to help determine situational stimuli that might trigger them. |
| **Exposure** | A program of gradual exposure to situations in which panic attacks have occurred. During exposure trials, a person engages in self-relaxation and rational self-talk to prevent anxiety from spiraling out of control. In some programs, participants learn to tolerate changes in bodily sensations associated with panic attacks by experiencing these sensations within the controlled setting of the treatment clinic. A person may be spun around in a chair to induce feelings of dizziness, learning in the process that such sensations are not dangerous or signs of imminent harm. |
| **Development of Coping Responses** | Developing coping skills to interrupt the vicious cycle in which overreactions to anxiety cues or cardiovascular sensations culminate in panic attacks. Behavioral methods focus on deep, regular breathing and relaxation training. Cognitive methods focus on modifying catastrophic misinterpretations of bodily sensations. Breathing retraining may be used to help an individual avoid hyperventilation during panic attacks. |

are common after patients discontinue medication. Reemergence of panic is likely unless cognitive-behavioral treatment is provided to help patients modify their cognitive overreactions to their bodily sensations (Clark, 1986).

Cognitive-behavioral therapists use a variety of techniques in treating panic disorder, including training in coping skills for handling panic attacks, breathing retraining and relaxation training to reduce states of heightened bodily arousal, and direct exposure to situations linked to panic attacks and to the bodily cues associated with panicky symptoms (Gloster et al., 2014). The therapist may help clients think differently about changes in bodily cues, such as sensations of dizziness or heart palpitations. By recognizing that these cues are fleeting sensations rather than signs of an impending heart attack or other catastrophe, clients learn to cope with them without panicking. Clients learn to replace catastrophizing thoughts and self-statements ("I'm having a heart attack!") with calming, rational alternatives ("Calm down. These are panicky feelings that will soon pass."). Panic attack sufferers may also be reassured by having a medical examination to ensure that they are physically healthy and their physical symptoms are not signs of heart disease.

*Breathing retraining* is a technique that aims to restore a normal level of $CO_2$ in the blood. Clients breathe slowly and deeply from the abdomen, avoiding the shallow, rapid breathing that leads to breathing out too much carbon dioxide. In some treatment programs, people with panic disorder are encouraged to intentionally induce panicky symptoms in order to learn how to cope with them—for example, by hyperventilating in the controlled setting of the treatment clinic or spinning around in a chair (Antony et al., 2006; Katon, 2006). Through firsthand experiences with panicky symptoms, patients learn to calm themselves and cope with these sensations rather than overreact. Some elements commonly used in CBT for panic disorder are shown in Table 5.3.

You need not suffer recurrent panic attacks and fears about loss of control. If your attacks are persistent or frightening, consult a professional. When in doubt, see a professional.

Michael, whom we introduced at the beginning of the chapter, was 30 when he suffered his first panic attack. Michael first sought a medical consultation with a cardiologist to rule out any underlying heart condition. He was relieved when he received a clean bill of health. Although the attacks continued for a time, Michael learned to gain a better sense of control over them. He describes what the process was like in this first-person account.

"I"

### "Glad They're Gone"

For me, it came down to not fearing them. Knowing that I was not going to die gave me confidence that I could handle them. When I began to feel an attack coming on, I would practice relaxation and talk myself through the attack. It really seemed to take the steam out of them. At first I was having an attack every week or so, but after a few months, they whittled down to about one a month, and then they were gone completely. Maybe it was how I was coping with them, or maybe they just disappeared as mysteriously as they began. I'm just glad they're gone.

*"The Case of Michael," from the Author's Files*

## A CLOSER Look

### COPING WITH A PANIC ATTACK

People who have panic attacks usually feel their hearts pounding such that they are overwhelmed and unable to cope. They typically feel an urge to flee the situation as quickly as possible. If escape is impossible, however, they may become immobilized and freeze until the attack dissipates. What can you do if you suffer a panic attack or an intense anxiety reaction? Here are a few coping responses:

- Don't let your breathing get out of hand. Breathe slowly and deeply.
- Try breathing into a paper bag. The carbon dioxide in the bag may help you calm down by restoring a more optimal balance between oxygen and carbon dioxide.
- Talk yourself down: Tell yourself to relax. Tell yourself you're not going to die. Tell yourself that no matter how painful the attack, it is likely to pass soon.
- Find someone to help you through the attack. Call someone you know and trust. Talk about anything at all until you regain control.
- Don't fall into the trap of making yourself housebound to avert future attacks.
- If you are uncertain about whether sensations such as pain or tightness in the chest have physical causes, seek immediate medical assistance. Even if you suspect your attack may "only" be one of anxiety, it is safer to have a medical evaluation than to diagnose yourself.

A number of well-controlled studies attest to the effectiveness of CBT in treating panic disorder (e.g., Craske et al., 2009; Gloster et al., 2014; Gunter & Whittal, 2010). Investigators report average response rates to CBT treatment of more than 60% of cases (Schmidt & Keough, 2010). Despite the common belief that panic disorder is best treated with psychiatric drugs, CBT compares favorably to drug therapy in the short term and generally leads to better long-term results (Otto & Deveney, 2005; Schmidt & Keough, 2010).

Why does CBT produce longer-lasting results? In all likelihood, the answer is that CBT helps people acquire skills they can use even after treatment ends. Although psychiatric drugs can help quell panicky symptoms, they do not assist patients in developing new skills that can be used after drugs are discontinued. However, there are some cases in which a combination of psychological treatment and drug treatment is most effective. We should also note that other forms of psychological treatments may have therapeutic benefits. Evidence supports the treatment benefits of a form of psychodynamic therapy specifically designed to treat panic symptoms (Milrod et al., 2007).

# Phobic Disorders

The word **phobia** derives from the Greek *phobos*, meaning *fear*. The concepts of fear and anxiety are closely related. *Fear* is anxiety experienced in response to a particular threat, and a phobia is a fear of an object or situation that is disproportionate to the threat it poses. To experience a sense of gripping fear when your car is about to go out of control is not a phobia, because you truly are in danger. In phobic disorders, however, the fear exceeds any reasonable appraisal of danger. People with a driving phobia, for example, might become fearful even when they are driving well below the speed limit on a sunny day on an uncrowded highway, or they might be so afraid that they will not drive or even ride in a car. Most, but not all, people with phobic disorders recognize that their fears are excessive or unreasonable.

A curious thing about phobias is that they usually involve fears of ordinary events in life, such as taking an elevator or driving on a highway—not extraordinary events. Phobias can become disabling when they interfere with daily tasks such as taking buses, planes, or trains; driving; shopping; or even leaving the house.

Different types of phobias usually appear at different ages, as noted in Table 5.4. The ages of onset appear to reflect levels of cognitive development and life experiences. Fears of animals are frequent subjects of children's fantasies, for example. Agoraphobia, in contrast, often follows the development of panic attacks beginning in adulthood.

**Table 5.4** Typical Age of Onset for Various Phobias

| | Mean Age of Onset |
|---|---|
| Animal phobia | 7 |
| Blood phobia | 9 |
| Injection phobia | 8 |
| Dental phobia | 12 |
| Social phobia | 15 |
| Claustrophobia | 20 |
| Agoraphobia | 28 |

**SOURCE:** Adapted from Grant, Hasin, Blanco, et al., 2006; Grant, Hasin, Stinson, et al., 2006; Öst, 1987.

## Types of Phobic Disorders

**5.6 Describe the key features and specific types of phobic disorders.**

The *DSM* recognizes three distinct phobic disorders: *specific phobia, social anxiety disorder (social phobia)*, and *agoraphobia*.

**SPECIFIC PHOBIAS** A **specific phobia** is a persistent, excessive fear of a specific object or situation that is out of proportion to the actual danger these objects or situations pose. There are many types of specific phobias, including the following (American Psychiatric Association, 2013):

- Fear of animals, such as fear of spiders, insects, or dogs
- Fear of natural environments, such as fear of heights (*acrophobia*), storms, or water
- Fear of blood-injection injury, such as fear of needles or invasive medical procedures
- Fear of specific situations, such as fear of enclosed spaces (*claustrophobia*), elevators, or airplanes

The phobic person experiences high levels of fear and physiological arousal when encountering the phobic object, which prompts strong urges to avoid or escape the situation or to avoid the feared stimulus, as in the following case.

### Carla Passes the Bar but Not the Courthouse Staircase:

#### A CASE OF SPECIFIC PHOBIA

Passing the bar exam was a significant milestone in Carla's life, but it left her terrified at the thought of entering the county courthouse. She wasn't afraid of encountering a hostile judge or losing a case, but of climbing the stairs leading to the second-floor promenade where the courtrooms were located. Carla, 27, suffered from acrophobia, or fear of heights. "It's funny, you know," Carla told her therapist. "I have no problem flying or looking out the window of a plane at 30,000 feet, but the escalator at the mall throws me into a tailspin. It's just any situation where I could possibly fall, like over the side of a balcony or banister."

People with anxiety disorders try to avoid situations or objects they fear. Carla scouted out the courthouse before she was scheduled to appear. She was relieved to find a service elevator in the rear of the building she could use instead of the stairs. She told her fellow attorneys with whom she was presenting the case that she suffered from a heart condition and couldn't climb stairs. Not suspecting the real problem, one of the attorneys said, "This is great. I never knew this elevator existed. Thanks for finding it."

*From the Author's Files*

To rise to the level of a diagnosable disorder, the phobia must significantly affect the person's lifestyle or functioning or cause significant distress. You may have a fear of snakes, but unless your fear interferes with your daily life or causes you significant emotional distress, it would not warrant a diagnosis of phobic disorder.

Specific phobias often begin in childhood. Many children develop passing fears of specific objects or situations. Some, however, go on to develop chronic clinically significant phobias. Claustrophobia seems to develop later than most other specific phobias, with a mean age of onset of 20 years (see Table 5.4).

Specific phobias are among the most common psychological disorders, affecting about 12.5% of the general population at some point in their lives (see Table 5.1). The fear, anxiety, and avoidance associated with specific phobias typically persist for six months or longer, and often for years or even decades unless the phobia is successfully treated.

Anxiety disorders in general and phobic disorders in particular are more common in women than in men (McLean & Anderson, 2009). Gender differences in

**TWO TYPES OF PHOBIC DISORDERS.** The young woman in the left photo would like to join others but keeps to herself because of social anxiety, an intense fear of social criticism and rejection. The woman in the photo on the right has acrophobia, or a fear of heights, which makes her feel uncomfortable even on a second floor balcony.

development of phobias may reflect cultural influences that socialize women into more dependent roles in society—for example, to be timid rather than brave or adventurous. Examiners also need to be aware of cultural factors when making diagnostic judgments. Fears of magic or spirits are common in some cultures and should not be considered signs of a phobic disorder unless the fear is excessive for the culture in which it occurs and leads to significant emotional distress or impaired functioning.

People with specific phobias will often recognize that their fears are exaggerated or unfounded. However, they still are afraid, as in the case of a young woman who shares how her fear of medical injections almost prevented her from getting married. **T / F**

## TRUTH *or* FICTION

People with phobias believe their fears are well founded.

☑ **FALSE** Actually, many people with phobias recognize that their fears are exaggerated or unfounded, but they remain fearful.

**"I"** "This Will Sound Crazy, But..."

This will sound crazy, but I wouldn't get married because I couldn't stand the idea of getting the blood test [required to test for syphilis at the time]. I finally worked up the courage to ask my doctor if he would put me out with ether or barbiturates—taken by pills—so that I could have the blood test. At first he was incredulous. Then he became sort of sympathetic but said that he couldn't risk putting me under any kind of general anesthesia just to draw some blood. I asked him if he would consider faking the report, but he said that administrative procedures made that impossible.

Then he got me really going. He said that getting tested for marriage was likely to be one of my small life problems. He told me about minor medical problems that could arise and make it necessary for blood to be drawn, or to have an IV in my arm, so his message was I should try to come to grips with my fear. I nearly fainted while he was talking about these things, so he gave it up.

The story has half a happy ending. We finally got married in [a state] where we found out they no longer insisted on blood tests. But if I develop one of those problems the doctor was talking about, or if I need a blood test for some other reason, even if it's life-threatening, I really don't know what I'll do. But maybe if I faint when they're going to [draw blood], I won't know about it anyway, right?

People have me wrong, you know. They think I'm scared of the pain. I don't like pain—I'm not a masochist—but pain has nothing to do with it. You could pinch my arm till I turned black and blue and I'd tolerate it. I wouldn't like it, but I wouldn't start shaking and sweating and faint on you. But even if I didn't feel the needle at all—just the knowledge that it was in me is what I couldn't take.

*From the Author's Files*

STEVE: SOCIAL ANXIETY DISORDER (SOCIAL PHOBIA)

**SOCIAL ANXIETY DISORDER (SOCIAL PHOBIA)** It is not abnormal to experience some degree of fear or anxiety in social situations such as dating, attending parties or social gatherings, or giving a talk or presentation to a class or group. Yet people with **social anxiety disorder** (also called *social phobia*) have such an intense fear of social situations that they may avoid them altogether or endure them only with great distress. The underlying problem is an excessive fear of negative evaluations from others: fear of being rejected, humiliated, or embarrassed.

Imagine what it's like to have social anxiety disorder. You are always fearful of doing or saying something humiliating or embarrassing. You may feel as if a thousand eyes are scrutinizing your every move. You are probably your own harshest critic and are likely to become fixated on whether your performance measures up when interacting with others. Negative thoughts run through your mind: "Did I say the right thing? Do they think I'm stupid?" You may even experience a full-fledged panic attack in social situations.

Stage fright, speech anxiety, and dating fears are common forms of social anxiety. People with social anxiety may find excuses for declining social invitations. They may eat lunch at their desks to avoid socializing with coworkers and avoid situations in which they might meet new people, or they may find themselves in social situations and attempt a quick escape at the first sign of anxiety. Relief from anxiety negatively reinforces escape behavior, but escape prevents learning how to cope with fear-evoking situations. Leaving the scene while still feeling anxious only serves to strengthen the link between the social situation and anxiety. Some people with social anxiety are unable to order food in a restaurant for fear the server or their companions might make fun of the foods they order or how they pronounce them.

Social anxiety or fear can severely impair a person's daily functioning and quality of life. Fear may prevent people from completing educational goals, advancing in their careers, or even holding a job in which they need to interact with others. In some cases, social fears are limited to speaking or performing in front of others, such as in the case of stage fright or fear of public speaking situations. People with this form of social anxiety disorder do not fear nonperformance social situations, such as meeting new people or interacting with others in social gatherings.

**ANXIETY STRIKES OUT.** Zack Greinke, the National League starting pitcher in the 2015 All-Star Game, has battled social anxiety disorder through much of his baseball career. Working with a sports psychologist and taking antidepressant medication helped him get his career back on track. He says it may affect him again in the future, but it's not something he thinks about any longer or feels stressed about.

People with social anxiety often turn to tranquilizers or try to "medicate" themselves with alcohol when preparing for social interactions (see Figure 5.3). In extreme cases, they may become so fearful of interacting with others that they become essentially housebound.

Nationally representative surveys show that about 12.1% of U.S. adults are affected by social anxiety disorder at some point in their lives (see Table 5.1). The disorder is more common among women than men, perhaps because of the greater social or cultural pressures placed on young women to please others and earn their approval.

The average age of onset of social anxiety disorder is about 15 years (Grant, Hasin, Blanco, et al., 2006). About 80% of affected people develop the disorder by age 20 (Stein & Stein, 2008). Social anxiety is strongly associated with a

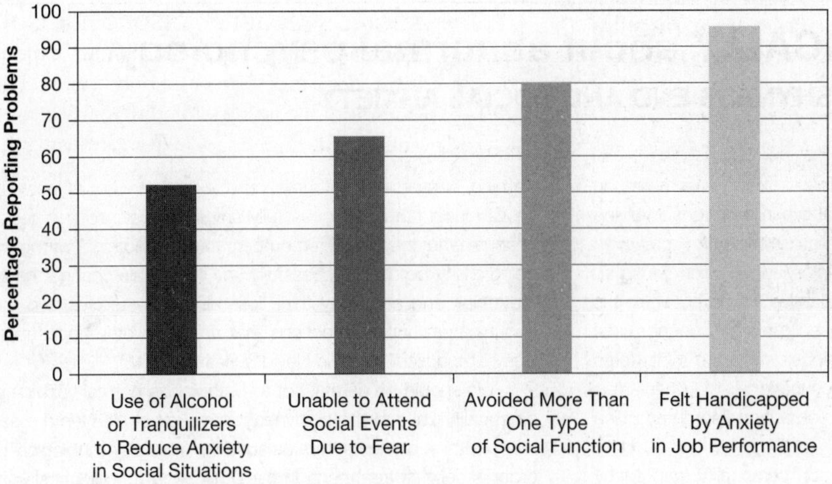


**Figure 5.3** Percentage of people with social anxiety reporting specific difficulties associated with their fears of social situations.

More than 90% of people with social anxiety feel handicapped by anxiety in their jobs.

**SOURCE:** Adapted from Turner & Beidel, 1989.

history of childhood shyness (Cox et al., 2004). Consistent with the diathesis–stress model (see Chapter 2), shyness may represent a diathesis or predisposition that makes a person more vulnerable to developing social anxiety in the face of stressful experiences, such as traumatic social encounters (e.g., being embarrassed in front of others). Although social anxiety disorder may have a short duration in some cases, it is typically a chronic, persistent disorder, lasting about 16 years on average (Grant, Hasin, Blanco, et al., 2006; Vriends, Bolt, & Kunz, 2014). Despite its early development and the many negative effects it has on social functioning, people with social anxiety disorder first receive help at an average age of 27 (Grant, Hasin, Blanco, et al., 2006).

**AGORAPHOBIA** The word *agoraphobia* is derived from Greek words meaning "fear of the marketplace," which suggests a fear of being out in open, busy areas. People with agoraphobia may fear shopping in crowded stores; walking through crowded streets; crossing a bridge; traveling by bus, train, or car; eating in restaurants; being in a movie theater; or even leaving the house. They may structure their lives around avoiding exposure to fearful situations and in some cases become housebound for months or even years, even to the extent of being unable to venture outside to mail a letter. Agoraphobia has the potential to become the most incapacitating type of phobia.

People with agoraphobia develop a fear of places and situations from which it might be difficult or embarrassing to escape in the event of panicky symptoms or a full-fledged panic attack or a fear of situations in which help may be unavailable if such problems should occur. Elderly people with agoraphobia may avoid situations in which they fear they might fall and not have help available. **T / F**

### TRUTH or FICTION

Some people are so fearful of leaving their homes that they are unable to venture outside even to mail a letter.

☑ TRUE Some people with agoraphobia become literally housebound and unable to venture outside even to mail a letter.

Women are about as likely as men to develop agoraphobia (American Psychiatric Association, 2013). Once agoraphobia develops, it tends to follow a persistent or chronic course. Frequently, it begins in late adolescence or early adulthood. It may occur either with or without accompanying panic disorder. Agoraphobia is often but not always associated with panic disorder. A person with panic disorder who develops agoraphobia may live in fear of recurrent attacks and avoid public places where attacks have occurred or might occur. Because panic attacks can seem to come out of nowhere, some people restrict their activities for fear of making public spectacles of themselves or finding themselves without help. Others venture outside only with a companion. Still others forge ahead despite intense anxiety.

## THINKING CRITICALLY about abnormal psychology

### @ISSUE: WHERE DOES SHYNESS END AND SOCIAL ANXIETY DISORDER BEGIN?

We began this chapter by noting that anxiety is a common emotional experience that may be adaptive in situations involving a threat to our safety or well-being. It is common and may even be expected to feel anxious on a job interview or when taking an important test. Anxiety becomes maladaptive, however, when it is either inappropriate to the situation (no real threat or danger exists) or excessive (beyond expectable reactions) and when it interferes significantly with a person's social, occupational, or other areas of functioning (e.g., turning down a job on a high floor in an office building because of a fear of heights).

But what about shyness, a common personality trait? Many of us are shy, but where should we draw a line between ordinary shyness and social anxiety disorder? As Bernardo Carducci, a prominent shyness researcher at Indiana University, points out, "shyness is not a disease, a psychiatric disorder, a character flaw, or a personality defect that needs to be 'cured'" (cited in Nevid & Rathus, 2013). Many famous people in history were reported to be shy, among them Charles Darwin, Albert Einstein, and Harry Potter creator J. K. Rowling (Cain, 2011). Carducci speaks of shy people becoming successfully shy, not by changing who they are but by accepting themselves and learning how to interact with others, such as by working in a volunteer organization, learning conversation starters, and expanding social networks. As Carducci notes, "successfully shy individuals do not need to change who they are—remember, there is nothing wrong with being a shy person. Successfully shy individuals change the way they think and act. They think less about themselves and more about others and take actions that are more other-focused and less self-focused" (cited in Nevid & Rathus, 2013).

We should be careful not to pathologize normal variations in personality traits such as shyness or make people who are naturally shy think of themselves as suffering from a psychological disorder in need of treatment. In the *DSM* system, a diagnosis of an anxiety disorder must be based on evidence of significant impairment of functioning or marked personal distress. Sometimes what the shy person needs is public speaking training, not psychotherapy or medication (Cain, 2011).

In thinking critically about the issue, consider the following questions:

- Think of someone you know who is painfully shy, perhaps even yourself. Does this person suffer from a diagnosable psychological disorder? Why or why not?
- What do you think it means to be successfully shy?

People with agoraphobia who have no history of panic disorder may experience mild panicky symptoms, such as dizziness, that lead them to avoid venturing away from places where they feel safe or secure. They, too, tend to become dependent on others for support. The following case of agoraphobia without a history of panic disorder illustrates the dependencies often associated with agoraphobia.

## Helen:

### A CASE OF AGORAPHOBIA

Helen, a 59-year-old widow, became increasingly agoraphobic 3 years after the death of her husband. By the time she came for treatment, she was essentially housebound, refusing to leave her home except under the strongest urging of her daughter, Mary, age 32, and only if Mary accompanied her. Her daughter and 36-year-old son, Pete, did her shopping and took care of her other needs as best they could. However, the burden of caring for their mother on top of their other responsibilities was becoming too great for them to bear. They insisted that Helen begin treatment, and Helen begrudgingly acceded to their demands.

Helen was accompanied to her evaluation session by Mary. Helen was a frail-looking woman who entered the office clutching Mary's arm and insisted that Mary stay throughout the interview. Helen recounted that she had lost her husband and mother within 3 months of one another; her father had died 20 years earlier. Although she had never experienced a panic attack, she always considered herself an insecure, fearful person. Even so, she had been able to function in meeting the needs of her family until the deaths of her husband and mother left her feeling abandoned and alone. She had now become afraid of "just about everything" and was terrified of being out on her own, lest something bad would happen and she wouldn't be able to cope with it. Even at home, she was fearful that she might lose Mary and Pete. She needed continual reassurance from them that they too wouldn't abandon her.

*From the Author's Files*

# Theoretical Perspectives

**5.7 Explain the role of learning, cognitive, and biological factors in the development of phobias.**

Theoretical approaches to understanding the development of phobias have a long history in psychology, beginning with the psychodynamic perspective.

**PSYCHODYNAMIC PERSPECTIVES** From the psychodynamic perspective, anxiety is a danger signal indicating that threatening impulses of a sexual or aggressive (murderous or suicidal) nature are nearing the level of awareness. To fend off these threatening impulses, the ego mobilizes its defense mechanisms. In phobias, the Freudian defense mechanism of *projection* comes into play. A phobic reaction is a projection of a person's own threatening impulses onto the phobic object. For instance, a fear of knives or other sharp instruments may represent the projection of one's own destructive impulses onto the phobic object. The phobia serves a useful function. Avoiding contact with sharp instruments prevents these destructive wishes toward the self or others from becoming consciously realized or acted on. The threatening impulses remain safely repressed. Similarly, people with acrophobia may harbor unconscious wishes to jump that are controlled by avoiding heights. The phobic object or situation symbolizes or represents these unconscious wishes or desires. The person is aware of the phobia, but not of the unconscious impulses it symbolizes.

**LEARNING PERSPECTIVES** The classic learning perspective on phobias was offered by psychologist O. Hobart Mowrer (1960). Mowrer's **two-factor model** incorporated roles for both classical and operant conditioning in the development of phobias. The fear component of phobia is believed to be acquired through classical conditioning, as previously neutral objects and situations gain the capacity to evoke fear by being paired with noxious or aversive stimuli. A child who is frightened by a barking dog may acquire a dog phobia. A child who receives a painful injection may develop a needle or syringe phobia. Many people with phobias had experiences in which the phobic object or situation was associated with aversive situations (e.g., getting trapped on an elevator).

Consider the case of Phyllis, a 32-year-old writer and mother of two sons who had not used an elevator in 16 years. Her life revolved around finding ways to avoid appointments and social events on high floors. She had suffered from a fear of elevators since the age of 8, when she had been stuck between floors with her grandmother. In conditioning terms, the unconditioned stimulus was the aversive experience of being stuck on the elevator and the conditioned stimulus was the elevator itself.

As Mowrer pointed out, the avoidance component of phobias is acquired and maintained by operant conditioning, specifically by *negative reinforcement*. That is, relief from anxiety *negatively reinforces* the avoidance of fearful stimuli, which thus serves to strengthen the avoidance response. Phyllis learned to relieve her anxiety over riding the elevator by opting for the stairs instead. Avoidance works to relieve anxiety, but at a significant cost. By avoiding the phobic stimulus (e.g., elevators), the fear may persist for years, even a lifetime. On the other hand, fear can be weakened and even eliminated by repeated, uneventful encounters with the phobic stimulus. In classical conditioning terms, *extinction* is the weakening of the conditioned response (e.g., the fear component of a phobia) when the conditioned stimulus (the phobic object or stimulus) is repeatedly presented in the absence of the unconditioned stimulus (an aversive or painful stimulus).

Conditioning accounts for some, but certainly not all, phobias. In many cases, perhaps even most, people with specific phobias can't recall any aversive experiences with the objects they fear. Learning theorists might counter that memories of conditioning experiences may be blurred by the passage of time or that the experience occurred too early in life

**AN INJECTION PHOBIA.** Many phobias are conditioned responses that are acquired based on pairings of painful or traumatic stimuli with previously neutral stimuli. A phobic response to injections may have been learned as the result of having received an unusually painful injection in the past.

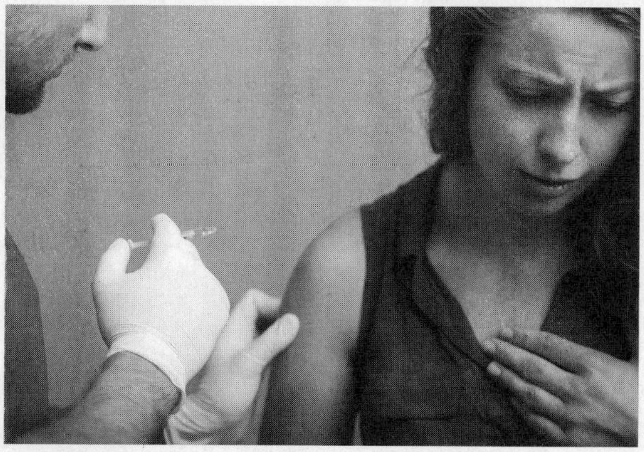

to be recalled verbally, but contemporary learning theorists highlight the role of another form of learning—*observational learning*—that does not require direct conditioning of fears. In this form of learning, observing parents or significant others model a fearful reaction to a stimulus can lead to the acquisition of a fearful response. In an illustrative study of 42 people with severe phobias for spiders, observational learning apparently played a more prominent role in fear acquisition than did conditioning (Merckelbach, Arnitz, & de Jong, 1991). Moreover, simply receiving information from others, such as hearing others speak about the dangers posed by a particular stimulus (e.g., spiders), can also lead to the development of phobias (Merckelbach et al., 1996).

Learning models help account for the development of phobias (Field, 2006)—but why do some people seem to acquire fear responses more readily than others? The biological and cognitive perspectives may offer some insights.

**BIOLOGICAL PERSPECTIVES** Genetic factors can predispose individuals to develop anxiety disorders, such as panic disorder and phobic disorder (Kendler, 2005; Smoller et al., 2008), but how do genes affect a person's likelihood of developing anxiety disorders?

For one thing, we've learned that people with variations of particular genes are more prone to develop fear responses and to have greater difficulty overcoming them (Lonsdorf et al., 2009). For example, people with a variation of a particular gene who are exposed to fearful stimuli show greater activation of a brain structure called the *amygdala*, an almond-shaped structure in the brain's limbic system (Hariri et al., 2002). Located below the cerebral cortex, the limbic system comprises a group of interconnected structures involved in memory formation and processing emotional responses.

The amygdala produces fear responses to triggering stimuli without conscious thought (Agren et al., 2012). It works as a kind of "emotional computer" that kicks into gear whenever we encounter a threat or danger (Wood, Ver Hoef, & Knight, 2014; see Figure 5.4). Higher brain centers, especially the *prefrontal cortex* in the frontal lobes of the cerebral cortex, have the job of evaluating threatening stimuli more carefully. As noted in Chapter 2, the prefrontal cortex, which lies directly under your forehead, is responsible for many higher mental functions, such as thinking, problem solving, reasoning, and decision making. Therefore, when you see an object in the road that resembles a snake, the amygdala bolts into action, inducing a fear response that makes you stop or jump backwards and sends quivers of fear racing through your body. A few moments later, the prefrontal cortex sizes up the threat more carefully, allowing you to breathe a sigh of relief ("It's only a stick. Relax.").

In people with anxiety disorders, however, the amygdala may become overly excitable, inducing fear in response to mildly threatening situations or environmental cues

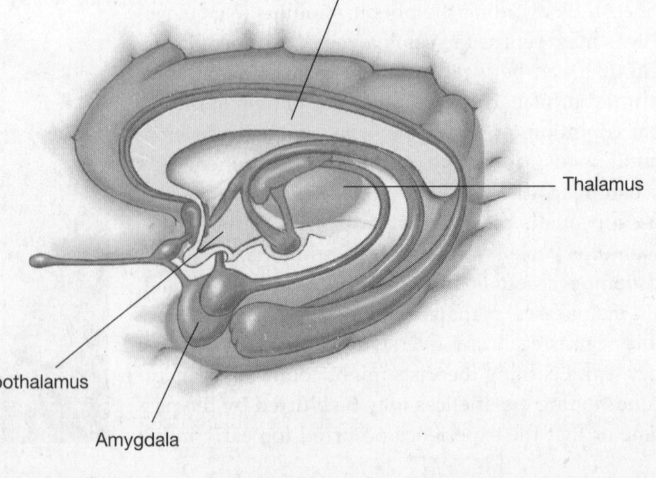


**Figure 5.4** The amygdala and limbic system.

The amygdala, the brain's fear-triggering center, is part of the brain's limbic system. This system comprises a group of interconnected structures located below the cerebral cortex, which also includes parts of the thalamus and hypothalamus and other nearby structures. The limbic system is involved in memory formation and emotional processing. Recent evidence links anxiety disorders to an overly excitable amygdala.

**Figure 5.5** Brain responses to criticism in people with generalized social anxiety.

Functional MRI scans of the brain in response to criticism showed greater activity in the amygdala (left) and parts of the prefrontal cortex (circled in black, right) in people with generalized social anxiety.

**SOURCE:** NIMH, 2008b.

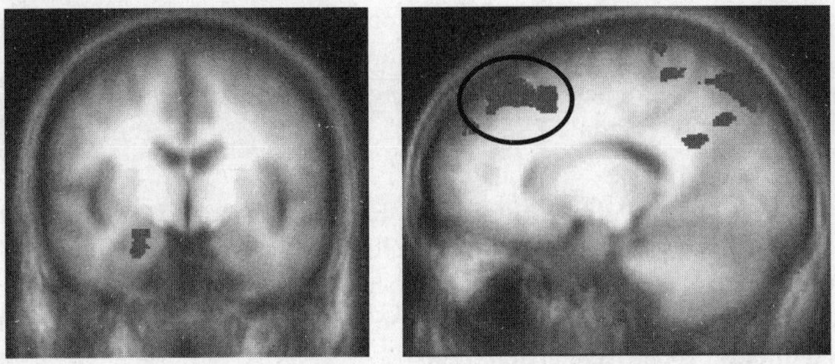

(Nitschke et al., 2009). Supporting this view, researchers find increased levels of activation of the amygdala in people with social anxiety and in combat veterans with PTSD (Stein & Stein, 2008). In another recent study, anxious adolescents showed a greater amygdala response to faces with fearful expressions than did nonpatient controls (Beesdo et al., 2009). For people with anxiety disorders, the amygdala may become overreactive to cues of threat, fear, and rejection.

In related research, investigators used functional magnetic resonance imaging (fMRI) to examine how the brain responds to negative social cues (Blair et al., 2008). Investigators compared brain responses to negative social comments (e.g., "You are ugly.") of people with a more generalized form of social anxiety and nonphobic controls. The socially phobic individuals showed greater levels of activation in the amygdala and in some parts of the prefrontal cortex (see Figure 5.5). The amygdala may trigger the initial fear response to negative social cues, like criticism, whereas the prefrontal cortex may be engaging processes relating to self-reflection about these cues ("Why did he say that about me? Am I really so ugly?").

Investigators have also used experimental animals, such as laboratory rats, to explore how the brain responds to fearful stimuli. An influential study showed that a part of the prefrontal cortex in the rat's brain sends a kind of "all-clear" signal to the amygdala, quelling fearful reactions (see Figure 5.6; Milad & Quirk, 2002). Investigators first conditioned rats to respond to a tone with fear by repeatedly pairing the tone with shock. The rats froze whenever they heard the tone. The investigators then extinguished the fear response by presenting the tone repeatedly without the shock. Following extinction, neurons in the middle of the prefrontal cortex fired up whenever the tone was sounded, sending signals through neural pathways to the amygdala. The more of these neurons that fired, the less the rats froze (NIH, 2002). The discovery that the prefrontal cortex sends a safety signal to the amygdala may eventually lead to new treatments for people with phobias. These treatments would work by turning on the brain's all-clear signal.

Research on the biological underpinnings of fear continues. For example, investigators are targeting particular types of neurons involved in fear memories. Destroying these types of neurons in laboratory mice literally erased memories of earlier learned fear responses (Han et al., 2009). Although extending laboratory research with mice to helping people overcome phobic responses is a stretch, experimental work with animals may lead to the development of drugs that might selectively block or interfere with fear responses in humans.

Are humans genetically predisposed to acquire phobic responses to certain classes of stimuli? People appear to be more likely to have fears of snakes and spiders than of rabbits, for example. This belief in a biological predisposition to

**Figure 5.6** The "all-clear" signal quells fear.

Evidence from animal studies shows that all-clear signals from the prefrontal cortex to the amygdala inhibit fear responses. This discovery may lead to treatments that can help quell fear reactions in humans.

**SOURCE:** Milad & Quirk, 2002. Figure reprinted from NIH, 2002.

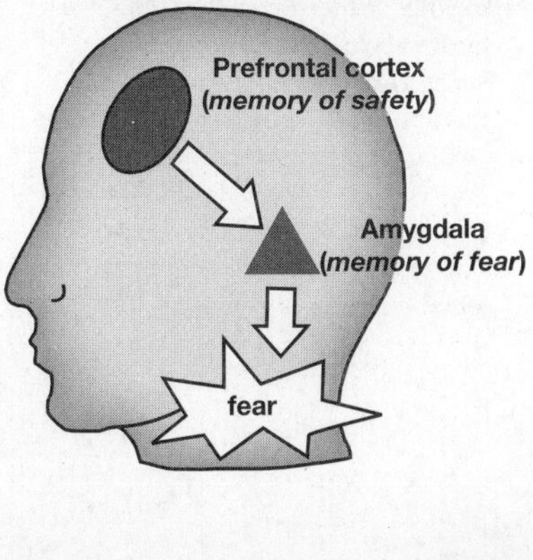

## TRUTH or FICTION

We may be genetically predisposed to acquire fears of objects that posed a danger to ancestral humans.

☑ **TRUE** Some theorists believe that we are genetically predisposed to acquire certain fears, such as fears of large animals and snakes. The ability to readily acquire these fears may have had survival value to ancestral humans.

acquire fears of certain types of objects or situations, called *prepared conditioning*, suggests that evolution favored the survival of human ancestors who were genetically predisposed to develop fears of potentially threatening objects, such as large animals, snakes, spiders, and other "creepy-crawlies"; of heights; of enclosed spaces; and even of strangers. This model may explain why we are more likely to develop fears of spiders or heights than of objects that appeared much later on the evolutionary scene, such as guns or knives, although these later-appearing objects pose more direct threats to our survival today. **T / F**

**COGNITIVE PERSPECTIVES** Recent research highlights the importance of cognitive factors in determining proneness to phobias, including factors such as oversensitivity to threatening cues, overpredictions of dangerousness, and self-defeating thoughts and irrational beliefs (e.g., Armfield, 2006; Schultz & Heimberg, 2008; Wenzel et al., 2005):

1. *Oversensitivity to threatening cues.* People with phobias tend to perceive danger in situations most people consider safe, such as riding elevators or driving over bridges. Similarly, people with social anxiety tend to be overly sensitive to social cues of rejection or negative evaluation from others (Schmidt et al., 2009).

   We all possess an internal alarm system—the "fight or flight" response—that is sensitive to cues of threat. The amygdala in the brain's limbic system plays a key role in this early warning system. This emergency alarm may have provided evolutionary advantages for ancestral humans by increasing the chances of survival in a hostile environment. Early humans who responded quickly to signs of threat, such as a rustling sound in the bush that may have indicated a lurking predator about to pounce, may have been better prepared to take defensive action (to fight it off or to flee to safety) than those with a less sensitive alarm system. Today, our emergency alarm system may be activated by a real physical threat (e.g., an attack by an assailant) or by psychological threats, such as taking an important exam or giving a speech in public. The emergency alarm is characterized by arousal of the autonomic nervous system, during which the body mobilizes its resources by increasing blood flow and oxygen to our muscles, allowing us to either fight or flee.

   The emotions of anxiety and fear are key components of the emergency alarm that may have served to motivate our early ancestors to take defensive action in the face of threats or predators, which in turn may have helped them survive. This emergency alarm system is wired into our nervous system. People with specific phobias or other anxiety-related disorders may have an alarm system that is overly sensitive to threatening cues. They are continually on high alert to threatening objects or situations. If there is a spider in the room, it's a safe bet that a spider phobic will be the first one in a group to notice it and point it out (Purkis, Lester, & Field, 2011). Researchers also find that the greater the fear of spiders, the bigger the person perceives them to be (Vasey et al., 2012). **T / F**

## TRUTH or FICTION

If there is a spider in the room, the spider phobic in the group will likely be the first to notice it and point it out.

☑ **TRUE** People with specific phobias tend to be on high alert for detecting fearful stimuli or objects.

2. *Overprediction of danger.* Phobic individuals tend to overpredict how much fear or anxiety they will experience in a fearful situation. A person with a snake phobia, for example, may expect to tremble when he or she encounters a snake in a cage. People with dental phobia may have exaggerated expectations of the pain they will experience during dental visits. Typically speaking, the actual fear or pain experienced during exposure to the phobic stimulus is a good deal less than what people expect. Yet the tendency to expect the worst encourages avoidance of feared situations, which in turn prevents an individual from learning to manage and overcome anxiety.

   Overprediction of dental pain and fear may also lead people to postpone or cancel regular dental visits, which can contribute to more serious dental problems down the road. Actual exposure to fearful situations may lead instead to more accurate predictions of the person's level of fear. A clinical implication is that with repeated exposure, people with anxiety disorders may come to anticipate their responses to fear-inducing stimuli more accurately, leading to reductions of fear expectancies. This in turn may reduce avoidance tendencies.

3. *Self-defeating thoughts and irrational beliefs.* Self-defeating thoughts can heighten and perpetuate anxiety and phobic disorders. When faced with fear-evoking stimuli, a person may think, "I've got to get out of here," or "My heart is going to leap out of my chest." Thoughts like these intensify autonomic arousal, disrupt planning, magnify the aversiveness of stimuli, prompt avoidance behavior, and decrease self-efficacy expectancies concerning a person's ability to control the situation. Similarly, people with social anxiety may think, "I'll sound stupid," whenever they have an opportunity to speak in front of a group of people (Hofmann et al., 2004). Such self-defeating thoughts may stifle social participation.

**"IT WAS AS BIG AS MY HEAD, I SWEAR!"** Investigators find that the more afraid people are of spiders, the larger they perceive them to be.

People with phobias also display more irrational beliefs of the type cataloged by Albert Ellis (see Chapter 2) than do nonfearful people. These irrational beliefs may involve exaggerated needs to be approved of by everyone they meet and to avoid any situation in which negative appraisal from others might arise. Consider these beliefs: "What if I have an anxiety attack in front of other people? They might think I'm crazy. I couldn't stand it if they looked at me that way." The results of an early study may hit close to home: College men who believed it was awful (not just unfortunate) to be turned down when requesting a date showed more social anxiety than those who were less likely to catastrophize rejection (Gormally et al., 1981).

Before going on, you may wish to review Figure 5.7, which illustrates a conceptual model for understanding phobias in terms of roles of learning influences and vulnerability factors, such as a genetic predisposition and cognitive factors.

## Treatment Approaches

**5.8 Evaluate methods used to treat phobic disorders.**

Traditional psychoanalysis fosters awareness of how clients' fears symbolize their inner conflicts so that the ego can be freed from expending its energy on repression. Modern psychodynamic therapies also foster clients' awareness of inner sources of conflict. They focus to a greater extent than do traditional approaches on exploring sources of anxiety that arise from current rather than past relationships, however, and they encourage clients to develop more adaptive behaviors. Such therapies are briefer and more directed toward specific problems than traditional psychoanalysis. Although psychodynamic therapies may prove to be helpful in treating some cases of anxiety disorders, there is little compelling empirical support documenting their overall effectiveness (USDHHS, 1999).

## Adam Learns to Overcome His Fear of Injections:

### A CASE OF SPECIFIC PHOBIA

Adam has a needle (injection) phobia. His behavior therapist treats him as he reclines in a comfortable padded chair. In a state of deep muscle relaxation, Adam observes slides projected on a screen. A slide of a nurse holding a needle has just been shown three times, 30 seconds at a time. Each time, Adam has shown no anxiety. Now, a slightly more discomforting slide is shown: one in which the nurse aims the needle toward someone's bare arm. After 15 seconds, our armchair adventurer notices twinges of discomfort and raises a finger as a signal (speaking might disturb his relaxation). The projector operator turns off the light, and Adam spends 2 minutes imagining his "safe scene"—lying on a beach beneath the tropical sun. Then the slide is shown again. This time Adam views it for 30 seconds before feeling anxiety.

**SOURCE:** *From Essentials of Psychology (6th ed.) by S. A. Rathus, p. 537. Copyright © 2001. Reprinted with permission of Brooks/Cole, an imprint of Wadsworth Group, a division of Thomson Learning.*

## Figure 5.7 A multifactorial model of phobia.

Learning influences play a key role in the acquisition of many phobias. But whether these learning experiences lead to the development of phobias may also depend on vulnerability factors, such as genetic predisposition and cognitive factors.

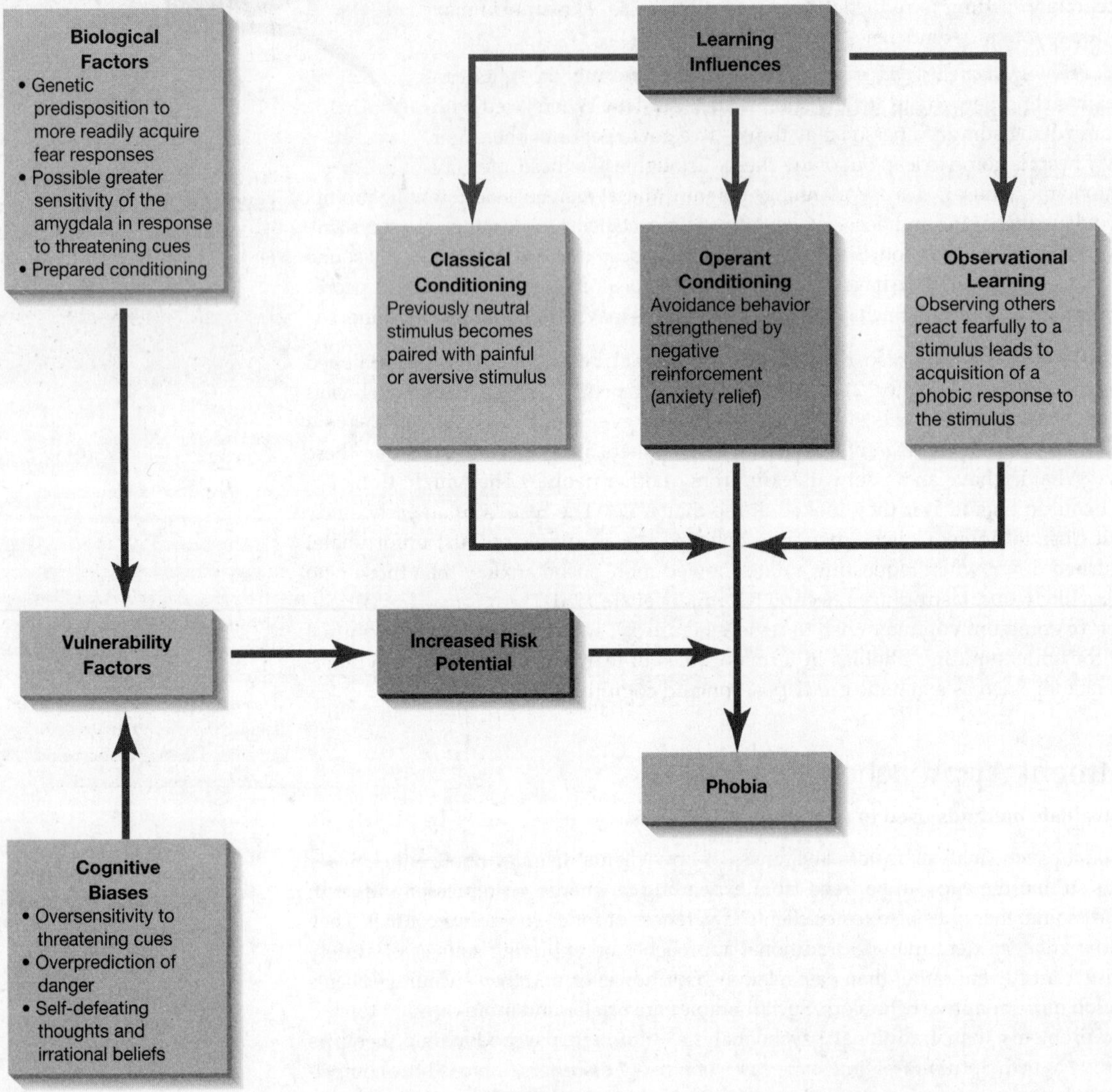


The major contemporary treatment approaches to specific phobias, as for other anxiety disorders, derive from the learning, cognitive, and biological perspectives.

**LEARNING-BASED APPROACHES** A substantial body of research demonstrates the effectiveness of learning-based approaches in treating a range of anxiety disorders. At the core of these approaches is the effort to help individuals cope more effectively with anxiety-provoking objects and situations. Examples of learning-based approaches include *systematic desensitization, gradual exposure,* and *flooding*.

Adam (whose case is covered earlier in the chapter) is undergoing **systematic desensitization**, a fear-reduction procedure originated by psychiatrist Joseph Wolpe (1958) in the 1950s. Systematic desensitization is a gradual process in which clients learn to handle progressively more disturbing stimuli while they remain relaxed. About 10 to 20 stimuli are arranged in a sequence or hierarchy—called a **fear-stimulus hierarchy**—according to their capacity to evoke anxiety. By using their imagination or by viewing photos, clients are exposed to the items in the hierarchy, gradually imagining themselves approaching the target behavior—be it the ability to receive an injection or to remain in an enclosed room or elevator—without undue anxiety.

Systematic desensitization is based on the assumption that phobias are learned or conditioned responses that can be unlearned by substituting an incompatible response to anxiety in situations that usually elicit anxiety (Rachman, 2000). Muscle relaxation is generally used as the incompatible response, and Wolpe's followers generally use the method of progressive relaxation (described in Chapter 6) to help clients acquire relaxation skills. For this reason, Adam's therapist is teaching Adam to experience relaxation in the presence of (otherwise) anxiety-evoking slides of needles.

Systematic desensitization creates a set of conditions that can lead to extinction of fear responses. The technique fosters extinction by providing opportunities for repeated exposure to phobic stimuli in the imagination without aversive consequences.

**Gradual exposure** uses a stepwise approach in which phobic individuals gradually confront the objects or situations they fear. Repeated exposure to a phobic stimulus in the absence of any aversive event (i.e., nothing bad happening) can lead to extinction or gradual weakening of the phobic response, even to the point that it is eliminated. Gradual exposure also leads to cognitive changes. A person comes to perceive the previously feared object or situation as harmless and perceives him- or herself as capable of handling the situation more effectively.

Exposure therapy can take several forms, including *imaginal exposure* (imagining oneself in the fearful situation) and *in vivo exposure* (actual encounters with phobic stimuli in real life). In vivo exposure may be more effective than imaginal exposure, but both techniques are often used in therapy. The effectiveness of exposure therapy for phobias is well established, making it the treatment of choice for many phobias (e.g., Gloster et al., 2011; Hofmann, 2008; McEvoy, 2008).

Consider social anxiety, for example. In exposure therapy, socially phobic clients may be instructed to enter increasingly stressful social situations (e.g., eating and conversing with coworkers in the cafeteria) and to remain in those situations until the anxiety and urge to escape lessen. The therapist may help guide them during exposure trials, gradually withdrawing direct support so that clients become capable of handling such situations on their own. Exposure therapy for agoraphobia generally follows a stepwise course in which the client is exposed to increasingly fearful stimulus situations, such as walking through congested streets or shopping in department stores. A trusted companion or perhaps the therapist may accompany the person undergoing therapy during the exposure trials. The eventual goal is for a person to be able to handle each situation alone and without discomfort or an urge to escape. Gradual exposure was used in treating the following case of claustrophobia.

**GRADUAL EXPOSURE.** The client confronts fearful stimuli in real-life situations in a step-by-step fashion and may be accompanied by a therapist or trusted companion serving in a supportive role. To encourage the person to accomplish the exposure tasks increasingly on his or her own, the therapist or companion gradually withdraws direct support. Gradual exposure is often combined with cognitive techniques that focus on helping the client replace anxiety-producing thoughts and beliefs with calming, rational alternatives.

## Kevin Combats His Fear of Elevators:

### A CASE OF CLAUSTROPHOBIA

Claustrophobia (fear of enclosed spaces) is not very unusual, although Kevin's case was. Kevin's claustrophobia took the form of a fear of riding on elevators. What made the case so unusual was Kevin's occupation: He worked as an elevator mechanic. Kevin spent his work days repairing elevators. Unless it was absolutely necessary, however, Kevin managed to complete the repairs without riding in the elevator. He would climb the stairs to the floor where an elevator was stuck, make repairs, and hit the down button. He would then race downstairs to see that the elevator had operated correctly. When his work required an elevator ride, panic would seize him as the doors closed. Kevin tried to cope by praying for divine intervention to prevent him from passing out before the doors opened.

Kevin related the origin of his phobia to an accident three years earlier in which he had been pinned in his overturned car for nearly an hour. He remembered feelings of helplessness and suffocation. Kevin developed claustrophobia—a fear of situations from which he could not escape, such as flying on an airplane, driving in a tunnel, taking public transportation, and, of course, riding in an elevator. Kevin's fear had become so incapacitating that he was seriously considering switching careers, although the change would require considerable financial sacrifice. Each night, he lay awake wondering whether he would be able to cope the next day if he were required to test-ride an elevator.

Kevin's therapy involved gradual exposure. He followed a stepwise program of exposure to increasingly fearful stimuli. A typical anxiety hierarchy for helping people overcome a fear of riding on elevators might include the following steps:

1. Standing outside the elevator
2. Standing in the elevator with the door open
3. Standing in the elevator with the door closed
4. Taking the elevator down one floor
5. Taking the elevator up one floor
6. Taking the elevator down two floors
7. Taking the elevator up two floors
8. Taking the elevator down two floors and then up two floors
9. Taking the elevator down to the basement
10. Taking the elevator up to the highest floor
11. Taking the elevator all the way down and then all the way up

Clients begin at step 1 and do not progress to step 2 until they are able to remain calm on the first. If they become anxious, they remove themselves from the situation and regain calmness by practicing muscle relaxation or focusing on soothing mental imagery. The encounter is then repeated as often as necessary to reach and sustain feelings of calmness. They then proceed to the next step, repeating the process.

Kevin was also trained to practice self-relaxation and to talk calmly and rationally to himself to help him remain calm during his exposure trials. Whenever he began to feel even slightly anxious, he would tell himself to calm down and relax. He was able to counter the disruptive belief that he was going to fall apart if he was trapped in an elevator with rational self-statements such as, "Just relax. I may experience some anxiety, but it's nothing that I haven't been through before. In a few moments, I'll feel relieved."

Kevin slowly overcame his phobia but still occasionally experienced some anxiety, which he interpreted as a reminder of his former phobia. He did not exaggerate the importance of these feelings. Now and then it dawned on him that an elevator he was servicing had once occasioned fear. One day following his treatment, Kevin was repairing an elevator, which serviced a bank vault 100 feet underground. The experience of moving deeper and deeper underground aroused fear, but Kevin did not panic. He repeated to himself, "It's only a couple of seconds and I'll be out." By the time he took his second trip down, he was much calmer.

*From the Author's Files*

**Flooding** is a form of exposure therapy in which subjects are exposed to high levels of fear-inducing stimuli either in the imagination or in real-life situations. *Why?* The belief is that anxiety represents a conditioned response to a phobic stimulus and should dissipate if the individual remains in the phobic situation for a long enough period of time without harmful consequences. Most individuals with phobias avoid confronting phobic stimuli or beat a hasty retreat at the first opportunity if they cannot avoid them. Consequently, they lack the opportunity to unlearn the fear response. In flooding, a person purposely engages a highly feared situation, such as in the case of a person with social anxiety sitting down at a lunch table where people have already gathered, and remains for a long enough period of time for anxiety to dissipate. Flooding has been used effectively in treating various anxiety disorders, including social anxiety and PTSD (Cusack et al., 2015; Moulds & Nixon, 2006).

**VIRTUAL THERAPY: THE NEXT BEST THING TO BEING THERE** In the movie *The Matrix*, the lead character played by Keanu Reeves comes to realize that the world he believes is real is merely an illusion, a complex virtual environment so lifelike that people cannot tell it isn't real. *The Matrix* is science fiction, but the use of virtual reality as a therapeutic tool is science fact.

**Virtual reality therapy (VRT)** is a behavior therapy technique that uses computer-generated simulated environments as therapeutic tools. Advances in digital technology are making it possible to create extremely lifelike simulated environments. By donning a specialized helmet and gloves that are connected to a computer, a person with a fear of heights, for example, can encounter frightening stimuli such as riding in a glass-enclosed elevator to the top floor of an imaginary hotel, peering over a railing on a balcony on the 20th floor, or crossing a virtual Golden Gate Bridge in the virtual world. By a process of exposure to a series of increasingly frightening virtual stimuli and progressing only when fear at each step diminishes, people can learn to overcome fears in virtual reality in much the same way they would had they followed a program of gradual exposure in real-life situations. **T / F**

## TRUTH or FICTION

Therapists have used virtual reality to help people overcome phobias.

☑ **TRUE** Virtual reality therapy has been used successfully in helping people overcome phobias, including fear of heights.

Virtual therapy can help people overcome phobias, such as fear of heights and fear of flying, and the gains they achieve can generalize to real-life situations (Morina et al., 2015; Turner & Casey, 2014). In an influential early research study, virtual reality was just shown to be just as effective as real-life exposure in treating fear of flying, with both treatments showing better results than an untreated (waiting list) control condition (Rothbaum et al., 2002). Ninety-two percent of VRT participants succeeded in flying on a commercial airliner in the year following treatment. A recent review article reported substantial benefits of VRT that were even larger than those from alternative behavioral treatments (Turner & Casey, 2014).

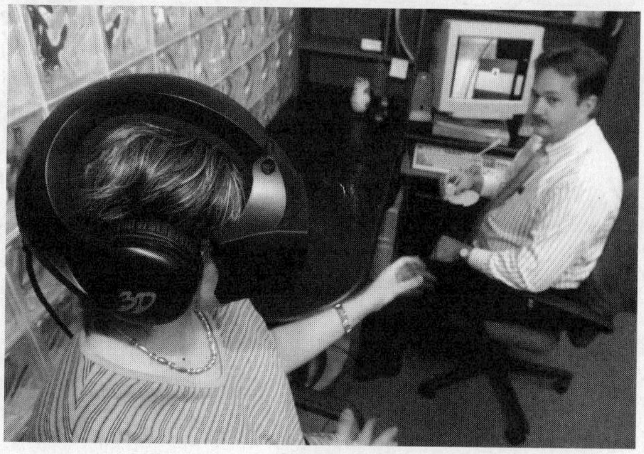

**OVERCOMING FEARS WITH VIRTUAL REALITY.** Virtual reality technology can be used to help people overcome phobias.

Virtual reality therapy offers certain advantages over traditional exposure-based treatments. For example, it is often difficult or even impossible to arrange real-life exposures that can be simulated in virtual reality, such as repeated airplane takeoffs and landings. Virtual therapy also gives a participant greater control over the stimulus environment, such as in controlling the intensity and range of stimuli during virtual exposure sessions. Individuals may also be more willing to perform certain fearful tasks in virtual reality than in real life.

In order for virtual therapy to be effective, says psychologist Barbara Rothbaum, an early pioneer in the use of the technique, a person must become immersed in the experience and believe at some level that it is real and not like watching a videotape. "If the first person had put the helmet on and said, 'This isn't scary,' it wouldn't have worked," Dr. Rothbaum said. "But you get the same physiological changes—the racing heart, the sweat—that you would in the actual place" (cited in Goleman, 1995, p. C11). Today, with advances in virtual reality technology, the simulated virtual environment is convincing enough to evoke intense anxiety in fearful people (Lubell, 2004).

**COGNITIVE THERAPY** Through rational emotive behavior therapy, Albert Ellis might have shown people with social anxiety how irrational needs for social approval and perfectionism produce unnecessary anxiety in social interactions. Eliminating exaggerated needs for social approval is apparently a key therapeutic factor.

Cognitive therapists seek to identify and correct dysfunctional or distorted beliefs. For example, people with social anxiety might think that no one at a party will want to talk with them and that they will wind up lonely and isolated for the rest of their lives. Cognitive therapists help clients recognize the logical flaws in their thinking and help them to view situations rationally. Clients may be asked to gather evidence to test their beliefs, which may lead them to alter beliefs they find are not grounded in reality. Therapists may encourage clients with social anxiety to test their beliefs that they are bound to be ignored, rejected, or ridiculed by others in social gatherings by attending a party, initiating conversations, and monitoring other people's reactions. Therapists may also help clients develop social skills to improve their interpersonal effectiveness and teach them how to handle social rejection, if it should occur, without catastrophizing.

One example of a cognitive technique is **cognitive restructuring**, a method in which therapists help clients pinpoint self-defeating thoughts and generate rational alternatives they can use to cope with anxiety-provoking situations. For example, Kevin (see earlier case study) learned to replace self-defeating thoughts with rational alternatives and to practice speaking rationally and calmly to himself during his exposure trials.

Cognitive-behavioral therapy is the general term applied to therapeutic approaches that combine behavioral and cognitive therapy techniques. CBT practitioners incorporate behavioral techniques, such as exposure, with techniques drawn from the cognitive therapies of Ellis, Beck, and others. For example, in treating social anxiety, therapists often combine exposure treatment with cognitive restructuring techniques that help clients replace anxiety-inducing thoughts with calming alternatives (Rapee, Gaston, & Abbott, 2009). Evidence supports the effectiveness of CBT in treating many types of phobia, including social anxiety and claustrophobia (e.g., Craske et al., 2014; Goldin et al., 2013; McEvoy et al., 2012; Rachman, 2009). That said, a recent large-scale study showed that a contemporary form of psychodynamic therapy was about equally effective as CBT in treating social anxiety disorder (Clarkin, 2014; Leichsenring et al., 2013, 2014).

**DRUG THERAPY** Evidence also supports the use of antidepressant drugs, including sertraline (Zoloft) and paroxetine (Paxil), in treating social anxiety (Liebowitz, Gelenberg, & Munjack, 2005; Schneier, 2006). A combination of psychotherapy and drug therapy in the form of antidepressant medication may be more effective in some cases than either treatment approach alone (Blanco et al., 2010).

# Generalized Anxiety Disorder

**Generalized anxiety disorder (GAD)** is characterized by excessive anxiety and worry that is not limited to any one object, situation, or activity. Normally, anxiety can be an adaptive response, a built-in bodily warning signal that a threat is perceived and requires immediate attention. However, for people with GAD, anxiety is excessive, becomes difficult to control, and is accompanied by physical symptoms such as restlessness, jumpiness, and muscle tension (Donegan & Dugas, 2012; Stein & Sareen, 2015).

## Features of GAD

**5.9 Describe generalized anxiety disorder and identify its key features.**

The central feature of GAD is excessive and uncontrollable worry (Stefanopoulou et al., 2014; Stein & Sareen, 2015). People with GAD tend to be chronic worriers—even lifelong worriers. They may worry about many things, including their health, their finances, the well-being of their children, and their social relationships. They tend to worry about everyday, minor things, such as getting stuck in traffic, and about unlikely future events, such as going bankrupt. They may avoid situations or events in which they expect that something "bad" might happen, or they might repeatedly seek reassurance from others that everything is okay. To reach a diagnostic level, GAD needs to be associated with either marked emotional distress or significant impairment in daily functioning. Children with GAD tend to worry about academics, athletics, and social aspects of school life.

PHILIP: GENERALIZED ANXIETY DISORDER (GAD)

The emotional distress associated with GAD interferes significantly with a person's daily life. GAD frequently occurs together with other disorders, including depression or other anxiety disorders such as agoraphobia and obsessive-compulsive disorder. Other related features include restlessness; feeling tense, keyed up, or on edge; becoming easily fatigued; having difficulty concentrating or finding one's mind going blank; irritability; muscle tension; and disturbances of sleep, such as difficulty falling asleep or staying asleep, or having restless and unsatisfying sleep.

GAD tends to be a stable disorder that initially arises in the mid-teens to mid-20s and then typically follows a lifelong course. The lifetime prevalence of GAD in the general U.S. population is estimated to be around 5.7% overall; it occurs about twice as often among women as among men (Stein & Sareen, 2015). About 3% of adults are affected by GAD in any given year. In the case of Earl, we find a number of features of GAD.

## "Worrying about Worrying":

### A CASE OF GENERALIZED ANXIETY DISORDER

Earl was a 52-year-old supervisor at an automobile plant. His hands trembled as he spoke. His cheeks were pale. His face was somewhat boyish, making his hair seem grayed with worry.

He was reasonably successful in his work, although he noted that he was not a "star." His marriage of nearly three decades was in "reasonably good shape," although sexual relations were "less than exciting—I shake so much that it isn't easy to get involved." The mortgage on the house was not a burden and would be paid off within five years, but "I don't know what it is; I think about money all the time." The three children were doing well. One was employed, one was in college, and one was in high school. But "with everything going on these days, how can you not worry about them? I'm up for hours worrying about them."

"But it's the strangest thing." Earl shook his head. "I swear I'll find myself worrying when there's nothing in my head. I don't know how to describe it. It's like I'm worrying first and then there's something in my head to worry about. It's not like I start thinking about this or that and I see it's bad and then I worry. And then the shakes come, and then, of course, I'm worrying about worrying, if you know what I mean. I want to run away; I don't want anyone to see me. You can't direct workers when you're shaking."

Going to work had become a major chore. "I can't stand the noises of the assembly lines. I just feel jumpy all the time. It's like I expect something awful to happen. When it gets bad like that I'll be out of work for a day or two with shakes."

Earl had been checked over "for everything; my doctor took blood, saliva, urine, you name it. He listened to everything, he put things inside me. He had other people look at me. He told me to stay away from coffee and alcohol. Then from tea. Then from chocolate and Coca-Cola, because there's a little bit of caffeine [in them]. He gave me Valium [an antianxiety drug or minor tranquilizer] and I thought I was in heaven for a while. Then it stopped working, and he switched me to something else. Then that stopped working, and he switched me back. Then he said he was 'out of chemical miracles' and I better see a shrink or something. Maybe it was something from my childhood."

*From the Author's Files*

## Theoretical Perspectives and Treatment Approaches

**5.10 Describe the theoretical perspective on GAD and identify two major ways of treating GAD.**

Freud characterized the type of anxiety we see in GAD as "free floating" because people seem to carry it from situation or situation. From a psychodynamic perspective, generalized anxiety represents the threatened leakage of unacceptable sexual or aggressive impulses or wishes into conscious awareness. The person is aware of the anxiety but not its underlying source. The problem with speculating about the unconscious origins of anxiety is that they lie beyond the reach of direct scientific tests. We cannot directly observe or measure unconscious impulses.

From a learning perspective, generalized anxiety is precisely that: generalization of anxiety across many situations. People concerned about broad life themes, such as finances, health, and family matters, are likely to experience apprehension or worry in a variety of settings. Anxiety would thus become connected with almost any environment or situation.

CHRISTY: GAD WITH INSOMNIA

The cognitive perspective on GAD emphasizes the role of exaggerated or distorted thoughts and beliefs, especially beliefs that underlie worry. People with GAD tend to worry just about everything. They also tend to be overly attentive to threatening cues in the environment (Amir et al., 2009), perceiving danger and calamitous consequences at every turn. Consequently, they feel continually on edge, as their nervous systems respond to the perception of threat or danger with activation of the sympathetic nervous system, leading to increased states of bodily arousal and the accompanying feelings of anxiety.

The cognitive and biological perspectives converge in evidence showing irregularities in the functioning of the amygdala in GAD patients and in its connections to the brain's thinking center, the prefrontal cortex (PFC; Etkin et al., 2009; see Figure 5.8). It appears that in people with GAD, the PFC may rely on worrying as a cognitive strategy for dealing with the fear generated by an overactive amygdala.

We also suspect irregularities in neurotransmitter activity in GAD. We mentioned earlier that antianxiety drugs such as the benzodiazepines *diazepam* (Valium) and *alprazolam* (Xanax) increase the effects of GABA, an inhibitory neurotransmitter that tones down central nervous system arousal. Similarly, irregularities of the neurotransmitter serotonin are implicated in GAD on the basis of evidence that GAD responds favorably to the antidepressant drug *paroxetine* (Paxil), which specifically targets serotonin (Sheehan & Mao, 2003). Neurotransmitters work on brain structures that regulate emotional states such as anxiety, so it is possible that an overreactivity of these brain structures (e.g., the amygdala) is involved.

## A CLOSER Look

### TAKE THIS PILL BEFORE SEEING YOUR THERAPIST

The drug *D-cycloserine* (DSQ), an antibiotic used to treat tuberculosis, might find another use in boosting the effects of exposure therapy in the treatment of anxiety-related disorders (Andersson et al., 2015; de Kleine et al., 2014). The drug acts on synaptic connections in the brain involved in processes of learning and memory, so investigators suspect that it might enhance the effects of learning-based treatments such as CBT. More about this in a moment, but first, let's look at some background information.

Experimental research with laboratory mice showed that DSQ boosted ability on tests of memory of particular objects seen earlier and places where these objects had been placed (Zlomuzica et al., 2007). Other research showed that DSQ sped up extinction of fear responses in rats (Davis et al., 2005). As you'll recall, extinction is the process by which a conditioned fear response is weakened as a result of repeated exposure to the conditioned stimulus (i.e., the fearful object or situation) in the absence of the aversive unconditioned stimulus (i.e., a painful or unpleasant stimulus).

The drug acts on a particular receptor for the neurotransmitter *glutamate*, a chemical in the brain that keeps the central nervous system aroused and kicking. The drug caffeine also increases glutamate activity, which explains why many people start their morning with a cup of caffeine-rich coffee or tea to increase their level of arousal and alertness.

The underlying brain mechanism explaining the effectiveness of DSQ in boosting extinction of fear responses remains unknown, but investigators suspect that the amygdala, the fear-triggering part of the brain, is involved (Davis et al., 2006). One possibility is that DSQ acts on glutamate receptors in the amygdala to speed up the process of extinction (Britton et al., 2007).

Might DSQ have similar effects on anxiety disorders in people? We don't yet know. Some evidence shows that DSQ boosts effectiveness of exposure therapy in treating PTSD, OCD, and social anxiety disorder (Andersson et al., 2105; Chasson et al., 2010; Difede et al., 2014; de Kleine et al., 2014; Smits et al., 2013). However, another large-scale study found that DSQ failed to enhance treatment effects in combat veterans with PTSD (e.g., Neylan, 2014; Rothbaum et al., 2014). Future research will hopefully sort out these inconsistencies. The use of drugs to boost psychological interventions is still in its infancy, but a day may come when popping a pill before seeing your behavior therapist becomes more or less routine.

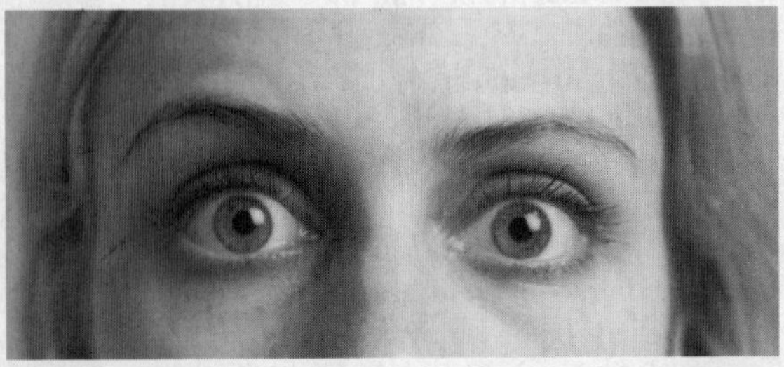

**CAN DRUGS BOOST THE EFFECTS OF BEHAVIOR THERAPY?** Investigators are exploring whether the drug D-cycloserine can boost the effects of behavior (learning-based) therapy of phobias and other anxiety disorders.

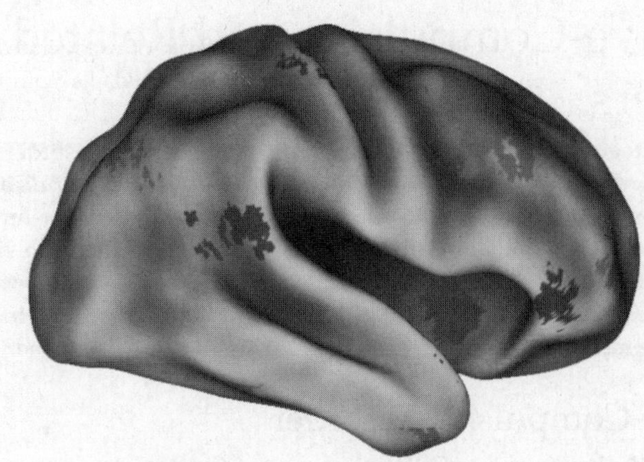

**Figure 5.8** Links between the prefrontal cortex and amygdala.

The areas in red in the front part of this brain image show parts of the prefrontal cortex that have stronger connections to the amygdala in the brains of GAD patients than in the brains of nonpatient controls. These areas are involved in processes relating to distraction and worry.

The major forms of treatment of GAD are psychiatric drugs and CBT. Antidepressant drugs, such as *sertraline* (Zoloft) and *paroxetine* (Paxil), can help relieve anxiety symptoms (Allgulander et al., 2004; Liebowitz et al., 2002). Bear in mind, however, that although psychiatric drugs may help relieve anxiety, they do not cure the underlying problem. Once the drugs are discontinued, the symptoms often return.

Cognitive-behavioral therapists use a combination of techniques to treat GAD, including training in relaxation skills; learning to substitute calming, adaptive thoughts for intrusive, worrisome thoughts; and learning skills of decatastrophizing (e.g., avoiding the tendency to think the worst). Evidence from controlled studies shows substantial therapeutic benefits from CBT in treating GAD (DiMauro et al., 2013; Wetherell et al., 2013). The effectiveness of CBT is comparable to that of drug therapy, but with lower dropout rates, which indicates that the psychological treatment is better tolerated by patients (Mitte, 2005). In one illustrative study, the great majority of GAD patients treated with either behavioral or cognitive methods, or the combination of these methods, no longer met diagnostic criteria for the disorder following treatment (Borkovec et al., 2002).

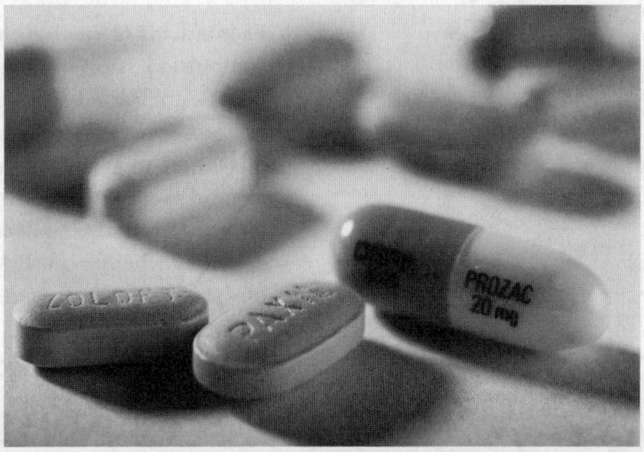


**ANTIDEPRESSANT OR ANTIANXIETY MEDICATION?**

Antidepressant medication such as the drugs Zoloft and Paxil may help quell anxiety. Although these drugs may treat the symptoms of anxiety, they do not resolve the underlying problems.

## TYING it together

Many psychologists believe that the origins of anxiety disorders involve a complex interplay of environmental, physiological, and psychological factors. Complicating matters further is that different causal pathways may be at work in different cases. Given that multiple causes are at work, it is not surprising that different approaches to treating anxiety disorders have emerged.

To illustrate, let's offer a possible causal pathway for panic disorder. Some people may inherit a genetic predisposition, or diathesis, that makes them overly sensitive to minor changes in bodily sensations. Cognitive factors may also be involved. Physical sensations associated with changing $CO_2$ levels, such as dizziness, tingling, or numbness, may be misconstrued as signs of an impending disaster—suffocation, heart attack, or loss of control. This in turn may lead, like dominoes falling in line, to an anxiety reaction that quickly spirals into a full-fledged panic attack.

Whether this happens may depend on another vulnerability factor: an individual's level of anxiety sensitivity. People with high levels of anxiety sensitivity may be more likely to panic in response to changes in their physical sensations. In some cases, a person's anxiety sensitivity may be so high that panic ensues even without a genetic predisposition. Over time, panic attacks may come to be triggered by exposure to internal or external cues (conditioned stimuli) that have been associated with panic attacks in the past, such as heart palpitations or boarding a train or elevator. As we saw in the case of Michael at the beginning of the chapter, changes in physical sensations may be misconstrued as signs of an impending heart attack, setting the stage for a cycle of physiological responses and catastrophic thinking that can result in a full-blown panic attack.

Helping panic sufferers develop more effective coping skills for handling anxiety symptoms without catastrophizing can help break this vicious cycle.

# Obsessive-Compulsive and Related Disorders

The *DSM-5* category of Obsessive-Compulsive and Related Disorders contains a hodgepodge of disorders that have in common a pattern of compulsive or driven repetitive behaviors associated with significant personal distress or impaired functioning in meeting demands of daily life (see Table 5.5). In the following sections, we focus on three major disorders in this category: *obsessive-compulsive disorder, body dysmorphic disorder*, and *hoarding disorder*. Two other related disorders, *trichotillomania (hair pulling disorder)* and *excoriation (skin picking) disorder*, are described in Table 5.5.

## Obsessive-Compulsive Disorder

**5.11 Describe the key features of obsessive-compulsive disorder and ways of understanding and treating it.**

People with **obsessive-compulsive disorder (OCD)** are troubled by recurrent obsessions, compulsions, or both that are time-consuming, such as lasting more than an hour a day, or cause significant distress or interfere with a person's normal routines or occupational or social functioning (American Psychiatric Association, 2013; Parmet, Lynm, & Golub, 2011). An **obsession** is a recurrent, persistent, and unwanted thought, urge, or mental image that seems beyond a person's ability to control. Obsessions can be potent and persistent enough to interfere with daily life and can engender significant distress and anxiety. One may wonder endlessly whether one has locked the doors and shut the windows, for example. One may be obsessed with the urge to do harm to one's spouse. One can have intrusive mental images or

**Table 5.5** Overview of Obsessive-Compulsive and Related Disorders

| Type of Disorder | Approximate Lifetime Prevalence in Population | Description | Associated Features |
|---|---|---|---|
| **Obsessive-Compulsive Disorder** | About 2% to 3% | Recurrent obsessions (recurrent, intrusive thoughts) and/or compulsions (repetitive behaviors the person feels compelled to perform) | • Obsessions generate anxiety that may be at least partially relieved by performance of the compulsive rituals |
| **Body Dysmorphic Disorder** | Unknown | Preoccupation with an imagined or exaggerated physical defect | • Person may believe that others think less of him or her as a person because of the perceived defect<br>• Person may engage in compulsive behaviors, such as excessive grooming, that aim to correct the perceived defect |
| **Hoarding Disorder (Compulsive Hoarding)** | 2% to 5% | Strong need to accumulate possessions, regardless of their value, and persistent difficulty or distress associated with discarding them | • Leads to cluttering the home with piles of collected materials, such as books, clothing, household items, and even junk mail<br>• Can have a range of harmful effects, including difficulty using living space and conflicts with family members and others<br>• Person may feel a sense of security from accumulating and retaining otherwise useless or unnecessary stuff<br>• Person may fail to recognize that the hoarding behavior is a problem, despite the obvious evidence |
| **Trichotillomania (Hair-Pulling Disorder)** | Unknown | Compulsive or repetitive hair pulling resulting in hair loss | • Hair pulling may involve the scalp or other parts of the body and may result in noticeable bald spots<br>• Hair pulling may have self-soothing effects and be used as a coping response in dealing with stress or anxiety |
| **Excoriation (Skin-Picking) Disorder** | 1.4% or higher (in adults) | Compulsive or repetitive picking of the skin, resulting in skin lesions or sores that may never completely heal because of repeated picking at scabs | • Skin picking may involve scratching, picking, rubbing, or digging into the skin<br>• Skin picking may be an attempt to remove slight imperfections or irregularities in the skin or used as a coping response to stress or anxiety |

**SOURCES:** American Psychiatric Association, 2013; Grant, 2014; Mataix-Cols et al., 2010; Snyder, 2015; and other sources.

fantasies, such as the recurrent fantasy of a young mother that her children had been run over by traffic on the way home from school. Obsessions generally cause anxiety or distress, but not in all cases (American Psychiatric Association, 2013).

**DAVE: OBSESSIVE-COMPULSIVE DISORDER (OCD)**

A **compulsion** is a repetitive behavior (e.g., hand washing or checking door locks) or mental act (e.g., praying, repeating certain words, or counting) that a person feels compelled or driven to perform (American Psychiatric Association, 2013). Compulsions typically occur in response to obsessional thoughts and are frequent and forceful enough to interfere with daily life or cause significant distress. Table 5.6 describes some relatively common obsessions and compulsions. In the following first-person account, a man describes his obsessive concerns about having caused harm to other people (and even insects) as the result of his actions.

"I"

**"Tormenting Thoughts and Secret Rituals"**

My compulsions are caused by fears of hurting someone through my negligence. It's always the same mental rigmarole: making sure the doors are latched and the gas jets are off; making sure I switch off the light with just the right amount of pressure, so I don't cause an electrical problem; making sure I shift the car's gears cleanly, so I don't damage the machinery.

I fantasize about finding an island in the South Pacific and living alone. That would take the pressure off; if I would harm anyone it would just be me. Yet even if I were alone, I'd still have my worries, because even insects can be a problem. Sometimes when I take the garbage out, I'm afraid that I've stepped on an ant. I stare down to see if there is an ant kicking and writhing in agony.

I realize that other people don't do these things. Mainly, it's that I don't want to go through the guilt of having hurt anything. It's selfish in that sense. I don't care about them as much as I do about not feeling the guilt.

**SOURCE:** *Osborn, 1998*

Most compulsions fall into two categories: cleaning rituals and checking rituals. Rituals can become the focal point of life. A compulsive hand washer, Corinne, engaged in elaborate hand-washing rituals. She spent 3 to 4 hours daily at the sink and complained, "My hands look like lobster claws." Some people literally take hours checking and rechecking that all the appliances are off before they leave home, and still remain in doubt.

Another woman with a checking compulsion described an elaborate ritual she insisted her husband perform to complete the simple act of taking out the garbage (Colas, 1998). The couple lived in an apartment and deposited their garbage in a common dumpster. The ritual was intended to keep the neighbors' germs out of her apartment. She insisted that after her husband tossed the garbage without ever touching the dumpster,

**Table 5.6** Examples of Obsessive Thoughts and Compulsive Behaviors

| Obsessive Thought Patterns | Compulsive Behavior Patterns |
|---|---|
| Thinking that one's hands remain dirty despite repeated washing | Rechecking one's work time and time again |
| Difficulty shaking the thought that a loved one has been hurt or killed | Rechecking the doors or gas jets before leaving home |
| Repeatedly thinking that one has left the door to the house unlocked | Constantly washing one's hands to keep them clean and germ free |
| Worrying constantly that the gas jets in the house were not turned off | |
| Repeatedly thinking that one has done terrible things to loved ones | |

he then needed to take his shoes off when returning to the apartment and wash his hands, using his clean hand to pump the soap dispenser so that it would not become contaminated. Her husband then needed to repeat the process 20 times, one time for each of 20 sealed bags of garbage. If she noticed a stain on his shirt, say a brown liquid stain, she insisted he go into the dumpster and find the bag matching the stain in order to identify the liquid. If he refused, she would hound him for hours until he relented.

Compulsions often accompany obsessions and may at least partially relieve the anxiety created by obsessional thinking. By washing their hands 40 or 50 times in a row each time they touch a public doorknob, compulsive hand washers may experience some relief from the anxiety engendered by the obsessive thought that germs or dirt still linger in the folds of skin. They may believe that the compulsive ritual will help prevent a dreaded event, such as germ contamination. However, the repetitive nature of the compulsive behavior far exceeds any reasonable steps one can take as a precaution. In effect, the solution (i.e., performing the compulsive ritual) becomes the problem (Salkovskis et al., 2003). A person becomes trapped in a vicious pattern of worrisome, intrusive thoughts, leading to compulsive rituals. People with OCD generally recognize that their obsessive concerns are excessive or irrational but feel incapable of stopping them (Belkin, 2005).

OCD affects between 2% and 3% of the general population at some point in their lives and may emerge as early as age 4 (American Psychiatric Association, 2013; Sookman & Fineberg, 2015; Snyder et al., 2015). It usually begins in adolescence or early adulthood, but may emerge in childhood. A Swedish study found that although most OCD patients eventually showed some improvement, most also continued to have some symptoms of the disorder through the course of their lives (Skoog & Skoog, 1999). The disorder occurs about equally often in men and women. The case example of Jack illustrates a checking compulsion.

## Jack's "Little Behavioral Quirks":

### A CASE OF OBSESSIVE-COMPULSIVE DISORDER

Jack, a successful chemical engineer, was urged by his wife, Mary, a pharmacist, to seek help for "his little behavioral quirks," which she had found increasingly annoying. Jack was a compulsive checker. When they left the apartment, he would insist on returning to check that the lights or gas jets were off or that the refrigerator doors were shut. Sometimes he would apologize at the elevator and return to the apartment to carry out his rituals; sometimes the compulsion to check struck him in the garage. He would return to the apartment, leaving Mary fuming. Going on vacation was especially difficult for Jack. The rituals occupied the better part of the morning of their departure. Even then, he remained plagued by doubts.

Mary had also tried to adjust to Jack's nightly routine of bolting out of bed to recheck the doors and windows. Her patience was running thin. Jack realized that his behavior was impairing their relationship as well as causing him distress. Yet he was reluctant to enter treatment. He gave lip service to wanting to be rid of his compulsive habits, but he also feared that surrendering his compulsions would leave him defenseless against the anxieties they helped to ease.

*From the Author's Files*

**THEORETICAL PERSPECTIVES** Within the psychodynamic tradition, obsessions represent leakage of unconscious urges or impulses into consciousness, and compulsions are acts that help keep these impulses repressed. Obsessive thoughts about contamination by dirt or germs may represent the threatened emergence of unconscious infantile wishes to soil oneself and play with feces. The compulsion (in this case, cleanliness rituals) helps keep such wishes at bay. The psychodynamic model remains largely speculative, in large part because of the difficulty (some would say impossibility) of arranging scientific tests to determine the existence of unconscious impulses and conflicts.

Vulnerability to OCD is partly determined by genetic factors (Mattheisen et al., 2014; Taylor & Jang, 2011). On a related note, many people with OCD, especially those who develop the disorder during childhood, have a history of tic disorders, which leads investigators to suspect there is a genetic link between tic disorders and OCD (Browne et al., 2015; Hirschtritt et al., 2015).

Another possibility is that the actions of particular genes affect chemical balances in the brain that lead to overarousal of a network of neurons called a *worry circuit*, a neural network that signals danger in response to perceived threats. In OCD, the brain may be continually sending messages through this worry circuit or neural circuit that something is wrong and requires immediate attention, leading to obsessional, worrisome thoughts and repetitive, compulsive behaviors. These signals may emanate from the brain's fear-triggering center, the amygdala, which is part of the limbic system. Normally, the prefrontal cortex modulates input from the amygdala and other lower brain structures. However, in people with OCD and other anxiety disorders, this process may break down as the PFC fails to control excess neural activity emanating from the amygdala, leading to anxiety and worry (Harrison et al., 2009; Monk et al., 2008).

Let's consider other intriguing possibilities regarding the biological underpinnings of OCD. One possibility requiring further study is that compulsive aspects of OCD result from abnormalities in brain circuits that normally serve to constrain repetitive behaviors. As a result, people with OCD may feel compelled to perform repetitive behaviors as though they were "stuck in gear" (Leocani et al., 2001).

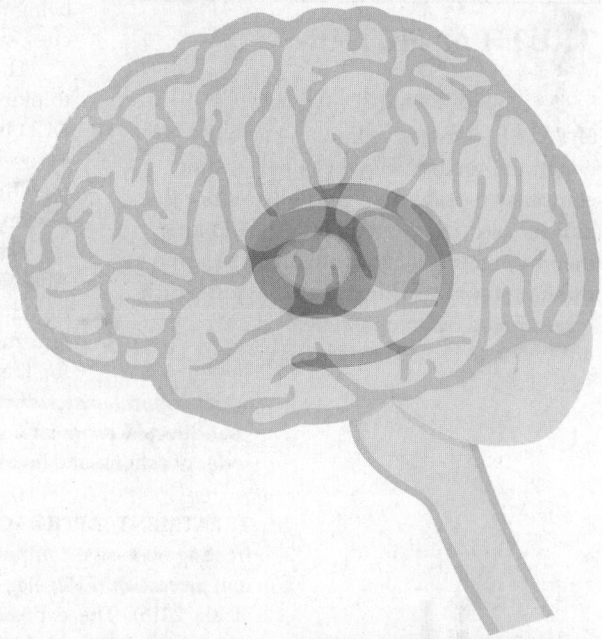

**PROBING THE BRAIN FOR CLUES TO OCD.** Scientists are probing deeper structures in the brain, including the basal ganglia (shown here), looking for abnormalities in brain mechanisms that control repetitive movements or habits.

The frontal lobes in the cerebral cortex regulate brain centers in the lower brain that control bodily movements. Brain imaging studies implicate abnormal patterns of activation of brain circuits involving the frontal lobes in OCD patients (Hsieh et al., 2014; Snyder et al., 2015). A disruption in these neural pathways may explain difficulties people with compulsive behavior have in inhibiting repetitive, ritualistic behaviors.

Other parts of the brain, including the basal ganglia, may also be involved in OCD. The basal ganglia are involved in controlling body movements, so it makes sense that a dysfunction in this region might help explain the ritualistic behaviors seen in OCD patients. Recently, investigators linked excessive habits or ritualized behaviors in OCD patients with overactivation in a part of the basal ganglia called the *caudate nucleus*, which is involved in regulating voluntary body movements (Gillan et al., 2015). By this account, OCD may involve a breakdown in how the brain controls repetitive body movements or habits.

Psychological models of OCD emphasize cognitive and learning-based factors. People with OCD tend to be overly focused on their thoughts (Taylor & Jang, 2011). They can't seem to break the mental loop in which the same intrusive, negative thoughts reverberate in their minds. They also tend to exaggerate the risk that unfortunate events will occur. Because they expect terrible things to happen, people with OCD engage in rituals to prevent them. For example, an accountant who imagines awful consequences for slight mistakes on a client's tax forms may feel compelled to repeatedly check her or his work. Rituals may provide an illusion of control over stressful events (Reuven-Magril, Dar, & Liberman, 2008).

**AN OBSESSIVE THOUGHT?** One type of obsession involves recurrent, intrusive images of a calamity occurring as the result of one's own carelessness. For example, a person may not be able to shake the image of his or her house catching fire because of an electrical short in an appliance inadvertently left on.

Another cognitive factor linked to the development of OCD is perfectionism, or belief that one must perform flawlessly (Moretz & McKay, 2009; Taylor & Jang, 2011). People who hold perfectionist beliefs exaggerate the consequences of turning in less-than-perfect work and may feel compelled to redo their efforts until every detail is flawless.

From a learning perspective, we can view compulsive behaviors as operant responses that are negatively reinforced by relief from anxiety triggered by obsessional thoughts. Put simply, "obsessions give rise to anxiety/distress and compulsions reduce it" (Franklin et al., 2002,). If a person obsesses that dirt or foreign bodies contaminate other people's hands, then shaking hands with another person or even touching a doorknob may evoke powerful anxiety. Compulsive hand washing following exposure to a perceived contaminant provides some degree of relief from anxiety. We know that reinforcement, be it positive or negative, strengthens the behavior it follows. Thus, anxiety relief from performing the compulsive ritual increases the likelihood of the ritual

## TRUTH or FICTION

Obsessive thinking helps relieve anxiety.

☑ **FALSE** Obsessive thinking actually engenders anxiety. However, performing compulsive rituals may partially reduce the anxiety associated with obsessive thinking, thereby creating a cycle in which obsessive thinking prompts ritualistic behavior, which is reinforced by anxiety relief.

being repeated the next time the person encounters anxiety-evoking cues, such as shaking hands or touching doorknobs. **T / F**

The question remains: Why do some people develop obsessive thinking, and others do not? Perhaps it's the case that people with OCD have an overly sensitive bodily alarm system that is activated by even minor cues of danger. Along these lines, we can speculate that the brain's worry circuit kicks into action whenever such a person senses a possible threat, whether it is real or imagined.

Deficits in memory may also play a role (Abramovitch, Abramowitz, & Mittelman, 2013). For example, compulsive checkers may have difficulty bringing to mind tasks they performed, such as remembering whether they had turned off toaster oven before leaving for the day. Evidence also shows that OCD patients have deficits in *executive functioning*, which is a cluster of cognitive abilities needed to control and regulate goal-directed behaviors, such as planning for the future, prioritizing and sequencing a series of actions, and breaking problem habits (Snyder et al., 2015).

**TREATMENT APPROACHES** Behavior therapists have achieved impressive results treating obsessive-compulsive disorder with a technique called *exposure with response* (ritual) *prevention* (ERP; e.g., Crino, 2015; Franklin & Foa, 2011; McKay et al., 2014; Wheaton et al., 2016). The exposure component involves repeated and prolonged exposure to stimuli or situations that evoke obsessive thoughts. For many people, such situations are hard to avoid. Leaving the house, for example, may trigger obsessive thoughts about whether the gas jets are turned off or the windows and doors are locked. Clients may be instructed to purposely induce obsessive thoughts by leaving the house messy or rubbing their hands in dirt. The *response prevention* component involves preventing the compulsive behavior or ritual from occurring. Clients who rub their hands in dirt must avoid washing them for a designated period of time. After locking the front door, the compulsive lock checker must avoid rechecking to see that the door is securely locked.

Through ERP, people with OCD learn to tolerate the anxiety triggered by their obsessive thoughts while they are prevented from performing their compulsive rituals. With repeated exposure trials, the anxiety eventually subsides, and the person feels less compelled to perform the accompanying rituals. The underlying principle, yet again, is extinction. When cues that trigger obsessive thoughts and accompanying anxiety are repeatedly presented but the person sees that nothing bad happens, the bonds between these cues and the anxiety response should weaken.

**DID I LOCK IT? OR DID I JUST THINK I LOCKED IT?** In ERP, the therapist assists the client in breaking the obsessive-compulsive disorder cycle by confronting stimuli, such as dirt, that evoke obsessive thoughts, but without performing the compulsive ritual (e.g., rechecking that the door is securely locked).

Cognitive techniques are often combined with ERP within a cognitive-behavioral treatment program (Abramowitz, 2008; Hassija & Gray, 2010). The cognitive component involves correcting distorted ways of thinking (cognitive distortions), such as tendencies to overestimate the likelihood or severity of feared consequences (Whittal et al., 2008).

SSRI antidepresssants (selective serotonin reuptake inhibitors; discussed in Chapter 2) also have therapeutic benefits in treating OCD (Grant, 2014). This class of drugs includes *fluoxetine* (Prozac), *paroxetine* (Paxil), and *clomipramine* (Anafranil). These drugs increase the availability of the neurotransmitter serotonin in the brain. The effectiveness of these drugs suggests that problems with serotonin transmission play an important role in the development of OCD, at least in some cases (Maia & Cano-Colino, 2015). However, we need to bear in mind that only a small percentage of people treated with SSRIs show full symptom relief (Grant, 2014). We should also note that many patients fail to respond fully to CBT (Fisher & Wells, 2005).

CBT produces greater benefits than antidepressant (SSRI) drugs in treating OCD and may lead to more lasting results (Franklin & Foa, 2011; Öst, Havnen, et al., 2015). Approximately 60% to 85% of people with OCD who are treated with exposure with response prevention show significant reductions in OCD symptoms (Holmes, Craske, & Graybiel, 2014; Grant, 2014). We also have learned that adding CBT to (SSRI) antidepressant treatment for OCD can boost the effectiveness of drug treatment alone (Grant, 2014; Ressler & Rothbaum, 2013; Simpson, 2014). *A Closer Look: A Pacemaker for the Brain?*

explores an experimental treatment for OCD and other psychological disorders involving electrical stimulation of structures deep within the brain.

## Body Dysmorphic Disorder

**5.12 Describe the key features of body dysmorphic disorder.**

People with **body dysmorphic disorder (BDD)** are preoccupied with an imagined or exaggerated physical defect in their appearance, such as skin blemishes, wrinkling or swelling of the face, body moles or spots, or facial swelling, causing them to feel they are ugly or even disfigured (Buhlmann, Marques, & Wilhelm, 2012; Fang, Schwartz, & Wilhelm, 2016). They fear others will judge them negatively on the basis of their perceived defect or flaw (Anson, Veale, & de Silva, 2012). They may spend hours examining themselves in the mirror and go to extreme measures to correct the perceived defect, even undergoing invasive or unpleasant medical procedures, including unnecessary plastic surgery. Some people with BDD

**CAN'T YOU SEE IT?** A person with body dysmorphic disorder may spend hours in front of a mirror obsessing about an imagined or exaggerated physical defect in appearance.

## A CLOSER Look

### A PACEMAKER FOR THE BRAIN?

Although psychosurgery remains an experimental and controversial treatment, emerging evidence points to a possible role for a surgical technique involving deep brain stimulation (DBS) in treating people with severe obsessive-compulsive disorder (Denys et al., 2010). DBS targets particular brain circuits linked to specific disorders, such as OCD (see Figure 5.9). In DBS, electrodes are surgically implanted in specific areas of the brain and attached to a small battery placed in the chest wall. When stimulated by a pacemaker-like device, the electrodes transmit electrical signals directly into surrounding brain tissue. We can't say exactly how DBS works, but it may involve interrupting aberrant brain signals.

One unanswered question in using deep brain stimulation is where to place the electrodes. As psychiatrist Wayne Goodman of the National Institute of Mental Health points out, "We're still not exactly sure where the sweet spot is in the brain to reduce the symptoms of OCD. Even if you think you're in the right neighborhood, you may be one block off. And one block off in the brain may be just 1 millimeter" (quoted in "Pacemaker for Brain," 2008).

Though DBS remains an experimental treatment, recent research points to its potential use in treating other disorders in addition to OCD. Investigators find encouraging results in using DBS to treat severely depressed people who fail to respond to other treatments (e.g., Blomsted et al., 2011; Hirschfeld, 2011; Holtzheimer et al., 2012; Keshtkar, Ghanizadeh, & Firoozabadi, 2012).

It is not too fanciful to conjecture that someday, perhaps someday soon, people with severe OCD, depression, or other psychological disorders may be able to self-administer bursts of electricity to precise areas of the brain to control their troublesome symptoms. On a related note, investigators are also evaluating whether brain stimulation from an MRI device might yield a therapeutic benefit similar to DBS. Preliminary results from this form of brain stimulation are promising, showing a reduction in depression in people with major depression (Vaziri-Bozorg et al., 2012).

**Figure 5.9 Deep brain stimulation for obsessive-compulsive disorder.**

This illustration shows the placement of the two electrodes inserted into nuclei of cell bodies that lie under the thalamus. These electrodes are used to stimulate the brain in patients with obsessive-compulsive disorder.

SOURCE: Luc Mallet, Research Director at Inserm, Centre of Research of the Brain & Spine Institute, France.

Used with Permission.

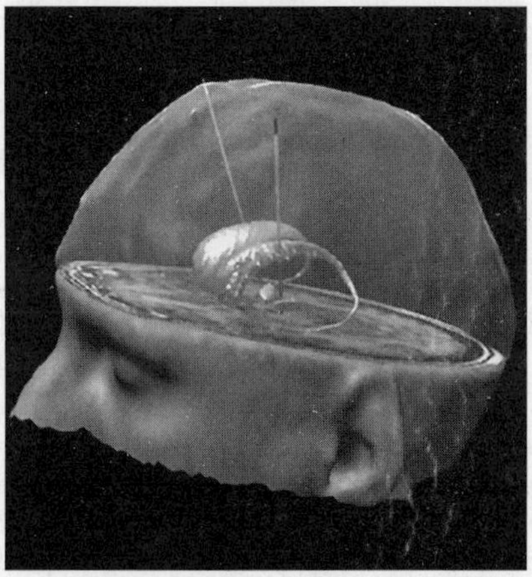

remove all the mirrors from their homes so as not to be reminded of the "glaring flaw" in their appearance. People with BDD may believe that others view them as ugly or deformed and treat them negatively because of their physical flaws.

BDD is classified within the obsessive-compulsive spectrum because people with the disorder often become obsessed with their perceived defect and often feel compelled to check themselves in the mirror or engage in compulsive behaviors aimed at fixing, covering, or modifying the perceived defect. In the case example of BDD on this page, compulsive behavior takes the form of repetitive grooming, washing, and styling of hair.

Although BDD is believed to be relatively common, we don't have specific data on the rates of the disorder because many people with the disorder fail to seek help or keep their symptoms a secret. Not surprisingly, people with BDD have lower self-esteem and higher levels of perfectionism, as compared to healthy controls (Hartmann et al., 2014). We should not underplay the emotional distress associated with BDD, as evidence shows high rates of suicidal thinking and suicide attempts among people with the disorder (Buhlmann, Marques, & Wilhelm, 2012; Phillips & Menard, 2006). More encouraging is evidence based on a small group of people with BDD indicating that most patients eventually recovered, although it often took five years or longer (Bjornsson et al., 2011). **T / F**

### TRUTH or FICTION

Having skin blemishes leads some people to consider suicide.

☑ **TRUE** People with BDD may become so consumed by their self-perceived flaws—even minor skin blemishes—that they think seriously of ending it all.

Cognitive-behavioral therapy, typically involving exposure therapy with response prevention, has demonstrated good results in treating BDD (Roy-Byrne, 2016; Fang, Schwartz, & Wilhelm, 2016; Greenberg, Mothi, & Wilhelm, 2016). Exposure can take the form of intentionally revealing the perceived defect in public, rather than concealing it with makeup or clothing. Response prevention may involve efforts to avoid mirror checking (e.g., by covering mirrors at home) and excessive grooming. ERP is generally combined with cognitive restructuring, in which therapists help clients challenge their distorted beliefs about their physical appearance and evaluate them in light of evidence (Phillips & Rogers, 2011).

## "When My Hair Isn't Right . . . I'm Not Right":

### A CASE OF BODY DYSMORPHIC DISORDER

For Claudia, a 24-year-old legal secretary, virtually every day was a "bad hair day." She explained to her therapist, "When my hair isn't right, which is like every day, I'm not right. Can't you see it?" she went on to explain. "It's so uneven. This piece should be shorter and this one just lies there. People think I'm crazy but I can't stand looking like this. It makes me look like I'm deformed. It doesn't matter if people can't see what I'm talking about. I see it. That's what counts." Several months earlier Claudia had a haircut she described as a disaster. Shortly thereafter, she had thoughts of killing herself: "I wanted to stab myself in the heart. I just couldn't stand looking at myself."

Claudia checked her hair in the mirror innumerable times during the day. She would spend two hours every morning doing her hair and still wouldn't be satisfied. Her constant pruning and checking had become a compulsive ritual. As she told her therapist, "I want to stop pulling and checking it, but I just can't help myself."

Having a bad hair day for Claudia meant that she would not go out with her friends and would spend every second examining herself in the mirror and fixing her hair. Occasionally she would cut pieces of her hair herself in an attempt to correct the mistakes of her last haircut. But cutting it herself inevitably made it even worse, in her view. Claudia was forever searching for the perfect haircut that would correct defects only she could perceive. Several years earlier she had what she described as a perfect haircut. "It was just right. I was on top of the world. But it began to look crooked when it grew in." Forever in search of the perfect haircut, Claudia had obtained a hard-to-get appointment with a world-renowned hair stylist in Manhattan, whose clientele included many celebrities. "People wouldn't understand paying this guy $375 for a haircut, especially on my salary, but they don't realize how important it is to me. I'd pay any amount I could." Unfortunately, even this celebrated hair stylist disappointed her: "My $25 haircut from my old stylist on Long Island was better than this."

Claudia reported other fixations about her appearance earlier in life: "In high school, I felt my face was like a plate. It was just too flat. I didn't want any pictures taken of me. I couldn't help thinking what people thought of me. They won't tell you, you know. Even if they say there's nothing wrong, it doesn't mean anything. They were just lying to be polite." Claudia related that she was taught to equate physical beauty with happiness: "I was told that to be successful you had to be beautiful. How can I be happy if I look this way?"

*From the Author's Files*

# Hoarding Disorder

**5.13 Describe the key features of hoarding disorder.**

Compulsive hoarding, which is classified by *DSM-5* as a newly recognized disorder called **hoarding disorder**, is characterized by extreme difficulty discarding stacks of unnecessary and seemingly useless possessions, which results in personal distress or in creating so much clutter that it makes a person's home unsafe to walk through or nearly uninhabitable (Muroff & Underwood, 2016; Roy-Byrne, 2013b).

In the general community, the percentage of people who say they have difficulty discarding worn or worthless useless possessions is larger than we might expect—21% of the population (Rodriguez, 2013). However, in hoarding disorder—affecting an estimated 2% to 5% of the general population, which is about the same percentage as suffers from OCD—the problem is more severe and negatively impacts daily functioning (Mataix-Cols et al., 2010; Woody, Kellman-McFarlane, & Welsted, 2014). In people with hoarding disorder, piles of unneeded objects, such as stacks of newspapers or magazines, can become a fire hazard or render most of their living space effectively unusable. Visitors must carefully navigate around mounds of clutter.

People who hoard cling to their possessions, leading to conflicts with family members and others who press them to discard the apparently useless junk. People with hoarding disorder tend to be older, poorer, and with more mental and physical health problems than nonhoarders (Nordsletten et al., 2013).

Hoarding disorder bears a close relationship to obsessive-compulsive disorder (Frost, Steketee, & Tolin, 2012). The obsessional features of hoarding disorder may involve recurring thoughts about acquiring objects and fears over losing them. The compulsive features may involve repeatedly rearranging stacks of possessions and

## A CLOSER Look

### "DON'T THEY SEE WHAT I SEE?" VISUAL PROCESSING OF FACES IN PEOPLE WITH BODY DYSMORPHIC DISORDER

Findings from a brain imaging study resonate with impressions many clinicians have about people with BDD. In the study, fMRI scans were taken of people with BDD and non-BDD (control) participants during a facial matching task (Feusner et al., 2007; see Figure 5.10). Participants were shown a series of male and female faces and asked to match each face with one of three comparison faces shown directly below the target face. Brain scans during the matching task showed different patterns of brain activation between BDD and control participants.

The major difference was that participants with BDD showed more activation in the left cerebral hemisphere than did control group members. For most people, the left hemisphere is dominant for tasks requiring analytic, evaluative processing, whereas the right hemisphere is dominant for holistic processing—the type of processing involved in recognizing faces. We typically perceive faces by holistic processing (i.e., recognizing faces as whole patterns) rather than by assembling the component parts of the face in a piecemeal fashion.

Among people with BDD, visual processing in the brain involves greater left hemisphere activation consistent with detailed or piecemeal analysis, in contrast to the more global or contextual processing of the control group. In other words, the BDD group was more prone to overattend to visual details in piecing together parts of the face rather than recognizing faces as whole patterns. This tendency to hone in on details of physical appearance is a key clinical feature of BDD. People with BDD may wrongly assume that other people are as detail-oriented in their perception of physical appearance as they are. This may help explain why they often assume that other people will notice the minor blemishes or physical defects that stand out so clearly in their perceptions of their own faces.

**Figure 5.10 Brain activation patterns of people with dysmorphic disorder.**

These are brain scans showing activation of parts of the brain (shown by areas of red) in BDD patients (top row) and controls (bottom row) in response to facial stimuli. BDD patients show activation in both the left and right prefrontal regions (top part of images), whereas controls show activation only in the right prefrontal regions.

**SOURCE:** Image provided courtesy of Dr. Jamie Feusner.

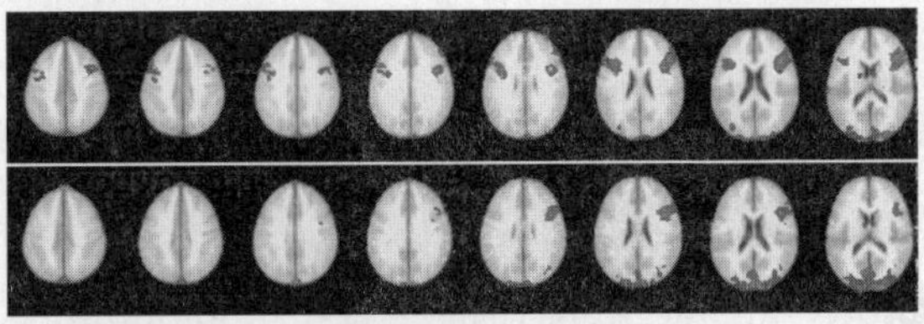

## The Neighbors Complain:
### A CASE OF COMPULSIVE HOARDING

The 55-year-old divorced man did not regard his hoarding as a problem, but felt pressured to come for treatment because of complaints filed by neighbors who were concerned about a fire hazard (his house was one of a series of attached row houses). A home visit revealed the extent of the problem: The rooms were filled with all kinds of useless objects, including out-of-date food cans, piles of newspapers and magazines, and stacks of papers and even pieces of cloth. Most of the furniture was completely hidden by the clutter. A narrow path around the clutter led to the bathroom and to the man's bed. The kitchen was so cluttered that no appliances were accessible. The man reported that he hadn't used the kitchen in quite a while and routinely went out for his meals. There was a pervasive stale and dusty smell throughout the house. When asked why he had kept all of this stuff, he replied that he felt fearful of discarding "important papers" and "things he might need." However, observers were at a loss to explain how any of these objects could be important or needed.

**SOURCE:** *Adapted from Rachman & DeSilva, 2009*

stubbornly refusing to avoid discarding them, even in the face of strong protests from other people. Despite the similarities to OCD, hoarding disorder in the *DSM-5* is a distinct disorder, not a subtype of OCD. There are important shades of difference between hoarding disorder and OCD. For one, obsessional thinking in hoarding disorder does not have the character of intrusive, unwanted thoughts that it does in OCD. These thoughts in people who hoard are typically experienced as a part of the normal stream of thoughts (Mataix-Cols et al., 2010). Moreover, people who hoard do not experience an urge to perform rituals to control disturbing thoughts. Distress associated with hoarding is not a result of intrusive, obsessive thinking but is the result of difficulty adjusting to living amidst all the clutter and conflicts with other people about the clutter. Another difference from OCD is that people who hoard typically experience pleasure or enjoyment from collecting possessions and thinking about them, which is unlike the anxiety associated with obsessional thinking in OCD.

**HOARDING.** People who hoard compulsively acquire and retain piles of useless or unneeded possessions. They become emotionally attached to their possessions and fearful of parting with them.

Underlying causal factors in hoarding behavior continue to be studied, but recent research is probing its neurological basis. When thinking about acquiring and discarding possessions, people who hoard show abnormal patterns of activation in parts of the brain involved in processes such as decision making and self-regulation (Tolin et al., 2012). Further research along these lines may help us better understand the difficulties of people who hoard in making decisions about accumulating objects and avoiding discarding them. Although hoarding has been difficult to treat, CBT shows promising results (Storch & Lewin, 2016; Tolin et al., 2015). CBT helps a person challenge underlying beliefs about the need to accumulate and retain useless possessions and provides training in skills needed for sorting and discarding them (Muroff & Underwood, 2016).

# Summing Up

## Overview of Anxiety Disorders

### Features of Anxiety Disorders

**5.1 Describe the prominent physical, behavioral, and cognitive features of anxiety disorders.**

Anxiety disorders are characterized by disturbed patterns of behavior in which anxiety is the most prominent feature. They are characterized by physical symptoms such as jumpiness, sweaty palms, and a pounding or racing heart; by behavioral features such as avoidance behavior, clinging or dependent behavior, and agitated behavior; and by cognitive features such as worry or a sense of dread or apprehension about the future and fear of losing control.

## Ethnic Differences in Anxiety Disorders

**5.2 Evaluate ethnic differences in rates of anxiety disorders.**

Evidence from nationally representative samples of U.S. adults showed generally lower rates of some anxiety disorders among ethnic minorities as compared to (non-Hispanic) White Americans.

# Panic Disorder

## Features of Panic Attacks

**5.3 Describe the key features of panic attacks.**

Panic attacks have intense, physical features, notably cardiovascular symptoms, that may be accompanied by feelings of sheer terror and fears of losing control, losing one's mind, or dying. Panic attack sufferers often limit their outside activities for fear of recurrent attacks. This can lead to agoraphobia, the fear of venturing into public places.

## Theoretical Perspectives

**5.4 Describe the leading conceptual model of panic disorder.**

The predominant model conceptualizes panic disorder in terms of a combination of cognitive factors (e.g., catastrophic misinterpretation of bodily sensations, anxiety sensitivity) and biological factors (e.g., genetic proneness, increased sensitivity to bodily cues). In this view, panic disorder involves physiological and psychological factors interacting in a vicious cycle that can spiral into full-blown panic attacks.

## Treatment Approaches

**5.5 Evaluate methods used to treat panic disorder.**

The most effective methods of treatment are cognitive-behavioral therapy and drug therapy. CBT for panic disorder incorporates techniques such as self-monitoring, controlled exposure to panic-related cues, including bodily sensations, and development of coping responses for handling panic attacks without catastrophic misinterpretations of bodily cues. Biomedical approaches incorporate use of antidepressant drugs, which have antianxiety and antipanic effects as well as antidepressant effects.

# Phobic Disorders

## Types of Phobic Disorders

**5.6 Describe the key features and specific types of phobic disorders.**

Phobias are excessive irrational fears of specific objects or situations. Phobias involve a behavioral component—the avoidance of the phobic stimulus—as well as physical and cognitive features of anxiety associated with exposure to the phobic stimulus. Specific phobias are excessive fears of particular objects or situations, such as mice, spiders, tight places, or heights. Social phobia (social anxiety disorder) involves an intense fear of being judged negatively by others. Agoraphobia involves fears of venturing into public places. Agoraphobia may occur with, or in the absence of, panic disorder.

## Theoretical Perspectives

**5.7 Explain the role of learning, cognitive, and biological factors in the development of phobias.**

Learning theorists explain phobias as learned behaviors that are acquired on the basis of the principle of conditioning and observational learning. Mowrer's two-factor model incorporates classical and operant conditioning in the explanation of phobias. Phobias appear to be moderated by cognitive factors, such as oversensitivity to threatening cues, overprediction of dangerousness, and self-defeating thoughts and irrational beliefs. Genetic factors also appear to increase proneness to development of phobias. Some investigators believe we are genetically predisposed to acquire certain types of phobias that may have had survival value for our prehistoric ancestors.

## Treatment Approaches

**5.8 Evaluate methods used to treat phobic disorders.**

The most effective methods of treatment are learning-based approaches, such as systematic desensitization and gradual exposure, as well as cognitive therapy and drug therapy, such as the use of antidepressants (e.g., Zoloft, Paxil) for treating social anxiety.

# Generalized Anxiety Disorder

## Features of GAD

**5.9 Describe generalized anxiety disorder and identify its key features.**

Generalized anxiety disorder is a type of anxiety disorder involving persistent anxiety that seems to be free floating or not tied to specific situations. The key features are worry and emotional distress.

## Theoretical Perspectives and Treatment Approaches

**5.10 Describe the theoretical perspective on GAD and identify two major ways of treating it.**

Psychodynamic theorists view anxiety disorders as attempts by the ego to control the conscious emergence of threatening impulses. Feelings of anxiety are seen as warning signals that threatening impulses are nearing awareness. Learning-based models focus on the generalization of anxiety across stimulus situations. Cognitive theorists seek to account for generalized anxiety in terms of faulty thoughts or beliefs that underlie worry. Biological models focus on irregularities in neurotransmitter functioning in the brain. The two major treatment approaches are CBT and drug therapy (typically *paroxetine*).

# Obsessive-Compulsive and Related Disorders

## Obsessive-Compulsive Disorder

**5.11 Describe the key features of obsessive-compulsive disorder and ways of understanding and treating it.**

Obsessive-compulsive disorder involves recurrent patterns of obsessions, compulsions, or a combination of the two. Obsessions are nagging, persistent thoughts that create anxiety and seem beyond a person's ability to control. Compulsions are apparently irresistible, repetitious urges to perform certain behaviors, such as repeated elaborate washing after using the bathroom.

Within the psychodynamic tradition, obsessions represent leakage of unconscious urges or impulses into consciousness, and compulsions are acts that help keep these impulses repressed. Research on biological factors highlights roles for genetics and for brain mechanisms involved in signaling danger and controlling repetitive behaviors. Research shows roles for cognitive factors, such as overfocusing on one's thoughts, exaggerated perceptions of risk of unfortunate events, and perfectionism. Learning theorists view compulsive behaviors as operant responses that are negatively reinforced by relief from anxiety produced by obsessional thinking.

The major contemporary treatment approaches include learning-based models (exposure with response prevention), cognitive therapy (correction of cognitive distortions), and use of SSRI-type antidepressants.

## Body Dysmorphic Disorder

**5.12 Describe the key features of body dysmorphic disorder.**

In body dysmorphic disorder, people are preoccupied with an imagined or exaggerated defect in their physical appearance. It is classified within the OCD spectrum because people with BDD typically experience obsessive thoughts related to their physical appearance and show compulsive checking behaviors and attempts to correct or cover up the problem.

## Hoarding Disorder

**5.13 Describe the key features of hoarding disorder.**

Hoarding disorder is characterized by excessive accumulation and retention of possessions to a point of causing personal distress or significantly interfering with a person's ability to maintain a safe and habitable living space. People who hoard have a strong attachment to objects they accumulate and have difficulty discarding them. Hoarding disorder shares characteristics with obsessive-compulsive disorder, such as obsessive thinking about acquiring objects and fears over losing them as well as compulsive behaviors involving rearranging possessions and rigidly resisting efforts to discard them.

# Critical Thinking Questions

On the basis of your reading of this chapter, answer the following questions:

- Anxiety may be a normal emotional reaction in some situations, but not in others. Think of a situation in which anxiety would be a normal reaction and one in which it would be a maladaptive reaction. What are the differences? What criteria would you use to distinguish between normal and abnormal anxiety reactions?
- Do you have any specific phobias, such as fears of small animals, insects, heights, or enclosed spaces? What factors may have contributed to the development of the phobia (or phobias)? How has the phobia affected your life? How have you coped with it?
- John has been experiencing sudden panic attacks on and off for the past few months. During the attacks, he has difficulty breathing and fears that his heart is racing out of control. His physician checked him out and told him the problem is with his nerves, not his heart. What treatment alternatives are available to John that might help him deal with this problem?
- Do you know anyone who has received treatment for an anxiety disorder or OCD? What was the outcome? What other treatment alternatives might be available? Which approach to treatment would you seek if you suffered from a similar problem?

# Key Terms

anxiety, p. 165
anxiety disorder, p. 165
panic disorder, p. 167
agoraphobia, p. 168
phobia, p. 175
specific phobia, p. 176
social anxiety disorder, p. 178
two-factor model, p. 181
systematic desensitization, p. 186
fear-stimulus hierarchy, p. 186
gradual exposure, p. 187
flooding, p. 188
virtual reality therapy (VRT), p. 188
cognitive restructuring, p. 189
generalized anxiety disorder (GAD), p. 190
obsessive-compulsive disorder (OCD), p. 194
obsession, p. 194
compulsion, p. 195
body dysmorphic disorder (BDD), p. 199
hoarding disorder, p. 201

# Chapter 6
# Dissociative Disorders, Somatic Symptom and Related Disorders, and Psychological Factors Affecting Physical Health

## Learning Objectives

**6.1** **Describe** the key features of dissociative identity disorder and **explain** why the concept of dissociative identity disorder is controversial.

**6.2** **Describe** the key features of dissociative amnesia.

**6.3** **Describe** the key features of depersonalization/derealization disorder.

**6.4** **Identify** two culture-bound syndromes with dissociative features.

**6.5** **Describe** different theoretical perspectives on dissociative disorders.

**6.6** **Describe** the treatment of dissociative identity disorder.

**6.7** **Describe** the key features of somatic symptom disorder.

**6.8** **Describe** the key features of illness anxiety disorder.

**6.9** **Describe** the key features of conversion disorder.

**6.10** **Explain** the difference between malingering and factitious disorder.

**6.11** **Describe** the key features of koro and dhat syndromes.

**6.12** **Describe** the theoretical understandings of somatic symptom and related disorders.

**6.13** **Describe** methods used to treat somatic symptom and related disorders.

**6.14** **Describe** the role of psychological factors in understanding and treating headaches.

**6.15** **Identify** psychological risk factors in coronary heart disease.

**6.16** **Identify** psychological factors that may trigger asthma attacks.

**6.17** **Identify** behavioral risk factors in cancer.

**6.18** **Describe** the role that psychologists play in prevention and treatment of HIV/AIDS.

## TRUTH *or* FICTION

**T☐ F☐** The term *split personality* refers to schizophrenia. (p. 209)

**T☐ F☐** People with multiple personalities typically have two different personalities. (p. 210)

**T☐ F☐** Very few of us have episodes in which we feel strangely detached from our own bodies or thought processes. (p. 216)

**T☐ F☐** A surprisingly high number of children who suffered severe physical or sexual abuse in childhood go on to develop multiple personalities as adults. (p. 220)

**T☐ F☐** Some people lose all feeling in their hands or legs, although nothing is medically wrong with them. (p. 226)

**T☐ F☐** Some men have a psychological disorder characterized by fear of the penis shrinking and retracting into the body. (p. 229)

**T☐ F☐** The term *hysteria* derives from the Greek word for testicle. (p. 230)

**T☐ F☐** People can relieve the pain of migraine headaches by raising the temperature in a finger. (p. 235)

**T☐ F☐** Deaths from coronary heart disease are rising in the United States, largely as a result of increased rates of smoking. (p. 238)

## CHAPTER INTRODUCTION: DISSOCIATIVE DISORDERS, SOMATIC SYMPTOM AND RELATED DISORDERS, AND PSYCHOLOGICAL FACTORS AFFECTING PHYSICAL HEALTH

### "I" "We Share a Single Body"

Writing under a pseudonym, "Quiet Storm," a woman posts a message on an online bulletin board to share her experience of what it is like to have multiple personalities residing within herself. She describes a personality that was so fractured because of severe childhood abuse that it had splintered into many pieces. Some of the pieces bear memories of the abuse, whereas others go about their business unaware of the pain and trauma. Now, imagine that these separate parts develop their own unique characteristics. Imagine too that these alter personalities become so compartmentalized that they don't know of each other's existence.

One personality, Sally,* is a nurse. Another, Diana, is a therapist, while Patty is a playful little girl who collects insects, which she keeps in a mayonnaise jar. There is also Claire, the shy one, and Cathy, an adolescent working hard to grow up. She refers to herself as "we," a collection of many different people who share the same body. These alter personalities have their own individual goals, fears, and memories. Some of them are still mired in the past, a dark past filled with shrouded memories of traumatic abuse and incest. These alters were born of abuse they suffered at the hands of their own father. There would be one alter, Nancy, who would go to father when he beckoned her to lay with him, shielding the others from having to do the things he demanded. Nancy protected the others, but at the cost of fracturing the sense of self that makes each of us a whole person.

*The names of the alter personalities have been changed.

**SOURCE:** *Adapted from "Quiet Storm," pseudonym used by a woman who claims to have several personalities residing within her.*

This is a description of *dissociative identity disorder*, known popularly as "multiple personality disorder," perhaps the most perplexing and intriguing of all psychological disorders. The diagnosis is officially recognized in the *DSM* system, although it remains controversial, with many professionals either doubting its existence altogether or ascribing it to a form of role-playing (Boysen & VanBergen, 2014). Dissociative identity disorder is classified as a type of *dissociative disorder*, a grouping of psychological disorders characterized by changes or disturbances in the functions of self—identity, memory, or consciousness—that make the personality whole.

Normally speaking, we know who we are. We may not be certain of ourselves in an existential, philosophical sense, but we know our names, where we live, and what we do for a living. We also tend to remember the salient events of our lives. We may not recall every detail, and we may confuse what we had for dinner on Tuesday with what we had on Monday, but we generally know what we have been doing for the past days, weeks, and years. Normally speaking, there is a unity to consciousness that gives rise to a sense of self. We perceive ourselves as progressing through space and time. In people with dissociative disorders, one or more of these aspects of daily living is disturbed—sometimes bizarrely so.

In this chapter, we explore the dissociative disorders as well as another class of puzzling disorders, *somatic symptom and related disorders*. People with these disorders may have physical complaints that defy medical explanation and so are believed to involve underlying psychological conflicts or issues. They may report blindness or numbness, although no organic basis can be detected. In other cases, people with somatic symptom and related disorders hold exaggerated beliefs about the seriousness of their physical symptoms, such as taking them as signs of life-threatening illnesses despite medical reassurances to the contrary.

In earlier versions of the *DSM*, dissociative and somatic symptom and related disorders were classified with the anxiety disorders under the general category of "neurosis." This grouping was based on the psychodynamic model, which holds that dissociative and somatic symptom and related disorders, as well as the anxiety disorders discussed in Chapter 5, involve maladaptive ways of managing anxiety. With anxiety disorders, disturbing levels of anxiety are expressed directly in behavior, such as the avoidance shown by a person with a phobic disorder toward the feared object or situation. By contrast, the role of anxiety in dissociative and somatic symptom and related disorders is *inferred* rather than directly *observed* in behavior. People with dissociative disorders have psychological problems, such as loss of memory or changes in identity, but don't typically show obvious signs of anxiety. From the psychodynamic model, we infer that dissociative symptoms serve a psychological purpose of shielding the self from the anxiety that would arise from conscious awareness of disturbing internal conflicts over sexual or aggressive wishes or impulses. Likewise, some people with conversion disorder, which is classified in the category of Somatic Symptom and Related Disorders, may show a strange indifference to physical problems such as loss of vision that would greatly concern most of us. Here too we can theorize that the "symptoms" mask unconscious sources of anxiety. Some theorists interpret indifference to symptoms to mean that those symptoms have an underlying benefit; that is, they help prevent anxiety from intruding into consciousness.

The *DSM-5* separates anxiety-related disorders from the other classical categories of neuroses—the dissociative and somatic symptom and related disorders—with which they were historically linked. Yet many practitioners continue to use the broad conceptualization of *neuroses* as a useful framework for grouping together anxiety-related disorders, dissociative disorders, and somatic symptom and related disorders.

# Dissociative Disorders

The major **dissociative disorders** include *dissociative identity disorder, dissociative amnesia,* and *depersonalization/derealization disorder*. In each case, there is a disruption or dissociation ("splitting off") of the functions of identity, memory, or consciousness that normally make us whole. Table 6.1 presents an overview of the dissociative disorders discussed in the text.

**Table 6.1** Overview of Dissociative Disorders

| Type of Disorder | Approximate Lifetime Prevalence in Population | Description | Associated Features |
|---|---|---|---|
| **Dissociative identity disorder** | Unknown | Emergence of two or more distinct personalities | • Alternates may vie for control<br>• May represent a psychological defense against severe childhood abuse or trauma |
| **Dissociative amnesia** | Unknown | Inability to recall important personal material that cannot be accounted for by medical causes | • Information lost to memory is usually of traumatic or stressful experiences<br>• Subtypes include localized amnesia, selective amnesia, and generalized amnesia<br>• May be associated with dissociative fugue, a rare condition in which a person may travel to a new location and start a new life under a different identity |
| **Depersonalization/ derealization disorder** | 2% | Episodes of feeling detached from one's self or one's body or having a sense of unreality about one's surroundings (derealization) | • Person may feel as if he or she is living in a dream or acting like a robot<br>• Episodes of depersonalization are persistent or recurrent and cause significant distress |

**SOURCE:** Prevalence rates derived from American Psychiatric Association, 2013.

# Dissociative Identity Disorder

**6.1 Describe the key features of dissociative identity disorder and explain why the concept of dissociative identity disorder is controversial.**

The Ohio State campus dwelled in terror as four college women were seized, coerced to cash checks or get money from ATMs, and then raped. A cryptic phone call led to the capture of Billy Milligan, a 23-year-old drifter who had been dishonorably discharged from the Navy.

Billy was diagnosed with multiple personality disorder, which is now called **dissociative identity disorder** (DID). In dissociative identity disorder, two or more personalities—each with its own distinctive traits, memories, mannerisms, and even style of speech—"occupy" one person. Dissociative identity disorder, which is often called *multiple personality* or *split personality* by laypeople, should not be confused with schizophrenia. Schizophrenia (which comes from Greek roots meaning *split mind*) occurs much more commonly than multiple personality and involves the "splitting" of cognition, affect, and behavior. In a person with schizophrenia, there may be little agreement between thoughts and emotions or between perceptions of reality and what is truly happening. A person with schizophrenia may become giddy when told of disturbing events or may experience hallucinations or delusions (see Chapter 11). In people with multiple personality, a personality apparently divides into two or more personalities, but each personality usually shows more integrated functioning on cognitive, affective, and behavioral levels than is true of people with schizophrenia. **T / F**

**TRUTH or FICTION**

The term *split personality* refers to schizophrenia.

☑ **FALSE** The term *split personality* refers to multiple personality, not schizophrenia.

Celebrated cases of multiple personality have been depicted in the popular media. One became the subject of the 1950s film *The Three Faces of Eve*. In the film, Eve White is a timid housewife who harbors two other personalities: Eve Black, a sexually provocative, antisocial personality; and Jane, a balanced, developing personality who can balance her sexual needs with the demands of social acceptability. The three faces eventually merged into one—Jane—providing a "happy ending." The real-life Eve, whose name was Chris Sizemore, failed to maintain this integrated personality. Her personality reportedly split into 22 subsequent personalities.

**CLINICAL FEATURES** DID is characterized by the emergence of two or more distinct personalities that may vie for control of the person. There may be one dominant or core personality and several subordinate personalities. The sudden transformation of one personality into another may be experienced as a form of possession. The more common alter personalities include children of various ages, adolescents of the opposite gender, prostitutes, and gay males and lesbians. Some of the personalities may show psychotic symptoms—a break with reality expressed in the form of hallucinations and delusional thinking.

In some cases, the host (main) personality is unaware of the existence of the other identities, whereas the other identities are aware of the existence of the host. In other cases, the different personalities are completely unaware of one another. In some isolated cases, alternate personalities (also called *alter personalities*) may even have different eyeglass prescriptions, different allergic reactions, and different responses to medication (e.g., Birnbaum, Martin, & Thomann, 1996; Spiegel, 2009). A person with DID may also have memory gaps, including events experienced by other alters and ordinary life events as well as important personal information (e.g., where the person attended high school or college) or prior traumatic experiences (American Psychiatric Association, 2013).

All in all, the clusters of alter personalities serve as a microcosm of conflicting urges and cultural themes. Themes of sexual ambivalence (sexual openness vs. restrictiveness) and shifting sexual orientations are particularly common. It is as if conflicting internal impulses cannot coexist or achieve dominance. As

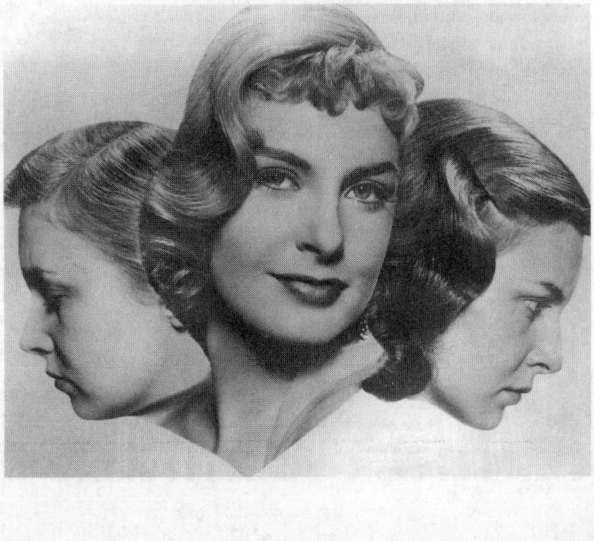

**THE THREE FACES OF EVE.** In the classic film *The Three Faces of Eve*, the actress Joanne Woodward (pictured here) won an Academy Award for playing Eve's three personalities: Eve White (left), a timid housewife, who harbors two alter personalities: Eve Black (middle), a libidinous and antisocial personality; and Jane (right), an integrated personality who can accept her sexual and aggressive urges but still engage in socially appropriate behavior. In the film, the therapist succeeded in helping Eve integrate her three personalities. In real life, however, Chris Sizemore, the woman portrayed by Joanne Woodward, reportedly split into 22 personalities later on.

## Not the Boy Next Door:

### A CASE OF DISSOCIATIVE IDENTITY DISORDER

Billy wasn't quite the boy next door. He tried twice to commit suicide while he was awaiting trial, so his lawyers requested a psychiatric evaluation. The psychologists and psychiatrists who examined Billy deduced that ten personalities dwelled inside of him. Eight were male and two were female. Billy's personality had been fractured by a brutal childhood. The personalities displayed diverse facial expressions, memories, and vocal patterns. They performed in dissimilar ways on personality and intelligence tests.

Arthur, a sensible but phlegmatic personality, conversed with a British accent. Danny, 14, was a painter of still lifes. Christopher, 13, was normal enough, but somewhat anxious. A 3-year-old English girl went by the name of Christine. Tommy, a 16-year-old, was an antisocial personality and escape artist. It was Tommy who enlisted in the Navy. Allen was an 18-year-old con artist. Allen also smoked. Adelena was a 19-year-old introverted lesbian. It was she who committed the rapes. It was probably David who made the mysterious phone call. David was an anxious 9-year-old who wore the anguish of early childhood trauma on his sleeve. After his second suicide attempt, Billy had been placed in a straitjacket. When the guards checked his cell, however, he was sleeping with the straitjacket as a pillow. Tommy later explained that he was responsible for Billy's escape.

The defense argued that Billy was afflicted with multiple personality disorder. Several alternate personalities resided within him. The alternate personalities knew about Billy, but Billy was unaware of them. Billy, the core or dominant personality, had learned as a child that he could sleep as a way of avoiding the sexual and physical abuse of his father. A psychiatrist claimed that Billy had likewise been "asleep"—in a sort of "psychological coma"—when the crimes were committed. Therefore, Billy should be judged innocent by reason of insanity.

Billy was decreed not guilty by reason of insanity. He was committed to a mental institution. In the institution, 14 additional personalities emerged. Thirteen were rebellious and labeled "undesirables" by Arthur. The fourteenth was the "Teacher," who was competent and supposedly represented the integration of all the other personalities. Billy was released 6 years later.

**SOURCE:** *Adapted from Keyes, 1982*

### TRUTH or FICTION

People with multiple personalities typically have two different personalities.

☑ FALSE Most report having several alters, sometimes even 20 or more.

a result, each is expressed as the cardinal or steering trait of an alternate personality. A clinician can sometimes elicit alternate personalities by inviting them to make themselves known, as in asking, "Is there another part of you that wants to say something to me?"

In many cases, the dominant personality remains unaware of the existence of the alter personalities. It thus seems that unconscious processes control the underlying mechanism that results in dissociation, or splitting off of awareness. There may even be "interpersonality rivalry," in which one personality aspires to do away with another, usually in ignorance of the fact that murdering an alternate would result in the death of all.

Although dissociative identity disorder is diagnosed more frequently in women, it is not clear whether there are gender differences in the prevalence of the disorder in the general population. Cases of DID typically present with several alter personalities, and sometimes with 20 or more alters. The key features of dissociative identity disorder are listed in Table 6.2. **T / F**

**DISSOCIATIVE IDENTITY DISORDER.** In dissociative identity disorder, multiple personalities emerge from within the same person, with each having its own well-defined traits and memories.

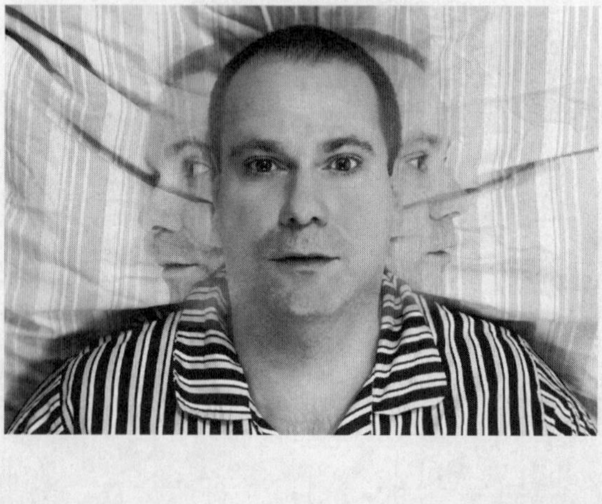

**CONTROVERSIES** Although multiple personality is generally considered rare, the very existence of the disorder continues to arouse debate. Many professionals continue to have doubts about the legitimacy of the diagnosis.

Only a handful of cases worldwide were reported from 1920 to 1970, but since then, the number of reported cases has skyrocketed into the thousands (Spanos, 1994). This may indicate that multiple personality is more common than was earlier believed. However, it is also possible that the disorder has been overdiagnosed in highly suggestible people who might simply be following suggestions that they might have the disorder. Increased public attention paid to the disorder in recent years may also account for the perception that its prevalence is greater than was commonly believed.

**Table 6.2 Key Features of Dissociative Identity Disorder (Formerly Multiple Personality Disorder)**

- Two or more distinct personalities exist within a person.
- Alter personalities may represent different ages, genders, interests, and ways of relating to others.
- Two or more alter personalities repeatedly take full control of the individual's behavior.
- Forgetfulness about ordinary life events and important personal information occurs that cannot be explained by ordinary forgetfulness.
- The main or dominant personality may or may not know of the existence of the alter personalities.

The disorder does appear to be culture-bound and largely restricted to North America (Spanos, 1994). Relatively few cases have been reported elsewhere, even in Western countries such as Great Britain and France. A recent survey in Japan failed to find even one case, and in Switzerland, 90% of the psychiatrists polled had never seen a case of the disorder (Modestin, 1992; Spanos, 1994). Even in North America, few psychologists and psychiatrists have ever encountered a case of multiple personality. Most cases are reported by a relatively small number of investigators and clinicians who strongly believe in the existence of the disorder. Critics wonder if they may be helping to manufacture that which they seek.

Some leading authorities, such as the late psychologist Nicholas Spanos, believe that to be the case. Spanos and others have challenged the existence of dissociative identity disorder (Reisner, 1994; Spanos, 1994). To Spanos, dissociative identity is not a distinct disorder but a form of role-playing in which individuals first come to construe themselves as having multiple selves and then begin to act in ways that are consistent with their conception of the disorder. Eventually, their role-playing becomes so ingrained that it becomes a reality to them. Perhaps their therapists or counselors unintentionally planted the idea in their minds that their confusing welter of emotions and behaviors may represent different personalities at work. Impressionable people may have learned how to enact the role of persons with the disorder by watching others on television and in the movies. Films such as *The Three Faces of Eve* and *Sybil* have given detailed examples of the behaviors that characterize multiple personalities. Or perhaps therapists provided cues about the features of multiple personality.

Once the role is established, it may be maintained through social reinforcement, such as attention from others and avoidance of accountability for unacceptable behavior. This is not to suggest that people with multiple personalities are "faking," any more than you are faking when you perform different daily roles as student, spouse, or worker. You may enact the role of a student (e.g., sitting attentively in class, raising your hand when you wish to talk) because you have learned to organize your behavior according to the nature of the role and because you have been rewarded for doing so. People with multiple personalities may have come to identify so closely with the role that it becomes real for them.

Relatively few cases of multiple personality involve criminal behavior, so the incentives for enacting a multiple personality role do not often relieve individuals of criminal responsibility for their behavior. However, there still may be perceived benefits to enacting the role of a multiple personality, such as a therapist's expression of interest and excitement at discovering a multiple personality. People with multiple personalities were often highly imaginative during childhood. Accustomed to playing games of make-believe, they may readily adopt alternate identities, especially if they learn how to enact the multiple personality role and there are external sources of validation, such as a clinician's interest and concern.

The social reinforcement model may help to explain why some clinicians seem to "discover" many more cases of multiple personality than others. These clinicians may unknowingly cue clients to enact the role of a multiple personality and then reinforce the performance with extra attention and concern. With the right set of cues, certain clients may adopt the role of a multiple personality to please their clinicians. Some authorities have challenged the role-playing model (e.g., Gleaves, 1996), and it remains to be seen how many cases of the disorder in clinical practice the model can explain. Whether dissociative identity disorder is a real phenomenon or a form of role-playing, there is no question that people who display this behavior have serious emotional and behavioral difficulties.

We have personally noted a tendency for claims of multiple personality to spread on inpatient units. In one case, Susan—a prostitute admitted for depression and suicidal thoughts—claimed that she could exchange sex for money only when "another person" inside her emerged and took control. Upon hearing this, another woman, Ginny—a child abuser who had been admitted for depression after her daughter had been removed from her home by social services—claimed that she abused her daughter only when another person inside of her assumed control of her personality. Susan's chart recommended that she be evaluated further for multiple personality disorder (the term used at the time to refer to the disorder), but Ginny was diagnosed with a depressive disorder and a personality disorder, not with multiple personality disorder.

Dissociative disorders are associated with an increased risk of suicide attempts, including multiple suicide attempts (Foote et al., 2008). Suicide attempts are especially common among people with multiple personalities. In one Canadian study, 72% of multiple personality patients had attempted suicide, and about 2% had succeeded (Ross, Norton, & Wozney, 1989).

# Dissociative Amnesia

**6.2 Describe the key features of dissociative amnesia.**

Dissociative amnesia is believed to be the most common type of dissociative disorder (Maldonado, Butler, & Spiegel, 1998). *Amnesia* derives from the Greek roots *a*, meaning *not*, and *mnasthai*, meaning *to remember*. In **dissociative amnesia** (formerly called *psychogenic amnesia*), a person becomes unable to recall important personal information, usually involving traumatic or stressful experiences, in a way that cannot be accounted for by simple forgetfulness. Nor can the memory loss be attributed to a particular organic cause, such as a blow to the head or a particular medical condition, nor to the direct effects of drugs or alcohol. Unlike some progressive forms of memory impairment (such as dementia associated with Alzheimer's disease; see Chapter 14), the memory loss in dissociative amnesia is reversible, although it may last for days, weeks, or even years. Recall of dissociated memories may happen gradually, but often occurs suddenly and spontaneously, as when the soldier who has no recall of a battle for several days afterward suddenly remembers being transported to a hospital away from the battlefield.

SHARON: DISSOCIATIVE AMNESIA

Memories of childhood sexual abuse are sometimes recovered during the course of psychotherapy or hypnosis. The sudden emergence of such memories has become a source of major controversy within the field and the general community, as we explore in *Thinking Critically: Are Recovered Memories Credible?* on page 215.

Amnesia is not ordinary forgetfulness, such as forgetting someone's name or where you left your car keys. Memory loss in amnesia is more profound or wide ranging. Dissociative amnesia is divided into five distinct types of memory problems:

1. *Localized amnesia.* Most cases take the form of *localized amnesia*, in which events occurring during a specific time period are lost to memory. For example, a person cannot recall events for a number of hours or days after a stressful or traumatic incident, such as a battle or a car accident.
2. *Selective amnesia.* In *selective amnesia*, people forget only the disturbing particulars that take place during a certain period of time. A person may recall the period of life during which he conducted an extramarital affair, but not the guilt-arousing affair itself. A soldier may recall most of a battle, but not the death of his buddy.

3. *Generalized amnesia.* In *generalized amnesia*, people forget their entire lives—who they are, what they do, where they live, whom they live with. This form of amnesia is very rare, although you wouldn't think so if you watch daytime soap operas. People with generalized amnesia cannot recall personal information, but they tend to retain their habits, tastes, and skills. If you had generalized amnesia, you would still know how to read, although you would not recall your elementary school teachers. You would still prefer French fries to baked potatoes—or vice versa.
4. *Continuous amnesia.* In this form of amnesia, a person forgets everything that occurred from a particular point in time up to and including the present.
5. *Systematized amnesia.* In *systematized amnesia*, memory loss is specific to a particular category of information, such as memory about one's family or particular people in one's life.

People with dissociative amnesia usually forget events or periods of life that were traumatic—that generated strong negative emotions, such as horror or guilt. Consider the case of Rutger, at the bottom of this page.

People sometimes claim they cannot recall certain events of their lives, such as criminal acts, promises made to others, and so forth. Falsely claiming amnesia as a way of escaping responsibility is called *malingering*, which refers to faking symptoms or making false claims for personal gain (such as avoiding work). Clinicians don't have any guaranteed methods for distinguishing people with dissociative amnesia from malingerers, but experienced clinicians can make reasonably well-educated guesses.

A rare subtype of dissociative amnesia is characterized by *fugue*, or "amnesia on the run." The word *fugue* derives from the Latin *fugere*, meaning *flight*. (The word *fugitive* has the same origin.) In dissociative fugue, the person may travel suddenly and unexpectedly from his or her home or place of work. The travels may either be purposeful, leading to a particular location, or involve bewildered wandering. During a fugue state, a person may be unable to recall past personal information and becomes confused about his or her identity or assumes a new identity (either partially or completely). Despite these odd behaviors, the person may appear "normal" and show no other signs of mental disturbance (Maldonado, Butler, & Spiegel, 1998). The person may not think about the past, or may report a past filled with false memories without recognizing them as false.

**"DOES ANYBODY KNOW ME"?** Diagnosed with dissociative amnesia, 40-year-old Jeffrey Ingram searched for more than a month for anyone who could tell him who he was. He was finally recognized by a family member who saw him on a TV news program. Even after returning home, he lacked any memory of his identity, but said that it felt like home to him. According to his mother, he had suffered earlier incidents of memory loss and had never fully recovered his memory.

## Rutger:

### A CASE OF DISSOCIATIVE AMNESIA

He was brought to the emergency room of a hospital by a stranger. He was dazed and claimed not to know who he was or where he lived, and the stranger had found him wandering in the streets. Despite his confusion, it did not appear that he had been drinking or abusing drugs or that his amnesia could be attributed to physical trauma. After staying in the hospital for a few days, he awoke in distress. His memory had returned. His name was Rutger and he had urgent business to attend to. He wanted to know why he had been hospitalized and demanded to leave. At the time of admission, Rutger appeared to be suffering from generalized amnesia: He could not recall his identity or the personal events of his life. But now that he was requesting discharge, Rutger showed localized amnesia for the period between entering the emergency room and the morning he regained his memory for prior events.

Rutger provided information about the events prior to his hospitalization that was confirmed by the police. On the day when his amnesia began, Rutger had killed a pedestrian with his automobile. There had been witnesses, and the police had voiced the opinion that Rutger—although emotionally devastated—was blameless in the incident. Rutger was instructed, however, to fill out an accident report and to appear at the inquest. Still nonplussed, Rutger filled out the form at a friend's home. He accidentally left his wallet and his identification there. After placing the form in a mailbox, Rutger became dazed and lost his memory.

Although Rutger was not responsible for the accident, he felt awful about the pedestrian's death. His amnesia was probably connected with feelings of guilt, the stress of the accident, and concerns about the inquest.

**SOURCE:** *Adapted from Cameron, 1963, pp. 355–356.*

## The Lady in the Water:
### A CASE OF DISSOCIATIVE AMNESIA

The captain of the Staten Island Ferry caught sight of the bobbing head in the treacherous waters about a mile off the southern tip of Manhattan. It was a woman floating face down in the water, and incredibly, she was alive. The crew rescued her from the river and she was taken to the hospital, where she was treated for hypothermia and dehydration. Stories likes these seldom end well: A young woman mysteriously disappears. A body is found floating in the water. The body matches the description of the missing woman. Police suspect foul play or suicide. But this case was different, very different.

This was the case of a 23-year-old schoolteacher in New York City, Hannah Emily Upp, who one day went out jogging and three weeks later ended up being rescued from the river. What happened during the three weeks in which she was missing remains a mystery. Her doctors supplied an explanation: dissociative fugue, a subtype of dissociative amnesia in which individuals suddenly lose their memory of their identity and may travel to other places, sometimes establishing whole new identities. The loss of personal memory may last for hours, days, or even years.

How did Hannah end up in the river? As best as we can tell, she hadn't jumped off a pier in an attempt to end her life, nor was she pushed. In a confused state, and suffering from a large blister on her foot from having walked around Manhattan for several weeks, she apparently sought relief by wading into the river on that warm August night. Hannah later reflected, "They think that just as I was wandering on land, I wandered in the water.... I don't think I had a purpose. But I had that really big blister, so maybe I just didn't want my shoes on anymore" (cited in Marx & Didziulis, 2009, p. CY7).

So many questions, so few answers. How had she survived for several weeks without any money or identification? (Her wallet, cell phone, and ID were found at her apartment.) Hannah herself could supply few answers. In her first interview some months after her rescue, she talked about her sense of responsibility for her disappearance: "How do you feel guilty for something you didn't even know you did? It's not your fault, but it's still somehow you. So it's definitely made me reconsider everything. Who was I before? Who was I then—is that part of me? Who am I now?" (cited in Marx & Didziulis, 2009, p. CY7). Months later, Hannah was reconnecting with friends and family, filling in the pieces of her past life and trying to come to terms with who she was.

Hannah Emily Upp, months after her rescue, in the park where she went jogging the night she disappeared.

Whereas people with amnesia appear to wander aimlessly, people in a fugue state act more purposefully. Some stick close to home. They spend the afternoon in the park or in a theater, or they spend the night at a hotel under another name, usually avoiding contact with others. The new identity is incomplete and fleeting, and the individual's former sense of self returns in a matter of hours or a few days. Less common is a pattern in which dissociative fugue lasts for months or years and involves travel to distant places and assumption of a new identity. These individuals may assume an identity that is more spontaneous and sociable than their former selves, which were typically "quiet" and "ordinary." They may establish new families and successful businesses. Although these events sound rather bizarre, the fugue state is not considered psychotic because people with the disorder can think and behave quite normally—in their new lives, that is. Then one day, quite suddenly, awareness of their past identity returns to them, and they are flooded with old memories. Now they typically do not recall the events that occurred during the fugue state. The new identity, the new life—including all its involvements and responsibilities—vanish from memory.

Dissociative amnesia is relatively uncommon, but is most likely to occur in wartime or in the wake of another kind of disaster or extremely stressful event. The underlying notion is that dissociation protects a person from traumatic memories or other sources of emotionally painful experiences or conflict (Maldonado, Butler, & Spiegel, 1998).

Dissociative amnesia can also be difficult to distinguish from malingering. That is, people who were dissatisfied with their former lives can claim to have amnesia when they are discovered in their new locations and new identities. Let's consider a case that could lead to varying interpretations (Spitzer et al., 1989).

## Burt or Gene?

### A CASE OF DISSOCIATIVE FUGUE?

A 42-year-old man had gotten into a fight at the diner where he worked. The police were called, and the man, who carried no ID, identified himself as Burt Tate. He said he had arrived in town a few weeks earlier, but could not remember where he had lived or worked before arriving in town. Although no charges were pressed against him, the police prevailed upon him to come to the emergency room for evaluation. "Burt" knew the town he was in and the current date and recognized that it was somewhat unusual that he couldn't remember his past, but he didn't seem concerned about it. There was no evidence of any physical injuries, head trauma, or drug or alcohol abuse. The police made some inquiries and discovered that Burt fit the profile of a missing person, Gene Saunders, who had disappeared a month earlier from a city some 2,000 miles away. Mrs. Saunders was called in and confirmed that Burt was indeed her husband. She reported that her husband, who had worked in middle-level management in a manufacturing company, had been having difficulty at work before his disappearance. He was passed over for promotion and his supervisor was highly critical of his work. The job stress apparently affected his behavior at home. Once easygoing and sociable, he withdrew into himself and began to criticize his wife and children. Then, just before his disappearance, he had a violent argument with his 18-year-old son. His son called him a "failure" and bolted out the door. Two days later, the man disappeared. When he came face to face with his wife again, he claimed he didn't recognize her, but appeared visibly nervous.

**SOURCE:** *Adapted from Spitzer et al., 1994, pp. 254–255*

Although the presenting evidence supported a diagnosis of dissociative fugue, clinicians can find it difficult to distinguish true amnesia from amnesia that is faked to allow a person to start a new life.

## THINKING CRITICALLY about abnormal psychology

### @ISSUE: ARE RECOVERED MEMORIES CREDIBLE?

A high-level business executive's comfortable life fell apart one day when his 19-year-old daughter accused him of having repeatedly molested her throughout her childhood. The executive lost his marriage as well as his $400,000-a-year job. However, he fought back against the allegations, which he insisted were untrue. He sued his daughter's therapists, who had helped her recover these memories. A jury sided with the businessman, awarding him $500,000 in damages from the two therapists.

This case is but one of many involving adults who claim to have only recently become aware of memories of childhood sexual abuse. Hundreds of people across the country have been brought to trial on the basis of recovered memories of childhood abuse, with many of these cases resulting in convictions and long jail sentences, even in the absence of corroborating evidence. The question of whether memories of traumatic experiences can be *repressed*—that is, forgotten because of the emotional pain associated with a painful experience—continues to be a subject of debate among professionals (see Brewin & Andrews, 2014; Patihis et al., 2014). However, the fact remains that many recovered memories occur following suggestive probing by a therapist or hypnotist. At the heart of the debate about recovered memories is the question, "Are they believable?" No one doubts that childhood sexual abuse is a major problem confronting our society—but should recovered memories be taken at face value?

Several lines of evidence lead us to question the validity of recovered memories. Experimental evidence shows that false memories can be created, especially under the influence of leading or suggestive questioning during hypnosis or psychotherapy (Gleaves et al., 2004; McNally & Geraerts, 2009). Memory for events that never happened actually may be created and seem just as genuine as memories of real events (Bernstein & Loftus, 2009). If anything, genuine traumatic events are highly memorable, even if people may be a little sketchy about the details (McNally & Geraerts, 2009). A leading memory expert, psychologist Elizabeth Loftus (1996, p. 356), writes of the dangers of taking recovered memories at face value:

**ELIZABETH LOFTUS.** Research by Loftus and others has demonstrated that false memories of events that never actually occurred can be induced experimentally. This research calls into question the credibility of reports of recovered memories.

After developing false memories, innumerable "patients" have torn their families apart, and more than a few innocent people have been sent to prison. This is not to say that people cannot forget horrible things that have happened to them; most certainly they can. But there is virtually no support for the idea that clients presenting for therapy routinely have extensive histories of abuse of which they are completely unaware, and that they can be helped only if the alleged abuse is resurrected from their unconscious.

Should we conclude then that recovered memories are bogus? Not necessarily. Both false memories and recovered true memories may exist (Gleaves et al., 2004). In all likelihood, some recovered memories are genuine, whereas others are undoubtedly false (Erdleyi, 2010).

In sum, we shouldn't think of the brain as a kind of mental camera that stores snapshots of events as they actually happened in the form of memories. Memory is more of a reconstructive process in which bits of information are pieced together in ways that can sometimes lead to a distorted recollection of events, although a person may be convinced a memory is accurate. Unfortunately, scientists don't have the tools needed to reliably distinguish true memories from false ones.

In thinking critically about the issue, answer the following questions:

1. Why should we not accept claims of recovered memories at face value?
2. How does human memory work differently than a camera in recording events and experiences?

# Depersonalization/Derealization Disorder

**6.3 Describe the key features of depersonalization/derealization disorder.**

**Depersonalization** is a temporary loss or change in the usual sense of our own reality. In a state of depersonalization, people feel detached from themselves and their surroundings. They may feel as if they are dreaming or acting like robots (Sierra et al., 2006). **Derealization**—a sense of unreality about the external world involving odd changes in the perception of one's surroundings or in the passage of time—may also be present. People and objects may seem to change in size or shape and sounds may seem different. Derealization may be associated with features of anxiety, such as dizziness and fears of going insane, or with depression.

Healthy people occasionally experience fleeting feelings of depersonalization or derealization. According to the *DSM*, about half of all adults experience single brief episodes of depersonalization, usually during times of extreme stress (American Psychiatric Association, 2013). People with depersonalization/derealization disorder have more recurrent and troubling episodes. **T / F**

## TRUTH or FICTION

Very few of us have episodes in which we feel strangely detached from our own bodies or thought processes.

☑ **FALSE** About half of all adults at some time experience an episode of depersonalization in which they feel detached from their own bodies or mental processes.

## Questionnaire

### AN INVENTORY OF DISSOCIATIVE EXPERIENCES

Brief dissociative experiences, such as momentary feelings of depersonalization, are quite common in the general population (Bernstein & Putnam, 1986; Michal et al., 2009). Many of us experience them from time to time. Fleeting dissociative experiences may be quite common, but those reported by people with dissociative disorders are more frequent and problematic than those experienced by the general population (Waller & Ross, 1997). Dissociative disorders involve persistent and severe dissociative experiences.

The following is a sampling of dissociative experiences similar to those experienced by many people in the general population. Bear in mind that transient experiences like these are reported in varying frequencies by both normal and abnormal groups. We suggest, however, that if these experiences become persistent or commonplace or cause you concern or distress, then it might be worthwhile to discuss them with a professional.

**Have You Ever Experienced the Following?**

1. Had a sense that objects or people around you seemed unreal.
2. Felt as if you were walking through a fog or a dream.
3. Weren't sure whether you were asleep or awake.

4. Not recognized yourself in a mirror.
5. Found yourself walking somewhere and not remembering where you were going or what you were doing.
6. Felt like you were watching yourself from a distance.
7. Felt detached or disconnected from yourself.
8. Didn't know who you were, or where you were, at a particular moment.
9. Felt distant or detached from what was happening around you.
10. Were in a familiar place that seemed unfamiliar or strange.
11. Found yourself in a place with no memory of how you got there.
12. Had such a vivid fantasy or daydream that it seemed like it was really happening at the moment.
13. Had a memory of an event that seemed like you were reliving it in the moment.
14. Felt like you were watching yourself doing something as if you were watching another person.
15. Spaced out when talking to someone and didn't know all or part of what the person was saying.
16. Became confused as to whether you had just done something or had just thought about doing it, such as wondering whether you had actually mailed a letter or just thought about mailing a letter.

**DEPERSONALIZATION.** Episodes of depersonalization are characterized by feelings of detachment from oneself. It may feel as if one is walking through a dream or observing the environment or oneself from outside one's body.

Although these sensations are strange, people with depersonalization/derealization disorder maintain contact with reality. They can distinguish reality from unreality, even during the depersonalization episode. In contrast to generalized amnesia and fugue, they know who they are. Their memories are intact and they know where they are—even if they do not like their present state. Feelings of depersonalization usually come on suddenly and fade gradually.

Given the commonness of occasional dissociative symptoms, Richie's experience, described in the following case study, is not atypical.

## Richie's Experience at Disney World:

### A CASE OF DEPERSONALIZATION/DEREALIZATION

We went to Orlando with the children after school let out. I had also been driving myself hard, and it was time to let go. We spent three days "doing" Disney World, and it got to the point where we were all wearing shirts with mice and ducks on them and singing Disney songs. On the third day, I began to feel unreal and ill at ease while we were watching these middle American, Ivory soap teenagers singing and dancing in front of Cinderella's Castle. The day was finally cooling down, but I broke into a sweat. I became shaky and dizzy and sat down on the cement next to the 4-year-old's stroller without giving [my wife] an explanation. There were strollers and kids and [adults'] legs all around me, and for some strange reason I became fixated on the pieces of popcorn strewn on the ground. All of a sudden it was like the people around me were all silly mechanical creatures, like the dolls in the "It's a Small World" [exhibit] or the animals on the "Jungle Cruise." Things sort of seemed to slow down, the way they do when you've smoked marijuana, and there was this invisible wall of cotton between me and everyone else.

Then, the concert was over, and my wife was like "What's the matter?" and did I want to stay for the Electrical Parade and the fireworks, or was I sick? Now, I was beginning to wonder if I was going crazy and I said I was sick, that my wife would have to take me by the hand and drive us back to the Sonesta Village [motel]. Somehow, we got back to the monorail and turned in the strollers. I waited in the herd [of people] at the station like a dead person, my eyes glazed over, looking out over kids with Mickey Mouse ears and Mickey Mouse balloons. The mechanical voice on the monorail almost did me in and I got really shaky.

I refused to go back to the Magic Kingdom. I went with the family to Sea World, and on another day I dropped [my wife] and the kids off at the Magic Kingdom and picked them up that night. My wife thought I was goldbricking or something, and we had a helluva fight about it, but we had a life to get back to, and my sanity had to come first.

*From the Author's Files*

Richie's depersonalization experience was limited to the one episode and would not qualify for a diagnosis of **depersonalization/derealization disorder**. The disorder is diagnosed only when these experiences become persistent or recurrent and cause significant distress or impairment in daily functioning. Depersonalization/derealization disorder can become a chronic or long-lasting problem. The *DSM* diagnoses depersonalization/derealization disorder according to the criteria shown in Table 6.3. Note the following case example.

## Feeling "Outside" Himself:

### A CASE OF DEPERSONALIZATION/DEREALIZATION DISORDER

A 20-year-old college student feared he was going insane. For 2 years, he had increasingly frequent experiences of feeling "outside" himself. During these episodes, he experienced a sense of "deadness" in his body, and felt wobbly, frequently bumping into furniture. He was more apt to lose his balance when he was out in public, especially when he felt anxious. During these episodes, his thoughts seemed "foggy," which reminded him of his state of mind when he was given shots of a pain-killing drug for an appendectomy 5 years earlier. He tried to fight off these episodes when they occurred, by saying "stop" to himself and by shaking his head. This would temporarily clear his head, but the feeling of being outside himself and the sense of deadness would shortly return. The disturbing feelings would gradually fade away over a period of hours. By the time he sought treatment, he was experiencing these episodes about twice a week, each one lasting from 3 to 4 hours. His grades remained unimpaired, and had even improved in the past several months, because he was spending more time studying. However, his girlfriend, in whom he had confided his problem, felt that he had become totally absorbed in himself and threatened to break off their relationship if he didn't change. She had also begun dating other men.

**SOURCE:** *Adapted from Spitzer et al., 1994, pp. 270–271*

**Table 6.3** Key Features of Depersonalization/Derealization Disorder

- Repeated episodes of depersonalization, derealization, or both.
- Episodes are characterized by feelings of detachment from one's thoughts, feelings, or sensations (depersonalization) or from one's surroundings (derealization).
- Episodes may produce the feeling of being an outside observer of oneself.
- Episodes may have a dreamlike quality.
- During these episodes, a person can still distinguish reality from unreality.

In terms of observable behavior and associated features, depersonalization and derealization may be more closely related to anxiety disorders such as phobias and panic disorder than to dissociative disorders. People with depersonalization/derealization disorder tend to make exaggerated or catastrophic interpretations of bodily symptoms, which can trigger anxiety (Hunter, Salkovskis, & David, 2014). Unlike other dissociative disorders that seem to protect the self from anxiety, depersonalization and derealization can lead to anxiety and in turn prompt avoidance behavior, as we saw in the case of Richie.

Cultural influences have an important bearing on the development and expression of abnormal behavior patterns, including dissociative disorders. For example, evidence suggests that depersonalization and derealization experiences may be more common in individualistic cultures that emphasize individualism or self-identity, such as the United States, than in collectivistic cultures, which emphasize group identity and responsibility to one's social roles and obligations (Sierra et al., 2006). As we explore next, dissociative disorders may also take very different forms in different cultures.

## Culture-Bound Dissociative Syndromes

**6.4 Identify two culture-bound syndromes with dissociative features.**

Similarities exist between the Western concept of dissociative disorder and certain culture-bound syndromes found in other parts of the world (Ross, Schroeder, & Ness, 2013). For example, *amok* is a culture-bound syndrome occurring primarily in Southeast Asian and Pacific Island cultures that involves a trancelike state in which a person suddenly becomes highly excited and violently attacks other people or destroys objects (see Table 3.2 in Chapter 3). People who "run amuck" may later claim to have no memory of the episode or recall feeling as if they were acting like robots. Another example is *zar*, a term used in countries in North Africa and the Middle East to describe people in dissociative states that are believed to reflect spirit possession. During these states, individuals engage in unusual behavior, ranging from shouting to banging their heads against the wall.

# Theoretical Perspectives

**6.5 Describe different theoretical perspectives on dissociative disorders.**

Dissociative disorders are fascinating and perplexing phenomena. How can one's sense of personal identity become so distorted that one develops multiple personalities, blots out large chunks of personal memory, or develops a new identity? Although these disorders remain mysterious in many ways, some clues provide insights into their origins. A history of trauma figures prominently in the development of dissociative disorders, although it is important to recognize that some cases occur without any history of trauma (Stein et al., 2014).

**PSYCHODYNAMIC VIEWS** To psychodynamic theorists, dissociative disorders involve the massive use of repression, resulting in the splitting off from consciousness of unacceptable impulses and painful memories, typically involving parental abuse (Ross & Ness, 2010). Dissociative amnesia may serve an adaptive function of disconnecting or dissociating one's conscious self from awareness of traumatic experiences or other sources of psychological pain or conflict. In dissociative amnesia and fugue, the ego protects itself from anxiety by blotting out disturbing memories or by dissociating threatening impulses of a sexual or aggressive nature. In dissociative identity disorder, people may express these unacceptable impulses through the development of alternate personalities. In depersonalization, people stand outside themselves—safely distanced from the emotional turmoil within.

**SOCIAL-COGNITIVE THEORY** From the standpoint of social-cognitive theory, we can conceptualize dissociation in the form of dissociative amnesia and fugue as a learned response involving the behavior of psychologically distancing oneself from disturbing memories or emotions. The habit of psychologically distancing oneself from these matters, such as by splitting them off from consciousness, is negatively reinforced by relief from anxiety or removal of feelings of guilt or shame. For example, shielding oneself from memories or emotions associated with past physical or sexual abuse by disconnecting (dissociating) them from ordinary consciousness is a way to avoid the anxiety or misplaced guilt these experiences may engender.

As noted earlier, some social-cognitive theorists, such as the late Nicholas Spanos, believe that dissociative identity disorder is a form of role-playing acquired through observational learning and reinforcement. This is not quite the same as pretending or malingering; people can honestly come to organize their behavior patterns according to particular roles they have observed. They might also become so absorbed in role-playing that they "forget" they are enacting a role.

**BRAIN DYSFUNCTION** Might dissociative behaviors be connected with underlying brain dysfunction? Research along these lines is still in its infancy, but preliminary evidence shows structural differences in brain areas involved in memory and emotion between patients with dissociative identity disorder and healthy controls (Vermetten et al., 2006). Although intriguing, the significance of these differences in explaining DID remains to be determined. Another study showed differences in brain metabolic activity between people with depersonalization/derealization disorder and healthy subjects (Simeon et al., 2000). These findings, which point to a possible dysfunction in parts of the brain involved in body perception, may help account for the feeling of being disconnected from one's body that is characteristic of depersonalization.

Recent evidence also points to another irregularity in brain functioning during sleep. Investigators suggest that disruption in the normal sleep-wake cycle may result in intrusions of dream-like experiences in the waking state that result in dissociative experiences, such as feeling detached from one's body (van der Kloet et al., 2012). Regulating the sleep-wake cycle may thus help prevent or treat dissociative experiences.

**IMAGINARY FRIENDS.** It is normal for children to play games of make-believe and even to have imaginary playmates. In the case of multiple personalities, however, games of make-believe and the invention of imaginary playmates may be used as psychological defenses against abuse. Research indicates that most people with multiple personalities were abused as children.

**DIATHESIS-STRESS MODEL** Despite widespread evidence of severe physical or sexual abuse in childhood in the great majority of cases of dissociative identity disorder, very few children who experience trauma go on to develop the disorder (Boysen & VanBergen, 2014; Dale et al., 2009; Spiegel, 2006). Consistent with the diathesis-stress model, people who are prone to fantasize, are highly hypnotizable, and are open to altered states of consciousness may be more likely than others to develop dissociative experiences in the face of traumatic abuse. (See *Tying It Together* on page 222.) These personality traits in themselves do not lead to dissociative disorders. They actually are quite common in the population. However, they may increase the risk that people who experience severe trauma will develop dissociative phenomena as a survival mechanism (Butler et al., 1996). Investigators continue to debate the role of fantasy proneness as a risk factor for dissociation in response to trauma (Dalenberg et al., 2012). However, one possibility is that people who are not prone to fantasize will experience anxious, intrusive thoughts associated with posttraumatic stress disorder (PTSD) following traumatic stress, rather than dissociative disorders (Dale et al., 2009). **T / F**

**TRUTH or FICTION**

A surprisingly high number of children who suffered severe physical or sexual abuse in childhood go on to develop multiple personalities as adults.

☑ **FALSE** Although the great majority of people with multiple personalities report experiencing severe physical or sexual abuse during childhood, very few children who suffer severe childhood trauma eventually develop dissociative identity disorder.

Perhaps most of us can divide our consciousness so that we become unaware of—at least temporarily—those events we normally focus on. Perhaps most of us can thrust the unpleasant from our minds and enact various roles—parent, child, lover, businessperson, and soldier—that help us meet the requirements of our situations. Perhaps the marvel is *not* that attention can be splintered, but that human consciousness is normally integrated into a meaningful whole.

## Treatment of Dissociative Disorders

**6.6 Describe the treatment of dissociative identity disorder.**

Dissociative amnesia and fugue are usually fleeting experiences that end abruptly. Episodes of depersonalization can be recurrent and persistent, and they are most likely to occur when people are undergoing periods of mild anxiety or depression. In such cases, clinicians usually focus on managing the anxiety or depression. Although research is limited, the available evidence shows that treating dissociative disorders does help reduce symptoms of dissociation, depression, and feelings of distress (Brand et al., 2009, 2012).

Much of the research interest in treating dissociative identity disorder focuses on integrating the alter personalities into a cohesive personality structure. To accomplish this end, therapists seek to help patients uncover and work through memories of early childhood trauma. In doing so, they often recommend establishing connections with the dominant and alter personalities (Chu, 2011b; Howell, 2011). A therapist may ask a client to close his or her eyes and wait for the alter personalities to emerge (Krakauer, 2001). Wilbur (1986) points out that the therapist can work with whatever personality dominates the therapy session. The therapist asks any and all personalities that come out to talk about their troubling memories and dreams and assures them that the therapist will help them make sense of their anxieties, safely "relive" traumatic experiences, and make them conscious. The disclosure of abuse is considered essential to the therapeutic process (Krakauer, 2001). Wilbur notes that anxiety experienced during a therapy session may lead to a switch in personalities, because alter personalities were presumably developed as a means of coping with intense anxiety. If therapy is successful, a person will be able to work through the traumatic memories and will no longer need to escape into alternate "selves" to avoid the anxiety associated with the trauma. Thus, reintegration of the personality becomes possible.

Through the process of integration, the disparate elements, or alters, are woven into a cohesive self. Here, a patient speaks about this process of "making mine" those parts of the self that had been splintered off.

**"I"** **"Everybody's Still Here"**

Integration made me feel alive for the first time. When I feel things now, I know I feel them. I'm slowly learning it's okay to feel all feelings, even unpleasant ones. The bonus is, I get to feel pleasurable feelings as well. I also don't worry about my sanity anymore.

It's difficult to explain even to people who try to understand what integration means to someone who has been "in parts" for a lifetime. I still talk in a "we" way sometimes. Some of my "before integration" friends assume I can now just get back to being "me"—whatever that is. They don't realize integration is like being three all over again. I don't know how to act in certain situations because "I" never did it before. Or I only know how to respond in fragmented ways. What does "sadness" mean to someone who doesn't feel it continually? I don't know sometimes when I feel sad if I really should. It's confusing and scary being responsible for me all by myself now.

The most comforting aspect of integration for me, and what I especially want other multiples to know is [this:] Nobody died. Everybody's still here inside me, in their correct place without controlling my body independently. There was not a scene where everybody left except one. I am a remarkably different "brand new" person. I've spent months learning how to access my alters' skills and emotions—and they are mine now. I have balance and perspective that never existed before. I'm happy and content. This isn't about dying. It's about celebrating living to the fullest extent possible.

**SOURCE:** *From Olson, 1997*

Wilbur describes the formation of another treatment goal in the case of a woman with dissociative identity disorder.

## The "Children" Should Not Feel Ashamed:

### A CASE OF DISSOCIATIVE IDENTITY DISORDER

A 45-year-old woman had suffered from dissociative identity disorder throughout her life. Her dominant personality was timid and self-conscious, rather reticent about herself. Soon after she entered treatment, a group of "little ones" emerged, who cried profusely. The therapist asked to speak with someone in the personality system who could clarify the personalities that were present. It turned out that they included several children, all of whom were under 9 years of age and had suffered severe, painful sexual abuse at the hands of an uncle, a great-aunt, and a grandmother. The great-aunt was a lesbian with several voyeuristic lesbian friends. They would watch the sexual abuse, generating fear, pain, rage, humiliation, and shame.

It was essential in therapy for the "children" to come to understand that they should not feel ashamed because they had been helpless to resist the abuse.

**SOURCE:** *Adapted from C. B. Wilbur, 1986.*

Does therapy for dissociative identity disorder work? We don't yet have sufficient empirical evidence to support any general conclusions (Brand et al., 2012). In an early work, Coons (1986) followed 20 "multiples" aged between 14 and 47 at time of intake for an average of 3.25 years. Only five of the subjects showed a complete reintegration of their personalities. Other therapists report significant improvement in measures of dissociative symptoms and depressive symptoms in treated patients, even in those who failed to achieve integration. However, greater symptom improvement is also reported for those who achieved integration (Ellason & Ross, 1997).

Reports of the effectiveness of psychodynamic and other forms of therapy, such as behavior therapy, rely on uncontrolled case studies. Controlled studies of treatments of dissociative identity disorder or other forms of dissociative disorder are yet to be reported. The relative infrequency of the disorder has hampered efforts to conduct controlled experiments that compare different forms of treatments with each other and with control groups. Nor do scientists have evidence showing psychiatric drugs or other biological approaches are effective in bringing about integration of various alternate personalities. Although psychiatric drugs such as the antidepressant Prozac have been used to treat depersonalization/derealization disorder, there is a lack of evidence that they are any more effective than placebos (Simeon et al., 2004; Sierra et al., 2012). This lack of responsiveness suggests that depersonalization/derealization disorder may not be a secondary feature of depression.

# TYING it together

Although scientists have different conceptualizations of dissociative phenomena, evidence points to a history of childhood abuse in a great many cases. The most widely held view of dissociative identity disorder is that it represents a means of coping with and surviving severe, repetitive childhood abuse, generally beginning before the age of 5 (Burton & Lane, 2001; Foote et al., 2005). The severely abused child may retreat into alter personalities as a psychological defense against unbearable abuse. The construction of these alter personalities allows these children to psychologically escape or distance themselves from their suffering. In the case example in the opening of the chapter, one alter personality, Nancy, bore the worst of the abuse for all the others. Dissociation may offer a means of escape when no other means is available. In the face of continued abuse, these alter personalities may become stabilized, making it difficult for a person to maintain a unified personality. In adulthood, people with multiple personalities may use their alter personalities to block out traumatic childhood memories and their emotional reactions to them, thus wiping the slate clean and beginning life anew in the guise of alter personalities. The alter identities or personalities may also help a person cope with stressful situations or express deep-seated resentments that the individual is unable to integrate within his or her primary personality. The diathesis-stress model, as represented in Figure 6.1, offers a conceptual framework for understanding the development of dissociative identity disorder on the basis of the combination of predisposing factors (a diathesis) and traumatic stress.

Compelling evidence indicates that exposure to childhood trauma, usually by a relative or caretaker, is involved in the development of dissociative disorders, especially dissociative identity disorder. Dissociative identity disorder is strongly linked to a history of sexual or physical abuse in childhood. In some samples, rates of reported childhood physical or sexual abuse have ranged from 76% to 95% (Ross et al., 1990; Scroppo et al., 1998). Evidence of cross-cultural similarity comes from a study in Turkey, which showed that the great majority of dissociative identity disorder patients in one research sample reported sexual or physical abuse in childhood (Sar, Yargic, & Tutkun, 1996). Childhood abuse is also linked to dissociative amnesia (Chu, 2011a).

Childhood abuse is not the only source of trauma linked to dissociative disorders. Trauma of warfare in both civilians and soldiers plays a part in some cases of dissociative amnesia. Significant life stress, such as severe financial problems and the wish to avoid punishment for socially unacceptable behavior, may precipitate episodes of dissociative amnesia or depersonalization.

**Figure 6.1 Diathesis-stress model of dissociative identity disorder.**

In this model, exposure to severe, recurrent trauma (stress), together with certain predisposing factors (diathesis), leads in some cases to the development of alter personalities, which over time become stabilized and strengthened by social reinforcement and blocking out of disturbing memories.

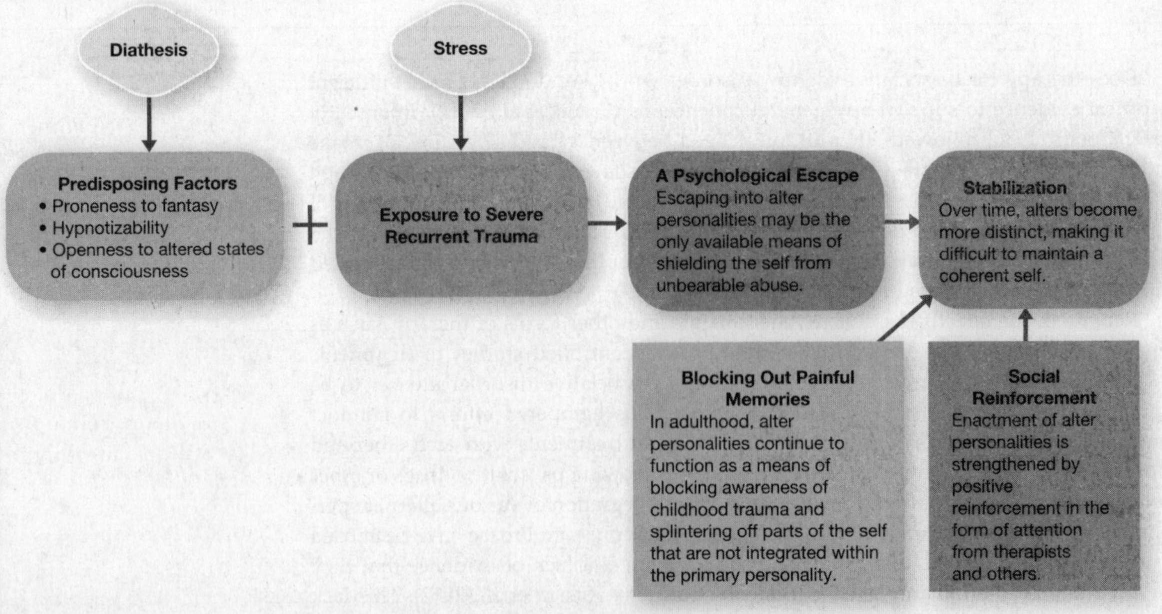

# Somatic Symptom and Related Disorders

The word *somatic* derives from the Greek *soma*, meaning *body*. People with **somatic symptom and related disorders** (formerly called *somatoform disorders*) may have physical (somatic) symptoms without an identifiable physical cause or have excessive concerns about the nature or meaning of their symptoms. The symptoms significantly interfere with the people's lives and often lead them to go "doctor shopping" in the hope of finding a medical practitioner who can explain and treat their ailments (Rief & Sharpe, 2004). Or they may hold the belief that they are gravely ill, despite reassurances from their doctors to the contrary. Some individuals fake or manufacture physical symptoms for no apparent reason other than to receive medical treatment.

The concept of somatic symptom and related disorders presumes that psychological processes affect physical functioning. For example, some people complain of problems in breathing or swallowing, or a "lump in the throat." Such problems can reflect overactivity of the sympathetic branch of the autonomic nervous system, which might result from anxiety. All in all, at least 20% of doctor visits involve complaints that cannot be explained medically (Rief & Sharpe, 2004).

There are several types of somatic symptom and related disorders. Here, we consider the following major types: *somatic symptom disorder, illness anxiety disorder, conversion disorder*, and *factitious disorder*. Table 6.4 provides an overview of these disorders.

**WHAT TO TAKE?** *Hypochondriasis* is a persistent concern or fear that one is seriously ill, although no organic basis can be found to account for one's physical complaints. People with this disorder tend to be heavy users of prescription and over-the-counter medications and find little if any reassurance in doctors' assertions that their health is not in jeopardy.

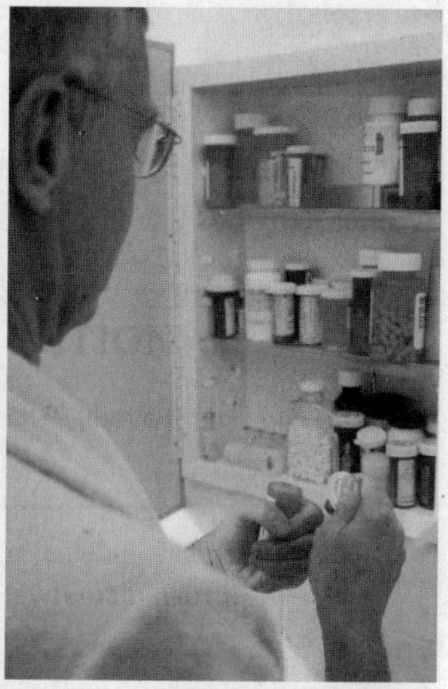

## Somatic Symptom Disorder

### 6.7 Describe the key features of somatic symptom disorder.

Most people have physical symptoms somewhere along life's course. It is normal to feel concerned about one's physical symptoms and to seek medical attention. However, people with **somatic symptom disorder** (SSD) not only have troubling physical symptoms but also are excessively concerned about their symptoms to the extent that it affects their thoughts, feelings, and behaviors in daily life. Thus, the diagnosis emphasizes the psychological features of physical symptoms, not whether the underlying cause or causes of the symptoms can be medically explained. The diagnosis of SSD requires that physical symptoms be persistent, lasting typically for a period of six months or longer (though any one symptom may not be continuously present), and that they are associated with

**Table 6.4** Overview of Major Somatic Symptom and Related Disorders

| Type of Disorder | Approximate Lifetime Prevalence in Population | Description | Associated Features |
|---|---|---|---|
| **Somatic symptom disorder** | Unknown, but may affect 5% to 7% of the general adult population | A pattern of abnormal behaviors, thoughts, or feelings relating to physical symptoms | • Symptoms prompt frequent medical visits or cause significant impairment of functioning. |
| **Illness anxiety disorder** | Unknown | Preoccupation with the belief that one is seriously ill | • Fear of illness persists despite medical reassurance to the contrary.<br>• Tendency to interpret physical sensations or minor aches and pains as signs of serious illness. |
| **Conversion disorder (functional neurological symptom disorder)** | Unknown, but reported in 5% of patients referred to neurology clinics | Change in or loss of a physical function without medical cause | • Emerges in context of conflicts or stressful experiences, which lends credence to its psychological origins.<br>• May be associated with *la belle indifférence* (indifference to symptoms). |
| **Factitious disorder** | Unknown, but an estimated 1% of medical patients in hospital settings may qualify for the diagnosis | Faking or manufacturing physical or psychological symptoms without any apparent motive | • Unlike malingering, the symptoms do not result in any obvious gain.<br>• There are two major types: factitious disorder imposed on self (fabricating or inducing symptoms in oneself, generally called Münchausen syndrome) and factitious disorder imposed on another (fabricating or inducing symptoms in others). |

**SOURCE:** Prevalence rates derived from American Psychiatric Association, 2013.

either significant personal distress or interference with daily functioning. The symptoms may include such complaints as gastric (stomach) distress and various aches and pains.

People with SSD may have excessive concerns about the seriousness of their symptoms. They may be bothered by nagging anxiety about what their symptoms might mean and spend a great deal of time running from doctor to doctor seeking a cure or confirmation that their worries are valid. Their concerns may last for years and become a source of continuing frustration both for themselves and for their families and physicians (Holder-Perkins & Wise, 2002). A study that tracked use of medical care by patients with excessive somatic concerns found them to be heavy users of medical services (Barsky, Orav, & Bates, 2005).

Previous versions of the *DSM* included a disorder called **hypochondriasis**, which applied to people with physical complaints who believed their symptoms were due to a serious, undetected illness, such as cancer or heart disease, despite medical reassurance to the contrary. For example, a person suffering from headaches may fear that they are a sign of a brain tumor and believe doctors are wrong when they say these fears are groundless. At the core of hypochondriasis is health anxiety, a preoccupation that one's physical symptoms are signs of something terribly wrong with one's health (Abramowitz & Braddock, 2011; Skritskaya et al., 2012). Hypochondriasis is believed to affect about 1% to 5% of the general population and about 5% of patients seeking medical care (Abramowitz & Braddock, 2011; Barsky & Ahern, 2004).

**HENRY: HYPOCHONDRIASIS**

The term *hypochondriasis* is still in widespread use but is no longer a distinct diagnosis in *DSM-5*. The great majority of cases previously diagnosed as hypochondriasis, perhaps as many as three-fourths, would now be diagnosed as somatic symptom disorder (American Psychiatric Association, 2013).

People with hypochondriasis do not consciously fake their symptoms. They feel real physical discomfort, often involving their digestive system or an assortment of aches and pains throughout the body. They may be overly sensitive to benign changes in physical sensations, such as slight changes in heartbeat and minor aches and pains (Barsky et al., 2001).

Anxiety about physical symptoms can produce its own physical sensations, however—for example, heavy sweating and dizziness, or even fainting. Thus, a vicious cycle may ensue. Patients may become resentful when their doctors tell them that their own fears may be causing their physical symptoms. They frequently go doctor shopping in the hope that a competent and sympathetic physician will heed them before it is too late. Physicians too can develop hypochondriasis, as we see in the following case example.

## The Doctor Feels Sick:

### A CASE OF HYPOCHONDRIASIS

Robert, a 38-year-old radiologist, had just returned from a 10-day stay at a famous diagnostic center where he had undergone extensive testing of his entire gastrointestinal tract. The evaluation proved negative for any significant physical illness, but rather than feel relieved, he appeared resentful and disappointed with the findings. He had been bothered for several months with a variety of physical symptoms, including mild abdominal pain, feelings of "fullness," "bowel rumblings," and a feeling of a "firm abdominal mass." He had become convinced that his symptoms were due to colon cancer and began testing his stool for blood on a weekly basis and carefully palpating his abdomen for "masses" every few days while lying in bed. He also secretly performed X-ray studies on himself. There was a history of a heart murmur that was discovered when he was 13, and his younger brother had died of congenital heart disease in early childhood. Although the evaluation of his murmur showed it to be benign, he began worrying that something might have been overlooked. He developed a fear that something was terribly wrong with his heart, and while the fear eventually subsided, it never entirely left him. In medical school, he worried about diseases he learned about in pathology. Since graduating, he repeatedly experienced concerns about his health that followed a typical pattern: noticing certain symptoms, becoming preoccupied with what the symptoms might mean, and undergoing physical evaluations that proved negative. His decision to seek a psychiatric consultation was prompted by an incident with his 9-year-old son. His son accidentally walked in on him while he was palpating his abdomen and asked, "What do you think it is this time, Dad?" He became tearful as he described this incident and reported feeling shame and anger—mostly at himself.

**SOURCE:** *Adapted from Spitzer et al., 1994, pp. 89–90*

People with hypochondriasis often report having been sick as children, having missed school because of health reasons, and having experienced childhood trauma, such as sexual abuse or physical violence (Barsky et al., 1994). Hypochondriasis and other forms of somatic symptom disorder can last for years and often occur together with other psychological disorders, especially major depression and anxiety disorders.

About one in four people with hypochondriasis complain of relatively minor or mild symptoms that they take to be signs of a serious undiagnosed illness. Because of the mildness of their symptoms, the diagnosis of somatic symptom disorder would not apply (American Psychiatric Association, 2013). However, these individuals express such a high level of health anxiety or concern about their medical condition that they would likely receive a diagnosis of a newly recognized disorder in *DSM-5* called *illness anxiety disorder*.

## Illness Anxiety Disorder

**6.8 Describe the key features of illness anxiety disorder.**

A common misconception is that physical symptoms in people with hypochondriasis are "made up" or "all in their heads." However, in the great majority of cases, people with hypochondriasis have real symptoms that cause real distress and so would warrant a diagnosis of somatic symptom disorder (SSD). However, there is a subgroup of people with hypochondriasis who complain of relatively minor or mild symptoms they take to be signs of a serious undiagnosed illness. The *DSM-5* introduced a new diagnostic category to apply to this subgroup, **illness anxiety disorder** (IAD), with the emphasis placed on the anxiety associated with illness rather than the distress the symptoms cause. For these patients, it's not the symptoms they find so troubling—symptoms such as vague aches and pains or a passing feeling of tightness in the abdomen or chest. Rather, it's the fear of what these symptoms might mean. In some cases, there are no reported symptoms at all, but the person still expresses serious concerns about having a serious undiagnosed illness.

In some cases of illness anxiety disorder, a person has a family history of a serious disease (e.g., Alzheimer's disease) but becomes preoccupied with an exaggerated concern that he or she is suffering from the disease or is slowly developing it. The person may become preoccupied with checking his or her body for signs of the feared disease.

There are two general subtypes of the disorder. One subtype, the *care-avoidant subtype*, applies to people who postpone or avoid medical visits or lab tests because of high levels of anxiety about what might be discovered. The second subtype, called the *care-seeking subtype*, describes people who go doctor shopping, basically jumping from doctor to doctor in the hope of finding the one medical professional who might confirm their worst fears. These individuals may become angry at doctors who try to convince them that their fears are unwarranted.

## Conversion Disorder

**6.9 Describe the key features of conversion disorder.**

**Conversion disorder** (called *functional neurological symptom disorder* in *DSM-5*) is characterized by symptoms or deficits that affect the ability to control voluntary movements (inability to walk or move an arm, for example) or that impair sensory functions, such as an inability to see, hear, or feel tactile stimulation (touch, pressure, warmth, or pain). What qualifies these problems as a psychological disorder is that the loss or impairment of physical functions is either inconsistent or incompatible with known medical conditions or diseases (Rickards & Silver, 2014). Consequently, conversion disorder is believed to involve the conversion or transformation of emotional distress into significant symptoms in the motor or sensory domains (Becker et al., 2013; Reynolds, 2012). In some cases, however, what appears to be conversion disorder actually turns out to be intentional fabrication or faking of symptoms for some external gain (malingering). Unfortunately, clinicians lack the ability to reliably determine that someone is faking.

The physical symptoms in conversion disorder usually come on suddenly in stressful situations. A soldier's hand may become "paralyzed" during intense combat, for example. The fact that conversion symptoms first appear in the context of or are aggravated by conflicts or stressors suggests a psychological connection. The prevalence of the disorder in the general population remains unknown, but the diagnosis is reported in about of 5% of patients referred to neurology clinics (American Psychiatric Association, 2013). Like dissociative identity disorder, conversion disorder is linked in many cases to a history of childhood trauma or abuse (Sobot et al., 2012).

Conversion disorder is so named because of the psychodynamic belief that it represents the channeling, or *conversion*, of repressed sexual or aggressive energies into physical symptoms. Conversion disorder was formerly called *hysteria* or *hysterical neurosis*, and it played an important role in Freud's development of psychoanalysis (see Chapter 2). Hysterical or conversion disorders seem to have been much more common in Freud's day than they are today.

**TRUTH or FICTION**

Some people lose all feeling in their hands or legs, although nothing is medically wrong with them.

☑ **TRUE** Some people with conversion disorder have lost sensory or motor functions even though there is nothing medically wrong with them. (However, some people who are assumed to have conversion disorders may actually have medical problems that go unrecognized.)

According to the *DSM*, conversion symptoms mimic neurological or general medical conditions involving problems with voluntary motor (movement) or sensory functions. Some classic symptom patterns take the form of paralysis, epilepsy, problems in coordination, blindness and tunnel vision, loss of the sense of hearing or of smell, or loss of feeling in a limb (anesthesia). The bodily symptoms found in conversion disorders often do not match the medical conditions they suggest. For example, *conversion epileptics*, unlike true epileptic patients, may maintain control over their bladders during an attack. People whose vision is supposedly impaired may walk through the physician's office without bumping into the furniture. People who become "incapable" of standing or walking may nevertheless perform other leg movements normally. Nonetheless, hysteria and conversion symptoms are sometimes incorrectly diagnosed in people who turn out to have underlying medical conditions (Stone et al., 2005). **T / F**

If you suddenly lost your vision, or if you could no longer move your legs, you would probably show understandable concern. But some people with conversion disorders, like those with dissociative amnesia, show a remarkable indifference to their symptoms, a phenomenon termed *la belle indifférence* (the beautiful indifference; Stone et al., 2006). The *DSM* advises against relying on indifference to symptoms as a factor in making the diagnosis, however, because many people cope with real physical disorders by denying or minimizing their pain or concerns, which relieves anxieties—at least temporarily.

## Factitious Disorder

**6.10 Explain the difference between malingering and factitious disorder.**

**Factitious disorder** is a puzzlement. People with this disorder fake or manufacture physical or psychological symptoms, but without any apparent motive. Sometimes, they are outright faking, claiming they cannot move an arm or a leg or claiming a pain that doesn't exist. Sometimes, they injure themselves or take medication that causes troubling, even life-threatening symptoms. The puzzlement involves the lack of a motive for these deceitful behaviors. Factitious disorder is not the same as **malingering**. Because malingering is motivated by external rewards or incentives, it is not considered a mental disorder within the *DSM* framework. People may feign physical illness to avoid work or to qualify for disability benefits. They may be deceitful and even dishonest, but they are not deemed to be suffering from a psychological disorder.

In factitious disorder, the symptoms do not bring about obvious gains or external rewards. Thus, factitious disorder serves an underlying psychological need involved in assuming a sick role; hence, it is classified as a type of mental or psychological disorder.

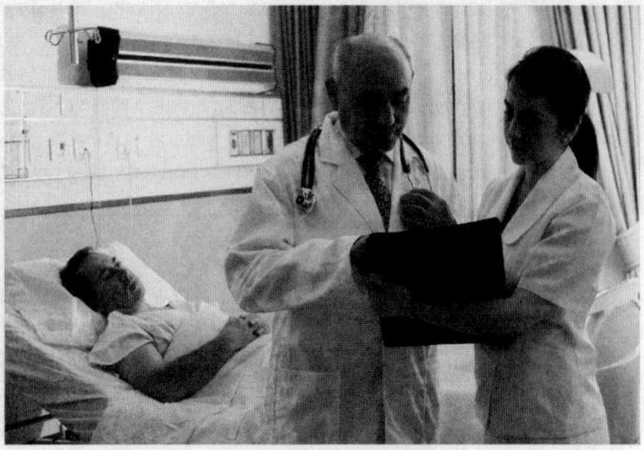

**IS THIS PATIENT REALLY SICK?** Münchausen syndrome is characterized by the fabrication of medical complaints for no other apparent purpose than to gain admission to hospitals. Some Münchausen patients may produce life-threatening symptoms in their attempts to deceive doctors.

The two major subtypes of factitious disorder are (1) *factitious disorder on self* (characterized by faking or inducing symptoms in oneself) and (2) *factitious disorder imposed on another* (characterized by inducing symptoms in others).

Factitious disorder imposed on onseself is the most common form of the disorder and is popularly referred to as **Münchausen syndrome**. The syndrome is a form of feigned illness in which a person either fakes being ill or makes him- or herself ill (by ingesting toxic substances, for example). Although people with somatic symptom disorder may reap some benefits from having physical symptoms (e.g., drawing sympathy from others), they do not purposefully produce them. They do not set out to deceive others. Münchausen syndrome, on the other hand, is a type of factitious disorder in which there is deliberate fabrication or inducement of seemingly plausible physical complaints for no obvious gain, apart from assuming the role of a medical patient and receiving sympathy and support from others.

Münchausen syndrome was named after Baron Karl von Münchausen, one of history's great fibbers. The good baron, an 18th-century German army officer, entertained friends with tales of outrageous adventures. In the vernacular, *Münchausenism* refers to tellers of tall tales. In clinical terms, Münchausen syndrome refers to patients who tell tall tales or outrageous lies to their doctors. People who have Münchausen syndrome usually suffer deep anguish as they bounce from hospital to hospital and subject themselves to unnecessary, painful, and sometimes risky medical treatments, even surgery. *A Closer Look: Münchausen Syndrome* explores this curious disorder in more depth.

## A CLOSER Look

### MÜNCHAUSEN SYNDROME

A woman staggered into the emergency room of a New York City hospital bleeding from the mouth, clutching her stomach, and wailing with pain (Lear, 1988). Even in that setting, forever serving bleeders and clutchers and wailers, there was something about her, some terrible star quality that held center stage. The story she told was one of horrible abuse and trauma. There was a man who had seduced her and then tied her, beaten her, and forced her to turn over her money and jewelry. She had other physical symptoms, including pain in her lower body and an intense headache. After she was admitted to the hospital, tests were run but to no avail. No physical cause of her bleeding and pain could be found—but a hospital aide noticed some objects on her bedside table, including a syringe and a blood thinner. Yes, she had injected herself before entering the hospital with the blood thinner, causing the bleeding. She denied it all, claiming the items on the bedside table were not hers. Someone had planted them on the table, she claimed. Finding no one who believed her, she soon checked herself out the hospital, claiming she would find other doctors who really cared. Later, it was discovered that she had been admitted recently to two other hospitals, reporting the same symptoms.

Münchausen patients may go to great lengths to seek a confirmatory diagnosis, such as agreeing to exploratory surgery, even though they know there is nothing wrong with them. Some inject themselves with drugs to produce symptoms such as skin rashes. When confronted with evidence of their deception, they may turn nasty and stick to their guns. They are also skillful enough actors to convince others that their complaints are genuine.

Why do patients with Münchausen syndrome fake illness or put themselves at risk by making themselves out to be sick or injured? Perhaps enacting the sick role in the protected hospital environment provides a sense of security that was lacking in childhood. Perhaps the hospital becomes a stage on which they can act out resentments against doctors and parents that have been brewing since childhood. Perhaps they are trying to identify with a parent who was often sick. Or perhaps they learned to enact a sick role in childhood to escape from repeated sexual abuse or other traumatic experiences and continue to enact the role to escape stressors in their adult lives. No one is really sure, and the disorder remains one of the more puzzling forms of abnormal behavior.

Julie's case highlights a most pernicious form of child maltreatment called *Münchausen syndrome by proxy*, which in the *DSM-5* is now called *factitious disorder imposed on another*. People with this disorder intentionally falsify or induce physical or emotional illness or injury in another person, typically (and shockingly) a child or dependent person (Feldman, 2003).

"I"

**Sickened: Factitious Disorder Imposed on Another**

In her memoir entitled *Sickened*, Julie Gregory recounts how she was subjected to numerous X-rays and operations as a child, not because there was anything wrong with her, but to find the cause of an illness that existed only in her mother's mind (Gregory, 2003). At age 13, Julie underwent an invasive medical procedure, a heart catheterization, because of her mother's insistence to "get to the bottom of this thing." When the cardiologist informed Julie's mother that the test results were within normal limits, her mother argued for an even more invasive test involving open-heart surgery. When the doctor refused, Julie's mother confronted him in Julie's presence:

"I can't believe it! I cannot believe this! You're not going to dig into this and do the open-heart? I thought we had agreed to follow this through to the end, Michael. I thought you said you were committed to me on this."

[The doctor responds] "I'm committed to finding Julie's illness, Ms. Gregory, but Julie doesn't need heart surgery. Usually parents are thrilled to—"

[Julie's Mom replies] "Oh, that's just it? That's all you're going to do? Just drop me like a hot potato? I mean, for crying out loud, why can't I just have a normal kid like other mothers? I mean I'm a good mom...."

[Julie observes] I'm standing behind my mother's left leg, my eyes glued to the doctor, boring an SOS into his eyes: "Don't make me go, don't let her take me."

[The doctor continues] "Ms. Gregory, I didn't say you weren't a good mother. But I can't do anything else here. You need to drop the heart procedures. Period."

And with that he turned on his heels.

"Well, you're the one who's going to be sorry," Mom screeches, "when this kid dies on you. That's what. Cause you're going to get sued out the yin-yang for being such an incompetent idiot. Can't even find out what's wrong with a thirteen-year-old girl! You are insane! This kid is sick, you hear me? She's sick!"

**SOURCE:** *Gregory, 2003*

Parents or caregivers who induce illness in their children may be trying to gain sympathy or experience the sense of control made possible by attending to a sick child. The disorder is controversial and remains under study by the psychiatric community. The controversy arises in large part because it appears to put a diagnostic label on abusive behavior. What is clear is that the disorder is linked to heinous crimes against children (Mart, 2003). In one sample case, a mother was suspected of purposely causing her 3-year-old's repeated bouts of diarrhea (Schreier & Ricci, 2002). Sadly, the child died before authorities could intervene. In another case, a foster mother is alleged to have brought about the deaths of three children by giving them overdoses of medicines containing potassium and sodium. The chemicals induced suffocation or heart attacks.

A review of 451 cases of Münchausen syndrome by proxy reported in the scientific literature showed that 6% of the victims died (Sheridan, 2003). Typical victims were 4 years of age or younger. Mothers were perpetrators in three out of four cases. Cases of Münchausen syndrome by proxy often involve mysterious high fevers in children, seizures of unknown cause, and similar symptoms. Doctors typically find the illnesses to be unusual, prolonged, and unexplained. They require some medical sophistication on the part of the perpetrator.

# Koro and Dhat Syndromes: Far Eastern Somatic Symptom Disorders?

**6.11 Describe the key features of koro and dhat syndromes.**

In the United States, it is common for people who develop hypochondriasis to be troubled by the idea that they have serious illnesses, such as cancer. The koro and dhat syndromes of the Far East share some clinical features with hypochondriasis. Although these syndromes may seem foreign to North American readers, each is connected with the folklore of its own culture.

**KORO SYNDROME** As discussed in Chapter 3, a culture-bound syndrome found primarily in China and some other southeast Asian countries, **koro syndrome** characterizes people who fear that their genitals are shrinking and retracting into their bodies, which they believe will result in death (Bhatia, Jhanjee, & Kumar, 2011). Though koro is classified as a culture-bound syndrome, some cases have been reported in other parts of the world (e.g., Alvarez et al., 2012; Ntouros et al., 2010). The syndrome has been identified mainly in young men, although some cases have also been reported in women. Koro syndrome tends to be short-lived and to involve episodes of acute anxiety about one's genitals retracting. Physiological signs of anxiety that approach panic are common, including profuse sweating, breathlessness, and heart palpitations. Men who suffer from koro have been known to use mechanical devices, such as chopsticks, to try to prevent the penis from retracting into the body (Devan, 1987).

Koro syndrome has been traced within Chinese culture as far back as 3000 B.C.E. Epidemics involving hundreds or thousands of people have been reported in China, Singapore, Thailand, and India (Tseng et al., 1992). In Guangdong Province in China, an epidemic of koro involving more than 2,000 people occurred during the 1980s. Guangdong residents who developed koro tended to be more superstitious, lower in intelligence, and more accepting of koro-related folk beliefs (such as the belief that shrinkage of the penis will be lethal) than those who did not fall victim to the epidemic. Medical reassurance that such fears are unfounded often quells koro episodes (Devan, 1987). Koro episodes among those who do not receive corrective information tend to pass with time but may recur. **T / F**

## TRUTH *or* FICTION

Some men have a psychological disorder characterized by fear of the penis shrinking and retracting into the body.

☑ **TRUE** This culture-bound syndrome found in the Far East may have existed in China for at least 5,000 years.

**DHAT SYNDROME** Found among young Asian Indian males, **dhat syndrome** involves excessive fears over the loss of seminal fluid in nocturnal emissions, in urine, or through masturbation (Bhatia, Jhanjee, & Kumar, 2011; Mehta, De, & Balachandran, 2009). Some men with this syndrome also believe (incorrectly) that semen mixes with urine and is excreted through urination. Men with dhat syndrome may roam from physician to physician seeking help to prevent nocturnal emissions or the (imagined) loss of semen mixed with excreted urine. There is a widespread belief within Indian culture (and other Near and Far Eastern cultures) that the loss of semen is harmful because it depletes the body of physical and mental energy. Like other culture-bound syndromes, dhat must be understood within its cultural context (Akhtar, 1988, p. 71). In traditional Indian culture, semen is believed to be a vital bodily fluid, an "elixir of life" needed to preserve health and enhance longevity. It is a commonly held Hindu belief that forty meals need to be consumed to create one droplet of blood, that forty droplets of blood are needed to create one droplet of bone marrow, and that forty droplets of bone marrow are needed to create but one droplet of semen (Akhtar, 1988).

On the basis of the cultural belief in the life-preserving nature of semen, it is not surprising that some Indian males experience extreme anxiety over the involuntary loss of the fluid through nocturnal emissions (Akhtar, 1988). Dhat syndrome has also been associated with difficulty in achieving or maintaining erection, apparently due to excessive concern about loss of seminal fluid through ejaculation (Singh, 1985).

# Theoretical Perspectives

**6.12 Describe the theoretical understandings of somatic symptom and related disorders.**

Conversion disorder, or "hysteria," was known to the great physician of ancient Greece, Hippocrates, who attributed the strange bodily symptoms to a wandering uterus (*hystera* in Greek), creating internal chaos. Hippocrates noticed that these complaints were less common among married than unmarried women. He prescribed marriage as a "cure" on the basis of these observations and also on the theoretical assumption that pregnancy would satisfy uterine needs and fix the organ in place. Pregnancy fosters hormonal and structural changes that are of benefit to some women with menstrual complaints, but Hippocrates's mistaken belief in the "wandering uterus" has contributed throughout the centuries to degrading interpretations of women's complaints of physical problems. Despite Hippocrates's belief that hysteria is exclusively a female concern, it also occurs in men. **T / F**

**TRUTH or FICTION**

The term *hysteria* derives from the Greek word for testicle.

☑ **FALSE** The term is derived from *hystera*, the Greek word for uterus.

Not much is known about the biological underpinnings of somatic symptom and related disorders. Brain-imaging studies of patients with hysterical paralysis (a limb the person claims to be unable to move, despite healthy muscles and nerves) points to possible disruptions occurring in brain circuitry responsible for controlling movement and emotional responses (Kinetz, 2006). These imaging studies suggest that normal control of movement may be inhibited by activation of brain circuits involved in processing emotions. We should caution that scientists are only at the beginning stages of understanding the biological bases of conversion disorder and much remains unknown. Like the dissociative disorders, the scientific study of conversion disorder and other forms of somatic symptom disorder has been largely approached from the psychological perspective, which is our focus here.

**THE WANDERING UTERUS.** The ancient Greek physician Hippocrates believed that hysterical symptoms were exclusively a female problem caused by a wandering uterus. However, Hippocrates did not have opportunity to treat male aviators during World War II who developed "hysterical night blindness" that prevented them from carrying out dangerous nighttime missions.

**PSYCHODYNAMIC THEORY** Hysterical disorders provided an arena for some of the debate between the psychological and biological theories of the 19th century. The alleviation—albeit often temporary—of hysterical symptoms through hypnosis by Charcot, Breuer, and Freud contributed to the belief that hysteria was rooted in psychological rather than physical causes and led Freud to the development of a theory of the unconscious mind (see Chapter 2). Freud held that the ego manages to control unacceptable or threatening sexual and aggressive impulses arising from the id through defense mechanisms such as repression. Such control prevents the anxiety that would occur if a person were to become aware of these impulses. In some cases, the leftover emotion that is strangulated, or cut off, from the threatening impulses becomes *converted* into a physical symptom, such as hysterical paralysis or blindness. Although the early psychodynamic formulation of hysteria is still widely held, empirical evidence has been lacking. One problem with the Freudian view is that it does not explain *how* energies left over from unconscious conflicts become transformed into physical symptoms (Miller, 1987).

According to psychodynamic theory, hysterical symptoms are functional: They allow a person to achieve *primary gains* and *secondary gains*. The primary gain of the symptoms is to allow an individual to keep internal conflicts repressed. The person is aware of the physical symptom but not of the conflict it represents. In such cases, the "symptom" is symbolic of, and provides the person with a "partial solution" for, the underlying conflict. For example, the hysterical paralysis of an arm might symbolize and also prevent an individual from acting on repressed unacceptable sexual (e.g., masturbatory) or aggressive (e.g., murderous) impulses. Repression occurs unconsciously, so the individual remains unaware of the underlying conflicts. *La belle indifférence*, first noted by Charcot, is believed to occur because the physical symptoms help relieve rather than cause anxiety. From the psychodynamic perspective, conversion disorders, like dissociative disorders, serve a purpose.

Secondary gains from the symptoms are those that allow individuals to avoid burdensome responsibilities and to gain the support—rather than condemnation—of those around them. For example, soldiers sometimes experience sudden "paralysis" of their hands, which prevents them from firing their guns in battle. They may then be sent to recuperate at a hospital rather than face enemy fire. The symptoms in such cases are not considered contrived, as would be the case in malingering. A number of bomber pilots during World War II suffered hysterical "night blindness" that prevented them from carrying out dangerous nighttime missions. In the psychodynamic view, their blindness may have achieved a primary gain of shielding them from guilt associated with dropping bombs on civilian areas. It may also have achieved a secondary purpose of helping them avoid dangerous missions.

**NIGHT BLINDNESS.** A number of bomber pilots during World War II complained of night blindness that prevented them from carrying out dangerous nighttime missions. Might this have been a form of hysterical behavior? How might the psychodynamic perspective interpret these symptoms?

**LEARNING THEORY** Theoretical formulations, including both psychodynamic theory and learning theory, focus on the role of anxiety in explaining conversion disorders. Psychodynamic theorists, however, seek the causes of anxiety in unconscious conflicts. Learning theorists focus on the more direct reinforcing properties of the symptom and its secondary role in helping an individual avoid or escape anxiety-evoking situations.

From the learning perspective, people with somatic symptom and related disorders may also carry the benefits, or reinforcing properties, of the "sick role." People with conversion disorders, for instance, may be relieved of chores and responsibilities such as going to work or performing household tasks. Being sick also usually earns sympathy and support. See Figure 6.2 for a schematic representation of the psychodynamic and learning theory conceptualizations of conversion disorder.

Differences in learning experiences may explain why conversion disorders were historically more often reported among women than men. It may be that women in Western culture are more likely than men to be socialized to cope with stress by enacting a sick role (Miller, 1987). We are not suggesting that people with conversion disorders are fakers. We are merely pointing out that people may learn to adopt roles that lead to reinforcing consequences, regardless of whether they deliberately seek to enact these roles.

Some learning theorists link hypochondriasis to obsessive–compulsive disorder (e.g., Weck et al., 2011). People with hypochondriasis, which is now labeled somatic symptom disorder or illness anxiety disorder, are often bothered by obsessive, anxiety-inducing thoughts about the state of their health. Running from doctor to doctor may be a form of compulsive behavior that is reinforced by the temporary relief from anxiety that comes from doctors reassuring them that their fears are unwarranted. Yet the troublesome thoughts eventually return, prompting repeated consultations. The cycle then repeats.

**COGNITIVE THEORY** From a cognitive perspective, we can think about hypochondriasis in some cases as a type of self-handicapping strategy, a way of blaming poor performance on failing health. In other cases, diverting attention to physical complaints may serve as a means of avoiding thinking about other life problems.

Another cognitive explanation focuses on the role of distorted thinking. People with hypochondriasis have a tendency to exaggerate the significance of minor physical complaints (Fulton, Marcus, & Merkey, 2011; Hofmann, Asmundson, & Beck, 2011). They misinterpret benign symptoms as signs of a serious illness, which creates anxiety, which leads them to chase down one doctor after another in an attempt to uncover the dreaded disease

**Figure 6.2 Conceptual models of conversion disorder.**

Psychodynamic and learning theories offer conceptual models of conversion disorder that emphasize the role of conversion symptoms that lead to escape or relief from anxiety.

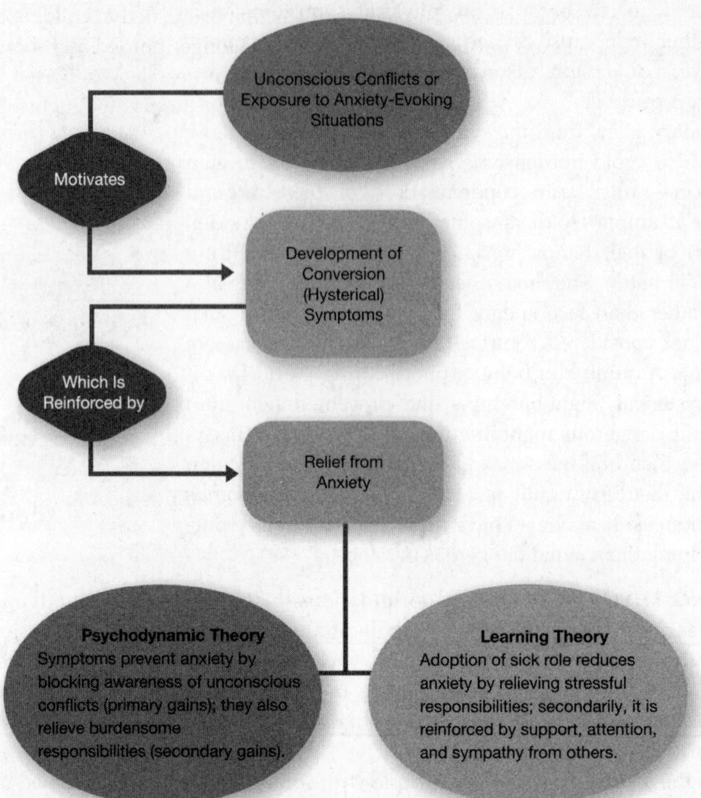


they fear they have. The anxiety itself may lead to unpleasant physical symptoms, which are likewise exaggerated in importance, leading to more worrisome cognitions.

Anxiety about health concerns is a common feature of hypochondriasis and panic disorder (Abramowitz, Olatunji, & Deacon, 2008). Theorists speculate that both disorders may share a common cause involving a distorted way of thinking that leads to misinterpreting minor changes in bodily sensations as signs of pending catastrophe (Salkovskis & Clark, 1993). The differences between the two disorders may hinge on whether the misinterpretation of bodily cues carries a perception of an imminent threat that leads to a rapid spiraling of anxiety (panic disorder) or of a longer-range threat that leads to fear of an underlying disease process (hypochondriasis). Given the prominent role of anxiety in hypochondriasis, investigators question whether it should be classified, as it is now, as a form of somatic symptom disorder or illness anxiety disorder, or be moved to the category of Anxiety Disorders (Creed & Barsky, 2004; Gropalis et al., 2012).

**BRAIN DYSFUNCTION** Recently, investigators proposed that conversion symptoms may involve a disconnect or impairment in the neural connections between parts of the brain that control certain functions (speech, for example) and other parts involved in regulating anxiety (Bryant & Das, 2012). Research into the biological underpinnings of somatic symptom and related disorders is in its infancy, but it promises to help elucidate connections between anxiety and brain functions.

# Treatment of Somatic Symptom and Related Disorders

**6.13 Describe methods used to treat somatic symptom and related disorders.**

The treatment approach that Freud pioneered, psychoanalysis, began with the treatment of hysteria, which is now termed *conversion disorder*. Psychoanalysis seeks to uncover and bring into conscious awareness unconscious conflicts that originated in childhood. Once a conflict is aired and worked through, the symptom is no longer needed and should disappear. The psychoanalytic method is supported by case studies, some reported by Freud and others by his followers. However, evidence supporting the therapeutic value of psychological treatment for conversion disorder remains sparse (Rickards & Silver, 2014). One reason for the lack of scientific studies is the infrequent occurrence of conversion disorders.

The behavioral approach to treatment focuses on removing sources of secondary reinforcement (or secondary gain) that may become connected with physical complaints. Family members and others, for example, often perceive individuals with these disorders as sickly and incapable of carrying out normal responsibilities. This reinforces dependent and complaining behaviors. The behavior therapist may teach family members to reward attempts to assume responsibility and to ignore nagging and complaining. The behavior therapist may also work directly with patients, helping them learn more adaptive ways of handling stress or anxiety (through relaxation and cognitive restructuring, for example).

Cognitive-behavioral therapy has achieved good results in treating somatic symptom disorders such as hypochondriasis (e.g., Olatunji et al., 2014; Weck & Neng, 2015; Weck et al., 2015). In treating hypochondriasis, for example, the cognitive technique of restructuring distorted beliefs helps people replace exaggerated illness-related beliefs with rational alternatives. The behavioral technique of exposure with response prevention, which is discussed in Chapter 5, can help people with hypochondriasis break the cycle of running to doctors for reassurance whenever they experience worrisome, health-related concerns. These individuals can also benefit from breaking problem habits, such as repeatedly checking the Internet for illness-related information and reading newspaper obituaries (Barsky & Ahern, 2004). Unfortunately, many people with somatic symptom and related disorders drop out of treatment when they are told that their problems are psychological in nature, not physical. As one leading expert, Dr. Arthur Barksy, put it: "They'll say, 'I don't need to talk about this, I need somebody to stick a biopsy needle in my liver, I need that CAT scan repeated'" ("Therapy and Hypochondriacs," 2004, p. A19).

Although CBT is the best established treatment for somatic symptom and related disorders, several studies also support the therapeutic value of antidepressants in treating these disorders, including somatic symptom disorder (hypochondriasis) and factitious disorder (Münchausen syndrome; Kroenke, 2009; Rief & Sharpe, 2004).

All in all, the dissociative disorders and somatic symptom and related disorders remain among the most intriguing and least understood patterns of abnormal behavior.

# Psychological Factors Affecting Physical Health

The somatic symptom and related disorders open a window to the role of disturbed thoughts, behaviors, and emotions in our physical health. In this section, we take a broader view of the role of psychological factors in physical health. Whereas somatic symptom and related disorders are behavioral or psychological in nature, physical disorders are affected by psychological factors, as we will consider next. Physical disorders in which psychological factors are believed to play a causal or contributing role have traditionally been termed **psychosomatic disorders**. The term *psychosomatic* is derived from the Greek roots *psyche*, meaning *soul* or *intellect*, and *soma*, which means *body*. Disorders such as asthma and headaches have traditionally been labeled as psychosomatic because of the belief that psychological factors play an important role in their development.

Ulcers are another ailment traditionally identified as a psychosomatic disorder. Ulcers affect about 1 in 10 people in the United States. However, their status as a psychosomatic disorder has been reevaluated in light of recent landmark research showing that a bacterium, *H. pylori*, not stress or diet, is the major cause of the types of ulcers called *peptic ulcers*, which are sores in the lining of the stomach or upper part of the small intestine (Jones, 2006). Ulcers may arise when the bacterium damages the protective lining of the stomach or intestines.

Treatment with a regimen of antibiotics may cure ulcers by attacking the bacterium directly. Scientists don't yet know why some people who harbor the bacterium develop ulcers and others do not. The virulence of the particular strain of *H. pylori* may determine whether infected people develop peptic ulcers. Stress may also play a role, although scientists lack definitive evidence that stress contributes to vulnerability (Jones, 2006).

The field of psychosomatic medicine explores health-related connections between the mind and the body. Today, evidence points to the importance of psychological factors in a much wider range of physical disorders than those traditionally identified as psychosomatic. In this section, we discuss several traditionally identified psychosomatic disorders, as well as other diseases in which psychological factors may play a role in the course or treatment of the disease: cardiovascular disease, cancer, and HIV/AIDS.

## Headaches

**6.14 Describe the role of psychological factors in understanding and treating headaches.**

Headaches are symptoms of many medical disorders. When they occur in the absence of other symptoms, however, they may be classified as stress-related. By far, the most frequent kind of headache is the *tension headache*. Stress can lead to persistent contractions of the muscles of the scalp, face, neck, and shoulders, giving rise to periodic or chronic tension headaches. Such headaches develop gradually and are generally characterized by dull, steady pain on both sides of the head and feelings of pressure or tightness.

*Migraines*, which affect an estimated 36 million Americans, are more than simple headaches (Gelfand, 2014). They are complex neurological disorders that last for hours or days. Although they can affect people of both genders and of all ages, about two out of three cases occur in women between 15 and 55 years of age. Migraines may occur as often as daily or as seldom as every other month. They are characterized by piercing or throbbing sensations on one side of the head only or centered behind an eye. They can be so intense that they seem intolerable. Sufferers may experience an *aura*, or cluster of warning sensations that precedes the attack. Auras are typified by perceptual distortions, such as flashing lights, bizarre images, or blind spots. Coping with the misery of brutal migraine attacks can take its toll, impairing quality of life and leading to disturbances of sleep, mood, and thinking processes.

**MIGRAINE!** Migraine headaches involve intense throbbing pain on one side of the head. They may be triggered by many factors, such as hormonal changes, exposure to strong light, changes in barometric pressure, hunger, exposure to pollen, red wine, and use of certain drugs and even monosodium glutamate.

**THEORETICAL PERSPECTIVES** The underlying causes of headaches remain unclear and subject to continued study. One factor contributing to tension headaches may be increased sensitivity of the neural pathways that send pain signals to the brain from the face and head (Holroyd, 2002). Migraine headaches may involve an underlying central nervous system disorder involving nerves and blood vessels in the brain. The neurotransmitter serotonin is also implicated. Falling levels of serotonin may cause blood vessels in the brain to contract (narrow) and then dilate (expand). This stretching stimulates sensitized nerve endings, giving rise to the throbbing, piercing sensations associated with migraines. Evidence also points to a strong genetic contribution to migraine ("Scientists Discover," 2003).

Many factors can trigger a migraine attack, including emotional stress; stimuli such as bright lights and fluorescent lights; menstruation; sleep deprivation; altitude; weather and seasonal changes; pollen; certain drugs; the chemical monosodium glutamate (MSG), which is often used to enhance the flavor of food; alcohol; hunger; and weather and seasonal changes (Sprenger, 2011; Zebenholzer et al., 2011). In women, hormonal changes associated with the menstrual cycle can also trigger attacks, so it is not surprising that the incidence of migraines among women is about twice that among men.

**TREATMENT** Commonly available pain relievers, such as aspirin, ibuprofen, and acetaminophen, may reduce or eliminate pain associated with tension headaches. Drugs that constrict dilated blood vessels in the brain or help regulate serotonin activity are used to treat the pain from migraine headache. Evidence shows that psychological interventions, such as mindfulness meditation (see *A Closer Look: Psychological Methods for Lowering Arousal*), can be helpful in treating headache pain (Wells et al., 2014).

Psychological treatment can also help relieve tension or migraine headache in many cases. These treatments include training in biofeedback, relaxation, coping skills training, and some forms of cognitive therapy (Holroyd, 2002; Nestoriuc & Martin, 2007). **Biofeedback training (BFT)** helps people gain control over various bodily functions, such as muscle tension and brain waves, by giving them information (feedback) about these functions in the form of auditory signals (e.g., "bleeps") or visual displays. People learn to make the signal change in the desired direction. Training people to use relaxation skills combined with biofeedback has also been shown to be effective. *Electromyographic* (EMG) biofeedback is a form of BFT that involves relaying information about muscle tension in the forehead. EMG biofeedback thus heightens awareness of muscle tension in this region and provides cues that people can use to learn to reduce it.

Some people have relieved the pain of migraine headaches by raising the temperature in a finger. This biofeedback technique, called *thermal BFT*, modifies patterns of blood flow throughout the body, including blood flow to the brain, helping to control migraine headaches (Smith, 2005). One way of providing thermal feedback is by attaching a temperature-sensing device to a finger. A console bleeps more slowly or rapidly as the temperature in the finger rises. The temperature rises when more blood flows to the fingers and away from the head. The client can imagine the finger growing warmer to bring about these desirable changes in the flow of blood in the body. **T / F**

**TRUTH or FICTION**

People can relieve the pain of migraine headaches by raising the temperature in a finger.

☑ **TRUE** Some people have relieved migraine headaches by raising the temperature in a finger. This biofeedback technique modifies patterns of blood flow in the body.

## A CLOSER Look

### PSYCHOLOGICAL METHODS FOR LOWERING AROUSAL

Stress induces bodily responses such as excessive levels of sympathetic nervous system arousal, which, if persistent, may impair our ability to function optimally and increase the risk of stress-related illnesses. Psychological treatments have been shown to lower states of bodily arousal that may be prompted by stress. Here, we consider two widely used psychological methods of lowering arousal: meditation and progressive relaxation.

#### Meditation

Meditation comprises several ways of narrowing consciousness to moderate the stressors of the outer world. Yogis (adherents to Yoga philosophy) study the design on a vase or a mandala. The ancient Egyptians riveted their attention on an oil-burning lamp, which is the inspiration for the tale of Aladdin's lamp. In Turkey, Islamic mystics called whirling dervishes fix on their motion and the cadences of their breathing. Meditation has measurable benefits in treating many psychological and physical disorders, especially those in which stress plays a contributing role, such as hypertension, chronic pain, and insomnia, as well as problems of anxiety, depression, and even eating disorders and substance abuse (see, for example, Armstrong & Rimes, 2016; Creswell & Lindsay, 2014; Davis & Zautra, 2013; Gu et al., 2015; Kocovskia et al., 2013; Meadows et al., 2014; Nyklíček et al., 2013; Slomski, 2014; Strauss et al., 2014; Sundquist et al., 2014; van der Velden et al., 2015; Williams et al., 2014).

A study of African American heart patients showed that daily meditation reduced the risk of heart attacks and deaths compared to a health education (control) condition (Schneider et al., 2012). Another important study with U.S. marines preparing for deployment showed that training in mindfulness meditation improved physiological markers of resilience to stress (Johnson et al., 2014).

Many thousands of Americans regularly practice *transcendental meditation* (TM), a simplified kind of Indian meditation brought to the United States in 1959 by Maharishi Mahesh Yogi. Practitioners of TM repeat *mantras*—relaxing sounds such as *ieng* and *om*. In *mindfulness meditation*, a form of meditation practiced by Tibetan Buddhists, a person focuses on increasing awareness of one's thoughts, feelings, and sensations on a moment-to-moment basis, without judging or evaluating them. We can liken it to observing the flow of a river. Meditation shows promise as a helpful treatment on its own or when combined with other psychological or medical treatments for problems such as hypertension, chronic pain, insomnia, anxiety, PTSD, and depression.

Functional magnetic resonance imaging (fMRI) shows that the brains of long-term practitioners of meditation, as compared to those of newly trained meditators, have higher levels of activity in the areas involved in attention and decision making (Brefczynski-Lewis et al., 2007; see Figure 6.3). These findings lead scientists to speculate that regular practice of meditation may alter brain functioning in ways that may be therapeutic to children with *attention deficit/hyperactivity disorder* (ADHD), who have trouble maintaining attention. (ADHD is discussed further in Chapter 13.)

One of the lead investigators in the fMRI study, University of Wisconsin psychologist Richard Davidson, points out that it may be possible to train the brain through regular practice to become more efficient in performing certain cognitive processes, including

## Figure 6.3 A well-trained brain.

Here, we see brain scans of groups of expert meditators and novice meditators during an attentional task. Areas of greater activation are shown in hues of orange and red. Row C shows areas of the brains that were significantly different between the groups, with more activation in several parts of the brain involved in attentional processes, including the prefrontal cortex (toward the right side of the brain image).

**SOURCE:** Adapted from Brefczynski-Lewis et al., 2007.

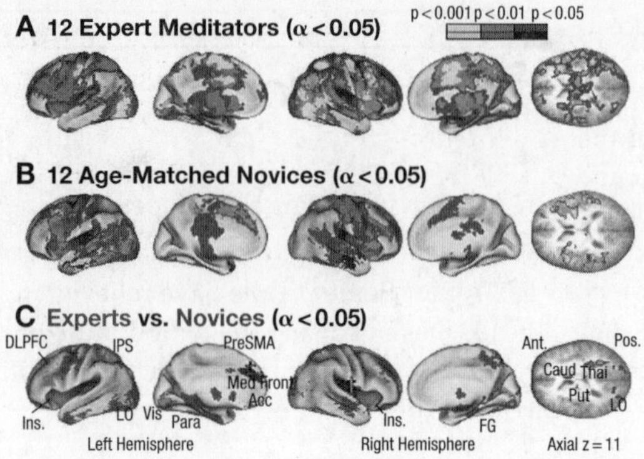

**GOING WITH THE FLOW.** Meditation is a popular method of managing the stresses of the outside world by reducing states of bodily arousal.

attention. We can train the body through regular exercise, so perhaps we can also train the brain through systematic practice of attentional skills. As promising as these research findings may be, we await systematic research to determine whether psychological techniques can change the brain's attentional processes.

Although there are differences among meditative techniques, the following suggestions illustrate some general guidelines:

1. Try meditation once or twice a day for 10 to 20 minutes at a time.
2. When you meditate, what you don't do is more important than what you do. Therefore, embrace a passive attitude: Tell yourself, "What happens, happens." In meditation, you take what you get; you don't strive for more. Striving of any kind hinders meditation.
3. Place yourself in a hushed, calming environment. For example, don't face a light directly.
4. Avoid eating for an hour before you meditate. Avoid caffeine (found in coffee, tea, many soft drinks, and chocolate) for at least two hours before meditation.
5. Get into a relaxed position. Modify it as needed. You can scratch or yawn if you feel the urge.
6. For a focusing device, you can concentrate on your breathing or sit in front of a serene object, such as a plant or burning incense. Benson suggests "perceiving" (not "mentally saying") the focus word once each time you breathe out. That is, think the word, but "less actively" than you normally would. Other researchers suggest thinking the word in as you breathe in and out, or ah-h-h, as you breathe out. They also suggest mantras, such as ah-nam, rah-mah, and shi-rim.
7. When preparing for meditation, repeat your mantra aloud many times—if you're using a mantra. Enjoy it. Then say it progressively more softly. Close your eyes. Focus on the mantra. Allow thinking the mantra to become more and more "passive" so that you perceive rather than think it. Again, embrace your "what happens, happens" attitude. Continue focusing on the mantra. It may become softer or louder or fade and then reappear.
8. If unsettling thoughts drift in while you're meditating, allow them to "pass through." Don't worry about squelching them, or you may become tense.
9. Remember to take what comes. You cannot force the relaxing effects of meditation. Like sleep, you can only set the stage for it and then permit it to happen.
10. Let yourself drift. (You won't get lost.) What happens, happens.

### Progressive Relaxation

Progressive relaxation was originated by University of Chicago physician Edmund Jacobson in 1938. Jacobson noticed that people tense their muscles under stress, intensifying their uneasiness. They tend to be unaware of these contractions, however. Jacobson reasoned that if muscle contractions contributed to tension, muscle relaxation might reduce tension. However, clients who were asked to focus on relaxing muscles often had no idea what to do.

Jacobson's method of progressive relaxation teaches people how to monitor muscle tension and relaxation. With this method, people first tense, then relax, selected muscle groups in the arms; the facial area; the chest, stomach, and lower back muscles; the hips, thighs, and calves; and so on. The sequence heightens awareness of muscle tension and helps people differentiate feelings of tension from relaxation. The method is progressive in that people progress from one group of muscles to another in practicing the technique. Since the 1930s, progressive relaxation has been used by a number of behavior therapists, including Joseph Wolpe and Arnold Lazarus (1966).

The following instructions from Wolpe and Lazarus (1966, pp. 177–178) illustrate how the technique is applied to relaxing the arms. Relaxation should be practiced in a favorable setting. Settle back on a recliner, a couch, or a bed with a pillow. Select a place and time when you're unlikely to be disturbed. Make the room warm and comfortable. Dim sources of light. Loosen tight clothing. Tighten muscles about two-thirds as hard as you could if you were trying your hardest. If you sense that a muscle could have a spasm, you are tightening too much. After tensing, let go of tensions completely.

**STRESS-RELATED IMPACTS ON HEALTH AND STRESS RELIEF TECHNIQUES**

**Relaxation of Arms (Time: 4–5 Minutes)**

Settle back as comfortably as you can. Let yourself relax to the best of your ability. . . . Now, as you relax like that, clench your right fist, just clench your fist tighter and tighter, and study the tension as you do so. Keep it clenched and feel the tension in your right fist, hand, forearm. . . . and now relax. Let the fingers of your right hand become loose, and observe the contrast in your feelings. . . . Now let yourself go and try to become more relaxed all over. . . . Once more, clench your right fist really tight. . . . hold it, and notice the tension again. . . . Now let go, relax; your fingers straighten out, and you notice the difference once more. . . . Now repeat that with your left fist. Clench your left fist while the rest of your body relaxes; clench that fist tighter and feel the tension. . . . and now relax. Again enjoy the contrast. . . . Repeat that once more, clench the left fist, tight and tense. . . . Now do the opposite of tension—relax and feel the difference. Continue relaxing like that for a while. . . . Clench both fists tighter and together, both fists tense, forearms tense, study the sensations. . . . and relax; straighten out your fingers and feel that relaxation. Continue relaxing your hands and forearms more and more. . . . Now bend your elbows and tense your biceps, tense them harder and study the tension feelings. . . . All right, straighten out your arms, let them relax and feel that difference again. Let the relaxation develop. . . . Once more, tense your biceps; hold the tension and observe it carefully. . . . Straighten the arms and relax; relax to the best of your ability. . . . Each time, pay close attention to your feelings when you tense up and when you relax. Now straighten your arms, straighten them so that you feel most tension in the triceps muscles along the back of your arms; stretch your arms and feel that tension. . . . And now relax. Get your arms back into a comfortable position. Let the relaxation proceed on its own. The arms should feel comfortably heavy as you allow them to relax. . . . Straighten the arms once more so that you feel the tension in the triceps muscles; straighten them. Feel that tension. . . . and relax. Now let's concentrate on pure relaxation in the arms without any tension. Get your arms comfortable and let them relax further and further. Continue relaxing your arms even further. Even when your arms seem fully relaxed, try to go that extra bit further; try to achieve deeper and deeper levels of relaxation.

# Cardiovascular Disease

**6.15 Identify psychological risk factors in coronary heart disease.**

Your cardiovascular system, the network that connects your heart and blood vessels, is your highway of life. Unfortunately, there are accidents along this highway in the form of **cardiovascular disease (CVD)** or heart and artery disease. CVD is the leading cause of death in the United States, claiming about 830,000 lives annually, which translates to about one in every three deaths, most often as the result of heart attacks or strokes (American Heart Association, 2009; Centers for Disease Control, 2015c). *Coronary heart disease* (CHD), the major form of cardiovascular disease, accounts for more than 500,000 of these deaths, mostly from heart attacks (Centers for Disease Control, 2015a). CHD is the leading cause of death for both men and women and claims more women's lives than all forms of cancer, including breast cancer.

In coronary heart disease, the flow of blood to the heart is insufficient to meet the heart's needs. The underlying disease process in CHD is called *arteriosclerosis*, or hardening of the arteries, a condition in which artery walls become thicker, harder, and less elastic, which makes it more difficult for blood to flow freely. The major underlying cause of arteriosclerosis is *atherosclerosis*, a process involving the buildup of fatty deposits along artery walls, which leads to the formation of artery-clogging plaque. If a blood clot should form in an artery narrowed by plaque, it may nearly or completely block the flow of blood to the heart. The result is a heart attack (also called a *myocardial infarction*), a life-threatening event in which heart tissue dies because of a lack of oxygen-rich blood. When a blood clot blocks the supply of blood in an artery serving the brain, a *stroke* can occur, leading to death of brain tissue, which can result in loss of function controlled by that part of the brain, coma, or even death.

We can lower our risks of developing cardiovascular disease by reducing risk factors we can directly control. Some risk factors are indeed beyond our control, such as age and family history. But other major risk factors are controllable through obtaining medical treatment and making healthy lifestyle changes: factors such as high blood levels of low-density (LDL) cholesterol, hypertension (high blood pressure), smoking, overeating, heavy drinking, consuming a high-fat diet, and leading a sedentary lifestyle (e.g., Bauchner, Fontanarosa, & Golub, 2013; Eckel et al., 2014; Foody, 2013; James et al., 2014; Mitka, 2013). Fortunately, adoption of healthier behaviors can have beneficial effects on the heart and circulatory system (Roger, 2009). Even seasoned couch potatoes can reduce their risk of cardiovascular disease by becoming more physically active (Borjesson & Dahlof, 2005). Additional good news is that deaths from CHD have been declining for several decades, thanks largely to improved medical care and reductions in risk factors such as smoking (Ma et al., 2015; McGinnis, 2015; National Center for Health Statistics, 2012a). **T / F**

## TRUTH *or* FICTION

Deaths from coronary heart disease are rising in the United States, largely as a result of increased rates of smoking.

☑ **FALSE** Just the opposite is the case.

**NEGATIVE EMOTIONS** Frequent emotional distress in the form of anger, anxiety, and depression may have damaging effects on the cardiovascular system (e.g., Allan & Fisher, 2011; Glassman, Bigger, & Gaffney, 2009; Lichtman et al., 2014). Here, we focus on the effects of chronic anger.

Occasional anger may not damage the heart in healthy people, but chronic anger—the type you see in people who appear to be angry much of the time—is linked to increased risk of CHD (Chida & Steptoe, 2009; Denollet & Pedersen, 2009). Anger is closely associated with hostility—a personality trait characterized by quickness to anger and by tendencies to blame others and to perceive the world in negative terms. Hostile people tend to have short fuses and are prone to getting angry easily. Hostility is a component of the **Type A behavior pattern (TABP)**, a style of behavior that characterizes people who are hard driving, ambitious, impatient, and highly competitive. Although earlier research linked the TABP to a higher risk of CHD, later research casts doubt on the relationship between this general behavior pattern and coronary risk (Geipert, 2007). On the other hand, evidence consistently links hostility, a component of the TABP, to increased risks of heart disease and other negative health outcomes (Chida & Steptoe, 2009; Eichstaedt et al., 2015; Everson-Rose et al., 2014; Kitayama et al., 2015). People high in hostility tend to be angry much of the time.

How might anger or other negative emotions translate into increased risk of coronary heart disease? Although we can't say with certainty, the stress hormones epinephrine and norepinephrine appear to play significant roles. Anxiety and anger trigger the release of these stress hormones by the adrenal glands. These hormones increase heart rate, breathing rate, and blood pressure, which results in pumping more oxygen-rich blood to the muscles to enable them to prepare for defensive action—to either fight or flee—in the face of a threatening stressor. In people who frequently experience strong negative emotions such as anger or anxiety, the body may repeatedly pump out these stress hormones, eventually damaging the heart and blood vessels.

**EMOTIONS AND THE HEART.** Emotional stress in the form of persistent negative emotions, such as anxiety and anger, is a risk factor in heart-related problems.

Episodes of acute anger can actually trigger heart attacks and sudden cardiac death in people with established heart disease (Clay, 2001). Moreover, people who are higher in the psychological trait of hostility tend to have more cardiovascular risk factors, such as obesity and smoking, than do less hostile people (Bunde & Suls, 2006). Anxiety and anger may also compromise the cardiovascular system by increasing blood levels of cholesterol, the fatty substance that clogs arteries and increases the risk of heart attacks (Suinn, 2001). Helping angry people learn to remain calm in provocative situations may have beneficial effects on the heart as well as the mind.

## A CLOSER Look

### CAN YOU DIE OF A BROKEN HEART?

You've probably heard the expression "a broken heart" used in relation to a failed romantic relationship. However, broken-heart syndrome is an actual medical condition that potentially can be deadly. Under high emotional stress, the body releases large amounts of stress hormones epinephrine and norepinephrine into the bloodstream. Physicians suspect that in broken-heart syndrome, these hormones effectively "stun" the heart, preventing it from pumping normally (Wittstein et al., 2006). The symptoms can be very similar to those of a true heart attack, including chest pain and problems breathing ("As Valentine's Day Approaches," 2012). Consider this case report:

> The patient's heart was failing. She was only 45, but showed all the signs of having a heart attack. But it wasn't a heart attack. Were it a heart attack, there would have been blockage of blood flow through the arteries that service the heart. However, blood flowed freely to her heart. No, in this case, the woman's heart was failing because of the emotional shock of losing her husband in a car crash two days earlier. She had rushed to the crash site and collapsed next to his body, crying inconsolably and trying desperately but unsuccessfully to wake him. Two days later, she was rushed to the hospital complaining of chest pain and difficulty breathing. This woman's heart was pumping only a fraction of the expected amount of blood. Fortunately, the woman survived, as the levels of stress hormones receded and the heart returned to pumping at a nearly normal level. Later, she told a reporter, "If anyone had told me that you could die of a broken heart . . . I'd never have believed it. But I almost did." (Sanders, 2006, p. 28)

Although broken-heart syndrome was so named because of its association with intense grief, it may also be triggered by stressful events associated with strong emotional reactions of anxiety, fear, or even sudden surprise (Naggiar, 2012). Fortunately, broken-heart syndrome is a rare occurrence, but it may explain isolated cases of sudden death following an emotional shock, such as the unexpected death of a spouse. For people without a prior history of heart disease, the symptoms are usually short-lived and, unlike true heart attacks, they do not permanently damage the heart ("As Valentine's Day Approaches," 2012). However, patients with established coronary heart disease may be especially susceptible to serious and even life-threatening coronary events in response to strong emotional stress (Strike et al., 2006).

Depression may also play a role in coronary heart disease, perhaps because it places additional stress on the body (Everson-Rose et al., 2014; Gordon et al., 2011). As Jeff Huffman of Harvard Medical School, a leading researcher in this area, puts it: "There is good evidence that if a person has depression after a heart attack, they are more likely to die from cardiac causes in the following months and years" (cited in "Depression Ups Risk," 2008). Even people without already established heart disease who suffered major depression appear to be at greater risk than nondepressed people of dying from heart-related causes (Penninx et al., 2000). All in all, taking care of our emotional health may yield additional benefits for our physical health.

**SOCIAL ENVIRONMENTAL STRESS** *Social environmental stress* also appears to heighten the risk of CHD (Krantz et al., 1988). Factors such as overtime work, assembly-line labor, and exposure to conflicting demands are linked to increased risk of CHD (Jenkins, 1988). The stress–CHD connection is not straightforward, however. For example, the effects of demanding occupations may be moderated by factors such as psychological hardiness and whether or not people find their work meaningful (Krantz et al., 1988).

Other forms of stress are also linked to increased cardiovascular risk (Walsh, 2011). Researchers in Sweden, for example, find that among women, marital stress triples the risk of recurrent cardiac events, including heart attacks and cardiac death (Foxhall, 2001; Orth-Gomér et al., 2000).

**ETHNICITY AND CHD** Coronary heart disease is not an equal opportunity destroyer. European Americans (non-Hispanic Whites) and African Americans (non-Hispanic Blacks) have the highest rates of death due to coronary heart disease (see Figure 6.4; Ferdinand & Ferdinand, 2009). Factors such as obesity, smoking, diabetes, and hypertension play important roles in determining relative risks of CHD and the rate of CHD-related deaths (CDC, 2011b; Taubes, 2012). For example, African Americans have higher

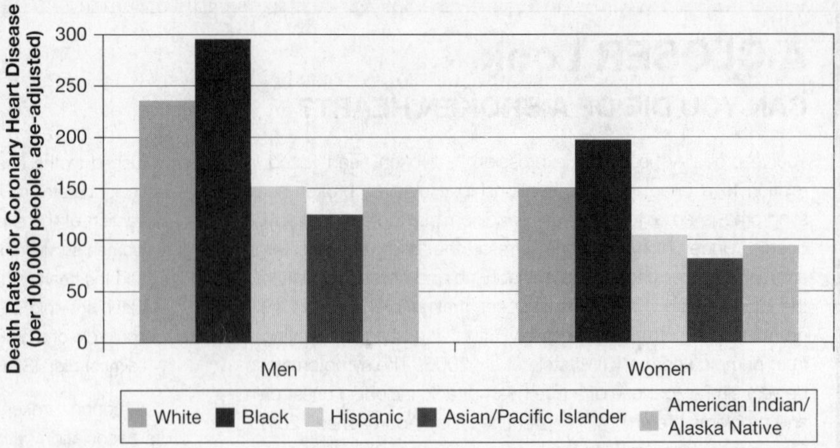


**Figure 6.4** Coronary heart disease death rates in relation to race and ethnicity.

Deaths due to CHD in our society fall disproportionately on Black (non-Hispanic) men and women.

**SOURCE:** National Center for Health Statistics, (2012b).

rates of hypertension relative to other U.S. population groups, as well as higher rates of obesity and diabetes. Moreover, a dual standard of care limits access to quality health care for minority group members. Black Americans with heart disease who suffer heart attacks, strokes, or heart failure generally do not receive the same level of care as Whites or have as much access to the latest cardiac care technologies, which likely contributes to their higher overall death rates due to cardiovascular disease (Chen et al., 2001; Peterson & Yancy, 2009). This dual standard of care may reflect both discrimination and cultural factors limiting utilization of services, such as mistrust among many African Americans toward the medical establishment.

We finish this section with encouraging news. Americans have begun to take better care of their cardiovascular health. The incidence of CHD and deaths from heart disease have been declining steadily during the past 50 years, thanks largely to reductions in smoking, improved treatment for coronary heart disease, and perhaps other lifestyle changes, such as reduced intake of dietary fat. Better-educated people are also more likely to modify unhealthy behavior patterns and reap the benefits of change. Is there a message here for you?

## Asthma

**6.16 Identify psychological factors that may trigger asthma attacks.**

*Asthma* is a respiratory disorder in which the main tubes of the windpipe—the bronchi—constrict and become inflamed, and large amounts of mucus are secreted. During asthma attacks, people wheeze, cough, and struggle to breathe in enough air. They may feel as though they are suffocating.

Asthma affects about 26 million people in the the United States (CDC, 2012b). Rates of asthma are on the rise, having more than doubled over the past 30 years. Attacks can last from just a few minutes to several hours and vary notably in intensity. A series of attacks can harm the bronchial system, causing mucus to collect and muscles to lose their elasticity. Sometimes, the bronchial system is weakened to the point at which a subsequent attack is lethal.

**THEORETICAL PERSPECTIVES** Many causal factors are implicated in asthma, including allergic reactions; exposure to environmental pollutants, including cigarette smoke and smog; and genetic and immunological factors. Asthmatic reactions in susceptible people can be triggered by exposure to allergens such as pollen, mold spores, and animal dander; by cold, dry air and by hot, humid air; and by emotional responses such as anger or even laughing too hard. Psychological factors such as stress, anxiety, and depression can increase susceptibility to asthmatic attacks (see Schreier & Chen, 2008; Voelker, 2012). Asthma, moreover, has psychological consequences. Some sufferers avoid strenuous activity, including exercise, for fear of increasing their demand for oxygen and tripping attacks.

**TREATMENT** Although asthma cannot be cured, it can be controlled by reducing exposure to allergens, by desensitization therapy (allergy shots) to help the body acquire more resistance to allergens, by use of inhalers, and by drugs that open bronchial passages during asthma attacks (called *bronchodilators*) and others (called *anti-inflammatories*) that reduce future attacks by helping to keep bronchial tubes open. Behavioral techniques may be used to help asthma sufferers develop breathing and relaxation skills to improve their breathing and cope more effectively with stress (e.g., Brody, 2009).

# Cancer

### 6.17 Identify behavioral risk factors in cancer.

The word *cancer* is arguably the most feared word in the English language, and rightly so: One out of every four deaths in the United States is caused by cancer. Cancer claims more than half a million lives in the United States annually, or about one every 60 seconds or so (Centers for Disease Control and Prevention, 2015c). Men have a one in two chance of developing cancer at some point in their lives; for women, the odds are one in three. Yet there is good news to report: The cancer death rate has been declining in recent years, in large part due to better screening and treatment (Hampton, 2015).

Cancer involves the development of aberrant, or mutant, cells that form growths (tumors) that spread to healthy tissue. Cancerous cells can take root anywhere: in the blood, bones, lungs, digestive tract, and reproductive organs. When it is not contained early, cancer may *metastasize*, or establish colonies throughout the body, leading to death.

There are many causes of cancer, including genetic factors, exposure to cancer-causing chemicals, and even exposure to some viruses. Yet more than half of all cancers could be prevented if people adopted healthier behaviors, especially avoiding smoking, limiting fat intake, controlling excess body weight, curtailing alcohol consumption, exercising regularly, and limiting exposure to the sun (i.e., ultraviolet light causes skin cancer; see, e.g., Colditz, Wolin, & Gehlert, 2012; Li et al., 2009). Consider, for example, that death rates from cancer are much lower in Japan than in the United States, where people ingest more fat, especially animal fat. The difference is not genetic or racial, but one of lifestyle and diet; Japanese Americans whose dietary intake of saturated fat approximates that of the typical American diet show similar death rates from cancer as other Americans.

**STRESS AND CANCER** A weakened or compromised immune system may increase susceptibility to cancer. We've seen that psychological factors, such as exposure to stress, may affect the immune system, so it stands to reason that exposure to stress might increase a person's risk of developing cancer. However, links between stress and cancer remain inconclusive and in need of further study (Cohen, Janicki-Deverts, & Miller, 2007).

On the other hand, we have ample evidence that psychological counseling and group support programs can improve the quality of life of patients and help them cope with the serious emotional consequences of cancer, which often include depression, anxiety, and feelings of hopelessness (e.g., Cleary & Stanton, 2015; de la Torre-Luque et al., 2015; Hopko et al., 2015; Stanton et al., 2013). Combining cognitive therapy with mindfulness meditation training can also help relieve depression and anxiety in cancer patients (Foley et al., 2010). We also have promising findings from an Ohio State University study that showed that participation in coping skills training and stress-management techniques increased survival rates in women with breast cancer (Anderson, Liu, & Kryscio, 2008).

Cancer patients may also benefit from coping skills training programs aimed at relieving the stress and pain of coping with cancer, such as dealing with the unpleasant side effects of chemotherapy. Cues associated with chemotherapy, such as the hospital environment itself, may become conditioned stimuli that elicit nausea and vomiting even before drugs are administered. Pairing relaxation, pleasant imagery, and attention distraction with these cues may help reduce nausea and vomiting associated with chemotherapy.

# Acquired Immunodeficiency Syndrome

**6.18 Describe the role that psychologists play in prevention and treatment of HIV/AIDS.**

Acquired immunodeficiency syndrome (AIDS) is a disease caused by the *human immunodeficiency virus* (HIV). HIV attacks the immune system, leaving it helpless to fend off diseases it normally would hold in check. HIV/AIDS is one of history's worst epidemics. Worldwide, HIV/AIDS has claimed more than 39 million lives and currently infects about 35 million people (WHO, 2014). Approximately 50,000 new cases of HIV infection are reported annually in the United States (CDC, 2015e).

There are two primary reasons for including HIV/AIDS in our discussion of psychological factors in physical illness. First, people living with HIV/AIDS often develop significant psychological problems in adjusting to living with the disease. Second, behavioral patterns such as unsafe sexual and injection practices play the dominant role in determining the risk of contracting and transmitting the virus.

HIV can be transmitted by sexual contact—that is, vaginal and anal intercourse or oral–genital contact; by direct infusion of contaminated blood, as from transfusions of contaminated blood, accidental pricks from needles used previously on an infected person, or needle sharing among injecting drug users; or from an infected mother to a child during pregnancy or childbirth or through breast-feeding. AIDS is not contracted by donating blood; by airborne germs; by insects; or by casual contact, such as using public toilets, holding or hugging infected people, sharing eating utensils with them, or living or going to school with them. Routine screening of the blood supply for HIV has reduced the risk of infection from blood transfusions to virtually nil. There is no cure or vaccine for HIV infection, but the introduction of highly effective antiretroviral drugs has revolutionized treatment of the disease (Thompson et al., 2012). Although not a cure, these drugs can keep the disease at bay for decades (Cohen, 2012). Fortunately, the number of AIDS-related deaths worldwide has declined in recent years as antiviral therapies become more widely available. However, the lack of a cure or effective vaccine means that prevention programs focusing on reducing or eliminating risky sexual and injection practices represent our best hope for controlling the epidemic.

**ADJUSTMENT OF PEOPLE WITH HIV AND AIDS** Given the nature of the disease and the stigma suffered by people with HIV and AIDS, it is not surprising that many people with HIV, although certainly not all, develop psychological problems—most commonly anxiety and depression.

Psychologists and other mental health professionals are involved in providing treatment services to people affected by HIV/AIDS. Coping skills training and cognitive-behavioral therapy can improve immune response, reduce feelings of depression and anxiety, enhance ability to handle stress, and improve quality of life in patients with HIV/AIDS (McCain et al., 2008; Scott-Sheldon et al., 2008; Stout-Shaffer & Page, 2008). Treatment may incorporate stress-management techniques, such as relaxation training and use of positive mental imagery, as well as cognitive strategies to control intrusive negative thoughts and preoccupations.

Antidepressant medication may also help patients with HIV/AIDS cope with a frequent emotional consequence of living with the disease—depression. Whether treatment of depression or stress-management training can improve immunological functioning or prolong life in people with HIV and AIDS remains an open question.

**PSYCHOLOGICAL INTERVENTIONS TO REDUCE RISKY BEHAVIORS** Providing information about risk reduction alone is not sufficient to induce widespread changes in sexual behavior. Despite awareness of the dangers, many people continue to practice unsafe sexual and injection behaviors. Fortunately, psychological interventions are effective in helping people alter risky behaviors (e.g., Albarracín, Durantini, & Ear, 2006; Carey et al., 2004). These programs raise awareness about risky behaviors and help people practice more adaptive behaviors, such as assertively refusing invitations to engage in unsafe sex and communicating more effectively with partners about safer sexual practices. The likelihood of engaging in safer sexual practices is also linked to the avoidance of alcohol and drugs before sex and to the perception that practicing safer sex represents a social norm (expected behavior) within one's peer group.

We have focused on relationships between stress and health and on the psychological factors involved in health. Psychology has much to offer in the understanding and treatment of physical disorders. Psychological approaches may help in the treatment of physical disorders such as headaches and coronary heart disease. Psychologists can also help people develop healthier behaviors that reduce their risks of developing serious health problems such as cardiovascular disorders, cancer, and AIDS. Emerging fields such as psychoneuroimmunology promise to further enhance our knowledge of the intricate relationships between mind and body.

# Summing Up

## Dissociative Disorders

### Dissociative Identity Disorder

**6.1 Describe the key features of dissociative identity disorder and explain why the concept of dissociative identity disorder is controversial.**

In dissociative identity disorder, two or more distinct personalities, each possessing well-defined traits and memories, exist within a person and repeatedly take control of the person's behavior. Some theorists question whether dissociative identity disorder is a true disorder or rather an elaborate form of role-playing of a "multiple personality" that is reinforced by attention and interest from others, including therapists.

### Dissociative Amnesia

**6.2 Describe the key features of dissociative amnesia.**

In dissociative amnesia, a person experiences a loss of memory for personal information that cannot be accounted for by organic causes. In dissociative amnesia with fugue, a person suddenly travels away from home or the workplace, shows a loss of memory for his or her personal past, and experiences identity confusion or takes on a new identity.

### Depersonalization/Derealization Disorder

**6.3 Describe the key features of depersonalization/derealization disorder.**

In depersonalization/derealization disorder, a person experiences persistent or recurrent episodes of depersonalization or derealization of sufficient severity to cause significant distress or impairment in functioning.

### Culture-Bound Dissociative Syndromes

**6.4 Identify two culture-bound syndromes with dissociative features.**

Two culture-bound syndromes with dissociative features are amok, which has trancelike features, and zar, which involves people who show dissociative behaviors that are attributed within the folk culture to spirit possession.

### Theoretical Perspectives

**6.5 Describe different theoretical perspectives on dissociative disorders.**

Psychodynamic theorists view dissociative disorders as a form of psychological defense by which the ego defends itself against troubling memories and unacceptable impulses by blotting them out of consciousness. There is increasing documentation of a link between dissociative disorders and early childhood trauma, which lends support to the view that dissociation may serve to protect the self from troubling memories. To learning and cognitive theorists, dissociative experiences involve ways of learning not to think about certain troubling behaviors or thoughts that might lead to feelings of guilt or shame. Relief from anxiety negatively reinforces this pattern of dissociation. Some social-cognitive theorists suggest that multiple personality may represent a form of role-playing behavior.

### Treatment of Dissociative Disorders

**6.6 Describe the treatment of dissociative identity disorder.**

The major form of treatment is psychotherapy aimed at achieving a reintegration of the personality by focusing on helping people with dissociative identity disorder uncover and integrate dissociated painful experiences from childhood.

## Somatic Symptom and Related Disorders

### Somatic Symptom Disorder

**6.7 Describe the key features of somatic symptom disorder.**

Somatic symptom disorder describes cases of excessive concern about physical symptoms to the extent that such concern affects one's thoughts, feelings, and behaviors in daily life.

## Illness Anxiety Disorder

**6.8 Describe the key features of illness anxiety disorder.**

Illness anxiety disorder describes cases of minor physical symptoms in which a person becomes preoccupied with the belief that such symptoms reflect serious underlying illness despite medical evidence to the contrary.

## Conversion Disorder

**6.9 Describe the key features of conversion disorder.**

Conversion disorder describes cases of people with physical symptoms or deficits in motor or sensory functioning that cannot be accounted for by known medical conditions or diseases.

## Factitious Disorder

**6.10 Explain the difference between malingering and factitious disorder.**

Malingering involves deliberate efforts to fake or exaggerate symptoms to reap personal gain or avoid unwanted responsibilities and so is not considered a mental or psychological disorder. The symptoms in factitious disorder are also fabricated. However, because of the absence of any obvious gain, the symptoms in factitious disorder are believed to reflect underlying psychological needs, and hence they represent the features of a mental or psychological disorder. Münchausen syndrome is the major form of factitious disorder and is characterized by deliberate fabrication of physical symptoms for no apparent reason other than to assume a patient role.

## Koro and Dhat Syndromes: Far Eastern Somatic Symptom Disorders?

**6.11 Describe the key features of koro and dhat syndromes.**

These are two examples of culture-bound syndromes. Koro disorder, which is found primarily in China, is characterized by excessive fear that one's genitals are shrinking and retracting into the body. Dhat syndrome, found primarily in India, involves excessive fears in men concerning the loss of seminal fluid.

## Theoretical Perspectives

**6.12 Describe the theoretical understandings of somatic symptom and related disorders.**

Much of the theoretical focus on somatic symptom and related disorders has centered on hypochondriasis, which is now classified as either somatic symptom disorder or illness anxiety disorder. One learning theory model likens hypochondriasis to obsessive–compulsive behavior. Cognitive factors in hypochondriasis include possible self-handicapping strategies and cognitive distortions involving exaggerated perceptions of the status of one's health. The psychodynamic model of conversion disorder holds that it represents the conversion into physical symptoms of leftover emotion or energy cut off from unacceptable or threatening impulses that the ego has prevented from reaching awareness. The symptom is functional in the sense that it allows a person to achieve both primary gains and secondary gains. Learning theorists focus on reinforcements associated with conversion disorders, such as the reinforcing effects of adopting a "sick role."

## Treatment of Somatic Symptom and Related Disorders

**6.13 Describe methods used to treat somatic symptom and related disorders.**

Psychodynamic therapists attempt to uncover and bring to the level of awareness underlying unconscious conflicts originating in childhood, believed to be at the root of somatic symptom and related disorders. Once conflicts are uncovered and worked through, symptoms should disappear because they are no longer needed as a partial solution to the underlying conflict. Behavioral approaches focus on removing underlying sources of reinforcement that may be maintaining the abnormal behavior pattern. More generally, behavior therapists help people with somatic symptom and related disorders learn to handle stressful or anxiety-arousing situations more effectively. In addition, a combination of cognitive-behavioral techniques, such as exposure with response prevention and cognitive restructuring, may be used in treating hypochondriasis. Antidepressant medication may prove to be helpful in treating some cases of somatic symptom and related disorders.

# Psychological Factors Affecting Physical Health

## Headaches

**6.14 Describe the role of psychological factors in understanding and treating headaches.**

The most common headache is the tension headache, which is often stress-related. Behavioral methods of relaxation training and biofeedback help in treating various types of headaches.

## Cardiovascular Disease

**6.15 Identify psychological risk factors in coronary heart disease.**

Psychological factors that increase the risk of coronary heart disease include unhealthy patterns of consumption, leading a sedentary lifestyle, and persistent negative emotions.

## Asthma

**6.16 Identify psychological factors that may trigger asthma attacks.**

Psychological factors such as stress, anxiety, and depression may trigger asthma attacks in susceptible individuals.

## Cancer

**6.17 Identify behavioral risk factors in cancer.**

Although relationships between stress and risk of cancer remain under study, behavioral risk factors for cancer include unhealthy dietary practices (especially high fat intake), heavy alcohol use, smoking, and excessive sun exposure.

## Acquired Immunodeficiency Syndrome

**6.18 Describe the role that psychologists play in prevention and treatment of HIV/AIDS.**

Psychologists are involved in prevention programs to reduce risky behaviors that can lead to HIV infection and in developing treatment programs, such as coping-skills training and cognitive-behavioral therapy, designed to help people affected by HIV/AIDS.

# Critical Thinking Questions

On the basis of your reading of this chapter, answer the following questions:

- Why is the diagnosis of dissociative identity disorder controversial? Do you believe that people with dissociative identity disorder are merely playing a role they have learned? Why or why not?
- How are dissociative and somatic symptom and related disorders distinguished from malingering? What difficulties arise in trying to make these determinations?
- Why is conversion disorder considered a treasure trove in the annals of abnormal psychology? What role did the disorder play in the development of psychological models of abnormal behavior?
- Does koro or dhat syndrome seem strange to you? How might your reaction depend on the culture in which you were raised? Can you give an example of a behavioral pattern in your culture that might be viewed as strange by members of other cultures?

# Key Terms

dissociative disorders, p. 208
dissociative identity disorder, p. 209
dissociative amnesia, p. 212
depersonalization, p. 216
derealization, p. 216
depersonalization/derealization disorder, p. 217
somatic symptom and related disorders, p. 223
somatic symptom disorder, p. 223
hypochondriasis, p. 224
illness anxiety disorder, p. 225
conversion disorder, p. 225
factitious disorder, p. 226
malingering, p. 227
Münchausen syndrome, p. 227
koro syndrome, p. 229
dhat syndrome, p. 229
psychosomatic disorders, p. 233
biofeedback training (BFT), p. 235
cardiovascular disease (CVD), p. 237
Type A behavior pattern (TABP), p. 238

Chapter 7

# Mood Disorders and Suicide

## Learning Objectives

**7.1** **Describe** the key features of major depressive disorder and **evaluate** factors that may account for the higher rate of depression among women.

**7.2** **Describe** the key features of persistent depressive disorder (dysthymia).

**7.3** **Describe** the key features of premenstrual dysphoric disorder.

**7.4** **Describe** the key features of bipolar disorder.

**7.5** **Describe** the key features of cyclothymic disorder.

**7.6** **Evaluate** the role of stress in depression.

**7.7** **Describe** psychodynamic models of depression.

**7.8** **Describe** the humanistic model of depression.

**7.9** **Describe** learning theory models of depression.

**7.10 Describe** Beck's cognitive model and the learned helplessness model of depression.

**7.11 Identify** biological factors in depression.

**7.12 Identify** causal factors in bipolar disorders.

**7.13 Describe** psychological methods used to treat depression.

**7.14 Describe** biomedical approaches to treating depression.

**7.15 Identify** risk factors in suicide.

**7.16 Identify** the major theoretical perspectives on suicide.

**7.17 Apply** your knowledge of factors in suicide to steps you can take if someone you know experiences suicidal thoughts.

## TRUTH *or* FICTION

T☐ F☐ Feeling sad or depressed is abnormal. (p. 249)

T☐ F☐ Major depression affects millions of Americans, but fortunately most get the help they need. (p. 251)

T☐ F☐ Exposure to bright artificial light can help relieve depression in some cases. (p. 254)

T☐ F☐ Men are about twice as likely as women to develop major depression. (p. 257)

T☐ F☐ Physical exercise not only helps tone the body, but also can help combat depression. (p. 268)

T☐ F☐ High levels of fish oil in the diet are linked to increased risk of bipolar disorder. (p. 277)

T☐ F☐ Placing a powerful electromagnet on the scalp can help relieve depression. (p. 284)

T☐ F☐ The ancient Greeks and Romans used a chemical to curb turbulent mood swings that is still used today. (p. 285)

T☐ F☐ People who threaten suicide basically are attention seekers. (p. 291)

**CHAPTER INTRODUCTION: MOOD DISORDERS AND SUICIDE**

## "I" Darkness Visible

At age 60, William Styron (1925–2006), the celebrated author of *The Confessions of Nat Turner* and *Sophie's Choice*, suffered from depression so severe that he planned to commit suicide. In a 1990 memoir, he spoke about this period of personal darkness in his life and about reclaiming his commitment to living:

"I watched myself in mingled terror and fascination as I began to make the necessary preparation: going to see my lawyer in the nearby town—there rewriting my will—and spending part of a couple of afternoons in a muddled attempt to bestow upon posterity a letter of farewell. It turned out that putting together a suicide note... was the most difficult task of writing that I had ever tackled.

Late one bitterly cold night, when I knew that I could not possibly get myself through the following day... I had forced myself to watch the tape of a movie... At one point in the film... the characters moved down the hallway of a music conservatory, beyond the walls of which, from unseen musicians, came a contralto voice, a sudden soaring passage from the Brahms Alto Rhapsody.

This sound, which like all music—indeed, like all pleasure—I had been numbly unresponsive to for months, pierced my heart like a dagger, and in a flood of swift recollection I thought of all the joys the house had known: the children who had rushed through its rooms, the festivals, the love and work, the honestly earned slumber, the voices and the nimble commotion, the perennial tribe of cats and dogs and birds.... All this I realized was more than I could ever abandon... And just as powerfully I realized I could not commit this desecration on myself. I drew upon some last gleam of sanity to perceive the terrifying dimensions of the mortal predicament I had fallen into. I woke up my wife and soon telephone calls were made. The next day I was admitted to the hospital."

**SOURCE:** *From Darkness Visible by William Styron*

**WILLIAM STYRON.** The celebrated author William Styron suffered from severe depression—a "darkness visible" that led him to the precipice of suicide.

A distinguished author stood at the precipice of taking his own life. The depression that enshrouded him and that nearly cost him his life—this "darkness visible"—is an unwelcome companion for millions of people. Depression is a disturbance of mood that casts a long, deep shadow over many facets of life.

*Moods* are feeling states that color our psychological lives. Most of us experience changes in mood: We feel elated when we have earned high grades, a promotion, or the affections of Ms. or Mr. Right. We feel down or depressed when we are rejected by a date, flunk a test, or suffer financial reverses. It is normal and appropriate to be happy about uplifting events. It is just as normal, just as appropriate, to feel depressed by dismal events. It might very well be *abnormal* not to feel down or depressed in the face of tragic or deeply disappointing events or circumstances. However, people with **mood disorders** experience disturbances in mood that are unusually severe or prolonged and impair their ability to function in meeting their normal responsibilities. Some people become severely depressed even when things appear to be going well or when they encounter mildly upsetting events that others take in stride. Still others experience extreme mood swings: They ride an emotional roller coaster to dizzying heights and abysmal depths when the world around them remains largely on an even keel. Let's begin our study of these emotional problems by examining the different types of mood disorders.

**WHEN ARE CHANGES IN MOOD CONSIDERED ABNORMAL?** Although changes in mood in response to the ups and downs of everyday life may be quite normal, persistent or severe changes in mood or cycles of extreme elation and depression may suggest the presence of a mood disorder.

# Types of Mood Disorders

This chapter explores the two major forms of mood disorders: depressive disorders and bipolar disorders (mood swing disorders). Unlike previous editions of the *DSM*, the *DSM-5* does not include a general category of mood disorders. Instead, mood disorders are now classified in separate categories called *Depressive Disorders* and *Bipolar and Related Disorders*. Our study of mood disorders breaks down into a study of twos; that is, there are two major types of depressive disorders, *major depressive disorder* and *persistent depressive disorder*, and two major types of bipolar disorders, *bipolar disorder* and *cyclothymic disorder* (also called *cyclothymia*). We'll also see that bipolar disorder is comprised of two distinct disorders, *bipolar I disorder* and *bipolar II disorder*.

Depressive disorders are also called *unipolar* disorders because the mood disturbance goes in only one emotional direction or pole: down. By contrast, mood swing disorders are called *bipolar* disorders because they involve states of both depression and elation, which often appear in an alternating pattern. Table 7.1 provides an overview of these disorders, and a convenient way of conceptualizing differences in mood states corresponding to these disorders is shown in the form of a mood thermometer in Figure 7.1.

Many of us—probably most of us—have periods of sadness from time to time. We may feel down in the dumps, cry, lose interest in things, have trouble concentrating, expect the worst to happen, and even consider suicide. For most of us, mood changes pass quickly or are not severe enough to interfere with our lifestyles or ability to function. Among people with mood disorders, including depressive disorders and bipolar disorders, mood changes are more severe or prolonged and affect daily functioning. **T / F**

**TRUTH or FICTION**

Feeling sad or depressed is abnormal.

☑ **FALSE** Feeling depressed is not abnormal in the context of depressing events or circumstances.

## Table 7.1 Overview of Mood Disorders

| | Type of Disorder | Approximate Lifetime Prevalence Rates* | Major Features or Symptoms | Additional Comments |
|---|---|---|---|---|
| **Depressive Disorders** | Major depressive disorder (MDD) | 12% in men; 21% in women; 16.5% overall | Episodes of severe depression characterized by downcast mood, feelings of hopelessness and worthlessness, changes in sleep patterns or appetite, loss of motivation, loss of pleasure in usual activities | Following a depressive episode, a person may return to his or her usual state of functioning, but recurrences are common. Seasonal affective disorder is a type of major depression. |
| | Persistent depressive disorder (dysthymia) | 4.3% | A chronic pattern of depression | A person experiences chronic mild or major depression or feels "down in the dumps" most of the time. |
| | Premenstrual dysphoric disorder (PMDD) | Unknown | Marked changes in mood during a woman's premenstrual period | A new diagnostic category in *DSM-5*, PMDD remains controversial; critics claim it unfairly stigmatizes women who have significant premenstrual symptoms by labeling them with a mental or psychological disorder. |
| **Bipolar Disorders** | Bipolar disorder | About 1% | Periods of shifting moods, energy level, and level of activity between mania and depression, perhaps with intervening periods of normal mood; two general subtypes are bipolar I disorder (occurrence of one or more manic episodes) and bipolar II disorder (major depressive episode and hypomanic episode, but no full manic episode) | Manic episodes are characterized by pressured speech, greatly increased energy or activity, flight of ideas, poor judgment, high levels of restlessness and excitability, and inflated mood and sense of self. |
| | Cyclothymic disorder | About 0.4% to 1.0% | Mood swings that are milder in severity than those in bipolar disorder | Cyclothymia usually begins in late adolescence or early adulthood and tends to persist for years. |

**Lifetime prevalence* refers to the percentage of people in the population affected by the disorder at some point in their lives.

**SOURCES:** Prevalence rates derived from American Psychiatric Association, 2013; Conway, Compton, Stinson & Grant, 2006; Merikangas et al., 2007; Merikangas & Pato, 2009; Van Meter, Youngstrom, & Findling, 2012. Table updated and adapted from J. S. Nevid (2013). *Psychology: Concepts and Applications* (Fourth Ed., p. 585). Belmont, CA: Wadsworth, Cengage Learning. Reprinted with permission.

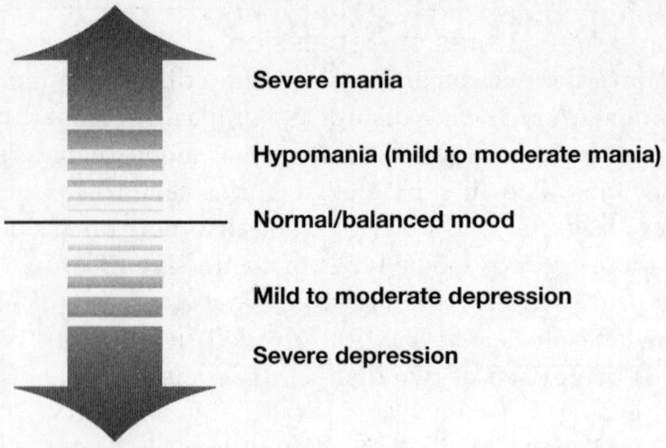


**Figure 7.1** A mood thermometer.

Mood states can be conceptualized as varying along a spectrum or continuum. One end represents severe depression and the other end severe mania, which is a cardinal feature of bipolar disorder. Mild or moderate depression is often called "the blues," but is classified as *dysthymia* when it becomes chronic. In the middle of the spectrum is normal or balanced mood. Mild or moderate mania is called *hypomania* and is characteristic of cyclothymic disorder.

**SOURCE:** NIMH.

# Major Depressive Disorder

**7.1 Describe the key features of major depressive disorder and evaluate factors that may account for the increased rates of depression among women.**

The diagnosis of **major depressive disorder** (also called *major depression*) is based on the occurrence of at least one *major depressive episode* (MDE) in the absence of a history of **mania** or **hypomania**. A major depressive episode includes a clinically significant change in functioning involving a range of depressive symptoms, including depressed mood (feeling sad, hopeless, or "down in the dumps") and/or loss of interest or pleasure in all or virtually all activities for a period of at least two weeks (American Psychiatric Association, 2013). Table 7.2 lists some of the common features of depression. The diagnostic criteria for a major depressive episode are listed in the *DSM* diagnostic table on page 252.

Major depression is not simply a state of sadness or the blues. People with *major depressive disorder* (MDD) may have poor appetite, lose or gain substantial amounts of weight, have trouble sleeping or sleep too much, and become physically agitated or—at the other extreme—show a marked slowing down in their motor (movement) activity. Here, a woman recounts how depression—the "beast" as she calls it—affects every fiber of her being.

**"I"** "The Beast Is Back"

My body aches intermittently, in waves, as if I had malaria. I eat with no appetite, simply because the taste of food is one of my dwindling number of pleasures. i am tired, so tired. Last night I lay like a pile of old clothes, and when David came to bed I did not stir. Sex is a foreign notion. At work today I am forgetful; I have trouble forming sentences, I lose track of them halfway through, and my words keep getting tangled. I look at my list of things to do today, and keep on looking at it; nothing seems to be happening. Things are sad to me. This morning I thought of the woman who used to live in my old house, who told me she went to Sears to buy fake lace curtains. It seemed a forlorn act—having to save your pennies, not being able to afford genuine lace. (Why? A voice in my head asks. The curtains she bought looked perfectly nice.) I feel as if my brain were a lump of protoplasm with tiny circuits embedded in it, and some of the wires keep shorting out. There are tiny little electrical fires up there, leaving crispy sections of neurons smoking and ruined.

I don't even know when this current siege began—a week ago? A month ago? The onset is so gradual, and these things are hard to tell. All I know is, the Beast is back.

It is called depression, and my experiences with it have shaped my life—altered my personality, affected my most intimate relationships, changed the course of my career—in ways I will probably never be fully aware of.

**SOURCE:** *From Thompson, 1995*

Major depression impairs people's ability to meet the ordinary responsibilities of everyday life. People with major depression may lose interest in most of their usual activities and pursuits, have difficulty concentrating and making decisions, have pressing thoughts of death, and attempt suicide. They even show impaired driving skills in driving simulation tests (Bulmash et al., 2006).

**Table 7.2** Common Features of Depression

| | |
|---|---|
| **Changes in emotional states** | • Changes in mood (persistent periods of feeling down, depressed, sad, or blue)<br>• Evidence of tearfulness or crying<br>• Increased irritability, jumpiness, or loss of temper |
| **Changes in motivation** | • Feeling unmotivated, or having difficulty getting going in the morning or even getting out of bed<br>• Reduced level of social participation or interest in social activities<br>• Loss of enjoyment or interest in pleasurable activities<br>• Reduced interest in sex<br>• Failure to respond to praise or rewards |
| **Changes in functioning and motor behavior** | • Moving about or talking more slowly than usual<br>• Changes in sleep habits (sleeping too much or too little, or awakening earlier than usual and having trouble getting back to sleep in early morning hours—so-called early morning awakening)<br>• Changes in appetite (eating too much or too little)<br>• Changes in weight (gaining or losing weight)<br>• Functioning less effectively at work or school; failing to meet responsibilities and neglecting one's physical appearance |
| **Cognitive changes** | • Difficulty concentrating or thinking clearly<br>• Thinking negatively about oneself and one's future<br>• Feeling guilty or remorseful about past misdeeds<br>• Lack of self-esteem or feelings of inadequacy<br>• Thinking of death or suicide |

Mired in the depths of depression in 1841, Abraham Lincoln said of himself, "I am now the most miserable man living. If what I feel were equally distributed to the whole human family, there would not be one cheerful face on the earth" (Lincoln 1841/1953, p. 230). These words of despair poignantly express just how disabling depression can be (Forgeard et al., 2012).

Many people don't seem to understand that people who are clinically depressed can't simply "shake it off" or "snap out of it." Many people still view depression as a sign of weakness, not a diagnosable disorder. Many people with major depression believe they can handle the problem themselves. These attitudes may help explain why, despite the availability of safe and effective treatments, about half of Americans with major depression fail to receive help from a mental health professional (González et al., 2010). Latinos and African Americans are less likely than other groups to receive care. Another factor explaining the lack of care is that many depressed patients seek help from their family physicians, who often fail to either detect depression or make referrals to mental health professionals (Simon et al., 2004). **T / F**

**THE MELANCHOLIC PRESIDENT.** Abraham Lincoln struggled with depression through much of his life.

MDD is the most common type of diagnosable mood disorder. Based on nationally representative surveys in the United States, researchers report a lifetime prevalence rate for MDD of about 12% for men, 21% for women, and about 16.5% overall (Conway et al., 2006; Forgeard et al., 2012; see Figure 7.2). Nearly 8% of U.S. adults currently suffer from the disorder (National Center for Health Statistics, 2012a).

Major depression is a major public health problem, not only affecting psychological functioning but also impairing a person's ability to meet school, work, family, and social responsibilities. As you can

## TRUTH or FICTION

Major depression affects millions of Americans, but fortunately most get the help they need.

☑ **FALSE** According to recent studies, only about half of Americans with major depression receive any form of professional treatment.

MARTHA: MAJOR DEPRESSIVE DISORDER

## Criteria for *DSM-5*

### MAJOR DEPRESSIVE DISORDER

A. Five (or more) of the following symptoms have been present during the same 2-week period and represent a change from previous functioning; at least one of the symptoms is either (1) depressed mood or (2) loss of interest or pleasure.

**Note:** Do not include symptoms that are clearly attributable to another medical condition.

1. Depressed mood most of the day, nearly every day, as indicated by either subjective report (e.g., feels sad, empty, hopeless) or observation made by others (e.g., appears tearful). (**Note:** In children and adolescents, can be irritable mood.)
2. Markedly diminished interest or pleasure in all, or almost all, activities most of the day, nearly every day (as indicated by either subjective account or observation).
3. Significant weight loss when not dieting or weight gain (e.g., a change of more than 5% of body weight in a month), or decrease or increase in appetite nearly every day. (**Note:** In children, consider failure to make expected weight gain.)
4. Insomnia or hypersomnia nearly every day.
5. Psychomotor agitation or retardation nearly every day (observable by others, not merely subjective feelings of restlessness or being slowed down).
6. Fatigue or loss of energy nearly every day.
7. Feelings of worthlessness or excessive or inappropriate guilt (which may be delusional) nearly every day (not merely self-reproach or guilt about being sick).
8. Diminished ability to think or concentrate, or indecisiveness, nearly every day (either by subjective account or as observed by others).
9. Recurrent thoughts of death (not just fear of dying), recurrent suicidal ideation without a specific plan, or a suicide attempt or a specific committing suicide.

B. The symptoms cause clinically significant distress or impairment in social, occupational, or other important areas of functioning.

C. The episode is not attributable to the physiological effects of a substance or to another medical condition.

**Note:** Criteria A–C represent a major depressive episode.

**Note:** Responses to a significant loss (e.g., bereavement, financial ruin, losses from a natural disaster, a serious medical illness or disability) may include the feelings of intense sadness, rumination about the loss, insomnia, poor appetite, and weight loss noted in Criterion A, which may resemble a depressive episode. Although such symptoms may be understandable or considered appropriate to the loss, the presence of a major depressive episode in addition to the normal response to a significant loss should also be carefully considered. This decision inevitably requires the exercise of clinical judgment based on the individual's history and the cultural norms for the expression of distress in the context of loss.

D. The occurrence of the major depressive episode is not better explained by schizoaffective disorder, schizophrenia, schizophreniform disorder, delusional disorder, or other specified and unspecified schizophrenia spectrum and other psychotic disorders.

E. There has never been a manic episode or a hypomanic episode.

**Note:** This exclusion does not apply if all of the manic-like or hypomanic-like episodes are substance-induced or are attributable to the physiological effects of another medical condition.

Reprinted with permission from the Diagnostic and Statistical Manual of Mental Disorders, Fifth Edition (Copyright American Psychiatric Association, 2013). American Psychiatric Association.

see in Figure 7.3, nearly 80% of people with moderate to severe depression report impaired work, family, or social functioning.

The economic costs of depression are staggering, costing billions of dollars in lost productivity due to time taken away from work. Major depression costs the average worker about 27.2 lost workdays per year; for bipolar disorder, about 65 days are lost on average (Kessler et al., 2006). The average worker suffering from depression earns about 10% less than unaffected workers in similar jobs (McIntyre, Liauw, & Taylor, 2011). Worldwide, depression is the leading disease-related cause of disability (Monroe & Anderson, 2015). On the other hand, effective treatment for depression leads not only to psychological improvement but also to more stable employment and increased income, because people are able to return to a more productive level.

Major depression, particularly in more severe episodes, may be accompanied by psychotic features, such as delusions that one's body is rotting from illness. People with major depression may also exhibit psychotic behaviors, such as hallucinations—for example, "hearing" voices condemning them for perceived misdeeds.

The following case illustrates the range of features connected with major depressive disorder.

**Figure 7.2** Lifetime prevalence rates for major depressive disorder.

Major depressive episodes affect about twice as many women as men.

**SOURCE:** Conway et al., 2006.

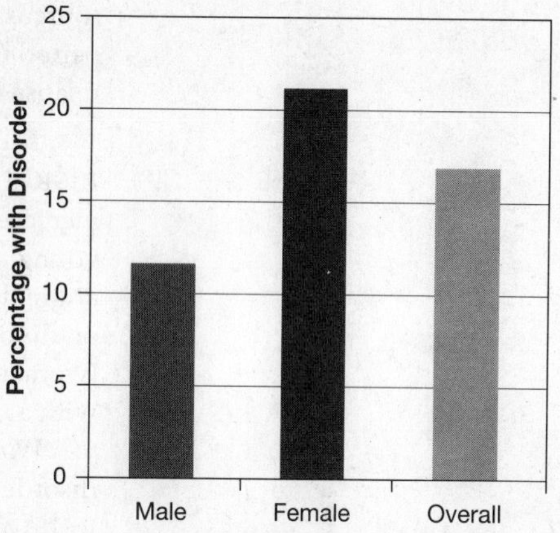


## Slowly Killing Herself:

### A CASE OF MAJOR DEPRESSIVE DISORDER

A 38-year-old female clerical worker has suffered from recurrent bouts of depression since she was about 13 years of age. Most recently, she has been troubled by crying spells at work, sometimes occurring so suddenly she wouldn't have enough time to run to the ladies' room to hide her tears from others. She has difficulty concentrating at work and feels a lack of pleasure from work she used to enjoy. She harbors severe pessimistic and angry feelings, which have been more severe lately because she has been putting on weight and has been neglectful in taking care of her diabetes. She feels guilty that she may be slowly killing herself by not taking better care of her health. She sometimes feels that she deserves to be dead. She has been bothered by excessive sleepiness for the past year and a half, and her driving license has been suspended because of an incident the previous month in which she fell asleep while driving, causing her car to hit a telephone pole. She wakes up most days feeling groggy and just "out of it" and remains sleepy throughout the day. She has never had a steady boyfriend and lives quietly at home with her mother, with no close friends outside of her family. During the interview, she cried frequently and answered questions in a low monotone, staring downward continuously.

**SOURCE:** *Adapted from Spitzer et al., 1989, 59–62*

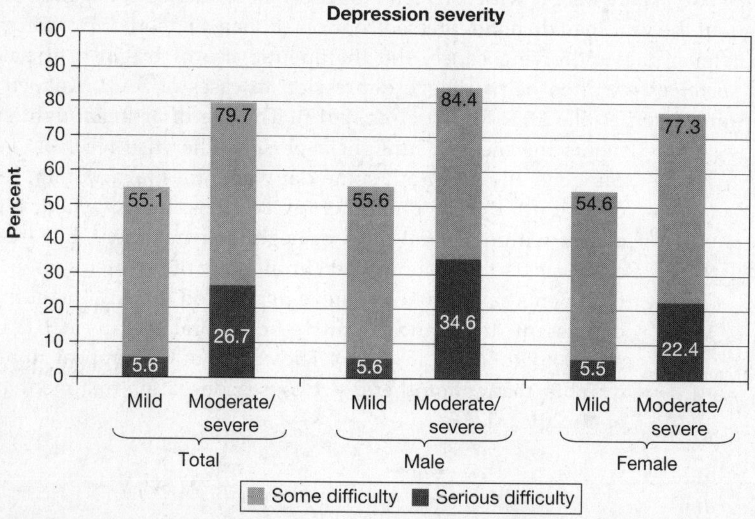


**Figure 7.3** Percentage of persons 12 years of age and older reporting difficulty with their work, home, and social activities by sex and depression severity.

Depression affects people in many ways. Most people (55.1% with mild depression; 79.7% with moderate or severe depression) report difficulties with work, home, or social activities.

**SOURCE:** Pratt & Brody, 2008.

Major depressive episodes may resolve in a matter of months or last for a year or more. Some people experience a single episode of major depression and then return to their earlier state of normal psychological functioning (Eaton et al., 2008). Yet most people with MDD have episodes of major depression occurring from time to time (Hölzel et al., 2011; Reifler, 2006). Evidence shows that risk of repeat episodes is related to genetic influences and the presence of other significant medical or psychiatric illnesses (Burcusa & Iacono, 2007; Richards, 2011). However, the good news is that the longer the period of recovery from an episode of major depression, the lower the risk of eventual relapse (Solomon et al., 2000).

**RISK FACTORS IN MAJOR DEPRESSION** Many factors are associated with an increased risk of major depression, including age (initial onset is most common among young adults); socioeconomic status (people lower down the socioeconomic ladder are at greater risk than those who are better off); marital status (people who are separated or divorced have higher rates than married or never-married people); and gender (women have higher rates). People with a family history of major depression and those with a childhood history of sexual abuse are also at higher risk (Klein et al., 2013).

Women are about twice as likely as men to be diagnosed with major depressive disorder. The greater risk of depression in women begins in early adolescence (ages 13 to 15) and persists at least through middle age (Costello et al., 2008; Hyde, Mezulis, & Abramson, 2008). Noting the existence of a gender gap in the diagnosis of depression is one thing; explaining it is quite another (see *Thinking Critically: What Accounts for the Gender Gap in Depression?* on page 256).

**SEASONAL AFFECTIVE DISORDER** Are you glum on gloomy days? Is your temper short during the brief days of winter? Are you dismal during the long, dark winter nights and sunny when spring and summer return?

Although our moods may vary with the weather, the changing of the seasons from summer to fall and winter can lead to a type of depression called *seasonal affective* (mood) *disorder* (SAD). In most SAD cases, the depression lifts in the spring. SAD is not a diagnostic category in its own right but is a specifier or subcategory of major depression. For example, major depressive disorder that occurs seasonally would be diagnosed as *major depressive disorder with seasonal pattern*. Although the causes of SAD remain unknown, one possibility drawing attention is that seasonal changes in light may alter the body's underlying biological rhythms that regulate processes such as body temperature and sleep-wake cycles (Oren, Koziorowski, & Desan, 2013). Another possibility is that seasonal changes might affect the availability or use in the brain of the mood-regulating neurotransmitter serotonin during winter months. Cognitive factors also may play a part; people with SAD tend to report more automatic negative thoughts throughout the year than do nondepressed controls (Rohan, Sigmon, & Dorhofer, 2003).

Whatever the underlying cause, the therapeutic use of bright artificial light, called *phototherapy*, often helps relieve depression in cases of SAD (Knapen et al., 2014; Mårtensson et al., 2015; Rohan et al., 2015). The use of artificial light supplements the meager sunlight a person otherwise receives. Patients can generally carry out some daily activities (e.g., eating, reading, or writing) during phototherapy sessions. Improvement typically occurs within several days of beginning treatment, but treatment often needs to be continued throughout the winter season. Other treatments can also help relieve depression in SAD, including antidepressant drugs and cognitive-behavioral therapy (CBT; Lam et al., 2006; Rohan et al., 2016). The effects of CBT appear to be more durable than phototherapy two seasons after treatment (Rohan et al., 2015). **T / F**

## TRUTH *or* FICTION

Exposure to bright artificial light can help relieve depression in some cases.

☑ **TRUE** Exposure to bright light is an effective treatment for seasonal affective disorder (SAD).

**POSTPARTUM DEPRESSION** Many new mothers, perhaps as many as 80%, experience mood changes following childbirth (Friedman, 2009; Payne, 2007). These mood changes are commonly called the "maternity blues," "postpartum blues," or "baby blues." They usually last for a few days and may be a normal response to hormonal changes associated with childbirth. Given these turbulent hormonal shifts, it might be considered "abnormal" for most women *not* to experience some mood changes shortly following childbirth. However, for some new mothers, severe mood changes that occur around the time of childbirth are classified as a type of major depression called **postpartum depression (PPD**; sometimes called *perinatal depression*).

**LIGHT THERAPY.** Exposure to bright artificial light for a few hours a day during the fall and winter months can often bring relief from seasonal affective disorder.

The word *postpartum* derives from the Latin roots *post*, meaning *after*, and *papere*, meaning *to bring forth*. PPD affects 10% to 15% of U.S. women in the first year following childbirth (CDC, 2008). It may persist for months or even a year or more. PPD is often accompanied by disturbances in appetite and sleep, low self-esteem, and difficulties in maintaining concentration or attention.

Postpartum depression is a form of major depression in which the onset of the depressive episode begins within 4 weeks after childbirth (American Psychiatric Association, 2013). Although depression tends to lessen over time, evidence shows that nearly one in three women with PPD continue to struggle with depression through the first three years after childbirth (Vliegen, Casalin, & Luyten, 2014). In some cases, postpartum depression can even lead to suicide. There may also be bipolar forms of PPD (Dudek et al., 2013).

Women with a history of depression or anxiety prior to pregnancy face an increased risk of PPD (Norhayatia et al., 2015; Patton et al., 2015). Genetic factors may also contribute to increased vulnerability (Figueiredo et al., 2015; Zhang et al., 2014). Other identified risk factors include the following (Helle et al., 2015; Kornfeld et al., 2012; Norhayatia et al., 2015; Viguera et al., 2011):

- Being a single or first-time mother
- Having financial problems or a troubled marriage
- Stressful life experience
- Having a very low birthweight baby
- Suffering domestic violence
- Lacking social support from partners and family members
- Having unwanted, sick, or temperamentally difficult infants

PPD increases the risk that a woman will experience future depressive episodes. Fortunately, effective treatments are available, including cognitive-behavioral therapy and antidepressant drugs (Molyneaux, Trevillion, & Howard, 2015; Sockol, 2015).

Postpartum depression is not limited to American culture. Researchers find high rates of PPD among South African women (Cooper et al., 1999) and Chinese women from Hong Kong (Lee et al., 2001). In the South African sample, a lack of psychological and financial support from the baby's father was associated with an increased risk of the disorder, mirroring findings with U.S. samples.

Postpartum depression needs to be distinguished from a much less common but more severe reaction, called *postpartum psychosis*, in which a new mother loses touch with reality and experiences symptoms such as hallucinations, delusions, and irrational thinking. Postpartum psychosis occurs in about one to two women in 1,000 childbirths and can become a life-threatening disorder that warrants immediate treatment (Vergink & Kushner, 2014). Questions remain about whether to diagnose these reactions as psychotic disorders or as forms of bipolar disorder with psychotic features.

# THINKING CRITICALLY about abnormal psychology

## @ISSUE: WHAT ACCOUNTS FOR THE GENDER GAP IN DEPRESSION?

Women are about twice as likely as men to suffer from clinical depression: about 12% for men versus about 21% for women (Conway et al., 2006; Hyde, Mezulis, & Abramson, 2008). A greater prevalence of depression among women was found in each of 15 countries from various parts of the world in a cross-national study by the World Health Organization (Seedat et al., 2009). The question is, *why*?

We need to take a number of factors into account (Eagly et al., 2012). Hormonal fluctuations may contribute to depression in some cases, as might gender differences in neurotransmitter functioning (Gray et al., 2015). As research on these fronts continues, we also need to account for the disproportionate stress burden women in our society tend to carry, as well as each individual's own way of coping with emotional distress. Women are more likely than men to experience stressful life factors such as physical and sexual abuse, poverty, single parenthood, and sexism, all of which may increase vulnerability to depression. Depressed women, especially those in young adulthood, tend to report more negative life events than depressed men—events such as the loss of loved one or changes in life circumstances (Harkness et al., 2010). On the other hand, a World Health Organization cross-national study showed that a narrowing of gender differences in major depression may be occurring, perhaps because of a loosening of traditional female gender roles in many cultures (Seedat et al., 2009).

The late psychologist Susan Nolen-Hoeksema focused on gender differences in coping styles. She proposed that women tend to ruminate or brood more about their problems, whereas men are more likely to distract themselves by doing something they enjoy, such as going to a favorite hangout to get their minds off their problems (Nolen-Hoeksema, 2006, 2012). Rumination increases emotional distress, setting the stage for depression and other negative emotions, such as anxiety (Mor & Daches, 2015). However, distracting oneself from one's problems by turning to alcohol or other drugs can lead to substance-related psychological and social problems.

Another view of the gender gap in depression is that women's self-esteem—how they view themselves—may hinge more than men's on their interpersonal relationships with their peers, friends, and romantic partners (Cambron, Acitelli, & Pettit, 2009). Evidence shows that depression in women is more often connected with problems in close, caring relationships (Weissman, 2014). Positive events in relationships may bolster their self-esteem, but when problems arise (arguments, rejection, etc.), self-esteem may plummet. This in turn may give rise in women to rumination about what's wrong with them and to negative interpersonal behaviors, such as excessive demands for reassurance of their self-worth, which in turn may lead to depression.

Rumination is not limited to women. For men and women, rumination or brooding about one's problems is associated with greater proneness to depression and longer and more severe depression (Joormann, Levens, & Gotlib, 2011; Mandell et al., 2014). People who continually mull over their problems tend to get stuck on bad thoughts. As University of Miami psychologist Jutta Joormann puts it, "They basically get stuck in a mindset where they relive what happened to them over and over again ... Even though they think, oh, it's not helpful, I should stop thinking about this, I should get on with my life—they can't stop doing it" (cited in "People with Depression," 2011).

Rumination tends to aggravate whatever moods people are experiencing at the time, making them feel sadder or more depressed if they are feeling down or angrier if they are feeling angry or irritated (Nolen-Hoeksema, 2008). Rumination may also play a role in other forms of abnormal behavior, including anxiety disorders and binge eating (Nolen-Hoeksema, Wisco, & Lyubomirksy, 2008).

Might the gender difference in depression be at least partially explained by a reporting bias that leads men to underreport depression? In our culture, men are expected to be tough and resilient. Consequently, they are less likely to report depression or seek treatment for it. Even physicians are not immune from these social expectations. As one male physician put it, "I'm the John Wayne generation.... I thought depression was a weakness—there was something disgraceful about it. A real man would just get over it" (cited in Wartik, 2000, p. MH1). The stigma associated with depression shows signs of lessening—but not disappearing. Although depression was long viewed by men as

**GENDER DIFFERENCES IN DEPRESSION.** Women are about twice as likely to suffer from major depression as men. The question is, *why?*

a sign of personal weakness, more men are coming forward to get help. The male ego has likely been battered by assaults from economic crises and growing financial insecurity. **T / F**

### TRUTH or FICTION

Men are about twice as likely as women to develop major depression.

☑ **FALSE** Actually, women are nearly twice as likely as men to develop major depression.

More research is needed to fully understand the gender gap in depression. Hopefully, research into factors such as hormonal influences, stress burdens, and ruminative styles will lead to the development of more specifically targeted interventions for treating depression in women. Likewise, by understanding men's culturally instilled resistance to reporting depression, clinicians can help destigmatize the disorder so that more men suffering from depression will be willing seek help rather than suffer in silence (Cochran & Rabinowitz, 2003).

In thinking critically about the issue, answer the following questions:

- How might a theorist in the biopsychosocial tradition account for gender differences in depression?
- Give an example of how more knowledge about the causes of gender differences in depression can lead to improved treatment approaches.
- What can be done about the other side of the gender gap in depression—that is, why so many depressed men seem reluctant to seek help?

# Persistent Depressive Disorder (Dysthymia)

**7.2 Describe the key features of persistent depressive disorder (dysthymia).**

Major depressive disorder is severe and characterized by a relatively abrupt change from a person's preexisting mental state and is followed by remission after a few weeks or months. However, some forms of depression are chronic conditions that can last for years. The diagnosis of **persistent depressive disorder** applies to cases of chronic depression lasting for at least two years. Persons with persistent depressive disorder may have either a chronic major depressive disorder or a chronic but milder form of depression called *dysthymia*. Dysthymia typically begins in childhood or adolescence and tends to follow a chronic course through adulthood. The word *dysthymia* derives from Greek roots *dys*, meaning *bad* or *hard*, and *thymos*, meaning *spirit*.

People with dysthymia feel "bad spirited" or "down in the dumps" most of the time, but they are not as severely depressed as those with major depressive disorder. Whereas major depressive disorder tends to be severe and time limited, dysthymia is relatively mild and nagging, typically lasting for years. The risk of relapse is quite high, as is the risk of major depressive disorder: 90% of people with dysthymia eventually develop major depression (Friedman, 2002).

Dysthymia affects about 4% of the general population at some point in their lifetimes (Conway et al., 2006). Like major depressive disorder, dysthymia is more common in women than in men (see Figure 7.4). It is diagnosed only in people who have never had episodes of either mania or hypomania, which are characteristics of bipolar disorder (American Psychiatric Association, 2013).

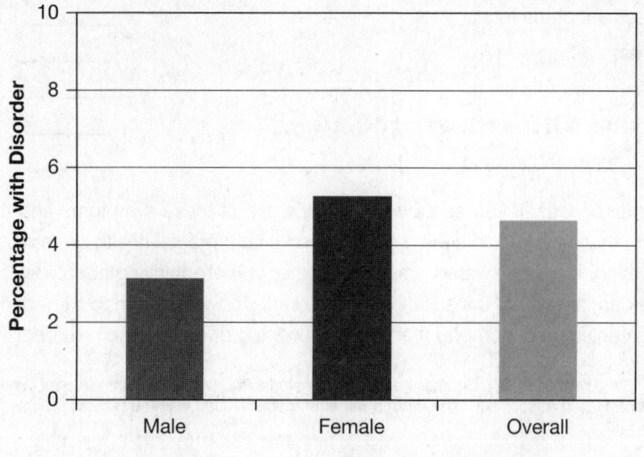


**Figure 7.4** Lifetime prevalence rates for dysthymia.

Like major depression, dysthymia occurs in about twice as many women as men.

**SOURCE OF DATA:** Conway et al., 2006.

In dysthymia, complaints of depression may become such a fixture of people's lives that they seem to feel it's a natural part of their personality, of who they are. They may not realize they are suffering from a diagnosable mood disorder. The persistence of complaints may lead others to perceive a person with dysthymia as whining and complaining. Although dysthymia is less severe than major depressive disorder, persistent depressed mood and low self-esteem can affect a person's occupational and social functioning, as in the following case.

## Dissatisfaction with All Facets of Life:

### A CASE OF DYSTHYMIA

A woman, a 28-year-old junior executive, complained of chronic feelings of depression since the age of 16 or 17. Despite doing well in college, she brooded about how other people were "genuinely intelligent." She felt she could never pursue a man she might be interested in dating because she felt inferior and intimidated. Although she had extensive therapy through college and graduate school, she could never recall a time during those years when she did not feel somewhat depressed. She was married shortly after college graduation to the man she was dating at the time, although she didn't think that he was anything "special." She just felt she needed the companionship of a husband, and he was available. But they soon began to quarrel, and she has lately begun to feel that marrying him was a mistake. She has had difficulties at work, turning in "slipshod" work, never seeking anything more than what was basically required of her and showing little initiative. Although she dreams of acquiring status and money, she doesn't expect that she or her husband will rise in their professions because they lack "connections." Her social life is dominated by her husband's friends and their spouses, and she doesn't think that other women would find her interesting. She lacks interest in life in general and expresses dissatisfaction with all facets of her life—her marriage, her job, her social life.

**SOURCE:** *Adapted from Spitzer et al., 1994, pp. 110–112*

## Questionnaire

### ARE YOU DEPRESSED?

This self-screening test can be used as an aid to understanding whether you may be suffering from depression. It is not intended for you to diagnose yourself, but should be used to raise awareness of concerns you may want to discuss further with a professional.

| | Yes | No |
|---|---|---|
| 1. I feel extremely sad all or most of the time. | ______ | ______ |
| 2. I have no energy. | ______ | ______ |
| 3. I cry a lot when I'm alone. | ______ | ______ |
| 4. I've lost interest in most of the activities I used to enjoy. | ______ | ______ |
| 5. I sleep much more (or much less) than usual. | ______ | ______ |
| 6. I have suddenly gained (or lost) a lot of weight. | ______ | ______ |
| 7. I have trouble concentrating, remembering, and making decisions. | ______ | ______ |
| 8. I feel hopeless about the future. | ______ | ______ |
| 9. I feel worthless. | ______ | ______ |
| 10. I feel anxious. | ______ | ______ |
| 11. I'm often irritable, and I never used to be that way. | ______ | ______ |
| 12. I think about death and suicide. | ______ | ______ |

*Evaluating your responses:* If you agree with two or more of these symptoms and they last for at least two weeks, then you should seek a consultation with a mental health professional for a more complete evaluation. If you answered "yes" to whether you are thinking about death and suicide, you should seek an immediate consultation. If you don't know to whom to turn, contact your college counseling center, neighborhood mental health center, or health care provider.

**SOURCE:** D. Blum & M. Kirchner (1997). Depression at work. *Customs Today*, Winter issue. Quotes used with permission of the National Mental Health Association. The Blum & Kirchner article is used with the authors' permission.

Some people are affected by both dysthymia and major depression at the same time. The term **double depression** applies to those who have a major depressive episode superimposed on a longer-standing dysthymia. People suffering from double depression generally have more severe depressive episodes than do people with major depression alone (Klein et al., 2000).

# Abnormal Psychology in the Digital Age

## DOES FACEBOOK MAKE YOU SADDER? THE UNINTENDED CONSEQUENCES OF SOCIAL COMPARISON

Facebook, which started as a social experiment in a Harvard dormitory, has become a worldwide phenomenon, with some 1.5 billion current users. When social media sites first arrived on the scene, many observers expressed concerns that they might cause loneliness or lead to a generation of social isolates whose social activities were limited to online interactions. These concerns proved to be unfounded; evidence shows that more active users of social networking sites like Facebook actually have more friends in both the online and real worlds (Lönnqvista & Deters, 2016). Moreover, social networking sites can have beneficial effects, such as helping people maintain and strengthen social relationships and perhaps assisting socially anxious people in building self-confidence (Indian & Grieve, 2014; Wilson, Gosling, & Graham, 2012). Most people use Facebook to maintain and strengthen relationships they have developed in the real world, not as a substitute for real-life relationships or to form new relationships (Lönnqvista & Deters, 2016). However, social networking can also have a dark side.

**DOES FACEBOOK BRING YOU DOWN?** What effects might frequent profile checking on Facebook have on your emotional health and well-being?

We're beginning to see some of the fallout associated with maladaptive use of social networking sites (SNSs). For example, a recent study in Germany showed that Internet addiction associated with heavy SNS use was linked to poorer mental health outcomes among adolescents (Müller et al., 2016). Other investigators in Europe, where most of the research to date has been conducted, found that heavier use of SNSs was associated with poorer academic performance, largely as the result of time taken away from studying (Tsitsika et al., 2014). These results dovetail with those of a recent study in the United States, which showed that college freshmen who were more frequent users of Facebook tended to have poorer grades than less frequent users (Junco, 2015). But is Facebook to blame for poor grades? Because studies relating Facebook use to grades are based on correlational evidence, their findings cannot pinpoint cause-and-effect relationships. The professor who conducted the U.S. study believes that Facebook may be no different than any other source of distraction that drains time away from academic work, such as watching TV. Drilling down deeper into the data, the professor found that some uses of Facebook, such as checking up on friends and sharing links, were actually connected to higher grades. Rather than indicting social networking in general, we need to better understand how maladaptive use of these services lead to adverse outcomes.

Investigators exploring the dark side of using Facebook and other social networking sites are also focusing on the unintended consequences of social comparison, which can lead SNS users to feel sadder after logging off. Although people may expect that social networking will make them feel better, it often makes them feel worse about themselves. As one researcher put it, "When you're on a site like Facebook, you get lots of posts about what people are doing. That sets up social comparison—you maybe feel your life is not as full and rich as those people you see on Facebook" (cited in Hu, 2013). Unfavorable social comparisons of self versus others may set the stage for diminished self-esteem and possibly even depression.

Research evidence shows that longer use of Facebook is linked to more negative moods afterwards, so perhaps the dosage (exposure) level is a critical determinant of the adverse effects of profile checking (Sagioglou & Greitemeyer, 2014). We've also learned that greater use of social media sites is associated with increased risk of depression, but the precise causal linkages remain to be determined (Lin et al., 2016).

The challenge for users of Facebook and other SNS services is not to get caught up in the practice of comparing themselves to others. The potentially damaging effects of social comparisons from online activity are also linked to the development of eating disorders, as we explore in Chapter 10. Another form of compulsive Internet use, cybersex addiction, is also discussed in Chapter 10.

# Premenstrual Dysphoric Disorder

**7.3 Describe the key features of premenstrual dysphoric disorder.**

**Premenstrual dysphoric disorder (PMDD)** was introduced as a diagnostic category in *DSM-5* (Epperson, 2013). It had been classified in the previous edition of the *DSM* as a proposed diagnosis requiring further study. The inclusion of this new diagnostic category is intended to draw greater attention to the problem of mood swings associated with the premenstrual period and increase delivery of services to women suffering from these types of problems.

PMDD is a more severe form of *premenstrual syndrome* (PMS), which is a cluster of physical and mood-related symptoms occurring during a woman's premenstrual period. The diagnosis of PMDD is intended to apply to women who experience a range of significant psychological symptoms in the week before menses (and improvement beginning within a few days following the onset of menses). A range of symptoms need to be present to diagnose PMDD, including symptoms such as mood swings, sudden tearfulness or feelings of sadness, depressed mood or feelings of hopelessness, irritability or anger, feelings of anxiety, tension, being on edge, greater sensitivity to cues of rejection, and negative thoughts about oneself. These symptoms also need to be associated with significant emotional distress or interference with a woman's ability to function on the job, in school, or in usual social activities.

The diagnosis of PMDD brings into focus the difficulty establishing clear lines between normal and abnormal behavior. Most women have some mood-related premenstrual symptoms, with many women (upwards of 50%) experiencing moderate to severe symptoms (Freeman, 2011). Investigators report that nearly one in five women have premenstrual physical or mood-related symptoms that are severe enough to interfere with their daily functioning, such as causing absenteeism from work or producing significant emotional distress (Halbreich et al., 2006; Heinemann et al., 2010).

The cause or causes of both PMS and premenstrual dysphoric disorder remain unclear. Investigators suspect that PMS involves a complex interaction between female sexual hormones and neurotransmitters (Bäckström et al., 2003; Kiesner, 2009). Psychological factors, such as a woman's attitudes about menstruation, may also play a role. Recent research suggests that normal levels of female sexual hormones may trigger negative emotional reactions in women with PMDD, but not in healthy women (Baller et al., 2013; Epperson, 2013).

The diagnosis of PMDD remains controversial. Critics fear it will pathologize a woman's natural menstrual cycle and may stigmatize women who have serious premenstrual complaints by labeling them with a psychiatric diagnosis. Although the new diagnosis of PMDD has been estimated to apply to perhaps only 2% to 5% of women overall ("PMDD Proposed," 2012), the question remains whether the diagnosis will become overextended to a much larger percentage of women who suffer from a wider range of premenstrual symptoms. Moreover, even if relatively few women are diagnosed with PMDD, is it fair to characterize them as suffering from a mental disorder when they may be suffering from a physical condition? Mental health professionals will need to contend with these questions as the PMDD diagnosis becomes more widely used in clinical practice.

Moving on, we noted previously that major depressive disorder and dysthymia are *depressive disorders* in the sense that the disturbance of mood is only in one direction—down. Yet people with mood disorders may have fluctuations in mood in both directions that exceed the usual ups and downs of everyday life. These types of disorders are called *bipolar disorders*. Next, we focus on the major types of mood swing disorders: bipolar disorder and cyclothymic disorder.

# Bipolar Disorder

**7.4 Describe the key features of bipolar disorder.**

Picture someone with **bipolar disorder**, a psychological disorder characterized by extreme swings of mood and changes in energy and activity levels. The person's mood swings shift between the heights of elation and the depths of depression over the span of a few weeks or months. The person's first episode may have been manic or depressive. A manic episode typically lasts a few weeks or perhaps a month or two, but is generally much shorter and ends more abruptly than major depressive episodes.

Despite what people may think, most people with bipolar disorder do not cycle between mania and depression from day to day. However, there are cases of bipolar disorder involving *mixed states* that are characterized by episodes of both mania and depression (American Psychiatric Association, 2013). During mixed states, a person's mood may rapidly shift between mania and depression (Swann et al., 2013). Some people with major depressive disorder also experience mixed states in which they show some symptoms of mania but not of a sufficient number or magnitude to merit a diagnosis of a bipolar disorder.

We need to be concerned about the risk of suicide "on the way down" from a manic phase. A person may report a willingness to do almost anything, including perhaps ending it all, to escape the depths of depression that lie ahead. Life for a person with bipolar disorder is like living on an emotional roller coaster.

**ANN: BIPOLAR DISORDER**

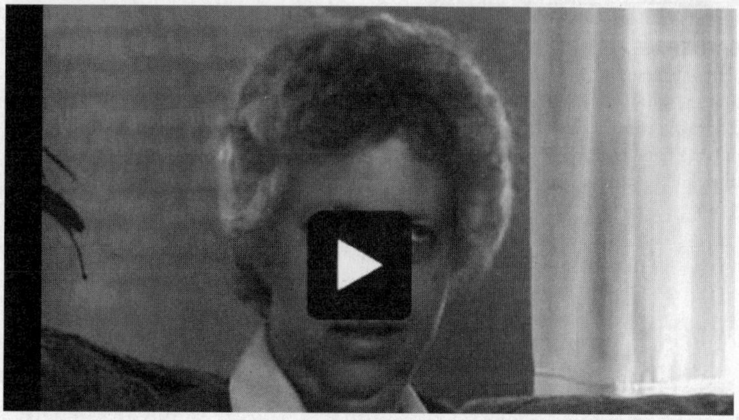

Kay Redfield Jamison, a psychologist and leading authority on the treatment of bipolar disorder, suffers from the disorder herself. Within three months of beginning her first professional appointment as an assistant professor in the Department of Psychiatry at UCLA, she became, in her own words, "ravingly psychotic." Jamison has suffered from bipolar disorder since her teens, but wasn't diagnosed until she was 28 (Ballie, 2002).

### "I" An Unquiet Mind

In her 1995 memoir, *An Unquiet Mind*, Jamison described her early and milder episodes of mania as "absolutely intoxicating states that gave rise to great personal pleasure, an incomparable flow of thoughts, and a ceaseless energy that allowed the translation of new ideas into papers and projects" (p. 5). But then:

"As night inevitably goes after the day, my mood would crash, and my mind again would grind to a halt. I lost all interest in my schoolwork, friends, reading, wandering, or daydreaming. I had no idea of what was happening to me, and I would wake up in the morning with a profound sense of dread that I was going to have to somehow make it through another entire day. I would sit for hour after hour in the undergraduate library, unable to muster up enough energy to go to class. I would stare out the window, stare at my books, rearrange them, shuffle them around, leave them unopened, and think about dropping out of college.... I understood very little of what was going on, and I felt as though only dying would release me from the overwhelming sense of inadequacy and blackness that surrounded me" (p. 44).

**SOURCE:** *From Jamison, 1995*

The *DSM 5* distinguishes between two types of bipolar disorder: *bipolar I disorder* and *bipolar II disorder*. The differences can be confusing, so let's try to clarify.

The distinction is based on whether a person has ever experienced a full-blown manic episode (Youngstrom, 2009). The diagnosis of bipolar I disorder applies to people who have had at least one *full manic episode* at some point in their lives. Typically, bipolar I disorder involves extreme mood swings between manic episodes and major depression,

**CATHERINE ZETA-JONES.** The actress Catherine Zeta-Jones revealed that she suffers from a form of bipolar disorder. She said she hopes that making her condition known will draw public attention to the problem.

with intervening periods of normal mood—but it is possible for bipolar I disorder to apply to a person who does not have a history of a major depressive episode. It is assumed in these cases that major depression may have been overlooked in the past or will develop in the future.

Bipolar II disorder applies to people who have had both *hypomanic episodes* (from the Greek prefix *hypo*, meaning *under* or *less than*) and a history of at least one major depressive episode, but have never had a full-blown manic episode. Hypomanic episodes are less severe than manic episodes and are not accompanied by the extreme social or occupational problems associated with full-blown mania (Tomb et al., 2012). During a hypomanic episode, a person might may feel unusually charged with energy and show a heightened level of activity and an inflated sense of self-esteem, and may be more alert, restless, and irritable than usual. Such a person may be able to work long hours with little fatigue or need for sleep.

Some but not all bipolar II patients go on to develop bipolar I disorder (Nusslock et al., 2012). The question of whether bipolar I and bipolar II disorders should be considered two distinct disorders or simply different points along a continuum of severity of a single bipolar disorder remains, however. About 1% of the adult population in the United States are affected by bipolar I disorder or bipolar II disorder at some point in their lives (Kupfer, 2005; Merikangas et al., 2007). Bipolar disorder typically develops around age 20 in both men and women and tends to become a chronic, recurring condition requiring long-term treatment (Frank & Kupfer, 2003; Tohen et al., 2003).

Unlike major depression, rates of bipolar I disorder appear about equal in men and women (Merikangas & Pato, 2009). In men, however, the onset of bipolar I disorder typically begins with a manic episode, whereas with women it usually begins with a major depressive episode. The underlying reason for this gender difference remains unknown. It remains unclear whether there is a gender difference in rates of bipolar II disorder (American Psychiatric Association, 2013).

In some cases of bipolar disorder, a pattern of "rapid cycling" occurs in which an individual experiences two or more full cycles of mania and depression within a year without any intervening normal periods. Rapid cycling is relatively uncommon, but occurs more often in women than men (Schneck et al., 2004, 2008). It is usually limited to a year or less, but is linked to poorer outcomes and is associated with a greater number of suicide attempts (Valentí et al., 2015).

**IS THERE A THIN LINE BETWEEN GENIUS AND MADNESS?** Many creative individuals, including the famed novelist Ernest Hemingway (pictured here) and the artist Vincent van Gogh, suffered from mood disorders. Whatever the links between creativity and mood disorders may be, we should bear in mind that the great majority of creative writers and artists did not suffer from serious mood disturbances.

Many writers draw attention to possible links between mood disorders, especially bipolar disorder, and creativity (e.g., Kyaga, 2015; Johnson et al., 2011; Power et al., 2015). Many distinguished writers, artists, and composers seem to have suffered from major depression or bipolar disorder. The list of luminaries who suffered from mood disorders stretches from artists Michelangelo and Vincent van Gogh to composers William Schumann and Peter Tchaikovsky to novelists Virginia Woolf and Ernest Hemingway and to poets Alfred Lord Tennyson, Emily Dickinson, Walt Whitman, and Sylvia Plath.

Links between creativity and psychological disorders remain unexplained. One possible connection is that some people with bipolar disorders channel the seemingly boundless energy and rapid stream of thoughts associated with mania into creative expressions. However, we should recognize that the vast majority of writers and artists did not suffer from serious mood disorders and that creativity does not typically spring from psychological disturbance. Moreover, not all studies find links between psychological disorders and creativity, so it's best to withhold judgment on how closely the two may be linked (Bailey, 2003).

MANIC EPISODE A **manic episode** typically begins abruptly, gathering force within days. A hallmark feature of a manic episode, as well as a hypomanic episode, is increased activity or energy (American Psychiatric Association, 2013). A person may seem to be on overdrive and to have boundless energy. The basic difference between a full manic episode and a hypomanic episode is one of degree or severity. During a manic episode, a person experiences a sudden elevation or expansion of mood and feels unusually cheerful, euphoric, or optimistic. That person may become extremely sociable, although perhaps to the point of becoming overly demanding and overbearing toward others. Other people recognize the sudden shift in mood to be excessive in light of the person's life situation. It is one thing to feel elated if one has just won the state lottery. It is another to feel euphoric because it's Wednesday. Here, a young man with bipolar disorder who dubbed himself "Electroboy" describes what a manic episode is like for him (Behrman, 2002).

"I" Electroboy

Manic depression is about flying from Zurich to the Bahamas and back to Zurich in three days to balance the hot and cold weather (my "sweet and sour" theory of bipolar disorder), carrying $20,000 in $100 bills in your shoes into the country on your way back to Tokyo, and picking out the person sitting six seats away at the bar to have sex with only because he or she happens to be sitting there. Most days I need to be as manic as possible to come as close as I can to destruction, to get a real good high—a $25,000 shopping spree, a four-day drug binge, or a trip around the world. Other days a simple high from a shoplifting excursion at Duane Reade for a toothbrush or a bottle of Tylenol is enough. I'll admit it: There's a great deal of pleasure to mental illness, especially to the mania associated with manic depression. It's an emotional state similar to Oz, full of excitement, color, noise, and speed—an overload of sensory stimulation—whereas the sane state of Kansas is plain and simple, black and white, boring and flat.

Mania is about desperately seeking to live life at a more passionate level, taking second and sometimes third helpings on food, alcohol, drugs, sex, and money, trying to live a whole life in one day. Pure mania is as close to death as I think I have ever come. The euphoria is both pleasurable and frightening. My manic mind teems with rapidly changing ideas and needs; my head is cluttered with vibrant colors, wild images, bizarre thoughts, sharp details, secret codes, symbols, and foreign languages. I want to devour everything—parties, people, magazines, books, music, art, movies, and television.

**SOURCE:** *From Electroboy by Andy Behrman*

People in a manic episode tend to show poor judgment and to be argumentative, sometimes going so far as to destroy property. Roommates may find them abrasive and keep a distance from them. They may become extremely generous and make large charitable contributions they can ill afford or give away costly possessions.

People in a manic episode tend to speak very rapidly (with *pressured speech*). Their thoughts and speech may jump from topic to topic in a rapid *flight of ideas*. Others find it difficult to get a word in edgewise. They typically experience an inflated sense of self-esteem that may range from extreme self-confidence to wholesale delusions of grandeur (Schulze et al., 2005). They may feel capable of solving the world's problems or of composing symphonies, despite a lack of any special knowledge or talent. They may spout off about matters of which they know little, such as how to eliminate world hunger or create a new world order. It soon becomes clear that they are disorganized and incapable of completing their projects. They also become highly distractible. Their attention is easily diverted by irrelevant stimuli, like the sounds of a ticking clock or people talking in the next room. They tend to take on multiple tasks, more than they can handle. They may suddenly quit their jobs to enroll in law school, wait tables at night, organize charity drives on weekends, and work on the great American novel in their "spare time." They may not be able to sit still and almost always show decreased need for sleep. They tend to awaken early yet feel well rested and full of energy. They sometimes go for days without sleep but without feeling tired. Although they may have abundant stores of energy, they seem unable to organize their efforts constructively. Their elation impairs their ability to work and to maintain normal relationships.

People in manic episodes fail to weigh the consequences of their actions. They may get into trouble as a result of lavish spending, reckless driving, or sexual escapades. In severe cases, they may experience hallucinations or become grossly delusional—believing, for example, that they have a special relationship with God.

**FELIZIANO: LIVING WITH BIPOLAR DISORDER**

## Cyclothymic Disorder

**7.5 Describe the key features of cyclothymic disorder.**

*Cyclothymia* is derived from the Greek *kyklos*, which means *circle*, and *thymos*, meaning *spirit*. The notion of a circular-moving spirit is an apt description, because this disorder represents a chronic cyclical pattern of mood disturbance characterized by mild mood swings lasting at least two years (one year for children and adolescents).

**Cyclothymic disorder** (also called *cyclothymia*) usually begins in late adolescence or early adulthood and persists for years. For people with this disorder, few, if any, periods of normal mood last for more than a month or two. However, the periods of elevated or depressed mood are not severe enough to warrant a diagnosis of bipolar disorder. Although reported prevalence rates of cyclothymic disorder range from about 0.4% to 1.0%, it tends to be underdiagnosed in clinical practice (American Psychiatric Association, 2013).

During a period of at least two years, the adult with cyclothymia has numerous periods of hypomanic symptoms that are not severe enough to meet the criteria for a hypomanic episode and numerous periods of mild depressive symptoms that do not measure up to a major depressive episode (American Psychiatric Association, 2013). In effect, the person fluctuates between periods of mildly high "highs" and mildly low "lows." When they are "up," people with cyclothymic disorder show elevated activity levels, which they direct toward accomplishing various professional or personal projects—and when their moods reverse, they may leave their projects unfinished. Then, they enter a mildly depressed mood state and feel lethargic and depressed, but not to the extent typical of a major depressive episode. Social relationships may become strained by shifting moods, and work may suffer. Sexual interest waxes and wanes with the person's moods.

The boundaries between bipolar disorder and cyclothymic disorder are not clearly established. Some forms of cyclothymic disorder may represent a mild, early type of bipolar disorder. Although cyclothymia is milder than bipolar disorder, it can significantly impair a person's daily functioning (Van Meter, Youngstrom, & Findling, 2012). Estimates are that about one in three people with cyclothymic disorder eventually go on to develop bipolar disorder (U.S. Department of Health and Human Services, 1999). Clinicians presently lack the ability to distinguish those with cyclothymia who are likely to develop bipolar disorder. The following case presents an example of the mild mood swings that typify cyclothymic disorder.

## "Good Times and Bad Times":

### A CASE OF CYCLOTHYMIC DISORDER

A 29-year-old car salesman reports that since the age of 14 he has experienced alternating periods of "good times and bad times." During his "bad" periods, which generally last between four and seven days, he sleeps excessively and feels a lack of confidence, energy, and motivation, as if he were "just vegetating." Then, his moods abruptly shift for a period of three or four days, usually upon awakening in the morning, and he feels aflush with confidence and sharpened mental ability. During these "good periods," he engages in promiscuous sex and uses alcohol, in part to enhance his good feelings and in part to help him sleep at night. The good periods may last upwards of 7 to 10 days at times, before shifting back into the bad periods, generally following a hostile or irritable outburst.

**SOURCE:** *Adapted from Spitzer et.al., 1994, pp. 155–157*

# Causal Factors in Mood Disorders

Depressive disorders are best understood in terms of complex interactions of biological and psychosocial influences. Although a full understanding of the causes of depressive and bipolar disorders presently lies beyond our grasp, researchers have begun to identify many of the important contributors to these disorders. In the next sections, we examine contemporary understandings of the causal factors in both depressive disorders and bipolar disorders. Many factors are implicated in the development of these disorders, including stressful life events and biological factors.

## Stress and Depression

**7.6 Evaluate the role of stress in depression.**

Stressful life events increase the risk of mood disorders such as bipolar disorder and major depression (Hammen, 2015; Kendler & Gardner, 2010; Koenders et al., 2014). Most people with major depression—perhaps as many as 80%—report experiencing a major source of life stress prior to the onset of the disorder (Monroe & Reid, 2009). Sources of life stress linked to depression include the loss of a loved one, breakup of a romantic relationship, prolonged unemployment and economic hardship, serious physical illness, marital or relationship problems, separation or divorce, exposure to racism and discrimination, and living in unsafe, distressed neighborhoods (e.g., Kõlves, Ide, & De Leo, 2010; National Center for Health Statistics, 2012b).

Any significant loss can lead to depression (American Psychiatric Association, 2013). The *DSM-5* considers grief to be an expectable response to a significant loss, but not a mental disorder. However, it recognizes that grief and depression may occur together after a loss and that some extreme or severe grief reactions (such as in the case of suicidal thinking or difficulty functioning) may indicate the presence of a major depressive disorder. However, it remains unclear whether practitioners will be able to distinguish between a normal or expectable grief reaction and a depressive disorder layered over the pain of grief in a bereaved individual.

A recent study suggests that stress associated with interpersonal problems with friends, family members, and romantic partners contributes to depression in young people, but only among those who tend to think negatively (Carter & Garber, 2011). This reminds us of the need to take multiple factors and their interactions into account—in this case, negative thinking and stress—in understanding causal pathways leading to mental disorders such as depression. For reasons that remain unclear, stressful life events are more closely connected to a first episode of major depression than to later episodes (Monroe et al., 2007; Stroud, Davila, & Moyer, 2008).

The relationship between stress and depression cuts both ways: Stressful life events may contribute to depression, whereas depressive symptoms may be stressful in themselves or lead to other sources of stress, such as divorce or loss of employment (Liu & Alloy, 2010; Uliaszek et al., 2012). For example, if you become depressed, you may find it more difficult to keep up with your work, which can lead to more stress as work backs up. Consider too that stress associated with unemployment and financial hardship may lead to depression, but depression may also lead to unemployment and lower income (Whooley et al., 2002).

Although stress is often implicated in depression, not everyone who encounters stress becomes clinically depressed. Factors such as coping skills, genetic endowment, and availability of social support may lessen the likelihood of depression in the face of stressful events. We also need to take into account gene–environment interactions in depression and suicidal behavior (Monroe & Reid, 2008; Shinozaki et al., 2013). Consistent with the *diathesis-stress model* outlined in Chapter 2, people who possess variants of certain genes may be more susceptible to developing depression if they have a history of severely stressful life experiences, such as maltreatment during childhood (Fisher et al., 2013).

**"GOTTA HAVE FRIENDS."** Social support from friends and family members appears to buffer the effects of stress and may reduce the risk of depression. People who lack important relationships and who rarely join in social activities are more likely to suffer from depression.

We need to consider further the role of early life experiences. A lack of secure attachments to parents during infancy or childhood may also contribute to greater vulnerability to depression in later life following disappointment, failure, or other stressful life events (Morley & Moran, 2011). Adverse experiences early in life, such as parental divorce or physical abuse, are also linked to greater vulnerability to depression in adulthood (Wainwright & Surtees, 2002).

Some psychosocial factors may act as buffers against stress, providing a cushion against depression. A strong marital relationship, for instance, may be a source of support during times of stress. Not surprisingly, divorced or separated people, who lack a supportive marital relationship, show higher rates of depression and suicide attempts than do married people (Weissman et al., 1991). People who live alone, and may thus have more limited social support available, also face a greater risk of depression (Pulkki-Raback et al., 2012).

## Psychodynamic Theories

**7.7 Describe psychodynamic models of depression.**

The classic psychodynamic theory of depression proposed by Freud (1917/1957) and his adherents (e.g., Abraham, 1916/1948) holds that depression represents anger directed inward rather than against significant others. Anger may become directed against the self following either the actual or the threatened loss of these important others.

Freud believed that mourning, or normal bereavement, is a healthy process by which one eventually comes to separate oneself psychologically from a person who has been lost through death, separation, divorce, or another reason. Pathological mourning, however, does not promote healthy separation. Rather, it fosters lingering depression. Pathological mourning is likely to occur in people who hold powerful ambivalent feelings—a combination of positive (love) and negative (anger, hostility) feelings—toward the person who has departed or whose departure is feared. Freud theorized that when people lose, or even fear losing, an important figure about whom they feel ambivalent, their feelings of anger turn to rage. Yet rage triggers guilt, which in turn prevents a person from venting anger directly at the lost person (called an *object*).

To preserve a psychological connection to the lost object, people *introject*, or bring inward, a mental representation of the object. They thus incorporate the other person into the self. Now, anger is turned inward, against the part of the self that represents the inward representation of the lost person. This produces self-hatred, which in turn leads to depression.

From the psychodynamic viewpoint, bipolar disorder represents shifting dominance of the individual's personality between the ego and superego. In the depressive phase, the superego is dominant, producing exaggerated notions of wrongdoing and flooding an individual with feelings of guilt and worthlessness. After a time, the ego rebounds and asserts supremacy, producing feelings of elation and self-confidence that characterize the manic phase. The excessive display of ego eventually triggers a return of guilt, once again plunging an individual into depression.

**LOSS AND DEPRESSION.** Psychodynamic theorists focus on the important role of loss in the development of depression.

Although they emphasize the importance of loss, more recent psychodynamic models shift the focus toward an individual's sense of self-worth or self-esteem. One model, called the *self-focusing model*, considers how people allocate their attentional processes after a loss, such as the death of a loved one or a personal failure or significant disappointment (Pyszczynski & Greenberg, 1987). In this view, depressed people have difficulty thinking about anything other than themselves and the loss they experienced.

Consider a person who must cope with the termination of a failed romantic relationship. The depression-prone individual becomes wrapped up in thinking about the relationship and hopes of restoring it, rather than recognizing the futility of the effort and getting on with life. Moreover, the lost partner was a source of emotional support on whom the depression-prone individual had relied to maintain self-esteem. Following the loss, the depression-prone individual feels stripped of hope and optimism because these positive feelings had depended on the lost object. The loss of self-esteem and of feelings of security, not the loss of the relationship per se, precipitates depression. Similarly, loss of a specific occupational goal may trigger self-focusing and consequent depression. Only by surrendering the object or lost goal and fostering alternate sources of identity and self-worth can the cycle be broken.

**RESEARCH EVIDENCE** Psychodynamic theorists focus on the role of loss in depression. Evidence shows loss of significant others (through death or divorce, for example) to be associated with increased risk of depression (Kendler et al., 2003). Personal losses may also lead to other psychological disorders. There is yet a lack of research to support Freud's view that repressed anger toward the departed loved one is turned inward in depression.

Evidence supports the view that a self-focusing style—an inward or self-absorbed focus of attention—is associated with depression, especially in women (Mor & Winquist, 2002; Muraven, 2005). Yet self-focused attention is not limited to depression and is often found in people with anxiety disorders and other psychological disorders. Thus, the general linkage between self-focused attention and psychopathology may limit the model's value as an explanation of depression.

## Humanistic Theories

### 7.8 Describe the humanistic model of depression.

From the humanistic framework, people become depressed when they cannot imbue their existence with meaning and make authentic choices that lead to self-fulfillment. The world becomes a drab place for them. People's search for meaning gives color and substance to their lives. Guilt may arise when people believe they have not lived up to their potential. Humanistic psychologists challenge us to take a long, hard look at our lives. Are they worthwhile and enriching? Or are they drab and routine? If the latter, perhaps we have frustrated our needs for self-actualization. We may be settling, coasting through life. Settling can give rise to a sense of dreariness that becomes expressed in depressive behavior: lethargy, sullen mood, and withdrawal.

Like psychodynamic theorists, humanistic theorists focus on the loss of self-esteem that can occur when people lose friends or family members or suffer occupational setbacks. We tend to connect our personal identity and sense of self-worth with our social roles as parents, spouses, students, or workers. When these role identities are lost—through the death of a spouse, the departure of children to college, or loss of a job, for example—our sense of purpose and self-worth can be shattered. Depression is a frequent consequence of such losses. It is especially likely when we base our self-esteem on our occupational role or success. Job loss, demotion, and failure to achieve a promotion are common precipitants of depression, especially for individuals who value themselves on the basis of occupational success.

## Learning Theories

### 7.9 Describe learning theory models of depression.

Whereas the psychodynamic perspectives focus on inner, often unconscious, causes, learning theorists emphasize situational factors, such as the loss of positive reinforcement. We perform best when levels of reinforcement are commensurate with our efforts. Changes in the frequency or effectiveness of reinforcement can shift the balance so that life becomes unrewarding.

**THE ROLE OF REINFORCEMENT** Learning theorist Peter Lewinsohn (1974) proposed that depression results from an imbalance between behavior and reinforcement. A lack of

**WORKING OUT TO WORK IT OUT.**
Recent evidence suggests that regular physical activity or exercise may be helpful in combating depression, especially in people facing significant life stressors.

reinforcement for one's efforts can sap motivation and induce feelings of depression. Inactivity and social withdrawal reduce opportunities for reinforcement; lack of reinforcement exacerbates withdrawal.

The low rate of activity typical of depressed individuals may also be a source of secondary reinforcement. Family members and other people may rally around people suffering from depression and release them from their responsibilities. Sympathy may thus become a source of reinforcement that helps maintain depressed behavior.

Reduction in reinforcement levels can occur for many reasons. A person who is recuperating at home from a serious illness or injury may find little that is reinforcing to do. Social reinforcement may plummet when people close to us, who were suppliers of reinforcement, die or leave us. People who suffer social losses are more likely to become depressed when they lack the social skills to form new relationships. Some first-year college students are homesick and depressed because they lack the skills to form rewarding new relationships. Widows and widowers may be at a loss as to how to start a new relationship.

Changes in life circumstances also may alter the balance of effort and reinforcement. A prolonged layoff may reduce financial reinforcement, which in turn may force painful cutbacks in lifestyle. A disability or an extended illness may also impair one's ability to ensure a steady flow of reinforcements. Lewinsohn's model is supported by research findings that connect depression to a low level of positive reinforcement and, importantly, by evidence that encouraging depressed patients to participate in rewarding activities and goal-oriented behaviors can help alleviate depression (Otto, 2006). Encouraging depressed patients to engage in regular physical activity or exercise also helps combat depression, especially in the face of major life stressors (Carneiro et al., 2015; Cecchini-Estrada et al., 2015; Lindwall et al., 2014). Regular physical activity may help prevent depression, which is yet another reason for all of us to get moving (Mammen & Faulkner, 2013). Some clinicians now recommend that regular exercise be included as part of a standard treatment plan for depression (Kerling et al., 2015). **T / F**

## TRUTH *or* FICTION

Physical exercise not only helps tone the body, but also can help combat depression.

☑ TRUE Evidence supports the benefits of regular physical activity or exercise in the treatment of depression.

**INTERACTIONAL THEORY** Problems in interpersonal relationships may help explain the lack of positive reinforcement. Interactional theory, developed by psychologist James Coyne (1976), proposes that the adjustment to living with a depressed person can become so stressful that the person's partner or family member becomes progressively less reinforcing.

Interactional theory is based on the concept of *reciprocal interaction*. Our behavior influences how other people respond to us, and how they respond to us influences how we respond to them in turn. The theory holds that depression-prone people react to stress by seeking or demanding reassurance and support from their partners and significant others (Evraire & Dozois, 2011; Rehman, Gollan, & Mortimer, 2008). At first, this effort to garner support may succeed—but over time, persistent demands for emotional support begin to elicit more anger and annoyance than expressions of support. Although loved ones may keep these negative feelings to themselves, these feelings may surface in subtle ways that spell rejection. Depressed people may react to cues of rejection with deeper feelings of depression and by making greater demands for reassurance, triggering a vicious cycle of further rejection and more profound depression. They may also feel guilty about causing distress in the family, which can exacerbate their negative feelings about themselves.

Family members may find it stressful to adjust to a depressed person's behavior, especially the latter's withdrawal, lethargy, despair, and constant demands for reassurance. Not surprisingly, evidence shows that people with spouses being treated for depression tend to report higher-than-average levels of emotional distress (Benazon, 2000; Kronmüller et al., 2011).

Evidence generally supports Coyne's model that depressed individuals' excessive needs for reassurance lead to rejection by the very people from whom they seek reassurance and support (Rehman, Gollan, & Mortimer, 2008; Starr & Davila, 2008). Lack of social skills may best explain this rejection. Depressed people tend to be unresponsive, uninvolved, and even impolite when they interact with others. For example, they tend to gaze very little at others, take an excessive amount of time to respond, show very little approval or validation of others, and dwell on their problems and negative feelings. They even dwell on negative feelings when interacting with strangers. In effect, they turn other people off, setting the stage for rejection. Yet relationships can work both ways; partners who fail to meet each other's psychological needs or are critical or hurtful toward each other can affect each other's emotional well-being (Ibarra-Rovillard & Kuiper, 2011).

## Cognitive Theories

**7.10 Describe Beck's cognitive model and the learned helplessness model of depression.**

Cognitive theorists relate the origin and maintenance of depression to the ways in which people see themselves and the world around them. One of the most influential cognitive theorists, psychiatrist Aaron Beck (Beck & Alford, 2009; Beck et al., 1979), links the development of depression to the adoption early in life of a negatively biased or distorted way of thinking—the **cognitive triad of depression** (see Table 7.3). The cognitive triad includes negative beliefs about oneself ("I'm no good"), the environment or the world at large ("This school is awful"), and the future ("Nothing will ever turn out right for me"). Cognitive theory holds that people who adopt this negative way of thinking are at greater risk of becoming depressed in the face of stressful or disappointing life experiences, such as getting a poor grade or losing a job.

Beck views these negative concepts of the self and the world as mental templates that are adopted in childhood on the basis of early learning experiences. Children may find that nothing they do is good enough to please their parents or teachers. As a result, they come to regard themselves as basically incompetent and to perceive their future prospects as dim. These beliefs may sensitize them later in life to interpret any failure or disappointment as a reflection of something basically wrong or inadequate about themselves. Even a minor disappointment becomes a crushing blow or a total defeat that can quickly lead to states of depression.

The tendency to magnify the importance of minor failures is an example of an error in thinking that Beck labels a *cognitive distortion*. He believes cognitive distortions set the stage for depression in the face of personal losses or negative life events. A colleague of Beck, psychiatrist David Burns (1980), identified a number of cognitive distortions associated with depression:

1. *All-or-nothing thinking:* Seeing events as either all good or all bad, or as either black or white with no shades of gray. For example, one may perceive a relationship that ended in disappointment as a totally negative experience, despite any positive feelings or experiences that may have occurred along the way. Perfectionism is an example of all-or-nothing thinking. Perfectionists judge any outcome other than perfect success to be complete failure. They may consider a grade of B or even an A– to be

### Table 7.3 The Cognitive Triad of Depression

| | |
|---|---|
| **Negative view of oneself** | Perceiving oneself as worthless, deficient, inadequate, unlovable, and lacking the skills necessary to achieve happiness. |
| **Negative view of the environment** | Perceiving the environment as imposing excessive demands and/or presenting obstacles that are impossible to overcome, leading to continual failure and loss. |
| **Negative view of the future** | Perceiving the future as hopeless and believing that one is powerless to change things for the better. One expects of the future only continuing failure and unrelenting misery and hardship. |

**Note:** According to Aaron Beck, depression-prone people adopt a habitual style of negative thinking—the so-called cognitive triad of depression.

**SOURCE:** Adapted from Beck & Young, 1985; Beck et al., 1979.

**"WHY DO I ALWAYS SCREW UP?"** Cognitive theorists believe a person's self-defeating or distorted interpretations of life events, such as tendencies to blame oneself without considering other factors, can set the stage for depression in the face of disappointing life experiences.

tantamount to an F. Perfectionism is connected both with an increased vulnerability to depression and to poor treatment outcomes (Blatt et al., 1998; Minarik & Ahrens, 1996).

2. *Overgeneralization:* Believing that if a negative event occurs, it is likely to occur again in similar situations in the future. One may interpret a single negative event as foreshadowing an endless series of negative events. For example, receiving a letter of rejection from a potential employer leads one to assume that all other job applications will be similarly rejected.
3. *Mental filter:* Focusing only on negative details of events, thereby rejecting the positive features of one's experiences. Like a droplet of ink that spreads to discolor an entire beaker of water, focusing only on a single negative detail can darken one's vision of reality. Beck called this cognitive distortion *selective abstraction*, meaning the individual selectively abstracts the negative details from events and ignores the events' positive features. One thus bases one's self-esteem on perceived weaknesses and failures rather than on positive features or on a balance of accomplishments and shortcomings. For example, a person receives a job evaluation that contains both positive and negative comments, but focuses only on the negative ones.
4. *Disqualifying the positive:* The tendency to snatch defeat from the jaws of victory by neutralizing or denying one's accomplishments. An example is dismissing congratulations for a job well done by thinking and saying, "Oh, it's no big deal. Anyone could have done it." As a matter of fact, taking credit where credit is due may help people overcome depression by increasing their belief that they can make changes that will lead to a positive future.
5. *Jumping to conclusions:* Forming a negative interpretation of events, despite a lack of evidence. Two examples of this style of thinking are mind reading and the fortune teller error. In *mind reading*, a person arbitrarily jumps to the conclusion that others don't like or respect him or her, as in interpreting a friend's not calling for a while as a rejection. The *fortune teller error* is the prediction that something bad is always about to happen. A person believes the prediction of calamity is factually based, even though there is no evidence to support it. For example, a person concludes that a passing tightness in the chest *must* be a sign of heart disease, discounting the possibility of more benign causes.
6. *Magnification and minimization:* The tendency to make mountains out of molehills. Also called *catastrophizing*, this type of distortion refers to exaggeration of the importance of negative events, personal flaws, fears, or mistakes. Minimization is the mirror image, a type of cognitive distortion in which one minimizes or underestimates one's good points.
7. *Emotional reasoning:* Basing reasoning on emotions. A person with this distortion thinks, for example, "If I feel guilty, it must be because I've done something really wrong." One interprets feelings and events on the basis of emotions rather than on fair consideration of evidence.
8. *"Should" statements:* Creating personal imperatives or self-commandments—"shoulds" or "musts." For example, "I *should* always get my first serve in!" or "I *must* make Chris like me!" By creating unrealistic expectations, *musterbation*—the label given to this form of thinking by Albert Ellis—can lead one to become depressed when one falls short.
9. *Labeling and mislabeling:* Explaining behavior by attaching negative labels to oneself and others. Students may explain a poor grade on a test by thinking they were "lazy" or "stupid" rather than simply unprepared for the specific exam—or, perhaps, ill. Labeling other people as "stupid" or "insensitive" can engender hostility toward them. Mislabeling involves the use of labels that are emotionally charged and inaccurate, such as calling oneself a "pig" because of a minor deviation from one's usual diet.
10. *Personalization:* Assuming that one is responsible for other people's problems and behavior. For example, an individual may feel blame if his or her partner or spouse is crying, rather than recognizing that other causes may be involved.

Consider the errors in thinking illustrated in the following case example.

## Christie's Errors in Thinking:

### A CASE OF COGNITIVE DISTORTION

Christie was a 33-year-old real estate sales agent who suffered from frequent episodes of depression. Whenever a deal fell through, she would blame herself: "If only I had worked harder, negotiated better, talked more persuasively, the deal would have been done." After several successive disappointments, each one followed by self-recriminations, she felt like quitting altogether. Her thinking became increasingly dominated by negative thoughts, which further depressed her mood and lowered her self-esteem: "I'm a loser; I'll never succeed; it's all my fault; I'm no good, and I'm never going to succeed at anything."

Christie's thinking included cognitive errors such as the following: (1) personalization (believing herself to be the sole cause of negative events); (2) labeling and mislabeling (labeling herself to be a loser); (3) overgeneralization (predicting a dismal future on the basis of a present disappointment); and (4) applying a mental filter (judging her personality entirely on the basis of her disappointments). In therapy, Christie learned to think more realistically about events and not to jump to conclusions that she was automatically at fault whenever a deal fell through or to judge her whole personality on the basis of disappointments or perceived flaws in herself. In place of this self-defeating style of thinking, she began to think more realistically when disappointments occurred, like telling herself, "Okay, I'm disappointed. I'm frustrated. I feel lousy. So what? It doesn't mean I'll never succeed. Let me discover what went wrong and try to correct it the next time. I have to look ahead, not dwell on disappointments in the past."

*From the Author's Files*

Distorted thinking tends to occur automatically, as if the thoughts just popped into one's head. Automatic thoughts are likely to be accepted as statements of fact rather than as opinions or habitual ways of interpreting events. Distorted thinking is not limited to particular cultures. Chinese researchers recently reported that among adolescents in Hunan Province, having a negative cognitive style (i.e., high levels of dysfunctional negative thinking) predicts greater depressive symptoms following negative life experiences (Abela et al., 2011).

Beck and his colleagues formulated a **cognitive-specificity hypothesis**, which proposes that different disorders are characterized by different types of automatic thoughts. Beck and his colleagues found some interesting differences in the types of automatic thoughts in people with depressive and anxiety disorders (Beck et al., 1987; see Table 7.4). People with diagnosable depression more often reported automatic thoughts concerning themes of loss, self-deprecation, and pessimism. People with anxiety disorders more often reported automatic thoughts concerning physical danger and other threats.

Research studies provide support for Beck's model of depression by finding that depressed patients tend to show more distorted or dysfunctional thinking than nondepressed controls (e.g., Beevers, Wells, & Miller, 2007; Carson, Hollon, & Shelton, 2010). People with bipolar disorder also tend to show higher levels of negative, dysfunctional thinking than nonpatient controls (Goldberg et al., 2008).

Other evidence supports the basic tenets of the cognitive-specificity hypothesis: that certain types of negative thoughts—those relating to themes of loss and failure—are strongly associated with depression, whereas negative thoughts relating to social threats of rejection or criticism are more strongly tied to anxiety symptoms (Schniering & Rapee, 2004). Depressed patients tend to feel inadequate and to blame themselves for their failures (Zahn et al., 2015).

However, investigators need to consider causal linkages. Although dysfunctional cognitions (negative, distorted, or pessimistic thoughts) tend to be more common among people who are depressed, underlying causal pathways remain unclear. Negative or distorted thinking may cause depression, or depression may cause negative, distorted thinking. Some evidence actually points to depression causing negative thinking rather than the reverse (LaGrange et al., 2011). However, other research suggests that distorted, negative thinking often precedes emotional distress and may indeed play a causal role in its development (Baer et al., 2012). Clearly, more research is needed to disentangle causes and effects.

## Table 7.4 Automatic Thoughts Associated with Depression and Anxiety

| Common Automatic Thoughts Associated with Depression | Common Automatic Thoughts Associated with Anxiety |
|---|---|
| 1. I'm worthless. | 1. What if I get sick and become an invalid? |
| 2. I'm not worthy of other people's attention or affection. | 2. I am going to be injured. |
| 3. I'll never be as good as other people are. | 3. What if no one reaches me in time to help? |
| 4. I'm a social failure. | 4. I might be trapped. |
| 5. I don't deserve to be loved. | 5. I am not a healthy person. |
| 6. People don't respect me anymore. | 6. I'm going to have an accident. |
| 7. I will never overcome my problems. | 7. Something will happen that will ruin my appearance. |
| 8. I've lost the only friends I've had. | 8. I am going to have a heart attack. |
| 9. Life isn't worth living. | 9. Something awful is going to happen. |
| 10. I'm worse off than they are. | 10. Something will happen to someone I care about. |
| 11. There's no one left to help me. | 11. I'm losing my mind. |
| 12. No one cares whether I live or die. | |
| 13. Nothing ever works out for me anymore. | |
| 14. I have become physically unattractive. | |

**SOURCE:** Adapted from Beck & Young, 1985; Beck et al., 1979.

We should also recognize that causal linkages may work both ways. In other words, thoughts may affect moods, and moods may affect thoughts. For example, depressed mood may induce negative, distorted thinking. The more negative and distorted depressed individuals' thinking becomes, the more depressed those individuals may feel, and the more depressed they feel, the more dysfunctional their thinking becomes. However, it is equally possible that dysfunctional thinking comes first in the cycle, perhaps in response to a disappointing life experience, which then leads to a downcast mood. This in turn may accentuate negative thinking, and so on. Investigators are still faced with the old "chicken or egg" dilemma of determining which comes first in the causal sequence: distorted thinking or depressed mood. In all likelihood, distorted cognitions and negative moods interact in the complex web of factors leading to depression.

**LEARNED HELPLESSNESS (ATTRIBUTIONAL) THEORY** The **learned helplessness** model proposes that people may become depressed because they learn to view themselves as helpless to change their lives for the better. The originator of the learned helplessness concept, Martin Seligman (1973, 1975), suggests that people learn to perceive themselves as helpless because of their experiences. The learned helplessness model therefore straddles the behavioral and the cognitive: Situational factors foster attitudes that lead to depression.

Seligman and his colleagues based the learned helplessness model on early laboratory studies of animals. In these studies, dogs exposed to an inescapable electric shock showed the *learned helplessness effect* by failing to learn to escape when escape became possible (Overmier & Seligman, 1967; Seligman & Maier, 1967). Exposure to uncontrollable forces apparently taught the animals that they were helpless to change the situation (Forgeard et al., 2012). Animals that developed learned helplessness showed behaviors similar to those of depressed people, including lethargy, lack of motivation, and difficulty acquiring new skills (Maier & Seligman, 1976).

Seligman (1975, 1991) proposed that some forms of depression in humans might result from exposure to apparently uncontrollable situations. Such experiences can instill the expectation that future outcomes are beyond one's ability to control ("Why try? I'll only wind up failing again"). A cruel, vicious cycle may come into play in cases of depression. A few failures may produce feelings of helplessness and expectations of further failure. Perhaps you know people who have failed certain subjects, such as mathematics. They may come to believe themselves incapable of succeeding in math. They may thus decide that studying for the quantitative section of the Graduate Record Exam is a waste of time. They then perform poorly, completing the self-fulfilling prophecy, which further intensifies feelings of helplessness, leading to lowered expectations, and so on, in a vicious cycle.

Although it stimulated much interest, Seligman's model failed to account for the low self-esteem typical of people who are depressed, and neither did it explain why depression persists in some people but not in others. Seligman and his colleagues (Abramson, Seligman, & Teasdale, 1978) offered a reformulation of the theory to meet such shortcomings. The revised theory held that perception of lack of control over future rewards or reinforcers did not by itself explain the persistence and severity of depression. It was also necessary to consider cognitive factors, especially ways in which people explain their failures and disappointments to themselves.

Seligman and his colleagues recast helplessness theory in terms of the social psychology concept of *attributional style*. An attributional style is a personal style of explanation. When disappointments or failures occur, we may explain them in various characteristic ways. We may blame ourselves (an internal attribution), or we may blame the circumstances we face (an external attribution). We may see bad experiences as typical events (a stable attribution) or as isolated events (an unstable attribution). We may see them as evidence of broader problems (a global attribution) or as evidence of precise and limited shortcomings (a specific attribution). The reformulated helplessness theory holds that people who explain the causes of negative events (such as failure in work, school, or romantic relationships) according to the following three types of attributions are most vulnerable to depression:

1. *Internal factors*, beliefs that failures reflect their personal inadequacies, rather than external factors, or beliefs that failures are caused by environmental factors
2. *Global factors*, beliefs that failures reflect sweeping flaws in personality, rather than specific factors, or beliefs that failures reflect limited areas of functioning
3. *Stable factors*, beliefs that failures reflect fixed personality factors, rather than unstable factors, or beliefs that the factors leading to failures are changeable

Let's illustrate this attributional style with the example of a college student who goes on a disastrous date. Afterward, he shakes his head in wonder and tries to make sense of his experience. An internal attribution for the calamity is characterized by self-blame, as in, "I really messed it up." An external attribution would place the blame elsewhere, as in, "Some couples just don't hit it off," or "She must have been in a bad mood." A stable attribution would suggest a problem that cannot be changed, as in, "It's my personality." An unstable attribution, on the other hand, would suggest a transient condition, as in, "It was probably the head cold." A global attribution for failure magnifies the extent of the problem, as in, "I really have no idea what I'm doing when I'm with people." A specific attribution, in contrast, chops the problem down to size, as in, "My problem is how to make small talk to get a relationship going."

The revised theory holds that each attributional dimension makes a specific contribution to feelings of helplessness. Internal attributions for negative events are linked to lower self-esteem. Stable attributions help explain the persistence—or, in medical terms, the *chronicity*—of helplessness cognitions. Global attributions are associated with the pervasiveness (generality) of feelings of helplessness following negative events. The adoption of a negative attributional style (i.e., attributing negative life events to internal, stable, and global factors) is a recognized risk factor not only for depression but also for anxiety disorders (Hamilton et al., 2015; Safford, 2008).

## Biological Factors

### 7.11 Identify biological factors in depression.

A large and growing body of evidence points to important roles for biological factors, especially genetics and neurotransmitter functioning, in the development of depressive disorders.

**"IS IT ME?"** According to reformulated helplessness theory, the kinds of attributions we make concerning negative events can make us more or less vulnerable to depression. Responding to the breakup of a relationship by internalizing ("It's me"), globalizing ("I'm totally worthless"), and stabilizing ("Things are always going to turn out badly for me") can lead to depression.

**GENETIC FACTORS** Genetic factors play a significant role in determining risk of developing mood disorders, including major depression and especially bipolar disorder (e.g., Duffy et al., 2014; Duric et al., 2010; Malhotra et al., 2011; Nes et al., 2012). Researchers are making progress in drilling down to particular genes linked to mood disorders (e.g., Zhang et al., 2014; Zhao et al., 2014).

An emerging model in the field focuses on interactions of genetic and environmental factors in major depression and other mood disorders (Jokela et al., 2007). Underscoring the importance of interactions between biological and psychosocial factors, investigators find that variations of particular genes involved in regulating serotonin are linked to greater risk of depression in the face of life stress (Karg et al., 2011). Serotonin is the neurotransmitter targeted by antidepressants such as Prozac and Zoloft, so it is not surprising that it may play a role in proneness to depression.

What we have come to understand is that the effects of life stressors on the development of depression are greater in people at high genetic risk (Lau & Eley, 2010). Developing a better understanding of the role that particular genes play in depression may lead to the use of gene therapy in treating depression by means of directly influencing the functioning of targeted genes (Alexander et al., 2010).

Let's look more closely at evidence supporting the role of genetic factors in major depression. Not only does major depression tend to run in families, but the closer the genetic relationship people share, the more likely they are to share a depressive disorder. Yet families share environmental as well as genetic similarities. To tease out the effects of genetic factors, investigators have turned to studies of twins. They examine the relative percentages of cases in which MZ, or identical, twins share a common trait or disorder, as compared with DZ, or fraternal, twins. The percentage of cases in which the twin of a person who is identified as having a given trait or disorder also has the trait or disorder is called the concordance (agreement) rate. As discussed in Chapter 1, because MZ twins have 100% of genes in common, as compared with the 50% among DZ twins, evidence of a higher concordance rate among MZ twins provides strong support for a genetic contribution.

Ground-breaking research along these lines showed more than double the concordance rate for major depression among MZ twins than among DZ twins (Kendler et al., 1993). This evidence provided strong support for a genetic component, but it was well short of the 100% concordance one would expect if genetics were solely responsible for these disorders. Although heredity appears to play an important role in major depression, it isn't the only determinant and may not even be the most important determinant. Environmental factors, as well as the interactions of genetic and environmental influences, may be even more important contributors to the development of major depression.

Before going further, we should note that different psychological disorders may share common genetic links. A breakthrough study reported in 2013 showed that five separate disorders—major depression, bipolar disorder, schizophrenia, autism, and attention-deficit/hyperactivity disorder—all share certain genetic variations in common (Cross-Disorder Group of the Psychiatric Genomics Consortium, 2013). Two people may share the same genetic risk factor but develop very different disorders depending on their particular life experiences or other factors (Kolata, 2013). Developing a better understanding of the common genetic risk factors that cut across various psychological disorders may lead to new ways of classifying disorders that take into account underlying genetic patterns as well as differences in symptom presentation.

**BIOCHEMICAL FACTORS AND BRAIN ABNORMALITIES** Research on the biological underpinnings of mood disorders has largely focused on abnormalities in neurotransmitter activity in the brain. Early research more than 50 years ago showed that drugs we now call *antidepressants*, which increase levels of the neurotransmitters serotonin and norepinephrine in the brain, often helped relieve depression.

Might the lack of certain neurotransmitters in the brain cause depression? Investigators discount this view, in part because antidepressants boost levels of neurotransmitters in the brain within a few days or even a few hours of use, but it usually takes weeks or months before therapeutic effects are achieved (Cryan & O'Leary, 2010; Shive, 2015). Also, evidence fails to show a lack of serotonin or norepinephrine in people with major depression (Belmaker & Agam, 2008). Consequently, it is unlikely that depression is caused by a mere deficiency in serotonin or that antidepressants work simply by boosting levels of neurotransmitters in the brain.

More complex views of the role of neurotransmitters in depression are emerging. Among the intriguing possibilities is that depression may involve irregularities in the numbers of receptors on receiving neurons where neurotransmitters dock (having too many or too few), abnormalities in the sensitivity of these receptors to particular neurotransmitters, or irregularities in how these chemicals bind to receptors (Oquendo et al., 2007; Sharp, 2006). It is conceivable that antidepressants work to relieve depression by altering the number or density of these receptors or their sensitivity to neurotransmitters, a process that takes time to unfold (hence the several weeks' lag time before the effects of antidepressants occur). Although irregularities in how serotonin is used in the brain appear to be linked to depression (Carver, Johnson, & Joormann, 2008, 2009), we don't yet have a final answer about the exact role that serotonin and other neurotransmitters play in depression or about the mechanisms that might explain the therapeutic effects of antidepressants.

Another avenue of research explores the biological underpinnings of mood disorders by focusing on abnormalities in the brain. Brain-imaging studies show reduced

## A CLOSER Look

### BRAIN INFLAMMATION, A POSSIBLE PATHWAY IN MOOD DISORDERS

An intriguing possibility drawing attention of researchers today is that some psychological disorders, including depression, bipolar disorder, and possibly schizophrenia and autism, may at least partly be caused by inflammation in the brain. Inflammation results when the body mobilizes its defenses against infection or injury. You are probably familiar with the signs of inflammation—the redness and swelling—that occur when you suffer an injury. When the body's immune system is overreactive, as in the case of autoimmune diseases such as arthritis and Crohn's disease, chronic states of inflammation may result, taking a toll on the body's joints, gastrointestinal system, and other bodily systems and structures, possibly including the brain.

Might inflammation play a role in psychological disorders such as mood disorders? This field of inquiry is still emerging, but investigators have identified biological markers of inflammation in both depressed and bipolar patients (Barbosa et al., 2014; Friedrich, 2014; Jokela, et al., 2016; Kiecolt-Glaser, Derry, & Fagundes, 2015). One line of inquiry focuses on whether brain inflammation may lead to a loss of ability to experience pleasure (Felger et al., 2015). A lively debate among researchers today focuses on whether inflammation is a causal factor in depression, whether depression causes inflammation, or whether the relationship cuts both ways. Investigations are underway to identify the particular brain pathways that may be susceptible to inflammation and to test anti-inflammatory drugs to see if they might be helpful in treating mood disorders (Ayorech et al., 2015; Kim et al., 2015). Certain dietary nutrients, such as the omega-3 fatty acids found in some types of fish oil, also have anti-inflammatory effects, which may help explain their beneficial effects in treating depression (see *A Closer Look: Something Fishy about This*).

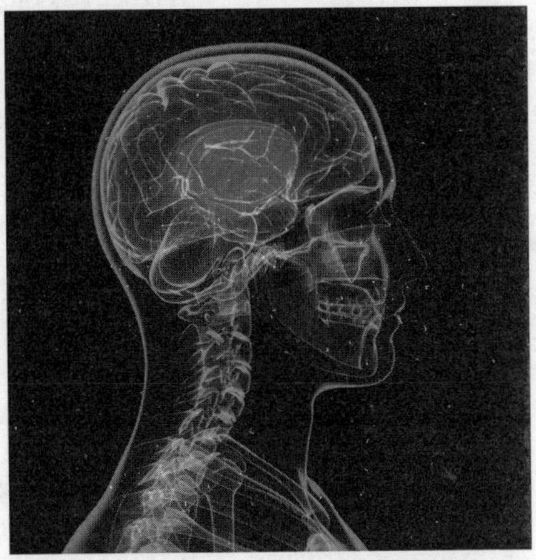

**MIGHT INFLAMMATION IN THE BRAIN BE A CAUSE OF DEPRESSION?** Evidence suggests that inflammation of neural pathways in the brain may be involved in psychological disorders such as mood disorders.

volume (size) and lower rates of metabolic activity in people with mood disorder in areas of the brain involved in regulating thinking processes, mood, and memory, including parts of the prefrontal cortex and the limbic system (e.g., Kaiser et al., 2015; Klauser et al., 2014; Lai & Wu, 2015; Schmaal et al., 2015). The prefrontal cortex, the part of the frontal lobes that lies in front of the motor cortex, is responsible for higher mental functions, such as thinking, problem solving and decision making, and organizing thoughts and behaviors. The neurotransmitters serotonin and norepinephrine play important roles in regulating nerve impulses in the prefrontal cortex, so it is not surprising that evidence points to irregularities in this region of the brain. Parts of the limbic system are involved in processing emotions and forming new memories, including those associated with emotional experiences.

As research using brain-imaging techniques continues, investigators will likely develop a clearer picture of how the brains of people with mood disorders differ from those of healthy individuals and perhaps even discover ways of better diagnosing these disorders and treating them. Other systems in the body, such as the endocrine system, may also play a role in the development of mood disorders in ways that future research may help clarify. As in other complex forms of abnormal behavior, such as anxiety disorders and schizophrenia, the underlying causes of depression in all likelihood involve multiple factors (Belmaker & Agam, 2008).

## Causal Factors in Bipolar Disorders

**7.12 Identify causal factors in bipolar disorders.**

Many investigators believe that multiple causes acting together contribute to the development of bipolar disorders. Brain-imaging studies find evidence of abnormalities in many regions of the brain in bipolar disorder patients, especially areas involved in emotional processing and regulation (Cullen & Lim, 2014; Nenadic et al., 2015; Phillips & Swartz, 2014).

Genetic factors play a major role in bipolar disorder (Hyman, 2011). In a large population-based study in Finland, investigators found the concordance rate to be seven times greater among MZ twins than DZ twins (43% versus 6%, respectively; Kieseppä et al., 2004). Genetics appears to play an even stronger role in bipolar disorder than it does in major depressive disorder (Belmaker & Agam, 2008).

Intriguing findings reported in 2008 from Sweden showed a connection between higher risk of bipolar disorder and greater paternal age at birth, especially father's age 55 and older (Frans et al., 2008). We should note that maternal age was less clearly connected to bipolar disorder in offspring. A possible explanation for the paternal link is that genetic errors tend to be more frequent in the sperm of older men, so it is possible that such defects predispose their offspring to certain psychological disorders, including bipolar disorder.

Investigators are actively tracking down specific genes in bipolar disorder (Lee et al., 2013). However, genes don't tell the whole story. If bipolar disorder were caused entirely by genetics, then an identical twin of someone having the disorder would always develop the disorder, but this isn't the case. Consistent with the diathesis-stress model, stressful life changes and underlying biological influences may interact with a genetic predisposition to increase a person's vulnerability to bipolar disorder. Moreover, investigators have learned that stressful life events can trigger mood episodes in people with bipolar disorder (Miklowitz & Johnson, 2009). Negative life events (e.g., loss of a job, marital conflicts) may precede depressive episodes, whereas both negative and positive life events (e.g., getting a new job) may precede a hypomanic or manic episode (Alloy et al., 2009).

Investigators are also learning more about the role of psychosocial factors in bipolar disorder (Bender & Alloy, 2011). For example, social support from family members and friends can enhance the level of functioning of bipolar patients by providing them with a buffer against negative effects of stress. Moreover, the availability of social support appears to play a role in helping speed recovery from mood episodes and reducing the likelihood of recurrent episodes (Alloy et al., 2005).

# A CLOSER Look

## SOMETHING FISHY ABOUT THIS

You may have heard that high concentrations of certain types of fish oil in the diet, especially those high in omega-3 fatty acids, are linked to lower rates of cardiovascular disease. But did you know that high dietary levels of fish oil are also linked to reduced risk of major depression and bipolar disorder (Rechenberg, 2016; Saunders et al., 2015)? Omega-3 fatty acids are essential nutrients the brain may need to function optimally. Although research in this area is in its infancy, early evidence points to possible therapeutic benefits of omega-3 fatty acids in treating depression (e.g., Lin et al., 2012; Rechenberg, 2016).

Population studies show that people who consume high levels of fish in their diet are less likely to experience depression than people with low levels of fish consumption (Li, Liu, & Zhang, 2015). This evidence is correlational, so we can't say whether eating fish prevents depression or whether people who are less likely to become depressed are also the type of people that like fish. Omega-3 fatty acids found in fish appear to boost serotonin activity in the brain, which may help explain its possible effects on depression (Patrick & Ames, 2015). Omega-3 also has anti-inflammatory effects, which help curb brain inflammation that researchers suspect may play a causal role in mood disorders such as depression and bipolar disorder (Ayorech et al., 2015). We presently lack a sufficient body of research to make any solid claims that omega-3 fatty acids or eating fish can prevent or combat depression, but all of this promising evidence to date justifies continued research on whether these dietary factors are involved in mood disorders (Rechenberg, 2016).

Omega-3 fatty acids are not the only nutrient drawing attention from researchers. *Curcumin*, a component of the spice turmeric that gives mustard and Indian curry their yellow color, may also affect underlying biological processes involved in depression. In a recent research trial, investigators found that curcumin supplements resulted in significantly greater improvement in mood-related symptoms than a placebo control (Lopresti et al., 2014). We should caution that studies on the antidepressant effects of dietary substances are in an early stage of development, so we should withhold judgment on whether nutritional supplements should become part of the therapeutic arsenal used in treating depression or other psychological disorders.

We also have evidence from cross-national studies showing a link between high consumption of seafood, which is rich in omega-3 fatty acids, and low rates of mood disorders (Parker et al., 2006). In one cross-national study, the country consuming the most seafood, Iceland, showed low rates of bipolar disorder, whereas countries with lower levels of seafood consumption, such as Germany, Switzerland, Italy, and Israel, showed higher rates (Noaghiul & Hibbeln, 2003). **T / F**

**GO FISH.** Might fish oil help combat mood disorders? We don't have a definitive answer, but some evidence suggests there may be a value in treating depression to adding certain types of fish oil to the diet, especially those high in omega-3 fatty acids.

### TRUTH or FICTION

High levels of fish oil in the diet are linked to increased risk of bipolar disorder.

☑ FALSE Actually, evidence links high levels of dietary fish oil to lower rates of mood disorders.

We should caution that causal linkages cannot be ascertained from observed relationships between eating fish and lower risks of mood disorders. Nevertheless, these linkages encourage researchers to explore further whether a dietary supplement may indeed live up to its popular billing as good brain food. In the meantime—salmon, anyone?

# Treatment of Mood Disorders

Just as different theoretical perspectives point to many factors that may be involved in the development of mood disorders, these models have spawned different approaches to treatment. Here, we focus on the leading contemporary approaches.

**INTERPERSONAL PSYCHOTHERAPY.** IPT is usually a brief, psychodynamically oriented therapy that focuses on issues in a person's current interpersonal relationships. Like traditional psychodynamic approaches, IPT assumes that early life experiences are key issues in adjustment, but IPT focuses on the present—the here and now.

# Psychological Treatment

**7.13 Describe psychological methods used to treat depression.**

Depressive disorders are typically treated with psychotherapy, in the form of psychodynamic therapy, behavior therapy, or cognitive therapy, or with biomedical treatments, such as antidepressant medication or electroconvulsive therapy (ECT). Sometimes, a combination of treatment approaches works best (Cuijpers et al., 2010, 2011; Maina, Rosso, & Bogetto, 2009). Here, we survey several of the leading psychological approaches to treatment.

**PSYCHODYNAMIC TREATMENT** Traditional psychoanalysis aims to help depressed people understand underlying ambivalent (conflicting) feelings toward important people (objects) in their lives whom they have lost or whose loss was threatened. By working through feelings of anger toward these lost objects, people can turn anger outward—through verbal expression of feelings, for example—rather than leave it to fester and turn inward.

It can take years of traditional psychoanalysis to uncover and deal with unconscious conflicts. Modern psychoanalytic approaches also focus on unconscious conflicts, but they are more direct, relatively brief, and focus on present as well as past conflicted relationships (Rosso, Martini, & Maina, 2012). Some psychodynamic therapists also use behavioral methods to help clients acquire the social skills needed to develop a broader social network. Recent analyses of outcome studies supports the effectiveness of short-term psychodynamic therapy in treating depression (Driessen et al., 2010, 2015).

One psychodynamic treatment model receiving a good deal of research attention is *interpersonal psychotherapy* (IPT). This is a relatively brief therapy (usually lasting no more than 9 to 12 months) that emphasizes the role of interpersonal issues in depression and helps clients make healthy changes in their relationships (Weissman, Markowitz, & Klerman, 2000). IPT has emerged as an effective treatment for major depression and shows promise in treating other psychological disorders, such as dysthymia, bulimia, and posttraumatic stress disorder (Lipsitz & Markowitz, 2013; Markowitz et al., 2015; Rieger et al., 2010; Weissman, 2007). Investigators also find IPT to be effective in treating depressed patients from other parts of the world, including sub-Saharan Africa (Bolton et al., 2003).

Although IPT shares some features with traditional psychodynamic approaches (principally the belief that early life experiences and rigid personality traits affect psychological adjustment), it differs from traditional psychodynamic therapy by focusing on the client's current relationships rather than on unconscious internal conflicts of childhood origin.

IPT helps clients deal with unresolved or delayed grief reactions following the death of a loved one as well as with role conflicts in present relationships. The therapist also helps clients identify areas of conflict in their present relationships, understand underlying issues, and consider ways of resolving them. If the problems in a relationship are beyond repair, the therapist helps the client consider ways of ending the relationship and establishing new ones. Take the case of 31-year-old Sal D., whose depression was associated with marital conflict.

## Sal Feels "Numb":

### A CASE OF DEPRESSION

Sal began to explore his marital problems in the fifth therapy session, becoming tearful as he recounted his difficulty expressing his feelings to his wife because of feelings of being "numb." He felt that he had been "holding on" to his feelings, which was causing him to become estranged from his wife. The next session zeroed in on the similarities between himself and his father—in particular, how he was distancing himself from his wife in a similar way as his father had kept a distance from him. By session 7, a turning point had been reached. Sal expressed how he and his wife had become "emotional" and closer to one another during the previous week and how he was able to talk more openly about his feelings, and how he and his wife had been able to make a joint decision concerning a financial matter that had been worrying them for some time. When later he was laid off from his job, he sought his wife's opinion, rather than picking a fight with her as a way of thrusting his job problems on her. To his surprise, he found that his wife responded positively—not "violently," as he had expected—to times when he expressed his feelings. In his last therapy session (session 12), Sal expressed how therapy had led to a "reawakening" within himself with respect to the feelings he had been keeping to himself—an openness that he hoped to create in his relationship with his wife.

**SOURCE:** *Adapted from Klerman et al., 1984, pp. 111–113*

**BEHAVIOR THERAPY** Behavior therapists generally focus on helping depressed patients develop more effective social or interpersonal skills and increasing their participation in pleasurable or rewarding activities. The most widely used behavioral treatment model, called *behavioral activation*, encourages patients to increase their frequency of rewarding or enjoyable activities (Chartier & Provencher, 2013). Behavioral activation can produce substantial effects in treating depression (Carlbring et al., 2013; Dimidjian et al., 2011; Hunnicutt-Ferguson, Hoxha, & Gollan, 2012). Behavioral approaches are often used along with cognitive therapy in a broader treatment model called *cognitive-behavioral therapy* (CBT; also called *cognitive behavior therapy*), which is perhaps the most widely used psychological treatment for depression today.

**COGNITIVE-BEHAVIORAL THERAPY** Cognitive therapists believe that distorted thinking or cognitive distortions play a key role in the development of depression. Depressed people typically focus on how badly they feel rather than the thoughts that trigger their negative feelings. Aaron Beck and his colleagues (Beck et al., 1979) developed *cognitive therapy*, a leading form of CBT that focuses on helping people recognize and correct dysfunctional thought patterns. Table 7.5 shows some common examples of distorted, automatic thoughts, the types of cognitive distortions they represent, and rational alternative responses that can be used to replace them.

Cognitive therapy, like behavior therapy, is relatively brief, lasting perhaps 14 to 16 weekly sessions. Therapists use a combination of behavioral and cognitive techniques to help clients change negative, dysfunctional thought patterns and develop more adaptive behaviors (Anthes, 2014). For example, they help clients connect thought patterns to negative moods by having them monitor the automatic negative thoughts they experience throughout the day using a thought diary or daily record. Clients note when and where negative thoughts occur and how they feel at the time. Then, the therapist helps the client challenge the negative thoughts and replace them with more adaptive thoughts. The following case example shows how a cognitive therapist works with a client to challenge the validity of thoughts that reflect the cognitive distortion of *selective abstraction* (the tendency to judge oneself entirely on the basis of specific weaknesses or flaws in character). The client judged herself to be totally lacking in self-control because she ate a single piece of candy while she was on a diet.

***COGNITIVE THERAPY FOR DEPRESSION***

CLIENT: I don't have any self-control at all.

THERAPIST: On what basis do you say that?

C: Somebody offered me candy and I couldn't refuse it.

T: Were you eating candy every day?

C: No, I just ate it this once.

T: Did you do anything constructive during the past week to adhere to your diet?

C: Well, I didn't give in to the temptation to buy candy every time I saw it at the store. Also, I did not eat any candy except that one time when it was offered to me and I felt I couldn't refuse it.

T: If you counted up the number of times you controlled yourself versus the number of times you gave in, what ratio would you get?

C: About 100 to 1.

T: So if you controlled yourself 100 times and did not control yourself just once, would that be a sign that you are weak through and through?

C: I guess not—not through and through. [Smiles.].

*Beck et al., 1979, p. 68*

Cognitive-behavioral therapies, including Beck's cognitive therapy, have produced impressive results in treating major depression and reducing risks of recurrent episodes (e.g., Hans & Hiller, 2013; Hollon & Ponniah, 2010; Lutz et al., 2015; Mondin et al., 2015; Rehm, 2010). The benefits of cognitive-behavioral therapy appear comparable to those of antidepressant medication in treating depression, even in treating moderate to severe depression (Beck & Dozois, 2011; Siddique et al., 2012; Weitz et al., 2015).

## Biomedical Treatment

### 7.14 Describe biomedical approaches to treating depression.

The most common biomedical approaches to treating mood disorders are the use of antidepressant drugs and electroconvulsive therapy for depression, and lithium carbonate for bipolar disorder.

**Table 7.5** Cognitive Distortions and Rational Responses

| Automatic Thought | Kind of Cognitive Distortion | Rational Response |
|---|---|---|
| I'm all alone in the world. | All-or-nothing thinking | It may feel like I'm all alone, but there are some people who care about me. |
| Nothing will ever work out for me. | Overgeneralization | No one can look into the future. Concentrate on the present. |
| My looks are hopeless. | Magnification | I may not be perfect looking, but I'm far from hopeless. |
| I'm falling apart. I can't handle this. | Magnification | Sometimes, I just feel overwhelmed—but I've handled things like this before. I'll just take it a step at a time and I'll be okay. |
| I guess I'm just a born loser. | Labeling and mislabeling | Nobody is destined to be a loser. I need to stop talking myself down. |
| I've only lost 8 pounds on this diet. I should just forget it. I can't succeed. | Negative focusing/minimization/ disqualifying the positive/jumping to conclusions/all-or-nothing thinking | Eight pounds is a good start. I didn't gain all this weight overnight, and I have to expect that it will take time to lose it. |
| I know things must really be bad for me to feel this awful. | Emotional reasoning | Feeling something doesn't make it so. If I'm not seeing things clearly, my emotions will be distorted too. |
| I know I'm going to flunk this course. | Fortune teller error | Just focus on getting through this course, not jumping to negative conclusions. |
| I know John's problems are really my fault. | Personalization | I need to stop blaming myself for everyone else's problems. There are many reasons why John's problems have nothing to do with me. |
| Someone my age should be doing better than I am. | Should statements | I need to stop comparing myself to others. All I can expect of myself is to do my best. What good does it do to compare myself to others? It only leads me to get down on myself rather than getting motivated. |
| I just don't have the brains for college. | Labeling and mislabeling | I'll stop calling myself names like "stupid." I can accomplish a lot more than I give myself credit for. |
| Everything is my fault. | Self-blaming | There I go again. I'll stop playing this game of pointing blame at myself. There's enough blame to go around. Better yet, forget placing blame and try to think through how to solve this problem. |
| It would be awful if Sue turns me down. | Magnification | It might be upsetting, but it needn't be awful unless I make it so. |
| If people really knew me, they would hate me. | Mind reader | What evidence is there for that? More people who get to know me like me than don't like me. |
| If something doesn't get better soon, I'll go crazy. | Jumping to conclusions/ magnification | I've dealt with these problems this long without falling apart. I just have to hang in there. Things are not as bad as they seem. |
| I can't believe I have another pimple on my face. This is going to ruin my whole weekend. | Mental filter | Take it easy. A pimple is not the end of the world. It doesn't have to spoil my whole weekend. Other people get pimples and seem to have a good time. |

**SOURCE:** Adapted from Beck et al., 1987.

**ANTIDEPRESSANT DRUGS** The use of antidepressant drugs has skyrocketed in recent years in the United States, so much so that more than 1 in 10 adults is now taking them (Kuehn, 2011a; B. J. Smith, 2012). Antidepressant use has mushroomed nearly 400% since 1988 (Hendrick, 2011). One statistic that seems to pop off the page is that nearly one in four (23%) American women in the 40- to 59-year age range are now taking antidepressants (Mukherjee, 2012). A significant consequence of the rising use of antidepressants is that fewer depressed patients today are receiving psychotherapy as compared to the 1990s (Dubovsky, 2012; Fullerton et al., 2011). Although antidepressants are mostly used to treat depression, they are also employed to combat other psychological disorders, including anxiety disorders (see Chapter 5) and bulimia (see Chapter 9).

Antidepressants increase the availability of certain neurotransmitters in the brain, but they do so in different ways (see Figure 7.5). As noted in Chapter 2, there are four major classes of antidepressant drugs: (1) *tricyclics* (TCAs); (2) *monoamine oxidase* (MAO) *inhibitors*; (3) *selective serotonin-reuptake inhibitors* (SSRIs); and (4) *serotonin–norepinephrine reuptake inhibitors* (SNRIs).

The tricyclics, which include *imipramine* (Tofranil), *amitriptyline* (Elavil), *desipramine* (Norpramin), and *doxepin* (Sinequan), are so named because of their three-ringed molecular structure. They increase brain levels of the neurotransmitters norepinephrine and serotonin by interfering with the process of reuptake (reabsorption by the transmitting cell) of these chemical messengers.

The MAO inhibitors, such as *phenelzine* (Nardil), increase the availability of neurotransmitters by inhibiting the action of monoamine oxidase, an enzyme that normally breaks down or degrades neurotransmitters in the synapse. MAO inhibitors are less widely used than other antidepressants because of potentially serious interactions with certain foods and alcoholic beverages.

**WHAT'S IN IT FOR ME? YOUR BRAIN ON DRUGS**

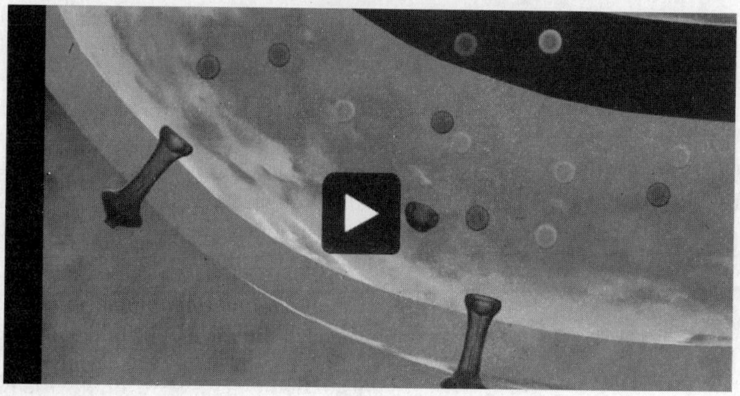

**Figure 7.5 The actions of various types of antidepressants at the synapse.**
Tricyclic antidepressants and selective reuptake inhibitors (SSRIs and NSRIs) increase the availability of neurotransmitters by preventing their reuptake by the presynaptic neuron. MAO inhibitors work by inhibiting the action of monoamine oxidase, an enzyme that normally breaks down neurotransmitters in the synaptic cleft.

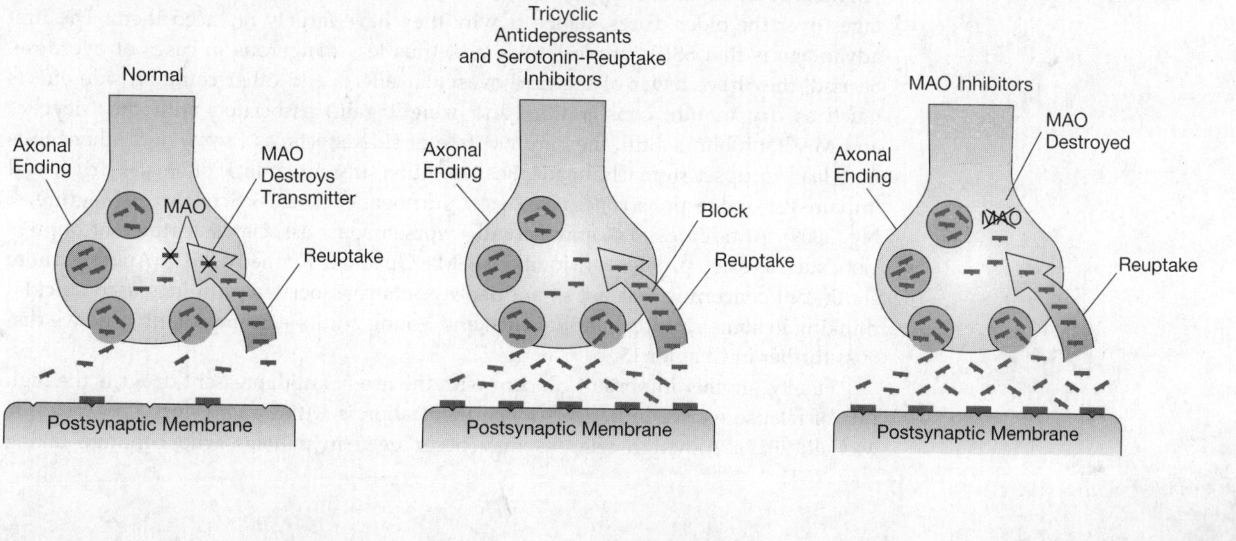

The SSRIs, such as *fluoxetine* (Prozac) and *sertraline* (Zoloft), work in a similar fashion as the TCAs by interfering with reuptake of neurotransmitters, but they have more specific effects on serotonin. The SNRIs, such as *venlafaxine* (Effexor), selectively target reuptake of both norepinephrine and serotonin, which increases levels of these neurotransmitters in the brain.

Investigators understand how antidepressants affect neurotransmitter levels, but, as noted earlier, the underlying mechanisms explaining how they work to relieve depression remains unclear. Potential side effects of tricyclics and MAO inhibitors include dry mouth, a slowing down of motor responses, constipation, blurred vision, sexual dysfunction, and, less frequently, urinary retention, paralytic ileus (a paralysis of the intestines, which impairs the passage of intestinal contents), confusion, delirium, and cardiovascular complications, such as reduced blood pressure. Tricyclics are also highly toxic, which raises the prospect of suicidal overdoses if the drugs are used without close supervision.

Research evidence shows that antidepressants help relieve symptoms of major depression and dysthymia (Imel et al., 2008; Kennedy, Lam et al., 2009; Kennedy, Milev et al., 2009; Mori, Lockwood, & McCall, 2015). However, despite the dramatic effects touted in drug company commercials on television, full symptom relief (remission) in clinical trials typically occurs in only about one in three patients treated with a first round of antidepressants (e.g., Kennedy, Young, & Blier, 2011; McClintock et al., 2011). Many patients continue to experience lingering symptoms such as insomnia, sadness, and problems with concentration. Moreover, investigators find that about two-thirds of the overall effects of antidepressants can be explained by placebo effects (Rief et al., 2009).

When one antidepressant doesn't bring about symptom relief, switching to another one or adding another antidepressant or other psychiatric drug (such as Abilify) may bring about a more favorable response (Casey et al., 2014; Coryell, 2011; Nelson et al., 2010). Among patients in a recent study who failed to respond to one antidepressant, adding cognitive-behavioral therapy together with switching to a different drug was more effective than switching drugs alone (Brent et al., 2008).

The severity of depression also needs to be considered when evaluating the effectiveness of antidepressants. A review of six large-scale randomized controlled studies showed the relative benefits of antidepressants compared to placebos (inert "sugar pills"); they were greater in treating severely depressed people than those with milder depression (Fournier et al., 2010). More recently, however, other investigators reported that antidepressants worked well in treating both milder and more severe depression (Gibbons et al., 2012). More research is needed to clarify whether the benefits of antidepressants depend on a person's level of depression.

Importantly, evidence shows comparable levels of effectiveness among different SSRIs and between SSRIs and the older generation of tricyclic antidepressants (Gartlehner et al., 2008; Roy-Byrne, 2013a). That said, SSRIs do hold two key advantages over the older drugs, which is why they have largely replaced them: The first advantage is that SSRIs are less toxic and thus less dangerous in cases of overdose. Second, they have fewer of the cardiovascular effects and other common side effects (such as dry mouth, constipation, and weight gain) associated with the tricyclics and MAO inhibitors. Still, they are not free of side effects, as Prozac and other SSRIs may lead to upset stomach, headaches, agitation, insomnia, lack of sexual drive, and impaired sexual responsiveness (see, e.g., Nurnberg et al., 2008; Schweitzer, Maguire, & Ng, 2009). Antidepressants may actually worsen some associated features of depression, such as sleep problems (Morehouse, MacQueen, & Kennedy, 2011). Another, more significant concern is that use of antidepressants is associated with increased suicidal thinking in some children, adolescents, and young adults—an important issue we discuss further in Chapter 13.

Finally, another important concern with the use of antidepressant drugs is the high rate of relapse we see in patients when medication is withdrawn (Mori, Lockwood, & McCall, 2015). Although relapses may occur even in patients who continue taking medication, the risk of relapse may be reduced when medication is continued for months after symptoms subside (Kim et al., 2011).

Cognitive-behavioral therapy typically provides greater protection against relapse than antidepressant medication, perhaps because psychotherapy patients—unlike patients receiving only medication—learn skills in therapy they can later use to handle life stressors and disappointments (Beshai et al., 2011; Clarke et al., 2015; Spielmans, Berman, & Usitalo, 2011). Adding psychotherapy to drug therapy not only helps boost treatment effects but also reduces the risk of relapse, even after psychiatric drugs are withdrawn (Friedman et al., 2004; Oestergaard & Møldrup, 2011). We can liken CBT to a kind of psychological inoculation that continues to bestow protection against depression long after the initial dose is given (Smith, 2009).

Overall, about 50% to 70% of depressed patients treated in outpatient settings respond favorably to either psychotherapy or antidepressant medication (U.S. Department of Health and Human Services, 1999). Some people who fail to respond to psychological approaches may respond to antidepressants, and the opposite is also true: Some people who fail to respond to drug therapy respond to psychological approaches. However, recent evidence points to the advantages of psychological therapy when added to drug therapy (Cuijpers, 2014). Adding psychotherapy to drug therapy not only helps boost treatment effects; it also reduces the risk of relapse, even after psychiatric drugs are withdrawn (Guidi, Tomba, & Fava, 2016; Friedman et al., 2004; Oestergaard & Møldrup, 2011). Also, an important, large-scale, multisite study showed that a combination of cognitive therapy and antidepressant medication achieved better outcomes than antidepressants alone in treating severe depression (Hollon et al., 2014; Thase, 2014).

**ELECTROCONVULSIVE THERAPY** *Electroconvulsive therapy* (ECT), more commonly called *shock therapy*, continues to evoke controversy. The idea of passing an electric current through someone's brain may seem barbaric, yet evidence supports ECT as

## A CLOSER Look

### MAGNETIC STIMULATION THERAPY FOR DEPRESSION

Mesmer would be proud. Franz Friedrich Mesmer (1734–1815) was the 18th-century Austrian physician from whose name the term *mesmerism* is derived. (We still sometimes speak of people being *mesmerized* by things.) He believed that hysteria was caused by an underlying imbalance in the distribution of a magnetic fluid in the body—a problem he believed he could correct by prodding the body with metal rods. A scientific commission of the time debunked Mesmer's claims and attributed any cures he obtained to the effects of natural recovery or self-delusion (what today we might call the power of suggestion). The chairperson of the commission was none other than Benjamin Franklin, who served at the time as the ambassador to France from the newly independent United States. Although Mesmer's theories and practices were discredited, recent evidence into the therapeutic use of magnetism suggests that he might have been on to something.

Fast-forward 200 years. Australian doctors identified 60 patients with major depression who had failed to respond to different types of antidepressants (Fitzgerald et al., 2003). In a landmark double-blind controlled design, they treated these patients with either strong magnetic stimulation to the head (called *transcranial magnetic stimulation*, or TMS) or a fake treatment that had all the trappings of the active treatment except that the magnet was angled away to prevent magnetic stimulation of the brain. With TMS, a powerful electromagnet placed on the scalp generates a strong magnetic field that passes through the skull and affects the electrical activity of the brain. After two weeks of treatment, patients receiving TMS showed clinical improvement in depression as opposed to the minimal change found in the control group. Improvement was modest and did not occur in all patients. The investigators believe that longer treatment (at least 4 weeks) may be necessary to produce more meaningful therapeutic benefits.

Investigators are adding to a growing body of evidence supporting the antidepressant effects of TMS (e.g., Holtzheimer & McDonald, 2014; Liu et al., 2014; Pallanti et al., 2014; Philip et al., 2015; Ren et al., 2014). The specific form and intensity of TMS needed to produce therapeutic effects remains under study. We should also note that TMS carries some potential risks, such as the possibility of seizures. However, the risk of seizures may be reduced by using low-frequency stimulation.

In sum, TMS shows promise as a new form of treatment for moderate depression. Although it has been approved for medical use in Canada, it is still considered experimental in the United States. It also appears promising as an alternative to ECT (electroconvulsive therapy) for people with major depression who fail to respond to pharmacological treatment. TMS may be particularly helpful in treating depression because the prefrontal cortex in the left cerebral hemisphere becomes less active in depressed patients, and this part of the brain can be directly affected by TMS (Henry, Pascual-Leone, & Cole, 2003). We should caution, however, that more evidence is needed to support its efficacy and safety and to determine whether it is more effective than alternative treatments, such as ECT, before it might be recommended for more general use in treating severe depression (Knapp et al., 2008). TMS may also have therapeutic benefits in treating other disorders, such as PTSD and OCD (Cohen et al., 2004; Nauczyciel et al., 2014). **T / F**

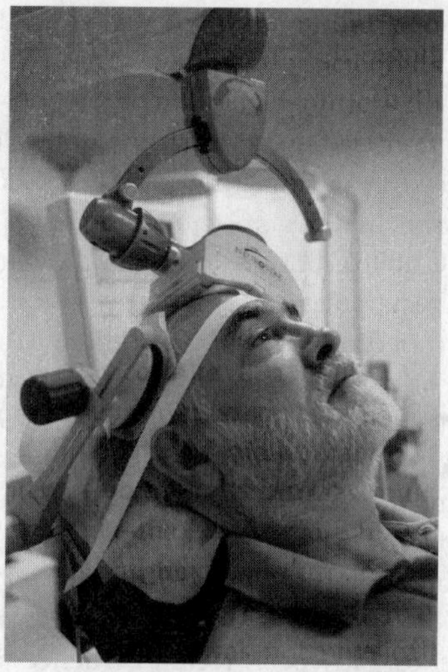

**TRANSCRANIAL MAGNETIC STIMULATION THERAPY.** TMS is a promising therapeutic approach in which powerful magnets are used to help relieve depression.

**SOURCE:** NIH Photo Library.

### TRUTH *or* FICTION

Placing a powerful electromagnet on the scalp can help relieve depression.

☑ TRUE In a number of research studies, magnetic stimulation of the head has been shown to have antidepressant effects.

a generally safe and effective treatment for severe depression and shows that it can help relieve major depression, even in cases in which drug treatments have failed (e.g., Mori, Lockwood, & McCall, 2015; Kellner et al., 2012; Oltedal et al., 2015). Estimates are that about 100,000 Americans undergo ECT annually (Dahl, 2008).

In ECT, an electrical current of between 70 and 130 volts is applied to the head to induce a convulsion that is similar to a *grand mal* epileptic seizure. ECT is usually administered in a series of six to 12 treatments, given three times per week over several weeks. The patient is put to sleep with a brief-acting general anesthetic and given a muscle relaxant to avoid wild convulsions that might result in injury. As a result, spasms may be barely perceptible to onlookers. The patient awakens soon after the procedure and generally remembers nothing of it. Although ECT had earlier been used in the treatment of a wide variety of psychological disorders, including schizophrenia and bipolar disorder, the American Psychiatric Association recommends that ECT be used only to treat major depressive disorder in people who do not respond to antidepressant medication.

ECT leads to significant improvement in a majority of people with major depression who had failed to respond to antidepressant medication (Hampton, 2012; Medda et al., 2009; Reifler, 2006). It can also have dramatic effects on relieving suicidal thinking (Kellner et al., 2005). No one knows exactly how ECT works, but one possibility is that ECT helps normalize neurotransmitter activity in the brain.

Although ECT can be an effective short-term treatment for severe depression, it is no panacea. There is understandable concern among patients, relatives, and professionals about possible risks, especially memory loss for events occurring around the time of treatment (Meeter et al., 2011). Another nagging problem with ECT is a high rate of relapse following treatment (Sackheim et al., 2001). Many professionals view ECT as a treatment of last resort, to be considered only after other treatment approaches have been tried and failed.

All in all, effective psychological and pharmacological treatments are available for treating depressive disorders. Evidence shows that psychological treatment and drug therapies generally are comparable in their level of effectiveness (Huhn et al., 2014; Wolf & Hopko, 2008). However, the combination of psychological treatment and antidepressant medication in some cases may be more effective than either treatment alone (Cuijpers et al., 2010). It's also clear that psychotherapy leads to more durable treatment effects than antidepressants alone (Karyotaki et al., 2016). More invasive treatment, such as ECT, is also available for people with severe depression who fail to respond to other approaches.

## TRUTH or FICTION

The ancient Greeks and Romans used a chemical to curb turbulent mood swings that is still used today.

☑ **TRUE** The ancient Greeks and Romans did use a chemical substance to control mood swings that is still widely used today: It is called *lithium*.

**LITHIUM AND OTHER MOOD STABILIZERS** Bipolar disorder is most commonly treated with drugs that aim to stabilize mood swings, including lithium and other mood stabilizers. The ancient Greeks and Romans were among the first to use lithium as a form of chemical treatment for mood disorders. They prescribed mineral water that contained lithium for people with turbulent mood swings. Today, the drug *lithium carbonate*, a powdered form of the metallic element lithium, is widely used in treating bipolar disorder. **T / F**

Lithium helps reduce mania and stabilize moods in bipolar patients and reduces the risk of relapse (Lichta, 2010; Shafti, 2010). People with bipolar disorder may be placed on lithium indefinitely to control their mood swings, just as diabetics may use insulin continuously to control their illness. Despite more than 40 years of use as a therapeutic drug, investigators still can't say with certainty how lithium works.

Despite its benefits, lithium is no panacea. Many patients either fail to respond to the drug or cannot tolerate it (Nierenberg et al., 2013). Lithium treatment must be closely monitored because of potential toxic effects and other side effects. Lithium can also lead to mild memory problems, which may lead people to stop taking it. Side effects may include weight gain, lethargy, and grogginess, as well as a general slowing down of motor functioning. Long-term use can produce gastrointestinal distress and lead to liver problems.

Although lithium is still widely used, the drug's limitations have prompted efforts to find alternative treatments. Anticonvulsant drugs used in the treatment of epilepsy can also help reduce manic symptoms and stabilize moods in people with bipolar disorder (Smith et al., 2010; van der Loos et al., 2009). These drugs include *carbamazepine* (Tegretol), *divalproex* (Depakote), and *lamotrigine* (Lamictal).

Anticonvulsant drugs may help people with bipolar disorder who fail to respond to lithium or cannot tolerate its side effects. Anticonvulsant drugs typically produce fewer or less severe side effects than lithium (Ceron-Litvoc et al., 2009; Reid, Gitlin, & Altshuler, 2013). Because most manic patients do not respond adequately to any one drug, a combination of drugs that may include antipsychotic drugs may sometimes be used to improve response (Ogawa et al., 2014; The Balance Investigators, 2010). More work needs to be focused on treating the depressive phase of bipolar disorder, which is the more enduring phase of bipolar cycles and is often resistant to drugs in present use. Clinicians sometimes use antidepressants to combat depression, but they do so cautiously because of the risk that they may trigger manic episodes (Pacchiarotti et al., 2013).

**ELECTROCONVULSIVE THERAPY.** ECT is helpful for many people with severe or prolonged depression who do not respond to other forms of treatment. Still, its use remains controversial.

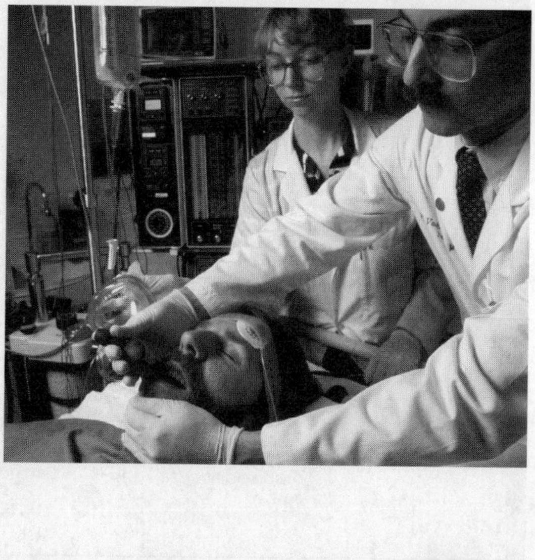

**PSYCHOLOGICAL TREATMENTS** Psychological treatments have an important role to play in treating bipolar disorders. Although use of mood stabilizers remains the primary treatment, the addition of psychosocial treatments, such as CBT, interpersonal therapy, and family therapy, can help enhance treatment effects (Alloy et al., 2005; Parikh et al., 2014; Reinares, Sánchez-Moreno, & Fountoulakis, 2014). Psychological treatment also helps boost adherence to a medication program in bipolar patients (Rougeta & Aubry, 2007).

# TYING it together

## MOOD DISORDERS

Mood disorders involve the interplay of multiple factors. Consistent with the *diathesis-stress model*, depression may reflect an interaction of biological factors (such as genetic factors, neurotransmitter irregularities, or brain abnormalities), psychological factors (such as cognitive distortions or learned helplessness), and social and environmental stressors (such as divorce or loss of a job).

Figure 7.6 illustrates a possible causal pathway on the basis of the diathesis-stress model. Let's break it down: Stressful life events, such as prolonged unemployment or a divorce, may produce a depressing effect by reducing neurotransmitter activity in the brain. These biochemical effects may be more likely to occur or may be more pronounced in people with a genetic predisposition, or diathesis, for depression. However, a depressive disorder may not develop, or may develop in a milder form, in people with more effective coping resources for handling stressful situations. For example, people who receive emotional support from others may be better able to withstand the effects of stress than those who have to go it alone. The same is true for people who make active coping efforts to meet the challenges they face in life.

Sociocultural factors can become sources of stress that influence the development or recurrence of mood disorders. These factors include poverty; overcrowding; exposure to racism, sexism, and prejudice; violence in the home or community; disproportionately high stressful burdens placed on women; and family disintegration. Other sources of stress that can contribute to mood disorders include negative life events, such as the loss of a job, the development of a serious illness, the breakup of a romantic relationship, and the loss of a loved one.

The diathesis for depression may take the form of a psychological vulnerability involving a depressive thinking style, one characterized by tendencies to exaggerate the consequences of negative events, to heap blame on oneself, and to perceive oneself as helpless to effect positive change. This cognitive diathesis may increase the risk of depression in the face of negative life events. These cognitive influences may also interact with a genetically based diathesis to further increase the risk of depression following stressful life events. The availability of social support from others may help bolster a person's resistance to stress during difficult times. People with more effective social skills may be better able to garner and maintain social reinforcement from others and thus be better able to resist depression than people lacking social skills. However, biochemical changes in the brain might make it more difficult for people to cope effectively and bounce back from stressful life events. Lingering biochemical changes and feelings of depression may exacerbate feelings of helplessness, compounding the effects of the initial stressor.

Gender-related differences in coping styles may also come into play. According to Nolen-Hoeksema and colleagues (Nolen-Hoeksema, 2006, 2008; Nolen-Hoeksema, Morrow, & Fredrickson, 1993), women are more likely to ruminate when facing emotional problems, whereas men are more likely to abuse alcohol. These or other differences in coping styles may propel longer and more severe bouts of depression in women while setting the stage for the development of drinking problems in men. As you can see, a complex web of contributing factors is likely involved in the development of mood disorders.

**Figure 7.6** Diathesis-stress model of depression.

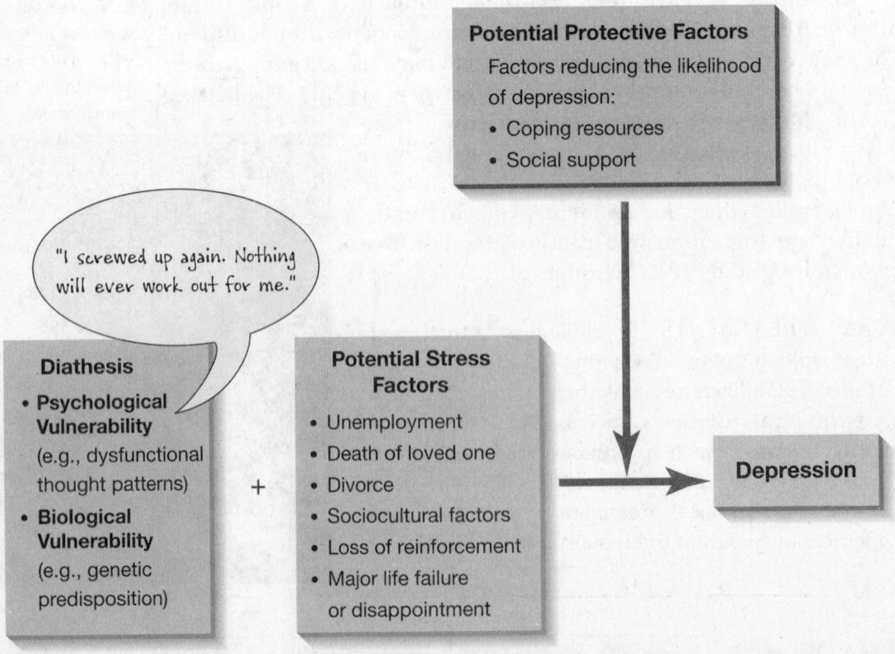

# Suicide

What do you think is the second leading cause of death among college students, after motor vehicle accidents? Drugs? Homicide? The answer is suicide, with an estimated 1,000 suicides and 24,000 suicide attempts annually among college students aged 18 to 24 (Lamberg, 2006; Rawe & Kingsbury, 2006). It's not just college students who are at risk; suicide is the second leading cause of death among young people overall in the 15- to 24-year age range and the 10th leading cause of death overall in the United States.

Suicidal thoughts are common enough. At times of great stress, many people have had fleeting thoughts of suicide. It is fortunate that most people who have suicidal thoughts do not act on them. Still, each year in the United States some 500,000 people are treated in hospital emergency rooms for attempted suicide, and about 41,000 people "succeed" in taking their lives (CDC, 2015d, 2015e). Worldwide, an estimated 800,000 people take their own lives annually (Insel & Cuthbert, 2015).

Suicide exacts a heavy toll on the nation, as you can see in statistics reported by the U.S. government (see Table 7.6). More Americans die from suicide than from motor vehicle crashes. More than half of completed suicides involve the use of firearms (Sederer & Sharfstein, 2014).

Suicidal behavior is not a psychological disorder per se, but the great majority of suicides are linked to psychological disorders—most often mood disorders such as major depression and bipolar disorder (Schaffer et al., 2015; Sederer & Sharfstein, 2014; Tondo et al., 2015)—which is why we discuss it in this chapter. Not surprisingly, suicide attempts are more likely in people with major depression during a major depressive episode than between episodes (Holma et al., 2010). Estimates are that about 60% of people who commit suicide suffer from a mood disorder (National Strategy for Suicide Prevention, 2001).

## Risk Factors in Suicide

**7.15 Identify risk factors in suicide.**

To many lay observers, suicide seems so extreme an act that they believe only "insane" people (meaning people who are out of touch with reality) would commit suicide. However, suicidal thinking does not necessarily imply loss of touch with reality, deep-seated unconscious conflict, or a personality disorder. Having thoughts about suicide generally reflects a narrowing of the range of options people think are available to them for dealing with their problems. That is, they are discouraged by their problems and see no other way out.

**SUICIDE IN OLDER ADULTS** Although attention is focused on the tragedy of young people and suicide, as well it should be, suicide rates are actually highest among middle-aged and older adults, especially older White males (CDC, 2009; Mills et al., 2013;

**Table 7.6** Suicide: The Cost to the Nation

**SOURCE:** U.S. Department of Health and Human Services, 2001; updated in CDC, 2015d, 2015e.

- Every 15 minutes, another life is lost to suicide. Every day, more than 100 Americans take their own lives and over 2,500 attempt suicide.
- Suicide is the 10th leading cause of death in Americans.
- There are about 2.5 times as many deaths from suicide as from homicide.
- There are now more than three times the number of deaths due to suicide as due to HIV/AIDS.
- In the month prior to their suicide, 75% of elderly persons had visited a physician.
- Over half of all suicides occur in adult men, ages 25 to 65.
- Many who make suicide attempts never seek professional care immediately after the attempt.
- Men are nearly four times more likely to commit suicide than are women.
- More teenagers and young adults die from suicide than from cancer, heart disease, AIDS, birth defects, stroke, pneumonia and influenza, and chronic lung disease combined.
- Suicide takes the lives of more than 40,000 Americans every year.

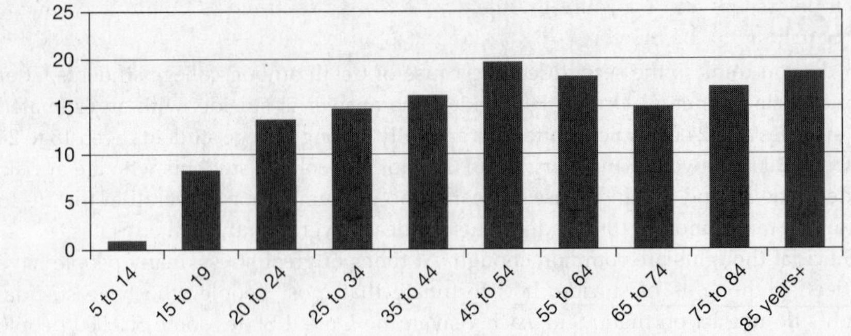


**Figure 7.7** Suicide rates according to age.

Although adolescent suicides may be more highly publicized, adults—especially older adults—have higher suicide rates.

**SOURCE:** CDC (2015e). *Health, United States, 2014.*

see Figure 7.7). (We discuss youth suicide further in Chapter 13.) Yet it turns out that suicide rates are rising most rapidly among women in the 60- to 74-year age range, pointing to a vulnerability to suicidal thinking in women in late middle age that has largely gone unnoticed (CDC, 2013a).

Despite life-extending advances in medical care, some older adults find the quality of their lives less than satisfactory. Older people are more susceptible to diseases such as cancer and Alzheimer's, which can leave them with feelings of helplessness and hopelessness that, in turn, can give rise to depression and suicidal thinking (Starkstein et al., 2005).

Many older adults also suffer a mounting accumulation of losses of friends and loved ones, leading to social isolation. These losses, as well as the loss of good health and of a responsible role in the community, may wear down the will to live. Not surprisingly, the highest suicide rates in older men are among those who are widowed or socially isolated. Society's increased acceptance of suicide in older people may also play a part. Whatever the causes, suicide has become an increased risk for elderly people. Perhaps society should focus its attention on the quality of life that is afforded to our elderly, in addition to providing them the medical care that helps make longer life possible.

**GENDER AND ETHNIC/RACIAL DIFFERENCES** More women attempt suicide, but more men "succeed" (Hawton et al., 2013). For every female suicide, there are about four male suicides. More males succeed in large part because they tend to choose quicker-acting and more lethal means, such as handguns.

Suicides are more common among (non-Hispanic) White Americans and Native Americans than among African Americans, Asian Americans, or Hispanic Americans (Garlow, Purselle, & Heninger, 2005; Gone & Trimble, 2012; O'Keefe et al., 2014; see Figure 7.8). White Americans are more than twice as likely to take their own lives as African Americans (Joe et al., 2006). Yet the highest suicide rates in the nation are found among Native American adolescent and young adult males (Meyers, 2007).

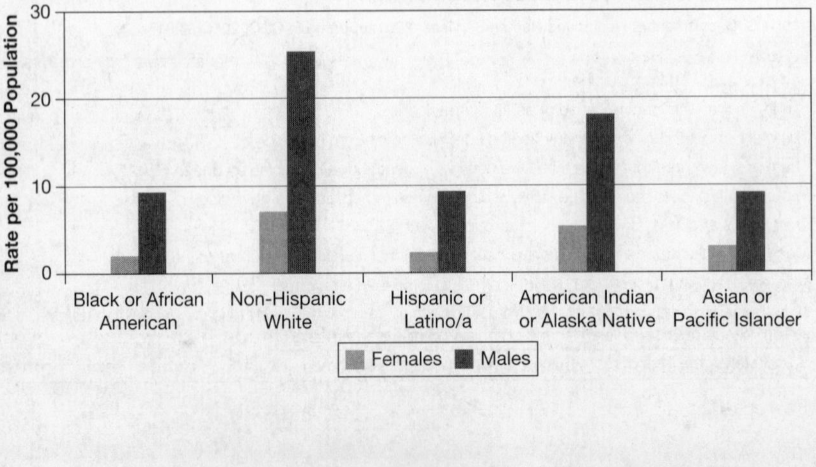


**Figure 7.8** Ethnicity and suicide rates.

Suicide rates are higher among males than females, and higher among non-Hispanic White Americans and Native Americans than other ethnicities.

**SOURCE:** CDC (2015e). *Health, United States, 2014.*

Hopelessness and exposure to others who have attempted or committed suicide may contribute to the increased risk of suicide among Native American youth. Native American youth at greatest risk tend to be reared in communities that are largely isolated from U.S. society. They perceive themselves as having relatively few opportunities to gain the skills necessary to join the workforce in the larger society and are also relatively more prone to substance abuse, including alcohol abuse. Knowledge that peers have attempted or completed suicide renders suicide a highly visible escape from psychological pain.

**SUICIDE AND PSYCHOLOGICAL DISORDERS** The risk of suicide is much higher among people with severe mood disorders, such as major depression and bipolar disorder (Gonda et al., 2012; Hawton et al., 2013). People who suffer from more severe and chronic mood disorders and those who have repeated episodes of major depression are at even greater risk (Witte et al., 2009). Compounding the risk of suicide attempts in persons with MDD are deep feelings of worthlessness (Jeon et al., 2014). However, we shouldn't think that suicide is limited to people with severe mood disorders. Suicide and attempted suicide are also linked to many other psychological problems, including alcoholism and drug dependence, anxiety disorders, anorexia, schizophrenia, and borderline personality disorder (e.g., Angelakis et al., 2015; Bentley et al., 2016; Conner et al., 2014; DeVylder et al., 2015; Jylhä et al., 2015; Pompili et al., 2013).

Not all suicides, however, are connected with psychological disorders. Some people suffering from intractable pain or terminal illness may seek to escape further suffering by taking their own lives. These suicides are sometimes labeled "rational suicides" in the belief that they are based on a rational decision that life is no longer worth living in light of continual suffering. However, in many of these cases, a person's judgment and reasoning ability may be colored by an underlying and potentially treatable psychological disorder, such as depression. Other suicides are motivated by deep-seated religious or political convictions, as in the case of people who sacrifice themselves in acts of protest against their governments or who kill themselves and others in suicide bombings in the belief that their acts will be rewarded in an afterlife.

**PRIOR SUICIDE ATTEMPTS** Past suicide attempts are an important predictor of later suicide attempts (Bolton et al., 2010; Kessler et al., 2014). Sadly, people who fail on a first attempt often succeed on a subsequent attempt. Those who survive an attempt but express to others that they wish they had died are more likely to go on to eventually complete suicide than those who express ambivalence about the attempt (Henriques et al., 2005). Adolescents who have a history of attempted suicide stand a risk of a later completed suicide that is 14 times higher in females and 22 times higher in males as compared to the general adolescent population (Olfson et al., 2005).

**ROLE OF STRESS** Stressful life events play an important role in prompting suicide attempts in vulnerable individuals, including "exit events" such as the death of a spouse, close friend, or relative; prolonged unemployment; significant financial setbacks; and divorce or separation (Barr et al., 2012; Liu & Miller, 2014; McFeeters, Boyda, & O'Neill, 2015). People who consider suicide in times of stress may lack problem-solving skills and may be unable to find alternative ways of coping with stressors.

# Theoretical Perspectives on Suicide

**7.16 Identify the major theoretical perspectives on suicide.**

The classic psychodynamic model views depression as the turning inward of anger against the internal representation of a lost love object. Suicide then represents inward-directed anger that turns murderous. Suicidal people, then, do not seek to destroy themselves. Instead, they seek to vent their rage against the internalized representation of the love object. In so doing, they destroy themselves as well, of course. In his later writings, Freud speculated that suicide may be motivated by the "death instinct," a tendency to return to the tension-free state that preceded birth. Existential and humanistic theorists relate suicide to the perception that life has become meaningless, empty, and essentially hopeless.

In the 19th century, social thinker Emile Durkheim (1897/1958) noted that people who experienced *anomie*—who feel lost, without identity, rootless—are more likely to commit suicide. Sociocultural theorists believe that alienation plays a role in many suicides. In our modern, mobile society, people frequently move hundreds or thousands of miles to schools and jobs. Many people are socially isolated or cut off from their support groups. Moreover, city dwellers tend to limit or discourage informal social contacts because of crowding, overstimulation, and fear of crime. It is thus understandable that many people find few sources of support in times of crisis. Supporting these links, suicidal thoughts occur less commonly among people with higher levels of social support (Kleiman & Liu, 2013). Yet in some cases, the availability of social support from family members may not helpful. Family members may be perceived as part of the problem, not part of the solution.

Learning theorists focus largely on the lack of problem-solving skills for handling significant life stress. According to Shneidman (1985), those who attempt suicide wish to escape unbearable psychological pain and may perceive no other way out. People who threaten or attempt suicide may also receive sympathy and support from loved ones and others, perhaps making future—and more lethal—attempts more likely. This is not to suggest that suicide attempts or gestures should be ignored. People who threaten suicide are *not* merely seeking attention. Although those who threaten suicide may not carry out the act, they should be taken seriously. People who commit suicide often tell others of their intentions or provide clues. Moreover, many people make aborted suicide attempts before they go on to make actual suicide attempts.

Social-cognitive theorists suggest that suicide may be motivated by personal expectancies, such as beliefs that one will be missed by others or that survivors will feel guilty for having mistreated him or her, or that suicide will solve one's own problems or even other people's problems (e.g., "He won't have to worry about me any longer") in one fell swoop.

**STARRY, STARRY NIGHT.** The famed artist Vincent van Gogh suffered from severe bouts of depression and eventually took his own life at the age of 37, dying of a self-inflicted gunshot wound. In this self-portrait, van Gogh strikes a melancholy pose that allows the viewer to sense the deep despair he endured.

Social-cognitive theorists also focus on the potential modeling effects of observing suicidal behavior in others, especially among teenagers who feel overwhelmed by academic and social stressors. A *social contagion*, or spreading of suicide in a community, may occur in the wake of suicides that receive widespread publicity. Teenagers seem especially vulnerable to these modeling effects and may even romanticize the suicidal act as one of heroic courage. Suicide clusters account for about 5% of teen suicides (Richtel, 2015). Copycat suicides may be more likely to occur when reports of suicides are sensationalized. Teenagers may come to expect their deaths will have a meaningful impact on their families and communities.

Biological factors are also implicated in suicide, including genetic factors and neurotransmitter imbalances involving the mood-regulating chemical serotonin (Petersen et al., 2014; Sullivan et al., 2015). Because serotonin is linked to depression, its relationship with suicide is not surprising. Yet serotonin also acts to curb or inhibit nervous system activity, so perhaps lowered serotonin activity leads to *disinhibition*, or release, of impulsive behavior that takes the form of a suicidal act in vulnerable individuals. Genes that affect the regulation of serotonin in the brain are also implicated in suicide (Crowell et al., 2008; Must et al., 2009).

Mood disorders in family members and parental suicide are also connected with suicide risk. But what are the causal connections? Do people who attempt suicide inherit vulnerabilities to mood disorders that are connected with suicide? Does the family atmosphere promote feelings of hopelessness? Does the suicide of one family member give others the idea of doing the same thing? Does one suicide create the impression that other family members are destined to kill themselves? These are all questions researchers need to address.

Suicide is often motivated by the desire to escape from unbearable emotional pain. Here, the late actress Patty Duke, who rose to acclaim in childhood by playing the role of Helen Keller in the movie *The Miracle Worker* and who battled bipolar disorder throughout much of her life, expresses how the desire to escape pain motivated many of the suicide attempts she had made in her life.

**"I"**

**"Please Make This Stop"**

I can't even remember how many times I tried to kill myself. Not all of them got as far as actually taking the pills or digesting the pills. And it was almost always pills, although I did make a show sometimes of trying to use razors. But I always chickened out. A couple of times I tried to jump out of a moving car. But I didn't seem willing to inflict physical pain on myself. Some of the attempts continued to be attention-getting devices. Others came out of so much pain. I just wanted it to stop. I wish I had a more colorful, more profound way to describe it, but the only thoughts that went through my head were "Please make this stop. Please make me brave enough to die so that this anguish will stop."

**SOURCE:** *Duke & Hochman, 1992, p. 12.*

Suicide involves a complex web of factors, and predicting it is not simple. Moreover, many myths about suicide abound (see Table 7.7). Yet it is clear that many suicides could be prevented if people with suicidal feelings received treatment for underlying disorders, including depression, bipolar disorder, schizophrenia, and alcohol and substance abuse. We also need strategies that emphasize the maintenance of hope during times of severe stress. **T / F**

**TRUTH or FICTION**

People who threaten suicide basically are attention seekers.

☑ **FALSE** Although people who threaten suicide may not carry out the act, their threats should be taken seriously. People who plan to commit suicide often leave clues or tell others of their intentions.

## Predicting Suicide

**7.17 Apply your knowledge of factors in suicide to steps you can take if someone you know experiences suicidal thoughts.**

*"I don't believe it. I just saw him last week and he looked fine."*

*"She sat here just the other day, laughing with the rest of us. How were we to know what was going on inside her?"*

*"I knew he was depressed, but I never thought he'd do something like this. I didn't have a clue."*

*"Why didn't she just call me?"*

Friends and family members often respond to news of a suicide with disbelief or guilt that they failed to pick up signs of the impending act. Yet even trained professionals find it difficult to predict who is likely to commit suicide.

Evidence points to the pivotal role of hopelessness about the future in predicting suicidal thinking and suicide attempts (Kaslow et al., 2002; Hawton et al., 2013). But *when* does hopelessness lead to suicide?

## Table 7.7 Myths about Suicide

| Myth | Fact |
|---|---|
| People who threaten suicide are only seeking attention. | Not so. Researchers report that most people who commit suicide gave prior indications of their intentions or consulted a health provider beforehand (Luoma, Martin, & Pearson, 2002). |
| A person must be insane to attempt suicide. | Most people who attempt suicide may feel hopeless, but they are not insane (i.e., out of touch with reality). |
| Talking about suicide with a depressed person may prompt the person to attempt it. | An open discussion of suicide with a depressed person does not prompt the person to attempt it. In fact, extracting a promise that the person will not attempt suicide before calling or visiting a mental health worker may well *prevent* a suicide. |
| People who attempt suicide and fail aren't serious about killing themselves. | Most people who commit suicide have made previous unsuccessful attempts. |
| If someone threatens suicide, it is best to ignore it so as not to encourage repeated threats. | Although some people do manipulate others by making idle threats, it is prudent to treat every suicide threat as genuine and to take appropriate action. |

**SOURCE:** Adapted from J. S. Nevid. (2013). *Psychology: Concepts and Applications* (Fourth Ed.). Belmont, CA: Cengage Learning. Reprinted by permission.

**SUICIDE HOTLINES.** Telephone hotlines provide emergency assistance and referral services to people experiencing suicidal thoughts or impulses. If you know someone experiencing suicidal thoughts or threatening suicide, speak to a mental health professional or call a suicide hotline in your community for advice.

People who commit suicide tend to signal their intentions, often quite explicitly, such as by telling others about their suicidal thoughts, yet some cloak their intentions. Behavioral clues may reveal suicidal intent. Edwin Shneidman, a leading researcher on suicide, found that 90% of the people who committed suicide had left clear clues, such as disposing of their possessions (Gelman, 1994). People contemplating suicide may also suddenly try to sort out their affairs, as in drafting a will or buying a cemetery plot. They may purchase a gun despite lack of prior interest in firearms. When troubled people decide to commit suicide, they may seem to be suddenly at peace; they feel relieved because they no longer have to contend with life problems. This sudden calm may be misinterpreted as a sign of hope. Other factors linked to increased suicidal risk include substance abuse, financial problems, a recent crisis, medical problems, and relationship problems (Logan, Hall, & Karch, 2011).

The prediction of suicide is not an exact science, even for experienced professionals. Many observable factors, such as hopelessness, seem to be connected with suicide, but we cannot accurately predict when a hopeless person will attempt suicide, if at all.

# A CLOSER Look

## SUICIDE PREVENTION

Imagine yourself having an intimate conversation with a close campus friend, Chris. You know that things have not been good. Chris's grandfather died six weeks ago, and the two had been very close. Chris's grades have been going downhill, and Chris's romantic relationship also seems to be coming apart at the seams. Still, you are unprepared when Chris says very deliberately, "I just can't take it anymore. Life is just too painful. I don't feel like I want to live anymore. I've decided that the only thing I can do is to kill myself."

When somebody discloses that he or she is contemplating suicide, you may feel bewildered and frightened, as if a great burden has been placed on your shoulders. It has been. If someone confides suicidal thoughts to you, your goal should be to persuade him or her to see a professional, or to get the advice of a professional yourself as soon as you can. But if the suicidal person declines to talk to another person and you sense you can't break away for such a conference, here are some things you can do then and there:

1. *Draw the person out*. Shneidman advises framing questions such as "What's going on?" "Where do you hurt?" or "What would you like to see happen?" (Shneidman, 1985, p. 11). Such questions may prompt people to verbalize thwarted psychological needs and offer some relief. They also grant you the time to appraise the risk and contemplate your next move.
2. *Be sympathetic*. Show that you fathom how troubled the person is. Don't say something like, "You're just being silly. You don't really mean it."

3. *Suggest that means other than suicide can be discovered to work out the person's problems, even if they are not apparent at the time.* Shneidman (1985) notes that suicidal people can usually see only two solutions to their predicaments: either suicide or some kind of magical resolution. Professionals try to help them see the available alternatives.
4. *Ask how the person expects to commit suicide.* People with explicit methods who also possess the means (e.g., a gun or drugs) are at greatest risk. Ask if you may hold on to the gun, drugs, or whatever, for a while. Sometimes, the person agrees.
5. *Propose that the person accompany you to consult a professional right away.* Many campuses, towns, and cities have hotlines that you or the suicidal individual can call anonymously. Other possibilities include the emergency room of a general hospital, a campus health center or counseling center, or the campus or local police. If you are unable to maintain contact with the suicidal person, get professional assistance as soon as you separate.
6. *Don't say something like, "You're talking crazy."* Such comments are degrading and injurious to the individual's self-esteem. Don't press the suicidal person to contact specific people, such as parents or a spouse. Conflict with these people may have given rise to the suicidal thoughts.

Above all, keep in mind that your primary goal is to confer with a helping professional. Don't go it alone any longer than you must.

# Summing Up

## Types of Mood Disorders

### Major Depressive Disorder

**7.1 Describe the key features of major depressive disorder and evaluate factors that may account for the higher rate of depression among women.**

Mood disorders are disturbances in mood that are unusually prolonged or severe and serious enough to impair daily functioning. Mood disorders are divided into two major types: (1) unipolar disorders (major depressive disorder, persistent depressive disorder, and premenstrual dysphoric disorder, all of which are characterized by a downward mood disturbance) and (2) bipolar disorders (bipolar disorder and cyclothymic disorder), which are characterized by mood swings.

In major depressive disorder, there is a profound change in mood that impairs a person's ability to function. The associated features of major depressive disorder include downcast mood; changes in appetite; difficulty sleeping; reduced sense of pleasure in formerly enjoyable activities; feelings of fatigue or loss of energy; sense of worthlessness; excessive or misplaced guilt; difficulties concentrating, thinking clearly, or making decisions; repeated thoughts of death or suicide; attempts at suicide; and even psychotic behaviors (hallucinations and delusions).

Women are nearly twice as likely as men to suffer from major depression. The reasons are complex, but a number of factors may be involved, including the greater stress burden many women shoulder, hormonal influences, gender differences in coping styles (rumination versus distraction), greater influence in women of interpersonal relationships on self-esteem, and underreporting of depression in men.

### Persistent Depressive Disorder (Dysthymia)

**7.2 Describe the key features of persistent depressive disorder (dysthymia).**

Persistent depressive disorder involves chronic forms of major depressive disorder or milder depression. These forms of depression vary in severity, but both are associated with impaired functioning in social and occupational roles.

### Premenstrual Dysphoric Disorder

**7.3 Describe the key features of premenstrual dysphoric disorder.**

Premenstrual dysphoric disorder is characterized by clinically significant changes in mood in women during the premenstrual period.

### Bipolar Disorder

**7.4 Describe the key features of bipolar disorder.**

In bipolar disorder, people experience fluctuating mood states that interfere with their ability to function. Bipolar I disorder is identified by one or more manic episodes and, typically, by alternating episodes of major depression. Manic episodes are characterized by sudden elevation or expansion of mood and sense of self-importance, feelings of almost boundless energy, hyperactivity, and extreme sociability, which often takes a demanding and overbearing form. People in manic episodes tend to exhibit pressured or rapid speech, rapid "flight of ideas," and decreased need for sleep. Bipolar II disorder is characterized by the occurrence of at least one major depressive episode and one hypomanic episode, but without any full-blown manic episodes.

### Cyclothymic Disorder

**7.5 Describe the key features of cyclothymic disorder.**

Cyclothymic disorder is characterized by a chronic pattern of mild mood swings that sometimes progresses to bipolar disorder.

## Causal Factors in Mood Disorders

### Stress and Depression

**7.6 Evaluate the role of stress in depression.**

Exposure to life stress is associated with an increased risk of development and recurrence of mood disorders, especially major depression. Yet some people are more resilient in the face of stress, perhaps because of psychosocial factors such as social support.

### Psychodynamic Theories

**7.7 Describe psychodynamic models of depression.**

In classic psychodynamic theory, depression is viewed in terms of inward-directed anger. People who hold strongly ambivalent feelings toward people they have lost or whose loss is threatened may direct unresolved anger toward the inward representations of these people whom they have incorporated or introjected within themselves, producing self-loathing and depression. Bipolar disorder is understood within psychodynamic theory in terms of the shifting balances between the ego and superego. More recent psychodynamic models, such as the self-focusing model, incorporate both psychodynamic and cognitive aspects in explaining depression in terms of self-absorption with the lost love object.

### Humanistic Theories

**7.8 Describe the humanistic model of depression.**

Humanistic theorists view depression as reflecting a lack of meaning and authenticity in a person's life.

### Learning Theories

**7.9 Describe learning theory models of depression.**

Learning theorists explain depression by focusing on situational factors, such as changes in the level of reinforcement. When reinforcement is reduced, a person may feel unmotivated and depressed, which can occasion inactivity and further reduce opportunities for reinforcement. Coyne's interactional theory focuses on the negative family interactions that can lead the family members of people with depression to become less reinforcing toward them.

### Cognitive Theories

**7.10 Describe Beck's cognitive model and the learned helplessness model of depression.**

Beck's cognitive model focuses on the role of negative or distorted thinking in depression. Depression-prone people hold negative beliefs about themselves, the environment, and the future. This cognitive triad of depression leads to specific errors in thinking (or cognitive distortions) in response to negative events, which in turn lead to depression.

The learned helplessness model is based on the belief that people may become depressed when they come to view themselves as helpless to control the reinforcements in their environment or to change their lives for the better. A reformulated version of the theory holds that the ways in which people explain events—their attributions—determine their proneness toward depression in the face of negative events. The combination of internal, global, and stable attributions for negative events renders a person most vulnerable to depression.

### Biological Factors

**7.11 Identify biological factors in depression.**

Genetics appears to play a role in explaining major depressive disorder, as do imbalances in neurotransmitter activity in the brain. The diathesis-stress model is an explanatory framework that illustrates how biological or psychological diatheses may interact with stress in the development of mood disorders such as major depression.

### Causal Factors in Bipolar Disorders

**7.12 Identify causal factors in bipolar disorders.**

Genetics appears to play an important role in bipolar disorder, but stressful life experiences also contribute. Bipolar disorders are perhaps best explained in terms of multiple causes acting together within a diathesis-stress framework. Social support may be important in speeding recovery from mood episodes and reducing the risks of recurrences.

## Treatment of Mood Disorders

### Psychological Treatment

**7.13 Describe psychological methods used to treat depression.**

Psychodynamic treatment of depression has traditionally focused on helping a depressed person uncover and work through ambivalent feelings toward a lost object, thereby lessening the anger directed inward. Modern psychodynamic approaches tend to be more direct and briefer and focus more on developing adaptive means of achieving self-worth and resolving interpersonal conflicts. Learning theory approaches have focused on helping people with depression increase the frequency of reinforcement in their lives through means such as increasing the rates of pleasant activities in which they participate. Cognitive therapists focus on helping people identify and correct distorted or dysfunctional thoughts and learn more adaptive behaviors.

### Biomedical Treatment

**7.14 Describe biomedical approaches to treating depression.**

Biomedical treatments have focused on the use of antidepressant drugs and other biological treatments, such as electroconvulsive therapy. Antidepressant drugs may help normalize neurotransmitter functioning in the brain. Bipolar disorder is commonly treated with either lithium or anticonvulsant drugs.

## Suicide

### Risk Factors in Suicide

**7.15 Identify risk factors in suicide.**

Mood disorders are often linked to suicide. Although women are more likely to attempt suicide, more men actually succeed, probably because they select more lethal means. Older adults—not the young—are more likely to commit suicide. People who attempt suicide are often depressed, but they are generally in touch with reality. They may, however, lack effective problem-solving skills and see no other way of dealing with life stress than suicide. A sense of hopelessness also figures prominently in suicides.

### Theoretical Perspectives on Suicide

**7.16 Identify the major theoretical perspectives on suicide.**

These draw on the classic psychodynamic model of anger turned inward; the role of social alienation; and learning, social-cognitive, and biologically based perspectives.

### Predicting Suicide

**7.17 Apply your knowledge of factors in suicide to steps you can take if someone you know experiences suicidal thoughts.**

You should never ignore a person's threat to commit suicide. Although not all people who threaten suicide go on to commit the act, many do. People who commit suicide often signal their intentions—for example, by telling others about their suicidal thoughts. If someone you know is thinking about suicide, draw him or her out to talk about his or her feelings, be sympathetic, suggest means other than suicide of coping with the problems at hand, ask about his or her intentions, and, most importantly, accompany him or her to get professional help—now.

## Critical Thinking Questions

On the basis of your reading of this chapter, answer the following questions:

- "Women are just naturally more prone to depression than men." Do you agree or disagree? Explain your answer.
- Jonathan becomes clinically depressed after losing his job and his girlfriend. On the basis of your review of the different theoretical perspectives on depression, explain how these losses may have figured in Jonathan's depression.
- If you were to become clinically depressed, which course of treatment would you prefer: medication, psychotherapy, or a combination? Explain.
- Did your reading of the text change your ideas about how you might deal with a suicide threat by a friend or loved one? If so, how?

## Key Terms

mood disorders, p. 248
major depressive disorder, p. 250
mania, p. 250
hypomania, p. 250
postpartum depression (PPD), p. 255
persistent depressive disorder, p. 257
double depression, p. 259
premenstrual dysphoric disorder (PMDD), p. 260
bipolar disorder, p. 260
manic episode, p. 262
cyclothymic disorder, p. 264
cognitive triad of depression, p. 269
cognitive-specificity hypothesis, p. 271
learned helplessness, p. 272

## Chapter 8

# Substance-Related and Addictive Disorders

## Learning Objectives

**8.1** **Identify** the major types of substance-related disorders in the *DSM-5* and **describe** their key features.

**8.2** **Describe** nonchemical forms of addiction or compulsive behavior.

**8.3** **Explain** the difference between physiological dependence and psychological dependence.

**8.4** **Identify** common stages in the pathway to drug dependence.

**8.5** **Describe** the effects of depressants and the risks they pose.

**8.6** **Describe** the effects of stimulants and the risks they pose.

**8.7** **Describe** the effects of hallucinogens and the risks they pose.

**8.8** **Describe** biological perspectives on substance use disorders and **explain** how cocaine affects the brain.

**8.9** **Describe** psychological perspectives on substance use disorders.

**8.10 Identify** biological treatments of substance use disorders.

**8.11 Identify** factors associated with culturally sensitive approaches to treatment.

**8.12 Identify** a nonprofessional support group for people with substance use disorders.

**8.13 Identify** two major types of residential treatment facilities for people with substance use disorders.

**8.14 Describe** the psychodynamic treatment of substance abusers.

**8.15 Identify** behavioral approaches to substance use disorders.

**8.16 Describe** relapse-prevention training.

**8.17 Describe** the key features of gambling disorder.

**8.18 Describe** ways of treating gambling disorder.

## TRUTH or FICTION

T☐ F☐ Legally available substances account for more deaths than all illegal substances combined. (p. 298)

T☐ F☐ You cannot become psychologically dependent on a drug without also becoming physically dependent on it. (p. 305)

T☐ F☐ More teenagers and young adults die from alcohol-related motor vehicle accidents than from any other cause. (p. 307)

T☐ F☐ It is safe to let someone who has passed out from drinking just sleep it off. (p. 310)

T☐ F☐ Even moderate use of alcohol increases the risk of heart attacks. (p. 313)

T☐ F☐ Heroin addiction primarily affects people in decaying, inner-city neighborhoods. (p. 314)

T☐ F☐ *Coca-Cola* originally contained cocaine. (p. 316)

T☐ F☐ Marijuana use has surpassed cigarette use among high school seniors today. (p. 319)

T☐ F☐ People who can "hold their liquor" better than most stand a lower risk of becoming problem drinkers. (p. 322)

T☐ F☐ A widely used treatment for heroin addiction involves substituting one addictive drug for another. (p. 330)

### CHAPTER INTRODUCTION: SUBSTANCE-RELATED AND ADDICTIVE DISORDERS

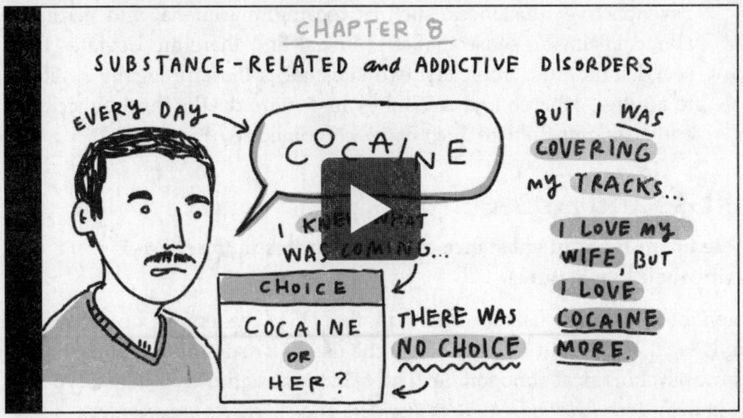

"I"

**"Nothing and Nobody Comes Before My Coke"**

She had just caught me with cocaine again after I had managed to convince her that I hadn't used in over a month. Of course I had been tooting (snorting) almost every day, but I had managed to cover my tracks a little better than usual. So she said to me that I was going to have to make a choice—either cocaine or her. Before she finished the sentence, I knew what was coming, so I told her to think carefully about what she was going to say. It was clear to me that there wasn't a choice. I love my wife, but I'm not going to choose anything over cocaine. It's sick, but that's what things have come to. Nothing and nobody comes before my coke.

**SOURCE:** *From Weiss & Mirin, 1987, p. 55*

These comments from Eugene, a 41-year-old architect, underscore the powerful effects that drugs like cocaine can have on people's lives. Our society is flooded with psychoactive substances that alter the mood and twist perceptions—substances that lift you up, calm you down, and turn you upside down. Many young people start using these substances because of peer pressure or because their parents and other authority figures tell them not to. For many others who become addicted to drugs, like Eugene, the pursuit and use of drugs take center stage in their lives and become even more important than family, work, or their own welfare.

In this chapter, we examine the physiological and psychological effects of the major classes of drugs. We explore how mental health professionals classify substance-related disorders and where they draw the line between use and abuse. We then examine contemporary understandings of the origins of these disorders and how mental health professionals help people who struggle to combat them.

# Classification of Substance-Related and Addictive Disorders

The use of psychoactive substances that affect a person's mental state is normal, at least as gauged by statistical frequency and social standards. In this sense, it is normal to start the day with caffeine in our coffee or tea, to consume wine or coffee with meals, to meet friends for a drink after work, and to end the day with a nightcap. Each of these substances affects our mental state, making us more alert, in the case of caffeine, or more relaxed, in the case of alcoholic beverages. Many of us take prescription drugs that calm us down or ease our pain. Flooding the bloodstream with nicotine through cigarette smoking is normal in the sense that about one in five Americans do it. However, use of some psychoactive substances, such as cocaine, marijuana, and heroin, is abnormal in the sense that it is illegal and therefore deviates from social standards. Ironically, two substances that are legally available to adults—tobacco and alcohol—cause more deaths through sickness and accidents than all illicit drugs combined. **T / F**

**TRUTH or FICTION**

Legally available substances account for more deaths than all illegal substances combined.

☑ **TRUE** Two legally available substances, alcohol and tobacco, cause far more deaths.

## Substance Use and Abuse

**8.1 Identify the major types of substance-related disorders in the *DSM-5* and describe their key features.**

The classification of substance use disorders in the *DSM* system is not based on whether a drug is legal or not, but rather on how the use of a drug impairs the person's physiological and psychological functioning. The *DSM-5* classifies two major types of substance-related disorders: *substance-induced disorders* and *substance use disorders.*

**SUBSTANCE-INDUCED DISORDERS** These disorders are characterized by abnormal behavior patterns that are directly induced by psychoactive substances. Two major types of **substance-induced disorders** are *substance intoxication* and *substance withdrawal.* Different substances have different effects, so some of these disorders may be induced by one, by a few, or by nearly all substances. In Chapter 14, we consider a substance-induced disorder called *Korsakoff's syndrome* that leads to irreversible memory loss after years of chronic alcohol abuse.

**Substance intoxication** is a substance-induced disorder involving a pattern of repeated episodes of intoxication, which is a state of drunkenness or being "high," brought about by use of a particular drug. The features of intoxication depend on which drug is ingested, the dose, the user's biological reactivity, and—to some degree—the user's expectations. Signs of intoxication often include confusion, belligerence, impaired judgment, inattention, and impaired motor and spatial skills.

It's important to note that overdoses of alcohol, cocaine, opioids (narcotics), and phencyclidine (PCP) can result in death (yes, you can die from alcohol overdoses), either because of a substance's biochemical effects or because of behavior patterns—such as suicide—that are connected with psychological pain or impaired judgment brought on by use of the drug. Accidental overdoses are the second-leading cause of accidental death (after motor vehicle accidents) in the United States, accounting for more than 27,000 deaths annually (Okie, 2010).

**Substance withdrawal** is a substance-induced disorder involving a cluster of symptoms that occur when a person abruptly stops using a particular substance following a period of prolonged and heavy use (or in the case of caffeine withdrawal, daily use) of the substance. Repeated use of a substance may alter the body's physiological reactions, leading to the development of physiological effects such as *tolerance* and a clearly defined *withdrawal syndrome* (also called an *abstinence syndrome*).

**Tolerance** is a state of physical habituation to a drug, resulting from frequent use, such that higher doses are needed to achieve the same effect. Withdrawal symptoms vary with the particular type of drug. Symptoms of alcohol withdrawal may include sweating or rapid pulse, tremors of the hand, fleeting hallucinations or illusions, insomnia, nausea or vomiting, agitated behavior, anxiety, and possible seizures. For caffeine withdrawal, the symptoms are generally milder and may include headache, significant drowsiness, depressed mood, problems with concentration, flu-like symptoms, nausea, and muscle stiffness or pain. People who experience a withdrawal syndrome often return to using the substance to relieve the discomfort associated with withdrawal, which thus serves to maintain the addictive pattern.

In some chronic, heavy users of alcohol, withdrawal produces a state of *delirium tremens* (DTs). The DTs are usually limited to chronic, heavy users of alcohol who dramatically lower their intake of alcohol after many years of heavy drinking. DTs involve intense autonomic hyperactivity (profuse sweating and tachycardia) and *delirium*—a state of mental confusion characterized by incoherent speech, disorientation, and extreme restlessness. Terrifying hallucinations—frequently of creepy, crawling animals—may also be present.

Regular or prolonged use of certain substances may lead to a **withdrawal syndrome**, which is a cluster of psychological and physical symptoms following abrupt cessation of use of the substance. Psychoactive substances that can lead to withdrawal syndromes include alcohol, opioids (opiate drugs), stimulants such as cocaine and amphetamine, sedatives and sleep-inducing drugs (hypnotics), marijuana, and tobacco (which contains the stimulant nicotine). Because abrupt withdrawal from hallucinogens such as LSD and phencyclidine (PCP) and inhalants (e.g., glues or aerosols) does not produce clinically significant withdrawal effects, they are not recognized as producing identifiable withdrawal syndromes (American Psychiatric Association, 2013).

SUBSTANCE USE DISORDERS **Substance use disorders** involve a pattern of maladaptive use of a psychoactive substance that results in significant personal distress or impaired functioning. The term *substance use disorder* is a general diagnostic classification, but for each individual case, the clinician provides a specific diagnosis—such as *alcohol use disorder*—that identifies the particular substance associated with problematic use. In addition to evidence of significant distress or impaired functioning resulting from problematic use of a psychoactive substance, the diagnosis of a substance use disorder requires two or more specific features or symptoms occurring during the preceding one-year period.

The particular features vary with the type of drug. For example, alcohol use disorder is characterized by features such as the following (not all need to be present):

- Spending an excessive amount of time seeking or using alcohol or recovering from overuse
- Having persistent problems cutting back or controlling alcohol use despite wanting to do so
- Using excessive amounts of alcohol beyond what the person intends
- Having difficulty fulfilling expectable roles as a student, employee, or family member because of alcohol use
- Continuing to use alcohol despite the social, interpersonal, psychological, or medical problems it causes
- Developing tolerance or a withdrawal syndrome associated with alcohol use
- Using alcohol in situations that pose a risk to the person's safety or the safety of others, such as repeatedly drinking and driving
- Having strong, persistent urges or cravings for alcohol
- Withdrawing from usual activities because of alcohol use

The previous version of the *DSM* distinguished between two types of substance use disorders: a milder form called *substance abuse disorder* and a more severe form called *substance dependence disorder*. However, because the lines between the two categories of disorders were never clearly stipulated, the *DSM-5* combined the two types of disorders into a single category of substance use disorders (Hasin et al., 2013). The *DSM-5* allows clinicians to designate the severity of the disorder by specifying whether it is mild, moderate, or severe.

People can develop substance use disorders involving a wide range of psychoactive substances, including alcohol, opioids (opiates such as heroin and morphine), sedatives and sleep-inducing or hypnotic drugs, stimulants such as cocaine and amphetamines, and tobacco. Yet the most widely used psychoactive drug, caffeine (the mild stimulant found in coffee, tea, colas, and even chocolate), is not identified with a recognized substance use disorder because it has not been reliably linked to problematic use leading to impaired functioning or personal distress. However, the *DSM-5* lists caffeine use disorder in the appendix of the diagnostic manual as a proposed diagnosis in need of further study. The *DSM-5* also recognizes that regular use of caffeine can lead to a substance withdrawal disorder following the abrupt cessation of caffeine intake after a prolonged period of daily use.

Not all nor even most of the associated features or symptoms of a substance use disorder need to be present for a diagnosis to be made. Consequently, not all persons with the same diagnosis fit the same symptom profile. For example, Henry may show clear signs of a withdrawal syndrome and have persistent difficulty curtailing use of alcohol despite multiple attempts, whereas Jessica's drinking may lead to recurrent problems at work or school and continue despite knowledge of these harmful consequences, even though she shows no evidence of a tolerance or of withdrawal symptoms when she goes without alcohol for a time.

Where does the use of a drug or psychoactive substance end and substance abuse begin? The *DSM-5* draws the line at the point at which a pattern of substance use significantly impairs a person's occupational, social, or daily functioning or causes significant personal distress. Examples of impaired functioning include the following:

- Problems meeting one's role responsibilities as a student, worker, or parent
- Engaging in behavior that is physically dangerous (e.g., mixing driving and substance use)
- Repeated social or interpersonal problems (e.g., repeatedly getting into fights when drinking)

**TWO OF THE MANY FACES OF ALCOHOL USE—AND ABUSE.** Alcohol is our most widely used—and abused—drug. Many people use alcohol to celebrate achievements and happy occasions, as in the photograph on the left. Unfortunately, like the man in the photograph on the right, some people use alcohol to drown their sorrows, which may only compound their problems. Where exactly does substance use end and abuse begin? Use becomes abuse when it leads to damaging consequences.

When people repeatedly miss school or work because they are drunk or "sleeping it off," their behavior may show signs of developing a substance use disorder. A single incident of excessive drinking at a friend's wedding would not qualify for a diagnosis. Nor would regular consumption of low to moderate amounts of alcohol be considered abusive so long as it is not connected with any impairment in functioning. Neither the amount nor the type of drug ingested, nor whether the drug use is legal or illegal, is the key to defining whether a substance use disorder is present. Rather, the determining feature of substance use disorder is whether a pattern of drug-using behavior continues even though it causes significant problems in daily functioning or personal distress.

Although public concern is largely focused on problems relating to use of illicit drugs, the most widely used substances linked to adverse consequences are legally available substances, alcohol and tobacco. To put this in context, while about 10% of adults develop substance use disorders involving illicit drugs at some point in their lives, the lifetime rates of substance use disorders involving alcohol is estimated to be as high as 29% of American adults (Compton et al., 2005; Grant et al., 2015, 2016). Also, despite significant gains in reducing smoking, about 18% of Americans continue to smoke.

Although a popular stereotype exists that drug-related problems are more frequent among ethnic minorities, this belief is not supported by evidence. To the contrary, African Americans and Latinos have comparable or even lower rates of substance use disorders than do European Americans (non-Hispanic Whites; Breslau et al., 2005; Compton et al., 2005).

# Nonchemical Addictions and Other Forms of Compulsive Behavior

**8.2 Describe nonchemical forms of addiction or compulsive behavior.**

The *DSM-5* introduced a new diagnostic category, *Substance Use and Addictive Disorders*, that includes both substance use disorders and *gambling disorder* (previously called *pathological gambling*), which is considered a nonchemical form of addiction. Pathological or compulsive gambling was previously classified in the *DSM-4* in a diagnostic category called *Impulse Control Disorders*, which included other problem behaviors also characterized by difficulties controlling or restraining impulsive behavior, such as *kleptomania* (compulsive stealing) and *pyromania* (compulsive fire setting).

The change in diagnostic classification stems from the understanding that certain compulsive or addictive patterns of behavior share important features with drug-related problems. Compulsive gambling, compulsive shopping, and even compulsive Internet use share some hallmark features of drug addiction or dependence, such as impaired control over the behavior and the development of withdrawal symptoms like anxiety and depression if the problem behavior stops abruptly. Future versions of the *DSM-5* may incorporate other behavioral addictions such as compulsive shopping and compulsive Internet use (see boxed feature below) as recognized disorders, but for now these types of disorders are considered proposed disorders requiring further study.

## Abnormal Psychology in the Digital Age

### INTERNET ADDICTION

How many hours a day do you spend looking at an electronic screen? If you are like the average young adult in the United States today, you probably clock upwards of 10 hours of screen time a day (Statista Inc., 2015). Young people today are members of a texting, Googling, and Facebooking generation who have never known a time without cell phones or the Internet (Nevid, 2011). They have been plugged into one or another electronic device since they were toddlers. These technologies have become a way of life today—and not just for the Millennial generation. The use of electronic devices has become as woven into the fabric of our daily lives today as working, eating, or even breathing. Many of us would sooner leave home without our pants than leave without our cell phones. Texting has become the preferred method of communication among young adults.

College students are especially heavy users of technology, especially smartphones (Roberts, Yaya, & Manolis, 2014). The smartphone has largely replaced the personal computer as the major channel for connecting to the Internet for many young people today, just as cell phones have come to replace land lines for telephony for many people. Of course, we should point out that very little time spent using smartphones actually involves telephony, as most young adults use smartphones mostly for texting, emailing, and checking websites and social networking sites. A recent study of six European countries found that 40% of adolescents spent more than 2 hours daily on social networking sites (Tsitsika et al., 2014).

As ingrained as the Internet has become in our daily lives, is there a point at which use of the Internet becomes so excessive or maladaptive that it crosses a threshold to addiction and poses a threat to mental health and emotional well-being? For an alarming number of people today, excessive use of the Internet is associated with a range of psychological problems (Müller et al., 2016). The term **Internet addiction disorder** (IAD) is widely used to describe a form of nonchemical addiction characterized by maladaptive use of the Internet (Young, 2015). IAD may involve excessive or maladaptive use of social networking sites, Internet chat rooms, online gaming, and online porn sites. IAD also encompasses the various ways in which people access the Internet, including via laptops, desktop computers, tablets, and smartphones.

Prevalence rates for IAD remain unknown. Estimates from cross-cultural studies vary widely, from as little as 1% in some countries to 20% or higher in others (Kuss et al., 2014; Müller et al., 2016; Wallace, 2014). Although we certainly need more definitive studies of the prevalence of the disorder, it is clear that IAD is a growing concern, especially among heavy users of the Internet such as high school and college students and and even younger students in grade school.

IAD is not an officially recognized disorder by the psychiatric profession, not yet at least. The current edition of the diagnostic manual, the *DSM-5*, lists in its appendix a related disorder, *Internet gaming disorder*, classifying it as a potential disorder requiring further study. Investigators recognize that Internet gaming has a high addictive potential, especially gaming that involves massive-user role-playing games (Billieux et al., 2014). Many users become so caught up in a virtual world that they begin to withdraw from life activities in their real lives. However, Internet gaming is only one facet of a larger problem of Internet addiction.

In conceptualizing Internet addiction as a form of abnormal behavior, we need to revisit our criteria for determining the boundaries between normal and abnormal behavior, discussed in Chapter 1. The concept of Internet addiction does not hinge on the amount of time spent in front of a display screen, as spending many hours a day using the Internet—even spending most of the waking day surfing, using online media, and connecting to social networking sites—has become normative in our society, at least among younger adults. Recall that behavior that falls within the social norm is by definition normal. We need to rely on other criteria in determining abnormal behavior, such as whether the behavior becomes maladaptive or associated with personal distress. In the college survey cited previously, 60% of students felt they were addicted to their cell phones, with some reporting feeling upset or agitated whenever their cell phones were out of sight. Feelings of distress are also observed in laboratory studies; investigators report that college students felt more anxious and performed more poorly on a puzzle-solving task when they were physically separated from their cell phones than when their phones were in their possession (Clayton, Leshner, & Almond, 2015). Signs of personal distress that might point to Internet addiction include experiencing agitation or anxiety when temporarily separated from one's cell phone (or having a dead battery) and having a lack of access to the Internet. People with Internet addiction may feel compelled to continually check status updates and text messages. Maladaptive use of the Internet may involve loss of sleep from late night online activity or excessive gaming, lower grades due to distraction during studying or attending class, or interpersonal problems caused by frequent checking of smartphones during social interactions.

*Dangerousness* is yet another criterion we can use to classify behavior as abnormal. A problem related to Internet addiction is excessive or maladaptive texting. Texting can certainly be a dangerous source of distraction when it is combined with driving or when using other mechanical equipment, or even while walking down the street or through an intersection. Compulsive texting is a maladaptive form of behavior characterized by the need to continually check text messages and to respond instantly regardless of social circumstances.

Investigators note a gender difference in the effects of compulsive texting on academic performance. A study of teens in a Midwestern community found that compulsive texting was more strongly linked to poorer academic performance in girls than boys (Lister-Landman, Domoff, & Dubow, 2015). The researchers suspect that girls may become more preoccupied and hence distracted by texting because they tend to text more than boys to maintain and bolster relationships rather than just to convey information (American Psychological Association, 2015).

Although we are still at an early stage of research on Internet addiction, brain-imaging studies of youths with Internet addiction show patterns of brain activity and neurotransmitter functioning similar to those found in people with chemical addictions and gambling disorder (Hong, Zalesky, et al., 2013; Hong, Kim, et al., 2013; Lin & Lei, 2015; Wallace, 2014). As we come to better understand Internet addiction, we need to distinguish more clearly between different forms of problematic use of the Internet, such as differences between compulsive use of online gaming sites and social networking sites (SNSs; Müller et al., 2016).

Only one form of nonchemical compulsive behavior—compulsive gambling—is presently recognized as a diagnosable addictive disorder. Not all experts believe that Internet addiction should be recognized as a distinct disorder, arguing that it may simply be a feature of other diagnosable disorders, such as obsessive–compulsive disorder (OCD) or impulse-control disorders. More research is needed to determine whether Internet addiction should be codified as a distinct diagnosis.

We are only beginning to study the risk factors associated with Internet addiction (Wallace, 2014). Higher rates are reported among males—especially adolescent and young adults males—compared to females. People with lower self-esteem and other emotional problems, such as depression and emotional instability, appear to be at higher risk, perhaps because they are more likely to use the Internet to temporarily escape from their real-life problems by entering an online fantasy world. Impulsivity is a frequently occurring personality factor associated with excessive use of the Internet, as it is with other forms of addictive behavior, such as substance abuse and gambling disorder (Burnay et al., 2015).

**INTERNET ADDICTION.** What are the signs of Internet addiction? Are you or is someone you know at risk?

The personality traits associated with overuse of SNSs differ from those we see in youths with problematic Internet gaming. For example, extraversion emerges as a predictor of both greater Facebook use and greater likelihood of developing Internet addiction involving use of SNSs (Wang et al., 2015). On the other hand, traits of aggression, hostility, and sensation-seeking may be more closely connected to gaming addiction (Wallace, 2014).

Extraversion also predicts greater Facebook use in general, so we should be careful to distinguish between general use of SNSs and problematic use. People who are high in extraversion tend to be more active users of Facebook than more introverted peers, posting more photos and status updates and having more Facebook friends (Eftekhar, Fullwood, & Morris, 2014; Lee, Ahn, & Kim, 2014). Yet people who show traits of emotional instability are more likely to post idealized profiles of themselves on Facebook, because either they lack self-esteem or don't believe that others would interact with them online if they posted a profile typical of their true selves (Michikyan, Subrahmanyam, & Dennis, 2014).

To be sure, not all Internet use is problematic. However, as we come to understand better the features of Internet addiction, we can begin to identify people who may need help controlling their use of the Internet. The self-assessment presented in Table 8.1 may give you some insight into whether Internet use may be posing a problem for you.

## Table 8.1 Are You at Risk of Internet Addiction?

Internet addiction is a not an officially recognized diagnosis, but problems associated with maladaptive use of the Internet are attracting greater attention among researchers and clinicians. The following checklist contains some dimensions investigators associate with Internet addiction. If you endorse any of these problem behaviors, you may want to consult with a college counselor or mental health professional for a more thorough evaluation to assess how your use of the Internet is affecting your life.

| Signs of Internet Addiction | Examples |
|---|---|
| Negative outcomes of Internet use | My Internet use is affecting my schoolwork or job performance.<br>Having my smartphone near my bed all the time is costing me sleep.<br>I find myself checking my phone all the time, even in the middle of the night when I should be sleeping. |
| Salience | I am always thinking about my online activity—what I posted or didn't post, or what I need to do in my next online session.<br>I can't seem to wait to get online, even when I'm at work or school or interacting with other people. |
| Mood regulation | I go online to make myself feel better.<br>When I'm feeling down or anxious, I go online to try to snap out of it. |
| Social comfort | I feel more comfortable interacting with people online than face-to-face.<br>Relating to people online is easier than dealing with them in real life. |
| Withdrawal symptoms | Whenever I'm away from the Internet for a period of time, I begin feeling agitated or anxious.<br>Not being able to get online makes me feel down or depressed. |
| Escapism | I use the Internet to escape from my negative feelings.<br>I use the Internet to escape from my life. |
| Deception/concealment | I try to hide my online behavior from others.<br>I try to conceal how much I use the Internet.<br>I have lied to others about my online activity. |

**SOURCE:** Adapted from Wallace, 2014, and other sources.

# Clarifying Terms

**8.3 Explain the difference between physiological dependence and psychological dependence.**

What is physical or chemical dependence? What do we mean by the term *drug addiction*? What is psychological dependence? A confusing medley of terms used by professionals and laypeople exists to describe problem drug use. Let's take a moment to clarify how we use such terms in this text.

We use the term **physiological dependence** (also called *chemical dependence* or *physical dependence*) to refer to a pattern of drug use behavior in which a person's body has changed as a result of regular use of the drug such that the person now requires larger amounts of the drug to achieve the same effects (tolerance) or has troubling withdrawal symptoms upon cutting back or stopping use of the drug (a withdrawal syndrome).

However, physiological dependence is not the same thing as **addiction**. Scientists lack any universally accepted definition of *addiction*. For our purposes, we define *addiction* as compulsive use of a drug accompanied by signs of physiological dependence. Addiction involves a loss of control over use of a drug despite knowledge of the harmful consequences it causes. People who are addicted to drugs have difficulty controlling how much or how often they use these drugs. They may have made many unsuccessful attempts to cut down or cut out their use of the drug or have a persistent desire to do so, but without following through.

The developers of the *DSM-5* decided to use the term *substance use disorder* for diagnostic purposes, rather than the term *addictive disorder*. They believed that the more neutral term *substance use disorder* is less stigmatizing and pejorative than the term *addiction*. They do use the term *addictive* to apply to nonchemical forms of compulsive behavior such as problem gambling. That said, the use of the term *addiction* is widespread among both professionals and laypeople alike.

People may become physically (or chemically) dependent on a drug but not become addicted. For example, people recuperating from surgery are often given narcotics derived from opium as painkillers. Some may develop signs of physiological dependence, such as tolerance and a withdrawal syndrome, but not develop impaired control over the use of these drugs. They can stop when they no longer need the drug to control pain. You (and your authors as well) may become chemically dependent on caffeine if you regularly use the substance (say, in your morning coffee) and may feel "out of sorts" or have a headache if you go a day or two without it. However, you have no difficulty controlling how much or how often you use the drug and can stop if you put your mind (and heart) to it.

Let's also consider people who develop a *nonchemical addiction*, such as compulsive gambling. They show impaired control over the problem behavior in a similar way that people with a chemical addiction have difficulty controlling their drug use. They may also show evidence of withdrawal symptoms if they cut back or stop performing the behavior. However, their withdrawal symptoms are typically psychological (e.g., anxiety, irritability, or restlessness) rather than physiological (e.g., tremors, shaking hands, nausea) in nature.

Another pattern of problem drug use involves **psychological dependence** on a drug. People who become psychologically dependent use a drug compulsively to meet their psychological needs, such as relying on a drug to combat daily stress or anxiety. They may or may not be chemically or physiologically dependent or addicted to the drug. We can think of people who feel compelled to use marijuana (or caffeine or other drugs) to cope with the stresses of daily life, but do not require larger amounts of the substance to get high or experience distressing withdrawal symptoms when they cease using it. **T / F**

**TRUTH *or* FICTION**

You cannot become psychologically dependent on a drug without also becoming physically dependent on it.

☑ **FALSE** You can become psychologically dependent on a drug without developing a physiological dependence.

## Pathways to Addiction

**8.4 Identify common stages in the pathway to drug dependence.**

No one sets out to become addicted to drugs. What may have started as experimentation can progress through a series of stages to drug dependence or addiction. Just as there are different routes to follow to arrive at the same destination, there are different pathways to addiction. Here, we consider a common pathway in the road to addiction that involves three stages (based on Weiss & Mirin, 1987):

1. *Experimentation*. During the stage of experimentation, or occasional use, the drug temporarily makes users feel good, even euphoric. Users feel in control and believe they can stop at any time.
2. *Routine use*. During the next stage, a period of routine use, people begin to structure their lives around the pursuit and use of drugs. Denial plays a major role at this stage, as users mask the negative consequences of their behavior to themselves and others. Values change. What had formerly been important, such as family and work, comes to matter less than the drugs.

   A case example illustrates how denial can mask reality (Weiss & Mirin, 1987). A 48-year-old business owner was brought for a consultation by his wife. She complained that his once-successful business was jeopardized by his erratic behavior, that he was grouchy and moody, and had spent $7,000 in the previous month on cocaine. He also had missed more than a third of his workdays during the previous 2 months due to cocaine use. Yet he continued to deny that he had a problem with cocaine, telling the interviewer that missing so many days from work was not a big deal and that his company could run itself. When pressed further on the point, he still was unwilling to admit to his drug problem, but confessed that he just didn't want to think about it.

   As routine drug use continues, problems mount. Users devote more resources to drugs. They ravage family bank accounts, seek "temporary" loans from friends and family for trumped-up reasons, and sell family heirlooms and jewelry for a fraction of

**ADDICTION.** Although no one sets out to become addicted to drugs, routine drug use can lead to addiction when users feel powerless to control their use of drugs.

their value. Lying and manipulation become a way of life to cover up the drug use. A husband sells the TV set and forces the front door open to make it look like a burglary. A wife claims to have been robbed at knifepoint to explain the disappearance of a gold chain or engagement ring. Family relationships become strained as the mask of denial shatters and the consequences of drug abuse become apparent: days lost from work, unexplained absences from home, rapid mood shifts, depletion of family finances, failure to pay bills, stealing from family members, and missing family gatherings or children's birthday parties.

3. *Addiction or dependence*. Routine use becomes addiction or dependence when users feel powerless to resist drugs, either because they want to experience their effects or to avoid the consequences of withdrawal. Little or nothing else matters at this stage, as we saw in the case of Eugene that opened the chapter.

Now, let's examine the effects of different types of drugs of abuse and the consequences associated with their use and abuse.

# Drugs of Abuse

Drugs of abuse are generally classified within three major groupings: (a) depressants, such as alcohol and opioids; (b) stimulants, such as amphetamines and cocaine; and (c) hallucinogens, such as mescaline and LSD.

## Depressants

**8.5 Describe the effects of depressants and the risks they pose.**

A **depressant** is a drug that slows down or curbs the activity of the central nervous system. It reduces feelings of tension and anxiety, slows movement, and impairs cognitive processes. In high doses, depressants can arrest vital functions and cause death. The most widely used depressant, alcohol, can cause death when taken in large amounts because of its depressant effects on breathing. Other effects are specific to the particular kind of depressant. For example, some depressants, such as heroin, produce a "rush" of pleasure. Let's consider several major types of depressants.

**ALCOHOL** Alcohol is the most widely abused substance in the United States and worldwide. You might not think of alcohol as a drug, perhaps because it is so common, or perhaps because it is ingested by drinking rather than by smoking or injection. However, alcoholic beverages—such as wine, beer, and hard liquor—contain a depressant drug called *ethyl alcohol* (or *ethanol*). The concentration of the drug varies with the type of beverage (wine and beer have less pure alcohol per ounce than distilled spirits such as rye, gin, or vodka). Alcohol is classified as a depressant because it has biochemical effects similar to those of a class of antianxiety agents or minor tranquilizers, the *benzodiazepines*, which includes the well-known drugs *diazepam* (Valium) and *chlordiazepoxide* (Librium). We can think of alcohol as an over-the-counter tranquilizer.

Most American adults drink alcohol at least occasionally and do so in moderation—but many people develop significant problems with alcohol. As you can see in Figure 8.1, about three in ten American adults overall develop an alcohol use disorder during their lifetime, but as you can also see, the disorder is much more prevalent among men than women (Grant et al., 2015). Figure 8.1 shows both lifetime and current (past-year) rates of alcohol use disorder in the general population.

Many laypeople and professionals use the terms **alcoholism** and *alcohol dependence* interchangeably, and we will do the same. We use either term to refer to a pattern of impaired control over the use of alcohol in someone who has become physiologically

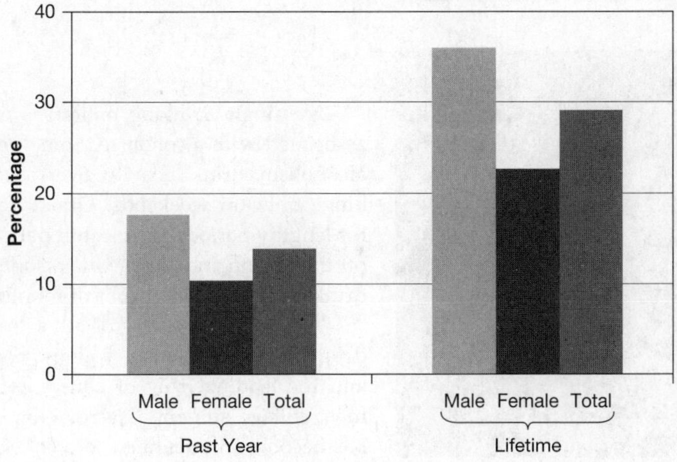


**Figure 8.1** Past Year and Lifetime Prevalence of Alcohol Use Disorders in the General Population

**SOURCE:** Grant et al., 2015.

dependent on the drug. An estimated eight million U.S. adults suffer from alcoholism (Kranzler, 2006).

The most widely held view of alcoholism is the disease model, the belief that alcoholism is a medical illness or disease. From this perspective, once a person with alcoholism takes a drink, the biochemical effects of the drug on the brain create an irresistible physical craving for more. The disease model holds that alcoholism is a chronic, permanent condition. The peer-support group Alcoholics Anonymous (AA) subscribes to this view, which is expressed in their slogan, "Once an alcoholic, always an alcoholic." AA views people suffering from alcoholism as either drinking or "recovering," never "cured." Although some health care providers believe that at least some alcohol abusers can learn to drink responsibly without "falling off the wagon," the belief remains a source of controversy in the field.

The personal and social costs of alcoholism exceed those of all illicit drugs combined. Alcohol abuse is connected with lower productivity, loss of jobs, and downward movement in socioeconomic status. Alcohol plays a role in many violent crimes, including assaults and homicides, and more than 180,000 rapes and sexual attacks annually in the United States (Bartholow & Heinz, 2006; Buddie & Testa, 2005). About one in three suicides in the United States and about the same proportion of deaths due to unintentional injury (e.g., from motor vehicle accidents) are linked to alcohol use (Sher, 2005; Shneidman, 2005). More teenagers and young adults die from alcohol-related motor vehicle accidents than from any other cause. All told, about 88,000 people in the United States die from alcohol-related causes each year, with most of these deaths resulting from alcohol-related motor vehicle crashes and diseases ("Heavy Toll," 2014; Kleiman, Caulkins, & Hawken, 2012). Deaths due to alcohol-related causes account for about one in 10 deaths among all working-age adults in the United States. **T / F**

### TRUTH *or* FICTION

More teenagers and young adults die from alcohol-related motor vehicle accidents than from any other cause.

☑ **TRUE** Alcohol-related motor vehicle accidents are the leading cause of death among teenagers and young adults.

Despite the popular image of the person who develops alcoholism as a skid row drunk, only a small minority of people with alcoholism fit the stereotype. The great majority of people with alcoholism are quite ordinary: your neighbors, coworkers, friends, and members of your own family. They are found in all walks of life and every social and economic class. Many have families, hold good jobs, and live fairly comfortably. Yet alcoholism can have just as devastating an effect on the well-to-do as on the indigent, leading to wrecked careers and marriages, to motor vehicle and other accidents, and to severe, life-threatening physical disorders, as well as exacting an enormous emotional toll. Alcoholism is also linked to domestic violence and increased risk of divorce (Foran & O'Leary, 2008).

CHRIS: ALCOHOLISM

No single drinking pattern is exclusively associated with alcoholism. Some people with alcoholism drink heavily every day; others binge only on weekends. Others can abstain for lengthy periods of time, but periodically go off the wagon and engage in episodes of binge drinking that last for weeks or months.

Alcohol, not cocaine or other drugs, is the drug of choice among young people today and the leading drug of abuse. Even though most college students are underage, drinking has become so integrated into college life that it is essentially normative, as much a part of the college experience as attending a weekend football or basketball game. Alcohol, not cocaine, heroin, or even marijuana, is the BDOC—the big drug on campus.

Drinking among college students tends to be limited to weekends and to be heavier early in the semester when academic demands are relatively light (Del Boca et al., 2004). College students tend to drink more than their peers who do not attend college (Slutske, 2005). Researchers describe a continuum of alcohol-related problems among college students, ranging from mild problems, such as missing class, to extreme problem behaviors, such as arrests resulting from drinking (Ham & Hope, 2003). In *A Closer Look: Binge Drinking, a Dangerous College Pastime,* we focus on a form of problem drinking that has become a leading issue on college campuses today.

## Questionnaire

### ARE YOU HOOKED?

Are you dependent on alcohol? If you shake and shiver and undergo the tortures of "Hell" when you go without a drink for a while, the answer is clear enough. However, sometimes the clues are more subtle. For the following quiz, place a check mark in the Yes or No column for each item. Then, check the key at the end of the chapter.

| | Yes | No |
|---|---|---|
| 1. Do you skip meals when you are drinking or eat only junk food? | ______ | ______ |
| 2. Do you feel down in the dumps after you've been drinking? | ______ | ______ |
| 3. Do you drink more than most people you know? | ______ | ______ |
| 4. Are you drinking more than usual? | ______ | ______ |
| 5. Do you binge drink on occasion? | ______ | ______ |
| 6. Are you sleeping it off in the morning after going out drinking the night before? | ______ | ______ |
| 7. Have you missed work or school, or come in late, because of your drinking? | ______ | ______ |
| 8. Have you been avoiding friends or family because you are embarrassed or feeling guilty about your drinking? | ______ | ______ |
| 9. Do you find it difficult to go a day or two without drinking? | ______ | ______ |
| 10. Do you need to drink more and more, just to get drunk? | ______ | ______ |
| 11. Have you become more irritable because of your drinking? | ______ | ______ |
| 12. Have you done things when you've been drinking that you later regretted? | ______ | ______ |

***Risk Factors for Alcoholism*** A number of factors place people at increased risk for developing alcoholism and alcohol-related problems. These include the following:

1. *Gender*. Men are more than twice as likely as women to develop alcoholism (Hasin et al., 2006). One possible reason for this gender difference is sociocultural; perhaps tighter cultural constraints are placed on women. Yet it may also be that alcohol hits

## A CLOSER Look

### BINGE DRINKING, A DANGEROUS COLLEGE PASTIME

Binge drinking is a major drug problem on college campuses today. Binge drinking is generally defined as consuming five or more drinks (for men) or four or more drinks (for women) on a single occasion. More than two out of five college students report binge drinking episodes during the prior month (Patrick & Schulenberg, 2011; Squeglia et al., 2012). Binge drinking is also reported by about one in four high school students (24%; Johnston et al., 2012). Overall, nearly one in five American adults (17%) reported a binge drinking episode during the past month (CDC, 2012c).

Concerns about binge drinking are well founded. Binge drinking is associated with a wide range of problems, including getting into trouble with the police, engaging in unprotected sexual activity, serious motor vehicle and other accidents, unintended pregnancies, violent behavior, getting poorer grades, and developing alcoholism and other drug use problems (e.g., CDC, 2012c; Wechsler & Nelson, 2008). Things can get even worse, as they did in the tragic case of Leslie, a young college student at the University of Virginia. An art major whose work her professors found promising, Leslie had maintained a 3.67 GPA and was completing her senior essay on a Polish-born sculptor (Winerip, 1998). She never finished it, because one day, after binge drinking, she fell down a flight of stairs and died. We may hear more about the deaths of young people due to heroin or cocaine overdoses, but more than 1,000 college-age students, like Leslie, die each year from alcohol-related causes such as overdoses and alcohol-related accidents (Yaccino, 2012).

Binge drinking is quite common, even ritualized in some cases, such as in the celebration of reaching the legal drinking age of 21 (Neighbors et al., 2012). A survey at the University of Missouri showed that about one third of college men and about one fourth of college women reported consuming at least 21 drinks or more on their 21st birthday. This represents a level of severe intoxication that can result in significant health risks, including coma and even death (Rutledge, Park, & Sher, 2008). The findings of the Missouri study likely generalize to many college campuses.

In an influential review article, psychologists Lindsay Ham and Debra Hope (2003) identified two general subtypes of college students who appear most clearly at risk of becoming problem drinkers. The first type includes students who drink mostly for social or enjoyment purposes. They tend to be male, European American, and participate in Greek organizations or other social organizations in which heavy drinking is socially acceptable. The second type includes students who drink due to pressures to conform or who use alcohol to soothe negative feelings. They more often tend to be female and to be troubled by problems with anxiety or depression. Generating these profiles may help counselors and health care providers identify young people at increased risk of developing problem drinking patterns.

**A DANGEROUS PASTIME.** Beer chugging and binge drinking can quickly lead to an alcohol overdose, a medical emergency that can have lethal consequences. Many college officials cite binge drinking as the major drug problem on campus.

Binge drinking and related drinking games (such as beer chugging) can place people at significant risk of death from alcohol overdose. Many students who play these games don't stop until they become too drunk or too sick to continue. What should you do if you see a friend or acquaintance become incapacitated or pass out from heavy drinking? Should you just let the person sleep it off? Can you tell whether a person has had too much to drink? Should you just mind your own business or turn to others for help?

You cannot tell simply by looking at a person whether he or she has overdosed on alcohol, but a person who becomes unconscious or unresponsive is in need of immediate medical attention. Don't assume that the person will simply sleep it off: He or she may never wake up. Be aware of the signs of potential overdose, such as the following (adapted from Nevid & Rathus, 2013):

- Nonresponsive when talked to or shouted at
- Nonresponsive to being pinched, shaken, or poked
- Unable to stand up on his or her own
- Failure to wake up or gain consciousness
- Purplish color or clammy-feeling skin
- Rapid pulse rate or irregular heart rhythms, low blood pressure, or difficulty breathing

**DEATH BY ALCOHOL.** Samantha Spady, a 19-year-old Colorado State University student, blacked out when drinking with her friends and never woke up. Samantha died of an alcohol overdose from heavy drinking. Would you recognize the signs of an alcohol overdose? What steps could you take—should you take—to help a friend or acquaintance who shows signs of an overdose?

If you suspect an overdose, do not leave the person alone. Summon medical help or emergency assistance and remain with the person until help arrives. If the person is responsive, find out if he or she has taken any medication or other drugs that might be interacting with the effects of the alcohol. Also, find out whether the person has an underlying illness that may contribute to the problem, such as diabetes or epilepsy. **T / F**

## TRUTH *or* FICTION

It is safe to let someone who has passed out from drinking just sleep it off.

☑ **FALSE** Sadly, the person may never wake up. Passing out from drinking needs to be treated as a medical emergency.

It may be easier to just pass by without taking action, but ask yourself: What you would like someone else to do if you showed signs of overdosing on alcohol? Wouldn't you want one of your friends to intervene to save your life?

**WOMEN AND ALCOHOL.** Women are less likely to develop alcoholism, in part because of greater cultural constraints on excessive drinking by women, and perhaps because women absorb more pure alcohol into the bloodstream than men, making them more biologically sensitive to the effects of alcohol at the same level of intake as men.

women harder, and not only because women usually weigh less than men. Alcohol seems to "go to women's heads" more rapidly than to men's. One reason may be that women have less of an enzyme that metabolizes alcohol in the stomach than men do. Ounce for ounce, women absorb more alcohol into their bloodstreams than men do. As a result, they are likely to become inebriated on less alcohol than men. Consequently, women's bodies may put the brakes on excessive drinking more quickly than men's.

2. *Age*. The great majority of cases of alcohol dependence develop in young adulthood, typically between the ages of 20 and 40. Although alcohol use disorders tend to develop somewhat later in women than in men, women who develop these problems experience similar health, social, and occupational problems by middle age as their male counterparts.
3. *Antisocial personality disorder*. Antisocial behavior in adolescence or adulthood increases the risk of later alcoholism. On the other hand, many people with alcoholism showed no antisocial tendencies in adolescence, and many antisocial adolescents do not abuse alcohol or other drugs as adults.
4. *Family history*. The best predictor of problem drinking in adulthood appears to be a family history of alcohol abuse. Family members who drink may act as models ("set a poor example"). Moreover, the biological relatives of people with alcohol dependence may also inherit a predisposition that makes them more likely to develop problems with alcohol.
5. *Sociodemographic factors*. Alcohol dependence is generally more common among people of lower income and educational levels, as well as among people living alone.

***Ethnicity and Alcohol Use and Abuse*** Rates of alcohol use and alcoholism vary among American ethnic and racial groups. Some groups—Jews, Italians, Greeks, and Asians—have relatively low rates of alcoholism, largely as the result of tight social controls placed on excessive and underage drinking. Asian Americans, in general, drink less heavily than other population groups (Adelson, 2006). Not only do Asian families place strong cultural constraints on excessive drinking, but an underlying biological factor may be at work in curbing alcohol use. Asian Americans are more likely than other groups to show a *flushing* response to alcohol (Peng et al., 2010). Flushing is characterized by redness and feelings of warmth on the face and, at higher doses, nausea, heart palpitations, dizziness, and headaches. Genes that control the metabolism of alcohol are believed to be responsible for regulating the flushing response (Luczak, Glatt, & Wall, 2006). Because people like to avoid these unpleasant experiences, flushing may serve as a natural defense against alcoholism by curbing excessive alcohol intake.

Hispanic American men and non-Hispanic White men have similar rates of alcohol consumption and alcohol-related physical problems. Hispanic American women, however, are much less likely to use alcohol and to develop alcohol use disorders than non-Hispanic White women. *Why?* An important factor may be cultural expectations. Traditional Hispanic American cultures place severe restrictions on the use of alcohol by women, especially heavy drinking. However, with increasing acculturation, Hispanic American women in the United States apparently are becoming more similar to European American women with respect to alcohol use and abuse.

Alcohol abuse is taking a heavy toll on African Americans (Zapolski et al., 2014). For example, the prevalence of *cirrhosis of the liver*, an alcohol-related, potentially fatal liver disease, is nearly twice as high in African Americans as in non-Hispanic White Americans. Yet African Americans show lower rates of alcohol abuse and dependence than do (non-Hispanic) White Americans. Why, then, do African Americans suffer more from alcohol-related problems?

Socioeconomic factors may help explain these differences. African Americans are more likely to encounter the stresses of unemployment and economic hardship, and stress may compound the damage to the body caused by heavy alcohol consumption. African Americans also tend to lack access to medical services and may be less likely to receive early treatment for the medical problems caused by alcohol abuse.

Rates of alcohol abuse and dependence vary from tribe to tribe, but Native Americans overall have higher rates of alcoholism and suffer from more alcohol-related problems than any other ethnic group—problems such as cirrhosis of the liver, fetal abnormalities, and automobile and other accident-related fatalities (Henry et al., 2011; Spillane & Smith, 2009). A recent national survey of adolescents found the highest rates of substance use and substance use disorders involving alcohol and drugs to be among Native American youth (Wu et al., 2011).

Many Native Americans believe the loss of their traditional culture is largely responsible for their high rates of drinking-related problems (Beauvais, 1998). The disruption of traditional Native American culture caused by the appropriation of Indian lands and by attempts by European American society to sever Native Americans from their cultural traditions while denying them full access to the dominant culture resulted in severe cultural and social disorganization (Kahn, 1982). Beset by such problems, Native Americans are also prone to child abuse and neglect. Abuse and neglect contribute to feelings of hopelessness and depression among adolescents, who may seek escape from their feelings by using alcohol and other drugs.

**ALCOHOL AND ETHNIC DIVERSITY.** The damaging effects of alcohol abuse appear to be taking the heaviest toll on African Americans and Native Americans. The prevalence of alcohol-related cirrhosis of the liver is nearly twice as high among African Americans as among White Americans, even though African Americans are less likely to develop alcohol abuse or dependence disorders. Jewish Americans have relatively low incidences of alcohol-related problems, perhaps because they tend to expose children to the ritual use of wine in childhood and impose strong cultural restraints on excessive drinking. Asian Americans tend to drink less heavily than most other Americans, in part because of cultural constraints and possibly because they have less biological tolerance for alcohol, as shown by a greater flushing response to alcohol.

***Psychological Effects of Alcohol*** The effects of alcohol or other drugs vary from person to person. By and large, they reflect the interaction of (a) the physiological effects of the substances and (b) our interpretations of those effects. What do most people expect from alcohol? People frequently hold stereotypical expectations that alcohol will reduce tension, enhance pleasurable experiences, wash away worries, and enhance social skills. But what does alcohol *actually* do?

At a physiological level, alcohol appears to work like the benzodiazepines (a family of antianxiety drugs) by heightening activity of the neurotransmitter GABA (see Chapter 5). Because GABA is an inhibitory neurotransmitter (it tones down nervous system activity), increasing GABA activity produces feelings of relaxation. As people drink, their senses become clouded, and balance and coordination suffer. Still higher doses act on the parts of the brain that regulate involuntary vital functions, such as heart rate, respiration rate, and body temperature.

People may do many things when drinking that they would not do when sober, in part because of expectations concerning the drug and in part because of the drug's effects on the brain. For example, they may become more flirtatious or sexually aggressive or say or do things they later regret. Their behavior may reflect their expectation that alcohol has liberating effects and provides an external excuse for questionable behavior. Later, they can claim, "It was the alcohol, not me." The drug may also impair the brain's ability to curb impulsive, risk-taking, or violent behavior, perhaps by interfering with information-processing functions. Investigators find strong links between alcohol use and many forms of violent behavior, including domestic violence and sexual assaults (Abbey et al., 2004; Fals-Stewart, 2003; Marshal, 2003).

Alcohol may lead people to feel more relaxed and self-confident, but it also impairs judgment, making it more difficult for people to weigh the consequences of their behavior. Under the influence of alcohol, people may make choices they might ordinarily reject, such as engaging in risky sexual behavior (Bersamin et al., 2012; Orchowski, Mastroleo, & Borsari, 2012; Ragsdale et al., 2012). Chronic alcohol abuse can impair cognitive abilities, such as memory, problem solving, and attention.

One of the lures of alcohol is that it induces short-term feelings of euphoria and elation that can drown self-doubts and self-criticism. Alcohol also makes people less capable of perceiving the unfortunate consequences of their behavior.

Alcohol use can dampen sexual arousal or excitement and impair sexual performance. As an intoxicant, alcohol also hampers coordination and motor ability. These effects help explain why alcohol use is implicated in about one in three accidental deaths in the United States.

***Physical Health and Alcohol*** Chronic, heavy alcohol use affects virtually every organ and body system, either directly or indirectly. Heavy alcohol use is linked to increased risk of many serious health concerns, including liver disease, increased risk of some forms of cancer, coronary heart disease, and neurological disorders. Two of the major forms of alcohol-related liver disease are *alcoholic hepatitis*, a serious and potentially life-threatening inflammation of the liver, and cirrhosis of the liver, a potentially fatal disease in which healthy liver cells are replaced with scar tissue.

Habitual drinkers tend to be malnourished, which can put them at risk of complications arising from nutritional deficiencies. Chronic drinking is thus associated with nutritionally linked disorders such as cirrhosis of the liver (linked to protein deficiency) and *Korsakoff's syndrome* (connected with vitamin B deficiency), the latter of which is characterized by glaring confusion, disorientation, and memory loss for recent events (see Chapter 14).

Pregnant women who drink place their fetuses at risk for infant mortality, birth defects, central nervous system dysfunctions, and later academic problems. Children whose mothers drink during pregnancy may also develop *fetal alcohol syndrome* (FAS), a syndrome characterized by facial features such as a flattened nose and widely spaced eyes and by mental retardation and social skills deficits. As many as 5% of U.S. children are believed to be affected to some degree by FAS ("Fetal Alcohol Spectrum," 2014; May et al., 2014). Although the risk of FAS is greater among women who drink heavily during pregnancy, the syndrome has also been found among children of mothers who drank as little as a drink and a half per week (Carroll, 2003). As there is no established "safe" limit for alcohol use by pregnant women, the safest course for women who know or suspect they are pregnant is not to drink (Feldman et al., 2012; Stein, 2012). *Period.* The fact remains that FAS is an entirely preventable birth defect.

***Moderate Drinking: Is There a Health Benefit?*** Despite this list of adverse effects associated with heavy drinking, correlational evidence links moderate use of alcohol (about one drink per day for women, about two drinks for men) to lower risks of heart attacks and strokes, as well as to lower death rates overall (Bollmann et al., 2014; Gémes et al., 2015; Ronksley et al., 2011). That said, we should point out that higher doses of alcohol used on a regular basis are associated with higher mortality (death) rates. **T / F**

Although it is possible that moderate alcohol use has a protective effect on the heart and circulatory system, public health officials have not endorsed use of alcohol for this reason, based largely on concerns that such an endorsement might increase risks of problem drinking. Also, investigators lack definitive evidence from experimental research that alcohol use is causally related to lower health risks (Rabin, 2009). We should also recognize that even moderate drinking has a modest effect on increasing the risk of breast cancer in women (Jayasekara et al., 2015; Kaunitz, 2011; Narod, 2011). Health promotion efforts might be better directed toward finding safer ways of achieving the health benefits associated with moderate drinking than by encouraging alcohol consumption, such as by quitting smoking, lowering dietary intake of fat and cholesterol, and exercising more regularly.

## TRUTH or FICTION

Even moderate use of alcohol increases the risk of heart attacks.

☑ **FALSE** Findings from recent studies show that moderate intake of alcohol is associated with a lower risk of heart attacks and lower death rates.

**BARBITURATES** About 1% of adult Americans develop a substance use disorder involving use of barbiturates, sleep medication (hypnotics), or antianxiety agents at some point in their lives. **Barbiturates** such as *amobarbital, pentobarbital, phenobarbital,* and *secobarbital* are depressants, or *sedatives.* These drugs have several medical uses, including easing anxiety and tension, dulling pain, and treating epilepsy and high blood pressure. Barbiturate use quickly leads to psychological and physiological dependence in the form of both tolerance and development of a withdrawal syndrome.

Barbiturates are also popular street drugs because they are relaxing and produce a mild state of euphoria, or a high. High doses of barbiturates, like alcohol, produce drowsiness, slurred speech, motor impairment, irritability, and poor judgment—a particularly deadly combination of effects when their use is combined with operation of a motor vehicle. The effects of barbiturates last from three to six hours.

Because of synergistic effects, a mixture of barbiturates and alcohol is about four times as powerful as either drug used alone. A combination of barbiturates and alcohol was implicated in the deaths of the actresses Marilyn Monroe and Judy Garland. Even such widely used antianxiety drugs as Valium and Librium, which have a wide margin of safety when used alone, can be dangerous and lead to overdoses when combined with alcohol.

Physiologically dependent people need to be withdrawn carefully from sedatives, barbiturates, and antianxiety agents, and only under medical supervision. Abrupt withdrawal can produce states of delirium that may involve visual, tactile, or auditory hallucinations and disturbances in thought processes and consciousness. The longer the period of use and the higher the doses used, the greater the risk of severe withdrawal effects. Epileptic (grand mal) seizures and even death may occur if an individual undergoes untreated, abrupt withdrawal.

**OPIOIDS** Opioids are classified as **narcotics**—strongly addictive drugs that have pain-relieving and sleep-inducing properties. Opioids include both naturally occurring opiates (morphine, heroin, codeine) derived from the poppy plant and synthetic drugs (e.g., Demerol, Vicodin) that have opiate-like effects. The ancient Sumerians named the poppy plant *opium,* meaning "plant of joy."

Opioids produce a *rush,* or intense feelings of pleasure, which is the primary reason for their popularity as street drugs. They also dull awareness of one's personal problems, which is attractive to people seeking a mental escape from stress. Their pleasurable effects derive from their ability to directly stimulate the brain's pleasure circuits—the same brain networks responsible for feelings of sexual pleasure or pleasure from eating a satisfying meal.

The major medical application of opioids—natural or synthetic—is the relief of pain, or *analgesia.* Medical use of opioids, however, is carefully regulated, because overdoses can lead to coma and even death. Street use of opioids is associated with many fatal overdoses and accidents. In a number of American cities, young men are more likely to die of a heroin overdose than in an automobile accident.

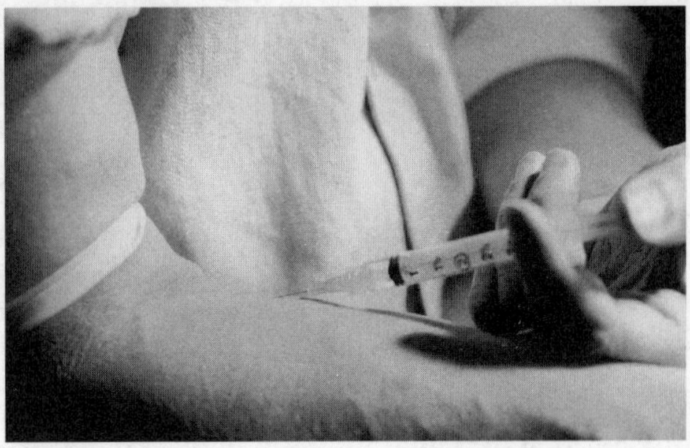

**SHOOTING UP.** Heroin users often inject the substance directly into their veins. Heroin is a powerful depressant that provides a euphoric rush. Users often claim that heroin is so pleasurable that it obliterates any thought of food or sex.

About 1.6 percent of Americans aged 12 or older report using heroin at some point in their lives and about 0.2% (2 in 1,000) report using the drug during the prior year (SAMHSA, 2012). Once dependence sets in, it usually becomes chronic, relieved only by brief periods of abstinence. Physical dependence often develops within a few weeks of regular use (Brady, McCauley, & Back, 2016).

Adding to the problem is that prescription opioids, which are prescribed medically for pain relief, can become drugs of abuse when they are used illicitly as street drugs. Many young adults have become dependent on prescription opioids (such as Oxycontin and Vicodin), which they obtain from physicians who overprescribe them or illicitly from street dealers (Bakes, 2013; Whiteside et al., 2013).

Two discoveries made in the 1970s show that the brain produces chemicals of its own that have opiate-like effects. One discovery was that neurons in the brain have receptor sites in which opiates fit like a key in a lock. The second was that the human body produces its own opiate-like substances that dock at the same receptor sites as opiates do. These natural substances, or **endorphins**, play important roles in regulating natural states of pleasure and pain. Opioids mimic the actions of endorphins by docking at receptor sites intended for endorphins, dulling pain and stimulating brain centers that produce pleasurable sensations. This helps explain why use of narcotic drugs produces feelings of pleasure (release of dopamine is yet another factor). Investigators have recently learned that drinking alcohol stimulates release of endorphins in the brain as well, which may help to account for why alcohol makes people feel good (Mitchell et al., 2012).

The withdrawal syndrome associated with opioids can be severe. It begins within four to six hours of the last dose. Flu-like symptoms are accompanied by anxiety, feelings of restlessness, irritability, and cravings for the drug. Within a few days, symptoms progress to rapid pulse, high blood pressure, cramps, tremors, hot and cold flashes, fever, vomiting, insomnia, and diarrhea, among others. Although these symptoms can be uncomfortable, they are usually not devastating, especially when other drugs are prescribed to relieve them. Moreover, unlike withdrawal from barbiturates, the withdrawal syndrome rarely results in death.

***Morphine*** **Morphine**—which receives its name from Morpheus, the Greek god of dreams—was introduced at about the time of the American Civil War. This powerful opium derivative was used liberally to deaden pain from wounds. Physiological dependence on morphine became known as the "soldier's disease." There was little stigma attached to dependence until morphine became a restricted substance.

***Heroin*** **Heroin**, the most widely used opiate, is a powerful depressant that can create a euphoric rush. Users of heroin claim that it is so pleasurable it can eradicate any thought of food or sex. Heroin was developed in 1875 during a search for a drug that would relieve pain as effectively as morphine, but without causing addiction. Chemist Heinrich Dreser transformed morphine into a drug believed to have "heroic" effects in relieving pain without addiction, which is why it was called *heroin*. Unfortunately, heroin does lead to a strong physiological dependence.

About four million Americans have used heroin at some point in their lives, and some 300,000 are current users (SAMHSA, 2012). More than half of current users are addicted to heroin. Most heroin users are men over the age of 25. The average age of first use is about 22 years. Heroin addiction is not limited to decaying, inner-city neighborhoods; in fact, it is now primarily affecting Caucasian men and women in their late 20s who live outside large urban areas (Cicero et al., 2014). **T / F**

## TRUTH *or* FICTION

Heroin addiction primarily affects people in decaying, inner-city neighborhoods.

☑ FALSE Heroin addiction is now more common in communities outside large urban areas.

Heroin is usually injected either directly beneath the skin (skin popping) or into a vein (mainlining). The effects are immediate. There is a powerful rush that lasts from 5 to 15 minutes and a state of satisfaction, euphoria, and well-being that lasts from 3 to 5 hours. In this state, all positive drives seem satisfied. All negative feelings of guilt, tension, and anxiety disappear. With prolonged usage, addiction can develop. Many heroin-dependent people support their habits through dealing (selling heroin), prostitution, or selling stolen goods. Heroin is a depressant, however, and its chemical effects do not directly stimulate criminal or aggressive behavior.

# Stimulants

**8.6 Describe the effects of stimulants and the risks they pose.**

**Stimulants** are psychoactive substances that increase the activity of the central nervous system, which enhances states of alertness, and can produce feelings of pleasure or even euphoric highs. The effects vary with the particular drug.

**AMPHETAMINES** The **amphetamines** are a class of synthetic stimulants. Street names for stimulants include speed, uppers, bennies (for *amphetamine sulfate*; trade name Benzedrine), meth (for *methamphetamine*; trade name Methedrine), and dexies (for *dextroamphetamine*; trade name Dexedrine).

Amphetamines are used in high doses for their euphoric rush. They are often taken in pill form or smoked in a relatively pure form called ice or crystal meth. The most potent form of amphetamine, liquid methamphetamine, is injected directly into the veins and produces an intense and immediate rush. Some users inject methamphetamine for days on end to maintain an extended high. Eventually, such highs come to an end. People who have been on extended highs sometimes "crash" and fall into a deep sleep or depression. Some people commit suicide on the way down. High doses can cause restlessness, irritability, hallucinations, paranoid delusions, loss of appetite, and insomnia.

About 5% of Americans aged 12 or older report using meth at some point in their lives and about 0.3% (3 in 1,000) report using the drug in the past year (SAMHSA, 2012). In all, more than 12 million Americans have used meth at some point in their lives (Jefferson, 2005). Physiological dependence can develop from using amphetamines, leading to an abstinence syndrome characterized by depression and fatigue, as well as by unpleasant, vivid dreams, insomnia or hypersomnia (excessive sleeping), increased appetite, and either a slowing down of motor behavior or agitation (American Psychiatric Association, 2013). Psychological dependence is seen most often in people who use amphetamines as a way of coping with stress or depression.

Methamphetamine abuse can cause brain damage, producing deficits in learning and memory in addition to other effects (Thompson et al., 2004; Toomey et al., 2003). Chronic use is also associated with increased depression, aggressive behavior, and social isolation (Homer et al., 2008). Impulsive acts of violence may also occur, especially when the drug is smoked or injected intravenously. The hallucinations and delusions of **amphetamine psychosis** mimic those of paranoid schizophrenia, which has encouraged researchers to study the chemical changes induced by amphetamines as possible clues to the underlying causes of schizophrenia.

**ECSTASY** The drug *ecstasy*, or MDMA (3,4-methylenedioxymethamphetamine), is a *designer drug*, a chemical knockoff similar in chemical structure to amphetamine. It produces mild euphoria and hallucinations. Teen use of ecstasy dropped significantly in the early years of the new millennium and then rose for a few years before declining again (Johnston et al., 2012). Perhaps the message about the dangers of ecstasy is beginning to get across to young people.

Ecstasy can produce adverse psychological effects, including depression, anxiety, insomnia, and even paranoia and psychosis. The drug can cause brain damage that impairs cognitive performance on tasks involving attention, learning, and memory

(Di Iorio et al., 2011; de Win et al., 2008). The greater the amount people use, the greater their risk of suffering long-lasting changes in the brain. Scientists suspect the drug kills or damages the neurons that produce the neurotransmitters dopamine and serotonin, key chemicals in the brain involved in regulating mood states and ability to reap pleasure from everyday life (Di Iorio et al., 2011; van Zessen et al., 2012). Physical side effects include higher heart rate and blood pressure, a tense or chattering jaw, and body warmth and/or chills. The drug can be lethal when taken in high doses.

**TRUTH or FICTION**

*Coca-Cola* originally contained cocaine.

☑ **TRUE** The original formula for *Coca-Cola* contained an extract of cocaine.

**COCAINE** It might surprise you to learn that the original formula for *Coca-Cola* contained an extract of **cocaine**. In 1906, however, the Coca-Cola company withdrew cocaine from its secret formula. The drink was originally described as a "brain tonic and intellectual beverage," in part because of its cocaine content. Cocaine is a natural stimulant extracted from the leaves of the coca plant—the plant from which the soft drink obtained its name. *Coca-Cola* is still flavored with an extract from the coca plant, but one that is not known to have psychoactive effects. **T / F**

It was long believed that cocaine was not physically addicting. However, the drug produces a tolerance effect and an identifiable withdrawal syndrome, which is characterized by depressed mood and disturbances in sleep and appetite. Intense cravings for the drug and loss of ability to experience pleasure may also be present. Withdrawal symptoms are usually brief in duration and may involve a crash, or period of intense depression and exhaustion, following abrupt withdrawal.

Cocaine is usually snorted in powder form or smoked in the form of **crack**, a hardened form of cocaine that may be more than 75% pure. Crack "rocks"—so called because they look like small white pebbles—are available in small, ready-to-smoke amounts and are considered to be the most habit-forming street drug available. Crack produces a prompt and potent rush that wears off in a few minutes. The rush from snorting powdered cocaine is milder and takes a while to develop, but it tends to linger longer than the rush of crack.

*Freebasing* also intensifies the effects of cocaine. In freebasing, cocaine in powder form is heated with ether, freeing the psychoactive chemical base of the drug, and then smoked. Ether, however, is highly flammable.

Next to marijuana, cocaine is the most widely used illicit drug in the United States. Nearly 15% of Americans aged 12 and older have used cocaine, and about 2% reported using it during the prior year (SAMHSA, 2012).

***Effects of Cocaine*** Like heroin, cocaine directly stimulates the brain's reward or pleasure circuits. It also produces a sudden rise in blood pressure and an accelerated heart rate that can cause potentially dangerous, even fatal, irregular heart rhythms. Overdoses can produce restlessness, insomnia, headaches, nausea, convulsions, tremors, hallucinations, delusions, and even sudden death due to respiratory or cardiovascular collapse. Regular snorting of cocaine can lead to serious nasal problems, including ulcers in the nostrils.

Repeated use and high-dose use of cocaine can lead to depression and anxiety. Depression may be severe enough to prompt suicidal behavior. Both initial and routine users report episodes of crashing (feelings of depression after a binge), although crashing is more common among long-term, high-dose users. Psychotic behaviors, which can be induced by cocaine use as well as by use of amphetamines, tend to become more severe with continued use. Psychotic symptoms may include intense visual and auditory hallucinations and delusions of persecution.

**NICOTINE** Smoking is not merely a bad habit: It is a physical addiction to the stimulant drug *nicotine*, which is found in tobacco products such as cigarettes, cigars, and smokeless tobacco. Smoking is deadly, claiming more than 480,000 lives annually in the United States, and is recognized as the leading preventable cause of death in the nation (CDC, 2015a). Most smoking-related deaths result from lung cancer and other lung diseases, as well as cardiovascular (heart and artery) disease. Yet smoking also causes a wide range of other serious disorders, from diabetes to colorectal cancer and liver cancer and even erectile dysfunction and ectopic pregnancy (Tavernisejan, 2014).

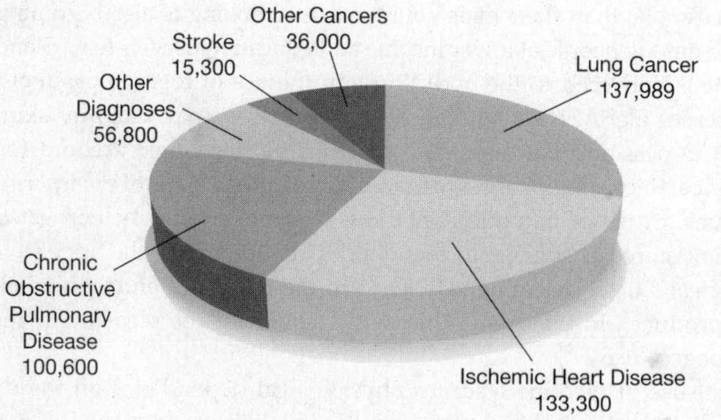


**Figure 8.2** U.S. deaths attributable each year to cigarette smoking.

Cigarette smoking claims the lives of more than 480,000 Americans annually, mostly from lung cancer, heart disease, and chronic obstructive pulmonary disease.

**SOURCE:** CDC, 2016.

All in all, smoking is the nation's leading health risk and is responsible for more premature deaths than any other cause, shaving about 10 years off the lifespan of the average smoker (Jha et al., 2013; Schroeder, 2013). Overall, smoking accounts for about one in five deaths of Americans and doubles the risk of dying before age 79 (Benowitz, 2010; Jha et al., 2013). Figure 8.2 shows the breakdowns of causes of death resulting from cigarette smoking in the United States. The good news is that quitting smoking at any age greatly reduces (but does not eliminate) the increased risk of smoking-related deaths (Jha & Peto, 2014; Thun et al., 2013).

Worldwide, about one in three adults smoke, and more than three million die each year from smoking-related causes (Ng, Freeman, et al., 2014; Schroeder & Koh, 2014). The additional good news is that the percentage of smokers both worldwide and in the United States has declined dramatically over the last several decades. In the United States, the percentage of adult smokers dropped from more than 40% in the mid-1960s to about 18% today (CDC, 2015a; Frieden, 2014). Smoking among teens is also on the decline, but still remains too high among high school seniors (18% for boys and girls; CDC, 2015a; Lanza et al., 2015).

The reduction in smoking in the United States is credited with preventing an estimated eight million premature deaths (Holford et al., 2014). That said, the public health challenge of smoking remains, as nearly one in five adult Americans continue to smoke, and the rate of decline in smoking rates is slowing down (CDC, 2015a; Koh & Sebelius, 2012). It may surprise you to learn that more women die of lung cancer than any other type of cancer, including breast cancer. Although quitting smoking clearly has health benefits for women and men, it unfortunately does not reduce the risks to normal (nonsmoking) levels. The lesson is clear: If you don't smoke, don't start; if you do smoke, quit.

Ethnic differences in smoking rates are shown in Figure 8.3. With the exception of Native Americans (American Indian/Alaskan Native), women in each ethnic group are

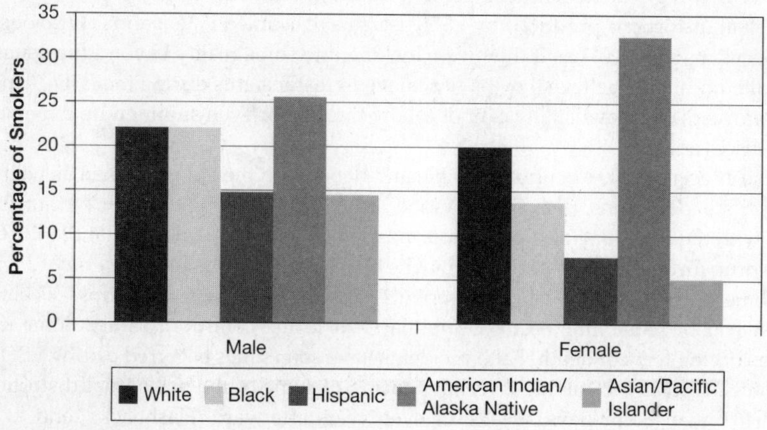


**Figure 8.3** Ethnic and gender differences in rates of cigarette smoking among U.S. adults.

Smoking rates are higher among men than women and among Native Americans (American Indian and Alaska Native) than other major racial/ethnic groups in the United States.

**SOURCE:** CDC, 2015h.

less likely to smoke than their male counterparts. Smoking is also becoming increasingly concentrated among people at lower income and educational levels (e.g., Blanco et al., 2008).

Nicotine is delivered to the body through the use of tobacco products. As a stimulant, it increases alertness, but it can also give rise to cold, clammy skin, nausea and vomiting, dizziness and faintness, and diarrhea—all of which account for the discomforts of novice smokers. Nicotine also stimulates the release of *epinephrine*, a hormone that generates a rush of autonomic nervous system activity, including rapid heartbeat and release of stores of sugar into the blood. Nicotine quells the appetite and provides a psychological "kick." Nicotine also leads to the release of endorphins, the opiate-like hormones produced in the brain. This may account for the pleasurable feelings associated with tobacco use.

Habitual use of nicotine leads to physiological dependence on the drug. Nicotine dependence is associated with both tolerance (intake rises to a level of a pack or two a day before leveling off) and a characteristic withdrawal syndrome. The withdrawal syndrome for nicotine includes a wide range of features, such as lack of energy, depressed mood, irritability, frustration, nervousness, impaired concentration, lightheadedness and dizziness, drowsiness, headaches, fatigue, insomnia, cramps, lowered heart rate, heart palpitations, increased appetite, weight gain, sweating, tremors, and strong craving for cigarettes. About 50% of tobacco users who quit for two or more days show evidence of tobacco withdrawal disorder (American Psychiatric Association, 2013).

Smoking gives an almost instant "hit" of the stimulant nicotine. The nicotine in cigarette smoke begins to occupy nicotine receptors in the brain from the first several puffs.

## Hallucinogens

**8.7 Describe the effects of hallucinogens and the risks they pose.**

**Hallucinogens**, also known as *psychedelics*, are a class of drugs that produce sensory distortions or hallucinations, including major alterations in color perception and hearing. Hallucinogens may also have other effects, such as relaxation and euphoria or, in some cases, panic.

Hallucinogens include lysergic acid diethylamide (LSD), psilocybin, and mescaline. Psychoactive substances that are similar in effect to psychedelic drugs are marijuana (*cannabis*) and *phencyclidine* (PCP). Mescaline is derived from the peyote cactus and has been used for centuries by Native Americans in the Southwest, Mexico, and Central America in religious ceremonies, as has psilocybin, which is derived from certain mushrooms. LSD, PCP, and marijuana are the most commonly used hallucinogens in the United States.

Although tolerance to hallucinogens may develop, investigators lack evidence of a consistent or clinically significant withdrawal syndrome associated with their use (American Psychiatric Association, 2013). However, cravings following withdrawal may occur.

**LSD** LSD is a synthetic hallucinogenic drug. In addition to the vivid parade of colors and visual distortions produced by LSD, users have claimed it "expands consciousness" and opens new worlds—as if they were looking into some reality beyond the usual reality. Sometimes, they believe they have achieved great insights during the LSD "trip," but when it wears off, they usually cannot follow through or even summon up a memory of these discoveries.

The effects of LSD are unpredictable and depend on the amount taken as well as on the user's expectations, personality, mood, and surroundings. The user's prior experiences with the drug may also play a role, as users who have learned to handle the effects of the drug through past experience may be better prepared than new users.

Some users have unpleasant experiences with the drug, or "bad trips." Feelings of intense fear or panic may occur. Users may fear losing control or sanity. Some experience terrifying fears of death. Fatal accidents have sometimes occurred during LSD trips. *Flashbacks*, typically involving a reexperiencing of some of the perceptual distortions of the "trip," may occur days, weeks, or even years afterward. Flashbacks tend to occur suddenly and often without warning. Perceptual distortions may involve geometric forms, flashes of color, intensified colors, afterimages, or appearances of halos around objects, among others. They likely stem from chemical changes in the brain caused by the prior use of the drug. Triggers for flashbacks include entry into darkened environments, drug use, anxiety or fatigue, or stress. Psychological factors, such as underlying personality problems, may also explain why some users experience flashbacks. In some cases, a flashback may involve an imagined reenactment of the LSD experience.

**PHENCYCLIDINE** *Phencyclidine*—which is referred to as "angel dust" on the street—was developed as an anesthetic in the 1950s, but its use was discontinued when its hallucinatory side effects were discovered. A smokable form of PCP became popular as a street drug in the 1970s. However, its popularity has since waned, largely because of its unpredictable effects.

The effects of PCP, like most drugs, are dose related. In addition to causing hallucinations, PCP accelerates the heart rate and blood pressure and causes sweating, flushing, and numbness. PCP is classified as a *deliriant*—a drug capable of producing states of delirium. It also has dissociating effects, causing users to feel as if there is some sort of invisible barrier between them and their environment. Dissociation can be experienced as pleasant, engrossing, or frightening, depending on the user's expectations, mood, setting, and so on. Overdoses can give rise to drowsiness and a blank stare, convulsions, and, now and then, coma; paranoia and aggressive behavior; and tragic accidents resulting from perceptual distortion or impaired judgment during states of intoxication.

**MARIJUANA** **Marijuana** is derived from the *Cannabis sativa* plant. Marijuana is generally classified as a hallucinogen because it can produce perceptual distortions or mild hallucinations, especially in high doses or when used by susceptible individuals. The psychoactive substance in marijuana is *delta-9-tetrahydrocannabinol*, or THC for short. THC is found in branches and leaves of the plant but is highly concentrated in the resin of the female plant. *Hashish*, or hash, also derived from the resin, is more potent than marijuana but has similar effects.

Did you know that more 12th graders today (21.4%) report using marijuana during the past month than smoking cigarettes (19.2%) (Lanza et al., 2015; MMWR, 2015)? The increased use of marijuana stands in sharp contrast to sharp declines in the use of cocaine and cigarettes among teens. **T / F**

## TRUTH *or* FICTION

Marijuana use has surpassed cigarette use among high school seniors today.

☑ TRUE More 12th graders today report having recently used marijuana than cigarettes.

Overall, about 10% of American adults report using marijuana during the prior year (Hasin et al., 2015; SAMHSA, 2012). Marijuana use among adults is on the rise, having doubled since the start of the 2000s (Hasin et al., 2015). Moreover, nearly 3% of U.S. adults currently suffer from a diagnosable cannabis (marijuana) use disorder, a rate that is nearly twice what it was at the beginning of the new millennia (Hasin et al., 2015). Men are more likely than women to develop a cannabis use disorder, and the rates of these disorders are greatest among people aged 18 to 30.

**LEGALIZED MARIJUANA.** In 2013, Colorado became the first state in the union to legalize marijuana. Do you believe marijuana should be a legally available but regulated substance like alcohol or tobacco? Why or why not?

Low doses of the drug can produce relaxing feelings similar to those from drinking alcohol. Some users report that at low doses, the drug makes them feel more comfortable at social gatherings. Higher doses, however, often lead users to withdraw into themselves. Some users believe the drug increases their capacity for self-insight or creative thinking, although the insights achieved under its influence may not seem so insightful once the drug's effects have passed. People may turn to marijuana, and to other drugs as well, to help them cope with life problems or to help them function when they are under stress. Strongly intoxicated people perceive time as passing more slowly. A song of a few minutes may seem to last an hour. There is increased awareness of bodily sensations, such as heartbeat. Smokers also report that strong intoxication heightens sexual sensations. Visual hallucinations may occur.

**ON THE PATH TO LOSING IQ POINTS?** Recent evidence shows that regular use of marijuana beginning in adolescence is linked to loss of IQ points by midlife.

Strong intoxication can cause smokers to become disoriented. If their moods are euphoric, disorientation may be construed as harmony with the universe. Yet some smokers find strong intoxication disturbing. An accelerated heart rate and sharpened awareness of bodily sensations cause some smokers to fear their hearts will "run away" with them. Some smokers are frightened by disorientation and the fear that they will not "come back." High levels of intoxication occasionally induce nausea and vomiting.

Marijuana use is associated with more compulsive use or psychological dependence than physiological dependence. Although tolerance to the drug may occur with chronic use, some users report reverse tolerance, or *sensitization*, making them more sensitive to the drug's effects with repeated use. Although a clear-cut withdrawal syndrome has not been reliably demonstrated, evidence does point to a definable withdrawal syndrome in long-term, heavy users who abruptly stop using the drug (Allsop et al., 2012; Mason et al., 2012). Investigators also find that when marijuana users who are dependent on the drug are put in an fMRI device and exposed to drug-related cues (handling a marijuana pipe), the parts of the brain that become activated are similar to those that become activated in cocaine users in response to cocaine cues (Filbey & Dunlop, 2014). This suggests that heavy use of marijuana may share a common neural pathway as addictive drugs like cocaine.

Brain scans also show worrisome signs of brain abnormalities in long-term marijuana users (Filbey et al., 2014). Regular use of marijuana use can lead to impaired learning and memory, especially in heavier or more persistent users (Bossong et al., 2012; Han et al., 2012; Meier et al., 2012). Marijuana may also disrupt memory functioning and ability to focus attention for about 24 hours after it is used, which might affect a student's ability to learn and a worker's ability to perform on the job the day after the drug is used (Moore, 2014). Even more troubling is evidence linking persistent use of marijuana beginning in adolescence to loss of IQ points by midlife (Meier et al., 2012).

Evidence also links marijuana use to later use of harder drugs such as heroin and cocaine (Kandel, 2003). Whether marijuana use is a causal factor leading to use of harder drugs remains unclear. It is clear, however, that marijuana impairs perception and motor coordination and thus makes driving and the operation of other heavy machinery dangerous. Recent evidence shows that drivers who used marijuana within three hours of driving were nearly twice as likely to cause a crash as those who were unimpaired by drug use (Asbridge, Hayden, & Cartwright, 2012).

Although marijuana use induces positive mood changes in many users, some people report anxiety and confusion; there are also occasional reports of paranoia or psychotic reactions. Marijuana elevates heart rate and blood pressure and is linked to an increased risk of heart attacks in people with heart disease. Like cigarettes, smoking marijuana can damage lung tissue and lead to serious respiratory diseases, such as chronic bronchitis, and may increase the risk of lung cancer (Singh et al., 2009; Zickler, 2006).

# Theoretical Perspectives

People begin using psychoactive substances for various reasons. Some adolescents start using drugs because of peer pressure or because they believe drugs make them seem more sophisticated or grown up. Some use drugs as a way of rebelling against their parents or society at large. Regardless of why people get started with drugs, they continue to use them because drugs produce pleasurable effects or because they find it difficult to stop. Most adolescents, however, drink alcohol to get high, not to establish that they are adults. Many people smoke cigarettes for the pleasure they provide. Others smoke to help them relax when they are tense and, paradoxically, to give them a kick or a lift when they are tired. Many would like to quit but find it difficult to break their addiction.

People who are anxious about their jobs or social lives may be drawn to the calming effects of alcohol, marijuana (in certain doses), tranquilizers, and sedatives. People with low self-confidence and self-esteem may be drawn to the ego-bolstering effects of amphetamines and cocaine. Many poor young people attempt to escape the poverty, anguish, and tedium of inner-city life through use of heroin and similar drugs. More well-to-do adolescents may rely on drugs to manage the transition from dependence to independence and major life changes concerning jobs, college, and lifestyles. In the next sections, we consider several major theoretical perspectives on drug use and abuse.

## Biological Perspectives

**8.8 Describe biological perspectives on substance use disorders and explain how cocaine affects the brain.**

Investigators are beginning to learn much more about the biological underpinnings of drug use and addiction. Much of the recent research has focused on the roles of neurotransmitters, especially dopamine, and genetic factors.

**NEUROTRANSMITTERS** Many drugs of abuse, including nicotine, alcohol, heroin, marijuana, and especially cocaine and amphetamines, produce pleasurable effects by increasing the availability of the neurotransmitter *dopamine*, a key brain chemical involved in activation of the brain's reward or pleasure circuits—the networks of neurons that produce feelings of pleasure (Flagel et al., 2011; Whitten, 2009). When we eat because we are hungry or drink because we are thirsty, reward pathways in the brain become flooded with dopamine, producing feelings of pleasure associated with engaging in these life-sustaining activities. Neuroscientists find that in people with alcohol dependence, even the mere exposure to words associated with alcohol can activate reward pathways in the brain, which are networks of interconnected neurons that produce feelings of pleasure (see Figure 8.4).

The role of dopamine is yet more complex; it motivates us to pay attention to objects linked to rewarding behaviors and basic survival needs, such as food when we're hungry or threatening animals or other dangers (Angier, 2009). For addicts, the steady influx of dopamine from using drugs makes it difficult for them to focus on anything other than attaining and using drugs, even if the drugs no longer produce feelings of pleasure.

Over time, regular use of drugs such as cocaine, alcohol, and heroin may sap the brain's own production of dopamine. Consequently, the brain's natural reward system—the "feel good" circuitry that produces states of pleasure associated with the ordinarily rewarding activities of life, such as consuming a satisfying meal and engaging in pleasant activities—becomes blunted (Dubovsky, 2006). Evidence based on brain imaging shows lower levels of naturally produced dopamine in the brains of cocaine-dependent individuals (Martinez et al., 2009). The addict's brain may come to depend on having a supply of the drug available in order to produce any feelings of pleasure or satisfaction (Denizet-Lewis, 2006). Without drugs, life may not seem to be worth living.

Changes in the dopamine system may help explain the intense cravings and anxiety that accompany drug withdrawal and the difficulty people have in maintaining abstinence. However, other neurotransmitters, including serotonin and endorphins, also appear to play important roles in drug abuse and dependence (Addolorato et al., 2005; Buchert et al., 2004).

Consider the role of *endorphins*, a class of neurotransmitters that have pain-blocking properties similar to those of opioids such as heroin. As we discussed earlier, endorphins and opiates dock at the same receptor sites in the brain. Normally, the brain produces a certain level of endorphins that maintains a psychological steady state of comfort and potential to experience pleasure. However, when the body becomes habituated to a supply of opioids, it may stop producing endorphins. This makes a user dependent on opiates for comfort, relief from pain, and pleasure. When the habitual user stops using heroin or other opiates, feelings of discomfort and little aches and pains may be magnified until the body resumes adequate production of endorphins. This discomfort may account, at least in part,

**Figure 8.4** Your brain in response to alcohol words.

In an fMRI study, a group of alcohol-dependent women showed greater levels of brain activation in parts of the limbic system and frontal lobes (indicated by yellow/orange colors) in response to alcohol cue words (e.g., *keg*, *binge*) than did a group of women who were light social drinkers. These parts of the brain are involved in reward pathways activated by use of alcohol and other drugs. These findings suggest that in people with alcohol dependence, the mere exposure to words associated with alcohol may produce similar effects in the brain as the drug itself.

**SOURCE:** Tapert et al., 2004.

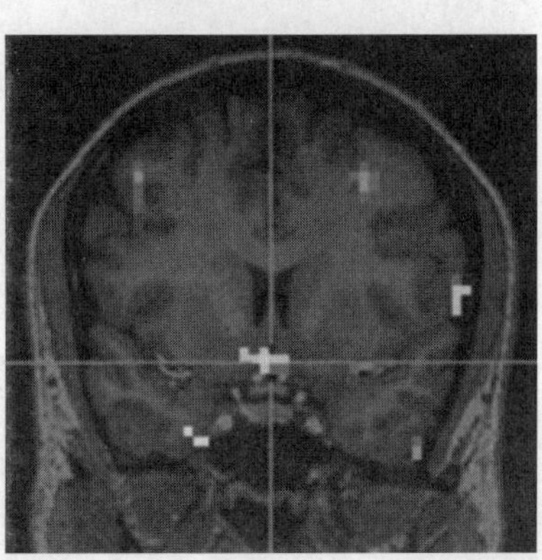

for the unpleasant withdrawal symptoms that people who are addicted to heroin or other opiates experience. However, this model remains speculative, and more research is needed to document direct relationships between endorphin production and withdrawal symptoms.

**GENETIC FACTORS** Evidence points to an important role for genetic factors in a range of substance use disorders involving alcohol, amphetamines, cocaine, heroin, and even tobacco (e.g., Ducci et al., 2011; Frahm et al., 2011; Hartz et al., 2012; Kendler et al., 2012; Ray, 2012). People who have a family history of substance use disorders stand a four to eight times greater chance of developing these disorders themselves (Urbanoski & Kelly, 2012). Environmental factors, such as family influences and peer pressure, appear to play a more important role in the initiation of drug use in early adolescence, whereas genetic factors play a prominent role in explaining continuation of drug use through early and middle adulthood (Kendler et al., 2008).

Investigators have begun to hunt for specific genes involved in alcohol and drug abuse and dependence (e.g., Anstee et al., 2013; Ray, 2012; Sullivan et al., 2013). Our focus here is on the genetic underpinnings of alcohol dependence, because this has been the area of greatest research interest. However, it appears that some genes involved in alcoholism are also involved in other forms of addiction, such as addiction to cocaine, nicotine (regular smoking), and heroin (Ming & Burmeister, 2009).

Alcoholism tends to run in families. The closer the genetic relationship, the greater the risk. Familial patterns provide only suggestive evidence of genetic factors, because families share a common environment as well as common genes. More definitive evidence comes from twin and adoptee studies.

Monozygotic (MZ) twins have identical genes, whereas fraternal or dizygotic (DZ) twins share only half of their genes. If genetic factors are involved, we would expect MZ twins to have higher concordance (agreement) rates for alcoholism than DZ twins. We have converging evidence that points to an important genetic contribution to alcoholism (MacKillop, McGeary, & Ray, 2010). First, there is a large body of evidence showing higher concordance rates for alcoholism among MZ twins than among DZ twins, which is consistent with a genetic contribution to alcoholism. Second, among adopted children raised in nonalcoholic families, those with a family history of alcoholism are more prone to develop alcoholism themselves than are those without alcoholism in their families.

If problem drinking and alcoholism are influenced by genetic factors, what exactly is inherited? Some clues have emerged (e.g., Corbett et al., 2005; Radel et al., 2005). Alcoholism, nicotine dependence, and opioid addiction are linked to genes that determine the structure of dopamine receptors in the brain. As we've noted, dopamine is involved in regulating states of pleasure, so one possibility is that genetic factors enhance feelings of pleasure derived from alcohol.

The genetic vulnerability to alcoholism most probably involves a combination of factors, such as reaping greater pleasure from alcohol and a capacity for greater biological tolerance for the drug. People who can tolerate larger doses of alcohol without incurring upset stomachs, dizziness, and headaches may have difficulty knowing when to stop drinking. Thus, people who are better able to "hold their liquor" may be at greater risk of developing drinking problems. They may need to rely on other cues, such as counting their drinks, to limit their drinking. Other people whose bodies more readily "put the brakes" on excess drinking may be less likely to develop problems in moderating their drinking. **T / F**

## TRUTH *or* FICTION

People who can "hold their liquor" better than most stand a lower risk of becoming problem drinkers.

☑ **FALSE** A high physical tolerance for liquor may lead a person to drink excessively, which may set the stage for problem drinking.

Whatever role genetics may play in alcohol dependence and other forms of substance dependence, genes do not dictate behavior. Environment also plays a role, as do interactions of genetic and environmental factors. For example, investigators report that drug use among a sample of young people at heightened genetic risk of developing drug abuse problems was reduced for those who had highly supportive parents

(Brody et al., 2009). Similarly, other investigators reported that being raised by parents free of alcoholism was associated with a lower risk of developing alcohol-related disorders in people at high genetic risk of alcohol-related problems (Jacob et al., 2003). In effect, good parenting can reduce the influence of bad genes. In sum, we can say that genetic factors act together with environmental and psychological factors in contributing to the development of substance use disorders.

## A CLOSER Look

### HOW COCAINE AFFECTS THE BRAIN

Cocaine works on the brain's use of dopamine (see Figure 8.5). Cocaine interferes with the process of *reuptake*, by which excess molecules of dopamine are reabsorbed by the transmitting neuron. As a result, high levels of dopamine remain active in the synaptic gaps between neurons in brain networks that control feelings of pleasure, overstimulating neurons that produce states of pleasure, including the euphoric high associated with cocaine use. In effect, cocaine and other drugs such as heroin and alcohol that also affect dopamine feel good because of the effects they have on the availability of dopamine in the brain's reward or pleasure networks. However, regular use of cocaine over time makes the brain less capable of producing dopamine on its own. Consequently, cocaine abusers crash when they stop using the drug because the brain is stripped of its own supply of this pleasure-producing chemical.

**Figure 8.5** Cocaine's effects on the brain.

**SOURCE:** Adapted from National Institute on Drug Abuse, U.S. Department of Health and Human Services, National Institutes of Health. Research Report Series: Cocaine Abuse and Addiction. NIH Publication Number 99-4342, revised November 2004. Reprinted from J. S. Nevid, *Psychology: Concepts and Applications*, 2009, with permission of Cengage Learning.

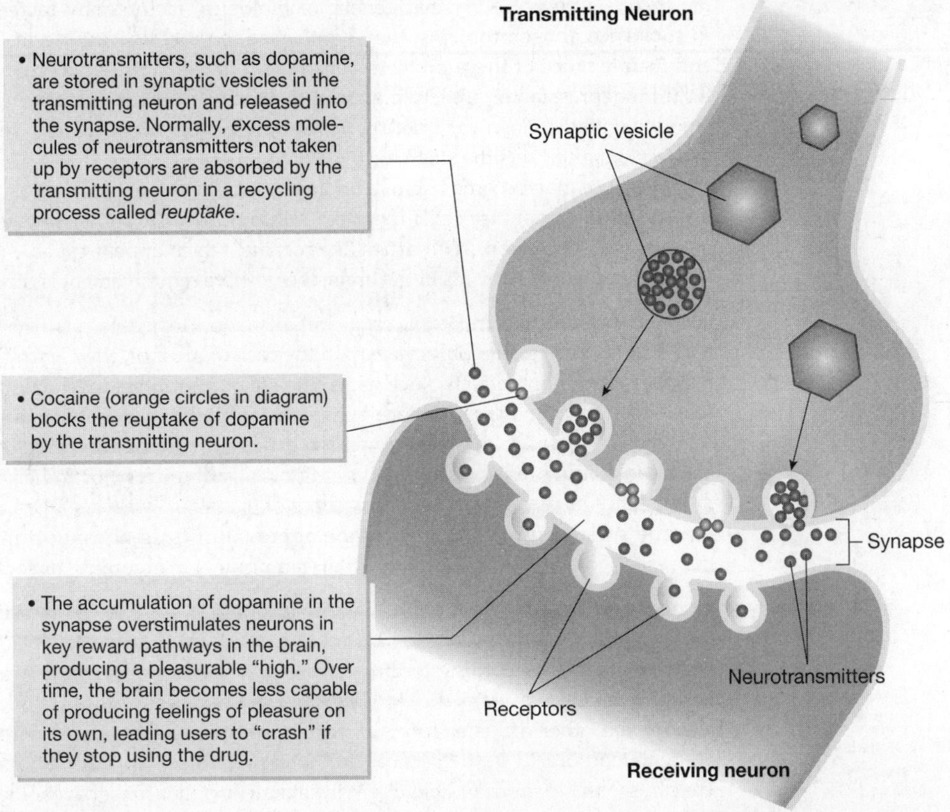

IN THE REAL WORLD: NEUROTRANSMITTERS

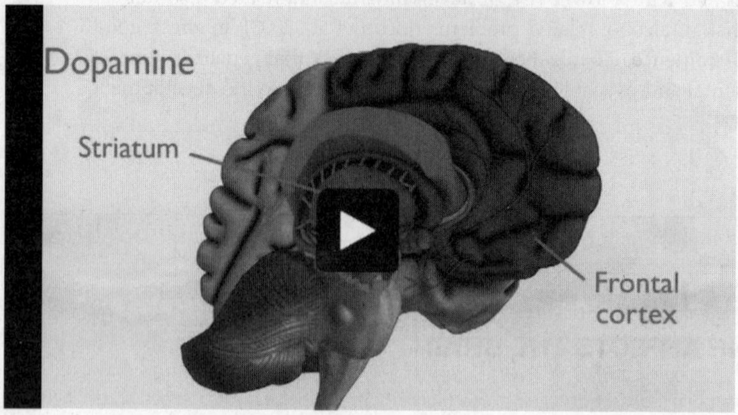


## Psychological Perspectives

**8.9 Describe psychological perspectives on substance use disorders.**

Psychological approaches to understanding substance use and abuse largely draw upon learning theories, cognitive theories, psychodynamic theories, and sociocultural theories.

**LEARNING THEORY PERSPECTIVES** Learning theorists propose that substance use behaviors are largely learned and can, in principle, be unlearned. They focus on the roles of operant and classical conditioning and observational learning. Drug-related problems are not regarded as symptoms of disease but rather as problem habits. Although learning theorists do not deny that genetic or biological factors may increase susceptibility to substance abuse problems, they emphasize the role of learning in the development and maintenance of these problem behaviors. They also recognize that people who suffer from depression or anxiety may turn to alcohol as a way of relieving these troubling emotional states, however brief the relief may be. Emotional stress, such as anxiety or depression, often sets the stage for the development of drug-related problems.

Drug use may become habitual because it produces feelings of pleasure (positive reinforcement) or temporary relief (negative reinforcement) from negative emotions, such as anxiety and depression. With drugs like cocaine, which appear capable of directly stimulating pleasure mechanisms in the brain, the positive reinforcement is direct and powerful.

***Operant Conditioning*** People may initially use a drug because of social influence, trial and error, or social observation. In the case of alcohol, they learn that the drug can produce reinforcing effects, such as feelings of euphoria, and reductions in anxiety and tension. Alcohol may also reduce behavioral inhibitions. Alcohol can thus be reinforcing when it is used to combat depression (by producing euphoric feelings, even if short lived), to combat tension (by functioning as a tranquilizer), or to help people sidestep moral conflicts (e.g., by dulling awareness of moral prohibitions). Drug abuse may also provide social reinforcers, such as the approval of drug-abusing companions and, in the cases of alcohol and stimulants, the (temporary) overcoming of social shyness.

***Alcohol and Tension Reduction*** Learning theorists have long maintained that one of the primary reinforcers for use of alcohol is relief from states of tension or unpleasant states of arousal. According to the *tension-reduction theory*, the more often one drinks to reduce tension or anxiety, the stronger the habit becomes. We can think of these uses of alcohol and other drugs as forms of *self-medication*—as a means of using the pill or the bottle to temporarily ease psychological pain (Cludius et al., 2013; Robinson et al., 2009). We can see this pattern of negative reinforcement (relief from psychological pain) in the following case example.

### "I" "Taking Away the Hurt I Feel"

"I use them [the pills and alcohol] to take away the hurt I feel inside." Joceyln, a 36-year-old mother of two, was physically abused by her husband, Phil. "I have no self-esteem. I just don't feel I can do anything," she told her therapist. Joceyln had escaped from an abusive family background by getting married at age 17, hoping that marriage would offer her a better life. The first few years were free of abuse, but things changed when Phil lost his job and began to drink heavily. By then, Jocelyn had two young children and felt trapped. She blamed herself for her unhappy family life, for Phil's drinking, for her son's learning disability. "The only thing I can do is drink or do pills. At least then I don't have to think about things for a while." Although drug use temporarily dulled her emotional pain, it came with a greater long-term cost in terms of the burden of addiction.

*From the Author's Files*

Although nicotine, alcohol, and other drugs may temporarily alleviate emotional distress, they cannot resolve underlying personal or emotional problems. Rather than learning to resolve these problems, people who turn to alcohol or other drugs as forms of self-medication often find themselves facing additional substance use problems.

**SELF-MEDICATION?** People who turn to alcohol or other drugs to quell disturbing emotions can compound their problems by developing a substance use disorder.

***Negative Reinforcement and Withdrawal*** Once people become physiologically dependent, negative reinforcement comes into play in maintaining the drug habit. In other words, people may resume using drugs to gain relief from unpleasant withdrawal symptoms. In operant conditioning terms, relief from unpleasant withdrawal symptoms is a *negative reinforcer* for resuming drug use (Higgins, Heil, & Lussier, 2004). For example, the addicted smoker who quits cold turkey may shortly return to smoking to fend off the discomfort of withdrawal.

***The Conditioning Model of Cravings*** Classical conditioning may help explain some forms of drug cravings. In some cases, cravings may represent a conditioned response to environmental cues associated with prior use of the substance (Kilts et al., 2004). In people with drug-related problems, exposure to cues such as the sight or aroma of an alcoholic beverage or the sight of a needle and syringe can become conditioned stimuli that elicit the conditioned response of strong drug cravings. For example, socializing with certain companions ("drinking buddies") or even passing a liquor store may elicit conditioned cravings for alcohol. In support of this theory, people who suffer from alcoholism show distinctive changes in brain activity in areas of the brain that regulate emotion, attention, and appetitive behavior when shown pictures of alcoholic beverages (George et al., 2001). Social drinkers, by comparison, do not show this pattern of brain activation.

Negative emotional states such as anxiety and depression that have been paired with the use of alcohol or drugs in the past may also elicit cravings. The following case illustrates cravings conditioned to environmental cues.

## Each Time the Subway Doors Opened:

### A CASE OF CONDITIONED DRUG CRAVINGS

A 29-year-old man was hospitalized for the treatment of heroin addiction. After four weeks of treatment, he returned to his former job, which required him to ride the subway past the stop at which he had previously bought his drugs. Each day, when the subway doors opened at this location, [he] experienced enormous craving for heroin, accompanied by tearing, a runny nose, abdominal cramps, and gooseflesh. After the doors closed, his symptoms disappeared, and he went on to work.

**SOURCE:** *From Weiss & Mirin, 1987.*

Similarly, some people are primarily "stimulus smokers." They reach for a cigarette in the presence of smoking-related stimuli, such as seeing someone else smoke or smelling smoke. Smoking becomes a strongly conditioned habit because it is paired repeatedly with many situational cues—watching TV, finishing dinner, driving in the car, studying, drinking or socializing with friends, sex, and, for some, using the bathroom.

The conditioning model of craving is supported by early research showing that people with alcoholism tend to salivate more than others at the sight and smell of alcohol (Monti et al., 1987). Pavlov's classic experiment conditioned a salivation response in dogs by repeatedly pairing the sound of a bell (a conditioned stimulus) with the presentation of food powder (an unconditioned stimulus). Salivation among people who develop alcoholism can also be viewed as a conditioned response to alcohol-related cues. People with drinking problems who show the greatest salivary response to alcohol cues may be at highest risk of relapse. They may also profit from conditioning-based treatments designed to extinguish responses to alcohol-related cues.

In a form of treatment for alcoholism called *cue exposure training*, a person is seated in front of alcohol-related cues, such as open alcoholic beverages, but is prevented from imbibing (Dawe et al., 2002). The pairing of the cue (alcohol bottle) with nonreinforcement (by dint of preventing drinking) may lead to extinction of the conditioned cravings. However, cravings can return after treatment, and often do return when people go back to their usual environments (Havermans & Jansen, 2003).

***Observational Learning*** Modeling or observational learning plays an important role in determining risk of drug-related problems. Parents who model inappropriate or excessive drinking or use of illicit drugs may set the stage for maladaptive drug use in their children (Kirisci, Vanyukov, & Tarter, 2005). Evidence shows that adolescents who have a parent who smokes face a substantially higher risk of smoking than do their peers in families in which neither parent smokes (Peterson et al., 2006). Other investigators find that having friends who smoke influences adolescents to begin smoking (Bricker et al., 2006).

**COGNITIVE PERSPECTIVES** Evidence supports the role of cognitive factors in drug use—especially positive expectancies, such as beliefs that drinking will boost one's popularity or eliminate states of tension or anxiety (Pabst et al., 2014). Holding positive expectancies about drug use, such as believing that drinking alcohol makes you more popular or outgoing, increases the likelihood of use of these substances (e.g., Cable & Sacker, 2007; Mitchell, Beals, & The Pathways of Choice Team, 2006). Outcome expectancies in teens—what they expect a drug's effects will be—are strongly influenced by the beliefs held by others in their social environment, including friends and parents (e.g., Donovan, Molina, & Kelly, 2009; Gunn & Smith, 2010).

Alcohol or other drug use may also boost *self-efficacy expectations*—personal expectancies we hold about our ability to successfully perform tasks. If we believe we need a drink or two (or more) to "get out of our shell" and relate socially to others, we may come to depend on alcohol in social situations.

Expectancies may account for the "one-drink effect"—the tendency of chronic alcohol abusers to binge once they have a drink. The late psychologist G. Alan Marlatt (1978) explained the one-drink effect as a type of self-fulfilling prophecy. If people with alcohol-related problems believe that just one drink will cause a loss of control, they may perceive the outcome as predetermined when they drink. Having even one drink may thus escalate into a binge. This type of expectation is an example of what Aaron Beck calls *absolutist thinking*. When we insist on seeing the world in black and white rather than shades of gray—seeing outcomes as either complete successes or complete failures—we may interpret one bite of dessert as proof that we are off our diets, or one cigarette as proof that we are hooked again. Rather than telling ourselves, "Okay, I goofed, but that's it. I don't have to have more," we encode our lapses as catastrophes and transform them into relapses. Still, alcohol-dependent people who believe they may go on a drinking binge if they have just one drink are well advised to abstain.

**PSYCHODYNAMIC PERSPECTIVES** According to traditional psychodynamic theory, alcoholism reflects an *oral-dependent personality*. Psychodynamic theory also associates excessive alcohol use with other oral traits, such as dependence and depression, and traces the origins of these traits to fixation in the oral stage of psychosexual development during infancy. Excessive drinking or smoking in adulthood symbolizes an individual's efforts to attain oral gratification.

Research support for these psychodynamic concepts is mixed. Although people who develop alcoholism often show dependent traits, it is unclear whether dependence contributes to or stems from problem drinking. Chronic drinking, for example, is connected with loss of employment and downward movement in social status, both of which would render drinkers more reliant on others for support. Moreover, an empirical connection between dependence and alcoholism does not establish that alcoholism represents an oral fixation that can be traced to infant development.

Then, too, many—but certainly not all—people who suffer from alcoholism have antisocial personalities characterized by independence-seeking as expressed through rebelliousness and rejection of social and legal codes. All in all, there doesn't appear to be any single alcoholic personality.

**SOCIOCULTURAL PERSPECTIVES** Drinking is determined, in part, by where we live, whom we worship with, and the social or cultural norms that regulate our behavior. Cultural attitudes can encourage or discourage problem drinking. As we have already seen, rates of alcohol abuse vary across ethnic and religious groups. Let's note some other sociocultural factors. Church attendance, for example, is generally connected with abstinence from alcohol. Perhaps people who are more willing to engage in culturally sanctioned activities, such as churchgoing, are also more likely to adopt culturally sanctioned prohibitions against excessive drinking.

Peer pressure and exposure to a drug subculture are important influences in determining substance use among adolescents and young adults (Dishion & Owen, 2002; Hu, Davies, & Kandel, 2006). Children who start drinking before age 15 stand a fivefold higher risk of developing alcohol dependence in adulthood as compared with those who began drinking at a later age (Kluger, 2001). Yet studies of Hispanic and African American adolescents show that support from family members can reduce the negative influence of drug-using peers on the adolescent's use of tobacco and other drugs (Farrell & White, 1998; Frauenglass et al., 1997).

# Treatment of Substance Use Disorders

There is a vast array of nonprofessional, biological, and psychological approaches to treating problems with substance abuse and dependence. However, treatment has often been a frustrating endeavor. In many (perhaps most) cases, drug-dependent people may not be ready or motivated to change their drug use behavior or may not seek treatment on their own. Substance abuse counselors may use techniques such as *motivational interviewing* to first increase their clients' readiness to make changes in their lives (Martins & McNeil, 2009; Miller & Rollnick, 2002). In a supportive rather than confrontational manner, counselors help clients recognize the problems caused by their drug use and the risks they face in continuing to use drugs. They then focus on raising clients' awareness of the differences between their present circumstances and how they want their lives to be and the steps they need to take to make these changes.

When drug-dependent people are ready to break free of drugs, the process of helping them through the withdrawal syndrome is an important first step. However, helping them pursue a life devoid of their preferred substances is more problematic. Treatment takes place in a setting—such as the therapist's office, a support group, a residential center, or a hospital—in which abstinence is valued and encouraged. Then, the individual returns to the work, family, or street settings in which abuse and dependence were instigated and maintained. The problem of relapse can thus be more troublesome than the problems involved in initial treatment.

## A CLOSER Look

### SUBLIMINAL CUES TRIGGER BRAIN RESPONSES IN COCAINE-ABUSING PATIENTS

We've noted that exposure to drug-related cues, such as the sight of a bottle of Scotch whiskey or of a needle and syringe, can elicit drug cravings in people with drug-related problems—but a recent study with cocaine-abusing patients goes a step further. Investigators flashed cocaine-related images at blinding speeds that the patients could not consciously perceive (see Figure 8.6). Yet these "unseen" cues activated parts of the brain's *limbic system*—the interconnected parts of the inner brain involved in processing basic emotional responses—which is implicated in drug cravings and drug-seeking behavior (Childress et al., 2008; see Figure 8.7). Dr. Nora Volkow, the director of the National Institute on Drug Abuse (NIDA), observed, "This is the first evidence that cues outside one's awareness can trigger rapid activation of the circuits driving drug-seeking behavior" (cited in "Subconscious Signals," 2008).

This research underscores the problems faced by patients with cocaine and other substance abuse problems. They may be exposed daily to images—even mere glimpses of images—that activate networks in the brain that prompt craving responses. As NIDA director Volkow puts it, "Patients often can't pinpoint when or why they start craving drugs. Understanding how the brain initiates that overwhelming desire for drugs is essential to treating addiction."

Compounding the problem further is that parts of the brain activated by drug-related subliminal cues are those that also become active in response to sexual images. Drug cravings may tap into the same reward systems as those involved in basic rewards, such as sexual gratification and food consumption.

**Figure 8.7** Limbic system response to "unseen" drug-related stimuli.

Parts of the limbic system in the brain, including the amygdala (denoted here by *amyg*), become active in response to cocaine-related images flashed at such a high speed that they are not consciously perceived. A similar pattern of activation was found for "unseen" sexual cues, suggesting that drug-related cues activated similar reward pathways in the brain as sexual cues.

**SOURCE:** Childress et al., 2008.

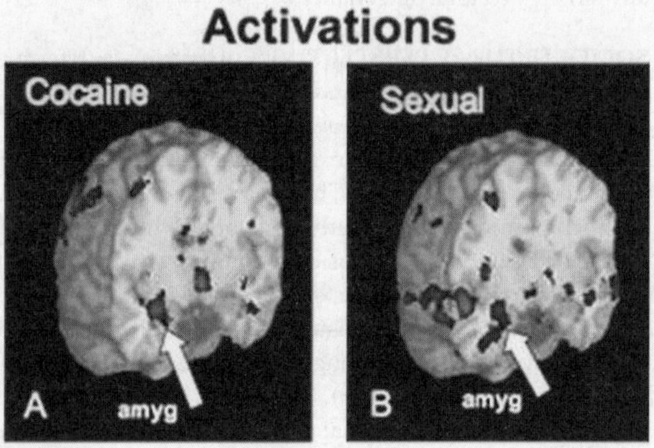


**Figure 8.6** Visual stimuli used in subliminal cue study.

These are examples of visual cues flashed to male cocaine patients to determine whether brain circuits involved in reward pathways of the brain would respond even if the stimuli themselves remained unseen.

**SOURCE:** Childress et al., 2008.

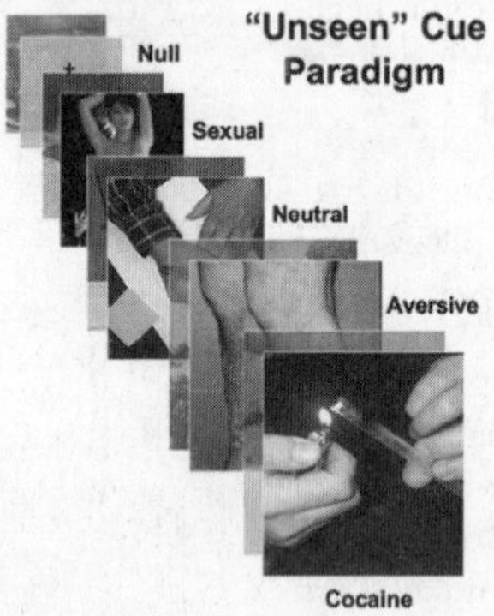


Another complication is that many people with drug-related problems have other psychological disorders as well. However, most clinics and treatment programs focus on the drug or alcohol problem, or the other psychological disorders, rather than treating all these problems simultaneously. This narrow focus results in poorer treatment outcomes, including more frequent rehospitalizations among those with these *dual diagnoses*.

## Biological Approaches

**8.10 Identify biological treatments of substance use disorders.**

An increasing range of biological approaches are being used in treating substance use disorders (Quenqua, 2012; Wessell & Edwards, 2010). For people with chemical dependencies, biological treatment typically begins with **detoxification**—that is, helping them through withdrawal from addictive substances.

**DETOXIFICATION** Detoxification often is more safely carried out in a hospital setting. In the case of addiction to alcohol or barbiturates, hospitalization allows medical personnel to monitor and treat potentially dangerous withdrawal symptoms such as convulsions. Antianxiety drugs, such as the benzodiazepines Librium and Valium, may help block severe withdrawal symptoms, such as seizures and delirium tremens. Detoxification to alcohol takes about a week. Detoxification is an important step toward staying clean, but it is only a start. Approximately half of all drug abusers relapse within a year of detoxification (Cowley, 2001). Continuing support and structured therapy—such as behavioral counseling—and possible use of therapeutic drugs increase the chances of long-term success.

A number of therapeutic drugs are used to treat people with chemical dependencies, and more chemical compounds are in the testing stage. Here, we survey some of the major therapeutic drugs in use today.

**DISULFIRAM** The drug *disulfiram* (Antabuse) discourages alcohol consumption because the combination of the two—the drug and the alcohol—produces a violent response consisting of nausea, headache, heart palpitations, and vomiting. In some extreme cases, combining disulfiram and alcohol can produce such a dramatic drop in blood pressure that an individual goes into shock or even dies. Although disulfiram has been used widely in alcoholism treatment, its effectiveness is limited because many patients who want to continue drinking simply stop using the drug. Others stop taking the drug because they believe they can remain abstinent without it. Unfortunately, many return to uncontrolled drinking. Another drawback is that the drug has toxic effects in people with liver disease, a frequent ailment of people who suffer from alcoholism. Little evidence supports the efficacy of the drug in the long run.

**SMOKING CESSATION DRUGS** The antidepressant drug *bupropion* (Zyban) is used to blunt cravings for nicotine, but the drug has only a modest benefit in helping people quit smoking successfully (Croghan et al., 2007). Another drug, *varenicline* (brand name Chantix), works by binding to nicotine receptors in the brain, blunting the pleasurable effects of nicotine and helping prevent withdrawal symptoms. The drug has shown mixed results in research studies, so we should withhold judgment on its effectiveness (e.g., Ebbert et al., 2015; Müller et al., 2014). Combining varenicline with nicotine replacement therapy may boost its effectiveness (Koegelenberg et al., 2014). However, use of varenicline is linked to serious complications, including increased risk of depression and suicidal behaviors when compared to other smoking-cessation treatments ("Chantix Unsuitable," 2011; Moore et al., 2011).

**IS THE PATH TO ABSTINENCE FROM SMOKING SKIN DEEP?** Nicotine replacement therapy in the form of a transdermal (skin) patch, as shown here, as well as nicotine chewing gum and lozenges, allows people to continue to take in nicotine when they quit smoking. Although nicotine replacement therapy is more effective than a placebo in helping people quit smoking, it does not address the behavioral components of addiction to nicotine, such as the habit of smoking while drinking alcohol. For this reason, nicotine replacement therapy may be more effective if it is combined with behavior therapy that focuses on changing smoking habits.

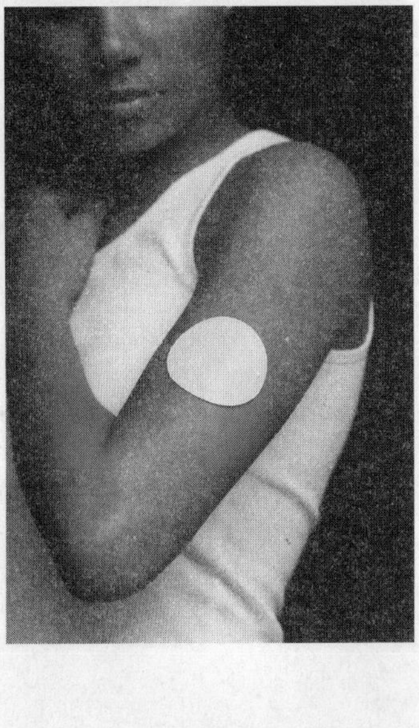

**NICOTINE REPLACEMENT THERAPY** Most regular smokers, perhaps the great majority, are nicotine dependent. The use of nicotine replacements in the form of prescription gum (Nicorette), transdermal (skin) patches, lozenges, gum, and nasal sprays can help smokers avoid unpleasant withdrawal symptoms and cravings for cigarettes (Strasser et al., 2005). After quitting smoking, ex-smokers can gradually wean themselves from the nicotine replacement. However, despite the successes touted on TV commercials for these products, quit rates a year later for smokers who used nicotine replacement methods are only about 20% or less (Baker et al., 2016; Siu, 2015). We should also add that while nicotine replacement can help quell the physiological components of withdrawal, it has no effect on behavioral patterns of addiction, such as the habit of smoking while drinking alcohol or socializing. As a result, nicotine replacement may be ineffective in promoting long-term changes unless it is combined with behavior therapy that focuses on fostering adaptive behavioral changes.

**METHADONE MAINTENANCE PROGRAMS** **Methadone** is a synthetic opiate that blunts cravings for heroin and helps curb the unpleasant symptoms that accompany withdrawal. Because methadone in normal doses does not produce a high or leave the user feeling drugged, it can help heroin addicts hold jobs and get their lives back on track (Schwartz et al., 2006). However, like other opioids, methadone is highly addictive. For this reason, people treated with methadone are, in effect, substituting dependence on one drug for dependence on another. Yet because most methadone programs are publicly financed, they relieve people addicted to heroin of the need to resort to criminal activity to support their drug habit. Although methadone is safer than heroin, its use needs to be strictly monitored because overdoses can be lethal and it may become abused as a street drug (Veilleux et al., 2010).

Since the introduction of methadone treatment, the annual death rate from opioid dependence has declined significantly (Krantz & Mehler, 2004). One frequent criticism of methadone treatment is that many participants continue to take the drug indefinitely, potentially even for a lifetime, rather than be weaned from it. However, proponents of methadone treatment point out that the measure of success should be whether people are able to take care of themselves and their families and act responsibly, not how long they continue to receive treatment (Marion, 2005). Even so, not everyone succeeds in treatment. Some patients turn to other drugs, such as cocaine, to get a high or return to using heroin. Others drop out of methadone programs and resume using heroin.

*Buprenorphine*, another synthetic opiate drug that is chemically similar to morphine, blocks withdrawal symptoms and cravings without producing a strong narcotic high (D'Onofrio et al., 2015; Ling et al., 2011). Many treatment providers prefer buprenorphine to methadone because it produces less of a sedative effect and can be taken in pill form only three times a week, whereas methadone is given in liquid form daily. *Levomethadyl*, another synthetic anti-opiate, also lasts longer than methadone and can be dispensed three times per week. The inclusion of psychosocial treatments, such as counseling and rehabilitation services, can help boost adherence to treatment with methadone or other therapeutic drugs (Veilleux et al., 2010). **T / F**

## TRUTH *or* FICTION

A widely used treatment for heroin addiction involves substituting one addictive drug for another.

☑ **TRUE** Methadone, a synthetic narcotic, is widely used in treating heroin addiction.

**NALTREXONE** **Naltrexone** is a drug that helps block the high or feelings of pleasure produced by alcohol, opioids such as heroin, and amphetamines. The drug doesn't prevent a person from taking a drink or using another drug, but it seems to blunt cravings for these drugs (Anton, 2008; Myrick et al., 2008). Blocking the pleasure produced by alcohol or other drugs may help break the vicious cycle in which one drink or use of a drug creates a desire for more. However, evidence on the effectiveness of naltrexone is mixed, and the drug appears to produce only modest effects at best (e.g., Anton et al., 2011; Harris et al., 2015; Mann et al., 2014; Oslin et al., 2015).

A nagging problem with drugs such as naltrexone, disulfiram, and methadone is that people who are suffering from drug addiction may drop out of treatment programs or simply stop using the drugs and soon return to their substance-abusing behavior. Such drugs also do not provide alternative sources of positive reinforcement that can replace the pleasurable states produced by drugs of abuse. These therapeutic drugs are effective only in the context of a broader treatment program consisting of

## THINKING CRITICALLY about abnormal psychology

### @ISSUE: SHOULD WE USE DRUGS TO TREAT DRUG ABUSE?

A variety of therapeutic drugs are used to treat drug addiction, including disulfiram for alcoholism, nicotine replacement for smoking dependence, antidepressants for cocaine dependence, and, the most controversial of all, the opioid methadone to treat dependence on the opioid heroin. It may seem ironic—indeed, paradoxical—to use drugs to treat problems with drugs.

In thinking critically about the issue of using therapeutic drugs to treat problems of drug abuse, answer the following questions:

- What drawbacks, if any, do you see in using therapeutic drugs to treat drug addiction?
- Should heroin addicts be given free opiates in the form of methadone by the government? Why or why not?
- Should there be limits placed on methadone treatment requiring people to be weaned from the drug after a certain period of time, or should they be permitted to take methadone as long as they feel they need it?

psychological counseling and life skills components, such as job and stress-management training. These treatments provide people with the skills they need to embark on a life in the mainstream culture and to find drug-free means of coping with stress (Fouquereau et al., 2003).

**CULTURALLY SENSITIVE TREATMENT.** Culturally sensitive therapy or treatment addresses all aspects of a person, including ethnic factors and the nurturing of pride in one's cultural identity. Ethnic pride may help people resist the temptation to cope with stress through alcohol and other substances.

## Culturally Sensitive Treatment of Substance Use Disorders

**8.11 Identify factors associated with culturally sensitive approaches to treatment.**

Members of ethnic minority groups may resist traditional treatment approaches because they feel excluded from full participation in society. Native American women, for example, tend to respond less favorably to traditional alcoholism counseling than White women (Rogan, 1986). Hurlburt and Gade (1984) attribute this difference to the resistance of Native American women to "White man's" authority, suggesting that Native American counselors might be more successful in overcoming this resistance.

The use of counselors from a client's own ethnic group is an example of a *culturally sensitive treatment approach*. Culturally sensitive programs address all facets of the human being, including racial and cultural identity, that nurture pride and help people resist the temptation to cope with stress through chemicals. Culturally sensitive treatment approaches have been extended to other forms of drug dependence, including programs for smoking cessation (e.g., Nevid & Javier, 1997; Nevid, Javier, & Moulton, 1996).

We need to understand the culturally specific factors that predict treatment response in ethnic minority groups. For example, a recent study points to the importance of social support in predicting success in achieving abstinence among American Indians and Alaska Natives in alcohol and drug treatment programs (Spear et al., 2013). Investigators also highlight the importance of incorporating values and cultural beliefs that represent a client's ethnic background in motivating the client to make efforts to change problem drinking behaviors (Field, Cochran, & Caetano, 2013). One example is the Hispanic value of *familism*, or emphasis on family-related consequences of problem drinking behaviors.

Treatment providers may also be more successful if they recognize and incorporate indigenous forms of healing into treatment. For example, spirituality is an important aspect of traditional Native American culture, and spiritualists have played important roles as natural healers. Seeking the assistance of a spiritualist may improve the counseling relationship. Likewise, given the importance of the church in African American and Hispanic American cultures, counselors working with people with alcohol use disorders from these groups may be more successful when they draw on clergy and church members as resources.

**A PATH TOWARD RECOVERY.** Self-help groups such as Alcoholics Anonymous provide support to people struggling with problems of alcohol and drug abuse.

## Nonprofessional Support Groups

**8.12 Identify a nonprofessional support group for people with substance use disorders.**

Despite the complexity of the factors contributing to drug abuse, drug treatment services are frequently provided by laypeople or nonprofessionals. Such people often have or have had the same problems themselves. For example, self-help group meetings are sponsored by organizations such as Alcoholics Anonymous, Narcotics Anonymous, and Cocaine Anonymous. These groups promote abstinence and provide members an opportunity to discuss their feelings and experiences in a supportive group setting. More experienced group members (sponsors) support newer members during periods of crisis or potential relapse. The meetings are sustained by nominal voluntary contributions.

Alcoholics Anonymous, the most widely used nonprofessional program, is based on the belief that alcoholism is a disease, not a sin. The AA philosophy holds that people suffering from alcoholism will never be cured, regardless of how long they abstain from alcohol; rather, people with alcoholism who remain "clean and sober" are seen as "recovering alcoholics." It is also assumed that people who suffer from alcoholism cannot control their drinking and need help to stop drinking. AA has more than 50,000 chapters in North America. The organization is so deeply embedded in the consciousness of helping professionals that many of them automatically refer newly detoxified people to AA as the follow-up agency. About half of AA members have problems with illicit drugs as well as alcohol.

The AA experience is in part spiritual, in part group supportive, and in part cognitive. AA follows a 12-step approach that focuses on accepting one's powerlessness over alcohol and turning one's will and life over to a higher power. This spiritual component may be helpful to some participants but distasteful to others. (Other lay organizations, such as Rational Recovery, adopt a nonspiritual approach.) The later steps in AA's approach focus on examining one's character flaws, admitting one's wrongdoings, being open to a higher power for help to overcome one's character defects, making amends to others, and, in step 12, bringing the AA message to other people suffering from alcoholism. Members are urged to pray or meditate to help them get in touch with their higher power. The meetings themselves provide group support, as does the buddy, or sponsor, system, which encourages members to call each other for support when they feel tempted to drink.

The success rate of AA remains in question, in large part because AA does not keep records of its members, but also because of an inability to conduct randomized clinical trials in AA settings. However, we do have evidence that participation in AA or 12-step programs is linked to better outcomes, including lower frequency and intensity of drinking (Bergman et al., 2013; Ferri, Amato, & Davoli, 2006; Ilgen et al., 2008). Even so, many people drop out of AA, as well as from other treatment programs. People who are more likely to do well with AA tend to be those who make a commitment to abstinence, who express intentions to avoid high-risk situations associated with alcohol use, and who stay longer with the program (e.g., McKellar, Stewart, & Humphreys, 2003; Moos & Moos, 2004).

Al-Anon, begun in 1951, is a spin-off of AA that supports the families and friends of people suffering from alcoholism. Another spin-off of AA, Alateen, provides support to children whose parents have alcoholism, helping them see that they are not to blame for their parents' drinking and are thus undeserving of the guilt they may feel.

## Residential Approaches

**8.13 Identify two major types of residential treatment facilities for people with substance use disorders.**

A residential approach to treatment requires a stay in a hospital or therapeutic residence. Hospitalization is recommended when substance abusers cannot exercise self-control in their usual environments, cannot tolerate withdrawal symptoms, or behave self-destructively or dangerously. Less costly outpatient treatment is indicated when withdrawal symptoms are less severe, clients are committed to changing their behavior, and support systems, such as families, can help clients make the transition to a drug-free lifestyle. The great majority of alcohol-dependent patients are treated on an outpatient basis.

Most inpatient programs use an extended 28-day detoxification period. For the first few days, treatment focuses on helping clients with withdrawal symptoms. Then the emphasis shifts to counseling about the destructive effects of alcohol and combating distorted ideas or rationalizations. Consistent with the disease model, abstinence is the goal.

Most people with alcohol use disorders, however, do not require hospitalization. A classic review article showed that outpatient and inpatient programs achieved about the same relapse rates (Miller & Hester, 1986). However, because medical insurance does not always cover outpatient treatment, many people who might benefit from outpatient treatment admit themselves for inpatient treatment instead.

A number of residential therapeutic communities are also in use. Some have part- or full-time professional staffs. Others are run entirely by laypeople. Residents are expected to remain free of drugs and take responsibility for their actions. They are often challenged to take responsibility for themselves and to acknowledge the damage caused by their drug abuse. They share their life experiences to help one another develop productive ways of handling stress.

As with AA, there is a lack of evidence from controlled studies demonstrating the efficacy of residential treatment programs. Also like AA, therapeutic communities have high numbers of early dropouts. Moreover, many residents relapse upon returning to the world outside.

## Psychodynamic Approaches

**8.14 Describe the psychodynamic treatment of substance abusers.**

Psychoanalysts view alcohol and drug problems as symptoms of conflicts rooted in childhood experiences. The therapist attempts to resolve the underlying conflicts, assuming that abusive behavior will then subside as the client seeks more mature forms of gratification. Although there are many successful psychodynamic case studies of people with substance use problems, there is a dearth of controlled and replicable research studies. The effectiveness of psychodynamic methods for treating alcohol and drug-related problems thus remains unsubstantiated.

## Behavioral Approaches

**8.15 Identify behavioral approaches to substance use disorders.**

Behavioral approaches to treating alcohol- and drug-related problems focus on modifying abusive and dependent behavior patterns. The key question for behaviorally oriented therapists is not whether alcohol- and drug-related problems are diseases, but whether abusers can learn to change their behavior when they are faced with temptation.

**SELF-CONTROL STRATEGIES** *Self-control training* helps abusers develop skills they can use to change their abusive behavior. Behavior therapists focus on three components—the ABCs of substance abuse:

1. The *antecedent* cues or stimuli (As) that prompt or trigger abuse
2. The abusive *behaviors* (Bs) themselves
3. The reinforcing or punishing *consequences* (Cs) that maintain or discourage abuse

Table 8.2 shows the kinds of strategies used to modify the ABCs of substance abuse.

**CONTINGENCY MANAGEMENT PROGRAMS** Learning theorists believe that our behavior is shaped by rewards and punishments. Consider how virtually everything you do, from attending class to stopping at red lights to working for a paycheck, is influenced by the flow of reinforcements or rewards (money, praise, approval) and punishments (traffic tickets, rebukes). *Contingency management* (CM) programs provide reinforcements (rewards) contingent on performing desirable behaviors, such as producing drug-negative urine samples (Petry et al., 2005; Poling et al., 2006; Roll et al., 2006). In one example, a group of patients had the opportunity to draw from a bowl and win monetary rewards or prize money (rewards) ranging from $1 to $100 in value (Petry & Martin, 2002). The monetary reward was contingent on submitting clean urine samples for cocaine and opioids. On average, the contingency management (reward) group achieved longer periods of continual abstinence than the standard methadone treatment group. Investigators find that even modest rewards for abstinence can help improve therapeutic outcomes in treating substance abusers (Dutra et al., 2008; Higgins, 2006).

**AVERSIVE CONDITIONING** In *aversive conditioning*, painful or aversive stimuli are paired with substance abuse or abuse-related stimuli to condition a negative emotional response to drug-related stimuli. In the case of problem drinking, tasting alcoholic beverages is usually

## Table 8.2 Self-Control Strategies for Modifying the ABCs of Substance Abuse

1. **Controlling the As (Antecedents) of Substance Abuse**

   People who abuse or become dependent on psychoactive substances become conditioned to a wide range of external (environmental) and internal (bodily states) stimuli. They may begin to break these stimulus–response connections by:

   - Removing drinking and smoking paraphernalia from the home—including all alcoholic beverages, beer mugs, carafes, ashtrays, matches, cigarette packs, lighters, and so on.
   - Restricting the stimulus environment in which drinking or smoking is permitted by using the substance only in a stimulus-deprived area of their homes, such as the garage, bathroom, or basement. All stimuli that might be connected to using the substance are removed from this area—for example, there is no TV, reading material, radio, or telephone. In this way, substance abuse becomes detached from many controlling stimuli.
   - Not socializing with others with substance abuse problems, by avoiding situations linked to abuse—bars, the street, bowling alleys, and so on.
   - Frequenting substance-free environments—lectures or concerts, a gym, museums, evening classes—and socializing with nonabusers, and eating in restaurants without liquor licenses.
   - Managing the internal triggers for abuse. This can be done by practicing self-relaxation or meditation and not taking the substance when tense; by expressing angry feelings by writing them down or by self-assertion, not by taking the substance; by seeking counseling, not alcohol, pills, or cigarettes, for prolonged feelings of depression.

2. **Controlling the Bs (Behaviors) of Substance Abuse**

   People can prevent and interrupt substance abuse by:

   - Using response prevention—breaking abusive habits by physically preventing them from occurring or making them more difficult (e.g., by not bringing alcohol home or keeping cigarettes in the car).
   - Using competing responses when tempted; by being prepared to handle substance use situations with appropriate ammunition: mints, sugarless chewing gum, and so on; by taking a bath or shower, walking the dog, walking around the block, taking a drive, calling a friend, spending time in a substance-free environment, practicing meditation or relaxation, or exercising when tempted, rather than using the substance.
   - Making abuse more laborious: buying one can of beer at a time; storing matches, ashtrays, and cigarettes far apart; wrapping cigarettes in foil to make smoking more cumbersome; pausing for 10 minutes when struck by the urge to drink, smoke, or use another substance and asking oneself, "Do I really need *this* one?"

3. **Controlling the Cs (Consequences) of Substance Abuse**

   Substance abuse has immediate positive consequences, such as pleasure, relief from anxiety and withdrawal symptoms, and stimulation. People can counter these intrinsic rewards and alter the balance of power in favor of nonabuse by:

   - Rewarding themselves for nonabuse and punishing themselves for abuse.
   - Switching to brands of beer and cigarettes they don't like.
   - Setting gradual substance reduction schedules and rewarding themselves for sticking to them.
   - Punishing themselves for failing to meet substance reduction goals. People with substance abuse problems can assess themselves, say, by setting aside a specific cash penalty for each slip and donating the cash to an unpalatable cause, such as a disliked brother-in-law's birthday present.
   - Rehearsing motivating thoughts or self-statements—such as writing reasons for quitting smoking on index cards. For example:
     - Each day I don't smoke adds another day to my life.
     - Quitting smoking will help me breathe deeply again.
     - Foods will smell and taste better when I quit smoking.
     - Think how much money I'll save by not smoking.
     - Think how much cleaner my teeth and fingers will be by not smoking.
     - I'll be proud to tell others that I kicked the habit.
     - My lungs will become clearer each and every day I don't smoke.
   - Smokers can carry a list of 20 to 25 such statements and read several of them at various times throughout the day. They can become parts of one's daily routine, a constant reminder of one's goals.

paired with drugs that cause nausea and vomiting or with electric shock. As a consequence, alcohol may come to elicit an unpleasant emotional or physical reaction. Unfortunately, aversive conditioning effects are often temporary and fail to generalize to real-life settings in which aversive stimuli are no longer administered. However, it may be useful as a treatment component in a broader-based treatment program.

**SOCIAL SKILLS TRAINING** Social skills training helps people develop effective interpersonal responses in social situations that prompt substance abuse. Assertiveness training, for example, may be used to train alcohol abusers to fend off social pressures to drink. Behavioral marital therapy seeks to improve marital communication and problem-solving skills with the goal of relieving marital stresses that can trigger abuse. Couples may learn how to use written behavioral contracts. For example, the person with a substance abuse problem might agree to abstain from drinking or to take Antabuse, while the spouse agrees to refrain from commenting on past drinking and the probability of future lapses.

**CONTROLLED DRINKING: A VIABLE GOAL?** According to the disease model of alcoholism, having even one drink causes people with alcoholism to lose control and go on a binge. Some professionals, however, argue that many people with alcohol abuse or dependence can develop self-control techniques that allow them to engage in *controlled drinking*—to have a drink or two without necessarily falling off the wagon (Sobell & Sobell, 1973a, 1973b, 1984). This contention, however, remains controversial. The proponents of the disease model of alcoholism strongly oppose attempts to teach controlled social drinking. However, controlled drinking programs may represent a pathway to abstinence for people who would not otherwise enter abstinence-only treatment programs (Glaser, 2014; Tatarsky & Kellogg, 2010). That is, a controlled drinking program can be a first step toward giving up drinking completely. By offering moderation as a treatment goal, controlled drinking programs may reach many people who refuse to participate in abstinence-only treatment programs.

## Relapse-Prevention Training

**8.16 Describe relapse-prevention training.**

The word *relapse* derives from Latin roots meaning *to slide back*. Because of the high rates of relapse in substance abuse treatment programs, cognitive-behavioral therapists have devised a number of methods referred to as *relapse-prevention training*. This training is designed to help substance abusers identify high-risk situations and learn effective coping skills for handling these situations without turning to alcohol or drugs (Witkiewicz & Marlatt, 2004). High-risk situations include negative mood states, such as depression, anger, or anxiety; interpersonal conflict, such as marital problems or conflicts with employers; and socially conducive situations, such as "the guys getting together" (Chung & Maisto, 2006). Participants learn to cope with these situations—for example, by learning relaxation skills to counter anxiety and by learning to resist social pressures to drink. They also learn to avoid practices that might prompt a relapse, such as keeping alcohol on hand for friends.

Relapse-prevention training also focuses on preventing *lapses* from turning into full-blown *relapses*. Clients learn about the importance of their *interpretations* of any lapses or slips that may occur, such as smoking a first cigarette or taking a first drink following quitting. They are taught not to overreact to a lapse by changing how they think about lapses. For example, they learn that people who lapse are more likely to relapse if they attribute their slip to personal weakness, and experience shame and guilt, than if they attribute the slip to an external or transient event. Consider a skater who slips on the ice (Marlatt & Gordon, 1985). Whether the skater gets back up and continues to perform depends largely on whether the skater sees the slip as an isolated and correctable event or as a sign of utter failure. Because lapses in ex-smokers often occur in response to withdrawal symptoms, it is important to help smokers develop ways of coping with these symptoms without resuming smoking (Piasecki et al., 2003). Participants in relapse-prevention training programs learn to view lapses as temporary setbacks that provide opportunities to learn what kinds of situations lead to temptation and to either avoid them or learn to cope with them. If they can learn to think, "Okay, I had a slip, but that doesn't mean all is lost unless I believe it is," they are less likely to relapse.

All in all, efforts to treat people with alcohol and drug problems have had mixed results at best. Many abusers really do not want to discontinue use of these substances, although they would prefer, if possible, to avoid their negative consequences. Yet many treatment approaches, including 12-step and cognitive-behavioral approaches, can work well when they are well delivered and when individuals desire change (DiClemente, 2011; Moos & Moos, 2005).

Effective treatment programs include multiple approaches that match the needs of substance abusers. They also address *comorbidity* (co-occurrence) of other psychological disorders. Problems such as anxiety disorders, mood disorders, and personality disorders is now the rule in treatment facilities for substance abuse rather than the exception (Arias et al., 2014; Pettinati, O'Brien, & Dundon, 2013; Vorspan et al., 2015). As noted in the following first-person narrative, the co-occurrence of substance abuse greatly complicates the treatment of other psychological disorders.

## "Surely They Can't Mean Beer!":

### A CASE OF ALCOHOLISM AND BIPOLAR DISORDER

A 30-year-old man who suffered from both bipolar disorder and alcoholism struggled with giving up alcohol, which he used to treat himself for symptoms of depression and mania. He later recounted how alcohol, especially beer, had become his best friend during those dark years when he was repeatedly hospitalized for recurrent manic episodes. It was during one of those hospital stays that he was told he needed to give up alcohol. He clearly remembered his response: "Surely they can't mean beer!" He was in complete denial about how alcohol was damaging his body and preventing him from benefiting from medication for bipolar disorder. It wasn't until his parents threatened to withdraw their emotional and financial support if his drinking contributed to yet another hospitalization that he finally decided to take action by participating in meetings of Alcoholics Anonymous. Over time, he eventually achieved abstinence, making it possible for his bipolar medication to work effectively. Stopping his use of alcohol, including beer, was an important step toward successful recovery, enabling him to work with his doctors to control his mood swings.

**SOURCE:** *Adapted from a testimonial posted on an online support site, NYC Voices.*

Although effective treatment programs are available, only a minority of people with alcohol dependence ever receive treatment, even when treatment is defined broadly enough to include AA (Kranzler, 2006). Echoing these findings, a study based on a sample of more than 1,000 people in Ontario, Canada, who had with alcohol abuse or dependence disorders found that only about one in three had ever received any treatment for their disorder (Cunningham & Breslin, 2004). Clearly, much more needs to be done in helping people with drug-related problems.

In the case of inner-city youth who have become trapped within a milieu of street drugs and hopelessness, culturally sensitive drug counseling and job training would be of considerable benefit in helping them to assume more productive social roles. The challenge is clear: to develop cost-effective ways of helping people recognize the negative effects of substances and forgo the powerful and immediate reinforcements they provide.

## TYING it together

### A BIOPSYCHOSOCIAL MODEL OF SUBSTANCE DEPENDENCE

Substance use disorders involve maladaptive patterns of substance abuse and dependence and reflect the interplay of biological, psychological, and environmental factors. These problems are best understood by investigating the distinctive constellation of factors that apply to each individual case. No single model or set of factors will explain each case, which is why therapists need to understand each individual's unique characteristics and personal history and direct treatment accordingly. Figure 8.8 illustrates a biopsychosocial model of substance dependence, showing how these causal factors interact.

As you can see in Figure 8.8, genetic factors can create a predisposition or diathesis for the development of drug-related problems (Young-Wolff, Enoch, & Prescott, 2011). Some people may be born with a greater tolerance for alcohol, which can make it difficult for them to regulate use of alcohol—to know "when to say when." Others have genetic tendencies that can lead them to become unusually tense or anxious. Perhaps they turn to alcohol or other drugs to quell their nervousness. Genetic predispositions can interact with environmental factors to increase the potential for drug abuse and dependence—factors such as pressure from peers to use drugs, parental modeling of excessive drinking or drug use, and family disruption that results in a lack of effective guidance or support. Cognitive factors, especially positive drug expectancies (e.g., beliefs that using drugs will enhance one's social skills or sexual prowess), raise the potential for alcohol or drug use problems. In adolescence and adulthood, these positive expectations, together with social pressures and a lack of cultural constraints, affect a young person's decision to begin using drugs and to continue to use them. Echoing the importance of interactions between genetic and environmental factors in explaining abnormal behavior patterns, investigators believe that genetic factors may increase the risk of people turning to alcohol or other drugs when they are under stress (Dong et al., 2011; Yager, 2011).

Sociocultural and biological factors are also included in this matrix of factors: the availability of alcohol and other drugs; the presence or absence of cultural constraints; the glamorizing of drug use in popular media; and genetic tendencies (such as among Asians) to flush more readily following alcohol intake (Luczak, Glatt, & Wall, 2006).

Learning factors also play important roles. Drug use may be *positively* reinforced by pleasurable effects (mediated perhaps by release of dopamine in the brain or by activation of endorphin

**Figure 8.8** A biopsychosocial model of substance dependence.

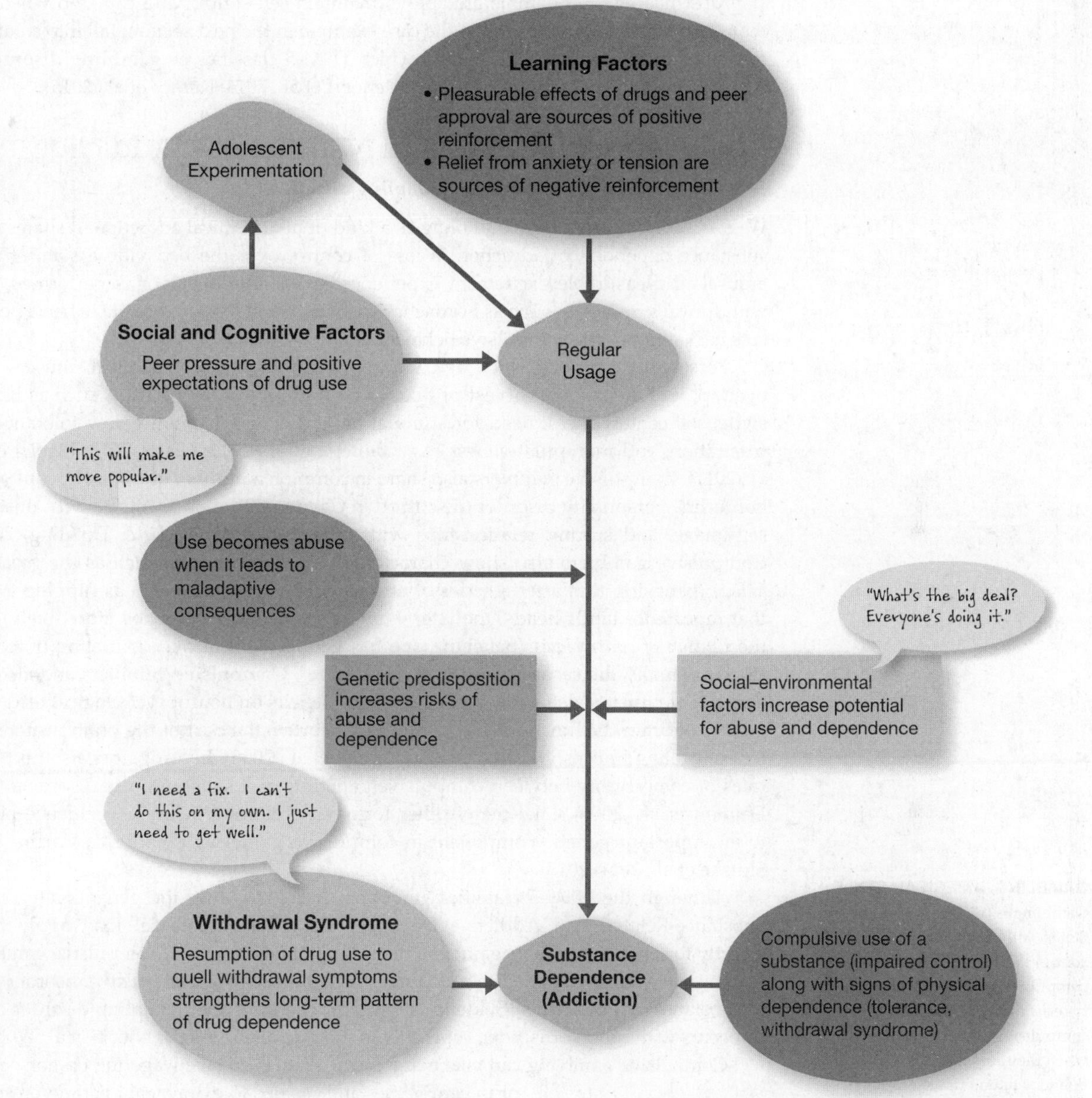


receptors). It may also be *negatively* reinforced by the reduction of tension and anxiety that depressant drugs such as alcohol, heroin, and tranquilizers can produce. In a sad but ironic twist, people who become dependent on drugs may continue to use them solely because of the relief from the withdrawal symptoms and cravings they encounter when they go without the drugs.

# Gambling Disorder

Gambling may never have been more popular in the United States than it is today. Legalized gambling encompasses many forms, such as state lotteries, offtrack betting (OTB) parlors, casino nights sponsored by religious and fraternal organizations, and gambling meccas like Atlantic City and Las Vegas. There has been a proliferation of online gambling opportunities—including Internet betting on sports and horse races and online card games—in recent years, despite crackdowns by legal authorities (e.g., Hodgins, Stea, & Grant, 2011; King et al., 2013).

Most people who gamble are able to maintain self-control and can stop whenever they wish. Others, like the man in the case example in the next section, fall into a pattern of problem or compulsive gambling, which *DSM-5* classifies as **gambling disorder**, a type of nonchemical addictive disorder (Rennert et al., 2014; Rumpf et al., 2015).

## Compulsive Gambling as a Nonchemical Addiction

**8.17 Describe the key features of gambling disorder.**

We can think of compulsive gambling as a kind of nonchemical addiction. It shares with substance dependence (addiction) a loss of control over the behavior, a state of high arousal or pleasurable excitement experienced when the behavior is performed, and withdrawal symptoms, such as headaches, insomnia, and loss of appetite, when a person cuts back or stops the compulsive behavior.

Personality characteristics of compulsive gamblers and chemical abusers also overlap, with psychological test profiles of both groups showing traits such as impulsivity, self-centeredness, need for stimulation, emotional instability, low tolerance for frustration, and manipulativeness (e.g., Billieux et al., 2012; Clark, 2012; MacLaren et al., 2011). Compulsive gamblers also share in common a number of traits of people with borderline personality disorder (discussed in Chapter 12), such as impulsivity, unstable self-image, and stormy relationships with others (Brown, Allen, & Dowling, 2014). Compulsive gamblers also show characteristic cognitive errors, such as the *gambler's fallacy* (believing that after a series of one particular outcome, such as flipping a coin that repeatedly lands heads, the alternative outcome, tails, becomes more likely) and the *illusion of control bias* (believing one has greater control over gambling outcomes than is actually the case; Goodie & Fortune, 2013). Compulsive gamblers and alcohol-dependent patients also show similar kinds of deficits on neuropsychological tests suggestive of brain dysfunctions in the prefrontal cortex, the part of the brain responsible for controlling impulsive behavior (Goudriaan et al., 2006). Investigators also find high rates of comorbidity between compulsive gambling and substance use disorders (e.g., Dannon et al., 2006). Like many other forms of abnormal behavior, evidence points to an important genetic component in compulsive gambling (Shaffer & Martin, 2011; Slutske et al., 2011, 2013).

Although the *DSM-5* classifies gambling disorder within the general category of Substance-Related and Addictive Disorders, the addiction model may apply more directly to some compulsive gamblers than others. Some forms of compulsive gambling may be more closely aligned to mood disorders or obsessive–compulsive disorder than to substance use disorders. Evidence shows, for example, that gambling disorder often co-occurs with bipolar disorder, especially in more severe cases (Di Nicola et al., 2014).

Compulsive gambling can take many forms, from excessive wagering on horse races or in card games and casinos to extravagant betting on sporting events to chancy stock picks. Many compulsive gamblers seek treatment only during a financial or emotional crisis, such as a bankruptcy or divorce.

The first national survey of its kind on problem gambling showed that about 2% of young Americans aged 14 to 21 (some 750,000 people in total) engaged in problem gambling during the prior year (Welte et al., 2008). Problem gambling was represented by such behaviors as gambling more money than one had intended or stealing money to gamble. About 0.4% to 1.0% of the general population will develop a gambling disorder at some point in their lives (American Psychiatric Association, 2013). Compulsive or problem gambling is on the rise, due in part to the increasing spread of legalized forms of gambling (Carlbring & Smit, 2008;

**GAMBLING, AMERICAN STYLE.** Gambling is big business in the United States. Although most gamblers can control their gambling behavior, compulsive gamblers are unable to resist impulses to gamble. Many compulsive gamblers seek help only when their losses throw them into financial or emotional crisis.

Hodgins, Stea, & Grant, 2011). The question is, where should we draw the line between recreational gambling and compulsive gambling?

Compulsive or pathological gamblers often report that they experienced a big win, or a series of winnings, early in their gambling careers. Eventually, however, their losses begin to mount, and they feel driven to bet with increasing desperation to reverse their luck and recoup their losses. Losses sometimes begin with the first bet, and compulsive gamblers often become trapped in a negative spiral of betting yet more frequently to recover losses even as their losses—and their debts—multiply. At some point, most compulsive gamblers hit rock bottom, a state of despair characterized by loss of control over gambling, financial ruin, suicide attempts, and shattered family relationships. They may attempt to reduce their mounting losses by gambling more frequently, hoping for the one "big score" that will put them "into the black." They may sometimes be bouncing with energy and overconfidence and at other times feel anxious and filled with despair. A compulsive gambler named Ed recounts, in his own words, how he sought the one big score to dig himself out of a financial hole.

**"I"**

**"The Big Hit"**

I looked at the amount of money I owed and thought there's no way I can go out and get a job and pay this off. I've got to have a big hit in order to do this. And you keep chasing and chasing not realizing you get further into a hole all the time. When gambling takes control of what you're doing rather than you controlling it, life became unmanageable. I was borrowing money. You shouldn't have to do that. I was lying about my gambling. You shouldn't have to do that. It [gambling] was taking away from other things in my life, my home life, my professional life, all those things were suffering because I was gambling.

**SOURCE:** *Excerpted from Speaking Out: Videos in Abnormal Psychology, Pearson Education, 2008.* *All rights reserved.*

Many compulsive gamblers suffer from low self-esteem and were rejected or abused as children by their parents (Hodgins et al., 2010). Gambling may become a means of boosting their self-esteem by proving that they are winners. Far too often, however, winnings are elusive and losses mount. Losing only strengthens their negative self-image, which can lead to depression and even suicide. Here, Ed comments on how winning boosted his self-esteem and how losses were explained away.

**"I"**

**"I Was Smarter Than Other People"**

There were a couple of things I know today were deficient in my character. I had failed as an athlete, I had failed as a student. I had failed in my original goal—I was going to be a priest. What was I going to be successful at? I was going to be successful as a handicapper (of greyhound dog races). I pursued that with a passion. I felt that [I]… would be successful and I would be an outstanding handicapper and make a lot of money at it.

The biggest rush of all was not so much winning fantastic sums of money or anything like that, but was being right. People would ask, how did you pick that? And it was my intelligence, that I was smarter than other people. I felt a definite sense of excitement, almost like a nervous anticipation … before the greyhounds were put in the box. While it's going on, you're almost in a nervous trance sensing what's going to happen and then depending on the final result, it was either one of ecstasy because you won or dejection because something had happened. It wasn't as if you made the wrong choice, but it was something that happened that impacted what would have gone your way.… I wanted people to look at me and say, "Wow, how did you do this, look at how smart you are." … They heard about my winnings, but they never heard about my losings.

**SOURCE:** *Excerpted from Speaking Out: Videos in Abnormal Psychology, Pearson Education, 2008.* *All rights reserved.*

ED: GAMBLING DISORDER

## Treatment of Compulsive Gambling

**8.18 Describe ways of treating gambling disorder.**

Treatment of compulsive gambling (gambling disorder) remains a challenge. Helping professionals face an uphill battle in working with compulsive gamblers who, like people with personality disorders and substance use disorders, make maladaptive choices but show little insight into the causes of their problems. They are reluctant to enter treatment and may resist efforts to help them, only seeking treatment when driven to do so by financial problems or emotional problems resulting from gambling (Valdivia-Salas et al., 2014). Despite these challenges, successful treatment efforts are reported, including cognitive-behavioral programs that focus on helping gamblers correct cognitive biases (e.g., beliefs that they can control gambling outcomes that are actually governed by chance, and tendencies to credit themselves for their wins and explain away their losses; see, e.g., Gooding & Tarrier, 2009; Okuda et al., 2009; Petry et al., 2008; Shaffer & Martin, 2011). Promising results are also reported from use of antidepressants and mood-stabilizing drugs, which suggests that compulsive gambling and mood disorders may share common features (e.g., Dannon et al., 2006; Grant, Williams, & Kim, 2006).

Many treatment programs involve peer support programs—like Gamblers Anonymous (GA), which models itself on Alcoholics Anonymous. This program emphasizes personal responsibility for one's behavior and ensures anonymity of group members so as to encourage participation and sharing of experiences. Within a supportive group setting, members gain insight into their self-destructive behaviors. In some cases, hospital-based or residential treatment programs may be used to sequester compulsive gamblers so that they can help break away from their usual destructive routines. Upon release, they are encouraged to continue treatment by participating in GA or similar programs. To ensure anonymity, lay programs like GA do not keep records of participants, so it is difficult to appraise success. Still, it appears that GA can be helpful in many cases, but abstinence rates among attendees are unfortunately low (Petry et al., 2006; Tavares, 2012).

Some compulsive gamblers show improvement on their own; indeed, some become free of symptoms, even without receiving any formal treatment. The problem is that investigators don't know which problem gamblers are likely to improve on their own. An analysis of data from two nationally representative samples in the United States showed that about 4 out of 10 compulsive gamblers were symptom-free during the previous year (Slutske, 2006).

# Summing Up

## Substance-Related and Addictive Disorders

### Substance Use and Abuse

**8.1 Identify the major types of substance-related disorders in the *DSM-5* and describe their key features.**

The *DSM-5* classifies substance-related disorders in two major diagnostic categories, substance-induced disorders (repeated episodes of drug intoxication or development of a withdrawal syndrome), and substance use disorders (maladaptive use of a substance leading to psychological distress or impaired functioning).

### Nonchemical Addictions and Other Forms of Compulsive Behavior

**8.2 Describe nonchemical forms of addiction or compulsive behavior.**

Patterns of compulsive behavior, such as compulsive gambling and shopping, and perhaps even excessive Internet use, may represent nonchemical forms of addiction. These behavior patterns are associated with classic signs of drug dependence or addiction—including impaired control over the behavior and withdrawal symptoms such as anxiety or depression—upon abrupt cessation of use.

### Clarifying Terms

**8.3 Explain the difference between physiological dependence and psychological dependence.**

Physiological dependence involves changes in the body as the result of regular use of a substance, such as the development of tolerance and a withdrawal syndrome. Psychological dependence involves habitual use of a substance to meet a psychological need, either with or without physiological dependence.

### Pathways to Addiction

**8.4 Identify common stages in the pathway to drug dependence.**

Three commonly identified stages in the pathway to drug dependence are (1) experimentation, (2) routine use, and (3) addiction or dependence.

## Drugs of Abuse

### Depressants

**8.5 Describe the effects of depressants and the risks they pose.**

Depressants are drugs that depress or slow down nervous system activity. They include alcohol, sedatives and minor tranquilizers, and opioids. Their effects include intoxication, impaired coordination, slurred speech, and impaired intellectual functioning. Chronic alcohol abuse is associated with health risks including Korsakoff's syndrome, cirrhosis of the liver, fetal alcohol syndrome, and other physical health problems. Barbiturates are depressants or sedatives that have been used medically for short-term relief of anxiety and treatment of epilepsy, among other uses. Like alcohol, they can impair driving ability and also can be dangerous in overdose situations, especially when use of barbiturates is combined with alcohol. Opioids such as morphine and heroin are derived from the opium poppy, and others are synthesized. Opioids are used medically for relief of pain, are strongly addictive, and can result in lethal overdoses.

### Stimulants

**8.6 Describe the effects of stimulants and the risks they pose.**

Stimulants increase activity in the central nervous system. Amphetamines and cocaine are stimulants that increase the availability of neurotransmitters in the brain, leading to heightened states of arousal and pleasurable feelings. High doses can produce psychotic reactions that mimic features of paranoid schizophrenia. Habitual cocaine use can lead to a variety of health problems, and an overdose can cause sudden death. Repeated use of nicotine, a mild stimulant found in tobacco, leads to physiological dependence.

### Hallucinogens

**8.7 Describe the effects of hallucinogens and the risks they pose.**

Hallucinogens are drugs that distort sensory perceptions and can induce hallucinations. They include LSD, psilocybin, and mescaline. Other drugs with similar effects are cannabis (marijuana) and phencyclidine, the latter a deliriant that can induce a state of mental confusion or delirium. Although hallucinogens may not lead to physiological dependence, psychological dependence may occur. Concerns exist about the potential for brain damage that affects learning and memory ability in heavier users of marijuana.

## Theoretical Perspectives

### Biological Perspectives

**8.8 Describe biological perspectives on substance use disorders and explain how cocaine affects the brain.**

The biological perspective focuses on uncovering the biological pathways that may explain mechanisms of physiological dependence. The biological perspective spawns the disease model, which posits that alcoholism and other forms of substance dependence are disease processes. Cocaine blocks the reuptake of dopamine by the transmitting neuron, which means that more dopamine remains in the synaptic gap, creating a euphoric high by overstimulating receiving neurons in brain networks that regulate feelings of pleasure.

## Psychological Perspectives

**8.9 Describe psychological perspectives on substance use disorders.**

Learning perspectives view problems with substance abuse as learned patterns of behavior, with roles for classical and operant conditioning and observational learning. Cognitive perspectives focus on roles of attitudes, beliefs, and expectancies in accounting for substance use and abuse. Sociocultural perspectives emphasize the cultural, group, and social factors that underlie drug use patterns, including the role of peer pressure in determining adolescent drug use. Psychodynamic theorists view problems of substance abuse, such as excessive drinking and habitual smoking, as signs of an oral fixation.

# Treatment of Substance Use Disorders

## Biological Approaches

**8.10 Identify biological treatments of substance use disorders.**

Biological treatments of substance use disorders include detoxification; the use of therapeutic drugs such as disulfiram, methadone, naltrexone, and antidepressants; and nicotine replacement therapy.

## Culturally Sensitive Treatment of Alcoholism

**8.11 Identify factors associated with culturally sensitive approaches to treatment.**

Factors that are highlighted in the text include the use of counselors from a person's own ethnic group, providing social support, incorporating culturally specific values and indigenous forms of healing in the treatment program, and drawing upon clergy and church members.

## Nonprofessional Support Groups

**8.12 Identify a nonprofessional support group for people with substance use disorders.**

A leading example of a nonprofessional support group is Alcoholics Anonymous, which promotes abstinence within a supportive group setting.

## Residential Approaches

**8.13 Identify two major types of residential treatment facilities for people with substance use disorders.**

Residential treatment approaches include hospitals that provide specialized services for substance abusers and therapeutic residences.

## Psychodynamic Approaches

**8.14 Describe the psychodynamic treatment of substance abusers.**

Psychodynamic treatment focuses on uncovering and working through the inner conflicts originating in childhood that may lie at the root of substance abuse problems.

## Behavioral Approaches

**8.15 Identify several behavioral approaches to substance use disorders.**

Behavior therapists focus on helping people with substance use problems help clients change problem behaviors by using techniques such as self-control training, aversive conditioning, and skills training approaches.

## Relapse-Prevention Training

**8.16 Describe relapse-prevention training.**

Regardless of the initial success of a treatment technique, relapse remains a pressing problem in treating people with substance abuse problems. Relapse-prevention training employs cognitive-behavioral techniques to help recovering substance abusers cope with high-risk situations and prevent lapses from becoming relapses by interpreting lapses in less damaging ways.

# Gambling Disorder

## Compulsive Gambling as a Nonchemical Addiction

**8.17 Describe the key features of gambling disorder.**

Gambling disorder or compulsive gambling can be likened to a type of nonchemical addiction in which people experience a loss of control over the behavior, a state of high arousal or pleasurable excitement when the behavior is performed, and withdrawal symptoms when they stop gambling. People with the disorder frequently have comorbid conditions, especially substance use disorders and mood disorders.

## Treatment of Compulsive Gambling

**8.18 Describe ways of treating gambling disorder.**

Promising treatment approaches for compulsive gambling have been developed, including antidepressants and mood-stabilizing drugs and cognitive-behavioral therapy, which is used to correct cognitive biases that may contribute to compulsive gambling. Many compulsive gamblers participate in peer support groups, such as Gamblers Anonymous, that help them gain insight into their self-defeating behavior and change their compulsive behavior patterns.

## Critical Thinking Questions

On the basis of your reading of this chapter, answer the following questions:

- What is the basis for determining when drug use becomes abuse or dependence? Have you or has someone you've known crossed the line between use and abuse? On what evidence do you base this judgment?
- Do you or does someone you know show evidence of nonchemical forms of addiction, such as compulsive shopping, gambling, or sexual behavior? How is this behavior affecting your (or his or her) life? What can you (or he or she) do about overcoming it?
- What do you think of the concept of using methadone, a narcotic drug, to treat addiction to another narcotic drug, heroin? What are the advantages and disadvantages of this approach? Do you believe the government should support methadone maintenance programs? Why or why not?
- Many teenagers today have parents who themselves smoked marijuana or used other drugs when they were younger. If you were one of those parents, what would you tell your children about drugs?

## Key Terms

substance-induced disorders, p. 299
substance intoxication, p. 299
substance withdrawal, p. 299
tolerance, p. 299
withdrawal syndrome, p. 299
substance use disorders, p. 299
Internet addiction disorder, p. 302
physiological dependence, p. 304
addiction, p. 304
psychological dependence, p. 305
depressant, p. 306
alcoholism, p. 306
barbiturates, p. 313
narcotics, p. 313
endorphins, p. 314
morphine, p. 314
heroin, p. 314
stimulants, p. 315
amphetamines, p. 315
amphetamine psychosis, p. 315
cocaine, p. 316
crack, p. 316
hallucinogens, p. 318
marijuana, p. 319
detoxification, p. 329
methadone, p. 329
naltrexone, p. 330
gambling disorder, p. 338

## Scoring Key for "Are You Hooked?" Questionnaire

*Any Yes* answer suggests that you may be dependent on alcohol. If you have answered any of these questions in the affirmative, we suggest you seriously examine what your drinking means to you and talk things over with a counselor or health care provider.

Chapter 9

# Eating Disorders and Sleep-Wake Disorders

## Learning Objectives

**9.1** **Describe** the key features of anorexia nervosa.

**9.2** **Describe** the key features of bulimia nervosa.

**9.3** **Describe** causal factors involved in anorexia nervosa and bulimia nervosa.

**9.4** **Evaluate** methods used to treat anorexia nervosa and bulimia nervosa.

**9.5** **Describe** the key features of binge-eating disorder and **identify** effective treatments for binge-eating disorder.

**9.6** **Describe** the key features of insomnia disorder.

**9.7** **Describe** the key features of hypersomnolence disorder.

**9.8** **Describe** the key features of narcolepsy.

**9.9** **Describe** the key features of breathing-related sleep disorders.

**9.10** **Describe** the key features of circadian rhythm sleep-wake disorders.

**9.11** **Identify** the major types of parasomnias and **describe** their key features.

**9.12** **Evaluate** methods used to treat sleep-wake disorders and **apply** your knowledge to identify more adaptive sleep habits.

## TRUTH *or* FICTION

T☐ F☐ Although others see them as extremely thin, young women with anorexia nervosa still see themselves as too fat. (p. 348)

T☐ F☐ Although anorexia nervosa is a serious psychological disorder, women with anorexia are actually less likely to attempt suicide than are women in general. (p. 349)

T☐ F☐ Women with bulimia nervosa induce vomiting only after binges. (p. 354)

T☐ F☐ Antidepressants can be used to treat bulimia nervosa. (p. 358)

T☐ F☐ Obesity is one of the most common psychological disorders in the United States. (p. 359)

T☐ F☐ When people start losing significant amounts of weight, their bodies respond as though they were starving. (p. 361)

T☐ F☐ After Santa Claus, the most recognizable figure to children is Ronald McDonald. (p. 361)

T☐ F☐ Many people suffer from sleep attacks in which they suddenly fall asleep without any warning. (p. 368)

T☐ F☐ Some people literally gasp for breath hundreds of times during sleep without realizing it. (p. 368)

CHAPTER INTRODUCTION: EATING DISORDERS AND SLEEP-WAKE DISORDERS

"I" "What's Up with That?"

Every night that I throw up I can't help but be afraid that my heart might stop or something else will happen. I just pray and hope I can stop this throwing up before it kills me. I hate this bulimia and I won't stop. It's hard for me to binge and throw up now (refrigerator is locked) and I just can't do it anymore. I just can't race through so much food so fast and then throw it up. I don't really want to.

Julie picked me up from class the other day, and she was eating dry sugar cookie mix from a bowl with a huge spoon. I panicked. I shook, perspired, had trouble taking full breaths, and couldn't focus or concentrate with all the thoughts rushing through my head. I wasn't eating it, but I could smell it and see it and heard the sugar crystals crunch as she chewed big mouthfuls of it. Then she started eating a cupcake. I couldn't handle it. She offered me some and I became severely nauseated by the mere thought of her offer. When she dropped me off, I raced into the house to gain control of this incredible binge. I was horrified and sick, saw myself gaining weight through my distorted vision, and immediately took laxatives to rid myself of all that forbidden food I felt inside, even though I hadn't eaten a thing.

After I calmed down, I realized the reality of the situation, and I felt stupid and crazy and like a total failure ... I don't even need a binge to have my purging cycle triggered to an intense degree. What's up with that?

**SOURCE:** *Costin, 1997, pp. 62–63*

The young woman who wrote this vignette has *bulimia nervosa*, an eating disorder characterized by repeated episodes of binge eating and purging. How can we explain eating disorders like *bulimia nervosa*—or like *anorexia nervosa*, a psychological disorder of self-starvation that can lead to serious medical consequences, even death? Eating disorders primarily affect young people of high school or college age, especially young women. Even if you don't know anyone with a diagnosable eating disorder, chances are you know people with disturbed eating behaviors such as occasional binge eating and excessive dieting. You probably also know people who suffer from obesity, a major health problem that affects increasing numbers of Americans.

This chapter explores the three major types of eating disorders: anorexia nervosa, bulimia nervosa, and binge-eating disorder. We also examine factors that contribute to obesity, a health problem that has reached epidemic proportions in our society. Our focus in this chapter also extends to another set of problems that commonly affects young adults: sleep-wake disorders. The most common form of sleep-wake disorder, insomnia disorder, affects many young people who are making their way in the world and who tend to bring their worries and concerns to bed with them.

# Eating Disorders

In a nation of plenty, some people literally starve themselves—sometimes to death. They are obsessed with their weight and they want to achieve an exaggerated image of thinness. Others engage in repeated cycles in which they binge on food and then attempt to purge their excess eating—for example, by inducing vomiting. These dysfunctional patterns are, respectively, the two major types of eating disorders: **anorexia nervosa** and **bulimia nervosa**.

**Eating disorders** involve disordered eating behaviors and maladaptive ways of controlling body weight. Eating disorders often occur together with other psychological disorders, such as depression, anxiety disorders, and substance abuse disorders (Jenkins et al., 2011). Table 9.1 provides an overview of the three types of eating disorders we examine in this chapter.

The great majority of cases of anorexia nervosa and bulimia nervosa occur among young women. Although eating disorders may develop in middle or even late adulthood, they typically begin during adolescence or early adulthood when the pressures to be thin are the strongest. As these social pressures have increased, so too have rates of eating disorders. Evidence from a large community-based survey indicates that anorexia nervosa affects about 0.9% of women (nearly 1 in 100; Hudson, Lalonde, et al., 2006). Bulimia nervosa is believed to affect about 0.9% to 1.5% of women (Smink, van Hoeken, & Hoek, 2012). There are also many cases of people with some anorexic or bulimic behaviors that are not at a level that would warrant a diagnosis of an eating disorder.

**Table 9.1** Overview of Eating Disorders

| Type of Disorder | Lifetime Prevalence in Population (Approx.) | Description | Associated Features |
|---|---|---|---|
| **Anorexia nervosa** | 0.9%, or 9 in 1,000 women; about 0.3%, or 3 in 1,000 men | Self-starvation, resulting in abnormally low body weight for one's age, gender, height, and physical health and developmental level | • Strong fears of gaining weight or becoming fat<br>• Distorted self-image (perceiving oneself as fat despite extreme thinness)<br>• Two general subtypes: binge eating/purging type and restricting type<br>• Potentially serious, even fatal, medical complications<br>• Typically affects young, European American women |
| **Bulimia nervosa** | 0.9% to 1.5% in women; 0.1% to 0.5% in men | Recurrent episodes of binge eating followed by purging | • Weight is usually maintained within a normal range<br>• Overconcern about body shape and weight<br>• Binge/purge episodes may result in serious medical complications<br>• Typically affects young European American women |
| **Binge-eating disorder** | 3.5% in women; 2% in men | Recurrent binge eating without compensatory purging | • Individuals with binge-eating disorder are frequently described as compulsive overeaters<br>• Typically affects obese women who are older than those affected by anorexia or bulimia |

**SOURCES:** Prevalence rates derived from Hudson, Hiripi, et al., 2006; Smink, van Hoeken, & Hoek, 2012.

Rates of anorexia nervosa and bulimia nervosa among men are estimated at about 0.3% (3 in 1,000) for anorexia and 0.1% to 0.5% (1 to 5 in 1,000) for bulimia (Hudson et al., 2006; Smink, van Hoeken, & Hoek, 2012). Many men with anorexia nervosa participate in sports such as wrestling that impose pressures on maintaining weight within a narrow range.

# Anorexia Nervosa

**9.1 Describe the key features of anorexia nervosa.**

The word *anorexia* derives from the Greek roots *an*, meaning *without*, and *orexis*, meaning *a desire for. Anorexia* thus means *without desire for [food]*, which is something of a misnomer, because people with anorexia nervosa rarely lose their appetite. However, they may be repelled by food and refuse to eat more than is absolutely necessary to maintain

## Anorexia Nervosa:

### THE CASE OF KAREN

Karen was the 22-year-old daughter of a renowned English professor. She had begun her college career full of promise at the age of 17, but 2 years ago, after "social problems" occurred, she had returned to live at home and taken progressively lighter course loads at a local college. Karen had never been overweight, but about a year ago, her mother noticed that she seemed to be gradually "turning into a skeleton."

Karen spent literally hours every day shopping at the supermarket, butcher, and bakeries conjuring up gourmet treats for her parents and younger siblings. Arguments over her lifestyle and eating habits had divided the family into two camps. The camp led by her father called for patience; that headed by her mother demanded confrontation. Her mother feared that Karen's father would "protect her right into her grave" and wanted Karen placed in residential treatment "for her own good." The parents finally compromised on an outpatient evaluation.

At an even 5 feet, Karen looked like a prepubescent 11-year-old. Her nose and cheekbones protruded crisply. Her lips were full, but the redness of the lipstick was unnatural, as if too much paint had been dabbed on a corpse for the funeral. Karen weighed only 78 pounds, but she had dressed in a stylish silk blouse, scarf, and baggy pants so that not one inch of her body was revealed.

Karen vehemently denied that she had a problem. Her figure was "just about where I want it to be" and she engaged in aerobic exercise daily. A deal was struck in which outpatient treatment would be tried as long as Karen lost no more weight and showed steady gains back to at least 90 pounds. Treatment included a day hospital with group therapy and two meals a day. But word came back that Karen was artfully toying with her food—cutting it up, sort of licking it, and moving it about her plate—rather than eating it. After 3 weeks, Karen had lost another pound. At that point, her parents were able to persuade her to enter a residential treatment program in which her eating behavior could be more carefully monitored.

*From the Author's Files*

**HOW DO I SEE MYSELF?** A distorted body image is a common feature of eating disorders.

a minimal weight for their ages and heights. Often, they starve themselves to the point at which they become dangerously emaciated. Anorexia nervosa (commonly referred to as *anorexia)* usually develops between the ages of 12 and 18, although earlier and later onsets are sometimes found.

The most prominent sign of anorexia nervosa is severe weight loss due to significant restriction of calorie intake or self-starvation. Other common features include the following:

- Excessive fears of gaining weight or becoming fat, despite being abnormally thin
- A distorted body image, as reflected in self-perception of one's body, or of parts of one's body, as fat, even though others perceive the person as thin
- Failure to recognize the risks posed by maintaining body weight at abnormally low levels

One common pattern of anorexia begins after menarche when the girl notices added weight and insists it must come off. The addition of body fat is normal in adolescent females: In an evolutionary sense, fat is added in preparation for childbearing and nursing. However, women with anorexia seek to rid their bodies of any additional weight and so turn to extreme dieting and, often, excessive exercise. However, these efforts continue unabated after the initial weight loss goal is achieved, even after family and friends express concern. Another common pattern occurs when young women leave home to attend college and encounter difficulties adjusting to the demands of college life and independent living. Anorexia nervosa is also common among young women involved in dance or modeling, both fields that place strong emphasis on maintaining an unrealistically thin body shape (Tseng et al., 2013).

**NATASHA: ANOREXIA**

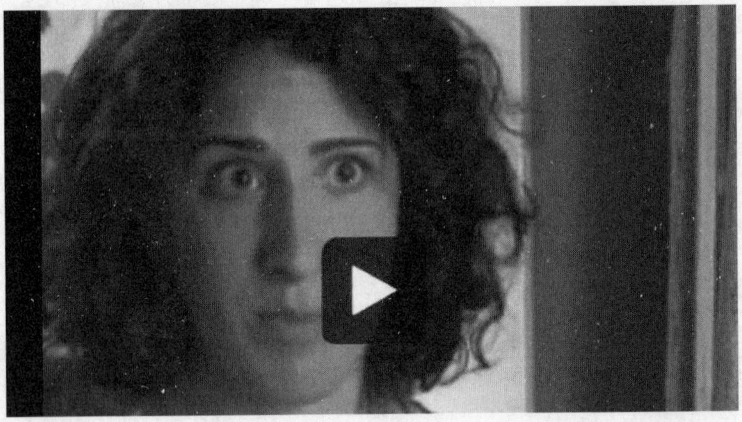

Adolescent girls and women with anorexia nervosa almost always deny that they are losing too much weight. They may argue that their ability to engage in stressful exercise demonstrates their fitness. Women with eating disorders are more likely than normal women to have a distorted body image. Other people may see them as nothing but "skin and bones," but women with anorexia still see themselves as too fat. Although they literally starve themselves, they may spend much of the day thinking and talking about food and even preparing elaborate meals for others. **T / F**

## TRUTH *or* FICTION

Although others see them as extremely thin, young women with anorexia nervosa still see themselves as too fat.

☑ TRUE Others may see them as nothing but "skin and bones," but anorexic women have a distorted body image and may still see themselves as too fat.

**SUBTYPES OF ANOREXIA NERVOSA** There are two general subtypes of the disorder, a binge-eating/purging type and a restricting type. The binge-eating/purging type is characterized by frequent episodes during the prior 3-month period of binge eating or purging (such as by self-induced vomiting or overuse of laxatives, diuretics, or enemas);

the restrictive type does not have bingeing or purging episodes. The distinction between the subtypes of anorexia nervosa is supported by differences in personality patterns. Individuals with the binge-eating/purging type tend to have difficulties with impulse control, which may lead to problems with substance abuse. They tend to alternate between periods of rigid control and impulsive behavior. Those with the restrictive type tend to rigidly, even obsessively, control their diet and appearance.

**MEDICAL COMPLICATIONS OF ANOREXIA NERVOSA** Anorexia nervosa can lead to serious medical complications that in extreme cases can be fatal (Franko et al., 2013). Losses of as much as 35% of body weight may occur, and anemia may develop. Females suffering from anorexia nervosa are also likely to encounter dermatological problems such as dry, cracking skin; fine, downy hair; even a yellowish discoloration of the skin that may persist for years after weight is regained. Cardiovascular complications include heart irregularities, hypotension (low blood pressure), and associated dizziness upon standing, sometimes causing blackouts. Decreased food ingestion can cause gastrointestinal problems such as constipation, abdominal pain, and obstruction or paralysis of the bowels or intestines. Menstrual irregularities in women are common in cases of anorexia, as is amenorrhea (absence or suppression of menstruation). Muscular weakness and abnormal growth of bones may occur, causing loss of height and osteoporosis.

Then, sadly, there is an increased risk of death, which is pegged at 5% to 20% of cases of anorexia nervosa, due either to suicide or to malnutrition due to starvation (Arcelus et al., 2011; Haynos, & Fruzzetti, 2011). Young women with anorexia nervosa are eight times more likely to commit suicide than are young women in the general population (Yager, 2008). In a study of several hundred people who had suffered from anorexia or were suffering still—95% of whom were female—nearly one in five (17%) had made a suicide attempt (Bulik et al., 2008). **T / F**

### TRUTH or FICTION

Although anorexia nervosa is a serious psychological disorder, women with anorexia are actually less likely to attempt suicide than are women in general.

☑ **FALSE** Actually, the rate of suicide attempts in young women with anorexia nervosa is much higher than that of young women in the general population.

## Bulimia Nervosa

**9.2 Describe the key features of bulimia nervosa.**

Nicole suffers from bulimia nervosa (commonly referred to as *bulimia*). The word *bulimia* derives from the Greek roots *bous*, meaning *ox* or *cow*, and *limos*, meaning *hunger*. The distressing picture inspired by the origin of the term is one of continuous eating, like a cow chewing its cud. Bulimia nervosa is an eating disorder characterized by recurrent episodes of gorging on large quantities of food, followed by use of inappropriate ways to compensate for overeating to prevent weight gain.

The defining feature of bulimia nervosa is the occurrence of frequent episodes of binge eating (gorging), followed by compensatory behaviors such as self-induced vomiting; abuse of laxatives, diuretics, or enemas; or fasting or excessive exercise. Other commonly occurring features of bulimia nervosa include the following:

- Feelings of lack of control over eating during binge-eating episodes
- Excessive fear of gaining weight
- Excessive emphasis on body shape and body weight on self-image

A *DSM-5* diagnosis of bulimia nervosa requires that binge-eating episodes and the accompanying compensatory behaviors occur at an average frequency of at least once a week for three months (American Psychiatric Association, 2013). A person with bulimia may use two or more strategies for purging, such as vomiting and laxatives. Although people with anorexia nervosa are extremely thin, those with bulimia nervosa generally maintain their weight within a healthy range (Bulik et al., 2012). However, they have an excessive concern about their shape and weight and may rely on purging to avoid gaining weight.

People with bulimia nervosa typically purge by gagging themselves to induce vomiting. Most attempt to conceal their behavior. Fear of gaining weight is a constant factor.

## Bulimia Nervosa:

### THE CASE OF NICOLE

Nicole has only opened her eyes, but already she wishes it was time for bed. She dreads going through the day, which threatens to turn out like so many other recent days. Each morning she wonders if this will be the day that she will be able to get by without being obsessed by thoughts of food. Or will she spend the day gorging herself? Today is the day she will get off to a new start, she promises herself. Today, she will begin to live like a normal person. Yet she is not convinced that it is really up to her.

Nicole starts the day with eggs and toast. Then she goes to work on cookies; doughnuts; bagels smothered with butter, cream cheese, and jelly; granola; candy bars; and bowls of cereal and milk—all within 45 minutes. Then she cannot take in any more food and turns her attention to purging what she has eaten. She goes to the bathroom, ties back her hair, turns on the shower to mask any noise she will make, drinks a glass of water, and makes herself vomit. Afterward, she vows, "Starting tomorrow, I'm going to change." But she suspects that tomorrow may be just another chapter of the same story.

**SOURCE:** *Adapted from Boskind-White & White, 1983, p. 29*

However, people with bulimia nervosa do not pursue the extreme thinness characteristic of anorexia nervosa. Their ideal weights are similar to those of women who do not suffer from eating disorders.

Eating binges often occur in secret, typically during unstructured afternoon or evening hours. A binge may last from 30 to 60 minutes and involves consumption of forbidden foods that are generally sweet and rich in fat. Binge eaters typically feel a lack of control over their bingeing and may consume as many as 5,000 to 10,000 calories. One young woman described eating everything available in the refrigerator, even to the point of scooping out margarine from its container with her finger. The episode continues until the binger is spent or exhausted, suffers painful stomach distention, induces vomiting, or runs out of food. Drowsiness, guilt, and depression usually ensue, but bingeing is initially pleasant because of release from dietary constraints.

Bulimia nervosa typically affects women in late adolescence or early adulthood, when concerns about dieting and dissatisfaction with body shape or weight are at their height. Despite the widespread belief that eating disorders are most common among more affluent people, the available evidence shows no strong linkages between these disorders and socioeconomic level (Mitchison & Hay, 2014; Swanson et al., 2011). Beliefs that eating disorders are associated with high socioeconomic status may reflect the tendency for more affluent patients to seek and obtain treatment. Alternatively, it may be that the social pressures on young women to strive to achieve an ultrathin ideal have now generalized across all socioeconomic levels.

**MEDICAL COMPLICATIONS OF BULIMIA NERVOSA** Like anorexia nervosa, bulimia nervosa is associated with many medical complications. Many of these stem from repeated vomiting: skin irritation around the mouth due to frequent contact with stomach acid, blockage of salivary ducts, decay of tooth enamel, and dental cavities. The acid from the vomit may damage taste receptors on the palate, making a person less sensitive to the taste of vomit with repeated purging. Decreased sensitivity to the aversive taste of vomit may help maintain the purging behavior. Cycles of bingeing and vomiting may cause abdominal pain, hiatal hernia, and other abdominal complaints, as well as disturbed menstrual functioning. Stress on the pancreas may produce pancreatitis (inflammation of the pancreas), which is a medical emergency. Excessive use of laxatives may cause bloody diarrhea and laxative dependency so that a person cannot have normal bowel movements without laxatives. In extreme cases, the bowel can lose its reflexive eliminatory response to pressure from waste material. Bingeing on large quantities of salty food may cause convulsions and swelling. Repeated vomiting or abuse of laxatives can lead to potassium deficiency, producing muscular weakness, cardiac irregularities, and even sudden death—especially when diuretics are used. As with anorexia, menstruation may come to a halt. Also like patients with anorexia, those with bulimia have high rates of early deaths as compared to the general population, with deaths resulting from various causes, such as suicide, substance abuse, and medical disorders (Crow et al., 2009). Although patients with bulimia show a shockingly high rate of suicide attempts, estimated at 25% to 35%, it's not yet clear whether their rate of completed suicide is higher than average (Franko & Keel, 2006).

**BODY DISSATISFACTION STARTS EARLY.** Investigators find greater levels of body dissatisfaction in girls than boys as young as 8 years of age.

## Causes of Anorexia Nervosa and Bulimia Nervosa

**9.3 Describe causal factors involved in anorexia nervosa and bulimia nervosa.**

Like other psychological disorders, anorexia nervosa and bulimia nervosa involve a complex interplay of factors. Perhaps most significant are social pressures that lead young women to base their self-worth on their physical appearance, especially their weight.

**SOCIOCULTURAL FACTORS** Sociocultural theorists point to social pressures and expectations placed on young women in our society as contributing factors in eating disorders (The McKnight Investigators, 2003; Mendez, 2005). The drive for thinness and body dissatisfaction figure prominently in eating disorders (Brannan & Petrie, 2011; Chernyak & Lowe, 2010). Comparing one's own body unfavorably to others in terms of appearance can lead to body dissatisfaction (Myers & Crowther, 2009). Young women begin measuring themselves against unrealistic standards of thinness—the "body perfect"— represented in media images of ultrathin models and performers, setting the stage for body dissatisfaction (Bell & Dittmar, 2011; Rodgers, Salès, & Chabrol, 2010). Body dissatisfaction, in turn, may lead to excessive dieting and disturbed eating behaviors. Even in children as young as 8 years, investigators find that girls express more dissatisfaction with their bodies than boys do (Ricciardelli & McCabe, 2004). Pressures to achieve a thin ideal are underscored by findings from a college sample that one in seven women (14%) said they would feel embarrassed buying a single chocolate bar in a store (Rozin, Bauer, & Catanese, 2003). Peer pressure from friends to adhere to a thin body shape also emerges as a strong predictor of bulimic behavior in young women (Young, McFatter, & Clopton, 2001). Body dissatisfaction is also linked to eating disorders in young men (Olivardia et al., 2004).

The idealization of thinness in women can be illustrated by the changes in the **body mass index (BMI)** of winners of the Miss America pageant from 1920 through 1990 (Rubinstein & Caballero, 2000; see Figure 9.1). BMI is a measure of

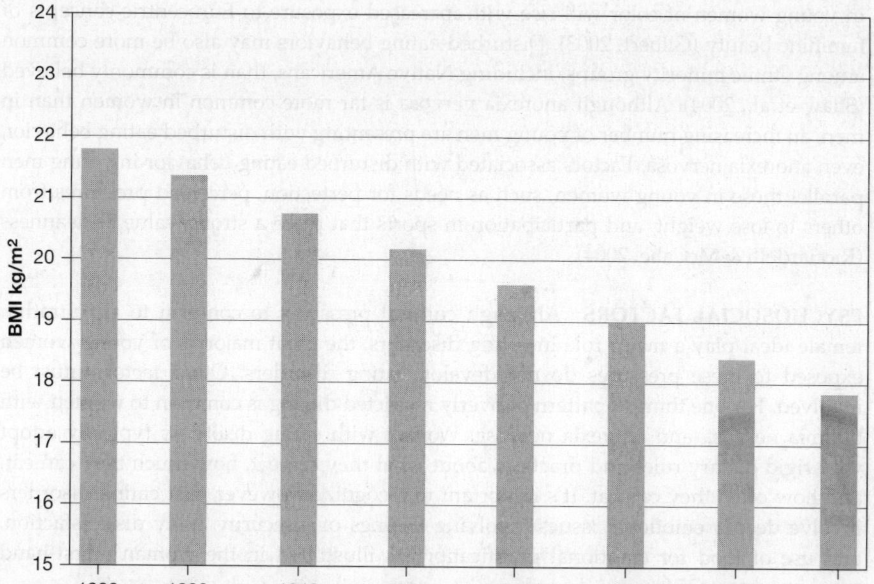


**Figure 9.1 Thinner and thinner.**

Note the downward trend in the BMI levels of Miss America contest winners over time. What might these data suggest about changes in society's view of the ideal female form?

**SOURCE:** Rubinstein & Caballero, 2000.

height-adjusted weight, and a level of 18.5 is considered the minimal standard of healthy weight. Notice the downward trend. By 2010, the average BMI of Miss America winners had dropped even further, to 16.9, a level well below the 18.5 standard considered the minimal level of a normal or healthy weight (Mapes, 2013). (To check your own BMI, use one of the many BMI calculators you can find online.) What messages about feminine beauty might this trend be conveying to young women and young men about female beauty?

The pressure to be thin is so prevalent that dieting has become the normative pattern of eating among young American women. Four out of five young women in the United States have gone on a diet by the time they reach their 18th birthdays. A survey of college women showed that regardless of how much they weighed, the great majority, about 80%, reported dieting (Malinauskas et al., 2006). Concerns about social pressures to be thin bring to light the idealized body images to which girls are exposed, including perhaps the most famous of all ultrathin ideals: Barbie (see *Thinking Critically: Should Barbie Be Banned?* on page 353).

In support of the sociocultural model, evidence shows that eating disorders are much less common in non-Western countries that do not associate thinness with female beauty (Giddens, 2006). Yet even in non-Western cultures, such as those in East Africa, the level of exposure to Western media and travel in Western countries is associated with a higher rate of eating disorder symptoms in young women (Eddy, Hennessey, & Thompson-Brenner, 2007). Investigators also find high levels of both body dissatisfaction and disordered eating behaviors in male and female middle-school children in Korea (Jung, Forbes, & Lee, 2009). In Taiwan, investigators find that body dissatisfaction among young women is predictive of intentions to lose weight (Lu & Hou, 2009).

Eating disorders in developing countries may be linked to factors other than obsessive concerns about weight. For example, among young women in the African country of Ghana, researchers found that extreme thinness was linked to fasting for religious reasons rather than for weight concerns (Bennett et al., 2004).

Rates of disordered eating behaviors and eating disorders also vary in the United States among ethnic groups, with higher rates found among Euro-American adolescents than among African American and other ethnic minority adolescents (Lamberg, 2003; Striegel-Moore et al., 2003). One likely reason for this discrepancy is that body image and body dissatisfaction are less closely tied to body weight among minority women (Angier, 2000). That said, investigators expect that the prevalence of eating disorders in young women of color will rise with increased exposure to Eurocentric concepts of feminine beauty (Gilbert, 2003). Disturbed eating behaviors may also be more common among ethnic minority groups, including Native Americans, than is commonly believed (Shaw et al., 2004). Although anorexia nervosa is far more common in women than in men, an increasing number of young men are presenting with disturbed eating behavior, even anorexia nervosa. Factors associated with disturbed eating behavior in young men parallel those in young women, such as needs for perfection, perceived pressures from others to lose weight, and participation in sports that place a strong value on leanness (Ricciardelli & McCabe, 2004).

**PSYCHOSOCIAL FACTORS** Although cultural pressures to conform to an ultrathin female ideal play a major role in eating disorders, the great majority of young women exposed to these pressures do not develop eating disorders. Other factors must be involved. For one thing, a pattern of overly restricted dieting is common to women with bulimia nervosa and anorexia nervosa. Women with eating disorders typically adopt very rigid dietary rules and practices about what they can eat, how much they can eat, and how often they can eat. It's important to recognize, however, that eating disorders involve deeper emotional issues involving feelings of insecurity, body dissatisfaction, and use of food for emotional gratification, as illustrated in the woman's first-hand account on page 354.

# THINKING CRITICALLY about abnormal psychology

## @ISSUE: SHOULD BARBIE BE BANNED?

We're not suggesting that Barbie and her entourage be thrown overboard in some modern-day version of the Boston Tea Party or that stores be prohibited from selling the popular toys. However, by raising such a provocative question, we hope to encourage you to think critically about the effects that these anatomically incorrect figurines may have on the psyches of young women. Lest you think that Barbie, now more than 50 years old, is merely a quaint relic of an earlier generation, 92% of American girls today between the ages of 3 and 12 have owned a Barbie doll (NBC News, 2016).

As writer Laura Vanderkam (2003) notes in her article "Barbie and Fat as a Feminist Issue," Barbie was designed to fit the idealized male fantasy of a bosomy but impossibly thin female form and then sold to girls who grew up wanting to look like her. Social worker Abigail Natenshon, author of *When Your Child Has an Eating Disorder*, argues that images of Barbie and ultrathin female models and actresses create expectations in the minds of young women about how they are supposed to look. Although many factors undoubtedly contribute to eating disorders, should parents keep Barbie at bay and not bring the doll into their homes? Or should they welcome Barbie but help their daughters see that her ultrathin form is not a female ideal, and help them understand that self-esteem should not be measured by a bathroom scale?

Although the unrealistically thin Barbie still sells in the millions, in 2016, the doll's manufacturer, Mattel, introduced several alternative versions of Barbie, including a fuller-figure Barbie ("Curvy Barbie") and others with darker skin tones. Will a Barbie that looks more like the rest of us come to replace the original? What's your prediction?

For that matter, should parents inform their sons that bulked-up wrestlers, muscularized movie heroes, and even action figures in video games are not exemplars of what they should aspire to? Even GI Joe–type action figures (i.e., dolls) appear more muscular today than in earlier versions.

Exposure to overly masculinized male images may create pressures on boys that can lead to disturbed eating behaviors. Evidence shows that many men express dissatisfaction with their bodies (Murray et al., 2013; Tiggemann, Martins, & Kirkbride, 2007). For both men and women, it appears that exposure to "perfect" bodies in the media and advertising reinforces the idea that "normal" bodies are not acceptable.

On the other hand, Vanderkam cautions us not to the throw the Barbie out with the bathwater (apologies for the pun). In light of the epidemic of obesity facing our society, perhaps we should champion the active, energetic lifestyle that Barbie embodies. What do you think?

In thinking critically about the issue, answer the following questions:

- Assume that you are a parent of a young boy or girl. Would you restrict the kinds of toys you buy based on considerations of appropriate body size and weight? Why or why not?
- What messages should parents convey to children regarding the overly slenderized and masculinized images that children regularly see?

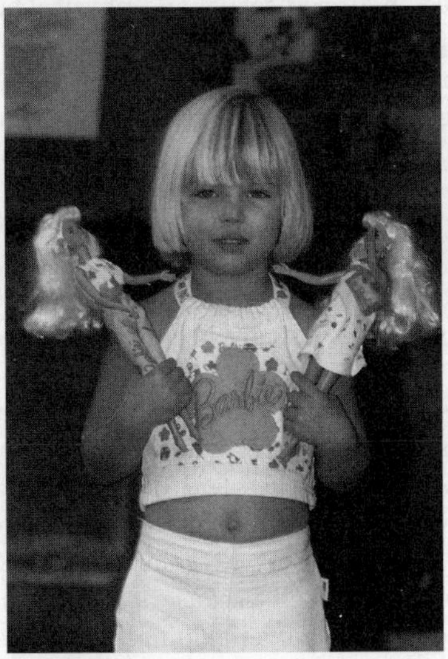


**TO BE LIKE BARBIE.** The Barbie doll has long represented a symbol of the buxom but ultrathin feminine form that has become idealized in our culture. What message do you think the classic Barbie-doll figure conveys to young girls? Might the 2016 introduction of fuller-figure Barbies change the message?

**IS THIS NORMAL?** Body dissatisfaction is not limited to young women. Regular exposure to overly muscularized masculine images may reinforce the idea that "normal" bodies are not acceptable.

## "I" "My Voice, My Cry for Help"

I started dieting when I was 13. As I look back now, I can see that I had feelings of insecurity that were surfacing as I struggled with relationships, my identity, and my sexuality. Back then it just felt like I was too fat. As my body began to change from a normal undeveloped child to a rounder, curvier woman, I held on to the ideals I saw in the media of the very thin, tall, hard bodies that defined beauty. My body was wrong. All my emotional struggles and insecurities became placed on my body. The first day I put myself on a diet, I stopped listening to the wisdom and truth of my own body. I began instead the pattern of forcing myself to conform to cultural standards that were impossible for me to obtain. My soul was crying out for love, for reassurance, security, and emotional soothing during a very overwhelming, confusing period in my life. The only way I knew how to soothe myself was to eat. The only way I knew how to be accepted was to diet. My voice, my cry for help was buried under the obsession and compulsion of dieting and bingeing, bingeing and purging.

**SOURCE:** *Normandi & Rorak, 1998, p. 3.*

Bulimia nervosa is also linked to problems in interpersonal relationships. Women with bulimia tend to be shy and have few if any close friends. Enhancing the social skills of women with bulimia may increase the quality of their relationships and perhaps reduce their tendencies to use food in maladaptive ways.

**EMOTIONAL FACTORS** People with anorexia nervosa may restrict their food intake in a misguided attempt to relieve upsetting emotions by seeking mastery or control over their bodies (Merwin, 2011). Young women with bulimia nervosa often have more emotional problems and lower self-esteem than other dieters (Jacobi et al., 2004). Negative emotional states such as anxiety and depression can trigger episodes of binge eating (Reas & Grilo, 2007). Bulimia nervosa is often accompanied by other diagnosable disorders, such as depression, obsessive–compulsive disorder, and substance-related disorders. This suggests that some forms of binge eating represent attempts at coping with emotional distress. Unfortunately, cycles of bingeing and purging exacerbate emotional problems rather than relieve them. Women with bulimia are also more likely than other women to have experienced childhood sexual and physical abuse (Kent & Waller, 2000). In some cases, bulimia nervosa may develop as an ineffective means of coping with abuse. Binge eating may represent an attempt to manage or soothe negative feelings, as evidence links negative emotional states to binge-eating episodes (Haedt-Matt & Keel, 2011).

**LEARNING PERSPECTIVES** From a learning perspective, we can conceptualize eating disorders as a type of weight phobia. In this model, relief from anxiety acts as negative reinforcement. Women with bulimia tend to have been slightly overweight before they developed bulimia, and the binge–purge cycle usually begins after a period of strict dieting to lose weight.

In a typical scenario, the rigid dietary controls fail, leading to a loss of inhibitions (disinhibition), which prompts a binge-eating episode. The binge eating induces fear of weight gain, which in turn prompts self-induced vomiting or excessive exercise. Some people with bulimia even resort to vomiting after every meal. Purging is negatively reinforced because it produces relief, or at least partial relief, from anxiety over gaining weight. As in anorexia, food-rejecting behavior (and purging in cases of the binge-eating/purging subtype) is negatively reinforced by relief from anxiety about weight gain. **T / F**

### TRUTH *or* FICTION

Women with bulimia nervosa induce vomiting only after binges.

☑ **FALSE** Some bulimic women induce vomiting after every meal.

Dietary restraint appears to play a more prominent role in bulimia nervosa for women at high genetic risk of the disorder (Racine et al., 2011). This again illustrates the need to examine interactions of psychosocial factors (dietary restraint) and genetic factors in the development of psychological disorders.

**COGNITIVE FACTORS** Perfectionism and overconcern about making mistakes figure prominently in many cases of eating disorders (Boone, Soenens, & Luyten, 2014; Martinez & Craighead, 2015; Wade et al., 2015). People with eating disorders tend to impose perfectionistic pressures on themselves to achieve a "perfect body" and get down on themselves whenever they fail to meet their impossibly high standards. They also tend to have a strong need for control, which takes the form of extreme dieting. This gives them a sense of control and independence that they feel is lacking in other areas of their lives. In the following account, a young woman with anorexia nervosa speaks about the feelings of power she experienced by deciding to go without food.

"I"

**"I Felt the Power"**

I was constantly comparing myself to people...that was just the absolutely unavoidable thing...Just looking at everybody and thinking to myself, "Oh my gosh, do I look like that?" I would only find the skinniest people...that's just where my eyes went, to the thinnest people and...that's where I would be like, "I want to be like them." I wasn't scared of gaining weight, I...just wanted to keep on losing weight and if I wasn't, then there was something wrong. Or if my jeans didn't fit just right or if they weren't baggy enough...or my thighs touched together—that was a big thing of mine—or my arms jiggling...But my idea of arms jiggling was my skin moving....(And if your body jiggled, what did that mean?)...That I was fat...if my body was moving, then that means I wouldn't eat for the day, or the night, or the weekend, whatever I decided, and that's where I felt the power that people talk about, the control, it's what I decided to do.

**SOURCE:** *Excerpted from Speaking Out: Videos in Abnormal Psychology, Pearson Education, 2008.* *All rights reserved.*

People who struggle with bulimia tend to think in dichotomous or "black or white" terms. Thus, they expect to adhere perfectly to their rigid dietary rules and judge themselves as complete failures when they deviate even slightly. They also judge themselves harshly for episodes of binge eating and purging. They may also hold exaggerated beliefs about the negative consequences of gaining weight, which further contributes to disordered eating. Investigators find that women with eating disorders tend to heap blame on themselves for negative events in general, and self-blame most probably contributes to maintaining their disordered eating behavior (Morrison, Waller, & Lawson, 2006).

Body dissatisfaction is also an important factor in eating disorders. Body dissatisfaction may lead to maladaptive attempts—through self-starvation and purging—to attain a desired body weight or shape. Women with eating disorders tend to be extremely concerned about their body weight and shape (Jacobi et al., 2004). Excessive weight-related concerns even affect many young children and may possibly set the stage for development of eating disorders in adolescence or early adulthood.

**PSYCHODYNAMIC PERSPECTIVES** Psychodynamic theorists suggest that girls with anorexia nervosa have difficulty separating from their families and consolidating separate, individuated identities (e.g., Bruch, 1973; Minuchin, Rosman, & Baker, 1978). Perhaps anorexia represents a girl's unconscious effort to remain a prepubescent child. By maintaining the veneer of childhood, pubescent girls may avoid dealing with adult issues such as increased independence and separation from their families, sexual maturation, and assumption of adult responsibilities.

**FAMILY FACTORS** Eating disorders frequently develop against a backdrop of family problems and conflicts. Some theorists focus on the brutal effect of self-starvation on parents. They suggest that some adolescents refuse to eat to punish their parents for feelings of loneliness and alienation they experience in the home.

Young women with eating disorders often come from dysfunctional family backgrounds characterized by high levels of family conflict and by parents who tend to be overprotective on the one hand but less nurturing and supportive on the other

**DEATH BY STARVATION.** A leading fashion model, Brazilian Ana Carolina Reston, was just 21 when she died in 2006 from complications due to anorexia. At the time of her death, the 5′7″ Reston weighed only 88 pounds. Anorexia nervosa continues to be a widespread problem among fashion models today.

(e.g., Giordano, 2005; Holtom-Viesel & Allan, 2014). Parents often seem less capable of promoting independence, or even permitting autonomy, in their daughters. Yet it remains uncertain whether these family patterns contribute to eating disorders or whether eating disorders disrupt family dynamics in these ways. The truth probably lies in an interaction between the two. Might binge eating, as suggested by Humphrey (1986), be a metaphoric effort to gain the nurturance and comfort through food that the daughter is lacking from her family?

From a systems perspective, families are systems that regulate themselves in ways that minimize the open expression of conflict and reduce the need for change. Within this perspective, girls who develop anorexia nervosa may be seen as helping maintain the shaky balances and harmonies found in dysfunctional families by displacing attention from family conflicts and marital tensions onto themselves. The girl may become the *identified patient*, although it is actually the family unit that is dysfunctional.

Regardless of the factors that initiate eating disorders, social reinforcers may maintain them. Children with eating disorders may quickly become the focus of attention in their families, receiving attention from their parents that is otherwise lacking.

**BIOLOGICAL FACTORS** Scientists suspect that abnormalities in brain mechanisms controlling hunger and satiety are involved in bulimia nervosa, most probably involving the brain chemical serotonin. Serotonin plays a key role in regulating mood and appetite, especially cravings for carbohydrates (Hildebrandt et al., 2010). Irregularities in the levels of serotonin or how it is used in the brain may contribute to binge-eating episodes. This line of thinking is buttressed by findings that antidepressants that specifically target serotonin, such as Prozac and Zoloft, help decrease binge-eating episodes in bulimia (Walsh et al., 2004). We also know that many women with eating disorders are depressed or have a history of depression, and imbalances of serotonin are implicated in depressive disorders.

Genetics appears to play an important role in the development of eating disorders (Baker et al., 2009; Kaye, 2009). We know that eating disorders tend to run in families, which is consistent with a genetic contribution (Hitti, 2006). We also have evidence of genetic factors from an important early study of more than 2,000 female twins (Kendler et al., 1991). The investigators found a much higher concordance rate for bulimia nervosa, 23% versus 9%, among monozygotic (MZ) twins than among dizygotic (DZ) twins. (Recall that *concordance rate* refers to the percentage of twins in which both twins have a given trait or disorder in common.) A greater concordance for anorexia nervosa is also found among MZ twins than among DZ twins, 50% versus 5% (Holland, Sicotte, & Treasure, 1988). Nonetheless, genetic factors cannot fully account for the development of eating disorders. Consistent with the diathesis–stress model, a genetic predisposition affecting the regulation of neurotransmitter activity in the brain may interact with stress associated with social and family pressures to increase the risk of eating disorders.

## Abnormal Psychology in the Digital Age

### HOW DO I SHAPE UP? POTENTIAL RISKS POSED BY USE OF SOCIAL NETWORKING SITES ON BODY IMAGE

*"Mirror, mirror on the wall, who is the fairest of them all?"* The mirror on the wall these days may be the one on the Facebook "wall" that reflects images of other people in your social network. Social networking sites may be a great way of keeping up with friends and acquaintances, but there may be an emotional cost to continually comparing yourself to others. In Chapter 7, we considered the unintended emotional consequences of social comparison associated with checking online profiles and status updates of friends. We saw that using social networking sites might lead people to feel worse about themselves and possibly even set the stage for depression if they are continually bombarded with images of others who seem to be leading richer, more exciting lives.

**FACEBOOKING AND BODY DISSATISFACTION.** Investigators have raised concerns that time spent comparing oneself to others on social networking sites might affect how people feel about their own bodies. What do you think?

Social comparison can also take a toll on body image. Recently, investigators studied the Facebook use of a sample of 232 college women over a four-week period. The women who said they used Facebook to compare themselves to others reported higher levels of body dissatisfaction, and higher levels of body dissatisfaction were in turn linked to a higher frequency of bulimic behaviors and overeating (Smith, Hames, & Joiner, 2013). We also learned from the results of another recent study of 960 college women that those who spent more time Facebooking had higher levels of disordered eating behaviors (Mabe, Forney, & Keel, 2014). We can draw from these findings a suggestion that limiting the time spent on social networking sites might help reduce the risk of body dissatisfaction and problem eating behaviors. We should also note again the challenge faced by users of social networking sites to not get caught up in the practice of comparing themselves to others.

# Treatment of Anorexia Nervosa and Bulimia Nervosa

**9.4 Evaluate methods used to treat anorexia nervosa and bulimia nervosa.**

Anorexia and bulimia nervosa are often difficult to treat, and outcomes remain less than satisfactory in many cases (Galsworthy-Francis, 2014; Pennesi & Wade, 2016). However, significant progress has been made in treating these challenging disorders (Grave et al., 2016; Holmes, Craske, & Graybiel, 2014; Thompson-Brenner, 2013). Unfortunately, most people with eating disorders do not receive appropriate medical or mental health treatment for their specific disorders (Hart et al., 2011; Labbe, 2011).

Treatment of anorexia nervosa may involve hospitalization, especially in cases in which weight loss becomes severe or body weight falls rapidly (Martinez & Craighead, 2015). In the hospital, patients are usually placed on a closely monitored refeeding regimen. Behavioral therapy is commonly used, with rewards made contingent on adherence to the refeeding protocol. Commonly used reinforcers include ward privileges and social opportunities. However, relapses are common, and upward of 50% of inpatients treated for anorexia nervosa are rehospitalized within a year of discharge (Haynos & Fruzzetti, 2011). Individual or family therapy is recommended to provide continuing care after hospitalization.

Research evidence supports the benefits of CBT in treating bulimia nervosa (Byrne et al., 2011; Glasofer & Devlin, 2013; Masheb, Grilo, & Rolls, 2011). A recent large-scale study showed that CBT resulted in the elimination of bingeing episodes in about two out of three eating disorder patients who presented with bingeing as a core symptom (Striegel-Moore et al., 2010).

Cognitive-behavioral therapy (CBT) is used to counter maladaptive beliefs about eating and body image (Galsworthy-Francis, 2014). CBT therapists help people with bulimia challenge self-defeating thoughts and beliefs, such as unrealistic, perfectionistic expectations regarding dieting and body weight. Another common dysfunctional thought pattern is dichotomous (all-or-nothing) thinking, which predisposes people to purge when they slip even a little from their rigid diets. CBT also challenges tendencies to overemphasize appearance in determining self-worth. To control self-induced vomiting, therapists may use the behavioral technique of *exposure with response prevention,* which was developed for treatment of people with obsessive-compulsive disorder. In this technique, the person with bulimia nervosa is exposed to eating forbidden foods while the therapist stands by to prevent vomiting until the urge to purge passes. Individuals with bulimia thus learn to tolerate violations of their rigid dietary rules without resorting to purging.

Psychodynamic therapy may also be used to probe for psychological conflicts (Zipfel et al., 2013), and family therapy may also be used to help resolve underlying family conflicts (Agras et al., 2014; Ciao et al., 2015; Le Grange et al., 2015). Hospitalization may sometimes be helpful in breaking the binge–purge cycle in bulimia nervosa, but it appears to be necessary only when eating behaviors are clearly out of control and outpatient treatment has failed, or when there are severe medical complications, suicidal thoughts or attempts, or substance abuse.

Interpersonal psychotherapy (IPT), a structured form of psychodynamic therapy, is also helpful in treating bulimia nervosa and may be useful in cases that fail to respond to CBT (Rieger et al., 2010). IPT focuses on resolving interpersonal problems based on the belief that more effective interpersonal functioning will lead to the adoption of healthier food habits and attitudes.

**TRUTH or FICTION**

Antidepressants can be used to treat bulimia nervosa.

☑ **TRUE** True, but their effectiveness is limited.

SSRI-type antidepressant drugs, such as Prozac and Zoloft, have also demonstrated therapeutic benefits in treating bulimia nervosa, but their effectiveness is limited (Mitchell, Roerig, & Steffen, 2013). These drugs decrease the urge to binge by normalizing levels of serotonin—the brain chemical involved in regulating appetite. Use of antidepressants and other drugs in treating anorexia nervosa has yielded either poor or mixed results, with many patients showing a lack of response (Miniati et al., 2015; Mitchell, Roerig, & Steffen, 2013). **T / F**

Although progress has been made in treating eating disorders, there is considerable room for improvement. Even CBT, which is recognized as the most effective form of treatment for bulimia, fails to succeed with a substantial proportion of patients (Wilson, Grilo, & Vitousek, 2007). Drug therapy with the use of antidepressants can also be helpful in patients with bulimia who fail to respond to cognitive-behavioral treatment (Walsh et al., 2000). We can't yet say whether a combination CBT/medication approach is more effective than either component alone.

Eating disorders can be tenacious and enduring problems, especially when excessive fears about body weight and distortions in body image persist beyond active treatment (Fairburn et al., 2003). Although recovery from anorexia tends to be a long and uncertain process, we are encouraged by evidence that cognitive-behavioral therapy can help delay or even prevent relapse (Carter et al., 2009). Difficulties in treating eating disorders only confirm the need to develop effective prevention programs. Recent studies demonstrate progress along these lines, with reduced risks of eating disorders following participation in programs targeting disordered eating behaviors and attitudes (e.g., Becker et al., 2008; Stice, Marti, & Cheng, 2014).

## Binge-Eating Disorder

**9.5 Describe the key features of binge-eating disorder and identify effective treatments for the disorder.**

People with **binge-eating disorder (BED)** have repeated binge-eating episodes, but unlike bulimia nervosa, there is no compensatory behavior afterward to reduce weight—no self-induced vomiting, excessive laxative use, or exercise, for example. Binge-eating episodes in BED occur on an average of at least once a week for a period of three months (American Psychiatric Association, 2013). These episodes are characterized by a lack of control over eating and by consuming far greater amounts of food than people typically eat in the same span of time. During a binge, a person may eat much more quickly than usual and continue eating despite feeling uncomfortably full. The person may binge alone because of embarrassment over excessive eating in front of others. Afterward, they may feel disgusted with themselves, be depressed, or be plagued by feelings of guilt.

BED is more common than either anorexia or bulimia, affecting about 3.5% of women and 2% of men at some point in their lives (Hudson et al., 2006). An estimated 8 million Americans struggle with BED (Ellin, 2012). People with BED tend to be older than those with anorexia or bulimia, and the disorder tends to develop later in life, often in a person's thirties or forties. Compared to overweight individuals, people with BED tend to have higher levels of depression and more disturbed eating behaviors

(Grilo et al., 2008). Although people with bulimia nervosa typically fall within a normal weight range, many (but not all) BED patients are either overweight or obese (Bulik et al., 2012; Hudson et al., 2006). BED is also linked to depression and to a history of unsuccessful attempts at losing excess weight and keeping it off. Like other eating disorders, it occurs more often among women and may have a genetic component. However, BED occurs more frequently among men than is the case with other eating disorders. Here, a 39-year-old man with BED relates his binge eating to negative feelings about himself: "Ultimately, it was about numbing out and self-loathing...There was this voice in my head that said, 'You're no good, worthless,' and I turned to food" (cited in Ellin, 2012).

BED may fall within a broader domain of compulsive behaviors characterized by impaired control over maladaptive behaviors, such as compulsive gambling and substance use disorders. A history of dieting may play a role in some cases of BED, but probably not to the extent that it does with bulimia.

Cognitive-behavioral therapy has become the treatment of choice for binge-eating disorder (e.g., Fischer et al., 2014; Hilbert et al., 2015). Antidepressants, especially SSRIs such as Prozac, may also be used to reduce binge-eating episodes by helping to normalize serotonin levels in the brain (Mitchell, Roerig, & Steffen, 2013). However, CBT showed even better results than antidepressant medication at a follow-up evaluation 12 months after treatment (Grilo, Masheb, & Crosby, 2012). Researchers recently reported promising results in using stimulant medication typically used to treat ADHD in children to reduce binge eating in people with BED (McElroy et al., 2015; Slomski, 2015).

**STACY: BINGE-EATING DISORDER**

In *A Closer Look: Obesity: A National Epidemic*, we focus on a health problem closely identified with binge eating: *obesity*.

# A CLOSER Look

## OBESITY: A NATIONAL EPIDEMIC

The problem of **obesity** once again brings into context the complex interrelationships between mind and body. Obesity is classified as a medical condition, not a psychological or mental disorder, but psychological factors play important roles in its development and treatment, which is why it is the focus of our attention here. **T / F**

Obesity has reached epidemic proportions not only in the United States, but throughout the world. The number of obese

### TRUTH or FICTION

Obesity is one of the most common psychological disorders in the United States.

☑ **FALSE** Obesity is a medical disorder, not a psychological disorder.

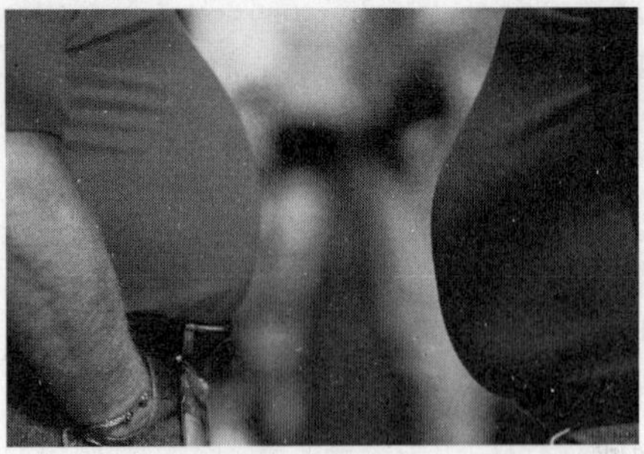

**HAZARDOUS WAIST.** Obesity is indeed a hazard to health and longevity.

people worldwide exceeds 2 billion (Ng, Gakidou, et al., 2014). More Americans are overweight today than at any time since the government started tracking obesity in the 1960s. About 69% of adult Americans are classified by health officials as overweight or obese; about 35% fit criteria for obesity (CDC, 2015e; Yang & Colditz, 2015). Along with our body weight, our collective waistlines have also increased in recent years (Ford, Maynard, & Li, 2014). Among American youth, about one in three children and teens in the United States is either overweight or obese (Tavernise, 2012; Weir, 2012a).

Health officials are rightly concerned about obesity because it is a risk factor in many chronic and potentially life-threatening diseases, including heart disease, stroke, diabetes, respiratory disease, and some forms of cancer (Gorman, 2012; Khoo et al., 2011; Taubes, 2012). All told, obesity accounts for more than 160,000 excess deaths in the United States every year and shaves 6 or 7 years off the average person's life expectancy (Flegal et al., 2005; Fontaine et al., 2003; Freedman, 2011). Evidence also shows that underweight people face about as high a risk of dying prematurely as obese people (Cao et al., 2014). What about people who are overweight but not obese? The answer is not entirely clear; recent findings indicate that overweight people who were not clinically obese actually have a lower risk of early death than people of normal weight (Flegal et al., 2013; Heymsfield & Cefalu, 2013).

Body weight is essentially a function of energy balance. When caloric intake exceeds energy output, the excess calories are stored in the body in the form of fat, leading to obesity (see Figure 9.2). Despite all the money and effort spent on weight-loss products and programs, our collective waistlines are getting larger—a result, health experts believe, of Americans consuming too many calories and exercising too little (Lamberg, 2006; Pollan, 2003). The reasons? A diet containing too much high-fat, high-calorie, and supersized portions that are growing ever larger and spending more time in sedentary activities.

The key to preventing obesity is to bring energy expenditure in line with energy (caloric) intake. Unfortunately, this is easier said than done. Research suggests that a number of factors contribute to the imbalance between energy intake and expenditure that underlies obesity, including genetics, metabolic factors, lifestyle factors, psychological factors, and socioeconomic factors. There is some good news to report: The average American diet in recent years shows reductions in both calories consumed and dietary fat (Beck & Schatz, 2014). Perhaps Americans are getting the message and taking a healthful turn that may stem the obesity epidemic.

## Figure 9.2 Weight—a balancing act.

Body weight is determined by the balance between energy consumed in the form of food calories and energy used in the course of the day through physical activity and maintenance of bodily processes. When calories consumed in food exceed calories used, we gain weight. To lose weight, we need to take in fewer calories than we expend. Weight control involves a balance between calories consumed and calories used.

**SOURCE:** Physical Activity and Weight Control, National Institutes of Diabetes and Digestive and Kidney Diseases (NIDDK).

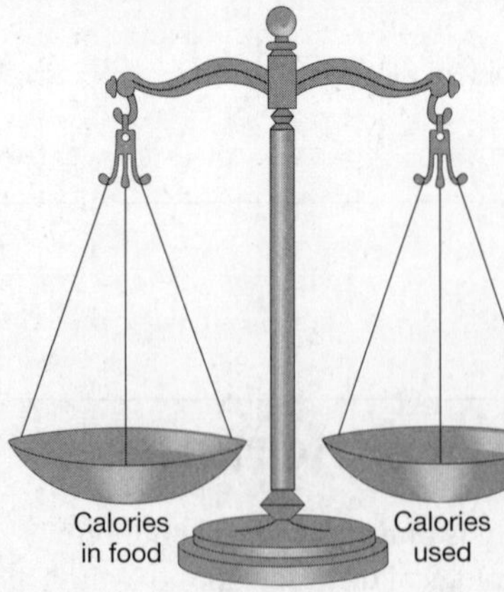


### Genetic Factors

Obesity is a complex condition in which multiple causes are involved (Hamre, 2013). Evidence points to a role for genetics, but genes don't tell the whole story (Freedman, 2011; Small et al., 2011). Environmental factors (diet and exercise patterns) are also important contributors.

### Metabolic Factors

Genetic differences in *metabolic rate* (the rate at which the body burns calories) may play an important role in determining risk of obesity. Also, when people start to lose significant amounts of weight, the body reacts as if it were starving by slowing the metabolic rate to preserve energy resources (Freedman, 2011). This makes it difficult to continue losing more weight or even to maintain weight that was lost. Mechanisms in the brain control the body's metabolism to keep body weight around a genetically influenced *set point*. The ability of the body to adjust the metabolic rate downward when calorie intake declines may have helped ancestral humans survive times of famine. However, this mechanism is a bane to people today who are trying to lose weight and keep it off. **T / F**

**TRUTH or FICTION**

When people start losing significant amounts of weight, their bodies respond as though they were starving.

☑ TRUE The body responds by slowing the metabolic rate, making it more difficult for dieters to lose additional weight or keep off the weight they lost.

People may be able to offset this metabolic adjustment by losing weight more gradually and by following a more vigorous exercise regimen. Vigorous exercise burns calories directly and may increase the metabolic rate by replacing fat tissue with muscle, especially if the exercise program involves weight-bearing activity. Also, ounce for ounce, muscle tissue burns more calories than fat tissue. Before starting an exercise regimen, check with your physician to determine which types of activity are best suited to your overall health condition.

### Fat Cells

Fat cells, which are cells that store fat, comprise the fatty tissue in the body (also called *adipose tissue*). Obese people have more fat cells than people who are not obese. Severely obese people may have some 200 billion fat cells, as compared to 25 or 30 billion in normal weight individuals. Why does this matter? As time passes after eating, the blood sugar level declines, drawing out fat from these cells to supply more nourishment to the body. The hypothalamus in the brain triggers hunger when it detects depletion of fat in these cells. Hunger is a drive that motivates eating, which thereby replenishes the fat cells. Unfortunately, even if we lose weight, we do not shed fat cells (Hopkin, 2008). In people who have more fatty tissue and hence higher numbers of fat cells, the body sends more signals of fat depletion to the brain than in people with fewer fat cells; as a result, they feel food-deprived sooner, making it more difficult for them to lose weight or to maintain the weight they have lost.

### Lifestyle Factors

Eating habits are changing, and not for the better. The constant bombardment of food-related cues in television commercials, print advertising, and the like can take a toll on our individual and collective waistlines. Restaurants today are competing with each other in terms of who can pile the most food on ever-larger dinner plates. Pizzerias are using larger pans, and fast-food restaurants are supersizing meals—all of which takes a toll on the waistline. That "big gulp" 64-ounce soft drink packs an incredible 800 calories (Smith, 2003)! A recent study showed that diners at a Chinese buffet served themselves 52% more and ate 45% more when food was served on larger plates (Wansink & van Ittersum, 2013). Diners at fast food restaurants also tend to underestimate the calorie counts of meals they consume (Block et al., 2013). Can you guess which character, after Santa Claus, children recognize most often? The answer: Ronald McDonald (Parloff, 2003). **T / F**

**TRUTH or FICTION**

After Santa Claus, the most recognizable figure to children is Ronald McDonald.

☑ TRUE Ronald is the second-most recognizable figure among children. What might his popularity have to do with our fast-food-obsessed culture?

Another contributing factor to our expanding waistlines is America's growing suburbs and the car-dependent culture this entails (McKee, 2003). City dwellers may burn off some extra calories hiking around town, but suburbanites must rely on their cars to get from place to place in spread-out communities in the suburban sprawl. Investigators suspect that reduced physical activity and exercise over the past 20 years is more to blame for America's expanding waistline than consuming more calories (Ladabaum et al., 2014).

### Psychological Factors

According to psychodynamic theory, eating is the cardinal oral activity. Psychodynamic theorists believe that people who were fixated in the oral stage by conflicts concerning dependence and independence are likely to regress in times of stress to excessive oral activities such as overeating. Other psychological factors connected with overeating and obesity include low self-esteem, lack of self-efficacy expectancies, family conflicts, and negative emotions. Emotions such as anger, fear, and sadness can prompt excessive eating.

### Socioeconomic Factors

Obesity is more prevalent among people of lower-income levels. Because people of color in our society are as a group lower in socioeconomic status than (non-Hispanic) White Americans, we should not be surprised that rates of obesity are higher among Black and Hispanic adults. (see Figure 9.3).

Why are people on the lower rungs of the socioeconomic ladder at greater risk of obesity? One reason is that more affluent people have greater access to information about nutrition and health and are more likely to take health education courses. They may also have greater access to quality health care. Poorer people also exercise less regularly than more affluent people do. More affluent people are more likely to have the time, the income, and the space to exercise. Many poor people in the inner city also turn to food as a way of coping with the stresses of poverty, discrimination, crowding, and crime.

Acculturation may also contribute to obesity, at least when it involves adopting the unhealthful dietary practices of the host culture. Consider that Japanese American men living in California and Hawaii eat a higher-fat diet than Japanese men do. Not surprisingly, the prevalence of obesity is two to three times higher among Japanese American men than among men living in Japan (Curb & Marcus, 1991).

### Facing the Challenge of Obesity

Despite their appeal, quickie diets don't work. The great majority of people who diet, perhaps more than 9 out of 10 people, regain any weight they lose. Nor are antiobesity or diet drugs the answer, as they offer temporary benefits at best and can have significant side effects. Long-term success in the "battle of the bulge" requires a continuing commitment to following a sensible, lower-calorie and lower-fat diet combined with regular physical activity or exercise (Bray, 2012; Van Horn, 2014; Wadden et al., 2014). Even people with genetics working against them can learn to control their weight within some broad limits by adopting a sensible diet, increasing activity and exercise levels, and developing healthier eating habits.

**Figure 9.3** Rates of obesity (age 20 or higher).

This figure shows the rates of obesity among U.S. adults in relation to race and ethnicity.

**SOURCE:** *Health, United States, 2015*, CDC, 2015g, National Center for Health Statistics, Office of Analysis and Epidemiology.

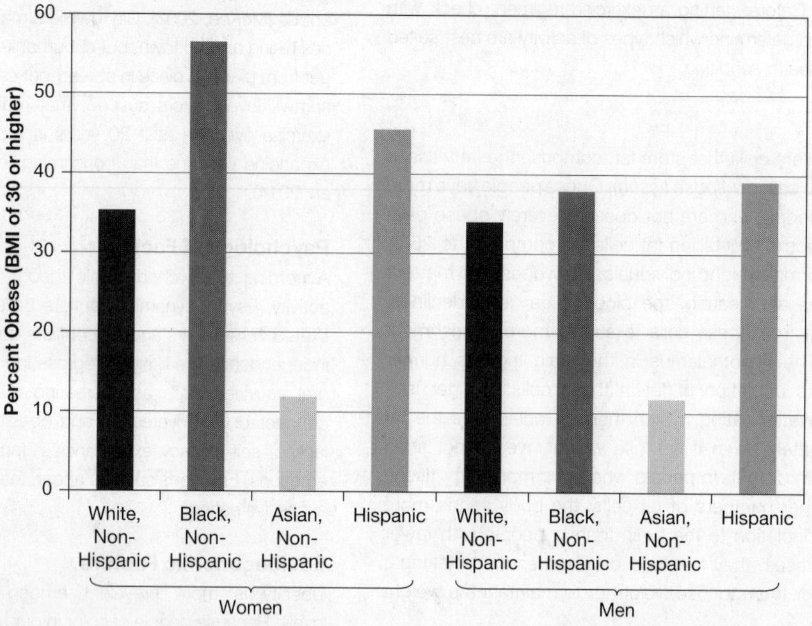


# TYING it together

## EATING DISORDERS

We can conceptualize eating disorders within a multifactorial framework in which psychosocial and biological influences interact in the development of disturbed eating behaviors. Figure 9.4 illustrates a potential causal pathway for explaining the development of bulimia nervosa. Note that negative reinforcement in the form of relief from anxiety about gaining weight plays a pivotal role in strengthening and maintaining maladaptive ways of controlling body weight through food-rejecting behavior in the case of anorexia nervosa and purging in the case of bulimia nervosa. Unfortunately, negative reinforcement is a powerful influence that contributes to maintaining these maladaptive behaviors.

**Figure 9.4** A potential causal pathway in bulimia nervosa.

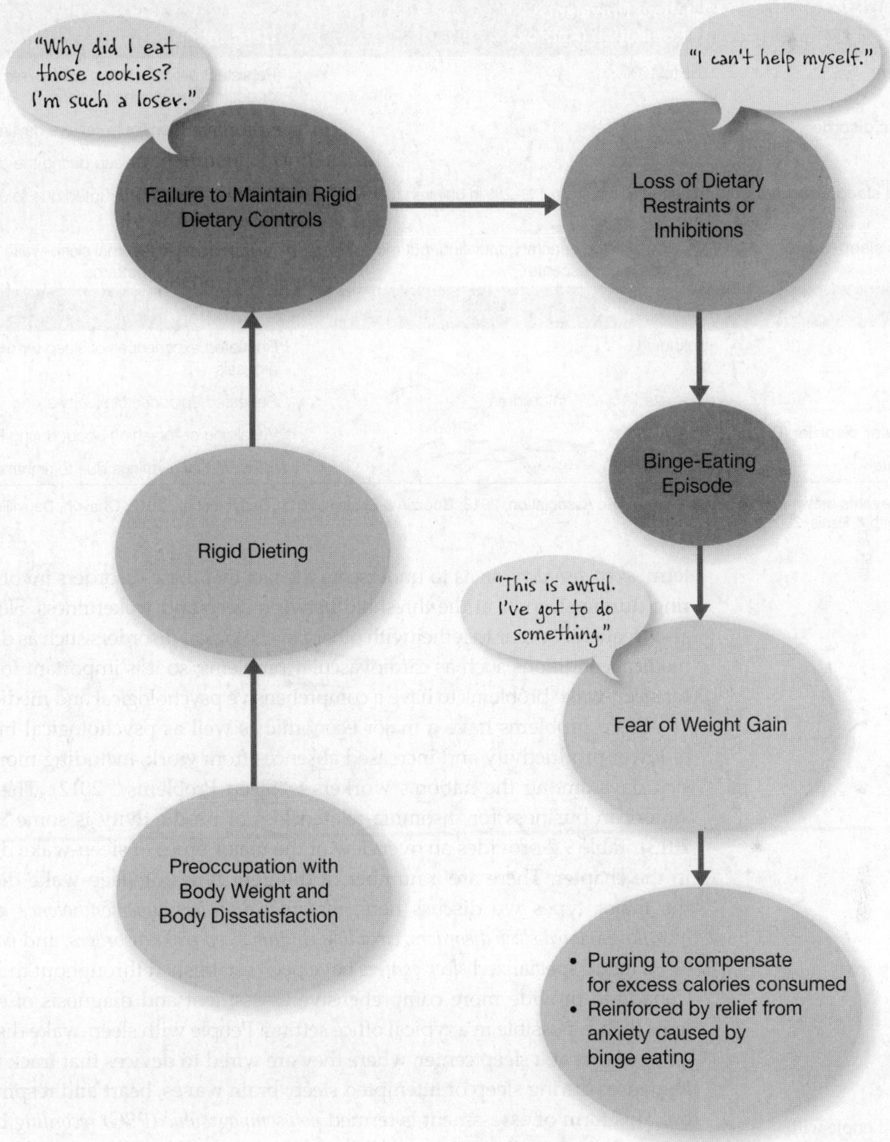


# Sleep-Wake Disorders

Sleep is a biological function that remains in some ways a mystery. We know that sleep is restorative and that most of us need 7 or more hours of sleep a night to function at our best. Yet we cannot identify the specific biochemical changes occurring during sleep that account for its restorative function. We also know that many of us are troubled by sleep problems, although the causes of some of these problems remain obscure. Sleep problems of sufficient severity and frequency that they lead to significant personal distress or impaired functioning in social, occupational, or other roles are classified in the *DSM* system as **sleep-wake disorders** (Reynolds & O'Hara, 2013). The term *sleep-wake disorders* replaces the earlier diagnostic

**Table 9.2** Overview of Major Sleep-Wake Disorders

| Type of Disorder | Lifetime Prevalence in Population (Approx.) | Description |
|---|---|---|
| **Insomnia disorder** | 6% to 10% | Persistent difficulty falling asleep, remaining asleep, or getting enough restful sleep |
| **Hypersomnolence disorder** | 1.5% | Persistent pattern of excessive daytime sleepiness |
| **Narcolepsy** | 0.05% (1 in 2,000) | Sudden attacks of sleep during the day |
| **Breathing-related sleep disorders** | Varies with age, from 1%–2% in children to more than 20% in older adults | Sleep repeatedly interrupted due to difficulties breathing |
| **Circadian rhythm sleep-wake disorders** | 1% or less in the general population, but more common in adolescents | Disruption of the internal sleep-wake cycle due to time changes in sleep patterns |
| | **Parasomnias** | |
| **Sleep terrors** | Unknown | Repeated experiences of sleep terrors resulting in sudden arousals |
| **Sleepwalking** | Estimated 1%–5% in children | Repeated episodes of sleepwalking |
| **REM sleep behavior disorder (RBD)** | 0.38%–0.5% | Vocalizing or thrashing about during REM sleep |
| **Nightmare disorder** | Unknown | Repeated awakenings due to nightmares |

SOURCES: Prevalence rates drawn from American Psychiatric Association, 2013; Bootzin & Epstein, 2011; Ohayon et al., 2012; Ohayon, Dauvilliers, & Reynolds, 2012; Scammell, 2015; Smith & Perlis, 2006.

term, *sleep disorders*, so as to underscore the fact that these disorders involve problems occurring during sleep or at the threshold between sleep and wakefulness. Sleep-wake disorders also frequently occur together with other psychological disorders such as depression and with medical conditions such as cardiovascular problems, so it is important for people evaluated for sleep-wake problems to have a comprehensive psychological and medical evaluation.

Sleep problems have a major economic as well as psychological impact as the result of lower productivity and increased absences from work, including more than 250 million sick days among the nation's workers ( "Sleep Problems," 2012). The estimated cost to American business for insomnia-related loss of productivity is some $63 billion (Weber, 2013). Table 9.2 provides an overview of the major types of sleep-wake disorders discussed in the chapter. There are a number of different types of sleep-wake disorders, including the major types we discuss here: *insomnia disorder, hypersomnolence disorder, narcolepsy, breathing-related sleep disorders, circadian rhythm sleep-wake disorders*, and *parasomnias*.

Highly specialized *sleep centers* have been established throughout the United States and Canada to provide more comprehensive assessment and diagnosis of sleep-related problems than is possible in a typical office setting. People with sleep-wake disorders may spend a few nights at a sleep center, where they are wired to devices that track their physiological responses during sleep or attempted sleep: brain waves, heart and respiration rates, and so on. This form of assessment is termed *polysomnographic (PSG) recording* because it involves simultaneous measurement of diverse physiological response patterns, including brain waves, eye movements, muscle movements, and respiration. Information obtained from physiological monitoring of sleep patterns is combined with that obtained from medical and psychological evaluations, subjective reports of sleep disturbance, and sleep diaries (i.e., daily logs compiled by the problem sleeper that track the length of time between retiring to bed and falling asleep, number of hours slept, nightly awakenings, daytime naps, and so on). Multidisciplinary teams of physicians and psychologists sift through this information to arrive at a diagnosis and suggest treatment approaches to address the presenting problem.

**SLEEP CENTER.** People with sleep-wake disorders are often evaluated in sleep centers, where their physiological responses can be monitored as they sleep.

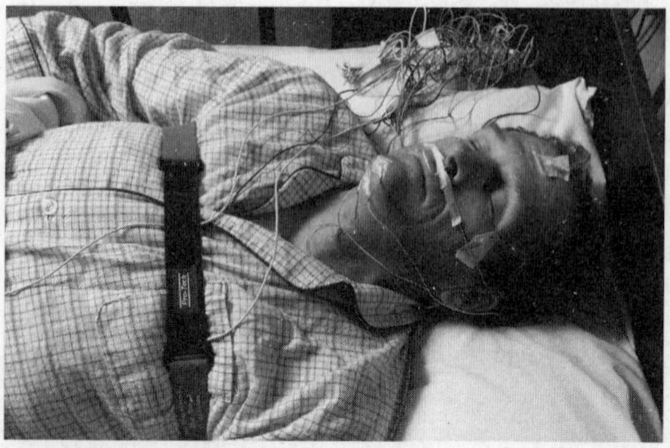

# Insomnia Disorder

**9.6 Describe the key features of insomnia disorder.**

The term **insomnia** derives from the Latin *in*, meaning *not* or *without*, and, of course, *somnus*, meaning *sleep*. Occasional bouts of insomnia, especially during times of stress, are not abnormal—but persistent insomnia characterized by recurrent difficulty getting to sleep or remaining asleep is an abnormal behavior pattern (Harvey & Tang, 2012). An estimated 6% to 10% of U.S. adults suffer from the most commonly occurring sleep-wake disorder: **insomnia disorder** (formerly called *primary insomnia*; Bootzin & Epstein, 2011; Smith & Perlis, 2006). A diagnosis of insomnia disorder requires that the problem has been present for at least three months and that it occurs at least three nights per week (American Psychiatric Association, 2013). Chronic insomnia may also be a feature of an underlying physical problem or psychological disorder, such as depression, substance abuse, or physical illness. If the underlying problem is treated successfully, chances are that normal sleep patterns will be restored. Although problems with recurrent insomnia mostly affect people over age 40, many adolescents and young adults are also affected (Roberts, 2008). People with insomnia disorder complain about the amount or quality of their sleep. They have persistent difficulty falling asleep, remaining asleep, achieving restorative sleep (sleep that leaves the person feeling refreshed and alert), or waking up very early in the morning and being unable to get back to sleep. The disorder is accompanied by significant personal distress or impaired functioning in meeting daily responsibilities—complaints such as regularly feeling fatigued, feeling sleepy, or having low energy; having difficulty with memory or paying attention or concentrating at school or work; feeling down; or perhaps showing behavioral disturbance such as hyperactivity, impulsivity, or aggression. All in all, problems with insomnia can exact a significant toll on the quality of life (Karlson et al., 2013).

Young people with insomnia disorder usually complain that it takes too long to get to sleep. Older people are more likely to complain of waking frequently during the night or of waking too early in the morning. Interestingly, many insomnia patients underestimate how much sleep they actually get—thinking they were lying awake when they actually had nodded off (Harvey & Tang, 2012).

There's a price to be paid for sleep deprivation associated with insomnia. Research evidence shows the sleep-deprived brain is less able to concentrate, pay attention, respond quickly, solve problems, and remember recently acquired information (Florian et al., 2011; Lim & Dinges, 2010). Chronic sleep deprivation—regularly getting too little sleep—is linked to a range of serious physical health problems, including poorer immune system functioning (Carpenter, 2013). The immune system protects the body against disease, so it is not surprising that researchers report that people who sleep less than 7 hours a night had a threefold higher risk of developing the common cold after exposure to cold viruses than those who sleep 8 or more hours nightly (Cohen et al., 2009; Reinberg, 2009).

If we miss a few hours of sleep, we may feel a little groggy the next day, but we will probably be able to muddle through. But over time, continued sleep deprivation takes a toll on our ability to function at our best, leading to daytime fatigue and creating difficulties performing our usual social, occupational, student, or other roles. Not surprisingly, people with insomnia disorder often have other psychological problems as well, especially anxiety and depression.

Psychological factors contribute to primary insomnia. People troubled by insomnia tend to bring their anxieties and worries to bed with them, which raises their bodily arousal to a level that can prevent natural sleep. Another source of anxiety comes in the form of *performance anxiety*, or pressure felt from thinking one must get a full night's sleep to be able to function the next day (Sánchez-Ortuño & Edinger, 2010). People who are struggling with insomnia may try to force themselves to sleep, which typically backfires by creating more anxiety and tension, thus making sleep even less likely to occur. It's well worth recognizing that sleep cannot be forced. We can only set the stage for sleep by going to bed when tired and relaxed and allowing sleep to occur naturally.

The principles of classical conditioning can help explain the development of persistent insomnia (Pollack, 2004b). After pairing a few anxious, sleepless nights with stimuli associated with the bedroom, simply entering the bedroom for the night may be sufficient to elicit bodily arousal that impairs sleep onset. Thus, states of heightened arousal become conditioned responses elicited by the conditioned stimuli of the bedroom—even the mere sight of bed.

## Hypersomnolence Disorder

**9.7 Describe the key features of hypersomnolence disorder.**

The word *hypersomnolence* is derived from the Greek *hyper*, meaning *over* or *more than normal*, and the Latin *somnus*, meaning *sleep*. There are several major types of "more than normal sleep" or *hypersomnolence disorder*, but they have in common complaints of excessive sleepiness or sudden sleep episodes during daytime hours.

**Hypersomnolence disorder** (formerly called *primary hypersomnia*), which is sometimes referred to as *sleep drunkenness*, is a pattern of excessive sleepiness during daytime hours occurring at least three days a week for a period of at least three months (American Psychiatric Association, 2013). People with hypersomnolence disorder may sleep 9 or more hours a night but still not feel refreshed upon awakening. They may have repeated episodes during the day of feeling an irresistible need to sleep, or napping repeatedly or falling asleep when they need to remain awake, or inadvertently dozing off while watching TV (Ohayon, Dauvilliers, & Reynolds, 2012). The daytime naps often last an hour or more, but the sleep does not leave the person feeling refreshed. The disorder cannot be accounted for by inadequate amounts of sleep during the night, by another psychological or physical disorder, or by drug or medication use.

Although many of us feel sleepy during the day from time to time, and may even drift off occasionally while reading or watching TV, people with hypersomnolence disorder have persistent periods of sleepiness that cause personal distress or difficulties in daily functioning, such as missing important meetings. About 1.5% of the general population meet the general criteria for hypersomnia (oversleeping), according to a recent estimate (Ohayon, Dauvilliers, & Reynolds, 2012).

The disorder may involve a defect in the sleep-wake mechanism in the brain and is often treated with stimulant medication to help the person maintain daytime wakefulness. A recent discovery suggests that in some cases of hypersomnia, a substance in the brain acts like a natural sleeping pill by increasing activity of GABA (gamma-aminobutyric acid), a neurotransmitter in the brain that induces feelings of drowsiness. GABA is the brain chemical affected by use of antianxiety drugs like Valium and Xanax (see Chapter 5; Rye et al., 2012).

## Narcolepsy

**9.8 Describe the key features of narcolepsy.**

The word **narcolepsy** derives from the Greek *narke*, meaning *stupor*, and *lepsis*, meaning *an attack*. People with narcolepsy experience an irresistible need to sleep or sudden sleep attacks or naps occurring at least three times a week over three months. During a sleep attack, a person suddenly falls asleep without warning and remains asleep for about 15 minutes. The person may be in the midst of a conversation at one moment and slump to the floor fast asleep a moment later.

Narcoleptic attacks are associated with an almost immediate transition from wakefulness to rapid eye movement (REM) sleep—the stage of sleep primarily associated with dreaming. REM sleep is so named because the sleeper's eyes tend to dart about rapidly under the closed lids. Normally, a person who falls asleep transitions through other sleep stages before entering REM. The most common type of narcolepsy, called *narcolepsy/hypocretin deficiency syndrome*, involves a deficiency in the brain of *hypocretin* (also called *orexin*), a protein-like molecule produced by the hypothalamus that plays an important role in regulating the sleep-wake cycle.

Narcolepsy is often associated with **cataplexy**, a medical condition in which a person experiences a loss of muscle tone ranging from mild weakness in the legs to complete loss of muscle control, causing the person to collapse. Cataplexy most often (but not always) occurs in people with narcolepsy. It is triggered by strong emotional reactions such as joy, crying, anger, sudden terror, or intense laughter. Like narcolepsy, cataplexy involves deficiency of the brain chemical hypocretin. In a cataplectic episode, a person may slump to the floor and be unable to move for a period of seconds to perhaps a few minutes, but remain conscious. People experiencing cataplectic episodes experience blurry vision, but are able to hear and understand what is happening around them. In some cases, however, a person having a cataplectic episode may suddenly lapse into REM sleep. Mali, a woman with long-standing narcolepsy, describes her cataplectic episodes in the following account.

"I"

"Like a Marionette"

Cataplexy is the sudden loss of muscle tone in response to (strong) emotion.... It's actually the same loss of muscle tone that everyone has when they are in REM sleep. It's almost like a marionette whose strings have been cut. You don't fall like a board... typically people won't hurt themselves, but it's more of a crumple, almost like somebody flipped the switch on the light switch and you lose all your muscle tone and it [then] comes back a few seconds, maybe a few minutes later. I hear absolutely everything that everyone says and can repeat everything when I come out of cataplexy, so it's an alert state, although [to] someone watching [a person] with cataplexy it seems like the person checked out and just went to sleep.

**SOURCE:** *Excerpted from Speaking Out: Videos in Abnormal Psychology, Pearson Education, 2010.* *All rights reserved.*

People with narcolepsy may also experience **sleep paralysis**, a temporary state following awakening in which they feel incapable of moving or talking. They may also report **hypnagogic hallucinations**, which are often frightening hallucinations occurring just before the onset of sleep or shortly upon awakening. Here, Mali describes her experience with both sleep paralysis and hypnagogic hallucinations.

"I"

"A Normal Thing at an Abnormal Time"

Sleep paralysis is that same loss of muscle tone that's normal in REM sleep, but what's unusual in sleep paralysis is that you are conscious and awake but all of your muscles are paralyzed and you are unable to talk or move.... It became fairly normal for me, [but] it was still scary for me. For me, sleep paralysis often went hand in hand with the hypnagogic hallucinations, which again is a normal thing at an abnormal time. When [you] are in REM sleep... you are unconscious and dreaming and if you [later] remember your dream it's a memory of the dream that you have. People with narcolepsy are sort of able to navigate these two worlds at the same time. So even though you're dreaming, there's a part of your brain that's conscious and awake, making the dream very, very realistic. And if you are having a negative or a scary dream, it can be kind of terrifying... For me, rather than having a lot of scary dreams I had a lot of dreams... that [left me wondering] whether I really had that conversation with someone... [or] did I really do that, did I really say that... I used to wake up in the morning and shake my head a bit and wondering what was real and what wasn't real.

**SOURCE:** *Excerpted from Speaking Out: Videos in Abnormal Psychology, Pearson Education, 2010.* *All rights reserved.*

Thankfully, narcolepsy is uncommon, affecting an estimated 1 in 2,000 people (0.05%; Scammell, 2015). Men and women are affected about equally. Unlike hypersomnia, in which daytime sleep episodes follow a period of increasing sleepiness, narcoleptic attacks occur abruptly, and the person awakes feeling refreshed. The attacks can be dangerous and frightening, especially if they occur when the person is driving or using heavy equipment or sharp implements.

**MALI: NARCOLEPSY**

About two out of three people with narcolepsy have fallen asleep while driving, and four out of five have fallen asleep on the job (Aldrich, 1992). Not surprisingly, the disorder is often associated with poor daily functioning. Household accidents resulting from falls are also common. The cause or causes of

## TRUTH *or* FICTION

Many people suffer from sleep attacks in which they suddenly fall asleep without any warning.

☑ **FALSE** Sleep attacks are relatively uncommon. They are characteristic of a disorder called *narcolepsy*.

narcolepsy remain unknown, but suspicion focuses on genetic factors and loss of brain cells in the hypothalamus responsible for producing hypocretin (Goel et al., 2010; Hor et al., 2011). Recently, investigators uncovered evidence that suggests that narcolepsy may be a type of autoimmune disease in genetically susceptible individuals in which the body's immune system mistakenly attacks brain cells that manufacture hypocretin (De la Herran-Arita et al., 2014). **T / F**

# Breathing-Related Sleep Disorders

**9.9 Describe the key features of breathing-related sleep-wake disorders.**

People with **breathing-related sleep disorders** experience repeated disruptions of sleep due to respiratory problems. These frequent disruptions of sleep result in insomnia or excessive daytime sleepiness.

The subtypes of the disorder are distinguished in terms of the underlying causes of the breathing problem. The most common subtype, **obstructive sleep apnea hypopnea syndrome** (more commonly called *obstructive sleep apnea*), typically involves repeated episodes during sleep of snorting or gasping for breath, pauses of breath, or abnormally shallow breathing. (The word *apnea* derives from the Greek prefix *a*, meaning *not* or *without*, and *pneuma*, meaning *breath*.) *Hypopnea* (literally *under breathing*) refers to shallow or reduced breathing that is not as severe as full apnea.

## TRUTH *or* FICTION

Some people literally gasp for breath hundreds of times during sleep without realizing it.

☑ **TRUE** People with sleep apnea may gasp for breath hundreds of times during the night without realizing it.

Obstructive sleep apnea is generally accompanied by loud snoring and is a relatively common problem, affecting an estimated 28 million Americans (Moloo, 2014; O'Connor, 2012). Sleep apnea may result from either complete or partial obstruction of breathing during sleep. The disorder leads to excessive daytime sleepiness, fatigue, and complaints of unrefreshing sleep. Obstructive sleep apnea occurs most commonly among middle age and older adults and affects racial minorities more often than whites (Chen, Wang, et al., 2015). It tends to affect men more frequently up to about the age of 50, at which point the rates are similar for men and women. The disorder occurs more commonly among obese people, apparently because their upper airways tend to be narrowed due to an enlargement of soft tissue.

The breathing difficulty results from the blockage of airflow in the upper airways, which is often caused by a structural defect, such as an overly thick palate or enlarged tonsils or adenoids. In cases of complete obstruction, the sleeper may literally stop breathing for periods of 15 to 90 seconds as many as 500 times during the night! When these lapses of breathing occur, the sleeper may suddenly sit up, gasp for air, take a few deep breaths, and fall back asleep without awakening or realizing that breathing was interrupted. **T / F**

**SLEEP APNEA.** Loud snoring may be a sign of obstructive sleep apnea, a breathing-related sleep disorder in which a person may temporarily stop breathing as many as 500 times during a night's sleep. Loud snoring, described by bed partners as reaching levels of industrial noise pollution, may alternate with momentary silences when breathing is interrupted or suspended.

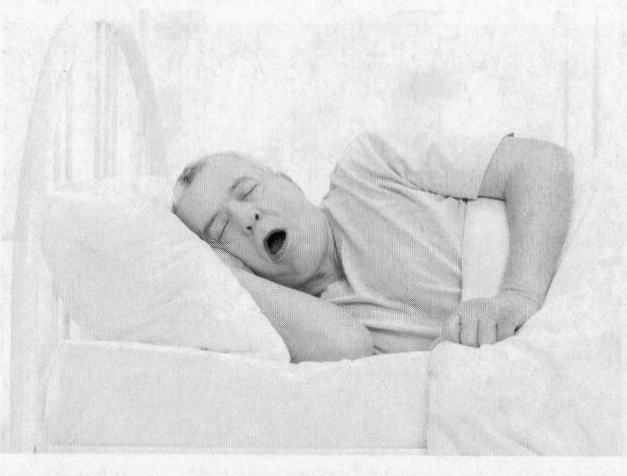

Although a biological reflex kicks in to force a gasping breath after these brief interruptions of breathing, the frequent disruptions of normal sleep resulting from apneas can leave people feeling sleepy the following day, making it difficult for them to function effectively.

Not surprisingly, people who have sleep apnea generally report an impaired quality of life. They also tend to have higher levels of depression than nonaffected individuals (Peppard et al., 2006). Sleep apnea is also a health concern because it is linked to increased risk of serious health problems, such as hypertension and other cardiovascular problems, as well as diabetes (Bratton et al., 2015; Campos-Rodriguez et al., 2012; Kapur & Weaver, 2012; Kendzerska et al., 2014; Macey et al., 2013).

Research points to yet another cause for concern: Repeated lapses of oxygen during episodes of apnea may lead to subtle forms of brain damage that affect psychological functioning, including thinking ability (Macey et al., 2008; Thorpy, 2008). Another concern is that people with sleep apnea also stand a higher risk of developing cancer (O'Connor, 2012). Unfortunately, about three out of four cases of sleep apnea remain untreated (Minerd & Jasmer, 2006).

Another subtype of breathing-related sleep disorder is *central sleep apnea*, in which breathing problems during sleep are less dependent on respiratory resistance (blocked airways) and may involve heart-related problems or chronic use of opioid drugs. Yet another subtype, *sleep-related hypoventilation* (*hypoventilation* means *low breathing*) is characterized by breathing problems that often trace to lung diseases or neuromuscular problems that affect lung functioning.

**SLEEP DEPRIVATION.** Frequent changes in work shifts can disturb the body's natural sleep-wake cycle, resulting in a circadian rhythm sleep-wake disorder that can leave a person feeling sleep deprived.

## Circadian Rhythm Sleep-Wake Disorders

**9.10 Describe the key features of circadian rhythm sleep-wake disorders.**

Most bodily functions follow a cycle or an internal rhythm—called a *circadian rhythm*—that lasts about 24 hours (Azzi et al., 2014; Dubovsky, 2014a; Sanchez-Romera et al., 2014). Even when people are relieved of scheduled activities and work duties and placed in environments in which they are not aware of the time of day, they usually follow relatively normal sleep-wake schedules.

**Circadian rhythm sleep-wake disorders** involve a persistent disruption of the person's natural sleep-wake cycle. This disruption in normal sleep patterns can lead to insomnia or hypersomnolence and result in daytime sleepiness. The disorder causes significant levels of distress or impairs a person's ability to function in social, occupational, or other roles. The jet lag that accompanies travel between time zones does not qualify because it is usually temporary. However, frequent changes of time zones or frequent changes of work shifts (as encountered by nurses, for example) can induce more persistent or recurrent problems, resulting in a diagnosis of circadian rhythm sleep-wake disorder. Treatment may include a program of gradual adjustments in the sleep schedule to allow a person's circadian system to become aligned with changes in the sleep-wake schedule.

## Parasomnias

**9.11 Identify the major types of parasomnias and describe their key features.**

Sleep typically runs in cycles of about 90 minutes each that progress in stages from light sleep to deep sleep and then to REM sleep, when most dreams occur. For some people, however, sleep is interrupted by partial or incomplete arousals during sleep. During these partial arousals, a person may appear confused, detached, or disconnected from the environment. The sleeper may be unresponsive to attempts by other people to awaken them or comfort them. The sleeper typically gets up the next day without any memory of these episodes of partial arousal.

*DSM-5* characterizes abnormal behavior patterns associated with partial or incomplete arousals as **parasomnias**, a category of sleep-wake disorders that is further divided into disorders associated with REM sleep and those associated with non-REM sleep. The word *parasomnia* literally means *around sleep* and signifies that abnormal behaviors involving partial or incomplete arousals occur around the boundary between wakefulness and sleep. As with other sleep-wake disorders, parasomnias cause significant levels of personal distress or interfere with a person's ability to perform expected social, occupational, or other important life roles. Here, we consider the major types of parasomnias associated with non-REM sleep (*sleep terrors, sleepwalking*) and REM sleep (*rapid eye movement sleep behavior disorder* and *nightmare disorder*).

**SLEEP TERRORS** **Sleep terrors** are characterized by repeated episodes of terror-induced arousals that usually begin with a panicky scream (American Psychiatric

Association, 2013). The arousal typically begins with a loud, piercing cry or scream in the night. Even the most soundly sleeping parent will be summoned to a child's bedroom as if shot from a cannon. The child (most cases involve children) may be sitting up, appearing frightened and showing signs of extreme arousal—profuse sweating with rapid heartbeat and respiration. The child may start talking incoherently or thrashing about wildly but is not fully awake. If the child does awaken fully, he or she may not recognize the parent or may attempt to push the parent away. After a few minutes, the child falls back into a deep sleep and upon awakening in the morning remembers nothing of the experience. These terrifying attacks or *sleep terrors* are more intense than ordinary nightmares. Unlike nightmares, sleep terrors tend to occur during the first third of nightly sleep and during deep, non-REM sleep.

If awakening occurs during a sleep terror episode, a person will usually appear confused and disoriented for a few minutes. The person may feel a vague sense of terror and report some fragmentary dream images, but not the sort of detailed dreams typical of nightmares. Most of the time, the person falls back asleep and remembers nothing of the experience the following morning.

Most young children with sleep terrors outgrow them by adolescence (Petit et al., 2015). More boys than girls are affected, but among adults, the gender ratio is about even. In adults, the disorder tends to follow a chronic course during which the frequency and intensity of the episodes wax and wane over time. Prevalence data on the disorder are lacking, but individual episodes of sleep terror are estimated to occur in about 37% of 18-month-old children, 20% of 30-month-old children, and about 2% of adults (American Psychiatric Association, 2013). The cause of sleep terrors remains a mystery, but a genetic contribution is suspected (Geller, 2015).

**SLEEPWALKING** In **sleepwalking**, people who are sleeping have repeated episodes in which they walk about the house while remaining asleep. During these episodes, a person is partially awake and can perform complex motor responses, such as getting out of bed and walking to another room. These motor behaviors are performed without conscious awareness and the person typically does not remember the incident upon fully awakening the following morning. Because these episodes tend to occur during the deeper (non-REM) stages of sleep in which there is an absence of dreaming, sleepwalking episodes do not seem to involve the enactment of a dream.

A sleepwalking disorder is most common in children, affecting 1% to 5% of children according to some estimates (American Psychiatric Association, 2013). Between 10% and 30% of children are believed to have had at least one episode of sleepwalking. The prevalence of the disorder among adults is unknown, as are its causes. Occasional episodes of sleepwalking are not unusual. About 4% of adults report experiencing a sleepwalking episode during the preceding year (Ohayon et al., 2012). However, persistent or recurrent episodes may occasion a diagnosis of a sleepwalking disorder. In the following account, a man recounts an episode of sleepwalking from his childhood, which was one of many such incidents.

"I"

**"He's Only Sleepwalking"**

All five of my sisters remember me as the family sleepwalker. [My sister] Shannon recalls helping Mom fold clothes in the den late one night when I appeared. Perhaps it was the fragrant smell of laundry, like incense, that drew me. I stopped in front of the TV in my pj's, eyes open, and began yelling. It was gibberish, Shannon remembers, but the choking anger behind it was alarming. While that behavior alone is odd, the aspect of her story I find most fascinating is my mother's reaction: unfazed, "He's only sleepwalking," she murmured, as though it were as common as the evening paperboy's late delivery. I imagine her then saying calmly, "Okay, Shannon, let's start on the towels."

**SOURCE:** *From Hayes, 2001, p. 99*

We don't know what causes sleepwalking, but investigators believe that a combination of genetic and (unspecified) environmental factors are involved (Brooks & Kushida, 2002; Geller, 2015). Sleepwalkers tend to have a blank stare on their faces. Although they typically avoid walking into things, accidents do occasionally happen. Sleepwalkers are generally unresponsive to others and difficult to awaken. Upon awakening the following morning, they typically have little, if any, recall of their sleepwalking experience. If they are awakened during an episode, they may be disoriented or confused for a few minutes (as is the case with sleep terrors), but full alertness is soon restored. There is no basis to the belief that it is harmful to sleepwalkers to awaken them during episodes. Isolated incidents of violent behavior have been associated with sleepwalking, but these are rare and may well involve other forms of psychopathology.

**RAPID EYE MOVEMENT SLEEP BEHAVIOR DISORDER** **REM sleep behavior disorder** (RBD) involves repeated episodes of acting out one's dreams during REM sleep in the form of vocalizing parts of the dream or thrashing about. Normally, muscle activity is blocked during REM sleep to the point that the body's muscles, except those needed for breathing and other vital bodily functions, are essentially paralyzed. This is fortunate because the muscle paralysis prevents injuries that might occur if the dreamer suddenly acts out the dream. However, in cases of RBD, muscle paralysis is absent or incomplete and a person may suddenly kick or flail the arms during REM sleep, potentially causing injuries to the self or the person's bed partner.

RBD affects about 0.5% of the adult population and occurs most often among older adults, generally as the result of neurodegenerative disorders such as Parkinson's disease (Sixel-Döring et al., 2011). In fact, RBD in some cases may be an early sign of the development of Parkinson's disease (Postuma et al., 2012). RBD may also be caused by withdrawal from alcohol or develop as a complication from using certain drugs. Medication may be used to help control symptoms of RBD (Aurora et al., 2010).

**NIGHTMARE DISORDER** People with **nightmare disorder** have recurrent episodes of disturbing and well-remembered nightmares during REM sleep. These nightmares are lengthy, story-like dreams in which the dreamer attempts to avoid imminent threats or physical danger, such as in the case of being chased, attacked, or injured. A person usually recalls the nightmare vividly upon awakening. Although fear is the most common emotional effect, the disturbing dreams may occasion other negative reactions, such as anger, sadness, frustration, guilt, disgust, or confusion. The dreamer may suddenly awaken during the nightmare, but have trouble getting back to sleep because of lingering feelings of fear resulting from the terrifying dream. These nightmarish dreams or the disruption of sleep they cause lead to significant personal distress or interfere with important areas of daily functioning.

Although many people have occasional nightmares, the percentage of people having the kind of intense, recurrent nightmares that lead to a diagnosis of nightmare disorder remains unknown. Nightmares are often associated with traumatic experiences and generally occur when an individual is under stress.

Nightmares generally occur during REM sleep, the stage of sleep in which most dreams occur. Periods of REM sleep tend to become longer and the dreams occurring during REM more intense in the latter half of nightly sleep, so nightmares usually occur late at night or toward morning. Although nightmares may involve a great deal of agitated movement in the dream itself, as in nightmares of fleeing from an assailant, dreamers show little muscle activity. The biological processes that activate dreams—including nightmares—inhibit body movement, causing a type of paralysis. This is indeed fortunate, as it prevents the dreamer from jumping out of bed and running into a dresser or a wall in an attempt to elude the pursuing assailants from the dream.

## Treatment of Sleep-Wake Disorders

**9.12 Evaluate methods used to treat sleep-wake disorders and apply your knowledge to identify more adaptive sleep habits.**

The most common method for treating sleep-wake disorders in the United States is the use of sleep medications. However, because of problems associated with these drugs, nonpharmacological treatment approaches—principally CBT—have come to the fore.

**BIOLOGICAL APPROACHES** Antianxiety drugs are often used to treat insomnia, including the class of antianxiety drugs called *benzodiazepines* (e.g., Valium and Ativan). (These psychiatric drugs are also widely used in the treatment of anxiety disorders, as we saw in Chapter 5.) Other sleep-inducing agents include the drug *zolpidem* (trade name Ambien), which is effective in both reducing the length of time it takes people with insomnia to fall asleep and increasing sleep duration (Roth et al., 2006).

When used for the short-term treatment of insomnia, sleep medications generally reduce the time it takes to get to sleep, increase total length of sleep, and reduce nightly awakenings. They work by reducing arousal and inducing feelings of calmness, thereby making a person more receptive to sleep. Sleep medications primarily work by increasing the activity of GABA, a neurotransmitter that dampens the activity of the central nervous system (see Chapter 5; Pollack, 2004a).

Despite their benefits, sleep medications have significant drawbacks in treating insomnia. They tend to suppress REM sleep, which may interfere with some of the restorative functions of sleep. They can also lead to a carryover or "hangover" the following day, which is associated with daytime sleepiness and reduced performance. Rebound insomnia can also follow discontinuation of the drug, causing worse insomnia than was originally the case. Rebound insomnia may be lessened, however, by tapering off the drug rather than abruptly discontinuing it. These drugs quickly lose their effectiveness at a given dosage level, so progressively larger doses must be used to achieve the same effect. High doses can be dangerous, especially if they are mixed with alcoholic beverages at bedtime.

Sleep medications can also produce chemical dependence if used regularly over time and can lead to tolerance (Pollack, 2004a). Once dependence is established, people experience withdrawal symptoms when they stop using the drugs, including agitation, tremors, nausea, headaches, and, in severe cases, delusions or hallucinations.

Users can also become *psychologically* dependent on sleeping pills. That is, they can develop a psychological need for the medication and assume that they will not be able to get to sleep without it. Because worry heightens bodily arousal, such self-doubts are likely to become self-fulfilling prophecies. Moreover, users may attribute their success in falling asleep to the pill and not to themselves, which strengthens reliance on the drugs and makes it harder to forgo using them.

Reliance on sleeping pills does nothing to resolve the underlying cause of the problem or help a person learn more effective ways of coping. If they are used at all, sleep medications such as benzodiazepines should only be used for a brief period of time, a few weeks at most. The aim of treatment should be to provide a temporary respite so the therapist can help the client find more effective ways of handling sources of stress and anxiety that contribute to insomnia.

Many people with sleep problems turn to alcohol to help them sleep. Using alcohol may help induce sleep, but it impairs the quality of sleep, reducing REM sleep—the stage of sleep in which dreams occur that may be needed for fully restorative and refreshing sleep (Ebrahim et al., 2013). Moreover, regular use of alcohol as a sleep aid can lead to alcohol dependence.

Antianxiety drugs of the benzodiazepine family and tricyclic antidepressants are also used to treat deep-sleep disorders, such as sleep terrors and sleepwalking. They seem to have a beneficial effect of decreasing the length of time spent in deep sleep and reducing partial arousals between sleep stages. As with primary insomnia, use of sleep medications for these disorders incurs the risk of physiological and psychological dependence. Therefore, sleep medications should be used only in severe cases and only as a temporary means of "breaking the cycle."

Stimulant drugs are often used to enhance wakefulness in people with narcolepsy and, as noted earlier, to combat daytime sleepiness in people suffering from hypersomnolence (Morgenthaler et al., 2007). Daily naps of 10 to 60 minutes and coping support from mental health professionals or self-help groups may also be helpful in treating narcolepsy.

The first-line treatment for sleep apnea is use of mechanical devices that help maintain breathing during sleep by keeping the upper airway passages open (Marin et al., 2012; Strollo et al., 2014). Surgery may be used to widen the upper airways in some cases.

**WHAT'S WRONG WITH THIS PICTURE?** People who use their beds for many other activities besides sleeping, including eating, reading, and watching television, may find that lying in bed loses its value as a cue for sleeping. Behavior therapists use stimulus control techniques to help people with insomnia create a stimulus environment associated with sleeping.

**PSYCHOLOGICAL APPROACHES** Psychological approaches have, by and large, been limited to treatment of primary insomnia. Cognitive-behavioral techniques are short term in emphasis and focus on lowering bodily arousal, establishing regular sleep habits, and replacing anxiety-producing thoughts with more adaptive thoughts. Cognitive-behavioral therapists typically use a combination of techniques, including stimulus control, adopting a regular sleep-wake cycle, relaxation training, and rational restructuring.

*Stimulus control* involves changing the environment associated with sleeping. We normally associate the bed and bedroom with sleep so that exposure to these stimuli induces feelings of sleepiness. However, when people use their beds for many other activities—such as eating, reading, planning the day's activities, and watching television—the bed loses its association with sleepiness. Moreover, the longer the person with insomnia lies in bed tossing and turning and worrying about not sleeping, the more the bed becomes a cue for anxiety and frustration.

Stimulus control techniques strengthen the connection between the bed and sleep by restricting the activities in bed as much as possible to sleeping. In other words, the bed should be reserved for sleep (and sex) to establish healthier sleep habits (Bootzin & Epstein, 2011). Typically, a person is instructed not to spend more than about 10 to 20 minutes in bed trying to fall asleep. If sleep does not occur during this time, the person should leave the bed and go to another room to regain a relaxed frame of mind before returning to bed—for example, by sitting quietly, reading, or practicing relaxation exercises.

Cognitive-behavioral therapists help clients program their bodies by establishing a consistent sleep-wake cycle. This involves going to bed and waking up at about the same time each day, including weekends and holidays. Relaxation techniques used before bedtime (such as the technique of progressive relaxation described in Chapter 6) help reduce states of physiological arousal to a level conducive to sleep.

*Rational restructuring* involves substituting rational alternatives for self-defeating, maladaptive thoughts or beliefs (see *A Closer Look: To Sleep, Perchance to Dream*). The belief that failing to get a good night's sleep will lead to unfortunate, even disastrous, consequences the next day reduces the chances of falling asleep because it raises the level of anxiety. Most of us function reasonably well if we lose sleep or even miss a night of sleep.

Cognitive-behavioral therapy is recognized as a first-line treatment for insomnia (Trauer et al., 2015). A large and growing body of evidence shows substantial therapeutic benefits from CBT for insomnia, as measured by reductions in the time it takes to get to sleep and also improved sleep quality (e.g., Blom et al., 2015; Harvey et al., 2014; Järnefelt et al., 2014; Kaldo et al., 2015; McCrae et al., 2014; Trockel et al., 2014; Wu, Appleman, et al., 2015). CBT also produces better results in the long term than sleep medications. After all, taking a pill does not help people with insomnia learn more adaptive sleep habits. Sleep medication may produce faster results, but behavioral treatment typically produces longer-lasting results (Pollack, 2004a, 2004b). However, adding sleep medication to CBT in the short term may increase the benefits of treatment in some cases over CBT alone, but not if sleep medication is continued for months at a time (Morin et al., 2009).

# A CLOSER Look

## TO SLEEP, PERCHANCE TO DREAM

Many of us have difficulty from time to time falling asleep or remaining asleep. Although sleep is a natural function and cannot be forced, we can develop more adaptive sleep habits that help us become more receptive to sleep. However, if insomnia or other sleep-related problems persist or become associated with difficulties functioning during the day, it is worthwhile to have a professional evaluate the problem. Here are some steps you can take to develop healthier sleeping patterns:

1. *Establish a regular sleep-wake cycle.* Go to bed and wake up about the same time every day. Sleeping late to make up for lost sleep can throw off your body's internal clock. Set your alarm for the same time each morning and get up, regardless of how many hours you have slept.
2. *Limit your activities in bed as much as possible to sleeping.* Avoid watching TV or reading in bed.
3. *Don't lie awake in bed too long.* If after 10 to 20 minutes of lying in bed you are unable to fall asleep, get out of bed, go to another room, and put yourself in a relaxed mood by reading, listening to calming music, or practicing self-relaxation.
4. *Avoid naps during the daytime.* You'll feel less sleepy at bedtime if you catch some z's during the afternoon.
5. *Avoid ruminating in bed.* Don't focus on problems as you attempt to sleep. Tell yourself that you'll think about tomorrow when tomorrow comes. Help yourself enter a more sleepful frame of mind by engaging in a mental fantasy or mind trip, or just let all thoughts slip away from consciousness. If an important idea comes to you, don't rehearse it in your mind. Jot it down on a handy pad so you won't lose it. If thoughts persist, get up and follow them elsewhere.
6. *Put yourself in a relaxed frame of mind before sleep.* Some people unwind before bed by reading; others prefer watching TV or just resting quietly. Do whatever you find most relaxing. You may find it helpful to incorporate within your regular bedtime routine the techniques for lowering your level of arousal discussed earlier in this text, such as meditation or progressive relaxation.
7. *Establish a regular daytime exercise schedule.* Regular exercise during the day (not directly before bedtime) can help induce sleepiness upon retiring.
8. *Avoid use of caffeinated beverages, such as coffee and tea, in the evening and late afternoon.* Also, avoid drinking alcoholic beverages. Alcohol can interfere with normal sleep patterns (reduced total sleep, REM sleep, and sleep efficiency), even when consumed upwards of 6 hours before bedtime.
9. *Reduce the lighting before bed.* Any source of lighting, including light emitted from smartphones, e-readers, tablets, and TVs, and even bright bathroom lights, can interfere with your body's circadian rhythm. Put your body in a receptive mood to sleep by turning off electronic devices and reducing the ambient lighting before going to bed.
10. *Practice rational restructuring.* Substitute rational alternatives for self-defeating thoughts. Here are some examples:

| Self-Defeating Thoughts | Rational Alternatives |
|---|---|
| "I must fall asleep right now or I'll be a wreck tomorrow." | "I may feel tired, but I've been able to get by with little sleep before. I can make up for it tomorrow by getting to bed early." |
| "What's the matter with me that I can't seem to fall sleep?" | "I can't blame myself for not being able to fall asleep. I can't control sleep. I'll just let whatever happens happen." |
| "If I don't get to sleep right now, I won't be able to concentrate on the exam (conference, meeting, etc.) tomorrow." | "My concentration may be off a bit, but I'm not going to fall apart. There's no point blowing things out of proportion. I might as well get up for a while and watch a little TV rather than lie here dwelling on this." |

# Summing Up

## Eating Disorders

### Anorexia Nervosa

**9.1 Describe the key features of anorexia nervosa.**

Anorexia nervosa is characterized by self-starvation and failure to maintain normal body weight, intense fears of becoming overweight, and distorted body image.

### Bulimia Nervosa

**9.2 Describe the key features of bulimia nervosa.**

Bulimia nervosa involves preoccupation with weight control and body shape, repeated binges, and regular purging to keep weight down.

### Causes of Anorexia Nervosa and Bulimia Nervosa

**9.3 Describe causal factors involved in anorexia nervosa and bulimia nervosa.**

Eating disorders typically begin in adolescence and affect more females than males. Anorexia nervosa and bulimia nervosa are linked to preoccupations with weight control and maladaptive ways of trying to keep weight down. Many other factors are implicated in their development, including social pressures on young women to adhere to unrealistic standards of thinness, issues of control, underlying psychological problems, and conflict within the family, especially over issues of autonomy.

## Treatment of Anorexia Nervosa and Bulimia Nervosa

**9.4 Evaluate methods used to treat anorexia nervosa and bulimia nervosa.**

Severe cases of anorexia are often treated in an inpatient setting in which a refeeding regimen can be closely monitored. Behavior modification and other psychological interventions, including psychotherapy and family therapy, may also be helpful. Most cases of bulimia are treated on an outpatient basis, with evidence supporting the therapeutic benefits of cognitive-behavioral therapy (CBT), interpersonal psychotherapy, and antidepressant medication.

## Binge-Eating Disorder

**9.5 Describe the key features of binge-eating disorder and identify effective treatments for the disorder.**

Binge-eating disorder (BED) involves a recurrent pattern of binge eating that is not accompanied by compensatory behaviors such as purging. People with BED tend to be older than those with anorexia or bulimia and are more likely to be obese. CBT and antidepressant medication have been shown to be effective in treating BED.

# Sleep-Wake Disorders

## Insomnia Disorder

**9.6 Describe the key features of insomnia disorder.**

Insomnia disorder involves a pattern of difficulty falling asleep or remaining asleep and is often associated with worry and anxiety, especially performance anxiety associated with overconcern about not getting enough sleep.

## Hypersomnolence Disorder

**9.7 Describe the key features of hypersomnolence disorder.**

Hypersomnolence disorder involves excessive daytime sleepiness in people who, despite adequate amounts of sleep, feel unrefreshed upon awakening and sleepy during the day.

## Narcolepsy

**9.8 Describe the key features of narcolepsy.**

Narcolepsy is characterized by abrupt sleep attacks during waking hours that may involve genetic factors and loss of brain cells in the hypothalamus that produce a wakefulness-regulating chemical.

## Breathing-Related Sleep Disorders

**9.9 Describe the key features of breathing-related sleep disorders.**

Breathing-related sleep-wake disorders involve recurrent episodes of momentary cessation of breathing during sleep and are often associated with daytime sleepiness. Obstructive sleep apnea hypopnea syndrome, the most common type of breathing-related sleep disorder, is typically caused by respiratory problems that interfere with normal breathing during sleep.

## Circadian Rhythm Sleep-Wake Disorders

**9.10 Describe the key features of circadian rhythm sleep-wake disorders.**

People with circadian rhythm sleep-wake disorders have irregular sleep-wake cycles, which occur often as a result of frequent shifts in work schedule or travel between time zones that disrupt the body's natural sleep-wake cycle.

## Parasomnias

**9.11 Identify the major types of parasomnias and describe their key features.**

Parasomnias involve abnormal behavior patterns associated with partial or incomplete arousals during sleep. They include two disorders occurring during non-REM sleep—sleep terrors (repeated episodes of sheer terror during sleep) and sleepwalking (repeatedly walking about in one's sleep)—and two disorders associated with sleep disturbances during REM sleep—REM sleep behavior disorder (RBD; nighttime thrashings or vocalizations during REM sleep) and nightmare disorder (persistent nightmares).

## Treatment of Sleep-Wake Disorders

**9.12 Evaluate methods used to treat sleep-wake disorders and apply your knowledge to identify more adaptive sleep habits.**

The most common form of treatment for sleep-wake disorders involves the use of antianxiety drugs. However, use of these drugs should be time limited because of the potential for psychological and/or physical dependence, among other problems. Cognitive-behavioral interventions have emerged as the treatment of choice for people with chronic insomnia.

Healthy sleep habits include the following: (1) Establish a regular sleep-wake cycle; (2) limit activities in bed as much as possible to sleeping; (3) get out of bed after 10 to 20 minutes if you are unable to fall asleep and restore a restful state of mind; (4) avoid daytime naps and avoid ruminating in bed; (5) establish a regular daytime exercise schedule; (6) avoid use of caffeinated beverages in the late afternoon and evening; and (7) replace self-defeating thoughts with adaptive alternatives.

# Critical Thinking Questions

Based on your reading of this chapter, answer the following questions:

- Why do you think people with anorexia nervosa and bulimia nervosa continue their self-defeating behaviors despite the medical complications of these conditions? Explain.
- What role do sociocultural factors play in eating disorders? How might we change societal attitudes and social pressures placed on young women that may lead to disordered eating habits?
- Do you believe that obesity results from a lack of willpower? Why or why not?
- Do your sleep habits help or hinder your sleep? Explain.

# Key Terms

anorexia nervosa, p. 346
bulimia nervosa, p. 346
eating disorders, p. 346
body mass index BMI, p. 351
binge-eating disorder BED, p. 358
obesity, p. 359
sleep-wake disorders, p. 363
insomnia, p. 364
insomnia disorder, p. 365
hypersomnolence disorder, p. 366
narcolepsy, p. 366
cataplexy, p. 366
sleep paralysis, p. 367
hypnagogic hallucinations, p. 367
breathing-related sleep disorders, p. 368
obstructive sleep apnea hypopnea syndrome, p. 368
circadian rhythm sleep-wake disorders, p. 369
parasomnias, p. 369
sleep terrors, p. 369
sleepwalking, p. 370
REM sleep behavior disorder, p. 371
nightmare disorder, p. 371

Chapter 10

# Disorders Involving Gender and Sexuality

## Learning Objectives

**10.1** **Describe** the key features of gender dysphoria and **explain** the difference between gender dysphoria and homosexuality.

**10.2** **Evaluate** psychological outcomes of sex reassignment surgery.

**10.3** **Describe** major theoretical perspectives on transgender identity.

**10.4** **Define** the term *sexual dysfunction* and **identify** the three major categories of sexual dysfunctions and the specific disorders within each type.

**10.5** **Describe** causal factors involved in sexual dysfunctions.

**10.6** **Describe** methods used to treat sexual dysfunctions.

**10.7** **Define** the term *paraphilia* and **identify** the major types.

**10.8** **Describe** theoretical perspectives on paraphilias.

**10.9** **Identify** methods for treating paraphilic disorders.

## TRUTH or FICTION

T☐ F☐ Gay males and lesbians have a gender identity of the opposite sex. (p. 381)

T☐ F☐ Orgasm is a reflex. (p. 386)

T☐ F☐ Obesity is linked to erectile dysfunction. (p. 390)

T☐ F☐ Walking at a brisk pace for two miles a day may cut the risk of erectile dysfunction in men by half. (p. 391)

T☐ F☐ Using antidepressants can interfere with a person's orgasmic response. (p. 391)

T☐ F☐ Wearing revealing bathing suits is a form of exhibitionism. (p. 398)

T☐ F☐ Some people cannot become sexually aroused unless they are subjected to pain or humiliation. (p. 402)

T☐ F☐ College women are more likely to be raped by strangers than by men they know. (p. 408)

T☐ F☐ Rapists are mentally ill. (p. 410)

**CHAPTER INTRODUCTION: DISORDERS INVOLVING GENDER AND SEXUALITY**

**"I"**

**"Paralyzed with Anxiety"**

At work, I have control over what I do. With sex, you don't have control over your sex organ. I know that my mind can control what my hands do—but the same is not true of my penis. I had begun to view sex as a basketball game. I used to play in college. When I would prepare for a game, I'd always be thinking, "Who was I guarding that night?" I'd try to psych myself up, sketching out in my mind how to play this guy, thinking through all possible moves and plays. I began to do the same thing with sex. If I were dating someone, I'd be thinking the whole evening about what might happen in bed. I'd always be preparing for the outcome. I'd sketch out in my mind how I was going to touch her, what I'd ask her to do. But all the time, right through dinner or the movies, I'd be worrying that I wouldn't get it up. I kept picturing her face and how disappointed she'd be. By the time we did go to bed, I was paralyzed with anxiety.

*"A Case of Erectile Disorder" from the Author's Files*

Disorders involving gender and sexuality touch upon the most intimate aspects of our psychological functioning. They involve problems relating to lack of sexual interest or difficulties with sexual performance, distress relating to our gender identity, and atypical patterns of sexual attraction. In sexual behavior, as in other types of behavior, the lines between the normal and the abnormal are not always agreed upon or precisely drawn. Sex, like eating, is a natural function. Also like eating, sexual behavior varies greatly among individuals and cultures. Our sexual behavior is profoundly affected by cultural, religious, and moral beliefs, custom, folklore, and superstition. In the realm of sexual behavior, our conceptions of what is normal or abnormal are influenced by cultural learning imparted through the family, school, and religious institutions.

Many patterns of sexual behavior, such as masturbation, premarital intercourse, and oral–genital sex, are normal in contemporary American society, if frequency of occurrence is any indication. However, frequency is not the only yardstick of normal behavior. Behavior is frequently labeled abnormal when it deviates from the norms of a society. For example, kissing is highly popular in Western cultures, but is considered deviant behavior in some preliterate societies in South America and Africa (Rathus, Nevid, & Fichner-Rathus, 2014). Members of the Thonga tribe of Africa were shocked when they first observed European visitors kissing. One man exclaimed, "Look at them—they eat each other's saliva and dirt." We will see that some sex-related activities are considered as abnormal in the eyes of mental health professionals as kissing seemed to the Thonga—for example, being more sexually aroused by articles of clothing than by one's partner, or losing interest in sex or being unable to become sexually aroused despite adequate stimulation.

We may also consider behavior to be abnormal when it is self-defeating, harms others, or causes personal distress. We shall see how psychological disorders discussed in this chapter meet one or more of these standards of abnormality. In exploring these disorders, we touch on questions that probe the boundaries between abnormality and normality. For example, is it abnormal to have difficulty becoming sexually aroused or reaching orgasm? How do mental health professionals define *exhibitionism* and *voyeurism*? When is it normal to watch another person disrobe, and when is it abnormal? Where do we draw the lines?

In this chapter, we explore a wide range of psychological disorders involving gender and sexuality. We will also consider a form of abnormal behavior that is not classified as a psychological disorder but that can have devastating emotional and physical effects on the people it victimizes: rape.

We begin with *gender dysphoria*, a diagnosable disorder that touches on the most basic part of our experience as sexual beings—our sense of being male or female.

# Gender Dysphoria

**Gender identity** is the psychological sense of being male or female. For most people, gender identity is consistent with their physical or genetic sex. The diagnosis of **gender dysphoria** (previously called *gender identity disorder*) applies to people who experience significant personal distress or impaired functioning as a result of a conflict between their anatomic sex and their gender identity—their sense of maleness or femaleness. The word *dysphoria* (from the Greek *dysphoros*, meaning *difficult to bear*) refers to feelings of dissatisfaction or discomfort, which in this case involves discomfort with one's designated gender.

To clarify our terms, *gender* is a psychosocial concept distinguishing maleness from femaleness, as in *gender roles* (societal expectations of behaviors appropriate for men and women) and *gender identity*—our psychological sense of ourselves as females or males. The terms *sex* or *sexual* refer to the biological division between males and females of a species, as in *sexual organs* (not gender organs).

TRAVIS: GENDER DYSPHORIA PART 1

# Features of Gender Dysphoria

**10.1 Describe the key features of gender dysphoria and explain the difference between gender dysphoria and homosexuality.**

People with a **transgender identity** have a psychological sense of belonging to one gender while possessing the sexual organs of the other. Not all people with transgender identity have gender dysphoria or any other diagnosable disorder. The diagnosis of gender dysphoria only comes into play in cases of significant discomfort associated with having a transgender identity (Zucker, 2015). These deep feelings of discomfort are accompanied by significant emotional distress or impaired functioning. The diagnosis of gender dysphoria is controversial, especially among transgender people who believe the mismatch between their gender identity and their anatomical sex is a mistake of nature and should not be treated as a mental health problem (see *Thinking Critically: Are People with a Transgender Identity Suffering from a Mental Disorder?*).

**CAITLYN JENNER.** At age 65, Bruce Jenner—Olympics gold medal winner and former member of the Kardashian clan reality TV series—took the name *Caitlyn* and announced to the world, "I am a woman."

The diagnosis of gender dysphoria may apply to children or adults, although it often begins in childhood. Children with gender dysphoria find their anatomical sex to be a source of persistent and intense distress. The diagnosis is not used simply to label "tomboyish" girls and "sissyish" boys. Rather, it is intended to apply to children who repudiate their biologic and associated characteristics in a number of ways, as described in Table 10.1.

We don't have reliable knowledge about how common gender dysphoria may be, but it is reasonable to assume that it is relatively uncommon. We do know that gender dysphoria can follow different paths. Gender dysphoria in childhood may end before adolescence, as children become more accepting of their biologic sex or come to terms with having a transgender identity; or it may persist into adolescence or adulthood as they continue to struggle with their transgender identity. Many transgender people also suffer from depression as the result of living in a world in which they are stigmatized, mistreated, and discriminated against (Bockting et al., 2015).

Gender identity should not be confused with sexual orientation. Gay males and lesbians have erotic interests in members of their own sex, but their gender identity (their sense of being male or female) is consistent with their anatomical sex. They do not desire

## Table 10.1 Key Features of Gender Dysphoria in Childhood

- Strong desire to be a member of the other gender or strongly expressing the belief that one is a member of the other gender (or of some alternative gender)
- Strong preferences for playing with members of the other gender and for toys, games, and activities associated with the other gender
- Strong feelings of disgust and personal distress about one's sexual anatomy
- Strong desires to have physical characteristics (i.e., primary or secondary sexual characteristics) associated with one's experienced gender
- Strong preferences for assuming roles of the other gender in make-believe or fantasy play
- Strong preferences for wearing clothing typically associated with the other gender and rejection of clothing associated with one's own gender

to become members of the other sex nor despise their own genitals, as we typically find in people with gender dysphoria. **T / F**

## Sex Reassignment Surgery

**10.2 Evaluate psychological outcomes of sex reassignment surgery.**

Not all people with gender dysphoria seek sex reassignment surgery. For those who do, surgeons attempt to construct external genital organs that closely resemble those of the opposite sex. Male-to-female surgery is generally more successful than female-to-male. Hormone treatments promote the development of secondary sex characteristics

### TRUTH *or* FICTION

Gay males and lesbians have a gender identity of the opposite sex.

☑ **FALSE** Gender identity should not be confused with sexual orientation. Gay males and lesbians have erotic interest in members of their own gender, but their gender identity is consistent with their anatomic sex.

## THINKING CRITICALLY about abnormal psychology

### @ISSUE: ARE PEOPLE WITH A TRANSGENDER IDENTITY SUFFERING FROM A MENTAL DISORDER?

One of the most controversial issues that has long plagued the *DSM* system is whether to classify transgender identity as a mental disorder. The previous edition of the *DSM*, the *DSM-4*, diagnosed people with transgender identity as having *gender identity disorder* (GID) if they experienced significant discomfort with their designated gender or gender roles. However, many people—including many advocates in the transgender community—argue that "difference" should not be equated with "disease" and that the term *gender identity disorder* unfairly stigmatizes people whose identity is different than the norm by implying that they suffer from a mental disorder by dint of their gender identity.

We noted that the term *gender identity disorder* was replaced in the *DSM-5* with a new diagnostic term: *gender dysphoria.* This new diagnosis emphasizes the intense discomfort or distress that transgender people may experience due to a mismatch between their gender identity and their designated gender. This change in labeling underscores the view that we shouldn't consider gender identity itself to be a mental disorder. Rather, the emphasis is now placed on the discomfort that may accompany the perceived mismatch between one's gender identity and one's assigned or designated gender. However, it remains unclear whether the use of the more neutral term *gender dysphoria* will quell the debate. Some people argue that whatever distress people with transgender identity may experience does not reflect a personal struggle with their gender identity so much as it does the many stresses and difficulties they face adjusting to living in a society that stigmatizes and discredits them.

Let's consider the broader implications of perceiving gender identity through the lens of mental illness. Conceptions of gender differ both across and within cultures, and they also vary across time in a given culture. For example, there was a time when women in our society were barred from many Ph.D. programs because the higher echelons of education were perceived to be a privileged male domain. Today, however, women comprise a majority of students in many graduate and professional schools, including doctoral programs in psychology. Most assumptions we make about gender identity are based on the social construction of gender as a dichotomous, mutually exclusive category in which people are either male or female. Yet this assumption is challenged by studies of cultures that have a recognized social identity for persons who do not fit typical male or female roles or gender identities. These individuals have an accepted role in their societies and are not deemed to be disordered or undesirable.

For example, well into the late 1800s, the Plains Indians and many other Western tribes accepted young members of the tribe who adopted roles typically assigned to the opposite sex (Carocci, 2009; Tafoya, 1996). In more than half of the surviving native languages, there are words to describe individuals who are assigned a third gender that is neither male nor female. Native tribal members believed that all human beings have both male and female elements. In many tribes, the term *two-spirit* was used for persons who embody a higher level of integration of their male and female spirits. Sometimes, a two-spirit person was a biological male who took on the tribe's female gender roles but was not considered either a male or a female. On the other hand, a female could take on the role and behaviors associated with tribal males. She could be initiated into puberty as a male and could adopt male roles and activities, including marrying a female.

These cultural variations highlight the importance of taking cultural contexts into account when making judgments about disordered behavior. Given the malleability of gender roles and identities we observe across cultures, we may question the validity of conceptualizing a transgender identity as a type of psychological disorder.

People who are dissatisfied with their biologic sex may be atypical or different from the majority, but does that mean their behavior is a form of psychopathology? Perhaps the emotional distress they experience is a result of the hostile treatment they receive in a society that insists that people fit into one of two arbitrarily designated categories and then treats harshly those who do not. Much of the distress that transgender children experience comes from difficulties getting along with other kids and being accepted by them, not from their gender identity per se.

The plight of transgender individuals may be compared with that of lesbians and gay men. The distress that many lesbians

**WHAT IS NORMAL AND WHAT IS ABNORMAL?** The cultural context must be considered in defining what is normal and what is abnormal in the realm of sexual and sexually related behavior. There is a wide range of variation in sexual practices across cultures and even in the ways people cloak or expose their bodies.

and gay men experience in reference to their sexual orientation may be a function of the hostility and abuse they encounter in the broader society. From this perspective, their distress is not a direct consequence of inner conflicts over their sexual orientation, but is an understandable response to the negative treatment they receive from others, even their loved ones. Similarly, critics of the psychiatric diagnostic system contend that clinicians should not use dissatisfaction with one's biologic sex as a basis for diagnosing a psychological disorder. Rather, they argue that ill treatment of people with atypical patterns of gender identity creates emotional distress, not gender identity per se (Reid & Whitehead, 1992). Absent the social construction of mutually exclusive gender categories, the disorder would no longer exist. Just as beliefs about sexual orientation have changed over time, perhaps greater tolerance of transgender individuals and greater appreciation of the diversity of gender expression in human beings will lead us to conceptualize gender identity with greater flexibility. Until that happens, however, the medical/psychiatric and transgender communities may well continue to battle each other.

In thinking critically about the issue, answer the following questions:

- Do you believe that dissatisfaction with one's biologic sex should be considered abnormal behavior or a variation in gender expression? Explain your answer.
- Should the diagnosis of gender dysphoria be retained in the *DSM* system, changed (and if so, how?), or simply dropped? Explain.

of the reassigned sex, such as growth of fatty tissue in the breasts in male-to-female cases and the growth of the beard and body hair in female-to-male cases.

People who undergo sex reassignment surgery can participate in sexual activity and even reach orgasm, but they cannot conceive or bear children because they lack the internal reproductive organs of their newly reconstructed sex. Investigators generally find positive effects on psychological adjustment and quality of life of transgender individuals (also called *transsexuals*) who undergo sex reassignment surgery (Cohen-Kettenis & Klink, 2015; Rolle et al., 2015; Wierck et al., 2011). A recent study of 32 patients who completed sex reassignment surgery showed that none regretted it and nearly all were generally satisfied with the results (Johansson et al., 2010).

Postoperative adjustment tends to be more favorable for female-to-male reassignment (Parola et al., 2010). One reason may be that society tends to be more accepting of women who desire to become men than the reverse (Smith et al., 2005). Female-to-male transgender individuals also may be better adjusted before surgery, so their superior postoperative adjustment may also represent a selection factor.

Men seeking sex reassignment outnumber women by about three to one (Spack, 2013). Most female-to-male individuals do not seek complete sex reassignment surgery. Instead, they may remove their internal sex organs (ovaries, fallopian tubes, and uterus) along with the fatty tissue in their breasts (Bockting & Fung, 2006). Testosterone (male sex hormone) treatments increase muscle mass and growth of the beard. Only a few female-to-male transgender individuals have the series of operations necessary to construct an artificial penis, largely because the constructed penises do not work very well and the surgery is expensive. Therefore, most female-to-male transgender individuals limit their physical alteration to hysterectomies, mastectomies, and testosterone treatment (J. M. Bailey, 2003a).

**TRAVIS: GENDER DYSPHORIA PART 2**

# Theoretical Perspectives on Transgender Identity

**10.3 Describe major theoretical perspectives on transgender identity.**

The origins of transgender identity remain unclear. Psychodynamic theorists point to extremely close mother–son relationships, empty relationships with parents, and fathers who were absent or detached. These family circumstances may foster strong identification with the mother in young males, leading to a reversal of expected gender roles and identity. Girls with weak, ineffectual mothers and strong masculine fathers may overly identify with their fathers and develop a psychological sense of themselves as "little men."

Learning theorists similarly point to father absence in the case of boys—that is, to the unavailability of a strong male role model. Children who were reared by parents who had wanted children of the other gender and who strongly encouraged cross-gender dressing and patterns of play may learn socialization patterns and develop a gender identity associated with the opposite sex.

Nonetheless, the great majority of people with the types of family histories described by psychodynamic and learning theorists do not develop a transgender identity. It may be the case that psychosocial influences interact with a biological predisposition in influencing the development of transgender identity. We know that many adults with a transgender identity showed cross-gender preferences in toys, games, and clothing very early in childhood (Zucker, 2005a, 2005b). If critical early learning experiences play a part, they most probably occurred very early in life.

Some male transgender people recall that, as children, they preferred playing with dolls, enjoyed wearing frilly dresses, and disliked rough-and-tumble play. Some female transgender people report that, as children, they disliked dresses and acted like tomboys. They preferred playing "boys' games" and playing with boys. Female transgender individuals may have an easier time adjusting than their male counterparts, as "tomboys" generally find acceptance more easily than "sissy boys." Even in adulthood, it may be easier for a female transsexual to wear male clothes and "pass" as a slightly built man than it is for a brawny man to pass for a large woman.

The development of transgender identity may largely be the result of variations in male sexual hormones acting upon the developing brain during prenatal development (Diamond, 2011; R. A. Friedman, 2015; Savic, Garcia-Falgueras, & Swaab, 2010). We can speculate that a disturbance in the endocrine (hormonal) environment during gestation leads the brain to become differentiated with respect to gender identity in one direction while the genitals develop normally in the other direction. Investigators find differences in the brains of transgender people, but what these differences mean for the development of transgender identity remains to be determined (Kranz et al., 2014). Importantly, we continue to lack direct evidence of abnormal hormonal balances during prenatal development that could explain the development of transgender identity. Even if such hormonal factors were demonstrated, they are unlikely to be the sole cause.

In sum, a combination of genetic and hormonal influences may create a disposition that interacts with early life experiences in leading to the development of transgender identity (Glicksman, 2013). However, explanations of the development of transgender identity do not directly teach us about factors that determine gender dysphoria. Many transgender individuals do not warrant a diagnosis of gender dysphoria, as they show no evidence of the significant distress or impairment in daily functioning needed to meet diagnostic criteria. We presently lack the knowledge base needed to understand the developmental trajectory in transgender individuals that leads to gender dysphoria.

# Sexual Dysfunctions

**Sexual dysfunctions** are persistent problems with sexual interest, arousal, or response. Table 10.2 provides an overview of the sexual dysfunctions reviewed in this chapter.

Reports of sexual problems are widespread. A recent worldwide review estimated that sexual dysfunctions affect 40% to 45% of adult women and 20% to 30% of adult men at some point in their lives (Lewis et al., 2010). Estimates of the prevalence of specific types of sexual problems are shown in Table 10.2.

Women more often report problems regarding painful sex, inability to attain orgasm, and lack of sexual desire. Men are more likely to report reaching orgasm too quickly (early or premature ejaculation). We should note that reports of sexual problems shown in the table mean that a significant problem was reported, and not that a diagnosable disorder is necessarily present. We continue to lack clear evidence of underlying rates of diagnosable sexual dysfunctions in the general community.

Sexual dysfunctions may be classified according to two general categories: lifelong versus acquired and situational versus generalized. Cases of sexual dysfunction that have existed for the individual's lifetime are called *lifelong dysfunctions. Acquired dysfunctions* begin following a period of normal functioning. In *situational dysfunctions*, the problems occur in some situations (e.g., with one's spouse), but not in others (e.g., with a lover or when masturbating), or at some times but not others. *Generalized dysfunctions* occur in all situations and every time the individual engages in sexual activity.

Despite the fact that sexual dysfunctions are believed to be widespread, relatively few people seek treatment for these problems. People may not know that effective

**Table 10.2** Overview of Sexual Dysfunctions

| Type of Disorder | Approximate Prevalence in Population | Description |
|---|---|---|
| **Disorders Involving Lack of Sexual Interest or Lack of Sexual Excitement or Arousal** | | |
| Male hypoactive sexual desire disorder | Ranging from about 8% to about 25% across age ranges, with greater prevalence among older men | Deficiency or lack of sexual interest or desire for sexual activity |
| Female sexual interest/arousal disorder | About 10% to 55% across age ranges, with greater prevalence in older women | Deficiency or lack of sexual interest or drive and problems achieving or sustaining sexual arousal |
| Erectile disorder | Varies widely with age; estimated at 1% to 10% under age 40, 20% to 40% in men in their 60s, and even higher among older men | Difficulty achieving or maintaining erection during sexual activity |
| **Disorders Involving Impaired Orgasmic Response** | | |
| Female orgasmic disorder | 10% to 42% across studies | Difficulty achieving orgasm in females |
| Delayed ejaculation | Less than 1% to 10% across studies | Difficulty achieving orgasm or ejaculation in males |
| Premature (early) ejaculation | Upwards of 30% of men across studies report problems with rapid ejaculation, including about 1% to 2% reporting ejaculation within one minute of penetration | Climaxing (ejaculating) too early in males |
| **Disorders Involving Pain During Intercourse or Penetration (in women)** | | |
| Genito-pelvic pain/penetration disorder | Varies across studies, but about 15% of women in North America report experiencing recurrent pain during intercourse | Pain during intercourse or attempts at penetration, or fear of pain associated with intercourse or penetration, or tensing or tightening of the pelvic muscles, making penetration difficult or painful |

SOURCE: Prevalence rates derived from Lewis et al., 2010, and based on most recent review of studies worldwide, and updated based on the *DSM-5* (American Psychiatric Association, 2013).

**Note**: Prevalence rates reflect percentages of adults reporting problems and may not correspond to clinical diagnosis of sexual dysfunctions. Reports of sexual pain and climaxing too early were based on individuals who were sexually active during the past 12-month period.

treatments are available or where to obtain help, or they may avoid seeking help because of the long-standing stigma attached to admitting a sexual difficulty.

# Types of Sexual Dysfunctions

**10.4 Define the term *sexual dysfunction* and identify the three major categories of sexual dysfunctions and the specific disorders within each type.**

As shown in Table 10.2, we can group sexual dysfunctions within three general categories:

1. Disorders involving problems with sexual interest, desire, or arousal
2. Disorders involving problems with orgasmic response
3. Problems involving pain during sexual intercourse or penetration (in women)

In making a diagnosis of a sexual dysfunction, the clinician must determine that the problem is not due to the use of drugs or medications; other medical conditions; severe relationship distress, such as partner violence; or other serious stressors. The disorder must also cause significant levels of personal distress or impairment in daily functioning.

**DISORDERS OF INTEREST AND AROUSAL** These disorders involve deficiencies in either sexual interest or arousal. Men with **male hypoactive sexual desire disorder** (MHSDD) persistently have little, if any, desire for sexual activity or may lack sexual or erotic thoughts or fantasies. Lack of sexual desire is more common among women than men (Géonet, De Sutter, & Zech, 2012). Nevertheless, the belief that men are always eager for sex is a myth.

Women with **female sexual interest/arousal disorder** (FSIAD) experience either a lack of or a greatly reduced level of sexual interest, drive, or arousal. Women with problems becoming sexually aroused may lack feelings of sexual pleasure or excitement that normally accompany sexual arousal, or they may experience little or no sexual interest or pleasure. They may also have few if any genital sensations during sexual activity. A study of women with low levels of sexual interest or drive showed that they generally had a less active sex life and experienced less satisfaction with their sexual relationships than women without the disorder (Leiblum et al., 2006).

Clinicians do not necessarily agree on criteria for determining the level of sexual desire considered "normal." They may weigh various factors in reaching a diagnosis of FSIAD, such as the client's lifestyle (e.g., parents contending with the demands of young children may lack energy for interest in sex), sociocultural factors (culturally restrictive attitudes may restrain sexual desire or interest), the quality of the relationship (problems in a relationship may contribute to lack of interest in sex), and the client's age (desire normally declines with age; McCarthy, Ginsberg, & Fucito, 2006; West et al., 2008).

Sex researchers continue to debate how to define sexual dysfunctions, especially in women. For example, some researchers argue that labeling a lack of sexual desire in women as a dysfunction imposes on women a male model of what should be normal (Bean, 2002). Researchers also debate whether to diagnose female sexual dysfunction on the basis of a lack of desire or difficulty achieving orgasm or by the woman's perceptions of these experiences as causing distress (Clay, 2009). Bear in mind that lack of desire usually does not come to the health practitioner's attention unless one partner is more interested in sex than the other. That is when the less-interested partner may be labeled with a dysfunction—but questions remain about where to draw the line between "normal" and "abnormal" levels of sexual drive or interest.

Problems with sexual arousal in men typically take the form of failure to achieve or maintain an erection sufficient to engage in sexual activity through completion. Almost all men have occasional difficulty achieving or maintaining erection during sex, but men with persistent erectile difficulties may

**SEXUAL DYSFUNCTIONS.** What are the different types of sexual dysfunctions? What treatments are available to help people with sexual problems?

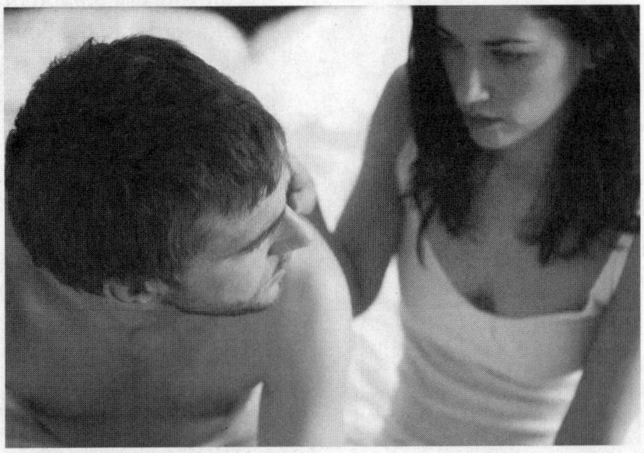

be diagnosed with **erectile disorder** (ED; also called *erectile dysfunction*). They may have difficulty achieving an erection or maintaining an erection to the completion of sexual activity, or have erections that lack the rigidity needed to perform effectively. The diagnosis requires the problem to be present for a period of about six months or longer and for it to occur on all or almost all (approximately 75% to 100%) occasions of sexual activity.

Occasional problems in achieving or maintaining erection are common enough, due to factors such as fatigue, alcohol, or anxiety with a new partner. The more concerned the man becomes about his sexual ability, the more likely he is to suffer *performance anxiety*. As we will explore further, performance anxiety can contribute to repeated failure, and a vicious cycle of anxiety and failure may develop.

The risks of erectile disorder increase with age. Approximately 50% of men in the 40- to 70-year age range experience some degree of erectile dysfunction (Saigal, 2004). Overall, an estimated 16 to 20 million men in the United States are affected by erectile dysfunction (Fang et al., 2015).

## TRUTH or FICTION

Orgasm is a reflex.

☑ **TRUE** People cannot will or force an orgasm. Nor can they will or force other sexual reflexes, such as erection and vaginal lubrication. Trying to force these responses generally backfires and only increases anxiety.

**ORGASM DISORDERS** *Orgasm* or *sexual climax* is an involuntary reflex that results in rhythmic contractions of the pelvic muscles and is usually accompanied by feelings of intense pleasure. In men, these contractions are accompanied by expulsion of semen. There are three types of disorders involving problems with achieving orgasm: **female orgasmic disorder**, **delayed ejaculation**, and **premature (early) ejaculation**. **T / F**

In *female orgasmic disorder* and *delayed ejaculation*, there is a marked delay in reaching orgasm (in women) or ejaculation (in men) or an infrequency or absence of orgasm or ejaculation. Diagnosis of these disorders requires that the problem be present for about six months or longer, that the symptoms cause a significant level of distress, and that the symptoms occur on all or almost all occasions of sexual activity (and for men, without a desire to delay ejaculation). The clinician needs to make a judgment about whether there is an "adequate" amount and type of stimulation needed to achieve orgasm, taking into account the wide variation that exists in normal sexual responsiveness (Ishak et al., 2010). Might a woman's difficulty achieving orgasm with her partner result from a lack of effective stimulation rather than an orgasmic disorder? Many women, for example, require direct clitoral stimulation (by their own hand or their partner's) to achieve orgasm during vaginal intercourse. This should not be considered abnormal because it is the *clitoris*, not the *vagina*, that is the woman's most erotically sensitive organ.

The *DSM-5* expanded the criteria for female orgasmic disorder to include cases in which women experience a sharp reduction in the intensity of orgasmic sensations. The drafters of the *DSM-5* argue that orgasm is not an "all or nothing" experience and that some women have a diminished level of orgasmic intensity that may become a problem for them.

Delayed ejaculation has received little attention in the clinical literature. Men with this problem are generally able to ejaculate through masturbation but have difficulty achieving ejaculation during intercourse with a partner or are unable to do so. Although the disorder may allow a man to prolong the sexual act, the experience is usually one of frustration for both partners (Althof, 2012).

Premature (early) ejaculation (PE) involves a recurrent pattern of ejaculation occurring within about one minute of vaginal penetration and before the man desires it (American Psychiatric Association, 2013). Men with PE perceive a lack of control over the ability to delay ejaculation (Althof et al., 2014). In some cases, rapid ejaculation occurs prior to penetration or following only a few penile thrusts. Occasional experiences of rapid ejaculation, such as when the man is with a new partner, has had infrequent sexual contacts, or is very highly aroused, are not considered abnormal. It is only when the problem becomes persistent and causes emotional distress or relationship problems that a diagnosis is rendered.

**GENITO-PELVIC PAIN/PENETRATION DISORDER** This disorder applies to women who experience sexual pain and/or difficulty engaging in vaginal intercourse or penetration. In some cases, women experience genital or pelvic pain during vaginal intercourse or attempts at penetration. The pain cannot be explained by an underlying medical condition and so is believed to have a psychological component. However, because many, if not most, cases of pain during intercourse are traceable to an underlying medical condition that may go undiagnosed, such as insufficient lubrication or a urinary tract infection, controversy persists over whether sexual pain during intercourse or penetration should be classified as a mental disorder (van Lankveld et al., 2010).

Some cases of **genito-pelvic pain/penetration disorder** involve **vaginismus**, a condition in which the muscles surrounding the vagina involuntarily contract whenever vaginal penetration is attempted, making sexual intercourse painful or impossible. Vaginismus is not a medical condition, but a conditioned response in which penile contact with the woman's genitals elicits an involuntary spasm of the vaginal musculature, preventing penetration or causing pain upon attempts at penetration.

# Theoretical Perspectives

**10.5 Describe causal factors involved in sexual dysfunctions.**

Many factors are implicated in the development of sexual dysfunctions, including factors representing psychological, biological, and sociocultural perspectives.

**PSYCHOLOGICAL PERSPECTIVES** The major contemporary psychological views of sexual dysfunctions emphasize the roles of anxiety, lack of sexual skills, irrational beliefs, perceived causes of events, and relationship problems. Here, we consider several potential causal pathways.

Physically or psychologically traumatic sexual experiences may lead to sexual contact producing anxiety rather than arousal or pleasure. Conditioned anxiety resulting from a history of sexual trauma or rape may lead to problems with sexual arousal or achieving orgasm or may lead to pain in women during penetration (Colangelo & Keefe-Cooperman, 2012; Ishak et al., 2010). Women who have problems becoming sexually aroused may also harbor deep-seated anger and resentment toward their partners. Underlying feelings of guilt about sex and ineffective stimulation by one's partner may also contribute to difficulties with sexual arousal.

Sexual trauma early in life may make it difficult for men or women to respond sexually when they develop intimate relationships. People with a history of sexual trauma may be flooded with feelings of helplessness, unresolved anger, or misplaced guilt. They may also experience flashbacks of the abusive experiences when they engage in sexual relations, preventing them from becoming sexually aroused or achieving orgasm. They may also develop other psychological problems that frequently co-occur with sexual dysfunctions, especially depression and anxiety (Rajkumar & Kumaran, 2015). The emotional disorders may contribute to sexual problems in some cases or result from them in others.

Another principal form of anxiety in sexual dysfunctions is *performance anxiety*, which represents an excessive concern about the ability to perform successfully. Performance anxiety can develop when people experience problems performing sexually and begin to doubt their abilities. People troubled by performance anxiety become spectators during sex rather than participants. Their attention is focused on how their bodies are responding (or not responding) to sexual stimulation. They are plagued by disruptive thoughts about the anticipated negative consequences of failing to perform adequately ("What will she think of me?") rather than focusing on their erotic experiences. Men with performance anxiety may have difficulty achieving or maintaining an erection or may ejaculate prematurely (Althof et al., 2014); women may fail to become adequately aroused or have difficulty achieving orgasm (McCabe & Connaughton, 2014). A vicious cycle may ensue in which each failure experience instills deeper doubts, which leads to more anxiety during sexual encounters, which occasions repeated failure, and so on. This vicious cycle is illustrated in Figure 10.1.

**Figure 10.1** Performance anxiety and sexual dysfunctions: a vicious cycle.

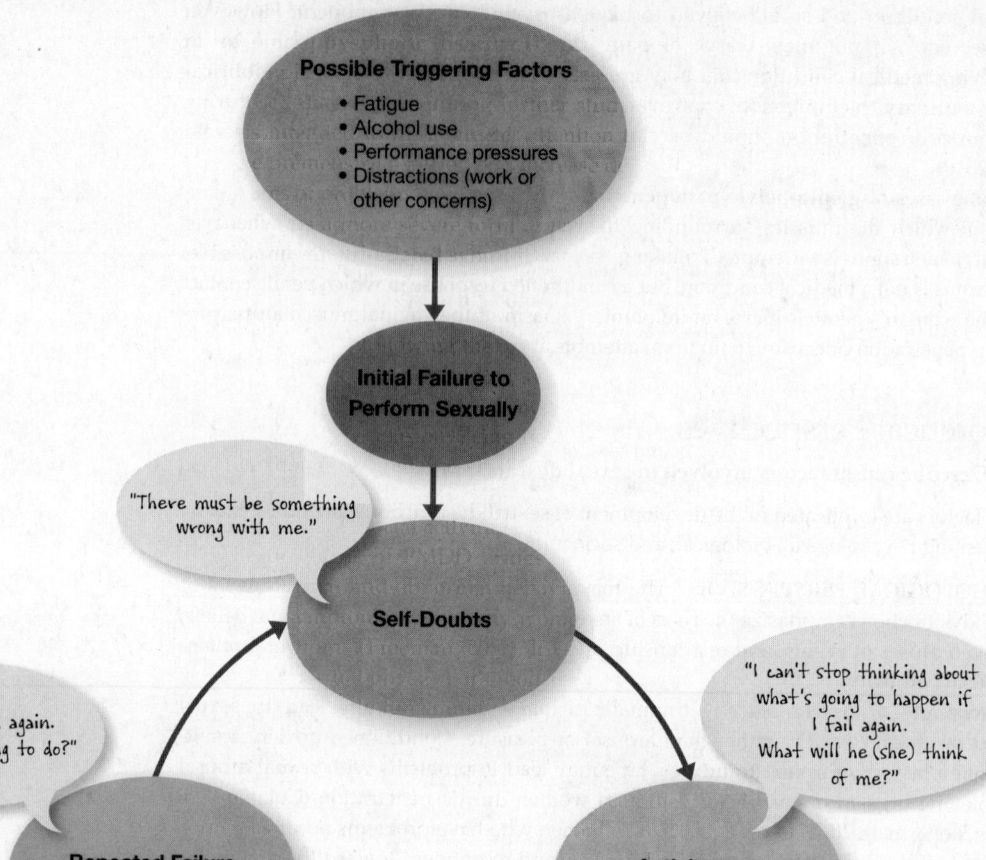


In Western cultures, there is a deeply ingrained connection between a man's sexual performance and his sense of manhood. The man who repeatedly fails to perform sexually may suffer a loss of self-esteem, become depressed, or feel he is no longer a man. He may see himself as a total failure, despite other accomplishments in life. Sexual opportunities are construed as tests of his manhood, and he may respond to them by bearing down and trying to will (force) an erection. Willing an erection may backfire because erection is a reflex that cannot be forced. With so much of his self-esteem on the line whenever he makes love, it is little wonder that performance anxiety may mount to a point that it inhibits erection. The erectile reflex is controlled by the parasympathetic branch of the autonomic nervous system. Activation of the sympathetic nervous system, which occurs when we are anxious or under stress, can block parasympathetic control, preventing the erectile reflex from occurring. Ejaculation, in contrast, is under sympathetic nervous system control, so heightened levels of arousal, as in the case of performance anxiety, can trigger rapid (premature) ejaculation (Althof et al., 2014). The relationship between performance anxiety and sexual dysfunction can become a vicious cycle. One client who suffered from erectile dysfunction described his feelings of sexual inadequacy this way:

> I always felt inferior, like I was on probation, having to prove myself. I felt like I was up against the wall. You can't imagine how embarrassing this was. It's like you walk out in front of an audience that you think is a nudist convention and it turns out to be a tuxedo convention.
>
> *From the Author's Files*

At the beginning of the chapter, you read about another client whose performance anxiety led him to prepare for sexual relations as though he were psyching himself up for a big game.

Women, too, may equate their self-esteem with their ability to reach frequent and intense orgasms. Yet when men and women try to will arousal or lubrication or to force an orgasm, they may find that the harder they try, the more these responses elude them. Several generations ago, the pressures concerning sex often revolved around the issue of "Should I or shouldn't I?" Today, however, the pressures for both men and women are often based more on achieving performance goals relating to reaching orgasm and satisfying one's partner's sexual needs. We noted that performance anxiety can impair sexual performance in both men and women. However, a recent study in Australia showed that performance anxiety was more closely tied to sexual problems in men, whereas relationship problems were more strongly linked to female sexual problems (McCabe & Connaughton, 2014).

Sexual fulfillment is also based on learning sexual skills. Sexual skills or competencies, like other types of skills, are acquired through opportunities for new learning. We learn about how our own and our partner's bodies respond sexually in various ways, including trial and error with our partners, by learning about our own sexual responses through self-exploration (as in masturbation), by reading about sexual techniques, and perhaps by talking to others or viewing sex films or videotapes. Yet children who are raised to feel guilty or anxious about sex may have lacked opportunities to develop sexual knowledge and skills and so remain ignorant about the types of stimulation they need to achieve sexual gratification. They may also respond to sexual opportunities with feelings of anxiety and shame rather than arousal and pleasure.

Cognitive theorists such as Albert Ellis (1977) point out that underlying irrational beliefs and attitudes can contribute to sexual dysfunctions. Consider two such irrational beliefs: (a) We must have the approval at all times of everyone who is important to us and (b) we must be thoroughly competent at everything we do. If we cannot accept the occasional disappointment of others, we may catastrophize the significance of a single frustrating sexual episode. If we insist that every sexual experience be perfect, we set the stage for inevitable failure.

How we appraise situations in terms of the perceived causes of events also plays a role. Attributing the cause for erectile difficulty to oneself ("What's wrong with me?") rather than to the situation ("It was the alcohol" or "I was tired") can undermine future sexual functioning.

Relationship problems can also contribute to sexual dysfunctions, especially when they involve long-simmering resentments and conflicts. The strain of a troubled relationship can take a toll on sexual desire, as can other stressful life events, such as job loss, family crisis, or serious illness (Heiman, 2008). The quality of sexual relations is usually no better than other facets of relationships or marriages. Couples who harbor resentments toward one another may choose the sexual arena for combat. Communication problems, moreover, are linked to general marital dissatisfaction. Couples who find it difficult to communicate their sexual desires may lack the means to help each other become more effective lovers.

The following case illustrates how sexual arousal disorder may be connected with problems in the relationship.

## Pete and Paula:

### A CASE OF SEXUAL AROUSAL DISORDER

After living together for 6 months, Pete and Paula are thinking seriously about getting married. But a problem has brought them to a sex therapy clinic. Paula explains to the therapist that for the past two months, Pete has been unable to sustain an erection during intercourse. Pete is 26 years old and a lawyer; Paula, 24, is a buyer for a large department store. They both grew up in middle-class, suburban families, were introduced through mutual friends, and began having intercourse, without difficulty, a few months into their relationship. At Paula's urging, Pete moved into her apartment, although he wasn't sure he was ready for such a step. A week later, he began to have difficulty maintaining his erection during intercourse, although he felt strong desire for his partner. When his erection waned, he would try again, but would lose his desire and be unable to achieve another erection. After a few times like this, Paula would become so angry that she began striking Pete in the chest and screaming at him. Pete, who at 200 pounds weighed more than twice as much as Paula, would just walk away, which angered Paula even more. It became clear that sex was not the only trouble spot in their relationship. Paula complained that Pete preferred to spend time with his friends and go to baseball games rather than spend time with her. When together at home, he would become absorbed in watching sports events on television and showed no interest in activities she enjoyed—attending the theater, visiting museums, and so on. Because there was no evidence that the sexual difficulty was due to either organic problems or depression, a diagnosis of male erectile disorder was given. Neither Pete nor Paula was willing to discuss their nonsexual problems with a therapist. Although the sexual problem was treated successfully with a form of sex therapy modeled after techniques developed by Masters and Johnson (as discussed later), and the couple later married, Pete's ambivalences continued, even well into their marriage, and there were future recurrences of sexual problems as well.

**SOURCE:** *Adapted from Spitzer et al., 1994, pp. 198–200*

**BIOLOGICAL PERSPECTIVES** Biological factors such as low testosterone levels and disease can dampen sexual desire and reduce responsiveness. Testosterone, the male sex hormone, plays a pivotal role in energizing sexual desire and sexual activity in both men and women (Davis et al., 2008). Both men and women produce testosterone in their bodies, although women produce smaller amounts. In men, a decline in testosterone production can lead to a loss of sexual interest and activity and difficulty achieving erections (Maggi, 2012; Montorsi et al., 2010). The adrenal glands and ovaries are the sites in the woman's body where testosterone is produced (Buvat et al., 2010). Women who have these organs surgically removed because of invasive disease no longer produce testosterone and may gradually lose sexual interest or develop a reduced capacity for sexual response (Davis & Braunstein, 2012; Wierman et al., 2010). We also have evidence linking low testosterone levels to some cases of depression in males, and depression may dampen sexual desire (Stephenson, 2008). However, people with sexual dysfunctions typically have normal levels of sex hormone circulating in their bodies.

Cardiovascular problems involving impaired blood flow both to and through the penis can cause erectile disorder—a problem that becomes more common as men age (Miner, 2011). Erectile disorder may share common risk factors with cardiovascular disorders (heart and artery diseases), which should alert physicians that erectile dysfunction may be an early warning sign of underlying heart disease that should be medically evaluated.

Erectile dysfunction is linked to obesity (as are cardiovascular problems) and prostate and urinary problems (Martin et al., 2014; Tan, Tong, & Ho, 2012). Obesity is associated with circulatory problems, so its connection to erectile disorder is not surprising. The good news is that obese men who lose weight and increase their activity levels may experience improved erectile functioning (Martin et al., 2014). **T / F**

### TRUTH or FICTION

Obesity is linked to erectile dysfunction.

☑ **TRUE** Yes, it's true: Obesity is a risk not only to physical health, but also to erectile functioning in men.

Men with diabetes mellitus also stand an increased risk of ED (Skeldon et al., 2015). Diabetes can damage blood vessels and nerves, including those serving the penis. Men with ED are more than twice as likely to have diabetes as men without ED (Sun et al., 2006). In one recent study, 39% of a sample of diabetic men had ED (Chakraborty et al., 2014).

Erectile disorder and delayed ejaculation may also result from multiple sclerosis (MS), a disease in which nerve cells lose the protective coatings that facilitate the smooth transmission of nerve impulses (Baranzini et al., 2010). Other forms of nerve damage, as well as chronic kidney disease, hypertension, cancer, and emphysema, can impair erectile response, as can endocrine disorders that suppress testosterone production (Koehler et al., 2012; Miner, 2011).

An influential study of 2,000 men by Eric Rimm (2000) of the Harvard School of Public Health found that erectile dysfunction was associated with having a large waist, physical inactivity, and drinking too much alcohol (or not drinking at all). The common link among these factors may be high levels of cholesterol. Cholesterol can impede blood flow to the penis, just as it can impede blood flow to the heart. Exercise, weight loss, and moderate alcohol intake all help lower cholesterol levels, but we are not recommending that abstainers begin drinking to avert or treat erectile problems. However, the findings of the Massachusetts Male Aging Study suggest that regular exercise may reduce the risk of erectile dysfunction (Derby et al., 2001). In this study, men who burned 200 calories or more a day in physical activity, an amount that can be achieved by taking a daily walk at a brisk pace for two miles, had about half the risk of erectile dysfunction than did more sedentary men. Exercise may help prevent clogging of arteries, keeping them clear for the flow of blood into the penis. **T / F**

## TRUTH *or* FICTION

Walking at a brisk pace for two miles a day may cut the risk of erectile dysfunction in men by about half.

☑ **TRUE** Results of a recent study showed that men who exercised regularly at a level comparable to taking a brisk walk for two miles a day had about half the risk of erectile dysfunction as sedentary men.

Women also develop vascular or nervous disorders that impair genital blood flow, reducing lubrication and sexual excitement, rendering intercourse painful, and reducing their ability to reach orgasm. As with men, these problems become more likely as women age.

Before we move on to discuss psychological factors, we need to note that prescription drugs and psychoactive drugs, including antidepressants and antipsychotics, can impair erectile functioning and cause orgasmic disorders (Olfson et al., 2005). About one in three women who use selective serotonin reuptake inhibitor (SSRI) antidepressants (such as Zoloft or Paxil) experience impaired orgasmic response or complete lack of orgasm (Ishak et al., 2010). Tranquilizers such as Valium and Xanax may cause orgasmic disorder in either men or women. Some medicinal drugs used to treat high blood pressure and high blood cholesterol levels can also interfere with erectile response. **T / F**

## TRUTH *or* FICTION

Using antidepressants can interfere with a person's orgasmic response.

☑ **TRUE** Use of SSRI-type antidepressants can impair orgasmic responsiveness.

Depressant drugs such as alcohol, heroin, and morphine can reduce sexual desire and impair sexual arousal. Narcotics, such as heroin, also depress testosterone production, which can diminish sexual desire and lead to erectile failure. Regular use of cocaine can cause erectile disorder or delayed ejaculation and reduce sexual desire in both women and men. Some people report increased sexual pleasure from initial use of cocaine, but repeated use can lead to dependency on the drug for sexual arousal, and long-term use may lessen sexual pleasure.

**SOCIOCULTURAL PERSPECTIVES** At around the turn of the 20th century, an Englishwoman was quoted as saying she would "close her eyes and think of England" when her husband approached her to perform her "marital duties." This old-fashioned stereotype suggests that sexual pleasure was once considered exclusively a male preserve—that sex, for women, was primarily a duty. Mothers usually informed their daughters of the conjugal duties before the wedding, and girls encoded sex as just one of the ways in which women serviced the needs of others.

Women who harbor such stereotypical attitudes toward female sexuality are unlikely to become aware of their own sexual potential. In addition, sexual anxieties may transform negative expectations into self-fulfilling prophecies. Sexual dysfunctions in men, too, may be linked to extremely strict sociocultural beliefs and sexual taboos. Other negative beliefs about sexuality may interfere with sexual desire, such as the belief that sexual desire is not appropriate for older adults past childbearing age (Géonet, De Sutter, & Zech, 2012).

Our colleague, psychologist Rafael Javier (2010), takes note of the idealization within many Hispanic cultures of the *marianismo* stereotype, which derives its name from the Virgin Mary. From this sociocultural perspective, the ideal virtuous woman "suffers in silence" as she submerges her needs and desires to those of her husband and children. She is the provider of joy, even in the face of her own pain or frustration. It is not difficult to imagine that women who adopt these stereotypical expectations find it difficult to assert their own needs for sexual gratification and may express resistance to this cultural ideal by becoming sexually unresponsive.

Sociocultural factors play an important role in erectile dysfunction as well. Investigators find a greater incidence of erectile dysfunction in cultures with more restrictive sexual attitudes toward premarital sex among females, toward sex in marriage, and toward extramarital sex (Welch & Kartub, 1978). Men in these cultures may be prone to developing sexual anxiety or guilt that interferes with sexual performance.

In India, cultural beliefs that link the loss of semen to a draining of the man's life energy underlie the development of *dhat syndrome*, an irrational fear of loss of semen (discussed in Chapter 6). Men with this condition sometimes develop erectile dysfunction because their fears about wasting precious seminal fluid interfere with their ability to perform sexually (Shukla & Singh, 2000).

## Treatment of Sexual Dysfunctions

**10.6 Describe methods used to treat sexual dysfunctions.**

Until the groundbreaking research of the famed sex researchers William Masters and Virginia Johnson in the 1960s, there was no effective treatment for most sexual dysfunctions. Psychoanalytic therapy approached sexual dysfunctions indirectly. It was assumed that sexual dysfunctions represented underlying conflicts, and so treatment focused on resolving those conflicts through psychoanalysis. A lack of evidence about the efficacy of this approach led to development of methods that focus more directly on the sexual problems.

**MASTERS AND JOHNSON.** Sex therapists William Masters and Virginia Johnson.

Most contemporary sex therapists assume that sexual dysfunctions can be treated by directly modifying a couple's sexual interactions. Pioneered by Masters and Johnson (1970), *sex therapy* uses cognitive-behavioral techniques in a brief therapy format to help individuals enhance their sexual competencies (sexual knowledge and skills) and relieve performance anxiety. Although therapists today may not strictly adhere to Masters and Johnson's techniques, they continue to incorporate many of their methods (Althof, 2010). When feasible, both partners are involved in therapy. In some cases, however, individual therapy may be preferable, as we shall see.

Before we turn to consider these specific methods, we should note that because sexual problems are often embedded in a context of troubled relationships, therapists may also use couple therapy to help couples share power in their relationships, improve communication skills, and negotiate differences (Coyle, 2006; McCarthy, Ginsberg, & Fucito, 2006).

Significant changes have occurred in the treatment of sexual dysfunctions in the past 25 years. Today, there is greater emphasis on biological or organic factors in the development of sexual problems and the use of medical treatments, such as the drug *sildenafil* (Viagra), to treat male erectile dysfunction. Erectile drugs have become so popular that they now represent a revenue source of $5 billion for drug makers and are used by tens of millions of men (Wilson, 2011). Let's survey some of the more common techniques used to treat sexual dysfunctions.

**WHEN A SOURCE OF PLEASURE BECOMES A SOURCE OF MISERY.** Sexual dysfunctions can be a source of intense personal distress and lead to friction between partners. Lack of communication is a major contributor to the development and maintenance of sexual dysfunctions.

**LOW SEXUAL DRIVE OR DESIRE** Sex therapists may try to help people with low sexual desire kindle their sexual appetites through the use of self-stimulation (masturbation) exercises together with erotic fantasies. When working with couples, therapists prescribe mutual pleasuring exercises that the couple can perform at home or encourage them to expand their sexual repertoire to add novelty and excitement to their sex life. When a lack of sexual desire is connected with depression, the treatment focuses on treating the underlying depression. Couple therapy might be needed in order to resolve problems in the relationship that may be contributing to lack of sexual desire (Carvalho & Nobre, 2010). When problems of low sexual desire or interest appear to stem from deep-seated causes, some sex therapists use insight-oriented (psychodynamic) approaches to help uncover and resolve underlying issues.

Some cases of low sexual desire are associated with hormonal deficiencies, especially lack of the male sex hormone, testosterone. The use of a testosterone gel patch attached to the skin for administering the hormone can increase sexual desire and improve sexual function in men with abnormally low levels of testosterone (Granata et al., 2012; Montorsi et al., 2010). Testosterone treatments can have potentially serious complications, such as liver damage and possible prostate cancer, and so should be undertaken cautiously. The long-term safety of testosterone treatment is not fully determined (Heiman, 2008).

Testosterone can also help boost sexual drive and interest in menopausal women with low sexual desire, but its effectiveness in premenopausal women remains unclear (Brotto et al., 2010; Kingsberg, 2010). However, because the long-term effects of testosterone therapy on raising the risk of breast cancer and other medical conditions in women are unknown, women seeking testosterone treatment need to consult with their medical care providers to weigh the potential risks and benefits. These hormonal treatments may also lead to growth of facial hair and acne.

**DISORDERS OF SEXUAL AROUSAL** Sexual arousal results in the pooling of blood in the genital region, causing erection in the male and vaginal lubrication in the female. These changes in blood flow occur as a reflexive response to sexual stimulation; they cannot be willed. Women who have difficulty becoming sexually aroused and men with erectile problems are first educated about the fact that they need not "do" anything to become aroused. As long as their problems are psychological, not organic, they need only expose themselves to sexual stimulation under relaxed, unpressured conditions so that disruptive thoughts and anxiety do not inhibit reflexive responses.

Masters and Johnson have a couple counter performance anxiety by engaging in *sensate focus exercises*. These are nondemanding sexual contacts—sensuous exercises that do not demand sexual arousal in the form of vaginal lubrication or erection. Partners begin by massaging one another without touching the genitals. The partners learn to "pleasure" each other and to "be pleasured" by following and giving verbal instructions and by guiding each other's hands. This method fosters both communication and sexual skills and countermands anxiety because there is no demand for sexual arousal. After several sessions, direct massage of the genitals is included in pleasuring. Even when obvious signs of sexual excitement are produced (lubrication or erection), the couple does not engage in intercourse straightaway, because intercourse might create performance demands. After excitement is achieved consistently, the couple engages in a relaxed sequence of other sexual activities, culminating eventually in intercourse.

Success rates in treating individual cases of erectile disorder with sex therapy techniques vary, and we still lack firm evidence from methodologically rigorous studies supporting the effectiveness of these techniques (Frühauf et al., 2013). In the following case example, we illustrate the use of sex therapy techniques in treating erectile dysfunction.

## Victor:

### A CASE OF ERECTILE DYSFUNCTION

Victor, a 44-year-old concert violinist, was eager to show the therapist reviews of his concert tour. A solo violinist with a distinguished orchestra, Victor's life revolved around practice, performances, and reviews. He dazzled audiences with his technique and the energy of his performance. As a concert musician, Victor had exquisite control over his body, especially his hands. Yet he could not control his erectile response in the same way. Since his divorce 7 years earlier, Victor had been troubled by recurrent episodes of erectile failure. Time and time again, he had become involved in a new relationship only to find himself unable to perform sexually. Fearing repetition, he would sever the relationship. He was unable to face an audience of only one. For a while he dated casually, but then he met Michelle.

Michelle was a writer who loved music. They were a perfect match because Victor, the musician, loved literature. Michelle, a 35-year-old divorcée, was exciting, earthy, sensual, and accepting. The couple soon grew inseparable. He would practice while she would write—poetry mostly, but also short magazine pieces. Unlike some women Victor met who did not know Bach from Bartok, Michelle held her own in conversations with Victor's friends and fellow musicians over late-night dinner at Sardi's, a famous New York restaurant. They kept their own apartments; Victor needed his own space and solitude for practice.

In the 9 months of their relationship, Victor was unable to perform on the stage that mattered most to him—his canopied bed. It was just so frustrating, he said. "I would become erect and then just as I approach her to penetrate, pow! It collapses on me." Victor's history of nocturnal erections and erections during light petting suggested that he was basically suffering from performance anxiety. He was bearing down to force an erection, much as he might try to learn the fingering of a difficult violin piece. Each night became a command performance in which Victor served as his own severest critic. Rather than focus on his partner, his attention was riveted on the size of his penis. As noted by the late, great pianist Vladimir Horowitz, the worst thing a pianist can do is watch his fingers; perhaps the worst thing a man with erectile problems can do is watch his penis.

To break the vicious cycle of anxiety, erectile failure, and more anxiety, Victor and Michelle followed a sex therapy program (Rathus & Nevid, 1977) modeled after the Masters and Johnson treatment. The aim was to restore the pleasure of sexual activity, unfettered by anxiety. The couple was initially instructed to abstain from attempts at intercourse to free Victor from any pressure to perform. The couple progressed through a series of steps:

1. Relaxing together in the nude without any touching, such as when reading or watching TV together.
2. Sensate focus exercises.
3. Genital stimulation of each other manually or orally to orgasm.
4. Nondemand intercourse (intercourse performed without any pressure on the man to satisfy his partner). The man may afterward help his partner achieve orgasm by using manual or oral stimulation.
5. Resumption of vigorous intercourse (intercourse involving more vigorous thrusting and use of alternative positions and techniques that focus on mutual satisfaction). The couple is instructed not to catastrophize occasional problems that may arise.

The therapy program helped Victor overcome his erectile disorder. Victor was freed of the need to prove himself by achieving erection on command. He surrendered his post as critic. Once the spotlight was off the bed, he became a participant and not a spectator.

*From the Author's Files*

**DISORDERS OF ORGASM** Women with orgasmic disorder often harbor underlying beliefs that sex is dirty or sinful. They may have been taught not to touch themselves. They feel anxious about sex and have not learned, through trial and error, what kinds of sexual stimulation will arouse them and help them reach orgasm. Treatment in these cases includes modification of negative attitudes toward sex. When orgasmic disorder reflects the woman's feelings about or relationship with her partner, treatment also involves enhancing the relationship.

Whether or not relationships issues are involved, Masters and Johnson preferred to work with the couple and first used sensate focus exercises to lessen performance anxiety, open channels of communication, and help the couple acquire sexual skills. In using this technique, the woman directs her partner to use caresses and techniques that stimulate her. By taking charge, the woman becomes psychologically freed from the stereotype of the passive, submissive female role.

Masters and Johnson also preferred working with the couple in cases of female orgasmic dysfunction, but other sex therapists prefer to work with the woman individually by directing her to practice masturbation in private. Directed masturbation provides women opportunities to learn about their own bodies at their own pace and has a success rate of 70% to 90% (Leiblum & Rosen, 2000). It frees women of the need to rely on or please partners. Once women can reliably masturbate to orgasm, couple-oriented treatment may facilitate transfer of training to orgasm with a partner. More recent evidence shows good support for the effectiveness of psychological treatment of orgasmic dysfunction in women (Frühauf et al., 2013).

Delayed ejaculation has received little attention in the clinical literature, but may involve psychological factors such as fear, anxiety, hostility, and relationship difficulties (Rowland et al., 2010). The standard treatment, barring underlying organic problems, focuses on increasing sexual stimulation and reducing performance anxiety (Althof, 2012).

The most widely used behavioral approach to treating premature (early) ejaculation, called the *stop-start* or *stop-and-go* technique, was introduced in 1956 by a urologist with the intriguing name of James Semans. The treatment focuses on helping men acquire sexual skills that enable them to delay ejaculation (Althof et al., 2014). Typically, the partners are instructed to suspend sexual activity when the man is about to ejaculate and then resume stimulation when his sensations subside. Repeated practice enables the man to better regulate ejaculation by sensitizing him to cues that precede the ejaculatory reflex, making him more aware of his "point of no return," the point at which the ejaculatory reflex is triggered. Therapists have reported high levels of success with the stop-start method, but more evidence based on controlled research trials remains sparse (Althof et al., 2014; Frühauf et al., 2013).

**GENITAL PAIN DISORDERS** Treatment of painful intercourse generally requires medical intervention to determine and treat any underlying physical problems, such as urinary tract infections, that might be causing pain (van Lankveld et al., 2010). In cases in which vaginismus contributes to pain, psychological treatment of vaginismus may help relieve pain.

*Vaginismus* is a conditioned reflex involving the involuntary constriction of the vaginal opening. It represents a psychologically based fear of penetration rather than a medical problem. Treatment for vaginismus may include a combination of behavioral methods, including relaxation techniques and the gradual exposure method, which desensitizes the vaginal musculature to penetration over the course of a few weeks by having the woman insert fingers or plastic dilators of increasing sizes into the vagina while she remains relaxed (Reissing, 2012; ter Kuile et al., 2013). Although therapists often report good results using gradual exposure, evidence supporting its effectiveness based on controlled research trials is limited or lacking, as is the case for many types of sexual dysfunctions (Frühauf et al., 2013; van Lankveld et al., 2010). Because many women with sexual pain or vaginismus have histories of rape or sexual abuse, psychotherapy is often part of a more comprehensive treatment program to help them cope with the psychological consequences of traumatic experiences.

**BIOLOGICAL TREATMENTS OF SEXUAL DYSFUNCTION** Erectile disorder frequently has organic causes, and so it is not surprising that treatment is becoming increasingly medicalized.

Sexual arousal in both men and women depends on engorgement of blood in the genitals. Drugs that increase blood flow to the penis, such as Viagra and Cialis, are safe and effective in helping men with ED achieve more reliable erections (Lue et al., 2010; Qaseem et al., 2009). However, combining psychotherapy with medications like Viagra can be more effective than medication alone (Aubin et al., 2009). When taking pills is ineffective, alternatives such as self-injection in the penis of a drug that increases penile blood flow or use of a vacuum erection device that works like a penis pump may prove more helpful (Montorsi et al., 2010).

Investigators are exploring biomedical therapies for female sexual dysfunctions, including use of erectile dysfunction (ED) drugs such as Viagra. Research on the effectiveness of these drugs in treating female orgasmic dysfunction has yielded mixed results, but the drugs may be helpful in some cases (Ishak et al., 2010).

**ERECTILE DISORDER DRUGS.** Viagra and other erectile disorder drugs are advertised widely on television and even on billboards. Do you believe these drugs should be advertised so heavily in popular media? Why or why not?

As noted, the male sex hormone testosterone may increase sexual drive in men and postmenopausal women with diminished sexual drive or interest. However, we shouldn't think that all cases of low sexual desire should be treated with hormones. As one leading sexual health expert put it, "if someone is unhappy with her spouse, no amount of testosterone is going to fix that" (cited in Clay, 2009, p. 34). Problems of sexual desire should not be treated in isolation but in a larger context that takes into account psychological, cultural, and interpersonal contexts (Leiblum, 2010b). For example, lack of sexual desire may reflect problems in a relationship, in which case couple therapy may be used to focus more on the relationship itself. As it stands, treatment of sexual desire problems is often more complex and less effective than treatment of other types of sexual dysfunction (LoPiccolo, 2011). Although a new drug for treating low sexual desire in women that works on neurotransmitters in the brain was approved for use in 2015, significant concerns remain about its safety and effectiveness (Clarke & Pierson, 2015; Fox, 2015a).

Surgery may be effective in rare cases in which blocked blood vessels prevent blood flow to the penis or in which the penis is structurally defective. SSRIs, such as the antidepressants *fluoxetine* (Prozac), *paroxetine* (Paxil), and *sertraline* (Zoloft), work by increasing the action of the neurotransmitter serotonin. Increased availability of serotonin in the brain can have the side effect of delaying ejaculation, which can help men with early ejaculation problems (Althof et al., 2014; Mohee & Eardley, 2011).

The medicalization of treatments for sexual dysfunctions holds great promise, but no pill or biomechanical device will enhance the quality of a relationship. If individuals have serious problems with their partners, popping a pill or applying a cream is unlikely to solve them. All in all, the success rates reported for treating sexual dysfunctions through psychological or biological approaches are quite encouraging, especially when we remember that only a few generations ago there were no effective treatments.

# Paraphilic Disorders

The word *paraphilia* was coined from the Greek roots *para*, meaning *to the side of*, and *philos*, meaning *loving*. People with **paraphilias** have unusual or atypical patterns of sexual attraction that involve sexual arousal ("loving") in response to atypical stimuli ("to the side of" normally arousing stimuli). These atypical patterns of sexual arousal may be labeled by others as deviant, bizarre, or "kinky" (Lehne, 2009). Paraphilias involve strong and recurrent sexual arousal to atypical stimuli, as evidenced by fantasies, urges, or behaviors (acting upon the urges). The range of stimuli considered "atypical" include nonhuman objects, such as underwear, shoes, leather, or silk; humiliation or experience of pain in oneself or one's partner; or children and other persons who do not or cannot grant consent (Fisher et al., 2011).

The *DSM-5* classifies these patterns of abnormal behavior within a class of mental disorders called *paraphilic disorders*. Yet there is an important distinction between a paraphilia itself and a paraphilic *disorder*. In some cases, paraphilic behaviors are not associated with disturbing or distressing consequences to oneself or others. Consequently, they would not be classified as mental or psychological disorders. An example is a shoe fetishist who practices the fetishistic behavior privately at home without any negative consequences. To be diagnosed as a paraphilic disorder, the paraphilic behavior must either cause personal distress or impairment in important areas of daily functioning, or—and this is different from other diagnostic categories—involve behaviors either presently *or in the past* in which satisfaction of the sexual urge involved harm or risk of harm to other people (American Psychiatric Association, 2013). Thus, the presence of paraphilia itself is a necessary but not a sufficient condition for a diagnosis of a paraphilic disorder.

For some individuals, engaging in paraphilic acts becomes the only means of achieving sexual gratification (Lehne, 2009). They cannot become sexually aroused unless certain stimuli are used, in actuality or in fantasies. Others resort to these atypical or deviant stimuli occasionally or when under stress. Although the prevalence rates of paraphilias and paraphilic disorders are unknown, we do know that these behaviors are almost never diagnosed in women, with the exception of some cases of sexual masochism and some isolated cases of other disorders.

## Types of Paraphilias

**10.7 Define the term *paraphilia* and identify the major types.**

Paraphilic disorders lie at the interface of mental health and the law (Calvert, 2014). Some paraphilias involve behaviors that are criminal acts, as in the case of exhibitionism, pedophilia, sexual sadism, and voyeurism. These paraphilias involve acts that can cause harm against nonconsenting victims, sometimes grievous harm. Other paraphilias are victimless and relatively harmless and so do not involve violations of the law. Among these are fetishism and transvestic fetishism. Here, we focus on the paraphilias themselves, but bear in mind that a diagnosis of a paraphilic disorder requires that the paraphilia causes personal distress, impaired functioning, or harm or risk of harm to others either presently or in past episodes of paraphilic behavior.

**EXHIBITIONISM** The paraphilia of **exhibitionism** ("flashing") is characterized by strong and recurrent urges, fantasies, or behaviors of exposing of one's genitals to unsuspecting individuals for the purpose of sexual arousal. Typically, a person seeks to surprise, shock, or sexually arouse a victim. The person may masturbate while fantasizing about or actually exposing himself (almost all cases involve men). The victims are almost always women.

Relatively few cases are reported to the police and even fewer lead to an arrest, as perpetrators tend to quickly flee the scene. One case that led to capture was that of a 25-year-old man who had been exposing himself to unsuspecting women for several years (Balon, 2015). He would typically expose himself while he was in his car, either to women in parking lots or those who passed by on the street. On one occasion, the woman he victimized jotted down his license plate as he drove off and reported it to police, which led to his capture. When he was arrested, the claimed he felt hopeless because he couldn't stop himself.

A national survey found that about 4% of men (and 2% of women) reported exposing their genitals for purposes of sexual arousal (Murphy & Page, 2008). The person diagnosed with exhibitionism usually does not seek sexual contact with the victim. Nevertheless, some people who expose their genitals progress to more serious crimes of sexual aggression (McLawsen, Scalora, & Darrow, 2012). Whether or not the exhibitionist seeks physical contact, the victim may believe herself to be in danger and be traumatized by the act. Victims are probably best advised to show no reaction to a flasher, but to just continue on their way, if possible. It would be unwise to insult the exhibitionist, lest it provoke a violent reaction (McNally & Fremouw, 2014). Nor do we recommend an exaggerated show of shock or fear, which tends to reinforce the behavior.

Men who engage in exhibitionistic acts do so as a means of indirectly expressing hostility toward women, perhaps because of perceptions of mistreatment (rejection) by women in the past. Men who perform exhibitionistic acts tend to be shy, lonely, dependent, and lacking in interpersonal skills and may have had difficulty relating to women or establishing relationships with women (Griffee et al., 2014; Murphy & Page, 2008). Some doubt their masculinity and harbor feelings of inferiority. Their victims' revulsion or fear boosts their sense of mastery of the situation and heightens their sexual arousal. Consider the following case example of exhibitionism.

**EXHIBITIONISM.** Exhibitionism is a type of paraphilia that characterizes people who seek sexual arousal or gratification through exposing themselves to unsuspecting victims. People who expose themselves are usually not interested in actual sexual contact with their victims.

## Michael:
### A CASE OF EXHIBITIONISM

Michael was a 26-year-old, handsome, boyish-looking married male with a 3-year-old daughter. He had spent about one quarter of his life in reform schools and in prison. As an adolescent, he had been a fire-setter. As a young adult, he had begun to expose himself. He came to the clinic without his wife's knowledge because he was exposing himself more and more often—up to three times a day—and he was afraid that he would eventually be arrested and thrown into prison again.

Michael said he liked sex with his wife, but it wasn't as exciting as exposing himself. He couldn't prevent his exhibitionism—especially now, when he was between jobs and worried about where the family's next month's rent was coming from. He loved his daughter more than anything and couldn't stand the thought of being separated from her.

Michael's method of operation was as follows: He would look for slender adolescent females, usually near the junior high school and the senior high school. He would take his penis out of his pants and play with it while he drove up to a girl or a small group of girls. He would lower the car window, continuing to play with himself, and ask them for directions. Sometimes the girls didn't see his penis. That was okay. Sometimes they saw it and didn't react. That was okay, too. When they saw it and became flustered and afraid, that was best of all. He would start to masturbate harder, and now and then he managed to ejaculate before the girls had departed.

Michael's history was unsettled. His father had left home before he was born, and his mother had drunk heavily. He was in and out of foster homes throughout his childhood. Before he was 10 years old, he was involved in sexual activities with neighborhood boys. Now and then the boys also forced neighborhood girls into petting, and Michael had mixed feelings when the girls got upset. He felt bad for them, but he also enjoyed it. A couple of times girls seemed horrified at the sight of his penis, and it made him "really feel like a man. To see that look, you know, with a girl, not a woman, but a girl—a slender girl, that's what I'm after."

*From the Author's Files*

### TRUTH or FICTION

Wearing revealing bathing suits is a form of exhibitionism.

☑ **FALSE** Wearing revealing bathing suits is not a form of exhibitionism in the clinical sense of the term. People diagnosed with the disorder—virtually all are men—are motivated by the wish to shock and dismay unsuspecting observers, not to show off the attractiveness of their bodies.

Although some cases are reported among women, virtually all cases of exhibitionism involve men (Hugh-Jones, Gough, & Littlewood, 2005). People who engage in exhibitionism are motivated by the wish to shock and dismay unsuspecting observers, not to show off the attractiveness of their bodies. Therefore, wearing skimpy bathing suits or other revealing clothing is not a form of exhibitionism in the clinical sense of the term. Nor do exotic dancers or strippers typically meet the clinical criteria for exhibitionism. They are generally not motivated by the desire to expose themselves to unsuspecting strangers in order to arouse them or shock them. The chief motive of the exotic dancer is usually to earn a living (Philaretou, 2006). **T / F**

**FETISHISM** The French word *fétiche* is thought to derive from the Portuguese *feitico*, referring to a "magic charm." In this case, the "magic" lies in the object's ability to arouse sexually. The chief feature of **fetishism** is recurrent, powerful sexual urges, fantasies, or behaviors involving inanimate objects, such as an article of clothing (bras, panties, hosiery, boots, shoes, leather, silk, and the like; Kafka, 2010). It is not abnormal for men to become sexually aroused by the sight, feel, and smell of their lovers' undergarments. Men with fetishism, however, may prefer the object to the person and may not be able to become sexually aroused without it. They often experience sexual gratification by masturbating while fondling the object, rubbing it, or smelling it or by having their partners wear it during sexual activity.

The origins of fetishism can be traced to early childhood in many cases. Most individuals with a rubber fetish in an early research sample were able to recall first experiencing a fetishistic attraction to rubber sometime between the ages of 4 and 10 (Gosselin & Wilson, 1980).

**TRANSVESTISM** The paraphilia of **transvestism** (also called *transvestic fetishism*) refers to individuals who have recurrent and powerful urges, fantasies, or behaviors in which they become sexually aroused by cross-dressing. Although other men with fetishes can be satisfied by handling objects such as women's clothing while they masturbate, transvestite men want to wear them. They may wear full feminine attire and makeup or favor one particular article of clothing, such as women's stockings. Although some transvestite men are gay, transvestism is usually found among heterosexual men (Långström &

Zucker, 2005; Taylor & Rupp, 2004). The man typically cross-dresses in private and imagines himself to be a woman whom he is stroking as he masturbates. Some frequent transvestite clubs or become involved in a transvestic subculture. Some transvestite men are sexually stimulated by fantasies that their own bodies are female (J. M. Bailey, 2003a).

Men with a transgender identity may cross-dress to "pass" as women or because they are not comfortable dressing in male clothing. Some gay men also cross-dress, perhaps to make a statement about overly rigid gender roles, but not because they seek to become sexually aroused. Because cross-dressing among gay men and transgender individuals is performed for reasons other than sexual arousal or gratification, their behavior is not classified as transvestic fetishism. Nor are female impersonators who cross-dress for theatrical purposes considered to have a form of transvestism.

Most men with transvestism are married and engage in sexual activity with their wives, but they seek additional sexual gratification through dressing as women, as in the following case.

## Archie:

### A CASE OF TRANSVESTIC FETISHISM

Archie was a 55-year-old plumber who had been cross-dressing for many years. There was a time when he would go out in public as a woman, but as his prominence in the community grew, he became more afraid of being discovered. His wife, Myrna, knew of his "peccadillo," especially because he borrowed many of her clothes, and she also encouraged him to stay at home, offering to help him with his "weirdness." For many years, his paraphilia had been restricted to the home.

The couple came to the clinic at the urging of the wife. Myrna described how Archie had imposed his will on her for 20 years. Archie would wear her undergarments and masturbate while she told him how disgusting he was. (The couple also regularly engaged in "normal" sexual intercourse, which Myrna enjoyed.) The cross-dressing situation had come to a head because a teenaged daughter had almost walked into the couple's bedroom while they were acting out Archie's fantasies.

With Myrna out of the consulting room, Archie explained that he grew up in a family with several older sisters. He described how underwear had been perpetually hanging all around the one bathroom to dry. As an adolescent, Archie experimented with rubbing against articles of underwear, then with trying them on. On one occasion, a sister walked in while he was modeling panties before the mirror. She told him he was a "dredge to society," and he straightaway experienced unparalleled sexual excitement. He masturbated when she left the room, and his orgasm was the strongest of his young life.

Archie did not think that there was anything wrong with wearing women's undergarments and masturbating. He was not about to give it up, regardless of whether his marriage was destroyed as a result. Myrna's main concern was finally separating herself from Archie's "sickness." She didn't care what he did anymore, so long as he did it by himself. "Enough is enough," she said.

That was the compromise the couple worked out in marital therapy. Archie would engage in his fantasies by himself. He would choose times when Myrna was not at home, and she would not be informed of his activities. He would also be very, very careful to choose times when the children were not around.

Six months later, the couple was together and content. Archie had replaced Myrna's input into his fantasies with transvestic-sadomasochistic magazines. Myrna said, "I see no evil, hear no evil, smell no evil." They continued to have sexual intercourse. After a while, Myrna even forgot to check to see which underwear had been used.

*From the Author's Files*

**VOYEURISM** The paraphilia of **voyeurism** ("peeping") involves strong and recurrent sexual urges, fantasies, or behaviors in which a person becomes sexually aroused by watching unsuspecting people, generally strangers, who are naked, disrobing, or engaging in sexual activity. The person who engages in voyeurism does not typically seek sexual activity with the person or persons being observed, but becomes sexually aroused by the act of watching. Like exhibitionism, virtually all cases of voyeurism occur among men (Langstrom, 2010).

Are acts of watching your partner disrobe or viewing sexually explicit films forms of voyeurism? The answer is no. The people who are observed know they are being observed by their partners or will be observed by film audiences. Nor is attending a strip club for purposes of sexual stimulation considered abnormal, as it does not involve seeking sexual arousal by watching unsuspecting persons. People may also frequent strip clubs for reasons other than sexual gratification, such as bonding experiences with friends.

The voyeur usually masturbates while watching or while fantasizing about watching. Voyeurs are often lacking in sexual experiences and may harbor deep feelings of inferiority or inadequacy (Leue, Borchard, & Hoyer, 2004). Peeping may be the voyeur's only sexual outlet. Some people engage in voyeuristic acts in which they place themselves in risky situations. The prospect of being discovered or injured apparently heightens their excitement.

**FROTTEURISM** The French word *frottage* refers to the artistic technique of making a drawing by rubbing against a raised object. The chief feature of the paraphilia of **frotteurism** is recurrent, powerful sexual urges, fantasies, or behaviors in which a person becomes sexually aroused by rubbing against or touching a nonconsenting person. Frotteurism, which is also called "mashing," often occurs in crowded places, such as subway cars or platforms, buses, or elevators (Clark et al., 2014). The rubbing or touching, not the coercive aspect of the act, sexually arouses the man. He may imagine himself enjoying an exclusive, affectionate sexual relationship with the victim. Because the physical contact is brief and furtive, people who perform acts of frotteurism stand only a small chance of being caught by authorities. Even victims may not realize at the time what has happened or register much protest. In the following case, a man victimized about 1,000 women over several years but was arrested only twice.

## Bumping on the Subway:
### A CASE OF FROTTEURISM

A 45-year-old man was seen by a psychiatrist following his second arrest for rubbing against a woman in the subway. He would select as his target a woman in her 20s as she entered the subway station. He would position himself behind her on the platform and wait for the train to enter the station. He would then follow her into the subway car and when the doors closed, would begin bumping against her buttocks, while fantasizing that they were enjoying having intercourse in a loving and consensual manner. About half of the time, he would reach orgasm. He would then continue on his way to work. Sometimes, when he hadn't reached orgasm, he would change trains and seek another victim. Although he felt guilty for a time after each episode, he would soon become preoccupied with thoughts about his next encounter. He never gave any thought to the feelings his victims might have about what he had done to them. Although he was married to the same woman for 25 years, he appeared to be rather socially inept and unassertive, especially with women.

**SOURCE:** *Adapted from Spitzer et al., 1994, pp. 164–165*

**WHAT DID HE JUST DO?** Mashing, or unwelcome sexual rubbing or touching, occurs most often in tight crowded places, such as on a subway car at rush hour.

**PEDOPHILIA** The word **pedophilia** derives from the Greek *paidos*, meaning *child*. People with pedophilia have recurrent and powerful sexual urges or fantasies or behaviors involving sexual activity with children (typically 13 years old or younger). To be diagnosed with pedophilic disorder, a person must be at least 16 years of age and at least 5 years older than the child or children toward whom the person is sexually attracted or whom the person has victimized. However, the diagnosis does not apply to a person in late adolescence who has a continuing relationship with a 12- or 13-year-old (American Psychiatric Association, 2013). In some cases, the person with pedophilia is attracted only to children. In others, the person is attracted to both children and adults.

Although most cases of pedophilic disorder involve men who are sexually attracted to children, pedophilia may involve men or women who seek sexual contact with either boys or girls. Some people with pedophilia restrict their deviant activities to looking at or undressing children, whereas others engage in exhibitionism, kissing, fondling, oral sex, and anal intercourse and, in the case of girls, vaginal intercourse. Not being worldly wise, children are often taken advantage of by molesters, who inform them they are "educating" them, "showing them something," or doing something they will "like."

Some pedophilic men limit their sexual activity with children to incestuous relations with family members; others only molest children outside the family. Sexual molestation of children is a criminal act and deservedly so. However, not all child molesters have pedophilic disorder, and not all people with pedophilic disorder molest children (Berlin, 2015). Some individuals diagnosed with the disorder have recurrent urges and fantasies about sexual activity with children and may masturbate while fantasizing, but they do not act out on their urges by molesting children. On the other hand, some child molesters experience only occasional pedophilic urges, perhaps during times of opportunity, and so would not meet the criterion of recurrent urges to warrant a clinical diagnosis of pedophilic disorder.

Despite the stereotype, most cases of pedophilia do not involve "dirty old men" who hang around schoolyards in raincoats. Men with this disorder (virtually all cases involve men) are usually (otherwise) law-abiding, respected citizens in their 30s or 40s. Most are married or divorced and have children of their own. They are usually well acquainted with their victims, who are typically either relatives or friends of the family. Many cases of pedophilia are not isolated incidents. They often begin when children are very young and continue for years until they are discovered or the relationship is broken off.

The origins of pedophilia are complex and varied. Some cases fit the stereotype of the shy, passive, socially inept, and isolated man who is threatened by relationships with adult women and so turns to children, who are less critical and demanding. Researchers find that pedophilic men tend to have fewer romantic relationships than other men, and the relationships they do have tend to be less satisfying (Seto, 2008). In some cases, childhood sexual experiences with other children may have been so enjoyable that the man, as an adult, attempts to recapture the excitement of earlier years. In some cases, men who were sexually abused in childhood reverse the situation in an effort to establish feelings of mastery.

***Effects of Sexual Abuse on Children*** High-profile cases in the news in recent years, such as the conviction of former Penn State assistant football coach Jerry Sandusky, have highlighted the problem of child sexual abuse. The occurrence of child sexual abuse is much more common than many people suspect.

A recent review of existing research showed that nearly 8% of adult males and nearly 20% of adult females reported some form of sexual abuse before the age of 18 (Pereda et al., 2009). Other recent estimates peg the frequency of sexual abuse during childhood at even higher levels—30% of girls and 15% of boys (Irish, Kobayashi, & Delahanty, 2010). The typical abuser is not the proverbial stranger lurking in the shadows, but a relative or step-relative of the child, a family friend, or a neighbor—someone who has held and then abused the child's trust (Beauregard, Proulx, & LeClerc, 2014; LeClerc et al., 2014).

Sexual abuse can inflict great psychological harm, whether it is perpetrated by a family member, an acquaintance, or a stranger. Abused children may suffer from a litany of psychological problems involving anger, anxiety, depression, eating disorders, inappropriate sexual behavior, aggressive behavior, drug abuse, suicide attempts, posttraumatic stress disorder, low self-esteem, sexual dysfunction, and feelings of detachment (e.g., Castellini, Maggi, & Ricca, 2014) Adults who were sexually abused as children stand a higher risk of developing psychological disorders and significant physical health problems, as well as problems with memory and cognitive functioning (Gould et al., 2012; Irish, Kobayashi, & Delahanty, 2010). A U.K. study showed that people with a history of child sexual abuse were between 6 and 10 times more likely to engage in suicidal behavior (threatening suicide or making suicide attempts) in adulthood (Bebbington et al., 2009).

We should also note that psychological effects of sexual abuse on children are variable, and no single pattern applies in all cases (Whitelock, Lamb, & Rentfrow, 2013). Sexual abuse may also cause genital injuries and psychosomatic problems such as stomachaches and headaches.

Younger children sometimes react with tantrums or aggressive or antisocial behavior. Older children often develop substance abuse problems. Some abused children become socially withdrawn and retreat into fantasy or refuse to leave the house. Abused children may also show regressive behaviors, such as thumb sucking, fear of the dark, and fear of strangers. Many survivors of childhood sexual abuse develop posttraumatic stress disorder. They suffer flashbacks, nightmares, emotional numbing, and feel alienated from other people (Herrera & McCloskey, 2003).

The sexual development of abused children may veer off in dysfunctional directions. For example, abused children may become prematurely sexually active or promiscuous in adolescence and adulthood (Herrera & McCloskey, 2003). Adolescent girls who have been sexually abused tend to be more sexually active than their peers.

The effects of childhood sexual abuse tend to be similar in boys and girls (Maikovich-Fong & Jaffee, 2010). Both tend to become fearful and have trouble sleeping, for example. However, some investigators report finding gender differences in the effects of abuse, with the most pronounced difference being that boys more often externalize their problems, often through physical aggression. Girls more often internalize their difficulties—for example, by becoming depressed (Edwards et al., 2003).

Psychological problems may continue into adolescence and adulthood in the form of posttraumatic stress disorder, anxiety, depression, substance abuse, and relationship problems. Late adolescence and early adulthood are particularly difficult times for survivors of child sexual abuse, because unresolved feelings of anger and guilt and a deep sense of mistrust can prevent the development of intimate relationships. Evidence shows that women who blame themselves for the abuse experience relatively lower self-esteem and greater depression than those who do not (Edwards et al., 2003). Childhood sexual abuse is also linked to later development of borderline personality disorder, a psychological disorder discussed in Chapter 12.

**SEXUAL MASOCHISM** **Sexual masochism** derives its name from the Austrian novelist Ritter Leopold von Sacher Masoch (1835–1895), who wrote stories and novels about men who sought sexual gratification from women by inflicting pain on themselves, often in the form of flagellation (being beaten or whipped). Sexual masochism involves strong and recurrent sexual urges, fantasies, or behaviors in which a person becomes sexually aroused by being humiliated, bound, flogged, or made to suffer in other ways. In cases of sexual masochism disorder, the urges either are acted on or cause significant personal distress. In some cases of sexual masochism, a person cannot attain sexual gratification in the absence of pain or humiliation. Sexual masochism is the one form of paraphilia found with some frequency in women, although it is more common among men (Logan, 2008).

## TRUTH *or* FICTION

Some people cannot become sexually aroused unless they are subjected to pain or humiliation.

☑ **TRUE** These people have a form of paraphilia called *sexual masochism.*

In some cases, sexual masochism involves binding or mutilating oneself during masturbation or sexual fantasies. In others, a partner is engaged to restrain (bondage), blindfold (sensory bondage), paddle, or whip the person. Some partners are prostitutes; others are consensual partners who are asked to perform the sadistic role. In some cases, a person may desire, for purposes of sexual gratification, to be urinated or defecated upon or be subjected to verbal abuse. **T / F**

A most dangerous expression of sexual masochism is **hypoxyphilia**, in which participants become sexually aroused by being deprived of oxygen—for example, by using a noose, plastic bag, chemical, or pressure on the chest during a sexual act, such as masturbation. The oxygen deprivation is usually accompanied by fantasies of asphyxiating or being asphyxiated by a lover. People who engage in this activity generally discontinue it before they lose consciousness, but occasional deaths due to suffocation are reported.

**SEXUAL SADISM** **Sexual sadism** is named after the infamous Marquis de Sade, the 18th-century Frenchman who wrote stories about the pleasures of achieving sexual gratification by inflicting pain or humiliation on others. Sexual sadism is the flip side of sexual masochism. It is characterized by recurrent, powerful sexual urges, fantasies, or behaviors in which a person becomes sexually aroused by inflicting physical or psychological suffering or humiliation on another person.

People with sexually sadistic fantasies sometimes recruit consenting partners, who may be lovers or wives with masochistic interests or prostitutes who are paid to play a masochistic role. However, some sexual sadists—a small minority—stalk and assault nonconsenting victims and become aroused by inflicting pain or suffering on them (Yates, Hucker, & Kingston, 2008). Sadistic rapists fall into this group. Laboratory evidence shows that sexual sadists tend to become genitally aroused by scenes of violence or injury to a victim in a sexual context (Seto et al., 2012). Let us note, however, that most rapists do not become sexually aroused by inflicting pain; many even lose sexual interest when they see their victims in pain.

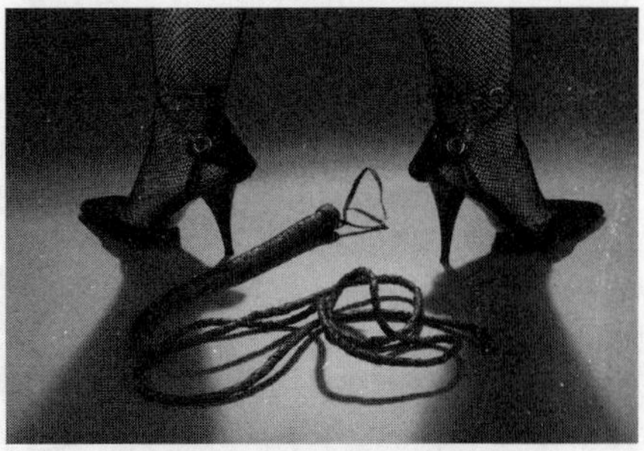

**ROLE-PLAYING OR PARAPHILIA?** Sadomasochism is a form of sexual role-playing between consensual partners. When does this behavior cross the line and become a paraphilia?

Many people have occasional sadistic or masochistic fantasies or engage in sex play involving simulated or mild forms of **sadomasochism** with their partners. Sadomasochism refers to a practice of mutually gratifying sexual interactions involving both sadistic and masochistic acts. Stimulation may take the form of using a feather brush to "strike" one's partner, so that no actual pain is administered. This and other variations, such as love bites, hair pulls, and mild scratching in the context of mutually consensual relationships, are considered to fall within the normal spectrum of human sexual interactions (Laws & O'Donohue, 2012). Rituals such as the "master and slave" game are staged, as though they were scenes in a play. People who engage in sadomasochism frequently switch roles. The clinical diagnosis of *sexual masochism disorder* or *sexual sadism disorder* is not brought to bear unless these sexual behaviors, urges, or fantasies cause personal distress or negatively impact a person's ability to function in meeting social, occupational, or other roles or risked or caused harm to others.

**JOCELYN: EXPLORING SADISM AND MASOCHISM**

**OTHER PARAPHILIAS** There are many other paraphilias. These include making obscene phone calls (telephone scatologia), necrophilia (sexual urges or fantasies involving contact with corpses), partialism (sole focus on part of the body, such as the breasts), zoophilia (sexual urges or fantasies involving contact with animals), and sexual arousal associated with feces (coprophilia), enemas (klismaphilia), and urine (urophilia).

We discuss what may be a new psychological disorder of modern times in *Abnormal Psychology in the Digital Age: Cybersex Addiction—A New Psychological Disorder?*

## Theoretical Perspectives

**10.8 Describe theoretical perspectives on paraphilias.**

As in the case of so many psychological disorders, approaches to understanding the causes of paraphilias emphasize psychological and biological factors.

**PSYCHOLOGICAL PERSPECTIVES** Psychodynamic theorists see many of the paraphilias as defenses against leftover castration anxiety from the phallic period of psychosexual development (see Chapter 2; Friedman & Downey, 2008). In Freudian theory, a young boy develops a sexual desire for his mother and perceives his father as a rival. Castration anxiety—the unconscious fear that the father will retaliate by removing the organ that

# Abnormal Psychology in the Digital Age

## CYBERSEX ADDICTION—A NEW PSYCHOLOGICAL DISORDER?

"How can I compete with hundreds of anonymous others who are now in our bed, in his head? Our bed is crowded with countless faceless strangers, where once we were intimate."

—A 34-year-old woman, married 14 years to a minister

"Porn sites get more visitors each month than Netflix, Amazon and Twitter combined."

—The Huffington Post

"Sex on the 'Net is like heroin. It grabs [people] and takes over their lives. And it's very difficult to treat because the people affected don't want to give it up."

—Mark Schwartz, Masters and Johnson Institute

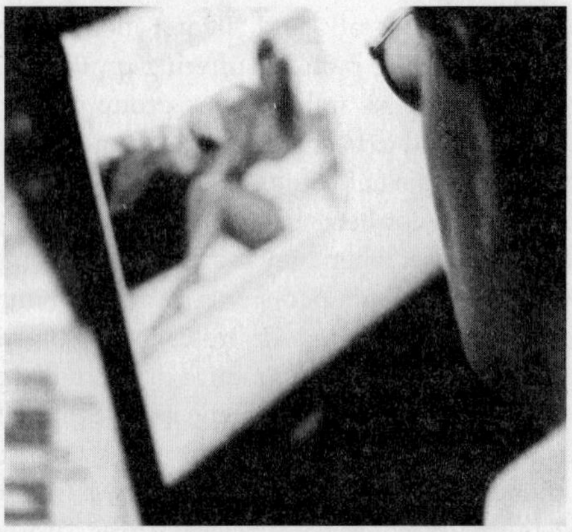

**CYBERSEX ADDICTION.** Easy access to cybersex may be feeding a new psychological disorder called *cybersex addiction*. Many compulsive users of online sexual content deny that they have a problem, even though their behavior can seriously disrupt their work and home lives.

Internet use has exploded in recent years, and cybersex is a major factor accounting for this growth. *Cybersex* includes such behaviors as surfing Internet porn sites, engaging in online sex with people in Internet chat rooms, and progressing to real-life sexual encounters with people who advertise their services online. Many people, mostly men, spend dozens of hours each week viewing Internet porn (Cooper et al., 2004; Daneback, Ross, & Månsson., 2006). People in intimate romantic relationships who peruse Internet porn may not see what they are doing as cheating or infidelity (Jones & Hertlein, 2012).

For some, the attraction to cybersex may be a relatively harmless recreational pursuit. However, experts express concern that for others, easy access to cybersex is feeding a new type of psychological disorder called *cybersex addiction* (Green, Carnes, & Carnes, 2012). An estimated 6% of adult users of the Internet show evidence of sexual compulsiveness in their online behavior, such as experiencing withdrawal symptoms when they are away from the Internet for a length of time (J. M. Bailey, 2003b). People with cybersex addiction may develop problems becoming sexually aroused by their flesh-and-blood partners, whom they see as less sexually desirable than porn actors and actresses (Griffiths, 2012).

People with cybersex compulsions can be likened to drug addicts, using the Internet for gratification in much the same way that a drug addict uses a drug of choice (Ayres & Haddock, 2009; Schneider, 2005). Based on a survey of 9,265 men and women who admitted online surfing for sex, psychologist Al Cooper and his colleagues (Cooper, Delmonico, & Burg, 2000) concluded that the web is "the crack cocaine of sexual compulsivity," with at least 1% of respondents strongly addicted to online sex. Although some studies find that men who become addicted to online sex have ample sexual opportunities in the real world, other studies find them to be lonelier than other men (Yoder, Virden, & Amin, 2005).

Physician Jennifer Schneider (2003, 2004) conducted a survey of 94 family members affected by cybersex addiction and found that it can arise even among people who are in good relationships and who have an abundance of sexual opportunities. "Sex on the 'Net is just so seductive and it's so easy to stumble upon it [that] people who are vulnerable can get hooked before they know it" (cited in Brody, 2000, p. F7).

Schneider (2005) defends the view that cybersex addiction is a true addiction, characterized by "loss of control, continuation of the behavior despite significant adverse consequences, and preoccupation or obsession with obtaining the drug or pursuing the behavior" (p. 76). Although behavioral addictions do not involve taking drugs, they may cause changes in the brain, such as releasing endorphins—brain chemicals whose actions mimic those of the narcotic morphine—that maintain the behavior.

Sexual arousal and orgasm also reinforce the behavior. As researcher Mark Schwartz noted: "Intense orgasms from the minimal investment of a few keystrokes are powerfully reinforcing. Cybersex affords easy, inexpensive access to a myriad of ritualized encounters with idealized partners" (cited in Brody, 2000, p. F7).

As with other addictions, tolerance to cybersex stimulation can develop, prompting a person to take more and more risks to recapture the initial high. Online viewing that began as a harmless recreation can become all-consuming and even lead to real sexual encounters with people met online. People with cybersex compulsions sometimes ignore their partners and children and risk their jobs. Many companies monitor employees' online activities, and visits to sexual sites can cost employees their jobs. Schneider reports other adverse consequences, including broken relationships. Partners often report feeling betrayed, ignored, and unable to compete with the online fantasies.

A 34-year-old woman married 14 years wondered how she could possibly compete with all the anonymous women her husband brought into bed with her in his mind. She felt that her bed, which once had been a place of intimacy for them, was now crowded with all these faceless strangers (Brody, 2000).

Cybersex addiction is not yet recognized as an official diagnostic category, nor can we clearly determine where recreational use of sexual material on the Internet ends and sexual compulsion begins. Yet the problem of cybersex compulsion continues to grow, especially with expanded broadband availability that allows streaming of explicit sexual video programming to computer screens around the world.

has become associated with sexual pleasure through masturbation—motivates the boy to give up his incestuous yearnings for his mother and identify with the aggressor, his father. However, a failure to successfully resolve the conflict may lead to leftover castration anxiety in adulthood. The unconscious mind equates the disappearance of the penis during genital intercourse with adult women with the risk of castration. At an unconscious level, leftover castration anxiety prompts the man to displace his sexual arousal onto "safer" sexual activities, such as having sexual contact with women's undergarments, surreptitiously viewing others disrobing, or having sex with children he can easily control. In exposing his genitals, the exhibitionist may be unconsciously seeking reassurance that his penis is secure, as if he were proclaiming, "Look! I have a penis!" Psychodynamic views of the origins of paraphilias remain speculative and controversial. We lack any direct evidence that men with paraphilias are handicapped by unresolved castration anxiety.

More recently, theorists speculated that paraphilias such as sexual masochism may represent a temporary escape from ordinary selfhood (Knoll & Hazelwood, 2009). Focusing on painful and pleasant sensations in the moment and on the experience of being a sexual object may provide a temporary reprieve from the responsibilities of maintaining a mature, responsible sense of self.

Learning theorists explain paraphilias in terms of conditioning and observational learning. Some object or activity becomes inadvertently associated with sexual arousal. The object or activity then gains the capacity to elicit sexual arousal. For example, Kinsey Institute researcher June Reinisch (1990) speculated that the earliest awareness of sexual arousal or response (such as erection) may have been connected with rubber pants or diapers. A person makes an association between the two, setting the stage for the development of a rubber fetish, or a boy who glimpses his mother's stockings on the towel rack while he is masturbating goes on to develop a fetish for stockings (Breslow, 1989). Orgasm in the presence of the object reinforces the erotic connection, especially when it occurs repeatedly. Yet if fetishes were acquired by mechanical association, we might expect people to develop fetishes to stimuli that are inadvertently and repeatedly connected with sexual activity, such as bed sheets, pillows, or even ceilings. But they do not. The *meaning* of the stimulus plays a primary role. The development of fetishes may depend on eroticizing certain types of stimuli (like women's undergarments) by incorporating them within sexual fantasies and masturbation rituals.

Family relationships may play a role. Some transvestite men report a history of "petticoat punishment" during childhood. That is, they were humiliated by being dressed in girls' attire. Perhaps the adult transvestite male is attempting psychologically to convert humiliation into mastery by achieving an erection and engaging in sexual activity despite being attired in female clothing.

**BIOLOGICAL PERSPECTIVES** Researchers are investigating the possible role of biological factors in paraphilic behavior. Investigators find evidence of higher-than-average sex drives in men with paraphilias, as evidenced by a higher frequency of sexual fantasies and urges and a shorter *refractory period* after orgasm by masturbation (i.e., length of time needed to become rearoused; Haake et al., 2003; Jordan et al., 2011). Some professionals refer to the heightened sex drive that may apply to some cases of paraphilia as *hypersexual arousal disorder*—the opposite of hypoactive sexual desire disorder. In such cases, a person may have repeated difficulty controlling urges to engage in illegal or maladaptive behaviors, such as frequenting prostitutes, masturbating in public, or uncontrolled use of pornography (Levine, 2012).

Other investigators find differences between paraphilic men and male control subjects in brainwave patterns in response to paraphilic (fetishistic and sadomasochistic) images and control images (nude women, genital intercourse, oral sex; Waismann et al., 2003). The meaning of these differences is not yet clear, but it is possible that in paraphilic men, the brain responds differently to different types of sexual stimuli than it does in other men. Recently, investigators found they could distinguish men with pedophilia from (nonpedophilic) healthy men with near 100% accuracy by examining brain responses, as measured by an fMRI scan, to images of nude children versus nude women (Ponseti et al., 2012). Although further research is needed, it is conceivable that disturbances in brain networks involved in sexual arousal may increase susceptibility to pedophilia in general or perhaps in men with a history of childhood trauma or abuse.

With time, we can expect to learn more about the biological underpinnings of paraphilic behavior. Like other sexual patterns, paraphilias may have multiple biological, psychological, and sociocultural origins. Might our understanding of them thus be best approached from a theoretical framework that incorporates multiple perspectives? Sex researcher John Money (2000), for example, traced the origins of paraphilias to childhood. He suggested that childhood experiences etch a pattern in the brain, which he called a *lovemap*. A lovemap determines the types of stimuli and activities that become sexually arousing (Goldie, 2014). In the paraphilias, lovemaps may become distorted or "vandalized" by early traumatic experiences. Evidence does tie early childhood emotional or sexual trauma to later development of paraphilias in many cases (Barbaree & Blanchard, 2008). As researcher Gregory Lehne notes, "A boy who is sexually abused may develop paraphilic fantasies involving sexual activity with a boy.... Being punished or embarrassed by being cross-dressed as a young boy may lead to some boys eroticizing the experience, which later is expressed as transvestism" (2009, p. 15).

# Treatment of Paraphilic Disorders

**10.9 Identify methods for treating paraphilic disorders.**

A major problem with treating paraphilic disorders is that many people who engage in these behaviors are generally not motivated to change. They may not want to alter their behavior unless they believe that treatment will relieve them from serious punishment, such as imprisonment or loss of a family life. Consequently, they don't typically seek treatment on their own. They usually receive treatment in prison after they have been convicted of a sexual offense, such as exhibitionism, voyeurism, or child molestation, or they are referred to a treatment provider by the courts. Under these circumstances, it is not surprising that sex offenders resist treatment. Therapists recognize that treatment may be futile when clients lack the motivation to change their behavior. Nonetheless, some forms of treatment, principally cognitive-behavioral therapy, may be helpful to sex offenders who seek to change their behavior (Abracen & Looman, 2004).

**PSYCHOANALYSIS** Psychoanalysts attempt to bring childhood sexual conflicts (typically of an Oedipal nature) into awareness so they can be resolved in light of an individual's adult personality (Laws & Marshall, 2003). Favorable results from individual case studies appear in the literature from time to time, but there is a dearth of controlled investigations to support the efficacy of psychodynamic treatment of paraphilias.

**COGNITIVE-BEHAVIORAL THERAPY** Traditional psychoanalysis involves a lengthy process of exploration of the childhood roots of the problem. Cognitive-behavioral therapy is briefer and focuses directly on changing the problem behavior. Cognitive-behavioral therapy includes a number of specific techniques, such as aversive conditioning, covert sensitization, and social skills training, to help eliminate paraphilic behaviors and strengthen appropriate sexual behaviors (Kaplan & Krueger, 2012; Marshall & Marshall, 2015). In many cases, a combination of methods is used.

The goal of *aversive conditioning* (also called *aversive therapy*) is to induce a negative emotional response to unacceptable stimuli or fantasies. Applying a conditioning model, sexual stimuli involving children are repeatedly paired with an aversive stimulus (e.g., an unpleasant smell, such as ammonia) in the hope that a person will develop a conditioned aversion toward the paraphilic stimulus (Seto, 2008). Aversive conditioning can reduce sexual arousal in response to children as stimuli, but questions remain about how lasting these effects may be (Marshall & Marshall, 2015; Seto, 2008).

*Covert sensitization* is a variation of aversion therapy in which paraphilic fantasies are paired with aversive stimuli in imagination. In a landmark study, men with pedophilia and men who had engaged in exhibitionism were first instructed to fantasize pedophilic or exhibitionistic scenes (Maletzky, 1980). Then:

> At a point ... when sexual pleasure is aroused, aversive images are presented.... Examples might include a pedophiliac fellating a child, but discovering a festering sore on the boy's penis, an exhibitionist exposing to a woman but suddenly being discovered by his wife or the police, or a pedophiliac laying a young boy down in a field, only to lie next to him in a pile of dog feces. (Maletzky, 1980, p. 308)

In a 25-year follow-up study of 7,275 sex offenders who received similar treatment, Maletzky and Steinhauser (2002) found that benefits were maintained for many men with exhibitionism but few with pedophilia. However, fewer than 50% of the original participants could be contacted after this amount of time had elapsed.

*Social skills training* helps an individual improve his ability to develop and maintain relationships with adult partners. The therapist might first model a desired behavior, such as asking a woman out on a date or handling rejection. The client might then rehearse the behavior, with the therapist playing the woman's role. The therapist provides feedback and additional guidance and modeling to help the client further improve his social skills.

Although research on the effectiveness of treatment for cybersex addiction or other forms of sexual addiction is limited by the absence of controlled studies (Rosenberg, Carnes, & O'Connor, 2015), some promising results from psychological and pharmacological treatment of individual cases are reported (Dhuffar & Griffiths, 2015).

**BIOMEDICAL THERAPIES** There is no magic pill or other medical cure for paraphilic disorders. Yet progress is reported in treating exhibitionism, voyeurism, and fetishism with SSRI antidepressants, such as Prozac (Assumpcao et al., 2014; Thibaut, 2012) Why SSRIs? We noted in Chapter 5 that SSRIs are often helpful in treating obsessive-compulsive disorder, a psychological disorder characterized by recurrent obsessions and compulsions. Paraphilias appear to mirror these behavioral patterns, which suggests that they may fall within an obsessive-compulsive spectrum of behaviors. People with paraphilias often experience obsessive thoughts or images of the paraphilic object or stimulus, such as intrusive and recurrent mental images of young children. Many also feel compelled to repeatedly carry out the paraphilic acts.

*Antiandrogen* drugs reduce levels of testosterone in the bloodstream. Testosterone energizes sexual drives, so the use of antiandrogens may reduce sexual drives and urges, including urges to sexually offend and related fantasies, especially when they are used in combination with psychological treatment (Assumpção et al., 2014; Fisher & Maggi, 2014; Kellar & Hignite, 2014). However, antiandrogens do not completely eliminate paraphilic urges, nor do they change the types of erotic stimuli to which the client is attracted.

Before moving on, you may want to review Table 10.3, which provides an overview of paraphilias, and Table 10.4, which provides an overview of causal factors and treatment approaches.

## Table 10.3 Overview of Paraphilias

| Major Types of Paraphilias: Atypical or deviant patterns of sexual gratification; excepting masochism, these disorders occur almost exclusively among males | |
|---|---|
| **Exhibitionism** | Sexual gratification from exposing one's genitals in public |
| **Voyeurism** | Sexual gratification from observing unsuspecting others who are naked, undressing, or engaging in sexual arousal |
| **Sexual masochism** | Sexual gratification associated with the receipt of humiliation or pain |
| **Fetishism** | Sexual attraction to inanimate objects or particular body parts |
| **Frotteurism** | Sexual gratification associated with acts of bumping or rubbing against nonconsenting strangers |
| **Sexual sadism** | Sexual gratification associated with inflicting humiliation or pain on others |
| **Transvestic fetishism** | Sexual gratification associated with cross-dressing |
| **Pedophilia** | Sexual attraction to children |

## Table 10.4 Overview of Paraphilias: Causal Factors and Treatment Approaches

| | |
|---|---|
| **Causal Factors: Multiple causes may be involved** | |
| **Learning perspective** | • Atypical stimuli become conditioned stimuli for sexual arousal as the result of prior pairing with sexual activity<br>• Atypical stimuli may become eroticized by incorporating them within erotic and masturbatory fantasies |
| **Psychodynamic perspective** | • Unresolved castration anxiety from childhood leads to sexual arousal being displaced onto safer objects or activities |
| **Multifactorial perspective** | • Sexual or physical abuse in childhood may corrupt normal sexual arousal patterns |
| **Treatment Approaches: Results remain questionable** | |
| **Biomedical treatment** | • Drugs to help individuals control deviant sexual urges or reduce sexual drives |
| **Cognitive-behavioral therapy** | • Includes aversive conditioning (pairing deviant stimuli with aversive stimuli), covert sensitization (pairing the undesirable behavior with an aversive stimulus in imagination), and nonaversive methods, such as social skills training that helps individuals acquire more adaptive behaviors |

# A CLOSER Look

## ARE RAPISTS MENTALLY ILL?

The prevalence of **rape** is shockingly high in the United States. According to the U.S. Department of Justice, 284,350 forcible rapes were reported in the United States in 2014, the most recent year for which statistics were available (Truman & Langton, 2015). However, these statistics greatly underreport the actual incidence of rape, because the great majority of rapes are not reported to authorities or prosecuted. Many women do not report rape because they fear being humiliated by the criminal justice system. Some fear reprisal from their families or from the rapist himself. Many women mistakenly believe that coercive sex is rape only when the rapist is a stranger or uses a weapon.

According to the federal Centers for Disease Control and Prevention, 19.3% of women and 1.7% of men report they have been raped (Breiding et al., 2014). Although women of all ages are at risk of being raped, two of three rapes involve young women between the ages of 11 and 24, and about 80% involve girls and young women under the age of 25 (CDC, 2011a).

According to the U.S. Department of Justice, about five in six rapes (83%) are *acquaintance rapes*—rapes committed by people known to the victim (Truman & Langton, 2015). Survivors of rape may not perceive sexual assaults by acquaintances as rapes. Even if a police report is filed, it may be treated as "misunderstanding" or "lovers' quarrel," rather than a violent crime. Only about one quarter of the women in a large-scale national college survey who were sexually assaulted viewed themselves as victims of rape (Koss & Kilpatrick, 2001; Rozee & Koss, 2001). This bears repeating: Only about one in four college women labeled what happened to them when they were sexually assaulted as rape.

Figure 10.2 shows the relationship patterns of rapist and victim based on the same large-scale national survey of college women. The great majority of rapes of college women were committed by men with whom the women were acquainted, including dates, nonromantic acquaintances, and family members. In nearly 90% of the rapes in the college sample, the woman was acquainted with the assailant. In any given year, about 3% of college women in the United States suffer rape or attempted rape (Fisher et al., 2003). **T / F**

**Figure 10.2** Relative percentages of stranger rapes and acquaintance rapes.

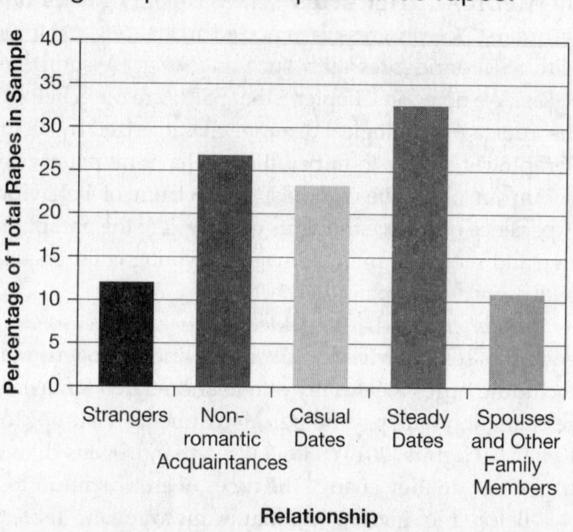


### TRUTH or FICTION

College women are more likely to be raped by strangers than by men they know.

☑ **FALSE** According to a large-scale college survey, most rapes of college women are committed by men with whom they are acquainted.

A young woman, Ann, offered the following account of how she was raped by a man she met at a college party.

**"I" "I Never Thought It Would Happen to Me"**

I first met him at a party. He was really good looking and he had a great smile. I wanted to meet him but I wasn't sure how. I didn't want to appear too forward. Then he came over and introduced himself. We talked and found we had a lot in common. I really liked him. When he asked me over to his place for a drink, I thought it would be OK. He was such a good listener, and I wanted him to ask me out again.

When we got to his room, the only place to sit was on the bed. I didn't want him to get the wrong idea, but what else could I do? We talked for a while and then he made his move. I was so startled. He started by kissing. I really liked him so the kissing was nice. But then he pushed me down on the bed. I tried to get up and I told him to stop. He was so much bigger and stronger. I got scared and I started to cry. I froze and he raped me.

It took only a couple of minutes and it was terrible, he was so rough. When it was over he kept asking me what was wrong, like he didn't know. He had just forced himself on me and he thought that was OK. He drove me home and said he wanted to see me again. I'm so afraid to see him. I never thought it would happen to me.

*"The Case of Ann" from the Author's Files*

Like Ann, thousands of women on college campuses have been raped by dates or acquaintances. Here, we consider comments from Jim, the man who raped Ann.

**"I" "Why Did She Put Up Such a Big Struggle?"**

I first met her at a party. She looked really hot, wearing a sexy dress that showed off her great body. We started talking right away. I knew that she liked me by the way she kept smiling and touching my arm while she was speaking. She seemed pretty relaxed so I asked her back to my place for a drink.... When she said yes, I knew that I was going to be lucky!

When we got to my place, we sat on the bed kissing. At first, everything was great. Then, when I started to lay her down on the bed, she started twisting and saying she didn't want to. Most women don't like to appear too easy, so I knew that she was just going through the motions. When she stopped struggling, I knew that she would have to throw in some tears before we did it.

She was still very upset afterwards, and I just don't understand it! If she didn't want to have sex, why did she come back to the room with me? You could tell by the way she dressed and acted that she was no virgin, so why she had to put up such a big struggle I don't know.

*"The Case of Jim" from the Author's Files*

From the standpoint of male privilege, men often perceive dating as an adversarial contest between a man and a woman, with overcoming a woman's resistance a part of the expected dating ritual. However, forced sexual penetration is not a game, nor is it a dating ritual; it is an act of sexual violence. Nor is it excusable on the basis of misinterpreting the other person's cues or intentions.

Are rapists mentally ill? Rape is not classified as a mental disorder in the *DSM* system, and many rapists do not suffer from any diagnosable mental disorder. Although some rapists do show evidence of psychopathology on psychological tests, especially antisocial or psychopathic traits, many do not (Lalumière et al., 2005). Psychological tests such as the Minnesota Multiphasic Personality Inventory (MMPI; see Chapter 3) fail to identify any particular rapist profile based on a set of personality traits (Gannon et al., 2008). The very normality of many rapists on psychological instruments suggests that socialization of young men plays an important role in creating a climate of sexual aggression.

Although rape is not a symptom of a mental disorder, it is a form of violent sexual behavior that places it squarely within the broader context of abnormal behavior. Moreover, rape survivors often experience a range of mental and physical health problems.

## TRUTH *or* FICTION

Rapists are mentally ill.

☑ **FALSE** Rape is a violent crime, not a symptom of a mental disorder. Many rapists do not show evidence of psychopathology. Rape is a form of social deviance, and rapists should be held accountable under the law for their violent acts.

Many rape survivors are traumatized by the experience (e.g., Bryant-Davis, 2011; Senn et al., 2015). They may have trouble sleeping and cry frequently. They may report eating problems, cystitis, headaches, irritability, mood changes, anxiety and depression, and menstrual irregularity. Survivors may become withdrawn, sullen, and mistrustful. Women who are raped may at least partly blame themselves, which can lead to feelings of guilt and shame. Emotional distress tends to peak by about three weeks following the attack and generally remains high for a month or so, before beginning to decline (Duke et al., 2008; Littleton & Henderson, 2009). Many survivors encounter lingering problems that last decades. Some survivors suffer physical injuries and sexually transmitted infections, even HIV/AIDS. **T / F**

Investigators report that 10% to 14% of married women suffer *marital rape* (Martin, Taft, & Resick, 2007). A traditional-minded husband may think he is entitled to have sex with his wife whenever he wishes. He may see sex as his wife's duty, even when she is unwilling. However, rape is rape, regardless of a woman's marital status. Men who are better educated and less accepting of traditional stereotypes about relationships between men and women are less likely to commit marital rape (Basile, 2002).

A commonly held myth is that men cannot be victims of rape (Peterson et al., 2010). Although women are much more likely to be raped, recent estimates indicate that some 1% to 3% of men at some point in their lives become victims of rape—defined as forced oral or anal penile penetration (Rabin, 2011). Most men who engage in male rape are heterosexual. Their motives often include domination and control, revenge and retaliation, sadism and degradation, and—when the rape is carried out by a gang member—status and affiliation (Krahe, Waizenhofer, & Moller, 2003). Sexual motives are often minimal or absent. As with women who are raped, male rape survivors often suffer serious physical and psychological effects (Peterson et al., 2010; Rabin, 2011).

Some date rapists mistakenly believe that acceptance of a date implies willingness to engage in sexual relations. They may believe that a woman they take out to dinner should pay with sex. Men may think that women who frequent singles bars and similar places are automatically willing to have sex. Some date rapists believe that women who resist advances are simply trying not to look "easy." These men misinterpret resistance as a ploy in the "battle of the sexes." Like Jim, who raped Ann in his dorm room, they may believe that when a woman says no, she means yes, especially when a sexual relationship has been established.

Social attitudes and cultural myths also contribute to the high incidence of rape (Davies, Gilston, & Rogers, 2012). Many people believe myths about rape, such as "Women say no when they mean yes." Yet another myth is that deep down inside, women want to be raped. Certainly, the popular media contribute to this belief when they portray a woman as first resisting a man's advances but then yielding to his overpowering masculinity. These myths have the effect of blaming the victim for the assault and legitimizing rape in the eyes of the public. Although both women and men believe some rape myths, researchers find that college men are more likely than college women to hold such beliefs (Osman, 2003; Stewart, 2014). Even after date rape education classes designed to challenge these views, men tend to cling more stubbornly to date myths than do women (Maxwell & Scott, 2014). The nearby questionnaire will help you evaluate whether you subscribe to beliefs that have the effect of legitimizing rape.

**MISREADING CUES?** Many date rapists misperceive social cues, such as assuming that women who frequent singles bars and similar places are signaling their willingness to have sex.

Many motives underlie rape. Feminists see rape as an expression of men's desire to dominate and degrade women, to establish unquestioned power and superiority over them. Other theorists argue that sexual motivation plays a key role in many kinds of rape, particularly acquaintance rape, date rape, and marital rape (Baumeister, Catanese, & Wallace, 2002; Bushman et al., 2003). In such cases, the motive may be largely sexual, but make no mistake—coerced sex in any form is an act of violence. Rape often occurs in a context of other forms of violent behavior (Gannon et al., 2008). For some rapists, violent cues appear to enhance sexual arousal, so they are motivated to combine sex with aggression. Some rapists who were abused as children may humiliate women as a way of expressing anger and power over women and of taking revenge.

Perhaps, as some researchers contend, our society breeds rapists by socializing men into socially and sexually dominant roles (Malamuth, Huppin, & Paul, 2005; Steinfeldt & Steinfeldt, 2012). Men are often reinforced from childhood for aggressive and competitive behavior. They may learn to "score" at all costs, whether they are on the ball field or in the bedroom. Such socialization influences may also lead men to reject "feminine" traits such as tenderness and empathy that might restrain aggression. Adding alcohol to the mix further increases the risk of sexual assault. A rapist may be just like the boy next door; in fact, he may be the boy next door. In light of the apparent normality of many men who commit rape, let us end by posing two questions to provoke some thoughtful discussion: *What are we teaching our sons? How can we teach them differently?*

## Questionnaire

### RAPE BELIEFS SCALE

Indicate whether you believe each of the following statements is true or false by circling the letters T or F. Then use the scoring key at the end of the chapter to interpret your responses.

| | | | |
|---|---|---|---|
| 1. | T | F | A woman who has a drink in a bar with a guy is just asking for sex. |
| 2. | T | F | Women cry rape when they can't admit to themselves that they wanted sex. |
| 3. | T | F | When a woman touches a man in a certain way, she should let him go all the way. |
| 4. | T | F | Women who dress seductively are basically just "asking for it." |
| 5. | T | F | Most women can prevent a man from taking advantage of them if they really wanted to. |
| 6. | T | F | When a woman says "no," it's generally because she doesn't want the man to think she is easy. |
| 7. | T | F | Women may have a hard time admitting it, but they really want a man to overpower them. |
| 8. | T | F | Date rape is basically a problem of miscommunication between a man and a woman. |
| 9. | T | F | Many women who say they really don't want sex are just not honest with themselves. |
| 10. | T | F | A woman wouldn't accompany a man back to his room after a date unless she really wanted to have intercourse. |

# Summing Up

## Gender Dysphoria

**10.1 Describe the key features of gender dysphoria and explain the difference between gender dysphoria and homosexuality.**

People with gender dysphoria experience their biologic sex as a source of persistent and intense distress. They may seek to change their sex organs to resemble those of the other sex, undergoing hormone treatments and/or surgery to achieve this end.

In gender dysphoria, there is a mismatch between one's psychological sense of being male or female and one's anatomic sex that is associated with significant distress or discomfort. Sexual orientation relates to the direction of one's sexual attraction—toward members of one's own sex or the other sex. Unlike people with gender dysphoria, people with a gay male or lesbian sexual orientation have a gender identity that is consistent with their biologic sex.

## Sex Reassignment Surgery

**10.2 Evaluate psychological outcomes of sex reassignment surgery.**

Evidence shows positive effects of surgery on psychological adjustment and high levels of satisfaction. Outcomes may be more favorable for female-to-male assignments.

## Theoretical Perspectives on Transgender Identity

**10.3 Describe major theoretical perspectives on transgender identity.**

Although the causes of transgender identity remain unknown, psychodynamic theorists emphasize the role of extremely close mother–son relationships and fathers who were absent or detached, whereas learning theorists focus on socialization patterns encouraging the development of cross-gender behavior. Biological explanations focus on genetic factors influencing the release of sex hormones in prenatal development that are involved in sculpting the brain along masculine or feminine lines. Biological factors operating during prenatal development may create a predisposition that interacts with early life experiences in leading to the development of transgender identity.

# Sexual Dysfunctions

## Types of Sexual Dysfunctions

**10.4 Define the term *sexual dysfunction* and identify the three major categories of sexual dysfunctions and the specific disorders within each type.**

A sexual dysfunction is a persistent or recurrent pattern involving lack of sexual desire, problems in becoming sexually aroused, and/or problems in reaching orgasm. Sexual dysfunctions can be classified in three general categories: (1) disorders involving low sexual desire or impaired arousal (female sexual interest/arousal disorder, male hypoactive sexual desire disorder, erectile disorder); (2) disorders involving impaired orgasmic response (female orgasmic disorder, delayed ejaculation, and premature or early ejaculation); and (3) disorders involving sexual pain (genito-pelvic pain/penetration disorder).

## Theoretical Perspectives

**10.5 Describe causal factors involved in sexual dysfunctions.**

Sexual dysfunctions can stem from biological factors (such as fatigue, disease, the effects of aging, or the effects of alcohol and other drugs), psychological factors (such as performance anxiety, lack of sexual skills, disruptive cognitions, or relationship problems), and sociocultural factors (such as sexually restrictive cultural learning).

## Treatment of Sexual Dysfunctions

**10.6 Describe methods used to treat sexual dysfunctions.**

Sex therapy is a cognitive-behavioral approach that helps people overcome sexual dysfunctions by enhancing self-efficacy expectancies, teaching sexual skills, improving communication, and reducing performance anxiety. Biomedical approaches include hormone treatments and, most commonly, the use of drugs to facilitate blood flow to the genital region (Viagra and its chemical cousins) or to delay ejaculation (SSRIs).

# Paraphilic Disorders

## Types of Paraphilias

**10.7 Define the term *paraphilia* and identify the major types.**

A paraphilia is a sexual deviation involving patterns of arousal to atypical stimuli, such as nonhuman objects (e.g., shoes or clothes), humiliation or the experience of pain in oneself or one's partner, or children. Paraphilias include exhibitionism, fetishism, transvestic fetishism, voyeurism, frotteurism, pedophilia, sexual masochism, and sexual sadism. Although some paraphilias are essentially harmless (such as fetishism), others, such as pedophilia and sexual sadism with nonconsenting individuals, certainly do harm victims.

## Theoretical Perspectives

**10.8 Describe theoretical perspectives on paraphilias.**

Psychoanalysts see many paraphilias as defenses against castration anxiety. Learning theorists attribute paraphilias to early learning experiences in which inappropriate stimuli were paired with sexual arousal. Biological factors may also be implicated, such as higher-than-normal sex drives and corrupted sexual arousal patterns.

## Treatment of Paraphilic Disorders

**10.9 Identify methods for treating paraphilic disorders.**

Methods of treating paraphilia include psychoanalytic therapy; cognitive-behavioral therapy involving aversive conditioning, covert sensitization, and social skills training; and biological therapies, including use of SSRI antidepressants and antiandrogen drugs.

## Critical Thinking Questions

Based on your reading of this chapter, answer the following questions:

- What is the difference between transgender identity and a gay male or lesbian sexual orientation?
- Do you believe people who engage in exhibitionism, voyeurism, and sexual acts with children should be punished, treated, or both? Explain.
- Can you think of examples in your own life in which you have been affected by performance anxiety? What did you do about it?
- If you had a sexual dysfunction, would you be willing to seek help for it? Why or why not?

## Key Terms



## Scoring Key for the Rape Beliefs Scale

This scale comprises a set of commonly held myths about rape. If you answered "true'" to any of these items, you may wish to use your critical thinking skills to reexamine your beliefs. For example, the belief that women truly want to be overpowered by a man is a common rationalization rapists use to justify their behavior. How can a person possibly know what another person truly wants unless the other person expresses it? Rape myths are often used as self-serving justifications to explain away unacceptable behavior. To be perfectly clear, when someone says "no" in a sexual context, it means "no." Not maybe, not perhaps, not in a few minutes—but simply *no*. In addition, consenting to some forms of intimate contact, whether kissing, fondling, or oral sex, does not imply consent to genital intercourse or other sexual activities. Consent must be expressed directly, not assumed or taken for granted. Also, a person always retains the right at any time to say "no" or to place limits on what he or she is willing to do.

Chapter 11

# Schizophrenia Spectrum Disorders

## Learning Objectives

**11.1** **Describe** the course of development of schizophrenia.

**11.2** **Describe** the key features and prevalence of schizophrenia.

**11.3** **Describe** psychodynamic, learning theory, biological, and family perspectives on schizophrenia.

**11.4** **Identify** and **evaluate** methods used to treat schizophrenia.

**11.5** **Describe** the key features of brief psychotic disorder.

**11.6** **Describe** the key features of schizophreniform disorder.

**11.7** **Describe** the key features of delusional disorder.

**11.8** **Describe** the key features of schizoaffective disorder.

## TRUTH or FICTION

T☐ F☐ Visual hallucinations ("seeing things") are the most common type of hallucinations in people with schizophrenia. (p. 424 )

T☐ F☐ Despite concerns about command hallucinations, most auditory hallucinations of patients with schizophrenia are experienced as friendly and supportive voices. (p. 425)

T☐ F☐ It is normal for people to hallucinate nightly. (p. 425)

T☐ F☐ If you have both parents with schizophrenia, it's nearly certain that you will develop schizophrenia yourself. (p. 429)

T☐ F☐ If you are an adopted child raised by a parent with schizophrenia, you have about the same chance of developing schizophrenia as biological children of parents with schizophrenia. (p. 430)

T☐ F☐ Scientists believe that a defect on one particular gene causes schizophrenia, but they haven't yet been able to identify the defective gene. (p. 431)

T☐ F☐ Although schizophrenia is widely believed to be a brain disease, we still lack evidence of abnormal functioning in the brains of people with schizophrenia. (p. 433)

T☐ F☐ We now have drugs that not only treat schizophrenia but also can cure it in many cases. (p. 441)

T☐ F☐ Some people have delusions that they are loved by a famous person. (p. 447)

**CHAPTER INTRODUCTION: SCHIZOPHRENIA SPECTRUM DISORDERS**

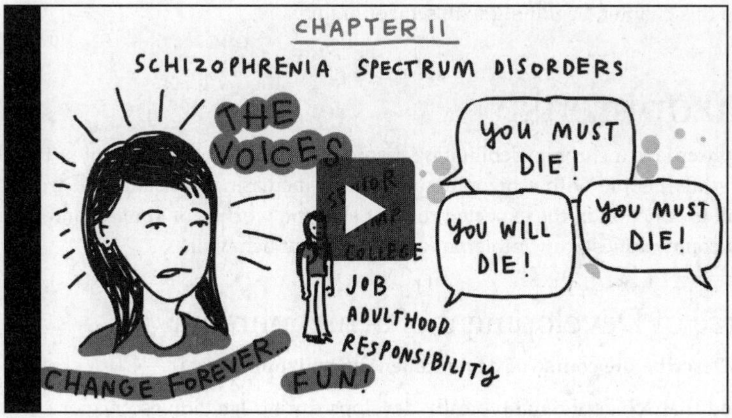


Schizophrenia typically develops in late adolescence or early adulthood, at the very time that young people are making their way from the family into the outside world (Dobbs, 2010; Tandon, Nasrallah, & Keshavan, 2009). For a young woman named Lori Schiller, the first *psychotic episode* or break with reality ("first break") came during her last year at summer camp.

**"I"** **"I Hear Something You Can't Hear"**

It was a hot night in August 1976, the summer of my seventeenth year, when, uninvited and unannounced, the Voices took over my life.

I was going into my senior year in high school, so this was to be my last year at summer camp. College, a job, adulthood, responsibility—they were all just around the corner. But for the moment I wasn't prepared for anything more than a summer of fun. I certainly wasn't prepared to have my life change forever....

"You must die!" Other Voices joined in. "You must die! You will die!"

At first I didn't realize where I was. Was I at the lake? Was I asleep? Was I awake? Then I snapped back to the present. I was here at camp, alone. My summertime fling was long gone, two years gone. That long-ago scene was being played out in my mind, and in my mind alone. But as soon as I realized that I was in my bunk, and awake—and that my roommate was still sleeping peacefully—I knew I had to run. I had to get away from these terrible, evil Voices....

Since that time, I have never been completely free of those Voices. At the beginning of that summer, I felt well, a happy, healthy girl—I thought—with a normal head and heart. By summer's end, I was sick, without any clear idea of what was happening to me or why. And as the Voices evolved into a full-scale illness, one that I only later learned was called schizophrenia, it snatched from me my tranquility, sometimes my self-possession, and very nearly my life.

Along the way I have lost many things: the career I might have pursued, the husband I might have married, the children I might have had. During the years when my friends were marrying, having their babies and moving into the houses I once dreamed of living in, I have been behind locked doors, battling the Voices who took over my life without even asking my permission.

**SOURCE:** *From Schiller & Bennett, 1994*

*Schizophrenia* is perhaps the most puzzling and disabling psychological disorder. It is the condition that best corresponds to popular conceptions of madness or lunacy. Although researchers are probing the psychological and biological foundations of schizophrenia, the disorder remains largely a mystery. In this chapter, we consider what we know about schizophrenia and what remains to be learned. Schizophrenia is not the only type of psychotic disorder in which a person experiences a break with reality: In this chapter, we also consider other psychotic disorders, including *brief psychotic disorder*, *schizophreniform disorder*, *schizoaffective disorder*, and *delusional disorder*. These disorders along with schizophrenia and a type of personality disorder called *schizotypal personality disorder* are classified in the *DSM-5* within a spectrum of schizophrenia-related disorders called Schizophrenia Spectrum and Other Psychotic Disorders. These disorders—excepting schizotypal personality disorder, which is discussed in Chapter 12— are the focus of our study in this chapter, beginning with schizophrenia.

**COURSE OF DEVELOPMENT.** Schizophrenia typically develops during late adolescence or early adulthood, a time of life when young people are beginning to make their way into the world.

# Schizophrenia

**Schizophrenia** is a chronic, debilitating disorder that touches every facet of the affected person's life. People with schizophrenia become increasingly disengaged from society. They fail to function in the expected roles of student, worker, or spouse, and their families and communities grow intolerant of their deviant behavior.

## Course of Development of Schizophrenia

**11.1 Describe the course of development of schizophrenia.**

We noted that schizophrenia typically develops during late adolescence or early adulthood. In some cases, the onset of the disorder is acute, as it was in the case of Lori Schiller. It occurs suddenly, within a few weeks or months. The individual may have been well adjusted and may have shown few signs of behavioral disturbance. Then, a rapid transformation in personality and behavior leads to an acute psychotic episode.

In most cases, there is a slower, more gradual decline in functioning, as was the case with Ian Chovil, a young man who has been living with schizophrenia since the age of 17. He shares his story with the hope that the next generation of people affected by this debilitating disorder will be spared some of the experiences he has endured.

"I"

### "I and I, Dancing Fool, Challenge You the World to a Duel"

Insidious is an appropriate word to describe the onset of schizophrenia I experienced. I gradually lost all my human relationships, first my girlfriend, then my immediate family, then friends and coworkers. I experienced a lot of emotional turmoil and social anxiety. Somehow I graduated from Trent University in Peterborough, Ontario, Canada, but the last year I was smoking marijuana almost every day. I was creative but found it increasingly difficult to actually read anything. My career aspirations were to become a Rastafarian sociobiologist. I had become incapable of long-term romantic relationships after the demise of my first one. At graduate school in Halifax I was hospitalized for a couple of weeks, a nervous breakdown I thought. Although I was prescribed *chlorpromazine* and then *trifluoperazine* [two types of antipsychotic drugs], no one mentioned schizophrenia to me or my father, a family physician. I tried to complete my year, but some courses went unfinished and I was kicked out of graduate school.

Within two years I was one of the homeless in Calgary, sleeping in a city park or the single men's hostel, hungry because I didn't get to eat very often. A World War II hero wanted to hurt me because I had discovered the war was caused by the influenza of 1918. Tibetan Buddhists read my mind everywhere I went because I had caused the Mount Saint Helens eruption for them earlier that year with my natural tantric abilities. For 10 years I lived more or less like that, in abject poverty, without any friends, quite delusional. At first I was going to be a Buddhist saint, then I was a pawn in a secret war between the sexuals and the antisexuals that would determine the fate of humanity, then I realized I was in contact with aliens of the future. There was going to be a nuclear holocaust that would break up the continental plates, and the oceans would evaporate from the lava. The aliens had come to collect me and one woman. All life here was about to be destroyed. My future wife and I were going to become aliens and have eternal life.

My actual situation by then was a sharp contrast. I was living in a downtown Toronto rooming house with only cockroaches for friends, changing light bulbs as they burnt out in a large department store. It was a full time job I could do, but I hated it intensely. I worried about my enemies who were trying to turn me into a homosexual, and I was in constant telepathic conversation with my future wife, listening to rock and roll songs for messages from aliens in my spare time. I ran into trouble with the law one night after becoming furious with the aliens for not transferring my mind to another body. The judge sentenced me to 3 years of probation with the condition I see a psychiatrist for that time....

I wrote a poem as an undergraduate that was published in the student newspaper. The first line was "I and I, dancing fool, challenge you the world to a duel." I intend to challenge the world to the best of my ability, until people like me have the quality of life possible with the most effective treatment strategies available.

**SOURCE:** *From Chovil, 2000. Reprinted with permission of the National Institute of Mental Health.*

As in this case, psychotic behaviors may emerge gradually over several years, although early signs of deterioration may be observed. This period of gradual deterioration is called the **prodromal phase** or *prodrome*. It is characterized by subtle symptoms involving unusual thoughts or abnormal perceptions (but not outright delusions or hallucinations), as well as waning interest in social activities, difficulty meeting responsibilities of daily living, and impaired cognitive functioning involving problems with memory and attention, use of language, and ability to plan and organize one's activities.

One of the first signs of a prodrome is often a lack of attention to one's appearance. A person may fail to bathe regularly or wear the same clothes repeatedly. Over time, the person's behavior becomes increasingly odd. There are lapses in job performance or schoolwork. Speech becomes vague and rambling. These changes in personality may be so gradual that they raise little concern at first among friends and family. The changes may be attributed to "a phase" the person is passing through. However, as behavior becomes more bizarre—such as hoarding food, collecting garbage, or talking to oneself on the street—the acute phase of the disorder begins. Frankly psychotic symptoms then develop, such as wild hallucinations, delusions, and increasingly bizarre behavior.

Following acute episodes, some people with schizophrenia enter the **residual phase**, in which their behavior returns to the level of the prodromal phase. Flagrant psychotic behaviors are absent, but the person is still impaired by significant cognitive, social, and emotional deficits, such as a deep sense of apathy and difficulties in thinking or speaking clearly, and by harboring unusual ideas, such as beliefs in telepathy or clairvoyance. These cognitive and social deficits can make it difficult for patients with schizophrenia to function effectively in their social and occupational roles (Hartmann et al., 2015; Harvey, 2010). In the following first-person account, Ian Chovil observes that despite improvement following treatment with the antipsychotic drug *olanzapine*, his functioning was still impaired by these deficits—the "poverties," as he calls them.

**"I"**

**"The Poverties"**

My life has been improving a little each year, and noticeably on *olanzapine*, but I am still quite unsure of myself. I still have what I call "the poverties," like poverty of thought, emotion, friends, and hard cash. My social life seems to be the slowest to improve. I have three or four recreational friends, only one without a mental illness, only one that I see fairly often. I lived for a while with Rosemary, whom I still see often, in a two-bedroom apartment until the government changed its regulations on cohabitation and we had to separate or lose almost $400 a month in income. Now I'm in a very nice subsidized apartment, fairly happy on my own for the first time thanks to *olanzapine* and my position at the Homewood, which brings me into contact with a lot of people.

**SOURCE:** *From Chovil, 2000. Reprinted with permission of the National Institute of Mental Health.*

Although schizophrenia is a chronic disorder, as many as one half to two-thirds of patients with schizophrenia improve significantly over time (USDHHS, 1999). However, a full return to normal behavior is uncommon, although it does occur in some cases. Typically, patients develop a chronic pattern characterized by occasional acute episodes and continued cognitive, emotional, and motivational impairment between psychotic episodes.

## Key Features of Schizophrenia

**11.2 Describe the key features and prevalence of schizophrenia.**

Acute episodes of schizophrenia involve a break with reality marked by the appearance of symptoms such as delusions, hallucinations, illogical thinking, incoherent speech, and bizarre behavior. Between acute episodes, people with schizophrenia may have lingering deficits, such as being unable to think clearly, speaking only in a flat tone, having difficulty perceiving facial expressions of emotion in others, and showing little if any facial expression of emotions themselves (Comparelli et al., 2013; Gold et al., 2012; Yalcin–Siedentop et al., 2014). Persistent deficits in cognitive and emotional functioning make it difficult for patients with schizophrenia to meet responsibilities of daily life, including holding a job. On a more positive note, 40% or more of schizophrenia patients have long periods of remission (i.e., no disturbing symptoms and ability to work in some capacity) that last a year or longer (Jobe & Harrow, 2010). Although some patients remain free of disturbing symptoms for a number of years even without medication, we still lack specific predictors to know which patients are likely to do well on their own and which need to take their medication continually to reduce the risk of relapse (De Hert et al., 2015).

Schizophrenia affects about 1% of the world's population, which in the United States translates to more than 2 million people (Balter, 2014; Carey, 2015). Nearly 1 million people are treated for schizophrenia each year in the United States, with about a third of those requiring hospitalization.

Men have a slightly higher risk of developing schizophrenia than women and also tend to develop the disorder at an earlier age (Tandon, Keshavan, & Nasrallah, 2008). The peak period of life when psychotic symptoms first appear is the early to middle twenties for men and the late twenties for women (American Psychiatric Association, 2013). Women tend to have a higher level of functioning before the onset of the disorder and to have a less severe course of illness than men. Men with schizophrenia tend to have more cognitive impairment, greater behavioral deficits, and a poorer response to drug therapy than do women with the disorder. These gender differences have led researchers to speculate that men and women may tend to develop different forms of schizophrenia. Perhaps schizophrenia affects different areas of the brain in men and women, which may explain the differences in the form or features of the disorder.

Although schizophrenia likely occurs universally across cultures, the course of the disorder and its particular symptoms can vary from culture to culture. For example, visual hallucinations appear to be most common in some non-Western cultures (Ndetei & Singh, 1983). Moreover, the themes expressed in delusions or hallucinations, such as particular religious or racial themes, vary across cultures.

Schizophrenia often elicits fear, misunderstanding, and condemnation rather than sympathy and concern. It strikes at the heart of a person, stripping the mind of the intimate connections between thoughts and emotions and filling it with distorted perceptions, false ideas, and illogical conceptions, as in the following case example.

## Angela's "Hellsmen":

### A CASE OF SCHIZOPHRENIA

Angela, 19, was brought to the emergency room by her boyfriend, Jaime, because she had cut her wrists. When she was questioned, her attention wandered. She seemed transfixed by creatures in the air, or by something she might be hearing. It seemed as if she had an invisible earphone.

Angela explained that she had slit her wrists at the command of the "hellsmen." Then she became terrified. Later she related that the hellsmen had cautioned her not to disclose their existence. Angela feared that the hellsmen would punish her for her indiscretion.

Jaime related that Angela and he had been living together for nearly a year. They had initially shared a modest apartment in town, but Angela did not like being around other people and persuaded Jaime to rent a cottage in the country. There, Angela spent much of her time making fantastic sketches of goblins and monsters. She occasionally became agitated and behaved as though invisible beings were issuing directions. Her words would become jumbled.

Jaime would try to persuade her to go for help, but she would resist. Then, about nine months ago, the wrist-cutting began. Jaime believed that he had made the bungalow secure by removing all knives and blades—but Angela always found a sharp object.

Then he would bring Angela to the hospital against her protests. Stitches would be put in, she would be held under observation for a while, and she would be medicated. She would recount that she cut her wrists because the hellsmen had informed her that she was bad and had to die. After a few days in the hospital, she would disavow hearing the hellsmen and insist on discharge.

Jaime would take her home. The pattern would repeat.

*From the Author's Files*

Schizophrenia is a pervasive disorder that affects a wide range of psychological processes involving cognition, affect, and behavior. *DSM* criteria for schizophrenia require that psychotic behaviors be present at some point during the course of the disorder and that signs of the disorder be present for at least six months and must have been active and prominent for at least one month (if not treated successfully). People with briefer forms of psychosis receive other diagnoses, such as brief psychotic disorder (discussed later in the chapter).

Table 11.1 provides an overview of schizophrenia. The diagnostic features of schizophrenia are listed in the boxed feature on page 420 (Criteria for *DSM-5*). Note that the diagnosis of schizophrenia in the *DSM-5* requires that at least two features of the disorder be present (not just an isolated delusional belief or hallucination) and that at least one of these features must include the cardinal symptoms of delusions, hallucinations, or disorganized (loosely connected, incoherent, or bizarre) speech.

People with schizophrenia show a marked decline in occupational and social functioning (Ekinci, Albayrak, & Ekinci, 2012; Kim, Park, & Blake, 2011). They may have difficulty

**Table 11.1** Clinical Features of Schizophrenia

| | |
|---|---|
| **Disturbed thought processes** | Delusions (fixed false ideas) and thought disorder (disorganized thinking and incoherent speech) |
| **Attentional deficiencies** | Difficulty attending to relevant stimuli and screening out irrelevant stimuli |
| **Perceptual disturbances** | Hallucinations (sensory perceptions in the absence of external stimulation) |
| **Emotional disturbances** | Flat (blunted) or inappropriate emotions |
| **Other types of impairments** | Confusion about personal identity, lack of volition, excitable behavior or states of stupor, odd gestures or bizarre facial expressions, impaired ability to relate to others, or possible catatonic behavior or gross disturbance in motor activity and orientation in which a person's behavior may slow to a stupor but then abruptly shift to a highly agitated state |

**A BEAUTIFUL MIND.** In the movie *A Beautiful Mind*, actor Russell Crowe portrayed Nobel Prize winner John Nash (1928–2015), a brilliant mathematician whose mind captured the exquisite intricacies of mathematical formulations but also was twisted by the delusions and hallucinations of schizophrenia. Nash is shown here in a photo from 1994.

holding a conversation, forming friendships, holding a job, or taking care of their personal hygiene. Yet no one behavior pattern is unique to schizophrenia. People with schizophrenia may exhibit delusions, problems with associative thinking, and hallucinations at one time or another, but not necessarily all at once. The diversity or heterogeneity of symptoms leads some investigators to suspect that what we call *schizophrenia* is actually a range of schizophrenia syndromes or schizophrenias (Arnedo et al., 2014; Tandon, Nasrallah, & Keshavan, 2009; Yager, 2014).

Schizophrenia is associated with a wide range of abnormal behaviors involving thinking, speech, attentional and perceptual processes, emotional processes, and voluntary behavior. A common way of grouping features of schizophrenia is to distinguish between positive and negative symptoms (Kring et al., 2013; Strauss et al., 2012):

- ***Positive symptoms*** are atypical excesses of behavior involving a break with reality, include hallucinations and delusional thinking.
- ***Negative symptoms*** are behavioral deficits or absences of typical behaviors and affect a person's ability to function in daily life. These include a lack of emotional responses or expression (maintaining a blank expression), loss of motivation, loss of pleasure in normally pleasant activities, lack of social relationships or withdrawal or isolation, and limited verbal expression ("poverty of speech"). Negative symptoms tend to persist even when positive symptoms lessen and often have a greater effect on the person's ability to adjusting to daily living than positive symptoms (Barch, 2013; Fusar-Poli et al., 2014). Negative symptoms are also less responsive than positive symptoms to antipsychotic drugs.

Let's take a closer look at several key features or symptoms associated with schizophrenia.

# Criteria for *DSM-5*

## SCHIZOPHRENIA

A. Two (or more) of the following, each present for a significant portion of time during a 1-month period (or less if successfully treated). At least one of these must be (1), (2), or (3):
   1. Delusions.
   2. Hallucinations.
   3. Disorganized speech (e.g., frequent derailment or incoherence).
   4. Grossly disorganized or catatonic behavior.
   5. Negative symptoms (i.e., diminished emotional expression or avolition).

B. For a significant portion of the time since the onset of the disturbance, level of functioning in one or more major areas, such as work, interpersonal relations, or self-care, is markedly below the level achieved prior to the onset (or when the onset is in childhood or adolescence, there is failure to achieve expected level of interpersonal, academic, or occupational functioning).

C. Continuous signs of the disturbance persist for at least 6 months. This 6-month period must include at least 1 month of symptoms (or less if successfully treated) that meet Criterion A (i.e., active-phase symptoms) and may include periods of prodromal or residual symptoms. During these prodromal or residual periods, the signs of the disturbance may be manifested by only negative symptoms or by two or more symptoms listed in Criterion A present in an attenuated form (e.g., odd beliefs, unusual perceptual experiences).

D. Schizoaffective disorder and depressive or bipolar disorder with psychotic features have been ruled out because either 1) no major depressive or manic episodes have occurred concurrently with the active-phase symptoms, or 2) if mood episodes have occurred during active-phase symptoms, they have been present for a minority of the total duration of the active and residual periods of the illness.

E. The disturbance is not attributable to the physiological effects of a substance (e.g., a drug of abuse, a medication) or another medical condition.

F. If there is a history of autism spectrum disorder or a communication disorder of childhood onset, the additional diagnosis of schizophrenia is made only if prominent delusions or hallucinations, in addition to the other required symptoms of schizophrenia, are also present for at least 1 month (or less if successfully treated).

**SOURCE:** Reprinted with permission from the Diagnostic and Statistical Manual of Mental Disorders, Fifth Edition, (Copyright 2013). American Psychiatric Association.

**DISTURBED THOUGHT AND SPEECH** Schizophrenia is characterized by positive symptoms involving disturbances in thinking and expression of thoughts through coherent, meaningful speech. Aberrant thinking may be found in both the content and form of thought.

***Aberrant Content of Thought*** Delusions involve disturbed content of thought in the form of false beliefs that remain fixed in a person's mind despite their illogical bases and lack of evidence to support them. They tend to remain unshakable even in the face of disconfirming evidence. Delusions may take many forms. Some of the most common types include the following:

- *Delusions of persecution or paranoia* (e.g., "The CIA is out to get me")
- *Delusions of reference* ("People on the bus are talking about me," or "People on TV are making fun of me")
- *Delusions of being controlled* (believing that one's thoughts, feelings, impulses, or actions are controlled by external forces, such as agents of the devil)
- *Delusions of grandeur* (believing oneself to be Jesus or believing one is on a special mission, or having grand but illogical plans for saving the world)

Other delusions include beliefs that one has committed unpardonable sins, that one is rotting away from a horrible disease, that the world or oneself does not really exist, or, as in the following case, that one desperately needs to help people.

**A PAINTING BY A MAN WITH SCHIZOPHRENIA.** Paintings or drawings by patients with schizophrenia often reflect the bizarre quality of their thought patterns and withdrawal into a private fantasy world.

## The Hospital at the North Pole:
### A CASE OF SCHIZOPHRENIA

Although people with schizophrenia may feel hounded by demons or earthly conspiracies, Mario's delusions had a messianic quality. "I need to get out of here," he said to his psychiatrist. "Why do you need to leave?" the psychiatrist asked. Mario responded, "My hospital. I need to get back to my hospital." "Which hospital?" he was asked. "I have this hospital. It's all white and we find cures for everything wrong with people." Mario was asked where his hospital was located. "It's all the way up at the North Pole," he responded. His psychiatrist asked, "But how do you get there?" Mario responded, "I just get there. I don't know how. I just get there. I have to do my work. When will you let me go so I can help the people?"

*From the Author's Files*

Other commonly occurring delusions include *thought broadcasting* (believing one's thoughts are somehow transmitted to the external world so that others can overhear them), *thought insertion* (believing one's thoughts have been planted in one's mind by an external source), and *thought withdrawal* (believing that thoughts have been removed from one's mind). Mellor (1970) offers the following examples:

- *Thought broadcasting*: A 21-year-old student reported, "As I think, my thoughts leave my head on a type of mental ticker tape. Everyone around has only to pass the tape through their mind and they know my thoughts."
- *Thought insertion*: A 29-year-old housewife reported that when she looks out of the window, she thinks, "The garden looks nice and the grass looks cool, but the thoughts of [a man's name] come into my mind. There are no other thoughts there, only his.... He treats my mind like a screen and flashes his thoughts on it like you flash a picture."
- *Thought withdrawal*: A 22-year-old woman experienced the following: "I am thinking about my mother, and suddenly my thoughts are sucked out of my mind by a phrenological vacuum extractor, and there is nothing in my mind, it is empty."

***Aberrant Forms of Thought*** Unless we are engaged in daydreaming or purposefully letting our thoughts wander, our thoughts tend to be tightly knit together. The connections (or associations) between our thoughts tend to be logical and coherent. In contrast, people with schizophrenia tend to think in a disorganized, illogical fashion. In schizophrenia, the form or structure of thought processes, as well as their content, is often disturbed. Clinicians label this type of disturbance a **thought disorder**.

Thought disorder is a positive symptom of schizophrenia involving a breakdown in the organization, processing, and control of thoughts. Looseness of associations is a cardinal sign of thought disorder. The speech pattern of people with schizophrenia is often disorganized or jumbled, with parts of words combined incoherently or words strung together to make meaningless rhymes. Their speech may jump disconnectedly from one topic to another. People with thought disorder are usually unaware that their thoughts and behavior appear abnormal. In severe cases, their speech may become completely incoherent or incomprehensible.

Another common sign of thought disorder is *poverty of speech* (speech that is coherent but so slow, limited in quantity, or vague that little information is conveyed). Less commonly occurring signs include *neologisms* (made-up words that have little or no meaning to others), *perseveration* (inappropriate but persistent repetition of the same words or train of thought), *clanging* (stringing together of words or sounds on the basis of rhyming, such as, "I know who I am but I don't know Sam"), and *blocking* (involuntary, abrupt interruption of speech or thought).

Many people with schizophrenia, but not all, show evidence of thought disorder. Some appear to think and speak coherently but have disordered content of thought, as seen by the presence of delusions. Nor is disordered thought unique to schizophrenia; it is even found in milder form among people without psychological disorders, especially when they are tired or under stress. Disordered thought is also found among other diagnostic groups, such as persons with mania. However, thought disorders in people experiencing a manic episode tend to be short lived and reversible. In people with schizophrenia, thought disorder tends to be more persistent or recurrent. Thought disorder occurs most often during acute episodes, but may linger into residual phases.

## A CLOSER Look

### IS SCHIZOPHRENIA A COGNITIVE DISORDER?

We tend to think of schizophrenia in terms of psychotic symptoms such as hallucinations and delusions, but many researchers today suspect that underlying cognitive deficits may be at the core of the disorder (Haut et al., 2015). People with schizophrenia tend to show a range of cognitive deficits, such as problems with memory, perception, learning, problem solving, reasoning, and attention. These deficits often emerge in childhood long before the more dramatic symptoms of schizophrenia—the hallucinations, delusions, and thought disorder—first appear. Researchers suspect that at its core, schizophrenia may be cognitive disorder and that psychotic behaviors emerge as secondary features from a breakdown in the brain's ability to perform basic cognitive processes that permit us to think clearly and perceive reality (Heckers, 2013). A shift in thinking about schizophrenia as a cognitive disorder may lead to a greater emphasis on developing interventions or early treatments when signs of cognitive problems appear in childhood or adolescence, perhaps years before psychotic symptoms emerge (Kahn & Keefe, 2013).

**ATTENTIONAL DEFICIENCIES** To read this book, you must screen out background noises and other environmental stimuli. Attention, the ability to focus on relevant stimuli and ignore irrelevant ones, is basic to learning and thinking. People with schizophrenia often have difficulty filtering out irrelevant stimuli, making it nearly impossible for them to focus their attention, organize their thoughts, and filter out unessential information. The mother of a son who had schizophrenia described her son's difficulties in filtering out extraneous sounds:

> His hearing is different when he's ill. One of the first things we notice when he's deteriorating is his heightened sense of hearing. He cannot filter out anything. He hears each and every sound around him with equal intensity. He hears the sounds from the street, in the yard, and in the house, and they are all much louder than normal.
>
> *Anonymous, as cited in Freedman et al., 1987, p. 670*

People with schizophrenia also appear to be *hypervigilant*, or acutely sensitive to extraneous sounds, especially during the early stages of the disorder. During acute episodes, they may become flooded by these stimuli, overwhelming their ability to make sense of their environments. Brain abnormalities associated with schizophrenia may lead to a deficit in the ability to filter out distracting sounds and other extraneous stimuli. Genetic factors may account for a sensory filtering deficit in people with schizophrenia.

Links between attentional deficits and schizophrenia are supported by various studies focusing on the psychophysiological aspects of attention. Here, we review some of this research.

***Eye Movement Dysfunction*** Many people with schizophrenia have some form of *eye movement dysfunction*, such as difficulty tracking a slow-moving target across their field of vision ("Eye Movements," 2012). Rather than the eyes steadily tracking the target, they fall back and then catch up in a kind of jerky movement. Eye movement dysfunctions appear to involve defects in the brain's control of visual attention.

Eye movement dysfunctions are common in people with schizophrenia and in their first-degree relatives (parents, children, and siblings). This suggests it might be a genetically transmitted trait, or *biomarker*, associated with genes linked to schizophrenia (Keshavan et al., 2008). Recently, investigators reported 98% accuracy in discriminating people with schizophrenia from healthy control subjects based on a set of eye movement indicators (Benson et al., 2012). However, the role of eye movement dysfunction as a biological marker for schizophrenia is limited because it is not unique to schizophrenia. People with other psychological disorders, such as bipolar disorder, sometimes show the dysfunction. Nor do all people with schizophrenia or their family members show eye movement dysfunctions. What we're left with is the understanding that eye movement dysfunction may be a biomarker for one of the many different genetic pathways leading to schizophrenia.

***Abnormal Event-Related Potentials*** Researchers have also studied brain wave patterns, called *event-related potentials* (ERPs), that occur in response to external stimuli such as sounds and flashes of light. ERPs can be broken down into various components that emerge at different intervals following the presentation of a stimulus (Guillaume et al., 2012). Normally, a sensory gating mechanism in the brain inhibits or suppresses ERPs to a repeated stimulus occurring within the first hundredth of a second after a stimulus is presented. This gating mechanism allows the brain to disregard irrelevant stimuli, such as the sound of a ticking clock, but it doesn't seem to work effectively in many people with schizophrenia (Kéri, Beniczky, & Kelemen, 2010; Sánchez-Morla et al., 2013). As a result, people with schizophrenia may have greater difficulty filtering out distracting stimuli, leading to *sensory overload* and resulting in a jumbling of sensations.

People with schizophrenia also show weaker ERPs occurring around 300 milliseconds (three-tenths of a second) after a sound or a flash of light is presented (e.g., Turetsky et al., 2014; Xiong et al., 2010). These ERPs are involved in processes of focusing attention to a stimulus to extract meaningful information from it.

**FILTERING OUT EXTRANEOUS STIMULI.** You probably have little difficulty filtering out unimportant stimuli, such as street sounds—but people with schizophrenia may be distracted by irrelevant stimuli and be unable to filter them out. Consequently, they may have difficulty focusing their attention and organizing their thoughts.

What we take away from these studies of ERPs is an understanding that many people with schizophrenia appear to be flooded with high levels of sensory information that impinge on their sensory organs but have great difficulty extracting useful information from these stimuli. As a result, they may become confused and find it difficult to filter out distracting stimuli.

**PERCEPTUAL DISTURBANCES**

## Voices, Devils, and Angels:
### A CASE OF PERCEPTUAL DISTURBANCES

Every so often during the interview, Sally would look over her right shoulder in the direction of the office door and smile gently. When asked why she kept looking at the door, she said that the voices were talking about the two of us just outside the door and she wanted to hear what they were saying. "Why the smile?" Sally was asked. "They were saying funny things," she replied, "like maybe you thought I was cute or something."

Tom was flailing his arms wildly in the hall of the psychiatric unit. Sweat seemed to pour from his brow, and his eyes darted about with agitation. He was subdued and injected with haloperidol (brand name Haldol) to reduce his agitation. When he was about to be injected, he started shouting, "Father, forgive them for they know not…forgive them…father." His words became jumbled. Later, after he had calmed down, he reported that the ward attendants had looked to him like devils or evil angels. They were red and burning, and steam issued from their mouths.

*From the Author's Files*

The most common perceptual disturbances in schizophrenia are **hallucinations**, which are sensory perceptions experienced in the absence of external stimulation. They are difficult to distinguish from reality. For Sally, the voices coming from outside the consulting room were real enough, although no one was there. Hallucinations may involve various senses. A person may see things, feel things, hear things, and smell things that are not there. Auditory hallucinations ("hearing voices") are the most common form of hallucination, affecting about three of four patients with schizophrenia (Goode, 2003). Tactile hallucinations (such as tingling, electrical, or burning sensations) and somatic hallucinations (such as feeling like snakes are crawling inside one's belly) are also common. Visual hallucinations (seeing things that are not there), gustatory hallucinations (tasting things that are not present), and olfactory hallucinations (sensing odors that are not present) are rarer. **T / F**

### TRUTH or FICTION

Visual hallucinations ("seeing things") are the most common type of hallucinations in people with schizophrenia.

☑ **FALSE** Auditory, not visual, hallucinations are the most common type of hallucinations among people with schizophrenia.

People with schizophrenia may experience auditory hallucinations as female or male voices and as originating inside or outside their heads. Hallucinators may hear voices conversing about them in the third person, debating their virtues or faults. They are often repetitive and may take the form of a running commentary (McCarthy-Jones et al., 2014). Some voices are experienced as supportive and friendly, but most are critical or even terrorizing.

**LARRY: SCHIZOPHRENIA**

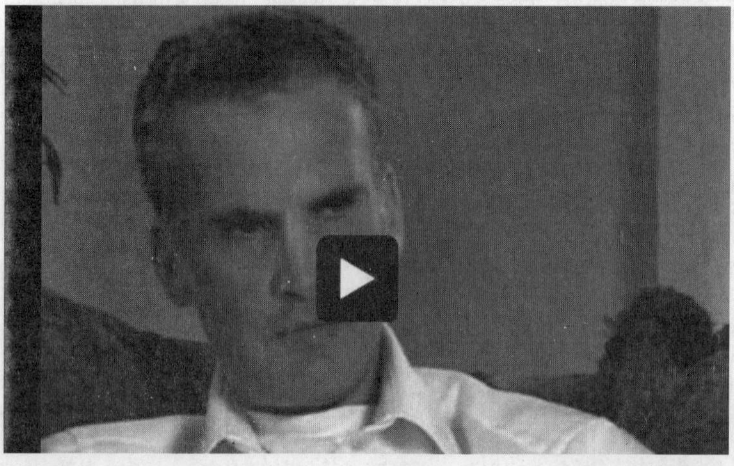

Some patients with schizophrenia experience *command hallucinations*, voices that instruct them to perform certain acts, such as harming themselves or others. Angela, for example, was instructed by the "hellsmen" to commit suicide. People with schizophrenia who experience command hallucinations are often hospitalized out of concern they may harm themselves or others. There is a good reason for this, as evidence shows that command hallucinations are linked to a higher risk of violent behavior (Shawyer et al., 2008). Some people who experience voices issuing commands to harm others do indeed act on them (Braham, Trower, & Birchwood, 2004). Yet command hallucinations often go undetected by professionals, because patients deny them or are unwilling to discuss them. **T / F**

### TRUTH *or* FICTION

Despite concerns about command hallucinations, most auditory hallucinations of patients with schizophrenia are experienced as friendly and supportive.

☑ FASLE Most voices are critical or even terrorizing.

Hallucinations are not unique to schizophrenia. People with major depression or bipolar disorder or other mental disorders may sometimes experience auditory hallucinations, as do some people without psychiatric diagnoses (Woods et al., 2015). Hallucinations in people without psychiatric conditions are often associated with high fevers, states of bereavement (hearing the voice of the departed loved one), and unusually low levels of sensory stimulation, such as when lying in the dark in a soundproof room for an extended time or facing the monotony of driving through the desert or an empty road (Sacks, 2012). The experience of a "mirage" in people traveling through a desert is one such example. These types of unusual experiences are temporary and not persistent, as they are in the case of patients with schizophrenia or other psychotic conditions. Also, people in the general population who experience fleeting hallucinations recognize that they are not real. All told, about 5% of people in the general population have experienced auditory or visual hallucinations at some point in their lives (McGrath et al., 2015). **T / F**

### TRUTH *or* FICTION

It is normal for people to hallucinate nightly.

☑ TRUE Hallucinations—perceptual experiences such as visual images, odors, and so on, in the absence of external stimulation—occur nightly in the form of dreams.

People may sometimes experience hallucinations during the course of religious experiences or rituals. They may report fleeting trancelike states with visions or other strange perceptual experiences. Then too, we all hallucinate nightly during dreams in which we hear and see things in the theater of our minds without any external stimulation.

Hallucinations during waking states can also occur in response to hallucinogenic drugs, such as LSD. Drug-induced hallucinations tend to be visual and often involve abstract shapes such as circles, stars, or flashes of light. Schizophrenic hallucinations, in contrast, tend to be more fully formed and complex. Hallucinations (e.g., of bugs crawling on one's skin) may also arise during *delirium tremens* (the DTs), which often occur as part of the withdrawal syndrome of chronic alcoholism. Hallucinations may also occur as side effects of medications or in neurological disorders, such as Parkinson's disease.

***Causes of Hallucinations*** The causes of psychotic hallucinations remain unknown, but speculations abound. Disturbances in brain chemistry are suspected. The neurotransmitter dopamine is implicated, largely because antipsychotic drugs that block dopamine activity also reduce hallucinations. Conversely, drugs that lead to increased production of dopamine, such as cocaine, can induce hallucinations. Because hallucinations resemble dreamlike states, they may be connected to a failure of brain mechanisms that normally prevent dream images from intruding on waking experiences.

Auditory hallucinations in patients with schizophrenia may represent a type of inner speech (silent self-talk; Alderson-Day & Fernyhough, 2015). Many of us, perhaps all of us, talk to ourselves from time to time, although we usually keep our mutterings under our breath (subvocal) and recognize the voice we "hear" as our own. Might auditory hallucinations in the patient with schizophrenia be a projection of one's own internal voice or self-speech onto an external source?

An intriguing possibility is that the brain of the hallucinating patient mistakes inner speech for external sounds. Investigators find that the auditory cortex—the part of the brain that processes auditory stimulation—becomes active during auditory hallucinations in the absence of real sounds (Allen et al., 2012). Auditory hallucinations may be a form of inner speech that for unknown reasons becomes attributed to external sources

**HEARING VOICES.** Auditory hallucinations—hearing voices—is the most common form of hallucination in patients with schizophrenia. Recent evidence suggests that auditory hallucinations may involve inner speech that becomes projected onto external sources.

rather than to one's own thoughts (Alderson-Day & Fernyhough, 2015; Arguedas, Stevenson, & Langdon, 2012). This line of research has led to a form of treatment in which cognitive-behavioral therapists attempt to teach hallucinators to reattribute their voices to themselves and to change how they respond to the voices (Turkington & Morrison, 2012; e.g., "My voices do not make me angry, it is how I think about the voices"). Patients are also trained to recognize the situational cues associated with their hallucinations—for example:

> one patient...recognized that her voices tended to become worse following family arguments. She became aware that the content of her voices reflected the things that she was feeling and thinking about her family but that she was unable to express. Specific targets and goals were then set to allow her to address these difficulties with her family, and techniques such as rehearsal, problem solving and cognitive restructuring were employed to help her work towards these goals.
>
> *Bentall, Haddock, & Slade, 1994, p. 58*

Cognitive-behavioral therapy has become a useful addition to drug therapy in helping control hallucinations and delusional thinking of patients with schizophrenia (e.g., Grant, Fathalli, et al., 2012; Turner et al., 2014; Waller et al., 2012). However, even if theories linking inner speech to auditory hallucinations stand up to further scientific inquiry, they cannot account for hallucinations in other sensory modalities, such as visual, tactile, or olfactory hallucinations.

The brain mechanisms responsible for hallucinations probably involve a number of interconnected systems. One intriguing possibility is that defects in deeper brain structures may lead the brain to create its own reality. This alternative reality goes unchecked because the higher thinking centers in the brain, located in the frontal lobes of the cerebral cortex, may fail to perform a "reality check" on these images to determine whether they are real, imagined, or hallucinated. Consequently, people may misattribute their own internally generated voices to outside sources.

Scientists suspect that abnormalities in connections among neurons in the brain may disrupt brain circuits that normally allow us to distinguish reality from fantasy. As we'll see later, evidence from brain-imaging studies points to abnormalities in the prefrontal cortex of the frontal lobes in people with schizophrenia. Another line of research indicates that abnormalities in synaptic connections among neurons in the brain may disrupt the communication needed within networks of neurons that normally allow us to think clearly and distinguish what is real from what is not (Dhindsa & Goldstein, 2016; Sekar et al., 2016; Zalesky et al., 2015).

**EMOTIONAL DISTURBANCES** Disturbed emotional response in schizophrenia may involve negative symptoms, such as loss of normal emotional expression, labeled as blunted affect or *flat affect*. In people showing flat affect, we observe an absence of emotional expression in the face and voice. People with schizophrenia may speak in a monotone and maintain an expressionless face, or "mask." They may not experience a normal range of emotional response to people and events. They may also display positive symptoms, which involve exaggerated or inappropriate affect. For example, they may laugh for no reason or giggle at bad news.

However, it is not clear whether emotional blunting in people with schizophrenia is a disturbance in their ability to express emotions, to report the presence of emotions, or to actually experience emotions. Recent research shows that patients with schizophrenia tend to show less facial expression of emotions but are similar to others in the internal experience of emotional states (Mote, Stuart, & Kring, 2014). In other words, schizophrenia patients may inwardly experience emotions while their outward expression of emotions remains blunted. Laboratory-based evidence also shows that patients with schizophrenia experience more intense negative emotions, but less intense positive emotions, than controls (Myin-Germeys, Delespaul, & deVries, 2000). In other words, schizophrenia patients may experience strong emotions (especially negative emotions), even if their experiences are not communicated to the world outside through their facial expressions or behavior. People with schizophrenia may lack the capacity to express their emotions outwardly.

**CATATONIA.** People in a catatonic state may remain in unusual, difficult positions that can last for hours, even though their limbs become stiff or swollen. They may seem oblivious to their environment during these episodes and fail to respond to people who are talking to them.

**OTHER TYPES OF IMPAIRMENTS** People who suffer from schizophrenia may become confused about their personal identities—the cluster of attributes and characteristics that define them as individuals and give meaning and direction to their lives. They may fail to recognize themselves as unique individuals and be unclear about how much of what they experience is part of themselves. In psychodynamic terms, this phenomenon is sometimes referred to as loss of *ego boundaries*. They may also have difficulty adopting a third-party perspective; they fail to perceive their own behavior and verbalizations as socially inappropriate in a given situation because they cannot see things from another person's point of view (Carini & Nevid, 1992). They also have difficulty recognizing or perceiving emotions in others or recognizing their facial expressions of emotions (Csukly et al., 2014).

*Disturbances of volition* are most often seen in the residual or chronic state. These negative symptoms are characterized by *apathy*, which involves a loss of motivation or initiative to pursue goal-directed activities (Hartmann et al., 2015). People with schizophrenia may be unable to carry out plans and lack interest or drive. Ambivalence may also play a part, as difficulty in choosing among different courses of action may block goal-directed activities. Patients with schizophrenia appear to be stuck in limbo, unable to translate desires and goals into effective goal-directed actions. Evidence from fMRI scans shows deficits in brain mechanisms in patients with schizophrenia, affecting their ability to convert desires and goals into actions, which may help explain difficulties they have completing basic life tasks like finding work, making friends, and pursuing an education (Morris et al., 2014).

In some cases, patients with schizophrenia show may show *catatonic behaviors*, which involve severely impaired cognitive and motor functioning. People with **catatonia** may become unaware of the environment and maintain a fixed or rigid posture—even a bizarre, apparently strenuous position for hours at a time, even as their limbs become stiff or swollen. They may exhibit odd gestures and bizarre facial expressions or become unresponsive and curtail spontaneous movement. They may show highly excited but seemingly purposeless behavior or slow down to a state of *stupor*. Although catatonia was recognized as a distinct subtype of schizophrenia in previous versions of the diagnostic manual, the *DSM-5* uses it as a type of specifier to further describe the psychiatric conditions in which it occurs (American Psychiatric Association, 2013).

A striking but less common feature of catatonia is *waxy flexibility*, which involves adopting a fixed posture into which they have been positioned by others. They will not respond to questions or comments during these periods, which can last for hours. Later, however, they may report that they heard what others were saying at the time.

## "What is Your Name?":
### A CASE OF CATATONIA

A 24-year-old man had been brooding about his life. He professed that he did not feel well but could not explain his bad feelings. While hospitalized, he initially sought contact with people, but a few days later he was found in a statuesque position, his legs contorted awkwardly. He refused to talk to anyone and acted as if he couldn't see or hear. His face was an expressionless mask. A few days later, he began to talk, but in an echolalic or mimicking way. For example, he would respond to the question, "What is your name?" by saying, "What is your name?" He could not care for his needs and had to be fed.

**SOURCE:** *Adapted from Arieti, 1974, p. 40*

Catatonia is not unique to schizophrenia. It can occur in other disorders, including brain disorders, drug intoxication, and metabolic disorders. In fact, it is found more often in people with mood disorders than in those with schizophrenia (Grover et al., 2015; Taylor & Fink, 2003).

People with schizophrenia also show significant impairment in interpersonal relationships. They withdraw from social interactions and become absorbed in private thoughts and fantasies, or they cling so desperately to others that they make them uncomfortable. They may become so dominated by their own fantasies that they essentially lose touch with the outside world. They also tend to be introverted and peculiar even before the appearance of psychotic behaviors. These early signs may be associated with a vulnerability to schizophrenia, at least in people with a genetic risk of developing the disorder.

# Theoretical Perspectives

**11.3 Describe psychodynamic, learning theory, biological, and family perspectives on schizophrenia.**

Schizophrenia has been approached from each of the major theoretical perspectives. Although the underlying causes of schizophrenia remain elusive, they are presumed to involve brain abnormalities in combination with psychological, social, and environmental influences (USDHHS, 1999). First, however, let's consider the viewpoints of psychodynamic and learning theories.

**PSYCHODYNAMIC PERSPECTIVES** Within the psychodynamic perspective, schizophrenia represents the overwhelming of the ego by primitive sexual or aggressive drives or impulses arising from the id. These impulses threaten the ego and give rise to intense intrapsychic conflict. Under such a threat, the person regresses to an early period in the oral stage, referred to as *primary narcissism*. In this period, the infant has not yet learned that the world is distinct from itself. Because the ego mediates the relationship between the self and the outer world, this breakdown in ego functioning accounts for the detachment from reality that is typical of schizophrenia. Input from the id causes fantasies to become mistaken for reality, giving rise to hallucinations and delusions. Primitive impulses may also carry more weight than social norms and be expressed in bizarre, socially inappropriate behavior.

Some of Freud's followers, such as Harry Stack Sullivan, placed more emphasis on interpersonal than on intrapsychic factors. Sullivan (1962), who devoted much of his life's work to schizophrenia, emphasized that impaired mother–child relationships can set the stage for gradual withdrawal from other people. In early childhood, anxious and hostile interactions between the child and the parent lead the child to take refuge in a private fantasy world. A vicious cycle ensues: The more the child withdraws, the less opportunity there is to develop a sense of trust in others and the social skills necessary to establish intimacy. Then the weak bonds between the child and others prompt social anxiety and further withdrawal. This cycle continues until young adulthood. Then, faced with increasing demands at school or work and in intimate relationships, the person becomes overwhelmed with anxiety and withdraws completely into a world of fantasy.

Critics of Freud's views point out that schizophrenic behavior and infantile behavior are different, so schizophrenia cannot be explained by regression. Critics of Freud and modern psychodynamic theorists note that psychodynamic explanations are post hoc, or retrospective. Early child–adult relationships are recalled from the vantage point of adulthood rather than observed longitudinally. Psychoanalysts have not been able to demonstrate that hypothesized early childhood experiences or family patterns lead to schizophrenia.

**LEARNING PERSPECTIVES** Although learning theory does not offer a complete explanation of schizophrenia, the development of some forms of schizophrenic behavior can be understood in terms of the principles of conditioning and observational learning.

From this perspective, people with schizophrenia learn to exhibit certain bizarre behaviors when these are more likely to be reinforced than normal behaviors.

Consider a classic case study of operant conditioning. Haughton and Ayllon (1965) conditioned a 54-year-old woman with chronic schizophrenia to cling to a broom. A staff member first gave her the broom to hold, and when she did, another staff member gave her a cigarette (a reinforcement). This pattern was repeated several times. Soon the woman could not be parted from the broom. However, the fact that reinforcement can influence people to engage in peculiar behavior does not demonstrate that the bizarre behaviors characteristic of schizophrenia are shaped by reinforcement.

Social-cognitive theorists suggest that modeling of schizophrenic behavior can occur within the mental hospital, where patients may begin to model themselves after fellow patients who act strangely. Hospital staff may also inadvertently reinforce schizophrenic behavior by paying more attention to patients who exhibit bizarre behavior. This understanding is consistent with the observation that schoolchildren who disrupt the class garner more attention from their teachers than well-behaved children do.

Perhaps some types of schizophrenic behaviors can be explained by the principles of modeling and reinforcement. However, many people display schizophrenic behavior patterns without prior exposure to other people with schizophrenia. In fact, the onset of schizophrenic behavior patterns is more likely to lead to hospitalization than to result from hospitalization.

**BIOLOGICAL PERSPECTIVES** Although we still have much to learn about the biological underpinnings of schizophrenia, investigators recognize that biological factors play a key role in the development of the disorder.

***Genetic Factors*** A wealth of evidence points to an important role for genetics in the development of schizophrenia (e.g., Cannon, 2016; Franke et al., 2016; Pocklington et al., 2015; Ruzzo & Geschwind, 2016). The closer the genetic relationship between people with schizophrenia and their family members, the greater the likelihood that their relatives will also have schizophrenia. Overall, first-degree relatives of people with schizophrenia (parents, children, or siblings) have about a tenfold greater risk of developing schizophrenia than do members of the general population (American Psychiatric Association, 2000).

Figure 11.1 shows the pooled results of European studies conducted from 1920 to 1987 on family incidence of schizophrenia. However, the fact that families share common environments as well as common genes requires that we dig deeper to examine the genetic underpinnings of schizophrenia.

More direct evidence of a genetic factor in schizophrenia comes from twin studies showing *concordance rates* (percentage sharing the disorder) among identical or MZ twins of about 48%, or more than twice the rate found among fraternal or DZ twins (about 17%; Gottesman, 1991; Pogue-Geile & Yokley, 2010). We should be careful, however, not to overinterpret the results of twin studies. Not only do MZ twins share 100% genetic similarity, but others may treat them more similarly than they would DZ twins. Consequently, environmental factors may contribute to the higher concordance rates found among MZ twins. **T / F**

**TRUTH or FICTION**

If you have both parents with schizophrenia, it's nearly certain that you will develop schizophrenia yourself.

☑ **FALSE** Children of parents who both have schizophrenia have less than a 50% chance of developing the disorder (see Figure 11.1, lowest bar).

To sort out environmental from genetic factors, investigators have turned to adoption studies in which high-risk children (of one or more biological parents with schizophrenia) were adopted shortly after birth and reared apart from their biological parents by adoptive parents who did not have schizophrenia (Wicks, Hjern, & Dalman, 2010). It turns out that the risk of schizophrenia was related to the presence of schizophrenia in the biological parents of the adopted children, not the adoptive parents (Tandon, Keshavan, & Nasrallah, 2008). Supporting the view that both genetics and environment play a part in schizophrenia, high-risk children who were adopted away but raised in economically disadvantaged homes

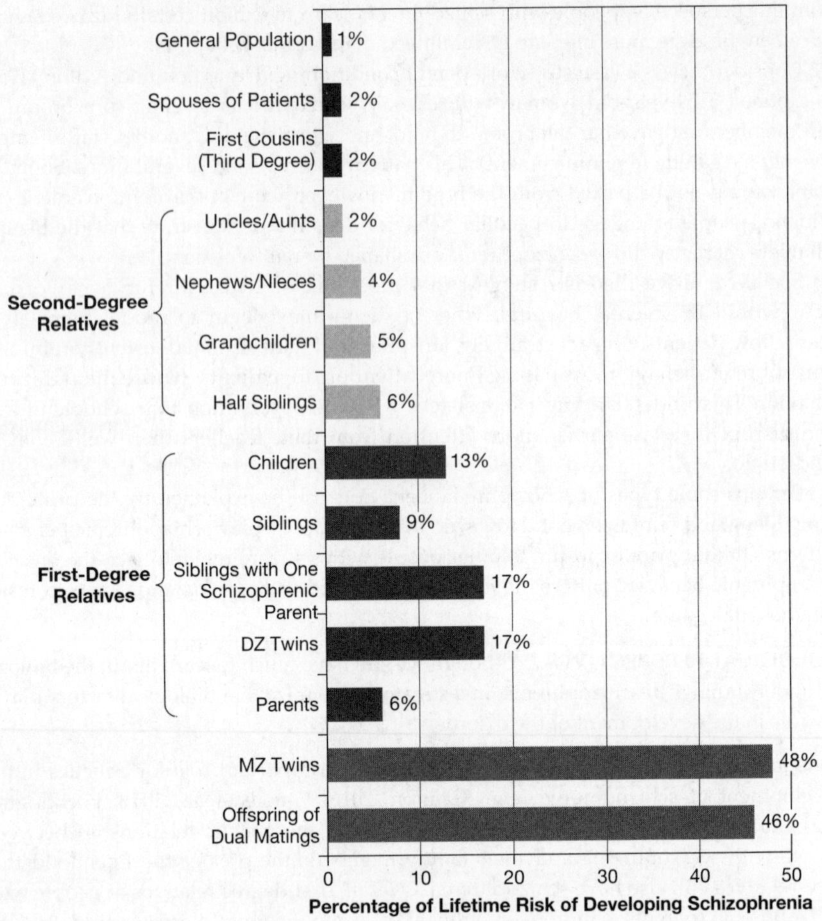


**Figure 11.1** The familial risk of schizophrenia.

Generally speaking, the more closely one is related to people who have developed schizophrenia, the greater the risk of developing schizophrenia oneself. Monozygotic (MZ) or identical twins, whose genetic heritages are identical, are much more likely than dizygotic (DZ) or fraternal twins, whose genes overlap by 50%, to be concordant for schizophrenia.

**SOURCE:** Adapted from Gottesman, McGuffin, & Farmer, 1987.

## TRUTH or FICTION

If you are an adopted child raised by a parent with schizophrenia, you have about the same chance of developing schizophrenia as biological children of parents with schizophrenia.

☑ **FALSE** Among adopted children whose biological parents do not have schizophrenia, those raised by adoptive parents with schizophrenia stand no greater chance of developing schizophrenia than do those of nonschizophrenic adoptive parents.

(single-parent homes or families with parental unemployment) stand a much higher risk than high-risk children raised in more comfortable circumstances (Wicks, Hjern, & Dalman, 2010). **T / F**

Other investigators have approached the question of heredity from the opposite direction. In a classic study, American researcher Seymour Kety, together with Danish colleagues (Kety et al., 1975, 1978), used official records in Denmark to find 33 index cases of children who had been adopted early in life and were later diagnosed with schizophrenia. They compared the rates of diagnosed schizophrenia in the biological and adoptive relatives of the index cases with those of the relatives of a matched reference group of adoptees with no psychiatric history. The results strongly supported the genetic explanation. The incidence of diagnosed schizophrenia was greater among biological relatives of adoptees who had schizophrenia than among biological relatives of control adoptees. Adoptive relatives of both index cases and control cases showed similar, *low* rates of schizophrenia. These findings and others show that family linkages in schizophrenia follow shared genes, not shared environments.

Another method for teasing out genetic from environmental influences, called the *cross-fostering study*, compares the incidence of schizophrenia among children whose biological parents either had or didn't have schizophrenia and who were reared by adoptive parents who either had or didn't have schizophrenia. In a classic study conducted in Denmark, Wender and his colleagues (Wender et al., 1974) found the risk of schizophrenia related to the presence of schizophrenia in the children's biological parents, but not in their adoptive parents. High-risk children (whose biological parents had schizophrenia) were almost twice as likely to develop schizophrenia as those of nonschizophrenic biological parents, regardless of whether they were reared by a parent with schizophrenia. It is also notable that adoptees whose biological parents did not suffer from schizophrenia were placed at no greater risk of developing schizophrenia by being reared by an adoptive parent with schizophrenia than by a nonschizophrenic parent. In sum, a genetic relationship with a person with schizophrenia seems to be the most prominent risk factor for developing the disorder.

Fast-forward to the present: A number of investigators are now zeroing in on particular genes linked to schizophrenia (e.g., Dickinson et al., 2014; Greenhill et al., 2015; Schizophrenia Working Group, 2014; Siegert et al., 2015). But let's be clear on this point: There is no single gene responsible for schizophrenia (Escudero & Johnstone, 2014; Walker et al., 2010). Rather, many different genes contribute to the development of brain abnormalities that, together with stressful environmental influences, lead to schizophrenia (Agerbo et al., 2015; International Schizophrenia Consortium, 2009). Any one of these genes may have only a small effect individually, but when the effects of multiple genes are combined, a person stands a much greater risk of developing the disorder. **T / F**

**TRUTH or FICTION**

Scientists believe that a defect on one particular gene causes schizophrenia, but they haven't yet been able to identify the defective gene.

☑ **FALSE** Scientists believe that many genes, not any one gene, are involved in complex processes that increase the likelihood that schizophrenia will develop.

Increased vulnerability to schizophrenia may involve an unlucky combination of common variations of particular genes or perhaps genetic mutations or defects on genes that affect various brain functions (Levinson et al., 2011; Li et al., 2011; Pocklington et al., 2015). Scientists also find that offspring of older fathers stand an increased risk of developing schizophrenia and autism, presumably because sperm of older men are more prone to mutations (D'Onofrio et al., 2014; Kong et al., 2012). However, no increased risks of genetic mutations are found in older mothers (Carey, 2012c).

Before we move on, let's note that genetics alone does not fully determine a person's risk of developing schizophrenia. Environmental influences also play important roles. Consider the fact that many people at high genetic risk of developing schizophrenia do not develop the disorder. In fact, the rate of concordance among MZ twins, as we noted earlier, is well below 100%, even though identical twins carry identical genes. The prevailing view of schizophrenia today is represented by the diathesis-stress model (see *Tying It Together* later in the chapter), which holds that some people inherit a predisposition or vulnerability to developing schizophrenia in the face of stressful life experiences. For example, a combination of genetic defects or variations in particular genes, together with stressful experiences early in life, may lead to abnormal brain development that increases the risk of later development of schizophrenia (Kim et al., 2012; Walker et al., 2010).

Let's now consider the roles of other biological factors in schizophrenia, including biochemical factors, possible viral infections, and brain abnormalities.

***Biochemical Factors*** Evidence points to irregularities in the use of dopamine in complex networks of neurons in the brain (Howes et al., 2012; Keshavan, Nasrallah, & Tandon, 2011). The leading biochemical model of schizophrenia, the **dopamine hypothesis**, posits that schizophrenia involves overactivity of dopamine transmission in the brain.

The major source of evidence for the dopamine model is found in the effects of antipsychotic drugs called *neuroleptics*. The first generation of neuroleptics belong to a class of drugs called *phenothiazines*, which includes drugs such as Thorazine, Mellaril, and Prolixin. Neuroleptic drugs block dopamine receptors, thereby reducing the level of dopamine activity. As a consequence, neuroleptics inhibit excessive transmission of neural impulses that may give rise to positive features of schizophrenia, such as hallucinations and delusional thinking.

Another source of evidence for the role of dopamine in schizophrenia is based on the actions of amphetamines, a class of stimulant drugs. These drugs increase the concentration of dopamine in the synaptic cleft by blocking its reuptake by presynaptic neurons. When given in large doses to normal people, these drugs cause symptoms that mimic paranoid schizophrenia.

Overall, the available evidence points to irregularities in neural pathways that utilize dopamine in the brains of people with schizophrenia—irregularities that may be genetically determined (Huttunen et al., 2008). The specific nature of this abnormality remains under study. It doesn't appear that the brain of a people with schizophrenia has too much dopamine, but rather that the dopamine system in the brain is overactive or too responsive to stimulation of dopamine receptors (Grace, 2010; Valenti et al., 2011). Another possibility deserving further study is that overreactivity of dopamine receptors may be responsible for positive symptoms, whereas decreased dopamine reactivity may help explain the development of negative symptoms. We also have evidence pointing to roles for other neurotransmitters, including serotonin, acetylcholine, glutamate, and gamma-aminobutyric acid (GABA; e.g., Dobbs, 2010; Rasmussen et al., 2010; Walker et al., 2010). The specific roles for these neurotransmitters in schizophrenia need to be explored further.

**SCHIZOPHRENIA**

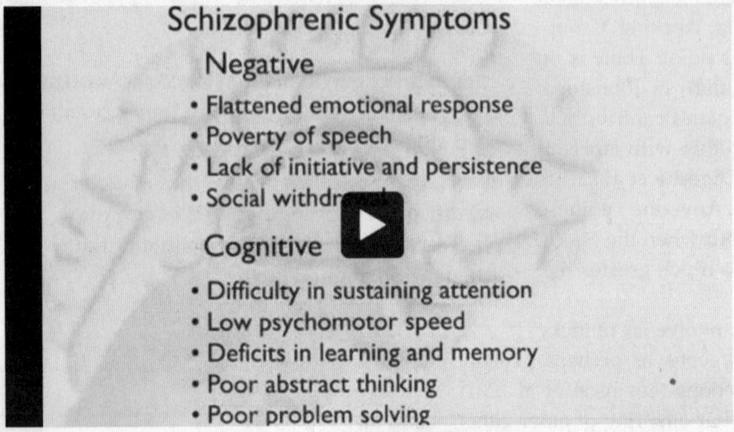


***Viral Infections*** Is it possible that at least some forms of schizophrenia are caused by a slow-acting virus that attacks the developing brain of a fetus or newborn child? Prenatal rubella (German measles), a viral infection, is a cause of intellectual disability. Could another virus give rise to schizophrenia? We don't yet know, but intriguing evidence points to links between prenatal infections and later development of schizophrenia (Brown et al., 2009; Canetta et al., 2014). For example, investigators report finding a sevenfold greater risk of schizophrenia in individuals who had been exposed to the influenza virus (the flu) during the first three months of prenatal development (Brown et al., 2004). Moreover, the risk of schizophrenia is greater in people who are born in the winter and early spring months in the northern hemisphere, a time of the year associated with a greater risk of the flu (King, St-Hilaire, & Heidkamp, 2010). It is possible that viral agents act on the developing brain during prenatal development in ways that increase the risk of developing schizophrenia later in life. Recent evidence from a large-scale study in Sweden suggests that the risk posed by prenatal infections may be limited to offspring whose mothers had psychiatric disorders, perhaps because of the interaction of a prenatal infection and a genetic vulnerability (Blomström et al., 2015). However, even if a viral basis for schizophrenia were discovered, it would probably account for only a small fraction of cases.

**Figure 11.2** Loss of brain tissue in adolescents with early-onset schizophrenia.

The brains of adolescents with early-onset schizophrenia (right image) show a substantial loss of gray matter. Some shrinkage of gray matter occurs normally during adolescence (left image), but the loss is more pronounced in adolescents with schizophrenia.

**SOURCE:** Thompson et al., 2001.

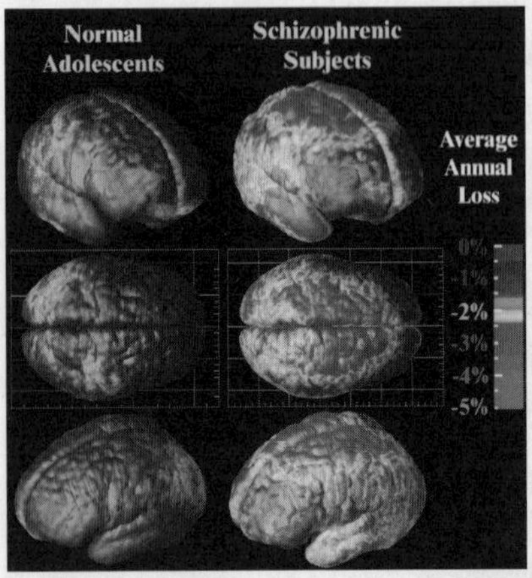


***Brain Abnormalities*** Brain scans of people with schizophrenia show evidence of both structural abnormalities and disturbed brain functioning (e.g., Hulshoff Pol et al., 2012; Kubota et al., 2013; Sun et al., 2015). The most prominent structural abnormality is the loss or thinning of brain tissue (gray matter) in schizophrenia patients (e.g., Guo, Liu, et al., 2015; Zhang et al., 2015). Figure 11.2 presents a visual representation of the brains of adolescents with early-onset (childhood) schizophrenia. The clearest sign of deterioration of brain tissue is the presence of abnormally enlarged ventricles, which are hollow spaces in the brain (see Figure 11.3; Kempton et al., 2010).

In schizophrenia, the brain may have been damaged or failed to develop normally during prenatal development as the result of genetic factors or environmental influences (e.g., viral infections, inadequate fetal nutrition) or perhaps birth traumas or complications (King, St-Hilaire, & Heidkamp, 2010; Walker et al., 2010). One indication of possible prenatal complications is the finding of an association between low birth weight—a marker for problems in prenatal development—and later schizophrenia (Abel et al., 2010). We need to keep in mind, however, that not all cases of schizophrenia involve structural damage to brain tissue. There may be several forms of schizophrenia that have different causal processes.

The picture beginning to emerge from brain scans of people with schizophrenia is of abnormal functioning and loss of brain tissue, especially in the prefrontal cortex (PFC; Kong, Bachmann, et al., 2012; Mechelli et al., 2011; Zhang et al., 2015). The PFC is the thinking, planning, and organizing center of the brain, which is why it is often called the brain's "executive center."

**Figure 11.3** Brain ventricles.

Individuals with schizophrenia typically have abnormally enlarged ventricles in the brain, which is a sign of deterioration or loss of brain tissue. Ventricles are hollow cavities containing a fluid that buffers or cushions the brain. Here, we see the location of brain ventricles on the left side of the brain.

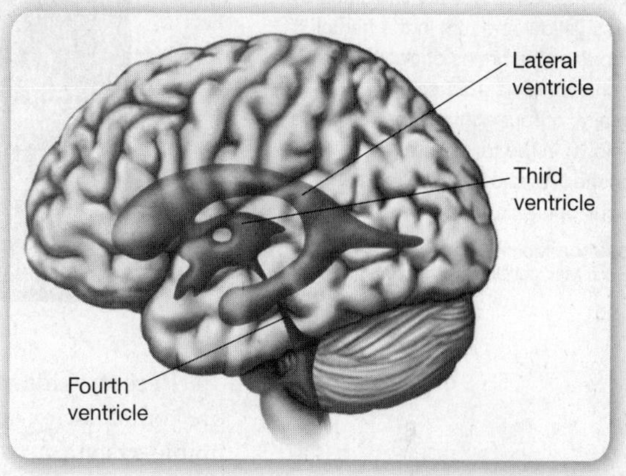


The prefrontal cortex lies directly behind the forehead in the frontal lobes of the cerebral cortex and directly in front of the motor cortex (the part of the brain that controls voluntary body movements). It is responsible for many higher-order or executive-type functions of the brain, such as regulating attention, organizing thoughts and behavior, prioritizing information, and formulating goals—the very types of deficits often found in people with schizophrenia. Investigators believe that prefrontal abnormalities may largely have a genetic origin (Bakken et al., 2011). We now have evidence linking genetic variations in schizophrenia to a thinning or pruning of synaptic connections in the prefrontal cortex of people with schizophrenia (Dhindsa & Goldstein, 2016; Sekar et al., 2016; see *Closer Look: The Hunt for Endophenotypes in Schizophrenia* on page 434).

The prefrontal cortex serves as a kind of mental clipboard for holding information needed to guide and organize behavior. Prefrontal abnormalities may explain why people with schizophrenia often have difficulty with *working memory*—the memory system we use to hold information in mind and work on that information (Heck et al., 2014; Kaller et al., 2014; Slifstein et al., 2015). We regularly use working memory to juggle information in our heads, such as when performing mental arithmetic or holding sounds in our minds just long enough to convert them into recognizable words in order to carry on a conversation. Impairment of working memory can lead to confusion and disorganized behavior of the type often seen in people with schizophrenia. Deficits in working memory and abnormalities in brain circuitry involving working memory often emerge before the first clinical symptoms of the disorder appear (Schmidt et al., 2013). **T / F**

## TRUTH or FICTION

Although schizophrenia is widely believed to be a brain disease, we still lack evidence of abnormal functioning in the brains of people with schizophrenia.

☑ **FALSE** Mounting evidence points to both structural and functional abnormalities in the brains of many people with schizophrenia.

Brain-imaging studies also show underactivation of the prefrontal cortex in people with schizophrenia as compared to healthy controls (e.g., Minzenberg et al., 2009; see Figure 11.4). For example, the prefrontal cortex in people with schizophrenia as compared to healthy controls shows lower neural activity while the person performs arithmetic problems (Hugdahl et al., 2004). Reduced neural activity in the prefrontal cortex, or *hypofrontality* (*hypo* means *under*), may reflect structural damage, such as loss of brain tissue. Investigators recently proposed yet another possibility—that the brains of people with schizophrenia may have relatively few pathways (think of them as roadways) in the prefrontal cortex for information to pass from one neuron to another (Cahill et al., 2009). As a result, messages may become bottled up in a veritable "traffic jam" in the brain (like drivers on an interstate needing to squeeze into a single lane because of construction). This, in turn, may result in confused and disorganized thinking.

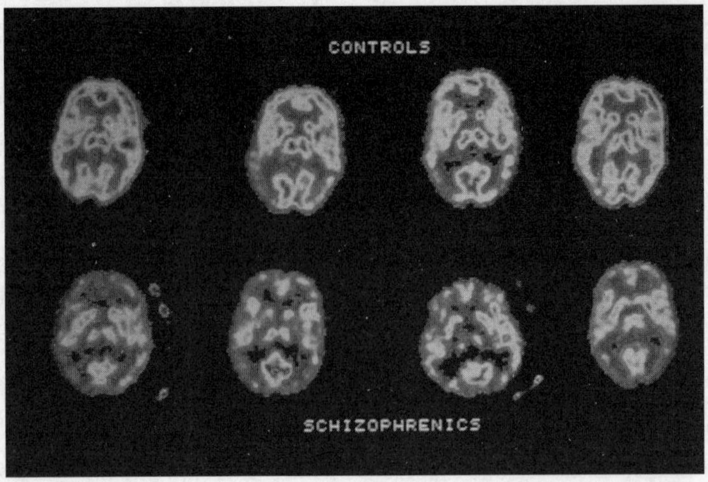


**Figure 11.4** PET scans of people with schizophrenia versus normals.

Positron emission tomography (PET) scan evidence of the metabolic processes of the brain shows relatively less metabolic activity (indicated by less yellow and red) in the frontal lobes of the brains of people with schizophrenia. PET scans of the brains of four controls (normals) are shown in the top row, and PET scans of the brains of four people with schizophrenia are shown below.

**SOURCE:** Monte Buchsbaum, M.D., Mt. Sinai Medical Center, New York, NY.

Recent evidence also points to abnormalities in brain circuitry connecting the prefrontal cortex and lower brain structures, including the thalamus and parts of the limbic system involved in regulating emotions and memory (e.g., Baker et al., 2014; Kubota et al., 2013). There may be a disconnect between the "thinking parts" of the brain (the prefrontal cortex) and lower regions of the brain involved in regulating emotions and memory processes (Freedman, 2012; Park & Thakkar, 2010). Problems in connectivity of neural networks may impair the transfer of information across brain regions, leading to a breakdown of higher mental functions and information processing needed to focus attention, think clearly, plan effectively, organize activities, and process emotions (Bohlken et al., 2016). These brain abnormalities may already be present early in life in people who later go on to develop schizophrenia (Anticevic, Murray, & Barch, 2015).

To summarize, a growing body of evidence indicates that schizophrenia is a neurodevelopmental disorder involving abnormalities in complex networks of neurons affecting different parts of the brain. Evidence is converging that genetic factors contribute to defects in connectivity between neurons in neuronal networks in the brain that render the person with schizophrenia less capable of thinking clearly, organizing and carrying out goal-directed activities, and distinguishing reality from fantasy. Although evidence of the biological underpinnings of schizophrenia continues to mount, we should be aware of a divergent view long associated with a psychiatrist, Dr. Thomas Szasz, who for many years before his death argued vociferously against the very concept of mental illness (see *Thinking Critically: Is Mental Illness a Myth?* later in the chapter).

**FAMILY PERSPECTIVES** What role do disturbed family relationships play in the development and course of schizophrenia? An early—but since discredited—theory focused on the role of the *schizophrenogenic mother* (Fromm-Reichmann, 1948, 1950).

## A CLOSER Look

### THE HUNT FOR ENDOPHENOTYPES IN SCHIZOPHRENIA

Although still in its infancy, the scientific search for **endophenotypes** is gathering momentum among researchers (Greenwood et al., 2016; Lowe et al., 2015; Riesel et al., 2015). What is an endophenotype? Think of it as an underlying process or mechanism, unseen by the unaided human eye, that explains how genetic instructions encoded in an organism's DNA influence an observable characteristic of the organism, or *phenotype* (Gottesman & Gould, 2003). Phenotypes are outward expressions of traits, such as eye color or observed behavior. Think of endophenotypes as mechanisms or critical links by which genes become expressed in behavioral or physical traits or disorders.

To better understand the role of genes in the development of schizophrenia or other disorders, we need to dig under the surface to uncover the specific processes or mechanisms—the endophenotypes—that explain how genes lead to the development of particular disorders. Investigators are now investigating possible endophenotypes for disorders such as schizophrenia, depression, bipolar disorder, and obsessive–compulsive disorder (e.g., Fears et al., 2014; Goldstein & Klein, 2014; Hamilton, 2015; Peterson, Wang, et al., 2014; Roussos et al., 2015; Yao et al., 2015). Figure 11.5 shows a model representing links between candidate genes and possible endophenotypes, leading to increased vulnerability to schizophrenia.

The hunt for endophenotypes in schizophrenia has largely focused on disturbances in brain circuitry, deficits in working memory, impaired attentional and cognitive processes, and abnormalities in neurotransmitter functioning (e.g., Hill et al., 2013; Ivleva et al., 2013; Turetsky et al., 2014). Consider abnormalities in brain circuitry as a possible endophenotype. Brain circuits connecting the prefrontal cortex and lower brain regions, including the limbic system, are involved in organizing thoughts, perceptions, emotions, and attentional processes. Defects in this circuitry may lead to a breakdown in these processes, resulting in positive features of schizophrenia, such as hallucinations, delusions, and thought disorder.

Researchers are beginning to shed light on underlying processes leading to defective brain circuitry. A landmark study in 2016 linked genetic variations associated with schizophrenia to excessive thinning of synaptic connections between neurons in the prefrontal cortex of the brain, a process likened to pruning a tree (Dhindsa & Goldstein, 2016; Sekar et al., 2016). The brain normally sheds some synaptic connections that become redundant or weak as it matures (Carey, 2016). This new research indicates that excessive shedding of synaptic connections in the brain of people with schizophrenia may lead to communication problems between networks of brain neurons responsible for thinking, attention, perception, and emotional processing. Further supporting this view, other evidence shows brain abnormalities associated with a breakdown in communication and signaling between different parts of the brain in people with schizophrenia as well those with bipolar disorder (Skudlarski et al., 2013).

As the search for hidden mechanisms in schizophrenia continues, we should understand that scientists haven't found any one brain abnormality that is present in every person suffering from schizophrenia. Perhaps a "one size fits all" model doesn't apply. Schizophrenia is a complex disorder characterized by different subtypes and symptom complexes. Different causal processes in the brain may explain different forms of schizophrenia. What we now call *schizophrenia* may actually turn out to be more than one disorder.

**Figure 11.5** From genes to vulnerability.

**SOURCE:** Adapted from Gottesman & Gould, 2003.

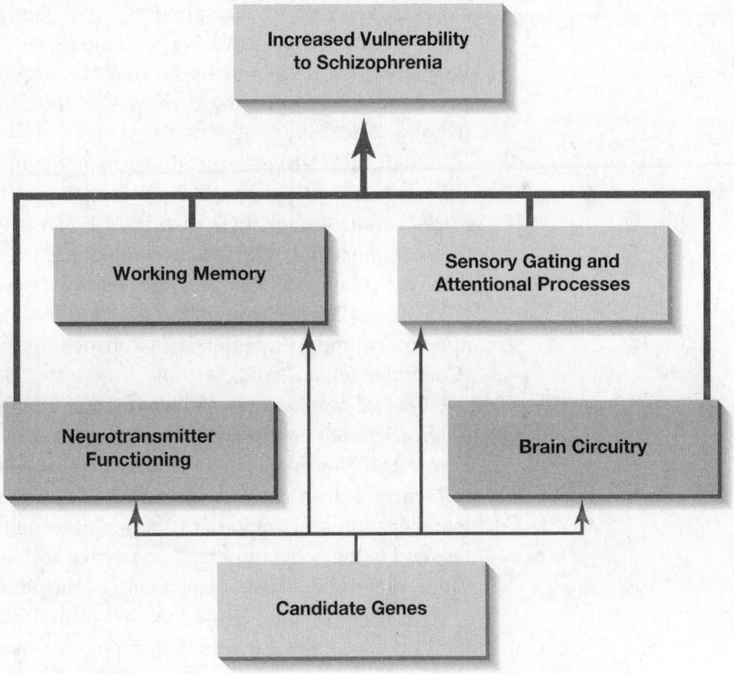


In what some feminists view as historic psychiatric sexism, the schizophrenogenic mother was described as cold, aloof, overprotective, and domineering. She was characterized as stripping her children of self-esteem, stifling their independence, and forcing them into dependency on her. Children reared by such mothers were believed to be at special risk for developing schizophrenia if their fathers were passive and failed to counteract the mother's pathogenic influences. Thankfully, the concept of the "schizophrenogenic mother" was discredited as investigators showed that mothers of people who develop schizophrenia do not fit this stereotypical pattern (e.g., Hirsch & Leff, 1975).

Today, investigators interested in family influences have turned to considering the effects of deviant patterns of communication within the family as well as intrusive, negative comments directed toward the schizophrenic family member.

***Communication Deviance*** Communication deviance (CD) is a pattern of unclear, vague, disruptive, or fragmented communication that is often found among parents and family members of people with schizophrenia. CD is speech that is hard to follow and from which it is difficult to extract any shared meaning. High CD parents often have difficulty focusing on what their children are saying. They verbally attack their children rather than offer constructive criticism. They may also interrupt the child with intrusive, negative comments. They are prone to telling the child what she or he "really" thinks rather than allowing the child to formulate her or his own thoughts and feelings. Evidence shows that parents with high levels of CD stand a higher than average of risk of having offspring with schizophrenia spectrum disorders (Roisko et al., 2014).

We should note that the causal pathway between CD and schizophrenia may work in both directions. On the one hand, CD may increase the risk of schizophrenia in genetically vulnerable individuals. However, CD also may be a parental reaction to the behavior of disturbed children. Parents may learn to use odd language as a way of coping with children who continually interrupt and confront them.

***Expressed Emotion*** Another form of disturbed family communication, *expressed emotion* (EE), is a pattern of responding to the family member with schizophrenia in hostile, critical, and unsupportive ways (Banerjee & Retamero, 2014; von Polier et al., 2014). People with schizophrenia who live in a high EE family environment have more than twice the risk of suffering a relapse as those from low EE (more supportive) families (Hooley, 2010).

High EE relatives typically show less empathy, tolerance, and flexibility than low EE relatives and tend to believe that their relatives with schizophrenia can exercise greater control over their disturbed behavior (Weisman et al., 2006). EE in relatives is also associated with poorer outcomes in people with other psychological disorders, including major depression, eating disorders, and posttraumatic stress disorder (PTSD; e.g., Barrowclough, Gregg, & Tarrier, 2008). Living with a high EE relative appears to impose greater stress on people who are challenged by mental disorders (Chambless et al., 2008).

Low EE families may actually protect, or buffer, the family member with schizophrenia from the adverse impact of outside stressors and help prevent recurrent episodes (see Figure 11.6). Yet family interactions are a two-way street: Family members and patients influence each other and are influenced in turn. Disruptive behaviors by the family member with schizophrenia frustrate other members of the family, prompting them to respond to the person in a less supportive and more critical and hostile way. This, in turn, can lead to more disruptive behavior of the person with schizophrenia.

We need to take a close look at cultural differences in both the frequency of EE in family members of patients with schizophrenia and the effects these behaviors have on the patients. Investigators find high EE families to be more common in industrialized countries, such as the United States and Canada, than in developing countries, such as India (Barrowclough & Hooley, 2003).

Cross-cultural evidence shows that Mexican American, Anglo American, and Chinese families with high levels of EE are more likely than low EE families to view the psychotic behavior of a family member with schizophrenia as within the person's control (Weisman et al., 1998). The anger and criticism of high EE family members may stem from the perception that patients can and should exert greater control over their aberrant behavior.

In a study of cultural differences in EE, investigators found that high levels of EE in family members were linked to more negative outcomes in patients with schizophrenia

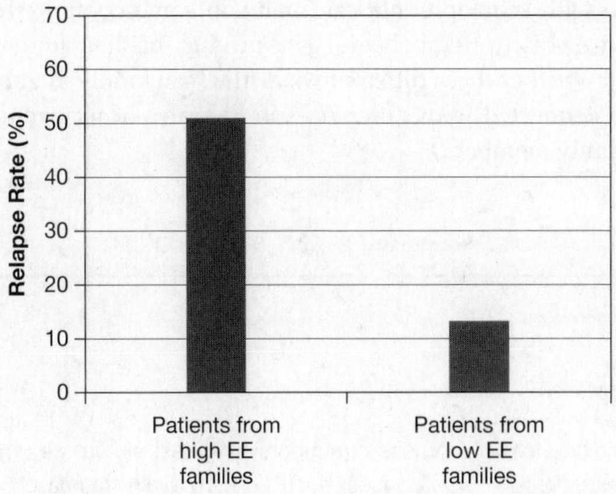


**Figure 11.6** Relapse rates of people with schizophrenia in high and low EE families.

People with schizophrenia whose families are high in EE are at greater risk of relapse than those whose families are low in EE. Whereas low EE families may help protect the family member with schizophrenia from environmental stressors, high EE families may impose additional stress.

**SOURCE:** Adapted from King & Dixon, 1999.

among Anglo American families, but not among Mexican American families (Lopez et al., 2004). For Mexican American families, the degree of family warmth, not EE per se, was related to a more positive course of schizophrenia in the affected family members, whereas for Anglo American patients, family warmth did not relate to such outcomes. In another study, investigators reported that among African American patients, high levels of EE were actually associated with better outcomes (Rosenfarb, Bellack, & Aziz, 2006). What might be the reason for this apparent contradiction? The study investigators suggested that for African Americans, intrusive critical comments during family interactions may be perceived as signs of caring and concern rather than rejection. These results underscore the importance of looking at abnormal behavior patterns through a cultural lens.

Families of people with schizophrenia typically have little if any preparation for coping with the stress of caring for them. Rather than focusing so much attention on the negative influence of high EE family members, perhaps we should seek to help family members learn more constructive ways of relating to and supporting one another. As part of a comprehensive treatment program, therapists need to work with the family of patients with schizophrenia to reduce the level of EE.

***Family Factors in Schizophrenia: Causes or Sources of Stress?*** Evidence fails to support the belief that negative family interactions directly cause schizophrenia. Rather, people who have a genetic vulnerability to schizophrenia may be more likely to develop the disorder if they live in a family environment wracked by stressful family and social relationships (Reiss, 2005; Tienari et al., 2004).

How families conceptualize mental disorders has a bearing on how they relate to relatives who suffer from them. For example, the term *schizophrenia* carries a stigma in our society and comes with the expectation that the disorder is enduring. In contrast, to many Mexican Americans, a person with schizophrenia is perceived as suffering from *nervios* ("nerves"), a cultural label attached to a wide range of troubling behaviors, including anxiety, schizophrenia, and depression, and one that carries less stigma and more positive expectations than the label of *schizophrenia*. The label *nervios* may have the effect of destigmatizing family members with schizophrenia.

**WHAT'S IN A NAME?** Quite a lot, apparently. Many Mexican Americans perceive people with schizophrenia to be suffering from *nervios* ("nerves"). The label *nervios* carries less stigma and more positive expectations than the label of *schizophrenia*.

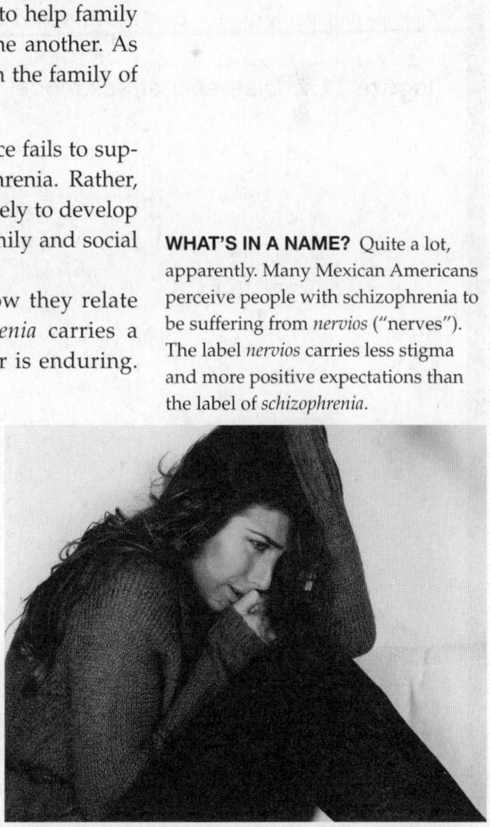

Family members may respond differently to relatives who have schizophrenia if they ascribe aspects of their behavior to a temporary or curable condition, which they believe can be altered by willpower, than if they believe the behavior is caused by a permanent brain abnormality. The degree to which relatives perceive family members with schizophrenia as having control over their disorders may be a critical factor in how they respond to them. Families may cope better with a family member with schizophrenia by taking a balanced view acknowledging that while people with schizophrenia can maintain some control over their behavior, some of their odd or disruptive behavior is a product of their underlying disorder. It remains to be seen whether these different ways in which family members conceptualize schizophrenia are connected with differences in the rates of recurrence of the disorder among affected family members.

# TYING it together

## THE DIATHESIS-STRESS MODEL

In 1962, psychologist Paul Meehl proposed an integrative model for schizophrenia that led to the development of the diathesis-stress model. Meehl suggested that certain people possess a genetic predisposition to schizophrenia that is expressed behaviorally only if they are reared in stressful environments (Meehl, 1962, 1972).

Later, Zubin and Spring (1977) formulated the diathesis-stress model, which views the development of schizophrenia in terms of an interaction or combination of a *diathesis*, or genetic predisposition to develop the disorder, and stressful life factors, especially environmental stress that exceeds the individual's stress threshold or coping resources (see Figure 11.7 for a representation of the diathesis-stress model of schizophrenia). Also note that the presence of protective factors may potentially buffer the effects of life stress, thereby reducing the likelihood that a genetic predisposition for schizophrenia will be expressed in the development of the disorder.

Environmental stressors may include psychological factors, such as family conflict, child abuse, emotional deprivation, or loss of supportive figures, as well as physical environmental influences, such as early brain trauma or injury. On the other hand, if environmental stress remains below the person's stress threshold, schizophrenia may never develop, even in persons at genetic risk.

### Research Evidence Supporting the Diathesis-Stress Model

Several lines of evidence support the diathesis-stress model. One is the fact that schizophrenia tends to develop in late adolescence or early adulthood, around the time that young people typically face the increased stress associated with establishing independence and finding a role in life. Other evidence shows that psychosocial stress, such as EE, worsens symptoms in people with schizophrenia and increases risks of relapse. Other stressors, such as economic hardship and living in distressed neighborhoods, may also interact with genetic vulnerability in the causal matrix leading to schizophrenia. However, whether stress directly

**Figure 11.7** Diathesis-stress model of schizophrenia.

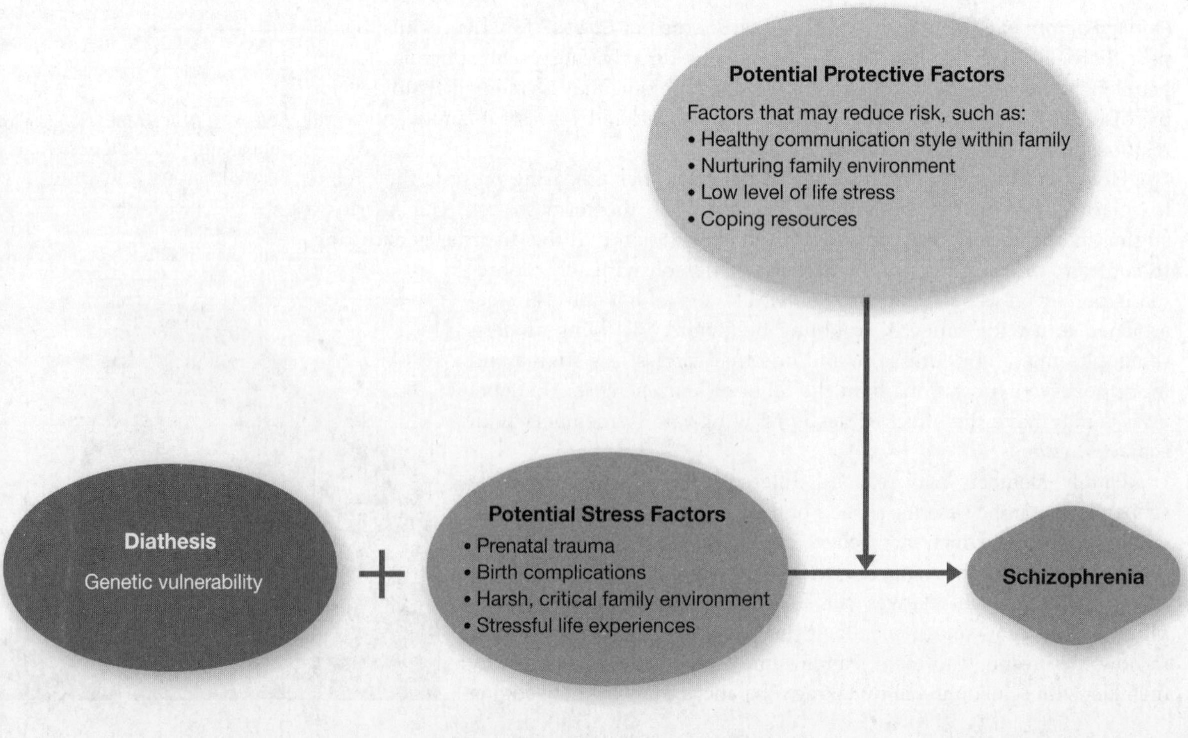

**PROTECTIVE FACTORS IN HIGH-RISK CHILDREN.** A supportive and nurturing environment may reduce the likelihood of developing schizophrenia among high-risk children.

triggers the initial onset of schizophrenia in genetically vulnerable individuals remains an open question.

More direct support for the diathesis-stress model comes from longitudinal studies of high-risk children who are at increased genetic risk of developing the disorder by virtue of having one or both parents with schizophrenia. Longitudinal studies of high-risk children support the central tenet of the diathesis-stress model: that heredity interacts with environmental influences in determining vulnerability to schizophrenia. Longitudinal studies track individuals over extended periods of time. Ideally, they begin before the emergence of the disorder or the behavior pattern in question and follow its course. In this way, investigators may identify early characteristics that predict the later development of a disorder. These studies require a commitment of many years and substantial cost. Because schizophrenia occurs in only about 1% of the general adult population, researchers have focused on high-risk children. Children with one parent with schizophrenia have about a 10% to 25% chance of developing schizophrenia, and those with both parents with schizophrenia have about a 45% risk (Erlenmeyer-Kimling et al., 1997; Gottesman, 1991).

The best-known longitudinal study of high-risk children was undertaken by Sarnoff Mednick and his colleagues in Denmark. In 1962, the Mednick group identified 207 high-risk children (whose mothers had schizophrenia) and 104 reference subjects who were matched for factors such as gender, social class, age, and education but whose mothers did not have schizophrenia (Mednick, Parnas, & Schulsinger, 1987). The children from both groups ranged in age from 10 to 20 years, with a mean of 15 years. None showed signs of disturbance when first interviewed.

Five years later, at an average age of 20, the children were reexamined. By then, 20 of the high-risk children were found to have demonstrated abnormal behavior, although not necessarily a schizophrenic episode (Mednick & Schulsinger, 1968). The children who showed abnormal behavior, referred to as the high-risk "sick" group, were then compared with a matched group of 20 high-risk children from the original sample who remained well-functioning (a high-risk "well" group) and a matched group of 20 low-risk subjects. It turned out that the mothers of the high-risk "well" offspring had experienced easier pregnancies and deliveries than those of the high-risk "sick" group or the low-risk group. Seventy percent of the mothers of the high-risk "sick" children had serious complications during pregnancy or delivery. Perhaps, consistent with the diathesis-stress model, stressful factors such as complications during pregnancy, childbirth, or shortly after birth may cause brain damage that, in combination with a genetic vulnerability, leads to severe mental disorders later in life.

In another classic research project, Finnish researchers also found links between fetal and postnatal abnormalities and the development of schizophrenia in adulthood (Jones et al., 1998). The low rate of complications during pregnancy and birth in the high-risk "well" group in the Danish study suggests that normal pregnancies and births may help protect high-risk children from developing abnormal behavior patterns (Mednick, Parnas, & Schulsinger, 1987).

Again from Denmark, evidence from tracking nearly 1.4 million births showed an interesting connection supporting the role of maternal stress during prenatal development. The offspring of mothers who experienced a highly stressful event—the death of a relative—during the first trimester showed higher than average rates of schizophrenia (Khashan et al., 2008). This evidence suggests that severe stressors during early pregnancy may adversely affect brain development in the fetus.

Positive environmental factors, such as good parenting, may help prevent the disorder in children who stand an increased genetic risk. In support of the role of early environmental influences, Mednick and his colleagues found that high-risk children who later developed schizophrenia had poorer relationships with their parents than did high-risk children who did not develop the disorder (Mednick, Parnas, & Schulsinger 1987). The presence of childhood behavior problems may also be a marker for the later development of schizophrenia-related disorders in high-risk children (Amminger et al., 1999).

# Treatment Approaches

**11.4 Identify and evaluate methods used to treat schizophrenia.**

There is no cure for schizophrenia. Treatment is generally multifaceted, incorporating pharmacological, psychological, and rehabilitative approaches. Most people treated for schizophrenia in organized mental health settings receive some form of antipsychotic medication, which is intended to control symptoms such as hallucinations and delusions and decrease the risk of recurrent episodes.

**BIOLOGICAL APPROACHES** The advent in the 1950s of antipsychotic drugs—also referred to as *major tranquilizers* or *neuroleptics*—revolutionized the treatment of schizophrenia and provided the impetus for large-scale releases of mental patients into the community (deinstitutionalization). Antipsychotic medication helps control the more flagrant behavior patterns of schizophrenia, such as delusional thinking and hallucinations, and reduces the need for long-term hospitalization.

For many patients with chronic schizophrenia, entering a hospital is like going through a revolving door; they are repeatedly admitted and discharged. Many are simply discharged to the streets once they are stabilized on medication and receive little, if any, follow-up care. This often leads to a pattern of chronic homelessness punctuated by brief stays in the hospital.

The first generation of antipsychotic drugs included the phenothiazines *chlorpromazine* (Thorazine), *thioridazine* (Mellaril), *trifluoperazine* (Stelazine), and *fluphenazine* (Prolixin). *Haloperidol* (Haldol), which is chemically distinct from the phenothiazines, produces similar effects.

Antipsychotic drugs block dopamine receptors in the brain, which reduces dopamine activity in the brain and helps quell the more obvious symptoms, such as hallucinations and delusions. The effectiveness of antipsychotic drugs has been repeatedly demonstrated in double-blind, placebo-controlled studies (Geddes, Stroup, & Lieberman, 2011; Nasrallah et al., 2009). Even so, these drugs don't help all patients with schizophrenia, and relapses can and do occur in patients, even in some patients who continue taking medication.

The major risk of long-term use of neuroleptics is a potentially disabling side effect called **tardive dyskinesia** (TD). TD can take different forms, the most common of which is frequent eye blinking. Common signs of the disorder include involuntary chewing and eye movements, lip smacking and puckering, facial grimacing, and involuntary movements of the limbs and trunk. In some cases, the movement disorder is so severe that patients have difficulty breathing, talking, or eating. In many cases, the disorder persists even when the neuroleptic medication is withdrawn.

TD is most common among older people and among women. Although TD tends to improve gradually or stabilize over a period of years, many people with TD remain persistently and severely disabled. We presently lack an effective and safe treatment for this very troubling side effect. The risk of this potentially disabling side effect requires physicians to carefully weigh the risks and benefits of long-term drug treatment.

A second generation of antipsychotic drugs, referred to as *atypical antipsychotics*, has largely replaced the earlier generation of antipsychotics. Atypical antipsychotics have about the same level of effectiveness as first-generation antipsychotics but have the advantage of carrying fewer neurological side effects and a lower risk of tardive dyskinesia (e.g., Harvey, James, & Shields, 2016; Rosenheck & Lin, 2014; Yu et al., 2015).

The more commonly used atypical antipsychotics include *clozapine* (brand name Clozaril), *risperidone* (brand name Risperdal), and *olanzapine* (brand name Zyprexa). For Lori Schiller, the woman who experienced her first psychotic break during summer camp, the voices became softer when she was treated with *clozapine*.

"I"

**The Voices Grow Softer**

It was as if it [my brain] were draining out from the inside. My head had been filled with sticky stuff, like melted rubber or motor oil. Now all that sticky stuff was dripping out, leaving only my brain behind. Slowly I was beginning to think more clearly.

And the Voices? The Voices were growing softer. Were the Voices growing softer? They were growing softer! They began moving around, from outside my skull, to inside, to outside again. But their decibel level was definitely falling.

It was happening. I was being set free. I had prayed to find some peace, and my prayers were finally being answered.... I want to live. I want to live.

**SOURCE:** *From Schiller & Bennett, 1994*

Over time, the voices receded into the background and then disappeared. Lori needed to learn to live without the voices and to build a life for herself. She began venturing beyond the confines of the hospital. She entered a halfway house and began to move toward a more independent life. Lori spent three and a half years at a halfway house and is now living independently.

Antipsychotic drugs help control symptoms of schizophrenia, but they are not a cure. People with chronic schizophrenia typically receive maintenance doses of antipsychotic drugs once their acute symptoms abate. However, many patients relapse even if they keep taking medication. The risk of relapse is even greater for patients who stop taking medication. Still, not all people with schizophrenia require antipsychotic medication to live independently (Jobe & Harrow, 2010). Unfortunately, we cannot yet predict which patients can manage effectively without continued medication. **T / F**

## TRUTH *or* FICTION

We now have drugs that not only treat schizophrenia but also can cure it in many cases.

☑ **FALSE** Antipsychotic drugs help control the symptoms of schizophrenia but cannot cure the disorder.

Atypical antipsychotics also carry risks of significant side effects, including such serious medical complications as sudden cardiac death, substantial weight gain, and metabolic disorders associated with increased risks of death due to heart disease and stroke (e.g., Abbott, 2010). In addition, the atypical antipsychotic drug clozapine carries a risk of a potentially lethal disorder in which the body produces inadequate supplies of white blood cells. Because of the seriousness of this risk, patients receiving the drug need to have their blood checked regularly. In sum, doctors face a difficult choice, having to balance the benefits of treatment with the attendant risks of potentially serious side effects (Stroup et al., 2016).

Whatever the benefits of antipsychotic medication may be, drugs alone cannot meet the multifaceted needs of people with schizophrenia. Psychiatric drugs may improve the more flagrant symptoms but have only a limited impact on the person's general social functioning, quality of life, and remediation of negative symptoms (Friedman, 2012; Turkington & Morrison, 2012). Consequently, drug therapy needs to be supplemented with psychological treatment, rehabilitation, cognitive (memory and attention) training, social skills training (including helping patients read emotional expressions in other people's faces), and social services designed to help patients with schizophrenia adjust to the many demands of community living (e.g., Hooker et al., 2012; LeVine, 2012; Strauss, 2014). A wide array of treatment components are needed within a comprehensive model of care, including the use of antipsychotic medication, medical care, psychological treatment, family therapy, social skills training, crisis intervention, rehabilitation services, and housing and other social services. Treatment programs must also ensure a continuity of care between the hospital and the community.

**SOCIOCULTURAL FACTORS IN TREATMENT** Response to psychiatric medications and dosage levels may vary with patient ethnicity (USDHHS, 1999). Asians and Hispanics, for example, may require lower doses of neuroleptics than European Americans do. Asians also tend to experience more side effects from the same dosage. Racial disparities also exist in how patients with schizophrenia are treated; for example, African American patients in one study were less likely to receive the newer generation of atypical antipsychotics than were European American patients (Kuno & Rothbard, 2002).

Ethnicity may also play a role in the family's involvement in treatment. In a study of 26 Asian Americans and 26 non-Hispanic White Americans with schizophrenia, family members of the Asian American patients were more frequently involved in the treatment program (Lin et al., 1991). For example, family members were more likely to accompany the Asian American patients to their medication evaluation sessions. The greater family involvement among Asian Americans may reflect the relatively stronger sense of family responsibility in Asian cultures. Non-Hispanic White Americans are more likely to emphasize individualism and self-responsibility.

Maintaining connections between the person with schizophrenia and the family and larger community is part of the cultural tradition in many Asian cultures, as well as in other parts of the world, such as Africa. The seriously mentally ill of China, for instance, retain strong supportive links to their families and workplaces, which helps increase their chances of being reintegrated into community life (Liberman, 1994). In traditional healing centers for the treatment of schizophrenia in Africa, the strong support that patients receive from their family and community members and a community-centered lifestyle are important elements of successful care (Peltzer & Machleidt, 1992).

**PSYCHODYNAMIC THERAPY** Freud did not believe that traditional psychoanalysis was well suited to the treatment of schizophrenia. The withdrawal into a fantasy world that typifies schizophrenia prevents the individual with schizophrenia from forming a meaningful relationship with the psychoanalyst. The techniques of classical psychoanalysis, Freud wrote, must "be replaced by others; and we do not know yet whether we shall succeed in finding a substitute" (as cited in Arieti, 1974, p. 532).

Other psychoanalysts, such as Harry Stack Sullivan and Frieda Fromm-Reichmann, adapted psychoanalytic techniques specifically for the treatment of schizophrenia. However, research has failed to demonstrate the effectiveness of psychoanalytic or psychodynamic therapy for treating schizophrenia. Although less extensively studied than learning-based therapies, promising results are reported for a modified form of psychodynamic therapy grounded in the diathesis-stress model that helps patients cope with stress and build social skills, such as learning how to deal with criticism from others (Bustillo et al., 2001).

**LEARNING-BASED THERAPIES** Although few behavior therapists believe that faulty learning causes schizophrenia, learning-based interventions have proved to be effective in modifying schizophrenic behavior and in helping people with the disorder develop behaviors that can help them adjust more effectively to living in the community. Therapy methods include the following:

1. *Selective reinforcement of behavior*, such as providing attention for appropriate behavior and extinguishing bizarre verbalizations through withdrawal of attention
2. *Token economy*, in which individuals in inpatient units are rewarded for appropriate behavior with tokens, such as plastic chips, that can be exchanged for tangible reinforcers, such as desirable goods or privileges
3. *Social skills training*, in which clients are taught conversational skills and other appropriate social behaviors through coaching, modeling, behavior rehearsal, and feedback

Although token economies can help increase desirable behaviors of psychiatric inpatients, they have largely fallen out of favor in mental hospitals in recent years (Dickerson, Tenhula, & Green-Paden, 2005). Part of the problem is that they are time- and staff-intensive. For such methods to be successful, they must have strong administrative support, skilled treatment leaders, extensive staff training, and continuous quality control, all of which can limit their practicality.

Social skills training (SST) programs help individuals acquire a range of social and vocational skills. People with schizophrenia are often deficient in basic social skills needed for community living, such as assertiveness, interviewing skills, and general conversational skills. SST can help them to improve their social skills and general level of social functioning (e.g., Granholm et al., 2014; Hooley, 2010; Lecomte et al., 2014). However, SST has only a modest effect on reducing rates of relapse once patients leave the hospital.

**BUILDING SKILLS.** Social skills training groups help patients with schizophrenia develop the social and vocational skills they need to adapt to more independent life in the community.

The basic model for social skills training incorporates role-playing exercises within a group format. Participants practice skills such as starting or maintaining conversations with new acquaintances and receive feedback and reinforcement from the therapist and other group members. The first step might be a dry run in which the participant role-plays the targeted behavior, such as asking strangers for bus directions. The therapist and other group members then praise the effort and provide constructive feedback. Role-playing is augmented by techniques such as modeling (observation of the therapist or other group members enacting the desired behavior), direct instruction (specific directions for enacting the desired behavior), shaping (reinforcement for successive approximations to the target behavior), and coaching (use of verbal or nonverbal prompts to elicit a particular desired behavior in the role-play).

Participants are given homework assignments to practice the behaviors in the settings in which they live, such as in the hospital ward or in the community. The aim is to generalize the training or transfer it to other settings. Training sessions may also be run in stores, restaurants, schools, and other real-life settings.

Another learning-based approach coming into wider practice in treating schizophrenia as an adjunct to drug therapy is cognitive-behavioral therapy (CBT; Turkington et al., 2014; Turner et al., 2014; Wykes, 2014). CBT focuses on changing thinking patterns to help patients with schizophrenia control their hallucinations by means of reattributing their voices to their internal voice or self. CBT therapists also help patients avoid cognitive errors, such as jumping to conclusions; replace delusional beliefs with alternative explanations; and combat negative symptoms, such as lack of motivation and apathy, that make it difficult for them to adjust to demands of community living. A large and growing body of evidence shows therapeutic benefits from using CBT and similar techniques in treating patients with schizophrenia (e.g., Hazell et al., 2016; Lecomte et al., 2014; Morrison et al., 2014; Shiraishi et al., 2014). The focus in CBT on helping schizophrenia patients develop adaptive skills of living brings us to consider the role of psychosocial rehabilitation as part of a multifaceted treatment approach.

**PSYCHOSOCIAL REHABILITATION** People with schizophrenia typically have difficulties functioning in social and occupational roles and performing work that depends on basic cognitive abilities involving attention and memory. These problems limit their ability to adjust to community life, even in the absence of overt psychotic behavior. Promising results are reported for cognitive rehabilitation training in helping patients with schizophrenia strengthen cognitive skills such as attention and memory (Moritz et al., 2014; Wykes, 2014).

A number of self-help clubs (commonly called clubhouses) and rehabilitation centers have sprung up to help people with schizophrenia find a place in society. Many centers were launched by nonprofessionals or by people with schizophrenia themselves, largely because mental health agencies often failed to provide comparable services. A clubhouse is not a home; rather, it serves as a self-contained community that provides members with social support and help finding educational opportunities and paid employment.

Multiservice rehabilitation centers typically offer housing, as well as job and educational opportunities. These centers often make use of skills training approaches to help clients learn how to handle money, resolve disputes with family members, develop friendships, take buses, cook their own meals, shop, and so on.

**FAMILY INTERVENTION PROGRAMS** Family conflicts and negative family interactions can heap stress on family members with schizophrenia, increasing the risk of recurrent episodes. Researchers and clinicians have worked with families of people with schizophrenia to help them cope with the burdens of care and to assist them in developing more cooperative, less confrontational ways of relating to others. The specific components of family interventions vary, but they usually share some common features, such as a focus on the practical aspects of everyday living, educating family members about schizophrenia, teaching them how to relate in a less hostile way to family members with schizophrenia, improving communication, and fostering effective problem-solving and coping skills. Structured family intervention programs can reduce friction in the family, improve social functioning in patients with schizophrenia, and even reduce relapse rates (Addington, Piskulic, & Marshall, 2010; Guo et al., 2010). However, the benefits appear to be relatively modest, and questions remain about whether relapses are prevented or merely delayed.

**A CONSENSUS EMERGES—COMBINED APPROACHES ARE NEEDED** A large-scale influential study of 404 first-episode patients with schizophrenia showed what many clinicians had long recognized, that drug therapy combined with psychological approaches is more effective than standard drug therapy alone (Carey, 2015; Kane et al., 2015). Patients in the study were randomized to receive either standard drug therapy with antipsychotic drugs or a combined regimen consisting of lower-dose medication (to minimize side effects), vocational and academic assistance, educating family members about schizophrenia, and individual, one-on-one psychotherapy. In psychotherapy, patients learned various skills, such as ways of coping with the voices in their heads—for

## THINKING CRITICALLY about abnormal psychology

### @ISSUE: IS MENTAL ILLNESS A MYTH?

In 1961, the psychiatrist Thomas Szasz (1920–2012) shocked the psychiatric establishment by making a bold claim that mental illness does not exist. In his controversial book *The Myth of Mental Illness*, Szasz, a long-time critic of the psychiatric establishment, argued that mental illness is a myth, a convenient fiction society uses to stigmatize and subjugate people whose behavior it finds to be deviant, odd, or bizarre (Szasz, 1960, 2011). To Szasz, the so-called mental illnesses are really "problems in living," not diseases in the same way that influenza, hypertension, and cancer are diseases. Szasz did not dispute that the behavior of people diagnosed with schizophrenia or other mental disorders is peculiar or disturbed, nor did he deny that these individuals suffer emotional problems or have difficulties adjusting to society. However, he challenged the conventional view that strange or eccentric behavior is a product of an underlying disease. Szasz argued that treating problems as "diseases" empowers psychiatrists to put socially deviant people away in medical facilities. To Szasz, involuntary hospitalization is a form of tyranny disguised as therapy. It deprives people of human dignity and strips them of the most essential human right: liberty.

**THOMAS SZASZ.** The late psychiatrist Thomas Szasz waged a long-standing battle with institutional psychiatry. Arguing that mental illness is a myth, Szasz believed that mental health problems are problems in living, not medical diseases.

Are the myriad problems of people with schizophrenia—the deluded thoughts and hallucinations and incoherent speech—merely "problems in living," or are they symptoms of an underlying disease process? The belief that mental illness is a myth or a social construction is difficult to reconcile with a large body of evidence showing structural and functional differences in the brains of patients with schizophrenia and of genetic factors that increase the risk of developing the disorder.

We've learned a great deal about the biological underpinnings of mental or psychological disorders since Szasz claimed that mental illness doesn't exist, although we still have much to learn. Our knowledge of the causes of many diseases, including cancer and Alzheimer's disease, is also incomplete, but a lack of knowledge does not make them any less diseases. Many professionals believe that radical theorists like Szasz go too far in arguing that mental illness is merely a fabrication invented by society to stigmatize social deviants.

Evidence supports a prominent role for biological factors in many abnormal behavior patterns, including schizophrenia, mood disorders, and autism. How far should we extend the disease model? Is antisocial personality disorder an illness? Or attention deficit hyperactivity disorder? Or specific phobias, such as fear of flying? What are the implications of treating abnormal behavioral patterns as diseases versus viewing them as problems in living?

The *DSM* itself does not take a position on which mental disorders, if any, are biologically based. It recognizes that the causes of most mental disorders remain uncertain: Some disorders may have purely biological causes. Some may have psychological causes. Still others, probably most, involve an interaction of biological, psychological, and social–environmental causes.

All in all, the views of Szasz and other critics of the mental health establishment have helped bring about much-needed improvements in the protection of the rights of patients in psychiatric institutions. They have also directed our attention to the social and political implications of our responses to deviant behavior. Perhaps most importantly, they have challenged us to examine our assumptions when we label and treat undesirable behaviors as signs of illness rather than as problems of adjustment.

In thinking critically about the issue, answer the following questions:

- What would it mean to say that schizophrenia is a problem of living rather than a disease? What would be the implications for treatment? In what way does society respond to people who behave in unusual ways?
- Based on knowledge that has accumulated since Szasz first wrote his book, which mental illnesses should be classified as problems of living? Which as diseases?

example, by talking back to them or ignoring them—and acquired social skills needed to build social relationships and learned to manage depressive symptoms.

In sum, no single treatment approach meets all the needs of people with schizophrenia. The conceptualization of schizophrenia as a lifelong disability underscores the need for long-term treatment interventions that integrate the use of antipsychotic medication, family therapy, supportive or cognitive-behavioral forms of therapy, vocational training, and housing and other social support services. To help an individual reach maximal social adjustment, these interventions should be coordinated and integrated within a comprehensive model of treatment.

# Other Schizophrenia Spectrum Disorders

The *DSM-5* classifies a range of psychological disorders within the schizophrenia spectrum of disorders. They range from milder forms of disorganized or unusual thinking and difficulties relating to others associated with schizotypal personal disorder (discussed in Chapter 12) to frankly psychotic disorders, including brief psychotic disorder, schizophreniform disorder, delusional disorder, and schizoaffective disorder, as well as schizophrenia itself.

## Brief Psychotic Disorder

**11.5 Describe the key features of brief psychotic disorder.**

Some brief psychotic episodes do not progress to schizophrenia. The diagnostic category of **brief psychotic disorder** applies to a psychotic disorder that lasts from a day to a month and is characterized by at least one of the following features: delusions, hallucinations, disorganized speech, or grossly disorganized or catatonic behavior. Eventually, there is a full return to the individual's prior level of functioning. Brief psychotic disorder is often linked to a significant stressor or stressors, such as the loss of a loved one or exposure to brutal traumas in wartime. Women sometimes experience the disorder after childbirth.

## Schizophreniform Disorder

**11.6 Describe the key features of schizophreniform disorder.**

**Schizophreniform disorder** consists of abnormal behaviors identical to those in schizophrenia that have persisted for at least 1 month but less than 6 months. They thus do not yet justify the diagnosis of schizophrenia. Although some cases have good outcomes, in others the disorder persists beyond 6 months and may be reclassified as schizophrenia or perhaps another form of psychotic disorder, such as schizoaffective disorder. However, questions remain about the validity of the diagnosis. It may be more appropriate to diagnose people who show psychotic features of recent origin with a classification that does not specify a specific type of psychotic disorder until additional information clearly indicates which specific disorder applies.

## Delusional Disorder

**11.7 Describe the key features of delusional disorder.**

Many of us, perhaps even most of us, feel suspicious of other people's motives at times. We may feel that others have it in for us or believe that others are talking about us behind our backs. For most of us, however, paranoid thinking does not take the form of outright delusions. The diagnosis of **delusional disorder** applies to people who hold persistent, clearly delusional beliefs, often involving paranoid themes. Delusional disorder is rare, affecting an estimated 20 people in 10,000 during their lifetimes (American Psychiatric Association, 2013).

In delusional disorder, the delusional beliefs may be bizarre (e.g., believing that aliens have implanted electrodes in the person's head) or may fall within a range of seeming plausibility, such as unfounded beliefs concerning the infidelity of a spouse, persecution by others, or attracting the love of a famous person. The apparent plausibility of some of these beliefs may lead other people to take them seriously and check them out before concluding that they are unfounded. Apart from the delusion, the individual's behavior may not show evidence of obviously bizarre or odd behavior, as we see in the following case example.

**IS SOMEONE OUT TO GET YOU?** People with delusional disorder often weave paranoid fantasies in their minds that they confuse with reality.

## Hit Men:
### A CASE OF DELUSIONAL DISORDER

Mr. Polsen, a married 42-year-old postal worker was brought to the hospital by his wife because he had been insisting that there was a contract out on his life. He told the doctors that the problem started about four months ago when his supervisor accused him of tampering with a package, an offense that could have cost him his job. Although the supervisor was exonerated at a formal hearing, he was furious and felt publicly humiliated. The man went on to say that his coworkers soon began avoiding him, turning away from him when he walked by, as if they didn't want to see him. He began to think that they were talking about him behind his back, although he could never clearly make out what they were saying. He gradually became convinced that his coworkers were avoiding him because his boss had put a contract on his life. He said he had noticed several large white cars cruising up and down the street where he lived. He believed there were hit men in these cars and refused to leave his home without a companion. Other than reporting that his life was in danger, his thinking and behavior appeared entirely normal on interview. He denied any hallucinations and excepting his unusual beliefs about his life being in danger, he showed no other signs of psychotic behavior. The diagnosis of delusional disorder, persecutory type seemed the most appropriate, because there was no evidence that a contract had been taken on his life (hence, it was deemed a persecutory delusion) and there were no other clear signs of psychosis that might support a diagnosis of schizophrenia.

**SOURCE:** *Adapted from Spitzer et al., 1994, pp. 177–179*

Mr. Polsen's delusional belief that "hit teams" were pursuing him was treated with antipsychotic medication in the hospital and faded in about three weeks. His belief that he had been the subject of an attempted "hit" stuck in his mind, however. A month following admission, he stated, "I guess my boss has called off the contract. He couldn't get away with it now without publicity" (Spitzer et al., 1994, p. 179).

Although delusions frequently occur in schizophrenia, delusional disorder is believed to be distinct from schizophrenia. Persons with delusional disorder do not exhibit confused or jumbled thinking. Hallucinations, when they occur, are not as prominent. Delusions in schizophrenia are embedded within a larger array of disturbed thoughts, perceptions, and behaviors. In delusional disorders, the delusion itself may be the only clear sign of abnormality.

Various types of delusional disorders in the *DSM-5* are described in Table 11.2. Like other forms of psychosis, delusional disorders often respond to antipsychotic medication (Morimoto et al., 2002; Sammons, 2005). However, once the delusion is established, it may persevere, although the individual's concern about it may wax and wane over the years. In other cases, the delusion may disappear entirely for periods of time and then recur. Sometimes, the disorder permanently disappears.

**Table 11.2** Types of Delusional Disorders

| Type | Description |
|---|---|
| **Erotomanic type** | Delusional beliefs that someone else, usually a person of higher social status such as a movie star or a political figure, is in love with you; also called *erotomania*. |
| **Grandiose type** | Inflated beliefs about one's own worth, importance, power, knowledge, or identity, or beliefs that one has a special relationship to a deity or to a famous person. Cult leaders who believe they have special mystical powers of enlightenment may have delusional disorders of this type. |
| **Jealous type** | Delusions of jealousy in which the person may become convinced, without due cause, of the infidelity of his or her partner. The delusional person may misinterpret certain clues as signs of unfaithfulness, such as spots on the bed sheets. |
| **Persecutory type** | The most common type of delusional disorder, persecutory delusions, involve themes of being conspired against, followed, cheated, spied on, poisoned or drugged, or otherwise maligned or mistreated. People with these delusions may repeatedly bring legal actions against those whom they perceived to be responsible for their mistreatment, or may even commit acts of violence against them. |
| **Somatic type** | Delusions involving the person's physical or medical condition. People with these delusions may believe that foul odors are emanating from their bodies or that internal parasites are eating away at them. |
| **Mixed type** | Delusions typify more than one of the other types with no single predominant theme. |

# A CLOSER Look

## THE LOVE DELUSION

**Erotomania**, or the love delusion, is a rare delusional disorder in which an individual believes that he or she is loved by someone else, usually someone famous or of high social status. In reality, the individual has only a passing or nonexistent relationship with the alleged lover. People with erotomania are often unemployed and socially isolated (Kennedy et al., 2002). Although the love delusion was once thought to be predominantly a female disorder, recent reports suggest it may not be a rarity among men. Although women with erotomania may have a potential for violence when their attentions are rebuffed, men with this condition appear more likely to threaten or commit acts of violence in the pursuit of the objects of their unrequited desires (Goldstein, 1986). These disorders are difficult to treat, and evidence supporting the use of antipsychotic medications is limited largely to case reports (Roudsari, Chun, & Manschreck, 2015). We also lack sufficient evidence that psychotherapy helps people with erotomania. The prognosis thus is bleak, and people with erotomania may harass their love objects for many years. Mental health professionals need to be aware of the potential for violence in the management of people who possess these delusions of love. The following cases provide some examples of the love delusion. **T / F**

### TRUTH or FICTION

Some people have delusions that they are loved by a famous person.

☑ TRUE Some people do suffer from the delusion that they are loved by a famous person. They are said to have a delusional disorder, erotomanic type.

### Three Cases of Erotomania

Mr. A., a 35-year-old man, was described as a "love-struck" suitor of a daughter of a former president of the United States. He was arrested for repeatedly harassing the woman in an attempt to win her love, although they actually were perfect strangers. Refusing to adhere to the judge's warnings to stop pestering the woman, he placed numerous phone calls to her from prison and was later transferred to a psychiatric facility, still declaring they were very much in love.

Mr. B. was arrested for breaching a court order to stop pestering a famous pop singer. A 44-year-old farmer, Mr. B. had followed his love interest across the country, constantly bombarding her with romantic overtures. He was committed to a psychiatric hospital, but maintained the belief that she'd always wait for him.

Then there was Mr. C., a 32-year-old businessman, who believed a well-known woman lawyer had fallen in love with him following a casual meeting. He constantly called and sent flowers and letters, declaring his love. Although she repeatedly rejected his advances and eventually filed criminal charges for harassment, he felt that she was only testing his love by placing obstacles in his path. He abandoned his wife and business and his functioning declined. When the woman continued to reject him, he began sending her threatening letters and was committed to a psychiatric facility.

**SOURCE:** *Adapted from Goldstein, 1986, p. 802*

# Schizoaffective Disorder

**11.8 Describe the key features of schizoaffective disorder.**

**Schizoaffective disorder** is sometimes referred to as a "mixed bag" of symptoms because it includes psychotic behaviors associated with schizophrenia (e.g., hallucinations and delusions) occurring at the same time as a major mood disorder (major depressive episode or manic episode). At some point in the course of the disorder, delusions or hallucinations occur for a period of at least two weeks without the presence of a major mood disorder (so as to distinguish the disorder from a mood disorder with psychotic features).

In terms of severity of disturbed behavior, schizoaffective disorder falls between mood disorders on the lower end and schizophrenia on the higher end (Rink et al., 2016). The lifetime prevalence of the disorder is estimated to be 0.3% of the general population (American Psychiatric Association, 2013). Like schizophrenia, schizoaffective disorder tends to follow a chronic course characterized by persistent difficulties adjusting to the demands of adult life. Also like schizophrenia, the psychotic features of schizoaffective disorder often respond well to antipsychotic drugs (McEvoy et al., 2013).

Schizoaffective disorder and schizophrenia appear to share a genetic link (Cardno & Owen, 2014). We need to discover why this common genetic substrate or predisposition leads to one disorder and not the other. Yet questions remain about whether schizoaffective disorder should remain a distinct diagnosis, or whether it would be more useful to apply separate diagnoses of schizophrenia and mood disorder in cases that present with both sets of symptoms (Kotov et al., 2013).

# Summing Up

## Schizophrenia

### Course of Development of Schizophrenia

**11.1 Describe the course of development of schizophrenia.**

Schizophrenia usually develops in late adolescence or early adulthood. Its onset may be abrupt or gradual. Gradual onset involves a prodromal phase, a period of gradual deterioration that precedes the onset of acute symptoms. Acute episodes, which may occur periodically throughout life, are typified by clear psychotic symptoms, such as hallucinations and delusions. Between acute episodes, the disorder is characterized by a residual phase in which the person's level of functioning is similar to that which was present during the prodromal phase, but deficits still remain in cognitive, emotional, and social areas of functioning.

### Key Features of Schizophrenia

**11.2 Describe the key features and prevalence of schizophrenia.**

Schizophrenia is a chronic psychotic disorder characterized by acute episodes involving a break with reality, as manifested by symptoms such as delusions, hallucinations, illogical thinking, incoherent speech, and bizarre behavior. The key diagnostic features include disturbed content of thought (delusions) and form of thought (thought disorder), as well as perceptual distortions (hallucinations) and emotional disturbances (flattened or inappropriate affect). There are also underlying dysfunctions in brain processes regulating attention to stimuli from the external world. Schizophrenia affects about 1% of the general population.

### Theoretical Perspectives

**11.3 Describe psychodynamic, learning theory, biological, and family perspectives on schizophrenia.**

In the traditional psychodynamic model, schizophrenia represents a regression to a psychological state corresponding to early infancy in which the prodding of the id produces bizarre, socially deviant behavior and gives rise to hallucinations and delusions. Learning theorists propose that some forms of schizophrenic behavior may result from lack of social reinforcement, which leads to gradual detachment from the social environment and increased attention to an inner world of fantasy. Modeling and selective reinforcement of bizarre behavior may explain some schizophrenic behaviors in the hospital setting. Evidence based on psychodynamic and learning-based models of schizophrenia have limited value in explaining the development of schizophrenia.

Compelling evidence for a strong genetic component in schizophrenia comes from studies of family patterns of schizophrenia, twin studies, and adoption studies. The mode of genetic transmission remains unknown. Most researchers believe the neurotransmitter dopamine plays a role in schizophrenia, especially in explaining the more flagrant features of the disorder, such as hallucinations and delusions. Viral factors may also be involved, but definite proof of viral involvement is lacking. Evidence also demonstrates that schizophrenia involves both structural and functional abnormalities in the brain. The diathesis-stress model posits that schizophrenia results from an interaction of a genetic predisposition (the diathesis) and environmental stressors (e.g., family conflict, child abuse, emotional deprivation, loss of supportive figures, and early brain trauma).

Family factors such as CD and EE may act as sources of stress that may increase the risk of development or recurrence of schizophrenia among people with a genetic predisposition to the disorder.

### Treatment Approaches

**11.4 Identify and evaluate methods used to treat schizophrenia.**

Contemporary treatment approaches tend to be multifaceted, incorporating pharmacological and psychosocial approaches. Antipsychotic medication is not a cure, but it can help control the more flagrant features of the disorder and reduce the need for hospitalization and the risk of recurrent episodes. Psychosocial interventions such as token economy systems, social skills training, and structured forms of psychotherapy can help patients learn to cope more effectively and develop more adaptive behaviors. Psychosocial rehabilitation can help patients adapt more successfully to occupational and social roles in the community. Family intervention programs help families cope with the burdens of care, communicate more clearly, and learn more helpful ways of relating to the patient.

## Other Schizophrenia Spectrum Disorders

### Brief Psychotic Disorder

**11.5 Describe the key features of brief psychotic disorder.**

Brief psychotic disorder is a schizophrenia spectrum disorder lasting less than a month that may be reactive to a significant stressor.

### Schizophreniform Disorder

**11.6 Describe the key features of schizophreniform disorder.**

Schizophreniform disorder is a schizophrenia spectrum disorder with symptoms identical to those of schizophrenia but lasting for a month to less than 6 months.

### Delusional Disorder

**11.7 Describe the key features of delusional disorder.**

Delusional disorder is a schizophrenia spectrum disorder marked by the presence of specific delusions—often of a paranoid nature—that may be the only sign of disturbed thinking or behavior.

### Schizoaffective Disorder

**11.8 Describe the key features of schizoaffective disorder.**

Schizoaffective disorder is a schizophrenia spectrum disorder characterized by a combination of psychotic symptoms and significant mood disturbance.

## Critical Thinking Questions

Based on your reading of this chapter, answer the following questions:

- Schizophrenia is perhaps the most disabling type of mental or psychological disorder. What makes it so?
- What do you think it would be like to hear voices? Have you ever known anyone who heard voices? How would you like others to treat you if you were diagnosed with schizophrenia?
- Have you known anyone who was diagnosed with schizophrenia? What information do you have about the person's family history, family relationships, and stressful life events that might shed light on the development of the disorder?
- How does the diathesis-stress model attempt to account for the development of schizophrenia? What evidence supports the model?
- What are the relative risks and benefits of antipsychotic medication? Why is medication alone not sufficient to treat schizophrenia? Do you believe that people with schizophrenia should be treated indefinitely with antipsychotic drugs? Why or why not?

## Key Terms

schizophrenia, p. 416
prodromal phase, p. 417
residual phase, p. 417
positive symptoms, p. 420
negative symptoms, p. 420
thought disorder, p. 422
hallucinations, p. 424
catatonia, p. 427
dopamine hypothesis, p. 431
endophenotypes, p. 434
tardive dyskinesia, p. 440
brief psychotic disorder, p. 445
schizophreniform disorder, p. 445
delusional disorder, p. 445
erotomania, p. 447
schizoaffective disorder, p. 447

Chapter 12

# Personality Disorders and Impulse-Control Disorders

## Learning Objectives

**12.1** **Identify** three clusters of personality disorders used in the *DSM* system.

**12.2** **Describe** the key features of personality disorders characterized by odd or eccentric behavior.

**12.3** **Describe** the key features of personality disorders characterized by dramatic, emotional, or erratic behavior.

**12.4** **Describe** the key features of personality disorders characterized by anxious or fearful behavior.

**12.5** **Evaluate** problems associated with the classification of personality disorders.

**12.6** **Describe** psychodynamic perspectives on the development of personality disorders.

**12.7** **Describe** learning theory perspectives on the development of personality disorders.

**12.8** **Describe** the role of family relationships in the development of personality disorders.

**12.9** **Describe** biological perspectives on the development of personality disorders.

**12.10** **Describe** sociocultural perspectives on the development of personality disorders.

**12.11** **Describe** psychodynamic approaches to treating personality disorders.

**12.12** **Describe** cognitive-behavioral approaches to treating personality disorders.

**12.13** **Describe** drug therapy approaches to treating personality disorders.

**12.14** **Describe** the key features of impulse-control disorders.

**12.15** **Describe** the key features of kleptomania.

**12.16** **Describe** the key features of intermittent explosive disorder.

**12.17** **Describe** the key features of pyromania.

## TRUTH or FICTION

**T☐ F☐** People with schizoid personalities may have deeper feelings for animals than they do for people. (p. 456)

**T☐ F☐** People we call psychopaths are psychotic. (p. 458)

**T☐ F☐** People with antisocial personalities inevitably run afoul of the law. (p. 458)

**T☐ F☐** Recent research findings support the popular image of psychopathic murderers as "cold-blooded" killers. (p. 461)

**T☐ F☐** Many notable figures in history, from Lawrence of Arabia to Adolf Hitler and even Marilyn Monroe, showed signs of borderline personality. (p. 461)

**T☐ F☐** Inflicting pain on oneself is sometimes used as a means of escaping from mental distress. (p. 462)

**T☐ F☐** People with dependent personality disorder have so much difficulty making independent decisions that they may allow their parents to decide whom they will marry. (p. 468)

**T☐ F☐** Despite years of trying, we still lack evidence that psychotherapy can help people with borderline personality disorder. (p. 483)

**T☐ F☐** Kleptomania, or compulsive stealing, is usually motivated by poverty. (p. 485)

## CHAPTER INTRODUCTION: PERSONALITY DISORDERS AND IMPULSE-CONTROL DISORDERS

"I" "My Dark Place"

She wrote about herself on an online bulletin board, sharing her personal anguish with strangers, wanting others to know just how deeply she had suffered. She wrote there were times when she entered a "dark place" in which she would experience an urge to cut herself at different places on her body, mostly on her arms and legs. She later learned that her self-mutilation or cutting was a symptom of borderline personality disorder (BPD). She could not run or hide from these urges to cut herself and felt powerless to control them. She recounted how she had battled depression since she was a young girl and had begun cutting herself at the age of 8. The cutting would bring a momentary sense of relief, blotting out the negative feelings. Strangely, it became a way in which she could comfort herself and block the deeper pain she felt inside. Now as a young adult, she realizes she must find other ways of relieving her emotional pain, but recognizes it will be a long process that will take a great deal of work and therapy.

**SOURCE:** *Adapted from an anonymous posting on an online support site, New York City Voices*

Like this person, people with borderline personality disorder are often severely depressed and turn to self-mutilation in a twisted attempt to escape from emotional pain—but their problems lie deeper than depression. They involve the kinds of rigid, inflexible, and maladaptive behavior patterns that clinicians classify as *personality disorders*. These behavior patterns involve maladaptive expressions of personality traits, which have far-reaching consequences for a person's psychological adjustment and relationships with others.

All of us have particular styles of behavior and ways of relating to others. Some of us are orderly, others sloppy. Some of us prefer solitary pursuits; others are more social. Some of us are followers; others are leaders. Some of us seem immune to rejection by others, whereas others avoid social initiatives for fear of getting shot down. When behavior patterns become so inflexible or maladaptive that they cause significant personal distress or impair people's social or occupational functioning, they may be classified as *personality disorders*.

Later in the chapter, we discuss another class of disorders, called *impulse-control disorders*, which are also characterized by maladaptive patterns of behavior. With impulse-control disorders, such as kleptomania and intermittent explosive disorder, the maladaptive behaviors take the form of failure to resist impulses that lead to harmful consequences. Another feature that personality disorders and impulse disorders have in common is that people diagnosed with these disorders often fail to see how their own behaviors are seriously disrupting their lives.

As a historical note, gambling was recognized in earlier editions of the *DSM* as a type of impulse-control disorder (called *pathological gambling*), as it is characterized by difficulty controlling an impulse to gamble. However, the close relationships between compulsive gambling and addictive disorders led to its reclassification as a type of addictive disorder in *DSM-5* that is called *gambling disorder* (see Chapter 8).

# Types of Personality Disorders

> In most of us by the age of thirty, the character has set like plaster, and will never soften again.
>
> —*William James*

The core features of **personality disorders** are overly rigid and maladaptive patterns of behavior and ways of relating to others that reflect extreme variations on underlying personality traits, such as undue suspiciousness, excessive emotionality, and impulsivity. These problem traits become evident by adolescence or early adulthood. They continue through much of adult life and become so deeply ingrained that they are often highly resistant to change. The warning signs of personality disorders may emerge in childhood based on problem behaviors involving disturbed conduct, depression, anxiety, and immaturity. An estimated 6% to 10% of the general population is believed to have personality disorders (Samuels, 2011).

People with personality disorders often fail to see how their own behaviors are seriously disrupting their lives. They may blame others for the problems they have, rather than take a long, hard look in the mirror. Take a moment to think about the person who stares back at you in the bathroom mirror. What is that person like? How would you describe that person's traits or behavioral characteristics? How do these attributes influence the person's behavior and ways of relating to others? Is the person shy or outgoing? Reliable and conscientious, or lax and undependable? Anxious or calm? What makes this person unique? What accounts for the consistency in the person's behavior from place to place and time to time?

Let's first define what we mean by the term *personality*. Psychologists use the term *personality* to describe the set of distinctive psychological traits and behavioral characteristics that make each of us unique and help account for the consistency of our behavior. No two people are completely alike, not even identical twins. We each have our own distinctive ways of relating to others and interacting with the world at large. However, people with personality disorders have exaggerated or excessive personality traits that lead to personal distress or significantly interfere with their ability to function effectively in their home, school, or work environments and the communities in which they live.

Despite the self-defeating consequences of their behavior, people with personality disorders typically don't believe they need to change. Using psychodynamic terms, the *DSM* notes that people with personality disorders tend to perceive their traits as **ego syntonic**—as natural parts of themselves. Consequently, people with personality disorders are more likely to be brought to the attention of mental health professionals by others than to seek services themselves. In contrast, people with anxiety disorders (Chapter 5) or mood disorders (Chapter 7) tend to view their disturbed behaviors as **ego dystonic**. They do not see their behaviors as parts of their self-identities and are thus more likely to seek help to relieve the distress caused by these behaviors. Although personality traits may not be as hardened after the age of 30 as the famed early psychologist William James held, the extreme variations of personality traits that we find in personality disorders tend to be stable over time.

# Classification of Personality Disorders

**12.1 Identify three clusters of personality disorders used in the *DSM* system.**

The *DSM* classifies personality disorders in three categories, called clusters:

- *Cluster A:* People who are perceived as odd or eccentric. This cluster includes paranoid, schizoid, and schizotypal personality disorders.
- *Cluster B:* People whose behavior is overly dramatic, emotional, or erratic. This grouping consists of antisocial, borderline, histrionic, and narcissistic personality disorders.
- *Cluster C:* People who often appear anxious or fearful. This cluster includes avoidant, dependent, and obsessive-compulsive personality disorders.

Table 12.1 provides an overview of the personality disorders discussed in this chapter. We should also note that people with personality disorders often have other diagnosable psychological disorders. For example, a person may be diagnosed with major depression and with a personality disorder such as borderline personality disorder.

# Personality Disorders Characterized by Odd or Eccentric Behavior

**12.2 Describe the key features of personality disorders characterized by odd or eccentric behavior.**

This group of personality disorders includes paranoid, schizoid, and schizotypal disorders. People with these disorders often have difficulty relating to others or show little or no interest in developing social relationships. Here, we consider paranoid and schizoid personality disorders.

**PARANOID PERSONALITY DISORDER** The defining trait of the **paranoid personality disorder** is pervasive suspiciousness—the tendency to interpret other people's behavior as deliberately threatening or demeaning. People with the disorder are excessively

**Table 12.1** Overview of Personality Disorders

| Disorder | Lifetime Prevalence in Population (Approx.) | Description |
|---|---|---|
| **Personality Disorders Characterized by Odd or Eccentric Behavior** | | |
| Paranoid personality disorder | 2.3% to 4.4% across samples | Pervasive suspiciousness of the motives of others but without outright paranoid delusions |
| Schizoid personality disorder | 3.1% to 4.9% across samples | Social aloofness and shallow or blunted emotions |
| Schizotypal personality disorder | 4.6% (based on U.S. sample) | Persistent difficulty forming close social relationships and odd or peculiar beliefs and behaviors without clear psychotic features |
| **Personality Disorders Characterized by Dramatic, Emotional, or Erratic Behavior** | | |
| Antisocial personality disorder | Upward of 6% in men, 1% in women | Chronic antisocial behavior, callous treatment of others, irresponsible behavior, and lack of remorse for wrongdoing |
| Borderline personality disorder | 1.6% to 5.9% | Tumultuous moods and stormy relationships with others, unstable self-image, and lack of impulse control |
| Histrionic personality disorder | 1.8% | Overly dramatic and emotional behavior; demands to be the center of attention; excessive needs for reassurance, praise, and approval |
| Narcissistic personality disorder | Under 1% to 6.2% across samples | Grandiose sense of self; extreme needs for admiration |
| **Personality Disorders Characterized by Anxious or Fearful Behavior** | | |
| Avoidant personality disorder | 0.5% to 1% | Chronic pattern of avoiding social relationships due to fears of rejection |
| Dependent personality disorder | Less than 1% | Excessive dependence on others and difficulty making independent decisions |
| Obsessive-compulsive personality disorder | 2.1% to 7.9% across samples | Excessive needs for orderliness and perfectionism, excessive attention to detail, rigid ways of relating to others |

**SOURCES:** Prevalence rates derived from American Psychiatric Association, 2013; Cale & Lilienfeld, 2002; Kessler et al., 1994.

mistrustful of others, and their relationships suffer for it. Although they may be suspicious of coworkers and supervisors, they can generally maintain employment.

The following case illustrates the unwarranted suspicion and reluctance to confide in others that typifies people with paranoid personalities.

## Always Suspicious of Others:

### A CASE OF PARANOID PERSONALITY DISORDER

An 85-year-old retired businessman was interviewed by a social worker to determine health care needs for himself and his wife. The man had no history of treatment for a mental disorder. He appeared to be in good health and mentally alert. He and his wife had been married for 60 years, and it appeared that his wife was the only person he'd ever really trusted. He had always been suspicious of others. He would not reveal personal information to anyone but his wife, believing that others were out to take advantage of him. He had refused offers of help from other acquaintances because he suspected their motives. When called on the telephone, he would refuse to give out his name until he determined the nature of the caller's business. He'd always involved himself in "useful work" to occupy his time, even during his 20 years of retirement. He spent a good deal of time monitoring his investments and had altercations with his stockbroker when errors on his monthly statement prompted suspicion that his broker was attempting to cover up fraudulent transactions.

**SOURCE:** *Adapted from Spitzer et al., 1994, pp. 211–213*

People who have paranoid personality disorder tend to be overly sensitive to criticism, whether real or imagined. They take offense at the smallest slight. They are readily angered and hold grudges when they think they have been mistreated. They are unlikely to confide in others because they believe that personal information may be used against them. They question the sincerity and trustworthiness of friends and associates. A smile or a glance may be viewed with suspicion. As a result, they have few friends and intimate relationships. When they do form an intimate relationship, they may suspect infidelity, even without evidence. They tend to remain hypervigilant, as if they must be on the lookout against harm. They deny blame for misdeeds, even when warranted, and are perceived by others as cold, aloof, scheming, devious, and humorless. They tend to be argumentative and may launch repeated lawsuits against those who they believe have mistreated them.

Clinicians need to weigh cultural and sociopolitical factors when arriving at a diagnosis of paranoid personality disorder. For example, members of immigrant or ethnic minority groups, political refugees, or people from other cultures may seem guarded or defensive, but this behavior may reflect unfamiliarity with the language, customs, or rules and regulations of the majority culture or cultural mistrust arising from a history of neglect or oppression. Such behavior should not be confused with paranoid personality disorder.

Although people with paranoid personality disorder harbor exaggerated and unwarranted suspicions, they do not have the outright paranoid delusions that characterize the thought patterns of people with paranoid schizophrenia (e.g., believing the FBI is out to get them). People who have paranoid personalities are unlikely to seek treatment; they see others as causing their problems. The reported prevalence of paranoid personality disorder in the general population ranges from 2.3% to 4.4% across samples (American Psychiatric Association, 2013). The disorder is diagnosed more often in men than in women among people receiving mental health treatment.

**SCHIZOID PERSONALITY DISORDER** Social isolation is the cardinal feature of **schizoid personality disorder**. Often described as a loner or an eccentric, the person with a schizoid personality lacks interest in social relationships. The person's emotions usually appear shallow or blunted, but not to the degree found in schizophrenia (see Chapter 11). People with this disorder rarely, if ever, experience strong anger, joy, or sadness. They may appear distant from others or aloof. Their

**SCHIZOID PERSONALITY.** It is normal to be reserved about displaying one's feelings, especially when one is among strangers, but people with schizoid personalities rarely express emotions and are distant and aloof. Yet the emotions of people with schizoid personalities are not as shallow or blunted as those of people with schizophrenia.

faces tend to show no emotional expression, and they rarely exchange social smiles or nods. They seem indifferent to criticism or praise and appear to be wrapped up in abstract ideas rather than in thoughts about people. Although they prefer to remain distant from others, they maintain better contact with reality than people with schizophrenia do. The prevalence of the disorder in the general population remains unknown. Men with this disorder rarely date or marry. Women with the disorder are more likely to accept romantic advances passively and to marry, but they seldom initiate relationships or develop strong attachments to their partners.

We may find inconsistencies between the outer appearances and the inner lives of people with schizoid personalities. For example, they may appear to have little appetite for sex, but harbor voyeuristic wishes or become absorbed with pornography. However, the apparent social distance and aloofness of people with schizoid personalities may be somewhat superficial. They may harbor exquisite sensitivity, deep curiosities about people, and wishes for love that they cannot express. In some cases, sensitivity is expressed in deep feelings for animals rather than people. **T / F**

**TRUTH *or* FICTION**

People with schizoid personalities may have deeper feelings for animals than they do for people.

☑ **TRUE** People with a schizoid personality may show little or no interest in people but develop strong feelings for animals.

## Schizotypal Personality Disorder

People with **schizotypal personality disorder (SPD)** have persistent difficulties in forming close relationships with others and display behaviors, mannerisms, and thought patterns that seem peculiar or odd, but not disturbed enough (not a "break with reality") to merit a diagnosis of schizophrenia (Garakani & Siever, 2015).

People with schizotypal personality disorder lack a coherent sense of self. They may have a distorted self-concept or lack self-direction (e.g., not knowing where they are going in life). They may also lack the capacity for empathy, showing a lack of understanding for how their own behavior affects others or misinterpreting other people's behaviors or motives. They may be especially anxious in social situations, even when interacting with familiar people. They have difficulty forming close relationships, or even any relationships, a finding we also see reported with schizotypal patients in other cultures, such as in a Chinese population in Singapore (Guoa et al., 2010). The social anxiety of schizotypal patients is often linked to paranoid thinking (e.g., fears that others mean them harm) rather than to concerns about being rejected or evaluated negatively by others. People with schizotypal personality disorder often have other co-occurring emotional disorders, such as major depression and anxiety disorders, as well as an increased risk of suicidal behavior (Lentz, Robinson, & Bolton, 2010).

People with schizotypal personality disorder may experience unusual perceptions or illusions, such as feeling the presence of a deceased family member in the room. They realize, however, that the person is not actually there. They may become unduly suspicious of others or paranoid in their thinking. They may develop *ideas of reference*, such as believing that others are talking about them behind their backs. They may engage in *magical thinking*, such as believing they possess a "sixth sense" (e.g., can foretell the future) or that others can sense their feelings. They may attach unusual meanings to words. Their own speech may be vague or unusually abstract, but it is not incoherent or filled with the loose associations that characterize schizophrenia. They may appear unkempt, display unusual mannerisms, and engage in unusual behaviors, such as talking to themselves in the presence of others. Their thought processes also appear odd and are marked by vague, metaphorical, or stereotyped thinking. Their faces may register little emotion. They may fail to exchange smiles with or nod at others, or they may appear silly and smile and laugh at the wrong times. They tend to be socially withdrawn and aloof, with few, if any, close friends or confidants. They seem to be especially anxious around unfamiliar people. We can see evidence of the social aloofness and illusions that are often associated with schizotypal personality disorder in the following case example.

## Jonathan:
### A CASE OF SCHIZOTYPAL PERSONALITY DISORDER

Jonathan, a 27-year-old auto mechanic, had few friends and preferred reading science fiction novels to socializing with other people. He seldom joined in conversations. At times, he seemed to be lost in his thoughts, and his coworkers would have to whistle to get his attention when he was working on a car. He often showed a weird expression on his face. Perhaps the most unusual feature of his behavior was his reported intermittent experience of "feeling" his deceased mother standing nearby. These illusions were reassuring to him, and he looked forward to their occurrence. Jonathan realized they were not real. He never tried to reach out to touch the apparition, knowing it would disappear as soon as he drew closer. It was enough, he said, to feel her presence.

*From the Author's Files*

Schizotypal personality disorder may be slightly more common in males than in females and is believed to affect about 4.6% of the general population (American Psychiatric Association, 2013). Investigators also find higher rates of the disorder among African Americans than among Caucasians or Hispanic Americans (Chavira et al., 2003). However, clinicians need to be careful not to label as schizotypal certain behavior patterns that reflect culturally determined beliefs or religious rituals, such as beliefs in voodoo and other magical beliefs.

As discussed in Chapter 11, schizotypal personality disorder is conceptualized by *DSM-5* as part of the schizophrenia spectrum of disorders. Schizophrenia and schizotypal personality disorder appear to share a common genetic basis and certain brain abnormalities (Chemerinski et al., 2012; Ettinger et al., 2014). One exception is that the prefrontal cortex—the brain's thinking center—appears to be spared in SPD but not in schizophrenia (Ettinger et al., 2014; Hazlett et al., 2014). This leads to the intriguing possibility that preservation of prefrontal function in SPD may protect a person from the flagrant psychotic behaviors and cognitive impairment associated with schizophrenia (Hazlett et al., 2014). Another line of speculation is that the emergence of schizophrenia in people with this shared genetic predisposition may be determined by other factors, such as stressful life experiences. What we do know with greater certainty is that relatively few people diagnosed with schizotypal personality disorder eventually develop schizophrenia or other psychotic disorders (American Psychiatric Association, 2000).

# Personality Disorders Characterized by Dramatic, Emotional, or Erratic Behavior

**12.3 Describe the key features of personality disorders characterized by dramatic, emotional, or erratic behavior.**

This cluster of personality disorders includes the antisocial, borderline, histrionic, and narcissistic types. People with these disorders exhibit behavior patterns that are excessive, unpredictable, or self-centered; they also have difficulty forming and maintaining relationships and show antisocial behavior.

**ANTISOCIAL PERSONALITY DISORDER** People with **antisocial personality disorder** are *antisocial* in the sense that they often violate the rights of others, disregard social norms and conventions, and, in some cases, break the law. They show a lack of concern or callous indifference about violating the rights of others and using other people for their own gain. We should note they are not "antisocial" in the colloquial sense of seeking to avoid people.

People with antisocial personalities tend to be impulsive and fail to live up to their commitments to others (Swann et al., 2009). Yet they often show a superficial charm and possess at least average intelligence. They frequently have little, if any, anxiety when faced with threatening situations and lack feelings of guilt or remorse following wrongdoing (Kiehl, 2006). Punishment

**ANTISOCIAL PERSONALITY.** Serial killer Ted Bundy, shown here shortly before his execution, killed without feeling or remorse but also displayed some of the superficial charm seen in some people with antisocial personality disorder.

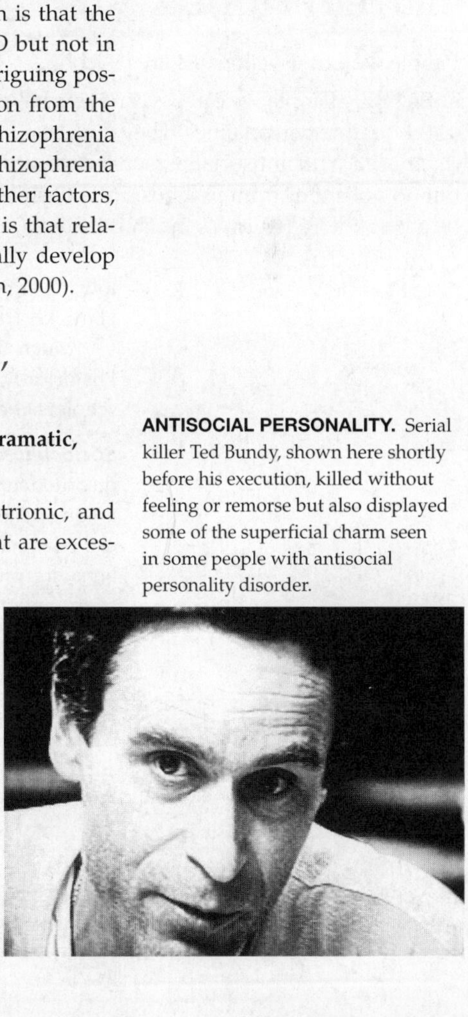

**Figure 12.1 Lifetime prevalences of antisocial personality disorder by gender.**

Antisocial personality disorder is more than five times as common among men as among women. However, the prevalence of the disorder has been rising more rapidly among women in recent years.

**SOURCE:** National Comorbidity Survey (Kessler et al., 1994).

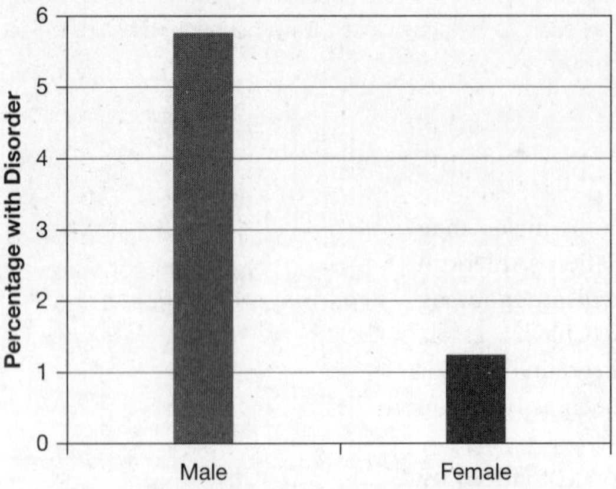


## TRUTH or FICTION

People we call psychopaths are psychotic.

☑ **FALSE** People we call psychopaths have psychopathic personalities. They may be diagnosed with antisocial personality disorder, but do not suffer from psychosis (manifested by a break with reality, as in schizophrenia).

may have little or no effect on their behavior. Although parents and others have usually punished them for their misdeeds, they persist in leading irresponsible and impulsive lives.

Antisocial personality disorder occurs more commonly in men than in women, with prevalence rates based on community samples ranging from about 1% in women to nearly 6% in men (see Figure 12.1). The diagnosis is limited to people 18 years of age or older. However, the pattern of antisocial behavior that characterizes antisocial personality disorder begins in childhood or adolescence, typically by the age of 8, and extends into adulthood. A pattern of antisocial behaviors before age 18 is usually diagnosed as *conduct disorder* (discussed further in Chapter 13). If the antisocial behavior persists beyond age 18, the diagnosis is converted to antisocial personality disorder. Early forms of antisocial behavior we see in childhood and adolescence often include truancy, running away, initiating physical fights, use of weapons, forcing someone into sexual activities, physical cruelty to people or animals, deliberate destruction of property or fire setting, lying, stealing, robbery, and assaulting others.

Clinicians once used terms such as *psychopath* and *sociopath* to refer to people who today are classified as having antisocial personalities—people whose behavior is amoral, asocial, and impulsive, and who lack remorse and shame. Some clinicians continue to use these terms interchangeably with *antisocial personality*. The roots of the word *psychopath* focus on the idea that there is something amiss (pathological) in the individual's psychological functioning. The roots of *sociopath* center on the person's social deviance. **T / F**

Over time, antisocial and criminal behavior associated with the disorder tends to decline with age and may disappear by the time the person reaches the age of 40, but not so for the underlying personality traits associated with the disorder—traits such as egocentricity; manipulativeness; lack of empathy, guilt, or remorse; and callousness toward others. These appear to be relatively stable even with increasing age (Harpur & Hare, 1994).

Much of our attention in this chapter focuses on antisocial personality disorder. Historically, this is the personality disorder that has been most extensively studied by scholars and researchers.

***Sociocultural Factors and Antisocial Personality Disorder*** Antisocial personality disorder cuts across all racial and ethnic groups. The disorder is most common, however, among people in lower socioeconomic groups. One explanation is that people with antisocial personality disorder drift downward occupationally, perhaps because their antisocial behavior makes it difficult for them to hold steady jobs or to progress upward. People from lower socioeconomic levels may also be more likely to have parents who modeled antisocial behavior. However, the diagnosis may also be misapplied to people living in hard-pressed communities who engage in seemingly antisocial behaviors as a survival strategy (American Psychiatric Association, 2013).

## TRUTH or FICTION

People with antisocial personalities inevitably run afoul of the law.

☑ **FALSE** Not all criminals show signs of psychopathy and not all people with psychopathic personalities become criminals.

***Antisocial Behavior and Criminality*** We tend to think of antisocial behavior as synonymous with criminal behavior. Although antisocial personality disorder is associated with an increased risk of criminality (Kosson, Lorenz, & Newman, 2006), not all criminals have antisocial personalities, nor do all people with antisocial personality disorder become criminals. Many people with antisocial personality disorders are law abiding and successful in their careers, even though they may treat others in a callous and insensitive manner. **T / F**

Investigators have begun to view antisocial personality as composed of two somewhat independent dimensions. The first is a *personality dimension*: It consists of traits such as superficial charm, selfishness, lack of empathy, callous and remorseless use of others, and disregard for others' feelings and welfare. This type of psychopathic personality applies to people who have these kinds of psychopathic traits but don't become lawbreakers.

The second dimension is a *behavioral dimension*: It is characterized by the adoption of a generally unstable and antisocial lifestyle, including frequent problems with the law, poor employment history, and unstable relationships. These two dimensions are not entirely separate; many antisocial individuals show evidence of both sets of traits.

**CRIMINALITY OR ANTISOCIAL PERSONALITY DISORDER?**
It is likely that many prison inmates could be diagnosed with antisocial personality disorder; however, people may become criminals or delinquents not because of a disordered personality but because they were raised in environments or exposed to subcultures that both encouraged and rewarded criminal behavior.

We should also note that some people do not become criminals or delinquents because of a disordered personality but because they were reared in environments or subcultures that rewarded criminal behavior. Although criminal behavior is deviant to society at large, it is normal by the standards of the subculture. Also, lack of remorse, which is a cardinal feature of antisocial personality disorder, does not characterize all criminals. Some criminals regret their crimes, and judges and parole boards consider evidence of remorse when passing sentence or recommending a prisoner for parole.

Despite the popular impression that criminals are all psychopaths, and vice versa, only about half of prison inmates could be diagnosed with antisocial personality disorder (Robins, Locke, & Reiger, 1991). Moreover, only a minority of people diagnosed with antisocial personality disorder run afoul of the law. Many fewer (thankfully!) fit the stereotype of the psychopathic killer popularized in films such as *The Silence of the Lambs*.

***Profile of the Antisocial Personality*** Antisocial personality or psychopathy is associated with a wide range of traits, including failure to conform to social norms, irresponsibility, aimlessness and lack of long-term goals or plans, impulsive behavior, outright lawlessness, violence, chronic unemployment, marital problems, lack of remorse or empathy, substance abuse or alcoholism, and a disregard for the truth and for the feelings and needs of others. In a classic work in the field originally published in 1941, Hervey Cleckley (1976) argued that the characteristics that define the psychopathic or antisocial personality—self-centeredness, irresponsibility, impulsivity, and insensitivity to the needs of others—exist not only among criminals but also among many respected members of the community, including doctors, lawyers, politicians, and business executives.

**A "HUMAN SNAKE" IN A THREE-PIECE SUIT?** Not all psychopathic personalities are violent criminals. The disgraced financier Bernie Madoff never committed a violent crime but is serving a life sentence in federal prison for having pilfered the life savings of scores of individuals while showing no apparent remorse or concern for the people he harmed.

Investigators in the field believe that psychopathic traits can be grouped in four basic factors or dimensions (Mokros et al., 2015; Neumann & Hare, 2008): (1) an *interpersonal factor* characterized by superficiality, grandiosity, and deceitfulness; (2) an *affective factor* characterized by lack of remorse and empathy and a failure to accept responsibility for misbehavior; (3) a *lifestyle factor* characterized by impulsivity and lack of goals; and (4) an *antisocial factor* characterized by poor behavioral control and antisocial behavior.

Irresponsibility, a common trait among people with antisocial personalities, may be seen in a personal history dotted by repeated, unexplained absences from work, abandonment of jobs without having other job opportunities to fall back on, or long stretches of unemployment. Irresponsibility often extends to financial matters, where there may be repeated failure to repay debts, to pay child support, or to meet other financial responsibilities to one's family and dependents. The key clinical features of antisocial personality disorder are shown in Table 12.2. Not all of these behaviors need to be present in every case.

## Table 12.2 Key Features of Antisocial Personality Disorder

| Features | Examples |
|---|---|
| Failure to adhere to social rules, social norms, or legal codes | Engaging in criminal behavior that may result in arrest, such as destruction of property, engaging in unlawful occupations, stealing, or harassing others |
| Aggressive or hostile behavior | Repeatedly getting into physical confrontations and fights with others or assaulting others, even one's own children or spouse |
| Lack of responsible behavior | Failure to maintain regular employment due to chronic absences or lateness or failure to seek gainful employment when it is available; failure to honor financial obligations, such as failing to meet child support responsibilities or defaulting on debts; failure to establish or maintain a stable monogamous relationship |
| Impulsive behavior | Acting on impulse and failing to plan ahead or consider consequences; traveling around without any clear employment opportunities or goals |
| Lack of truthfulness | Repeatedly lying, conning others, or using aliases for personal gain or pleasure |
| Reckless behavior | Taking undue risks to one's safety or the safety of others, such as by driving at unsafe speeds or driving while intoxicated |
| Lack of remorse for misdeeds | Lack of concern or remorse for the harm done to others by one's behavior, or rationalizing harm to others |

The following case represents a number of these antisocial characteristics.

## "Twisted Sister":

### A CASE OF ANTISOCIAL BEHAVIOR

The 19-year-old male is brought by ambulance to the hospital emergency room in a state of cocaine intoxication. He's wearing a T-shirt that reads "Twisted Sister" on the front, and he sports a punk-style haircut. His mother is called and sounds groggy and confused on the phone; the doctors must coax her to come to the hospital. She later tells the doctors that her son has arrests for shoplifting and for driving while intoxicated. She suspects that he takes drugs, although she has no direct evidence. She believes that he is performing fairly well at school and has been a star member of the basketball team.

It turns out that her son has been lying to her. In actuality, he never completed high school and never played on the basketball team. A day later, his head cleared, the patient tells his doctors, almost boastfully, that his drug and alcohol use started at the age of 13, and that by the time he was 17, he was regularly using a variety of psychoactive substances, including alcohol, speed, marijuana, and cocaine. Lately, however, he has preferred cocaine. He and his friends frequently participate in drug and alcohol binges. At times, they each drink a case of beer in a day along with downing other drugs. He steals car radios from parked cars and money from his mother to support his drug habit, which he justifies by adopting a (partial) "Robin Hood" attitude—that is, taking money only from people who have lots of it.

**SOURCE:** *Adapted from Spitzer et al., 1994, pp. 81–83*

Although this case is suggestive of antisocial personality disorder, the diagnosis was maintained as provisional because the interviewer could not determine whether the deviant behavior (lying, stealing, skipping school) began before the age of 15.

**BORDERLINE PERSONALITY DISORDER** **Borderline personality disorder (BPD)** is characterized by features such as a deep sense of emptiness, an unstable self-image, a history of turbulent and unstable relationships, dramatic mood changes, impulsivity, difficulty regulating negative emotions, self-injurious behavior, and recurrent suicidal behaviors (e.g., Krause-Utz et al., 2013; Lazarus et al., 2014; Santangelo et al., 2014; Schulze, Schmahl, & Niedtfeld, 2015).

People with BPD tend to be uncertain about their personal identities—their values, goals, careers, perhaps even their sexual orientations. This instability in self-image or personal identity leaves them with nagging feelings of emptiness and boredom. They cannot tolerate being alone and make desperate attempts to avoid feelings of abandonment. Fear of abandonment leads them to become clingy and demanding in their personal relationships, but their clinging often pushes away the very people on whom they depend. Rejection may enrage them, putting further strain on their relationships. Their feelings toward others are intense and shifting. They alternate between extremes of adulation (when their needs are met) and loathing (when they feel scorned). They tend to view other

## A CLOSER Look

### "IN COLD BLOOD": PEERING INTO THE MINDS OF PSYCHOPATHIC MURDERERS

The popular image we hold of the psychopathic murderer is of a "cold-blooded" killer, someone motivated by external goals in carrying out calculated, premeditated murder. Is this image supported by hard evidence?

In an influential study that peered into the minds of 125 incarcerated murderers, Canadian researchers compared homicides committed by psychopathic offenders with those committed by nonpsychopathic offenders (Woodworth & Porter, 2002). They expected that homicides committed by the psychopathic offenders would fit the profile of a cold-blooded killing, whereas those committed by nonpsychopathic offenders would be "crimes of passion" (impulsive, "hot-headed," angry reactions to provocative situations).

The sample was drawn from two Canadian federal institutions, one in British Columbia and the other in Nova Scotia. The investigators administered a widely used and well-validated measure of psychopathy to classify offenders as psychopathic. The results supported the hypothesis that psychopathic offenders were more likely to have committed cold-blooded homicides—intentional acts motivated by goals such as obtaining drugs, money, sex, or revenge but without any emotional trigger. More than 90% (93%) of the homicides committed by the psychopathic offenders fit this profile, as compared to 48% of the murders committed by offenders who were not psychopathic.

Interestingly, the image of the "cold-blooded" psychopathic killer does not square with the long-recognized belief that psychopathic personalities often engage in impulsive, acting-out behavior. The investigators suggest that psychopathic offenders may engage in *selective impulsivity* by constraining their impulses to perform such an extreme act as murder. With such high stakes involved (e.g., lifetime incarceration if convicted), the psychopathic offender may adopt a more calculated role when carrying out these acts.

However chilling the results of this study, they help us to better understand the psychological aspects of homicide. In that respect, they may help homicide investigators narrow the scope of their investigations by focusing on personality profiles of offenders who are likely to commit particular types of crimes. **T / F**

### TRUTH *or* FICTION

Recent research findings support the popular image of psychopathic murderers as "cold-blooded" killers.

☑ **TRUE** Canadian researchers found that psychopathic murderers incarcerated for homicide were more likely than other incarcerated murderers to have committed cold-blooded homicides.

people as either all good or all bad and abruptly shift in their appraisals of others from one extreme to the other. As a result, they may flit from partner to partner in a series of brief and stormy relationships. People they had idealized are treated with contempt when relationships end or when they feel that other people fail to meet their needs.

Borderline personality disorder is believed to affect about 1.6% to 5.9% of the general adult population (American Psychiatric Association, 2013; Kernberg & Michels, 2009; Paris, 2010). Although women more frequently receive the diagnosis than men, it remains undetermined whether this gender difference reflects diagnostic practices or underlying differences in the prevalence rates of the disorder for men and women. The disorder appears to be more common among Latino Americans than White European Americans and African Americans (Chavira et al., 2003). The factors accounting for these ethnic differences require further investigation. Many notable figures have been described as having personality features associated with BPD, including Marilyn Monroe, Lawrence of Arabia, Adolf Hitler, and the philosopher Sören Kierkegaard. **T / F**

### TRUTH *or* FICTION

Many notable figures in history, from Lawrence of Arabia to Adolf Hitler and even Marilyn Monroe, showed signs of borderline personality.

☑ **TRUE** Many notable public figures have shown personality traits associated with borderline personality disorder.

The term *borderline personality* was originally used to refer to individuals whose behavior appeared to be on the border between neuroses and psychoses. People with borderline personality disorder generally maintain better contact with reality than people with psychoses, although they may show fleeting psychotic behaviors during times of stress. Generally speaking, they are more severely impaired than most people with neuroses but not as dysfunctional as those with psychotic disorders.

A central feature of BPD is difficulty regulating emotions (Baer et al., 2012). People with BPD have mood changes that run the gamut from anger and irritability to depression and anxiety (Köhling et al., 2015; Zimmerman & Morgan, 2014). They tend to be troubled by intense emotional pain and chronic feelings of anger, which often gives rise to angry outbursts. Feelings of emptiness and shame are common, together with a long-standing negative self-image (Gunderson, 2011). They often lack the ability to thoughtfully plan their actions in advance and will act impulsively without considering the consequences (Gvirts et al., 2012; Millon, 2011). They may be prone to fighting others or smashing things. They may fly into a rage at the slightest sign of rejection or for little or no reason at all, as a woman recounts about her husband in the following account.

### "I" Walking on Eggshells

They may fly into a rage at the slightest sign of rejection or for little or no reason at all.

Living with a borderline person, as one woman put it, is like "walking on eggshells." She described her borderline husband as having two personalities, a "Jovial Jekyll" and a "Horrible Hyde." Living with him, she said, was heaven one minute but hell the next. He would often explode at a moment's notice, sometimes because she spoke too quickly or too soon, or in the wrong tone of voice, or even with the wrong facial expression. Just about anything would set him off on an emotional tirade. We should recognize that rage in borderline personalities masks deeper emotional pain. It may cover up deep-seated fears of abandonment or rejection or a need to hurt others because they themselves have been hurt or abused by others.

**SOURCE:** *Adapted from Mason & Kreger, 1998*

### TRUTH *or* FICTION

Inflicting pain on oneself is sometimes used as a means of escaping from mental distress.

☑ **TRUE** People with borderline personalities may inflict pain on themselves in the attempt to escape from mental anguish.

People with borderline personalities often act on impulse, such as eloping with someone they have just met. Impulsive and unpredictable behavior is often self-destructive, involving self-mutilation (e.g., cutting) and suicidal gestures or actual attempts, especially when underlying fears of abandonment are kindled (Gunderson, 2011, 2015; Leichsenring et al., 2011). Maladaptive behaviors such as cutting, substance use, and lashing out in anger may be attempts at controlling intense negative feelings (Baer et al., 2012). About three out of four people with borderline personality disorder make suicide attempts, and about one in 10 eventually commits suicide. **T / F**

Women with borderline personality disorder tend to show more inwardly directed aggression, such as cutting or other forms of self-mutilation. Men with borderline personality disorder tend to show more outward expressions of aggression (Schmahl & Bremner, 2006). Suicide attempts and nonsuicidal self-injuries may be motivated by the desire to escape from troubling emotions.

**LIZ: BORDERLINE PERSONALITY**

Borderline personality disorder is usually diagnosed in early adulthood, although signs of the disorder are often seen in adolescence (Gunderson, 2011). Impulsive behavior may include spending sprees, gambling, drug abuse, unsafe sexual activity, reckless driving, binge eating, or shoplifting. Impulsive acts of self-mutilation, such as the self-inflicted cutting described at the opening of this chapter, may also involve scratching the wrists or even touching burning cigarettes on the arms. The following dialogue illustrates this type of behavior.

CLIENT: I've got such repressed anger in me; what happens is... I can't *feel* it; I get anxiety attacks. I get very nervous, smoke too many cigarettes. So what happens to me is I tend to *explode*. Into tears or hurting myself or whatever... because I don't know how to contend with all those mixed-up feelings.

INTERVIEWER: What was the more recent example of such an "explosion"?

CLIENT: I was alone at home a few months ago; I was frightened! I was trying to get in touch with my boyfriend and I couldn't.... He was nowhere to be found. All my friends seemed to be busy that night and I had no one to talk to.... I just got more and more nervous and more and more agitated. Finally, *bang!*... I took out a cigarette and lit it and stuck it into my forearm. I don't know why I did it because I didn't really care for him all that much. I guess I felt I had to do something dramatic....

—*Adapted from Stone, 1980, p. 400*

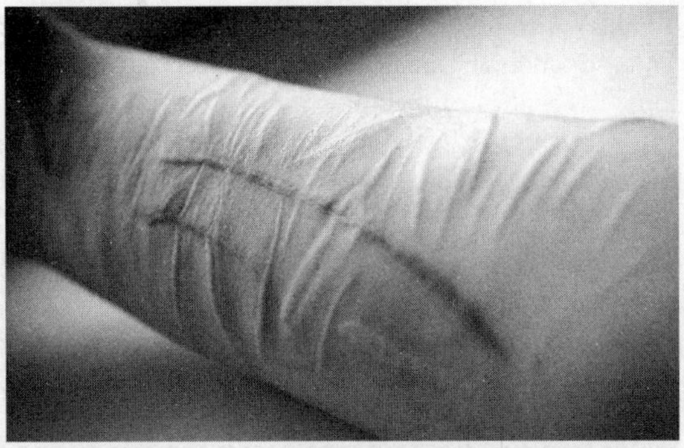

**CUTTING.** People with borderline personalities may engage in impulsive acts of self-mutilation, such as cutting themselves, perhaps as a means of temporarily blocking or escaping from deep, emotional pain.

Self-mutilation is sometimes an expression of anger or a means of manipulating others. Such acts may be intended to counteract self-reported feelings of "numbness," particularly in times of stress. Individuals with borderline personality disorder often have very troubled relationships with their families and others (Gratz et al., 2008; Johnson et al., 2006). They often had troubling childhood experiences, such as parental losses or separations, harsh punishment or maltreatment, parental neglect or lack of nurturing, or witnessing violence. They tend to view their relationships as rife with hostility and to perceive others as rejecting and abandoning. They also tend to be difficult to work with in psychotherapy (Silk, 2008). They tend to demand a great deal of support from therapists, calling them at all hours or acting suicidal to elicit support, or dropping out of therapy prematurely. Their feelings toward therapists, as toward other people, undergo rapid alterations between idealization and outrage. Psychoanalysts interpret these abrupt shifts in feelings as signs of **splitting**, or inability to reconcile the positive and negative aspects of one's experience of oneself and others.

People with borderline personality disorder may cling desperately to others whom they first idealize, but then shift abruptly to utter contempt when they perceive the other person—a therapist, lover, family member, close friend—as rejecting them or failing to meet their emotional needs. The unfortunate irony is that their desperate attempts to obtain emotional support place unreasonable demands on others, which can result in pushing others away, leading to perceptions of rejection and a belief that the other person never truly was "there for them." Perceptions of rejection are thus linked to rage (Berenson et al., 2011).

A saving grace is that many features of borderline personality, including suicidal thinking, turbulent emotions, self-harm, and impulsivity, tend to improve over a period of years (Bateman, 2012; Gunderson et al., 2012). Investigators also comment that impulsivity tends to "burn out" with increasing age (Stevenson, Meares, & Comerford, 2003).

**MARY: NONSUICIDAL SELF-INJURY**

**HISTRIONIC PERSONALITY DISORDER** **Histrionic personality disorder** is characterized by excessive emotionality and an overwhelming need to be the center of attention. The term is derived from the Latin *histrio*, which means *actor*. People with histrionic personality disorder tend to be dramatic and emotional, but their emotions seem shallow, exaggerated, and volatile. The disorder was formerly called *hysterical personality*. The following case example illustrates the excessively dramatic behaviors typical of someone with histrionic personality disorder.

## Marcella:
### A CASE OF HISTRIONIC PERSONALITY DISORDER

Marcella was a 36-year-old, attractive, but overly made-up woman who was dressed in tight pants and high heels. Her hair was in a bird's nest of the type that had been popular when she was a teenager. Her social life seemed to bounce from relationship to relationship, from crisis to crisis. Marcella sought help from the psychologist at this time because her 17-year-old daughter, Nancy, had just been hospitalized for cutting her wrists. Nancy lived with Marcella and Marcella's current boyfriend, Morris, and there were constant arguments in the apartment. Marcella recounted the disputes that took place with high drama, waving her hands, clanging the bangles that hung from her bracelets, and then clutching her breast. It was difficult having Nancy live at home because Nancy had expensive tastes, was "always looking for attention," and flirted with Morris as a way of "flaunting her youth." Marcella saw herself as a doting mother and denied any possibility that she was in competition with her daughter.

Marcella came for a handful of sessions, during which she basically ventilated her feelings and was encouraged to make decisions that might lead to a reduction of some of the pressures on herself and her daughter. At the end of each session she said, "I feel so much better" and thanked the psychologist profusely. At termination of "therapy," she took the psychologist's hand and squeezed it endearingly. "Thank you so much, Doctor," she said and made her exit.

*From the Author's Files*

The supplanting of *hysterical* with *histrionic* and the associated exchange of the roots *hystera* (meaning *uterus*) and *histrio* allow professionals to distance themselves from the notion that the disorder is intricately bound up with being female. Although some studies using structured interview methods find similar rates of occurrence among men and women, in clinical practice the disorder is diagnosed more frequently in women than men (American Psychiatric Association, 2013). Whether the gender discrepancy in clinical practice reflects true differences in the underlying rates of the disorder, diagnostic biases, or unseen factors remains an open question.

**OVER THE TOP?** Not all people who dress outrageously or flamboyantly have histrionic personalities. What other personality features characterize people with histrionic personality disorder?

People with histrionic personalities may become unusually upset by news of a sad event and exude exaggerated delight at a pleasant occurrence. They may faint at the sight of blood or blush at a slight faux pas. They tend to demand that others meet their needs for attention and play the victim when others fall short. They also tend to be self-centered and intolerant of delays of gratification: They want what they want when they want it. They grow quickly restless with routine and crave novelty and stimulation. They are drawn to fads. Others may see them as putting on airs or playacting, although they may evince a certain charm. They tend to be flirtatious and seductive but are too wrapped up in themselves to develop intimate relationships or have deep feelings toward others. As a result, their associations tend to be stormy and ultimately ungratifying. They tend to use their physical appearance as a means of drawing attention to themselves. Men with the disorder may act and dress in an overly "macho" way, and women may choose very frilly, feminine clothing. Glitter supersedes substance.

People with histrionic personalities may be attracted to professions like modeling or acting, where they can hog the spotlight. Despite outward successes, they lack self-esteem and strive to impress others to boost their self-worth. If they suffer setbacks or lose their place in the limelight, depressing inner doubts may emerge.

**NARCISSISTIC PERSONALITY DISORDER** *Narkissos* was a handsome youth who, according to Greek myth, fell in love with his reflection in a spring. Because of his excessive self-love, the gods transformed him into the flower we know as the *narcissus*.

People with **narcissistic personality disorder** have an inflated or grandiose sense of themselves and an extreme need for admiration. They brag about their accomplishments and expect others to shower them with praise. They expect others to notice their special qualities, even when their accomplishments are ordinary, and they enjoy basking in the light of adulation. They are self-absorbed and lack empathy for others. Although they share certain features with histrionic personalities, such as demanding to be the center of attention, they have a much more inflated view of themselves and are less melodramatic than people with histrionic personality disorder. As compared to people with borderline personality disorder, those with narcissistic personality disorder are generally better able to organize their thoughts and actions. They tend to be more successful in their careers and are better able to rise to positions of status and power. Their relationships also tend to be more stable than those of people with borderline personality disorder.

## Abnormal Psychology in the Digital Age

### ARE YOU A FACEBOOK EXTRAVERT? OR A TWITTER NARCISSIST?

What we present to the world on Facebook may be a representation of the ideal person we wish we would be, especially for people struggling with issues relating to self-esteem and emotional instability in their real lives. Less well-adjusted young adults (i.e., those higher in the trait of *neuroticism*) tend to present more of an ideal or false self on their Facebook profiles, perhaps because of an inner lack of self-esteem or because they don't believe other Facebook users would want to interact with them if their profiles reflected their true selves (Michikyan, Subrahmanyam, & Dennis, 2014). On the other hand, extraverted young adults who tend to have more social confidence and self-esteem also tend to be more active users of Facebook. On the average, they post more photos and status updates and have more Facebook friends than introverted users (Eftekhar, Fullwood, & Morris, 2014; Lee, Ahn, & Kim, 2014).

**AN EXTROVERT ONLINE, OFFLINE, OR BOTH?** Extraverted people tend to interact more with others in both the real and virtual worlds.

Investigators examining personality traits associated with the use of Twitter wonder if the site was designed with narcissists in mind. People with narcissistic traits tend to think very highly of themselves and relish followers who prop up their self-image—a perfect fit, or so it would seem, for sites like Twitter. A recent study supported this view, showing that Twitter was the preferred method of social networking among college-age narcissists (Davenport et al., 2014). By contrast, more active use of Facebook was unrelated to narcissism in the college-age sample.

**SOURCE:** *Reprinted from Nevid & Rathus, 2016, with permission of John Wiley & Sons, Inc.*

More people diagnosed with narcissistic personality disorder are men, but as we discuss later in the chapter, we cannot say whether there is an underlying gender difference in prevalence rates in the general population. A certain degree of narcissism may represent a healthful adjustment to insecurity, a shield from criticism and failure, or a motive for achievement. Excessive narcissistic qualities can become unhealthful, especially when the cravings for adulation are insatiable. Up to a point, self-interest fosters success and happiness. In more extreme cases, as with narcissism, it can compromise relationships and careers.

People with narcissistic personalities tend to be preoccupied with fantasies of success and power, ideal love, or recognition for brilliance or beauty. Like people with histrionic personalities, they may gravitate toward careers in modeling, acting, or politics. Although they tend to exaggerate their accomplishments and abilities, many people with narcissistic personalities are quite successful in their occupations—but they envy those who achieve even greater success. Insatiable ambition may prompt them to devote themselves tirelessly to work. They are driven to succeed, not so much for money as for the adulation that comes with success.

People with narcissistic personalities are extremely sensitive to the slightest hint of rejection or criticism. These *narcissistic injuries*, as they are called, hurt so deeply because they reopen very old psychological wounds. Even a seemingly trivial comment can throw a person into a tailspin, as in the following example of a woman, Stephanie, whose husband's criticism exposed old wounds of inadequacy. Moreover, instead of making the pain go away, his mild rebuke added insult to injury.

"I" **Rubbing Salt into a Wound**

"Watch the ball," she told herself [during a game of tennis], "get sideways, hit through, finish up."... For a few precious moments, she was in that "zone" that athletes cherish when everything comes together and there are no mistakes.

She was smiling secretly, enjoying an illicit high, wondering if her husband, Doug, had also noticed how well she was hitting today, when a heavily underspun return angled into her backhand. She lunged, stabbed, and caught the ball on her racquet rim, sending it flying out of the court. "You never read that spin," Doug scolded from the far court. "Never," Stephanie echoed, suddenly feeling as though she had just blown an internal tire. Pain washed over her and settled in the middle of her chest.... "I'll never be any good at this game," she thought miserably, smashing the next three balls into the net. The elation of only moments before had evaporated, replaced by a hopeless feeling of ineptitude. Stephanie swallowed the tears rising in her throat and gave herself a mental kick in the backside. "You're such a baby," she muttered to herself as she prepared to pack up and go home. "You wimping out on me again?" Doug called out. He was only teasing, trying to goad her back into the drill, but his words were like salt on a fresh abrasion. There would be no more tennis this day.

**SOURCE:** *Hotchkiss, 2002.*

Interpersonal relationships are invariably strained by the demands that people with narcissistic personality impose on others and by their lack of empathy with, and concern for, other people. They seek the company of flatterers and, although they are often superficially charming and friendly, their interest in people is one-sided: They seek people who will serve their interests and nourish their sense of self-importance. They have feelings of entitlement that lead them to exploit others. They tend to adopt a game-playing style in romantic relationships rather than seeking true intimacy, apparently because of their needs for power and autonomy (Campbell, Foster, & Finkel, 2002). They treat sex partners as devices for their own pleasure or to brace their self-esteem, as in the case of Bill.

## Bill:
### A CASE OF NARCISSISTIC PERSONALITY DISORDER

Most people agreed that Bill, a 35-year-old investment banker, had a certain charm. He was bright, articulate, and attractive. He possessed a keen sense of humor that drew people to him at social gatherings. He would always position himself in the middle of the room, where he could be the center of attention. The topics of conversation invariably focused on his "deals," the "rich and famous" people he had met, and his outmaneuvering of opponents. His next project was always bigger and more daring than the last. Bill loved an audience. His face would light up when others responded to him with praise or admiration for his business successes, which were always inflated beyond their true measure. When the conversation shifted to other people, he would lose interest and excuse himself to make a drink or to call his answering machine. When hosting a party, he would urge guests to stay late and feel hurt if they had to leave early; he showed no sensitivity to, or awareness of, the needs of his friends.

The few friends he had maintained over the years had come to accept Bill on his own terms. They recognized that he needed to have his ego fed or that he would become cool and detached.

Bill had also had a series of romantic relationships with women who were willing to play the adoring admirer and make the sacrifices that he demanded—for a time. However, they inevitably tired of the one-sided relationship or grew frustrated by Bill's inability to make a commitment or feel deeply toward them. Lacking empathy, Bill was unable to recognize other people's feelings and needs. His demands for constant attention from willing admirers did not derive from selfishness, but from a need to ward off underlying feelings of inadequacy and diminished self-esteem. It was sad, his friends thought, that Bill needed so much attention and adulation from others and that his many achievements were never enough to calm his inner doubts.

*From the Author's Files*

# Personality Disorders Characterized by Anxious or Fearful Behavior

**12.4 Describe the key features of personality disorders characterized by anxious or fearful behavior.**

This cluster of personality disorders includes the avoidant, dependent, and obsessive-compulsive types. Although the features of these disorders differ, they share a component of fear or anxiety.

**AN AVOIDANT PERSONALITY?** People with avoidant personalities often keep to themselves because of fear of rejection.

**AVOIDANT PERSONALITY DISORDER** People with **avoidant personality disorder** (APD) are so terrified of rejection and criticism that they may be unwilling to develop relationships with others without ardent reassurances of acceptance. As a result, they may have few close relationships outside their immediate families. They also tend to avoid group occupational or recreational activities for fear of rejection. They prefer to lunch alone at their desks. They shun company picnics and parties, unless they are perfectly sure of acceptance. Avoidant personality disorder appears to be equally common in men and women and is believed to affect between 0.5% and 1.0% of the general population (American Psychiatric Association, 2013).

Unlike people with schizoid qualities, with whom they share the feature of social withdrawal, individuals with avoidant personalities have interest in, and feelings of warmth toward, other people. However, fear of rejection prevents them from striving to meet their needs for affection and acceptance. In social situations, they tend to hug the walls and avoid conversing with others. They fear public embarrassment, the thought that others might see them blush, cry, or act nervously. They tend to stick to their routines and exaggerate the risks or effort involved in trying new things. They may refuse to attend a party that is an hour away on the pretext that the late drive home would be too taxing. Consider the following case example.

## Harold:
### A CASE OF AVOIDANT PERSONALITY DISORDER

Harold, a 24-year-old accounting clerk, had dated but a few women, and he had met them through family introductions. He never felt confident enough to approach a woman on his own. Perhaps it was his shyness that first attracted Stacy, a 22-year-old secretary who worked alongside Harold and asked him if he would like to get together sometime after work. At first Harold declined, claiming some excuse, but when Stacy asked again a week later, Harold agreed, thinking she must really like him if she was willing to pursue him. The relationship developed quickly, and soon they were dating virtually every night. The relationship was strained, however. Harold interpreted any slight hesitation in her voice as a lack of interest. He repeatedly requested reassurance that she cared about him, and he evaluated every word and gesture for evidence of her feelings. If Stacy said that she could not see him because of fatigue or illness, he assumed she was rejecting him and sought further reassurance. After several months, Stacy decided she could no longer accept Harold's nagging, and the relationship ended. Harold assumed that Stacy had never truly cared for him.

*From the Author's Files*

Avoidant personality disorder is often comorbid (co-occurring) with social phobia (Friborg et al., 2013). The overlap between the two disorders suggests they may share common genetic factors (Torvik et al., 2016). It may turn out that avoidant personality disorder is actually a more severe form of social phobia rather than a distinct diagnosis.

Consistent with this view, evidence shows heightened amygdala activity in people with APD as compared to healthy controls in social situations in which the person anticipates negative feedback (Denny et al., 2015). (Recall that the amygdala is activated in response to threatening stimuli.) For the time being, however, social phobia and avoidant personality disorder remain distinct diagnostic diagnoses in the *DSM-5*.

**DEPENDENT PERSONALITY DISORDER** **Dependent personality disorder** describes people who have an excessive need to be taken care of by others. This leads them to be overly submissive and clingy in their relationships and extremely fearful of separation. People with this disorder find it very difficult to do things on their own. They seek advice in making even the smallest decision. Children or adolescents with the problem may look to their parents to select their clothes, diets, schools or colleges, or even their friends. Adults with the disorder allow others to make important decisions for them. Sometimes, they are so dependent on others that they allow their parents to determine whom they will marry, as in the case of Matthew.

## Matthew:

### A CASE OF DEPENDENT PERSONALITY DISORDER

Matthew, a 34-year-old single accountant who lives with his mother, sought treatment when his relationship with his girlfriend came to an end. His mother had objected to marriage because his girlfriend was of a different religion, and—because "blood is thicker than water"—Matthew acceded to his mother's wishes and ended the relationship. Yet he is angry with himself and at his mother because he feels that she is too possessive to ever grant him permission to get married. He describes his mother as a domineering woman who "wears the pants" in the family and is accustomed to having things her way. Matthew alternates between resenting his mother and thinking that perhaps she knows what's best for him.

Matthew's position at work is several levels below what would be expected of someone of his talent and educational level. Several times he has declined promotions in order to avoid increased responsibilities that would require him to supervise others and make independent decisions. He has maintained close relationships with two friends since early childhood and has lunch with one of them on every working day. On days his friend calls in sick, Matthew feels lost. Matthew has lived his whole life at home, except for one year away at college. He returned home because of homesickness.

**SOURCE:** *Adapted from Spitzer et al., 1994, pp. 179–180*

## TRUTH or FICTION

People with dependent personality disorder have so much difficulty making independent decisions that they may allow their parents to decide whom they will marry.

☑ **TRUE** People with dependent personality disorder in our culture may be so dependent on others for making decisions that they allow their parents to determine whom they will marry.

After marriage, people with dependent personality disorder may rely on their spouses to make decisions such as where they should live, which neighbors they should cultivate, how they should discipline the children, what jobs they should take, how they should budget money, and where they should vacation. Like Matthew, individuals with dependent personality disorder avoid positions of responsibility. They turn down challenges and promotions and work beneath their potential. They tend to be overly sensitive to criticism and preoccupied with fears of rejection and abandonment. They may be devastated by the end of a close relationship or by the prospect of living on their own. Because of fear of rejection, they often subordinate their wants and needs to those of others. They may agree with outlandish statements about themselves and do degrading things to please others. **T / F**

Before going further, we should note that dependence needs to be examined through the lens of culture. Arranged marriages are the norm in some traditional cultures, so people from those cultures who let their parents decide whom they will marry would not be classified as having dependent personality disorder. Similarly, in strongly patriarchal cultures, women may be expected to defer to their fathers and husbands in making many life decisions, even small everyday decisions.

However, we needn't look beyond our own society to consider the role of culture. Evidence shows that dependent personality disorder in our culture is diagnosed more frequently in women than in men (American Psychiatric Association, 2013). The diagnosis is often applied to women who, for fear of abandonment, tolerate husbands who openly cheat on them, abuse them, or gamble away the family's resources. Underlying feelings of inadequacy and helplessness discourage them from taking effective action. In a vicious cycle, their passivity encourages further abuse, leading them to feel yet more inadequate and helpless. Applying the diagnosis to women with this pattern is controversial and may be seen as unfairly "blaming the victim," because women in our society are often socialized to dependent roles. Women typically encounter greater stress than men in contemporary life as well as greater social pressures to be passive, demure, or deferential. Therefore, dependent behaviors in women may reflect cultural influences rather than an underlying personality disorder.

Investigators link dependent personality disorder to increased risk of psychological disorders such as mood disorders and social phobia, as well as to suicide and health problems such as hypertension, cardiovascular disorder, and gastrointestinal disorders like ulcers and colitis (e.g., Disney, 2013; Samuels, 2011). There also appears to be a link between dependent personality and what psychodynamic theorists refer to as "oral" behavior problems, such as smoking, eating disorders, and alcoholism (Bornstein, 1999). Psychodynamic theorists trace dependent behaviors to the utter dependence of the newborn baby and the baby's seeking of nourishment through oral means (suckling). Food may come to symbolize love, and people with dependent personalities may overeat to ingest love symbolically. People with dependent personalities often attribute their problems to physical rather than emotional causes and seek support and advice from medical experts rather than psychologists or counselors.

**A PLACE FOR EVERYTHING, AND EVERYTHING IN ITS PLACE?**
People with obsessive-compulsive personalities may have invented this maxim. Many such people have excessive needs for orderliness in their environments, as suggested by this Laurie Simmons photograph, *Red Library #2*.

**OBSESSIVE-COMPULSIVE PERSONALITY DISORDER** The defining features of **obsessive-compulsive personality disorder** include excessive orderliness, perfectionism, rigidity, and need for control over one's environment (Pinto, 2016). Estimates of the prevalence of the disorder vary from 2.1% to 7.9% of the population (American Psychiatric Association, 2013). The disorder is about twice as common in men as in women. Unlike obsessive-compulsive anxiety disorder, people with obsessive-compulsive personality disorder do not necessarily experience outright obsessions or compulsions. If they do, both diagnoses may be deemed appropriate.

People with obsessive-compulsive personality disorder are so preoccupied with the need for perfection that they cannot complete work on time. Their efforts inevitably fall short of their expectations, so they redo their work, or they ruminate about how to prioritize their work and never seem to start working. They focus on details that others perceive as trivial. As the saying goes, they fail to see the forest for the trees. Their rigidity impairs their social relationships; they insist on doing things their way rather than compromising. Their zeal for work keeps them from participating in or enjoying social and leisure activities. They tend to be stingy with money. They find it difficult to make decisions and postpone or avoid them for fear of making the wrong choice. They tend to be inflexible and overly rigid in issues of morality and ethics, to be overly formal in relationships, and to find it difficult to express feelings. It is hard for them to relax and enjoy pleasant activities; they worry about the costs of such diversions. Consider the following case example.

## Jerry:
### A CASE OF OBSESSIVE-COMPULSIVE PERSONALITY DISORDER

Jerry, a 34-year-old systems analyst, was perfectionistic, overly concerned with details, and rigid in his behavior. Jerry was married to Marcia, a graphic artist. He insisted on scheduling their free time hour by hour and became unnerved when they deviated from his agenda. He would circle a parking lot repeatedly in search of just the right parking spot to ensure that another car would not scrape his car. He refused to have the apartment painted for over a year because he couldn't decide on the color. He had arranged all the books in their bookshelf alphabetically and insisted that every book be placed in its proper position.

Jerry never seemed to relax. Even on vacation, he was bothered by thoughts of work that he had left behind and by fears that he might lose his job. He couldn't understand how people could lie on the beach and let all their worries evaporate in the summer air. Something can always go wrong, he figured, so how can people let themselves go?

*From the Author's Files*

# Problems with the Classification of Personality Disorders

**12.5 Evaluate problems associated with the classification of personality disorders.**

Questions remain about the classification of personality disorders in the *DSM* system and the criteria used to diagnose them. Here, we focus on major concerns that clinicians and researchers have raised about how these patterns of behavior are classified and diagnosed.

**DIMENSIONS OR CATEGORIES?**
A major point of controversy is whether personality disorders should be conceptualized as extreme variations of personality traits found in the general population or as discrete categories of abnormal behavior.

**PERSONALITY DISORDERS: CATEGORIES OR DIMENSIONS?** Are personality disorders best understood as distinct categories of psychological disorders marked by particular symptoms or behavioral features? Or should we think of them as extreme variations of common personality dimensions found in the general population? The *DSM* adopts a categorical model for classifying abnormal behavior patterns into specific diagnostic categories based on particular diagnostic criteria.

Let's use antisocial personality disorder as an example. To warrant a diagnosis of antisocial personality disorder, a person must show a range of clinical features similar to those outlined in Table 12.2—but just how many of the seven features listed in the table need to be present for a diagnosis of antisocial personality disorder? Three of them, four of them, or perhaps all of them? The answer, according to the diagnostic manual, is that three or more of these criteria need to be present. Why *three*? Basically, this determination represents a consensus of the authors of the *DSM*. A person may exhibit two of these features in abundance, but still not be diagnosed with antisocial personality disorder, whereas someone showing three of the features in a milder form would merit a diagnosis. The problem of where to draw the line when applying diagnostic categories ripples throughout the *DSM* system, raising concerns of many critics that the system relies too heavily on an arbitrary set of cutoffs or diagnostic criteria.

Another concern with the categorical model is that many of the features associated with personality disorders and with many other diagnostic categories (e.g., mood disorders, anxiety disorders) are found to some degree in the general population. Thus, it may be difficult to distinguish between normal variations of these features (or traits) and abnormal variations (Skodol & Bender, 2009). People with antisocial personality disorder, for example, may fail to plan ahead, show impulsive behavior, or lie for personal gain—but so do many people without antisocial personality disorder.

The dimensional model of personality disorders offers an alternative to the traditional categorical model of the *DSM* (e.g., Suzuki et al., 2015; Widiger, Livesley, & Clark, 2009). The dimensional model depicts personality disorders as maladaptive and extreme variations of personality traits commonly found within the general population, rather than as discrete diagnostic categories.

You may recall that psychologist Thomas Widiger discussed the dimensional approach to the diagnosis of personality disorder in Chapter 3. Widiger and his colleagues propose that personality disorders can be represented as extreme or maladaptive variations of the five basic traits of personality that comprise the Five-Factor Model of personality (the so-called Big Five): (1) *neuroticism* or emotional instability, (2) *extraversion*, (3) *openness to experience*, (4) *agreeableness* or friendliness, and (5) *conscientiousness* (Widiger & Mullins-Sweatt, 2009). In the dimensional model, a disorder like antisocial personality disorder might be characterized in part by extremely low levels of conscientiousness and agreeableness (Lowe & Widiger, 2008). People with this combination of traits are often described as aimless and unreliable, as well as manipulative and exploitive of others. In a similar way, other personality disorders can be mapped onto extreme ends of the Big Five dimensions. A growing body of evidence shows links between the dimensions underlying personality disorders and the Big Five personality traits (e.g., Gore & Widiger, 2013). One limitation of the dimensional model is that we lack clear guidelines for setting cutoff scores on personality scales to determine just how extreme a trait needs to be for it to be deemed clinically meaningful (Skodol, 2012).

The developers of the *DSM-5* are currently reviewing just how best to diagnose personality in preparation for the next version of the *DSM-5*, to be called *DSM-5.1*. Several alternative models are under consideration, including a hybrid dimensional–categorical model that is part categorical and part dimensional. The dimensional model is based on the Big Five personality traits. Under the proposed plan, a diagnosis of a personality disorder would be based on meeting specified criteria for particular disorders (the categorical approach) together with ratings of extreme or pathological traits (the dimensional approach). This hybrid model is consistent with methods used to diagnose medical illnesses, which rely on both specific criteria (e.g., findings of cancerous cells on biopsies, symptoms of infectious diseases) and extreme measures on continuous dimensions (e.g., a diagnosis of hypertension based on high blood pressure readings). An advantage of the dimensional component in assessment and diagnosis is that it allows the examiner to make a judgment of the severity of the problem based on the degree of extremity of pathological traits, as opposed to merely a yes/no or dichotomous judgment of whether a particular disorder is present or not.

Many proponents of the dimensional model believe the proposed hybrid model does not go far enough in representing dysfunctional personality in a dimensional framework. They claim that it continues to endorse an overriding categorical model. We hope that as the debate continues to unfold about whether the *DSM* should be categorical, dimensional, or a kind of hybrid of the two models, it will be informed by evidence pertaining to the utility and validity of different models of classification.

**PROBLEMS DISTINGUISHING PERSONALITY DISORDERS FROM OTHER CLINICAL SYNDROMES** One nagging question is whether personality disorders can be reliably differentiated from other clinical syndromes. For example, clinicians often have difficulty distinguishing between obsessive-compulsive disorder and obsessive-compulsive personality disorder. Clinical syndromes are believed to be variable over time, whereas personality disorders are held to be generally more enduring patterns of disturbance. Yet the features of personality disorders may vary over time with changes in circumstances, while some other clinical syndromes (e.g., dysthymia) follow a more or less chronic course.

**OVERLAP AMONG DISORDERS** A high degree of overlap exists among the personality disorders. Most people receiving a diagnosis of a personality disorder meet criteria for more than one (Skodol, 2012). Although some personality disorders have distinct features, many share common traits, such as problems in interpersonal relationships. For example, a person may have traits suggestive of both antisocial personality disorder and borderline personality disorder (e.g., impulsivity, unstable relationship patterns). People may also have traits suggestive of both dependent personality disorder (inability to make decisions or initiate activities independently) and avoidant personality disorder (extreme social anxiety and heightened sensitivity to criticism).

Co-occurrence (called *comorbidity*) of different personality disorders is quite common (Grant et al., 2005). This suggests that the specific types of personality disorders in the *DSM* system may not be clearly distinct from each other. Some personality disorders actually may not be distinct disorders, but rather subtypes or variations of other personality disorders.

**DIFFICULTY IN DISTINGUISHING BETWEEN NORMAL AND ABNORMAL BEHAVIOR** Another problem with the diagnosis of personality disorders is that they involve personality traits that in lesser degrees describe the behavior of most normal individuals. Feeling suspicious now and then does not mean you have a paranoid personality disorder. The tendency to exaggerate your own importance does not mean you are narcissistic. You may avoid social interactions for fear of embarrassment or rejection without having an avoidant personality disorder, and you may be especially conscientious in your work without having an obsessive-compulsive personality disorder. Because the defining attributes of these disorders are common personality traits, clinicians should only apply these diagnostic labels when the patterns are so pervasive that they interfere with the individual's functioning or cause significant personal distress. We still lack the evidence we need to determine the particular points at which personality traits become maladaptive and to justify a diagnosis of a personality disorder.

**CONFUSING LABELS WITH EXPLANATIONS** It may seem obvious that we should not confuse diagnostic labels with explanations, but in practice the distinction is sometimes clouded. If we confuse labeling with explanation, we may fall into the trap of circular reasoning. For example, what is wrong with the logic of the following statements?

1. John's behavior is antisocial.
2. Therefore, John has antisocial personality disorder.
3. John's behavior is antisocial because he has antisocial personality disorder.

The statements demonstrate circular reasoning because they (a) use behavior to make a diagnosis, and then (b) use the diagnosis as an explanation for the behavior. We may be guilty of circular reasoning in our everyday speech. Consider the following statements: "John never gets his work in on time; therefore, he is lazy. John doesn't get his work in because he's lazy." The label may be acceptable in everyday conversation, but it lacks scientific rigor. For a construct such as *laziness* to have scientific rigor, we need to understand the causes of laziness and the factors that help maintain it. We should not confuse the label we attach to a behavior with the cause of the behavior.

Moreover, labeling people with disturbing behavior as having personality disorders overlooks the social and environmental contexts of the behavior. The impact of traumatic life events, which may occur with a greater range or intensity among members of a particular gender or cultural group, is an important underlying factor in maladaptive behavior. However, the conceptual underpinnings of the personality disorders do not consider cultural differences, social inequalities, or power differences between genders or cultural groups. For example, many women diagnosed with personality disorders have a history of childhood physical and sexual abuse. The ways in which people cope with abuse may come to be viewed as flaws in their character rather than as reflections of the dysfunctional societal factors that underlie abusive relationships.

Personality disorders are convenient labels for identifying common patterns of ineffective and self-defeating behavior, but labels do not explain the behaviors they name. Still, the development of an accurate descriptive system is an important step toward scientific explanation. The establishment of reliable diagnostic categories sets the stage for valid research into causation and treatment.

**SEXIST BIASES** The construction of certain personality disorders may have sexist underpinnings. The diagnostic criteria seem to label stereotypical feminine behaviors as pathological with greater frequency than stereotypical masculine behaviors. Take the example of histrionic personality, which seems a caricature of the traditional stereotype of the feminine personality: flighty, emotional, shallow, seductive, attention-seeking.

If the feminine stereotype corresponds to a diagnosable mental disorder, shouldn't we also have a diagnostic category that reflects the masculine stereotype of the "macho male"? We might argue that overly masculinized traits can be associated with significant distress or impairment in social or occupational functioning in certain males. For example, highly masculinized males may get into fights and experience difficulties working for female bosses. Yet there is presently no personality disorder corresponding to the "macho male" stereotype.

Does the diagnosis of dependent personality disorder unfairly stigmatize women who have been socialized into dependent roles by attaching to them a label of a personality disorder? Women may be at greater risk of receiving diagnoses of histrionic or dependent personality disorders simply because clinicians perceive these patterns as common among women or because women are more likely than men to be socialized into these behavior patterns.

**ARE THERE SEXIST BIASES IN THE CONCEPTION OF PERSONALITY DISORDERS?** The concept of the histrionic personality disorder seems to be a caricature of the highly stereotyped feminine personality. Why, then, is there not also something akin to a macho male personality disorder, which caricatures the highly stereotyped masculine personality?

Borderline, histrionic, and dependent personality disorders are more often diagnosed in women, whereas narcissistic and antisocial personality disorders are more often diagnosed in men. Is this because of gender differences in the prevalence of these disorders, or might it be the case that some personality disorders are diagnosed in one or the other gender more often because of societal expectations and underlying biases? We don't have a final answer to this question, but we do have evidence of gender biases in diagnoses. Recently, investigators asked psychologists in training to make diagnostic judgments of hypothetical cases presenting with ambiguous symptoms (Braamhorst et al., 2015). These future psychologists showed gender biases, more often diagnosing hypothetical cases with borderline personality disorder when the patient was identified as female and with narcissistic personality disorder when the case was male. Sexist biases are also found in judging women as having histrionic personality disorder and men as having antisocial personality disorder, even when they demonstrate the same symptoms (Garb, 1997). Consider your own attitudes: Have you ever assumed that women are "just dependent or hysterical" or that men are "just narcissists or antisocial"?

# Theoretical Perspectives

In this section, we consider theoretical perspectives on the personality disorders. Many theoretical accounts of disturbed personality derive from the psychodynamic model. We thus begin with a review of traditional and modern psychodynamic models.

## Psychodynamic Perspectives

**12.6 Describe psychodynamic perspectives on the development of personality disorders.**

Traditional Freudian theory focused on problems arising from the Oedipus complex as the foundation for abnormal behaviors, including personality disorders. Freud believed that children normally resolve the Oedipus complex by forsaking incestuous wishes for the parent of the opposite gender and identifying with the parent of the same gender. As a result, they incorporate the parent's moral principles in the form of a personality structure called the *superego*. Many factors may interfere with appropriate identification and sidetrack the normal developmental process, preventing children from developing moral constraints and the feelings of guilt or remorse that normally follow antisocial behavior. Freud's account of moral development focused mainly on the development of males. He has been criticized for failing to account for the moral development of females.

More recent psychodynamic theories have generally focused on the earlier, pre-Oedipal period of about 18 months to 3 years, during which infants begin to develop identities separate from those of their parents. These theories focus on the development of the sense of self in explaining disorders such as narcissistic and borderline personality disorders.

**HANS KOHUT** One of the principal shapers of modern psychodynamic concepts is Hans Kohut, whose theory is labeled *self psychology* because of its emphasis on processes in the development of a cohesive sense of self. Freud believed that the resolution of the Oedipus complex was central to the development of the adult personality. Kohut disagreed, arguing that what matters most is how the self develops—whether the person is able to develop self-esteem, values, and a cohesive and realistic sense of self as opposed to an inflated, narcissistic personality (Anderson, 2003; Goldberg, 2003).

Kohut (1966) believed that people with narcissistic personalities mount a facade of self-importance to cover up deep feelings of inadequacy. The narcissist's self-esteem is like a reservoir that needs to be constantly replenished with a steady stream of praise and attention lest it run dry. A sense of grandiosity helps people with a narcissistic personality mask their underlying feelings of worthlessness. Failures or disappointments threaten to expose these feelings and drive the person into a state of depression, so as a defense against despair, the person attempts to diminish the importance of disappointments or failures.

People with narcissistic personalities may become enraged by others whom they perceive have failed to protect them from disappointment or have declined to shower them with reassurance, praise, and admiration. They may become infuriated by even the slightest criticism, no matter how well intentioned. They may mask feelings of rage and humiliation by adopting a facade of cool indifference. They can make difficult psychotherapy clients because they may become enraged when therapists puncture their inflated self-images to help them develop more realistic self-concepts.

To Kohut, early childhood involves a normal stage of *healthy narcissism*. Infants feel powerful, as though the world revolves around them. Infants also normally perceive their parents as idealized towers of strength and wish to be one with them and to share their power. Empathic parents reflect their child's inflated perceptions by making them feel that anything is possible and by nourishing their self-esteem (e.g., telling them how terrific and precious they are). Even empathic parents are critical from time to time, however, and puncture their children's grandiose sense of self or fail to measure up to their children's idealized views of them. Gradually, unrealistic expectations dissolve and are replaced by more realistic appraisals of oneself and others. In adolescence, childhood idealization is transformed into realistic admiration for parents, teachers, and friends. In adulthood, these ideas develop into a set of internal ideals, values, and goals.

Lack of parental empathy and support, however, sets the stage for *pathological narcissism*. Children who are not prized by their parents fail to develop a sturdy sense of self-esteem. They develop damaged self-concepts and feel incapable of being loved and admired. Pathological narcissism involves the construction of a grandiose facade of self-perfection that cloaks perceived inadequacies. The facade is always on the brink of crumbling, however, and must be shored up by a constant flow of reassurance that one is special and unique. This leaves a person vulnerable to painful blows to self-esteem following failure to achieve social or occupational goals.

Kohut's approach to therapy provides clients who have a narcissistic personality with an initial opportunity to express their grandiose self-images and to idealize the therapist. Over time, however, the therapist helps them explore the childhood roots of their narcissism and gently points out imperfections in both client and therapist to encourage clients to form more realistic images of the self and others.

**OTTO KERNBERG** Otto Kernberg (1975), a leading psychodynamic theorist, views borderline personality in terms of a failure in early childhood to develop a sense of constancy and unity in one's image of oneself and others. From this perspective, borderline individuals cannot synthesize contradictory (positive and negative) elements of themselves and others into complete, stable wholes. Rather than viewing important people in their lives as sometimes loving and sometimes rejecting, they shift back and forth between pure idealization and utter hatred. This rapid shifting back and forth between viewing others as either "all good" or "all bad" is referred to as *splitting*.

Kernberg tells of a woman in her 30s whose attitude toward him vacillated in such a way. The woman would respond to him in one session as the most wonderful therapist and feel that all her problems were solved; several sessions later, she would turn against him and accuse him of being unfeeling and manipulative, become dissatisfied with treatment, and threaten to drop out (cited in Sass, 1982).

In Kernberg's view, parents, even excellent parents, invariably fail to meet all their children's needs. Infants, therefore, face the early developmental challenge of reconciling images of the nurturing, comforting "good mother" with those of the withholding, frustrating "bad mother." Failure to reconcile these opposing images into a realistic, unified, and stable parental image may have the effect of psychologically fixating the child in the pre-Oedipal period of psychosexual development. Consequently, as an adult, a person may continue to have rapidly shifting attitudes toward therapists and others, idealizing them one moment and rejecting them the next.

**MARGARET MAHLER** Margaret Mahler, another influential modern psychodynamic theorist, explained borderline personality disorder in terms of childhood separation from the mother figure. Mahler and her colleagues (Mahler & Kaplan, 1977; Mahler, Pine, & Bergman, 1975) believed that during the first year, infants develop a symbiotic attachment to their mothers. *Symbiosis*, or interdependence, is a biological term derived from Greek roots meaning *to live together*. In psychology, symbiosis is a state of oneness in which the child's identity is fused with the mother's. Normally, children gradually differentiate their own identities or senses of self from those of their mothers. The process, *separation-individuation*, is the development of a separate psychological and biological identity from the mother (separation) and recognition of personal characteristics that define one's self-identity (individuation). Separation-individuation may be a stormy process. Children may vacillate between seeking greater independence and moving closer to, or "shadowing," the mother, which is seen as a wish for reunion. The mother may disrupt normal separation-individuation by refusing to let go of the child or by too quickly pushing the child toward independence. The tendencies of people with borderline personalities to react to others with ambivalence and to alternate between love and hate are suggestive of earlier ambivalences during the separation-individuation process. Borderline personality disorder may arise from the failure to master this developmental challenge.

Psychodynamic theory provides ways of understanding the development of several types of personality disorders. However, a limitation of the theory is that it is based largely on inferences drawn from behavior and retrospective accounts of adults rather than on observations of children. We may also question whether it is valid to compare normal childhood experiences with abnormal behaviors in adulthood. For example, the ambivalences that characterize the adult borderline personality may bear only a superficial relationship, if any, to children's vacillations between closeness and separation during separation-individuation.

Links between abuse in childhood and later development of personality disorders suggest that failure to form close bonding relationships with parental caretakers in childhood plays a critical role in the development of personality disorders. We will explore the links between abuse and personality disorders later in this chapter.

**SEPARATION-INDIVIDUATION.** According to the influential psychodynamic theorist Margaret Mahler, young children undergo a process of separation-individuation in which they learn to differentiate their own identities from those of their mothers. She believed that a failure to successfully master this developmental challenge may lead to the development of a borderline personality.

## Learning Theory Perspectives

**12.7 Describe learning theory perspectives on the development of personality disorders.**

Learning theorists focus on maladaptive behaviors rather than disorders of personality. They are interested in identifying the learning histories and environmental factors that give rise to maladaptive behaviors associated with diagnoses of personality disorders and the reinforcers that maintain them.

Learning theorists suggest that childhood experiences shape the pattern of maladaptive habits of relating to others that constitute personality disorders. For example, children who are regularly discouraged from speaking their minds or exploring their environments may develop a dependent behavior pattern. Excessive parental discipline may lead to obsessive-compulsive behaviors. Psychologist Theodore Millon (1981) suggests that children whose behavior is rigidly controlled and punished by parents, even for slight transgressions, may develop inflexible, perfectionistic standards. As these children mature, they strive to develop themselves in an area in which they excel, such as schoolwork or athletics, as a way of avoiding parental criticism or punishment—but because of overattention to a single area of development, they do not become well rounded. Thus, they squelch expressions of spontaneity and avoid risks. They may also place perfectionistic demands on themselves to avoid punishment or rebuke, or develop other behaviors associated with the obsessive-compulsive personality pattern.

Millon suggests that histrionic personality disorder may be rooted in childhood experiences in which social reinforcers, such as parental attention, are connected to a child's appearance and willingness to perform for others, especially when reinforcers are dispensed inconsistently. Inconsistent attention teaches children not to take approval for granted and to strive for it continually. People with histrionic personalities may also identify with parents who are dramatic, emotional, and attention-seeking. Extreme sibling rivalry would further heighten motivation to perform for attention from others.

Social-cognitive theories emphasize the role of reinforcement in explaining the origins of antisocial behaviors. In an early influential work, Ullmann and Krasner (1975) proposed that people with antisocial personalities failed to learn to respond to other people as potential reinforcers. Most children learn to treat others as reinforcing agents because others reinforce them with praise for good behavior and punishment for bad. Reinforcement and punishment provide feedback that helps children modify their behavior to maximize the chances of future rewards and minimize the risks of future punishments. As a consequence, children become sensitive to the demands of powerful others, usually parents and teachers, and learn to regulate their behavior accordingly. They thus adapt to social expectations: They learn what to do and what to say, how to dress and how to act to obtain praise and approval (social reinforcement) from others.

People with antisocial personalities, by contrast, may not have become socialized in this way because their early learning experiences lacked consistency and predictability.

Perhaps they were sometimes rewarded for doing the "right thing," but just as often not. They may have borne the brunt of harsh physical punishments, delivered at random. As adults, they do not place much value on what other people expect, because as children, they saw no connection between their own behavior and reinforcement. Although Ullmann and Krasner's views may account for some features of antisocial personality disorder, they may not adequately address the development of the "charming" type of antisocial personality; people in this group are skillful at reading the social cues of others and using them for personal advantage. Some people with psychopathy are remarkably successful in their lines of work and appear to be more conscientious and reliable in their work habits than other psychopathic personalities (Mullins-Sweatt et al., 2010). However, as pointed out by psychologists Paul Babiak and David Hare in their book *Snakes in Suits*, the numbers of psychopathic personalities who attain executive positions in business, in which they can control others and use guile, manipulation, and charm to cause damage to others, far exceed the numbers in prisons or in society at large (Babiak & Hare, 2006).

Social-cognitive theorist Albert Bandura has studied the role of observational learning in aggressive behavior, a common component of antisocial behavior. In a classic study, he and his colleagues (Bandura, Ross, & Ross, 1963) showed that children acquire skills, including aggressive skills, by observing the behavior of others. Exposure to aggression may come from watching violent television programs or observing parents who behave violently. Bandura, however, does not believe that children and adults display aggressive behaviors in a mechanical way. Rather, people usually do not imitate aggressive behavior unless they are provoked and believe they are more likely to be rewarded than punished for it. Children are most likely to imitate violent role models who get their way with others by acting aggressively. Children may also acquire antisocial behaviors such as cheating, bullying, or lying by direct reinforcement if they find that those behaviors help them avoid blame or manipulate others.

Social-cognitive psychologists have also shown that the ways in which people with personality disorders interpret their social experiences influences their behavior. Aggressive, antisocial (psychopathic) individuals, as compared to healthy controls, are more likely to read ambiguous facial expressions in others as signs of hostile intentions (Schönenberg & Jusyte, 2014). Interpreting other people's intentions as hostile primes them to respond aggressively in social situations. Antisocial adolescents also tend to have hostile cognitive biases; they incorrectly interpret other people's behavior as threatening (Dodge et al., 2002). Often, perhaps because of their family and community experiences, they presume that others intend them ill when they do not. Therapists often use a form of *problem-solving therapy* to help aggressive, antisocial children and adolescents reconceptualize conflict situations as problems to be solved rather than as threats to be responded to aggressively. Children learn to generate nonviolent solutions to social confrontations and, like scientists, to test the most promising ones. In the section on biological perspectives, we also see that there may be a physiological basis explaining why people with antisocial personalities may fail to learn from punishing experiences.

All in all, learning approaches to personality disorders, like the psychodynamic approaches, have their limitations. They are grounded in theory rather than in observations of family interactions that presage the development of personality disorders. Research is needed to determine whether childhood experiences proposed by psychodynamic and learning theorists actually lead to the development of particular personality disorders as hypothesized.

**WHAT ARE THE ORIGINS OF ANTISOCIAL PERSONALITY DISORDER?** Are youth who develop antisocial personalities largely "unsocialized" because their early learning experiences lack the consistency and predictability that help other children connect their behavior with rewards and punishments? Or are they very "socialized," but socialized to imitate the behavior of other antisocial youth? To what extent does criminal behavior or membership in gangs overlap with antisocial personality disorder?

## Family Perspectives

**12.8 Describe the role of family relationships in the development of personality disorders.**

Many theorists have argued that disturbances in family relationships underlie the development of personality disorders. Consistent with psychodynamic formulations, people with borderline personality disorder tend to think of their parents as more controlling and less caring than do people with other psychological disorders (Zweig-Frank & Paris, 1991). When people with borderline personality disorder recall their earliest memories, they are more likely than other people to paint significant others as malevolent or evil. They portray their parents and others close to them as likely to injure them or as failing to protect them (Nigg et al., 1992).

Evidence links childhood physical or sexual abuse or neglect to development of personality disorders, including BPD (e.g., Martín-Blanco et al., 2014). Perhaps the splitting observed in people with BPD is the result of learning to cope with unpredictable and harsh behavior from parental figures or other caregivers. Moreover, loss of parental figures through death or divorce is also common in people with BPD.

Also consistent with psychodynamic theory, family factors such as parental overprotection and authoritarianism (a "do what I said because I said so" style of parenting) are implicated in the development of dependent personality traits (Bornstein, 1992). Extreme fears of abandonment may also be involved, perhaps resulting from a failure to develop secure bonds with parental attachment figures in childhood due to parental neglect, rejection, or death. Subsequently, these individuals develop a chronic fear of abandonment by significant others, leading to the clinginess that typifies dependent personality disorder. Theorists also suggest that obsessive-compulsive personality disorder may emerge within a strongly moralistic and rigid family environment, which does not permit even minor deviations from expected roles or behavior (e.g., Oldham, 1994).

As with borderline personality disorder, researchers find that childhood abuse, parental neglect, or lack of parental nurturing are important risk factors in the development of antisocial personality disorder in adulthood (Johnson et al., 2006; Lobbestael & Arntz, 2009). In an early but influential view that straddled the psychodynamic and learning theories, the McCords (McCord & McCord, 1964) focused on the role of parental rejection or neglect in the development of antisocial personality disorder. They suggest that children normally learn to associate parental approval with conformity to parental practices and values and disapproval with disobedience. When tempted to transgress, children feel anxious about losing parental love. Anxiety signals the child to inhibit antisocial behavior. Eventually, the child identifies with parents and internalizes these social controls in the form of a conscience. When parents do not show love for their children, this identification does not occur. Children do not fear loss of love, because they have never had it. The anxiety that might have served to restrain antisocial and criminal behavior is absent.

Children who are rejected or neglected by their parents may not develop warm feelings of attachment to others. They may lack the ability to empathize with the feelings and needs of others, developing instead an attitude of indifference, or perhaps they retain a wish to develop loving relationships but lack the ability to experience genuine feelings.

Although family factors may be implicated in some cases of antisocial personality disorder, many neglected children do not later show antisocial or other abnormal behaviors. We are left to develop other explanations to predict which deprived children will develop antisocial personalities or other abnormal behaviors and which will not.

**CHILD MALTREATMENT.** Child abuse and neglect figure prominently in cases of people with personality disorders, including borderline personality disorder. What are some of the emotional consequences associated with childhood abuse and neglect?

## Biological Perspectives

**12.9 Describe biological perspectives on the development of personality disorders.**

Much remains to be learned about the biological underpinnings of personality disorders. Most of the attention in the research community has centered on antisocial personality disorder and the personality traits that underlie the disorder, which is the focus of much of our discussion.

**GENETIC FACTORS** Evidence points to genetic factors playing a role in several types of personality disorders, including antisocial, narcissistic, paranoid, and borderline types (Ficks, Dong, & Waldman, 2014; Gunderson, 2011; Kendler et al., 2008; Meier et al., 2011; Reichborn-Kjennerud et al., 2013). Parents and siblings of people with personality disorders, such as antisocial, schizotypal, and borderline types, are more likely to be diagnosed with these disorders themselves than are members of the general population (American Psychiatric Association, 2013). Genetic factors also appear to be involved in the development of personality traits that underlie the psychopathic personality, such as callousness, antisocial behavior, impulsivity, and irresponsibility (Larsson, Andershed, & Lichtenstein, 2006; Van Hulle et al., 2009). Investigators also report finding genetic indicators in a particular chromosome linking to features of borderline personality disorder (Distel et al., 2008).

Although we have evidence of genetic contributions to personality traits associated with personality disorders, it is important to recognize that environmental factors play an important contributing role. For example, exposure to environmental influences, such as being raised in a dysfunctional or troubled family, may predispose individuals to develop personality disorders, such as antisocial or borderline personality disorders. We should also note that personality traits associated with particular personality disorders may represent interactions of genetic factors and life experiences. Along these lines, investigators found that a variant of a particular gene was associated with antisocial behavior in adult men, but only in those who were maltreated in childhood (Caspi et al., 2002).

**LACK OF EMOTIONAL RESPONSIVENESS** According to a leading theorist, Hervey Cleckley (1976), people with antisocial personalities can maintain their composure in stressful situations that would induce anxiety in most people. Lack of anxiety in response to threatening situations may help explain the failure of punishment to induce antisocial people to relinquish antisocial behavior. For most of us, the fear of getting caught and being punished is sufficient to inhibit antisocial impulses. People with antisocial personalities, however, often fail to inhibit behavior that has led to punishment in the past, perhaps because they experience little, if any, fear or anticipatory anxiety about being caught and punished.

When people get anxious, their palms tend to sweat. This skin response, called the *galvanic skin response* (GSR), is a sign of activation of the sympathetic branch of the autonomic nervous system (ANS). In an early study, Hare (1965) showed that people with antisocial personalities had lower GSR levels when they were expecting painful stimuli than normal controls did. Apparently, the people with antisocial personalities experienced little anxiety in anticipation of impending pain.

Hare's findings of a weaker GSR response in people with antisocial personalities has been replicated a number of times in studies showing lower levels of physiological responsiveness in people with psychopathic or antisocial personalities (e.g., Fung et al., 2005; Zimak, Suhr, & Bolinger, 2014). This lack of emotionality may help explain why the threat of punishment seems to have so little effect on deterring their antisocial behavior. It is conceivable that the ANS of people with antisocial personalities is underresponsive to threatening stimuli.

**THE CRAVING-FOR-STIMULATION MODEL** Other investigators have attempted to explain the antisocial personality's lack of emotional response in terms of the levels of stimulation necessary to maintain an *optimum level of arousal*, the degree of arousal at which a person feels best and functions most efficiently.

People with antisocial or psychopathic personalities tend to crave excitement or stimulation (Prins, 2013). Perhaps they require a higher-than-normal threshold of stimulation to maintain an optimum state of arousal. In other words, they may need more stimulation than other people to maintain interest and function normally.

A need for higher levels of stimulation may explain why people with antisocial personality traits tend to become bored easily and gravitate to stimulating but potentially dangerous activities, like the use of alcohol and other drugs, motorcycling, skydiving, high-stakes gambling, or high-risk sexual adventures. A higher-than-normal threshold for stimulation would not directly cause antisocial or criminal behavior; after all, astronauts, soldiers, police officers, and firefighters must also exhibit this trait to some respect. However, the threat of boredom and the inability to tolerate monotony may influence some sensation seekers to drift into crime or reckless behavior.

## Questionnaire

### THE SENSATION-SEEKING SCALE

Do you crave stimulation or seek sensation? Are you satisfied by reading or by watching television, or must you ride the big wave or bounce your motorbike over desert dunes? Psychologist Marvin Zuckerman (2007) uses the term *sensation seeker* to describe people with a high need for arousal and constant stimulation. They have a strong need to pursue thrill and adventure and are easily bored by routine. Although some sensation seekers abuse drugs or get into trouble with the law, many limit their sensation-seeking behaviors to sanctioned activities. Thus, sensation seeking should not be interpreted as criminal or antisocial in itself.

The following questionnaire can help you assess whether you are a sensation seeker. For each of the following items, select the choice, A or B, that best describes you. Then compare your responses to those in the key at the end of the chapter.

1. _____ **a.** I prefer to go out on the town at all hours of the night.
or _____ **b.** I prefer spending a quiet evening at home.
2. _____ **a.** I like scary amusement park rides.
or _____ **b.** I avoid scary amusement park rides.
3. _____ **a.** I'm the type of person who craves thrilling experiences.
or _____ **b.** I'm the type of person who likes quiet, relaxing activities.
4. _____ **a.** I have been skydiving or would like to go skydiving.
or _____ **b.** Skydiving is not for me.
5. _____ **a.** Every so often, I like to stir up a little excitement in my life.
or _____ **b.** I prefer keeping things calm and mellow.
6. _____ **a.** When traveling, I prefer to follow a planned itinerary.
or _____ **b.** When traveling, I like going places without any definite plans.
7. _____ **a.** I'm basically a creature of habit.
or _____ **b.** I get bored easily with routines.
8. _____ **a.** I would do practically anything on a dare.
or _____ **b.** I avoid risky situations if at all possible.
9. _____ **a.** I enjoy loud parties.
or _____ **b.** I prefer to relax at home or going out with friends.
10. _____ **a.** I believe you should live life to the max.
or _____ **b.** I prefer things to be slow and steady.
11. _____ **a.** I love going out in really cold, brisk weather just for the feel of it against my skin.
or _____ **b.** I prefer staying indoors when it gets really cold.
12. _____ **a.** I'm the kind of person that prefers peace and tranquility.
or _____ **b.** I'm the kind of person that needs a high level of stimulation to feel alive.

**BRAIN ABNORMALITIES** Brain-imaging studies link borderline personality disorder and antisocial personality disorder to dysfunctions in parts of the brain involved in regulating emotions and restraining impulsive behaviors, especially aggressive behaviors (Calzada-Reyes et al., 2012; Carrasco et al., 2012; Schiffer et al., 2014).

Areas of the brain most directly implicated in these disorders are the prefrontal cortex (located in the front or anterior part of the frontal lobes) and deeper brain structures in the limbic system. The prefrontal cortex is involved in controlling impulsive behavior, weighing consequences of actions, and solving problems. It serves as a kind of "emergency brake" to keep impulses from becoming expressed in violent or aggressive behavior (Raine, 2008). The limbic system is involved in processing emotional responses and forming new memories.

There may also be a neurological basis to the lack of empathy and concern for others we see in people with antisocial personality disorder or psychopathy. When people with psychopathic personalities were asked in a laboratory study to imagine someone in

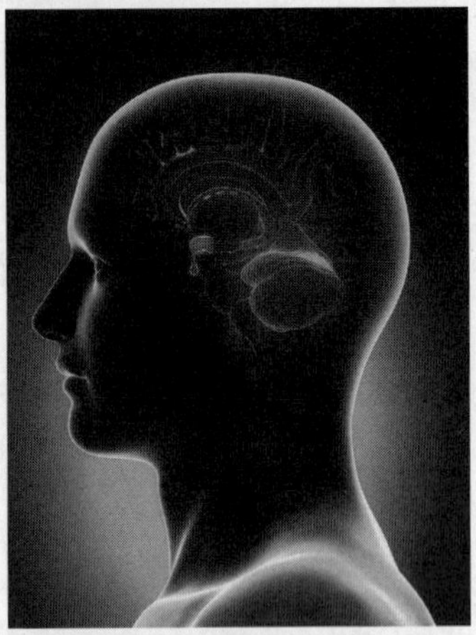

**BRAIN CIRCUITRY.** Abnormalities in brain circuitry between the prefrontal cortex, the brain's thinking center, and the limbic system may contribute to impulse control problems in people with borderline and antisocial personality disorders. The limbic system is a primitive part of the brain involved in regulating emotional processing and memory formation. The amygdala, a part of the limbic system involved in triggering fear, is highlighted here (one on each side of the brain).

pain, the parts of the brain that normally become active when people experience empathy remained inactive, and parts of the brain involved in states of pleasure showed a pattern of increased activation (Decety et al., 2013). These findings suggest that psychopathic personalities may actually reap pleasure from imagining someone in pain.

A developing area of research involves attempts to identify neural networks in the brain that may underlie personality disorders, which may give us a better understanding of these disorders and possibly lead to more effective treatments. Recent studies using brain-imaging techniques show differences in the brains of people with antisocial personalities involving brain circuitry that connects the amygdala, the fear-generating center in the limbic system, with the prefrontal cortex, the part of the brain responsible for weighing the consequences of behavior (Bøen et al., 2014; Motzkin et al., 2011). These abnormalities may help explain difficulties with impulse-control problems that we see in many people with borderline personality and antisocial personality disorders. In the case of borderline personality disorder, an intriguing possibility is that the prefrontal cortex fails to inhibit or restrain impulsive behaviors in the face of strong negative emotions (Silbersweig et al., 2008).

## Sociocultural Perspectives

**12.10 Describe sociocultural perspectives on the development of personality disorders.**

Social conditions may contribute to the development of personality disorders. Because antisocial personality disorder is reported most frequently among people from lower socioeconomic classes, the kinds of stressors encountered by disadvantaged families may contribute to antisocial behavior patterns. Many inner-city neighborhoods are beset with social problems such as alcohol and drug abuse, teenage pregnancy, and disorganized and disintegrating families. These stressors are associated with an increased likelihood of child abuse and neglect, which may in turn contribute to lower self-esteem and breed feelings of anger and resentment in children. Neglect and abuse may become translated into the lack of empathy and callous disregard for the welfare of others that are associated with antisocial personalities.

Children reared in poverty are also more likely to be exposed to deviant role models, such as neighborhood drug dealers. Maladjustment in school may lead to alienation and frustration with the larger society, leading to antisocial behavior. Addressing the problem of antisocial personality may thus require attempts at a societal level to redress social injustice and improve social conditions.

Little information is available about the rates of personality disorders in other cultures. One initiative in this direction involved a joint program sponsored by the World Health Organization (WHO) and the U.S. Alcohol, Drug Abuse, and Mental Health Administration (ADAMHA). The goal of the program was to develop and standardize diagnostic instruments that could be used to arrive at psychiatric diagnoses worldwide. One result of this effort was the development of the International Personality Disorder Examination (IPDE), a semistructured interview protocol for diagnosing personality disorders (Carcone, Tokarz, & Ruocco, 2015).

## TYING it together

### A MULTIFACTORIAL PATHWAY IN THE DEVELOPMENT OF ANTISOCIAL PERSONALITY DISORDER

Throughout the text, we've endorsed the value of a multifactorial model of abnormal behavior, the view that psychological disorders result from a complex web of psychological, sociocultural, and biological factors. Our understanding of personality disorders is no exception. A history of childhood abuse, neglectful or punitive parents, and learning experiences that breed fear of social interactions rather than self-confidence may underlie the development of personality disorders, such as antisocial personality disorder. Social-cognitive factors, such as the effects of modeling aggressive behavior and cognitive biases that predispose people to misconstrue other people's behavior as threatening, also influence the development of maladaptive ways of relating to others that become identified with personality disorders. Genetic factors also contribute to the matrix of causal factors.

Other biological factors implicated specifically in antisocial personality disorder include a lack of emotional responsiveness to threatening cues, excessive need for stimulation, and underlying brain abnormalities. Sociocultural factors, such as social stressors associated with poverty and living in a disintegrating, crime-ridden neighborhood, are linked to a greater likelihood of child abuse and neglect, which in turn sets the stage for the lingering resentments and lack of empathy for others that typify the antisocial personality.

How are these factors linked together? Typically, we find common themes in the development of specific personality disorders, such as harsh or punitive parenting in the case of antisocial personality. However, we need to allow for different combinations of factors and causal pathways to come into play. For example, some people with antisocial personality disorder were raised in economically deprived conditions and lacked consistent parenting. Others were raised in middle-class families but experienced neglectful or harsh parenting. Clinicians need to evaluate how each person's developmental history may have shaped his or her way of relating to others.

Figure 12.2 illustrates a potential causal pathway leading to the development of antisocial personality disorder based on a multifactorial model. This is but one of many possible causal pathways leading to the same outcome. In this causal pathway, poor parenting and modeling influences in the family lead to poor socialization in the child, but whether the child goes on to develop antisocial personality disorder may depend on the presence of particular vulnerability risk factors that increase the risk potential for the disorder.

**Figure 12.2** A multifactorial model of antisocial personality disorder.

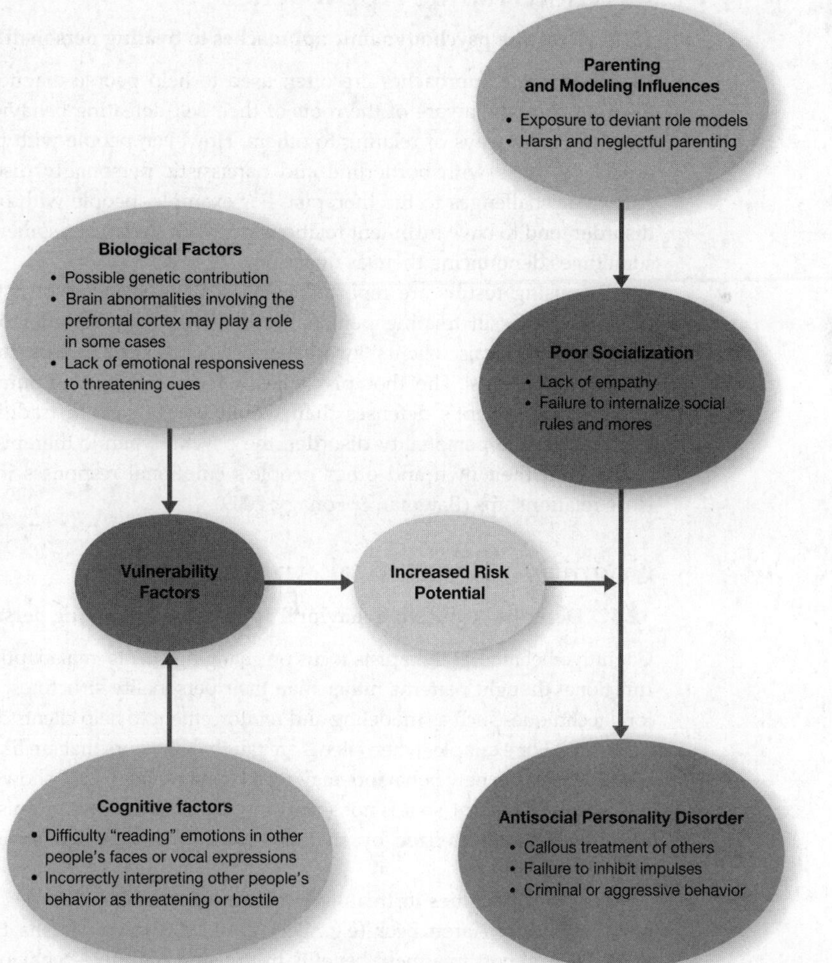

# Treatment of Personality Disorders

We began the chapter with a quote from the eminent psychologist William James, who suggested that people's personalities seem to be "set in plaster" by a certain age. James's view is applicable to many people with personality disorders, who are typically highly resistant to change.

People with personality disorders usually see their behaviors, even maladaptive, self-defeating behaviors, as natural parts of themselves. Even when unhappy and distressed, they are unlikely to perceive their own behavior as causative. Like Marcella, whom we described as showing features of a histrionic personality disorder, they may condemn others for their problems and believe that others, not they, need to change. Thus, they usually do not seek help on their own, or they begrudgingly acquiesce to treatment at the urging of others but drop out or fail to cooperate with the therapist. Even if they go for help, they commonly feel overwhelmed by anxiety or depression and terminate treatment as soon as they find some relief, rather than probing more deeply for the underlying causes of their problems. Despite these obstacles, evidence supports the effectiveness of psychotherapy in treating personality disorders, and some of these treatment approaches are described in the following sections (e.g., Muran, Eubanks-Carter, & Safran, 2010; Paris, 2012).

## Psychodynamic Approaches

**12.11 Describe psychodynamic approaches to treating personality disorders.**

Psychodynamic approaches are often used to help people diagnosed with personality disorders become aware of the roots of their self-defeating behavior patterns and learn more adaptive ways of relating to others. However, people with personality disorders, especially those with borderline and narcissistic personality disorders, often present particular challenges to the therapist. For example, people with borderline personality disorder tend to have turbulent relationships with therapists, sometimes idealizing them, sometimes denouncing them as uncaring.

Promising results are reported using structured forms of psychodynamically oriented therapies in treating personality disorders (e.g., Gunderson, 2011; Paris, 2008). These therapies raise clients' awareness of how their behaviors cause problems in their close relationships. The therapist takes a more direct, confrontational approach that addresses the client's defenses than would be the case in traditional psychoanalysis. With borderline personality disorder, the psychodynamic therapist helps clients better understand their own and other people's emotional responses in the context of their close relationships (Bateman & Fonagy, 2009).

## Cognitive-Behavioral Approaches

**12.12 Describe cognitive-behavioral approaches to treating personality disorders.**

Cognitive-behavioral therapists focus on changing clients' maladaptive behaviors and dysfunctional thought patterns rather than their personality structures. They may use behavioral techniques such as modeling and reinforcement to help clients develop more adaptive behaviors. For example, when clients are taught behaviors that are likely to be reinforced by other people, the new behaviors may well be maintained. CBT shows good results in treating anxiety disorders, so it is not surprising that it also shows promise in treating personality disorders characterized by anxiety, especially avoidant personality disorder (Rees & Pritchard, 2015).

Despite difficulties in treating borderline personality disorder, two groups of therapists headed by Aaron Beck (e.g., Beck et al., 2003) and Marsha Linehan (e.g., Linehan et al., 2006) report treatment benefits from using cognitive-behavioral techniques. Beck's approach focuses on helping an individual identify and correct distorted thinking, such as tendencies to see oneself as completely defective, bad, and helpless. Linehan's technique, called *dialectical behavior therapy* (DBT), is specifically designed to treat borderline personality disorder. DBT combines cognitive-behavioral therapy and Buddhist mindfulness meditation (discussed in Chapter 6) to help people with borderline personality disorder accept and tolerate strong negative emotions and learn more adaptive ways of relating to others. DBT has consistently shown therapeutic benefits in treating people with BPD (e.g., Linehan et al., 2015; Neacsiu et al., 2014; Wilks et al., 2016). DBT also appears to help adolescents with borderline features who repeatedly engage in acts of self-harm (cutting or injuring themselves; Courtney-Seidler, Klein, & Miller, 2014; Mehlum et al., 2014). **T / F**

### TRUTH or FICTION

Despite years of trying, we still lack evidence that psychotherapy can help people with borderline personality disorder.

☑ **FALSE** Several methods of treatment for borderline personality disorder, including psychodynamic therapy, cognitive behavior therapy, and DBT, have shown treatment benefits.

The word *dialectic* is drawn from classical philosophy and applies to a form of reasoning in which you consider both sides of an argument, an argument and a counterargument, and try to reconcile them through rational discussion. As applied to DBT, the dialectical approach involves the attempt to reconcile the opposites or contradictions of *acceptance* and *change*. DBT therapists recognize the need to show acceptance of people with borderline personalities by validating their feelings while also gently encouraging them to make adaptive changes in their behavior. Therapists help patients recognize how their feelings and behaviors cause problems in their lives, and encourage them to identify alternative ways of relating to others. The tension between acceptance and mild encouragement of change constitutes the dialectical approach.

DBT incorporates behavioral techniques to help clients improve their relationships with others, develop problem-solving skills, and learn more adaptive ways of handling confusing feelings. It also involves cognitive-behavioral techniques focused on helping people learn to regulate their emotions and mindfulness techniques (see Chapter 4) intended to help people accept and tolerate their disturbing emotions. Because people with borderline personality disorder tend to be overly sensitive to even the slightest cues of rejection, therapists offer acceptance and support, even when clients become manipulative or overly demanding.

Some antisocial adolescents have been placed, often by court order, in residential and foster-care programs that contain numerous behavioral treatment components. These programs have concrete rules and clear rewards for obeying them. Some residential programs rely on *token economies*, in which prosocial behaviors are rewarded with tokens such as plastic chips that can be exchanged for privileges. Although participants in such programs often show improved behavior, it remains unclear whether such programs reduce the risk that adolescent antisocial behavior will continue into adulthood.

### "I" "I Cannot Die a Coward"

In 2011 at the age of 68, the renowned psychologist Marsha Linehan, developer of one of the leading treatments for borderline personality disorder—dialectical behavior therapy—stood before a group of friends, family, and fellow professionals to reveal a dark secret: that she too had suffered from borderline personality disorder. She began by explaining her reason for finally coming out: "So many people have begged me to come forward, and I just thought—well, I have to do this. I owe it to them. I cannot die a coward" (cited in B. Carey, 2011, p. A1).

The faded burns, cuts, and welts on her arms attested to the personal pain she carried with her from her youth, from her psychiatric hospitalization at age 17, during which she was placed in seclusion and repeatedly inflicted herself with cigarette burns on her wrists, banging her head, and cutting her arms and other parts of her body. She received electroshock therapy, but nothing seemed to work to relieve her deep inner pain. She was hospitalized for 26 months and was one of the most disturbed patients in the hospital. Looking back, she told a reporter, "I was in hell . . . And I made a vow: when I get out, I'm going to come back and get others out of here." It wasn't an easy road to follow. There were later suicide attempts and another hospitalization. She eventually turned to her Catholic faith, finding the inner strength to put her life on track, getting a job in an insurance company, taking college classes, and eventually completing a doctoral program in clinical psychology and from there entering a long, distinguished career as a leading researcher and clinician, and through her development of DBT, providing help to a great many people struggling with suicidal thinking and the inner anguish of BPD. Looking back on her life, she told the interviewer that she is a very happy person now. She went on to say that, yes, she still has her ups and downs, "but I think no more than anyone else."

## Biological Approaches

**12.13 Describe drug therapy approaches to treating personality disorders.**

Drug therapy does not directly treat personality disorders. However, antidepressant and antianxiety drugs are sometimes used to treat depression and anxiety in people with personality disorders. Neurotransmitter activity also is implicated in aggressive behavior of the type seen in individuals with borderline personality disorder. The neurotransmitter serotonin helps put the brakes on impulsive behaviors, including acts of impulsive aggression (Carver, Johnson, & Joormann, 2008; Seo, Patrick, & Kennealy, 2008). Antidepressants of the selective serotonin reuptake inhibitor (SSRI) class (e.g., Prozac) increase the availability of serotonin in synaptic connections between neurons and can help temper feelings of anger and rage. However, we've yet to see antidepressant medication produce any substantial benefits relative to placebo in treating borderline personality disorder (Gunderson, 2011). Atypical antipsychotics (discussed in Chapter 11) may have benefits in controlling aggressive and self-destructive behavior in people with borderline personality disorder, but the effects are modest and the drugs carry serious potential side effects (Gunderson, 2011; Stoffers & Lieb, 2015). Moreover, drugs alone do not target the long-standing patterns of maladaptive behavior that are the defining features of personality disorders.

Much remains to be learned about working with people who have personality disorders. The major challenges involve recruiting people who do not see themselves as being disordered into treatment and prompting them to develop insight into their self-defeating or injurious behaviors. Current efforts to help such people are too often reminiscent of the old couplet:

*He that complies against his will,*
*Is of his own opinion still.*

—Samuel Butler, *Hudibras*

# Impulse-Control Disorders

People with borderline personalities often have difficulty controlling their impulses. But problems with impulse control are not limited to people with personality disorders. The *DSM* includes a category of mental disorders called **impulse-control disorders** that are characterized by difficulties in controlling or restraining impulsive behavior.

## Features of Impulse-Control Disorders

**12.14 Describe the key features of impulse-control disorders.**

Have you ever blown your budget on a sale item? Have you ever made a bet you could not afford? Have you ever lost it and screamed at someone, even though you knew you should be keeping your cool? Most of us keep our impulses under control most of the time. Although we may sometimes surrender to a tempting dessert or occasionally blurt out an obscenity in anger, we generally hold our impulsive behaviors in check. People with impulse-control disorders, however, have persistent difficulty resisting harmful impulses, temptations, or drives. They experience a rising level of tension or arousal just prior to the impulsive act, followed by a sense of relief or release after the act is completed. They often have other psychological disorders, especially mood disorders, a fact that leads investigators to question whether these disorders should be classified within a broader spectrum of mood disorders.

Impulse-control disorders in *DSM-5* are grouped in a broader category of disruptive, impulse-control, and conduct disorders that also include conduct disorder and oppositional defiant disorder. Other impulse-control problems such as compulsive Internet use and compulsive shopping are presently under consideration for inclusion in later versions of the diagnostic manual. Our focus here is on three types of impulse-control disorders: *kleptomania, intermittent explosive disorder*, and *pyromania*.

# Kleptomania

**12.15 Describe the key features of kleptomania.**

**Kleptomania**, which derives from the Greek *kleptes*, meaning *thief*, and *mania*, meaning *madness* or *frenzy*, is characterized by repeated acts of compulsive stealing. The stolen objects are typically of little value or use to the person who takes them. The person may give them away, return them secretly, discard them, or just keep them hidden at home. In most cases, people with kleptomania can easily afford the items they steal. Even wealthy people have been known to be compulsive shoplifters. The thefts are apparently unmotivated by anger or vengeance. These crimes typically result from a momentary impulse, are poorly planned, and sometimes lead to arrests.

Although shoplifting is common, kleptomania is a recurring pattern of compulsive stealing. Kleptomania is considered a rare condition, affecting less than 1% of the general population, but occurring more frequently in women by a ratio of about three to one (American Psychiatric Association, 2013; Shoenfeld & Dannon, 2012). We have little scientific evidence on kleptomania to guide our understanding of the disorder. The presence of an irresistible, repetitive pattern in kleptomania suggests common features with obsessive-compulsive disorder. However, there is an important distinction. People with obsessive-compulsive anxiety disorder experience only temporary relief from anxiety when they perform compulsive acts; by contrast, people with kleptomania experience pleasurable excitement or gratification when they engage in compulsive stealing. Another difference is that kleptomania appears to be an end in itself, whereas compulsions in obsessive-compulsive anxiety disorder are performed to avoid potential unfortunate events (like repeatedly checking the gas jets to prevent a gas explosion). **T / F**

> **TRUTH or FICTION**
>
> Kleptomania, or compulsive stealing, is usually motivated by poverty.
>
> ☑ **FALSE** People with kleptomania typically steal items of little value to them, not necessities they cannot afford to buy.

All in all, some forms of kleptomania may be like obsessive-compulsive anxiety disorder, whereas others forms may have more in common with substance use or mood disorders (Grant, Odlaug, & Kim, 2012). Perhaps the thrill of theft is a way in which some people attempt to fend off feelings of depression. By coming to better understand the subtypes, we may learn to be better equipped to tailor more effective treatment approaches. As it stands, the few isolated treatment studies are limited to a few cases.

Traditional psychodynamic formulations viewed kleptomania as a defense against unconscious penis envy in women and castration anxiety in men. The classic psychodynamic belief is that people with kleptomania are motivated to steal phallic objects (symbols of the penis) as a magical way of protecting themselves against the apparent loss (in females) or threatened loss (in males) of the penis (Fenichel, 1945). Whether this theoretical speculation has merit remains uncertain, as we lack any supportive evidence of these unconscious processes.

There is little formal research on the treatment of kleptomania. In the following case example, we describe a behavioral approach to treating kleptomania.

## "Baby Shoes":

### A CASE OF KLEPTOMANIA

The client was a 56-year-old woman, who had shoplifted every day of the preceding 14 years. Her compulsive urges to steal fit the clinical criteria that may distinguish kleptomania from other types of shoplifting, although her booty had no apparent meaning to her. Typical loot examples might include a pair of baby shoes, although there was no baby in her family to whom she could give the shoes. The compulsion to steal was so strong that she felt powerless to resist it. She told her therapist that she wished she could be "chained to a wall" (Glover, 1985, p. 213) in order to prevent her from acting out. She expressed anger that it was so easy to steal from a supermarket, in effect blaming the store for her own misconduct.

Her treatment, called covert sensitization, involved the pairing in imagination of an aversive stimulus with the undesired behavior. The therapist directed the woman to imagine feeling nauseous and vomiting while stealing. She was instructed to picture herself in the supermarket, approaching an object she intends to steal, and becoming nauseated and vomiting as she attempts to remove it, which draws the scowling attention of other shoppers. She is then directed to imagine herself replacing the object and consequently feeling relief from the nausea.

In a subsequent session, she imagined the nausea starting as she approached the object, but the nausea disappeared when she turned away rather than removing it. She was also asked to practice the imaginal scenes on her own throughout the week as a homework assignment. She reported a decline in stealing behavior during the treatment program. She reported only one instance of shoplifting between the completion of treatment and a 19-month follow-up evaluation.

**SOURCE:** *Adapted from Glover, 1985*

Was the treatment effective? Perhaps. Then again, uncontrolled case studies cannot ascertain cause-and-effect relationships. For example, we cannot know whether the treatment itself or other factors, such as the client's motivation to change her life, were responsible for the changes in her behavior. Controlled studies are needed to evaluate the effectiveness of treatment.

# Intermittent Explosive Disorder

**12.16 Describe the key features of intermittent explosive disorder.**

*Rage*: This is the very first word of *The Iliad*, Homer's epic poem about the Trojan War, establishing a theme for the entire work. Homer's poem, believed to have been written about 750 B.C.E, chronicles the tragic consequences that unfold as unrestrained rage leads to war, killing, and destruction.

People have been concerned about the human capacity for rage and the violent behavior it often provokes for time immemorial. Rage is not a criterion used to diagnose mental or psychological disorders in the *DSM*. However, rage is often a feature of **intermittent explosive disorder** (IED), a type of impulse-control disorder characterized by repeated episodes of impulsive, uncontrollable aggression in which people strike out at others or destroy property (Kessler, Coccaro, et al., 2012). The core feature of IED is impulsive aggression, the tendency to lose control of aggressive impulses (Coccaro, 2010).

People with IED have episodes of violent rage in which they suddenly lose control and hit or try to hit other people or smash objects. One man with IED had episodes of explosive rage in which he would smash anything he could lay his hands on, including cell phones, keyboards, remote controls, tables, and even drywall. Even minor provocations or perceived insults can lead to aggressive outbursts that are grossly out of proportion to the situation. People with IED typically experience a state of tension before their violent outbursts and a sense of relief afterwards. Typically, people with IED attempt to justify their behavior, but they also feel genuine remorse or regret because of the harm their behavior causes. Incidents of road rage and domestic violence often occur in cases of IED. Early studies suggested that IED may be a rare condition, but more recent work indicates it may be as common as many other psychiatric disorders (Coccaro, 2012; Tamam, Eroğlu, & Paltacı, 2011). There also appear to be links between childhood trauma, violent behaviors, and development of IED (Lee, Meyerhoff, & Coccaro, 2014).

Recent research on IED has largely focused on its biological underpinnings and particularly on the possible role of the neurotransmitter serotonin. You'll recall from earlier in the chapter that serotonin serves to put the brakes on impulsive behaviors, including acts of impulsive aggression associated with IED. Research in this area is preliminary, but it points toward possible irregularities in serotonin transmission in the brains of people with IED (Coccaro, Lee, & Kavoussi, 2010). Supporting this view is evidence that treatment with antidepressant drugs that boost serotonin availability, such as Prozac, has shown promise in treating impulsive aggression associated with IED (Coccaro & McCloskey, 2010). Functioning of the prefrontal cortex, the part of the brain that curbs impulsive behavior, may also be impaired. Psychological treatment in the form of anger-management training may be used to help individuals with IED develop better control over anger outbursts that lead to impulsive acts of aggression and learn to stop and think before they act.

Anger and rage are often a feature of psychological disorders, but the *DSM* does not include a category of anger disorders. In *Thinking Critically: Anger Disorders and the DSM*, a leading researcher, Jerry Deffenbacher of Colorado State University, takes up the controversial question of whether the *DSM* should include a category of anger disorders.

## THINKING CRITICALLY about abnormal psychology

### @ISSUE: ANGER DISORDERS AND THE *DSM*: WHERE HAS ALL THE ANGER GONE?—JERRY DEFFENBACHER

You may recall from Chapter 4 that research evidence links chronic anger to serious health problems, including coronary heart disease. Anger also contributes to a range of problem behaviors, such as the following (e.g., Dahlen et al., 2012; Deffenbacher, Stephens, & Sullman, in press; Shorey, Cornelius, & Idema, 2011; Spector, 2011):

- Abusive parenting
- Aggressive behaviors, including intimate partner violence and aggressive (as well as risky) driving
- Problems at work
- Negative feelings about oneself

Anger is also a "red flag" for predicting poorer outcomes in psychotherapy and greater risk of relapse after successful treatment of substance abuse (Patterson et al., 2008). However, anger is not necessarily problematic. When it is mild or moderate in degree and expressed constructively, anger can lead to positive outcomes, such as standing up for oneself, setting appropriate limits, and mobilizing one's efforts to resolve problems in personal relationships. Problems occur when anger becomes too intense or is expressed inappropriately. These forms of maladaptive anger can lead to many kinds of negative outcomes, such as states of personal distress (e.g., embarrassment, guilt, self-recrimination), negative physical outcomes (e.g., injury to self and others), legal and financial problems (e.g., arrests for assault or disturbing the peace, legal bills, and property damage), educational problems (e.g., dismissal from college), vocational problems (e.g., losing a job), interpersonal problems (e.g., damaged or terminated relationships), and impaired role behaviors (e.g., abusive or dysfunctional parenting). The personal suffering and costs associated with maladaptive anger more than meet the threshold for abnormal behavior.

With so many negative consequences linked to anger, you might think that anger figures prominently in the classification of abnormal behavior patterns, but this is not the case. It is true that anger is often part of the clinical profile of certain psychological disorders, including major depressive disorder, bipolar disorder, posttraumatic stress disorder, and personality disorders such as antisocial and borderline personality disorders. However, anger is not a necessary diagnostic feature of any of these disorders. Some people with these diagnoses show problems with anger, but many do not. People who display impulsive acts of aggression toward others that result in serious personal harm or destruction of property may receive a diagnosis of IED. As discussed in this chapter, IED is a type of impulse-control disorder in which a person shows impaired ability to control impulses. In people with IED, acts of uncontrolled aggression are grossly out of proportion to any provocation or precipitating stressors. The aggressive behavior must be impulsive or anger-based and not premeditated or committed to achieve some objective (e.g., coercion of others, pursuit of power or money). However, although intense anger is often associated with IED, the diagnosis is based on failure to control aggressive impulses, not on anger per se.

Simply put, there are no purely anger-based disorders in the *DSM* system that apply to adults: no diagnosable disorders in which anger is the cardinal feature and must be present to make a diagnosis. Compare the absence of anger-related disorders in adulthood to the wide range of diagnosable disorders that involve two other major negative emotions—anxiety and depression. Anxiety, of course, is the chief feature of anxiety disorders such as panic disorder, generalized anxiety disorder, and phobic disorders, as well as a key feature of obsessive-compulsive disorder. Depression is the keynote feature of mood disorders such as major depressive disorder and persistent depressive disorder (dysthymia). The absence of anger disorders in the *DSM* system does not mean these problems do not exist. People do indeed suffer from anger-related problems, and in some cases these problems bring considerable suffering to others.

I have argued (e.g., Deffenbacher, 2003) along with others in the field that anger disorders affecting adults should be included in the *DSM* system. In the scheme I proposed, dysfunctional anger involves at least four types of triggering events:

1. A specific situation, such as driving
2. Different types of situations, such as problems at work and at home
3. An identifiable psychosocial stressor, such as the breakup of a relationship
4. Unclear triggers in which anger wells up quickly and intensely

We can then use this scheme to classify four types of corresponding anger disorders: (1) situational anger disorder, (2) generalized anger disorder, (3) adjustment disorder with anger, and (4) anger attacks. Because maladaptive anger may be associated with aggressive behavior, we could also elaborate each of these anger disorders in terms of the presence of significant aggression that is likely in need of attention. This diagnostic scheme might help legitimize the pain and suffering of people with anger-related problems and provide the basis for insurance reimbursement of clinical services to treat these problems and funds for much-needed research on their causes and treatments (Fernandez, 2013).

Not every professional agrees that the diagnostic system should be expanded to include anger disorders. Some argue that including these disorders in the *DSM* system may excuse aggressive or violent behaviors committed in anger by labeling them as forms of mental illness and that bringing these behaviors under the umbrella of the diagnostic system will lead to cases in which people who commit violent acts are not held fully accountable for their behavior. A related concern is that diagnosing anger disorders might undermine efforts to reduce intimate partner violence.

It remains to be seen if future revisions of the diagnostic manual will include anger-related disorders.

In thinking critically about whether anger-related disorders should be included in the diagnostic manual, answer the following questions:

- Do you know someone who has a serious anger problem? Should his or her behavior be considered abnormal? What are the legal, moral, and ethical consequences of diagnosing these problems as types of mental or psychological disorders?
- If a person with anger-related problems entered therapy for anger reduction, should insurance companies be required to reimburse treatment at a rate comparable to that of treatment for anxiety or depression? If yes, why? If no, why not?
- Should a person who acts out violently against someone else in a state of anger be held fully responsible for his or her behavior? Why or why not?

**JERRY L. DEFFENBACHER, PH.D., ABPP.** Dr. Deffenbacher is professor emeritus and formerly professor laureate and director of clinical training in the Department of Psychology at Colorado State University. He routinely taught large undergraduate classes in abnormal psychology. In discussing how he became interested in anger-related problems, he noted that he essentially stumbled into it more than 30 years ago during clinical supervision. Graduate students wanted help in treating angry clients, but he recognized that he knew little about the treatment of anger. When he and students searched the scientific literature, they found very little guidance. He then became curious about helping people with anger problems and has been involved in the study of problematic anger ever since.

## Pyromania

**12.17 Describe the key features of pyromania.**

**Pyromania**, from the Latin root *pyr*, meaning *fire*, and the Greek word *mania*, meaning *madness* or *frenzy*, is characterized by repeated acts of compulsive fire setting in response to irresistible urges. Only a small percentage of arsonists are diagnosed with pyromania. The most common motives for fire setting appear to be anger and revenge rather than a psychiatric disorder (Grant & Odlaug, 2009). Other instances of arson may be motivated by financial incentives, as in cases of owners of failing businesses who arrange to have their premises torched in order to illicitly collect insurance settlements. Intentional fire setting also occurs among some youths with *conduct disorder* (a psychological disorder affecting children and adolescents, discussed in Chapter 13). Fire setting associated with conduct disorder is part of a larger pattern of antisocial and intentionally cruel or harmful behavior.

Pyromania is considered a rare disorder, which may help explain why it remains so poorly understood. People with pyromania feel a sense of release or psychological relief when setting fires and perhaps feelings of empowerment as the result of prompting firefighters to rush to the scene of the blaze, along with the heavy firefighting equipment they bring. The fire setter may also experience pleasurable excitement by watching or even participating in the firefighting effort. The origins of pyromania remain obscure, but there does appear to have been a morbid fascination with fire from an early age (Lejoyeux & Germain, 2012). In the following account, a female college student who was committed to a mental hospital for compulsive fire setting recounts her experiences.

**"I" "A Part of My Vocabulary"**

Fire became a part of my vocabulary in preschool days… Each summer, I would look forward to the beginning of fire season as well as the fall…. I may feel abandoned, lonely, or bored, which triggers feelings of anxiety or emotional arousal before the fire…. I want to see the chaos as well as the destruction that I or others have caused…. [After the fire is out] I feel sadness and anguish and the desire to set another fire.

**SOURCE:** *Wheaton, 2001, as quoted in Lejoyeux & Germain, 2012, p. 139.*

Treatment of pyromania may involve cognitive-behavioral therapy focused on helping a person identify thoughts and situational cues that prompt fire-setting urges and practice in using coping responses to resist them. However, here again we lack controlled studies of treatment effectiveness.

# Summing Up

## Types of Personality Disorders

### Classification of Personality Disorders

**12.1 Identify three clusters of personality disorders used in the *DSM* system.**

Personality disorders in the *DSM* system are classified within three major clusters according to the following characteristics: (1) odd or eccentric behavior, (2) dramatic, emotional, or erratic behavior, and (3) anxious or fearful behavior.

### Personality Disorders Characterized by Odd or Eccentric Behavior

**12.2 Describe the key features of personality disorders characterized by odd or eccentric behavior.**

Personality disorders involving odd or eccentric behavior include paranoid personality disorder, schizoid personality disorders, and schizotypal personality disorder. People with paranoid personality disorder are unduly suspicious and mistrustful of others, to the point that their relationships suffer, but they do not hold the more flagrant paranoid delusions typical of schizophrenia. Schizoid personality disorder describes people who have little if any interest in social relationships, show a restricted range of emotional expression, and appear distant and aloof. People with schizotypal personalities appear odd or eccentric in their thoughts, mannerisms, and behavior, but not to the degree found in schizophrenia.

### Personality Disorders Characterized by Dramatic, Emotional, or Erratic Behavior

**12.3 Describe the key features of personality disorders characterized by dramatic, emotional, or erratic behavior.**

Personality disorders involving dramatic, emotional, or erratic behavior include antisocial personality disorder, borderline personality disorder, narcissistic personality disorder, and histrionic personality disorder. Antisocial personality disorder describes people who persistently engage in behavior that violates social norms and the rights of others and who tend to show no remorse for their misdeeds. Borderline personality disorder is defined in terms of instability in self-image, relationships, and mood. People with borderline personality disorder often engage in impulsive acts, which are frequently self-destructive. People with histrionic personality disorder tend to be highly dramatic and emotional in their behavior, whereas people diagnosed with narcissistic personality disorder have an inflated or grandiose sense of self, and like those with histrionic personalities, they demand to be the center of attention.

### Personality Disorders Characterized by Anxious or Fearful Behavior

**12.4 Describe the key features of personality disorders characterized by anxious or fearful behavior.**

Personality disorders involving anxious or fearful behavior include avoidant personality disorder, dependent personality disorder, and obsessive-compulsive personality disorder. Avoidant personality disorder describes people who are so terrified of rejection and criticism that they are generally unwilling to enter relationships without unusually strong reassurances of acceptance. People with dependent personality disorder are overly dependent on others and have extreme difficulty acting independently or making even the smallest decisions on their own. People with obsessive-compulsive personality disorder have various traits such as orderliness, perfectionism, rigidity, and overattention to detail, but are without the true obsessions and compulsions associated with obsessive-compulsive (anxiety) disorder.

### Problems with the Classification of Personality Disorders

**12.5 Evaluate problems associated with the classification of personality disorders.**

Various controversies and problems attend the classification of personality disorders, including overlap among the categories, difficulty in distinguishing between variations in normal behavior and abnormal behavior, confusion of labels with explanations, and possible underlying sexist biases.

## Theoretical Perspectives

### Psychodynamic Perspectives

**12.6 Describe psychodynamic perspectives on the development of personality disorders.**

Earlier Freudian theory focused on unresolved Oedipal conflicts in explaining normal and abnormal personality development. More recent psychodynamic theorists have focused on the pre-Oedipal period in explaining the development of personality disorders such as narcissistic and borderline personality.

## Learning Theory Perspectives

**12.7 Describe learning theory perspectives on the development of personality disorders.**

Learning theorists view personality disorders in terms of maladaptive patterns of behavior rather than personality traits. Learning theorists seek to identify the early learning experiences and present reinforcement patterns that explain the development and maintenance of personality disorders. Antisocial adolescents are more likely to interpret social cues as provocations or intentions of ill will. This cognitive bias may lead them to be confrontational in their relationships with peers.

## Family Perspectives

**12.8 Describe the role of family relationships in the development of personality disorders.**

Many theorists argue that disturbed family relationships play formative roles in the development of personality disorders. For example, theorists connect antisocial personality to parental rejection or neglect and parental modeling of antisocial behavior.

## Biological Perspectives

**12.9 Describe biological perspectives on the development of personality disorders.**

Biological explanations of antisocial personality focus on the possible role of lack of emotional responsiveness to physically threatening stimuli and reduced levels of ANS reactivity and the need for higher levels of stimulation to maintain optimal levels of arousal in people with antisocial personalities.

## Sociocultural Perspectives

**12.10 Describe sociocultural perspectives on the development of personality disorders.**

Sociocultural theorists focus on the roles of poverty, urban blight, and drug abuse in leading to family disorganization and disintegration that makes it less likely that children will receive the nurturance and support they need to develop more socially adaptive personalities. Sociocultural theorists believe that such factors may underlie the development of personality disorders, especially antisocial personality disorder.

# Treatment of Personality Disorders

## Psychodynamic Approaches

**12.11 Describe psychodynamic approaches to treating personality disorders.**

Psychodynamic therapists seek to help people with personality disorders become aware of the underlying roots of their self-defeating behavior patterns and learn more adaptive ways of relating to others in the context of their close relationships.

## Cognitive-Behavioral Approaches

**12.12 Describe cognitive-behavioral approaches to treating personality disorders.**

CBT focuses on helping clients change their maladaptive behaviors and dysfunctional thought patterns rather than their personality structures. Two major forms of cognitive-behavioral treatment for personality disorders have emerged: Beck's cognitive therapy approach and Linehan's dialectical behavior therapy approach.

## Biological Approaches

**12.13 Describe drug therapy approaches to treating personality disorders.**

Drug therapy is limited to helping people with personality disorders control troubling emotional states such as depression and anxiety, temper feelings of anger or rage, and help control aggressive and self-destructive behavior. However, it does not directly help people with personality disorders change long-standing patterns of maladaptive behavior.

# Impulse-Control Disorders

## Features of Impulse-Control Disorders

**12.14 Describe the key features of impulse-control disorders.**

Impulse-control disorders are psychological disorders characterized by a pattern of repeated failure to resist impulses to perform acts that lead to harmful consequences to self or others. People affected by these disorders experience a rising level of tension or arousal just before the act, then a sense of relief or release when the act is committed.

## Kleptomania

**12.15 Describe the key features of kleptomania.**

Kleptomania is characterized by a compulsion to steal, usually involving items of little value to the person.

## Intermittent Explosive Disorder

**12.16 Describe the key features of intermittent explosive disorder.**

Intermittent explosive disorder (IED) involves acts of impulsive aggression and may involve irregularities in serotonin transmission in the brain.

## Pyromania

**12.17 Describe the key features of pyromania.**

Pyromania, or compulsive fire setting, is poorly understood but may be motivated in part by the desire to control the response of firefighters and even assist them in their work.

## Critical Thinking Questions

Based on your reading of this chapter, answer the following questions:

- How is psychopathic behavior different from psychotic behavior? How is this distinction sometimes confused in the movies or on television shows?
- Are some personality disorders more likely to be diagnosed in men or in women because of gender-based societal expectations? Have you ever assumed that women are "just dependent or hysterical" or that men are "just narcissists or antisocial"? What kinds of problems do underlying assumptions like these pose for clinicians and researchers?
- Have you known people whose personality traits or behaviors caused significant difficulties in their personal relationships? In what ways? Do you think that any of the personality disorders discussed in this chapter might apply to this person or persons? Explain your answer. Did the person ever seek help from a mental health professional? If so, what was the outcome? If not, why not?
- What factors make it difficult for therapists to treat people with personality disorders? If you were a therapist, how might you attempt to overcome these difficulties?

## Key Terms

personality disorders, p. 453
ego syntonic, p. 453
ego dystonic, p. 453
paranoid personality disorder, p. 454
schizoid personality disorder, p. 455
schizotypal personality disorder, p. 456
antisocial personality disorder, p. 457
borderline personality disorder (BPD), p. 460
splitting, p. 463
histrionic personality disorder, p. 464
narcissistic personality disorder, p. 465
avoidant personality disorder, p. 467
dependent personality disorder, p. 468
obsessive-compulsive personality disorder, p. 469
impulse-control disorders, p. 484
kleptomania, p. 485
intermittent explosive disorder, p. 486
pyromania, p. 488

## Key for Sensation-Seeking Scale

Although we don't have any applicable norms, answers that agree with the following key are suggestive of sensation seeking. The more answers keyed in this direction, the stronger your sensation-seeking needs are likely to be.

| | | | |
|---|---|---|---|
| 1. A | 4. A | 7. B | 10. A |
| 2. A | 5. A | 8. A | 11. A |
| 3. A | 6. B | 9. A | 12. B |

Chapter 13

# Abnormal Behavior in Childhood and Adolescence

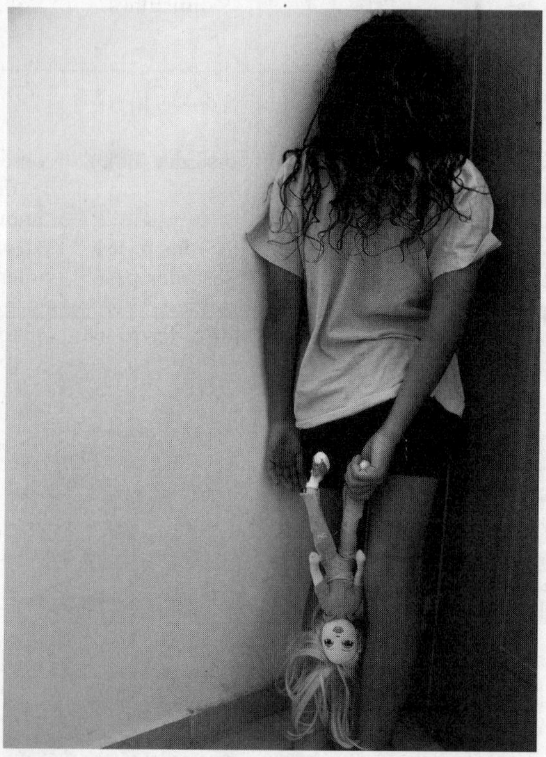

## Learning Objectives

**13.1** **Explain** the differences between normal and abnormal behavior in childhood and adolescence and the role of cultural beliefs in determining abnormality.

**13.2** **Describe** the prevalence of psychological disorders in children and adolescents.

**13.3** **Identify** risk factors for psychological disorders in childhood and adolescence and **describe** the effects of child abuse.

**13.4** **Describe** key features of autism.

**13.5** **Identify** possible causal factors in autism.

**13.6** **Describe** the treatment of autism.

**13.7** **Describe** the key features and causes of intellectual disability.

**13.8** **Describe** interventions used to help children with intellectual disability.

**13.9** **Identify** the types of deficits associated with learning disorders and **describe** ways of understanding and treating learning disorders.

**13.10** **Describe** the key features of language disorder.

**13.11** **Describe** the key features of psychological disorders involving problems with speech.

**13.12** **Describe** the key features of social (pragmatic) communication disorder.

**13.13** **Describe** the key features of attention-deficit/hyperactivity disorder, identify causal factors, and evaluate treatment methods.

**13.14** **Describe** the key features of conduct disorder.

**13.15** **Describe** the key features of oppositional defiant disorder.

**13.16** **Describe** the key features of anxiety-related disorders in children and adolescents.

**13.17** **Describe** common features of depression in childhood and **identify** cognitive biases associated with childhood depression and ways of treating childhood depression.

**13.18** **Identify** risk factors for suicide in adolescents.

**13.19** **Describe** the key features of enuresis and **evaluate** methods of treating bed-wetting.

**13.20** **Describe** the key features of encopresis.

## TRUTH or FICTION

T☑ F☑ Many behavior patterns considered normal for children would be considered abnormal in adults. (p. 495)

T☐ F☑ About one in 10 cases of adult psychological disorders began before age 18. (p. 496) one in 2 by 14

T☑ F☐ Boys are more likely than girls to develop anxiety and mood disorders. (p. 497)

T☑ F☐ When it comes to child maltreatment, it's not just "sticks and stones" that do damage. (p. 498)

T☐ F☑ Childhood vaccines cause autism. (p. 501)

T☐ F☑ A former vice president of the United States had such difficulty with arithmetic that he could never balance a checkbook. (p. 510) he had dyslexia (Nelson Rockefeller)

T☐ F☑ Children who are hyperactive are often given depressants to help calm them down. (p. 517)

T☑ F☐ Difficulties at school, problem behaviors, and physical complaints may actually be signs of depression in children. (p. 524)

T☑ F☐ Principles of classical conditioning can be applied to treat bed-wetting in children. (p. 531)

## CHAPTER INTRODUCTION: ABNORMAL BEHAVIOR IN CHILDHOOD AND ADOLESCENCE

An autistic woman, Donna Williams, reflects on what it is like to be an autistic child. In this excerpt from her memoir *Nobody Nowhere*, she speaks about her need to keep the world out. She was about 3 years old when her parents took her to a doctor out of concern that she appeared malnourished.

**"I"** **"A World of My Own Creation"**

"My parents thought I had leukemia and took me for a blood test. The doctor took some blood from my earlobe. I cooperated. I was intrigued by a multicolored cardboard wheel the doctor had given me. I also had hearing tests because, although I mimicked everything, it appeared that I was deaf. My parents would stand behind me and make sudden loud noises without my so much as blinking in response. 'The world' simply wasn't getting in.... The more I became aware of the world around me, the more I became afraid. Other people were my enemies, and reaching out to me was their weapon, with only a few exceptions—my grandparents, my father, and my Aunty Linda."

Donna also recalled how, for her, people became things and things existed to offer her protection and shield her from a fear of vulnerability:

"I collected scraps of colored wool and crocheted bits and would put my fingers through the holes so that I could fall asleep securely. For me, the people I liked were things, and those things (or things like them) were my protection from the things I didn't like—other people.

The habits I adopted of keeping and manipulating these symbols were my equivalent of magic spells cast against the nasties who could invade me if I lost my cherished objects or had them taken away. My strategies were not the result of insanity or hallucination, but simply harmless imagination made potent by my overwhelming fear of vulnerability....

People were forever saying that I had no friends. In fact my world was full of them. They were far more magical, reliable, predictable, and real than other children, and they came with guarantees. It was a world of my own creation where I didn't need to control myself or the objects, animals, and nature, which were simply being in my presence."

**SOURCE:** *Williams, 1992, pp. 5, 6, 9*

Psychological disorders of childhood and adolescence often have a special poignancy—perhaps none more than autism. These disorders affect children at ages when they have little capacity to cope. Some of these problems, such as autism and intellectual disability (formerly called *mental retardation*), prevent children from fulfilling their developmental potentials. Some psychological problems in children and adolescents mirror those found in adults—problems such as mood disorders and anxiety disorders. In some cases, the problems are unique to childhood, such as separation anxiety; in others, such as attention-deficit/hyperactivity disorder (ADHD), the problem manifests itself differently in childhood than in adulthood.

# Normal and Abnormal Behavior in Childhood and Adolescence

Determining whether a child's behavior is abnormal depends on our expectations about what is normal for a child of a given age in a given culture. We need to consider whether a child's behavior falls outside the range of developmental and cultural norms. For example, determining that 7-year-old Jimmy is hyperactive depends on the types of behaviors deemed reasonable for children of the same age and cultural background (Drabick & Kendall, 2010; Kendall & Drabick, 2010).

Many problems are first identified when a child enters school. Although these problems may have existed earlier, they may have been tolerated or not seen as "problems" in the home. Sometimes, the stress of starting school contributes to their onset. However, keep in mind that what is socially acceptable at a particular age, such as intense fear of strangers at about nine months, may be socially unacceptable at more advanced ages.

*"Pop, am I experiencing a normal childhood?"*

**SOURCE:** © Lee Lorenz/The New Yorker Collection/www.cartoonbank.com

Many behavior patterns we might consider abnormal among adults—such as intense fear of strangers and lack of bladder control—are perfectly normal for children at certain ages. Many children are misdiagnosed when clinicians fail to take developmental expectations into account. Researchers estimate that nearly 1 million American children may have been misdiagnosed with ADHD in kindergarten and treated with medication simply because they were the youngest (and hence least mature) children in their classes ("Nearly One Million," 2010). As the lead researcher, Todd Edler, told a reporter, "If a child is behaving poorly, if he's inattentive, if he can't sit still, it may simply be because he's 5 and the other kids are 6." **T / F**

**TRUTH or FICTION**

Many behavior patterns considered normal for children would be considered abnormal in adults.

☑ **TRUE** Many behavior patterns that would be considered abnormal among adults—such as intense fear of strangers and lack of bladder control—are perfectly normal for children at certain ages.

Many of the psychological disorders affecting children and adolescents are classified in the *DSM-5* category of **neurodevelopmental disorders**. These disorders involve an impairment of brain functioning or development that affects a child's psychological, cognitive, social, or emotional development. This category of mental disorders includes the following types of disorders we discuss in this chapter:

- Autism spectrum disorder
- Intellectual disability
- Specific learning disorder
- Communication disorders
- Attention-deficit/hyperactivity disorder

In this chapter, we also review other disorders affecting children and adolescents, including disruptive behavior disorders (oppositional defiant disorder and conduct disorder), problems relating to anxiety and depression, and elimination disorders.

## Cultural Beliefs about What Is Normal and Abnormal

**13.1 Explain the differences between normal and abnormal behavior in childhood and adolescence and the role of cultural beliefs in determining abnormality.**

Cultural beliefs help determine whether people view behavior as normal or abnormal. Because children rarely label their own behavior as abnormal, definitions of *normality* depend largely on how a child's behavior is filtered through a cultural lens (Callanan & Waxman, 2013; Norbury & Sparks, 2013). Cultures vary with respect to the types of behaviors they classify as unacceptable or abnormal as well as the threshold for labeling child behaviors as deviant. In an illustrative study, groups of American and Thai parents were presented with vignettes depicting two children, one with problems of "overcontrol"

**PLAY THERAPY.** In play therapy, children may enact scenes with dolls or puppets that symbolically represent conflicts occurring within their own families.

(e.g., shyness and fears) and one with problems of "undercontrol" (e.g., disobedience and fighting). Thai parents rated both types of problems as less serious and worrisome than American parents did (Weisz et al., 1988). Thai parents also rated the children in the vignettes as more likely to improve over time, even without treatment. These viewpoints are embedded within traditional Thai-Buddhist beliefs and values, which tolerate broad variations in children's behavior and assume that change is inevitable.

Like definitions of *abnormality*, methods of treatment differ for children. Children may not have the verbal skills to express their feelings through speech or the attention span required to sit through a typical therapy session. Therapy methods must be tailored to the level of the child's cognitive, physical, social, and emotional development. For example, psychodynamic therapists have developed techniques of *play therapy* in which children enact family conflicts symbolically through their play activities, such as by playacting with dolls or puppets. Or they might be given drawing materials and asked to draw pictures, in the belief that their drawings will reflect their underlying feelings.

As with other forms of therapy, child therapy needs to be offered in a culturally sensitive framework. Therapists need to tailor their interventions to the cultural backgrounds and social and linguistic needs of children in order to establish effective therapeutic relationships.

## Prevalence of Mental Health Problems in Children and Adolescents

**13.2 Describe the prevalence of psychological disorders in children and adolescents.**

> **TRUTH or FICTION**
>
> About one in 10 cases of adult psychological disorders began before age 18.
>
> ☑ **FALSE** Actually, about one in two cases of adult disorders began by age 14.

Just how common are mental health problems among America's children and adolescents? Unfortunately, quite common. Approximately four of 10 adolescents (40.3%) have experienced a diagnosable mental disorder during the past year (Kessler, Avenevoli, et al., 2012). About one in 10 children suffer from a mental disorder severe enough to impair development ("A Children's Mental Illness 'Crisis,'" 2001). Another reason to be concerned about mental health problems in childhood and adolescents is that among adults, half of the cases of psychological disorders started by age 14 (Insel, 2014). **T / F**

In children 6 to 17 years of age, the most commonly diagnosed psychological disorders are learning disorders (11.5%) and attention-deficit/hyperactivity disorder (8.8%; Blanchard, Gurka, & Blackman, 2006). If we limit our scope to adolescents, anxiety-related disorders top the list of the most commonly diagnosed disorders (Kessler, Avenevoli, et al., 2012). Depression too is all too common, as seen in the results of a telephone survey that was based on a national probability sample of American youth ages 12 to 17. The survey found that 7% of the boys and 14% of the girls had suffered from major depression in the preceding 6-month period of time (Kilpatrick et al., 2003).

**NEEDING BUT NOT GETTING TREATMENT.** Sadly, most children and adolescents with diagnosable psychological disorders, even those who have severely disturbed behavior, do not receive mental health treatment. Fewer than half get the help they need.

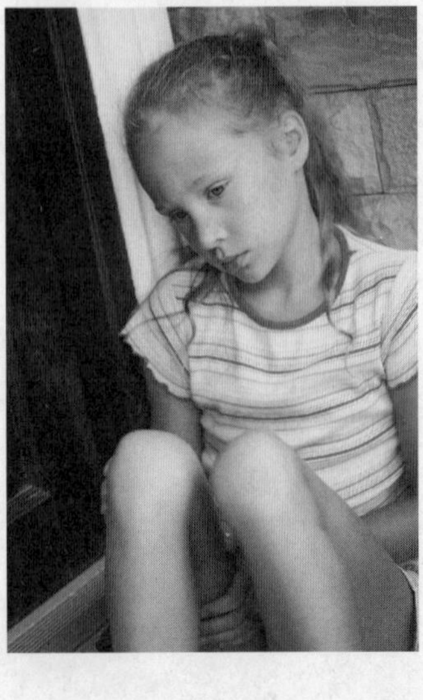

Despite the prevalence of childhood psychological disorders, the great majority of children with psychological disorders fail to get the treatment they need. Only about one third of adolescents with diagnosable mental disorders and fewer than half of children and adolescents with severe impairment or disturbed behavior receive any form of mental health treatment (Merikangas et al., 2011; Olfson, Druss, & Marcus, 2015). Children with *internalized* problems, especially anxiety and depression, are at higher risk of going untreated than those with *externalized* problems (problems involving acting out or aggressive behavior) that are disruptive or annoying to others.

## Risk Factors for Childhood Disorders

**13.3 Identify risk factors for psychological disorders in childhood and adolescence and describe the effects of child abuse.**

Many factors contribute to increased risk of developmental disorders, including genetic susceptibility, prenatal influences on the developing brain, environmental stressors (such as low socioeconomic level and living in decaying neighborhoods), and family factors (such as inconsistent or harsh discipline, neglect, or physical or sexual abuse; e.g., Hicks et al., 2013; Lewis et al., 2013; Plasschaert & Bartolomei, 2013; Salvatore et al., 2015). Children of depressed parents also stand a higher risk of developing psychological disorders, perhaps because parental depression contributes to greater levels of family stress (Essex et al., 2006; Weissman et al., 2006). Children with behavior problems from poorer, economically disadvantaged families are more likely to be labeled "bad kids" than to receive a diagnosis and professional help.

Ethnicity and gender are other discriminating factors. For reasons that remain unclear, ethnic minority children stand a higher risk of developing problems such as ADHD and anxiety and depressive disorders (Anderson & Mayes, 2010; Miller, Nigg, & Miller, 2009). Boys are at greater risk for developing many childhood disorders, ranging from autism to hyperactivity to elimination disorders. Problems of anxiety and depression also affect boys proportionally more often than girls. In adolescence, however, anxiety and mood disorders become more common in girls and remain so throughout adulthood (USDHHS, 1999). **T / F**

## TRUTH or FICTION

Boys are more likely than girls to develop anxiety and mood disorders.

☑ TRUE However, anxiety and mood disorders become more common among women beginning in adolescence.

Child maltreatment—which involves neglect or physical, sexual, or emotional abuse—is linked to a wide range of physical and psychological problems in both childhood and adulthood (e.g., Fuller-Thomson, West, & Baird, 2015; Geller, 2013; Herringa et al., 2013; Paul & Eckenrode, 2015; Whitelock, Lamb, & Rentfrow, 2013). (Effects of childhood sexual abuse are discussed in Chapter 10.)

Despite the common belief that physical and sexual abuse is more harmful to children than emotional abuse and neglect, evidence shows that these different forms of child maltreatment have the same, broad, negative effects on children's behavior and emotional well-being (Vachon et al., 2015). In fact, a recent major review showed that emotional abuse and neglect was even more strongly connected to the development of depression than were other forms of maltreatment (Infurna et al., 2016). Also important to consider is that even milder forms of physical punishment in childhood that may not rise to the level of physical abuse or neglect, such as spanking, smacking, and pushing, increase the risk of the later development of anxiety or mood disorders in adulthood (Afifi et al., 2012).

Physically abused or neglected children often have difficulty forming healthy peer relationships and healthy attachments to others. They may lack the capacity for empathy or fail to develop a sense of conscience or concern about the welfare of others. They may act out in ways that mirror the cruelty they've experienced in their lives, such as by torturing or killing animals, setting fires, or picking on smaller, more vulnerable children. Other common psychological effects of neglect and abuse include lowered self-esteem, depression, immature behaviors such as bed-wetting or thumb-sucking, suicide attempts and suicidal thinking, poor school performance, behavior problems, and failure to venture beyond the home to explore the outside world. The behavioral and emotional consequences of child abuse often extend into adulthood, increasing the likelihood of depression and other mental health problems (Miller-Perrin, Perrin, & Kocur, 2009; Nakai et al., 2014).

Child sexual and physical abuse is hardly an isolated problem. About 3.5 million cases of child abuse are reported to authorities annually in the United States An international study of data drawn from the United States and 21 other countries showed that about 8% of men and 20% of women reported suffering sexual abuse before the age of 18 (Pereda et al., 2009). In the United States, one in eight children (12%) suffer documented maltreatment involving neglect or physical, emotional, or sexual abuse before age 18 (Wildeman et al., 2014). Sadly, between 1,000 and 2,000 children in the United States die each year as the result of abuse or neglect, more than twice the rate (adjusted for population size) of Great Britain, France, Canada, or Japan (Koch, 2009). As horrific as these numbers are, they greatly understate the problem, as most incidents of child maltreatment are never publicly reported.

Concerns about physical abuse are understandable, but we should not lose sight of the emotional consequences of psychological abuse and maltreatment—of parents harshly scolding, belittling, or swearing at their children or making them feel unloved or unwanted. Yes, "sticks and stones" can break bones, but damaging words can do extensive emotional harm. The damaging effects of psychological maltreatment equal or surpass those of physical or sexual abuse (Spinazzola et al., 2015). Exposure to domestic violence or spousal abuse is also associated with higher levels of behavioral and emotional problems in children (Evans, Davies, & DiLillo, 2008). **T / F**

## TRUTH or FICTION

When it comes to child maltreatment, it's not just "sticks and stones" that do damage.

☑ TRUE Verbal abuse can lead to extensive emotional harm.

We now consider the specific types of psychological disorders in childhood and adolescence. We will examine the features of these disorders, their causes, and the treatments used to help children who suffer from them. First, you may wish to review Table 13.1, which provides an overview of these disorders.

**Table 13.1** Overview of Psychological Disorders in Childhood and Adolescence

| Types of Disorders | Description | Major Types/Estimated Prevalence Rates, If Known | Features |
|---|---|---|---|
| **Autism spectrum disorder** | A spectrum of autism-related disorders varying in level of severity | • 1% to 2% | • Impaired functioning; marked deficits relating to others; impaired language and cognitive functioning; restricted range of activities and interests |
| **Intellectual disability (intellectual developmental disorder)** | A broad-based delay in the development of cognitive and social functioning | • Deficits vary with level of severity from mild to profound (about 1% overall) | • Diagnosed on the basis of low IQ score and poor adaptive functioning |
| **Specific learning disorder** | Deficiencies in specific learning abilities in the context of at least average intelligence and exposure to learning opportunities | • May involve deficiencies in mathematics, writing, reading, or executive functions; for deficiencies in reading, writing, and mathematics, 5% to 15% of school-age children | • For mathematics deficiencies, difficulties understanding basic mathematical or arithmetical operations<br>• For writing deficiencies, grossly deficient writing skills<br>• For reading deficiencies, difficulties recognizing words or comprehending written text<br>• For executive function deficiencies, difficulties with planning and organizing skills |
| **Communication disorders** | Difficulties in understanding or using language | • Language disorder<br>• Speech sound disorder (formerly phonological disorder)<br>• Childhood-onset fluency disorder (stuttering; 1%)<br>• Social (pragmatic) communication disorder | • Difficulty understanding or using spoken language<br>• Difficulty articulating sounds of speech<br>• Difficulty speaking fluently without interruption<br>• Problems communicating with others in conversations or social contexts |
| **Attention-deficit/hyperactivity disorder and disruptive behavior disorders** | Patterns of disturbed behavior that are generally disruptive to others and to adaptable social functioning | • Attention-deficit/hyperactivity disorder approx. 10%<br>• Conduct disorder (12% males; 7% females)<br>• Oppositional defiant disorder (1% –11%) | • Problems of impulsivity, inattention, and hyperactivity<br>• Antisocial behavior that violates social norms and the rights of others<br>• Pattern of noncompliant, negativistic, or oppositional behavior |
| **Anxiety and mood disorders** | Emotional disorders affecting children and adolescents | • Separation anxiety disorder (4%–5%)<br>• Specific phobia<br>• Social phobia<br>• Generalized anxiety disorder<br>• Major depressive disorder (5% in children to upward of 20% in adolescents)<br>• Bipolar disorder | • Anxiety and depression often have similar features in children as in adults, but some differences exist<br>• Children may suffer from school phobia as a form of separation anxiety<br>• Depressed children may fail to label their feelings as depression or may show behaviors, such as conduct problems and physical complaints, that mask depression |
| **Elimination disorders** | Persistent problems with controlling urination or defecation that cannot be explained by organic causes | • Enuresis (lack of control over urination; 5%–10% among 5-year-olds)<br>• Encopresis (lack of control over defecation; 1% of 5-year-olds) | • Nighttime-only enuresis (bed-wetting) is the most common type<br>• Occurs most often during daytime hours |

**SOURCES:** Prevalence rates derived from American Psychiatric Association, 2013; CDC, 2012a; Frick & Silverthorn, 2001; Galanter, 2013; Kasper, Alderson, & Hudec, 2012; Masi, Mucci, & Millipiedi, 2001; Nock et al., 2006; Rohde et al., 2013; Shear et al., 2006; Wingert, 2000; Yeargin-Allsopp et al., 2003.

# Autism and Autism Spectrum Disorder

Autism is one of the most severe behavioral disorders of childhood. It is a chronic, lifelong condition. Children with autism, like Peter, seem utterly alone in the world, despite parental efforts to bridge the gulf that divides them.

Eugen Bleuler + Leo Kanner

## Peter:

### A CASE OF AUTISM

Peter nursed eagerly, sat and walked at the expected ages. Yet some of his behavior made us vaguely uneasy. He never put anything in his mouth. Not his fingers nor his toys—nothing....

More troubling was the fact that Peter didn't look at us, or smile, and wouldn't play the games that seemed as much a part of babyhood as diapers. He rarely laughed, and when he did, it was at things that didn't seem funny to us. He didn't cuddle, but sat upright in my lap, even when I rocked him. But children differ and we were content to let Peter be himself... Although Peter was a first child, he was not isolated. I frequently put him in his playpen in front of the house, where the schoolchildren stopped to play with him as they passed. He ignored them, too.

Peter's babbling had not turned into speech by the time he was 3. His play was solitary and repetitious. He tore paper into long thin strips, bushel baskets of it every day. He spun the lids from my canning jars and became upset if we tried to divert him. Only rarely could I catch his eye, and then saw his focus change from me to the reflection in my glasses....

[Peter's] adventures into our suburban neighborhood had been unhappy. He had disregarded the universal rule that sand is to be kept in sandboxes, and the children themselves had punished him. He walked around a sad and solitary figure, always carrying a toy airplane, a toy he never played with. At that time, I had not heard the word that was to dominate our lives, to hover over every conversation, to sit through every meal beside us. That word was autism.

**SOURCE:** *Adapted from Eberhardy, 1967*

The word *autism* derives from the Greek *autos*, meaning *self*. The term was first used in 1906 by the Swiss psychiatrist Eugen Bleuler to refer to a peculiar style of thinking among people with schizophrenia. Autistic thinking is the tendency to view oneself as the center of the universe, to believe that external events somehow refer to oneself. In 1943, another psychiatrist, Leo Kanner, applied the diagnosis "early infantile autism" to a group of disturbed children who seemed unable to relate to others, as if they lived in their own private worlds. Unlike children with intellectual disability, these children seemed to shut out any input from the outside world, creating a kind of "autistic aloneness" (Kanner, 1943).

**XAVIER: AUTISM SPECTRUM DISORDERS**

The *DSM-5* places autism (previously called *autistic disorder*) in a broader diagnostic category called **autism spectrum disorder** (ASD), which includes a range of autism-related disorders that vary in severity. *DSM-5* identifies ASD on the basis of a common set of behaviors representing persistent deficits in communication and social interactions and restricted or fixated interests and repetitive behaviors (see Table 13.2). Not all of these problem behaviors need to be present, but there must be evidence of problem behaviors across a range of settings or contexts. Clinicians need to rate the severity of ASD as severe, moderate, or mild. The more severe the disorder, the greater the level of support that is needed.

## Table 13.2 Key Features of Autism Spectrum Disorder (ASD)

| Problem Behaviors | Examples |
|---|---|
| Impaired social interactions and communication | • Unable to maintain normal back and forth conversations<br>• Does not initiate or respond to social interactions<br>• Fails to engage in give-and-take of social interactions or to share feelings or thoughts with others or engage in imaginary play with others<br>• Language deficits that may range from complete lack of speech to delays in use of spoken language to speaking only in simple sentences<br>• Abnormalities in speech may be present, such as stereotyped or repetitive speech, as in echolalia; idiosyncratic use of words; speaking about the self in the second or third person (using "you" or "he" to mean "I")<br>• Difficulties interacting nonverbally with others, such as failure to maintain eye contact, or use of odd body language or gestures<br>• Lack of interest in peer interactions or difficulty making friends or maintaining relationships, or understanding the bases of relationships |
| Restricted, repetitive, and stereotyped behavior patterns | • Shows restricted range of interests or becomes fixated on particular interests or unusual objects (e.g., carrying a piece of string)<br>• Insists on sameness or routines (e.g., always uses same route to go from one place to another, eating the same foods every day, or insisting on lining up toys), becomes extremely upset at small changes in routines, has difficulty shifting focus or activities<br>• Shows stereotyped or repetitive movements (e.g., hand flicking, head banging, rocking, spinning)<br>• Shows preoccupation with parts of objects (e.g., repetitive spinning of wheels of toy car)<br>• Shows either little or excessive reactivity to environmental stimuli (e.g., may fail to respond to pain or changes in temperature, may become fascinated with lights, may show extreme distress to certain sounds or noises) |

Asperger's disorder was a distinct diagnosis in the previous edition of the *DSM* but is now classified in the *DSM-5* as a form of autism spectrum disorder—but only if diagnostic criteria for ASD are met. *Asperger's disorder* refers to a pattern of abnormal behavior involving social awkwardness and stereotyped or repetitive behaviors but without the significant language or cognitive deficits associated with more severe forms of autistic spectrum disorder. Children with Asperger's don't show the profound deficits in intellectual, verbal, and self-care skills we find in children with the classic form of autism (Harmon, 2012). They may have remarkable verbal skills, such as reading newspapers at age 5 or 6, and may develop an obsessive interest in, and body of knowledge about, an obscure or narrow range of topics, like the interstate highway system, or, as in one case, vacuum cleaners (Osborne, 2002; Wallis, 2009). Many parents of children with Asperger's are understandably concerned that their children may not qualify for the *DSM-5* diagnosis of autism spectrum disorder and therefore not receive the treatment services they need or be eligible for reimbursement for these services (Carey, 2012a; Mestel, 2012).

**AUTISM.** Children with autism lack the ability to relate to others and seem to live in their own private worlds.

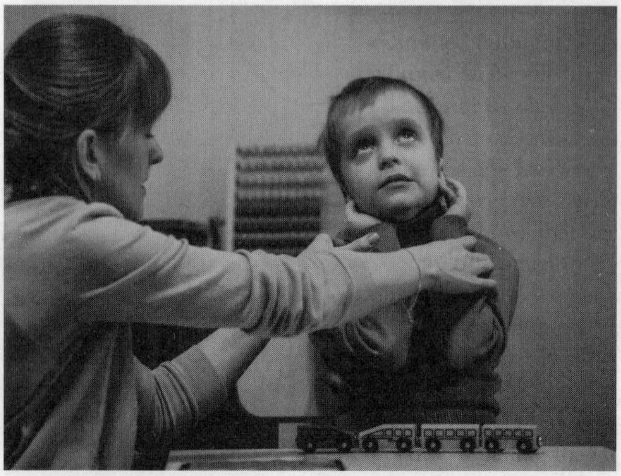

The reported prevalence of ASD has been rising steadily over the past 20 years or so (CDC, 2014a). Government researchers estimate that about one in 50 children (2%)—more than 1 million U.S. children—are affected by autism spectrum disorder, up from one in 86 reported in 2007 (Blumberg et al., 2013). The estimate is based on a nationwide phone survey of parents, not on careful diagnosis of cases. However, government officials believe the estimate reflects the proportion of American families struggling with some form of autism. The jump in reported cases of autism in recent years does not mean the disorder is occurring more often. Experts attribute much of the rise in reported cases to changes in diagnostic practices and greater awareness of the disorder among health care professionals (Blumberg et al., 2016; Hansen, Schendel, & Parner, 2014).

Scientists are investigating whether other factors—perhaps prenatal or childhood infections, or environmental factors such as exposure to environmental toxins—may be contributing to increased rates of autism (Weintraub, 2011; Xiang et al., 2015). As reported in Chapter 11, investigators find an increased risk of both autism and schizophrenia in children of older fathers (but, curiously, not in children of older mothers; Kong, Frigge, et al., 2012). The link to paternal age is explained by a greater prevalence of random genetic mutations in the sperm of older men, which may be contributing to a true increase in the rates of autism because couples today are more likely to postpone having children than those in earlier generations (Carey, 2012c). Still, the risks remain relatively low in offspring of older men, about 2% for fathers in their 40s or older.

One source of concern about the risk of autism is the widespread suspicion among parents of affected children regarding possible contamination from a chemical preservative in the widely used MMR (measles, mumps, rubella) vaccine. However, investigators find no relationship between autism and use of childhood vaccines (Jain et al., 2015; King, 2015; Weintraub, 2011). **T / F**

**TRUTH or FICTION**

Childhood vaccines cause autism.

☑ **FALSE** Investigators find no links between autism and childhood vaccines.

Autism is nearly five times as common in boys as girls (CDC, 2014a). Scientists suspect that the male brain may be more sensitive than the female brain to harmful genetic alterations or variations that can lead to these types of neurodevelopmental disorders (Jacquemont et al., 2014). Recent evidence also shows that autistic boys tend to show more severe repetitive and restrictive behaviors than girls—behaviors such as demands for holding to routines and repetitive movements, such as repeated flapping of the hands (Supekar & Menon, 2015).

Children with autism are often described by their parents as having been "good babies" early in infancy. This generally means they were not demanding. As they develop, however, they begin to reject physical affection, such as cuddling, hugging, and kissing. Their speech development begins to fall behind the norm. Signs of social detachment often begin during the first year of life, such as failure to look at other people's faces. Although ASD can be diagnosed reliably by around age 2 or 3, the average autistic child doesn't receive a diagnosis until about age 6. Delays in diagnosis can be detrimental, because the earlier children with autism are diagnosed and treated, the better they generally do. Signs of the disorder, such as lack of nonverbal communication, may first be observed as early as 12 to 18 months of age (CDC, 2014a; Norton, 2012; Pramparo et al., 2015).

## Features of Autism

**13.4 Describe key features of autism.**

Perhaps the most poignant feature of autism is the child's utter aloneness. Other features include profound deficits in social skills, language, and communication and ritualistic or stereotyped behavior. The child may also be mute, or if some language skills are present they may be characterized by peculiar usage, as in *echolalia* (parroting back what the child has heard in a high-pitched monotone); pronoun reversals (using "you" or "he" instead of "I"); use of words that have meaning only to those who have intimate knowledge of the child; and tendencies to raise the voice at the end of sentences, as if asking a question. Nonverbal communication may also be impaired or absent. For example, autistic children may avoid eye contact and show an absence of any facial expressions. They are also slow to respond to adults who try to grab their attention, if they respond at all. Although they may be unresponsive to others, they display strong emotions, especially strong negative emotions, such as anger, sadness, and fear.

One of the primary features of autism is repetitive, purposeless, stereotyped movements—interminably twirling, flapping the hands, or rocking back and forth with the arms around the knees (Leekam, Prior, & Uljarevic, 2011). Some children with autism mutilate themselves, even as they cry out in pain. They may bang their heads, slap their faces, bite their hands and shoulders, or pull out their hair. They may also throw sudden tantrums or panics. Another feature of autism is aversion to environmental changes—a feature termed *preservation of sameness*. When familiar objects are moved even slightly from their usual places, children with autism may throw tantrums or cry continually. Children with autism may insist on eating the same food every day.

Children with autism are bound by ritual. The teacher of a 5-year-old girl with autism learned to greet her every morning by saying, "Good morning, Lily, I am very, very glad to see you" (Diamond, Baldwin, & Diamond, 1963). Although Lily would not respond to the greeting, she would shriek if the teacher omitted even one of the *verys*.

Like Donna Williams, the woman whose childhood experiences opened this chapter, autistic children often view people as a threat. Reflecting back on his childhood, a high-functioning autistic young man speaks about his needs for sameness and for performing repetitive, stereotyped behaviors in the following account. For this young man, people were a threat because they were not always the same and were made up of pieces that didn't quite fit together.

**"I"**

**"I Didn't Know What They Were For"**

I loved repetition. Every time I turned on a light I knew what would happen. When I flipped the switch, the light went on. It gave me a wonderful feeling of security because it was exactly the same each time. Sometimes there were two switches on one plate, and I liked those even better; I really liked wondering which light would go on from which switch. Even when I knew, it was thrilling to do it over and over. It was always the same.

People bothered me. I didn't know what they were for or what they would do to me. They were not always the same and I had no security with them at all. Even a person who was always nice to me might be different sometimes. Things didn't fit together to me with people. Even when I saw them a lot, they were still in pieces, and I couldn't connect them to anything.

**SOURCE:** *Barron & Barron, 2002, pp. 20–21*

Autistic children appear to lack a differentiated self-concept, a sense of themselves as distinct individuals. Despite their unusual behavior, they are often quite attractive and have an "intelligent look" about them. However, as measured by scores on standardized tests, their intellectual development tends to lag well below the norm (Matson & Shoemaker, 2009). Although some autistic children have normal IQs, many show evidence of intellectual disability (Mefford, Batshaw, & Hoffman, 2012). Even those without intellectual impairment have difficulty acquiring the ability to symbolize, such as recognizing emotions, engaging in symbolic play, and solving problems conceptually. They also display difficulty in performing tasks that require interaction with other people. The relationship between autism and intelligence is clouded, however, by difficulties in administering standardized IQ tests to these children. Testing requires cooperation, a skill that is dramatically lacking in children with autism. At best, we can only estimate their intellectual ability.

# Theoretical Perspectives on Autism

**13.5 Identify possible causal factors in autism.**

An early and now discredited belief held that the autistic child's aloofness was a reaction to parents who were cold and detached—"emotional refrigerators" who lacked the ability to establish warm relationships with their children.

Psychologist O. Ivar Lovaas and his colleagues (Lovaas, Koegel, & Schreibman, 1979) offered a cognitive learning perspective on autism. They suggest that children with autism have perceptual deficits that limit them to processing only one stimulus at a time. As a result, they are slow to learn by means of classical conditioning (association of stimuli). From the learning theory perspective, children become attached to their primary caregivers through associations with primary reinforcers such as food and hugging. Autistic children, however, attend either to the food or to the cuddling and do not connect it with the parent.

Autistic children often have difficulties integrating information from various senses. At times, they seem unduly sensitive to stimulation. At other times, they become so insensitive that an observer might wonder whether they are deaf. Perceptual and cognitive deficits seem to diminish their capacity to make use of information—to comprehend and apply social rules.

We don't yet know what causes autism, but mounting evidence points to a neurological basis involving abnormalities in the brain in the connections between neurons as well as loss of brain tissue (e.g., Cheng et al., 2015; Ecker et al., 2013). One strong possibility is that prenatal influences lead to abnormal wiring in the circuitry of the developing brain that sets the stage for autistic behavior (Valasquez-Manoff, 2012; Wolff et al., 2012).

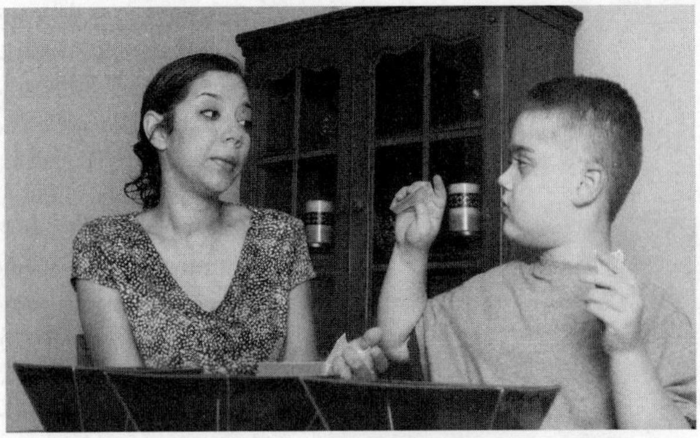

**ESTABLISHING CONTACT.** One of the principal therapeutic tasks in working with children with autism is the establishment of interpersonal contact. Behavioral therapists use reinforcers to increase adaptive social behaviors, such as paying attention to the therapist and playing with other children. Behavioral therapists may also use mild punishments to inhibit self-mutilation.

The brain of the autistic child appears to develop abnormally due to a combination of genetic factors and (presently unknown) environmental factors (e.g., Colvert et al., 2015; Gori et al., 2015; Meek et al., 2013; Pramparo et al., 2015; Yi et al., 2015). Well before symptoms emerge, we begin to see evidence of abnormal brain development in infant children who go on to develop autism (Wolff et al., 2012). Abnormal brain development may even begin before birth (Stoner et al., 2014). Prenatal risk factors, such as maternal infections during pregnancy, may increase the risk of autistic behaviors in genetically at-risk offspring (Atladóttir et al., 2012; Mazina et al., 2015). These factors may adversely affect the developing brain in the fetus.

Parts of the brain responsible for language and social behavior may grow much more slowly in children with autism than other children (Hua et al., 2011). As researcher Xua Hua explained, "Because the brain of a child with autism develops more slowly during this critical period of life, these children may have an especially difficult time struggling to establish personal identity, develop social interactions and refine emotional skills" (cited in "Autistic Brains," 2011). Delays in brain development may continue into adolescence.

Multiple genes are involved in determining susceptibility to autism. Research is progressing in laboratories across the world to track down the responsible genes (e.g., Campbell, 2015; Deriziotis et al., 2014; Griesi-Oliveira et al., 2014). Researchers have already discovered mutations on particular genes that are linked to at least some cases of autism (Carey, 2012b; Sanders et al., 2012). Scientists are also beginning to make headway in understanding the effects of autism-related genes on brain functioning—that is, how the expression of certain genes leads to abnormalities in the brain associated with autism (e.g., Clarke, Lupton, et al., 2015; King, Yandava, et al., 2013; Willsey et al., 2013).

# Treatment of Autism

### 13.6 Describe the treatment of autism.

Although there is no cure for autism, intensive and early behavioral treatment programs based on learning principles can significantly improve the learning and language skills and socially adaptive behaviors of autistic children (Eikeseth et al., 2012; Howard et al., 2014; MacDonald et al., 2014). These learning-based approaches involve *applied behavior analysis* (ABA) treatment models. No other treatment approach has produced comparable results. These methods apply learning principles of operant conditioning, with therapists and parents performing painstaking work, systematically using rewards and mild punishments to increase the child's ability to attend to others, play with other children, develop academic skills, and reduce or eliminate self-mutilation.

The most widely used behavioral treatment programs are highly intensive and structured, offering a great deal of individual, one-to-one instruction. In a classic study,

Lovaas (1987) demonstrated impressive gains in autistic children who received more than 40 hours of one-to-one behavioral treatment each week for at least 2 years. Subsequent research shows favorable gains in autistic children receiving long-term, intensive behavioral treatment with respect to language development, intellectual functioning, social functioning, and other adaptive behaviors (Eikeseth et al., 2012; Virués-Ortega, 2010). The earlier the treatment is started (before age 5) and the more intensive the treatment, the better the results tend to be (Vismara & Rogers, 2010).

Autistic toddlers also benefit from early training that focuses on building imitation skills, helping lay the foundation for social interactions (Kuehn, 2011b; Landa et al., 2011). Unfortunately, intensive one-to-one treatment is very expensive, and parents seeking publically subsidized programs can expect to deal with long waiting lists.

We don't have a drug cure or effective treatment for autism. Biomedical treatments are limited largely to the use of antipsychotic drugs to control disruptive behavior, such as tantrums, aggression, self-injurious behavior, and stereotyped behavior in autistic children. Antipsychotic drugs work better when treatment includes parents in a training program that teaches them how to respond to their child's disruptive behavior (Scahill et al., 2012).

Autism typically follows a chronic course and continues to affect a person's functioning through adulthood (Frith, 2013). Some autistic children go on to earn college degrees and function independently, but others need continuing treatment throughout their lives, even institutionalized care. There appears to be a small subset of autistic children who overcome the disorder. An influential 2013 study showed that a small but significant minority of children with previously diagnosed autism had no symptoms of the disorder when evaluated in later childhood or adolescence (Carey, 2013; Fein et al., 2013). Although these findings offer hope to autistic children and their families, we should caution that only a small minority of autistic children show this level of improvement.

## Abnormal Psychology in the Digital Age

### HELPING AUTISTIC CHILDREN COMMUNICATE: WE'VE GOT AN APP FOR THAT

There are mobile apps today for virtually anything, including, as it turns out, helping autistic children communicate. One example, iMean™, is the brainchild of Michael Bergmann, whose son Daniel suffers from autism ("iPad App Helps Autistic," 2010). The app converts the iPhone into a large-button keyboard with a word prediction feature. Many autistic children lack the fine motor control needed to type on a regular keyboard or phone display. The app's large letter display allows the user to point at particular letters and see predictions of the full word on the display screen. The autistic child can work independently to gradually build communication skills. A later version of the app includes speech-recognition capabilities.

iPads offer another means for autistic children to communicate with the outside world and to access educational programming. A parent of a 9-year-old autistic boy was amazed by his son's reaction to the iPad (Kendrick, 2010). His son immediately took to working with the device and with only a little training began using a wide range of educational tools, such as spelling and counting games and features. Electronic devices like the iPad herald potentially revolutionary new ways of reaching and teaching autistic children.

**YES, THERE'S AN APP FOR THAT.** The creator of the iMean app, Michael Bergmann, holding an iPad displaying the app. He's shown here with his son Daniel, who uses the letterboard to work with abstract thoughts.

# Intellectual Disability

About 1% of the general population is affected by **intellectual disability** (ID; also called *intellectual developmental disorder* [IDD]). The primary feature of ID is a general deficit in intellectual development. Formerly called *mental retardation*, intellectual disability is the diagnostic term applied to individuals who have significant and broad-ranging limitations or deficits in intellectual functioning and adaptive behaviors (e.g., lack of basic conceptual, social, and practical skills of daily living). Children with ID tend to have deficits in reasoning and problem-solving ability, abstract thinking skills, judgment, and school performance.

Intellectual disability begins before the age of 18 during child development and follows a lifelong course. However, many children with ID improve over time, especially if they receive support, guidance, and enriched educational opportunities. Those who are reared in impoverished environments may fail to improve or may deteriorate further.

## Features and Causes of Intellectual Disability

**13.7 Describe the key features and causes of intellectual disability.**

Intellectual disability is diagnosed on the basis of a low IQ score and impaired adaptive functioning occurring before the age of 18 that results in significant impairments in meeting expected standards of independent functioning and social responsibility. These impairments may involve difficulty performing common tasks of daily life expected of someone of the same age in a given cultural setting in three domains: (1) conceptual (skills relating to use of language, reading, writing, math, reasoning, memory, and problem solving), (2) social (skills relating to awareness of other people's experiences, ability to communicate effectively with others, and ability to form friendships, among others), and (3) practical (ability to meet personal care needs, fulfill job responsibilities, manage money, and organize school and work tasks, among others). Although earlier versions of the *DSM* required an IQ score of less than 70 (100 is the average score) for a diagnosis of intellectual disability, *DSM-5* does not set any particular IQ score for the diagnosis of ID. The diagnosis is based on a person's level of adaptive functioning rather than solely on an IQ score.

The level of severity depends upon the child's adaptive functioning, or ability to meet the expectable demands children face at school and in the home. Most children with ID (about 85%) fall into the mild range. These children are generally capable of meeting basic academic demands, such as learning to read simple passages. As adults, they are generally capable of independent functioning, although they may require some guidance and support. Table 13.3 provides a description of the adaptive skills and needs for continuing support associated with various degrees of ID.

**Table 13.3** Levels of Intellectual Disability and Types of Adaptive Behaviors

| Level of Severity | Typical Levels of Adaptive Functioning and Needs for Support |
|---|---|
| **Mild** (about 85% of cases; typical IQ range of 50–70) | Able to acquire practical skills and reading and arithmetic competence to about a third- to sixth-grade level; can hold jobs, be self-sufficient, and live independently in the community with minimal supports, such as assistance with more complex life skills involving personal budgeting and nutritional planning. |
| **Moderate** (about 10% of cases, typical IQ range of 35–49) | Show clear delays in speech and motor development, but able to learn basic communication skills; able to respond to training in safety habits and simple manual skills, but may not progress to functional levels in reading and arithmetic; may lack social judgment and ability to make independent life decisions, and continue to need instruction and support; may be able to work independently in settings that don't require conceptual or social skills or in sheltered workshop settings; may also be able to live independently and care for themselves, but may require moderate levels of support, such as living in group homes. |
| **Severe** (3%–4% of cases; typical IQ range of 20–34) | Marked delays in motor and speech development, but able to develop basic communication skills and to respond to training in elementary self-care skills—e.g., self-feeding; needs continuing support and safety supervision in protective environments, but may be capable of performing routine repetitive tasks; requires supportive housing. |
| **Profound** (1%–2% of cases; typical IQ range below 20) | Gross intellectual disability; minimal capacity for functioning in all areas of development; lack the ability to live independently and usually requires round-the-clock care and support with close supervision; may have rudimentary speech and communication skills and be able to participate in physical and social activities, but lack ability to care for themselves; have other physical limitations or congenital abnormalities. |

The causes of ID include biological factors, psychosocial factors, or a combination of these factors. Biological causes include chromosomal and genetic disorders, infectious diseases, and maternal alcohol use during pregnancy. Psychosocial causes include exposure to an impoverished home environment marked by a lack of intellectually stimulating activities during childhood.

**DOWN SYNDROME AND OTHER CHROMOSOMAL ABNORMALITIES** The most frequently identified cause of ID is **Down syndrome** (formerly called *Down's syndrome*), which is characterized by an extra chromosome on the 21st pair of chromosomes, resulting in 47 chromosomes rather than the normal complement of 46 (Einfeld & Brown, 2010; Mefford, Batshaw, & Hoffman, 2012). Down syndrome occurs in about one in 800 births. It usually occurs when the 21st pair of chromosomes in either the egg or the sperm fails to divide normally, resulting in an extra chromosome. Chromosomal abnormalities become more likely as parents age, so expectant couples in their mid-30s or older often undergo prenatal genetic tests to detect Down syndrome and other genetic abnormalities. Down syndrome can be traced to the mother's egg cell in about 90% of cases, with about 10% attributable to the father's sperm (Genetic Science Learning Center, 2012).

People with Down syndrome are recognizable by distinctive physical features: a round face; broad, flat nose; and small, downward-sloping folds of skin at the inside corners of the eyes, which give the impression of slanted eyes; as well as a protruding tongue; small, squarish hands and short fingers; a curved fifth finger; and disproportionately small arms and legs in relation to their bodies. Nearly all of these children have ID and many suffer from physical problems, such as malformations of the heart and respiratory difficulties. The average life expectancy of Down syndrome patients has been rising over the past few decades, from 25 years in 1983 to 60 years today (National Down Syndrome Society, 2015). In their later years, people with Down syndrome tend to suffer memory losses and experience childish emotions that represent a form of dementia. Unfortunately, we don't have a treatment for Down syndrome, but scientists are hopeful that learning more about the affected genes on chromosome 21 may lead to ways of regulating them to improve brain functioning (Einfeld & Brown, 2010).

Children with Down syndrome suffer various deficits in learning and development (Sanchez et al., 2012). They tend to be uncoordinated and to lack proper muscle tone, which makes it difficult for them to carry out physical tasks and play like other children. Down syndrome children suffer memory deficits, especially for information presented verbally, which makes it difficult for them to learn in school. They also have difficulty following instructions from teachers and expressing their thoughts or needs clearly in speech. Despite their disabilities, most can learn to read, write, and perform simple arithmetic, if they receive appropriate schooling and encouragement.

Although less common than Down syndrome, chromosomal abnormalities on the sex chromosome may also result in intellectual disabilities, such as in Klinefelter syndrome and Turner syndrome. *Klinefelter syndrome*, which only occurs among males, is characterized by the presence of an extra X chromosome, resulting in an XXY chromosomal pattern rather than the normal XY pattern. Estimates of the prevalence of Klinefelter syndrome are one to two cases per 1,000 male births (Morris et al., 2008). These men fail to develop appropriate secondary sex characteristics, resulting in small, underdeveloped testes, low sperm production, enlarged breasts, poor muscular development, and infertility. ID and learning disorders (also called *learning disabilities*) are also common. Men with Klinefelter syndrome often don't discover they have the condition until they undergo tests for infertility.

*Turner syndrome* occurs only in females and is characterized by the presence of a single X chromosome instead of the normal two (or only a partial second X chromosome; Freriks et al., 2015; Hong, Dunkin, & Reiss, 2011). Girls with Turner syndrome develop normal external genitals, but their ovaries remain poorly developed, producing reduced amounts of estrogen. As women, they are generally of short stature and infertile, and have endocrine and cardiovascular problems. They also tend to show evidence of mild retardation, especially in skills relating to math and science.

**FRAGILE X SYNDROME AND OTHER GENETIC ABNORMALITIES** Scientists have identified several genetic causes of ID (formerly mental retardation). The most commonly identified genetic cause is **Fragile X syndrome**, which affects about one out of 1,000 to 1,500 males and about one out of 2,000 to 2,500 females (Hall et al., 2008; Maher, 20077). The syndrome is the second most common form of ID overall, after Down syndrome. It is caused by a mutation on a single gene in an area of the X chromosome that appears fragile—hence the name (Hall et al., 2013).

The effects of Fragile X syndrome range from mild learning disorders to ID so profound that those affected can hardly speak or function. Females normally have two X chromosomes, whereas males have only one. For females, having two X chromosomes seems to provide some protection against the disorder if the defective gene turns up on one of the two chromosomes, which generally results in a milder form of intellectual disability. This may explain why the disorder usually has more profound effects on males than on females. Yet the mutation does not always manifest itself. Many males and females carry the Fragile X mutation without showing any clinical signs. Such carriers can still pass the syndrome to their offspring.

A genetic test can detect the defect that causes Fragile X syndrome. Although there is currently no available treatment for the syndrome, genetic research focused on identifying the molecular cause of the disorder may someday lead to an effective treatment (Bar-Nur, Caspi, & Benvenisty, 2012; Colak et al., 2014; Jacquemont et al., 2011).

**STRIVING TO ACHIEVE.** Most children with Down syndrome can learn basic academic skills if they are afforded opportunities to learn and are provided with encouragement.

**Phenylketonuria (PKU)** is a genetic disorder that occurs in about one in 10,000 to 15,000 births (Widaman, 2009). It is caused by a recessive gene that prevents a child from metabolizing the amino acid phenylalanine, which is found in many foods. Consequently, phenylalanine and its derivative, phenylpyruvic acid, accumulate in the body, causing damage to the central nervous system, resulting in severe intellectual disability. PKU can be detected in newborns by analyzing blood or urine samples. Although there is no cure for PKU, children with the disorder may suffer less damage or develop normally if they are placed on a diet low in phenylalanine soon after birth. These children receive protein supplements that compensate for their nutritional loss.

Today, various prenatal tests can detect chromosomal abnormalities and genetic disorders. In *amniocentesis*, which is usually conducted about 14 to 15 weeks following conception, a sample of amniotic fluid is drawn with a syringe from the amniotic sac that contains the fetus. Cells from the fetus can then be separated from the fluid, allowed to grow in a culture, and examined for abnormalities, including Down syndrome. Blood tests are used to detect carriers of other disorders.

**PRENATAL FACTORS** Some cases of ID are caused by maternal infections or substance abuse during pregnancy. Rubella (German measles) in the mother, for example, can be passed along to the unborn child, causing brain damage that results in intellectual disability. It may also play a role in autism. Although the mother may experience mild symptoms or none at all, the effects on the fetus can be tragic. Other maternal infections that may cause retardation in the child include syphilis, cytomegalovirus, and genital herpes.

Widespread programs that immunize women against rubella before pregnancy and tests for syphilis during pregnancy have reduced the risk of transmission of these infections to children. Most children who contract genital herpes from their mothers do so during delivery by coming into contact with the herpes simplex virus in the birth canal. Therefore, delivery by cesarean section (C-section) can prevent viral transmission during childbirth.

Drugs that the mother ingests during pregnancy may pass through the placenta to the child. Some can cause severe birth deformities and ID. Children whose mothers take alcohol during pregnancy are often born with *fetal alcohol syndrome* (described in Chapter 8), one of the most prominent causes of ID.

Birth complications, such as oxygen deprivation or head injuries, place children at increased risk for neurological disorders, including ID. Prematurity also places children at risk of intellectual disability and other developmental problems. Brain infections, such as encephalitis and meningitis, or traumas during infancy and early childhood, can result in ID and other health problems. Children who ingest toxins, such as paint chips containing lead, may also suffer brain damage that leads to ID.

**CULTURAL-FAMILIAL CAUSES** Most cases of ID fall in the mild range of severity and have no apparent biological cause or distinguishing physical features. These cases typically have cultural-familial roots, such as being raised in an impoverished home or social or cultural environment lacking in intellectually stimulating activities or wracked by neglect or abuse.

Children in impoverished families may lack toys, books, or opportunities to interact with adults in intellectually stimulating ways. Consequently, they may not develop appropriate language skills or acquire any motivation to learn. Economic burdens, such as the need to hold multiple jobs, may prevent their parents from spending time reading to them, talking to them at length, and exposing them to creative play or activities. The children may spend most of their days glued to the TV set. The parents, most of whom were also reared in poverty, may lack the reading or communication skills to help their children develop these skills. A vicious cycle of poverty and impoverished intellectual development is repeated from generation to generation.

## A CLOSER Look

### THE SAVANT SYNDROME

Got a minute? Try the following:

1. Without referring to a calendar, calculate the day of the week that March 15, 2079, will fall on.
2. List the prime numbers between 1 and 1 billion. (Hint: The list starts 1, 2, 3, 5, 7, 11, 13, 17....)
3. Repeat verbatim the newspaper stories you read over coffee this morning.
4. Sing accurately every note played by the first violin in Beethoven's Ninth Symphony.

Give up? Don't feel bad about yourself, because very few people can perform such mental feats. Ironically, the people most likely to be able to accomplish these tasks suffer from autism, intellectual disability, or both. Clinicians use the label *savant syndrome* to refer to someone with severe mental deficiencies who possesses some remarkable mental abilities. Commonly, these people are called *savants* (the term *savant* is derived from the French *savoir*, meaning *to know*). People with savant syndrome have shown remarkable though circumscribed mental skills, such as calendar calculating and rare musical talents, which stand in contrast to their limited general intellectual abilities. Some people with the syndrome engage in lightning calculations, such as calendar calculating. One young man could tell you in a few seconds the day of the week of any given date—for example, what day of the week October 23, 1996, was (Thioux et al., 2006). Another savant could make extraordinary drawings as a child but could barely speak (Selfe, 2011).

There have also been cases of savants who were blind but could play back any musical piece, no matter how complex, or repeat long passages of foreign languages without losing a syllable. Others could make exact estimates of elapsed time. One could reportedly repeat verbatim the contents of a newspaper he had just read; another could repeat backward what he had just read (Tradgold, 1914, cited in Treffert, 1988).

The savant syndrome phenomenon occurs more frequently in males by a ratio of about six to one. The special skills of people with the savant syndrome tend to appear out of the blue and may disappear as suddenly.

**SAVANT SYNDROME.** Leslie Lemke, a blind autistic savant musician, played music he heard verbatim and composed his own music, even though he had no music education. One day when he was about 14, he played the entirety of Tchaikovsky's Piano Concerto no. 1 flawlessly after having heard it once the night before.

Many theories have been proposed to explain the savant syndrome, but scientists have yet to reach a consensus. One theory is that people with savant syndrome may inherit two sets of hereditary factors, one for intellectual disability and the other for special memory abilities. Other theorists speculate that the brains of savants are wired with specialized circuitry that allows them to perform concrete and narrowly defined tasks, such as perceiving number relationships (Treffert, 1988). An environment that reinforces savant abilities and provides opportunities for practice and concentration would give further impetus to the development of these unusual abilities. Still, the savant syndrome remains a mystery.

Children with this form of intellectual disability may respond dramatically when provided with enriched learning experiences, especially at an early age. Social programs, such as Head Start, have helped many children at risk of cultural-familial intellectual disability to function within the normal range of mental ability.

## Interventions for Intellectual Disability

**13.8 Describe interventions used to help children with intellectual disability.**

The services that children with ID need depend on the level of severity and type of intellectual disability. With appropriate training, children with mild forms of intellectual disability may approach a sixth-grade level of competence. They can acquire vocational skills and prepare for meaningful work. Many of these children can be mainstreamed in regular classes. At the other extreme, children with severe or profound ID may need institutional care or placement in a residential care facility in the community, such as a group home. Placement in an institution is often based on the need to control destructive or aggressive behavior, not the severity of the individual's intellectual impairment. Consider the case of a child with moderate level of intellectual disability.

### Unable to Control His Behavior:

#### A CASE OF INTELLECTUAL DISABILITY (MODERATE SEVERITY)

The mother pleaded with the emergency room physician to admit her 15-year-old son, claiming that she couldn't take it anymore. Her son, a Down syndrome patient with an IQ of 45, had alternated since the age of 8 between living in institutions and at home. Each visiting day he pleaded with his mother to take him home, and after about a year at each placement, she would bring him home but find herself unable to control his behavior. During temper tantrums, he would break dishes and destroy furniture and had recently become physically assaultive toward his mother, hitting her on the arm and shoulder during a recent scuffle when she attempted to stop him from repeatedly banging a broom on the floor.

**SOURCE:** *Adapted from Spitzer et al., 1989, pp. 338–340*

Educators sometimes disagree about whether children with ID should be mainstreamed in regular classes or placed in special education classes. Although some children with mild intellectual disability achieve better when they are mainstreamed, others do not. They may find these classes overwhelming and withdraw from their schoolmates. There has also been a trend toward deinstitutionalization of people with more severe ID, motivated in large part by public outrage over the appalling conditions that formerly existed in many institutions serving this population. The Developmentally Disabled Assistance and Bill of Rights Act, which Congress passed in 1975, provided that people with mental retardation (now labeled ID) have the right to receive appropriate treatment in the least-restrictive treatment setting. Nationwide, the population of institutions for people with ID shrank by nearly two-thirds in the years following the legislation. People with ID who are capable of functioning in the community have the right to receive less restrictive care than is provided in large institutions. Many are capable of living outside the institution and have been placed in supervised group homes. Residents typically share household responsibilities and are encouraged to participate in meaningful daily activities, such as training programs or sheltered workshops. Others live with their families and attend structured day programs. Intellectually disabled adults often work in outside jobs and live in their own apartments or share apartments with other people with mild intellectual disability. Although the large-scale dumping of mental patients into the community from psychiatric institutions resulted in massive social problems and swelled the ranks of America's homeless population, deinstitutionalization of people with ID has largely been a success story that has been achieved with rare dignity (Hemmings, 2010; Lemay, 2009).

People with intellectual disability often develop other psychological disorders, such as anxiety and depression, as well as behavioral problems (Matson & Williams, 2013; Melville et al., 2016). Unfortunately, the emotional life of people with ID has received little attention in the literature. Many professionals even assumed (wrongly) that people with intellectual disability are somehow immune from psychological problems or that they lack the verbal skills needed to benefit from psychotherapy. However, evidence shows that people with intellectual disability can benefit from psychological treatment for depression and other emotional problems (McGillivray & Kershaw, 2013; Vereenooghe & Langdon, 2013).

People with ID often need psychological help dealing with adjustment to life in the community (McKenzie, 2011). Many have difficulty making friends and become socially isolated. Problems with self-esteem are also common, especially because people who have ID are often demeaned and ridiculed. Psychological counseling may be supplemented with behavioral techniques that help people acquire skills in areas such as personal hygiene, work, and social relationships. Structured behavioral approaches are used to teach people with more severe intellectual disability to master basic hygienic behaviors such as toothbrushing, self-dressing, and hair combing. Other behavioral treatment techniques include social skills training, which focuses on increasing the individual's ability to relate effectively to others, and anger-management training to help individuals develop effective ways of handling conflicts without acting out.

**TRUTH or FICTION**

A former vice president of the United States had such difficulty with arithmetic that he could never balance a checkbook.

☑ **FALSE** Nelson Rockefeller, vice president during the Ford administration in the 1970s, suffered from dyslexia and struggled with reading, not arithmetic.

# Learning Disorders

Nelson Rockefeller was a governor of New York State and a vice president of the United States. He was brilliant and well educated. However, despite the best of tutors, he always had trouble reading. Rockefeller suffered from **dyslexia**, a condition whose name is derived from the Greek roots *dys*, meaning *bad*, and *lexikon*, meaning *of words*. Dyslexia is the most common type of **learning disorder** (also called *learning disability*), accounting for perhaps 80% of cases. People with dyslexia have trouble reading despite the fact that they possess at least average intelligence **T / F**

## Features of Learning Disorders, Causal Factors, and Treatments

**13.9 Identify the types of deficits associated with learning disorders and describe ways of understanding and treating learning disorders.**

Learning disorders are typically chronic disorders that affect development well into adulthood. Children with learning disorders tend to perform poorly in school in relation to their level of intelligence and age. Their teachers and families often view them as failures. It is not surprising that children with learning disorders often have other psychological problems, such as low self-esteem. They also stand a higher risk of developing ADHD.

The *DSM-5* applies a single diagnosis of *specific learning disorder* to encompass various types of learning disorders or disabilities involving significant deficits in skills involved in reading, writing, arithmetic and math, and executive functions. These deficits significantly impact academic performance. They emerge during the grade-school years, but may not be recognized until academic demands exceed the individual's abilities, such as when timed tests are introduced. The diagnosis also requires that learning deficits cannot be better explained by a generalized delay in intellectual development (i.e., ID) or by underlying neurological or other medical conditions. The examiner needs to specify the particular learning deficit that interferes with academic, social or occupational functioning, or, as commonly is the case, a combination of specific deficits.

**PROBLEMS WITH READING** Children with specific learning disorders involving reading difficulties have persistent problems with basic reading skills. Although *DSM-5* does not use the term *dyslexia*, the term remains in widespread use among teachers, clinicians, and researchers to describe significant deficits in reading skills.

Children with dyslexia may struggle to understand or recognize basic words or comprehend what they read, or they may read unusually slowly or in a halting manner.

Dyslexia affects about 4% of school-age children and is much more common in boys than in girls (Rutter et al., 2004). Boys with dyslexia are also more likely than girls to show disruptive behavior in class and so are more likely to be referred for evaluation.

Children with dyslexia may read slowly and with great difficulty and may distort, omit, or substitute words when reading aloud. They have trouble decoding letters and letter combinations and translating them into the appropriate sounds (Meyler et al., 2008). They may also misperceive letters as upside down (e.g., confusing *w* for *m*) or in reversed images (*b* for *d*). Dyslexia is usually apparent by the age of 7, coinciding with the second grade, although it is sometimes recognized in 6-year-olds. Children and adolescents with dyslexia are prone to problems such as depression, low self-worth, and ADHD.

Rates of dyslexia vary with respect to native language. Rates are higher in English-speaking and French-speaking countries, where the language contains a large number of ways of spelling words containing the same sounds (e.g., the same *o* sound in the words *toe* and *tow*). Rates are low in Italy, where the language has a smaller ratio of sounds to letter combinations (Paulesu et al., 2001).

**PROBLEMS WITH WRITING** This deficiency is characterized by errors in spelling, grammar, or punctuation; by problems with legibility or fluent handwriting; or by difficulty composing clear, well-organized sentences and paragraphs. Severe writing difficulties generally become apparent by age 7 (second grade), although milder cases may not be recognized until the age of 10 (fifth grade) or later.

**PROBLEMS WITH ARITHMETIC AND MATHEMATIC REASONING SKILLS** Children may have problems understanding basic arithmetic facts, such as addition or subtraction operations, or performing calculations or learning multiplication tables or solving math reasoning problems. The problem may become apparent as early as the first grade (age 6) but is not generally recognized until about the second or third grade.

**PROBLEMS WITH EXECUTIVE FUNCTIONS** Executive function skills are a set of higher mental abilities involved in organizing, planning, and coordinating tasks needed to manage one's task or assignments. Although many children struggle with these types of challenges, children with executive function deficits have marked and sustained difficulties organizing and coordinating their school-related activities. They may frequently fall behind in school work, fail to keep track of homework assignments, or fail to plan ahead in order to complete assignments on time.

**UNDERSTANDING AND TREATING LEARNING DISORDERS** Much of the research on learning disorders focuses on dyslexia, with mounting evidence pointing to brain abnormalities that affect how visual information (printed words) and auditory information (spoken words) is processed (Golden, 2008; Nicolson & Fawcett, 2008; Underwood, 2013). People with dyslexia have difficulty connecting the sounds that correspond to particular letters (e.g., seeing an *f* or a *ph* or a *gh* and saying or hearing in their minds an *f* sound). They also have trouble distinguishing speech sounds, such as the sounds *ba* and *da*. Evidence points to a genetic influence in the development of these difficulties (Gabrieli, 2009; Paracchini et al., 2008).

Investigators speculate that dyslexia may take two general forms, one more genetically influenced and one more environmentally influenced (Morris, 2003; Shaywitz et al., 2003). The genetic form appears to involve defects in the neural circuitry in the brain that readers use to process speech sounds (Shaywitz, Mody, & Shaywitz, 2006). Dyslexic children with this genetic form of the disorder learn to compensate for these defects by relying on other brain capabilities, although they continue to read slowly. In the environmentally influenced form, neural circuitry is intact but people rely more on memory than on decoding strategies to understand written words. This second type may be more prevalent in children from disadvantaged educational backgrounds and is associated with more persistent reading disability (Kersting, 2003).

Linking learning disorders to defects in brain circuitry responsible for processing sensory (visual and auditory) information may point toward the development of treatment programs that help children adjust to their sensory capabilities (see Figure 13.1).

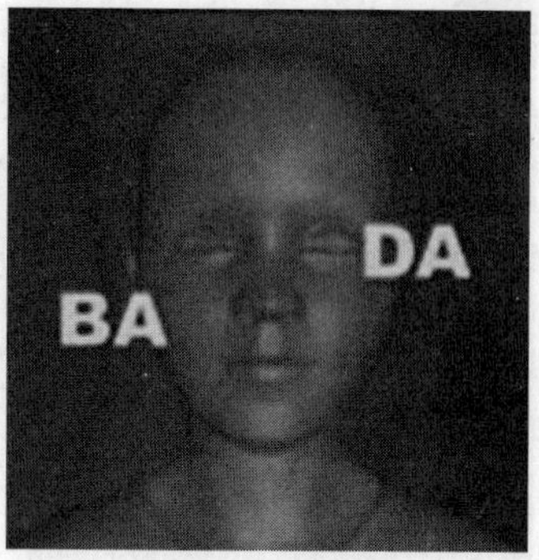


**DISTINGUISHING SPEECH SOUNDS.** Dyslexic children appear to have difficulty distinguishing basic speech sounds, such as *ba* and *da*, and connecting these sounds to particular letters in the alphabet.

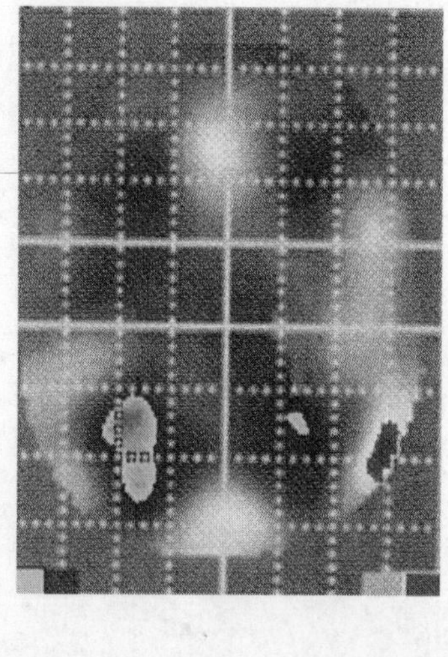

**Figure 13.1 Brain-imaging study of dyslexic adults.** Brain scans taken during a reading task show that stronger activation of the reading systems in the left hemisphere (shown here by areas tinted in yellow) is associated with better reading skills in nondyslexic readers. By contrast, more competent dyslexic readers rely more on the right hemisphere (as shown by blue-tinted areas). More capable dyslexic readers seem to rely on different neural pathways than normal readers. By examining differences in activation of particular areas of the brain, scientists hope to learn more about the neurological underpinnings of dyslexia.

## A CLOSER Look

### TRAINING THE BRAIN IN DYSLEXIC CHILDREN

Recent research evidence shows improved brain functioning in dyslexic children as the result of remedial reading instruction (Meyler et al., 2008). Before training, the parts of the cerebral cortex responsible for decoding the sounds of written letters and assembling them into words and sentences were less active in these children than in nondyslexic controls. However, after just 100 hours of intensive remedial instruction, these brain regions showed increased levels of neural activity. These gains in neural activity further strengthened over the next year, to the point that differences in brain activation between dyslexic and control children virtually disappeared (see Figure 13.2).

One of the investigators, Marcel Just of Carnegie Mellon University, points out that we can see actual evidence of how remedial training changes brain functioning. He elaborated by saying, "Any kind of education is a matter of training the brain. When poor readers are learning to read, a particular brain area is not performing as well as it might, and remedial instruction helps to shape that area up." As Professor Just puts it, these findings suggest that "poor readers can be helped to develop buff brains" (cited in "Remedial Instruction," 2008).

**Figure 13.2** Differences in brain activation of dyslexic and nondyslexic children.

Here we see areas of the brain showing greater activation (shown in yellow) in good readers versus poor readers. The right side of the brain is depicted on the left side of the figure and the left side of the brain is depicted on the right side. These differences virtually disappeared after remedial reading instruction (postremediation) and at a 1-year follow-up evaluation.

**SOURCE:** Image courtesy of Marcel Just of Carnegie Mellon University.

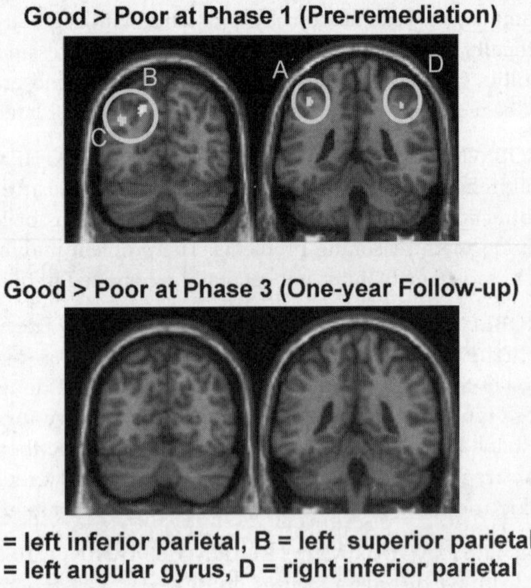


Therapists need to design strategies tailored to each child's particular type of disability and educational needs. For example, a child who can work better with auditory information than with visual information might be taught verbally—perhaps by using recordings rather than written materials. Other intervention approaches focus on evaluating children's learning competencies and designing strategies to help them acquire skills needed to perform basic academic tasks, such as arithmetic and reading skills (Solis et al., 2012). In addition, language specialists can help dyslexic children grasp the structure and use of words.

# Communication Disorders

**Communication disorders** are persistent difficulties in understanding or using language or speaking clearly and fluently. Because of the primacy of speech and language in daily life, these disorders can greatly interfere with a person's ability to succeed in school, the workplace, or in social situations. Here, we consider the major types of communication disorders.

## Language Disorder

**13.10 Describe the key features of language disorder.**

**Language disorder** involves impairments in the ability to produce or understand spoken language. There may be specific impairments, such as slow vocabulary development, errors in tenses, difficulties recalling words, and problems producing sentences of appropriate length and complexity for the individual's age. Affected children may also have a speech sound (articulation) disorder, compounding their speech problems.

Children with language disorder may also have difficulties understanding words or sentences. In some cases, they struggle with understanding certain word types (such as words expressing differences in quantity—*large, big,* or *huge*), spatial terms (such as *near* or *far*), or sentence types (such as sentences that begin with the word *unlike*). Other cases are marked by difficulties understanding simple words or sentences.

## Problems with Speech

**13.11 Describe the key features of psychological disorders involving problems with speech.**

Children may also have problems producing clear and fluent speech. In **speech sound disorder** (formerly called *phonological disorder*), there is persistent difficulty articulating the sounds of speech in the absence of defects in the oral speech mechanism or neurological impairment. Children with the disorder may omit, substitute, or mispronounce certain sounds—especially *ch, f, l, r, sh,* and *th,* which most children articulate properly by the time they reach the early school years. It may sound as if they are uttering "baby talk."

Children with more severe cases have problems articulating sounds usually mastered during the preschool years: *b, m, t, d, n,* and *h.* Speech therapy is often helpful, and mild cases often resolve themselves by the age of 8.

Persistent stuttering, which is characterized by impaired fluency of speech, is classified in *DSM-5* as a type of communication disorder called **childhood-onset fluency disorder**. People who stutter have difficulty speaking fluently with the appropriate timing of speech sounds. Stuttering usually begins between 2 and 7 years of age (American Psychiatric Association, 2013). The disorder is characterized by one or more of the following features: (a) repetitions of sounds and syllables; (b) prolongations of certain sounds; (c) interjections of inappropriate sounds; (d) broken words, such as pauses occurring within a spoken word; (e) blocking of speech; (f) circumlocutions (substitutions of alternative words to avoid problematic words); (g) displaying an excess of physical tension when emitting words; and (h) repetitions of monosyllabic whole words (e.g., "I-I-I-I am glad to meet you").

Stuttering occurs in three times as many males as females. The good news is that most children who stutter, upward of 80%, overcome the problem without any treatment, typically before age 16.

Although the specific causes of stuttering remain under study, genetic factors play an important role, perhaps involving genes that influence the control of the muscles involved in producing speech (Fibiger et al., 2010). Scientists recently reported discovering a mutation on a particular gene linked to persistent stuttering (Kang et al., 2010).

Stuttering also has an emotional component. Children who stutter tend to be more emotionally reactive than nonstutterers; when faced with stressful or challenging situations, they become more upset or excited (Karrass et al., 2006). They also tend to be troubled by social anxiety stemming from overconcern about how others evaluate them (Kraaimaat, Vanryckeghem, & Van Dam-Baggen, 2002). Stuttering is often accompanied by anxiety about speaking or avoidance of speaking situations, arising from embarrassment.

## Social (Pragmatic) Communication Disorder

**13.12 Describe the key features of social (pragmatic) communication disorder.**

**Social (pragmatic) communication disorder** is a newly recognized disorder in *DSM-5*. The diagnosis applies to children who have continuing and profound difficulties communicating verbally and nonverbally with other people in their natural contexts—in school, at home, or in play. These children have difficulty carrying on conversations and may fall silent when in a group of children. They have difficulty acquiring and using both spoken and written language. Yet they do not show a general low level of language or mental abilities that might explain their difficulties communicating with others. Their communication deficits make it difficult for them to participate fully in social interactions and adversely affects their school or work performance.

Treatment of communication disorders is generally approached with specialized speech and language therapy or with fluency training, which involves learning to speak more slowly and to regulate one's breathing and progressing from simpler to more complex words and sentences (NIDCD, 2010). Stuttering treatment may also include psychological counseling for the anxiety in speaking situations that is often experienced by people who struggle with stuttering.

# Behavior Problems: Attention-Deficit/Hyperactivity Disorder, Oppositional Defiant Disorder, and Conduct Disorder

We link these disorders together because they all involve problem behaviors that can seriously interfere with a child's functioning in school, at home, and on the playground. These disorders are socially disruptive and usually are more upsetting to other people than to the children who are diagnosed with these problems. The rate of comorbidity (co-occurrence) among these disorders is high (Beauchaine, Hinshaw, & Pang, 2010).

## Attention-Deficit/Hyperactivity Disorder

**13.13 Describe the key features of attention-deficit/hyperactivity disorder, identify causal factors, and evaluate treatment methods.**

Many parents believe that their children are not attentive toward them—that they run around on a whim and do things their own way. Some inattention, especially in early childhood, is normal enough. In **attention-deficit/hyperactivity disorder** (ADHD), however, children display impulsivity, inattention, and hyperactivity that are inappropriate to their developmental levels.

**JIMMY: ATTENTION-DEFICIT/HYPERACTIVITY DISORDER**

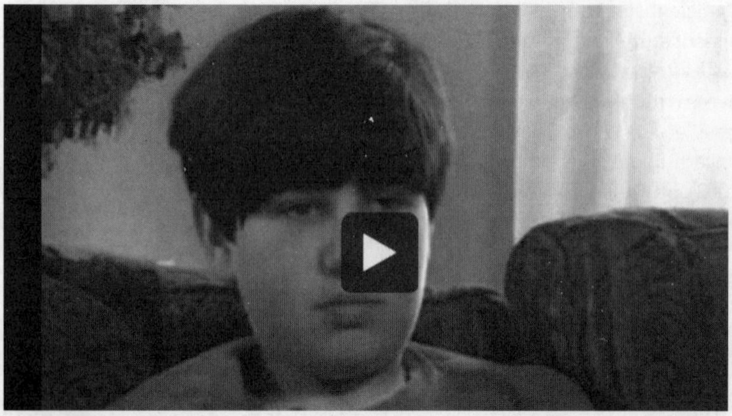

ADHD is the most widely diagnosed psychological disorder among U.S. children, affecting some 10% of young people age 6 to 17, amounting to more than 4 million children who have received the diagnosis (CDC, 2015f; Pastor et al., 2015). Nearly 70% of children diagnosed with ADHD take stimulant medication or other psychiatric drugs, which works out to about 3.5 million children in total (Stein, 2013; Visser et al., 2014). ADHD frequently occurs together with other disorders, especially learning disabilities, conduct disorder, anxiety and depressive disorders, and communication disorders (Harvey, Breaux, & Lugo-Candelas, 2016; Larson et al., 2011; Stein, 2011).

**ATTENTION-DEFICIT/ HYPERACTIVITY DISORDER.**
ADHD is more common in boys than girls and is characterized by attentional difficulties, restlessness, impulsivity, excessive motor behavior (continuous running around or climbing), and temper tantrums.

ADHD is diagnosed nearly three times as often in boys as in girls (CDC, 2015f). Black and Hispanic children are less likely to receive the diagnosis than Euro-American children (Pastor et al., 2015). The disorder is usually first diagnosed during elementary school, at an average age of 7, a time at which problems with attention or hyperactivity-impulsivity make it difficult for a child to adjust to school ("By the Numbers," 2015). However, the inattentive, hyperactive, and impulsive features of ADHD may begin any time before the age of 12.

In addition to inattention, associated problems in ADHD include inability to sit still for more than a few minutes, bullying, temper tantrums, stubbornness, and failure to respond to punishment. In some cases of ADHD, the problem is limited basically to attentional problems, whereas other cases predominantly involve hyperactive or impulsive behaviors, and still others involve a combination of attentional and hyperactive/impulsive problem behaviors. Children with ADHD also may present with other problems such as anxiety and depression (Meinzer, Pettit, & Viswesvaran, 2014). The key features or symptoms of ADHD are shown in Table 13.4.

Children with ADHD have problems adjusting to school. They seem incapable of sitting still. They fidget and squirm in their seats, butt into other children's games, have outbursts of temper, and may engage in dangerous behavior, such as running into the street without looking. All in all, they can drive parents and teachers to despair.

Where does "normal" age-appropriate overactivity end and hyperactivity begin? Assessment of the degree of hyperactive behavior is crucial, because many normal children are called "hyper" from time to time. Some critics of the ADHD diagnosis argue that it merely labels children who are difficult to control as mentally disordered or sick. Most children, especially boys, are highly active during the early school years. Proponents of the diagnosis counter that there is a difference in quality between normal overactivity and ADHD. Normally overactive children are usually goal directed and can exert voluntary control over their behavior, but children with ADHD appear hyperactive without reason and seem unable to conform their behavior to the demands of teachers and parents. Put another way, most children can sit still and concentrate for a while when they want to; children who are hyperactive seemingly cannot.

Children with ADHD tend to be of average or above-average intelligence, but they tend to underachieve in school. They are frequently disruptive in the classroom and tend to get into fights (especially the boys). They may fail to follow or remember instructions or complete assignments. Compared to children not diagnosed with ADHD, they are more likely to have learning disabilities, to repeat grades, and to be placed in special education classes. Inattention in elementary school tracks to poorer educational outcomes

## Table 13.4 Key Features of Attention-Deficit/Hyperactivity Disorder (ADHD)

| Problem Behaviors | Specific Behavior Pattern |
|---|---|
| Lack of attention | Fails to attend to details or makes careless errors in schoolwork<br>Has difficulty sustaining attention in schoolwork or play<br>Doesn't appear to pay attention to what is being said<br>Fails to follow through on instructions or to finish work<br>Has trouble organizing work and other activities<br>Avoids work or activities that require sustained attention<br>Loses work tools (e.g., pencils, books, assignments, toys)<br>Becomes readily distracted<br>Is forgetful in daily activities |
| Hyperactivity | Fidgets with hands or feet or squirms in his or her seat<br>Leaves seat in situations such as the classroom in which remaining seated is required<br>Is constantly running around or climbing on things<br>Has difficulty playing quietly |
| Impulsivity | Frequently "calls out" in class<br>Fails to wait his/her turn in line, games, etc. |

in adolescence and early adulthood, including increased risk of failing to complete high school by early adulthood (Gau, 2011; Pingault et al., 2011). Children with ADHD tend to have problems with working memory (holding information in mind in order to work on it), which makes it more difficult for them to keep their mind on the task at hand (Chiang & Gau, 2014; Kasper, Alderson, & Hudec, 2012).

Children with ADHD are also more likely to have mood disorders, anxiety disorders, and problems getting along with family members. Investigators find that boys with ADHD tend to lack empathy, or awareness of other people's feelings (Braaten & Rosén, 2000). Not surprisingly, children with ADHD tend to be less well liked by their classmates and more likely to be rejected than other children (Hoza et al., 2005). Compared to their peers, children with ADHD are more likely in adolescence and early adulthood to have problems with drugs; have difficulty holding a job and attaining higher educational levels; show more delinquent and antisocial behavior; and develop mood disorders, anxiety disorders, and, in young women, eating disorders (Biederman et al., 2010; Klein et al., 2012; Kuriyan et al., 2013; Lee et al., 2011; Sibley et al., 2011).

ADHD symptoms tend to decline with age, but the disorder may persist in milder forms into adolescence and adulthood. ADHD affects about 4% of U.S. adults at some point in their lives (Kessler et al., 2006). ADHD in adulthood usually takes the form of inattention, problems with working memory, and distractibility rather than hyperactivity—racing thoughts rather than racing around the room (Finke et al., 2011; Gonzalez-Gadea et al., 2013; B. L. Smith, 2012).

**THEORETICAL PERSPECTIVES** Increasing evidence points to a strong influence of genetic factors in ADHD (e.g., Colvert et al., 2015; Harold et al., 2013; Pingault et al., 2015; Stergiakouli et al., 2012). Consistent with a genetic contribution to the disorder, investigators find higher concordance rates for ADHD among monozygotic (MZ) than DZ (dizygotic) twins (Burt, 2009; Waldman & Gizera, 2006).

Genes do not operate in a vacuum; we need to consider the role of environmental influences and interactions of genetic and environmental factors in the development of ADHD. Environmental factors linked to ADHD include maternal smoking and emotional stress during pregnancy, high levels of family conflict, and poor parenting skills in handling children's misbehavior. Recently, investigators linked lead exposure in children to ADHD symptoms (hyperactivity and inattention; Goodlad, Marcus, & Fulton, 2013). Scientists are also seeking to track down the specific genes involved in ADHD and how environmental factors interact with genetic susceptibility. The emerging view among researchers today is that ADHD may be attributable to a breakdown in executive control functions of the brain, involving processes of attention and restraint of impulsive behaviors needed to organize and follow through on goal-directed behaviors (Casey & Durston, 2006; Winstanley, Eagle, & Robbins, 2006). This viewpoint is supported by evidence from brain-imaging studies that shows abnormalities or delayed maturation in parts of the brain in children with ADHD—especially in the prefrontal cortex, the part of the brain responsible for regulating attention and controlling impulsive behavior (e.g., Klein, 2011; Nakao et al., 2011; Shaw et al., 2011; see Figure 13.3). Another intriguing possibility is that the reward circuits in the brain may be less responsive in the ADHD child than in other children, which may account for ADHD children becoming easily bored with routine activities and in need of higher levels of stimulation than their peers (Friedman, 2014b).

**Figure 13.3** Parts of the prefrontal cortex.

Parts of the brain shown here in blue/purple, are thinner in ADHD children than in other children. These regions of the brain regulate processes of attention and motor activity that are often affected in children with ADHD. Note that the front of the brain is at top of this image.

**SOURCE:** National Institute of Mental Health, Image Library.

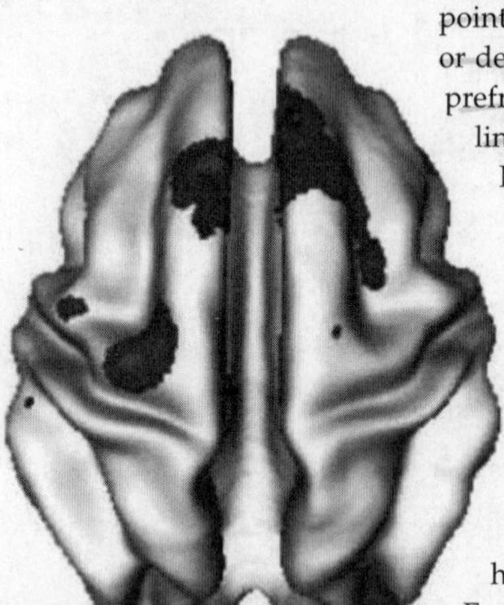

Investigators also find signs of abnormal brain development in preschool children with ADHD (Mahone et al., 2011). These brain abnormalities may set the stage for the development of attentional and learning problems these children later encounter in school.

**TREATMENT** At first glance, it may seem odd that many of the drugs used to help ADHD children calm down and attend better in school are actually stimulants. Examples include the widely used stimulant drug Ritalin and a longer-acting stimulant called Concerta, which is a one-dose-a-day drug. However, it's not odd that these drugs are effective if we consider the fact that stimulant drugs activate the prefrontal cortex, the part of the brain that regulates attentional processes and control of impulsive, acting-out behaviors associated with ADHD. **T / F**

## TRUTH or FICTION

Children who are hyperactive are often given depressants to help calm them down.

☑ **FALSE** Children with ADHD are often given stimulant drugs, such as Ritalin, not depressants. These stimulants have a paradoxical effect of calming them down and increasing their attention spans.

Stimulant drugs can reduce disruptive, hyperactive behavior and also improve attention spans of children with ADHD (Chronis, Jones, & Raggi, 2006; Van der Oord et al., 2008). Although use of stimulants is not without critics, these drugs help many children with ADHD calm down and concentrate better on tasks and schoolwork, perhaps for the first time in their lives. However, these drugs cannot teach children behavioral skills they need to succeed in school, especially organizational skills and effective study skills. Consequently, experts recognize the value of supplementing ADHD medication with behavioral therapies that emphasize skills training (Schwarz, 2013). We should also note a common problem with stimulant medication, as with other psychiatric drugs, is the high rate of relapse after the person stops taking the medication. Also, the range of effectiveness is limited, as in the following case example.

## Eddie Hardly Ever Sits Still:

### A CASE OF ADHD

Nine-year-old Eddie is a problem in class. His teacher complains that he is so restless and fidgety that the rest of the class cannot concentrate on its work. He hardly ever sits still. He is in constant motion, roaming the classroom and talking to other children while they are working. He has been suspended repeatedly for outrageous behavior, most recently swinging from a fluorescent light fixture and being unable to get himself down.

His mother reports that Eddie has been a problem since he was a toddler. He has never needed much sleep and always awakened before anyone else in the family, making his way downstairs and wrecking things in the living room and kitchen. He was continually restless and demanding. Once, at the age of 4, he unlocked the front door and wandered into traffic, but was rescued by a passerby.

Psychological testing shows Eddie to be average in academic ability but to have a "virtually nonexistent" attention span. He shows no interest in television or in games or toys that require concentration. He is unpopular with peers and prefers to ride his bike alone or to play with his dog. He has become disobedient at home and at school and has stolen small amounts of money from his parents and classmates.

Eddie has been treated with low doses of methylphenidate (Ritalin), but it was discontinued because it had no effect on his disobedience and stealing. However, it seemed to reduce his restlessness and increase his attention span at school.

**SOURCE:** *Adapted from Spitzer et al., 1989, pp. 315–317*

Then there's the matter of side effects. Although short-term side effects (e.g., loss of appetite or insomnia) usually subside within a few weeks or may be eliminated by lowering the dose, use of stimulant drugs may lead to other effects, including a slowdown of physical growth (DeNoon, 2006). Fortunately, children taking stimulant medication eventually catch up to their peers in physical stature.

The first nonstimulant drug approved for use in treating ADHD was Strattera (generic name *atomoxetine*). Strattera works differently from stimulant medication. It is a *selective norepinephrine reuptake inhibitor*, which means that it increases the availability of the neurotransmitter norepinephrine in the brain by interfering with the reuptake of the chemical by transmitting neurons. Although we don't know precisely how the drug works on ADHD, the increased availability of norepinephrine may enhance the brain's ability to regulate impulsive behavior and attention. Like the stimulant drug Ritalin, Strattera appears to be more effective than placebo drugs in treating ADHD, although it is perhaps not as effective as Ritalin (Newcorn et al., 2008).

Whatever the benefits of ADHD medication may be, drugs cannot teach new skills, so psychological interventions are needed to help the child develop more adaptive behaviors. For example, behavior modification programs to train parents and teachers to use contingent reinforcement for appropriate behaviors (e.g., a teacher praising the child for sitting quietly) may be combined with cognitive modification (e.g., training the child to silently talk him- or herself through the steps involved in solving challenging academic problems). Cognitive-behavioral therapists help ADHD children learn to "stop and think" before expressing angry impulses and acting out aggressively. Evidence backs up the effectiveness of cognitive-behavioral interventions in treating ADHD, although the effects may not be as strong as those of stimulant medication (Battagliese et al., 2015; Toplak et al., 2008).

Some children may do well with therapeutic drugs alone, others with cognitive-behavioral therapy (CBT) alone, and still others with a combination of both treatments (Pelham et al., 2005). Adults who are treated with medication for ADHD may also benefit from including CBT in their treatment program (Safren et al., 2010). Recently, investigators reported therapeutic benefits in treating adults with ADHD with a form of cognitive training that focused on building organizational, planning, and time-management skills (Solanto et al., 2010).

# Conduct Disorder

**13.14 Describe the key features of conduct disorder.**

Although it also involves disruptive behavior, **conduct disorder** (CD) differs in important ways from ADHD. Whereas children with ADHD seem literally incapable of controlling their behavior, children with CD purposefully engage in antisocial behavior that violates social norms and the rights of others. Whereas children with ADHD throw temper tantrums, children diagnosed as conduct disordered are intentionally aggressive and cruel. They are frequently aggressive toward others, bullying or threatening other children or starting physical altercations. Like antisocial adults, many conduct-disordered children are callous and apparently do not experience guilt or remorse for their misdeeds (Frick et al., 2014). They may lie or con others to obtain what they want, steal or destroy property, start fires, break into other people's houses, and, as they get older, commit serious crimes such as rape, armed robbery, or even homicide. They may cheat in school—when they bother to attend—and lie to cover their tracks. They frequently engage in substance abuse and early sexual activity.

Conduct disorder is a surprisingly common problem, affecting about 12% of males and 7% of females (9.5% overall; Nock et al., 2006). The disorder is not only more common among boys than among girls, but it also takes somewhat different forms. In boys, CD is more likely to be exhibited in stealing, fighting, vandalism, or disciplinary problems at school, whereas in girls, it is more likely to involve lying, truancy, running away, substance use, and prostitution. Children with CD often present with other disorders, including ADHD, major depression, and substance use disorders (Conner & Lochman, 2010). CD in childhood is also linked to antisocial behavior and development of antisocial personality disorder in adulthood (Burke, Waldman, & Lahey, 2010; Olino, Seeley, & Lewinsohn, 2010).

The average (median) age of onset of CD is 11.6 years, although it can develop at younger or older ages (Nock et al., 2006). CD is typically a chronic or persistent disorder. Although CD is closely linked to antisocial behavior, other commonly found traits include callousness (being uncaring, mean, and cruel) and an unemotional way of relating to others (Frick et al., 2014).

**OPPOSITIONAL DEFIANT DISORDER.** Children with ODD show negativistic and oppositional behavior in response to directives from parents, teachers, or other authority figures. They may act spitefully or vindictively toward others, but do not typically show the cruelty, aggressivity, and delinquent behavior associated with conduct disorder.

# Oppositional Defiant Disorder

**13.15 Describe the key features of oppositional defiant disorder.**

Conduct disorder and **oppositional defiant disorder** (ODD) are often combined under the general heading of "conduct problems." Although the disorders may be related, ODD is a separate diagnostic category, not merely a milder form of CD. ODD involves more nondelinquent (negativistic or oppositional) forms of conduct disturbance, whereas CD involves more outright delinquent behavior, such as truancy, stealing, lying, and aggression. Yet ODD, which typically develops earlier than CD, may lead to the development of CD at later ages. That said, only a minority of children with ODD go on to develop CD (Burke & Loeber, 2010).

Children with ODD tend to be overly negativistic or oppositional. They defy authority by frequently arguing with parents and teachers and refusing to follow requests or directives. They may deliberately annoy other people, become easily angered or lose their temper, become touchy or easily annoyed, blame others for their mistakes or misbehavior, feel resentful toward others, or act in spiteful or vindictive ways toward others. They tend to easily lose their temper and often display an angry or irritable mood. They also act in a spiteful or vindictive manner towards others they feel have wronged them. The disorder typically begins before 8 years of age and develops gradually over a period of months or years. It typically starts in the home environment but may extend to other settings, such as school.

ODD is one of the most common diagnoses among children. The disorder is estimated to affect from 1% to 11% of children and adolescents (American Psychiatric Association, 2013). ODD is more common among boys than girls before age 12, but it is unclear whether there is a gender difference among adolescents and adults (American Psychiatric Association, 2013). By contrast, most studies find CD to be more common in boys than in girls across all age groups.

**THEORETICAL PERSPECTIVES ON ODD AND CD** The causal factors in ODD remain obscure. Some theorists believe that oppositionality is an expression of an underlying temperament described as the "difficult child" type (Rey, 1993). Others believe that unresolved parent-child conflicts or overly strict parental control lie at the root of the disorder. Psychodynamic theorists look at ODD as a sign of fixation at the anal stage of psychosexual development, when conflicts between the parent and child emerge over toilet training. Leftover conflicts may later become expressed in the form of rebelliousness against parental wishes.

Learning theorists view oppositional behaviors as arising from parental use of inappropriate reinforcement strategies. In this view, parents may inappropriately reinforce oppositional behavior by giving in when the child refuses to comply with their wishes, which can become a pattern.

Family factors are also implicated in the development of CD. The disorder often develops in the context of negative parenting, such as failure to positively reinforce or praise the child for appropriate behavior and use of harsh and inconsistent discipline following misbehavior (Berkout, Young, & Gross, 2011). Family interactions of families of conduct-disordered children are often characterized by negative, coercive interactions.

Conduct-disordered children are often demanding and noncompliant with their parents and other family members. Family members often reciprocate by using inappropriate or harsh behaviors, such as threatening or yelling at the child or using physical means of coercion. Parental aggression against children with conduct behavior problems commonly includes pushing, grabbing, slapping, spanking, hitting, or kicking. It's not too much of a stretch to speculate that parental modeling of antisocial behaviors can lead to antisocial conduct in children. Some conduct-disordered children go on to develop antisocial personality disorder in adulthood (Burke, Waldman, & Lahey, 2010).

Conduct disorder often occurs in a context of parental distress, such as marital conflict. Coercive parental discipline and poor parental monitoring are also linked to increased risk of CD (Kilgore, Snyder, & Lentz, 2000). Poor parenting behaviors, such as harsh discipline and lack of monitoring, may foster the lack of empathy for others and the poor control over disruptive behavior we find in conduct-disordered children.

Children with disruptive behavior disorders such as CD or ODD also tend to show biased ways of processing social information (Crozier et al., 2008). For example, they may wrongly assume that others intend them ill. They are often quick to blame others for the scrapes they get into. They tend to view others as treating them unfairly regardless of the evidence. They may also show other cognitive deficits, such as an inability to generate alternative, nonviolent responses to social conflicts.

As with many psychological disorders, evidence points to a genetic contribution interacting with environmental influences in the development of CD (Jian et al., 2011; Kendler, Aggen, & Patrick, 2013; Lahey et al., 2011). For example, evidence shows that early experiences of physical abuse and harsh parenting increase the risk of CD, but only in children with a certain genetic profile (Dodge, 2009). Genetic factors may also be involved in the development of ODD.

**TREATMENT APPROACHES** Behaviorally based parent-training programs are often used to help parents reduce children's aggressive, disruptive, and oppositional behavior and increase their adaptive behavior (Battagliese et al., 2015). Treatment targets several goals, including helping parents use more consistent and clearer rules and effective discipline strategies, increase positive reinforcement (use of rewards and praise for desirable behaviors of the child), and increase positive interactions with the child (Rajwan, Chacko, & Moeller, 2012). Thus, parents must learn not only how to alter disruptive behaviors of their children but also to pay attention to their children and reward them when they act appropriately. Anger-control training may also be of value in treating children with anger problems and aggressive behavior (Sukhodolsky et al., 2005).

The following example illustrates the involvement of the parents in the behavioral treatment of a child with ODD.

## Billy:

### A CASE OF OPPOSITIONAL DEFIANT DISORDER

Billy was a 7-year-old second grader referred by his parents. The family was relocated frequently because the father was in the Navy. Billy usually behaved when his father was taking care of him, but he was noncompliant with his mother and yelled at her when she gave him instructions. His mother was incurring great stress in the effort to control Billy, especially when her husband was at sea.

Billy had become a problem at home and in school during the first grade. He ignored and violated rules in both settings. Billy failed to carry out his chores and frequently yelled at and hit his younger brother. When he acted up, his parents would restrict him to his room or the yard, take away privileges and toys, and spank him, but all of these measures were used inconsistently. He also played on the railroad tracks near his home, and twice the police brought him home after he had thrown rocks at cars.

A home observation showed that Billy's mother often gave him inappropriate commands. She interacted with him as little as possible and showed no verbal praise, physical closeness, smiles, or positive facial expressions or gestures. She paid attention to him only when he misbehaved. When Billy was noncompliant, she would yell back at him and then try to catch him to force him to comply. Billy would then laugh and run from her.

Billy's parents were informed that the child's behavior was a product of inappropriate cueing techniques (poor directions), a lack of reinforcement for appropriate behavior, and lack of consistent sanctions for misbehavior. They were taught the appropriate use of reinforcement, punishment, and time out. The parents then charted Billy's problem behaviors to gain a clearer idea of what triggered and maintained them. They were shown how to reinforce acceptable behavior and use time out as a contingent punishment for misbehavior. Billy's mother was also taught relaxation training to help desensitize her to Billy's disruptions. Biofeedback was used to enhance the relaxation response.

During a 15-day baseline period, Billy behaved in a noncompliant manner about four times per day. When treatment began, Billy showed an immediate drop to about one instance of noncompliance every two days. Follow-up data showed that instances of noncompliance were maintained at a bearable level of about one per day. Fewer behavioral problems in school were also reported, even though they had not been addressed directly.

**SOURCE:** *Adapted from Kaplan, 1986, pp. 227–230*

Conduct-disordered children are sometimes placed in residential treatment programs that establish explicit rules with clear rewards and mild punishments (e.g., withdrawal of privileges). Many conduct-disordered children, especially boys, display aggressive behavior and have problems controlling their anger. They can benefit from skills training programs to help them manage conflict without resorting to aggressive behavior. Many treatment programs today operate on a systems-based model that provides intensive treatment targeting the many systems that impact upon a child's functioning, including schools, neighborhoods, peer groups, and families (Weiss et al., 2013).

Cognitive-behavioral therapy is also used to teach aggressive children to reconceptualize social provocations as problems to be solved rather than as challenges to answer with violence. These children learn to use calming self-talk to inhibit impulsive behavior and control anger and to find and use nonviolent solutions to social conflicts.

# Childhood Anxiety and Depression

Anxieties and fears are a normal feature of childhood, just as they are a normal feature of adult life. Childhood fears—of the dark or of small animals—are common, and most children outgrow them naturally. Anxiety is abnormal, however, when it is excessive and interferes with normal academic or social functioning or becomes troubling or persistent. Many children suffer from anxiety and depressive disorders (Cummings, Caporino, & Kendall, 2014; Ginsburg et al., 2014; Usami et al., 2015). These disorders occur more frequently among ethnic minority children, which alerts us to the need to examine the kinds of stressors that may put minority children at greater risk for these problems (Anderson & Mayes, 2010).

## Anxiety-Related Disorders in Children and Adolescents

**13.16 Describe the key features of anxiety-related disorders in children and adolescents.**

Anxiety disorders are the most common psychological disorders affecting adolescents (Kessler, Avenevoli, et al., 2012). Children may suffer from anxiety-related disorders that also affect adults, including phobic disorders and generalized anxiety disorder (GAD), obsessive-compulsive disorder (OCD), and posttraumatic stress disorder (PTSD). They may also develop a type of anxiety disorder that typically develops during early childhood: separation anxiety disorder.

Anxiety in childhood often goes unrecognized and undertreated, in part because helping professionals may have difficulty distinguishing developmentally appropriate fears, worries, and shyness in children from the more extreme forms of these problems associated with anxiety disorders. Another problem with proper diagnosis is that many anxious children report only physical symptoms, such as headache and stomachache. They may be unable to express in words feeling states such as "worry" and "fear." Or their symptoms may be masked because they tend to avoid the objects or situations they fear. The socially phobic child, for instance, may avoid opportunities to socially interact with other children. The failure to detect anxiety disorders is unfortunate, in part because effective treatments are available and in part because undetected anxiety disorders in childhood increase the risk of anxiety disorders, depression, and substance abuse in later life (Emslie, 2008).

**SEPARATION ANXIETY DISORDER** It is normal for young children to show anxiety when they are separated from their caregivers. Famed attachment researcher Mary Ainsworth (1989) chronicled the development of attachment behaviors and found that separation anxiety normally begins during the first year. The sense of security normally provided by bonds of attachment apparently encourages children to explore their environments and become progressively independent of their caregivers. Having a strong attachment to the mother may help buffer the effects of later stressful life experiences. Compared to more securely attached infants, those who show insecure attachments are more prone to develop problem behaviors, such as anxiety, in later childhood in the face of negative life events experienced by the family (Dallaire & Weinraub, 2007).

**Separation anxiety disorder** in children is diagnosed when the level of fear or anxiety associated with separation from a caregiver or attachment figure is persistent and

**SOCIAL ANXIETY.** Socially anxious children tend to be excessively shy and withdrawn and have difficulty interacting with other children.

excessive or inappropriate for the child's developmental level. That is, 3-year-olds ought to be able to attend preschool without nausea and vomiting brought on by anxiety. Similarly, 6-year-olds ought to be able to attend first grade without persistent dread that something awful will happen to them or their parents. Children with separation anxiety disorder tend to cling to their parents and follow them around the house. They may voice concerns about death and dying and insist that someone stay with them while they are falling asleep. Other features of the disorder include nightmares, stomachaches, nausea and vomiting when separation is anticipated (as on school days), pleading with parents not to leave, or throwing tantrums when parents are about to depart. Children may refuse to attend school for fear that something will happen to their parents while they are away.

Separation anxiety disorder affects an estimated 4% to 5% of children and is the most common anxiety disorder affecting children under the age of 12 (American Psychiatric Association, 2013; Shear et al., 2006). The disorder occurs most often in girls and is often associated with school refusal. It also frequently occurs together with social anxiety (Ferdinand et al., 2006). The disorder may persist or even begin during adulthood, leading to an exaggerated concern about the well-being of one's children and spouse and difficulty tolerating any form of separation from them (Silove et al., 2015).

In the past, separation anxiety disorder was usually referred to as *school phobia.* However, separation anxiety disorder may occur at preschool ages. In young children, refusal to attend school is usually viewed as separation anxiety. In adolescents, however, refusal to attend school is frequently connected with academic and social concerns, so the label of *separation anxiety disorder* would not apply.

The development of separation anxiety disorder frequently follows a stressful life event, such as illness, the death of a relative or pet, or a change of school or home. In the following example, Alison's problems followed the death of her grandmother.

## Alison's Fear of Death:

### A CASE OF SEPARATION ANXIETY DISORDER

Alison's grandmother died when Alison was 7 years old. Her parents decided to permit her request to view her grandmother in the open coffin. Alison took a tentative glance from her father's arms across the room, then asked to be taken out of the room. Her 5-year-old sister took a leisurely close-up look, with no apparent distress.

Alison had been concerned about death for 2 or 3 years by this time, but her grandmother's passing brought on a new flurry of questions: "Will I die?," "Does everybody die?," and so on. Her parents tried to reassure her by saying, "Grandma was very, very old, and she also had a heart condition. You are very young and in perfect health. You have many, many years before you have to start thinking about death."

Alison could not be alone in any room in her house. She pulled one of her parents or her sister along with her everywhere she went. She also reported nightmares about her grandmother and, within a couple of days, insisted on sleeping in the same room with her parents. Fortunately, Alison's fears did not extend to school. Her teacher reported that Alison spent some time talking about her grandmother, but her academic performance was apparently unimpaired.

Alison's parents decided to allow Alison time to "get over" the loss. Alison gradually talked less and less about death, and by the time 3 months had passed, she was able to go into any room in her house by herself. She wanted to continue to sleep in her parents' bedroom, however—so her parents "made a deal" with her. They would put off the return to her own bedroom until the school year ended (a month away), if Alison would agree to return to her own bed at that time. As a further incentive, a parent would remain with her until she fell asleep for the first month. Alison overcame the anxiety problem in this fashion with no additional delays.

*From the Author's Files*

**UNDERSTANDING AND TREATING CHILDHOOD ANXIETY** Theoretical perspectives on anxiety in children parallel to some degree explanations of anxiety disorders in adults. Psychoanalytic theorists argue that childhood anxieties and fears, like their adult counterparts, symbolize unconscious conflicts. Cognitive theorists focus on the role of cognitive biases. Anxious children tend to show the types of cognitive distortions found in adults with anxiety disorders, including interpreting social situations as threatening and expecting bad things to happen (Dudeney, Sharpe, & Hunt, 2015; Micco et al., 2013; Muris & Field, 2013).

They also tend to engage in negative self-talk (Kendall & Treadwell, 2007). Expecting the worst, combined with having low self-confidence, encourages avoidance of feared activities—with friends, in school, and elsewhere. Negative expectations also heighten feelings of anxiety to the point that they impair performance in the classroom or the athletic field.

Learning theorists suggest that generalized anxiety may arise from fears of rejection or failure that carry across situations. Underlying fears of rejection or feelings of inadequacy generalize to most areas of social interaction and achievement. Genetic factors also appear to contribute to the development of anxiety disorders in children, including separation anxiety and specific phobias (Bolton et al., 2006).

Whatever the causes of anxiety disorders may be, anxious children can benefit from the types of cognitive-behavioral therapies used to treat anxiety in adults, such as gradual exposure to phobic stimuli and relaxation training (see Chapter 5 for a description of these techniques; e.g., Krebs & Heyman, 2014; Mohatt, Bennett, & Walkup, 2014; Öst, Cederlund, & Reuterskiöld, 2015). CBT incorporates cognitive techniques to help children identify anxiety-generating thoughts and replace them with calming alternative thoughts. Evidence supports the effectiveness of CBT in treating anxiety disorders in both children and adolescents (e.g., Holmes et al., 2014; Manassis, 2013; van Steensel & Bögels, 2015; Wu, Salloum, et al., 2015).

Antidepressants of the class of selective serotonin reuptake inhibitors (SSRIs), such as *fluvoxamine* (brand name Luvox), *sertraline* (Zoloft), and *fluoxetine* (Prozac), work well in treating anxious children and adolescents (Beidel et al., 2007; Dobson & Strawn, 2016). In a recent large-scale study, 488 children with diagnoses of separation anxiety disorder, GAD, or social phobia were randomly assigned to treatment conditions in which they received CBT, antidepressant medication (Zoloft), a combination of CBT and antidepressant medication, or a placebo drug. The investigators found superior effects for both CBT and medication as compared to the placebo, but greater effects still for the combination of CBT and antidepressant medication (Walkup et al., 2008). However, children receiving CBT reported less insomnia, fatigue, sedation, and restlessness than those receiving medication. Because of such side effects, parents may be reluctant to have their children treated with antidepressants.

## Childhood Depression

**13.17 Describe common features of depression in childhood and identify cognitive biases associated with childhood depression and ways of treating childhood depression.**

We may think of childhood as the happiest time of life. Most children are protected by their parents and are unencumbered by adult responsibilities. From the perspective of aging adults, their bodies seem made of rubber and free of aches. They have apparently boundless energy. However, many children and adolescents suffer from diagnosable mood disorders, including major depression and bipolar disorder. Major depression is the most common of these disorders, affecting about 5% of children aged 5 to 12.9 years and upward of 20% of adolescents from 13 to 17.9 years of age (Rohde et al., 2013). Major depression even occurs among preschoolers, although it is rare. Girls are more likely to experience a first episode of major depression during childhood or adolescence, but there does not appear to be a gender difference in the likelihood of having a recurrent episode (Rohde et al., 2013).

Like depressed adults, depressed children and adolescents typically have feelings of hopelessness; distorted thinking patterns and tendencies to blame themselves for negative events; and lower self-esteem, self-confidence, and perceptions of competence. They report episodes of sadness and crying, feelings of apathy, and insomnia and fatigue. They may experience loss of appetite or weight loss, but do not typically show weight gain or increased appetite (Cole et al., 2012). They may also experience suicidal thoughts or even attempt suicide.

Depression in children is also associated with some distinctive features, such as refusal to attend school, fears of parents' dying, and clinging to parents. Depression may also be masked by behaviors that appear unrelated. Conduct and academic problems, physical complaints,

## TRUTH or FICTION

Difficulties at school, problem behaviors, and physical complaints may actually be signs of depression in children.

☑ TRUE Children may not label what they are feeling as depression or be able to put into words how they feel. Depression is often masked by conduct problems, academic problems, and physical complaints.

and hyperactivity may stem from unrecognized depression. Among adolescents, aggressive and sexual acting out may also be signs of depression.

Depressed children or adolescents may not label what they are feeling as depression. They may not report feeling sad even though they appear sad to others. Part of the problem is cognitive-developmental. Children are not usually capable of recognizing internal feeling states until about the age of 7 years. They may not be able to identify negative feeling states, such as depression, in themselves. Some children appear bored or irritable rather than sad, at least in the early stages of depression. **T / F**

Children with relatively few friends are at increased risk of depression (Schwartz et al., 2008). Becoming isolated from friendship groups or cliques in late childhood predicts the development of depression in early adolescence (Witvliet et al., 2010). Depressed children often lack academic and athletic skills, as well as the social skills needed to form friendships. Depressed children may find it hard to concentrate in school and may suffer from impaired memory, making it difficult for them to keep their grades up. They often keep their feelings to themselves, which may prevent their parents from recognizing the problem and seeking help. Children may express negative feelings in the form of anger, sullenness, or impatience, leading to conflicts with parents that in turn can accentuate and prolong depression.

A major depressive episode in childhood or adolescence may last upward of a year or longer and may recur later in life. However, childhood depression rarely occurs by itself. Depressed children often have other significant psychological problems, including anxiety disorders, conduct or oppositional defiant disorders, and, among adolescent girls, eating disorders. About half of children who suffer from anxiety or depression in childhood go on to have similar problems in young adulthood (Patton et al., 2014).

**UNDERSTANDING AND TREATING CHILDHOOD DEPRESSION** Depression and suicidal behavior in childhood are frequently related to family problems and conflicts. Children and adolescents exposed to stressful life events affecting the family, such as parental conflict or unemployment, stand an increased risk of depression (Rudolph, Kurlakowsky, & Conley, 2001). Stressful life events, such as romantic breakups or strained friendships, diminish a person's sense of self-worth, competence, and desirability and can trigger depressive episodes in vulnerable adolescents (Hammen, 2009). In girls, disturbed eating behaviors and body dissatisfaction after puberty often predict the development of major depression during adolescence (Stice et al., 2000).

Negative thinking styles begin to enter the picture as children mature and their cognitive abilities develop (Garber, Keiley, & Martin, 2002). Like adults, depressed children and adolescents tend to show distorted patterns of thinking, such as the following:

- Expecting the worst (pessimism)
- Catastrophizing the consequences of negative events
- Blaming themselves for disappointments and negative outcomes, even when unwarranted
- Minimizing their accomplishments and focusing only on negative aspects of events

**IS THIS CHILD TOO YOUNG TO BE DEPRESSED?** Although we tend to think of childhood as the happiest and most carefree time of life, depression is actually quite common among older children and adolescents. Depressed children may report feelings of sadness and lack of interest in previously enjoyable activities. Many, however, do not report or are not aware of feelings of depression, even though they may look depressed to observers. Depression may also be masked by other problems, such as conduct or school-related problems, physical complaints, and overactivity.

Investigators also find distorted thinking patterns in depressed children in other cultures. For example, a study of 582 Chinese children in secondary schools in Hong Kong linked feelings of depression to distorted thinking patterns involving tendencies to minimize accomplishments and blow failures and shortcomings out of proportion (Leung & Poon, 2001). European researchers linked several thinking patterns to depression in young people, including blaming oneself for things that were not one's fault, ruminating about one's problems (mulling them over again and again in one's mind), and blowing problems out of proportion (Garnefski, Kraaij, & Spinhoven, 2001).

Although there are links between cognitive factors and depression, we do not know which comes first; that is, whether children become depressed because of a depressive mindset or whether depression leads to distorted, negative thoughts. Quite possibly, the relationship is reciprocal, with depression affecting thinking patterns and thinking patterns affecting emotional states.

Adolescent girls tend to show greater levels of depressive symptoms than adolescent boys do, a finding that mirrors the gender gap in depression among adults (Stewart et al., 2004). Girls who adopt a passive, ruminative coping style (e.g., brooding and obsessing about their problems) may be at greater risk of developing depression.

Evidence supports the effectiveness of CBT in treating depression in children and adolescents (Brunwasser, Gillham, & Kim, 2009; Chorpita et al., 2011). In one study, 75% of depressed youths treated with CBT no longer showed signs of depression by the end of treatment (Weisz et al., 2009). CBT typically involves social skills training (e.g., learning how to start a conversation and make friends), training in problem-solving skills, increasing frequency of rewarding activities, and countering depressive thoughts. In addition, family therapy may help families resolve underlying conflicts and reorganize their relationships so that members can become more supportive of each other.

SSRI-type antidepressant drugs such as *fluoxetine* (brand name Prozac), *sertraline* (Zoloft), and *citalopram* (brand name Celexa) show therapeutic benefits in treating depression in children and adolescents (Qin et al., 2014). The combination of CBT and antidepressants may be used to boost the effectiveness of either treatment alone (March & Vitiello, 2009). However, concerns have been raised that psychiatric drugs, including stimulants and antidepressants, are being prescribed much too widely in treating children with psychological problems, as we examine in *Thinking Critically: Are We Overmedicating Our Kids?*

## THINKING CRITICALLY about abnormal psychology

### @ISSUE: ARE WE OVERMEDICATING OUR KIDS?

The rising use of psychiatric drugs in recent years to treat ADHD, depression, and other psychological disorders in children has been nothing short of explosive. More than 6% of American children and teens take psychiatric medications, most commonly stimulant medication for ADHD ("By the Numbers," 2015; Mann, 2013; Olfson, Druss, & Marcus, 2015).

The use of stimulant drugs for treating ADHD has jumped dramatically in recent years—up about twentyfold since the 1980s (Sroufe, 2012). More than 70% of children with ADHD receive stimulant medication (CDC, 2015f). These drugs are also being used, and increasingly so, with preschoolers as young as 2 to 5 years of age (Novotney, 2015). Nearly 3% of youths are on antidepressants, which are used to treat depression, panic disorder, and eating disorders. Increasing numbers of young people are also receiving other psychiatric drugs, including mood stabilizers (anticonvulsants), antianxiety drugs, sleep medications, and even powerful antipsychotic drugs (Olfson, King, & Schoenbaum, 2015).

Two flashpoints in the controversy concern the use of powerful antipsychotic drugs and the use of Ritalin and other stimulant drugs to control hyperactivity. Antipsychotic drugs such as Risperdal and Zyprexa (discussed in Chapter 11) used to treat schizophrenia in adults have become more widely used in treating ADHD, even though these drugs are not approved for that purpose and their effects on brain development remain unclear (Correll & Blader, 2015; Olfson, King, & Schoenbaum, 2015). These drugs carry risks of serious side effects, including metabolic disorders that can lead to significant weight gain and high blood cholesterol levels and to potentially irreversible tic disorders, such as *tardive dyskinesia* (also discussed in Chapter 11). Potent antipsychotic drugs are also used to treat disruptive behaviors in children and teens, including aggressive and impulsive behavior (Correll & Blader, 2015). The fact that boys are more likely to be treated with antipsychotics than girls suggests they are being used more to control disruptive behaviors than to control psychotic symptoms (Olfson, King, & Schoenbaum, 2015). (See further discussion in *Thinking Critically: The Bipolar Kid* on page 528.)

With so many children receiving powerful psychiatric drugs, critics claim we are too ready to seek a "quick fix" for problem behavior rather than examining contributing factors, such as family conflicts, that may take more effort and time to treat. If a child is not sitting quietly at his or her desk doing schoolwork, there is pressure to find a chemical solution. Young people who become accustomed to using powerful psychiatric drugs to control negative feelings may be discouraged from finding other ways of managing them (Sharpe, 2012).

One pediatrician expressed concerns about overmedication in young patients by saying, "It takes time for parents and teachers to sit down and talk to kids.... It takes less time to get a child a pill" (Hancock, 1996, p. 52). A deputy director of the CDC, Ileana Arias, put it this way: "We do not know what the long-term effects of psychotropic medication are on the developing brains and bodies of little kids...Because behavioral therapy is the safest ADHD treatment for children under the age of 6, it should be used first, before ADHD medication for those children." (CDC, 2015f). That said, the CDC estimates that only about 44% of American children and teens with ADHD receive any form of behavioral treatment.

The two sides of the debate are clearly drawn. Critics contend that we are overusing psychiatric drugs, especially Ritalin. They point to the risk of potentially troubling side effects, such as weight loss and sleeplessness from Ritalin, and express concerns that we just don't know how stimulants and other powerful psychiatric drugs affect still-developing brains (e.g., Geller, 2006; Stambor, 2006). Nor can we rule out that ADHD drugs cause cardiovascular problems in children and adolescents (Kratochvil, 2012; Vitiello et al., 2012).

The effects of stimulant drugs are also limited—very limited. They may enhance a child's ability to concentrate for a short time, but become less effective over time and do not lead to general improvements in grades or academic performance (Sroufe, 2012). A leading researcher on ADHD, psychologist L. Alan Sroufe, commented that the fixation on finding a pill to fix behavior problems in children is shortsighted: "The illusion that children's behavior problems can be cured with drugs prevents us as a society from seeking the more complex solution that will be necessary" (cited in Sroufe, 2012, p. 6). As Sroufe points out, we cannot expect to solve all of the problems we face in life with a pill. Critics contend that while alternative treatments, such as CBT, are available to treat many of these problems, they remain underused in comparison with the prescription pad.

On the other side of the debate, proponents of drug therapy point to the therapeutic benefits of using drugs to treat disorders such as ADHD and depression. Stimulant drugs can help calm down hyperactive children and improve concentration, and antidepressants can combat anxiety and depression. However, we still lack evidence of the long-term effectiveness and safety of using psychiatric drugs with youths.

Clouding the picture further are warnings issued by the Food and Drug Administration (FDA) about a small increased risk of suicidal symptoms in youths and young adults treated with antidepressant medication. This increased risk seems to apply only to young people under the age of 25 (Stone et al., 2009). However small the increased risk may be, providers and family members need to carefully watch for warning signs of suicidal behavior in young patients (Reeves & Ladner, 2009). Clinicians also need to be aware of factors that may raise the risk of self-harm in adolescents treated with antidepressants, such as the presence of suicidal thinking, family conflict, and drug use (Brent et al., 2009; Sharma et al., 2016). We should recognize that risks of suicidal ideation and attempts are greater at higher SSRI dosage levels (Brent & Gibbons, 2013; Miller et al., 2014).

The FDA warnings are having an effect, as the numbers of prescriptions for antidepressants for adolescents have declined since the warnings went into effect (Clarke et al., 2012; Friedman, 2014a). Some clinicians express concern that the risk posed by failing to treat depressed children and adolescents with antidepressants may be far greater than the small increased risk of suicidal thinking associated with their use (Friedman, 2014a). Moreover, the reduced use of antidepressant medication has not been offset by increased use of alternative treatments, such as psychotherapy or other psychiatric drugs.

**SHOULD THIS CHILD BE MEDICATED?** The use of psychiatric drugs in children has skyrocketed in recent years. Do you know of any children who have benefited from psychiatric drugs? What concerns do the use of these drugs pose? What alternatives are available?

Not only are millions of children taking psychiatric drugs, but an estimated 1.6 million are taking two or more drugs, sometimes even three or more, at a time. For example, many kids are taking stimulants for ADHD and antidepressants or mood stabilizers for mood disorders. However, we have only minimal evidence to support the use of taking two psychiatric drugs at the same time and no evidence at all to support the use of three or more drugs (Harris, 2006). As psychiatrist Daniel Safer—a leading authority on the use of psychiatric drugs in children—put it, "No one has been able to show that the benefits of these combinations outweigh the risks in children" (cited in Harris, 2006, p. A28.)

One thing on which both sides seem to agree is that drug therapy alone is not sufficient to treat psychological problems in children and adolescents. The child with academic difficulties, problems at home, and low self-esteem needs more than a pill (or a combination of pills). Any use of therapeutic drugs needs to be supplemented by psychological interventions to help troubled children develop more adaptive behaviors. Perhaps drug therapy should be considered a second-line treatment when nonpharmacological approaches prove ineffective. Sometimes, a combination approach works best.

In thinking critically about the issue, answer the following questions:

- Why is the prescription of stimulant drugs and antidepressants in treating childhood disorders controversial?
- In many comparable countries, drugs are prescribed much less frequently for childhood disorders than they are in the United States. What does this suggest?

## Suicide in Children and Adolescents

### 13.18 Identify risk factors for suicide in adolescents.

Suicide is rare in childhood and early adolescence but becomes more common in late adolescence and early adulthood (Pelkonen & Marttunen, 2003). Among college students, suicide is the second leading cause of death, after motor vehicle accidents (Rawe &

Kingsbury, 2006). Among young people overall in the 15- to 24-year-old age group, suicide is the third most common cause of death, after accidents and homicides (NIMH, 2003; Winerman, 2004). Approximately one person per 10,000 (0.01%) in this age range commits suicide. Official statistics only account for reported suicides; some apparent accidental deaths, such as those due to falling from a window, may be suicides as well.

Despite the commonly held view that children and adolescents who talk about suicide are only venting their feelings, most young people who kill themselves send out signals beforehand (Bongar, 2002). In fact, those who discuss their plans are the ones most likely to carry them out. Unfortunately, parents tend not to take their children's suicidal talk seriously.

In addition to increasing age, other factors associated with heightened risk of suicide in children and adolescents include the following (e.g., Dervic, Brent & Oquendo, 2008; Fergusson & Woodward, 2002; NIMH, 2003; Pelkonen & Marttunen, 2003):

- *Gender.* Girls, like women, are three times more likely than boys to attempt suicide. However, boys, like men, are more likely to succeed, perhaps because boys, like men, are more apt to use lethal means, such as guns.
- *Geography.* Adolescents in less-populated areas are more likely to commit suicide. Adolescents in the rural western regions of the United States have the highest suicide rate.
- *Ethnicity.* The suicide rates for African American, Asian American, and Hispanic American youth are about 30% to 60% lower than that of (non-Hispanic) White youth. Yet, as noted in Chapter 7, the highest suicide rates in the United States are among Native American adolescent and young adult males (Meyers, 2007).
- *Depression and hopelessness.* Depression figures as prominently in youth suicide as it does in adult suicide, especially when it is combined with feelings of hopelessness and low self-esteem.
- *Previous suicidal behavior.* One quarter of adolescents who attempt suicide are repeaters. More than 80% of adolescents who take their lives have talked about it before doing so. Suicidal teenagers may carry lethal weapons, talk about death, make suicide plans, or engage in risky or dangerous behavior.
- *Prior sexual abuse.* In an Australian sample, young people with a history of childhood sexual abuse had rates of suicide more than 10 times higher than the national average (Plunkett et al., 2001). Moreover, about one third of young people who had been abused had attempted suicide, compared to none in a nonabused control group.
- *Family problems.* Family problems contribute to an increased risk of suicide attempts and actual suicides. These problems include family instability and conflict, physical or sexual abuse, loss of a parent due to death or separation, and poor parent–child communication.
- *Stressful life events.* Many suicides among young people are directly preceded by stressful or traumatic events, such as breaking up with a girlfriend or boyfriend, having an unwanted pregnancy, getting arrested, having problems at school, moving to a new school, or having to take an important test.
- *Substance abuse.* Addiction in the adolescent's family, or substance abuse by the adolescent, is a factor.
- *Social contagion.* Adolescent suicides sometimes occur in clusters, especially when a suicide or a group of suicides receives widespread publicity. Adolescents may romanticize suicide as a heroic act of defiance. There are often suicides or attempts among the siblings, friends, parents, or adult relatives of suicidal adolescents. Perhaps the suicide of a family member or schoolmate renders suicide a more "real" option for managing stress or punishing others. Perhaps the other person's suicide gives the adolescent the impression that he or she is "doomed" to commit suicide. Adolescent suicides may occur in bunches in a community, especially when adolescents are subjected to mounting academic pressures, such as competing for admission to college; note, for example, the case of Pam, Kim, and Brian.

## Pam, Kim, and Brian:

### A CASE OF MULTIPLE SUICIDES

Pam was an exceptionally attractive 17-year-old who was hospitalized after cutting her wrists. "Before we moved to [an upper-middle-class town in suburban New York]," she told the psychologist, "I was the brightest girl in the class. Teachers loved me. If we had a yearbook, I'd have been the most likely to succeed. Then we moved, and suddenly I was hit with it. Everybody was bright, or tried to be. Suddenly I was just another ordinary student planning to go to college.

"Teachers were good to me, but I was no longer special, and that hurt. Then we all applied to college. Do you know that 90% of the kids in the high school go on to college? I mean four-year colleges? And we all knew—or suspected—that the good schools had quotas on kids from here. I mean you can't have 30 kids from our senior class going to Yale or Princeton or Wellesley, can you? You're better off applying from Utah.

"Then Kim got her early-acceptance rejection from Brown. Kim was number one in the class. Nobody could believe it. Her father had gone to Brown and Kim had almost 1,500 SATs. Kim was out of commission for a few days—I mean she didn't come to school or anything—and then, boom, she was gone. She offed herself, kaput, no more, the end. Then Brian was rejected from Cornell. A few days later, he was gone, too. And I'm like, 'These kids were better than me.' I mean their grades and their SATs were higher than mine, and I was going to apply to Brown and Cornell. I'm like, 'What chance do I have? Why bother?'"

*From the Author's Files*

You can see how catastrophizing thoughts play a role in such tragic cases. Consistent with the literature on suicide among adults, young people who attempt suicide do not use active problem-solving strategies in handling stressful situations. They may see no other way out of their perceived failures or stresses. As with adults, one approach to working with suicidal children helps them to challenge distorted thinking and generate alternative strategies for handling problems and stressors. Promising prevention programs, including school-based skills training programs, have been developed, but evidence supporting their effectiveness remains to be gathered (Gould et al., 2003).

## THINKING CRITICALLY about abnormal psychology

### @ISSUE: THE BIPOLAR KID

There was a knock at her bedroom door. Six-year-old Claire had been happily watching goofy videos on her favorite website, *JibJab* (Egan, 2008). She had barricaded the door, using her toy chest and then piling on toys and other weighty objects. "If it's my brother," she said to a visiting journalist, "don't open it." She then said that she didn't care if she was being mean, but she couldn't trust her brother. Her brother, Claire said, always jumps out in a bad, scary way.

Her brother, 10-year-old James, had been diagnosed with bipolar disorder two years earlier. Like other children with a bipolar diagnosis, James had a history of aggressive behavior and episodes of explosive rage. There were times he would reach out to his mother, craving attention, but then suddenly explode into a rage, storming away from her, but later returning, seeking to connect, cuddle, and even cling to her. A decade or so ago, a child like James might have been diagnosed with ADHD or ODD—but in the 1990s, many professionals began diagnosing children like James with bipolar disorder, a diagnosis that previously had rarely been applied to children. As the diagnosis of childhood-onset bipolar disorder exploded in recent years, so too did the use of powerful drugs such as antipsychotics, anticonvulsives, and lithium that are used in treating adult forms of bipolar disorder.

By the early 2000s, as many as 1% of children and adolescents in the United States had received a bipolar disorder diagnosis, a rate that had jumped some fortyfold compared to the early 1990s (Holden, 2008; Moreno et al., 2007). Critics claim there is no real increase in the underlying rates of the disorder, but rather a tendency for mental health providers to relabel children who previously would have received another diagnosis, such as ADHD or CD (Holtmann, Bölte, & Poustka, 2008).

Underscoring concerns about overdiagnosis are findings from an important National Institute of Mental Health study that showed the great majority of children (80%) receiving a bipolar disorder diagnosis did not meet diagnostic criteria for the disorder (Carey, 2012d; Egan, 2008). On the other side of the debate are those who argue that bipolar disorder is more common in children than many mental health professionals suspect and that practitioners are only now recognizing a disorder that has been overlooked for many years.

Critics also claim that the pharmaceutical industry, which stands to profit enormously from medications used to treat bipolar disorder, has spurred overdiagnosis of the disorder by encouraging physicians to prescribe the latest drugs (Holden, 2008). As University of Washington psychiatrist Jack McClellan put it, "The treatment of bipolar disorder is meds first, meds second and meds third... whereas if these kids have a behavior disorder, then behavioral treatment should be considered the primary treatment" (cited in Carey, 2010, p. A17).

Bipolar disorder is characterized by clear-cut episodes of mania and depression, so professionals need to verify that children show both ends of the mood spectrum before reaching a diagnosis. Concerns about overdiagnosis of bipolar disorder in children and adolescents prompted changes in *DSM-5* to limit the diagnosis to children with clear signs of bipolar disorder. In the *DSM-5*, a new diagnosable disorder, *disruptive mood dysregulation disorder* (DMDD), applies to children with extreme irritability and severe and frequent temper outbursts (like those in the case of James described earlier), but who do not show the mood changes, inflated self-esteem, pressured speech, and other features of mania associated with bipolar disorder (Roy, Lopes, & Klein, 2014).

Children diagnosed with DMDD tend to fly off the handle, showing intense and prolonged rage reactions. Their frequent outbursts are greatly out of proportion to the situation and are accompanied by physical aggression against people or property or by verbal expressions of rage (Axelson, 2013). The diagnosis requires evidence of frequent behavior outbursts that occur at least three or more times a week for at least a year. A recent study of outcomes of children who receive a DMDD diagnosis showed they had elevated rates of depression and anxiety in early adulthood, which suggests that their impaired psychological functioning carries beyond adolescence (Copeland et al., 2014).

DMDD remains a controversial diagnosis in large part because of concerns that it may medicalize or pathologize common behavior problems in children, such as frequent temper tantrums. Such concerns may be overstated, as recent research shows that only about 1% of school-age children meet all criteria for the disorder (Copeland et al., 2013). However, we should recognize that explosive rage may be a sign of other disorders, such as ADHD, CD, and ODD, or even bipolar disorder. All in all, how the new DMDD disorder will play out in practice remains to be seen (Carey, 2012d).

Why does it matter whether children are diagnosed with bipolar disorder or another disorder like ADHD? The main reason is that diagnosis is used to guide treatment. Drugs used to treat ADHD, especially stimulant drugs like Ritalin, can trigger or exacerbate manic episodes, whereas bipolar drugs like lithium would be inappropriate and potentially harmful if used to treat ADHD.

Controversy also swirls around potential risks of treating children and adolescents with powerful antipsychotic drugs often used for adults with schizophrenia or bipolar disorder (Olfson, King, & Schoenbaum, 2015). Although atypical antipsychotics like Risperdal (generic name *risperidone*) can blunt anger and explosive rage, they are also associated with risk of significant weight gain (typically about 7% or more) and metabolic changes that may lead to diabetes and heart disease (Correll et al., 2009; Varley & McClellan, 2009). Other drugs, like lithium and anticonvulsive drugs used to treat epilepsy, also carry risks of significant side effects and complications. No one knows for certain what the long-term effects of these drugs may be on the developing brain of the child or adolescent (Kumra et al., 2008).

Another question is whether children who show frequent temper tantrums will now be medicated because a new diagnosis is rendered—*DMDD.* Many professionals believe the DMDD diagnosis will only exacerbate the overmedication of children, by focusing efforts on finding drugs that control disruptive behaviors rather than helping children learn to regulate their negative emotions and using behavioral techniques to help children learn more adaptive behaviors.

Clearly, children who receive a bipolar diagnosis have serious behavioral problems that can cause enormous difficulties for them and their families. As research continues, we hope to learn more about the best ways of conceptualizing and treating "bipolar kids."

In thinking critically about the issue, answer the following questions:

- What do you believe accounts for the surge in diagnoses of bipolar disorder in children in recent years?
- Should children with the types of behavior problems that lead to a bipolar diagnosis be treated with powerful psychiatric drugs or by other forms of treatment? Explain.

# Elimination Disorders

Fetuses and newborn children eliminate waste products reflexively. As children develop and undergo toilet training, they develop the ability to inhibit the natural reflexes that govern urination and bowel movements. For some children, however, problems with controlling elimination persist in the form of *enuresis* and *encopresis*, disorders of elimination that are not due to organic causes.

## Enuresis

**13.19 Describe the key features of enuresis and evaluate methods of treating bed-wetting.**

The term *enuresis* derives from the Greek roots *en*, meaning *in*, and *ouron*, meaning *urine*. **Enuresis** is failure to control urination after one has reached the "normal" age for attaining such control. Conceptions of what age is normal for achieving control vary among clinicians.

To be diagnosed with enuresis according to the *DSM*, the child must be at least 5 years of age or at an equivalent developmental level and meet the following criteria:

- Repeatedly wetting bedding or clothes (whether intentionally or involuntarily).
- Wetting occurs at least twice a week for three months or causes significant distress or impairment in functioning.
- There is no medical or organic basis to the disorder, nor is it caused by use of a drug or medication.

Enuresis, like so many other developmental disorders, is more common among boys. Bed-wetting affects upward of seven million children age 6 years and over in the United States (Lim, 2003). An estimated 5% to 10% of children meet diagnostic criteria for enuresis at age 5 (American Psychiatric Association, 2013). The disorder usually resolves itself by adolescence, if not earlier, although in about 1% of cases, the problem continues into adulthood.

As you might suspect, enuresis can be extremely distressing, especially to the older child (Butler, 2004). Wetting may occur during nighttime sleep only, during waking hours only, or during both nighttime sleep and waking hours. Nighttime-only enuresis is the most common type, and accidents occurring during sleep are referred to as *bed-wetting*. Achieving bladder control at night is more difficult than achieving daytime control. When asleep at night, children must learn to wake up when they feel the pressure of a full bladder and then go to the bathroom to relieve themselves. The younger the "trained" child is, the more likely she or he is to wet the bed at night. It is perfectly normal for children who have acquired daytime control over their bladders to have nighttime accidents for a year or more. Bed-wetting usually occurs during the deepest stage of sleep and may reflect immaturity of the nervous system. The diagnosis of enuresis applies in cases of repeated bed-wetting or daytime wetting of clothes by children of at least 5 years of age.

**THEORETICAL PERSPECTIVES** Psychodynamic explanations of enuresis suggest that it represents the expression of hostility toward children's parents because of harsh toilet training. It may represent regression in response to the birth of a sibling or some other stressor or life change, such as starting school or suffering the death of a parent or relative. Learning theorists point out that enuresis occurs most commonly in children whose parents attempted to train them early. Early failures may have connected anxiety with efforts to control the bladder. Conditioned anxiety, then, induces rather than curbs urination.

*Primary enuresis*, the most prevalent form of the disorder, characterizes children with persistent nocturnal bed-wetting who have never established urinary control through the night. It is due to maturational delays that have genetic underpinnings (Mast & Smith, 2012; Wei et al., 2010). We don't yet understand the genetic mechanism in enuresis, but one possibility implicates the genes that regulate the rate of development of motor control over eliminatory reflexes by the cerebral cortex. Although genetic factors appear to be involved in the transmission of primary enuresis, it is likely that environmental and behavioral factors also come into play in determining the development and course of the disorder. The other type of enuresis, *secondary enuresis*, is apparently not genetically influenced and characterizes children with occasional bed-wetting who developed the problem after having established urinary control.

**TREATMENT** Enuresis usually resolves itself as children mature. Behavioral methods have been shown to be helpful when enuresis endures or causes parents or children great distress, however. These methods condition children to wake up when their bladders are full. One dependable example is the use of a urine alarm method, a variation on a technique introduced by psychologist O. Hobart Mowrer in the 1930s.

The problem in bed-wetting is that children with enuresis continue to sleep despite bladder tension that awakens most other children (Butler, 2004). As a consequence, they reflexively urinate in bed. Mowrer pioneered the use of the urine alarm, which in its present form involves a moisture-activated alarm that is placed beneath the sleeping child. A sensor sounds the alarm when the child wets the bed, which awakens the child (Lim, 2003). After several repetitions, most children learn to awaken in response to bladder tension—*before* the alarm is sounded. The technique is usually explained through principles of classical conditioning. Tension in children's bladders is paired repeatedly with a stimulus (an alarm) that wakes them up when they wet the bed. The bladder tension (a conditioned stimulus) elicits the same response (waking up—the conditioned response) that is elicited by the alarm (the unconditioned stimulus). **T / F**

Treatment for enuresis, generally involving the urine alarm technique or drug therapy, is often helpful (Houts, 2010). Certain psychiatric drugs can also be helpful, such as *fluvoxamine* (brand name Luvox), an SSRI-type antidepressant that works on brain systems that control urination. However, the urine alarm technique has the highest cure rates and the lowest relapse rates among available treatments (Glazener, Evans, & Peto, 2000; Thiedke, 2003). The higher relapse rates associated with drug treatment underscores the fact that therapeutic drugs by themselves do not teach any new skills or adaptive behaviors that can be retained beyond the active treatment period.

**TRUTH or FICTION**

Principles of classical conditioning can be applied to treat bed-wetting in children.

☑ **TRUE** The use of a urine alarm can help condition the enuretic child to awaken to the pressure of a full bladder. In this paradigm, what is the unconditioned stimulus and what is the conditioned stimulus?

# Encopresis

**13.20 Describe the key features of encopresis.**

The term *encopresis* derives from the Greek roots *en*, meaning *in*, and *kopros*, meaning *feces*. **Encopresis** is lack of control over bowel movements that is not caused by an organic problem. The child must have a chronological age of at least 4 years, or in children with intellectual impairment, a mental age of at least 4 years. About 1% of 5-year-olds have encopresis (American Psychiatric Association, 2013). Like enuresis, this condition is most common among boys. Soiling may be voluntary or involuntary and is not caused by an organic problem, except in cases in which constipation is involved. Among the possible predisposing factors are inconsistent or incomplete toilet training and psychosocial stressors, such as the birth of a sibling or beginning school.

Soiling, unlike enuresis, is more likely to happen during the day than at night. It can thus be keenly embarrassing to the child. Classmates often avoid or ridicule soilers. Because feces have a strong odor, teachers may find it hard to act as though nothing has happened. Parents, too, are eventually galled by recurrent soiling and may increase their demands for self-control and employ powerful punishments for failure. As a result, children may hide soiled underwear, distance themselves from classmates, or feign sickness to stay at home. Their levels of anxiety concerning soiling increase. Because anxiety, which involves arousal of the sympathetic branch of the autonomic nervous system, promotes bowel movements, control may become yet more elusive. Not surprisingly, children who soil have more emotional and behavioral problems than those who do not soil (Joinson et al., 2006).

When soiling is involuntary, it is often associated with constipation, impaction, or retention that results in subsequent overflow. Constipation may be related to psychological factors, such as fears associated with defecating in a particular place or with a more general pattern of negativistic or oppositional behavior, or constipation may be related to physiological factors, such as complications from an illness or from medication. Much less frequently, encopresis is deliberate or intentional.

Soiling often appears to follow harsh punishment for an accident or two, particularly in children who are already highly stressed or anxious. Harsh punishment may rivet children's attention on soiling. They may then ruminate about soiling, raising their level of anxiety so that self-control is impaired.

Behavior therapy techniques are helpful in treating encopresis (Loening-Baucke, 2002). Treatment generally involves the parents rewarding (by praise and other means) successful attempts at self-control and using mild punishments for continued accidents (e.g., gentle reminders to attend more closely to bowel tension and having the child clean her or his own underwear). When encopresis persists, thorough medical and psychological evaluation is recommended to determine possible causes and appropriate treatments.

**URINE ALARM.** The urine alarm method is widely used in the treatment of nighttime enuresis. How does the method illustrate the principles of classical conditioning?

# Summing Up

## Normal and Abnormal Behavior in Childhood and Adolescence

### Cultural Beliefs about What Is Normal and Abnormal

**13.1 Explain the differences between normal and abnormal behavior in childhood and adolescence and the role of cultural beliefs in determining abnormality.**

In addition to the criteria described in Chapter 1 in distinguishing between normal and abnormal behavior in general, we need to take into account the child's age and cultural background in determining whether a child's or adolescent's behavior is abnormal with respect to deviating from developmental and normative standards. We also need to consider cultural norms in determining whether behavior in a given culture is deemed abnormal.

### Prevalence of Mental Health Problems in Children and Adolescents

**13.2 Describe the prevalence of psychological disorders in children and adolescents.**

Mental health disorders are unfortunately quite common in young people. Approximately 40% of adolescents have experienced a diagnosable psychological disorder during the past year, and about one in 10 children suffer from a psychological disorder significant enough to affect their development—yet the great majority of children with mental health problems fail to get the treatment they need.

### Risk Factors for Childhood Disorders

**13.3 Identify risk factors for psychological disorders in childhood and adolescence and describe the effects of child abuse.**

Among the factors associated with higher risk of psychological disorders in childhood and adolescence are genetic susceptibility; prenatal influences on the developing brain; environmental stressors (such as living in decaying neighborhoods); family factors, especially inconsistent or harsh discipline, neglect, or physical or sexual abuse; ethnic minority status for problems such as ADHD and anxiety and depressive disorders; and gender, with males more often affected by disorders such as autism, hyperactivity, and elimination disorders and problems in childhood involving anxiety and depression, whereas females more often develop problems with anxiety and depression in adolescence.

The effects of child abuse range from physical injuries or even death to emotional consequences, such as difficulties forming healthy attachments, low self-esteem, suicidal thinking, depression, and failure to explore the outside world, among other problems. The emotional and behavioral consequences of child abuse and neglect often extend into adulthood.

## Autism and Autism Spectrum Disorder

### Features of Autism

**13.4 Describe key features of autism.**

Children with autism spectrum disorder seem detached from others or utterly alone and show deficits in social interactions and ability to develop and maintain relationships, repetitive or restricted movements or behaviors, restricted or fixated interests, attempts to preserve sameness and routines, and peculiar speech habits such as repetitive speech, echolalia, pronoun reversals, and idiosyncratic speech.

### Theoretical Perspectives on Autism

**13.5 Identify possible causal factors in autism.**

The causes of autism remain unknown, but increasing evidence points to roles of genetic factors and brain abnormalities, perhaps in combination with as-yet-unspecified environmental influences.

### Treatment of Autism

**13.6 Describe the treatment of autism.**

Making contact or social interaction with an autistic child is key to implementing a therapeutic plan. Gains in academic and social functioning have been obtained through the use of an intensive behavioral approach called applied behavior analysis (ABA). These approaches rely on intensive, one-to-one behavioral treatment with the autistic child.

## Intellectual Disability

### Causes of Intellectual Disability

**13.7 Describe the key features and causes of intellectual disability.**

Intellectual disability (ID) is characterized by major impairment of intellectual and adaptive abilities. It is assessed by intelligence tests and measures of functional ability. Most cases fall in the mild range. ID is caused by chromosomal abnormalities, such as Down syndrome; genetic disorders, such as Fragile X syndrome and phenylketonuria; prenatal factors, such as maternal diseases and alcohol use; and familial-cultural factors associated with intellectually impoverished home or social environments.

### Interventions

**13.8 Describe interventions used to help children with intellectual disability.**

Interventions are geared to functional impairment and level of severity of the intellectual disability. Psychoeducational interventions are typically employed to help children with ID acquire vocational skills and prepare for meaningful work. Institutional or residential care facilities are limited to children with severe and profound ID.

# Learning Disorders

## Features of Learning Disorders, Causal Factors, and Treatments

**13.9 Identify the types of deficits associated with learning disorders and describe ways of understanding and treating learning disorders.**

Learning disorders (also called learning disabilities) are specific deficits in the development of reading, writing, math, or executive function skills. The causes remain under study but probably involve underlying brain dysfunctions that make it difficult to process or decode visual and auditory information. Intervention focuses mainly on attempts to remediate specific skill deficits.

# Communication Disorders

## Language Disorder

**13.10 Describe the key features of language disorder.**

Language disorder is characterized by significant difficulties producing or understanding spoken language. It may be associated with slow vocabulary development, errors in tenses, difficulties recalling words, and problems producing sentences of appropriate length and complexity for the individual's age.

## Problems with Speech

**13.11 Describe the key features of psychological disorders involving problems with speech.**

These disorders involve deficits in producing clear and fluent speech. Speech sound disorder involves a persistent difficulty articulating sounds of speech that cannot be explained by physiological defects. Childhood-onset fluency disorder, which is commonly called *stuttering*, involves difficulties speaking fluently and with the appropriate timing of speech sounds.

## Social (Pragmatic) Communication Disorder

**13.12 Describe the key features of social (pragmatic) communication disorder.**

Social (pragmatic) communication disorder applies to children who have persistent and profound difficulties communicating verbally and nonverbally with other people, including difficulty holding conversations with people at home, at school, or at play.

# Behavior Problems: Attention-Deficit/Hyperactivity Disorder, Oppositional Defiant Disorder, and Conduct Disorder

## Attention-Deficit/Hyperactivity Disorder

**13.13 Describe the key features of attention-deficit/hyperactivity disorder, identify causal factors, and evaluate treatment methods.**

Attention-deficit/hyperactivity disorder (ADHD) is characterized by impulsivity, inattention, and hyperactivity.

Causal factors in ADHD focus on an interaction of genetic and environmental factors, such as inconsistent or poor parenting behaviors, affecting the executive control functions of the brain. Stimulant medication is generally effective in reducing hyperactivity and increasing attention in ADHD children, but it has not led to general academic gains. Behavior therapy may help ADHD children adapt better to school. Behavior therapy can also be helpful in modifying behaviors of children with conduct disorders and oppositional defiant disorder.

## Conduct Disorder

**13.14 Describe the key features of conduct disorder.**

Children with conduct disorder intentionally engage in antisocial behavior and are frequently aggressive and cruel in their interactions with other children. They may engage in bullying or threatening behavior or start fights, and like antisocial adults, they show a callous disregard for others and lack feelings of guilt or anxiety over their wrongdoings.

## Oppositional Defiant Disorder

**13.15 Describe the key features of oppositional defiant disorder.**

Children with oppositional defiant disorder (ODD) show negativistic or oppositional behavior but not the outright delinquent or antisocial behavior characteristic of conduct disorder. However, ODD may lead to the development of conduct disorder.

# Childhood Anxiety and Depression

## Anxiety-Related Disorders in Children and Adolescents

**13.16 Describe the key features of anxiety-related disorders in children and adolescents.**

Anxiety disorders in children and adolescents commonly include specific phobias, social phobia, and GAD. Cognitive biases, such as expecting negative outcomes, negative self-talk, and interpreting ambiguous situations as threatening, figure prominently in anxiety disorders in children and adolescents, as they often do in adults.

Children with separation anxiety disorder show excessive anxiety for their developmental level when they are separated from their parents. The disorder may be accompanied by nightmares, stomachaches, and nausea and vomiting when separation is anticipated, as well as pleading with parents not to leave them, such as when dropping them off for school, or throwing tantrums when parents are about to depart. Cognitive biases, such as expecting negative outcomes, negative self-talk, and interpreting ambiguous situations as threatening, figure prominently in anxiety disorders in children and adolescents, as they often do in adults.

### Childhood Depression

**13.17 Describe common features of depression in childhood and identify cognitive biases associated with childhood depression and ways of treating childhood depression.**

Depressed children, especially younger children, may not report or be aware of feeling depressed. Depression may also be masked by seemingly unrelated behaviors, such as conduct disorders.

Depressed children tend to show negative thinking styles and cognitive biases commonly found among depressed adults, such a pessimistic explanatory style and negative, distorted thinking. Childhood depression may be treated with cognitive-behavioral treatment, antidepressant medication, or a combination of psychological and pharmacological approaches.

### Suicide in Children and Adolescents

**13.18 Identify risk factors for suicide in adolescents.**

Risk factors for adolescent suicide include gender, age, geography, race, depression, past suicidal behavior, strained family relationships, stress, substance abuse, and social contagion.

## Elimination Disorders

### Enuresis

**13.19 Describe the key features of enuresis and evaluate methods of treating bed-wetting.**

Enuresis involves persistent impaired control over urination that cannot be accounted for by organic causes and is not normative for the child's developmental level. The disorder is more common in boys. The best established method for treating bed-wetting is the urine alarm method, a technique that conditions children with enuresis to respond to bladder tension by awakening before urinating.

### Encopresis

**13.20 Describe the key features of encopresis.**

Encopresis involves persistent impairment in controlling bowel movements and is not normative for the child's developmental level. It may involve a history of inconsistent or incomplete toilet training and psychosocial stressors, such as the birth of a sibling or beginning school.

# Critical Thinking Questions

Based on your reading of this chapter, answer the following questions:

- Do you believe children with intellectual disability should be mainstreamed within regular classes? Why or why not?
- Do you believe people with learning disorders should be given special consideration, such as extra time, when taking standardized tests like the Scholastic Aptitude Test (SAT)? Why or why not?
- If you had a child with ADHD, would you consider using stimulant drugs like Ritalin? Why or why not?
- Do you know of any children who were treated for a psychological disorder? What treatments did they receive? What were the outcomes?

# Key Terms

neurodevelopmental disorders, p. 495
autism spectrum disorder, p. 499
intellectual disability, p. 505
Down syndrome, p. 506
Fragile X syndrome, p. 507
phenylketonuria (PKU), p. 507
dyslexia, p. 510
learning disorder, p. 510
communication disorders, p. 512
language disorder, p. 513
speech sound disorder, p. 513
childhood-onset fluency disorder, p. 513
social (pragmatic) communication disorder, p. 513
attention-deficit/hyperactivity disorder, p. 514
conduct disorder, p. 518
oppositional defiant disorder, p. 518
separation anxiety disorder, p. 521
enuresis, p. 529
encopresis, p. 531

Chapter 14

# Neurocognitive Disorders and Disorders Related to Aging

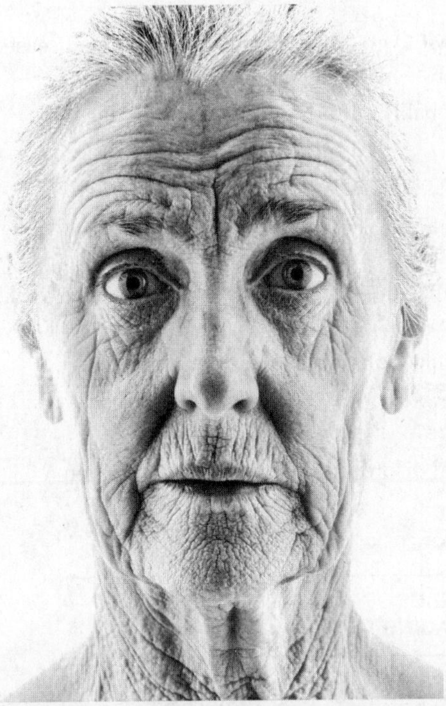

## Learning Objectives

**14.1** **Describe** the diagnostic features of neurocognitive disorders and **identify** three major types.

**14.2** **Describe** the key features and causes of delirium.

**14.3** **Describe** the key features and causes of major neurocognitive disorder.

**14.4** **Describe** the key features of mild neurocognitive disorder.

**14.5** **Describe** the key features and causes of Alzheimer's disease and **evaluate** current treatments.

**14.6** **Identify** other subtypes of neurocognitive disorders.

**14.7** **Identify** anxiety-related disorders and their treatments in older adults.

**14.8** **Identify** factors associated with depression in late adulthood and ways of treating it.

**14.9** **Identify** factors involved in late-life insomnia and ways of treating it.

## TRUTH or FICTION

T☐ F☐ Dementia is a normal part of the aging process. (p. 542)

T☐ F☐ Most older adults who develop mild cognitive impairment (MCI) go on to develop Alzheimer's disease within 5 to 10 years. (p. 543)

T☐ F☐ People who become occasionally forgetful as they age are probably suffering from the early stages of Alzheimer's disease. (p. 544)

T☐ F☐ Fortunately, we now have drugs that can halt the progression of Alzheimer's disease or even cure it in some cases. (p. 547)

T☐ F☐ Recent evidence shows that regular exercise protects the brain from Alzheimer's disease (AD). (p. 547)

T☐ F☐ After a motorcycle accident, a medical student failed to recognize the woman he had married a few weeks earlier. (p. 550)

T☐ F☐ A famous folksinger and songwriter was misdiagnosed with alcoholism and spent several years in mental hospitals until the correct diagnosis was made. (p. 553)

T☐ F☐ A form of dementia is linked to mad cow disease. (p. 554)

T☐ F☐ Anxiety-related disorders are the most common psychological disorders among older adults, even more common than depression. (p. 556)

### CHAPTER INTRODUCTION: NEUROCOGNITIVE DISORDERS AND DISORDERS RELATED TO AGING

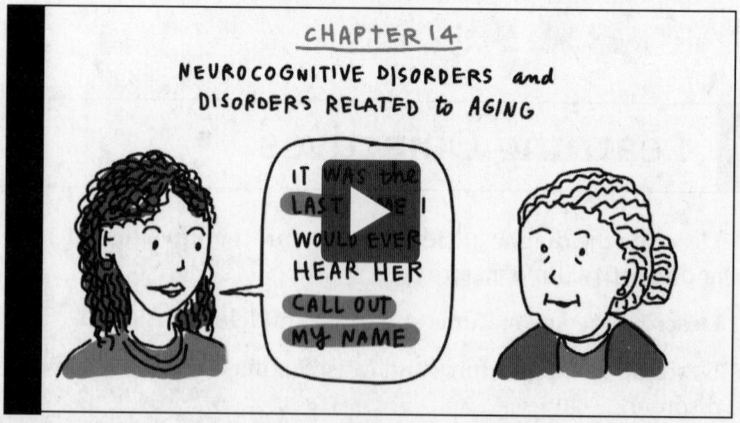


"You should pray for a sound mind in a sound body."

—Juvenal, Roman poet, 55–127 B.C.E.

In the following brief narrative, a woman who lost her mother to Alzheimer's after a 10-year struggle speaks of a moment of joy amidst the agony of daily losses exacted by this terrible disease.

**"I" "Mary's Story"**

Some part of me was ripped apart as I watched the daily losses Mom suffered as she slowly slipped away. Yet, as devastating as Alzheimer's is, our family somehow managed to grasp every bit of life, every bit of hope, and every bit of love that was possible....

Sitting with my mother at the piano, I would play her favorites. Some days the music would spark a memory and she would sing along. But more often than not, she would just smile....

If I had gone away...I might have shed less tears, but I wouldn't have the memory of one particular evening...I walked into the family room, kissed my dad, then walked over to my mom, gave her a big "Hi, Mom" and bent down to kiss her, just as I had done so many times before. But this evening, this one evening, she did more than just smile back and give me a little kiss. This evening, for the first time in a very long time, she clapped her hands and said, "Mary." And then she smiled and that was it. Not another word. Just Mary. It was the last time I would ever hear my mother call out my name. Mary. How wonderful it sounded to my ears! And as gut-wrenching as it felt years before when Mom didn't recognize me, it was somehow assuaged by how exhilarating this felt....And that moment lifted me higher than you could imagine.

**SOURCE:** *Excerpted from "Mary's Story," posted on the Alzheimer's Association website, www.alz.org*

Having a "sound mind in a sound body" is an ancient prescription for a healthy and happy life. However, brain diseases and injuries can make us unsound in both body and mind. When damage to the brain results from an injury or stroke, the deterioration in cognitive, social, and occupational functioning can be rapid and severe. In the case of a more gradual but progressive form of deterioration, such as in Alzheimer's disease (AD), the decline of mental functioning is more gradual but leads eventually to a state of virtual helplessness, as with Mary's mother.

In this chapter, we focus on the class of psychological disorders called *neurocognitive disorders*. These disorders arise from injuries or diseases that affect the brain. Some of these diseases, including AD, primarily affect older adults. Other neurocognitive disorders affect people of different age groups, not just older adults. We begin by reviewing various types of neurocognitive disorders.

# Neurocognitive Disorders

Our ability to perform cognitive functions—to think, reason, store, and recall information—depends on the functioning of the brain. **Neurocognitive disorders** arise when the brain is either damaged or impaired in its ability to function due to injury, illness, exposure to toxins, or use or abuse of psychoactive drugs. The more widespread the damage to the brain, the greater and more extensive the impairment in functioning.

Neurocognitive disorders are not psychologically based; they are caused by physical or medical diseases or drug use or withdrawal that affect the functioning of the brain. In some cases, the specific cause of the neurocognitive disorder can be pinpointed; in others, it cannot. Although these disorders are biologically based, psychological and environmental factors play key roles in determining the impact and range of disabling symptoms and in an individual's ability to cope with such symptoms.

## Types of Neurocognitive Disorders

**14.1 Describe the diagnostic features of neurocognitive disorders and identify three major types.**

Neurocognitive disorders are diagnosed based on deficits in cognitive functioning that represent marked changes in an individual's level of functioning, reflecting brain damage or dysfunction. The extent and location of impaired brain function largely determines the range and severity of cognitive problems. The location of the damage is also critical because many brain structures or regions perform specialized functions. Damage to the temporal lobe, for example, is associated with defects in memory and attention, whereas damage to the occipital lobe may result in visual–spatial deficits, as in the famous case of Dr. P., a distinguished musician and teacher who lost the ability to visually recognize objects, including faces.

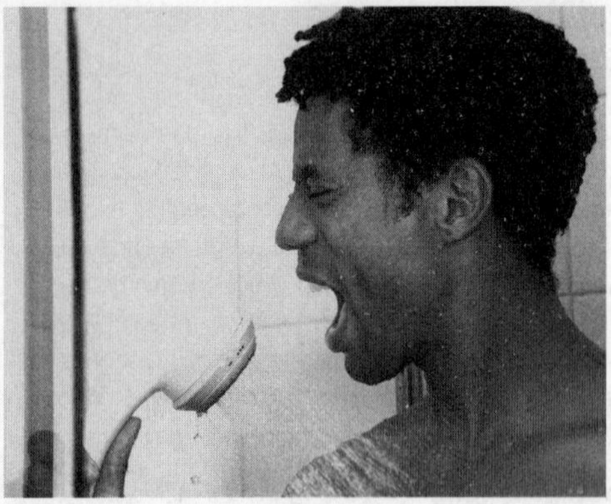

**DOES THIS MAN'S SINGING HELP HIM COORDINATE HIS ACTIONS?**
In a celebrated case study, famed neurologist Oliver Sacks discussed the case of "Dr. P.," who was discovered to be suffering from a brain tumor that impaired his ability to process visual cues. Yet he could still eat meals and wash and dress himself so long as he could sing to himself.

In *The Man Who Mistook His Wife for a Hat*, the late neurologist Oliver Sacks (1985) recounts how Dr. P. failed to recognize the faces of his students at the music school. When a student spoke, however, Dr. P. immediately recognized his or her voice. Not only did the professor fail to discriminate faces visually, but sometimes he perceived faces where none existed. He patted the heads of fire hydrants and parking meters, which he took to be children. He warmly addressed the rounded knobs on furniture. Dr. P. and his colleagues generally dismissed these peculiarities as jokes—after all, Dr. P. was well known for his oddball humor and jests. His music remained as accomplished as ever, and his general health seemed fine, so these misperceptions seemed little to be concerned about.

Not until 3 years later did Dr. P. seek a neurological evaluation. His ophthalmologist had found that although Dr. P.'s eyes were healthy, he had problems interpreting visual stimulation, so he made the referral to Dr. Sacks, a neurologist. When Dr. Sacks engaged Dr. P. in conversation, Dr. P.'s eyes fixated oddly on miscellaneous features of Dr. Sacks's face—his nose, then his right ear, then his chin, sensing parts of his face but apparently not connecting them in a meaningful pattern. When Dr. P. sought to put on his shoe after a physical examination, he confused his foot with the shoe. When preparing to leave, Dr. P. looked around for his hat, and then...

> [Dr. P.] reached out his hand, and took hold of his wife's head, tried to lift it off, to put it on. He had apparently mistaken his wife for a hat! His wife looked as if she was used to such things (Sacks, 1985, p. 10).

Dr. P.'s peculiar behavior may seem amusing to some, but his loss of visual perception was tragic. Although Dr. P. could identify abstract forms and shapes—a cube, for example—he no longer recognized the faces of his family, or his own. Some features of particular faces would strike a chord of recognition. For example, he could recognize a picture of Einstein from the distinctive hair and mustache and a picture of his own brother from the square jaw and big teeth—but he was responding to isolated features, not grasping the facial patterns as wholes.

As a final test on a particularly cold day in early spring, just as Dr. P. was about to leave the office, Sacks held up a glove and asked him, "What is this?" Dr. P. asked to examine it, and upon taking the glove and looking at it carefully, described it as though it were merely a geometric form, one having a "continuous surface infolded on itself." It seemed to possess, Dr. P. continued, "five outpouchings, if this is the word." "But what is it?" Sacks asked, to which Dr. P. replied, "a container." Sacks then asked what it would contain, to which Dr. P. replied with a laugh, "It would contain its contents!" Maybe, he went on to say, it's a purse for holding change, coins of different sizes. Sacks continued, but to no avail. Sacks concluded, sadly, that "No light of recognition dawned on his [Dr. P.'s] face. No child would have the power to see and speak of 'a continuous surface...infolded on itself,' but any child, any infant, would immediately know a glove as a glove, see it as familiar, as going with a hand. Dr. P. didn't. He saw nothing as familiar. Visually, he was lost in a world of lifeless abstractions" (Sacks, 1985, p. 13).

Later, we might add, Dr. P. accidentally put the glove on his hand, exclaiming, "My God, it's a glove!" (Sacks, 1985, p. 13). His brain immediately seized the pattern of tactile information, although his visual brain centers were powerless to interpret the shape as a whole. That is, Dr. P. showed lack of visual knowledge—a symptom referred to as visual **agnosia**, derived from Greek roots meaning *without knowledge*. Still, Dr. P.'s musical abilities and verbal skills remained intact. He was able to function, dress himself, take a shower, and eat his meals by singing various songs to himself—for example, eating songs and dressing songs—that helped him coordinate his actions. However, if his dressing song was interrupted while he was dressing himself, he would lose his train of thought and be unable to recognize not only the clothes his wife had laid out but also his own body. When the music stopped, so did his ability to make sense of the world. Sacks later learned that Dr. P. had a massive tumor in the area of the brain that processes visual information. Dr. P. was apparently unaware of his deficits, having filled his visually empty world with music to function and imbue his life with meaning and purpose.

Dr. P.'s case is unusual in the peculiarity of his symptoms, but it illustrates the universal dependence of psychological functioning on an intact brain. The case also shows how some people adjust—sometimes so gradually that the changes are all but imperceptible—to developing physical or organic problems. Dr. P.'s visual problems might have been relatively more debilitating in a person who was less talented or who had less social support to draw on. The tragic case of Dr. P. illustrates how psychological and environmental factors determine the impact and range of disabling symptoms as well as an individual's ability to cope with them.

People who suffer from neurocognitive disorders may become completely dependent on others to meet basic needs in feeding, toileting, and grooming. In other cases, although some assistance in meeting the demands of daily living may be required, people are able to function at a level that permits them to live semi-independently. The cognitive deficit that Dr. P. developed, *agnosia*, is often a feature of *dementia*, a severe neurocognitive disorder in which there is general deterioration of mental functioning.

The *DSM-5* restructured the "playing field" for classifying neurocognitive disorders, organizing them into three major types: delirium, major neurocognitive disorder, and mild neurocognitive disorder. Table 14.1 provides an overview of these disorders.

## Table 14.1 Overview of Neurocognitive Disorders

| Type of Disorder | Subtypes or Specifiers | Lifetime Prevalence in Population (Approx.) | Description | Associated Features |
|---|---|---|---|---|
| **Delirium** | • Delirium due to a general medical condition<br>• Substance intoxication delirium<br>• Substance withdrawal delirium<br>• Medication-induced delirium | Estimated to be 1% to 2% overall, but higher among older adults | States of extreme mental confusion interfering with concentration and ability to speak coherently | • Difficulty filtering out irrelevant stimuli or shifting attention; excited speech that conveys little meaning<br>• Disorientation as to time and place; frightening hallucinations or other perceptual distortions<br>• Motor behavior may slow to a stupor or fluctuate between states of restlessness and stupor<br>• Mental states may fluctuate between lucid intervals and periods of confusion |
| **Major neurocognitive disorder** | (specified below) | Estimated to be 1% to 2% at age 65, rising to as high as 30% by age 80 | Profound deterioration of mental functioning | • Most forms, such as dementia due to Alzheimer's disease, are irreversible and progressive<br>• Significant declines in cognitive abilities |
| **Mild neurocognitive disorder** | (specified below) | Estimated to be 2% to 10% at age 65 and between 5% and 25% by age 85 | Mild or modest decline in cognitive impairment over time; also called mild cognitive impairment (MCI) | • Complaints about cognitive declines must be supported by formal tests of cognitive functioning<br>• People with the disorder can function independently but find it more difficult to perform mental tasks they were accustomed to performing easily<br>• Some cases, but not most, eventually progress to Alzheimer's disease |
| **Subtypes of major and mild neurocognitive disorders** | • Neurocognitive disorder due to:<br>  • Alzheimer's disease<br>  • Traumatic brain injury<br>  • Parkinson's disease<br>  • HIV infection<br>  • Huntington's disease<br>  • Prion disease<br>• Vascular neurocognitive disorder<br>• Frontotemporal neurocognitive disorder<br>• Substance/medication-induced neurocognitive disorder<br>• Neurocognitive disorder with Lewy bodies | Varies with underlying condition | Cognitive impairment caused by a variety of underlying physical diseases or disorders that affect brain functioning | • Level of cognitive impairment can range from mild to severe (major)<br>• Treatment depends on the underlying cause of brain dysfunction |

**SOURCES:** Prevalence rates derived from American Psychiatric Association, 2000, 2013; Hebert et al., 2003.

# Delirium

**14.2 Describe the key features and causes of delirium.**

The word *delirium* derives from the Latin roots *de*, meaning *from*, and *lira*, meaning *line* or *furrow*. It means straying from the line or the norm, in perception, cognition, and behavior. **Delirium** is a state of extreme mental confusion in which people have difficulty focusing their attention, speaking clearly and coherently, and orienting themselves to the environment (see Table 14.2). People suffering from delirium may find it difficult to tune out irrelevant stimuli or to shift their attention to new tasks. They may speak excitedly, but their speech conveys little—if any—meaning. Disorientation as to time (not knowing the current date, day of the week, or time) and place (not knowing where one is) is common. Disorientation to person (the identities of oneself and others) is not. People in a state of delirium may experience terrifying hallucinations, especially visual hallucinations. The severity of symptoms tends to fluctuate during the course of the day (American Psychiatric Association, 2013).

Disturbances in perceptions often occur, such as misinterpretations of sensory stimuli (e.g., confusing an alarm clock for a fire bell) or illusions (e.g., feeling as if the bed has an electrical charge passing through it). There can be a dramatic slowing down of movement into a state resembling catatonia. There may be rapid fluctuations between restlessness and stupor. Restlessness is characterized by insomnia, agitated, aimless movements, or even bolting out of bed or striking out at nonexistent objects. This may alternate with periods in which a person has to struggle to stay awake.

There are many causes of delirium, including head trauma; high fevers due to infections; metabolic disorders, such as hypoglycemia (low blood sugar); adverse medication interactions; underlying medical conditions such as severe infections or heart failure; drug abuse or withdrawal; fluid or electrolyte imbalances; seizure disorders (epilepsy); deficiencies of the B vitamin thiamine; brain lesions; and stroke and diseases affecting the central nervous system, including Parkinson's disease, AD, viral encephalitis (a type of brain infection), liver disease, and kidney disease (e.g., Jones, 2014; Oldenbeuving et al., 2011).

The prevalence of delirium is estimated at about 1% to 2% in the general community, but rises to 14% among people over the age of 85 (Inouye, 2006). Delirium most often affects hospitalized patients, especially intensive care patients and elderly patients following surgical operations (Marcantonio et al., 2014; Mark et al., 2014; Reade & Finfer, 2014). Delirium in patients in intensive care is associated with poorer outcomes, including a higher risk of early death (Salluh et al., 2015).

Delirium may also occur due to exposure to toxic substances (such as eating certain poisonous mushrooms), as a side effect of using certain medications, or during states of drug or alcohol intoxication. Among young people, delirium is most commonly the result of abrupt withdrawal from psychoactive drugs, especially alcohol. However, among older patients, it is often a sign of a life-threatening medical condition (Inouye, 2006).

People with chronic alcoholism who abruptly stop drinking may experience a form of delirium called *delirium tremens*, or the DTs. The DTs are characterized by such symptoms as body tremors, states of agitation, irritability, confusion, and disorientation, and by wild and

## Table 14.2 Features of Delirium

| | Level of Severity | | |
|---|---|---|---|
| **Domain** | **Mild** | **Moderate** | **Severe** |
| **Emotion** | Apprehension | Fear | Panic |
| **Cognition and perception** | Confusion, racing thoughts | Disorientation, delusions | Meaningless mumbling, vivid hallucinations |
| **Behavior** | Tremors | Muscle spasms | Seizures |
| **Autonomic activity** | Abnormally fast heartbeat (tachycardia) | Perspiration | Fever |

**SOURCE:** Adapted from Freemon (1981), p. 82.

frightening hallucinations, such as "bugs crawling down walls" or on the skin. The DTs can last for a week or more and are best treated in a hospital, where the patient can be carefully monitored and the symptoms treated with mild tranquilizers and environmental support. Although there are many known causes of delirium, in many cases the specific cause cannot be identified.

Whatever the cause may be, delirium involves a widespread disruption of brain activity, possibly resulting from imbalances in the levels of certain neurotransmitters (Inouye, 2006). As a result, a person may be unable to process incoming information, leading to a state of general confusion. The person may not be able to speak or think clearly or to make sense of his or her surroundings. States of delirium may occur abruptly, as in cases resulting from seizures or head injuries, or gradually over hours or days, as in cases involving infections, fever, or metabolic disorders. During the course of delirium, the person's mental state often fluctuates between periods of clarity ("lucid intervals"), which are most common in the morning, and periods of confusion and disorientation. Delirium is generally worse in the dark and following sleepless nights.

Unlike dementia or other forms of major neurocognitive disorder (discussed later) in which there is a gradual deterioration of mental functioning, delirium develops rapidly, generally in a few hours to a few days and involves more clearly disturbed processes of attention and awareness (Wong et al., 2010). Also unlike dementia, which typically follows a chronic and progressive course, delirium tends to clear up spontaneously when the underlying medical or drug-related cause is resolved. Psychiatric medication may be used to reduce the symptoms. However, if the underlying cause persists or leads to further deterioration, delirium may progress to disability, coma, and even death (Inouye, 2006).

## Major Neurocognitive Disorder

**14.3 Describe the key features and causes of major neurocognitive disorder.**

**Major neurocognitive disorder** (commonly called *dementia*) is characterized by a profound decline or deterioration in mental functioning characterized by significant impairment of memory, thinking processes, attention, and judgment and by specific cognitive deficits such as those listed in Table 14.3. There are many causes of major neurocognitive disorder or dementia, but the most frequent cause is the disabling and degenerative brain disease called Alzheimer's disease. Other causes include brain diseases, such as Pick's disease, and infections or disorders affecting the functioning of the brain, such as meningitis, HIV infection, and encephalitis. In some cases, major neurocognitive disorder or dementia can be halted or reversed, especially if it is caused by certain types of

**Table 14.3** Cognitive Deficits Associated with Dementia

| Type of Cognitive Deficit | Description | Further Information |
|---|---|---|
| **Aphasia** | Impaired ability to comprehend and/or produce speech | There are several types of aphasia. In sensory or receptive aphasia, people have difficulty understanding written or spoken language, but retain the ability to express themselves through speech. In motor aphasia, the ability to express thoughts through speech is impaired, but a person can understand spoken language. A person with a motor aphasia may not be able to summon up the names of familiar objects or may scramble the normal order of words. |
| **Apraxia** | Impaired ability to perform purposeful movements despite an absence of any defect in motor functioning | There may be an inability to tie a shoelace or button a shirt, even though the affected person can describe how these activities should be performed and despite the fact that there is nothing wrong with the person's arm or hand. The person may have difficulty pantomiming the use of an object (e.g., combing one's hair). |
| **Agnosia** | Inability to recognize objects despite an intact sensory system | Agnosias may be limited to specific sensory channels. A person with a visual agnosia may not be able to identify a fork when shown a picture of the object, although he or she has an intact visual system and may be able to identify the object if allowed to touch it and manipulate it by hand. Auditory agnosia is marked by impairment in the ability to recognize sounds; in tactile agnosia, people are unable to identify objects (such as coins or keys) by holding them or touching them. |
| **Disturbance in executive functioning** | Deficits in planning, organizing, or sequencing activities or in engaging in abstract thinking | An office manager who formerly handled budgets and scheduling loses the ability to manage the flow of work in the office or adapt to new demands. An English teacher loses the ability to extract meaning from a poem or story. |

tumors, or by seizures, metabolic disturbances, or treatable infections, or when it results from depression or substance abuse. But sadly, the great majority of cases, including the most common form—dementia due to AD—follow a progressive and irreversible course.

A form of dementia caused by a bacterium had historical significance in the development of the medical model of mental disorders. This form of dementia was called **general paresis** (from the Greek *parienai*, meaning *to relax*), or "relaxation" of the brain in its most negative connotation. The dementia resulted from *neurosyphilis*, a form of later-stage syphilis, a sexually transmitted disease caused by the bacterium *Treponema pallidum*. In neurosyphilis, the bacterium directly attacks the brain, resulting in dementia. The 19th-century discovery of the connection between this form of dementia and a concrete physical illness, syphilis, strengthened the medical model and held out the promise that organic causes would eventually be found for other abnormal behavior patterns.

General paresis once accounted for upwards of 30% of admissions to psychiatric hospitals. However, advances in detection and the development of antibiotics that cure the infection have greatly reduced the incidence of late-stage syphilis and the development of general paresis. The effectiveness of treatment depends on when antibiotics are introduced and the extent of brain damage. In cases in which extensive tissue damage has occurred, antibiotics can stem the infection and prevent further damage, producing some improvement in intellectual performance; however, antibiotics cannot restore people to their original levels of functioning.

Impaired memory is the major feature of dementia due to AD, but other major neurocognitive disorders may entail different kinds of cognitive impairments, such as profound deficits in language use. The particular deficits depend largely on the part of the brain affected by the underlying condition. Although the term *dementia* is no longer used as a diagnostic label, it continues to be used widely in describing cognitive impairments in older adults. It has limited applicability to younger patients suffering from cognitive impairment. The developers of the *DSM-5* believe it is a pejorative term that carries an unfortunate stigma. Consequently, they decided to replace it in the diagnostic manual with a more descriptive term, *major neurocognitive disorder*, just as they did with another pejorative term, *mental retardation* (now labeled *intellectual disability*). However, because dementia continues to be widely used to describe some forms of cognitive impairment, especially in older adults, we continue to use the term where it applies.

**TRUTH or FICTION**

Dementia is a normal part of the aging process.

☑ **FALSE** Dementia is not a normal part of aging. It is caused by an underlying disease affecting brain functioning.

Dementia usually occurs in people over the age of 80. Dementia beginning after age 65 is called **late-onset dementia**. Dementia that begins at age 65 or earlier is termed **early-onset dementia**. Although the risk of dementia is greater in later life, dementia is not a consequence of normal aging. It is a sign of a degenerative brain disease, such as AD. **T / F**

## Mild Neurocognitive Disorder

**14.4 Describe the key features of mild neurocognitive disorder.**

**Mild neurocognitive disorder** is a newly recognized disorder in *DSM-5* that applies to people who suffer a mild or modest decline in cognitive functioning from their prior level. The decline is not of sufficient magnitude to justify a diagnosis of major neurocognitive disorder. Concerns about a person's cognitive functioning need to be evaluated by a clinician using formal neurocognitive tests measuring skills such as memory, attention, and problem solving. The clinician needs to be aware of the differences between normal cognitive aging, such as expected lapses in memory and ordinary forgetfulness, and the more severe cognitive deficits that characterize neurocognitive disorders. Cognitive aging is not a disease, but a naturally occurring process affecting every individual that begins at birth and continues through the lifespan (Jacob, 2015b).

Mild neurocognitive disorder is a new name for a clinical syndrome widely identified as *mild cognitive impairment* (MCI). People with mild neurocognitive disorder or MCI are able to function independently and complete tasks of daily living at home and on the job, but they need to apply more effort in completing tasks that used to come more easily. Or they may compensate in some ways to maintain their independence, such as shifting job responsibilities to others or using electronic devices to supplement their lagging memory. Clinicians struggle with determining the thresholds to use to distinguish MCI from normal age-related changes in cognitive abilities, especially memory for names and mental arithmetic.

**WHERE DID I LEAVE THOSE KEYS?** Forgetting where we left our keys is a form of ordinary forgetfulness that becomes more common as we age. Forgetting what keys are for is a sign of possible neurocognitive disorder that needs to be evaluated more thoroughly.

Mild impairment of cognitive functioning frequently occurs in the early stages of neurodegenerative diseases like AD and other conditions affecting the brain, such as traumatic brain injury, HIV infection, substance-use-related brain disorders, and diabetes. For example, Alzheimer's typically develops gradually over time, and most cases begin with the emergence of memory problems associated with mild cognitive impairment (MCI) that typically lasts for years before outright symptoms of Alzheimer's appear (Cooper et al., 2014; Vos et al., 2015). However, it is important to note that the majority of people with MCI do not go on to develop AD. **T / F**

The inclusion of a new diagnosis of mild neurocognitive disorder in *DSM-5* is important for several reasons. First, it highlights the need to identify cases of MCI that can be targeted for early intervention before more serious deficits emerge. Early intervention may involve treatment with drugs or cognitive retraining that is not effective once more severe levels of cognitive impairment develop. Second, diagnosing the disorder enables researchers to identify groups of possible research participants who may be willing to participate in research trials focusing on finding ways of preventing the progression from mild to severe forms of cognitive impairment.

We next focus on specific subtypes of neurocognitive disorders in which the level of cognitive impairment may range from mild in the case of mild neurocognitive disorders to severe in the case of major neurocognitive disorders. Our emphasis is on AD because it is the most prominent cause of major neurocognitive disorder.

**TRUTH or FICTION**

Most older adults who develop mild cognitive impairment (MCI) go on to develop Alzheimer's disease within 5 to 10 years.

☑ **FALSE** Sadly, some do, but most do not progress to Alzheimer's.

# Neurocognitive Disorder Due to Alzheimer's Disease

**14.5 Describe the key features and causes of Alzheimer's disease and evaluate current treatments.**

**Alzheimer's disease (AD)** is a degenerative brain disease that leads to progressive and irreversible dementia, characterized by memory loss and deterioration of other cognitive functions, including judgment and ability to reason. Alzheimer's is the sixth leading cause of death in the United States, accounting for about 85,000 deaths annually (CDC, 2015b, 2015c). The risk of AD increases dramatically with advancing age (Hebert et al., 2013; Querfurth & LaFerla, 2010). More than 99% of cases occur in people over the age of 65 (Alzheimer's Society, 2008). As the U.S. population continues to age, the disease is expected to affect as many as 16 million people by the year 2050. The forms of AD that strike before age 65 appear to involve a more severe form of the disease.

The great majority of cases of AD occur in people over the age of 65, most typically in those in their late 70s and 80s (see Figure 14.1). Women are at higher risk of developing the disease than men, although this may be because women tend to live longer. Yet it is important to note again that although AD is strongly connected with aging, it is a degenerative brain disease and not a consequence of normal aging.

**Figure 14.1** Prevalence of Alzheimer's disease among older adults.

Among older adults, the risk of Alzheimer's disease is much greater among people over the age of 75 than among those aged 65–74.

**SOURCE:** Hebert et al., 2003.

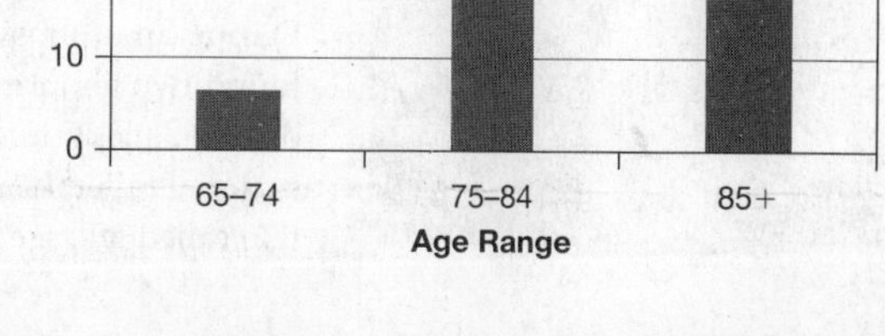

## TRUTH or FICTION

People who become occasionally forgetful as they age are probably suffering from the early stages of Alzheimer's disease.

☑ **FALSE** Occasional memory loss or forgetfulness is a normal consequence of the aging process.

Dementia associated with AD takes the form of progressive deterioration or loss of mental abilities involving memory, language, and problem solving. Occasional memory loss or forgetfulness in middle life (e.g., forgetting where one put one's glasses) is normal and not a sign of the early stages of AD. People in later life (and some of us not quite that advanced in years) complain of not remembering names as well as they used to or of forgetting names that were once well known to them. **T / F**

Forgetting where you put your keys is a normal occurrence; forgetting where you live is not. Here, a woman with early-onset Alzheimer's recounts how her memory began slipping away. She relates an experience that happened to her one day as she was driving home from her husband's office.

## "Living in the Labyrinth":

### A CASE OF EARLY-ONSET ALZHEIMER'S

I was hopelessly lost, and had no idea how to get home.... My body was shaking with fear and uncontrollable sobs. What was happening?

A few yards ahead, there was a park ranger building. Trembling, I wiped my eyes, and breathing deeply, tried to calm myself.... The guard smiled and inquired how he could assist me.

"I appear to be lost," I began....

"Where do you need to go?" the guard asked politely.

A cold chill enveloped me as I realized I could not remember the name of my street. Tears began to flow down my cheeks. I did not know where I wanted to go....

I felt panic wash over me anew as I searched my memory and found it blank. Suddenly, I remembered bringing my grandchildren to this park. That must mean I lived relatively nearby, surely.

"What is the closest subdivision?" I quavered.

The guard scratched his head thoughtfully.

"The closest Orlando subdivision would be Pine Hills, maybe," he ventured.

"That's right!" I exclaimed gratefully. The name of my subdivision had rung a bell....

I drove carefully in the exact direction he advised and searched each intersection.... Finally,... I recognized the entrance to the subdivision....

Once home, a wave of relief brought more tears.... I took refuge in the darkened master bedroom, and sat, curled up on my bed, my arms wrapped tightly around myself.

**SOURCE:** *McGowin, 1993*

**ALZHEIMER'S DISEASE.** AD has struck a number of notable people, including former President Ronald Reagan, shown here with his wife, Nancy, at his first public appearance after being diagnosed with AD. Reagan died of the disease in June 2004.

Suspicions of AD are raised when cognitive impairment is more severe and pervasive, affecting an individual's ability to meet the ordinary responsibilities of daily work and social roles. Over the course of the illness, people with AD may become lost in parking lots, in stores, or even in their own homes. The wife of an AD patient describes how AD affected her husband: "With no cure, Alzheimer's robs the person of who he is. It is painful to see Richard walk around the car several times because he can't find the door" (Morrow, 1998). Agitation, wandering behavior, depression, and aggressive behavior are common as the disease progresses.

People with AD may become depressed, confused, or even delusional when they sense their mental ability is slipping away but do not understand why. Depression, agitation, and apathy may precede the development of memory decline in people who go on to develop AD (Masters, Morris, & Roe, 2015). As the disease progresses, patients may experience hallucinations and other psychotic features. Bewilderment and fear may lead to paranoid delusions or beliefs that their loved ones have betrayed them, robbed them, or don't care about them. They may forget the names of their loved ones or fail to recognize them. They may even forget their own names.

AD was first described in 1907 by the German physician Alois Alzheimer (1864–1915). During an autopsy of a 56-year-old woman who had suffered from severe dementia, he found two abnormalities in the brain that are now regarded as characteristic signs of the disease: sticky masses of plaque (deposits of fibrous protein fragments composed of a material called *beta amyloid*) and neurofibrillary tangles (twisted bundles of fibers of a protein called *tau*; see Figure 14.2; Ossenkoppele et al., 2015; Underwood, 2015). Beta amyloid deposits in the brain may appear 20 or 30 years before symptoms of AD emerge (Belluck, 2015). The reddish areas in the set of photos at the bottom of Figure 14.2 show the presence of plaques in the brains of Alzheimer's patients.

**Figure 14.2** PET scans of healthy brains and those of Alzheimer's patients.

Note the areas in red in the brains of Alzheimer's patients that denote the presence of plaques.

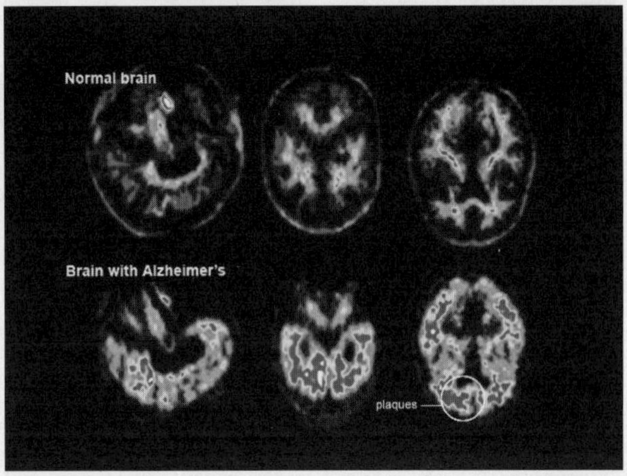


**ALZHEIMER'S DISEASE DIAGNOSIS** Various medical and psychological conditions sometimes mimic symptoms of AD, such as severe depression resulting in memory loss. Consequently, misdiagnoses may occur, especially in the early stages of the disease, and so doctors need to be careful in making a diagnosis of this dreadful disease. In 2012, new brain-scanning technology became available, allowing doctors for the first time to diagnose AD based on brain scans showing plaques associated with the disease together with clinical evidence of memory loss (Kolata, 2012). Brain-scanning techniques may soon be available to predict which patients with MCI are likely to progress to AD (Chen et al., 2011; Jack et al., 2011).

**SYMPTOMS OF ALZHEIMER'S DISEASE** The early stages of AD are marked by limited memory problems and subtle personality changes. People may at first have trouble managing their finances; remembering recent events or basic information, such as telephone numbers, area codes, zip codes, and the names of their grandchildren; and performing numerical computations. A business executive who once managed millions of dollars may become unable to perform simple arithmetic. There may be subtle personality changes, such as signs of withdrawal in people who had been outgoing or irritability in people who had been gentle. In these early stages, people with AD generally appear neat and well groomed and are generally cooperative and socially appropriate.

Some people with AD are not aware of their deficits. Others deny them. At first, they may attribute their problems to other causes, such as stress or fatigue. Denial may protect people with AD in the early or mild stages of the disease from recognizing that their intellectual abilities are declining, or the recognition that their mental abilities are slipping away may lead to depression.

In moderately severe AD, people require assistance in managing everyday tasks. At this stage, Alzheimer's patients may be unable to select appropriate clothes or recall their addresses or names of family members. When they drive, they begin making mistakes, such as failing to stop at stop signs or accelerating when they should be braking. They may encounter difficulties in toileting and bathing themselves. They often make mistakes in recognizing themselves in mirrors. They may no longer be able to speak in full sentences. Verbal responses may become limited to a few words.

ALVIN: DEMENTIA (ALZHEIMER'S TYPE)

Movement and coordination functions deteriorate further. People with AD at the moderately severe level may begin walking in shorter, slower steps. They may no longer be able to sign their names, even when assisted by others. They may have difficulty handling a knife and fork. Agitation becomes a prominent feature at this stage, and patients may act out in response to the threat of having to

**DO YOU KNOW WHO I AM?** Alzheimer's can devastate patients' families. Spouses usually provide the bulk of daily care and also bear the emotional cost of watching their loved ones slipping away day after day.

contend with an environment that no longer seems controllable. They may pace or fidget or display aggressive behavior such as yelling, throwing, or hitting. Patients may wander off because of restlessness and be unable to find their way back.

People with advanced AD may start talking to themselves or experience visual hallucinations or paranoid delusions. They may believe that someone is attempting to harm them or is stealing their possessions or that their spouses are unfaithful to them. They may even believe that their spouses are actually other people.

At the most severe stage, cognitive functions decline to the point where people become essentially helpless. They may lose the ability to speak or control body movement. They become incontinent; are unable to communicate, walk, or even sit up; and require assistance in toileting and feeding. In the end state, seizures, coma, and death result.

AD wreaks havoc not only on the affected person but also on the entire family. Families who helplessly watch their loved ones slowly deteriorate have been described as attending a "funeral that never ends" (Aronson, 1988). The symptoms of advanced AD, such as wandering away, aggressiveness, destructiveness, incontinence, screaming, and remaining awake at night, impose high levels of stress on caregivers. Living with a person with advanced AD may seem like living with a stranger—so profound are the changes in personality and behavior. Not surprisingly, caregivers tend to experience more health-related problems and higher levels of stress hormones than do noncaregivers (Vitaliano, Zhang, & Scanlan, 2003). Typically, the caretaking burden falls disproportionately on the adult daughters in the family, who are often middle-aged women feeling "sandwiched" between their responsibilities to their children and to their affected parents.

**CAUSAL FACTORS** We don't know what causes AD, but clues may lie in understanding the process by which plaques and tangled nerve fibers form in the brains of AD patients (Ossenkoppele et al., 2015; Zhao et al., 2015). A recent line of research suggests that build-up of amyloid plaques leads to inflammation in the brain, which in turn damages networks of neurons involved in memory formation and memory storage (Bie et al., 2014; ScienceDaily, 2014a).

**PLAQUES LINKED TO ALZHEIMER'S DISEASE.** In Alzheimer's disease, nerve tissue in the brain degenerates, forming steel-wool-like clumps or plaques composed of beta amyloid protein fragments, shown here as blue-stained areas in a section of the cerebral cortex.

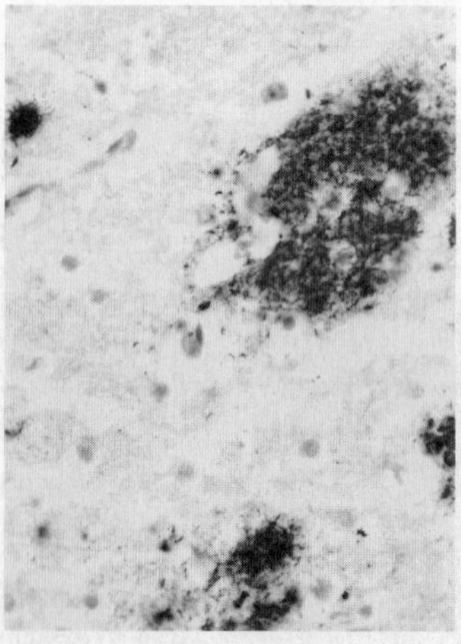

Scientists have discovered that AD starts in an area of the cerebral cortex that plays a key role in memory processes and then spreads to other parts of the cerebral cortex (Khan et al., 2013). Drilling down to the biochemical processes involved in AD gives scientists hope they will develop a better understanding of the molecular bases of AD that will lead to specific therapies to treat and perhaps even prevent the disease (Tsai & Madabhushi, 2014). Along these lines, abnormalities in AD patients in how the brain normally cleanses itself of toxic amyloid protein may play a role in the development of the brain plaques in AD (Keaney et al., 2015).

Another important line of inquiry focuses on genetic factors (Tanzi, 2015). Scientists have identified a number of genes linked to AD (e.g., Heck et al., 2015; Hooli et al., 2015; Lu et al., 2014). Different combinations of genes may be involved in different forms of the disease. Some forms of AD are associated with particular genes linked to the production of beta amyloid or to the abnormal build-up of amyloid plaques and neurofibrillary tangles in the brains of AD patients (Zhao et al., 2015). People with a genetic variant called the *ApoE4* gene stand a much higher risk of developing Alzheimer's disease, perhaps as much as three times greater risk than average (Bien-Ly et al., 2012).

Environmental factors may also be involved in AD (Sotiropoulos et al., 2011). We don't yet know which particular environmental factors may be involved, but stress is a suspected culprit. Scientists are working to develop a better understanding of how genes and environmental factors interact in the development of the disease.

**WORKING OUT IS GOOD FOR BODY AND MIND.** Following a healthy diet, avoiding smoking, engaging in mentally stimulating activities, and exercising regularly may boost cognitive functioning in late adulthood.

**TREATMENT AND PREVENTION** Presently available drugs for AD offer at best only modest benefits in slowing cognitive decline and boosting cognitive functioning. None is a cure. One widely used drug *donepezil* (brand name Aricept) increases levels of the neurotransmitter acetylcholine (ACh). AD patients show lower levels of ACh, possibly because of the death of brain cells in ACh-producing areas of the brain. However, the drug produces only small or modest improvements in cognitive functioning in people with moderate to severe AD (Howard et al., 2012; Kuehn, 2012a). Another drug, *memantine* (brand name Axura), blocks the neurotransmitter glutamate, a brain chemical found in abnormally high concentrations in AD patients (Rettner, 2011). High levels of glutamate may damage brain cells. Unfortunately, evidence fails to support the benefits of the drug over a placebo in treating milder forms of AD (Schneider et al., 2011). Antipsychotic medication may also be used to help control the aggressive or agitated behavior of dementia patients, but these drugs carry significant safety risks (Corbett & Ballard, 2012; Devanand et al., 2012). **T / F**

Inflammation in the brain appears to play a key role in the development of AD. Hence, investigators are evaluating the potential preventive effects of anti-inflammatory drugs, such as the common pain reliever *ibuprofen* (brand name Advil). Medical experts caution against widespread use of these drugs until it becomes clear whether they can reduce the risk of AD or delay its onset (Rogers, 2009). Unfortunately, we lack any drugs that can prevent or delay the development of AD (Kolata, 2010). Scientists suspect that the biological process involved in AD may begin more than 20 years before dementia develops (Bateman et al., 2012). Consequently, investigators are calling for greater attention to developing drugs that target the early stages of the disease rather than its end stage (Buchhave et al., 2012; Selkoe, 2012).

**TRUTH or FICTION**

Fortunately, we now have drugs that can halt the progression of Alzheimer's disease or even cure it in some cases.

☑ **FALSE** Although active research efforts are under way to develop such drugs, we lack drugs that can curb the progression of the disease or offer hope of a cure. At best, presently available drugs may slow the rate of cognitive decline.

Engaging in stimulating cognitive activities—solving puzzles, reading newspapers, playing word games, and so on—can help boost cognitive performance in people with mild to moderate AD (Woods et al., 2012). AD patients may also benefit from memory-training programs to help them make optimal use of their remaining abilities. Hopes for the future lie in the development of an effective vaccine to prevent this devastating disease (Michaud et al., 2013).

On the prevention front, observational studies link certain lifestyle factors to a lower risk of AD and general cognitive decline, such as maintaining a regular exercise program, avoiding smoking, and following a healthy diet that is low in animal fat and rich in vegetables and fish (Buchman et al., 2012; Nisbett et al., 2012; Smith et al., 2014; Gill & Seitz, 2015). Other evidence shows that a combination of healthy lifestyle adjustments, such as following a regular exercise program, adopting a healthy diet, and practicing challenging mental activities, can boost cognitive functioning in older adults (Eggenberger et al., 2015; Ngandu et al., 2015; Vidoni et al., 2015). We also have observational evidence linking physical fitness in middle adulthood to a lower risk of dementia in later adulthood (DeFina et al., 2013). Still, we need direct experimental evidence that programs designed to modify these lifestyle factors can protect the brain from AD. **T / F**

**TRUTH or FICTION**

Recent evidence shows that regular exercise protects the brain from Alzheimer's disease (AD).

☑ **FALSE** This may possibly be true, but for now we must count it as false, as we lack direct experimental evidence that exercise programs can actually prevent AD.

## A CLOSER Look

### TAKING A PAGE FROM FACEBOOK: NEUROSCIENTISTS EXAMINE BRAIN NETWORKS IN ALZHEIMER'S PATIENTS

Facebook, the popular social networking site, builds friendship networks based on connecting individuals to each other through common friends or interests. The common links between people are called *hubs*—for example, "Hey, I see we share a dog groomer together. Want to join our dog-walking group?" In this example, the dog groomer is a hub that connects two or more people together. You might eventually meet other customers of the same dog groomer, but Facebook hubs make communication faster and more reliable.

Neuroscientists at Stanford University School of Medicine compared networks of interconnected neurons or "hubs" in the brains of patients with AD with those in healthy people (Conger, 2008a, 2008b; Supekar et al., 2008). Functional magnetic imaging (fMRI) scans showed less well-connected neural networks in the brains of the Alzheimer's patients. In effect, the brains of Alzheimer's patients had fewer working hubs. A breakdown of hubs or connecting stations in the brain may help explain some of the memory loss and confusion of Alzheimer's patients (see Figure 14.3). Consequently, it becomes more difficult for neurons in the brain to communicate with each other because they are not as closely linked in active networks.

Analysis of these neural networks allowed investigators to correctly identify Alzheimer's patients and healthy controls about 75% of the time. This research may be a first step toward developing a new diagnostic tool that can distinguish early-stage AD from other brain disorders.

**Figure 14.3** Your brain on Facebook.

Facebook connects people through common links or hubs based on shared acquaintances or interest patterns. Neuroscientists find that the brains of Alzheimer's patients have less well-developed "hubs" or networks of interconnected neurons, which may help to explain cognitive impairments in memory and thinking processes.

**SOURCE:** www.thetechbrief.com/.../facebook_network_31.jpg.

# Other Neurocognitive Disorders

**14.6 Identify other subtypes of neurocognitive disorders.**

Although Alzheimer's disease is the most common form of neurocognitive disorder, there is a range of other disorders involving the brain that affect cognitive functioning. Our discussion of these other neurocognitive disorders begins with vascular neurocognitive disorder.

**VASCULAR NEUROCOGNITIVE DISORDER** The brain, like other living tissues, depends on the bloodstream to supply it with oxygen and glucose and to carry away its metabolic wastes. A stroke, also called a **cerebrovascular accident (CVA)**, occurs when part of the brain becomes damaged because of a disruption in its blood supply, usually as the result of a blood clot that becomes lodged in an artery that services the brain and obstructs circulation (Adler, 2004). Areas of the brain may be damaged or destroyed, leaving the victim with disabilities in motor, speech, and cognitive functions. Death may also occur.

**Vascular neurocognitive disorder** (formerly called vascular dementia or *multi-infarct dementia*) is a form of major or mild neurocognitive disorder resulting from cerebrovascular events (strokes) affecting the brain (Staekenborg et al., 2009). Vascular dementia, the second most common form of dementia after AD, most often affects people in later life, but at somewhat earlier ages than dementia due to AD. The disease affects more men than women and accounts for about one in five cases of dementia. Although any individual stroke may produce gross cognitive impairments, such as **aphasia**, strokes do not typically cause the more generalized cognitive declines associated with dementia. Vascular forms of dementia generally result from multiple strokes occurring at different times that have cumulative effects on a wide range of mental abilities.

The symptoms of vascular neurocognitive disorder are similar to those of dementia due to Alzheimer's, including impaired memory and language ability, agitation and emotional instability, and loss of ability to care for one's own basic needs. However, AD is characterized by an insidious onset and a gradual decline of mental functioning, whereas vascular dementia typically occurs abruptly and follows a stepwise course of deterioration involving rapid declines in cognitive functioning that are believed to reflect the effects of additional strokes. Some cognitive functions in people with vascular dementia remain relatively intact in the early course of the disorder, leading to a pattern of patchy deterioration in which islands of mental competence remain while other abilities suffer gross impairment, depending on the particular areas of the brain that have been damaged by multiple strokes.

**FRONTOTEMPORAL NEUROCOGNITIVE DISORDER** This neurocognitive disorder is characterized by deterioration (thinning or shrinkage) of brain tissue in the frontal and temporal lobes of the cerebral cortex. This typically takes the form of progressive dementia symptomatically similar to AD. Symptoms include memory loss and social inappropriateness, such as a loss of modesty or the display of flagrant sexual behavior. This form of dementia was originally known as **Pick's disease**, after the doctor who discovered abnormal structures now called *Pick's bodies* in the brains of some dementia patients. Diagnosis is confirmed only upon autopsy by the *absence* of the neurofibrillary tangles and plaques that are found in AD and by the presence of Pick's bodies in nerve cells. Pick's disease is believed to account for about 6% to 12% of all dementias (Kertesz, 2006). Unlike AD, the disease usually begins in middle age rather than late adulthood, but it occasionally affects young adults in their 20s (Love & Spillantini, 2011). The risk declines with advancing age after 70. Men are more likely than women to suffer from Pick's disease. Pick's disease often runs in families, and evidence points to a genetic component (Love & Spillantini, 2011).

**NEUROCOGNITIVE DISORDER DUE TO TRAUMATIC BRAIN INJURY** Head trauma resulting from jarring, banging, or cutting brain tissues, usually because of accident or assault, can injure the brain, sometimes severely so. Progressive dementia due to traumatic brain injury is more likely to result from multiple head traumas (as in the case of boxers who receive multiple blows to the head during their careers) than from a single blow or head trauma. Football players face a heightened risk of brain damage because of repetitive head injuries on the field. A widely cited study by the National Football League (NFL) found that reports of dementia and significant memory problems among retired football players were much higher than the rate in the general population (Schwarz, 2009). Another recent study found early signs of a degenerative brain condition in retired NFL players who had suffered concussions (Barrio et al., 2015). It's not just professional athletes who are at risk: According to a recent study, college football players had reduced volume in

**HEADED TOWARD DEMENTIA?**
A National Football League (NFL) study showed that former professional football players said they were diagnosed with Alzheimer's or other memory-related diseases at a much higher than average rate. Multiple blows to the head on the playing field may lead to dementia and other types of cognitive impairment.

parts of the brain involved in memory formation, and the more years they played, the greater the reductions (Singh et al., 2014).

Although risks of brain damage are greater with multiple head injuries, even a single head trauma can have psychological effects leading to neurocognitive disorder. If severe enough, a traumatic brain injury can lead to physical disability or death. Specific changes in personality following traumatic injury to the brain vary with the site and extent of the injury, among other factors. Damage to the frontal lobe, for example, is associated with a range of emotional changes involving alterations of mood and personality.

**Amnesia** (memory loss) frequently follows a traumatic event, such as a blow to the head, an electric shock, or a major surgical operation. A head injury may prevent people from remembering events that occurred shortly before the accident. An automobile accident victim may not remember anything that transpired after getting into the car. A football player who develops amnesia from a blow to the head during the game may not remember anything after leaving the locker room. In some cases, people retain memories of the remote past but lose those of recent events. For example, people with amnesia may be more likely to remember events from their childhood than last evening's dinner. Consider the following case.

## Who Is She?:

### A CASE OF AMNESIA

A medical student was rushed to the hospital after he was thrown from a motorcycle. His parents were with him in his hospital room when he awakened. As his parents were explaining what had happened to him, the door suddenly flew open and his flustered wife, whom he had married a few weeks earlier, rushed into the room, leaped onto his bed, began to caress him, and expressed her great relief that he was not seriously injured. After several minutes of expressing her love and reassurance, his wife departed and the flustered student looked at his mother and asked, "Who is she?"

**SOURCE:** *Adapted from Freemon, 1981, p. 96*

## TRUTH *or* FICTION

After a motorcycle accident, a medical student failed to recognize the woman he had married a few weeks earlier.

☑ TRUE After the accident, the student failed to recognize his wife of a few weeks, although he remembered his parents.

The medical student's long-term memory loss included memories dating not only to the accident but also farther back to the time before he was married or had met his wife. Like most victims of posttraumatic amnesia, the medical student recovered his memory fully. **T / F**

There are two general types of amnesia—**retrograde amnesia** (loss of memory of past events and personal information) and **anterograde amnesia** (inability or difficulty forming or storing new memories). A football player who does not remember anything after leaving the locker room has retrograde amnesia, but some cases are reported in the medical annals of people for whom information literally "goes in one ear and out the other" because they are unable to form new memories. These patients are experiencing anterograde amnesia. Problems with forming new memories may be revealed by an inability to remember the names of, or to recognize, people whom the person met 5 or 10 minutes earlier. Immediate memory, as measured by ability to repeat back a series of numbers, seems to be unimpaired in states of amnesia. The person is unlikely to remember the number series later, no matter how often it is rehearsed.

In a famous medical case, an epileptic patient known by the initials H.M. developed anterograde amnesia as a complication of surgery performed to control his seizures (Carey, 2009a). After the surgery, he became unable to learn any new information. Every time he would visit a store, it would be as if it were the first time. He would meet a new acquaintance time after time but would never recall having met the person before. He was quoted as saying, "Every day is alone by itself, whatever enjoyment I have had, whatever sorrow I have had."

People with amnesia may experience disorientation, more commonly involving disorientation to place (not knowing where one is at the time) and time (not knowing the day, month, and year) than disorientation to person (not knowing one's own name). They may not be aware of their memory loss or may attempt to deny or mask their memory deficits even when evidence of their impairment is presented to them. They may attempt to fill the gaps in their memories with imaginary events, or they may admit they have a memory problem but appear apathetic about it, showing a kind of emotional blandness.

Although amnesia patients may suffer profound memory losses, their general intelligence tends to remain within a normal range. In contrast, in progressive dementias such as AD, both memory and intellectual functioning deteriorate. Early detection and diagnosis of the causes of memory problems are critical because they are often curable if the underlying cause is treated successfully.

**H.M.** A patient with anterograde amnesia identified as H.M. in the neurology annals was among the most studied cases in medical history. The patient, Henry Molaison, pictured here outside his home in the 1970s, died in 2008. Had you met Henry and then walked away for a few minutes, he would later greet you as though he were meeting you for the first time.

In addition to brain trauma, other causes of amnesia include brain surgery; **hypoxia**, or sudden loss of oxygen to the brain; brain infection or disease; **infarction**, or blockage of the blood vessels supplying the brain; and chronic, heavy use of certain psychoactive substances, most commonly alcohol.

**SUBSTANCE/MEDICATION-INDUCED NEUROCOGNITIVE DISORDER** The use of, or withdrawal from, psychoactive substances or medications can impair brain functioning in many ways, leading to minor or major neurocognitive disorder. The most common example is **Korsakoff's syndrome**, which involves irreversible memory loss due to brain damage resulting from deficiency of vitamin B1 (thiamine). The disorder is associated with chronic alcoholism because people who abuse alcohol tend to take poor care of their nutritional needs and may not follow a diet rich enough in vitamin B1, or their alcohol-soaked livers may not be able to metabolize the vitamin efficiently. The memory deficits persist even years after the person stops drinking. However, Korsakoff's syndrome is not limited to people with chronic alcoholism. It has been reported in other groups that experience thiamine deficiencies during times of deprivation, such as prisoners of war.

People with Korsakoff's syndrome have major gaps in their memory of past experiences and significant difficulty learning new information. Despite their memory losses, patients with Korsakoff's syndrome may retain their general level of intelligence. They are often described as being superficially friendly but lacking in insight, unable to discriminate between actual events and wild stories they invent to fill the gaps in their memories. They sometimes become grossly disoriented and confused and require custodial care.

Korsakoff's syndrome often follows an acute attack of **Wernicke's disease**, another brain disorder caused by thiamine deficiency that occurs most often among people with alcoholism (Charness, 2009). Wernicke's disease is marked by confusion and disorientation; **ataxia**, or difficulty maintaining balance while walking; and paralysis of the muscles that control eye movements. These symptoms may pass, but a person is often left with Korsakoff's syndrome and enduring memory impairment. However, if Wernicke's disease is treated promptly with major doses of vitamin B1, Korsakoff's syndrome may not develop.

**ROBIN WILLIAMS.** The news of the suicide of famed entertainer Robin Williams in 2014 came as a shock to his many millions of fans. Williams was reported to have suffered from Lewy body dementia and depression. He gave no indications of his impending suicide.

**NEUROCOGNITIVE DISORDER WITH LEWY BODIES** Neurocognitive disorder due to Lewy body dementia is the second most common form of progressive dementia, after Alzheimer's disease, affecting about 1.3 million Americans (NINDS, 2012; ScienceDaily, 2014c). It accounts for about 10% of dementias in older adults. The disease has features of both AD and Parkinson's. **Lewy bodies** are abnormal protein deposits that form within the nucleus of cells in parts of the brain, disrupting brain processes that control memory and motor control. The distinguishing features of the disorder, in addition to profound cognitive decline similar to that of AD, is the appearance of fluctuating alertness and attention, marked by frequent periods of drowsiness and staring into space, as well as recurrent visual hallucinations and rigid body movements and stiff muscles typical of Parkinson's disease.

**BATTLING PARKINSON'S DISEASE.** Actor Michael J. Fox has been waging a personal battle against Parkinson's disease and has brought national attention to the need to fund research efforts to develop more effective treatments for this degenerative brain disease.

People with Lewy body dementia may also suffer from depression. The disease usually develops between the ages of 50 and 85, and unfortunately there is no cure, nor do scientists know why Lewy bodies accumulate in brain cells in some people.

**NEUROCOGNITIVE DISORDER DUE TO PARKINSON'S DISEASE** **Parkinson's disease** is a slowly progressing neurological disease of unknown cause affecting 500,000 to 1 million people in the United States, including such notable figures as former heavyweight champion Muhammad Ali and actor Michael J. Fox. The disease affects men and women about equally, most often strikes between the ages of 50 and 69, and affects more than 1% of people over 65 years. Dementia often occurs in Parkinson's disease, with estimates indicating that nearly 80% of Parkinson's disease patients will eventually develop dementia over the course of the illness (Shulman, 2010).

Parkinson's disease is characterized by uncontrollable shaking or tremors, rigidity, disturbances in posture (leaning forward), and lack of control over body movements. People with Parkinson's disease may be able to control their shaking or tremors, but only briefly. Some cannot walk at all. Others walk laboriously, in a crouch. Some execute voluntary body movements with difficulty, have poor control over fine motor movements, such as finger control, and have sluggish reflexes. They may look expressionless, as if they were wearing masks, a symptom that apparently reflects the degeneration of brain tissue that controls facial muscles. It is particularly difficult for patients to engage in sequences of complex movements, such as those required to sign their names. People with Parkinson's disease may be unable to coordinate two movements at the same time, as seen in this description of a Parkinson's patient who had difficulty walking and reaching for his wallet at the same time.

## Motor Impairment:

### A CASE OF PARKINSON'S DISEASE

A 58-year-old man was walking across the hotel lobby in order to pay his bill. He reached into his inside jacket pocket for his wallet. He stopped walking instantly as he did so and stood immobile in the lobby in front of strangers. He became aware of his suspended locomotion and resumed his stroll to the cashier; however, his hand remained rooted in his inside pocket, as though he were carrying a weapon he might display once he arrived at the cashier.

**SOURCE:** *Adapted from Knight, Godfrey, & Shelton (1988)*

Parkinson's disease involves the loss, due to unknown causes, of dopamine-producing nerve cells in the *substantia nigra* ("black substance"), an area of the brain that helps regulate body movement (Laguna et al., 2015; Palfreman, 2015). The underlying cause is unknown, but scientists suspect it involves an interaction between genetic influences and possible environmental factors, such as exposure to certain toxins (Dai et al., 2012; Mortiboys et al., 2015; NIH Research Matters, 2015). According to one expert, "Dopamine is like the oil in the engine of a car.... If the oil is there, the car runs smoothly. If not, it seizes up" (cited in Carroll, 2004, p. F5).

Despite the severity of motor disability, cognitive functions seem to remain intact during the early stages of the disease. Dementia is more common in the later stages or among those with more severe forms of the disease. The form of dementia associated with Parkinson's disease typically involves a slowing down of thinking processes, impaired ability to think abstractly or to plan or organize a series of actions, and difficulty in retrieving memories. Overall, the cognitive impairments associated with Parkinson's disease tend to be more subtle than those associated with AD. Parkinson's patients often become depressed (Torbey, Pachana, & Dissanayaka, 2015), perhaps because of the demands of coping with the disease or possibly due to underlying disturbances in the brain associated with the disease.

Whatever the underlying cause or causes of the disease may be, the symptoms of Parkinson's—the uncontrollable tremors, shaking, rigid muscles, and difficulty in walking—are tied to deficiencies in the amount of dopamine in the brain (Sahin & Kirik, 2012). The drug L-dopa, which increases dopamine levels, brought hope to Parkinson's patients when it was introduced in the 1970s. L-dopa is converted in the brain into dopamine (Devos, Moreau, & Destée, 2009).

Parkinson's remains an incurable and progressive disease, but L-dopa can help control the symptoms of the disease and slow its progress. After a few years of treatment, L-dopa begins to lose its effectiveness, and the disease continues to progress. Several other drugs are in the experimental stage, offering hope for further advances in treatment. Other sources of hope come from genetic studies that may one day lead to an effective gene therapy for Parkinson's disease and from experimental use of electrical stimulation of deep brain structures (Rezai et al., 2011; Weaver et al., 2009). Investigators report that deep brain electrical stimulation may help block tremors in some Parkinson patients (Schuepbach et al., 2013; Tanner, 2013).

**NEUROCOGNITIVE DISORDER DUE TO HUNTINGTON'S DISEASE** **Huntington's disease**, also known as *Huntington's chorea*, was first recognized by the neurologist George Huntington in 1872. In Huntington's disease, there is progressive deterioration of the basal ganglia, a part of the brain that helps regulate body movement and posture.

The most prominent physical symptoms of the disease are involuntary, jerky movements of the face (grimaces), neck, limbs, and trunk—in contrast to the poverty of movement that typifies Parkinson's disease. These twitches carry the label of *choreiform*, a word that derives from the Greek root *choreia*, meaning *dance*. Unstable moods, alternating with states of apathy, anxiety, and depression, are common in the early stages of the disease. As the disease progresses, paranoia may develop, and people may become "suicidally" depressed. Difficulties retrieving memories in the early course of the disease may later develop into dementia. Eventually, there is loss of control of bodily functions, leading to death occurring typically within 15 to 20 years after the onset of the disease ("Huntington's Disease Advance," 2011).

Huntington's disease afflicts about one in 10,000 people in the United States or about 30,000 in total ("A Step toward Controlling," 2011). The disease typically begins in the prime of adulthood, between the ages of 30 and 45. One of the victims of the disease was the famed folksinger Woody Guthrie, who gave us the beloved song "This Land Is Your Land," among many others. He died of Huntington's disease in 1967, after 22 years of battling the malady. Because of the odd, jerky movements associated with the disease, Guthrie, like many other Huntington's victims, was misdiagnosed as suffering from alcoholism. He spent several years in mental hospitals before the correct diagnosis was made. **T / F**

## TRUTH or FICTION

A famous folksinger and songwriter was misdiagnosed with alcoholism and spent several years in mental hospitals until the correct diagnosis was made.

☑ TRUE The folksinger and songwriter was Woody Guthrie, whose Huntington's disease went misdiagnosed for years.

Huntington's disease is caused by a genetic defect on a single gene (Chung et al., 2011). The defective gene produces abnormal protein deposits in nerve cells in the brain (Biglan et al., 2012; Tsunemi et al., 2012). The disease is transmitted genetically from either parent to children of either gender. People who have a parent with Huntington's disease stand a 50% chance of inheriting the gene. People who inherit the gene eventually contract the disease. Although there is no cure or effective treatment, scientists are attempting to block or counteract the effects of the defective gene, raising hopes for a potential breakthrough treatment (Aronin & Moore, 2012; Olson et al., 2011; Song et al., 2011).

A genetic test can determine whether a person carries the defective gene that causes Huntington's disease. Whether or not a person who has a parent with Huntington's undergoes genetic testing is a controversial and personally poignant question, as we explore in *Thinking Critically: The Danger Lurking Within—Would You Want to Know?* on page 555.

**NEUROCOGNITIVE DISORDER DUE TO HIV INFECTION** The human immunodeficiency virus (HIV), which causes AIDS, can invade the central nervous system and cause a minor or major neurocognitive disorder. The major cognitive effects of HIV infection include forgetfulness, impaired concentration, and problem-solving ability. Dementia is rare in people with HIV who have not yet developed full-blown AIDS. Common behavioral features of dementia associated with HIV disease are apathy and social withdrawal. As AIDS progresses, the dementia grows more severe, taking the form of delusions, disorientation, further impairments in memory and thinking processes, and perhaps even delirium. In its later stages, the dementia may resemble the profound deficiencies found among people with advanced AD (Clifford et al., 2009).

**NEUROCOGNITIVE DISORDER DUE TO PRION DISEASE** Prions are protein molecules found normally in body cells. In the case of prion disease, abnormal clusters of prions form and become infectious, converting other prion molecules to assume an abnormal, infectious form. Prion disease can cause brain damage when clusters of abnormal prion molecules spread within the brain. The best known example of prion disease is *Creutzfeldt-Jakob disease*, a rare but fatal brain disease. It is characterized by the formation of small cavities in the brain that resemble the holes in a sponge. The disease causes brain damage, which commonly results in dementia (major neurocognitive disorder). Symptoms of the disease usually begin in the late 50s. There are no treatments for the disease, and death usually results within months of the onset of symptoms. Most forms of Creutzfeldt-Jakob disease occur without any apparent cause, but in rare cases a genetic cause (inheriting an abnormal prion from a parent) is suspected. A variant of Creutzfeldt-Jakob disease is related to *mad cow disease*, a fatal illness spread by eating infected beef. **T / F**

### TRUTH *or* FICTION

A form of dementia is linked to mad cow disease.

☑ **TRUE** A form of dementia is caused by the human form of mad cow disease.

# Psychological Disorders Related to Aging

Many physical changes occur with aging. Changes in calcium metabolism cause the bones to grow brittle and heighten the risk of breaks from falls. The skin grows less elastic, creating wrinkles and folds. The senses become less keen, so older people see and hear less acutely. Older people need more time (called *reaction time*) to respond to stimuli, whether they are driving or taking intelligence tests. For example, older drivers require more time to react to traffic signals and other cars. The immune system functions less effectively with increasing age, so people become more vulnerable to illness.

Cognitive changes occur as well. It is normal for people in later life to experience some decline in memory functioning and general cognitive ability, as measured by tests of intelligence, or IQ tests. The decline is sharpest on timed items, such as the performance subtests of the Wechsler Adult Intelligence Scale (discussed in Chapter 3). Some abilities, such as vocabulary and accumulated store of knowledge, hold up well and may actually improve over time. However, people typically experience some reduction in memory as they age, especially memory for names or recent events. Apart from the occasional social embarrassment resulting from forgetting a person's name, in most cases cognitive declines do not significantly interfere with a person's ability to meet social or occupational responsibilities. Declines in cognitive functioning may also be offset to a certain extent by increased knowledge and life experience.

**WHAT CHANGES TAKE PLACE AS WE AGE, AND HOW DO THEY AFFECT OUR MOODS?** Although some declines in cognitive and physical functioning are connected with aging, older adults who remain active and engage in rewarding activities can be highly satisfied with their lives.

The important point here is that dementia is not the result of normal aging. Rather, it is a sign of degenerative brain disease. Screening and testing for neurological and neuropsychological deficits can help distinguish dementias from normal aging processes. Generally speaking, the decline in intellectual functioning in dementia is more rapid and severe.

## THINKING CRITICALLY about abnormal psychology

### @ISSUE: THE DANGER LURKING WITHIN—WOULD YOU WANT TO KNOW?

Until recently, children of patients with Huntington's disease had to wait until they developed symptoms themselves—usually in midlife—to know whether they had inherited the disease. A genetic test is now available that can detect carriers of the defective gene, those who will eventually develop the disease should they live long enough. Eventually, perhaps, genetic engineering may provide a means of modifying the defective gene or its effects. Because researchers have not yet developed ways to cure or control Huntington's disease, some potential carriers prefer not to know whether they have inherited the gene. A famous example is Arlo Guthrie, a folksinger like his father, Woody Guthrie, who is best remembered for the classic song, "This Land Is Your Land, This Land Is My Land," and who died from the disease in 1967. Arlo preferred not to know whether he carried the gene and never underwent genetic testing. Fortunately, he escaped his father's fate.

If you were in Arlo's position, would you want to know if you had inherited Huntington's? Or would you prefer keeping yourself in the dark and living your life as best you could?

What about AD? Would you want to know if you have AD or are carrying genes that put you at heightened risk? New brain-scanning technology makes it possible to diagnose the disease, but the effects of learning that you have Alzheimer's can be emotionally devastating. Without any effective treatment or means of slowing it down, is it worth knowing? People with positive brain scans for Alzheimer's also stand the risk of being denied long-term care insurance (Kolata, 2012). However, proponents of testing argue that providing information can help remove uncertainty, help people prepare as best they can, and identify candidates for experimental treatment programs that may lead to advances in treatment or prevention. When asked, most people in a recent study said they would prefer not knowing whether AD is imprinted in their genes (Miller, 2012).

In thinking critically about these questions, you may wish to challenge some common assumptions, such as the idea that knowledge is necessarily better than ignorance. Gaining knowledge is valuable when it can help stave off or limit the impact of disease, but what if the knowledge carries no health benefits? Might ignorance be better than knowledge? Deciding on genetic testing for defective genes is a personal choice, but controversy arises over whether people who may be potential carriers of genetic diseases have an ethical or moral responsibility to determine their genetic risk before deciding whether or not to bear children. We pose the question to encourage you to examine the issue critically. Do you believe that people at genetic risk have an obligation to determine their genetic risk before becoming parents? Going further, should people who discover they are carrying a potentially lethal or disabling gene be morally (or perhaps legally) obliged not to bear children?

**WOULD YOU WANT TO KNOW?** Folksinger Arlo Guthrie decided he did not. What do you think you would do if you had been in Arlo's place?

How might you look at this question differently if you were a fundamentalist Christian, an orthodox Jew, or a practicing Buddhist or Muslim?

Genetics plays an important role in many diseases discussed in this chapter, such as Parkinson's disease and AD. Genes are also implicated in many physical conditions, such as Tay-Sachs disease, sickle-cell disease, and cystic fibrosis. As we gain more knowledge and the ability to determine whether people carry many different conditions, insurance companies might require expectant parents to undergo genetic testing. Knowledge about the genetic causes of devastating diseases has deep ramifications for society.

In thinking critically about the issue, answer the following questions:

- Should people be required to be tested for genetic defects?
- Should we be required to reveal our relative risk of developing a wide range of diseases as a condition for obtaining health insurance or for getting a job? What are the effects of requiring such disclosure? Of not requiring it?

All told, about one in five older adults suffers from a mental disorder, including dementia as well as anxiety and mood disorders (Karel, Gatz, & Smyer, 2012). Here, we focus on several of these disorders, beginning with anxiety disorders, the most commonly experienced type of psychological disorder affecting older adults.

## Questionnaire

### EXAMINING YOUR ATTITUDES TOWARD AGING

What are your assumptions about late adulthood? Do you see older people as basically different from the young in their behavior patterns and their outlooks or just as more mature?

To evaluate the accuracy of your attitudes toward aging, mark each of the following items *true* or *false*, then turn to the answer key at the end of the chapter.

| | True | False |
|---|---|---|
| 1. By age 60, most couples have lost their capacity for satisfying sexual relations. | ____ | ____ |
| 2. Older people cannot wait to retire. | ____ | ____ |
| 3. With advancing age, people become more externally oriented, less concerned with the self. | ____ | ____ |
| 4. As individuals age, they become less able to adapt satisfactorily to a changing environment. | ____ | ____ |
| 5. General satisfaction with life tends to decrease as people become older. | ____ | ____ |
| 6. As people age, they tend to become more homogeneous; that is, all old people tend to be alike in many ways. | ____ | ____ |
| 7. For the older person, having a stable intimate relationship is no longer highly important. | ____ | ____ |
| 8. The aged are susceptible to a wider variety of psychological disorders than young and middle-aged adults. | ____ | ____ |
| 9. Most older people are depressed much of the time. | ____ | ____ |
| 10. Church attendance increases with age. | ____ | ____ |
| 11. The occupational performance of the older worker is typically less effective than that of the younger adult. | ____ | ____ |
| 12. Most older people are just not able to learn new skills. | ____ | ____ |
| 13. Compared to younger people, older people tend to think more about the past than about the present or the future. | ____ | ____ |
| 14. Most people in later life are unable to live independently and reside in nursing homes or similar institutions. | ____ | ____ |

**SOURCE:** Adapted from Nevid & Rathus (2013). *Psychology and the challenges of life: Adjustment and modern life* (12th ed.), p. 484. Hoboken, NJ: John Wiley and Sons. Reprinted with permission.

## TRUTH *or* FICTION

Anxiety-related disorders are the most common psychological disorders among older adults, even more common than depression.

☑ TRUE Problems relating to anxiety are the most common psychological disorders affecting older adults.

## Anxiety and Aging

**14.7 Identify anxiety-related disorders and their treatments in older adults.**

Although anxiety disorders may develop at any point in life, they tend to be less prevalent among older adults than among their younger counterparts. Still, anxiety disorders are the most commonly occurring psychological disorder among older adults, even more common than depression. Approximately one in 10 adults over the age of 55 suffer from a diagnosable anxiety disorder (USDHHS, 1999). Older women are more likely than older men to be affected by anxiety disorders (Bryant, Jackson, & Ames, 2008). **T / F**

The most frequently occurring anxiety-related disorders among older adults are generalized anxiety disorder (GAD) and phobic disorders. Although less common, panic disorder occurs in about one in 100 older adults (Chou, 2010). Most cases of agoraphobia affecting older adults tend to be of recent origin and may involve the loss of social support systems due to the death of a spouse or close friends. Then again, some older individuals who are frail may have realistic fears of falling on the street and may be misdiagnosed as agoraphobic if they refuse to leave the house alone. Generalized anxiety disorder may arise from the perception that one lacks control over one's life, which may be the case for older people contending with infirmity, loss of friends and loved ones, and lessened economic opportunities. Social anxiety disorder (also called social phobia) affects about 2% to 5% of older adults but does not appear to have a significant impact on the quality of late adulthood (Chou, 2009).

Antianxiety drugs such as benzodiazepines (Valium is one) and SSRI antidepressants (Zoloft, for example) are often used to treat anxiety disorders in older adults (Alaka et al., 2014; Wetherell et al., 2013). Psychological interventions, such as cognitive-behavioral therapy, show therapeutic benefits in treating anxiety in older adults but do not carry the risks of drug side effects or potential dependence (Mohlman, 2012; Zou et al., 2012).

# Depression and Aging

**14.8 Identify factors associated with depression in late adulthood and ways of treating it.**

Depression is a common problem affecting many older adults, especially those with a prior history of depression (Reppermund et al., 2011). For many older adults, late-life depression often involves a continuation of a lifelong pattern.

Estimates are that between 1% and 5% of older adults are currently suffering from a diagnosable major depressive episode (Fiske, Wetherell, & Gatz, 2009; Luijendijk et al., 2008). A much higher proportion of older adults, estimated to be as many as one in three, currently suffer from depressive symptoms that may not warrant a diagnosis but are significant enough to interfere with their quality of life (Meeks et al., 2011). Depression is higher among some groups of older adults, such as residents of nursing homes. Despite the fact that fewer older adults suffer from major depression than do younger adults, suicide is more frequent among older adults, especially among older white males (see Chapter 7; Bruce et al., 2004; Eddleston, 2006). Another reason for concern is that clinically significant depression that worsens over time in older adults is linked to increased risk of later development of dementia (Kaup et al., 2016).

Older people of color often carry an especially heavy stress burden. In one study, a sample of 127 elderly African Americans recruited from senior citizens' programs in two large urban centers in the northeastern United States were administered measures of race-related stress, satisfaction with life, and health concerns (Utsey et al., 2002). The investigators found that men reported experiencing higher levels of institutional and collective forms of racism than women did. The investigators commented that they weren't surprised by these findings, as African American men have traditionally been subjected to harsher experiences of societal racism and oppression. Going further, the investigators reported that institutional race-related stress was associated with poorer psychological well-being. Many of the elderly men in this sample had experienced institutional racism (i.e., government-sanctioned discrimination in housing, education, employment, health care, and public policy) during their early and middle lives. This study contributes to a growing body of literature showing links between race-related stress and mental health functioning of African Americans.

**AGORAPHOBIA OR A NEED FOR SUPPORT?** Some older adults may refuse to venture away from home on their own because of realistic fears of falling in the street. They may be in need of social support, not therapy.

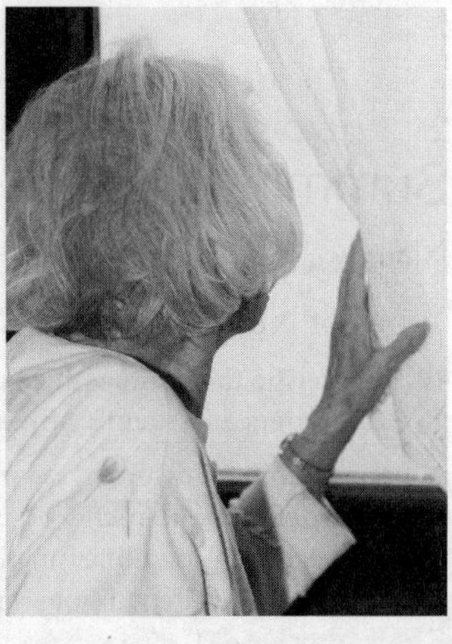

Other investigators have examined the role of acculturative stress in older adults from immigrant groups. A study of Mexican American older adults showed that those who were minimally acculturated to U.S. society had higher rates of depression than either highly acculturated or bicultural individuals (Zamanian et al., 1992).

Depressive disorders often occur in people suffering from various brain disorders, such as AD, Parkinson's disease, and stroke, which disproportionately affect older people (e.g., Bomasang-Layno et al., 2015; Even & Weintraub, 2012; Richard et al., 2012). In the case of Parkinson's disease, depression may result not only from coping with the disease but also from neurobiological changes in the brain caused by the disease.

Social support can help buffer the effects of stress, bereavement, and illness, thereby reducing the risk of depression. Social support is especially important to older people who are challenged because of physical disability. Participation in volunteer or religious organizations may also provide a sense of meaning and purpose as well as a needed social outlet.

Older people may be especially vulnerable to depression because of the stress of coping with life changes: retirement; physical illness or incapacitation; placement in a

**LATE-LIFE DEPRESSION.** Many older adults struggle with clinical depression. What factors contribute to depression in late adulthood?

residential facility or nursing home; the deaths of a spouse, siblings, lifetime friends, and acquaintances; or the need to care for a spouse whose health is declining. Retirement, whether voluntary or forced, may lead to a loss of role identity. Deaths of relatives and friends induce grief and remind older people of their own advanced age as well as reduce the availability of social support. Older adults may feel incapable of forming new friendships or finding new goals in life. The chronic strain of coping with a family member with AD can lead to depression in the caregiver, even without any prior vulnerability to depression (Mittelman et al., 2004).

Despite the prevalence of depression in older people, physicians often fail to recognize it or to treat it appropriately (Bosanquet et al., 2015). Health care providers may be less likely to recognize depression in older people because they tend to focus more on the older patient's physical complaints and because depression in older people is often masked by physical complaints and sleeping problems.

The good news about geriatric depression is that effective treatments are available, including antidepressant medication, cognitive-behavioral therapy, and interpersonal psychotherapy (e.g., Lavretsky et al., 2015; Sheline et al., 2012; Scogin & Shah, 2012; Thorlund et al., 2015; Titov et al., 2015). Evidence of treatment effectiveness should put to rest the erroneous belief that psychotherapy or psychiatric medication is not appropriate for people in late adulthood (Taylor, 2014). Moreover, the memory impairment that often accompanies late-life depression may lift once the underlying depression is resolved.

## Sleep Problems and Aging

**14.9 Identify factors involved in late-life insomnia and ways of treating it.**

Sleep problems are common among older people, affecting upwards of 50% of older adults (McCall & Winkelman, 2015). Insomnia is the most common sleep problem affecting older adults, and is actually more prevalent than depression. Sleep problems in older adults are often linked to other psychological disorders, such as depression, dementia, and anxiety disorders, as well as medical illness. Psychosocial factors, such as loneliness and the related difficulty of sleeping alone after the loss of a spouse, are also implicated in many cases. Dysfunctional thoughts, such as excessive concerns about lack of sleep and perceptions of hopelessness and helplessness about controlling sleep, are another contributor to sleep problems in later life.

Sleep medications are often used in treating late-life insomnia, but they can cause side effects and lead to dependence, as they can in younger adults (McCall & Winkelman, 2015). Fortunately, behavioral approaches, similar to those described in Chapter 9 provide a safe and effective alternative, producing therapeutic benefits that are as good as, if not better than, sleep medications and without risks of side effects or drug dependence (Bélanger, LeBlanc, & Morin, 2011; Bootzin & Epstein, 2011; Buysse et al., 2011). Moreover, older adults are as capable of benefiting from behavioral treatment as younger adults are.

# Summing Up

## Neurocognitive Disorders

### Types of Neurocognitive Disorders

**14.1 Describe the diagnostic features of neurocognitive disorders and identify three major types.**

A neurocognitive disorder involves a significant disturbance or deficit of thinking or memory that represents a marked decline in cognitive functioning. They are caused by physical or medical conditions or drug use or withdrawal affecting the functioning of the brain. The three major types identified in *DSM-5* are delirium, major neurocognitive disorder, and mild neurocognitive disorder.

### Delirium

**14.2 Describe the key features and causes of delirium.**

Delirium is a state of mental confusion characterized by symptoms such as impaired attention, disorientation, disorganized thinking and rambling speech, reduced level of consciousness, and perceptual disturbances. Delirium is most commonly caused by alcohol withdrawal, as in the form of DTs, but may also occur in hospitalized patients, especially after major surgery.

## Major Neurocognitive Disorder

**14.3 Describe the key features and causes of major neurocognitive disorder.**

Major neurocognitive disorder (e.g., dementia) is a significant cognitive deterioration or impairment, as evidenced by memory deficits, impaired judgment, personality changes, and disorders of higher cognitive functions, such as problem-solving ability and abstract thinking. Dementia is not a normal consequence of aging; rather, it is a sign of a degenerative brain disorder. There are various causes of major neurocognitive disorder, including Alzheimer's disease (AD) and Pick's disease, and brain infections and disorders.

## Mild Neurocognitive Disorder

**14.4 Describe the key features of mild neurocognitive disorder.**

Formerly called mild cognitive impairment (MCI), mild neurocognitive disorder refers to a milder decline in cognitive functioning. The person with the disorder is able to function but needs to expend greater effort or to use compensatory strategies to compensate for cognitive declines.

## Neurocognitive Disorder Due to Alzheimer's Disease

**14.5 Describe the key features and causes of Alzheimer's disease and evaluate current treatments.**

AD is a progressive brain disease characterized by progressive loss of memory and cognitive ability, as well as deterioration in personality functioning and self-care skills. There is neither a cure nor an effective treatment for AD. Currently available drug treatments offer only modest effects at best. Research into the causes of the disease points to roles for genetic factors and factors involved in the accumulation of amyloid plaques in the brain.

## Other Neurocognitive Disorders

**14.6 Identify other subtypes of neurocognitive disorders.**

Other medical conditions can lead to neurocognitive disorders, including vascular disease, Pick's disease, Parkinson's disease, Huntington's disease, prion disease, HIV infection, and head trauma.

# Psychological Disorders Related to Aging

## Anxiety and Aging

**14.7 Identify anxiety-related disorders and their treatments in older adults.**

Generalized anxiety disorder and phobic disorders are the most common anxiety disorders among older people. Problems with anxiety are often treated with antianxiety medical or psychological treatment, such as cognitive-behavioral therapy.

## Depression and Aging

**14.8 Identify factors associated with depression in late adulthood and ways of treating it.**

Factors include the challenge of coping with life changes, such as retirement, physical illness or incapacitation, placement in a residential facility or nursing home; lack of social support as the result of death of a spouse, siblings, lifetime friends, and acquaintances; and need to care for a spouse whose health is declining. Among immigrant groups and people of color, factors such as acculturative stress and coping with racism also play a role. Available treatments for depression in older as well as younger adults include antidepressant medication, cognitive-behavioral therapy, and interpersonal psychotherapy.

## Sleep Problems and Aging

**14.9 Identify factors involved in late-life insomnia and ways of treating it.**

Sleep problems, especially insomnia, are common among older adults—more common in fact than depression. Insomnia is often linked to other psychological disorders, medical illness, psychosocial factors such as loneliness and sleeping alone after losing a spouse, and dysfunctional thoughts. Behavioral techniques are effective for treating insomnia in older as well as younger adults.

# Critical Thinking Questions

Based on your reading of this chapter, answer the following questions:

- Do you expect people to develop dementia as they age? If so, what is the basis of your opinion?
- Why do you think depression is so common among older people? In what ways might depression be related to lowered role expectations placed on older people in our society? In what ways might society provide more meaningful social roles for people as they age?

- Should children be permitted to play physical contact sports that may lead to concussions or other head injuries? Why or why not? What precautions should be taken to protect children who participate in these sports?
- Have you known someone who was affected by AD? How was their behavior affected? What was done to help the person and the family? Do you think more could have been done or should have been done? Explain.

# Key Terms

neurocognitive disorders, p. 537
agnosia, p. 538
delirium, p. 540
major neurocognitive disorder, p. 541
general paresis, p. 542
late-onset dementia, p. 542
early-onset dementia, p. 542
mild neurocognitive disorder, p. 542
Alzheimer's disease (AD), p. 543
cerebrovascular accident (CVA), p. 548
vascular neurocognitive disorder, p. 549
aphasia, p. 549
Pick's disease, p. 549
amnesia, p. 550
retrograde amnesia, p. 550
anterograde amnesia, p. 550
hypoxia, p. 551
infarction, p. 551
Korsakoff's syndrome, p. 551
Wernicke's disease, p. 551
ataxia, p. 551
Lewy bodies, p. 551
Parkinson's disease, p. 552
Huntington's disease, p. 553

# Scoring Key for "Examining Your Attitudes toward Aging" Questionnaire

1. False. Most healthy couples continue to engage in satisfying sexual activities into their 70s and 80s.
2. False. This is too general a statement. Those who find their work satisfying are less anxious to retire.
3. False. In late adulthood, people tend to become more concerned with internal matters—their physical functioning and their emotions.
4. False. Adaptability remains reasonably stable throughout adulthood.
5. False. Age itself is not linked to noticeable declines in life satisfaction. Of course, people may respond negatively to disease and losses, such as the death of a spouse.
6. False. Although we can predict some general trends for older adults, we can also do so for younger adults. Older adults, like their younger counterparts, are heterogeneous in personality and behavior patterns.
7. False. Older adults with stable intimate relationships are more satisfied.
8. False. People are susceptible to a wide variety of psychological disorders at all ages.
9. False. Only a minority are depressed.
10. False. Actually, church attendance declines, but not verbally expressed religious beliefs.
11. False. Although reaction time may increase and general learning ability may undergo a slight decline, older adults usually have little or no difficulty at familiar work tasks. In most jobs, experience and motivation are more important than age.
12. False. Learning may just take a bit longer.
13. False. Older adults do not direct a higher proportion of thoughts toward the past than do younger people. Regardless of age, people may spend more time daydreaming if they have more time on their hands.
14. False. Fewer than 10% of older adults require some form of institutional care.

Chapter 15

# Abnormal Psychology and the Law

## Learning Objectives

**15.1** **Explain** the difference between civil commitment and criminal commitment.

**15.2** **Evaluate** the ability of mental health professionals to predict dangerousness.

**15.3** **Define** the duty to warn and **evaluate** the dilemma it poses for therapists.

**15.4** **Identify** major court cases establishing the rights of mental patients.

**15.5** **Describe** the history of the insanity defense, citing specific court cases and the guidelines proposed by the American Law Institute.

**15.6** **Describe** the legal basis for determining length of criminal commitment.

**15.7** **Describe** the legal basis for determining competency to stand trial.

## TRUTH or FICTION

T☐ F☐ People can be committed to psychiatric facilities because of odd or eccentric behavior. (p. 564)

T☐ F☐ Most people who are diagnosed with mental disorders commit violent crimes. (p. 567)

T☐ F☐ A surprisingly high percentage of violent crimes are committed by people with psychological disorders. (p. 569).

T☐ F☐ Therapists may not breach patient confidentiality, even when a patient makes a death threat against a specific person. (p. 570)

T☐ F☐ Patients in mental hospitals may be required to perform general housekeeping duties in a facility. (p. 572)

T☐ F☐ An attempt to assassinate the president of the United States was seen by millions of television viewers, but the would-be assassin was found not guilty by a court of law. (p. 574)

T☐ F☐ The insanity defense is used in a large number of trials, usually successfully. (p. 575)

T☐ F☐ People who are found not guilty of a crime by reason of insanity may be confined to a mental hospital for many years longer than they would have been sentenced to prison had they been found guilty. (p. 579)

T☐ F☐ A defendant may be held competent to stand trial but still be judged not guilty of a crime by reason of insanity. (p. 579)

**CHAPTER INTRODUCTION: ABNORMAL PSYCHOLOGY AND THE LAW**

### "I" "Point-Blank Range"

Congresswoman Gabrielle (Gabby) Giffords of Arizona was greeting constituents outside a supermarket on a sunny day in January 2011. A lone gunman approached from the rear. She had no warning and never saw the assailant. Shot through the head at point-blank range, Giffords was critically injured, but miraculously survived. Tragically, six bystanders were killed in the shooting and 13 others wounded. After her stay in a critical care facility, Giffords entered a rehabilitation facility, beginning a long and arduous process of recovery that is still ongoing. Yet she was able to return to the House of Representatives to receive the well-wishing of her colleagues and even led the Pledge of Allegiance at the 2012 Democratic National Convention. She later resigned from Congress to concentrate on her recovery, but she promised to return to public service at some point in the future.

What of the alleged shooter, 22-year-old Jared Loughner? A fellow student at the community college Loughner attended described him as a "troubled young man" whom no one wanted to sit next to in class (Lipton, Savage, & Shane, 2011). His behavior was so disturbing that his classmate wondered if he was taking hallucinogens. The portrait of Loughner that emerged in media reports was of an angry and deeply troubled young man who had become increasingly alienated from society and who displayed odd and even bizarre thoughts and behaviors. A series of short videos apparently posted on social media sites by Loughner were rambling and incoherent. In the videos, Loughner described himself as "treasurer of a new currency" and as controlling "English grammar structure." He also mentioned brainwashing and his belief that he had powers of mind control.

Appearing before a U.S. district court, Loughner was held to be incompetent to stand trial and remanded to a federal facility for further evaluation of his mental competency. Even his own attorneys described him as a "gravely mentally ill man" ("Ariz. Shooting Spree Suspect," 2011). We never had a formal determination of Loughner's mental status at the time of the shooting because he later pled guilty to the charges.

And what of James Holmes, the 24-year-old shooter in the movie theater massacre in 2012 in Aurora, Colorado, that left 12 people dead and 58 others wounded? Holmes reportedly received treatment from a University of Colorado psychiatrist while attending the university. In his first court appearance after the shooting, he appeared dazed and sported flaming orange hair. Although Holmes pleaded guilty by reason of insanity, the jury rejected his claim that he was legally insane at the time of the killings, finding him guilty for killing 12 people and wounding 70 others (CNN, 2015). He was sentenced to life in prison. Similarly, the insanity defense was rejected by the jury in the high-profile case in 2015 of Eddie Routh, who was convicted of the murder of two men, including Navy Seal Chris Kyle, whose life was featured in the movie *American Sniper* (Payne, Ford, & Morris, 2015).

The tragic events in Arizona and Colorado and in other mass murders highlight the interface between abnormal behavior and the law. They raise understandable concerns about the potential risks posed by people with severe mental disorders. What should society do when someone accused of a violent crime, even wanton killings, exhibits bizarre behavior, indicating a lack of mental competence to even understand the proceedings? What if the defendant can understand the proceedings and mount a credible defense, but claims the alleged criminal behavior is a product of a mental defect or disease? Should a defendant be held fully accountable regardless of his or her mental condition at the time of the act? Should someone judged not guilty by reason of insanity be punished by confinement in prison or treated in a mental institution, and for how long?

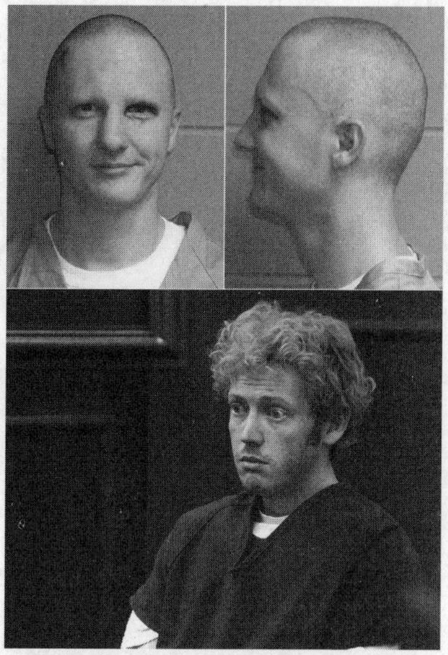

**JARED LOUGHNER (TOP) AND JAMES HOLMES (BOTTOM).** Punishment or treatment? Or both? What should society do about someone who is severely disturbed but commits a horrible crime?

In this chapter, we will discuss the insanity defense, its history in U.S. law, and the legal and moral arguments that underlie its use. We will also examine the legal rights of mental patients and the legal responsibility that falls on mental health care providers to warn third parties of threats made by patients. We will address questions that touch on the general issue of how to balance the rights of the individual with the rights of society. Do people who are obviously mentally disturbed have the right to refuse treatment? Do psychiatric institutions have the right to administer antipsychotic and other drugs to patients against their will? Should mental patients with a history of disruptive or violent behavior be hospitalized indefinitely or permitted to live in supervised residences in the community once their conditions are stabilized? When severely disturbed people break the law, should society respond to them with the criminal justice system or with the mental health system?

# Legal Issues in Mental Health Treatment

We begin our discussion of abnormal psychology and the law by examining the concept of civil or psychiatric commitment and the difference between civil commitment and criminal commitment. The commitment of individuals to psychiatric facilities without their consent brings into focus the interface between the rights of individuals and the rights of society. In Table 15.1, we list several landmark court cases that bear upon the rights of mental patients and society.

## Civil versus Criminal Commitment

**15.1 Explain the difference between civil commitment and criminal commitment.**

The legal placement of people in psychiatric institutions without their consent is called **civil commitment** (also called *psychiatric commitment*). Through civil commitment, individuals who are judged to be mentally ill and a threat to themselves or others can

**Table 15.1** Mental Health and the Law

| Case | Issue |
|---|---|
| *Durham v. United States*, 1954 | Insanity defense |
| *Wyatt v. Stickney*, 1972 | Minimum standard of care |
| *O'Connor v. Donaldson*, 1975 | Patients' rights |
| *Jackson v. Indiana*, 1972 | Competency to stand trial |
| *Tarasoff v. the Regents of the University of California*, 1976 | Duty to warn |
| *Rogers v. Okin*, 1979 | Right to refuse treatment |
| *Youngberg v. Romeo*, 1982 | Right to confinement in less-restrictive conditions |
| *Jones v. United States*, 1983 | Length of criminal commitment |
| *Medina v. California*, 1992 | Burden of proof for determining mental competency |
| *Sell v. United States*, 2003 | Forced medication of mentally ill defendants |

be involuntarily confined to psychiatric institutions to provide them with treatment and help ensure their own safety and that of others. Civil commitment should be distinguished from *voluntary hospitalization*, in which an individual voluntarily seeks treatment in a psychiatric institution and can, with adequate notice, leave the institution when she or he so desires. Even in such cases, however, when the hospital staff believes that a voluntary patient presents a threat to her or his own welfare or to others, they may petition the court to change the patient's legal status from voluntary to involuntary.

We also need to distinguish civil commitment from **criminal commitment**, in which an individual who is acquitted of a crime by reason of insanity is placed in a psychiatric institution for treatment. In criminal commitment, a defendant's unlawful act is judged by a court of law to result from a mental disorder or defect, and the defendant is committed to a psychiatric hospital where treatment can be provided rather than incarcerated in a prison.

Civil commitment in a psychiatric hospital usually requires that a relative or professional file a petition with the court, which empowers psychiatric examiners to evaluate a person. A judge hears the psychiatric testimony and decides whether or not to commit the individual. In the event of commitment, the law usually requires periodic legal review and recertification of the patient's involuntary status. The legal process is intended to ensure that people are not indefinitely "warehoused" in psychiatric hospitals. Hospital staff must demonstrate the need for continued inpatient treatment.

Legal safeguards protect people's civil rights in commitment proceedings. Defendants have the right to due process and to be assisted by an attorney, for example. However, when individuals are deemed to present a clear and imminent threat to themselves or others, the court may order immediate hospitalization until a formal commitment hearing can be held. Such emergency powers are usually limited to a specific period, usually 72 hours (Failer, 2002; Strachen, 2008). If a formal commitment petition is not filed with the court during this time, the individual has a right to be discharged.

Standards for psychiatric commitment have been tightened over the past generation, and the rights of individuals who are subject to commitment proceedings are more strictly protected. In the past, psychiatric abuses were more common. People were often committed without clear evidence that they posed a threat. Not until 1979, in fact, did the U.S. Supreme Court rule—in *Addington v. Texas*—that in order for individuals to be hospitalized involuntarily, they must be judged both to be mentally ill and to present a clear and present danger to themselves or others. Thus, people cannot be committed because of their odd behavior or eccentricity. **T / F**

## TRUTH *or* FICTION

People can be committed to psychiatric facilities because of odd or eccentric behavior.

☑ **FALSE** People cannot be committed because they are eccentric. The U.S. Supreme Court has determined that people must be judged mentally ill and present a clear and present danger to themselves or others to be committed to a psychiatric facility.

Few would argue that contemporary tightening of civil commitment laws protects the rights of the individual. Even so, some critics of the psychiatric system have called for the abolition of psychiatric commitment on the grounds that commitment deprives the individual of liberty in the name of therapy and that such a loss of liberty cannot be justified in a free society. Perhaps the most vocal and persistent critic of the civil commitment statutes was the psychiatrist Thomas Szasz, who died in 2012 (Szasz, 1970, 2003a, 2003b, 2007). Szasz argued that the label of *mental illness* is a societal invention that transforms social deviance into medical illness. In Szasz's view, people should not be deprived of their liberty because their behavior is perceived to be socially deviant or disruptive. Szasz likens involuntary hospitalization to institutional slavery (Szasz, 2003b). According to Szasz, people who violate the law should be prosecuted for criminal behavior, not confined to a psychiatric hospital. Although psychiatric commitment may prevent some individuals from acting violently, it does violence to many people who are innocent of any crime by depriving them of the fundamental right of liberty:

> The mental patient, we say, *may be* dangerous: he may harm himself or someone else. But we, society, *are* dangerous: we rob him of his good name and of his liberty, and subject him to tortures called "treatments."
>
> —*From Szasz, 1970*

> It is a fundamental principle of English and American law that only persons charged with and convicted of certain crimes are subject to imprisonment. Persons who respect other people's rights to life, liberty, and property have an inalienable right to their own life, liberty, and property.
>
> —*From Szasz, 2003a*

Szasz's strident opposition to institutional psychiatry and his condemnation of psychiatric commitment focused attention on abuses in the mental health system. Many people who have experienced psychiatric commitment rail against the practice.

Szasz was effective in persuading many professionals to question the legal, ethical, and moral bases of coercive psychiatric treatment in the forms of involuntary hospitalization and forced medication. Many caring and concerned professionals draw the line at abolishing psychiatric commitment, however. They argue that people may not be acting in their considered best interests when they threaten suicide or harm to others, or when their behavior becomes so disorganized that they cannot meet their basic needs (McMillan, 2003; Sayers, 2003). Most countries, including the United States and Canada, have laws that permit commitment of dangerous mentally ill people (Appelbaum, 2003). Yet the issue of psychiatric commitment continues to rouse debate, as we discuss in *Thinking Critically: What Should We Do About the "Wild Man of West 96th Street"?*

## THINKING CRITICALLY about abnormal psychology

### @ISSUE: WHAT SHOULD WE DO ABOUT THE "WILD MAN OF WEST 96TH STREET"?

The case of Larry Hogue touches on the problem of how society deals with the psychiatric homeless population. We first learned about Hogue—the "wild man of West 96th Street"—back in the early 1990s. Hogue was a homeless Vietnam War veteran who inhabited the alleyways and doorways of Manhattan's affluent Upper West Side. He went barefoot in winter, ate from garbage cans, and muttered to himself. He was described in newspaper reports as terrorizing the neighborhood, becoming especially violent when he smoked crack. Once, he was arrested for pushing a schoolgirl in front of a school bus (Shapiro, 1992). (Miraculously, she escaped injury.)

Hogue was shuttled in and out of state psychiatric hospitals and prisons more than 40 times. He popped up in the news again in 2009, having escaped from a Queens mental hospital and made his way back to West 96th Street in Manhattan, again frightening residents by his mere presence. As one resident told a reporter, "People called each other... saying, 'He's back.' Nobody, after 17 years, had to ask who" ("Wild Man," 2009).

We've lost track of Hogue, who sadly became the public face of the failure of the mental health system to care for people with severe and persistent mental illness who were left to fend for themselves on city streets. Larry Hogue became a national symbol of the many cracks in the system. There are many others like Hogue on our city streets and in rural towns throughout the country. For Hogue, the criminal justice, social services, and mental health systems were nothing but revolving doors. Typically, Hogue would improve during a brief hospital stay and be released, only to return to using crack instead of his psychiatric medication. His behavior would then deteriorate.

**THE WILD MAN OF WEST 96TH STREET.** Larry Hogue, the so-called wild man of West 96th Street in New York City, has become a symbol of the cracks in the mental health, criminal justice, and social services systems.

In 2008, the public spotlight focused again on the cracks in the mental health system in the wake of a vicious murder ("Queen's Man Arraigned," 2008). It also happened in New York, but it could have happened anywhere. The victim, Dr. Kathryn Faughey, a Manhattan psychologist, was found butchered to death in her office. She had been stabbed 15 times with a meat cleaver and a 9-inch knife. A suspect, David Tarloff, age 39, was soon arrested and held for trial. Tarloff appeared agitated and disturbed during his arraignment hearing. The police supplied a motive. Tarloff apparently came to the office to rob an office mate of the slain psychologist, another psychologist who had been treating him over the years. Tarloff told police he hadn't intended to harm Dr. Faughey and didn't realize at first that she was in the office. Later, the suspect's brother provided some background. The family, he told a reporter, had tried to get his brother help for many years. He had been hospitalized and released many times over the years. A neighbor of Tarloff described him as a "cuckoo" who had "some weird reactions from time to time."

Doesn't society have a right to protect itself from the likes of people like Hogue and Tarloff? What about those whose behavior may appear disturbed or deviant but who have not threatened or harmed others, such as people who sleep in the darkened corners of alleyways and over sidewalk heating vents, mumbling incoherently to themselves, but refusing psychiatric treatment?

Society certainly has a right to protect itself from people whose disturbed behavior causes physical harm to others or threatens harm. It may seem just as obvious that a humane society has the responsibility to provide care to people who seem unable to care for themselves. However, critics of the mental health system, such as Thomas Szasz, argue that by the very nature of a free society, people should be free to make their own decisions, even when those decisions are not in the best interests of their own health or welfare. Szasz argues that if they cause harm to others, or threaten harm, they should be subject to the criminal justice system, not psychiatric commitment.

Now let's extend the argument: If society has an obligation to protect individuals from themselves, as in the case of someone threatening suicide, does it not have a similar obligation to protect people whose behavior is harmful in other ways, such as those who smoke cigarettes, drink alcohol to excess, or become obese? Where would you draw that line?

And what about mental patients who commit violent crimes? Such cases, thankfully, are relatively uncommon, as only a small minority of people with mental disorders commit violent crimes. Later in the chapter, we consider the important question of whether mentally disturbed people who commit crimes should be held accountable, but first, let's discuss the more general issue of how to balance the rights of the individual with the rights of society and offer several questions that challenge us to think critically about these issues.

In thinking critically about the issue, answer the following questions:

- Do people in a free society have the right to live on the streets under unsanitary conditions?
- Do people who are obviously mentally disturbed have the right to refuse treatment?
- Should mental patients with a history of disruptive or violent behavior be hospitalized indefinitely or, once their conditions have stabilized, be permitted to live in supervised residences in the community?
- Do mentally ill people have a right to be left alone, so long as they do not break any laws? Or do you agree with psychiatrist E. Fuller Torrey and attorney Mary Zdanowicz (1999) that "for individuals whose brain is impaired by severe mental illness, defending their right to remain mentally ill is mindless"?
- When severely mentally disturbed people do break the law, should society respond to them with the criminal justice system or with the mental health system?

# Predicting Dangerousness

**15.2 Evaluate the ability of mental health professionals to predict dangerousness.**

Mental health professionals are often called on to judge whether patients are a danger to themselves or others as part of the legal proceedings to determine whether people should be involuntarily hospitalized or maintained involuntarily in the hospital. How accurate are the judgments of professionals when predicting dangerousness? Do professionals have special skills or clinical wisdom that renders their predictions accurate, or are their predictions no more accurate than those of laypeople? **T / F**

Unfortunately, psychologists and other mental health professionals who rely on their clinical judgments are not very accurate when it comes to predicting the dangerousness of the people they treat. Mental health professionals tend to overpredict dangerousness—that is, to label many individuals as dangerous when they are not. Clinicians tend to err on the side of caution in predicting the potential for dangerous behavior, perhaps because they believe that failure to predict violence may have more serious consequences than overprediction. However, overprediction of dangerousness does deprive many people of liberty. According to Szasz and other critics, the commitment of the many to prevent the violence of the few is a form of preventive detention that violates basic constitutional principles (Szasz, 2007).

## TRUTH or FICTION

Most people who are diagnosed with mental disorders commit violent crimes.

☑ **FALSE** Actually, only a small minority of people with mental disorders commit violent crimes.

The leading professional organizations, the American Psychological Association (1978) and the American Psychiatric Association (1998), have both gone on record as stating that neither psychologists nor psychiatrists, respectively, can reliably predict violent behavior. As a leading authority in the field, John Monahan of the University of Virginia, said, "When it comes to predicting violence, our crystal balls are terribly cloudy" (Rosenthal, 1993).

Clinician predictions are generally also less accurate than predictions based on evidence of past violent behavior (Odeh, Zeiss, & Huss, 2006). Basically, clinicians do not possess any special knowledge or ability for predicting violence beyond that of the average person. In fact, a layperson supplied with information concerning an individual's past violent behavior may predict the individual's potential for future violence more accurately than the clinician who bases a prediction solely on a clinical interview (Mossman, 1994). Unfortunately, although past violent behavior is the best predictor of future violence, hospital staff may not be permitted access to criminal records or may lack the time or resources to track down these records. The prediction problem has been cited by some as grounds for abandoning dangerousness as a criterion for civil commitment.

Why is predicting dangerousness so difficult? Investigators have identified a number of factors that lead to inaccurate predictions, including the following.

**THE POST HOC PROBLEM** Recognizing violent tendencies after a violent incident occurs (post hoc) is easier than predicting it beforehand. It is often said that hindsight is 20/20. Like Monday morning quarterbacking, it is easier to piece together fragments of people's prior behaviors as evidence of violent tendencies *after* they have committed acts of violence. Predicting a violent act before the fact is a more difficult task, however.

**THE PROBLEM IN LEAPING FROM THE GENERAL TO THE SPECIFIC** Generalized perceptions of violent tendencies may not predict specific acts of violence. Most people who have "general tendencies" toward violence never act on them. Nor is a diagnosis associated with aggressive or dangerous behavior, such as antisocial personality disorder, a sufficient basis for predicting specific violent acts by individuals.

**PROBLEMS IN DEFINING DANGEROUSNESS** One difficulty in predicting dangerousness is the lack of agreement over what types of behavior are violent or dangerous. Most people would agree that crimes such as murder, rape, and assault are acts of violence. There is less agreement, even among authorities, for labeling other acts—for example, driving recklessly, harshly criticizing one's spouse or children, destroying property, selling drugs, shoving into people at a tavern, or stealing cars—as violent or dangerous. Consider also the behavior of business owners and corporate executives who produce and market cigarettes despite widespread knowledge of the death and disease these substances cause. Clearly, the determination of which behaviors are regarded as dangerous involves moral and political judgments within a given social context.

**PREDICTING DANGEROUSNESS.** Should mental health professionals or school administrators have recognized signs of impending violence by Seung-Hui Cho, the man who went on a killing rampage at Virginia Tech? It is always easier after the fact to piece together fragments of a person's prior behaviors as signs of impending violent behavior. Predicting a violent act before it occurs is a much more difficult task, even for professionals.

**BASE-RATE PROBLEMS** The prediction of dangerousness is complicated by the fact that violent acts such as murder, assault, or suicide are infrequent within the general population, even if newspaper headlines sensationalize them regularly. Other rare events—such as earthquakes—are also difficult to predict with any degree of certainty concerning when or where they will strike.

The relative difficulty of making predictions about infrequent or rare events is known as the *base-rate problem.* Consider as an example the problem of suicide prediction. If the suicide rate in a given year has a low base rate of about 1% of a clinical population, the likelihood of accurately predicting that any given person in this population will commit suicide is very small. If you predicted that any given individual in this population would *not* commit suicide in a given year, you would be correct 99% of the time, but if you predict the nonoccurrence of suicide in every case, you would fail to predict the relatively few cases in which suicide does occur, even though virtually all your predictions would likely be correct. Therefore, predicting the one likely occurrence of suicide among those 100 people is likely to be tricky. When clinicians make predictions, they weigh the relative risks of a *false negative*—predicting that a violent behavior will not occur, but it does—and a *false positive*—predicting that a violent behavior will occur, but it does not. Clinicians often deliberately err on the side of the false positive and overpredict dangerousness. From their perspective, erring on the side of caution might seem like a no-lose situation. However, such a prediction practice results in many people being committed to an institution when they would not actually have acted violently against themselves or others, thereby denying them their liberty.

**THE UNLIKELIHOOD OF DISCLOSURE OF DIRECT THREATS OF VIOLENCE** How likely is it that truly dangerous people will disclose their violent intentions to a health professional who is evaluating them or to their own therapist? The client in therapy is not likely to inform a therapist of a clear threat, such as "I'm going to kill ________ next Wednesday morning." Threats are more likely to be vague and nonspecific, as in "I'm so sick of ________; I could kill her" or "I swear he's driving me to murder." In such cases, therapists must infer dangerousness from hostile gestures and veiled threats. Vague, indirect threats of violence are less reliable indicators of dangerousness than specific, direct threats.

**THE DIFFICULTY OF PREDICTING BEHAVIOR IN THE COMMUNITY FROM BEHAVIOR IN THE HOSPITAL** Mental health professionals fall well short of the mark when making long-term predictions of dangerousness. They are often wrong when predicting whether patients will become dangerous following release from the hospital. One reason is that they often base their predictions on patients' behavior in the hospital—but violent or dangerous behavior may be situation specific. A model patient who is able to adapt to a structured environment like that of a psychiatric hospital may be unable to cope with the pressures of independent community life. We can expect clinicians to be more accurate when they base their predictions on the patient's previous behavior in the community rather than in the controlled setting of a mental hospital.

Overall, although clinician predictions of dangerousness are significantly better than predictions based on chance alone, still they are often inaccurate (Kaplan, 2000). Although their crystal balls may be cloudy, mental health professionals who work in institutional settings continue to be called on to make predictions—deciding whom to commit and whom to discharge largely on the basis of how they judge the potential for violence (McNiel et al., 2003). Rather than expecting clinicians to rely only on their clinical judgment, investigators are developing better decision-making tools, such as more objective screening methods and violence rating scales to help guide assessment of violence risk (e.g., McNiel et al., 2003; Yang, Wong, & Coid, 2010).

These efforts help improve the ability of clinicians to predict the likelihood of violent behavior, at least with respect to short-term predictions (McNiel et al., 2003; Mills, Kroner, & Morgan, 2011). Clinicians may be more successful in predicting violence by basing predictions on a composite of factors, including evidence of past violent behavior, than on any single factor. Still, it's fair to say that predicting future violent behavior is difficult and that presently available methods are far from perfect (Yang, Wong, & Coid, 2010). Not surprisingly, the accuracy of clinician predictions of violence is generally greater when clinicians agree with one another than when they disagree (McNiel, Lam, & Binder, 2000). Accuracy also tends to be better when clinicians make shorter-term predictions of dangerousness (Mills, Kroner, & Morgan, 2011).

**VIOLENCE AND SEVERE MENTAL DISORDERS** The importance of developing tools to predict dangerousness is underscored by findings showing an increased risk of violence in people with severe mental disorders, such as schizophrenia and bipolar disorder, as compared to the general population (e.g., Douglas, Guy, & Hart, 2009; Friedman, 2014c). The risk of violent behavior is even greater among psychotic patients who remain untreated and have delusions of persecution and a history of violent behavior (Keer et al., 2013). That said, only a small number of patients with severe psychiatric disorders, even those who are untreated, commit violent acts (Torrey, 2011). Overall, fewer than 10% of violent crimes are linked to psychological disorders (Peterson, Skeem, et al., 2014). **T / F**

**TRUTH *or* FICTION**

A surprisingly high percentage of violent crimes are committed by people with psychological disorders.

☑ **FALSE** Recent evidence shows that fewer than 10% of violent crimes are linked to psychological disorders.

The general public's perception of the mentally ill as dangerous is greatly exaggerated by the disproportionate attention given to a few highly publicized cases in the media. Media reports of violence by a few people with severe mental disorders reinforces stereotypes and further contributes to stigmatization of people with mental disorders (Kuehn, 2012b). It is also important to recognize that alcohol and substance abuse play a much more important role than psychological disorders in predicting violent behavior (Friedman, 2014c; Luo & McIntire, 2013).

Digging deeper into the evidence reveals certain factors associated with an increased risk of violent behavior among schizophrenia patients (Elbogen & Johnson, 2009). The risk of violent crime is much higher, perhaps four or more times higher, among schizophrenia patients who also abuse alcohol or other drugs as compared to the general population (Fazel et al., 2009; Luo & McIntire, 2013; Volavka & Swanson, 2010). In addition, certain symptoms are associated with a greater risk of violence among schizophrenia patients—symptoms such as delusions of persecution and antisocial behavior (Bo et al., 2011; Harris & Lurigio, 2007; Swanson et al., 2006).

The risk of violent behavior among schizophrenia patients is also greater among those with command hallucinations—voices commanding them to harm themselves or others (McNiel, Lam, & Binder, 2000). The risk potential for violence is also greater among patients with severe mental illness who are living in economically distressed neighborhoods (Appelbaum, 2006). Having noted these increased risks of mental patients acting violently, let us also point out that people with severe psychiatric disorders actually stand a greater chance of becoming victims of violent crimes than people in the general population do (Teplin et al., 2005). People with mental disorders also are more likely to be victims of violent acts than perpetrators.

## The Duty to Warn

**15.3 Define the duty to warn and evaluate the dilemma it poses for therapists.**

The problem of predicting dangerousness also arises when therapists need to evaluate the seriousness of threats made by their patients against others. Do therapists have a *duty to warn*—a legal obligation to warn the intended targets of these threats? The duty to warn is one of many legal issues arising from society's response to problems of abnormal behavior. In the following sections, we discuss major legal issues, such as patients' rights, the insanity defense, and the right of mental patients to refuse treatment. *A Closer Look: The Duty to Warn* explores the dilemmas posed by the duty to warn standard.

# A CLOSER Look

## THE DUTY TO WARN

One of the most difficult dilemmas a therapist faces is whether to disclose confidential information that may protect third parties from harm. Part of the difficulty lies in determining whether the client has made a bona fide threat. The other part is that information a client discloses in psychotherapy is generally protected as privileged communication, which carries a right to confidentiality. However, this right is not absolute. State courts have determined that a therapist is obligated to breach confidentiality under certain conditions, such as when there is clear and compelling evidence that an individual poses a serious threat to others.

A 1976 court ruling in California in *Tarasoff v. the Regents of the University of California* established the legal basis for the therapist's **duty to warn** (Jones, 2003). In 1969, a graduate student at the University of California at Berkeley, Prosenjit Poddar, a native of India, became depressed when his romantic overtures toward a young woman, Tatiana Tarasoff, were rebuffed. Poddar entered psychotherapy with a psychologist at a student health facility and informed the psychologist that he intended to kill Tatiana when she returned from her summer vacation. The psychologist, concerned about Poddar's potential for violence, first consulted with his colleagues and then notified the campus police that Poddar was dangerous, recommending that he be taken to a facility for psychiatric treatment.

The campus police interviewed Poddar. They believed he was rational and released him after he promised to keep away from Tatiana. Poddar then terminated treatment with the psychologist and shortly afterward killed Tatiana. Poddar was found guilty of the lesser sentence of voluntary manslaughter rather than murder, on the basis of testimony of three psychiatrists that he suffered from diminished mental capacity and paranoid schizophrenia. Under California law, his diminished capacity prevented the finding of malice that was necessary for a murder conviction. Following a prison term, Poddar returned to India, where he reportedly made a new life for himself (Schwitzgebel & Schwitzgebel, 1980).

Tatiana's parents, however, sued the university. They claimed that the university health center had failed in its responsibility to warn Tatiana of the threat made against her by Poddar. The California Supreme Court agreed with the parents. The court ruled that a therapist who has reason to believe that a client poses a serious threat to another person is obligated to warn the potential victim, not merely to notify police. This ruling imposed on therapists a duty-to-warn obligation when their clients show the potential for violence by making threats against others. **T / F**

### TRUTH *or* FICTION

Therapists may not breach patient confidentiality even when a patient makes a death threat against a specific person.

☑ **FALSE** Therapists are actually obligated under some state laws to breach client confidentiality to warn people when threats of violence are made against them by their clients.

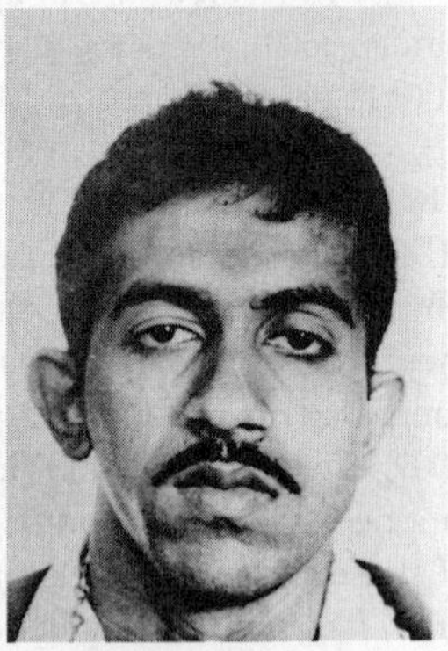

**TATIANA TARASOFF AND PROSENJIT PODDAR.** Poddar, Tatiana's killer, was a rejected suitor who had made threats against her to his therapist at a university health center. Poddar was subsequently convicted of voluntary manslaughter. A suit brought by Tatiana's parents against the university led to a landmark court ruling that established an obligation for therapists to warn third parties of threats made against them by their clients.

The ruling recognized that the rights of the intended victim outweigh the rights of confidentiality. Under *Tarasoff*, the therapist does not merely have a *right* to breach confidentiality and warn potential victims of danger, but is *obligated* by law to divulge such confidences to the potential victim.

The duty-to-warn provision poses ethical and practical dilemmas for clinicians. Under *Tarasoff*, therapists may feel obliged to protect their personal interests and those of others by breaching confidentiality on the mere suspicion that their clients harbor violent intentions. Because clients' threats are seldom carried out, the *Tarasoff* ruling may deny many clients their rights to confidentiality to prevent such rare instances. Although some clinicians may "overreact" to *Tarasoff* and breach confidentiality without sufficient cause, it can be argued that the interests of the few potential victims outweigh the interests of the many who may suffer a loss of confidentiality.

Another problem with applying the *Tarasoff* standard is the lack of any special ability on the therapist's part to predict dangerousness. Nevertheless, the *Tarasoff* ruling obliges therapists to judge whether or not their clients' disclosures indicate an imminent intent to harm others (VanderCreek & Knapp, 2001). In *Tarasoff*, the threat was obvious. In most cases, however, threats are not so clear-cut. There are no clear criteria for determining whether a therapist "should have known" that a client was dangerous before a violent act occurs. In the absence of guidelines that specify the criteria therapists should use to fulfill their duty to warn, they must rely on their best clinical judgment.

The ethical issues become even murkier when psychologists treat HIV-infected patients who put their sexual partners at risk by concealing their HIV status. Psychologists must balance their duty-to-warn obligations with their ethical responsibility to protect patient confidentiality. Presently, psychologists lack a clear set of professional standards they can apply to resolve these dilemmas (Huprich, Fuller, & Schneider, 2003). Psychologists must follow the laws of the states in which they practice regarding the requirements for maintaining confidentiality of their clients' HIV status and become aware of any exceptions that might exist for breaching confidentiality (Barnett, 2010).

The *Tarasoff* ruling and state laws implemented in its wake that mandate a duty to warn raise many concerns among clinicians who are trying to meet their legal responsibilities under *Tarasoff* provisions and their clinical responsibilities to their clients. Although the intent of the *Tarasoff* decision was to protect potential victims, it may inadvertently increase the risks of violence when applied to clinical practice, as in the following situations (Weiner, 2003):

1. *Clients may be less willing to confide in their therapists*, making it more difficult for therapists to help them diffuse violent feelings.
2. *Potentially violent people may be less likely to enter therapy*, fearing that disclosures made to a therapist will be revealed.
3. *Therapists may be less likely to probe violent tendencies*, seeking to avoid legal complications. Therapists may avoid asking clients about potential violence or may avoid treating patients who are believed to have violent tendencies.

The *Tarasoff* case was brought in California, and the decision applied only in that state. Other states have different statutes (Pabian, Welfel, & Beebe, 2009). As mentioned, therapists must be aware of the duty-to-warn laws in the particular states in which they practice. Some states permit therapists to breach confidentiality to warn third parties, but do not impose an obligation on therapists to do so. However, most states impose a duty to warn on therapists (or what is sometimes called a *duty to protect*) in some situations, such as when a client threatens a particular person and the threat of violence is imminent (American Psychological Association, 2012). In other states, however, a duty to warn is legally obligated even when there is no clearly identifiable victim, as when a client threatens to kill people at random or makes a threat to harm someone but does not identify the targeted person (American Psychological Association, 2011).

Laws in different states also specify how the duty to warn needs to be met, such as filing a report with the police or taking steps to prevent potential acts of violence, such as by hospitalizing the client.

Although therapists are under a legal obligation to follow the laws in the states in which they practice, they must also not lose sight of the primary therapeutic responsibility to their clients when legal issues arise. They must balance the obligation to meet their responsibilities under duty-to-warn provisions with the need to help their clients resolve the feelings of rage and anger that give rise to violent threats.

# Patients' Rights

**15.4 Identify major court cases establishing the rights of mental patients.**

We have considered issues regarding society's right to involuntarily hospitalize people who are judged to be mentally ill and to pose a threat to themselves or others, but what happens after commitment? Do involuntarily committed patients have the right to receive or demand treatment? Or can society just warehouse them in psychiatric facilities indefinitely without treating them? Consider the opposite side of the coin as well: May people who are involuntarily committed refuse treatment? Such issues—which have been brought into public light by landmark court cases—fall under the umbrella of *patients' rights*. Generally speaking, the history of abuses in the mental health system, as highlighted in popular books and movies such as *One Flew Over the Cuckoo's Nest*, has led to a tightening of standards of care and adoption of legal guarantees to protect patients' rights.

**RIGHT TO TREATMENT** We might assume that mental health institutions that accept people for treatment would provide them with treatment. Not until the 1972 landmark federal court case of *Wyatt v. Stickney*, however, did a federal court establish a minimum standard of care to be provided by hospitals. The case was a class action suit against Stickney, the commissioner of mental health for the state of Alabama, brought on behalf of Ricky Wyatt, an intellectually disabled young man, and other patients at a state hospital and school in Tuscaloosa.

The federal district court in Alabama held both that the hospital had failed to provide treatment to Wyatt and others and that living conditions at the hospital were inadequate and dehumanizing. The court described the hospital dormitories as "barnlike structures" that afforded no privacy to the residents. The bathrooms had no partitions between stalls, the patients were outfitted with shoddy clothes, the wards were filthy and crowded, the kitchens were unsanitary, and the food was substandard. In addition, the staff was inadequate in number and poorly trained. The case of *Wyatt v. Stickney* established certain patient rights,

**WHAT ARE THE RIGHTS OF MENTAL PATIENTS?** Popular books and films, such as *One Flew Over the Cuckoo's Nest*, starring Jack Nicholson, have highlighted many of the abuses occurring in mental hospitals. In recent years, a tightening of standards of care and the adoption of legal safeguards have led to better protection of the rights of patients in mental hospitals.

## TRUTH or FICTION

Patients in mental hospitals may be required to perform general housekeeping duties in a facility.

☑ **FALSE** The Alabama case of *Wyatt v. Stickney* established certain patient rights, including the right not to be required to perform work for the sake of maintaining the psychiatric hospital.

including the right not to be required to engage in work that is performed for the sake of maintaining the facility. The court held that mental hospitals must, at a minimum, provide the following (*Wyatt v. Stickney*, 1972):

1. A humane psychological and physical environment
2. Qualified staff in numbers sufficient to administer adequate treatment
3. Individualized treatment plans **T / F**

The court established that the state was obliged to provide adequate treatment for people who were involuntarily confined to psychiatric hospitals. The court further ruled that to commit people to hospitals for treatment involuntarily and then not to provide treatment violated their rights to due process under the law.

Table 15.2 lists some of the rights granted to institutionalized patients under the court's ruling. Although the ruling of the court was limited to Alabama, many other states have revised their mental hospital standards to ensure that involuntarily committed patients are not denied basic rights. Other court cases have further clarified patients' rights.

***O'Connor v. Donaldson*** The 1975 case of Kenneth Donaldson is another landmark in patients' rights. Donaldson, a former patient at a state hospital in Florida, sued two hospital doctors on the grounds that he had been involuntarily confined without receiving treatment for 14 years, although he posed no serious threat to himself or others. Donaldson had been originally committed on the basis of a petition filed by his father, who had perceived him as delusional. Although Donaldson received no treatment during his confinement and was denied grounds privileges and occupational training, his repeated requests for discharge were denied as well. He was finally released when he threatened to sue the hospital. Once discharged, Donaldson did sue his doctors and was awarded damages of $38,500 from O'Connor, the superintendent of the hospital. The case was eventually argued before the U.S. Supreme Court.

Court testimony established that although the hospital staff had not perceived Donaldson to be dangerous, they had refused to release him. The hospital doctors argued that continued hospitalization had been necessary because they had believed Donaldson was unlikely to adapt successfully to community living. The doctors had prescribed antipsychotic medications, but Donaldson had refused to take them because of his Christian Science beliefs. As a result, he received only custodial care.

In 1975, the Supreme Court held in *O'Connor v. Donaldson* that "mental illness [alone] cannot justify a State's locking a person up against his will and keeping him indefinitely

**Table 15.2** Partial Listing of the Patient's Bill of Rights under *Wyatt v. Stickney*

| | |
|---|---|
| 1. | Patients have rights to privacy and to be treated with dignity. |
| 2. | Patients shall be treated under the least-restrictive conditions that can be provided to meet the purposes that commitment was intended to serve. |
| 3. | Patients shall have rights to visitation and telephone privileges unless special restrictions apply. |
| 4. | Patients have the right to refuse excessive or unnecessary medication. In addition, medication may not be used as a form of punishment. |
| 5. | Patients shall not be kept in restraints or isolation except in emergency conditions in which their behavior is likely to pose a threat to themselves or others and less-restrictive restraints are not feasible. |
| 6. | Patients shall not be subject to experimental research unless their rights to informed consent are protected. |
| 7. | Patients have the right to refuse potentially hazardous or unusual treatments, such as lobotomy, electroconvulsive shock, or aversive behavioral treatments. |
| 8. | Unless it is dangerous or inappropriate to the treatment program, patients shall have the right to wear their own clothing and keep possessions. |
| 9. | Patients have rights to regular exercise and to opportunities to spend time outdoors. |
| 10. | Patients have rights to suitable opportunities to interact with the opposite gender. |
| 11. | Patients have rights to humane and decent living conditions. |
| 12. | No more than six patients shall be housed in a room, and screens or curtains must be provided to afford a sense of privacy. |
| 13. | No more than eight patients shall share one toilet facility, with separate stalls provided for privacy. |
| 14. | Patients have a right to nutritionally balanced diets. |
| 15. | Patients shall not be required to perform work that is performed for the sake of maintenance of the facility. |

in simple custodial confinement." There is no constitutional basis for confining such persons involuntarily if they are dangerous to no one and can live safely in freedom. The ruling addressed mentally ill patients who are not considered dangerous. It is not yet clear whether the same constitutional rights would be applied to committed patients who are judged to be dangerous.

In its ruling in *O'Connor v. Donaldson*, the Supreme Court did not deal with the larger issue of the rights of patients to receive treatment. The ruling does not directly obligate state institutions to treat involuntarily committed, nondangerous people because the institutions may elect to release them instead.

The Supreme Court did touch on the larger issue of society's rights to protect itself from individuals who are perceived as offensive. In delivering the opinion of the Court, Justice Potter Stewart wrote:

**KENNETH DONALDSON.** Donaldson points to the U.S. Supreme Court decision that ruled that people who are considered mentally ill but not dangerous cannot be confined against their will if they can be maintained safely in the community.

> May the State fence in the harmless mentally ill solely to save its citizens from exposure to those whose ways are different? One might as well ask if the State, to avoid public uneasiness, could incarcerate all who are physically unattractive or socially eccentric. Mere public intolerance or animosity cannot constitutionally justify the deprivation of a person's physical liberty.

***Youngberg v. Romeo*** In a 1982 case, *Youngberg v. Romeo*, the U.S. Supreme Court more directly addressed the issue of the patient's right to treatment. Even so, it seemed to retreat somewhat from the patients' rights standards established in *Wyatt v. Stickney*. Nicholas Romeo, a 33-year-old man with profound intellectual disability who was unable to talk or care for himself, had been institutionalized in a state hospital and school in Pennsylvania. While in the state facility, he had a history of injuring himself through his violent behavior and was often kept in restraints. The case was brought by the patient's mother, who alleged that the hospital was negligent in not preventing his injuries and in routinely using physical restraints for prolonged periods while not providing adequate treatment.

The Supreme Court ruled that involuntarily committed patients, such as Nicholas, have a right to be confined in less-restrictive conditions, such as being freed from physical restraints whenever it is reasonable to do so. The Supreme Court ruling also included a limited recognition of the committed patient's right to treatment. The court held that institutionalized patients have a right to minimally adequate training to help them function free of physical restraints, but only to the extent that such training can be provided in reasonable safety. Reasonableness, the court held, should be determined on the basis of the judgment of qualified professionals. The federal courts should not interfere with the internal operations of the facility, the court held, because "there's no reason to think judges or juries are better qualified than appropriate professionals in making such decisions." The courts should only second-guess the judgments of qualified professionals when such judgments depart from professional standards of practice. However, the Supreme Court did not address the broader issues of the rights of committed patients to receive training that might eventually enable them to function independently outside the hospital.

The related issue of whether people with severe psychological disorders who reside in the community have a constitutional right to receive mental health services (and whether states are obligated to provide these services) continues to be argued in the courts at both the state and federal levels.

**RIGHT TO REFUSE TREATMENT** Consider the following scenario. A person, John Citizen, is involuntarily committed to a mental hospital for treatment. The hospital staff determines that John suffers from a psychotic disorder, paranoid schizophrenia, and should be treated with antipsychotic medication. John, however, decides not to comply with treatment. He claims that the hospital has no right to treat him against his will. The hospital staff seeks a court order to mandate treatment, arguing that it makes little sense to commit people involuntarily unless the hospital is empowered to treat them as the staff deems fit.

Does an involuntary patient, such as John, have the right to refuse treatment? If so, does this right conflict with states' rights to involuntarily commit people to mental institutions to receive treatment? One might also wonder whether people who are judged in need of involuntary hospitalization are competent to make decisions about which treatments are in their best interests.

The right of committed patients to refuse psychotropic medications was tested in a 1979 case, *Rogers v. Okin*, in which a Massachusetts federal district court imposed an injunction on a Boston state hospital prohibiting the forced medication of committed patients except in emergency situations—for example, when patients' behaviors posed a significant threat to themselves or others. The court recognized that a patient may be unwise to refuse medication, but it held that a patient with or without a mental disorder has the right to exercise bad judgment so long as the effects of the "error" do not impose "a danger of physical harm to himself, fellow patients, or hospital staff."

Although statutes and regulations vary from state to state, cases in which hospitalized patients refuse medications are often first brought before an independent review panel. If the panel rules against the patient, the case may then be brought before a judge, who makes the final decision about whether the patient is to be forcibly medicated (Rolon & Jones, 2008). In practice, relatively few patients—perhaps only about 10%—refuse medication. Furthermore, the great majority of refusals that reach the review process are eventually overridden.

Our discussion of legal issues and abnormal behavior now turns to the controversy concerning the insanity defense.

### TRUTH *or* FICTION

An attempt to assassinate the president of the United States was seen by millions of television viewers, but the would-be assassin was found not guilty by a court of law.

☑ **TRUE** John Hinkley, who was seen by millions of TV viewers attempting to assassinate President Reagan, was found not guilty by reason of insanity by a court of law.

# The Insanity Defense

The 2011 shooting of Representative Gabby Giffords recalls another high-profile shooting in which the president of the United States, Ronald Reagan, was shot outside a hotel in Washington, D.C., in March 1981. Millions of Americans witnessed the shooting on their television screens, but the assailant, John Hinckley, a 25-year-old drifter, was found not guilty by reason of insanity and confined to a mental hospital. **T / F**

When gunshots rang out that cold day in March, Secret Service agents formed a human shield around the president; one shoved him into a waiting limousine, which sped to a hospital. The president was wounded, but fortunately recovered. James Brady, his press secretary, was hit by a stray bullet that shattered his spine and left him partially paralyzed. Federal agents seized the gunman, John Hinckley.

A letter Hinckley left in his hotel room, parts of which are reproduced ahead, revealed his hope that his assassination of the president would impress a young actress, Jodie Foster. Hinckley had never met Foster but had a crush on her.

At Hinckley's trial, there was never any question whether Hinckley had fired the wounding bullets, but the prosecutor was burdened to demonstrate beyond a reasonable doubt that Hinckley had the capacity to control his behavior and appreciate its wrongfulness. The defense presented testimony that portrayed Hinckley as an "incompetent schizophrenic" who suffered under the delusion that he would achieve a "magic union" with Foster as a result of killing the president. The jury sided with the defense and found Hinckley *not guilty by reason of insanity*. He was remanded to a federal psychiatric facility, St. Elizabeth's Hospital in Washington, D.C. In 2005, a federal judge ruled that the Hinckley, then 50 years old, was permitted home visits to be supervised by his parents for three or four nights at a time. By 2009, a federal court permitted him to extend his home visits to nine days at a time and in 2016 a judge ordered him released to the custody of his mother.

The idea that Hinckley or others found not guilty of heinous crimes by reason of insanity might one day be granted full release is unsettling to many people. Should he have been imprisoned rather than treated in a mental hospital? How should

**NOT GUILTY BY REASON OF INSANITY.** Was he insane when he shot the president? John Hinckley Jr. attempted to assassinate President Ronald Reagan in 1981 but was found not guilty by reason of insanity. The public outrage over the Hinckley verdict led to a reexamination of the insanity plea in many states.

society treat mentally disturbed individuals who commit crimes? Then again, had Hinckley been convicted of a crime, might he have already been set free or at least paroled?

**"I" "Please Look into Your Heart"**

Dear Jodie,

There is a definite possibility that I will be killed in my attempt to get Reagan. It is for this very reason that I am writing you this letter now.

As you well know by now I love you very much. Over the past seven months I've left you dozens of poems, letters and love messages in the faint hope that you could develop an interest in me....

Jodie, I would abandon this idea of getting Reagan in a second if I could only win your heart and live out the rest of my life with you, whether it be in total obscurity or whatever.

I will admit to you that the reason I'm going ahead with this attempt now is because I just cannot wait any longer to impress you. I've got to do something now to make you understand, in no uncertain terms, that I am doing all of this for your sake! By sacrificing my freedom and possibly my life, I hope to change your mind about me. This letter is being written only an hour before I leave for the Hilton Hotel. Jodie, I'm asking you to please look into your heart and at least give me the chance, with this historical deed, to gain your respect and love.

*John Hinckley's letter to actress Jodie Foster, written on March 31, 1981, shortly before he attempted to assassinate President Ronald Reagan*

**SOURCE:** *Linder, 2004, "The John Hinckley Trial"*

Perceptions of the use of the **insanity defense** tend to stray far from the facts. Contrary to the common perception that the insanity defense is widely and often successfully used, it is in fact used rarely and usually is unsuccessful. In actuality, it is raised in fewer than 1% of felony cases and succeeds in acquittals in a fraction of these cases, perhaps only about one quarter and far less in cases of homicide (Cevallos, 2015; L. Friedman, 2015). Thus, the use of the insanity defense is rare, and acquittals based on the defense are rarer still. **T / F**

**TRUTH or FICTION**

The insanity defense is used in a large number of trials, usually successfully.

☑ FALSE The insanity defense is used rarely in felony cases, and the rate of acquittals based on the defense is even rarer.

The public also overestimates the proportion of defendants acquitted on the basis of insanity who are set free rather than confined to mental health institutions and underestimates the length of hospitalization of those who are confined (Silver, Cirincione, & Steadman, 1994). People found not guilty of a crime on the basis of insanity are often confined to mental hospitals for longer periods of time than they would have otherwise served in prison (Lymburner & Roesch, 1999). The net result is that although changes in the insanity defense, or its abolition, might prevent a few flagrant cases of abuse, they would not afford the public much broader protection.

The Hinckley verdict led to a public outcry, with many calling for the abolition of the insanity defense. One objection focused on the fact that once the defense presented evidence to support a plea of insanity, the federal prosecutor had the responsibility of proving *beyond a reasonable doubt* that the defendant was sane. It can be difficult enough to demonstrate that someone is sane or insane in the present, so imagine the problems that attend proving someone was sane at the time a criminal act was committed.

In the aftermath of the Hinckley verdict, the federal government and many states changed their statutes to shift the burden of proof to the defense to prove insanity. Even the American Psychiatric Association went on record stating that psychiatric expert witnesses should not be called on to render opinions about whether defendants can control their behavior. In the opinion of the association, these are not medical judgments that psychiatrists are trained to provide.

In the wake of the Hinckley acquittal, a number of states adopted a new type of verdict, the *guilty-but-mentally-ill* (GBMI) verdict. The GBMI verdict offers juries the option of finding that a defendant is mentally ill but that the mental illness did not cause the defendant to commit the crime. People convicted under a GBMI statute go to prison but receive treatment while incarcerated.

The GBMI verdict has sparked considerable controversy. Although it was intended to reduce the number of not guilty by reason of insanity verdicts, it has failed to do so (Melville & Naimark, 2002; Slovenko, 2009). All in all, the GBMI verdict is widely seen as a social experiment that has failed to prove its usefulness (Palmer & Hazelrigg, 2000). Critics argue that the verdict merely stigmatizes defendants who are found guilty as also being mentally ill. Fewer than half of the states today permit a GBMI verdict (Kutys & Esterman, 2009).

## Legal Bases of the Insanity Defense

**15.5 Describe the history of the insanity defense, citing specific court cases and the guidelines proposed by the American Law Institute.**

Although the public outrage over the Hinckley and other celebrated insanity verdicts led to a reexamination of the insanity defense, society has long held to the doctrine of free will as a basis for determining responsibility for wrongdoing. The doctrine of free will, as applied to criminal responsibility, requires that people can be held guilty of a crime only if they are judged to have been in control of their actions at the time. Not only must a court of law determine, beyond a reasonable doubt, that a defendant had committed a crime, but it must also consider the individual's state of mind in determining guilt. The court must thus rule not only on whether a crime was committed but also on whether the defendant is morally responsible and deserving of punishment. The insanity defense is based on the belief that when a criminal act derives from a distorted state of mind, and not from the exercise of free will, the individual should not be punished but rather should be treated for the underlying mental disorder. The insanity defense has a long legal history.

Three major modern court rulings bear on the insanity defense. The first was an 1834 case in Ohio in which it was ruled that people could not be held responsible if they are compelled to commit criminal actions because of impulses they are unable to resist.

The second major legal test of the insanity defense is referred to as the M'Naghten rule, based on a case in England in 1843 of a Scotsman, Daniel M'Naghten, who had intended to assassinate the prime minister of England, Sir Robert Peel. Instead, he killed Peel's secretary, whom he had mistaken for the prime minister. M'Naghten claimed that the voice of God had commanded him to kill Peel. The English court acquitted M'Naghten on the basis of insanity, finding that the defendant had been "labouring under such a defect of reason, from disease of the mind, as not to know the nature and quality of the act he was doing; or, if he did know it, that he did not know he was doing what was wrong." The M'Naghten rule holds that people do not bear criminal responsibility if, by reason of a mental disease or defect, they either have no knowledge of their actions or are unable to tell right from wrong. The problem with the M'Naghten rule is that it focuses on lack of cognitive capacity to understand the difference between right and wrong and not on the ability to control one's actions (Cevallos, 2015).

The third major case that helped lay the foundation for the modern insanity defense was *Durham v. United States*, 1954. The verdict in this case held that the "accused [person] is not criminally responsible if his unlawful act was the product of mental disease or mental defect." Under the *Durham* rule, juries were expected to decide not only whether the accused suffered from a mental disease or defect but also whether this mental condition was causally connected to the criminal act. The U.S. Court of Appeals recognized that criminal intent is a precondition of criminal responsibility:

> The legal and moral traditions of the western world require that those who, of their own free will and with evil intent... commit acts which violate the law, shall be criminally responsible for those acts. Our traditions also require that where such acts stem from and are the product of a mental disease or defect... moral blame shall not attach, and hence there will not be criminal responsibility.

The intent of the *Durham* rule was to reject as outmoded the two earlier standards of legal insanity: the irresistible impulse rule and the right–wrong (or M'Naghten) principle. The court argued that the right–wrong test was outmoded because the concept of mental disease is broader than the ability to recognize right from wrong. The legal basis of insanity thus should not be judged on just one feature of a mental disorder, such as deficient reasoning ability. The irresistible impulse test was denied because the court recognized that in certain cases, criminal acts arising from "mental disease or defect" might occur in a cool and calculating manner rather than in the manner of a sudden, irresistible impulse. Defendants may have known they were committing criminal acts, but were not driven to do so by an irresistible impulse (Sokolove, 2003).

The *Durham* rule, however, has proved to be unsuccessful for several reasons, such as a lack of precise definitions for terms such as *mental disease* or *mental defect*. Courts were confused, for example, about whether a personality disorder (e.g., antisocial personality disorder) constituted a "disease." Also, juries found it difficult to draw conclusions about whether an individual's "mental disease" was causally connected to the criminal act. Without clear or precise definitions of terms, juries have come to rely on expert psychiatric testimony. In many cases, verdicts simply endorsed the testimony of expert witnesses. However, the psychiatrists juries relied upon as expert witnesses often disagreed with one another about a defendant's diagnosis, rendering the *Durham* rule unworkable (Bazelon, 2015).

By 1972, the *Durham* rule was replaced in many jurisdictions by legal guidelines formulated by the American Law Institute (ALI) to define the legal basis of insanity (Van Susteren, 2002). These guidelines, which essentially combine the M'Naghten principle with the irresistible impulse principle, include the following provisions (American Law Institute, 1962):

1. A person is not responsible for criminal conduct if at the time of such conduct as a result of mental disease or defect he lacks substantial capacity either to appreciate the criminality (wrongfulness) of his conduct or to conform his conduct to the requirements of law.
2. . . . The terms "mental disease or defect" do not include an abnormality manifested only by repeated criminal or otherwise antisocial conduct.

The first guideline incorporates aspects of the M'Naghten test (being unable to appreciate right from wrong) and the irresistible impulse test (being unable to conform one's behavior to the requirements of law) of insanity. The second guideline asserts that repeated criminal behavior (such as a pattern of drug dealing) is not sufficient in itself to establish a mental disease or defect that might relieve the individual of criminal responsibility. Although many legal authorities believe the ALI guidelines are an improvement over earlier tests, questions remain as to whether a jury composed of ordinary citizens can be expected to make complex judgments about the defendant's state of mind, even on the basis of expert testimony, especially in cases in which experts disagree with each other (Sadoff, 2011). Under the ALI guidelines, juries must determine whether defendants lack substantial capacity to be aware of, or capable of, conforming their behavior to the law. By adding the term *substantial capacity* to the legal test, the ALI guidelines broaden the legal basis of the insanity defense, implying that defendants need not be completely incapable of controlling their actions to meet the legal test of not guilty by reason of insanity.

Where things stand presently, there is no one standard determining the basis of the insanity defense from state to state. Individual states apply different legal standards, and five states have abolished the insanity defense altogether (Montana, Utah, Nevada, Idaho, and Kansas; Cevallos, 2015). Still, as we see next, there remain divergent perspectives on the insanity defense.

**PERSPECTIVES ON THE INSANITY DEFENSE** The insanity defense places special burdens on juries. In assessing criminal responsibility, the jury must determine not only that the accused committed a crime but also the defendant's state of mind at the time. In rejecting the *Durham* decision, courts have relieved psychiatrists and other expert witnesses from responsibility for determining whether the defendant's behavior is a product of a *mental disease or defect*. Is it reasonable to assume that juries are better able to assess defendants' states of mind than mental health professionals? In particular, how can a jury evaluate the testimony of conflicting expert witnesses? The jury's task is made even more difficult by the mandate to decide whether the defendant was mentally incapacitated *at the time of the crime*. The defendant's courtroom behavior may bear little resemblance to his or her behavior during the crime.

Thomas Szasz and others who deny the existence of mental illness have raised another challenge to the insanity defense: If mental illness does not exist, then the insanity defense becomes groundless. Szasz argues that the insanity defense is ultimately degrading because it strips people of personal responsibility for their behavior. People who break laws are criminals, Szasz argued, and should be prosecuted and sentenced accordingly. Acquittal of defendants by reason of insanity treats them as nonpersons, as unfortunates who are not deemed to possess the basic human qualities of free choice, self-determination, and personal responsibility. According to Szasz, we are responsible for our behavior and should each be held accountable for our misdeeds.

Szasz argued that the insanity defense has historically been invoked in crimes that were particularly heinous or perpetrated against persons of high social rank. When persons of low social rank commit crimes against persons of higher status, Szasz argued, the insanity defense directs attention away from the social ills that may have motivated the crime. Despite Szasz's contention, the insanity defense is invoked in many cases of less shocking crimes or in cases involving people from similar social classes.

How, then, are we to evaluate the insanity defense? To abolish it would reverse hundreds of years of legal tradition that recognizes that people are not to be held responsible for their criminal behavior when their ability to control themselves is impaired by a mental disorder or defect.

Consider a hypothetical example. John Citizen commits a crime, say a heinous crime such as murder, while acting on a delusional belief that the victim was intent on assassinating him. The accused claims that voices from his TV set informed him of the identity of the would-be assassin and commanded him to kill the person to save himself and other potential victims. Cases like this are thankfully rare. Few mentally disturbed people, even few people with psychotic features, commit violent crimes, and even fewer commit murder.

In reaching a judgment on the insanity plea, juries need to consider whether the law should apply special standards in cases such as John Citizen's, or whether one standard of criminal responsibility should apply to all. If lawmakers assert the legitimacy of the insanity defense in some cases, they still need a standard of insanity that can be interpreted and applied by juries of ordinary citizens. The furor over the Hinckley verdict suggests that issues concerning the insanity plea remain unsettled and are likely to continue to be so for a long period of time.

Under the U.S. system of justice, juries must struggle with the complex question of determining criminal responsibility, not merely criminal actions. What about those individuals who successfully plead not guilty by reason of insanity? Should they be committed to a mental institution for a fixed sentence, as they might have been had they been incarcerated in a penal institution? Or should their commitments be of an indeterminate term and their release dependent on their mental status? The legal basis for answering such questions was decided in the case of a man named Michael Jones.

## Determining the Length of Criminal Commitment

**15.6 Describe the legal basis for determining length of criminal commitment.**

The issue of determinate versus indeterminate commitment was addressed in the case of Michael Jones (*Jones v. United States*), who was arrested in 1975 and charged with petty larceny for attempting to steal a jacket from a Washington, D.C., department store. Jones was first committed to a public mental hospital, St. Elizabeth's Hospital (the same hospital where John Hinckley was committed). Jones was diagnosed as suffering from paranoid schizophrenia and was kept hospitalized until he was judged competent to stand trial, about six months later. Jones offered a plea of not guilty by reason of insanity, which the court accepted without challenge, remanding him to St. Elizabeth's. Although Jones's crime carried a maximum sentence of one year in prison, Jones's repeated attempts to obtain release were denied in subsequent court hearings.

The U.S. Supreme Court eventually heard his appeal seven years after Jones was hospitalized and reached its decision in 1983. It ruled against Jones's appeal and affirmed the decision of the lower courts that he was to remain in the hospital. The Supreme Court thereby established a principle that individuals who are acquitted by reason of insanity "constitute a special class that should be treated differently" from civilly committed individuals (Morris, 2002). They may be committed for an indefinite period to a mental institution under criteria that require a less stringent level of proof of dangerousness than is ordinarily applied in cases of civil commitment. Thus, people found not guilty by reason of insanity may remain confined to a mental hospital for many years longer than they would have been sentenced to prison had they been found guilty. **T / F**

Among other things, the Supreme Court ruling in *Jones v. United States* provides that the usual and customary sentences that the law provides for particular crimes have no bearing on criminal commitment. In the words of the Supreme Court:

> Different considerations underlie commitment of an insanity acquittee. As he was not convicted, he may not be punished. His confinement rests on his continuing illness and dangerousness. There simply is no necessary correlation between severity of the offense and length of time necessary for recovery.

**TRUTH or FICTION**

People who are found not guilty of a crime by reason of insanity may be confined to a mental hospital for many years longer than they would have been sentenced to prison had they been found guilty.

☑ **TRUE** People who are found not guilty of a crime by reason of insanity may remain confined in a mental hospital for many years longer than they would have served a prison term.

The Supreme Court ruling held that a person who is criminally committed may be confined "to a mental institution until such time as he has regained his sanity or is no longer a danger to society." As in the case of Michael Jones, people who are acquitted on the basis of insanity may remain confined for much longer periods of time than they would have been sentenced to prison. They may also be released earlier than they might have been released from prison, if their "mental condition" improves. However, public outrage over a speedy release, especially for a major crime, might prevent rapid release.

The indeterminateness of criminal commitment raises various questions. Is it reasonable to deny people such as Michael Jones their liberty for an indefinite and possibly lifelong term for a relatively minor crime, such as petty larceny? On the other hand, is justice served by acquitting perpetrators of heinous crimes by reason of insanity and then releasing them early if they are deemed by professionals to be able to rejoin society?

The Supreme Court's ruling in *Jones v. United States* seems to imply that we must separate the notion of legal sentencing from that of legal or criminal commitment. Legal sentencing rests on the principle that the punishment should fit the crime: The more serious the crime, the longer the punishment. In criminal commitment, however, persons acquitted of their crimes by reason of insanity are guiltless in the eyes of the law, and their length of confinement is determined by their mental state.

# Competency to Stand Trial

**15.7 Describe the legal basis for determining competency to stand trial.**

There is a basic rule of law that those who stand accused of crimes must be able to understand the charges and proceedings brought against them and be able to participate in their own defense. The concept of **competency to stand trial** should not be confused with the insanity defense. A defendant can be held competent to stand trial but still be judged not guilty of a crime by reason of insanity. A clearly delusional person, for example, may understand the court proceedings and be able to confer with defense counsel but still be acquitted by reason of insanity. On the other hand, a person may be incapable of standing trial at a particular time but be tried at a later time when competency is restored (Zapf & Roesch, 2011). Defendants who suffer from psychotic disorders, those who are unemployed, and those who have had a history of psychiatric hospitalization are more likely than those without these characteristics to be judged incompetent (Pirelli, Gottdiener, & Zapf, 2011). **T / F**

**TRUTH or FICTION**

A defendant may be held competent to stand trial but still be judged not guilty of a crime by reason of insanity.

☑ **TRUE** Yes, a defendant can be held competent to stand trial but then be found not guilty of a crime by reason of insanity at trial.

People are much more likely to be confined to mental institutions on the basis of the lack of mental competence to stand trial than on the basis of the insanity verdict (Roesch, Zapf, & Hart, 2010). People who are declared incompetent to stand trial are generally confined to a mental institution until they are deemed competent or until it is determined that they are unlikely to regain competency. Abuses may occur, however, if the accused are kept incarcerated for indefinite periods awaiting trial. In 1972, the U.S. Supreme Court

**NOT COMPETENT TO STAND TRIAL.** Jason Rodriguez, right—who was charged with one count of first-degree murder and five counts of attempted murder in an Orlando, Florida, office shooting—is shown here consulting with his public defender during a competency hearing. After hearing from three psychiatrists and a psychologist who testified that Rodriguez was currently incompetent to stand trial, the judge ordered him to a state mental hospital for treatment.

ruled, in the case of *Jackson v. Indiana*, that a person could not be kept in a mental hospital awaiting trial longer than it would take to determine whether treatment was likely to restore competency. Under *Jackson*, psychiatric examiners must determine whether there exists a substantial probability that the defendant would regain competency through treatment within the foreseeable future (Hubbard, Zapf, & Ronan, 2003). If it does not seem the person would ever become competent, even with treatment, the individual must either be released or committed under the procedures for civil commitment. However, compliance with the *Jackson* standard has been inconsistent, with some states imposing a minimum length of treatment (e.g., five years) before acknowledging that a defendant is deemed permanently incompetent (Morris, 2002).

A 1992 ruling by the U.S. Supreme Court, in the case of *Medina v. California*, held that the burden of proof for determining competency to stand trial lies with the defendant, not the state. Then, in 2003, the U.S. Supreme Court held in the case of *Sell v. United States* that mentally ill defendants could be forcibly medicated to render them competent to stand trial, at least under some limited circumstances (Bassman, 2005). The decision allows a defendant to be involuntarily medicated if it is deemed medically appropriate and would not cause side effects that would compromise the fairness of the trial (Heilbrun & Kramer, 2005). The effect of the *Sell* decision may be to bring to trial many defendants whose trials were delayed because of a lack of mental competence.

We opened this book by noting that despite the popular impression that abnormal behavior affects only a few of us, it actually affects every one of us in one way or another. Let us close by suggesting that if we all work together to foster research into the causes, treatment, and prevention of abnormal behavior, perhaps we can meet the multifaceted challenges that abnormal behavior poses to our society at large.

# Summing Up

## Legal Issues in Mental Health Treatment

### Civil versus Criminal Commitment

**15.1 Explain the difference between civil commitment and criminal commitment.**

The legal process by which people are placed in psychiatric institutions against their will is called *civil* or *psychiatric commitment*. Civil commitment is intended to provide treatment to people who are deemed to suffer from mental disorders and to pose a threat to themselves or others. Criminal commitment, by comparison, involves the placement of a person in a psychiatric institution for treatment who has been acquitted of a crime by reason of insanity. In voluntary hospitalization, people voluntarily seek treatment in a psychiatric facility and can leave of their own accord unless a court rules otherwise.

### Predicting Dangerousness

**15.2 Evaluate the ability of mental health professionals to predict dangerousness.**

Although people must be judged dangerous to be placed involuntarily in a psychiatric facility, mental health professionals have not demonstrated any special ability to predict dangerousness. Factors that may account for the failure to predict dangerousness include the following: (a) Recognizing violent tendencies post hoc is easier than predicting them; (b) generalized perceptions of violent tendencies may not predict specific acts of violence; (c) there is lack of agreement in defining *violence* or *dangerousness*; (d) base-rate problems make it difficult to predict rare events; (e) it is unlikely that potential offenders would directly disclose their violent intentions; and (f) predictions based on hospital behavior may not generalize to community settings.

### The Duty to Warn

**15.3 Define the duty to warn and evaluate the dilemma it poses for therapists.**

Although information disclosed by a client to a therapist generally carries a right to confidentiality, the *Tarasoff* ruling held that therapists have a duty or obligation to warn third parties of threats made against them by their clients. It poses ethical and practical dilemmas for therapists who need to determine whether to breach confidentiality on the basis of their judgment that patients have hostile intentions toward others and are likely to carry them out, even though therapists have no special ability to predict future dangerousness.

## Patients' Rights

**15.4 Identify major court cases establishing the rights of mental patients.**

In *Wyatt v. Stickney*, a court in Alabama imposed a minimum standard of care. In *O'Connor v. Donaldson*, the U.S. Supreme Court ruled that nondangerous mentally ill people could not be held in psychiatric facilities against their will if such people could be maintained safely in the community. In *Youngberg v. Romeo*, the Supreme Court ruled that involuntarily confined patients have a right to less-restrictive types of treatment and to receive training to help them function well. Court rulings, such as that of *Rogers v. Okin* in Massachusetts, have established that patients have a right to refuse medication, except in case of emergency.

# The Insanity Defense

## Legal Bases of the Insanity Defense

**15.5 Describe the history of the insanity defense, citing specific court cases and the guidelines proposed by the American Law Institute.**

Three court cases established legal precedents for the insanity defense. In 1834, a court in Ohio applied a principle of irresistible impulse as the basis of an insanity defense. The M'Naghten rule, based on a case in England in 1843, treated the failure to appreciate the wrongfulness of one's action as the basis of legal insanity. The *Durham* rule was based on a case in the United States in 1954, in which it was held that people did not bear criminal responsibility if their criminal behavior was the product of "mental disease or mental defect." Guidelines proposed by the American Law Institute are a set of standards that combines the M'Naghten principle of inability to ascertain the difference between right and wrong and the irresistible impulse principle of being unable to conform one's behavior to the requirements of law due to mental disease or defect.

## Determining the Length of Criminal Commitment

**15.6 Describe the legal basis for determining length of criminal commitment.**

The legal basis for determining length of criminal commitment holds that people who are criminally committed may be hospitalized for an indefinite period of time, with their eventual release dependent on a determination of their mental status.

## Competency to Stand Trial

**15.7 Describe the legal basis for determining competency to stand trial.**

People who are accused of crimes but are incapable of understanding the charges against them or of assisting in their own defense can be found incompetent to stand trial and remanded to a psychiatric facility. In the case of *Jackson v. Indiana*, the U.S. Supreme Court placed restrictions on the length of time a person judged incompetent to stand trial could be held in a psychiatric facility.

# Critical Thinking Questions

Based on your reading of this chapter, answer the following questions:

- Do you believe that psychiatric patients who wander city streets mumbling to themselves and living in cardboard boxes should be hospitalized against their will? Why or why not?
- If you were called on to evaluate whether an individual posed a danger to him- or herself or to others, on what criteria would you base your judgment? What evidence would you need to make your determination?
- Do you believe therapists should be obligated to breach confidentiality when their clients make threats against others? Why or why not? What concerns have therapists raised about the duty to warn? Do you believe their concerns are warranted?
- Do you believe the insanity verdict should be abolished or replaced with another type of verdict, like the guilty-but-mentally-ill verdict? Why or why not?

# Key Terms

civil commitment, p. 563
criminal commitment, p. 564
duty to warn, p. 570
insanity defense, p. 575
competency to stand trial, p. 579

# Glossary

## A

**Abnormal psychology.** The branch of psychology that deals with the description, causes, and treatment of abnormal behavior patterns.

**Acculturative stress.** Pressure to adjust to a host or mainstream culture.

**Acute stress disorder.** A traumatic stress reaction occurring during the month following exposure to a traumatic event.

**Addiction.** Impaired control over the use of a chemical substance despite the harmful consequences it causes.

**Adjustment disorder.** A maladaptive reaction to an identified stressor, characterized by impaired functioning or emotional distress that exceeds what would normally be expected.

**Adoptee studies.** Studies that compare the traits and behavior patterns of adopted children to those of their biological parents and their adoptive parents.

**Agnosia.** A disturbance of sensory perception, usually affecting visual perception.

**Agoraphobia.** Excessive, irrational fear of open or public places.

**Alarm reaction.** The first stage of the GAS, characterized by heightened sympathetic nervous system activity.

**Alcoholism.** Alcohol addiction or dependence resulting in serious personal, social, occupational, or health problems.

**Alzheimer's disease (AD).** A progressive brain disease characterized by gradual loss of memory and intellectual functioning, personality changes, and eventual loss of ability to care for oneself.

**Amnesia.** Memory loss that frequently follows a traumatic event, such as a blow to the head, an electric shock, or a major surgical operation.

**Amphetamine psychosis.** A psychotic state characterized by hallucinations and delusions, induced by ingestion of amphetamines.

**Amphetamines.** A class of synthetic stimulants that activate the central nervous system, producing heightened states of arousal and feelings of pleasure.

**Anorexia nervosa.** An eating disorder characterized by maintenance of an abnormally low body weight, a distorted body image, and intense fears of gaining weight.

**Anterograde amnesia.** Loss or impairment of ability to form or store new memories.

**Antianxiety drugs.** Drugs that combat anxiety and reduce states of muscle tension.

**Antidepressants.** Drugs used to treat depression that affect the availability of neurotransmitters in the brain.

**Antipsychotic drugs.** Drugs used to treat schizophrenia or other psychotic disorders.

**Antisocial personality disorder.** A personality disorder characterized by antisocial and irresponsible behavior and lack of remorse for misdeeds.

**Anxiety.** An emotional state characterized by physiological arousal, unpleasant feelings of tension, and a sense of apprehension or foreboding.

**Anxiety disorder.** A class of psychological disorders characterized by excessive or maladaptive anxiety reactions.

**Aphasia.** Impaired ability to understand or express speech.

**Archetypes.** According to Jung, primitive images or concepts that reside in the collective unconscious.

**Ataxia.** Loss of muscle coordination.

**Attention-deficit/hyperactivity disorder (ADHD).** A behavior disorder characterized by excessive motor activity and inability to focus one's attention.

**Autism spectrum disorder.** A developmental disorder characterized by significant deficits in communication and social interaction, as well as development of restricted or fixated interests and repetitive behaviors.

**Autonomic nervous system.** The division of the peripheral nervous system that regulates the activities of the glands and involuntary functions.

**Avoidant personality disorder.** A personality disorder characterized by avoidance of social relationships due to fears of rejection.

**Axon.** The long, thin part of a neuron along which nerve impulses travel.

## B

**Barbiturates.** Sedative drugs that are depressants with high addictive potential.

**Basal ganglia.** An assemblage of neurons at the base of the forebrain involved in regulating postural movements and coordination.

**Behavior therapy.** The therapeutic application of learning-based techniques to resolve psychological disorders.

**Behavioral assessment.** The approach to clinical assessment that focuses on the objective recording and description of problem behavior.

**Behaviorism.** The school of psychology that defines psychology as the study of observable behavior and that focuses on the role of learning in explaining behavior.

**Binge-eating disorder (BED).** An eating disorder characterized by recurrent eating binges without subsequent purging.

**Biofeedback training (BFT).** A method of giving an individual information (feedback) about bodily functions so that the person can gain some degree of control over them.

**Biopsychosocial model.** An integrative model for explaining abnormal behavior in terms of the interactions of biological, psychological, and sociocultural factors.

**Bipolar disorder.** A psychological disorder characterized by mood swings between states of extreme elation and depression.

**Blind.** A state of being unaware of whether one has received an experimental treatment or a placebo.

**Body dysmorphic disorder (BDD).** A psychological disorder characterized by preoccupation with an imagined or exaggerated physical defect in appearance.

**Body mass index (BMI).** A standard measure that takes both body weight and height into account.

**Borderline personality disorder (BPD).** A personality disorder characterized by abrupt shifts in mood, lack of a coherent sense of self, and unpredictable, impulsive behavior.

**Breathing-related sleep disorders.** Sleep disorders in which sleep is repeatedly disrupted by difficulty breathing normally.

**Brief psychotic disorder.** A psychotic disorder lasting from a day to a month that may follow exposure to a major stressor.

**Bulimia nervosa.** An eating disorder characterized by recurrent binge eating followed by self-induced purging, accompanied by overconcern with body weight and shape.

# C

**Cardiovascular disease (CVD).** A disease or disorder of the cardiovascular system, such as coronary heart disease or hypertension.

**Case studies.** Carefully drawn biographies based on clinical interviews, observations, and psychological tests.

**Cataplexy.** A physical condition triggered by a strong emotional reaction that involves loss of muscle tone and voluntary muscle control, which may result in a person slumping or collapsing to the floor.

**Catatonia.** Gross disturbances in motor activity and cognitive functioning, as in a catatonic state or stupor.

**Central nervous system.** The brain and spinal cord.

**Cerebellum.** A structure in the hindbrain involved in coordination and balance.

**Cerebral cortex.** The wrinkled surface area of the cerebrum responsible for processing sensory stimuli and controlling higher mental functions, such as thinking and use of language.

**Cerebrovascular accident (CVA).** A stroke or brain damage resulting from a rupture or blockage of a blood vessel supplying oxygen to the brain.

**Cerebrum.** The large mass of the forebrain, consisting of the two cerebral hemispheres.

**Childhood-onset fluency disorder.** Persistent stuttering, which is characterized by impaired fluency of speech.

**Circadian rhythm sleep-wake disorders.** Sleep-wake disorders characterized by a mismatch between the body's normal sleep-wake cycle and the demands of the environment.

**Civil commitment.** The legal process of placing a person in a mental institution, even against his or her will.

**Classical conditioning.** A form of learning in which a response to one stimulus can be made to occur in response to another stimulus by pairing or associating the two stimuli.

**Cocaine.** A stimulant derived from the leaves of the coca plant.

**Cognitive assessment.** Measurement of thoughts, beliefs, and attitudes that may be associated with emotional problems.

**Cognitive restructuring.** A cognitive therapy method that involves replacing irrational thoughts with rational alternatives.

**Cognitive therapy.** A form of therapy that helps clients identify and correct faulty cognitions (thoughts, beliefs, and attitudes) believed to underlie their emotional problems and maladaptive behavior.

**Cognitive triad of depression.** The view that depression derives from adopting negative views of oneself, the environment or world at large, and the future.

**Cognitive-behavioral therapy.** A learning-based approach to therapy incorporating cognitive and behavioral techniques.

**Cognitive-specificity hypothesis.** The belief that different emotional disorders are linked to particular kinds of automatic thoughts.

**Communication disorders.** A class of psychological disorders characterized by difficulties in understanding or using language.

**Competency to stand trial.** The ability of criminal defendants to understand the charges and proceedings brought against them and to participate in their own defense.

**Compulsion.** A repetitive or ritualistic behavior that the person feels compelled to perform.

**Conditional positive regard.** Valuing other people on the basis of whether their behavior meets one's approval.

**Conditioned response.** In classical conditioning, a learned response to a previously neutral stimulus.

**Conditioned stimulus.** A previously neutral stimulus that evokes a conditioned response after repeated pairings with an unconditioned stimulus that had previously evoked that response.

**Conduct disorder.** A psychological disorder in childhood and adolescence characterized by disruptive, antisocial behavior.

**Confidentiality.** Protection of research participants by keeping records secure and not disclosing their identities.

**Congruence.** The coherence or fit among one's thoughts, behaviors, and feelings.

**Conscious.** To Freud, the part of the mind that corresponds to our present awareness.

**Construct validity.** (1) In experimentation, the degree to which treatment effects can be accounted for by the theoretical mechanisms (constructs) represented in the independent variables; (2) in measurement, the degree to which a test measures the hypothetical construct that it purports to measure.

**Content validity.** The degree to which the content of a test or measure represents the the traits it purports to measure.

**Control group.** In an experiment, a group that does not receive the experimental treatment.

**Conversion disorder.** A somatoform disorder characterized by loss or impairment of physical function in the absence of any apparent organic cause.

**Correlation coefficient.** A statistical measure of the strength of the relationship between two variables expressed along a continuum that ranges between –1.00 and +1.00.

**Correlational method.** A scientific method of study that examines the relationships between factors or variables expressed in statistical terms.

**Countertransference.** In psychoanalysis, the transfer of the analyst's feelings or attitudes toward other persons in her or his life onto the client.

**Couple therapy.** A form of therapy that focuses on resolving conflicts in distressed couples.

**Crack.** The hardened, smokable form of cocaine.

**Criminal commitment.** The legal process of confining a person found not guilty by reason of insanity in a mental institution.

**Criterion validity.** The degree to which a test correlates with an independent, external criterion or standard.

**Critical thinking.** Adoption of a questioning attitude and careful scrutiny of claims and arguments in light of evidence.

**Culture-bound syndromes.** Patterns of abnormal behavior found predominantly in only one or a few cultures.

**Cyclothymic disorder.** A mood disorder characterized by a chronic pattern of less severe mood swings than are found in bipolar disorder.

# D

**Defense mechanisms.** The reality-distorting strategies used by the ego to shield the self from awareness of anxiety-provoking impulses.

**Deinstitutionalization.** The policy of shifting care for patients with severe or chronic mental health problems from inpatient facilities to community-based facilities.

**Delayed ejaculation.** Persistent or recurrent delay in achieving orgasm or inability to achieve orgasm despite a normal level of sexual interest and arousal. Formerly called *male orgasmic disorder*.

**Delirium.** A state of mental confusion, disorientation, and inability to focus attention.

**Delusional disorder.** A type of psychosis characterized by persistent delusions, often of a paranoid nature, that do not have the bizarre quality of the type found in paranoid schizophrenia.

**Dementia praecox.** The term given by Kraepelin to the disorder now called *schizophrenia*.

**Dendrites.** The rootlike structures at the ends of neurons that receive nerve impulses from other neurons.

**Dependent personality disorder.** A personality disorder characterized by difficulty making independent decisions and overly dependent behavior.

**Dependent variables.** Factors that are observed in order to determine the effects of manipulating an independent variable.

**Depersonalization/derealization disorder.** A dissociative disorder characterized by persistent or recurrent episodes of depersonalization and/or derealization.

**Depersonalization.** Feelings of unreality or detachment from one's self or one's body.

**Depressant.** A drug that lowers the level of activity of the central nervous system.

**Derealization.** A sense of unreality about the outside world.

**Detoxification.** The process of ridding the system of alcohol or other drugs under supervised conditions.

**Dhat syndrome.** A culture-bound disorder, found primarily among Asian Indian males, characterized by excessive fears over the loss of seminal fluid.

**Diathesis.** A vulnerability or predisposition to a particular disorder.

**Diathesis-stress model.** A model that posits that abnormal behavior problems involve the interaction of (1) a vulnerability or predisposition and (2) stressful life events or experiences.

**Dissociative amnesia.** A dissociative disorder in which a person experiences memory loss without any identifiable organic cause.

**Dissociative disorders.** Disorders characterized by disruption, or dissociation, of identity, memory, or consciousness.

**Dissociative identity disorder.** A dissociative disorder in which a person has two or more distinct, or alter, personalities.

**Dopamine hypothesis.** The prediction that schizophrenia involves overactivity of dopamine transmission in the brain.

**Double depression.** Concurrent major depressive disorder and dysthymia.

**Down syndrome.** A condition caused by the presence of an extra chromosome on the 21st pair and characterized by intellectual developmental disorder and various physical anomalies.

**Downward drift hypothesis.** A theory that attempts to explain the link between low socioeconomic status and behavior problems by suggesting that problem behaviors lead people to drift downward in social status.

**Duty to warn.** The therapist's obligation to warn third parties of threats made against them by clients.

**Dyslexia.** A learning disorder characterized by impaired reading ability.

# E

**Early-onset dementia.** Forms of dementia that begin before age 65.

**Eating disorders.** Psychological disorders characterized by disturbed patterns of eating and maladaptive ways of controlling body weight.

**Eclectic therapy.** An approach to psychotherapy that incorporates principles or techniques from various systems or theories.

**Ego.** The psychic structure that corresponds to the concept of the self, governed by the reality principle and characterized by the ability to tolerate frustration.

**Ego dystonic.** Referring to behaviors or feelings that are perceived to be alien to one's self-identity.

**Ego psychology.** Modern psychodynamic approach that focuses more on the conscious strivings of the ego than on the hypothesized unconscious functions of the id.

**Ego syntonic.** Referring to behaviors or feelings that are perceived as natural parts of the self.

**Electroconvulsive therapy (ECT).** A method of treating severe depression by administering electrical shock to the head.

**Emotion-focused coping.** A coping style that involves reducing the impact of a stressor by ignoring or escaping it rather than dealing with it directly.

**Empathy.** The ability to understand someone's experiences and feelings from that person's point of view.

**Encopresis.** Lack of control over bowel movements that is not caused by an organic problem in a child who is at least 4 years old.

**Endocrine system.** The system of ductless glands that secrete hormones directly into the bloodstream.

**Endophenotypes.** Measurable processes or mechanisms not apparent to the naked eye that explain how an organism's genetic code influences its observable characteristics or phenotypes.

**Endorphins.** Natural substances that function as neurotransmitters in the brain and are similar in their effects to opioids.

**Enuresis.** Failure to control urination after one has reached the expected age for attaining such control.

**Epidemiological method.** Research studies that track rates of occurrence of particular disorders among different population groups.

**Epigenetics.** The study of heritable changes in processes affecting gene expression that occur without changes in the DNA itself, the chemical material that houses the genetic code.

**Erectile disorder.** A sexual dysfunction in males characterized by difficulty achieving or maintaining erection during sexual activity.

**Erotomania.** A delusional disorder characterized by the belief that one is loved by someone of high social status.

**Exhaustion stage.** The third stage of the GAS, characterized by lowered resistance, increased parasympathetic nervous system activity, and eventual physical deterioration.

**Exhibitionism.** A type of paraphilia almost exclusively occurring in males, in which the man experiences persistent and recurrent sexual urges and sexually arousing fantasies involving the exposure of his genitals to unsuspecting strangers.

**Expectancies.** Beliefs about expected outcomes.

**Experimental group.** In an experiment, a group that receives the experimental treatment.

**Experimental method.** A scientific method that aims to discover cause-and-effect relationships by manipulating independent variables and observing the effects on the dependent variables.

**External validity.** The degree to which experimental results can be generalized to other settings and conditions.

**Eye movement desensitization and reprocessing (EMDR).** A controversial form of therapy for PTSD that involves the client's eye tracking of a visual target while holding images of the traumatic experience in mind.

# F

**Factitious disorder.** A disorder characterized by intentional fabrication of psychological or physical symptoms for no apparent gain.

**Family therapy.** A form of therapy in which the family, not the individual, is the unit of treatment.

**Fear-stimulus hierarchy.** An ordered series of increasingly fearful stimuli.

**Female orgasmic disorder.** A type of sexual dysfunction involving persistent difficulty achieving orgasm despite adequate stimulation.

**Female sexual interest/arousal disorder.** A type of sexual dysfunction in women involving difficulty becoming sexually aroused or lack of sexual excitement or pleasure during sexual activity.

**Fetishism.** A type of paraphilia in which a person uses an inanimate object as a focus of sexual interest and as a source of arousal.

**Fight-or-flight reaction.** The inborn tendency to respond to a threat by either fighting or fleeing.

**Fixation.** In Freudian theory, a constellation of personality traits associated with a particular stage of psychosexual development, resulting from either too much or too little gratification at that stage.

**Flooding.** A behavior therapy technique for overcoming fears by means of exposure to high levels of fear-inducing stimuli.

**Fragile X syndrome.** An inherited form of intellectual developmental disorder caused by a mutated gene on the X chromosome.

**Free association.** The method of verbalizing thoughts as they occur without a conscious attempt to edit or censor them.

**Frotteurism.** A type of paraphilia involving sexual urges or sexually arousing fantasies about bumping and rubbing against nonconsenting persons for sexual gratification.

## G

**Gambling disorder.** An addictive disorder characterized by a pattern of habitual gambling and impaired control over the behavior.

**Gender dysphoria.** A psychological disorder characterized by strong and persistent discomfort or distress about one's biologic or anatomic sex.

**Gender identity.** One's psychological sense of being female or being male.

**General adaptation syndrome (GAS).** The body's three-stage response to prolonged or intense stress, comprising the alarm reaction, the resistance stage, and the exhaustion stage.

**General paresis.** A form of dementia resulting from neurosyphilis.

**Generalized anxiety disorder (GAD).** A type of anxiety disorder characterized by general feelings of dread and foreboding and heightened states of bodily arousal.

**Genito-pelvic pain/penetration disorder.** Persistent or recurrent pain experienced during vaginal intercourse or penetration attempts.

**Genotype.** The set of traits specified by an individual's genetic code.

**Genuineness.** The ability to recognize and express one's true feelings.

**Gradual exposure.** (1) A behavior therapy technique for overcoming fears through direct exposure to increasingly fearful stimuli; (2) In behavior therapy, a method of overcoming fears through a stepwise process of exposure to increasingly fearful stimuli in imagination or in real-life situations.

**Group therapy.** A form of therapy in which a group of clients with similar problems meets together with a therapist.

## H

**Hallucinations.** Perceptions occurring in the absence of external stimuli that become confused with reality.

**Hallucinogens.** Substances that cause hallucinations.

**Health psychologist.** A psychologist who studies the interrelationships between psychological factors and physical health.

**Heroin.** A narcotic derived from morphine that has strong addictive properties.

**Histrionic personality disorder.** A personality disorder characterized by excessive need for attention, praise, reassurance, and approval.

**Hoarding disorder.** A psychological disorder characterized by strong needs to acquire, and resistance to discarding, large collections of seemingly useless or unneeded possessions.

**Hormones.** Substances secreted by endocrine glands that regulate body functions and promote growth and development.

**Humors.** According to the ancient Hippocratic belief system, the vital bodily fluids (phlegm, black bile, blood, yellow bile).

**Huntington's disease.** An inherited degenerative disease that is characterized by jerking and twisting movements, paranoia, and mental deterioration.

**Hypersomnolence disorder.** Persistent pattern of excessive sleepiness during the day.

**Hypnagogic hallucinations.** Hallucinations occurring at the threshold between wakefulness and sleep onset or shortly upon awakening.

**Hypochondriasis.** A pattern of abnormal behavior characterized by misinterpretation of physical symptoms as signs of underlying serious disease, now classified as a form of either somatic symptom disorder or illness anxiety disorder.

**Hypomania.** A relatively mild state of mania.

**Hypothalamus.** A structure in the forebrain involved in regulating body temperature, emotion, and motivation.

**Hypothesis.** A prediction that is tested through experimentation.

**Hypoxia.** Decreased supply of oxygen to the brain or other organs.

**Hypoxyphilia.** A paraphilia in which a person seeks sexual gratification by being deprived of oxygen by means of a noose, plastic bag, chemical, or pressure on the chest.

## I

**Id.** The unconscious psychic structure, present at birth, that contains primitive instincts and that is regulated by the pleasure principle.

**Illness anxiety disorder.** A somatic symptom disorder characterized by unduly high levels of anxiety or concerns about having a serious illness, even though physical symptoms are either absent or minor.

**Immune system.** The body's system of defense against disease.

**Impulse-control disorders.** Psychological disorders characterized by failure to control impulses, temptations, or drives, resulting in harm to oneself or others.

**Incidence.** The number of new cases of a disorder that occurs within a specific period of time.

**Independent variables.** Factors that are manipulated in experiments.

**Infarction.** The development of an infarct—or area of dead or dying tissue—resulting from the blocking of blood vessels that normally supply the tissue.

**Informed consent.** The principle that research participants should receive enough information about an experiment beforehand to decide freely whether to participate.

**Insanity defense.** A legal defense in which a defendant in a criminal case pleads not guilty on the basis of insanity.

**Insomnia.** Difficulties falling asleep, remaining asleep, or achieving restorative sleep.

**Insomnia disorder.** A sleep-wake disorder characterized by chronic or persistent insomnia not caused by another psychological or physical disorder or by the effects of drugs or medications.

**Intellectual disability.** A generalized delay or impairment in the development of intellectual and adaptive abilities.

**Intermittent explosive disorder.** A type of impulse-control disorder characterized by impulsive aggression.

**Internal validity.** The degree to which manipulation of the independent variables can be causally related to changes in the dependent variables.

**Internet addiction disorder.** A type of nonchemical addiction characterized by excessive or maladaptive use of the Internet.

## K

**Kleptomania.** A type of impulse-control disorder characterized by compulsive stealing.

**Koro syndrome.** A culture-bound disorder, found primarily in China, in which people fear that their genitals are shrinking and retracting into their bodies.

**Korsakoff's syndrome.** A syndrome associated with chronic alcoholism that is characterized by memory loss and disorientation.

## L

**Language disorder.** A type of communication disorder characterized by difficulties understanding or using language.

**Late-onset dementia.** Forms of dementia that begin after age 65.

**Learned helplessness.** A behavior pattern characterized by passivity and perceptions of lack of control.

**Learning disorder.** A deficiency in a specific learning ability in the context of normal intelligence and exposure to learning opportunities.

**Lewy bodies.** Abnormal protein deposits in brain cells that cause a form of dementia.

**Limbic system.** A group of forebrain structures involved in emotional processing, memory, and basic drives such as hunger, thirst, and aggression.

**Longitudinal study.** A research study in which subjects are followed over time.

## M

**Major depressive disorder.** A severe mood disorder characterized by major depressive episodes.

**Major neurocognitive disorder.** Profound deterioration of cognitive functioning, characterized by deficits in memory, thinking, judgment, and language use. Formerly called *dementia* in earlier versions of the *DSM*.

**Male hypoactive sexual desire disorder.** Persistent or recurrent lack of sexual interest or sexual fantasies in men.

**Malingering.** Faking illness to avoid work or duty.

**Mania.** A state of unusual elation, energy, and activity.

**Manic episode.** A period of unrealistically heightened euphoria, extreme restlessness, and excessive activity characterized by disorganized behavior and impaired judgment.

**Marijuana.** A hallucinogenic drug derived from the leaves and stems of the plant *Cannabis sativa*.

**Medical model.** A biological perspective in which abnormal behavior is viewed as symptomatic of underlying illness.

**Medulla.** An area of the hindbrain involved in regulation of heartbeat, respiration, and blood pressure.

**Mental status examination.** A structured clinical assessment to determine various aspects of a client's mental functioning.

**Methadone.** A synthetic opiate that does not produce a pleasurable high when used properly, but which can avert withdrawal symptoms in people with heroin addiction when they stop using heroin.

**Mild neurocognitive disorder.** Mild deterioration of cognitive functioning in which a person is able to perform tasks of daily living but needs to put in greater effort or compensate in other ways to maintain independent functioning.

**Modeling.** (1) Learning by observing and imitating the behavior of others; (2) in behavior therapy, a treatment technique for helping an individual acquire a target behavior by observing a therapist or another individual demonstrate the target behavior and then imitating it.

**Mood disorders.** Psychological disorders characterized by unusually severe or prolonged disturbances of mood.

**Morphine.** A strongly addictive narcotic derived from the opium poppy that relieves pain and induces feelings of well-being.

**Münchausen syndrome.** A type of factitious disorder characterized by the fabrication of medical symptoms.

**Myelin sheath.** The insulating layer or protective coating of the axon that helps speed transmission of nerve impulses.

## N

**Naltrexone.** A drug that blocks the high from alcohol as well as from opiates.

**Narcissistic personality disorder.** A personality disorder characterized by an inflated self-image and extreme needs for attention and admiration.

**Narcolepsy.** A sleep disorder characterized by sudden, irresistible episodes of sleep.

**Narcotics.** Drugs that are used medically for pain relief but that have strong addictive potential.

**Naturalistic observation method.** A research method in which behavior is observed and measured in its natural environment.

**Negative reinforcers.** Reinforcers that increase the frequency of the preceding behavior when removed.

**Negative symptoms.** Behavioral deficiencies associated with schizophrenia, such as social skills deficits, social withdrawal, flattened affect, poverty of speech and thought, psychomotor retardation, and failure to experience pleasure.

**Neurocognitive disorders.** A class of psychological disorders characterized by impairments in cognitive abilities and daily functioning that involve underlying brain disorders or abnormalities.

**Neurodevelopmental disorders.** A category of mental disorders in the *DSM-5* affecting children and adolescents that involve impaired brain functioning or development.

**Neurons.** Nerve cells.

**Neuropsychological assessment.** Measurement of behavior or performance that may be indicative of underlying brain damage or defects.

**Neurotransmitters.** Chemical substances that transmit messages from one neuron to another.

**Nightmare disorder.** A sleep-wake disorder characterized by recurrent awakenings due to frightening nightmares.

**Nonspecific treatment factors.** Factors not specific to any one form of psychotherapy, such as therapist attention and support and creating positive expectancies of change.

## O

**Obesity.** A condition of excess body fat; generally defined by a BMI of 30 or higher.

**Objective tests.** Self-report personality tests that can be scored objectively and that are based on a research foundation.

**Object-relations theory.** The psychodynamic viewpoint that focuses on the influences of internalized representations of the personalities of parents and other strong attachment figures (called *objects*).

**Obsession.** A recurring thought, image, or urge that the individual cannot control.

**Obsessive-compulsive disorder (OCD).** A type of anxiety disorder characterized by recurrent obsessions, compulsions, or both.

**Obsessive-compulsive personality disorder.** A personality disorder characterized by rigid ways of relating to others, perfectionistic tendencies, lack of spontaneity, and excessive attention to detail.

**Obstructive sleep apnea hypopnea syndrome.** A subtype of breathing-related sleep disorders more commonly called *obstructive sleep apnea*. It typically involves repeated episodes during sleep of snorting or gasping for breath, pauses of breath, or abnormally shallow breathing.

**Operant conditioning.** A form of learning in which behavior is acquired and strengthened when it is reinforced.

**Oppositional defiant disorder.** A psychological disorder in childhood and adolescence characterized by excessive oppositionality or tendencies to refuse requests from parents and others.

# P

**Panic disorder.** A type of anxiety disorder characterized by repeated episodes of intense anxiety or panic.

**Paranoid personality disorder.** A personality disorder characterized by undue suspiciousness of others' motives, but not to the point of delusion.

**Paraphilias.** Atypical patterns of sexual attraction in which one experiences recurrent sexual urges and sexually arousing fantasies involving nonhuman objects (such as articles of clothing), inappropriate or nonconsenting partners (e.g., children), or situations producing humiliation or pain to oneself or one's partner.

**Parasomnias.** Sleep-wake disorders involving abnormal behavior patterns associated with partial or incomplete arousals.

**Parasympathetic nervous system.** The division of the autonomic nervous system whose activity reduces states of arousal and regulates bodily processes that replenish energy reserves.

**Parkinson's disease.** A progressive disease characterized by muscle tremor and shakiness, rigidity, difficulty walking, poor control of fine motor movements, lack of facial muscle tone, and, in some cases, cognitive impairment.

**Pedophilia.** A type of paraphilia involving sexual attraction to children.

**Peripheral nervous system.** The somatic and autonomic nervous systems.

**Persistent depressive disorder.** A chronic type of depressive disorder.

**Personality disorders.** Excessively rigid behavior patterns, or ways of relating to others, that ultimately become self-defeating.

**Person-centered therapy.** The establishment of a warm, accepting therapeutic relationship that frees clients to engage in self-exploration and achieve self-acceptance.

**Phenotype.** An individual's actual or expressed traits.

**Phenylketonuria (PKU).** A genetic disorder that prevents the metabolization of phenylpyruvic acid, leading to intellectual developmental disorder unless the diet is strictly controlled.

**Phobia.** An excessive, irrational fear.

**Physiological dependence.** Bodily changes resulting from regular use of a drug, as denoted by the development of tolerance and/or a withdrawal syndrome (also called *chemical dependence*).

**Physiological assessment.** Measurement of physiological responses that may be associated with abnormal behavior.

**Pick's disease.** A form of dementia, similar to Alzheimer's disease, but distinguished by specific abnormalities (Pick's bodies) in nerve cells and the absence of neurofibrillary tangles and plaques.

**Placebo.** An inert medication or bogus treatment that is intended to control for expectancy effects.

**Pleasure principle.** The governing principle of the id, involving demands for immediate gratification of needs.

**Pons.** A structure in the hindbrain involved in body movements, attention, sleep, and respiration.

**Positive psychology.** A growing contemporary movement within psychology that focuses on the positive attributes of human behavior.

**Positive reinforcers.** Reinforcers that increase the frequency of the preceding behavior when introduced.

**Positive symptoms.** Flagrant symptoms of schizophrenia, such as hallucinations, delusions, bizarre behavior, and thought disorder.

**Postpartum depression (PPD).** Persistent and severe mood changes that occur after childbirth.

**Posttraumatic stress disorder (PTSD).** A prolonged maladaptive reaction to a traumatic event.

**Preconscious.** To Freud, the part of the mind whose contents lie outside present awareness but can be brought into awareness by focusing on them.

**Premature (early) ejaculation.** A type of sexual dysfunction involving a pattern of unwanted rapid ejaculation during sexual activity.

**Premenstrual dysphoric disorder (PMDD).** A psychological disorder characterized by significant changes in mood during a woman's premenstrual period.

**Presenile dementias.** Forms of dementia that begin at or before age 65.

**Prevalence.** The overall number of cases of a disorder in a population within a specific period of time.

**Proband.** The case first diagnosed with a given disorder.

**Problem-focused coping.** A coping style that involves confronting a stressor directly.

**Prodromal phase.** In schizophrenia, the period of decline in functioning that precedes the first acute psychotic episode.

**Projective test.** A psychological test that presents ambiguous stimuli onto which the examinee is thought to project his or her personality and unconscious motives.

**Psychoanalysis.** The method of psychotherapy developed by Sigmund Freud.

**Psychoanalytic theory.** The theoretical model of personality developed by Sigmund Freud, based on the belief that psychological problems are rooted in unconscious motives and conflicts from childhood; also called *psychoanalysis*.

**Psychodynamic model.** The theoretical model of Freud and his followers, in which abnormal behavior is viewed as the product of clashing forces within the personality.

**Psychodynamic therapy.** Therapy that helps individuals gain insight into and resolve deep-seated conflicts in the unconscious mind.

**Psychological dependence.** Compulsive use of a substance to meet a psychological need.

**Psychological disorder.** Abnormal behavior pattern that involves impairment of psychological functioning or behavior.

**Psychological hardiness.** A cluster of stress-buffering traits characterized by commitment, challenge, and control.

**Psychopharmacology.** The field of study that examines the effects of therapeutic or psychiatric drugs.

**Psychosis.** A severe form of disturbed behavior characterized by impaired ability to interpret reality and difficulty meeting the demands of daily life.

**Psychosomatic disorders.** Physical disorders in which psychological factors play a causal or contributing role.

**Psychotherapy.** A structured form of treatment derived from a psychological framework that consists of one or more verbal interactions or treatment sessions between a client and a therapist.

**Punishment.** Application of aversive or painful stimuli that reduces the frequency of the behavior it follows.

**Pyromania.** A type of impulse-control disorder characterized by compulsive fire setting.

## R

**Random assignment.** A method of assigning research subjects at random to experimental or control groups to balance the characteristics of people who comprise them.

**Random sample.** A sample that is drawn in such a way that every member of a population has an equal chance of being included.

**Rape.** Forced penetration of the vagina or anus by any body part or object, or of the mouth by a sexual organ (prior to 2012, the definition of *rape* used by law enforcement officials was limited to forced sexual intercourse).

**Rational emotive behavior therapy.** A therapeutic approach that focuses on helping clients replace irrational, maladaptive beliefs with alternative, more adaptive beliefs.

**Reality principle.** The governing principle of the ego, which involves considerations of social acceptability and practicality.

**Reality testing.** The ability to perceive the world accurately and to distinguish reality from fantasy.

**Rebound anxiety.** The experiencing of strong anxiety following withdrawal from a tranquilizer.

**Receptor site.** A part of a dendrite on a receiving neuron that is structured to receive a neurotransmitter.

**Reinforcement.** A stimulus or event that increases the frequency of the response that it follows.

**Reliability.** In psychological assessment, the consistency of a measure or diagnostic instrument or system.

**REM sleep behavior disorder.** A sleep-wake disorder characterized by vocalizing parts of a dream or thrashing about during a dream.

**Residual phase.** In schizophrenia, the phase that follows an acute phase, characterized by a return to the level of functioning of the prodromal phase.

**Resistance stage.** The second stage of the GAS, involving the body's attempt to withstand prolonged stress and preserve resources.

**Reticular activating system.** Brain structure involved in processes of attention, sleep, and arousal.

**Retrograde amnesia.** Loss or impairment of ability to recall past events.

**Reversal design.** An experimental design that consists of repeated measurement of a subject's behavior through a sequence of alternating baseline and treatment phases.

## S

**Sadomasochism.** Sexual activities between partners involving the attainment of gratification by means of inflicting and receiving pain and humiliation.

**Sanism.** The negative stereotyping of people who are identified as mentally ill.

**Schizoaffective disorder.** A type of psychotic disorder in which individuals experience both severe mood disturbance and features associated with schizophrenia.

**Schizoid personality disorder.** A personality disorder characterized by persistent lack of interest in social relationships, flattened affect, and social withdrawal.

**Schizophrenia.** A chronic psychotic disorder characterized by severely disturbed behavior, thinking, emotions, and perceptions.

**Schizophreniform disorder.** A psychotic disorder lasting less than 6 months in duration, with features that resemble schizophrenia.

**Schizotypal personality disorder.** A personality disorder characterized by lack of close personal relationships and eccentricities of thought and behavior, but without clearly psychotic features.

**Scientific method.** A systematic method of conducting scientific research in which theories or assumptions are examined in light of evidence.

**Selection factor.** A type of bias in which differences between experimental and control groups result from differences in the types of participants in the group, not from the influence of the independent variable.

**Self-actualization.** In humanistic psychology, the tendency to strive to become all that one is capable of being; the motive that drives one to reach one's full potential and express one's unique capabilities.

**Self-efficacy expectancies.** Beliefs in one's ability to cope with challenges and to accomplish particular tasks.

**Self-monitoring.** The process of observing or recording one's own behaviors, thoughts, or emotions.

**Semistructured interview.** A clinical interview in which the clinician follows a general outline of questions designed to gather essential information but is free to ask them in any order and to branch off in other directions.

**Separation anxiety disorder.** A childhood disorder characterized by extreme fear of separation from parents or other caretakers.

**Sexual dysfunctions.** Persistent or recurrent problems with sexual interest, arousal, or response.

**Sexual masochism.** A type of paraphilia characterized by sexual urges and sexually arousing fantasies about receiving humiliation or pain.

**Sexual sadism.** A type of paraphilia or sexual deviation characterized by recurrent sexual urges and sexually arousing fantasies about inflicting humiliation or physical pain on sex partners.

**Single-case experimental design.** A type of case study in which the subject is used as his or her own control.

**Sleep paralysis.** A temporary state of muscle paralysis upon awakening.

**Sleep terrors.** A sleep-wake disorder characterized by recurrent episodes of terror-induced arousals during sleep.

**Sleep-wake disorders.** Persistent or recurrent sleep-related problems that cause distress or impaired functioning.

**Sleepwalking.** A sleep-wake disorder involving repeated episodes of sleepwalking.

**Social (pragmatic) communication disorder.** A type of communication disorder characterized by difficulties communicating with others in social contexts.

**Social anxiety disorder.** Excessive fear of social interactions or situations. Also called *social phobia*.

**Social causation model.** A belief that social stressors, such as poverty, account for the increased risk of severe psychological disorders among people of lower socioeconomic status (SES) relative to those of higher SES levels.

**Social-cognitive theory.** A learning-based theory that emphasizes observational learning and incorporates roles for cognitive variables in determining behavior.

**Somatic nervous system.** The division of the peripheral nervous system that relays information from the sense organs to the brain and transmits messages from the brain to the skeletal muscles.

**Somatic symptom and related disorders.** A category of psychological disorders characterized by persistent emotional or behavioral problems relating to physical symptoms.

**Somatic symptom disorder.** A psychological disorder characterized by excessive concerns about one's physical symptoms.

**Specific phobia.** A phobia that is specific to a particular object or situation.

**Speech sound disorder.** A type of communication disorder characterized by difficulties in articulating speech.

**Splitting.** An inability to reconcile the positive and negative aspects of the self and others, resulting in sudden shifts between positive and negative feelings toward others.

**Stimulants.** Psychoactive substances that increase the activity of the central nervous system.

**Stress.** A demand made on an organism to adapt or adjust.

**Stressor.** A source of stress.

**Structured interview.** A clinical interview that follows a preset series of questions in a particular order.

**Substance intoxication.** A type of substance-induced disorder characterized by repeated episodes of intoxication.

**Substance use disorders.** Substance-related disorders characterized by maladaptive use of psychoactive substances, leading to significant impairment of functioning or personal distress.

**Substance withdrawal.** A type of substance-induced disorder characterized by a cluster of symptoms following the sudden reduction or cessation of use of a psychoactive substance after physical dependence has developed.

**Substance-induced disorders.** A category of substance-related disorders induced by using psychoactive substances.

**Superego.** The psychic structure that incorporates the values of our parents and important others and functions as a moral conscience.

**Survey method.** A research method in which samples of people are questioned by means of a survey instrument, such as a questionnaire or interview protocol.

**Sympathetic nervous system.** The division of the autonomic nervous system whose activity leads to heightened states of arousal.

**Synapse.** The junction between one neuron and another through which nerve impulses pass.

**Syndromes.** Clusters of symptoms that may be indicative of a particular disease or condition.

**Systematic desensitization.** A behavior therapy technique for overcoming phobias by means of exposure to progressively more fearful stimuli (in imagination or by viewing slides) while remaining deeply relaxed.

# T

**Tardive dyskinesia.** A disorder characterized by involuntary movements of the face, mouth, neck, trunk, or extremities caused by long-term use of antipsychotic medication.

**Terminals.** The small branching structures at the tips of axons.

**Thalamus.** A structure in the forebrain involved in relaying sensory information to the cortex and in regulating sleep and attention.

**Theory.** A formulation of the relationships underlying observed events.

**Thought disorder.** A disturbance in thinking characterized by the breakdown of logical associations between thoughts.

**Token economy.** A behavioral treatment program that creates a controlled environment in which desirable behaviors are reinforced by dispensing tokens that may be exchanged for desired rewards.

**Tolerance.** Physical habituation to a drug in which frequent use leads to higher doses being needed to achieve the same effects.

**Transdiagnostic model.** The understanding of abnormal behavior in terms of the common processes or features that extend across different diagnostic categories.

**Transference relationship.** In psychoanalysis, the client's transfer or generalization to the analyst of feelings and attitudes the client holds toward important figures in his or her life.

**Transgender identity.** A type of gender identity in which one's psychological experience of oneself as male or female is opposite to one's physical or genetic sex.

**Transvestism.** A type of paraphilia characterized by sexual urges and fantasies involving cross-dressing. Also called *transvestic fetishism.*

**Trephination.** A harsh, prehistoric practice of cutting a hole in a person's skull, possibly in an attempt to release demons.

**Two-factor model.** A theoretical model that accounts for the development of phobic reactions on the basis of classical and operant conditioning.

**Type A behavior pattern (TABP).** A behavior pattern characterized by a sense of time urgency, competitiveness, and hostility.

# U

**Unconditional positive regard.** Valuing other people as having basic worth regardless of their behavior at a particular time.

**Unconditioned response.** An unlearned response.

**Unconditioned stimulus.** A stimulus that elicits an unlearned response.

**Unconscious.** To Freud, the part of the mind that lies outside the range of ordinary awareness and that contains instinctual urges.

**Unstructured interview.** A clinical interview in which the clinician adopts his or her own style of questioning rather than following any standard format.

# V

**Vaginismus.** The involuntary spasm of the muscles surrounding the vagina when vaginal penetration is attempted, making sexual intercourse difficult or impossible.

**Validity.** The degree to which a test or diagnostic system measures the traits or constructs it purports to measure.

**Vascular neurocognitive disorder.** Dementia resulting from repeated strokes that cause damage in the brain.

**Virtual reality therapy (VRT).** A form of exposure therapy involving the presentation of phobic stimuli in a virtual reality environment.

**Voyeurism.** A type of paraphilia involving sexual urges and sexually arousing fantasies focused on acts of watching unsuspecting others who are naked, in the act of undressing, or engaging in sexual activity.

# W

**Wernicke's disease.** A brain disorder, associated with chronic alcoholism, characterized by confusion, disorientation, and difficulty maintaining balance while walking.

**Withdrawal syndrome.** A cluster of physical and psychological symptoms that arises following abrupt withdrawal from use of a psychoactive substance.

# Reference


Abbey, A., Zawackia, T., Bucka, O., Clinton, A. M., & McAuslan, P. (2004). Sexual assault and alcohol consumption: What do we know about their relationship and what types of research are still needed? *Aggression and Violent Behavior, 9*, 271–303. doi:10.1016/S1359-1789(03) 00011-9

Abbott, A. (2010). Schizophrenia: The drug deadlock. *Nature, 468*, 158–159. doi:10.1038/468158a

Abel, K. M., Wicks, S., Susser, E. S., Dalman, C., Pedersen, M. G., Mortensen, P. B., & Webb, R. T. (2010). Birth weight, schizophrenia, and adult mental disorder: Is risk confined to the smallest babies? *Archives of General Psychiatry, 67*, 923–930. doi:10.1001/archgenpsychiatry.2010.100

Abela, J. R. Z., Stolow, D., Mineka, S., Yao, S., Zhu, X. Z., & Hankin, B. L. (2011). Cognitive vulnerability to depressive symptoms in adolescents in urban and rural Hunan, China: A multiwave longitudinal study. *Journal of Abnormal Psychology, 120*, 765–778. doi:10.1037/a0025295escents

Abracen, J., & Looman, J. (2004). Treatment of sexual offenders with psychopathic traits: Recent research developments and clinical implications. *Trauma, Violence, & Abuse, 9*, 144–166.

Abraham, K. (1916/1948). The first pregenital stage of the libido. In D. Bryan & A. Strachey (Eds.), *Selected papers of Karl Abraham, M. D.* London: The Hogarth Press.

Abramovitch, A., Abramowitz, J. S., & Mittelman, A. (2013). The neuropsychology of adult obsessive-compulsive disorder: A meta-analysis. *Clinical Psychology Review, 33*, 1163–1171. doi:10.1016/j.cpr.2013.09.00

Abramowitz, J. S. (2008). Cognitive-behavioral therapy for OCD. *Clinical Psychology Review, 21*, 683–703.

Abramowitz, J. S., & Braddock, A. E. (2011). *Hypochondriasis and health anxiety: Advances in psychotherapy—evidence-based practice.* Cambridge, MA: Hogrefe Publishing.

Abramowitz, J. S., Olatunji, B. O., & Deacon, B. J. (2008). Health anxiety, hypochondriasis, and the anxiety disorders. *Behavior Therapy, 38*, 86–94. doi:10.1016/j.beth.2006.05.001

Abramson, L. T., Seligman, M. E. P., & Teasdale, J. D. (1978). Learned helplessness in humans: Critique and reformulation. *Journal of Abnormal Psychology, 87*, 49–74.

Achenbach, T. M., & Dumenci, L. (2001). Levent advances in empirically based assessment: Revised cross-informant syndromes and new DSM-oriented scales for the CBCL, YSR, and TRF: Comment on Lengua, Sadowski, Friedrich, and Fisher (2001). *Journal of Consulting and Clinical Psychology, 69*, 699–702. doi:10.1037/0022-006X.69.4.699

Adam, M. B., McGuire, J. K., Walsh, M., Basta, J., & LeCroy, C. (2005). Acculturation as a predictor of the onset of sexual intercourse among Hispanic and white teens. *Archives of Pediatrics & Adolescent Medicine, 159*, 261–265.

Addington, J., Piskulic, D., & Marshall, C. (2010). Psychosocial treatments for schizophrenia. *Current Directions in Psychological Science, 19*, 260–263. doi:10.1177/0963721410377743

Addolorato, G., Leggio, L., Abenavoli, L., Gasbarrini, G., & on behalf of the Alcoholism Treatment Study Group. (2005). Neurobiochemical and clinical aspects of craving in alcohol addiction: A review. *Addictive Behaviors, 30*, 1209–1224. doi:10.1016/j.addbeh.2004.12.011

Adelson, R. (2006, January). Cultural factors in alcohol abuse. *Monitor on Psychology, 37*(1), 32.

Adler, A. (2014). One in four high school students uses tobacco. *NEJM Journal Watch.* Retrieved from http://www.jwatch.org/fw109528/2014/11/14/one-four-high-school-students-uses-tobacco

Adler, J. (2004, March 8). The war on strokes. *Newsweek*, 42–48.

Afifi, T. O., Asmundson, G. J. G., Taylor, S., & Jang, K. L. (2010). The role of genes and environment on trauma exposure and posttraumatic stress disorder symptoms: A review of twin studies. *Clinical Psychology Review, 30*, 101–112. doi:10.1016/j.cpr.2009.10.002

Afifi, T. O., Mota, N. P., Dasiewicz, P., MacMillan, H. L., & Sareen, J. (2012). Physical punishment and mental disorders: Results from a nationally representative U.S. sample. *Pediatrics, 130*(2), 184–192. doi:10.1542/peds.2011-2947

Agerbo, E., Sullivan, P. F., Vilhjálmsson, B. J., Pedersen, C. B., Mors, O., Børglum, A. D.,… Mortensen, P. B. (2015). Polygenic risk score, parental socioeconomic status, family history of psychiatric disorders, and the risk for schizophrenia: A Danish population-based study and meta-analysis. *JAMA Psychiatry, 72*, 635–641. doi:10.1001/jamapsychiatry.2015.0346

Agras, W. S., Lock, J., Brandt, H., Bryson, S. W., Dodge, E., Halmi, K. A.,… Woodside, B. (2014). Comparison of 2 family therapies for adolescent anorexia nervosa: A randomized parallel trial. *JAMA Psychiatry, 71*, 1279–1286. doi:10.1001/jamapsychiatry.2014.1025

Agren, T., Engman, J. Frick, A., Bjorkstrand, J., Larsson, E.-M., Furmark, T., & Fredrikson, M. (2012). Disruption of reconsolidation erases a fear memory trace in the human amygdala. *Science, 337*, 1550. http://dx.doi.org/10.1126/science.1223006

Ainsworth, M. D. S. (1989). Attachments beyond infancy. *American Psychologist, 44*, 709–716.

Akhtar, S. (1988). Four culture-bound psychiatric syndromes in India. *The International Journal of Social Psychiatry, 34*, 70–74.

Alaka, K. J., Noble, W., Montejo, A., Dueñas, H., Munshi, A., Strawn, J. R.,… Ball, S. (2014). Efficacy and safety of duloxetine in the treatment of older adult patients with generalized anxiety disorder: A randomized, double-blind, placebo-controlled trial. *International Journal of Geriatric Psychiatry, 29*, 978–986. doi:10.1002/gps.4088

Alarcón, R. D., Becker, A. E., Lewis-Fernández, R., Like, R. C., Desai, P., Foulks, E.,… Primm, A. (2009). Issues for DSM-V: The role of culture in psychiatric diagnosis. *The Journal of Nervous and Mental Disease, 197*, 559–660. doi:10.1097/NMD.0b013e3181b0cbff

Alarcón, R. D., Oquendo, M. A., & Wainberg, M. L. (2014). Depression in a Latino man in New York. *American Journal of Psychiatry, 171*, 506–508. doi:10.1176/appi.ajp.2013.13101292

Albarracín, D., Durantini, M. R., & Ear, A. (2006). Empirical and theoretical conclusions of an analysis of outcomes of HIV-prevention interventions. *Current Directions in Psychological Science, 15*, 73–78.

Alderson-Day, B., & Fernyhough, C. (2015). Inner speech: Development, cognitive functions, phenomenology, and neurobiology. *Psychological Bulletin, 141*, 931–965. http://dx.doi.org/10.1037/bul0000021

Aldrich, M. S. (1992). Narcolepsy. *Neurology, 42*(7, Suppl. 6), 34–43.

Aleccia, J. (2014, March 5). Alzheimer's deaths may rival cancer, heart disease, study finds. Retrieved from msnbcnews.com

Alexander, B., Warner-Schmidt, J., Eriksson, T., Tamminga, C., Arango-Llievano, M., Ghose, S.,… Kaplitt, M. G. (2010). Reversal of depressed behaviors in mice by p11 gene therapy in the nucleus accumbens. *Science Translational Medicine, 2*, 54ra76. doi:1s0.1126/scitranslmed.3001079

Ali, M., Farooq, N., Bhatti, M. A., & Kuroiwa, C. (2012). Assessment of prevalence and determinants of posttraumatic stress disorder in survivors of earthquake in Pakistan using Davidson Trauma Scale. *Journal of Affective Disorders, 136*, 238–243.

Allan, R., & Fisher, J. (2011). *Heart and mind: The practice of cardiac psychology* (2nd ed.). Washington, DC: American Psychological Association.

Allderidge, P. (1979). Hospitals, madhouses and asylums: Cycles in the care of the insane. *British Journal of Psychiatry, 134*, 1476–1478.

Allen, D. N., Thaler, N. S., Ringdahl, E. N., Barney, S. J., & Mayfield, J. (2011). Comprehensive trail making test performance in children and adolescents with traumatic brain injury. *Psychological Assessment, 24*, 556–564. doi:10.1037/a0026263

Allen, P., Modinos, G., Hubl, D., Shields, G., Cachia, A., Jardri, R.,… Hoffman, R. (2012). Neuroimaging auditory hallucinations in schizophrenia: From neuroanatomy to neurochemistry and beyond. *Schizophrenia Bulletin, 38*, 695–703. http://dx.doi.org/10.1093/schbul/sbs066

Allgulander, C., Dahl, A. A., Austin, C., Morris, P. L. P., Sogaard, J. A., Fayyad, R.,… Clary, C. M. (2004). Efficacy of sertraline in a 12-week trial for generalized anxiety disorder. *American Journal of Psychiatry, 161*, 1642–1649.

Alloy, L. B., Abramson, L. Y., Urosevic, S., Bender, R. E., & Wagner, C. A. (2009). Longitudinal predictors of bipolar spectrum disorders: A behavioral approach system perspective. *Clinical Psychology: Science and Practice, 16*, 206–226. doi:10.1111/j.1468-2850.2009.01160.x

Alloy, L. B., Abramson, L. Y., Urosevic, S., Walshaw, P. D., Nusslock, R., & Neeren, A. M. (2005). The psychosocial context of bipolar disorder: Environmental, cognitive, and developmental risk factors. *Clinical Psychology Review, 25*, 1043–1075.

Allsop, D. J., Copeland, J., Norberg, M. M., Fu, S., Molnar, A., Lewis, J., & Budney, A. J. (2012). Quantifying the clinical significance of cannabis withdrawal. *PLOS ONE, 7*(9), e44864. doi:10.1371/journal.pone.0044864

Althof, S. E. (2010). What's new in sex therapy? *Journal of Sexual Medicine, 7*, 5–13.

Althof, S. E. (2012). Psychological interventions for delayed ejaculation/orgasm. *International Journal of Impotence Research, 24*, 131–136. doi:10.1038/ijir.2012.2

Althof, S. E., McMahon, C. G., Waldinger, M. D., Serefoglu, E. C., Shindel, A. W., Adaikan, P. G.,… Torres, L. O. (2014). An update of the International Society of Sexual Medicine's guidelines for the diagnosis and treatment of premature ejaculation (PE). *Journal of Sexual Medicine, 6*, 1392–1422. doi:10.1111/jsm.12504

Alvarez, P., Puente, V. M., Blasco, M. J., Salgado, P., Merino, A., & Bulbena, A. (2012). Concurrent Koro and Cotard syndromes in a Spanish male patient with a psychotic depression and cerebrovascular disease. *Psychopathology, 45*, 126–129. doi:10.1159/000329739

Alzheimer's Society. (2008, October). Genetics and dementia. Retrieved from http://alzheimers.org.uk/site/scripts/documents_info.php?documentID=

Ameli, R. (2014). *25 lessons in mindfulness: Now time for healthy living.* Washington, DC: American Psychological Association.

American Heart Association. (2009). Heart disease and stroke statistics 2009 update: A report from the American Heart Association Statistics Committee and Stroke Statistics Subcommittee. *Circulation, 119*, e21–e181. doi:10.1161/CIRCULATIONAHA.108.191261

American Law Institute. (1962). *Model penal code: Proposed official draft.* Philadelphia, PA: Author.

American Psychiatric Association. (1998). *Fact sheet: Violence and mental illness.* Washington, DC: Author.

American Psychiatric Association. (2000). *DSM-IV-TR: Diagnostic and statistical manual of mental disorders* (4th ed., Text Revision). Washington, DC: Author.

American Psychiatric Association. (2013). *DSM-5: Diagnostic and statistical manual of mental disorders* (5th ed.). Washington, DC: Author.

American Psychological Association. (1978). Report of the task force on the role of psychology in the criminal justice system. *American Psychologist, 33*, 1099–1113.

American Psychological Association. (2002). Ethical principles of psychologists and code of conduct. *American Psychologist, 57*, 1060–1073.

American Psychological Association. (2007a, October 24). Stress in America Survey. Retrieved from http://74.125.45.104/search?q=cache:UAeL3kDHQdoJ:apahelpcenter.mediaroom.com/file.php/138/Stress%2Bin%2BAmerica%2BREPORT%2BFINAL.doc+Stress+in+America+Survey&hl=en&ct=clnk&cd=1&gl=us

American Psychological Association. (2007b, October 25). Stress a major health problem in the U.S., warns APA. Retrieved from http://www.apa.org/releases/stressproblem.html

American Psychological Association. (2010). Stress in America 2011: Executive summary. Retrieved from http://www.apa.org/news/press/releases/stress-exec-summary.pdf
American Psychological Association. (2011). A matter of law: Psychologists' duty to protect. http://www.apapracticecentral.org/business/legal/professional/secure/duty-protect.aspx
American Psychological Association. (2012, Winter). Dealing with threatening client encounters: Good practice. Retrieved from www.apa.org
American Psychological Association. (2014, June 25). APA applauds landmark Illinois law allowing psychologists to prescribe medications. Retrieved from http://www.apa.org/news/press/releases/2014/06/prescribe-medications.aspx
American Psychological Association. (2015, October 2). Compulsive texting associated with poorer school performance among adolescent girls, study finds. Retrieved from http://www.sciencedaily.com/releases/2015/10/151005095738.htm
Amir, N., Beard, C., Burns, M., & Bomyea, J. (2009). Attention modification program in individuals with generalized anxiety disorder. *Journal of Abnormal Psychology, 118*, 28–33. doi:10.1037/a0012589
Amminger, G. P., Pape, S., Rock, D., Roberts, S. A., Ott, S. L., Squires-Wheeler, E.,... Erlenmeyer-Kimling, L. (1999). Relationship between childhood behavioral disturbance and later schizophrenia in the New York High-Risk Project. *American Journal of Psychiatry, 156*, 525–530.
Amstadter, A. B., Broman-Fulks, J., Zinzowa, H., Ruggiero, K. J., & Cercone, J. (2009). Internet-based interventions for traumatic stress-related mental health problems: A review and suggestion for future research. *Clinical Psychology Review, 29*, 410–420. doi:10.1016/j.cpr.2009.04.001
Andero, R., Heldt, S. A., Ye, K., Liu, X., Armario, A., & Ressler, K. J. (2011). Effect of 7,8-dihydroxyflavone, a small molecule TrkB agonist, on emotional learning. *American Journal of Psychiatry, 168*, 163–172. doi:10.1176/appi.ajp.2010.10030326
Anderson, E. M., & Lambert, M. J. (2001). A survival analysis of clinically significant change in outpatient psychotherapy. *Journal of Clinical Psychology, 57*, 875–888.
Anderson, E. R., & Mayes, L. C. (2010). Race/ethnicity and internalizing disorders in youth: A review. *Clinical Psychology Review, 30*, 338–348. doi:10.1016/j.cpr.2009.12.008
Anderson, J. W. (2003). "Mr. Psychoanalysis" breaks with Freud. *Contemporary Psychology: APA Review of Books, 48*, 855–857.
Anderson, J. W., Liu, C., & Kryscio, R. J. (2008). Blood pressure response to transcendental meditation: A meta-analysis. *American Journal of Hypertension, 21*, 310–316.
Anderson, P. L., Price, M., Edwards, S. M., Obasaju, M. A., Schmertz, S. K., Zimand, E.,... Calamaras, M. R. (2013). Virtual reality exposure therapy for social anxiety disorder: A randomized controlled trial. *Journal of Consulting and Clinical Psychology, 81*, 751–760. doi:10.1037/a0033559
Anderson, P. L., Price, M., Edwards, S., M., Obasaju, M. A., Schmertz, S. K., Stefan, K.,... Calamaras, M. R. (2013). *Journal of Consulting and Clinical Psychology, 81*, 751–760. doi:10.1037/a0033559
Andersson, E., Hedman, E., Enander, J., Djurfeldt, D. R., Ljótsson, B., Cervenka, S.,... Rück, C. (2015). D-cycloserine vs. placebo as adjunct to cognitive behavioral therapy for obsessive-compulsive disorder and interaction with antidepressants: A randomized clinical trial. *JAMA Psychiatry, 72*, 659–667. doi:10.1001/jamapsychiatry.2015.0546
Andersson. E. Hedman, E., Ljótsson, B., Wikström, M., Elveling, E., Lindefors, N.,... Rück, C. (2015). Cost-effectiveness of Internet-based cognitive behavior therapy for obsessive-compulsive disorder: Results from a randomized controlled trial. *Journal of Obsessive-Compulsive and Related Disorders, 4*, 47–53. doi:10.1016/j.jocrd.2014.12.004
Ang, R. P., Rescorla, L. A., Achenbach, T. M., Ooi, Y. P., Fung, D. S. S., & Woo, B. (2011). Examining the Criterion validity of CBCL and TRF problem scales and items in a large Singapore Sample. *Child Psychiatry & Human Development, 43*, 70–86. doi:10.1007/s10578-011-0253-2
Angelakis, I., Gooding, P., Tarrier, N., & Panagioti, M. (2015). Suicidality in obsessive compulsive disorder (OCD): A systematic review and meta-analysis. *Clinical Psychology Review, 39*, 1–15. doi:10.1016/j.cpr.2015.03.002
Angier, N. (2000, November 7). Who is fat? It depends on culture. *The New York Times*, pp. F1–F2.
Angier, N. (2009, October 26). A molecule of motivation, dopamine excels at its task. *The New York Times.* Retrieved from www.nytimes.com
Anson, M., Veale, D., & de Silva, P. (2012). Social-evaluative versus self-evaluative appearance concerns in body dysmorphic disorder. *Behaviour Research and Therapy, 50*, 753–760.
Anstee, Q. M., Knapp, S., Maguire, E. P., Hosie, A. M., Thomas, P., Mortensen, M.,... Thomas, H. C. (2013). Mutations in the Gabrb1 gene promote alcohol consumption through increased tonic inhibition. *Nature Communications, 4*, 2816. doi:10.1038/ncomms3816
Anthes, E. (2014). Depression: A change of mind. *Nature, 515*, 185–187. doi:10.1038/515185a
Anticevic, A., Murray, J. D., & Barch, D. M. (2015). Bridging levels of understanding in schizophrenia through computational modeling. *Clinical Psychological Science, 3*, 433–459. doi:10.1177/2167702614562041
Antidepressant medication augmented with cognitive-behavioral therapy for generalized anxiety disorder in older adults. *American Journal of Psychiatry, 170*, 782–789. doi:10.1176/appi.ajp.2013.12081104
Anton, R. F. (2008). Naltrexone for the management of alcohol dependence. *New England Journal of Medicine, 359*, 715–721.
Anton, R. F., Myrick, H., Wright, T. M., Latham, P. K., Baros, A. M., Waid, L. R.,... Randall, P. K. (2011). Gabapentin combined with naltrexone for the treatment of alcohol dependence. *American Journal of Psychiatry, 168*, 709–717.
Antony, M. M., Ledley, D. R., Liss, A., & Swinson, R. P. (2006). Responses to symptom induction exercises in panic disorder. *Behaviour Research and Therapy, 44*, 85–98.
APA Presidential Task Force on Evidence-Based Practice. (2006). Evidence-based practice in psychology. *American Psychologist, 61*, 271–285.
Appelbaum, P. S. (2003). Dangerous persons, moral panic, and the uses of psychiatry. *Psychiatric Services, 54*, 441–442.
Appelbaum, P. S. (2006). Violence and mental disorders: Data and public policy. *American Journal of Psychiatry, 163*, 1319–1321.
Arbisi, P. A., Ben-Porath, Y., S., & McNulty, J. A. (2002). A comparison of MMPI-2 validity in African American and Caucasian psychiatric inpatients. *Psychological Assessment, 14*, 3–15.
Arcelus, J., Mitchell, A. J., Wales, J., & Nielsen, S. (2011). Mortality rates in patients with anorexia nervosa and other eating disorders: A meta-analysis of 36 studies. *Archives of General Psychiatry, 68*, 724.
Arguedas, D., Stevenson, R., J., & Langdon, R. (2012). Source monitoring and olfactory hallucinations in schizophrenia. *Journal of Abnormal Psychology, 121*, 936–943. doi:10.1037/a0027174
Arias, F., Szerman, N., Vega, P., Mesias, B., Basurte, I., Morant, C.,... Babin, F. (2014). Alcohol abuse or dependence and other psychiatric disorders: Madrid study on the prevalence of dual pathology. *Mental Health and Substance Use, 4*, 122–129.
Arieti, S. (1974). *Interpretation of schizophrenia.* New York, NY: Basic Books.
Ariz. shooting spree suspect incompetent for trial. (2011, May 25). *MSNBC.com.* Retrieved from http://www.msnbc.msn.com/id/43165830/ns/us_news-crime_and_courts/
Armfield, J. M. (2006). Cognitive vulnerability: A model of the etiology of fear. *Clinical Psychology Review, 26*, 746–768.
Armstrong, L., & Rimes, K. A. (2016). Mindfulness-based cognitive therapy for neuroticism (stress vulnerability): A pilot randomized study. *Behavior Therapy*, in press.
Arnedo, J., Svrakic, D. M., del Val, C., Romero-Zaliz, R., Hernández-Cuervo, H., Fanous, A. H.,... Zwir, I. (2014). Uncovering the hidden risk architecture of the schizophrenias: Confirmation in three independent genome-wide association studies. *American Journal of Psychiatry,172*, 139–153. doi:10.1176/appi.ajp.2014.14040435
Arnow, B. A., Steidtmann, D., Blasey, C., Manber, R., Constantino, M. J., Klein, D. N.,... Kocsis, J. H. (2013). The relationship between the therapeutic alliance and treatment outcome in two, distinct psychotherapies for chronic depression. *Journal of Consulting and Clinical Psychology, 81*, 627–638. doi:10.1037/a0031530
Aronin, N., & Moore, M. (2012). Hunting down Huntingtin. *New England Journal of Medicine, 367*, 1753–1754. doi:10.1056/NEJMcibr1209595
Aronson, M. K. (1988). Patients and families: Impact and long-term-management implications. In M. K. Aronson (Ed.), *Understanding Alzheimer's disease* (pp. 74–78). New York, NY: Charles Scribners and Sons.
Asbridge, M., Hayden, J. A., & Cartwright, J. L. (2012). Acute cannabis consumption and motor vehicle collision risk: Systematic review of observational studies and meta-analysis. *British Medical Journal, 344*, e536.
Assumpção, A. A., Garcia, F. D., Garcia, H. D., Bradford, J. M. W., & Thibaut, F. (2014). Pharmacologic treatment of paraphilias. *Psychiatric Clinics of North America, 37*, 173–181.
Atladóttir, H. O., Henriksen, T. B., Schendel, D. E., & Parner, E. T. (2012). Autism after infection, febrile episodes, and antibiotic use during pregnancy: An exploratory study. *Pediatrics.* doi:10.1542/peds.2012-1107
Aubin, S., Heiman, J. R., Berger, R. E., Murallo, A. V., & Yung-Wen, L. (2009). Comparing sildenafil alone vs. sildenafil plus brief couple sex therapy on erectile dysfunction and couples' sexual and marital quality of life. *Journal of Sex and Marital Therapy, 35*(2), 122–143.
Aurora, R. N., Zak, R. S., Maganti, R. K., Auerbach, S. H., Casey, K. R., Chowdhuri, S.,... Standards of Practice Committee, American Academy of Sleep Medicine. (2010). Best practice guide for the treatment of REM sleep behavior disorder (RBD). *Journal of Clinical Sleep Medicine, 6*, 85–95.
Autistic brains develop more slowly than healthy brains, researchers say. (2011, October 20). *ScienceDaily.* Retrieved from www.sciencedaily.com
Axelson, D. (2013). Taking disruptive mood dysregulation disorder out for a test drive. *American Journal of Psychiatry, 170*, 136–139. doi:10.1176/appi.ajp.2012.12111434
Aybek, S., Nicholson, T. R., Zelaya, F., O'Daly, O. G., Craig, T. J., David, A. S.,... Kanaan, R. A. (2014). Neural correlates of recall of life events in conversion disorder. *JAMA Psychiatry, 71*, 52–60. doi:10.1001/jamapsychiatry.2013.2842
Ayers, J. W., Hofstetter, C. R., Usita, P., Irvin, V. L., Kang, S., & Hovell, M. F. (2009). Sorting out the competing effects of acculturation, immigrant stress, and social support on depression: A report on Korean women in California. *The Journal of Nervous and Mental Disease, 197*, 742–747. doi:10.1097/NMD.0b013e3181b96e9e
Ayorech, Z., Tracy, D. K., Baumeister, D., & Giaroli, G. (2015). Taking the fuel out of the fire: Evidence for the use of anti-inflammatory agents in the treatment of bipolar disorders. *Journal of Affective Disorders, 174C*, 467–478. doi:10.1016/j.jad.2014.12.015
Ayres, M. M., & Haddock, S. A. (2009). Therapists' approaches in working with heterosexual couples struggling with male partners' online sexual behavior. *Sexual Addiction & Compulsivity, 16*(1), 55–78.
Azrin, N. H., & Peterson, A. L. (1989). Reduction of an eye tick by controlled blinking. *Behavior Therapy, 20*, 467–473.
Azzi, A., Dallmann, R., Casserly, A., Rehrauer, H., Patrignani, A., Maier, B.,... Brown, S. A. (2014). Circadian behavior is light-reprogrammed by plastic DNA methylation. *Nature Neuroscience, 17*, 377. doi:10.1038/nn.3651
Babiak, P., & Hare, R. D. (2006). *Snakes in suits: When psychopaths go to work.* New York, NY: HarperBusiness.
Bäckström T., Andreen, L., Birzniece, V., Bjorn, I., Johansson, I. M., Nordenstam-Haghjo, M., Nyberg, S.,... Zhu, D. (2003). The role of hormones and hormonal treatments in premenstrual syndrome. *CNS Drugs, 17*(5), 325–342.
Baer, R. A., Peters, J. R., Eisenlohr-Moula, T. A., Geiger, P. J., & Sauer, S. E. (2012). Emotion-related cognitive processes in borderline personality disorder: A review of the empirical

literature. *Clinical Psychology Review, 32,* 359–369. doi:10.1016/j.cpr.2012.03.00

Bailey, D. S. (2003, November). The "Sylvia Plath" effect. *Monitor on Psychology, 34* (10), 42–43.

Bailey, J. M. (1999). Homosexuality and mental illness. *Archives of General Psychiatry, 56,* 883–884.

Bailey, J. M. (2003a). *The man who would be queen: The science of gender-bending and transsexualism.* Washington, DC: Joseph Henry Press.

Bailey, J. M. (2003b). Personal communication.

Baker, J. H., Maes, H. H., Lissner, L., Aggen, S. H., Lichtenstein, P., & Kendler, K. S. (2009). Genetic risk factors for disordered eating in adolescent males and females. *Journal of Abnormal Psychology, 118,* 576–578. doi:10.1037/a0016314

Baker, J. T., Holmes, A. J., Masters, G. A., Yeo, B. T. T., Krienen, F., Buckner, R. L., & Öngür, D. (2014). Disruption of cortical association networks in schizophrenia and psychotic bipolar disorder. *JAMA Psychiatry, 71,* 109–118. doi:10.1001/jamapsychiatry.2013.3469

Baker, T. B., Piper, M. E., Stein, J. H., Smith, S. S., Bolt, D. M., Fraser, D. L.,... Fiore, M. C. (2016). Effects of nicotine patch vs. varenicline vs. combination nicotine replacement therapy on smoking cessation at 26 weeks. *Journal of the American Medical Association, 315,* 371–379. doi:10.1001/jama.2015.19284

Bakes, K. (2013, December 12). Sedative and opioid abuse in adolescents. *NEJM Journal Watch Psychiatry.* Retrieved from http://www.jwatch.org/na32837/2013/12/12/sedative-and-opioid-abuse-adolescents?query=etoc_jwpeds

Bakken, T. E., Bloss, C. S., Roddey, J. C., Joyner, A. H., Rimol, L. M., Djurovic, S.,... Schork, N. J. (2011). Association of genetic variants on 15q12 with cortical thickness and cognition in schizophrenia. *Archives of General Psychiatry, 68,* 781–790. doi:10.1001/archgenpsychiatry.2011.81

Baldwin, D. S., Anderson, I. M., Nutt, D. J., Allgulander, C., Bandelow, B., den Boer, J.,... Wittchen, H.-U. (2014). Evidence-based pharmacological treatment of anxiety disorders, post-traumatic stress disorder and obsessive-compulsive disorder: A revision of the 2005 guidelines from the British Association for Psychopharmacology. *Journal of Psychopharmacology, 28,* 403–439. doi:10.1177/0269881114525674

Baller, E. B., Wei, S.-M., Kohn, P. D., Rubinow, D. R., Alarcón, G., Schmidt, P. J.,... Berman, K. F. (2013). Abnormalities of dorsolateral prefrontal function in women with premenstrual dysphoric disorder: A multimodal neuroimaging study. *American Journal of Psychiatry, 170,* 305.

Ballie, R. (2002, January). Kay Redfield Jamison receives $500,000 "genius award." *Monitor on Psychology.* Retrieved from http://www.apa.org/monitor/jan02/redfield.html

Balon, R. (2015). Paraphilic disorders. In L. W. Roberts & L. K. Louie (Eds.), *Study guide to DSM-5.* Washington, DC: American Psychiatric Association.

Balter, M. (2014). Talking back to madness. *Science, 343,* 1190–1193. doi:10.1126/science.343.6176.1190

Bandura, A. (1986). *Social foundations of thought and action: A social-cognitive theory.* Englewood Cliffs, NJ: Prentice Hall.

Bandura, A. (2004). Swimming against the mainstream: The early years from chilly tributary to transformative mainstream. *Behaviour Research and Therapy, 42,* 613–630.

Bandura, A. (2006). Toward a psychology of human agency. *Perspectives on Psychological Science, 1,* 164–180.

Bandura, A., Ross, S. A., & Ross, D. (1963). Imitation of film-mediated aggressive models. *Journal of Abnormal and Social Psychology, 66,* 3–11.

Bandura, A., Taylor, C. B., Williams, S. L., Medford, I. N., & Barchas, J. D. (1985). Catecholamine secretion as a function of perceived coping self-efficacy. *Journal of Consulting and Clinical Psychology, 53,* 406–414.

Banerjee, A., G., & Retamero, C. (2014). Expressed emotion—a determinant of relapse in schizophrenia: A case report and literature review. *Journal of Psychiatry and Brain Functions.* Retrieved from http://www.hoajonline.com/psychiatry/2055-3447/1/4#ref12

Baranzini, S. E., Mudge, J., van Velkinburgh, J C., Khankhanian, P., Khrebtukova, I., Miller, N. A.,... Kingsmore, S. F. (2010). Genome, epigenome and RNA sequences of monozygotic twins discordant for multiple sclerosis. *Nature, 464,* 1351. doi:10.1038/nature08990

Barbaree, H. E., & Blanchard, R. (2008). Sexual deviance over the lifespan. In D. R. Laws & W. T. O'Donohue (Eds.), *Sexual deviance: Theory, assessment, and treatment* (pp. 37–60). New York, NY: Guilford Press.

Barbosa, I. G., Morato, I. B., de Miranda, A. S., Bauer, M. E., Soares, J. C., & Teixeira, A. L. (2014). A preliminary report of increased plasma levels of IL-33 in bipolar disorder: Further evidence of pro-inflammatory status. *Journal of Affective Disorders, 157,* 41–44. doi:10.1016/j.jad.2013.12.042

Barch, D. M. (2013). The CAINS: Theoretical and practical advances in the assessment of negative symptoms in schizophrenia. *American Journal of Psychiatry, 170,* 133–135. doi:10.1176/appi.ajp.2012.12101329

Barnett, J. (2010, August 12). Is there a duty to warn when working with HIV-positive clients? *American Psychological Association, Division of Psychotherapy, Div. 29.* Retrieved from http://www.divisionofpsychotherapy.org/ask-the-ethicist-hiv/

Bar-Nur, O., Caspi, I., & Benvenisty, N. (2012). Molecular analysis of FMR1 reactivation in fragile-X induced pluripotent stem cells and their neuronal derivatives. *Journal of Molecular Cell Biology, 4,* 180–183. doi:10.1093/jmcb/mjs007

Barr, B., Taylor-Robinson, D., Scott-Samuel, A., McKee, M., & Stuckler, D. (2012). Suicides associated with the 2008–10 economic recession in England: Time trend analysis. *British Medical Journal, 345,* e5142. doi:10.1136/bmj.e5142

Barrio, C. J. R., Small, G. W., Wong, K.-P., Huang, S.-C., Liu, J., Merrill, D. A.,... Kepe, V. (2015). In vivo characterization of chronic traumatic encephalopathy using [F-18]FDDNP PET brain imaging. *Proceedings of the National Academy of Sciences, 112,* E2039–E2047. doi:10.1073/pnas.1409952112

Barron, J., & Barron, S. (2002). *There's a boy in here.* Arlington, TX: Future Horizons.

Barrowclough, C., Gregg, L. & Tarrier, N. (2008). Expressed emotion and causal attributions in relatives of posttraumatic stress disorder patients. *Behaviour Research and Therapy, 46,* 207–218.

Barrowclough, C., & Hooley, J. M. (2003). Attributions and expressed emotion: A review. *Clinical Psychology Review, 23,* 849–880.

Barsky, A. J., & Ahern, D. K. (2004). Cognitive behavior therapy for hypochondriasis: A randomized controlled trial. *Journal of the American Medical Association, 291,* 1464–1470.

Barsky, A. J., Ahern, D. K., Bailey, E. D., Saintfort, R., Liu, E. B., & Peekna, H. M. (2001). Hypochondriacal patients' appraisal of health and physical risks. *American Journal of Psychiatry, 158,* 783–787.

Barsky, A. J., Orav, E. J., & Bates, D. W. (2005). Somatization increases medical utilization and costs independent of psychiatric and medical comorbidity. *Archives of General Psychiatry, 62,* 903–910.

Barsky, A. J., Wool, C., Barnett, M. C., & Cleary, P. D. (1994). Histories of childhood trauma in adult hypochondriacal patients. *American Journal of Psychiatry, 151,* 397–401.

Bartholow, B. D., & Heinz, A. (2006). Alcohol and aggression without consumption alcohol cues, aggressive thoughts, and hostile perception bias. *Psychological Science, 17,* 30–37.

Basch, M. F. (1980). *Doing psychotherapy.* New York, NY: Basic Books.

Basile, K. C. (2002). Attitudes toward wife rape: Effects of social background and victim status. *Violence & Victims, 17(3),* 341–354.

Bassman, R. (2005). Mental illness and the freedom to refuse treatment: Privilege or right. *Professional Psychology: Research and Practice, 36,* 488–497.

Bateman, A., & Fonagy, P. (2009). Randomized controlled trial of outpatient mentalization-based treatment versus structured clinical management for borderline personality disorder. *American Journal of Psychiatry, 166(12),* 1355–1364. doi:10.1176/appi.ajp.2009.09040539

Bateman, A. W. (2012). Treating borderline personality disorder in clinical practice. *American Journal of Psychiatry, 169,* 560–563. doi:10.1176/appi.ajp.2012.12030341

Bateman, R. J., Xiong, C., Benzinger, T. L. S., Fagan, A. M., Goate, A., Fox, N. C.,... Morris, J. C. (2012). Clinical and biomarker changes in dominantly inherited Alzheimer's disease. *New England Journal of Medicine, 367,* 795–804. doi.org/10.1056/NEJMoa1202753

Battagliese, G., Caccetta, M., Luppino, O. I., Baglioni, C., Cardi, V., Mancini, F.,... Buonanno, C. (2015). Cognitive-behavioral therapy for externalizing disorders: A meta-analysis of treatment effectiveness. *Behaviour Research and Therapy, 75,* 60–71. doi:10.1016/j.brat.2015.10.008

Bauchner, H. (2011). A snapshot of children with ADHD. *Journal Watch Medicine.* Retrieved from http://general-medicine.jwatch.org/cgi/content/full/2011/317/4?q=etoc_jwgenmed

Bauchner, H., Fontanarosa, P. B., & Golub, R. M. (2013). Updated guidelines for management of high blood pressure: Recommendations, review, and responsibility [Editorial]. *Journal of the American Medical Association, 311,* 477–478. doi:10.1001/jama.2013.284432

Baucom, B. R., Atkins, D. C., Rowe, L. S., Doss, B. D., & Christensen, A. (2015a). Prediction of treatment response at 5-year follow-up in a randomized clinical trial of behaviorally based couple therapies. *Journal of Consulting and Clinical Psychology, 83,* 103–114. http://dx.doi.org/10.1037/a0038005

Baucom, B. R., Sheng, E., Christensen, A., Georgioud, P. G., Narayanand, S. S., & Atkins, D. C. (2015b). Behaviorally-based couple therapies reduce emotional arousal during couple conflict. *Behaviour Research and Therapy, 72,* 49–55.

Bauer, S., Okon, E., Meermann, R., & Kordy, H. (2012). Technology-enhanced maintenance of treatment gains in eating disorders: Efficacy of an intervention delivered via text messaging. *Journal of Consulting and Clinical Psychology, 80,* 700–706. doi:10.1037/a0028030

Baumeister, R. F., Catanese, K. R., & Vohs, K. D. (2001). Is there a gender difference in strength of sex drive? Theoretical views, conceptual distinctions, and a review of relevant evidence. *Personality & Social Psychology Review, 5,* 242–273.

Baumeister, R. F., Catanese, K. R., & Wallace, H. M. (2002). Conquest by force: A narcissistic reactance theory of rape and sexual coercion. *Review of General Psychology, 6,* 92–135. doi:10.1037/1089-2680.6.1.92

Bazelon, E. (2015, June 21). Better judgment. *The New York Times Magazine,* 46–51.

Beals, J., Novins, D. K., Whitesell, N. R., Spicer, P., Mitchell, C. M., & Manson, S. M. (2005). Prevalence of mental disorders and utilization of mental health services in two American Indian reservation populations: Mental health disparities in a national context. *American Journal of Psychiatry, 162,* 1723–1732.

Bean, J. L. (2002). Expressions of female sexuality. *Journal of Sex & Marital Therapy, 28*(Suppl. 1), 29–38.

Beauchaine, T. P. Hinshaw, S. P., & Pang, K. L. (2010). Comorbidity of attention-deficit/hyperactivity disorder and early-onset conduct disorder: Biological, environmental, and developmental mechanisms. *Clinical Psychology: Science and Practice, 17,* 327–336. doi:10.1111/j.1468-2850.2010.01224.x

Beauregard, E., Proulx, J., & LeClerc, B. (2014). Offending pathways: The role of lifestyle and precrime factors in extrafamilial child molesters. In E. Beauregard, J. Proulx, & B. LeClerc (Eds.), *Pathways to sexual aggression* (pp. 137–155). New York, NY: Routledge.

Beauvais, F. (1998). American Indians and alcohol. *Alcohol Health and Research World, 22,* 253–259.

Bebbington, P. E., Cooper, C., Minot, S., Brugha, T. S., Jenkins, R., Meltzer, H.,... Dennis, M. (2009). Suicide attempts, gender, and sexual abuse: Data from the 2000 British Psychiatric Morbidity Survey. *American Journal of Psychiatry, 166,* 1135–1140. doi:10.1176/appi.ajp.2009.09030310

Beck, A. T. (2005). The current state of cognitive therapy: A 40-year retrospective. *Archives of General Psychiatry, 62,* 953–959.

Beck, A. T., & Alford, B. A. (2009). *Depression: Causes and treatment* (2nd ed.). Baltimore, MD: University of Pennsylvania Press.

Beck, A. T., Brown, G., Steer, R. A., Eidelson, J. I., & Riskind, J. H. (1987). Differentiating anxiety and depression: A test of the cognitive content-specificity hypothesis. *Journal of Abnormal Psychology, 96,* 179–183.

Beck, A. T., & Dozois, D. J. A. (2011). Cognitive therapy: Current status and future directions.

*Annual Review of Medicine, 62,* 397–409. doi:10.1146/annurevmed-052209-100032

Beck, A. T., Freeman, A., Davis, D. D., & Associates. (2003). *Cognitive therapy of personality disorders* (2nd ed.). New York, NY: Guilford.

Beck, A. T., Rush, A. J., Shaw, B. F., & Emery, G. (1979). *Cognitive therapy of depression.* New York, NY: Guilford Press.

Beck, A. T., & Young, J. E. (1985). Depression. In D. H. Barlow (Ed.), *Clinical handbook of psychological disorders* (pp. 206–244). New York, NY: Guilford Press.

Beck A. T., & Weishaar, M. E. (2011). Cognitive therapy. In R. J. Corsini & D. Wedding (Eds.), *Current psychotherapies* (9th ed.). Belmont, CA: Brooks/Cole.

Beck, M., & Schatz, A. (2014, January 17). American eating habits take a healthier turn. *Wall Street Journal,* pp. A1, A3.

Becker, B., Scheele, D., Moessner, R., Maier, W., & Hurlemann, R. (2013). Deciphering the neural signature of conversion blindness. *American Journal of Psychiatry, 170,* 121–122. doi:10.1176/appi.ajp.2012.12070905

Becker, C. B., Bull, S., Schaumberg, K., Cauble, A., & Franco, A. (2008). Effectiveness of peer-led eating disorders prevention: A replication trial. *Journal of Consulting and Clinical Psychology, 76,* 347–354.

Beesdo, K., Lau, J. Y. F., Guyer, A. E., McClure-Tone, E. B., Monk, C. S., Nelson, E. E.,…Pine, D. S. (2009). Common and distinct amygdala-function perturbations in depressed vs. anxious adolescents. *Archives of General Psychiatry, 66,* 275–285.

Beevers, C. G., Wells, T. T., & Miller, I. W. (2007). Predicting response to depression treatment: The role of negative cognition. *Journal of Consulting and Clinical Psychology, 75,* 422–431.

Behrman, A. (2002). *Electroboy: A memoir of mania.* New York, NY: Random House.

Beidel, D. C., Turner, S. M., Sallee, F. R., Ammerman, R. T., Crosby, L. A., & Pathak, S. (2007). SET-C versus fluoxetine in the treatment of childhood social phobia. *Journal of American Academy of Child and Adolescent Psychiatry, 46,* 1622–1632.

Beitman, B. D., Goldfried, M. R., & Norcross, J. C. (1989). The movement toward integrating the psychotherapies: An overview. *American Journal of Psychiatry, 146,* 138–147.

Bélanger, L., LeBlanc, M., & Morin, C. M. (2011). Cognitive behavioral therapy for insomnia in older adults. *Cognitive and Behavioral Practice, 68,* 991–998. doi:10.1016/j.cbpra.2010.10.003

Belkin, L. (2005, May 22). Can you catch obsessive-compulsive disorder? *The New York Times.* Retrieved from http://www.nytimes.com

Bell, B. T., & Dittmar, H. (2011). Does media type matter? The role of identification in adolescent girls' media consumption and the impact of different thin-ideal media on body image. *Sex Roles, 65,* 478–490. doi:10.1007/s11199-011-9964-x

Belluck, P. (2015, May 19). Studies confirm brain plaque can help predict Alzheimer's. *The New York Times.* Retrieved from http://www.nytimes.com/2015/05/20/health/studies-confirm-brain-plaque-can-help-predict-alzheimers.html

Belmaker, R. H., & Agam, G. (2008). Major depressive disorder. *New England Journal of Medicine, 35,* 55–68.

Benazon, N. R. (2000). Predicting negative spousal attitudes toward depressed persons: A test of Coyne's interpersonal model. *Journal of Abnormal Psychology, 109,* 500–554.

Bender, R. E., & Alloy, L. B. (2011). Life stress and kindling in bipolar disorder: Review of the evidence and integration with emerging biopsychosocial theories. *Clinical Psychology Review, 31,* 383–398. doi:10.1016/j.cpr.2011.01.004

Bennett, D. (1985). Rogers: More intuition in therapy. *APA Monitor, 16,* 3.

Bennett, D., Sharpe, M., Freeman, C., & Carson, A. (2004). Anorexia nervosa among female secondary school students in Ghana. *British Journal of Psychiatry, 185,* 312–317.

Benowitz, N. L. (2010). Nicotine addiction. *New England Journal of Medicine, 362,* 2295–2303.

Benson, P. J., Beedie, S. A., Shephard, E., Giegling, I., Rujescu, D., & St. Clair, D. (2012). Simple viewing tests can detect eye movement abnormalities that distinguish schizophrenia cases from controls with exceptional accuracy. *Biological Psychiatry, 72,* 716. doi:10.1016/j.biopsych.2012.04.019

Bentall, R. P., Haddock, G., & Slade, P. (1994). Cognitive behavior therapy for persistent auditory hallucinations: From theory to therapy. *Behavior Therapy, 25,* 51–66.

Bentley, K. H., Franklin, J. C., Ribeiro, J. D., Kleiman, E. M., Fox, K. R., & Nock, M. K. (2016). Anxiety and its disorders as risk factors for suicidal thoughts and behaviors: A meta-analytic review. *Clinical Psychology Review, 43,* 30–46. doi:10.1016/j.cpr.2015.11.008

Berenson, K., R., Downey, G., Rafaeli, E., Coifman, K. G., & Paquin, N. L. (2011). The rejection–rage contingency in borderline personality disorder. *Journal of Abnormal Psychology, 120,* 681–690. doi:10.1037/a0023335

Berger, T., Boettcher, J., & Caspar, F. (2014). Internet-based guided self-help for several anxiety disorders: A randomized controlled trial comparing a tailored with a standardized disorder-specific approach. *Psychotherapy, 51,* 207–219. doi:10.1037/a0032527

Bergeron, J. Langlois, J., & Cheang, H. S. (2014). An examination of the relationships between cannabis use, driving under the influence of cannabis and risk-taking on the road. *Revue Européenne de Psychologie Appliquée/European Review of Applied Psychology, 4,* 101–109.

Bergman, B. G., Greene, M. C., Hoeppner, B. B., Slaymaker, V., & Kelly, J. F. (2013). Psychiatric comorbidity and 12-step participation: A longitudinal investigation of treated young adults. *Alcoholism: Clinical and Experimental Research, 38,* 501–510. doi:10.1111/acer.12249

Berkout, O. V., Young, J. N, & Gross, A. M. (2011). Mean girls and bad boys: Recent research on gender differences in conduct disorder. *Aggression and Violent Behavior, 16,* 503–511. doi:10.1016/j.avb.2011.06.001

Berle, D., Starcevic, V., Hannan, A., Milicevica, D., Lamplugh, C., & Fenech, P. (2008). Cognitive factors in panic disorder, agoraphobic avoidance and agoraphobia. *Behaviour Research and Therapy, 46,* 282–291.

Berlim, M. T., McGirr, A., den Eynde, F., Fleck, M. P. A., & Giacobbe, P. (2014). Effectiveness and acceptability of deep brain stimulation (DBS) of the subgenual cingulate cortex for treatment-resistant depression: A systematic review and exploratory meta-analysis. *Journal of Affective Disorders, 159,* 31–38.

Berlin, F. S. (2015). Pedophilia and DSM-5: The importance of clearly defining the nature of a pedophilic disorder. *Journal of the American Academy of Psychiatry and the Law, 42,* 404–407.

Bernstein, D. M., & Loftus, E. F. (2009). The consequences of false memories for food preferences and choices. *Perspectives on Psychological Science, 4,* 135–139. doi:10.1111/j.1745-6924.2009.01113

Bernstein, E. M., & Putnam, F. W. (1986). Development, reliability, and validity of a dissociation scale. *Journal of Nervous and Mental Disease,174,* 727–735.

Bersamin, M. M., Paschall, M. J., Saltz, R. F., & Zamboanga, B. L. (2012). Young adults and casual sex: The relevance of college drinking settings. *Journal of Sex Research, 49,* 274–281. doi:10.1080/00224499.2010.548012

Beshai, S., Dobson, K. S., Bockting, C. L. H., & Quigley, L. (2011). Relapse and recurrence prevention in depression: Current research and future prospects. *Clinical Psychology Review, 31,* 1349–1360.

Bhatia, M. S., Jhanjee, A., & Kumar, P. (2011). Culture bound syndromes: A cross-sectional study from India. *European Psychiatry, 26,* 448.

Bianchi, R., Schonfeld, I. S., & Laurent, E. (2015). Burnout–depression overlap: A review. *Clinical Psychology Review, 36,* 28–41.

Bie, B., Wu, J., Yang, H., Xu, J. J., Brown, D. L., & Naguib, M. (2014). Epigenetic suppression of neuroligin 1 underlies amyloid-induced memory deficiency. *Nature Neuroscience, 17,* 223–231. doi:10.1038/nn.3618

Biederman, J., Petty, C. R., Monuteaux, M. C., Fried, R., Byrne, D., Mirto, T., Faraone, S. V. (2010). Adult psychiatric outcomes of girls with attention deficit hyperactivity disorder: 11-year follow-up in a longitudinal case-control study. *American Journal of Psychiatry, 167,* 409–417. doi:10.1176/ appi.ajp.2009.09050736

Bien-Ly, N., Gillespie, A., K., Walker, D., Yoon, S. Y., & Huang, Y. (2012). Reducing human apolipoprotein e levels attenuates age-dependent Aβ Accumulation in mutant human amyloid precursor protein transgenic mice. *The Journal of Neuroscience, 32,* 4803–4811. doi:10.1523/JNEUROSCI.0033-12.2012

Biesheuvel-Leliefeld, K. E. M., Kok, G. D., Bockting, C. L., H., Cuijpers, P., Hollon, S. D., van Marwijka, H. W. J.,…Smit, F. (2015). Effectiveness of psychological interventions in preventing recurrence of depressive disorder: Meta-analysis and meta-regression. *Journal of Affective Disorders, 174,* 400–410.

Biglan, K. M., Dorsey, E. R., Evans, R. V. V., Ross, C. A., Hersch, S.,…Kieburtz, K. (2012). Plasma 8-hydroxy-2- deoxyguanosine levels in Huntington disease and healthy controls treated with coenzyme Q10. *Journal of Huntington's Disease, 1,* 65–69. doi:10.3233/JHD-2012-120007

Billieux, J., Deleuze, J., Griffiths, M. D., & Kuss, D. J. (2014). Internet gaming addiction: The case of massively multiplayer online role-playing games. In N. el-Guebaly, G. Carrà, & M. Galanter (Eds.), *Textbook of addiction treatment: International perspectives* (pp. 1515–1525). New York, NY: Springer-Verlag.

Billieux, J., Lagrange, G., Van der Linden, M., Lançon, C., Adida, M., & Jeanningros, R. (2012). Investigation of impulsivity in a sample of treatment-seeking pathological gamblers: A multidimensional perspective. *Psychiatry Research, 198*(2), 291–296.

Birnbaum, M. H., Martin, H., & Thomann, K. (1996). Visual function in multiple personality disorder. *Journal of the American Optometric Association, 67,* 327–334.

Bjornsson, A. S., Sibrava, N. J, Beard, C., Moitra, E., Weisberg, R. B., Benítez, C. I.,…Keller, M. B. (2014). Two-year course of generalized anxiety disorder, social anxiety disorder, and panic disorder with agoraphobia in a sample of Latino adults. *Journal of Consulting and Clinical Psychology, 82,* 1186–1192. Retrieved from http://dx.doi.org/10.1037/a0036565

Bjornsson, A., Dyck, I., Moitra, E., Stout, R. L., Weisberg, R. B., Keller, M. B., & Phillips, K. A. (2011). The clinical course of body dysmorphic disorder in the Harvard/Brown Anxiety Research Project (HARP). *Journal of Nervous & Mental Disease, 199,* 55–57. doi:10.1097/NMD.0b013e31820448f7

Black, B. S., Johnston, D., Rabins, P. V., Morrison, A., Lyketsos, C., & Samus, Q. M. (2013). Unmet needs of community-residing persons with dementia and their informal caregivers: Findings from the maximizing independence at home study. *Journal of the American Geriatrics Society, 61,* 2087. doi:10.1111/jgs.12549

Blair, K., Geraci, M., Devido, J., McCaffrey, D., Chen, G., Ng, M. V. P., Hollon, N.,…Pine, D. S. (2008). Neural response to self- and other referential praise and criticism in generalized social phobia. *Archives of General Psychiatry, 165,* 1176–1184.

Blanc, J., Bui, E., Mouchenik, Y., Derivois, D., & Birmes, P. (2015). Prevalence of post-traumatic stress disorder and depression in two groups of children one year after the January 2010 earthquake in Haiti. *Journal of Affective Disorders, 172,* 121–126.

Blanchard, E. B., & Hickling, E. J. (2004). *After the crash: Psychological assessment and treatment of survivors of motor vehicle accidents* (2nd ed.). Washington, DC: American Psychological Association.

Blanchard, L. T., Gurka, M. J., & Blackman, J. A. (2006). Emotional, developmental, and behavioral health of American children and their families: A report from the 2003 National Survey of Children's Health. *Pediatrics, 117,* 1202–1212.

Blanco, C., Heimberg, R. G., Schneier, F. R., Fresco, D. M., Chen, H., Turk, C. L., Liebowitz, M. R. (2010). A placebo-controlled trial of phenelzine, cognitive behavioral group therapy, and their combination for social anxiety disorder. *Archives of General Psychiatry, 7,* 286–295.

Blanco, C., Okuda, M., Wright, C., Hasin, D. S., Grant, B. F., Liu, S. M., & Olfson, M. (2008). Mental health of college students and their non–college-attending peers: Results from the National Epidemiologic Study on Alcohol and Related Conditions. *Archives of General Psychiatry, 65,* 1429–1437.

Blatt, S. J., Zuroff, D. C., Bondi, C. M., Sanislow, C. A., & Pilkonis, P. (1998). When and how perfectionism impedes the brief treatment of depression: Further analyses of the National Institute of Mental Health Treatment of Depression Collaborative Research Program. *Journal of Consulting and Clinical Psychology, 66,* 423–428.

Blessitt, E., Voulgari, S., & Eisler, I. (2015). Family therapy for adolescent anorexia nervosa. *Currrent Opinions in Psychiatry, 28*, 455–560. doi:10.1097/YCO.0000000000000193

Block, J. P., Condon, S. K., Kleinman, K., Mullen, J., Rifas-Shiman, S. & Gillman, M. W. (2013). Consumers' estimation of calorie content at fast food restaurants: Cross sectional observational study. *British Medical Journal, 346*, f2907.

Blom, K., Tillgren, H. T., Wiklund, T., Danlycke, E., Forssén, M., Söderström, A.,… Kaldo. V. (2015). Internet- vs. group-delivered cognitive behavior therapy for insomnia: A randomized controlled non-inferiority trial. *Behaviour Research and Therapy, 70*, 47–55. doi:10.1016/j.brat.2015.05.002

Blomsted, P., Sjoberg, R. L., Hansson, M., Bodlund, O., & Hariz, M. I. (2011). Deep brain stimulation in the treatment of depression. *Acta Psychiatrica Scandinavica, 123*, 4–11. doi:10.1111/j.1600-0447.2010.01625.x

Blomström, A., Karlsson, H., Gardner, R., Jörgensen, L., Magnusson, C., & Dalman, C. (2015). Associations between maternal infection during pregnancy, childhood infections and the risk of subsequent psychotic disorder: A Swedish cohort study of nearly 2 million individuals. *Schizophrenia Bulletin*. Retrieved from http://schizophreniabulletin.oxfordjournals.org/content/early/2015/08/23/schbul.sbv112.abstract

Blum, H. P. (2010). Object relations in clinical psychoanalysis. *International Journal of Psychoanalysis, 91*, 973–976.

Blumberg, S. J., Bramlett, M. D., Kogan, M. D., Schieve, L A., Jones, J. R., & Lu, M. (2013). Changes in prevalence of parent-reported autism spectrum disorder in school-aged U.S. children: 2007 to 2011–2012. *National Health Statistics Report, 65*, 1–12.

Blumberg, S. J., Clarke, T. C., & Blackwell, D. L. (2015, June). Racial and ethnic disparities in men's use of mental health treatments. *NCHS Data Brief, 206*. Retrieved from http://www.cdc.gov/nchs/data/databriefs/db206.htmJune 2015

Blumberg, S. J., Zablotsky, B., Avila, R. M., Colpe, L. J., Pringle, B. A., & Kogan, M. D. (2016). Diagnosis lost: Differences between children who had and who currently have an autism spectrum disorder diagnosis. *Autism*, in press.

Bo, S., Abu-Akel, A., Kongerslev, M., Haahrc, U. H., & Simonsen, E. (2011). Risk factors for violence among patients with schizophrenia. *Clinical Psychology Review, 31*, 711–726. doi:10.1016/j.cpr.2011.03.002

Boag, S. (2006). Freudian repression, the common view, and pathological science. *Review of General Psychology, 10*, 74–86.

Bockting, C. L., Hollon, S. D., Jarrett, R. B., Kuyken, W., & Dobson, K. (2015). A lifetime approach to major depressive disorder: The contributions of psychological interventions in preventing relapse and recurrence. *Clinical Psychology Review, 41*, 16–26. doi:10.1016/j.cpr.2015.02.003

Bockting, W. O., & Fung, L. C. T. (2006). Genital reconstruction and gender identity disorders. In D. B. Sarwer (Ed.), *Psychological aspects of reconstructive and cosmetic plastic surgery: Clinical, empirical, and ethical perspectives* (pp. 207–229). New York, NY: Lippincott Williams & Wilkins.

Bøen, E., Westlye, L. T., Elvsåshagen, T., Hummelen, B., Hol, P. K., Boye, B.,… Malt, U. F. (2013). Regional cortical thinning may be a biological marker for borderline personality disorder. *Acta Psychiatrica Scandinavica, 130*, 193–204. doi:10.1111/acps.12234

Bögels, S. M., Wijts, P., Oort, F. J., & Sallaerts, S. J. M. (2014). Psychodynamic psychotherapy versus cognitive behavior therapy for social anxiety disorder: An efficacy and partial effectiveness trial. *Depression and Anxiety, 31*, 5, 363–373. doi:10.1002/da.22246

Bohlken, M. M., Brouwer, R. M., Mandl, R. W., Van den Heuvel, M. P., Hedman, A. M., De Hert, M.,… Hulshoff Pol, H. E. (2016). Structural brain connectivity as a genetic marker for schizophrenia. *JAMA Psychiatry, 73*, 11–19. doi:10.1001/jamapsychiatry.2015.1925

Bollmann, F., Art, J., Henke, J., Schrick, K., Besche, V., Bros, M.,… Pautz, A. (2014). Resveratrol post-transcriptionally regulates pro-inflammatory gene expression via regulation of KSRP RNA binding activity. *Nucleic Acids Research, 42*, 12555–12569. doi:10.1093/nar/gku1033

Bolton, D., Eley, T. C., O'Connor, T. G., Perrin, S., Rabe-Hesketh, S., Rijsdijk, F.,… Smith, P. (2006). Prevalence and genetic and environmental influences on anxiety disorders in 6-year-old twins. *Psychological Medicine, 36*, 335–344.

Bolton, J. M., Pagura, J., Enns, M. W., Grant, B., & Sareen, J. (2010). A population-based longitudinal study of risk factors for suicide attempts in major depressive disorder. *Journal of Psychiatric Research*. Retrieved from http://www.ncbi.nlm.nih.gov/pubmed/20122697

Bolton, P., Bass, J., Neugebauer, R., Verdeli, H., Clougherty, K. F., Wickramaratne, P., Speelman, L.,… Weissman, M. (2003). Group interpersonal psychotherapy for depression in rural Uganda: A randomized controlled trial. *Journal of the American Medical Association, 289*, 3117–3124.

Bomasang-Layno, E., Fadlon, I., Murray, A. N., & Himelhoch, S. (2015). Antidepressive treatments for Parkinson's disease: A systematic review and meta-analysis. *Parkinsonism & Related Disorders, 21*, 833–842. doi:10.1016/j.parkreldis.2015.04.018

Bonanno, G. A., Galea, S., Bucciarelli, A., & Vlahov, D. (2006). Psychological resilience after disaster: New York City in the aftermath of the September 11th terrorist attack. *Psychological Science, 17*, 181–186.

Bongar, B. (2002). *The suicidal patient: Clinical and legal standards of care* (2nd ed.). Washington, DC: American Psychological Association.

Boodman, S. G. (2012). Docs: Antipsychotics often prescribed for "problems of living." Retrieved from http://vitals.msnbc.msn.com/_news/2012/03/18/10724080-docs-antipsychoticsoften-prescribed-for-problems-of-living

Boone, L., Soenens, B., & Luyten, P. (2014). When or why does perfectionism translate into eating disorder pathology? A longitudinal examination of the moderating and mediating role of body dissatisfaction. *Journal of Abnormal Psychology, 123*, 412–418. doi:10.1037/a0036254

Boot, E., Kant, S. G., Otter, M., Cohen, D., Nabanizadeh, A., & Baas, R. W. J. (2012). Overexpression of Chromosome 15q11-q13 gene products: A risk factor for schizophrenia and associated psychoses? *American Journal of Psychiatry, 169*, 96–97. doi:10.1176/appi.ajp.2011.11091382

Bootzin, R. R., & Epstein, D. R. (2011). Understanding and treating insomnia. *Annual Review of Clinical Psychology, 7*, 435–458. doi:10.1146/annurev.clinpsy.3.022806.091516

Borjesson, M., & Dahlof, B. (2005). Physical activity has a key role in hypertension therapy. *Lakartidningen, 102*, 123–124, 126, 128–129.

Borkovec, T. D., Newman, M. G., Pincus, A. L., & Lytle, R. (2002). A component analysis of cognitive-behavioral therapy for generalized anxiety disorder and role of interpersonal problems. *Journal of Consulting and Clinical Psychology, 70*, 288–298.

Bornstein, R. F. (1992). The dependent personality: Developmental, social, and clinical perspectives. *Psychological Bulletin, 112*, 3–23.

Bornstein, R. F. (1999). Dependent and histrionic personality disorders. In T. Millon, P. H. Blaney, & R. D. Davis (Eds.), *Oxford textbook of psychopathology* (*Oxford textbooks in clinical psychology*, Vol. 4, pp. 535–554). New York, NY: Oxford University Press.

Bosanquet, K., Mitchell, N., Gabe, R., Lewis, H., McMillan, D., Ekers, D.,… Gilbody, S. (2015). Diagnostic accuracy of the Whooley depression tool in older adults in UK primary care. *Journal of Affective Disorders, 182*, 39–43. doi:10.1016/j.jad.2015.04.020

Boskind-White, M., & White, W. C. (1983). *Bulimarexia: The binge–purge cycle*. New York, NY: W. W. Norton.

Bossong, M. G., Jansma, J. M., van Hell, H. H., Jager, G., Oudman, E., Saliasi, E.,… Ramsey, N. F. (2012). Effects of 9-tetrahydrocannabinol on human working memory function. *Biological Psychiatry, 71*, 693.

Bousman, C. A., Twamley, E. W., Vella, L., Gale, M., Norman, S. B., Judd, B.,… Heaton, R. K. (2011). Homelessness and neuropsychological impairment: Preliminary analysis of adults entering outpatient psychiatric treatment. *Journal of Nervous & Mental Disease, 198*, 790–794. doi:10.1097/NMD.0b013e3181f97dff

Boysen, G. A., & VanBergen, A. (2014). Simulation of multiple personalities: A review of research comparing diagnosed and simulated dissociative identity disorder. *Clinical Psychology Review, 34*, 14–28. doi:10.1016/j.cpr.2013.10.008

Braamhorst, W., Lobbestael, J., Emons, W. H. M., Arntz, A., Witteman, C. L. M., Cilia, L. M.,… Bekker, M. H. J. (2015). Sex bias in classifying borderline and narcissistic personality disorder. *Journal of Nervous & Mental Disease, 203*, 804–808. doi:10.1097/NMD.0000000000000371

Braaten, E. B., & Rosén, L. E. (2000). Self-regulation of affect in attention deficit–hyperactivity disorder (ADHD) and non-ADHD boys: Differences in empathic responding. *Journal of Consulting and Clinical Psychology, 68*, 313–321.

Brady, K. R., McCauley, J. L., & Back, S. E. (2016). Prescription opioid misuse, abuse, and treatment in the United States: An update. *American Journal of Psychiatry, 173*, 18–26.

Braham, L. G., Trower, P., & Birchwood, M. (2004). Acting on command hallucinations and dangerous behavior: A critique of the major findings in the last decade. *Clinical Psychology Review, 24*, 513–528.

Braje, S. E., & Hall, G. C. N. (2015). Cross-cultural issues in assessment. *The encyclopedia of clinical psychology*, 1–9. doi:10.1002/9781118625392.wbecp435

Brand, B. L., Classen, C. C., McNary, S. W., & Zaveri, P. (2009). A review of dissociative disorders treatment studies: Collapse box. *The Journal of Nervous and Mental Disease, 197*, 646–654. doi:10.1097/NMD.0b013e3181b3afaa

Brand, B. L., Lanius, R., Vermetten, E., Loewenstein, R. J., & Spiegel, D. (2012). Where are we going? An update on assessment, treatment, and neurobiological research in dissociative disorders as we move toward the DSM-5. *Journal of Trauma & Dissociation, 13*, 9–31. doi:10.1080/15299732.2011.620687

Brand, B. L., Myrick, A. C., Loewenstein, R. J., Classen, C. C., Lanius, R., McNary, S. W.,… Putnam, F. (2012). A survey of practices and recommended treatment interventions among expert therapists treating patients with dissociative identity disorder and dissociative disorder not otherwise specified. *Psychological Trauma: Theory, Research, Practice, and Policy, 4*, 490–500. doi:10.1037/a0026487

Brandt, M. J., IJzerman, H., Dijksterhuis, A. P., Farach, F. J., Geller, J., Giner-Sorolla, R.,… van 't Veer, A. (2013). The replication recipe: What makes for a convincing replication? *Journal of Experimental Social Psychology, 50*, 217–224. doi:10.1016/j.jesp.2013.10.005

Brannan, M. E., & Petrie, T. A. (2011). Psychological well-being and the body dissatisfaction-bulimic symptomatology relationship: An examination of moderators. *Eating Behaviors, 12*, 233–241. doi:10.1016/j.eatbeh.2011.06.002

Brannigan, G. G., & Decker, S. L. (2006). The Bender-Gestalt II. *American Journal of Orthopsychiatry, 76*, 10–12.

Bratton, D. J., Gaisl, T., Wons, A. M., & Kohler, M. (2015). CPAP vs. mandibular advancement devices and blood pressure in patients with obstructive sleep apnea: A systematic review and meta-analysis. *Journal of the American Medical Association, 314*, 2280. Retrieved from http://dx.doi.org/10.1001/jama.2015.16303

Bray, G. A. (2012). Diet and exercise for weight loss. *Journal of the American Medical Association, 307*, 2641–2642. doi:10.1001/jama.2012.7263

Brefczynski-Lewis, J. A., Lutz, A., Schaefer, H. S., Levinson, D. B., & Davidson, R. J. (2007). Neural correlates of attentional expertise in long-term meditation practitioners. *Proceedings of the National Academy of Sciences, 104*, 11483–11488.

Breiding, M. J., Smith, S. G., Basile, K. C., Walters, M. L., Chen, J., & Merrick, M. T. (2014, September 5). Prevalence and characteristics of sexual violence, stalking, and intimate partner violence victimization—National Intimate Partner and Sexual Violence Survey, United States, 2011. Surveillance Summaries, Centers for Disease Control and Prevention. *Morbidity and Mortality Weekly Report, 63*(SS08), 1–18.

Brent, D. A., & Gibbons, R. (2013). Initial dose of antidepressant and suicidal behavior in youth: Start low, go slow. *JAMA Internal Medicine, 174*, 909–911. doi:10.1001/jamainternmed.2013.14016

Brent, D. A., Emslie, G. J., Clarke, G. N., Asarnow, J., Spirito, A., Ritz, L.,… Keller, M. B. (2009). Predictors of spontaneous and systematically assessed

suicidal adverse events in the Treatment of SSRI-Resistant Depression in Adolescents (TORDIA) Study. *American Journal of Psychiatry, 166*, 418–426. doi:10.1176/appi.ajp.2008.08070976
Brent, D., Emslie, G., Clarke, G., Wagner, K. D., Asarnow, J. R., Keller, M.,... Zelazny, J. (2008). Switching to another SSRI or to venlafaxine with or without cognitive behavioral therapy for adolescents with SSRI-resistant depression: The TORDIA randomized controlled trial. *Journal of the American Medical Association, 299*, 901–913.
Breslau, J., Aguilar-Gaxiola, S., Kendler, K. S., Su, M., Williams, D., & Kessler, R. C. (2006). Specifying race-ethnic differences in risk for psychiatric disorder in a USA national sample. *Psychological Medicine, 36*, 57–68.
Breslau, J., Kendler, K. S., Su, M., Gaxiola-Aguilar, S., & Kessler, R. C. (2005). Lifetime risk and persistence of psychiatric disorders across ethnic groups in the United States. *Psychological Medicine, 35*, 317–327.
Breslow, N. (1989). Sources of confusion in the study and treatment of sadomasochism. *Journal of Social Behavior and Personality, 4*, 263–274.
Brewin C. R., & Andrews B. (2014). Why it is scientifically respectable to believe in repression: A response to Patihis, Ho, Tingen, Lilienfeld, and Loftus (2014). *Psychological Science, 25*, 1964–1966.
Bricker, J. B., Peterson, A. V., Jr., Andersen, M. R., Rajana, K. B., Leroux, B. G., & Sarasona, I. G. (2006). Childhood friends who smoke: Do they influence adolescents to make smoking transitions? *Addictive Behaviors, 31*, 889–900.
Brody, G. H., Beach, S. R. H., Philibert, R. A., Chen, Y.-F., Lei, M.-K., Murry, V. M., & Brown, A. C. (2009). Parenting moderates a genetic vulnerability factor in longitudinal increases in youths' substance use. *Journal of Consulting and Clinical Psychology, 77*, 1–11. doi:2283,35400018793225.0010
Brody, J. E. (2000, May 16). Cybersex gives birth to a psychological disorder. *The New York Times*, pp. F7, F12.
Brody, J. E. (2009, November 3). A breathing technique offers help for people with asthma. *The New York Times*, p. D7.
Brooks, S., & Kushida, C. (2002). Behavioral parasomnias. *Current Psychiatric Reports, 4*, 363–368.
Brotto L. A., Bitzer, J., Laan, E., Leiblum, S., & Luria, M. (2010). Women's sexual desire and arousal disorders. *Journal of Sexual Medicine, 7*, 586–614.
Brown, A. S., Begg, M. D., Gravenstein, S., Schaefer, C. A., Wyatt, R. J., Bresnahan, M.,... Susser, E. S. (2004). Serologic evidence of prenatal influenza in the etiology of schizophrenia. *Archives of General Psychiatry, 61*, 774–780.
Brown, A. S., Vinogradov, S., Kremen, W. S., Poole, J. H., Deicken, R. F., Penner, J. D.,... Schaefer, C. A. (2009). Prenatal exposure to maternal infection and executive dysfunction in adult schizophrenia. *American Journal of Psychiatry, 166*, 683–690. doi:10.1176/appi.ajp.2008.08010089
Brown, M. J. (2006). Hypertension and ethnic group. *British Medical Journal, 332*, 833–836.
Brown, M., Allen, J. S., & Dowling, N. A. (2014). The application of an etiological model of personality disorders to problem gambling. *Journal of Gambling Studies, 31*, 1179–1199. doi:10.1007/s10899-014-9504-z.1-21
Browne, H. A., Hansen, S. N., Buxbaum, J. D., Gair, S. L., Nissen, J. B., Nikolajsen, K. H.,... Grice, D. E. (2015). Familial clustering of tic disorders and obsessive-compulsive disorder. *JAMA Psychiatry, 72*, 359–366. doi:10.1001/jamapsychiatry.2014.2656
Bruce, M. L., Ten Have, T. R., Reynolds, C. F., III, Katz, I. I., Schulberg, H. C., Mulsant, B. H.,... Brown, G. K. (2004). Reducing suicidal ideation and depressive symptoms in depressed older primary care patients: A randomized controlled trial. *Journal of the American Medical Association, 291*, 1081–1091.
Bruch, H. (1973). *Eating disorders: Obesity, anorexia and the person within*. New York, NY: Basic Books.
Brunet, A., Orr, S. P., Tremblay, J., Robertson, K., Nader, K., & Pitman R. K. (2007). Effect of post-retrieval propranolol on psychophysiologic responding during subsequent script-driven traumatic imagery in post-traumatic stress disorder. *Journal of Psychiatric Research, 42*, 503–506.
Brunwasser, S. M., Gillham, J. E., & Kim, E. S. A. (2009). A meta-analytic review of the Penn Resiliency Program's effect on depressive symptoms. *Journal of Consulting and Clinical Psychology, 77*, 1042–1054.
Bryant, C., Jackson, H., & Ames, D. (2008). The prevalence of anxiety in older adults: Methodological issues and a review of the literature. *Journal of Affective Disorders, 109*, 233–250.
Bryant, R. A., Moulds, M. L., Guthrie, R. M., Dang, S. T., & Nixon, R. D. V. (2003). Imaginal exposure alone and imaginal exposure with cognitive restructuring in treatment of posttraumatic stress disorder. *Journal of Consulting and Clinical Psychology, 71*, 706–712.
Bryant, R., & Das, P. (2012). The neural circuitry of conversion disorder and its recovery. *Journal of Abnormal Psychology, 121*, 289–296. doi:10.1037/a0025076
Bryant-Davis, T. (Ed.). (2011). *Surviving sexual violence*. Lanham, MD: Rowman & Littlefield.
Buchert, R., Thomasius, R., Wilke, F., Petersen, K., Nebeling, B., Obrocki, J.,... Clausen, M. (2004). A voxel-based PET investigation of the long-term effects of "ecstasy" consumption on brain serotonin transporters. *American Journal of Psychiatry, 161*, 1181–1189.
Buchhave, P., Minthon, L., Zetterberg, H., Wallin, A. K., Blennow, K., & Hansson, O. (2012). Cerebrospinal fluid levels of b-Amyloid 1–42, but not of tau, are fully changed already 5 to 10 years before the onset of Alzheimer dementia. *Archives of General Psychiatry, 69*, 98–106. doi:10.1001/archgenpsychiatry.2011.155
Buchman, A. S., Boyle, P. A., Yu, L., Shah, R. C., Wilson, R. S., & Bennett, D. A. (2012). Total daily physical activity and the risk of AD and cognitive decline in older adults. *Neurology, 78*, 1323–1329. doi:10.1212/WNL.0b013e3182535d35
Buddie, A. M., & Testa, M. (2005). Rates and predictors of sexual aggression among students and nonstudents. *Journal of Interpersonal Violence, 20*, 713–724.
Buhlmann, U., Marques, L. M., & Wilhelm, S. (2012). Traumatic experiences in individuals with body dysmorphic disorder. *Journal of Nervous and Mental Disease, 200*, 95–98. doi:10.1097/NMD.0b013e31823f6775
Bulik, C. M., Marcus, M. D., Zerwas, S., Levine, M. D., & La Via, M. (2012). The changing "weightscape" of bulimia nervosa. *American Journal of Psychiatry, 169*, 1031–1036. doi:10.1176/appi.ajp.2012.12010147
Bulik, C. M., Thornton, L., Poyastro, Pinheiro A., Plotnicov, K., Klump, K. L.,... Brandt, H. (2008). Suicide attempts in anorexia nervosa. *Psychosomatic Medicine, 70*, 378.
Bullmore, E. (2012). The future of functional MRI in clinical medicine. *NeuroImage, 62*, 1267–1271. doi:10.1016/j.neuroimage.2012.01.026
Bulmash, E. L., Moller, H. J., Kayumov, L., Shen, J., Wang, X., & Shapiro, C. M. (2006). Psychomotor disturbance in depression: Assessment using a driving simulator paradigm. *Journal of Affective Disorders, 93*, 213–218.
Bunde, J., & Suls, J. (2006). A quantitative analysis of the relationship between the Cook-Medley Hostility Scale and traditional coronary artery disease risk factors. *Health Psychology, 25*, 493–500.
Burcusa, S. L., & Iacono, W. G. (2007). Risk for recurrence in depression. *Clinical Psychology Review, 27*, 959–985.
Burke, J. & Loeber, R. (2010). Oppositional defiant disorder and the explanation of the comorbidity between behavioral disorders and depression. *Clinical Psychology: Science and Practice, 17*, 319–326. doi:10.1111/j.1468
Burke, J. D., Waldman, I., & Lahey, B. B. (2010). Predictive validity of childhood oppositional defiant disorder and conduct disorder: Implications for the DSM-V. *Journal of Abnormal Psychology, 119*, 739–751. doi:10.1037/a0019708
Burnay, J., Billieux, J., Blairy, S., & Larøi, F. (2015). Which psychological factors influence Internet addiction? Evidence through an integrative model. *Computers in Human Behavior, 43*, 28–34. doi:10.1016/j.chb.2014.10.039
Burns, D. D. (1980). *Feeling good: The new mood therapy*. New York, NY: Morris.
Burrow-Sanchez, J. J, & Wrona, M. (2012). Comparing culturally accommodated versus standard group CBT for Latino adolescents with substance use disorders: A pilot study. *Cultural Diversity and Ethnic Minority Psychology, 18*, 373–383. doi:10.1037/a0029439
Burt, A. (2009). Rethinking environmental contributions to child and adolescent psychopathology: A meta-analysis of shared environmental influences. *Psychological Bulletin, 135*, 608–637. doi:10.1037/a0015702
Burton, N., & Lane, R. C. (2001). The relational treatment of dissociative identity disorder. *Clinical Psychology Review, 21*, 301–320.
Bushman, B. J., Bonacci, A. M., van Dijk, M., & Baumeister, R. F. (2003). Narcissism, sexual refusal, and aggression: Testing a narcissistic reactance model of sexual coercion. *Journal of Personality and Social Psychology, 84*, 1027–1040.
Busscher, B., Spinhoven, P., van Gerwen, L. J., & de Geus, E. J. C. (2013). Anxiety sensitivity moderates the relationship of changes in physiological arousal with flight anxiety during in vivo exposure therapy. *Behaviour Research and Therapy, 51*, 98–105
Bustillo, J., Lauriello, J., Horan, W., & Keith, S. (2001). The psychosocial treatment of schizophrenia: An update. *American Journal of Psychiatry, 158*, 163–175.
Butcher, J. N. (2011). *A beginner's guide to the MMPI-2* (3rd ed.). Washington, DC: American Psychological Association.
Butler, A. C., Chapman, J. E., Forman, E. M., & Beck, A. T. (2006). The empirical status of cognitive-behavioral therapy: A review of meta-analyses. *Clinical Psychology Review, 26*, 17–33.
Butler, L. D., Duran, R. E. F., Jasiukaitus, P., Koopman, C., & Spiegel, D. (1996). Hypnotizability and traumatic experience: A diathesis-stress model of dissociative symptomatology. *American Journal of Psychiatry, 153*(Suppl. 7), 42–63.
Butler, R. J. (2004). Childhood nocturnal enuresis: Developing a conceptual framework. *Clinical Psychology Review, 24*, 909–931.
Buvat, J., Maggi, M., Gooren, L., Guay, A.T., Kaufman, J., Morgentaler, A.,... Zitzmann, M. (2010). Endocrine aspects of male sexual dysfunctions. *Journal of Sexual Medicine, 7*, 1627–1656.
Buysse, D. J., Germain, A., Moul, D. E., Franzen, P. L., Brar, L. K., Fletcher, M. E.,... Monk, T. H. (2011). Efficacy of brief behavioral treatment for chronic insomnia in older adults. *Archives of Internal Medicine, 171*, 887–895.
By the numbers. (2015, September). *Monitor on Psychology, 46*(8), 13.
Byrne, S. M., Fursland, A., Allen, K. L., & Watson, H. (2011). The effectiveness of enhanced cognitive behavioural therapy for eating disorders: An open trial. *Behaviour Research and Therapy, 49*, 219–226. doi:10.1016/j.brat.2011.01.006
Cable News Network. (2015, August 8). James Holmes sentenced to life in prison for Colorado movie theater murders. Retrieved from http://www.cnn.com/2015/08/07/us/james-holmes-movie-theater-shooting-jury/
Cable, N., & Sacker, A. (2007). The role of adolescent social disinhibition expectancies in moderating the relationship between psychological distress and alcohol use and misuse. *Addictive Behaviors, 32*, 282–295.
Caetano, R. (1987). Acculturation and drinking patterns among U.S. Hispanics. *British Journal of Addiction, 82*, 789–799.
Cahill, M. E., Xie, Z., Day, M., Photowala, H., Barbolina, M. V., Miller, C. A.,... Penzes, P. (2009). Kalirin regulates cortical spine morphogenesis and disease-related behavioral phenotypes. *Proceedings of the National Academy of Sciences, 106*, 31, 13058–13063. doi:10.1073/pnas.0904636106
Cai, D., Pearce, K., Chen, S., & Glanzman, D. L. (2011). Protein kinase M maintains long-term sensitization and long-term facilitation in aplysia. *Journal of Neuroscience, 31*, 6421–6431. doi:10.1523/JNEUROSCI.4744-10.2011
Cain, S. (2011, June 25). Shyness: Evolutionary tactic? *The New York Times*. Retrieved from http://www.nytimes.com
Cale, E. M., & Lilienfeld, S. O. (2002). Sex differences in psychopathy and antisocial personality disorder: A review and integration. *Clinical Psychology Review, 22*, 1179–1207.
Callanan, M., & Waxman, S. (2013). Commentary on special section: Deficit or difference? Interpreting diverse developmental paths. *Developmental Psychology, 49*, 80–83. doi:10.1037/a0029741

Calvert, C. (2014). Voyeurism and exhibitionism. *The encyclopedia of criminology and criminal justice.* Retrieved from http://onlinelibrary.wiley.com/doi/10.1002/9781118517383.wbeccj009/abstract?userIsAuthenticated=false&deniedAccessCustomisedMessage=

Calzada, E. J., Fernandez, Y., & Cortes, D. E. (2010). Incorporating the cultural value of respeto into a framework of Latino parenting. *Cultural Diversity and Ethnic Minority Psychology, 16,* 77–86.

Calzada-Reyes, A., Alvarez-Amador, A., Galán-García, L., & Valdés-Sosa, M. (2012). Electroencephalographic abnormalities in antisocial personality disorder. *Journal of Forensic and Legal Medicine, 19,* 29–34. doi:10.1016/j.jflm.2011.10.002

Cambron, M. J., Acitelli, L. K., & Pettit, J. W. (2009). Explaining gender differences in depression: An interpersonal contingent self-esteem perspective. *Sex Roles, 61,* 751–894. doi:10.1007/s11199-009-9616-6

Cameron, N. (1963). *Personality development and psychopathology: A dynamic approach.* Boston, MA: Houghton Mifflin.

Campbell, B., Caine, K., Connelly, K., Doub, T., & Bragg, A. (2014). Cell phone ownership and use among mental health outpatients in the USA. *Personal and Ubiquitous Computing, 19,* 367. doi:10.1007/s00779-014-0822-z

Campbell, D. B. (2015). Genetic investigation of autism-related social communication deficits. *American Journal of Psychiatry, 172,* 212–213. Retrieved from http://dx.doi.org/10.1176/appi.ajp.2014.14121503

Campbell, T. (2000). First person account: Falling on the pavement. *Schizophrenia Bulletin, 26,* 507–509.

Campbell, W. K., Foster, C. A., Finkel, E. J. (2002). Does self-love lead to love for others?: A story of narcissistic game playing. *Journal of Personality and Social Psychology,* Vol 83(2), 340-354. Retrieved from http://dx.doi.org/10.1037/0022-3514.83.2.340

Campos-Rodriguez, F., Martinez-Garcia, M. A., de la Cruz-Moron, I., Almeida-Gonzalez, C., Catalan-Serra, P., & Montserrat, J. M. (2012). Cardiovascular mortality in women with obstructive sleep apnea with or without continuous positive airway pressure treatment: A cohort study. *Annals of Internal Medicine, 156,* 115.

Canetta, S. E., Bao, Y., Co, M. D. T., Ennis, F. A., Cruz, J., Terajima, M.,… Brown, A. S. (2014). Serological documentation of maternal influenza exposure and bipolar disorder in adult offspring. *American Journal of Psychiatry, 171,* 557–563. doi:10.1176/appi.ajp.2013.13070943

Cannon, T. D. (2016). Deciphering the genetic complexity of schizophrenia. *JAMA Psychiatry, 73,* 5–6. doi:10.1001/jamapsychiatry.2015.2111

Cao, S., Moineddin, R., Urquia, M. L., Razak, F., & Ray, J. G. (2014). J-shapedness: An often missed, often miscalculated relation: The example of weight and mortality. *Journal of Epidemiology and Community Health, 68,* 683–690. doi:10.1136/jech-2013-203439

Carcone, D., Tokarz, V. L., & Ruocco, A. C. (2015). A systematic review on the reliability and validity of semistructured diagnostic interviews for borderline personality disorder. *Canadian Psychology/Psychologie Canadienne, 56,* 208–226.

Cardeña, E., & Carlson, E. (2011). Acute stress disorder revisited. *Annual Review of Clinical Psychology, 7,* 245–267. doi:10.1146/annurev-clinpsy-032210-104502

Cardno, A. G., & Owen, M. J. (2014). Genetic relationships between schizophrenia, bipolar disorder, and schizoaffective disorder. *Schizophrenia Bulletin.* Retrieved from http://schizophreniabulletin.oxfordjournals.org/content/early/2014/02/21/schbul.sbu016.short

CareLoop. (2015). University of Manchester. Retrieved from http://www.population-health.manchester.ac.uk/healthinformatics/research/Careloop/

Carey, B. (2005, October 18). Can brain scans see depression? *The New York Times.* Retrieved from http://www.nytimes.com

Carey, B. (2009a, December 3). Dissection begins on famous brain. *The New York Times,* A27.

Carey, B. (2009b, November 26). Surgery for mental ills offers both hope and risk. *The New York Times.* Retrieved from http://www.nytimes.com/2009/11/27/health/research/27brain.html?_r=1&scp=1&sq=psychosurgery&st=cse

Carey, B. (2010, February 10). Revising book on disorders of the mind. *The New York Times.* Retrieved from www.nytimes.com

Carey, B. (2011). Expert on mental illness reveals her own fight. *The New York Times,* pp. A1, A17.

Carey, B. (2012a, January 19). New autism definition may exclude many, study suggests. *The New York Times.* Retrieved from www.nytimes.com

Carey, B. (2012b, April 4). Scientists link gene mutation to autism risk. *The New York Times.* Retrieved from nytimes.com

Carey, B. (2012c, August 23). Study finds risk of autism linked to older fathers. *The New York Times.* Retrieved from www.nytimes.com

Carey, B. (2012d, December 11). A tense compromise on defining disorders. *The New York Times,* pp. D1, D6.

Carey, B. (2013, January 16). Some with autism diagnosis can overcome symptoms, study finds. *The New York Times.* Retrieved from nytimes.com

Carey, B. (2015, October 2). Talk therapy found to ease schizophrenia. *The New York Times.* Retrieved from http://www.nytimes.com/2015/10/20/health/talk-therapy-found-to-ease-schizophrenia.html

Carey, B. (2016, January 28). Scientists home in on cause of schizophrenia. *The New York Times,* pp. A1, A17.

Carey, M. P., Carey, K. B., Maisto, S. A., Gordon, C. M., Schroder, K. E. E., & Vanable, P. A. (2004). Reducing HIV-risk behavior among adults receiving outpatient psychiatric treatment: Results from a randomized controlled trial. *Journal of Consulting and Clinical Psychology, 72,* 252–268.

Carini, M. A., & Nevid, J. S. (1992). Social appropriateness and impaired perspective in schizophrenia. *Journal of Clinical Psychology, 48,* 170–177.

Carlbring, P., & Smit, F. (2008). Randomized trial of Internet-delivered self-help with telephone support for pathological gamblers. *Journal of Consulting and Clinical Psychology, 76,* 1090–1094.

Carlbring, P., Hägglund, M., Luthström, A., Dahlin, M., Kadowaki, A., Vernmark, K., & Andersson, G. (2013). Internet-based behavioral activation and acceptance-based treatment for depression: A randomized controlled trial. *Journal of Affective Disorders,* 148, 331–337.

Carlsson, E., Frostell, A., Ludvigsson, J., & Faresjo, M. (2014). Psychological stress in children may alter the immune response. *The Journal of Immunology, 192,* 2071. doi:10.4049/jimmunol.1301713

Carneiro, L. S. Fl., Fonseca, A. M., Vieira-Coelho, M. A., Mota, M. P., & Vasconcelos-Raposo, J. (2015). Effects of structured exercise and pharmacotherapy vs. pharmacotherapy for adults with depressive symptoms: A randomized clinical trial. *Psychiatry Research, 71,* 48–55. doi:10.1016/j.jpsychires.2015.09.007

Carocci, M. (2009). Written out of history: Contemporary Native American narratives of enslavement. *Anthropology Today, 25,* 18–22. doi:10.1111/j.1467-8322.2009.00668.x

Carpenter, S. (2013, January). Awakening to sleep. *Monitor on Psychology, 44,* 40–45.

Carrasco, J. L., Tajima-Pozo, K., Díaz-Marsá, M., Casado, A., López-Ibor, J. J., Arrazola, J., & Yus, M. (2012). Microstructural white matter damage at orbitofrontal areas in borderline personality disorder. *Journal of Affective Disorders, 139,* 149–153. Retrieved from http://dx.doi.org/10.1016/j.jad.2011.12.019

Carroll, L. (2003, November 4). Fetal brains suffer badly from effects of alcohol. *The New York Times Online.* Retrieved from http://www.nytimes.com

Carroll., L. (2004, February 10). Parkinson's research focuses on links to genes and toxins. *The New York Times,* p. F5.

Carson, R. C., Hollon. S. D., & Shelton, R. C. (2010). Depressive realism and clinical depression. *Behaviour Research and Therapy, 48,* 257–265. doi:10.1016/j.brat.2009.11.011

Carter, J. C., McFarlane, T. L., Bewell, C., Olmsted, M. P., Woodside, D. B., Kaplan, A. S., & Crosby, R. D. (2009). Maintenance treatment for anorexia nervosa: A comparison of cognitive behavior therapy and treatment as usual. *International Journal of Eating Disorders, 42,* 202–207. doi:10.1002/eat.20591

Carter, J. D., Crowe M. T., Jordan, J., McIntosh, V. V. W., Frampton, C., & Joyce, P. R. (2015). Predictors of response to CBT and IPT for depression: The contribution of therapy process. *Behaviour Research and Therapy, 74,* 72–79. doi:10.1016/j.brat.2015.09.003

Carter, J. S., & Garber, J. (2011). Predictors of the first onset of a major depressive episode and changes in depressive symptoms across adolescence: Stress and negative cognitions. *Journal of Abnormal Psychology, 120,* 779–796. doi:10.1037/a0025441

Carvalho, J., & Nobre, P. (2010). Gender issues and sexual desire: The role of emotional and relationship variables. *Journal of Sexual Medicine, 7,* 2469–2478.

Carver, C. S. (2014). Dispositional optimism. *Trends in Cognitive Sciences, 18,* 293–299. Retrieved from http://dx.doi.org/10.1016/j.tics.2014.02.003

Carver, C. S., Johnson, S. L., & Joormann, J. (2008). Serotonergic function, two-mode models of self-regulation, and vulnerability to depression: What depression has in common with impulsive aggression. *Psychological Bulletin, 134,* 912–943.

Carver, C. S., Johnson, S. L., & Joormann, J. (2009). Two-mode models of self-regulation as a tool for conceptualizing effects of the serotonin system in normal behavior and diverse disorders. *Current Directions in Psychological Science, 18,* 195–199. doi:10.1111/j.1467-8721.2009.01635.x

Casey, B. J., & Durston, S. (2006). From behavior to cognition to the brain and back: What have we learned from functional imaging studies of attention deficit hyperactivity disorder? *American Journal of Psychiatry, 163,* 957–960.

Casey, D. E., Laubmeier, K. K., Eudicone, J. M., Marcus, R., Berman, R. M., Rahman, Z.,… Sheehan, T. (2014). Response and remission rates with adjunctive aripiprazole in patients with major depressive disorder who exhibit minimal or no improvement on antidepressant monotherapy. *International Journal of Clinical Practice, 68,* 1301–1308.

Casey, L. M., Oei, T. P. S., & Newcombe, P. A. (2004). An integrated cognitive model of panic disorder: The role of positive and negative cognitions. *Clinical Psychology Review, 24,* 529–555.

Casey, P., Maracy, M., Kelly, B. D., Lehtinend, V., Ayuso-Mateose, J.-L., Dalgard, O. S., & Dowrick, C. (2006). Can adjustment disorder and depressive episode be distinguished? Results from ODIN. *Journal of Affective Disorders, 92,* 291–297.

Caspi, A., McClay, J., Moffitt, T. E., Mill, J., Martin, J., Craig, I. W., Taylor, A.,… Poulton R. (2002). Role of genotype in the cycle of violence in maltreated children. *Science, 297,* 851–854.

Castellini, G., Maggi, M., & Ricca, V. (2014). Childhood sexual abuse and psychopathology. In G. Corona, E. A. Jannini, & M. Maggi (Eds.), *Emotional, physical and sexual abuse* (pp. 71–91). New York, NY: Springer.

Cecchini-Estrada, J.-A., Méndez-Giménez, A., Cecchini, C., Moulton, M., & Rodríguez, C. (2015). Exercise and Epstein's TARGET for treatment of depressive symptoms: A randomized study. *International Journal of Clinical and Health Psychology, 15,* 191–199.

Centers for Disease Control and Prevention. (2008, April 11). Prevalence of self-reported postpartum depressive symptoms: 17 states, 2004–2005. *Morbidity and Mortality Weekly Report, 57,* 361.

Centers for Disease Control and Prevention. (2009). Suicide: Facts at a glance, summer 2009. National Center for Injury Prevention and Control. Retrieved from www.cdc.gov/injury/wisqars/index.html

Centers for Disease Control and Prevention. (2011a, December 14). The National Intimate Partner and Sexual Violence Survey (NISVS). Retrieved from www.cdc.gov/ViolencePrevention/NISVS/index.html

Centers for Disease Control and Prevention. (2011b). Prevalence of coronary heart disease: United States, 2006–2010. *Morbidity and Mortality Weekly Report, 306,* 2084–2086.

Centers for Disease Control and Prevention. (2011c). Vital signs: Current cigarette smoking among adults aged ≥ 18 years: United States, 2005–2010. *Morbidity and Mortality Weekly Report, 60,* 1207–1212.

Centers for Disease Control and Prevention. (2011d). Vital signs: Prevalence, treatment, and control of hypertension: United States, 1999–2002 and 2005–2008. *Morbidity and Mortality Weekly Report, 305,* 1531–1534.

Centers for Disease Control and Prevention (2012a, March 29). CDC estimates 1 in 88 children in United States has been identified as having an autism spectrum disorder. Retrieved from www.cdc.gov/media/releases/2012/p0329_autism_disorder.html

Centers for Disease Control and Prevention. (2012b). Trends in asthma prevalence, health care use, and mortality in the United States, 2001–2010. Retrieved

from www.cdc.gov/nchs/data/databriefs/db94.htm
Centers for Disease Control and Prevention. (2012c). Vital signs: Binge drinking prevalence, frequency, and intensity among adults: United States, 2010. *Morbidity and Mortality Weekly Report*, *307*, 908–910.
Centers for Disease Control and Prevention. (2013a). Suicide among adults aged 35–64 years: United States, 1999–2010. *Morbidity and Mortality Weekly Report*, *62*, 321. Retrieved from www.cdc.gov/mmwr/preview/mmwrhtml/mm6217a1.htm?s_cid=mm6217a1_w
Centers for Disease Control and Prevention. (2013b). Suicide now claims more U.S. lives than vehicular crashes. *Journal of the American Medical Association*, *309*, 2432. doi:10.1001/jama.2013.6689
Centers for Disease Control and Prevention. (2014a). Autism spectrum disorder up by 30%. *Journal of the American Medical Association*, *311*, 2058. doi:10.1001/jama.2014.5107
Centers for Disease Control and Prevention. (2014b). Early release of selected estimates based on data from the National Health Interview Survey, January–March 2014. Retrieved from www.cdc.gov/nchs/data/nhis/earlyrelease/earlyrelease201409_08.pdf
Centers for Disease Control and Prevention. (2015a). Current cigarette smoking among adults in the United States. Retrieved from www. cdc.gov/tobacco/data_statistics/fact_sheets/adult_data/cig_smoking/index.htm
Centers for Disease Control and Prevention. (2015b, April 8). Fast stats: Alzheimer's disease. Retrieved from www.cdc.gov/nchs/fastats/alzheimers.htm
Centers for Disease Control and Prevention. (2015c, February 2). Fast stats: Deaths and mortality. Retrieved from www.cdc.gov/nchs/fastats/deaths.htm
Centers for Disease Control and Prevention. (2015d, April 29). Suicide – Facts at a Glance. Retrieved from www.cdc.gov/ViolencePrevention/pdf/Suicide-DataSheet-a.pdf
Centers for Disease Control and Prevention. (2015e). Health, United States, 2014 (Updated May 6, 2015). Retrieved from www.cdc.gov/nchs/hus.htm
Centers for Disease Control and Prevention. (2015f). Too little behavioral therapy for kids with ADHD. *Journal of the American Medical Association*, *313*, 2016. doi:10.1001/jama.2015.4969
Centers for Disease Control and Prevention, National Center for Health Statistics, Office of Analysis and Epidemiology. (2015g) Rates of obesity (age 20 or higher). Retrieved from www.cdc.gov/obesity/data/adult.html
Centers for Disease Control and Prevention. (2015h). Current Cigarette Smoking Among Adults—United States, 2005–2014. *Morbidity and Mortality Weekly Report, 64* (44), 1233–1240.
Centers for Disease Control and Prevention. (2016, February 18). Annual deaths attributable to cigarette smoking-United States, 2005–2009. Retrieved from www.cdc.gov/tobacco/data_statistics/tables/health/infographics/index.htm#annual-deaths
Centre for Addiction and Mental Health. (2014, March 31). Two new genes linked to intellectual disability discovered. *ScienceDaily*. Retrieved from www.sciencedaily.com/releases/2014/03/140331114332.htm
Ceron-Litvoc, D., Soares, B. G., Geddes, J., Litvoc, J., & de Lima, M. S. (2009). Comparison of carbamazepine and lithium in treatment of bipolar disorder: A systematic review of randomized controlled trials. *Human Psychopharmacology: Clinical and Experimental, 24,* 19–28. doi:10.1002/hup.990
Cesario, J. (2014). Priming, replication, and the hardest science. *Perspectives on Psychological Science*, *9*, 40–48. doi:10.1177/1745691613513470
Cevallos, D. (2015, July 17). Don't rely on insanity defense. *CNN.com.* Retrieved from http://www.cnn.com/2015/02/11/opinion/cevallos-insanity-defense/
Chakraborty, K., Mondal, M., Neogi, R., Chatterjee, S., & Makhal, M. (2014). Erectile dysfunction in patients with diabetes mellitus: Its magnitude, predictors and their bio-psycho-social interaction: A study from a developing country. *Asian Journal of Psychiatry, 7,* 58–65. http://dx.doi.org/10.1016/j.ajp.2013.10.012
Chambless, D. L., Floyd, F. J., Rodebaugh, T. L., & Steketee, F. S. (2008). Expressed emotion and familial interaction: A study with agoraphobic and obsessive-compulsive patients and their relatives. *Journal of Abnormal Psychology, 116,* 754–761.
Chantix unsuitable for first-line smoking cessation use, study finds. (2011, November 2). *ScienceDaily.* Retrieved from http://www.sciencedaily.com/
Charness, M. E. (2009). Functional connectivity in Wernicke encephalopathy. *Journal Watch Neurology.* Retrieved from http://neurology.jwatch.org/cgi/content/full/2009/623/4?q=etoc_jwneuro
Chartier, I. S., & Provencher, M. D. (2013). Behavioural activation for depression: Efficacy, effectiveness and dissemination. *Journal of Affective Disorders, 145,* 292–299.
Chasson, G. S., Buhlmann, U., Tolin, D. F., Rao, S. R., Reese, H. E., Rowley, T.,... Wilhelm, S. (2010). Need for speed: Evaluating slopes of OCD recovery in behavior therapy enhanced with d-cycloserine. *Behaviour Research and Therapy, 48,* 675–679. doi:10.1016/j.brat.2010.03.007
Chavira, D. A., Golinelli, D., Sherbourne, C., Stein, M. B., Sullivan, G., Bystritsky, A.,... Craske, M. (2014). Treatment engagement and response to CBT among Latinos with anxiety disorders in primary care. *Journal of Consulting and Clinical Psychology, 82,* 392-403. doi:10.1037/a0036365
Chavira, D. A., Grilo, C., Carlos, M., Shea, M. T., Yen, S., Gunderson, J. G.,... McGlashan, T. H. (2003). Ethnicity and four personality disorders. *Comprehensive Psychiatry, 44,* 483–491.
Chemerinski, E., Byne, W., Kolaitis, J. C., Glanton, C. F., Canfield, E. L., Newmark, R. E.,... Hazlett, E. A. (2012). Larger putamen size in antipsychotic-naïve individuals with schizotypal personality disorder. *Schizophrenia Research, 43,* 158–164. doi:10.1016/j.schres.2012.11.00
Chen, J., Rathore, S. S., Radford, M. J., Wang, Y., & Krumholz, H. M. (2001). Racial differences in the use of cardiac catheterization after acute myocardial infarction. *New England Journal of Medicine, 344,* 1443–1449.
Chen, L., Liu, Y.-H., Zheng, Q-W., Xiang, Y.-T., Duan, Y.-P., Yang, F.-D.,... Si, T. M. (2014). Suicide risk in major affective disorder: Results from a national survey in China. *Journal of Affective Disorders, 155,* 174–179. doi:10.1016/j.jad.2013.10.046
Chen, L., Zhang, G., Hu, M., & Liang, X. (2015). Eye movement desensitization and reprocessing versus cognitive-behavioral therapy for adult posttraumatic stress disorder: Systematic review and meta-analysis. *Journal of Nervous & Mental Disease, 203,* 443–451.
Chen, X., Wang, R., Zee, P., Lutsey, P. L., Javaheri, S., Alcántara, C.,... Redline, S. (2015). Racial/ethnic differences in sleep disturbances: The Multi-Ethnic Study of Atherosclerosis (MESA). *Sleep, 38,* 877.
Chen, Y., Wolk, D. A., Reddin, J. S., Korczykowski, M., Martinez, P. M., Musiek, E. S.,... Detre, J. A. (2011). Voxel-level comparison of arterial spin-labeled perfusion MRI and FDG-PET in Alzheimer disease. *Neurology, 77,* 1977–1985. doi:10.1212/WNL.0b013e31823a0ef7
Cheng, W., Rolls, E. T., Gu, H., Zhang, J., & Feng, J. (2015). Autism: reduced connectivity between cortical areas involved in face expression, theory of mind, and the sense of self. *Brain, 138,* 5, 1382–1393. doi:10.1093/brain/awv051
Chernyak, Y., & Lowe, M. R. (2010). Motivations for dieting: Drive for thinness is different from drive for objective thinness. *Journal of Abnormal Psychology, 119,* 276–281. doi:10.1037/a0018398
Cheung, F. M. (1991). The use of mental health services by ethnic minorities. In H. F. Myers, P. Wohlford, L. P. Guzman, & R. J. Echemendia (Eds.), *Ethnic minority perspectives on clinical training and services in psychology* (pp. 23–31). Washington, DC: American Psychological Association.
Cheung, F. M., Kwong, J. Y. Y., & Zhang, J. (2003). Clinical validation of the Chinese Personality Assessment Inventory. *Psychological Assessment, 15,* 89–100.
Chiang, H.-L., & Gau, S-F. (2014). Impact of executive functions on school and peer functions in youths with ADHD. *Research in Developmental Disabilities, 35,* 963-972. doi:10.1016/j.ridd.2014.02.010
Chida, Y., & Steptoe, A. (2009). The association of anger and hostility with future coronary heart disease: A meta-analytic review of prospective evidence. *Journal of the American College of Cardiology, 53,* 936–946. doi:10.1016/j.jacc.2008.11.044
A children's mental illness "crisis": Report: 1 in 10 children suffers enough to impair development. (2001, January 3). *MSNBC.com.* Retrieved from http://www.msnbc.com/news/510934.asp
Childress, A. R., Ehrman, R. N., Wang, Z., Li, Y., Sciortino, N., Hakun, J.,... O'Brien, C. P. (2008). Prelude to passion: Limbic activation by "unseen" drug and sexual cues. *PLOS ONE, 3*(1), e1506. Retrieved from http://www.plosone.org/article/info:doi/10.1371/journal.pone.0001506
Chioqueta, A.P., & Stiles, T.C. (2007). Dimensions of the Dysfunctional Attitude Scale and the Automatic Thoughts Questionnaire as cognitive vulnerability factors in the development of suicide ideation. *Behavioral and Cognitive Psychotherapy, 35,* 579–589.
Chorpita, B. F., Daleiden, E. L., Ebesutani, C., Young, J., Becker, K. D., Nakamura, B. J.,... Starace, N. (2011). Evidence-based treatments for children and adolescents: An updated review of indicators of efficacy and effectiveness. *Clinical Psychology: Science and Practice, 18,* 154–172. doi:10.1111/j.1468-2850.2011.01247.x
Chou, K.-L. (2009). Social anxiety disorder in older adults: Evidence from the National Epidemiologic Survey on Alcohol and Related Conditions. *Journal of Affective Disorders, 119,* 76–83.
Chou, K.-L. (2010). Panic disorder in older adults: Evidence from the National Epidemiologic Survey on Alcohol and Related Conditions. *International Journal of Geriatric Psychiatry, 25*(8), 822–832. doi:10.1002/gps.2424
Chou, T., Asnaani, A., & Hofmann, S. G. (2012). Perception of racial discrimination and psychopathology across three U.S. ethnic minority groups. *Cultural Diversity and Ethnic Minority Psychology, 18,* 74–81. doi:10.1037/a0025432
Chovil, I. (2000). First person account: I and I, dancing fool, challenge you the world to a duel. *Schizophrenia Bulletin, 26,* 745–747.
Chow, C. K., Redfern, J., Hillis, G. S., Thakkar, J., Santo, K., Hackett, M. L.,... Thiagalingam, A. (2015). Effect of lifestyle-focused text messaging on risk factor modification in patients with coronary heart disease: A randomized clinical trial. *Journal of the American Medical Association, 314,* 1255–1263. doi:10.1001/jama.2015.10945
Christensen, A., Atkins, D. C., Baucom, B., & Yi, J. (2010). Marital status and satisfaction five years following a randomized clinical trial comparing traditional versus integrative behavioral couple therapy. *Journal of Consulting and Clinical Psychology, 78,* 225–235. doi:10.1037/a0018132
Chronis, A. M., Jones, H. A., & Raggi, V. L. (2006). Evidence-based psychosocial treatments for children and adolescents with attention-deficit/hyperactivity disorder. *Clinical Psychology Review, 26,* 486–502.
Chu, J. A. (2011a). Falling apart: Dissociation and the dissociative disorders. In J. A. Chu (Ed.), *Rebuilding shattered lives: Treating complex PTSD and dissociative disorders* (2nd ed., pp. 41–64). Hoboken: John Wiley & Sons.
Chu, J. A. (2011b). The rational treatment of dissociative identity disorder. In J. A. Chu (Ed.), *Rebuilding shattered lives: Treating complex PTSD and dissociative disorders* (2nd ed., pp. 205–227). Hoboken: John Wiley & Sons.
Chung, D. W., Rudnicki, D. D., Yu, L., & Margolis, R. L. (2011). A natural antisense transcript at the Huntington's disease repeat locus regulates HTT expression. *Human Molecular Genetics, 20,* 3467–3477. doi:10.1093/hmg/ddr263
Chung, T., & Maisto, S. A. (2006). Relapse to alcohol and other drug use in treated adolescents: Review and reconsideration of relapse as a change point in clinical course. *Clinical Psychology Review, 26,* 149–161.
Church, D., Feinstein, D., Palmer-Hoffman, J., Stein, P. K., & Tranguch, A. (2014). Empirically supported psychological treatments: The challenge of evaluating clinical innovations. *Journal of Nervous & Mental Disease, 202,* 699–709. doi:10.1097/NMD.0000000000000188
Ciao, A. C., Accurso, E. C., Fitzsimmons-Craft, E. F., & Le Grange, D. (2015). Predictors and moderators

of psychological changes during the treatment of adolescent bulimia nervosa. *Behaviour Research and Therapy, 69*, 48–53. doi:10.1016/j.brat.2015.04.002

Cicero, T. J, Ellis, M. S., Surratt, H. L., & Kurtz, S. P. (2014). The changing face of heroin use in the United States: A retrospective analysis of the past 50 years. *JAMA Psychiatry, 71*, 821–826. doi:10.1001/jamapsychiatry.2014.366

Clark, D. M. (1986). A cognitive approach to panic. *Behaviour Research and Therapy, 24*, 461–470.

Clark, L. (2012). Epidemiology and phenomenology of pathological gambling. In J. E. Grant & M. N. Potenza (Eds.), *The Oxford handbook of impulse control disorders* (pp. 94–116). New York, NY: Oxford University Press.

Clark, R. (2006). Perceived racism and vascular reactivity in Black college women: Moderating effects of seeking social support. *Health Psychology, 25*, 20–25.

Clark, S. K., Jeglic, E. L., Calkins, C., & Tatar, J. R. (2014). More than a nuisance: The prevalence and consequences of frotteurism and exhibitionism. *Sexual Abuse, 4*, 3–19. doi:10.1177/1079063214525643

Clarke, J., Proudfoot, J., Birch, M. R., Whitton, A. E., Parker, G., Manicavasagar, V.,... Hadzi-Pavlovic, D. (2014). Effects of mental health self-efficacy on outcomes of a mobile phone and web intervention for mild-to-moderate depression, anxiety and stress: Secondary analysis of a randomised controlled trial. *BMC Psychiatry, 14*, 272. doi:10.1186/s12888-014-0272-1

Clarke, K., Mayo-Wilson, E., Kenny, J., & Pilling. S. (2015). Can non-pharmacological interventions prevent relapse in adults who have recovered from depression? A systematic review and meta-analysis of randomised controlled trials. *Clinical Psychology Review, 39*, 58–70. doi:10.1016/j.cpr.2015.04.002

Clarke, T., & Pierson, R. (2015, August 19). FDA approves "female Viagra" with strong warning. *Reuters News Service.* Retrieved from http://www.reuters.com/article/2015/08/19/us-pink-viagra-fda-idUSKCN0QN2BH20150819

Clarke, T.-K., Lupton, M. K., Fernandez-Pujals, A. M., Starr, J., Davies, G., Cox, S.,... McIntosh, A. M. (2015). Common polygenic risk for autism spectrum disorder (ASD) is associated with cognitive ability in the general population. *Molecular Psychiatry, 21*(3), 419–425. doi:10.1038/mp.2015.12

Clarke., G., Dickerson, J., Gullion, C. M., & Debar, L. L. (2012). Trends in youth antidepressant dispensing and refill limits, 2000 through 2009. *Journal of Child and Adolescent Psychopharmacology, 22*, 11–20.

Clarkin, J. (2014). Raising the bar in the empirical investigation of psychotherapy. *American Journal of Psychiatry, 171*, 1027–1030. doi:10.1176/appi.ajp.2014.14060792

Clay, R. A. (2001, January). Bringing psychology to cardiac care. *Monitor on Psychology, 32*(1), 46–49.

Clay, R. A. (2009). The debate over low libidos: Psychologists differ on how to treat a lack of desire among some women. *Monitor on Psychology, 40*(4), 32.

Clayton, R. B., Leshner, G., & Almond, A. (2015). The extended iSelf: The impact of iPhone separation on cognition, emotion, and physiology. *Journal of Computer-Mediated Communication, 20*, 119–135. doi:10.1111/jcc4.12109

Cleary, E. H., & Stanton, A. L. (2015). Mediators of an Internet-based psychosocial intervention for women with breast cancer. *Health Psychology, 34*, 477–485. Retrieved from http://dx.doi.org/10.1037/hea0000170

Cleckley, H. (1976). *The mask of sanity* (5th ed.). St. Louis, MO: Mosby.

Clifford, D. B., Fagan, A. M., Holtzman, D. M., Morris J. C., Teshome M., Shah, A. R.,... Kauwe, J. S. (2009). CSF biomarkers of Alzheimer disease in HIV-associated neurologic disease. *Neurology, 73*, 1982–1987.

Cloitre, M. (2014). Alternative intensive therapy for PTSD. *American Journal of Psychiatry, 171*, 249–251. doi:10.1176/appi.ajp.2013.13121695

Cloud, J. (2010, January 6). Why your DNA isn't your destiny. *Time Magazine.* Retrieved from http://www.time.com/time/magazine/article/0,9171,1952313-1,00.html

Clough, B. A., & Casey, L. M. (2011). Technological adjuncts to enhance current psychotherapy practices: A review. *Clinical Psychology Review, 31*, 279–292. doi:10.1016/j.cpr.2010.12.008

Clough, B. A., & Casey, L. M. (2015). The smart therapist: A look to the future of smartphones and mHealth technologies in psychotherapy. *Professional Psychology: Research and Practice, 46*, 147–153. Retrieved from http://dx.doi.org/10.1037/pro0000011

Cludius, B., Stevens, S., Bantin, T., Gerlach, A. L., & Hermann, C. (2013). The motive to drink due to social anxiety and its relation to hazardous alcohol use. *Psychology of Addictive Behaviors, 27*, 806–813. doi:10.1037/a0032295

Coccaro, E. F. (2010). A family history study of intermittent explosive disorder. *Journal of Psychiatric Research, 44*, 1101–1105.

Coccaro, E. F. (2012). Intermittent explosive disorder as a disorder of impulsive aggression for DSM-5. *American Journal of Psychiatry, 169*, 577–588. doi:10.1176/appi.ajp.2012.11081259

Coccaro, E. F., & McCloskey, M. S. (2010). Intermittent explosive disorder: Clinical aspects. In E. Aboujaoude & L. M. Koran (Eds.), *Impulse control disorders* (pp. 221–232). Cambridge, UK: Cambridge University Press.

Coccaro, E. F., Lee, R., & Kavoussi, R. J. (2010). Aggression, suicidality, and intermittent explosive disorder: Serotonergic correlates in personality disorder and healthy control subjects. *Neuropsychopharmacology, 35*, 435–444. doi:10.1038/npp.2009.148

Cochran, S. D., Sullivan, J. G., & Mays, V. M. (2003). Prevalence of mental disorders, psychological distress, and mental health services use among lesbian, gay, and bisexual adults in the United States. *Journal of Consulting and Clinical Psychology, 71*, 53–61.

Cochran, S. V., & Rabinowitz, F. E. (2003). Gender-sensitive recommendations for assessment and treatment of depression in men. *Professional Psychology: Research and Practice, 34*, 132–140.

Cohen, H., Kaplan, Z., Kotler, M., Kouperman, I., Moisa, R., & Grisaru, N. (2004). Repetitive transcranial magnetic stimulation of the right dorsolateral prefrontal cortex in posttraumatic stress disorder: A double-blind, placebo-controlled study. *American Journal of Psychiatry, 161*, 515–524.

Cohen, J. (2012). The many states of HIV in America. *Science, 6091*, 168–171. doi:10.1126/science.337.6091.168

Cohen, J. (2013, November). Breathing easier. *Monitor on Psychology, 44*(1), 42.

Cohen, S., & Janicki-Deverts, D. (2009). Can we improve our physical health by altering our social networks? *Perspectives on Psychological Science, 4*, 375–378. doi:10.1111/j.1745-6924.2009.01141

Cohen, S., Doyle, W. J., Alper, C. M., Janicki-Deverts, D., & Turner, R. B. (2009). Sleep habits and susceptibility to the common cold. *Archives of Internal Medicine, 169*, 62–66. doi:10.1001/archinternmed.2008.505

Cohen, S., Doyle, W. J., Turner, R., Alper, C. M., & Skoner, D. P. (2003). Sociability and susceptibility to the common cold. *Psychological Science, 14*, 389–395.

Cohen, S., Janicki-Deverts, D., & Miller, G. E. (2007). Psychological stress and disease. *Journal of the American Medical Association, 298*, 1685–1687. doi:10.1001/jama.298.14.1685

Cohen, S., Janicki-Deverts, D., Doyle, W. J., Miller, G. E., Frank, E., Rabin, B. S.,... Turner, R. B. (2012). Chronic stress, glucocorticoid receptor resistance, inflammation, and disease risk. *Proceedings of the National Academy of Sciences of the United States of America, 109*, 5995–5999. doi:10.1073/pnas.1118355109

Cohen, S., Kozlovsky, N., Matar, M. A., Kaplan, Z., Zohar, J., & Cohen, H. (2012). Post-exposure sleep deprivation facilitates correctly timed interactions between glucocorticoid and adrenergic systems, which attenuate traumatic stress responses. *Neuropsychopharmacology, 37*, 2388–2404. doi:10.1038/npp.2012.94

Cohen-Kettenis, P. Y., & Klink, D. (2015). Adolescents with gender dysphoria. *Best Practice & Research Clinical Endocrinology & Metabolism, 29*, 485–495.

Coila, B. (2009). What is epigenetics? Retrieved from http://bridget-coila.suite101.com/what-is-epigenetics-a104553

Colak, D., Zaninovic, N., Cohen, M. S., Rosenwaks, Z., Yang, W.-Y., Gerhardt, J.,... Jaffrey, S. R. (2014). Promoter-bound trinucleotide repeat mRNA drives epigenetic silencing in Fragile X Syndrome. *Science, 343*, 1002. doi:10.1126/science.1245831

Colangelo, J. J., & Keefe-Cooperman, K. (2012). Understanding the impact of childhood sexual abuse on women's sexuality. *Journal of Mental Health Counseling, 34*, 14–37.

Colas, E. (1998). *Just checking.* New York, NY: Simon & Schuster.

Colditz, G. A., Wolin, K. Y., & Gehlert, S. (2012). Applying what we know to accelerate cancer prevention. *Science Translational Medicine, 4*, 127. doi:10.1126/scitranslmed.3003218

Cole, D. A., Cho, S.-J., Martin, N. C., Youngstrom, E. A., March, J. S., Findling, R. L.,... Maxwell, M. A. (2012). Are increased weight and appetite useful indicators of depression in children and adolescents? *Journal of Abnormal Psychology, 121*, 838–851. doi:10.1037/a0028175

Collier, L. (2014, December). Envisioning healthy weight. *Monitor on Psychology, 45*(11), 58–59.

Colvert, E., Tick, B., McEwen, F., Stewart, C., Curran, S. R., Woodhouse, E., Gillan, N.,... Bolton, P. (2015). Heritability of autism spectrum disorder in a UK population-based twin sample. *JAMA Psychiatry, 72*, 415–423. doi:10.1001/jamapsychiatry.2014.3028

Comas-Diaz, L. (2011a). Multicultural psychotherapies. In R. J. Corsini & D. Wedding (Eds.), *Current psychotherapies* (9th ed., pp. 536–567). Belmont, CA: Brooks/Cole.

Comas-Diaz, L. (2011b). *Multicultural care: A clinician's guide to cultural competence.* Washington, DC: American Psychological Association.

Comas-Diaz, L., & Greene, B. (Eds.). (2013). *Psychological health of women of color: Interactions, challenges, and opportunities.* Santa Barbara, CA: ABC-CLIO.

Comparelli, A., Corigliano, V., De Carolis, A., Mancinelli, I., Trovini, G., Ottavi, G.,... Girardi, P. (2013). Emotion recognition impairment is present early and is stable throughout the course of schizophrenia. *Schizophrenia Research, 143*, 65–69.

Compton, W., Conway, K. P., Stinson, F. S., Colliver, J. D., & Grant, B. F. (2005). Prevalence and comorbidity of DSM-IV antisocial syndromes and specific drug use disorders in the United States: Results from the National Epidemiologic Survey on Alcohol and Related Conditions. *Journal of Clinical Psychiatry, 66*, 676–685.

Conger, K. (2008a, June 26). Facebook concepts indicate brains of Alzheimer's patients aren't as networked, Stanford study shows. *Stanford University School of Medicine News Release.* Retrieved from http://med.stanford.edu/news_releases/2008/june/alzheimers21.html

Conger, K. (2008b, July 9). Taking a page from Facebook: Researchers track brain networks in Alzheimer's. *Stanford University School of Medicine News Release.* Retrieved from http://med.stanford.edu/mcr/2008/alzheimers-0709.html

Connelly, M. (2013). Cognitive behavioral therapy for treatment of pediatric chronic migraine. *Journal of the American Medical Association, 310*, 2617–2618. doi:10.1001/jama.2013.282534

Conner, B. T., & Lochman, J. E. (2010). Comorbid conduct disorder and substance use disorders. *Clinical Psychology: Science and Practice, 17*, 337–349. doi:10.1111/j.1468-2850.2010.01225.x

Conner, K. R., Bossarte, R. M., Hea, H., Arora, J., Lu, N., Tua, X. M.,... Katz, I. R. (2014). Posttraumatic stress disorder and suicide in 5.9 million individuals receiving care in the veterans health administration health system. *Journal of Affective Disorders, 166*, 1–5. doi:10.1016/j.jad.2014.04.067

Connolly, B. S., & Lang, A. E. (2014). Pharmacological treatment of Parkinson disease: A review. *Journal of the American Medical Association, 311*, 1670–1683. doi:10.1001/jama.2014.3654

Conway, C. C., Rutter, L. A., & Brown, T. A. (2016). Chronic environmental stress and the temporal course of depression and panic disorder: A trait-state-occasion modeling approach. *Journal of Abnormal Psychology, 125*, 53–63. Retrieved from http://dx.doi.org/10.1037/abn0000122

Conway, K. P., Compton, W., Stinson, F. S., & Grant, B. F. (2006). Lifetime comorbidity of DSM-IV mood and anxiety disorders and specific drug use disorders: Results from the National Epidemiologic Survey on Alcohol and Related Conditions. *Journal of Clinical Psychiatry, 67*, 247–257.

Cook, J. M., Biyanova, T., & Coyne, J. C. (2009). Comparative case study of diffusion of eye movement desensitization and reprocessing in two clinical settings: Empirically supported treatment status is not enough. *Journal of Consulting and Clinical Psychology, 40,* 518–524.doi:10.1037/a0015144

Cooney, G. M., Dwan, K., Greig, C. A., Lawlor, D. A., Rimer, J., Waugh, F. R.,... Mead, G. E. (2013). Exercise for depression. *The Cochrane Library.* doi:10.1002/14651858.CD004366.pub6

Coons, P. M. (1986). Treatment progress in 20 patients with multiple personality disorder. *The Journal of Nervous and Mental Disease, 174,* 715–721.

Cooper, A., Delmonico, D. L., & Burg, R. (2000). Cybersex users, abusers, and compulsives: New findings and implications. *Sexual Addiction & Compulsivity, 7,* 5–29.

Cooper, A., Delmonico, D. L., Griffin-Shelley, E., & Mathy, R. M. (2004). Online sexual activity: An examination of potentially problematic behaviors. *Sexual Addiction & Compulsivity, 11*(3), 129–143.

Cooper, A., Scherer, C. R., Boies, S. C., & Gordon, B. L. (1999). Sexuality on the Internet: From sexual exploration to pathological expression. *Professional Psychology: Research & Practice, 30*(2), 154–164.

Cooper, C., Sommerlad, A., Lyketsos, C. G., & Livingston, G. (2014). Modifiable predictors of dementia in mild cognitive impairment: A systematic review and meta-analysis. *American Journal of Psychiatry, 172*(4), 323–334. doi:10.1176/appi.ajp.2014.1407087

Copeland, W. E., Angold, A., Costello, E. J., & Egger, H. (2013). Prevalence, comorbidity, and correlates of DSM-5 proposed disruptive mood dysregulation disorder. *American Journal of Psychiatry, 170,* 173–179.

Copeland, W. E., Shanahan, L, Egger, H., Angold, A., & Costello, E. J. (2014). Adult diagnostic and functional outcomes of DSM-5 disruptive mood dysregulation disorder. *American Journal of Psychiatry, 171,* 668-674. doi:10.1176/appi.ajp.2014.13091213

Corbett, A., & Ballard, C. (2012). Antipsychotics and mortality in dementia. *American Journal of Psychiatry, 169,* 7–9. doi:10.1176/appi.ajp.2011.11101488

Corbett, J., Saccone, N. L., Foroud, T., Goate, A., Edenberg, H., Nurnberger, J.,... Rice, J. P. (2005). Sex adjusted and age adjusted genome screen for nested alcohol dependence diagnoses. *Psychiatric Genetics, 15,* 25–30.

Coronado, S. F., & Peake, T. H. (1992). Culturally sensitive therapy: Sensitive principles. *Journal of College Student Psychotherapy, 7,* 63–72.

Correll, C. C., & Blader, J. C. (2015). Antipsychotic use in youth without psychosis: A double-edged sword. *JAMA Psychiatry, 72,* 859–860. doi:10.1001/jamapsychiatry.2015.0632

Correll, C. U., Manu, P., Olshanskiy, V., Napolitano, B., Kane, J. M., & Malhotra, A. K. (2009). Cardiometabolic risk of second-generation antipsychotic medications during first-time use in children and adolescents. *Journal of the American Medical Association, 302,* 1765–1773. doi:10.1001/jama.2009.1549

Cortina, L. M., & Kubiak, S. P. (2006). Gender and posttraumatic stress: Sexual violence as an explanation for women's increased risk. *Journal of Abnormal Psychology, 115,* 753–759.

Coryell, W. (2011). The search for improved antidepressant strategies: Is bigger better? *American Journal of Psychiatry, 168,* 664–666. doi:10.1176/appi.ajp.2011.11030510

Coryell, W., Pine, D., Fyer, A., & Klein, D. (2006). Anxiety responses to $CO_2$ inhalation in subjects at high risk for panic disorder. *Journal of Affective Disorders, 92,* 63–70.

Costello, D. M., Swendsen, J., Rose, J. S., & Dierkera, L. C. (2008). Risk and protective factors associated with trajectories of depressed mood from adolescence to early adulthood. *Journal of Consulting and Clinical Psychology, 76,* 173–183.

Costello, E. J., Compton, S. N., Keele, G., & Angold, A. (2003). Relationships between poverty and psychopathology: A natural experiment. *Journal of the American Medical Association, 290,* 2023–2029.

Costin, C. (1997). *Your dieting daughter: Is she dying for attention?* New York, NY: Brunner/Mazel.

Courtney-Seidler, E. A., Klein, D., & Miller, A. L. (2014). Borderline personality disorder in adolescents. *Clinical Psychology: Science and Practice, 20,* 425–444.

Cowley, G. (2001, February 12). New ways to stay clean. *Newsweek,* 45–47.

Cox, B. J., MacPherson, P. S., & Enns, M. W. (2005). Psychiatric correlates of childhood shyness in a nationally representative sample. *Behavior Research and Therapy, 43,* 1019–1027.

Cox, B. J., MacPherson, P. S., Enns, M. W., & McWilliams, L. A. (2004). Neuroticism and self-criticism associated with posttraumatic stress disorder in a nationally representative sample. *Behaviour Research and Therapy, 42*(1), 105–14.

Coyle, J. P. (2006). Treating difficult couples: Helping clients with coexisting mental and relationship disorders. *Family Relations: Interdisciplinary Journal of Applied Family Studies, 55*(1), 146–147.

Coyne, J. C. (1976). Toward an interactional description of depression. *Psychiatry, 39,* 14–27.

Cramer, P. (2000). Defense mechanisms in psychology today: Further processes for adaptation. *American Psychologist, 55,* 637–646.

Cramer, P. E., Cirrito, J. R., Wesson, D. W., Lee, D., Karlo, J. C., Zinn, A. E., Casali, B. T.,... Landreth, G. E. (2012). ApoE-directed therapeutics rapidly clear β-amyloid and reverse deficits in AD mouse models. *Science, 335*(6075), 1503–1506. doi:10.1126/science.1217697

Craske, M. G., Niles, A. N., Burklund, L. J., Wolitzky-Taylor, K. B., Vilardaga, J. C., Plumb, A.,... Lieberman, M. D. (2014). Randomized controlled trial of cognitive behavioral therapy and acceptance and commitment therapy for social phobia: Outcomes and moderators. *Journal of Consulting and Clinical Psychology, 82,* 1034–1048. Retrieved from http://dx.doi.org/10.1037/a0037212

Craske, M. G., Roy-Byrne, P. P., Stein, M. B., Sullivan, G., Sherbourne, C., & Bystritsky, A. (2009). Treatment for anxiety disorders: Efficacy to effectiveness to implementation. *Behaviour Research and Therapy, 47,* 931–937. doi:10.1016/j.brat.2009.07.012

Creed, F., & Barsky, A. (2004). A systematic review of the epidemiology of somatisation disorder and hypochondriasis. *Journal of Psychosomatic Research, 56,* 391–408.

Creswell, J. D., & Lindsay, E. K. (2014). How does mindfulness training affect health? A mindfulness stress buffering account. *Current Directions in Psychological Science, 23,* 401–407. doi:10.1177/0963721414547415

Crino, R. D. (2015). Psychological treatment of obsessive compulsive disorder: An update. *Australas Psychiatry, 23,* 347–349. doi:10.1177/1039856215590030

Critic calls American Psychiatric Association approval of DSM-V "a sad day for psychiatry." (2012, December 3). Retrieved from healthnewsreview.org

Crits-Christoph, P., Gibbons, M. B. C., Hamilton, J., Ring- Kurtz, S., & Gallop, R. (2011). The dependability of alliance assessments: The alliance–outcome correlation is larger than you might think. *Journal of Consulting and Clinical Psychology, 79,* 267–278. doi:10.1037/a0023668

Croghan, I. T., Hurt, R. D., Dakhil, S. R., Croghan, G. A., Sloan, J. A., Novotny, P. J.,... Loprinzi, C. L. (2007). Randomized comparison of a nicotine inhaler and bupropion for smoking cessation and relapse prevention. *Mayo Clinic Proceedings, 82,* 186–195.

Cross-Disorder Group of the Psychiatric Genomics Consortium. (2013, February 28). Identification of risk loci with shared effects on five major psychiatric disorders: A genome-wide analysis. *The Lancet.* Retrieved from http://press.thelancet.com/psychiatricdisorders.pdf

Crouse, K., & Pennington, B. (2012, November 13). Panic attack leads to hospital on way to golfer's first victory. *The New York Times,* pp. A1, A3.

Crow, S. J., Peterson, C. B., Swanson, S. A., Raymond, N. C., Specker, S., Eckert, E. D., & Mitchell, J. E. (2009). Increased mortality in bulimia nervosa and other eating disorders. *American Journal of Psychiatry, 166,* 1342–1346. doi:10.1176/appi.ajp.2009.09020247

Crowell, S. E., Beauchaine, T. P., McCauley, E., Smith, C. V., Vasilev, C. A., & Stevens, A. (2008). Parent-child interactions, peripheral serotonin, and self-inflicted injury in adolescents. *Journal of Consulting and Clinical Psychology, 76,* 15–21.

Crozier, J. C., Dodge, K. A., Fontaine, R. G., Lansford, J. E., Bates, J. E., Pettit, G. S.,... Levenson, R. W. (2008). Social information processing and cardiac predictors of adolescent antisocial behavior. *Journal of Abnormal Psychology, 117,* 253–267.

Cruchaga, C., Karch, C. M., Jin, S. C., Benitez, B. A., Cai, Y., Guerreiro, R., Harari, O.,... Goate, A. M. (2014). Rare coding variants in the phospholipase D3 gene confer risk for Alzheimer's disease. *Nature, 505,* 550–554.

Cryan, J. F., & O'Leary, O. F. (2010). A glutamate pathway to faster-acting antidepressants? *Science, 329,* 913–914. doi:10.1126/science.1194313

Csordas, T. J., Storck, M. J., & Strauss, M. (2008). Diagnosis and distress in Navajo healing. *Journal of Mental and Nervous Disease, 196,* 585–596.

Csukly, G., Stefanics, G., Komlósi, S., Czigler, I., & Czobor, P. (2014). Event-related theta synchronization predicts deficit in facial affect recognition in schizophrenia. *Journal of Abnormal Psychology, 123,* 178–189. doi:10.1037/a0035793

Cuijpers, P. (2014). Combined pharmacotherapy and psychotherapy in the treatment of mild to moderate major depression? *JAMA Psychiatry, 71,* 747–748. doi:10.1001/jamapsychiatry.2014.277

Cuijpers, P., Clignet, F., van Meijel, B., van Straten, A., Lid, J., & Andersson, G. (2011). Psychological treatment of depression in inpatients: A systematic review and meta-analysis. *Clinical Psychology Review, 31,* 353–360. doi:10.1016/j.cpr.2011.01.002

Cuijpers, P., Li, J., Hofmann, S. J., & Andersson, G. (2010). Self-reported versus clinician-rated symptoms of depression as outcome measures in psychotherapy research on depression: A meta-analysis. *Clinical Psychology Review, 30,* 768–778.

Cuijpers, P., Muñoz, R. F., Clarke, G. N., & Lewinsohn, P. M. (2009). Psychoeducational treatment and prevention of depression: The "Coping with Depression" course thirty years later. *Clinical Psychology Review, 29,* 449–458. doi:10.1016/j.cpr.2009.04.005

Cuijpers, P., Sijbrandij, M., Koole, S., Huibers, M., Berking, M., & Andersson, G. (2014). Psychological treatment of generalized anxiety disorder: A meta-analysis. *Clinical Psychology Review, 34,* 130–140.

Cuijpers, P., van Straten, A., Schuurmans, J., van Oppen, P., Hollon, S. D., & Andersson, G. (2010). Psychotherapy for chronic major depression and dysthymia: A meta-analysis. *Clinical Psychology Review, 30,* 51–62. doi:10.1016/j.cpr.2009.09.003

Cullen, K. R., & Lim, K. O. (2014). Toward understanding the functional relevance of white matter deficits in bipolar disorder. *JAMA Psychiatry, 71,* 362–364. doi:10.1001/jamapsychiatry.2013.4638

Cummings, C. M., Caporino, N. E., & Kendall, P. C. (2014). Comorbidity of anxiety and depression in children and adolescents: 20 years after. *Psychological Bulletin, 140,* 816–845. doi:10.1037/a0034733

Cummings, C. M., Caporino, N. E., Settipani, C. A., Read, K. L., Compton, S. N., March, J.,... Kendall, P. C. (2013). The therapeutic relationship in cognitive-behavioral therapy and pharmacotherapy for anxious youth. *Journal of Consulting and Clinical Psychology, 81,* 859–864. doi:10.1037/a0033294

Cunningham, J. A., & Breslin, F. C. (2004). Only one in three people with alcohol abuse or dependence ever seek treatment. *Addictive Behaviors, 29,* 221–223.

Curb, J. D., & Marcus, E. B. (1991). Body fat and obesity in Japanese-Americans. *American Journal of Clinical Nutrition, 53,* 1552S–1555S.

Cusack, K., Jonas, D. E., Forneris, C. A., Wines, C., Sonis, J., Middleton, J. C.,... Gaynes, B. N. (2015). Psychological treatments for adults with posttraumatic stress disorder: A systematic review and meta-analysis. *Clinical Psychology Review, 43,* 128–141. doi:10.1016/j.cpr.2015.10.003.

D'Onofrio, B. M., Rickert, M. E., Frans, E., Kuja-Halkola, R., Almqvist, C., Sjölander, A.,... Lichtenstein, P. (2014). Paternal age at childbearing and offspring psychiatric and academic morbidity. *JAMA Psychiatry, 71,* 432–438. doi:10.1001/jamapsychiatry.2013.4525

D'Onofrio, G., O'Connor, P. G., Pantalon, M. V., Chawarski, M. C., Busch, S. H., Owens, P. H.,... Fiellin, D. A. (2015). Emergency department–initiated buprenorphine/naloxone treatment for opioid dependence: A randomized clinical trial. *Journal of the American Medical Association, 313,* 1636–1644. doi:10.1001/jama.2015.3474

da Silva Costa, L., Alencar, A. P., Netoa, P. J. N., do Socorro Vieira dos Santos, M., Gleidiston, C., da Silva, L.,…Neto, M. L. R. (2014). Risk factors for suicide in bipolar disorder: A systematic review. *Journal of Affective Disorders, 170,* 237–254. doi:10.1016/j.jad.2014.09.003

Dahl, M. (2008, August 6). Shock therapy makes a quiet comeback. Retrieved from http://www.msnbc.msn.com/id/26044935/

Dahlen, E. R., Edwards, B. D., Tubre, T., Zyphur, M. J., & Warren, C. (2012). Taking a look behind the wheel: An investigation into personality predictors of aggressive driving. *Accident Analysis and Prevention, 45,* 1–9.

Dai, Y. B., Tan, X. J., Wu, W. F., Warner, M., & Gustafsson, J. A. (2012). Liver X receptor protects dopaminergic neurons in a mouse model of Parkinson disease. *Proceedings of the National Academy of Sciences, 109,* 13112. doi:10.1073/pnas.1210833109

Dale, K. Y., Berg, R., Elden, A., Ødegård, A., & Holte A. (2009). Testing the diagnosis of dissociative identity disorder through measures of dissociation, absorption, hypnotizability and PTSD: A Norwegian pilot study. *Journal of Trauma and Dissociation, 10,* 102–112. doi:10.1080/15299730802488478

Dalenberg, C. J., Brand, B. L., Gleaves, D. H., Dorahy, M. J., Loewenstein, R. J., Cardeña, E.,…Spiegel, D. (2012). Evaluation of the evidence for the trauma and fantasy models of dissociation. *Psychological Bulletin, 138,* 550–588. doi:10.1037/a0027447

Dallaire, D. H., & Weinraub, M. (2007). Infant-mother attachment security and children's anxiety and aggression at first grade. *Journal of Applied Developmental Psychology, 28,* 477–492.

Dalley, S. E., Buunk, A. P., & Umit, T. (2009). Female body dissatisfaction after exposure to overweight and thin media images: The role of body mass index and neuroticism. *Personality and Individual Differences, 45,* 47–51. doi:10.1016/j.paid.2009.01.044

Dalton, V. S., Kolshus, E., & McLoughlin, D. M. (2014). Epigenetics and depression: Return of the repressed. *Journal of Affective Disorders, 155,* 1–12.

Daneback, K., Ross, M. W., & Månsson, S. (2006). Characteristics and behaviors of sexual compulsives who use the Internet for sexual purposes. *Sexual Addiction & Compulsivity, 13*(1), 53–67.

Dannon, P. N., Lowengrub, K., Aizer, A., & Kotler, M. (2006). Pathological gambling: Comorbid psychiatric diagnoses in patients and their families. *Israel Journal of Psychiatry and Related Sciences, 43,* 88–92.

D'Astous, M., Cottin, S., Roy, M., Picard, C., & Cantin, L. (2013). Bilateral stereotactic anterior capsulotomy for obsessive-compulsive disorder: Long-term follow-up. *Journal of Neurology, Neurosurgery & Psychiatry, 84,* 1208–1213. doi:10.1136/jnnp-2012-303826

Davenport, S. W., Bergman, S. M., Bergman, J. Z., & Fearrington, M. E. (2014). Twitter versus Facebook: Exploring the role of narcissism in the motives and usage of different social media platforms. *Computers in Human Behavior, 32,* 212–220.

Davies, M., Gilston, J., & Rogers, P. (2012). Examining the relationship between male rape myth acceptance, female rape myth acceptance, victim blame, homophobia, gender roles, and ambivalent sexism. *Journal of Interpersonal Violence, 27,* 2807–2823.

Davis, A. W. (2014). Ethical issues for psychologists using communication technology: An Australian perspective on service provision flexibility. *Professional Psychology: Research and Practice, 45,* 303–308. Retrieved from http://dx.doi.org/10.1037/a0037081

Davis, M. C., & Zautra, A. J. (2013). An online mindfulness intervention targeting socioemotional regulation in fibromyalgia: Results of a randomized controlled trial. *Annals of Behavioral Medicine, 46,* 273–284. doi:10.1007/s12160-013-9513-7

Davis, M. C., & Zautra, A. J. (2013). An online mindfulness intervention targeting socioemotional regulation in fibromyalgia: Results of a randomized controlled trial. *Annals of Behavioral Medicine, 46,* 273–284. doi:10.1007/s12160-013-9513-7

Davis, M., Ressler, K., Rothbaum, B. O., & Richardson, R. (2006). Effects of D-cycloserine on extinction: Translation from preclinical to clinical work. *Biological Psychiatry, 60,* 369–375.

Davis, S. R., & Braunstein, G. D. (2012). Efficacy and safety of testosterone in the management of hypoactive sexual desire disorder in menopausal women. *The Journal of Sexual Medicine, 9,* 1134–1148.

Davis, S. R., Davison, S. L., Donath, S., & Bell, R. J. (2005). Circulating androgen levels and self-reported sexual function in women. *Journal of the American Medical Association, 294,* 91–96.

Davis, S. R., Moreau, M., Kroll, R., Bouchard, C., Panay, N., Gass, M.,…The APHRODITE Study Team. (2008). Testosterone for low libido in postmenopausal women not taking estrogen. *New England Journal of Medicine, 359,* 2005–2017.

Dawe, S., Rees, V. W., Mattick, R., Sitharthan, T., & Heather, N. (2002). Efficacy of moderation-oriented cue exposure for problem drinkers: A randomized controlled trial. *Journal of Consulting and Clinical Psychology, 70,* 1045–1050.

De Hert, M., Sermon, J., Geerts, P., Vansteelandt, K., Peuskens, J., &, Detraux, J. (2015). The use of continuous treatment versus placebo or intermittent treatment strategies in stabilized patients with schizophrenia: A systematic review and meta-analysis of randomized controlled trials with first- and second-generation antipsychotics. *CNS Drugs, 29,* 637–658. doi:10.1007/s40263-015-0269-4

de Kleine, R. A., Hendriks, G.-J., Smits, J. A. J., Broekman, T. G., & van Minnen, A. (2014). Prescriptive variables for d-cycloserine augmentation of exposure therapy for posttraumatic stress disorder. *Journal of Psychiatric Research, 48,* 40–46. doi:10.1016/j.jpsychires.2013.10.008

De la Cancela, V., & Guzman, L. P. (1991). Latino mental health service needs: Implications for training psychologists. In H. F. Myers, P. Wohlford, L. P. Guzman, & R. J. Echemendia (Eds.), *Ethnic minority perspectives on clinical training and services in psychology* (pp. 59–64). Washington, DC: American Psychological Association.

De la Herran-Arita, A. K., Kornum, B. R., Mahlios, J., Jiang, W., Lin, L., Hou, T.,…Mignot, M. (2014). CD4 T cell autoimmunity to hypocretin/orexin and cross-reactivity to a 2009 H1N1 influenza epitope in narcolepsy. *Science Translational Medicine, 5,* 216. doi:10.1126/scitranslmed.3007762

de la Torre-Luque, A., Gambara, H., López, E., & Cruzado, J. A. (2015). Psychological treatments to improve quality of life in cancer contexts: A meta-analysis. *International Journal of Clinical and Health Psychology, 26,* 660–667. doi:10.1037/0278-6133.26.6.660

De Raedt, R., Vanderhasselt, M.-A., & Baeken, C. (2015). Neurostimulation as an intervention for treatment resistant depression: From research on mechanisms towards targeted neurocognitive strategies. *Clinical Psychology Review, 41,* 61–69. doi:10.1016/j.cpr.2014.10.006

de Vries, A. L. C., McGuire, J. K., Steensma, T. D., Wagenaar, E. C., F., Doreleijers, T. A. H., &. Cohen-Kettenis, P. T. (2014). Young adult psychological outcome after puberty suppression and gender reassignment. *Pediatrics, 134,* 696. http://dx.doi.org/10.1542/peds.2013-2958

de Win, M. M. L., Jager, G., Booij, J., Reneman, L., Schilt, T., Lavini, C.,…van den Brink, W. (2008). Sustained effects of ecstasy on the human brain: A prospective neuroimaging study in novel users. *Brain, 131,* 2936.

DeAngelis, T. (2012a, March). Practicing distance therapy, legally and ethically. *Monitor on Psychology, 43*(3), 52.

DeAngelis, T. (2012b). A second life for practice? *Monitor on Psychology, 43*(3), 48.

Decety, J., Chen, C., Harenski, C., & Kiehl, K. A. (2013). An fMRI study of affective perspective taking in individuals with psychopathy: Imagining another in pain does not evoke empathy. *Frontiers in Human Neuroscience, 7,* 489. doi:10.3389/fnhum.2013.00489

Deffenbacher, J. L. (2003). Anger disorders. In E. F. Coccaro (Ed.), *Aggression psychiatric assessment and treatment* (pp. 89–111). New York, NY: Marcel Dekker.

Deffenbacher, J. L., Stephens, A. N., & Sullman, M. J. (in press). Driving anger as a psychological construct: Twenty years of research using the Driving Anger Scale. *Transportation Research Part F: Traffic Psychology and Behaviour.*

DeFina, L. F., Willis, B. L., Radford, N. B., Gao, A., Leonard, D., Haskell, W. L.,…Berry, J. D. (2013). The association between midlife cardiorespiratory fitness levels and later-life dementia: A cohort study. *Annals of Internal Medicine, 158,* 162–216.

Del Boca, F. K., Darkes, J., Greenbaum, P. E., & Goldman, M. S. (2004). Up close and personal: Temporal variability in the drinking of individual college students during their first year. *Journal of Consulting and Clinical Psychology, 72,* 155–164.

Delahanty, D. L. (2011a, November). Injury severity and posttraumatic stress. *Clinician's Research Digest,* p. 3.

Delahanty, D. L. (2011b). Toward the predeployment detection of risk for PTSD. *American Journal of Psychiatry, 168,* 9–11. doi:10.1176/appi.ajp.2010.10101519

Delgado, M. Y., Updegraff, K. A., Roosa, M. W., & Umaña-Taylor, A. J. (2010). Discrimination and Mexican-origin adolescents' adjustment: The moderating roles of adolescents', mothers', and fathers' cultural orientations and values. *Journal of Youth and Adolescence, 40,* 125–139. doi:10.1007/s10964-009-9467-z

Dempster, E. L., Pidsley, R., Schalkwyk, L. C., Owens, S., Georgiades, A., Kane, F.,…Mill, J. (2011). Disease-associated epigenetic changes in monozygotic twins discordant for schizophrenia and bipolar disorder. *Human Molecular Genetics, 43,* 969–976. doi:10.1093/hmg/ddr416

Denizet-Lewis, B. (2006, June 25). An anti-addiction pill? *The New York Times Magazine,* 48–53.

Dennis, E. L., Jahanshad, N., Rudie, J. D., Brown, J. A., Johnson, K., McMahon, K.,…Thompson, P. (2012). Altered structural brain connectivity in healthy carriers of the autism risk gene, CNTNAP2. *Brain Connectivity, 1,* 447–459. doi:10.1089/brain.2011.0064

Dennis, T. A., & O'Toole, L. J. (2014). Mental health on the go: Effects of a gamified attention-bias modification mobile application in trait-anxious adults. *Clinical Psychological Science, 2,* 576–590.

Denny, B. T., Fan, J., Liu, X., Ochsner, K. N., Guerreri, S., Mayson, S. J.,…Koenigsberg, H. W. (2015). Elevated amygdala activity during reappraisal anticipation predicts anxiety in avoidant personality disorder. *Journal of Affective Disorders, 172,* 1–7. doi:10.1016/j.jad.2014.09.017

Denollet, J., & Pedersen, S. S. (2009). Anger, depression, and anxiety in cardiac patients: The complexity of individual differences in psychological risk. *Journal of the American College of Cardiology, 53,* 947–949. doi:10.1016/j.jacc.2008.12.006

DeNoon, D. (2006, May 1). Do ADHD drugs stunt kids' growth? *WebMD Medical News.* Retrieved from http://www.webmd.com/content/article/121/114370

Denson, T. F., Spanovic, M., & Miller, N. (2009). Cognitive appraisals and emotions predict cortisol and immune responses: A meta-analysis of acute laboratory social stressors and emotion inductions. *Psychological Bulletin, 135,* 823–853. doi:10.1037/a0016909

Denys, D., Mantione, M., Figee, M., van den Munckhof, P., Koerselman, F., Westenberg, H.,…Schuurman, R. (2010). Deep brain stimulation of the nucleus accumbens for treatment-refractory obsessive-compulsive disorder. *Archives of General Psychiatry, 67,* 1061–1068. doi:10.1001/archgenpsychiatry.2010.122

Depping, M. S., Wolf, N. D., Vasic, N., Sambataro, F., Thomann, P. A., & Wolf, R. C. (2014). Specificity of abnormal brain volume in major depressive disorder: A comparison with borderline personality disorder. *Journal of Affective Disorders, 174,* 650–657.

Depression ups risk of complications following heart attack, study suggests. (2008, July 5). *ScienceDaily.* Retrieved from http://www.sciencedaily.com/releases/2008/07/080701194736.htm

Derby, C. A., Barbour, M. M., Hume, A. L. & McKinlay, J. B. (2001). Drug therapy and prevalence of erectile dysfunction in the Massachusetts Male Aging Study cohort. *Pharmacotherapy, 21,* 676–683.

Deriziotis, P., O'Roak, B. J., Graham, S. A., Estruch, S. B., Dimitropoulou, D., Bernier, R. A.,…Fisher, S. E. (2014). De novo TBR1 mutations in sporadic autism disrupt protein functions. *Nature Communications, 5*, 4954. doi:10.1038/ncomms5954

DeRubeis, R. J., Hollon, S. D., Amsterdam, J. D., Shelton, R. C., Young, P. R., Salomon, R.M.,... Gallop, R. (2005). Cognitive therapy vs. medications in the treatment of moderate to severe depression. *Archives of General Psychiatry, 62*, 409–416.

Dervic, K., Brent, D. A., & Oquendo, M. A. (2008). Completed suicide in childhood. *Psychiatric Clinics of North America, 31*, 271–291.

Devan, G. S. (1987). Koro and schizophrenia in Singapore. *British Journal of Psychiatry, 150*, 106–107.

Devanand, D. P., Mintzer, J., Schultz, S. K., Andrews, H. F., Sultzer, D. L., de la Pena, D., Gupta, S.,... Levin, B. (2012). Relapse risk after discontinuation of risperidone in Alzheimer's disease. *New England Journal of Medicine, 367*, 1497.

Devos, D., Moreau, C., & Destée, A. (2009). Levodopa for Parkinson's disease. *New England Journal of Medicine, 360*, 935–936.

DeVylder, J. E., Lukens, E. P., Link, B. G., & Lieberman, J. A. (2015). Suicidal ideation and suicide attempts among adults with psychotic experiences data from the collaborative psychiatric epidemiology surveys. *JAMA Psychiatry, 72*, 219–225. doi:10.1001/jamapsychiatry.2014.2663

Dhindsa, R. S., & Goldstein, D. B. (2016). Schizophrenia: From genetics to physiology at last. *Nature*, in press. doi:10.1038/nature16874

Dhuffar, M. K., & Griffiths, M. D. (2015). A systematic review of online sex addiction and clinical treatments using CONSORT evaluation. *Current Addiction Reports, 2*, 163–174.

Di Iorio, C. R., Watkins, T. J., Dietrich, M. S., Cao, A., Blackford, J. U., Rogers, B.,... Cowan, R. L. (2011). Evidence for chronically altered serotonin function in the cerebral cortex of female 3,4-methylenedioxymethamphetamine polydrug users. *Archives of General Psychiatry, 69*, 399–409. doi:10.1001/archgenpsychiatry.2011.156

Di Nicola, M., De Risio, L., Pettorruso, M., Caselli, G., De Crescenzo, G., Swierkosz-Lenart, K., & Janiri, L. (2014). Bipolar disorder and gambling disorder comorbidity: Current evidence and implications for pharmacological treatment. *Journal of Affective Disorders, 167*, 285–298. doi:10.1016/j.jad.2014.06.023

Diamond, M. (2011). Developmental, sexual and reproductive neuroendocrinology: Historical, clinical and ethical considerations. *Frontiers in Neuroendocrinology, 32*, 255–263.

Diamond, S., Baldwin, R., & Diamond, R. (1963). *Inhibition and choice*. New York, NY: Harper & Row.

Dick, D. M. (2011). Gene-environment interaction in psychological traits and disorders. *Annual Review of Clinical Psychology, 7*, 383–409. doi:10.1146/annurevclinpsy-032210-104518

Dickerson, F. B., Tenhula, W. N., & Green-Paden, L. D. (2005). The token economy for schizophrenia: Review of the literature and recommendations for future research. *Schizophrenia Research, 75*, 405–416.

Dickinson, D., Straub, R. E., Trampush, J. W., Gao, Y., Feng, N., Xie, B.,... Weinberger, D. R. (2014). Differential effects of common variants in SCN2A on general cognitive ability, brain physiology, and messenger RNA expression in schizophrenia cases and control individuals. *JAMA Psychiatry, 71*, 647–656. doi:10.1001/jamapsychiatry.2014.157

DiClemente, C. (2011). Project MATCH. In J. C. Norcross, G. R. VandenBos, & D. K. Freedheim (Eds.), *History of psychotherapy: Continuity and change* (2nd ed.) (pp. 395–401). Washington, DC: American Psychological Association.

Difede, J. A., Cukor, J., Wyka, K., Olden, M., Hoffman, H., Lee, F. S.,... Altemus, M. (2014). D-cycloserine augmentation of exposure therapy for post-traumatic stress disorder: A pilot randomized clinical trial. *Neuropsychopharmacology, 39*, 1052–1058. doi:10.1038/npp.2013.317

DiMauro, J., Domingues, J., Fernandez, G., & Tolina, D. F. (2012). Long-term effectiveness of CBT for anxiety disorders in an adult outpatient clinic sample: A follow-up study. *Behaviour Research and Therapy, 51*, 82–86. doi:10.1016/j.brat.2012.10.00

Dimeff, L. A., Paves, A. P., Skutch, J. M., & Woodcock E. A. (2011). Shifting paradigms in clinical psychology: How innovative technologies are shaping treatment delivery. In D. H. Barlow (Ed.), *The Oxford handbook of clinical psychology* (pp. 618–648). New York, NY: Oxford University Press.

Dimidjian, S., & Segal, Z. V. (2015). Prospects for a clinical science of mindfulness-based intervention. *American Psychologist, 70*, 593–620. Retrieved from http://dx.doi.org/10.1037/a0039589

Dimidjian, S., Barrera, M., Jr., Martell, C., Muñoz, R. F., & Lewinsohn, P. M. (2011). The origins and current status of behavioral activation treatments for depression. *Annual Review of Clinical Psychology, 7*, 1–38. doi:10.1146/annurevclinpsy-032210-104535

Dimsdale, J. E., & Levenson, J. (2013). What's next for somatic symptom disorder? *American Journal of Psychiatry, 170*, 1393–1395. doi:10.1176/appi.ajp.2013.13050589

Dishion, T. J., & Owen, L. D. (2002). A longitudinal analysis of friendships and substance use: Bidirectional influence from adolescence to adulthood. *Developmental Psychology, 38*, 480–491.

Disney, K. L. (2013). Dependent personality disorder: A critical review. *Clinical Psychology Review, 33*, 1184–1196. doi:10.1016/j.cpr.2013.10.001

Distel, M. A., Hottenga, J.-J., Trull, T. J., & Boomsma, D. I. (2008). Chromosome 9: Linkage for borderline personality disorder features. *Psychiatric Genetics, 18*, 302–307.

Dobbs, D. (2010). Schizophrenia appears during adolescence: But where does one begin and the other end? *Nature, 468*, 154–156. doi:10.1038/468154a

Dobson, E. T., & Strawn, J. R. (2016). Pharmacotherapy for pediatric generalized anxiety disorder: A systematic evaluation of efficacy, safety and tolerability. *Pediatric Drugs*, in press.

Dodge, K. A. (2009). Mechanisms of gene–environment interaction effects in the development of conduct disorder. *Perspectives on Psychological Science, 4*, 408–414. doi:10.1111/j.1745-6924.2009.01147.x

Dodge, K. A., Laird, R., Lochman, J. E., & Zelli, A. (2002). Multidimensional latent-construct analysis of children's social information processing patterns. *Psychological Assessment, 14*, 60–73.

Dohrenwend, B. P. (2006). Inventorying stressful life events as risk factors for psychopathology: Toward resolution of the problem of intracategory variability. *Psychological Bulletin, 132*, 477–495.

Dohrenwend, B. P., Turner, J. B., Turse, N. A., Adams, B. G., Koenen, K. C., & Marshall, R. (2006). The psychological risks of Vietnam for U.S. veterans: A revisit with new data and methods. *Science, 313*, 979–982.

Donaldson, S. I., Csikszentmihalyi, M., & Nakamura, J. (Eds.). (2011). *Applied positive psychology: Improving everyday life, health, schools, work, and society: Series in applied psychology*. New York, NY: Routledge/Taylor & Francis Group.

Donegan, E., & Dugas, M. J. (2012). Generalized anxiety disorder: A comparison of symptom change in adults receiving cognitive-behavioral therapy or applied relaxation. *Journal of Consulting and Clinical Psychology, 80*, 490–496. doi:10.1037/a0028132

Dong, L., Bilbao, A., Laucht, M., Henriksson, R., Yakovlev, T., Ridinger, M., Desrivieres, S.,... Schuman, G. (2011). Effects of the circadian rhythm gene period 1 (Per1) on psychosocial stress–induced alcohol drinking. *American Journal of Psychiatry, 168*, 1090–1098. doi.org/10.1176/appi.ajp.2011.10111579

Donovan, J. E., Molina, B. S. G., & Kelly, T. M. (2009). Alcohol outcome expectancies as socially shared and socialized beliefs. *Psychology of Addictive Behaviors, 23*, 248–259. doi:10.1037/a0015061

Doss, B. D., Mitchell, A., Georgia, E. J., Biesen, J. N., & Rowe, L. S. (2015). Improvements in closeness, communication, and psychological distress mediate effects of couple therapy for veterans. *Journal of Consulting and Clinical Psychology, 83*, 405–415. http://dx.doi.org/10.1037/a0038541

Douglas, K. S., Guy, L. S., & Hart, S. D. (2009). Psychosis as a risk factor for violence to others: A meta-analysis. *Psychological Bulletin, 135*, 679–706. doi:10.1037/a0016311

Drabick, D. A. G., & Kendall, P. C. (2010). Developmental psychopathology and the diagnosis of mental health problems among youth. *Clinical Psychology: Science and Practice, 17*, 272–280. doi:10.1111/j.1468-2850.2010.01219.x

Drieling, T., van Calker, D., & Hecht, H. (2006). Stress, personality and depressive symptoms in a 6.5-year follow-up of subjects at familial risk for affective disorders and controls. *Journal of Affective Disorders, 91*, 195–203.

Driessen, E., Cuijpers, P., de Maat, S. C. M., Abbass, A. A., de Jonghe, F., & Dekker, J. J. M. (2010). The efficacy of short-term psychodynamic psychotherapy for depression: A meta-analysis. *Clinical Psychology Review, 30*, 25–36. doi:10.1016/j.cpr.2009.08.010

Driessen, E., Hegelmaier, L. M., Abbass, A. A., Barber, J. P., Dekker, J. J. M., Vane, H. L.,... Cuijpers, P. (2015). The efficacy of short-term psychodynamic psychotherapy for depression: A meta-analysis update. *Clinical Psychology Review, 42*, 1–15. doi:10.1016/j.cpr.2015.07.004

Driscoll, M. W., & Torres, L. (2013). Acculturative stress and Latino depression: The mediating role of behavioral and cognitive resources. *Cultural Diversity and Ethnic Minority Psychology, 19*, 373–382. doi:10.1037/a0032821

Drum, K. B., & Littleton, H. L. (2014). Therapeutic boundaries in telepsychology: Unique issues and best practice recommendations. *Professional Psychology: Research and Practice, 45*, 309–315. Retrieved http://dx.doi.org/10.1037/a0036127

Dubovsky, S. (2006, February 12). An update on the neurobiology of addiction. *Journal Watch Psychiatry*. Retrieved from http://psychiatry.jwatch.org/cgi/content/full/2006/222/7?q=etoc

Dubovsky, S. (2012, January 13). How well are we treating depression? *Journal Watch Psychiatry*. Retrieved from http://psychiatry.jwatch.org/cgi/content/full/2012/113/2?q=etoc_jwpsych

Dubovsky, S. (2014a, March 14). How light alters circadian rhythms: An animal study. *NEJM Journal Watch*. Retrieved from http://www.jwatch.org/na33910/2014/03/14/how-light-alters-circadian-rhythms-animal-study?query=etoc_jwpsych

Dubovksy, S. (2014b, April 24). Searching for bipolar endophenotypes. *NEJM Watch Psychiatry*. Retrieved from http://www.jwatch.org/na34374/2014/04/24/searching-bipolar-endophenotypes?query=etoc_jwpsych

Dubovsky, S. (2015). How does deep brain stimulation work? *NEJM Journal Watch Psychiatry*. Retrieved from http://www.jwatch.org/na37868/2015/05/22/how-does-deep-brain-stimulation-work?query=etoc_jwpsych

Ducci, F., Kaakinen, M., Pouta, A., Hartikainen, A.-L., Veijola, J., Isohanni, M.,... Ekelund, J. (2011). TTC12-ANKK1-DRD2 and CHRNA5-CHRNA3-CHRNB4 influence different pathways leading to smoking behavior from adolescence to mid-adulthood. *Biological Psychiatry, 69*, 650–660. doi:10.1016/j.biopsych.2010.09.055

Dudek, D., Jaeschke, R., Siwek, M., Mączka, G., Topór-Mądry, R., & Rybakowski, J. (2013). Postpartum depression: Identifying associations with bipolarity and personality traits: Preliminary results from a cross-sectional study in Poland. *Psychiatry Research, 215*, 69–74. doi:10.1016/j.psychres.2013.10.013

Dudeney, J., Sharpe, L., & Hunt, C. (2015). Attentional bias towards threatening stimuli in children with anxiety: A meta-analysis. *Clinical Psychology Review, 40*, 66–75. doi:10.1016/j.cpr.2015.05.007

Duffy, A., Horrocks, J., Doucette, S., Keown-Stoneman, C., McCloskey, S., & Grof, P. (2014). The developmental trajectory of bipolar disorder. *The British Journal of Psychiatry, 204*, 122–128. doi:10.1192/bjp.bp.113.126706

Duke, L. A., Allen, R. N., Rozee, P., & Bommaritto, M. (2008). The sensitivity and specificity of flashbacks and nightmares to trauma. *Journal of Anxiety Disorders, 22*, 319–327.

Duke, P., & Hochman, G. (1992). *A brilliant madness*. New York, NY: Bantam Dell.

Dunn, E. C., Brown, R. C., Dai, Y., Rosand, J., Nugent, N. R., Amstadter, A. B.,... Smoller, J. W. (2015). Genetic determinants of depression. *Harvard Review of Psychiatry, 23*, 1. doi:10.1097/HRP.0000000000000054

Duran, B., Oetzel, J., Lucero, J., Jiang, Y., Novins, D. K., Manson, S., & Beals, J. (2005). Obstacles for rural American Indians seeking alcohol, drug, or mental health treatment. *Journal of Consulting and Clinical Psychology, 73*, 819–829.

Durham, R. C., Higgins, C., Chambers, J. A., Swan, J. S., & Dow, M. G. T. (2012). Long-term outcome of eight clinical trials of CBT for anxiety disorders: Symptom profile of sustained recovery and treatment-resistant groups. *Journal of Affective Disorders, 136,* 875–881.

Duric, V., Banasr, M., Licznerski, P., Schmidt, H. D., Stockmeier, C. A., Simen, A. S.,…Duman, R. S. (2010). A negative regulator of MAP kinase causes depressive behavior. *Nature Medicine, 16,* 1328–1332. doi:10.1038/nm.2219

Durkheim, E. (1958). *Suicide* (J. A. Spaulding & G. Simpson, Trans.). New York, NY: Free Press. (Original work published 1897)

Dutra, L., Stathopoulou, G., Basden, S. L., Leyro, T. M., Powers, M. B., & Otto, M. W. (2008). A meta-analytic review of psychosocial interventions for substance use disorders. *American Journal of Psychiatry, 165,* 179–187.

Dysken, M. W., Sano, M., Asthana, S., Vertrees, J. E., Pallaki, M., Llorente, M.,…Guarino, P. G. (2014). Effect of vitamin E and memantine on functional decline in Alzheimer disease: The TEAM-AD VA Cooperative Randomized Trial. *Journal of the American Medical Association, 311,* 33–44. doi:10.1001/jama.2013.282834

Dzokoto, V. A., & Adams, G. (2005). Understanding genital-shrinking epidemics in West Africa: Koro, juju, or mass psychogenic illness? *Culture, Medicine and Psychiatry, 29,* 53–78.

Eagly, A. H., Eaton, A., Rose, S. M., Riger, S., & McHugh, M. C. (2012). Feminism and psychology: Analysis of a half-century of research on women and gender. *American Psychologist, 67,* 211–230. doi:10.1037/a0027260

Eaton, W. W., Shao, H., Nestadt, G., Lee, B. H., Bienvenu, O. J., & Zandi, P. (2008). Population-based study of first onset and chronicity in major depressive disorder. *Archives of General Psychiatry, 65,* 513–520.

Ebbert, J. O., Hughes, J. R., West, R. J., Rennard, S. L., Russ, C., McRae, T. D.,…Park, P. W. (2015). Effect of varenicline on smoking cessation through smoking reduction: A randomized clinical trial. *Journal of the American Medical Association, 313,* 687–694. doi:10.1001/jama.2015.280

Eberhardy, F. (1967). The view from "the couch." *Journal of Child Psychological Psychiatry, 8,* 257–263.

Ebrahim, I. O., Shapiro, C. M., Williams, A. J., & Fenwick, P. B. (2013). Alcohol and sleep I: Effects on normal sleep. *Alcoholism: Clinical and Experimental Research, 37,* 539–549. doi:10.1111/acer.12006

Eckel, R. H., Jakicic, J. M., Ard, J. D., de Jesus, J., Miller, N. H., Hubbard, MD, V. S.,…Yanovski, S. Z. (2014). AHA/ACC prevention guideline 2013 AHA/ACC guideline on lifestyle management to reduce cardiovascular risk: A report of the American College of Cardiology/American Heart Association Task Force on Practice Guidelines. *Circulation, 129,* S76–S99. doi:10.1161/01.cir.0000437740.48606.d1

Ecker, C., Ginestet, C., Feng, Y., Johnston, P., Lombardo, M. V., Lai, M.-C.,…MRC AIMS Consortium. (2013). Brain surface anatomy in adults with autism: The relationship between surface area, cortical thickness, and autistic symptoms. *JAMA Psychiatry, 70,* 59–70. doi:10.1001/jamapsychiatry.2013.265

Eddleston, M. (2006). Physical vulnerability and fatal self-harm in the elderly. *British Journal of Psychiatry, 189,* 278–279.

Eddy, K. T., Hennessey, M., & Thompson-Brenner, H. (2007). Eating pathology in East African women: The role of media exposure and globalization. *The Journal of Nervous and Mental Disease, 195,* 196–202.

Edman, J. L., & Johnson, R. C. (1999). Filipino American and Caucasian American beliefs about the causes and treatment of mental problems. *Cultural Diversity and Ethnic Minority Psychology, 5,* 380–386.

Edwards, V. J., Holden, G. W., Felitti, V. J., & Anda, R. F. (2003). Relationship between multiple forms of childhood maltreatment and adult mental health in community respondents: Results from the Adverse Childhood Experiences Study. *American Journal of Psychiatry, 160,* 1453–1460.

Eftekhar, A., Fullwood, C., & Morris, N. (2014). Capturing personality from Facebook photos and photo-related activities: How much exposure do you need? *Computers in Human Behavior, 37,* 162–170. http://dx.doi.org/10.1016/j.chb.2014.04.048

Eftekhari, A., Ruzek, J. I., Crowley, J. J., Rosen, C. S., Greenbaum, M. A., & Karlin, B. E. (2013). Effectiveness of national implementation of prolonged exposure therapy in Veterans Affairs care. *JAMA Psychiatry, 70,* 949–955. doi:10.1001/jamapsychiatry.2013.36

Egan, J. (2008, September 14). The bipolar puzzle. *The New York Times Magazine,* 66, 75, 94–97.

Egan, S. J., Watson, H. J., Kane, R. T., McEvoy, P., Fursland, A., & Nathan, P. R. (2013). Anxiety as a mediator between perfectionism and eating disorders. *Cognitive Therapy and Research, 37,* 905–913. doi:10.1007/s10608-012-9516-x

Eggenberger, P., Schumacher, V., Angst, M., Theill, N., & de Bruin, E. D. (2015). Does multicomponent physical exercise with simultaneous cognitive training boost cognitive performance in older adults? A 6-month randomized controlled trial with a 1-year follow-up. *Journal of Clinical Interventions in Aging, 10,* 1335–1349. doi:10.2147/CIA.S87732

Ehlers, A., Grey, N., Wild, J., Stott, R., Liness, S., Deale, A.,…Clark, D. M. (2013). Implementation of cognitive therapy for PTSD in routine clinical care: Effectiveness and moderators of outcome in a consecutive sample. *Behaviour Research and Therapy, 51,* 742–752.

Ehlers, A., Hackmann, A., Grey, N., Wild, J., Liness, S., Albert, I.,…Clark, D. M. (2014). A randomized controlled trial of 7-day intensive and standard weekly cognitive therapy for PTSD and emotion-focused supportive therapy. *American Journal of Psychiatry, 171,* 294–304.

Ehlkes, T., Michie, P. T., & Schall, U. (2012). Brain imaging correlates of emerging schizophrenia. *Neuropsychiatry, 2,* 147–154. doi:10.2217/npy.12.13

Ehrenreich, B., Righter, B., Rocke, D. A., Dixon, L., & Himelhoch, S. (2011). Are mobile phones and handheld computers being used to enhance delivery of psychiatric treatment? A systematic review. *Journal of Nervous and Mental Disease, 199,* 886–891. doi:10.1097/NMD.0b013e3182349e90

Eichstaedt, J. C., Schwartz, H. A., Kern, M. L., Park, G., Labarthe, D. R., Merchant, R. M.,…Seligman, M. E. P. (2015). Psychological language on Twitter predicts county-level heart disease mortality. *Psychological Science, 26,* 159–169. doi:10.1177/0956797614557867

Eikeseth, S., Klintwall, L., Jahr, E., & Karlsson, P. (2012). Outcome for children with autism receiving early and intensive behavioral intervention in mainstream preschool and kindergarten settings. *Research in Autism Spectrum Disorders, 6,* 829–835. doi:10.1016/j.rasd.2011.09.002

Einfeld, S. L., & Brown, R. (2010). Down syndrome: New prospects for an ancient disorder. *Journal of the American Medical Association, 303,* 2525–2526.

Ekinci, O., Albayrak, Y., & Ekinci, A. (2012). Cognitive insight and its relationship with symptoms in deficit and nondeficit schizophrenia. *Journal of Nervous and Mental Disease, 200,* 44–50. doi:10.1097/NMD.0b013e31823e66af

El Alaoui, S., Hedman, E., Kaldo, V., Hesser, H., Kraepelien, M., Andersson, E.…Lindefors, N. (2015). Effectiveness of Internet-based cognitive–behavior therapy for social anxiety disorder in clinical psychiatry. *Journal of Consulting and Clinical Psychology, 83,* 902–914. http://dx.doi.org/10.1037/a0039198

Elbogen, E. B., & Johnson, S. C. (2009). The intricate link between violence and mental disorder: Results from the National Epidemiologic Survey on Alcohol and Related Conditions. *Archives of General Psychiatry, 66,* 152–161.

Eley, T. C., McAdams, T. A., Rijsdijk, F. V., Lichtenstein, P., Narusyte, J., Reiss, D.,…Neiderhiser, J. M. (2015). The intergenerational transmission of anxiety: A children-of-twins study. *American Journal of Psychiatry, 172,* 630–637. doi:10.1176/appi.ajp.2015.14070818

Ellason, J. W., & Ross, C. A. (1997). Two-year follow-up of inpatients with dissociative identity disorder. *American Journal of Psychiatry, 154,* 832–839.

Ellin, A. (2012, August 13). Binge eating among men steps out of the shadows. *The New York Times.* Retrieved from www.nytimes.com

Ellis, A. (1977). The basic clinical theory of rational-emotive therapy. In A. Ellis & R. Grieger (Eds.), *Handbook of rational-emotive therapy* (pp. 3–34). New York, NY: Springer.

Ellis, A. (1993). Reflections on rational-emotive therapy. *Journal of Consulting and Clinical Psychology, 61,* 199–201.

Ellis, A. (2001). *Overcoming destructive beliefs, feelings, and behaviors: New directions for rational emotive behavior therapy.* Amherst, NY: Prometheus Books.

Ellis, A. (2011). Rational emotive behavior therapy. In R. J. Corsini & D. Wedding (Eds.), *Current psychotherapies* (9th ed., pp. 196–234). Belmont, CA: Brooks/Cole.

Ellis, A., & Ellis, D. J. (2011). *Rational emotive behavior therapy: Theories of psychotherapy.* Washington, DC: American Psychological Association.

Elwood, L. S., Hahn, K. S., Olatunji, B. O., & Williams, N. L. (2009). Cognitive vulnerabilities to the development of PTSD: A review of four vulnerabilities and the proposal of an integrative vulnerability model. *Clinical Psychology Review, 29,* 87–100. doi:10.1016/j.cpr.2008.10.002

Emslie, G. J. (2008). Pediatric anxiety: Underrecognized and undertreated. *New England Journal of Medicine, 359,* 2835–2836.

Eonta, A. M., Christon, L. M., Hourigan, S. E., Ravindran, N., Vrana, S. R., & Southam-Gerow, M. (2011). Using everyday technology to enhance evidence-based treatments. *Professional Psychology: Research and Practice, 42,* 513–520. doi:10.1037/a0025825

Epperson, C. N. (2013). Premenstrual dysphoric disorder and the brain. *American Journal of Psychiatry, 170,* 248–252. doi:10.1176/appi.ajp.2012.1212155

Epping-Jordan, J. E., Compas, B. E., & Howell, D. C. (1994). Predictors of cancer progression in young adult men and women. *Health Psychology, 13,* 539–547.

Erdleyi, M. H. (2010). The ups and downs of memory. *American Psychologist, 65,* 622–633. doi:10.1037/a0020440

Erlenmeyer-Kimling, L., Adamo, U. H., Rock, D., Roberts, S. A., Bassett, A. S., Squires-Wheeler, E.,…Gottesman, I. I. (1997). The New York high-risk project: Prevalence and comorbidity of Axis I disorders in offspring of schizophrenic parents at 25-year follow-up. *Archives of General Psychiatry, 54,* 1096–1102.

Escudero, L., & Johnstone, M. (2014). Genetics of schizophrenia. *Current Psychiatry Reports, 16,* 502. doi:10.1007/s11920-014-0502-8.

Esman, A. H. (2011). Charcot, Freud, and the treatment of "nervous disorders." *Journal of Nervous & Mental Disease, 199,* 828–829. doi:10.1097/NMD.0b013e3182348cf9

Espay, A. J., Norris, M. M., Eliassen, J. C., Dwivedi, A., Smith, M. S., Banks, C.,…Szaflarski, J. P. (2015). Placebo effect of medication cost in Parkinson disease: A randomized double-blind study. *Neurology, 84,* 794–802. doi:10.1212/WNL.0000000000001282

Essex, M. J., Kraemer, H. C., Armstrong, J. M., Boyce, W. T., Goldsmith, H. H., Klein, M. H.,…Kupfer, D.J. (2006). Exploring risk factors for the emergence of children's mental health problems. *Archives of General Psychiatry, 63,* 1246–1256.

Etkin, A., Prater, K. E., Schatzberg, A. F., Menon, V., & Greicius, M. D. (2009). Disrupted amygdalar subregion functional connectivity and evidence of a compensatory network in generalized anxiety disorder. *Archives of General Psychiatry, 66,* 1361–1372.

Ettinger, U., Meyhöfer, I., Steffens, M., Wagner, M., & Koutsouleris, N. (2014). Genetics, cognition, and neurobiology of schizotypal personality: A review of the overlap with schizophrenia. *Frontiers in Psychiatry, 5,* 18. doi:10.3389/fpsyt.2014.00018

Evans, S. E., Davies, C., & DiLillo, D. (2008). Exposure to domestic violence: A meta-analysis of child and adolescent outcomes. *Aggression and Violent Behavior, 13,* 131–140.

Even, C., & Weintraub, D. (2012). Is depression in Parkinson's disease (PD) a specific entity? *Journal of Affective Disorders, 139,* 103–112. Retrieved from http://dx.doi.org/10.1016/j.jad.2011.07.002

Everson-Rose, S. A., Roetker, N. S., Lutsey, P. L., Kershaw, K. N., Longstreth, W. T., Sacco, R. L.,…Alonso, A. (2014). Chronic stress, depressive symptoms, anger, hostility, and risk of stroke and transient ischemic attack in the multi-ethnic study of atherosclerosis. *Stroke, 45,* 2318–2323. doi:10.1161/STROKEAHA.114.004815

Evraire, L. E., & Dozois, D. J. A. (2011). An integrative model of excessive reassurance seeking and negative feedback seeking in the development and maintenance of depression. *Clinical Psychology Review, 31,* 1291–1303. doi:10.1016/j.cpr.2011.07.014

Exner, J. E., Jr. (2002). Early development of the Rorschach test. *Academy of Clinical Psychology Bulletin, 8,* 9–24.

Eye movements and the search for biomarkers for schizophrenia. (2012, October 29). *ScienceDaily.* Retrieved from http://www.sciencedaily.com/releases/2012/10/121029081833.htm

Fabrega, H., Jr. (1990). Hispanic mental health research: A case for cultural psychiatry. *Journal of Behavioral Sciences, 12,* 339–365.

Failer, J. L. (2002). *Who qualifies for rights? Homelessness, mental illness, and civil commitment.* Ithaca, NY: Cornell University Press.

Fairburn, C. G., Cooper, Z., Doll, H. A., O'Connor, M. E., Bohn, K., Hawker, D. M.,... Palmer, R. L. (2009). Transdiagnostic cognitive-behavioral therapy for patients with eating disorders: A two-site trial with 60-week follow-up. *American Journal of Psychiatry, 166,* 311–319. doi:10.1176/appi.ajp.2008.08040608

Fairburn, C. G., Stice, E., Cooper, Z., Doll, H. A., Norman, P. A., & O'Connor, E. E. (2003). Understanding persistence in bulimia nervosa: A 5-year naturalistic study. *Journal of Consulting and Clinical Psychology, 71,* 103–109.

Fals-Stewart, W. (2003). The occurrence of partner physical aggression on days of alcohol consumption: A longitudinal diary study. *Journal of Consulting and Clinical Psychology, 71,* 41–52.

Fan, Y., Tang, Y., Lu, Q., Feng, S., Yu, Q., Sui, D.,... Song, L. (2009). Dynamic changes in salivary cortisol and secretory immunoglobulin A response to acute stress. *Stress and Health, 25,* 189–194. doi:10.1002/smi.1239

Fang, A., Schwartz, R. A., & Wilhelm, S. (2016). Treatment of an adult with body dysmorphic disorder. In E. A. Storch & A. B. Lewin (Eds.), *Clinical handbook of obsessive-compulsive and related disorders: A case-based approach to treating pediatric and adult populations* (pp. 259–271). New York, NY: Springer.

Fang, S. C., Rosen, R. C., Vita, J. A., Ganz, P., & Kupelian, V. (2015). Changes in erectile dysfunction over time in relation to Framingham cardiovascular risk in the Boston Area Community Health (BACH) Survey. *Journal of Sexual Medicine, 12,* 100–108. doi:10.1111/jsm.12715

Farr, C. B. (1994). Benjamin Rush and American psychiatry. *American Journal of Psychiatry, 151*(Suppl.), 65–73.

Farrell, A. D., & White, K. S. (1998). Peer influences and drug use among urban adolescents: Family structure and parent/adolescent relationship as protective factors. *Journal of Consulting and Clinical Psychology, 66,* 248–258.

Fava, G. A., Balon, R., & Rickels, K. (2015). Benzodiazepines in anxiety disorders. *JAMA Psychiatry, 72,* 733–734. doi:10.1001/jamapsychiatry.2015.0182

Fazel, S., Långström, N., Hjern, A., Grann, M., & Lichtenstein, P. (2009). Schizophrenia, substance abuse, and violent crime. *Journal of the American Medical Association, 301,* 2016–2023.

Fears, S. C., Service, S. K., Kremeyer, B., Araya, C., Araya, X., Bejarano, J.,... Bearden, C. E. (2014). Multisystem component phenotypes of bipolar disorder for genetic investigations of extended pedigrees. *JAMA Psychiatry, 71,* 375–387. doi:10.1001/jamapsychiatry.2013.4100

Fein, D., Barton, M., Eigsti, I.-M., Kelley, E., Naigles, L, Schultz, R. T.,... Tyson, K. (2013). Optimal outcome in individuals with a history of autism. *Journal of Child Psychology and Psychiatry, 54,* 195–205.

Feldman, H. S., Jones, K. L., Lindsay, S., Slymen, D., Klonoff-Cohen, H., Kao, K.,... Chambers, C. (2012). Prenatal alcohol exposure patterns and alcohol-related birth defects and growth deficiencies: A prospective study. *Alcoholism: Clinical and Experimental Research, 36,* 670–676. doi:10.1111/j.1530-0277.2011.01664.x

Feldman, M. D. (2003). Foreword. In J. Gregory (Ed.), *Sickened: The memoir of a Munchausen by proxy childhood* (pp. v–ix). New York, NY: Bantam.

Felger, J. C., Li, Z., Haroon, E., Woolwine, B. J., Jung, M. Y., Hu, X.,... Miller, A. H. (2015, November 10). Inflammation is associated with decreased functional connectivity within corticostriatal reward circuitry in depression. *Molecular Psychiatry.* doi:10.1038/mp.2015.168

Fenichel, O. (1945). *The psychoanalytic theory of neurosis.* New York, NY: W. W. Norton & Co.

Ferdinand, K. C., & Ferdinand, D. P. (2009). Cardiovascular disease disparities: Racial/ethnic factors and potential solutions. *Current Cardiovascular Risk Reports, 3,* 187–193. doi:10.1007/s12170-009-0030-y

Ferdinand, R. F., Bongersa, I. L., van der Ende, J., van Gastela, W., Tick, N., & Utens, E. (2006). Distinctions between separation anxiety and social anxiety in children and adolescents. *Behaviour Research and Therapy, 44,* 1523–1535.

Fergusson, D. M., & Woodward, L. J. (2002). Mental health, educational, and social role outcomes of adolescents with depression. *Archives of General Psychiatry, 59,* 225–231.

Fernandez, E. (2013). *Treatments for anger in specific populations: Theory, application, and outcome.* New York, NY: Oxford University Press.

Ferri, M., Amato, L., & Davoli, M. (2006). Alcoholics Anonymous and other 12-step programmes for alcohol dependence. *The Cochrane Database of Systematic Reviews.* Retrieved from http://dx.doi.org/10.1002/14651858.CD005032.pub2

Fetal alcohol spectrum disorders prevalence in U.S. revealed by study. (2014, October 14). *ScienceDaily.* Retrieved from http://www.sciencedaily.com/releases/2014/10/141030150632.htm

Feusner, J. D., Townsend, J., Bystritsky, A., & Bookheimer, S. (2007). Visual information processing of faces in body dysmorphic disorder. *Archives of General Psychiatry, 64,* 1417–1425.

Fibiger, S., Hjelmborg, V. B., Fagnani, C., &, Skytthe, A. (2010). Genetic epidemiological relations between stuttering, cluttering and specific language impairment. Proceedings of the *Sixth World Congress On Fluency Disorders,* August 5–8, 2009, Rio de Janeiro, Brazil. Retrieved from http://www.theifa.org/IFA2009

Ficks, C. A., Dong, L., & Waldman, I. D. (2014). Sex differences in the etiology of psychopathic traits in youth. *Journal of Abnormal Psychology, 123,* 406–411. doi:10.1037/a0036457

Field, A. P. (2006). Is conditioning a useful framework for understanding the development and treatment of phobias? *Clinical Psychology Review, 26,* 857–875.

Field, C. A., Cochran, G., & Caetano, R. (2013). Treatment utilization and unmet treatment need among Hispanics following brief intervention. *Alcoholism: Clinical and Experimental Research, 37,* 300–307. doi:10.1111/j.1530-0277.2012.01878.x

Fieve, R. R. (1975). *Moodswings: The third revolution in psychiatry.* New York, NY: Morrow.

Figueiredo, F. P., Parada, A. P., de Araujo, L. L., Jr., W. A. A., & Del-Bena, C. M. (2015). The influence of genetic factors on peripartum depression: A systematic review. *Journal of Affective Disorders, 172,* 265–273. doi:10.1016/j.jad.2014.10.016

Filbey, F. M., & Dunlop, J. (2014). Differential reward network functional connectivity in cannabis dependent and non-dependent users. *Drug and Alcohol Dependence, 140,* 101. doi:10.1016/j.drugalcdep.2014.04.002

Filbey, F. M., Aslan, S., Calhoun, V. D., Spence, J. S., Damaraju, E., Caprihan, A.,... Segall, J. (2014). Long-term effects of marijuana use on the brain. *Proceedings of the National Academy of Sciences, 111,* 16913–16918. doi:10.1073/pnas.1415297111

Finke, K., Schwarzkopf, W., Müller, U., Frodl, T., Müller, H. J., Schneider, W. X.,... Hennig-Fast, K. (2011). Disentangling the adult attention-deficit hyperactivity disorder endophenotype: Parametric measurement of attention. *Journal of Abnormal Psychology, 120,* 890–901. doi:10.1037/a0024944

Fischer, S., Meyer, A. H., Dremmel, D., Schlup, B., & Munsch, S. (2014). Short-term cognitive-behavioral therapy for binge eating disorder: Long-term efficacy and predictors of long-term treatment success. *Behaviour Research and Therapy, 58,* 36–42. doi:10.1016/j.brat.2014.04.007

Fisher, A. D., Bandini, E., Casale, H., & Maggi, M. (2011). Paraphilic disorders: Diagnosis and treatment. In M. Maggi (Ed.), *Hormonal therapy for male sexual dysfunction* (pp. 94–110). Hoboken, NJ: Wiley.

Fisher, A., D., & Maggi, M. (2014). Treatment of paraphilic sex offenders. In G. Corona, E. A. Jannini, & M. Maggi (Eds.), *Emotional, physical and sexual abuse* (pp. 17–31). New York, NY: Springer.

Fisher, B. S., Daigle, L. E., Cullen, F. T., & Turner, M. G. (2003). Reporting sexual victimization to the police and others: Results from a national-level study of college women. *Criminal Justice & Behavior, 30,* 6–38.

Fisher, H. L., Cohen-Woods, S., Hosang, G. M., Korszun, A., Owen, M., Craddock, N., Craig, I. W.,... Uher, R. (2013). Interaction between specific forms of childhood maltreatment and the serotonin transporter gene (5-HTT) in recurrent depressive disorder. *Journal of Affective Disorders, 145,* 136–141.

Fisher, P. L., & Wells, A. (2005). How effective are cognitive and behavioral treatments for obsessive–compulsive disorder? A clinical significance analysis. *Behaviour Research and Therapy, 43,* 1543–1558.

Fiske, A., Wetherell, J. L., & Gatz, M. (2009). Depression in older adults. *Annual Review of Clinical Psychology, 5,* 363–389. doi:10.1146/annurev.clinpsy.032408.153621

Fitzgerald, P. B., Brown, T. L., Marston, N. A. U., Daskalakis, J., de Castella, A., & Kulkarni, J. (2003). Transcranial magnetic stimulation in the treatment of depression: A double-blind, placebo-controlled trial. *Archives of General Psychiatry, 60,* 1002–1008.

Flagel, S. B., Clark, J. J., Robinson, T. E., Mayo, L., Czuj, A., Willuhn, I.,... Akil, H. (2011). A selective role for dopamine in stimulus–reward learning. *Nature, 469,* 53–57. doi:10.1038/nature09588

Flegal, K. M., Graubard, B. I., Williamson, D. F., & Gail, M. H. (2005). Excess deaths associated with underweight, overweight, and obesity. *Journal of the American Medical Association, 293,* 1861–1867.

Flegal, K. M., Kit, B., Orpana, H., & Graubard, B. I. (2013). Association of all-cause mortality with overweight and obesity using standard body mass index categories: A systematic review and meta-analysis. *Journal of the American Medical Association, 309,* 71–82. doi:10.1001/jama.2012.113905

Florian, C., Vecsey, C. G., Halassa, M. M., Haydon, P. G., & Abel, T. (2011). Astrocyte-derived adenosine and A1 receptor activity contribute to sleep loss-induced deficits in hippocampal synaptic plasticity and memory in mice. *Journal of Neuroscience, 31,* 6956.

Foa, E. B., McLean, C. P., Capaldi, S., & Rosenfield, D. (2013). Prolonged exposure vs. supportive counseling for sexual abuse–related PTSD in adolescent girls: A randomized clinical trial. *Journal of the American Medical Association, 310,* 2650–2657. doi:10.1001/jama.2013.282829

Foley, E., Baillie, A., Huxter, M., Price, M., & Sinclair, E. (2010). Mindfulness-based cognitive therapy for individuals whose lives have been affected by cancer: A randomized controlled trial. *Journal of Consulting and Clinical Psychology, 78,* 72–79. doi:10.1037/a0017566

Fontaine, K. R., Redden, D. T., Wang, C., Westfall, A. O., & Allison, D. B. (2003). Years of life lost due to obesity. *Journal of the American Medical Association, 289,* 187–193.

Foody, J. (2013, November 12). Guidelines for a heart-healthy lifestyle. *NEJM Journal Watch Psychiatry.* Retrieved from http://www.jwatch.org/na32827/2013/11/12/guidelines-heart-healthy-lifestyle?query=etoc_jwgenmed

Foote, B., Smolin, Y., Kaplan, M., Legatt, M. E., & Lipschitz, D. (2005). Prevalence of dissociative disorders in psychiatric outpatients. *American Journal of Psychiatry, 163,* 623–629.

Foote, B., Smolin, Y., Neft, D. I., & Lipschitz, D. (2008). Dissociative disorders and suicidality in psychiatric outpatients. *American Journal of Psychiatry, 163,* 623–629.

Foran, H. M., & O'Leary, K. D. (2008). Alcohol and intimate partner violence: A meta-analytic review. *Clinical Psychology Review, 28,* 1222–1234.

Ford, E. S., Maynard, L. M., & Li, C. (2014). Trends in mean waist circumference and abdominal obesity among U.S. adults, 1999–2012. *Journal of the American Medical Association, 312,* 1151. doi:10.1001/jama.2014.8362

Forgeard, M. J. C., & Seligman, M. E. P. (2012). Seeing the glass half full: A review of the causes and consequences of optimism. *Pratiques Psychologiques, 18,* 107–120. Retrieved http://dx.doi.org/10.1016/j.prps.2012.02.002

Forgeard, M. J. C., Haigh, E. A. P., Beck, A. T., Davidson, R. J., Henn, F. A., Maier, S. F.,... Seligman, M. (2012). Beyond depression: Toward a process-based approach to research, diagnosis, and treatment. *Clinical Psychology: Science and Practice, 18,* 275–299. doi:10.1111/j.1468-2850.2011.01259.x

Fouquereau, E., Fernandez, A., Mullet, E., & Sorum, P. C. (2003). Stress and the urge to drink. *Addictive Behaviors, 28,* 669–685.

Fournier, J. C., DeRubeis, R. J., Hollon, S. D., Dimidjian, S., Amsterdam, J. D., Shelton, R. C., & Fawcett, J. (2010). Antidepressant drug effects and depression severity: A patient-level meta-analysis. *Journal of the American Medical Association, 303,* 47–53.

Fox, M. (2014, January 9). What's in a sugar pill? Maybe more than you think. *NBC News.* Retrieved from http://www.nbcnews.com/health/whats-sugar-pill-maybe-more-you-think-2D11880962

Fox, M. (2015a, August 18). FDA approves flibanserin, "female Viagra" pill. *NBC News.* Retrieved from http://www.nbcnews.com/health/sexual-health/fda-approves-says-no-female-viagra-n411711

Fox, M. (2015b, November 12). "Real progress": Percentage of U.S. smokers plummets, CDC finds. *MSNBC.com.* Retrieved from www.msnbc.com

Foxhall, K. (2001, March). Study finds marital stress can triple women's risk of recurrent coronary event. *Monitor on Psychology, 32*(3), 14.

Frahm, S., Ślimak, M. A., Ferrarese, L., Santos-Torres, J., Antolin-Fontes, B., Auer, S.,... Ibañez-Tallon, I. (2011). Aversion to nicotine is regulated by the balanced activity of β4 and α5 nicotinic receptor subunits in the medial habenula. *Neuron, 70,* 522–535. doi:10.1016/j.neuron.2011.04.013

Frances, A. J., & Widiger, T. (2012). Psychiatric diagnosis: Lessons from the DSM-IV Past and cautions for the DSM-5 Future. *Annual Review of Clinical Psychology, 8,* 109–130. doi:10.1146/annurev-clinpsy-032511-143102

Frangou, S. (2013). Snipping at the endophenotypic space. *American Journal of Psychiatry, 170,* 1223–1225. doi:10.1176/appi.ajp.2013.13081116

Frank, E., & Kupfer, D. J. (2003). Progress in therapy of mood disorders: Scientific support. *American Journal of Psychiatry, 160,* 1207–1208.

Franke, B., Stein, J. L., Ripke, S., Anttila, V., Hibar, D. P., van Hulzen, K. J. E.,... Thalamuthu, A. (2016). Genetic influences on schizophrenia and subcortical brain volumes: Large-scale proof of concept. *Nature Neuroscience, 19,* 420–431. doi:10.1038/nn.4228

Franklin, M. E., & Foa, E. B. (2011). Treatment of obsessive compulsive disorder. *Annual Review of Clinical Psychology, 7,* 229–243. doi:10.1146/annurev-clinpsy-032210-104533x

Franklin, M. E., Abramowitz, J. S., Bux, D. A., Jr., Zoellner, L. A., & Feeny, N. C. (2002). Cognitive-behavioral therapy with and without medication in the treatment of obsessive-compulsive disorder. *Professional Psychology: Research and Practice, 33,* 162–168.

Franklin, T. B., Russig, H., Weiss, I. C., Gräff, J., Linder, N., Michalon, A.,... Mansuy, I. M. (2011). Epigenetic transmission of the impact of early stress across generations. *Biological Psychiatry, 68,* 408–415.

Franko, D. L., & Keel, P. K. (2006). Suicidality in eating disorders: Occurrence, correlates, and clinical implications. *Clinical Psychology Review, 26,* 769–782.

Franko, D. L., Keshaviah, A., Eddy, K. T., Krishna, M., Davis, M. C., Keel, P. K., & Herzog, D. B. (2013). A longitudinal investigation of mortality in anorexia nervosa and bulimia nervosa. *American Journal of Psychiatry, 170,* 917–925. doi:10.1176/appi.ajp.2013.12070868

Frans, E. M., Sandin, S., Reichenberg, A., Lichtenstein, P., Långström, N., & Hultman, C., M. (2008). Advancing paternal age and bipolar disorder. *Archives of General Psychiatry, 65,* 1034–1040.

Frauenglass, S., Routh, D. K., Pantin, H. M., & Mason, C. A. (1997). Family support decreases influence of deviant peers on Hispanic adolescents' substance use. *Journal of Clinical Child Psychology, 26,* 15–23.

Fredrickson, B. L., Tugade, M. M., Waugh, C. E., & Larkin, G. R. (2003). What good are positive emotions in crises? A prospective study of resilience and emotions following the terrorist attacks on the United States on September 11th, 2001. *Journal of Personality and Social Psychology, 84,* 365–376.

Free, C., Robertson, S., Whittaker, R., Edwards, P., Zhou, W., Rodgers, A.,... Roberts, I. (2011). Smoking cessation support delivered via mobile phone text messaging (txt2stop): A single-blind, randomised trial. *The Lancet, 378,* 49–55. Retrieved from http://dx.doi.org/10.1016/S0140-6736(11)60701-0

Freedman, D. H. (2011, February). How to fix the obesity crisis. *Scientific American.* Retrieved from http://www.scientificamerican.com/article.cfm?id=how-to-fix-the-obesitycrisis

Freedman, R. (2012). Brain development and schizophrenia. *American Journal of Psychiatry, 169,* 1019–1021. doi:10.1176/appi.ajp.2012.12081017

Freedman, R., Adler, L. E., Gerhardt, G. A., Waldo, M., Baker, N., Rose, G. M.,... Franks, R. (1987). Neurobiological studies of sensory gating in schizophrenia. *Schizophrenia Bulletin, 13,* 669–678.

Freeman, M. P. (2011, December 21). The menstrual cycle and mood: Premenstrual dysphoric disorder. *Journal Watch Women's Health.* Retrieved from http://womens-health.jwatch.org/cgi/content/full/2011/1221/1?q=etoc_jwwomen

Freemon, F. R. (1981). *Organic mental disease.* Jamaica, NY: Spectrum.

Freriks, K., Verhaak, C. M., Sas, T. C. J., Menke, L. A., Wit, J. M., Otten, B. J.,... Timmers, H. J. L. M. (2015). Long-term effects of oxandrolone treatment in childhood on neurocognition, quality of life and social-emotional functioning in young adults with Turner syndrome. *Hormones and Behavior, 69,* 59–67. doi:10.1016/j.yhbeh.2014.12.008

Freud, S. (1917/1957). Mourning and melancholia. In J. Rickman (Ed.), *A general selection from the works of Sigmund Freud.* Garden City, NY: Doubleday.

Freud, S. (1964). New introductory lectures. In *Standard edition of the complete psychological works of Sigmund Freud* (Vol. 22). London, UK: Hogarth Press. (Original work published 1933)

Friborg, O., Martinussen, M., Kaiser, S., Øvergårda, K. T., & Rosenvinge, J. H. (2013). Comorbidity of personality disorders in anxiety disorders: A meta-analysis of 30 years of research. *Journal of Affective Disorders, 45,* 143–155.

Frick, P. J., Ray, J. V., Thornton, L. C., & Kahn, R. E. (2014). Can callous-unemotional traits enhance the understanding, diagnosis, and treatment of serious conduct problems in children and adolescents? A comprehensive review. *Psychological Bulletin, 140,* 1–57. doi:10.1037/a0033076

Frick, P. J., & Silverthorn, P. (2001). Psychopathology in children and adolescents. In H. E. Adams (Ed.), *Comprehensive handbook of psychopathology* (3rd ed., pp. 879–919). New York, NY: Plenum Press.

Frieden, T. R. (2014). Tobacco control progress and potential. *Journal of the American Medical Association, 311,* 133–134. doi:10.1001/jama.2013.284534

Friedman, L. (2015, July 17). Op-Ed: Why juries reject the insanity defense. *The National Law Journal.* Retrieved from http://www.nationallawjournal.com/id=1202732457104/OpEd-Why-Juries-Reject-the-Insanity-Defense?slreturn=20151003164921

Friedman, M. A., Detweiler-Bedell, J. B., Leventhal, H. E., Horne, R., Keitner, G. I., & Miller, I. W. (2004). Combined psychotherapy and pharmacotherapy for the treatment of major depressive disorder. *Clinical Psychology: Science and Practice, 11,* 47–68.

Friedman, R. A. (2002, December 31). Born to be happy, through a twist of human hard wire. *The New York Times,* p. F5.

Friedman, R. A. (2012, September 25). A call for caution on antipsychotic drugs. *The New York Times,* p. D6.

Friedman, R. A. (2014a). Antidepressants' black-box warning: 10 years later. *New England Journal of Medicine, 371,* 1666–1668. doi:10.1056/NEJMp1408480

Friedman, R. A. (2014b, October 31). A natural fix for A.D.H.D. *The New York Times.* Retrieved from www.nytimes.com

Friedman, R. A. (2014c, May 27). Why can't doctors identify killers? *The New York Times.* Retrieved from nytimes.com

Friedman, R. A. (2015, August 22). How changeable is gender? *The New York Times.* Retrieved from www.nytimes.com

Friedman, R. C., & Downey, J. I. (2008). Sexual differentiation of behavior: The foundation of a developmental model of psychosexuality. *Journal of the American Psychoanalytic Association, 56*(1), 147–175.

Friedman, S. H. (2009). Postpartum mood disorders: Genetic progress and treatment paradigms. *American Journal of Psychiatry, 166,* 1201–1204. doi:10.1176/appi.ajp.2009.09081185

Friedrich, M. J. (2014). Research on psychiatric disorders targets Inflammation. *Journal of the American Medical Association, 312,* 474–476. doi:10.1001/jama.2014.8276

Frith, U. (2013). Autism and dyslexia: A glance over 25 years of research. *Perspectives on Psychological Science, 8,* 670–672. doi:10.1177/1745691613507457

Fromm-Reichmann, F. (1948). Notes on the development of treatment of schizophrenics by psychoanalytic psychotherapy. *Psychiatry, 11,* 263–273.

Fromm-Reichmann, F. (1950). *Principles of intensive psychotherapy.* Chicago, IL: University of Chicago.

Frost, R. O., Steketee, G., & Tolin, D. F. (2012). Diagnosis and assessment of hoarding disorder. *Annual Review of Clinical Psychology, 8,* 219–242.

Frühauf, S., Gerger, H., Schmidt, H. M., Munder, T., & Barth, J. (2013). Efficacy of psychological interventions for sexual dysfunction: A systematic review and meta-analysis. *Archives of Sexual Behavior, 42,* 915–933.

Fuertes, J. N., & Brobst, K. (2002). Clients' ratings of counselor multicultural competency. *Cultural Diversity and Ethnic Minority Psychology, 8,* 214–223.

Fuller-Thomson, E., West, J. S., & Baird, S. L. (2015). Childhood maltreatment is associated with ulcerative colitis but not Crohn's disease. *Inflammatory Bowel Diseases, 21*(11), 2640–2648. doi:10.1097/MIB.0000000000000551

Fullerton, C. A., Busch, A. B., Normand, S. L., McGuire, T. G., & Epstein, A. M. (2011). Ten-year trends in quality of care and spending for depression: 1996 through 2005. *Archives of General Psychiatry, 68,* 1218–1226.

Fulton, J. J., Marcus, D. K., & Merkey, T. (2011). Irrational health beliefs and health anxiety. *Journal of Clinical Psychology, 67,* 527–538. doi:10.1002/jclp.20769

Fung, M. T., Raine, A., Loeber, R., Lynam, D. R., Steinhauer, S., R., & Venables, P. H. (2005). Reduced electrodermal activity in psychopathy-prone adolescents. *Journal of Abnormal Psychology, 114,* 187–196.

Fusar-Poli, P., Papanastasiou, E., Stahl, D., Rocchetti, M., Carpenter, W., Shergill, S.,... McGuire, P. (2014). Treatments of negative symptoms in schizophrenia: Meta-analysis of 168 randomized placebo-controlled trials. *Schizophrenia Bulletin, 41,* 892–899. doi:10.1093/schbul/sbu170

Gabb, J., Sonderegger, L., Scherrer, S., & Ehlert, U. (2006). Psychoneuroendocrine effects of cognitive-behavioral stress management in a naturalistic setting: A randomized controlled trial. *Psychoneuroendocrinology, 31,* 428–438.

Gabbard, G. O. (2012). Clinical challenges in the Internet era. *American Journal of Psychiatry, 169,* 460–463. doi:10.1176/appi.ajp.2011.11101591

Gabert-Quillen, C. A., Fallon, W., & Delahanty, D. L. (2011). PTSD after traumatic injury: An investigation of the impact of injury severity and peritraumatic moderators. *Journal of Health Psychology, 16,* 678–687.

Gabrieli, J. D. E. (2009). Dyslexia: A new synergy between education and cognitive neuroscience. *Science, 325,* 280–283. doi:10.1126/science.1171999

Galanter, C. A. (2013). Limited support for the efficacy of nonpharmacological treatments for the core symptoms of ADHD. *American Journal of Psychiatry, 170,* 241–244. doi:10.1176/appi.ajp.2012.12121561

Galea, S., Nandi, A., & Vlahov, D. (2005). The epidemiology of post-traumatic stress disorder after disasters. *Epidemiologic Reviews, 27,* 78–91.

Galliher, R. V., Jones, M. D., & Dahl, A. (2011). Concurrent and longitudinal effects of ethnic identity and experiences of discrimination on psychosocial adjustment of Navajo adolescents. *Developmental Psychology, 47,* 509–526. doi:10.1037/a0021061

Galsworthy-Francis, L. (2014). Cognitive behavioral therapy for anorexia nervosa: A systematic review. *Clinical Psychology Review, 34,* 54–72. doi:10.1016/j.cpr.2013.11.001

Gannon, T. A., Collie, R. M., Ward, T., & Thakker, J. (2008). Rape: Psychopathology, theory and treatment. *Clinical Psychology Review, 28,* 982–1008.

Garakani, A., & Siever, L. J. (2015). Schizotypal personality disorder. *The encyclopedia of clinical psychology*. Retrieved from http://onlinelibrary.wiley.com/doi/10.1002/9781118625392.wbecp390/abstract?userIsAuthenticated=false&deniedAccessCustomisedMessage=

Garb, H. N. (1997). Race bias, social class bias, and gender bias in clinical judgment. *Clinical Psychology: Science and Practice, 4*, 99–120.

Garb, H. N. (2007). Computer-administered interviews and rating scales. *Psychological Assessment, 19*, 4–13.

Garb, H. N., Wood, J. M., Lilienfeld, S. O, & Nezworski, M. T. (2005). Roots of the Rorschach controversy. *Clinical Psychology Review, 25*, 97–118.

Garber, J., Keiley, M. K., & Martin, N. C. (2002). Developmental trajectories of adolescents' depressive symptoms: Predictors of change. *Journal of Consulting & Clinical Psychology, 70*, 79–95.

Garlow, S. J., Purselle, D., & Heninger, M. (2005). Ethnic differences in patterns of suicide across the life cycle. *American Journal of Psychiatry, 162*, 319–323.

Garnefski, N., Kraaij, V., & Spinhoven, P. (2001). De relatie tussen cognitieve copingstrategieen en symptomen van depressie, angst en suiecidaliteit. *Gedrag & Gezondheid: Tijdschrift voor Psychologie & Gezondheid, 29*, 148–158.

Gartlehner, G., Gaynes, B. N., Hansen, R. A., Thieda, P., DeVeaugh-Geiss, A., Krebs, E. E.,...Lohr, K. N. (2008). Comparative benefits and harms of second-generation antidepressants: Background paper for the American College of Physicians. *Annals of Internal Medicine, 149*, 734–750.

Gau, S. S. (2011). Childhood trajectories of inattention symptoms predicting educational attainment in young adults. *American Journal of Psychiatry, 168*, 1131–1133. doi:10.1176/appi.ajp.2011.11091328

Geddes, J. R., Stroup, S., & Lieberman, J. A. (2011). Comparative efficacy and effectiveness in the drug treatment of schizophrenia. In D. R. Weinberg & P. Harrison (Eds.), *Schizophrenia* (pp. 525–539). Hoboken, NJ: Wiley-Blackwell.

Gehar, D. R. (2009). *Mastering competencies in family therapy*. Belmont, CA: Brooks/Cole.

Geipert, N. (2007, January). Don't be mad: More research links hostility to coronary risk. *Monitor on Psychology, 38*(1), 50–51.

Gelfand, A. (2014, September 15). Finally, migraine-specific preventive therapy is on the horizon. *NEJM Journal Watch Neurology*. Retrieved from https://mail.google.com/mail/u/0/#inbox/14881317cf1e3506

Geller, B. (2006, October 16). Early use of methylphenidate: The jury on neuronal effects is still out. *Journal Watch Psychiatry*. Retrieved from http://psychiatry.jwatch.org/cgi/content/full/2006/1016/2

Geller, B. (2013, November 22). How childhood stress may lead to psychopathology. *NEJM Journal Watch Psychiatry*. Retrieved from http://www.jwatch.org/na32843/2013/11/22/how-childhood-stress-may-lead-psychopathology?query=etoc_jwpeds

Geller, B. (2015, May 22). It's all in the family: Children's parasomnias are often familial, decrease over time. *NEJM Journal Watch Psychiatry*. Retrieved from http://www.jwatch.org/na37906/2015/05/22/its-all-family-childrens-parasomnias-are-often-familial?query=etoc_jwpeds

Gelman, D. (1994, April 18). The mystery of suicide. *Newsweek*, 44–49.

Gémes, K., Janszky, I., Laugsand, L. E., László, K. D., Ahnve, S., Vatten, L. J., & Mukamal, K. J. (2015). Alcohol consumption is associated with a lower incidence of acute myocardial infarction: Results from a large prospective population-based study in Norway. *Journal of Internal Medicine, 14*. doi:10.1111/joim.12428

Genetic Science Learning Center, University of Utah. (2012). Down syndrome. Retrieved from http://learn.genetics.utah.edu/content/disorders/whataregd/down

Géonet, M., De Sutter, P., & Zech, E. (2012). Cognitive factors in women hypoactive sexual desire disorder. *Sexologies, 22*, e9–e15.

George, M. S., Anton, R. F., Bloomer, C., Teneback, C., Drobes, D. J., Lorberbaum, J. P.,...Vincent, D. J. (2001). Activation of prefrontal cortex and anterior thalamus in alcoholic subjects on exposure to alcohol-specific cues. *Archives of General Psychiatry, 58*, 345–352.

Gianaros, P. J., & Wager, T. D. (2015). Brain-body pathways linking psychological stress and physical health. *Current Directions in Psychological Science, 24*, 313–321.

Gibbons, M. B. C., Crits-Christoph, P., Barber, J. P., Wiltsey Stirman, S., Gallop, R., Goldstein, L. A., & Ring-Kurtz, S. (2009). Unique and common mechanisms of change across cognitive and dynamic psychotherapies. *Journal of Consulting and Clinical Psychology, 94*, 801–813. doi:10.1037/a0016596

Gibbons, R. D., Hur, K., Brown, C. H., Davis, J. M., & Mann, J. J. (2012). Benefits from antidepressants: Synthesis of 6-week patient-level outcomes from double-blind placebo-controlled randomized trials of fluoxetine and venlafaxine. *Archives of General Psychiatry, 69*, 572–579. doi:10.1001/archgenpsychiatry.2011.2044

Giddens, A. (2006). *Sociology* (5th ed.). Cambridge, UK: Polity.

Gil, K. M., Williams, D. A., Keefe, F. J., & Beckham, J. C. (1990). The relationship of negative thoughts to pain and psychological distress. *Behavior Therapy, 21*, 349–362.

Gilbert, S. C. (2003). Eating disorders in women of color. *Clinical Psychology: Science and Practice, 10*, 444–455.

Gill, S. S., & Seitz, D. P. (2015). Lifestyles and cognitive health: What older individuals can do to optimize cognitive outcomes. *Journal of the American Medical Association, 314*, 774–775. doi:10.1001/jama.2015.9526.

Gillan, C. M., Apergis-Schoute, A. M., Morein-Zamir, S., Urcelay, G. P., Sule, A., Fineberg, N. A.,...Robbins, T. W. (2015). Functional neuroimaging of avoidance habits in obsessive-compulsive disorder. *American Journal of Psychiatry, 172*, 284–293. doi:10.1176/appi.ajp.2014.14040525

Ginsburg, G. S., Becker, E. M., Keeton, C. P., Sakolsky, D., Piacentini, J., Albano, A. M.,...Kendall, P. C. (2014). Naturalistic follow-up of youths treated for pediatric anxiety disorders. *JAMA Psychiatry, 71*, 310–318. doi:10.1001/jamapsychiatry.2013.4186

Giordano, S. (2005). *Understanding eating disorders: Conceptual and ethical issues in the treatment of anorexia and bulimia nervosa*. Melbourne, Australia: Oxford University Press.

Glaser, G. (2014, January 2). Cold turkey isn't the only route. *The New York Times*, p. A19.

Glaser, R., Kiecolt-Glaser, J. K., Speicher, C. E., & Holliday, J. E. (1985). Stress, loneliness, and changes in herpes virus latency. *Journal of Behavioral≈Medicine, 8*, 249–260.

Glasofer, D. R., & Devlin, M. J. (2013). Cognitive behavioral therapy for bulimia nervosa. *Psychotherapy, 50*, 537–542. doi:10.1037/a0031939

Glassman, A. H., Bigger, T., Jr., & Gaffney, M. (2009). Psychiatric characteristics associated with long-term mortality among 361 patients having an acute coronary syndrome and major depression: Seven-year follow-up of SADHART participants. *Archives of General Psychiatry, 66*, 1022.

Glazener, C. M., Evans, J. H., & Peto, R. E. (2000). Tricyclic and related drugs for nocturnal enuresis in children. *Cochrane Database Systems Review, 3*, CD002117.

Gleaves, D. H. (1996). The sociocognitive model of dissociative identity disorder: A reexamination of the evidence. *Psychological Bulletin, 120*, 42–59.

Gleaves, D. H., Smith, S. M., Butler, L. D., & Spiegel, D. (2004). False and recovered memories in the laboratory and clinic: A review of experimental and clinical evidence. *Clinical Psychology: Science and Practice, 11*, 3–28.

Glicksman, E. (2013). Transgender terminology: It's complicated. *Monitor on Psychology, 44*(4), p. 39.

Gloster, A. T., Hauke, C., Höfler, M., Einsle, F., Fydrich, T., Hamm, A., Sthröhle, A., & Wittchen, H.-U. (2014). Long-term stability of cognitive behavioral therapy effects for panic disorder. *Behaviour Research and Therapy, 51*, 830–839. doi:10.1016/j.brat.2013.09.009

Gloster, A. T., Wittchen, H.-U., Einsle, F., Lang, T., Helbig-Lang, S., Fydrich, T.,...Aroltn, V. (2011). Psychological treatment for panic disorder with agoraphobia: A randomized controlled trial to examine the role of therapist-guided exposure in situ in CBT. *Journal of Consulting and Clinical Psychology, 79*, 406–420. doi:10.1037/a0023584

Glover, J. H. (1985). A case of kleptomania treated by covert sensitization. *British Journal of Clinical Psychology, 24*, 213–214.

Goddard, A. W., Mason, G. F., Almai, A., Rothman, D. L., Behar, K. L.,...Krystal, J. H. (2001). Reductions in occipital cortex GABA levels in panic disorder detected with 1h-magnetic spectroscopy. *Archives of General Psychiatry, 58*, 556–561.

Goel, N., Banks, S., Mignot, E., & Dinges, D. R. (2010). DQB1*0602 predicts interindividual differences in physiologic sleep, sleepiness, and fatigue. *Neurology, 75*, 1509–1519.

Goenjian, A. K., Noble, E. P., Walling, D. P., Goenjian, H. A., Karayan, I. S., Ritchie, T., & Bailey, J. N. (2008). Heritabilities of symptoms of posttraumatic stress disorder, anxiety, and depression in earthquake exposed Armenian families. *Psychiatric Genetics, 18*, 261–266.

Gold, R., Butler, P., Revheim, N., Leitman, D. I., Hansen, J. A., Gur, R. C.,...Javitt, D. C. (2012). Auditory emotion recognition impairments in schizophrenia: Relationship to acoustic features and cognition. *American Journal of Psychiatry, 169*, 424–432. doi:10.1176/appi.ajp.2011.11081230

Goldberg, A. (2003). Heinz Kohut, 1913–1981. *American Journal of Psychiatry, 160*, 670.

Goldberg, J. F., Gerstein, R. K., Wenze, S. J., Welker, T. M., & Beck, A. T. (2008). Dysfunctional attitudes and cognitive schemas in bipolar manic and unipolar depressed outpatients: Implications for cognitively based psychotherapeutics. *The Journal of Nervous and Mental Disease, 196*, 207–210.

Golden, G. S. (2008). Review of "Dyslexia, learning, and the brain." *New England Journal of Medicine, 359*, 2737.

Goldfried, M. R. (2012). On entering and remaining in psychotherapy. *Clinical Psychology: Science and Practice, 19*, 125–128. doi:10.1111/j.1468-2850.2012.01278.x

Goldie, T. (2014). *The man who invented gender*. Vancouver, Canada: UBC Press.

Goldin, P. R., Ziv, M., Jazaieri, H., Hahn, K., Heimberg, R., & Gross, J. J. (2013). Impact of cognitive behavioral therapy for social anxiety disorder on the neural dynamics of cognitive reappraisal of negative self-beliefs: Randomized clinical trial. *JAMA Psychiatry, 70*, 1048–1056. doi:10.1001/jamapsychiatry.2013.234

Goldstein, B. L., & Klein, D. N. (2014). A review of selected candidate endophenotypes for depression. *Clinical Psychology Review, 34*, 417–427.

Goldstein, R. L. (1986). Erotomania. *American Journal of Psychiatry, 143*, 802.

Goleman, D. (1995, June 21). "Virtual reality" conquers fear of heights. *The New York Times*, p. C11.

Gonda, X., Pompili, M., Serafini, G., Montebovi, F., Campi, S., Dome, P.,...Rihmer, Z. (2012). Suicidal behavior in bipolar disorder: Epidemiology, characteristics and major risk factors. *Journal of Affective Disorders, 143*, 16–26.

Gone, J. P., & Trimble, J. E. (2012). American Indian and Alaska Native mental health: Diverse perspectives on enduring disparities. *Annual Review of Clinical Psychology, 8*, 131–160.

González, H. M., Vega, W. A., Williams, D. R., Tarraf, W., West, B. T., & Neighbors, H. W. (2010). Depression care in the United States: Too little for too few. *Archives of General Psychiatry, 67*, 37–46.

Gonzalez, V. M., & Dulin, P. L. (2015). Comparison of a smartphone app for alcohol use disorders with an Internet-based intervention plus bibliotherapy: A pilot study. *Journal of Consulting and Clinical Psychology, 83*, 335–345. Retrieved from http://dx.doi.org/10.1037/a0038620

Gonzalez-Gadea, M. L., Baez, S., Torralva, T., Castellanos, F. X., Rattazzi, A., Bein, V.,...Ibanez, A. (2013). Cognitive variability in adults with ADHD and AS: Disentangling the roles of executive functions and social cognition. *Research in Developmental Disabilities, 34*, 817–830.

Goode, E. (2003). Experts see mind's voices in new light. *The New York Times*, pp. F1, F6.

Goodie, A. S., & Fortune, E. E. (2013). Measuring cognitive distortions in pathological gambling: Review and meta-analyses. *Psychology of Addictive Behaviors, 27*, 730–743. doi:10.1037/a0031892

Gooding, P., & Tarrier, N. (2009). A systematic review and meta-analysis of cognitive-behavioural interventions to reduce problem gambling: Hedging our bets? *Behaviour Research and Therapy, 47*, 592–560. doi:10.1016/j.brat.2009.04.002

Goodkind, M., Eickhoff, S. B., Oathes, D. J., Jiang, Y., Chang, A., Jones-Hagata, L. B., & Etkin, A. (2015). Identification of a common neurobiological substrate for mental illness. *JAMA Psychiatry, 2*, 305–315. doi:10.1001/jamapsychiatry.2014.2206

Goodlad, J. K., Marcus, D. K., & Fulton, J. J. (2013). Lead and attention-deficit/hyperactivity disorder (ADHD) symptoms: A meta-analysis. *Clinical Psychology Review, 33*, 417–425.

Gordon, J. L., Ditto, B., Lavoie, K. L., Pelletier, R., Campbell, T. S., Arsenault, A.,...Bacon, S. L. (2011). The effect of major depression on postexercise cardiovascular recovery. *Psychophysiology, 48*, 1605–1610. doi:10.1111/j.1469-8986.2011.01232.x

Gore, W. L., & Widiger, T. A. (2013). The DSM-5 dimensional trait model and five-factor models of general personality. *Journal of Abnormal Psychology, 122*, 816–821. doi:10.1037/a0032822

Gori, L., Giuliano, A., Muratori, F., Saviozzi, L., Oliva, P., Tancredi, R.,...Retico. A. (2015). Gray matter alterations in young children with autism spectrum disorders: Comparing morphometry at the voxel and regional level. *Journal of Neuroimaging, 73*, 25. doi:10.1111/jon.12280

Gormally, J., Sipps, G., Raphael, R., Edwin, D., & Varvil-Weld, D. (1981). The relationship between maladaptive cognitions and social anxiety. *Journal of Consulting and Clinical Psychology, 49*, 300–301.

Gorman, C. (2003, October 20). How to eat smarter. *Time*, 48–59.

Gorman, C. (2012, January). Five hidden dangers of obesity: Excess weight can harm health in ways that may come as a surprise. *Scientific American.* Retrieved from https://www.scientificamerican.com/article.cfm?id=five-hidden-dangersof-obesity

Gosselin, C., & Wilson, G. (1980). *Sexual variations.* New York, NY: Simon & Schuster.

Gothold, J. J. (2009). Peeling the onion: Understanding layers of treatment. *Annals of the New York Academy of Sciences, 1159*, 301–312.

Gottesman, I. I. (1991). *Schizophrenia genetics: The origins of madness.* New York, NY: Freeman.

Gottesman, I. I., & Gould, T. D. (2003). The endophenotype concept in psychiatry: Etymology and strategic intentions. *American Journal of Psychiatry, 160*, 636–645.

Gottesman, I. I., McGuffin, P., & Farmer, A. E. (1987). Clinical genetics as clues to the "real" genetics of schizophrenia. *Schizophrenia Bulletin, 13*, 23–47.

Goudriaan, A. E., Oosterlaan, J., de Beurs, E., & van den Brink, W. (2006). Neurocognitive functions in pathological gambling: A comparison with alcohol dependence, Tourette syndrome and normal controls. *Addiction, 101*, 534–547.

Gouin, J.-P., Glaser, R., Malarkey, W. B., Beversdorf, D., & Kiecolt-Glaser, J. (2012). Chronic stress, daily stressors, and circulating inflammatory markers. *Health Psychology, 31*, 264–268. doi:10.1037/a0025536

Gould, F., Clarke, J., Heim, C., Harvey, P. D., Majer, M., & Nemeroff, C. B. (2012). The effects of child abuse and neglect on cognitive functioning in adulthood. *Journal of Psychiatric Research, 46*, 500–506.

Gould, M. S., Greenberg, T., Velting, D. M., & Shaffer, D. (2003). Youth suicide risk and preventive interventions: A review of the past 10 years. *Journal of the American Academy of Child and Adolescent Psychiatry, 42*, 386–405.

Grace, A. A. (2010). Ventral hippocampus, interneurons, and schizophrenia: A new understanding of the pathophysiology of schizophrenia and its implications for treatment and prevention. *Current Directions in Psychological Science, 19*, 232–237. doi:10.1177/0963721410378032

Graham, J. R. (2011). *MMPI-2: Assessing personality and psychopathology* (5th ed.). New York, NY: Oxford University Press.

Granata, A. R., Pugni, V., Rochira, V., Zirilli, L., & Carani, C. (2012). Hormonal regulation of male sexual desire: The role of testosterone, estrogen, prolactin, oxytocin, and others. In M. Maggi (Ed.), *Hormonal therapy for male sexual dysfunction* (pp. 72–82). Hoboken, NJ: Wiley.

Granholm, E., Holden, J., Link, P. C., & McQuaid, J. R. (2014). Randomized clinical trial of cognitive behavioral social skills training for schizophrenia: Improvement in functioning and experiential negative symptoms. *Journal of Consulting and Clinical Psychology, 82*(6), 1173–1185. Retrieved from http://dx.doi.org/10.1037/a0037098

Grant, A., Fathalli, G., Rouleau, G., Joober, R., & Flores, C. (2012). Association between schizophrenia and genetic variation in DCC: A case–control study. *Schizophrenia Research, 137*, 26–31.

Grant, B. B., Saha, T. D., Ruan, W. J., Goldstein, R. B., Chou, S. P., Jung, J.,...Hasin, D. S. (2016). Epidemiology of DSM-5 drug use disorder: Results from the National Epidemiologic Survey on Alcohol and Related Conditions–III. *JAMA Psychiatry, 73*, 39–47. doi:10.1001/jamapsychiatry.2015.2132

Grant, B. F., Harford, T. C., Muthen, B. O., Yi, H. Y., Hasin, D. S., & Stinson, F. S. (2006). DSM-IV alcohol dependence and abuse: Further evidence of validity in the general population. *Drug and Alcohol Dependence, 86*, 154–166.

Grant, B. F., Hasin, D. S., Blanco, C., Stinson, F. S., Chou, S. P., Goldstein, R. B.,...Huang, B. (2006). The epidemiology of social anxiety disorder in the United States: Results from the National Epidemiologic Survey on Alcohol and Related Conditions. *Journal of Clinical Psychiatry, 66*, 1351–1361.

Grant, B. F., Hasin, D. S., Stinson, F. S., Dawson, D. A., Goldstein, R. B., Smith, S.,...Saha, T. D. (2006). The epidemiology of DSM-IV panic disorder and agoraphobia in the United States: Results from the National Epidemiologic Survey on Alcohol and Related Conditions. *Journal of Clinical Psychiatry, 67*, 363–374.

Grant, B. F., Hasin, D. S., Stinson, F. S., Dawson, D. A., Ruan, W. J. Goldstein, R. B.,...Huang, B. (2005). Prevalence, correlates, co-morbidity, and comparative disability of DSM-IV generalized anxiety disorder in the USA: Results from the National Epidemiologic Survey on Alcohol and Related Conditions. *Psychological Medicine, 35*, 1747–1759.

Grant, B. F., Stinson, F. S., Dawson, D. A., Chou, S. P., & Ruan, W. J. (2005). Co-occurrence of DSM-IV personality disorders in the United States: Results from the National Epidemiologic Survey on Alcohol and Related Conditions. *Comprehensive Psychiatry, 46*, 1–5.

Grant, B. R., Goldstein, R. B., Saha, T. D., Chou, S. P., Jung, J., Zhang, H.,...Hasin, D. S. (2015). Epidemiology of DSM-5 alcohol use disorder. *JAMA Psychiatry, 72*, 757–766. doi:10.1001/jamapsychiatry.2015.0584

Grant, J. E. (2014). Obsessive–compulsive disorder. *New England Journal of Medicine, 371*, 646–653. doi:10.1056/NEJMcp1402176

Grant, J. E., & Odlaug, B. L. (2009). Assessment and treatment of pyromania. In J. E. Grant & M. N. Potenza (Eds.), *The Oxford handbook of impulse control disorders* (pp. 353–359). Oxford, UK: Oxford University Press.

Grant, J. E., Odlaug, B. L., & Kim, S. W. (2012). Assessment and treatment of kleptomania. In J. E. Grant & M. N. Potenza (Eds.), *The Oxford handbook of impulse control disorders* (pp. 334–343). New York, NY: Oxford University Press.

Grant, J. E., Williams, K. A., & Kim, S. W. (2006). Update on pathological gambling. *Current Psychiatry Reports, 8*, 53–58.

Gratz, K. L., Tulla, M. T., Barucha, D. E., Bornovalova, M. A., & Lejuez, C. W. (2008). Factors associated with co-occurring borderline personality disorder among inner-city substance users: The roles of childhood maltreatment, negative affect intensity/reactivity, and emotion dysregulation. *Comprehensive Psychiatry, 49*, 603–615.

Grave, R. D., El Ghoch, M., Sartirana, M., & Calugi, S. (2016). Cognitive behavioral therapy for anorexia nervosa: An update. *Current Psychiatry Reports, 18*, 2.

Gray, A. L., Hyde, T. M., Deep-Soboslay, A., Kleinman, J. E., & Sodhi, M. S. (2015). Sex differences in glutamate receptor gene expression in major depression and suicide. *Molecular Psychiatry, 20*, 1057–1068. doi:10.1038/mp.2015.91

Gray, M. J., & Acierno, R. (2002) Posttraumatic stress disorder. In M. Hersen (Ed.), *Clinical behavior therapy: Adults and children* (pp. 106–124). New York, NY: John Wiley & Sons.

Gray-Little, B., & Hafdahl, A. R. (2000). Factors influencing racial comparisons of self-esteem: A quantitative review. *Psychological Bulletin, 126*, 26–54.

Green, B. A., Carnes, S., & Carnes, P. J. (2012). Cybersex addiction patterns in a clinical sample of homosexual, heterosexual, and bisexual men and women. *Sexual Addiction and Compulsivity, 19*(1–2), 77–98.

Greenberg, J. L., Mothi, S. S., & Wilhelm, S. (2016). Cognitive-behavioral therapy for body dysmorphic disorder by proxy. *Behavior Therapy*, in press.

Greene, B. (2009). The use and abuse of religious beliefs in dividing and conquering between socially marginalized groups: The same sex marriage debate. *American Psychologist, 64*(8), 698–709.

Greene, B. A. (1990). Sturdy bridges: The role of African American mothers in the socialization of African American children. *Women & Therapy, 10*, 205–225.

Greene, B. A. (1993a). African American women. In L. Comas-Diaz & B. Greene (Eds.), *Women of color and mental health* (pp. 13–25). New York, NY: Guilford Press.

Greene, B. A. (1993b, Spring). Psychotherapy with African American women: The integration of feminist and psychodynamic approaches. *Journal of Training and Practice in Professional Psychology, 7*, 49–66.

Greene, R. L., Robin, R. W., Albaugh, B., Caldwell, A., & Goldman, D. (2003). Use of the MMPI-2 in American Indians: II. Empirical correlates. *Psychological Assessment, 5*, 360–369.

Greenhill, S. D., Juczewski, K., de Haan, A. M., Seaton, G., Fox, K., & Hardingham, N. R. (2015). Adult cortical plasticity depends on an early postnatal critical period. *Science, 349*, 424. doi:10.1126/science.aaa8481

Greenwood, A. (2006, April 25). Natural killer cells power immune system response to cancer. *NCI Cancer Bulletin, 3*(17). Retrieved from http://www.cancer.gov/ncicancerbulletin/NCI_Cancer_Bulletin_042506/page4

Greenwood, T. A., Lazzeroni, L. C., Calkins, M. E., Freedman, R., Green, M. R., Gur, R. E.,...Braff, D. L. (2016). Genetic assessment of additional endophenotypes from the Consortium on the Genetics of Schizophrenia Family Study. *Schizophrenia Research, 170*, 30–40. http://dx.doi.org/10.1016/j.schres.2015.11.008

Gregory, J. (2003). *Sickened: The memoir of a Münchausen by proxy childhood.* New York, NY: Bantam.

Griesi-Oliveira, K., Acab, A., Gupta, A. R., Sunaga, D. Y., Chailangkarn, T., Nicol, X.,...Muotri, A. R. (2014). Modeling non-syndromic autism and the impact of TRPC6 disruption in human neurons. *Molecular Psychiatry, 20*, 1350–1365. doi:10.1038/mp.2014.141

Griffee, K., O'Keefe, S. L., Beard, K. W., Young, D. H., Kommord, M. J., Linz, T. D.,...Stroebelf, S. S. (2014). Human sexual development is subject to critical period learning: Implications for sexual addiction, sexual therapy, and for child rearing. *Sexual Addiction & Compulsivity, 21*(2), 114–169. doi:10.1080/10720162.2014.906012

Griffiths, M. D. (2012). Internet sex addiction: A review of empirical research. *Addiction Research & Theory, 20*, 111–124.

Grilo, C. M., Hrabosky, J. I., White, M. A., Allison, K. C., Stunkard, A. J., & Masheb, R. M. (2008). Overvaluation of shape and weight in binge eating disorder and overweight controls: Refinement of a diagnostic construct. *Journal of Abnormal Psychology, 117*, 414–419.

Grilo, C. M., Masheb, R. M., & Crosby, R. D. (2012). Predictors and moderators of response to cognitive behavioral therapy and medication for the treatment of binge eating disorder. *Journal of Consulting and Clinical Psychology, 80*, 897–906. doi:10.1037/a0027001

Grob, G. N. (1983). *Mental illness and American society, 1875–1940.* Princeton, NJ: Princeton University Press.

Grob, G. N. (1994). *The mad among us: A history of the care of America's mentally ill.* New York, NY: Free Press.

Grob, G. N. (2009). *Mental institutions in America: Social policy to 1875.* Piscataway, NJ: Transaction Publishers Rutgers—The State University of New Jersey.

Grogan, J. (2013). *Encountering America: Humanistic psychology, sixties culture and the shaping of the modern self*. New York, NY: HarperPerennial.

Gropalis, M., Bleichhardt, G., Witthöft, M., & Hiller, W. (2012). Hypochondriasis, somatoform disorders, and anxiety disorders: Sociodemographic variables, general psychopathology, and naturalistic treatment effects. *Journal of Nervous & Mental Disease, 200*, 406–412.

Grossman, L. (2003, January 20). Can Freud get his job back? *Time*, 48–51.

Grothe, K. B., Dutton, G. R., Jones, G. N., Bodenlos, J., Ancona, M., & Brantley, P. J. (2005). Validation of the Beck Depression Inventory-II in a low-income African American sample of medical outpatients. *Psychological Assessment, 17*, 110–114.

Grover, S., Chakrabarti, S., Ghormode, D., Agarwal, M., Sharma, A., & Avasthi, A. (2015). Catatonia in inpatients with psychiatric disorders: A comparison of schizophrenia and mood disorders. *Psychiatry Research, 229*, 919–925. doi:10.1016/j.psychres.2015.07.020

Gu, J., Strauss, C., Bond, R., & Cavanagh, K. (2015). How do mindfulness-based cognitive therapy and mindfulness-based stress reduction improve mental health and well-being? A systematic review and meta-analysis of mediation studies. *Clinical Psychology Review, 37*, 1–12.

Guidi, J., Tomba, E., & Fava, G. A. (2016). The sequential integration of pharmacotherapy and psychotherapy in the treatment of major depressive disorder: A meta-analysis of the sequential model and a critical review of the literature. *American Journal of Psychiatry, 173*, 128–137. Retrieved from http://dx.doi.org/10.1176/appi.ajp.2015.15040476

Guillaume, F., Guillem, F., Tiberghien, G., & Stip, E. (2012). ERP investigation of study-test background mismatch during face recognition in schizophrenia. *Schizophrenia Research, 134*, 101–109.

Gunderson, J. G. (2011). Borderline personality disorder. *New England Journal of Medicine, 364*, 2037–2042.

Gunderson, J. G. (2015). Reducing suicide risk in borderline personality disorder. *Journal of the American Medical Association, 314*, 181–182. doi:10.1001/jama.2015.4557

Gunderson, J. G., Stout, R. L., McGlashan, T. H., Shea, M., T., Morey, L. C., Grilo, C. M.,...Skodol, A. E. (2012). Ten-year course of borderline personality disorder: Psychopathology and function from the Collaborative Longitudinal Personality Disorders Study. *Archives of General Psychiatry, 68*, 827–837.

Gunn, R. L., & Smith, G. T. (2010). Risk factors for elementary school drinking: Pubertal status, personality, and alcohol expectancies concurrently predict fifth grade alcohol consumption. *Psychology of Addictive Behaviors, 24*, 617–627. doi:10.1037/a0020334

Gunter, R. W., & Whittal, M. L. (2010). Dissemination of cognitive-behavioral treatments for anxiety disorders: Overcoming barriers and improving patient access. *Clinical Psychology Review, 30*, 194–202. doi:10.1016/j.cpr.2009.11.001

Guo, J. Y., Huhtaniska, S. Miettunen, J., Jääskeläinen, E., Kiviniemi, V., Nikkinen, J.,...Murray, G. K. (2015). Longitudinal regional brain volume loss in schizophrenia: Relationship to antipsychotic medication and change in social function. *Schizophrenia Research, 168*, 297–304. doi:10.1016/j.schres.2015.06.016

Guo, W., Liu, F., Xiao, C., Yu, M., Zhang, Z., Liu, J.,... Zhao, J. (2015). Increased causal connectivity related to anatomical alterations as potential endophenotypes for schizophrenia. *Medicine (Baltimore), 94*, e1493. doi:10.1097/MD.0000000000001493

Guo, X., Zhai, J., Liu, Z., Fang, M., Wang, B., Wang, C.,...Zhao, J. (2010). Effect of antipsychotic medication alone vs. combined with psychosocial intervention on outcomes of early-stage schizophrenia: A randomized, 1-year study. *Archives of General Psychiatry, 67*, 895–904. doi:10.1001/archgenpsychiatry.2010.105

Guoa, M. E., Collinson, S. L., Subramaniam, M., & Chong. S. A. (2010). Gender differences in schizotypal personality in a Chinese population. *Personality and Individual Differences, 50*, 404–408. doi:10.1016/j.paid.2010.11.005

Gvirts, H. Z., Harari, H., Braw, Y., Shefet, D., Shamay-Tsoory, S. G. & Levkovitz, Y. (2012). Executive functioning among patients with borderline personality disorder (BPD) and their relatives. *Journal of Affective Disorders, 143*, 261–264.

H1N1-triggered narcolepsy may stem from "molecular mimicry." (2013, December 18). Stanford University Press Release. Retrieved from http://www.wakeupnarcolepsy.org/wp-content/uploads/Stanford-University-PRESS-RELEASE-Molecular-Mimicry.pdf

Haagen, J. F., Smid, G. E., Knipscheer, J. W., & Kleber, R. J. (2015). The efficacy of recommended treatments for veterans with PTSD: A metaregression analysis. *Clinical Psychology Review, 40*, 184–194. doi:10.1016/j.cpr.2015.06.008

Haake, P., Schedlowski, M., Exton, M. S., Giepen, C., Hartmann, U., Osterheider, M.,...Krüger, T. H. (2003). Acute neuroendocrine response to sexual stimulation in sexual offenders. *Canadian Journal of Psychiatry, 48*, 265–271.

Hadjistavropoulos, H. D., Pugh, N. E., Nugent, M. N., Hesser, H., Andersson, G., Ivanov, M.,...Austin, D. W. (2014). Therapist-assisted Internet-delivered cognitive behavior therapy for depression and anxiety: Translating evidence into clinical practices. *Journal of Anxiety Disorders, 28*, 884–893. doi:10.1016/j.janxdis.2014.09.018

Hadjistavropoulos, H. D., Thompson, M., Ivanov, M., Drost, C., Butz, C., Klein, B.,...Austin, D. W. (2011). Considerations in the development of a therapist-assisted Internet cognitive behavior therapy service. *Professional Psychology: Research and Practice, 42*, 463–471. doi:10.1037/a0026176

Haedt-Matt, A. A., & Keel, P. K. (2011). Revisiting the affect regulation model of binge eating: A meta-analysis of studies using ecological momentary assessment. *Psychological Bulletin, 137*, 660–681. doi:10.1037/a0023660

Hagen, S., & Carouba, M. (2002). *Women at ground zero: Stories of courage and compassion*. Indianapolis, IN: Alpha.

Halbreich, U., O'Brien, S., Eriksson, E., Bäckström, T., Yonkers, K. A., & Freeman, E. W. (2006). Are there differential symptom profiles that improve in response to different pharmacological treatments of premenstrual syndrome/premenstrual dysphoric disorder? *CNS Drugs, 20*, 523–547.

Hall, H. I., Song, R., Rhodes, P., Prejean, J., An, Q., Lee, L. M.,...Janssen, R. S. (2008). Estimation of HIV incidence in the United States. *Journal of the American Medical Association, 300*, 520–529.

Hall, S. S., Jiang, H., Reiss, A. J., & Greicius, M. D. (2013). Identifying large-scale brain networks in Fragile X Syndrome. *JAMA Psychiatry, 70*, 1215–1223. doi:10.1001/jamapsychiatry.2013.247

Ham, L. S., & Hope, D. A. (2003). College students and problematic drinking: A review of the literature. *Clinical Psychology Review, 23*, 719–759.

Hamani, C., Pilitsis, J., Rughani, A. I., Rosenow, J. M., Patil, P. G., Slavin, K. S.,...Kalkanis, S. (2014). Deep brain stimulation for obsessive-compulsive disorder. *Neurosurgery, 75*, 327. doi:0.1227/NEU.0000000000000499

Hamilton, J. L., Stange, J. P., Abramson, L. Y., & Alloy, L. B. (2015). Stress and the development of cognitive vulnerabilities to depression explain sex differences in depressive symptoms during adolescence. *Clinical Psychological Science, 3*, 702–714. doi:10.1177/2167702614545479

Hamilton, J. P. (2015). Amygdala reactivity as mental health risk endophenotype: A tale of many trajectories. *American Journal of Psychiatry, 172*, 214–215. http://dx.doi.org/10.1176/appi.ajp.2014.14121491

Hamilton, K. E., Wershler, J. L., Macrodimitris, S. D., Backs-Dermott, B. J., Ching, L. E., & Mothersill, K. J. (2012). Exploring the effectiveness of a mixed-diagnosis group cognitive behavioral therapy intervention across diverse populations. *Cognitive and Behavioral Practice, 19*, 472–482.

Hamilton, S. P. (2008). Schizophrenia candidate genes: Are we really coming up blank? *American Journal of Psychiatry, 165*, 420–423.

Hammen, C. (2009). Adolescent depression: Stressful interpersonal contexts and risk for recurrence. *Current Directions in Psychological Science, 18*, 200–204. doi:10.1111/j.1467-8721.2009.01636.x

Hammen, C. (2015). Stress sensitivity in psychopathology: Mechanisms and consequences. *Journal of Abnormal Psychology, 124*, 152–154. Retrieved from http://dx.doi.org/10.1037/abn0000040

Hampton, T. (2012). Effects of ECT. *Journal of the American Medical Association, 307*, 1790–1790. doi:10.1001/jama.2012.3723

Hampton, T. (2015). Report describes trends in U.S. cancer incidence and mortality rates. *Journal of the American Medical Association, 313*, 2014. doi:10.1001/jama.2015.4359

Hamre, K. (2013). Obesity: Multiple factors contribute. *Nature, 493*, 480. doi:10.1038/493480c

Han, J., Kesner, P., Metna-Laurent, M., Duan, T., Xu, L., Georges, G., Koehl, M.,...Ren, W. (2012). Acute cannabinoids impair working memory through astroglial CB1 receptor modulation of hippocampal LTD. *Cell, 148*(5), 1039–1050. doi:10.1016/j.cell.2012.01.037

Han, J.-H., Kushner, S. A., Yiu, A. P., Hsiang, H.-L., Buch, T., Waisman, A.,...Josselyn, S. (2009). Selective erasure of a fear memory. *Science, 323*, 1492–1496. doi:10.1126/science.1164139

Hancock, L. (1996, March 18). Mother's little helper. *Newsweek*, 51–56.

Hans, E., & Hiller, W. (2013). Effectiveness of and dropout from outpatient cognitive behavioral therapy for adult unipolar depression: A meta-analysis of nonrandomized effectiveness studies. *Journal of Consulting and Clinical Psychology, 81*, 75–88. doi:10.1037/a0031080

Hansen, N. B., Lambert, M. J., & Forman, E. M. (2002). The psychotherapy dose-response effect and its implications for treatment delivery services. *Clinical Psychology: Science and Practice, 9*, 329–343.

Hansen, N. D., Randazzo, K. V., Schwartz, A., Marshall, M., Kalis, D., Frazier, E. R.,...Norvig, G. (2006). Do we practice what we preach? An exploratory survey of multicultural psychotherapy competencies. *Professional Psychology: Research and Practice, 37*, 66–74.

Hansen, S. N., Schnendel, D. E., & Parner, E. T. (2014). Explaining the increase in the prevalence of autism spectrum disorders: The proportion attributable to changes in reporting practices. *JAMA Pediatrics, 169*, 56–62. doi:10.1001/jamapediatrics.2014.1893

Hare, R. D. (1965). Temporal gradient of fear arousal in psychopaths. *Journal of Abnormal Psychology, 70*, 442–445.

Hariri, A. R., Mattay, V. S., Tessitore, A., Kolachana, B., Fera, F., & Goldman, D. (2002). Serotonin transporter genetic variation and the response of the human amygdala. *Science, 19*, 400–403.

Harkness, K. L., Alavi, N., Monroe, S. M., Slavich, G. M., Gotlib, I. H., & Bagby, R. M. (2010). Gender differences in life events prior to onset of major depressive disorder: The moderating effect of age. *Journal of Abnormal Psychology, 119*, 791–803. doi:10.1037/a0020629

Harmon, A. (2012, April 8). The autism wars. *The New York Times*, p. SR3.

Harold, G. T., Leve, L. D., Barrett, D., Elam, K., Neiderhiser, J. M., Natsuaki, M. N.,...Thap, A. (2013). Biological and rearing mother influences on child ADHD symptoms: Revisiting the developmental interface between nature and nurture. *Journal of Child Psychology and Psychiatry, 54*, 1038–1046. doi:10.1111/jcpp.12100

Harpur, T. J., & Hare, R. D. (1994). Assessment of psychopathy as a function of age. *Journal of Abnormal Psychology, 103*, 604–609.

Harris, A. H., Bowe, T., Del Re, A. C., Finlay, A. K., Oliva, E., Myrick, H. L.,...Rubinsky, A. D. (2015). Extended release naltrexone for alcohol use disorders: Quasi-experimental effects on mortality and subsequent detoxification episodes. *Alcoholism: Clinical and Experimental Research, 39*, 79–83. doi:10.1111/acer.12597

Harris, A., & Lurigio, A. J. (2007). Mental illness and violence: A brief review of research and assessment strategies. *Aggression and Violent Behavior, 12*, 542–551.

Harris, E., & Younggren, J. N. (2011). Risk management in the digital world. *Professional Psychology: Research and Practice, 42*, 412–418. doi:10.1037/a0025139

Harris, G. (2006, November 23). Proof is scant on psychiatric drug mix for young. *The New York Times*, pp. A1, A28.

Harrison, B. J., Soriano-Mas, C., Pujol, J., Ortiz, H., Lopez-Sola, M., Hernandez-Ribas, Deus, J., & Cardoner, N. (2009). Altered corticostriatal functional connectivity in obsessive-compulsive disorder. *Archives of General Psychiatry, 66*, 1189–1200.

Hart, L. M., Granillo, M. T., Jorm, A. F., & Paxton, S. J. (2011). Unmet need for treatment in the eating disorders: A systematic review of eating disorder-specific treatment seeking among community cases. *Clinical Psychology Review, 31*, 727–735. doi:10.1016/j.cpr.2011.03.004

Hartmann, A., Thomas, J. J., Greenberg, J. L., Matheny, N., & Wilhelm, S. (2014). A comparison of self-esteem and perfectionism in anorexia nervosa and body dysmorphic disorder. *Journal of Nervous & Mental Disease, 202*, 883–888. doi:10.1097/NMD.0000000000000021570

Hartmann, M. N., Kluge, A., Kalis, A., Mojzisch, A., Tobler, P. N., & Kaiser, S. (2015). Apathy in schizophrenia as a deficit in the generation of options for action. *Journal of Abnormal Psychology, 124*, 309–318. http://dx.doi.org/10.1037/abn0000048

Hartz, S. M., Short, S. E., Saccone, N. L., Culverhouse, R., Chen, L., Schwantes-An, T.-H.,...Bierut, L. J. (2012). Increased genetic vulnerability to smoking at CHRNA5 in early-onset smokers. *Archives of General Psychiatry, 69*, 854–860. doi:10.1001/archgenpsychiatry.2012.124

Harvey, A. G., & Tang, N. K. Y (2012). (Mis)perception of sleep in insomnia: A puzzle and a resolution. *Psychological Bulletin, 138*, 77–101. doi:10.1037/a0025730

Harvey, A. G., Bélanger, L., Talbot, L., Eidelman, P., Beaulieu-Bonneau, S., Fortier-Brochu, E.,...Morin, C. M. (2014). Comparative efficacy of behavior therapy, cognitive therapy, and cognitive behavior therapy for chronic insomnia: A randomized controlled trial. *Journal of Consulting and Clinical Psychology, 82*, 670–683. doi:10.1037/a0036606

Harvey, E. A., Breaux, R. P., & Lugo-Candelas, C. I. (2016). Early development of comorbidity between symptoms of attention-deficit/hyperactivity disorder (ADHD) and oppositional defiant disorder (ODD). *Journal of Abnormal Psychology, 125*, 154–167. http://dx.doi.org/10.1037/abn0000090

Harvey, P. D. (2010). Cognitive functioning and disability in schizophrenia. *Current Directions in Psychological Science, 19*, 249–254. doi:10.1177/0963721410378033

Harvey, R. C., James, A. C., & Shields, G. E. (2016). A systematic review and network meta-analysis to assess the relative efficacy of antipsychotics for the treatment of positive and negative symptoms in early-onset schizophrenia. *CNS Drugs, 30*, 27–39. doi:10.1007/s40263-015-0308-1

Hashemi, J., Tepper, M., Spina, T. V., Esler, A., Morellas, V., Papanikolopoulos, N. P.,...Sapiro, G. (2014). Computer vision tools for low-cost and noninvasive measurement of autism-related behaviors in infants. *Autism Research and Treatment*. Retrieved from http://arxiv.org/pdf/1210.7014.pdf

Hasin, D., Hatzenbuehler, M. L., Keyes, K., & Ogburn, E. (2006). Substance use disorders: Diagnostic and Statistical Manual of Mental Disorders, fourth edition (DSM-IV) and International Classification of Diseases, tenth edition (ICD-10). *Addiction*, 101(Suppl. 1), 59–75.

Hasin, D. S., O'Brien, C. P., Auriacombe, M., Borges, G., Bucholz, K., Budney, A.,...Grant, B. F. (2013). DSM-5 criteria for substance use disorders: Recommendations and rationale. *American Journal of Psychiatry, 170*, 834–851. doi:10.1176/appi.ajp.2013.12060782

Hasin, D. S., Saha, T. D., Kerridge, B. T., Goldstein, R. B., Chou, S. P., Zhang, H.,...Grant, B. F. (2015). Prevalence of marijuana use disorders in the United States between 2001–2002 and 2012–2013. *JAMA Psychiatry, 72*, 1235–1242. doi:10.1001/jamapsychiatry.2015.1858

Hassija, C. M., & Gray, M. J. (2010). Are cognitive techniques and interventions necessary? A case for the utility of cognitive approaches in the treatment of PTSD. *Clinical Psychology: Science and Practice, 17*, 112–127. doi:10.1111/j.1468–2850.2010.01201.x

Haughton, E., & Ayllon, T. (1965) Production and elimination of symptomatic behavior. In L. P. Ullmann & L. Krasner (Eds.), *Case studies in behavior modification* (pp. 94–98). New York, NY: Holt, Rinehart and Winston.

Haut, K. M., van Erp, T. G. M., Knowlton, B., Bearden, C. E., Subotnik, K., Ventura, J.,...Cannon, T. D. (2015). Contributions of feature binding during encoding and functional connectivity of the medial temporal lobe structures to episodic memory deficits across the prodromal and first-episode phases of schizophrenia. *Clinical Psychological Science, 3*, 159–174. doi:10.1177/2167702614533949

Havermans, R. C., & Jansen, A. T. M. (2003). Increasing the efficacy of cue exposure treatment in preventing relapse of addictive behavior. *Addictive Behaviors, 28*, 989–994.

Hawton, K., Casañas i Comabella, C., Haw, C., & Saunders, K. (2013). Risk factors for suicide in individuals with depression: A systematic review. *Journal of Affective Disorders, 47*, 17–28.

Hayes, B. (2001). *Sleep demons: An insomniac's memoir.* New York, NY: Washington Square Press.

Hayes, S. C., Muto, T., & Masuda, A. (2011). Seeking cultural competence from the ground up. *Clinical Psychology: Science and Practice, 18*, 232–237. doi:10.1111/j.1468-2850.2011.01254.x

Haynos, A. F., & Fruzzetti, A. E. (2011). Anorexia nervosa as a disorder of emotion dysregulation: Evidence and treatment implications. *Clinical Psychology: Science and Practice, 18*, 183–202. doi:10.1111/j.1468-2850.2011.01250.x

Hays, P. A. (2009). Integrating evidenced-based practice, cognitive–behavior therapy, and multicultural therapy: Ten steps for culturally competent practice. *Professional Psychology: Research and Practice, 40*, 354–360.

Hazell, C. M., Hayward, M., Cavanagh, K., & Strauss, C. (2016). A systematic review and meta-analysis of low intensity CBT for psychosis. *Clinical Psychology Review*, in press.

Hazlett, E. A., Lamade, R. V., Graff, F. S., McClure, M. M., Kolaitis, J. C., Goldstein, K. E.,...Moshier, E. (2014). Visual-spatial working memory performance and temporal gray matter volume predict schizotypal personality disorder group membership. *Schizophrenia Research, 152*, 350–357. doi:10.1016/j.schres.2013.12.006

Heavy toll from alcohol. (2014). *Journal of the American Medical Association, 312*, 688. doi:10.1001/jama.2014.9637

Hebert, L. E., Scherr, P. A., Bienias, J. L., Bennett, D. A., & Evans, D. A. (2003). Alzheimer's disease in the U.S. population: Prevalence estimates using the 2000 census. *Archives of Neurology, 60*, 1119–1122.

Hebert, L. E., Weuve, J., Scherr, P. A., & Evans, D. A. (2013). Alzheimer disease in the United States (2010–2050) estimated using the 2010 census. *Neurology, 80*(19), 1778–1783. doi:10.1212/WNL.0b013e31828726f5

Heck, A., Fastenrath, M., Ackermann, S., Auschra, B., Bickel, H., Coynel, D.,...Papassotiropoulos, A. (2014). Converging genetic and functional brain imaging evidence links neuronal excitability to working memory, psychiatric disease, and brain activity. *Neuron, 81*, 1203–1213. doi:10.1016/j.neuron.2014.01.010

Heck, A., Fastenrath, M., Coynel, D., Auschra, B., Bickel, H., Freytag, V.,...Papassotiropoulos, A. (2015). Genetic analysis of association between calcium signaling and hippocampal activation, memory performance in the young and old, and risk for sporadic Alzheimer disease. *JAMA Psychiatry, 72*, 1029–1036. doi:10.1001/jamapsychiatr

Heckers, S. (2013). What is the core of schizophrenia? *JAMA Psychiatry, 70*, 1009–1010. doi:10.1001/jamapsychiatry.2013.2276

Hedman, E., Ljótsson, B., Kaldo, V., Hesser, H., El Alaoui, S., Kraepelien, M.,...Lindefors, N. (2014). Effectiveness of Internet-based cognitive behaviour therapy for depression in routine psychiatric care. *Journal of Affective Disorders, 155*, 49–58. doi:10.1016/j.jad.2013.10.023

Heilbrun, K., & Kramer, G. M. (2005). Involuntary medication, trial competence, and clinical dilemmas: Implications of *Sell v. United States* for psychological practice. *Professional Psychology: Research and Practice, 36*, 459–466.

Heiman, J. R. (2008). Treating low sexual desire: New findings for testosterone in women. *New England Journal of Medicine, 359*(19), 2047–2049.

Heinemann, L. A. J., Minh, T. D., Filonenko, A., & Uhl-Hochgräber, K. (2010). Explorative evaluation of the impact of severe premenstrual disorders on work absenteeism and productivity. *Women's Health Issues, 20*, 58–65. doi:10.1016/j.whi.2009.09.005

Heinrichs, M., Wagner, D., Schoch, W., Soravia, L. M., Hellhammer, D. H., & Ehlert, U. (2005). Predicting posttraumatic stress symptoms from pretraumatic risk factors: A 2-year prospective follow-up study in firefighters. *American Journal of Psychiatry, 162*, 2276–2286.

Helle, N., Barkmann, C., Bartz-Seel, J., Diehl, T., Ehrhardt, S., Hendel, A.,...Bindt, C. (2015). Very low birth-weight as a risk factor for postpartum depression four to six weeks postbirth in mothers and fathers: Cross-sectional results from a controlled multicentre cohort study. *Journal of Affective Disorders, 180*, 154–161.

Hemmings, C. (2010). Service use and outcomes. In N. Bouras (Ed.), *Mental health services for adults with intellectual disability: Strategies and solutions* (pp. 75–88). New York, NY: Psychology Press.

Hendrick, B. (2011, October 19). Use of antidepressants on the rise in the U.S. *WebMD Health*. Retrieved from http://www.webmd.com/depression/news/20111019/use-ofantidepressants-on-the-rise-in-the-us

Henig, R. M. (2012, September 30). Valium's contribution to our new normal. *The New York Times Sunday Review*, p. 9.

Henriques, G., Wenzel, A., Brown, G. K., & Beck, A. T. (2005). Suicide attempters' reaction to survival as a risk factor for eventual suicide. *American Journal of Psychiatry, 162*, 2180–2182.

Henry, K. L., McDonald, J. N., Oetting, E. R., Silk Walker, P., Walker, R. D., & Beauvais, F. (2011). Age of onset of first alcohol intoxication and subsequent alcohol use among urban American Indian adolescents. *Psychology of Addictive Behaviors, 25*, 48–56. doi:10.1037/a0021710

Henry, M., Pascual-Leone, A., & Cole, J. (2003). Electromagnetic stimulation shows promise for treatment-resistant depression. Retrieved from http://www.healthyplace.com/communities/depression/treatment/tms/index.asp

Hernandez, R., Kershaw, K. N., Siddique, J., Boehm, J. K., Kubzansky, L. D., Diez-Roux, A.,...Lloyd-Jones, D. M. (2015). Optimism and cardiovascular health: Multi-ethnic study of atherosclerosis (MESA). *Health Behavior and Policy Review, 2*, 62. doi:10.14485/HBPR.2.1.6

Herrera, V. M., & McCloskey, L. A. (2003). Sexual abuse, family violence, and female delinquency: Findings from a longitudinal study. *Violence & Victims, 18*, 319–334.

Herringa, R. J., Birna, P. M., Ruttle, P. L., Burghy, C. A., Stodola, D. E., Davidson, R. J.,...Essex, M. J. (2013). Childhood maltreatment is associated with altered fear circuitry and increased internalizing symptoms by late adolescence. *Proceedings of the National Academy of Sciences*. Retrieved from http://dx.doi.org/10.1073/pnas.1310766110

Heymsfield, S. B., & Cefalu, W. T. (2013). Does body mass index adequately convey a patient's mortality risk? *Journal of the American Medical Association, 309*, 87–88. doi:10.1001/jama.2012.185445

Hicks, B. M., Foster, K. T., Iacono, W. G., & McGue, M. (2013). Genetic and environmental influences on the familial transmission of externalizing disorders in adoptive and twin offspring. *JAMA Psychiatry, 70*, 1076–1083. doi:10.1001/jamapsychiatry.2013.258

Higgins, S. T. (2006). Extending contingency management to the treatment of methamphetamine use disorders. *American Journal of Psychiatry, 163*, 1870–1872.

Higgins, S. T., Heil, S. H., & Lussier, J. P. (2004). Clinical implications of reinforcement as a determinant of substance use disorders. *Annual Review of Psychology, 55*, 431–461.

Hilbert, A., Hildebrandt, T., Agras, W. S., Wilfley, D. E., & Wilson, G.T. (2015). Rapid response in psychological treatments for binge eating disorder. *Journal of Consulting and Clinical Psychology, 83*, 649–654. Retrieved from http://dx.doi.org/10.1037/ccp0000018

Hildebrandt, T., Alfano, L., Tricamo, M., & Pfaff, D. W. (2010). Conceptualizing the role of estrogens and serotonin in the development and maintenance of bulimia nervosa. *Clinical Psychology Review, 30*, 655–668. doi:0.1016/j.cpr.2010.04.011

Hill, C. E., Gelso, C. J., Gerstenblith, J., Chui, H., Pudasaini, S., Burgard, J.,…Huang, T. (2013). The dreamscape of psychodynamic psychotherapy: Dreams, dreamers, dream work, consequences, and case studies. *Dreaming, 23*, 1–45. doi:10.1037/a0032207

Hill, S. K., Reilly, J. L., Keefe, R. S. E., Gold, J. M., Bishop, J. R., Gershon, E. S.,…Sweeney, J. A. (2013). Neuropsychological impairments in schizophrenia and psychotic bipolar disorder: Findings from the Bipolar-Schizophrenia Network on Intermediate Phenotypes (B-SNIP) study. *American Journal of Psychiatry, 170*, 1275–1284.

Hinton, D. E., Park, L., Hsia, C., Hofmann, S., & Pollack, M. H. (2009). Anxiety disorder presentations in Asian populations: A review. *CNS Neuroscience & Therapeutics, 15*, 295–303. doi:10.1111/j.1755-5949.2009.00095.x

Hirsch, S. R., & Leff, J. P. (1975). *Abnormalities in parents of schizophrenics*. Oxford, UK: Oxford University Press.

Hirschfeld, R. M. A. (2011). Deep brain stimulation for treatment-resistant depression. *American Journal of Psychiatry, 168*, 455–456. doi:10.1176/appi.ajp.2011.11020231

Hirschtritt, M. E., Lee, P. C., Pauls, D. L., Dion, Y., Grados, M. A., Illmann, C., King, R. A.,…Mathews, C. A., for the Tourette Syndrome Association International Consortium for Genetics. (2015). Lifetime prevalence, age of risk, and genetic relationships of comorbid psychiatric disorders in Tourette Syndrome. *JAMA Psychiatry, 72*, 325–333. doi:10.1001/jamapsychiatry.2014.2650

Hispanics to total 30 percent of U.S. population by 2050. (2014, September 1). *MSNBC.com*. Retrieved from http://www.nbcnews.com/news/latino/hispanics-total-30-percent-us-population-2050-n193206

Hitti, M. (2006, March 6). Eating disorders may run in families. *Psychology Today*. Retrieved from http://psychologytoday.webmd.com/content/article/119/113378?src=rss_psychtoday

Hodgins, D. C., Schopflocher, D. P., el-Guebaly, N., Casey, D. M., Smith, G. J., Williams, R. J., & Wood, R. T. (2010). The association between childhood maltreatment and gambling problems in a community sample of adult men and women. *Psychology of Addictive Behaviors, 24*, 548–554. doi:10.1037/a0019946

Hodgins, D. C., Stea, J. N., & Grant, J. E. (2011). Gambling disorders. *The Lancet, 378*, 1874–1884. doi:10.1016/S0140-6736(10)62185-X

Hofmann, S. G. (2008). Cognitive processes during fear acquisition and extinction in animals and humans: Implications for exposure therapy of anxiety disorders. *Clinical Psychology Review, 28*, 200–211.

Hofmann, S. G., Asmundson, G. J. G., & Beck, A. T. (2011). The science of cognitive therapy. *Behavior Therapy, 44*, 199–212.

Hofmann, S. G., Asnaani, A., Vonk, I. J. J., Sawyer, A. T., & Fang, A. (2012). The efficacy of cognitive behavioral therapy: A review of meta-analyses. *Cognitive Therapy and Research, 36*, 427–440. doi:10.1007/s10608-012-9476-1

Hofmann, S. G., Moscovitch, D. A., Kim, H. J., & Taylor, A. N. (2004). Changes in self-perception during treatment of social phobia. *Journal of Consulting and Clinical Psychology, 72*, 588–596.

Hofmann, S. G., Smits, J. A. J., Rosenfield, D., Simon, N., Otto, M. W., Meuret, A. E.,…Pollack, M. H. (2013). D-cycloserine as an augmentation strategy with cognitive-behavioral therapy for social anxiety disorder. *American Journal of Psychiatry, 170*, 751–758. doi:10.1176/appi.ajp.2013.12070974

Holahan, C. J., Moos, R. H., Holahan, C. K., Brennan, P. L., & Schutte, K. K. (2005). Stress generation, avoidance coping, and depressive symptoms: A 10-year model. *Journal of Consulting and Clinical Psychology, 73*, 658–666.

Holbrook, T. L., Galarneau, M. R., Dye, J. L., Quinn, K., & Dougherty, A. L. (2010). Morphine use after combat injury in Iraq and post-traumatic stress disorder. *New England Journal of Medicine, 362*, 110–117.

Holden, C. (2008). Bipolar disorder: Poles apart. *Science, 321*, 193–195.

Holder-Perkins, V., & Wise, T. N. (2002). Somatization disorder. In K. A. Phillips (Ed.), *Somatoform and factitious disorders* (pp. 1–26). Washington, DC: American Psychiatric Association.

Holford, T. R., Meza, R., Warner, K. E., Meernik, C., Jeon, J., Moolgavkar, S. H.,…Levy, D. T. (2014). *Journal of the American Medical Association, 311*, 164–171. doi:10.1001/jama.2013.285112

Holland, A. J., Sicotte, N., & Treasure, J. (1988). Anorexia nervosa: Evidence of a genetic basis. *Journal of Psychosomatic Research, 32*, 561–571.

Hollingshead, A. B., & Redlich, F. C. (1958). *Social class and mental illness: Community study*. New York, NY: Wiley.

Hollon, S. D., & Ponniah, K. (2010). A review of empirically supported psychological therapies for mood disorders in adults. *Depression and Anxiety, 27*, 891–932.

Hollon, S. D., DeRubeis, R. J., Fawcett, J., Amsterdam, J. D., Shelton, R. C., Zajecka, J.,…Gallop, R. (2014). Effect of cognitive therapy with antidepressant medications vs. antidepressants alone on the rate of recovery in major depressive disorder: A randomized clinical trial. *JAMA Psychiatry, 7*, 1157–1164. doi:10.1001/jamapsychiatry.2014.1054

Hollon, S. D., & Kendall, P. C. (1980). Cognitive self-statements in depression: Development of an automatic thoughts questionnaire. *Cognitive Therapy and Research, 4*, 383–395.

Holma, K. M., Melartin, T. K., Haukka, J., Holma, I. A. K., Sokero, T. P., & Isometsä, E. T. (2010). Incidence and predictors of suicide attempts in DSM–IV major depressive disorder: A five-year prospective study. *American Journal of Psychiatry, 167*, 801–808.

Holmes, E. A., Craske, M. G., & Graybiel, A. M. (2014). Psychological treatments: A call for mental-health science. *Nature, 511*, 287–289. doi:10.1038/511287a

Holmes, M. C., Donovan, C. L., Farrell, L. J., & March, S. (2014). The efficacy of a group-based, disorder-specific treatment program for childhood GAD: A randomized controlled trial. *Behaviour Research and Therapy, 61*, 122–135.

Holroyd, K. A. (2002). Assessment and psychological management of recurrent headache disorders. *Journal of Consulting and Clinical Psychology, 70*, 656–677.

Holt-Lunstad, J., Smith, T. B., Baker, M., Harris, T., & Stephenson, D. (2015). Loneliness and social isolation as risk factors for mortality: A meta-analytic review. *Perspectives on Psychological Science, 10*, 227–237. doi:10.1177/1745691614568352

Holtmann, M., Bölte, S., & Poustka, F. (2008). Rapid increase in rates of bipolar diagnosis in youth: "True" bipolarity or misdiagnosed severe disruptive behavior disorders? *Archives of General Psychiatry, 65*, 477.

Holtom-Viesel, A., & Allan, S. (2014). A systematic review of the literature on family functioning across all eating disorder diagnoses in comparison to control families. *Clinical Psychology Review, 34*, 29–43. doi:10.1016/j.cpr.2013.10.005

Holtz, J. L. (2011). *Applied clinical neuropsychology*. New York, NY: Springer.

Holtzheimer, P. E., & McDonald, W. E. (Eds.). (2014). *A clinical guide to transcranial magnetic stimulation*. New York, NY: Oxford University Press.

Holtzheimer, P. E., Kelley, M. E., Gross, R. E., Filkowski, M. M., Garlow, S. J., Barrocas, A.,…Mayberg, H. S. (2012). Subcallosal cingulate deep brain stimulation for treatment-resistant unipolar and bipolar depression. *Archives of General Psychiatry, 69*, 150–158. doi:10.1001/archgenpsychiatry.2011.1456

Hölzel, L., Härter., M., Reese, C., & Kriston, L. (2011). Risk factors for chronic depression: A systematic review. *Journal of Affective Disorders, 129*, 1–13.

Homer, B. D., Solomon, T. M., Moeller, R. W., Mascia, A., DeRaleau, L., & Halkitis, P. N. (2008). Methamphetamine abuse and impairment of social functioning: A review of the underlying neurophysiological causes and behavioral implications. *Psychological Bulletin, 134*, 301–310.

Hong, D. S., Dunkin, B., & Reiss, A. L. (2011). Psychosocial functioning and social cognitive processing in girls with Turner syndrome. *Journal of Developmental & Behavioral Pediatrics, 7*, 512–520.

Hong, S., Kim, J., Choi, E., Kim, H., Suh, J., Kim, C.,…Yi, S. (2013). Reduced orbitofrontal cortical thickness in male adolescents with internet addiction. *Behavioral and Brain Functions, 9*, 11.

Hong, S., Zalesky, A., Cocchi, L., Fornito, A., Choi, E., Kim, H.,…Yi., S. (2013). Decreased functional brain connectivity in adolescents with internet addiction. *PLOS ONE, 8*, e57831.

Hongying, F., Xianbo, W., Fang, Y., Yang, B., & Beiguo, L. (2013). Oral immunization with recombinant *Lactobacillus acidophilus* expressing the adhesin hp0410 of *Helicobacter pylori* induces mucosal and systemic immune responses. *Clinical and Vaccine Immunology, 21*, 126–132. doi:10.1128/CVI.00434-13

Hooker, C. I., Bruce, L., Fisher, M., Verosky, S. C., Miyakawa, A., & Vinogradov, S. (2012). Neural activity during emotion recognition after combined cognitive plus social cognitive training in schizophrenia. *Schizophrenia Research, 39*, 53–59. doi:10.1016/j.schres.2012.05.009

Hooley, J. M. (2010). Social factors in schizophrenia. *Current Directions in Psychological Science, 19*, 238–242. doi:10.1177/0963721410377597

Hooli, B. V., Lill, C. M., Mullin, K., Qiao, D., Lange, C., Bertram, L., & Tanzi, R. E. (2015). PLD3 gene variants and Alzheimer's disease. *Nature, 520*, E7–E8. doi:10.1038/nature14040

Hopkin, M. (2008, May 5). Fat cell numbers stay constant through adult life. *Nature News*. doi:10.1038/ news.2008.800

Hopko, D. R., Cannity, K., McIndoo, C. C., File, A. A., Ryba, M. M., Clark, C. G.,…Bell, J. L. (2015). Behavior therapy for depressed breast cancer patients: Predictors of treatment outcome. *Journal of Consulting and Clinical Psychology, 83*, 225–231. http://dx.doi.org/10.1037/a0037704

Hor, H., Bartesaghi, L., Kutalik, Z., Vicário, J. L., de Andrés, C., Pfister, C.,…& Peraita-Adrados, R. (2011). A missense mutation in myelin oligodendrocyte glycoprotein as a cause of familial narcolepsy with cataplexy. *American Journal of Human Genetics, 89*, 474–479. doi:10.1016/j.ajhg.2011.08.007

Hotchkiss, S. (2002). *Saving yourself from the narcissists in your life*. New York, NY: Free Press.

Houts, A. C. (2010). Behavioral treatment for enuresis. In J. R. Weisz & A. E. Kazdin (Eds.), *Evidence-based psychotherapies for children and adolescents* (2nd ed., pp. 359–374). New York, NY: Guilford Press.

Howard, J. S., Stanislaw, H., Green, G., Sparkman, C. R., & Cohen, H. G. (2014). Comparison of behavior analytic and eclectic early interventions for young children with autism after three years. *Research in Developmental Disabilities, 35*, 3326–3344. doi:10.1016/j.ridd.2014.08.021

Howard, R., McShane, R., Lindesay, J., Ritchie, C., Baldwin, A., Barber, R.,…Phillips, P. (2012). Donepezil and memantine for moderate-to-severe Alzheimer's disease. *New England Journal of Medicine, 66*, 893–903.

Howell, E. F. (2011). *Understanding and treating dissociative identity disorder: A rational approach*. New York, NY: Routledge/Taylor & Francis.

Howes, O. D., Kambeitz, J., Kim, E., Stahl, D., Slifstein, M., Abi-Dargham, A., & Kapur, S. (2012). The nature of dopamine dysfunction in schizophrenia and what this means for treatment: Meta-analysis of imaging studies. *Archives of General Psychiatry, 69*, 776–786. doi:10.1001/archgenpsychiatry.2012.169

Hoza, B., Mrug, S., Gerdes, A. C., Hinshaw, S. P., Bukowski, W. M., Gold, J. A.,…Arnold, L. E. (2005). What aspects of peer relationships are impaired in children with attention-deficit/hyperactivity disorder? *Journal of Consulting and Clinical Psychology, 73*, 411–423.

Hsieh, H. J., Lue, K. H., Tsai, H. C., Lee, C. C., Chen, S. Y., & Kao, P. F. (2014). L-3,4-dihydroxy-6-[F-18] fluorophenylalanine positron emission tomography demonstrating dopaminergic system abnormality in the brains of obsessive-compulsive disorder patients. *Psychiatry and Clinical Neurosciences, 68*, 292–298. doi:10.1111/pcn.12139

Hu, E. (2013, August 20). Facebook makes us sadder and less satisfied, study finds. *NPR.org*. Retrieved from http://www.npr.org/blogs/alltechconsidered/2013/08/19/213568763/researchers-facebook-makes-us-sadder-and-less-satisfied

Hu, M.-C., Davies, M., & Kandel, D. B. (2006). Epidemiology and correlates of daily smoking and nicotine dependence among young adults in the United States. *American Journal of Public Health, 96*, 299–308.

Hua, X., Thompson, P. M., Leow, A. D., Madsen, S. K., Caplan, R., Alger, J. R.,…Levitt, J. G. (2011). Brain growth rate abnormalities visualized in adolescents with autism. *Human Brain Mapping*. Retrieved from http://onlinelibrary.wiley.com/doi/10.1002/hbm.21441/abstract

Huang, J., Ikeuchi, Y., Malumbres, M., & Bonni, A. (2014). A Cdh1-APC/FMRP ubiquitin signaling link drives mGluR-dependent synaptic plasticity in the mammalian brain. *Neuron, 86*, 726–739. doi:10.1016/j.neuron.2015.03.049

Hubbard, K. L., Zapf, P. A., & Ronan, K. A. (2003). Competency restoration: An examination of the differences between defendants predicted restorable and not restorable to competency. *Law and Human Behavior, 27*, 127–139.

Hudson, J. I., Hiripi, E., Pope, H. G., Jr., & Kessler, R. C. (2006). Prevalence and correlates of eating disorders in the National Comorbidity Survey Replication. *Biological Psychiatry, 61*, 348–358.

Hudson, J. I., Lalonde, J. K., Berry, J. M., Pindyck, L. J., Bulik, C. M., Crow, S. J.,... Pope, H. G., Jr. (2006). Binge-eating disorder as a distinct familial phenotype in obese individuals. *Archives of General Psychiatry, 63*, 313–319.

Hugdahl, K., Rund, B. R., Lund, A., Asbjørnsen, A., Egeland, J., Ersland, L.,... Thomsen, T. (2004). Brain activation measured with fMRI during a mental arithmetic task in schizophrenia and major depression. *American Journal of Psychiatry, 161*, 286–293.

Hugh-Jones, S., Gough, B., & Littlewood, A. (2005). Sexual exhibitionism as "sexuality and individuality": A critique of psychomedical discourse from the perspectives of women who exhibit. *Sexualities, 8*, 259–281.

Huhn, M., Tardy, M., Spineli, L. M., Kissling, W., Förstl, H., Pitschel-Walz, G.,... Leucht, S. (2014). Efficacy of pharmacotherapy and psychotherapy for adult psychiatric disorders: A systematic overview of meta-analyses. *JAMA Psychiatry, 71*, 706–715. doi:10.1001/jamapsychiatry.2014.112

Hulshoff Pol, H. E., van Baal, G. C., M., Schnack, H. G., Brans, R. G. H., van der Schot, A. C., Brouwer, R. M.,... Kahn, R. S. (2012). Overlapping and segregating structural brain abnormalities in twins with schizophrenia or bipolar disorder. *Archives of General Psychiatry, 69*, 349–359. doi:10.1001/archgenpsychiatry.2011.1615

Humphrey, L. L. (1986). Family dynamics in bulimia. In S. C. Feinstein, M. Sugar, A. H. Esman, & J. G. Looney (Eds.), *Adolescent psychiatry* (pp. 315–332). Chicago, IL: University of Chicago Press.

Hunnicutt-Ferguson, K., Hoxha, D., & Gollan, J. (2012). Exploring sudden gains in behavioral activation therapy for Major Depressive Disorder. *Behaviour Research and Therapy, 50*, 223–230.

Hunter, E. C. M., Phillips, M. L., Chalder, T., Sierra, M., & David, A. S. (2003). Depersonalisation disorder: A cognitive–behavioural conceptualization. *Behaviour Research and Therapy, 41*, 1451–1467.

Hunter, E. C. M., Salkovskis, P. M., & David, A. S. (2014). Attributions, appraisals and attention for symptoms in depersonalisation disorder. *Behaviour Research & Therapy, 253*, 20–29. doi:10.1016/j.brat.2013.11.005

Huntington's disease advance: Overactive protein triggers a chain reaction that causes brain nerve cells to die. (2011, February 23). *ScienceDaily*. Retrieved from http://www.sciencedaily.com/

Huprich, S. K., Fuller, K. M., & Schneider, R. B. (2003). Divergent ethical perspectives on the duty-to-warn principle with HIV patients. *Ethics & Behavior, 13*, 263–278.

Hurlburt, G., & Gade, E. (1984). Personality differences between Native American and Caucasian women alcoholics: Implications for alcoholism counseling. *White Cloud Journal, 3*, 35–39.

Huttunen, J., Heinimaa, M., Svirskis, T., Nyman, M., Kajander, J., Forsback, S.,... Hietala, J. (2008). Striatal dopamine synthesis in first-degree relatives of patients with schizophrenia. *Biological Psychiatry, 63*, 1814–1817. doi:10.1016/j.biopsych.2007.04.017

Huynh, Q.-L., Devos, T., & Dunbar, C. M. (2012). The psychological costs of painless but recurring experiences of racial discrimination. *Cultural Diversity and Ethnic Minority Psychology, 18*, 26–34. doi:10.1037/a0026601

Hwang, W.-C. (2006). The psychotherapy adaptation and modification framework: Application to Asian Americans. *American Psychologist, 61*, 702–715.

Hyde, J. S., Mezulis, A. H., & Abramson, L. Y. (2008). The ABCs of depression: Integrating affective, biological, and cognitive models to explain the emergence of the gender difference in depression. *Psychological Review, 115*, 291–313.

Hyman, S. E. (2011). The meaning of the Human Genome Project for neuropsychiatric disorders. *Science, 331*, 1026. doi:10.1126/science.1203544

Ibarra-Rovillard, M. S., & Kuiper, N. A. (2011). Social support and social negativity findings in depression: Perceived responsiveness to basic psychological needs. *Clinical Psychology Review, 31*, 342–352. doi:10.1016/j.cpr.2011.01.005

Ilgen, M. A., Wilbourne, P. L., Moos, B. S., & Moos, R. H. (2008). Problem-free drinking over 16 years among individuals with alcohol use disorders. *Drug and Alcohol Dependence, 92*, 116.

Imel, Z. E., Malterer, M. B., McKay, K. M., & Wampold, B. E. (2008). A meta-analysis of psychotherapy and medication in unipolar depression and dysthymia. *Journal of Affective Disorders, 110*, 197–206.

Indian, M., & Grieve, R. (2014). When Facebook is easier than face-to-face: Social support derived from Facebook in socially anxious individuals. *Personality and Individual Differences, 59*, 102–106.

Infurna, M. R., Reichl, C., Parzer, P., Schimmenti, A., Bifulco, A., & Kaess, M. (2016). Associations between depression and specific childhood experiences of abuse and neglect: A meta-analysis. *Journal of Affective Disorders, 190*, 47–55. doi:10.1016/j.jad.2015.09.006

Inman, A. G., & DeBoer Kreider, E. (2014). Multicultural competence: Psychotherapy practice and supervision. *Psychotherapy, 50*, 346–350. doi:10.1037/a0032029

Inouye, S. K. (2006). Delirium in older persons. *New England Journal of Medicine, 354*, 1157–1165.

Insel, T. R. (2014). Mental disorders in childhood: Shifting the focus from behavioral symptoms to neurodevelopmental trajectories. *Journal of the American Medical Association, 311*, 1727–1728. doi:10.1001/jama.2014.1193

Insel, T. R., & Cuthbert, B. N. (2015). Brain disorders? Precisely. *Science, 348*, 499–500. doi:10.1126/science.aab2358

Institute of Medicine. (April 2015). Cognitive aging: Progress in understanding and opportunities for action. *Report Brief*. Retrieved from http://www.iom.edu/~/media/Files/Report%20Files/2015/Cognitive_aging/Cognitive%20Aging%20report%20brief.pdf

International Schizophrenia Consortium, Purcell, S. M., Wray, N. R., Stone, J. L., Visscher, P. M., O'Donovan, M. C.,... Sklar, P. (2009). Common polygenic variation contributes to risk of schizophrenia and bipolar disorder. *Nature, 460*, 748–752. doi:10.1038/nature08185

iPad App helps autistic teen communicate. (2010, April 7). *Globe Newswire*. Retrieved from http://www.globenewswire.com/newsroom/news.html?d=188282

Irish, L., Kobayashi, I., & Delahanty, D. L. (2010). Long-term physical consequences of childhood sexual abuse: A meta-analytic review. *Journal of Pediatric Psychology, 35*, 450–461.

Ironson, G., O'Cleirigh, C., Leserman, J., Stuetzle, R., Fordiani, J., Fletcher, M. A., & Schneiderman, N. (2013). Gender-specific effects of an augmented written emotional disclosure intervention on posttraumatic, depressive, and HIV-disease-related outcomes: A randomized, controlled trial. *Journal of Consulting and Clinical Psychology, 81*, 284–298. doi:10.1037/a0030814

Ishak, W. W., Bokarius, A., Jeffrey, J. K., Davis, M. C., & Bakhta, Y. (2010). Disorders of orgasm in women: A literature review of etiology and current treatments. *Journal of Sexual Medicine, 7*, 3254–3268. doi:10.1111/j.1743-6109.2010.01928.x

Islam, L., Franzinia, A., Messina, G., Scaroneb, S., & Gambinib, O. (2015). Deep brain stimulation of the nucleus accumbens and bed nucleus of stria terminalis for obsessive-compulsive disorder: A case series. *World Neurosurgery, 83*, 657–663. http://dx.doi.org/10.1016/j.wneu.2014.12.024

Isles, A. R. (2015). Neural and behavioral epigenetics: What it is, and what is hype. *Genes, Brain and Behavior, 14*, 64–72, doi:10.1111/gbb.12184

Ivleva, E. I., Bidesi, A. S., Keshavan, M. S., Pearlson, G. D., Meda, S. A., Dodig D.,... Tamminga C. A. (2013). Gray matter volume as an intermediate phenotype for psychosis: Bipolar-schizophrenia network on intermediate phenotypes (B-SNIP). *American Journal of Psychiatry, 170*, 1285–1296.

Jablensky, A. V., Morgan, V., Zubrick, S. R., Bower, C., & Yellachich, L.-A. (2005). Pregnancy, delivery, and neonatal complications in a population cohort of women with schizophrenia and major affective disorders. *American Journal of Psychiatry, 162*, 79–91.

Jablensky, A., Sartorius, N., Ernberg, G., & Anker, M. (1992). Schizophrenia: Manifestations, incidence and course in different cultures: A World Health Organization ten-country study. *Psychological Medicine, 20*(Monograph Suppl.), 1–97.

Jack, C. R., Jr., Albert, M. S., Knopman, D. S., McKhann, G. M., Sperling, R. A., Carrillo, M. C.,... Phelps, C. H. (2011). Introduction to the recommendations from the National Institute on Aging and the Alzheimer's Association workgroup on diagnostic guidelines for Alzheimer's disease. *Alzheimers Dementia, 7*, 257–262.

Jackson, L. C., & Greene, B. A. (Eds.). (2000). *Psychotherapy with African American women: Innovations in psychodynamic perspectives and practice*. New York, NY: Guilford Press.

Jacob, J. (2015a). Anxiety disorders affect 4.3 million working U.S. adults. *Journal of the American Medical Association, 314*, 330. doi:10.1001/jama.2015.8411

Jacob, J. (2015b). IOM report on cognitive aging. *Journal of the American Medical Association, 313*, 2415. doi:10.1001/jama.2015.6577

Jacob, T., Waterman, B., Heath, A., True, W., Bucholz, K. K., Haber, R.,... Fu, Q. (2003). Genetic and environmental effects on offspring alcoholism: New insights using an offspring-of-twins design. *Archives of General Psychiatry, 60*, 1265–1272.

Jacobi, C., Hayward, C., de Zwaan, M., Kraemer, H. C., & Agras, W. S. (2004). Coming to terms with risk factors for eating disorders: Application of risk terminology and suggestions for a general taxonomy. *Psychological Bulletin, 130*, 19–65.

Jacquemont, S., Coe, B. P., Hersch, M., Duyzend, M. H., Krumm, N., Bergmann, S.,... Eichler, E. E. (2014). A higher mutational burden in females supports a "female protective model" in neurodevelopmental disorders. *The American Journal of Human Genetics, 34*, 415–425. doi:10.1016/j.ajhg.2014.02.001

Jacquemont, S., Curie, A., des Portes, V., Torrioli, M. G., Berry-Kravis, E., Hagerman, R. J.,... Gomez-Mancilla, B. (2011). Epigenetic modification of the fMRI gene in Fragile X Syndrome is associated with differential response to the mGluR5 antagonist AFQ056. *Science Translational Medicine, 3*, 64. doi:10.1126/scitranslmed.3001708

Jaffe, A. E., Gao, Y., Deep-Soboslay, A., Tao, R., Hyde, T. M., Weinberger, D. R., & Kleinman, J. E. (2016). Mapping DNA methylation across development, genotype and schizophrenia in the human frontal cortex. *Nature Neuroscience, 19*, 40–47. doi:10.1038/nn.4181

Jaffe, E. (2013, September). The link between personality and immunity. *APS Observer, 26*(7), 27–30.

Jain, A., Marshall, J., Buikema, A., Bancroft, T., Kelly, J. P., & Newschaffer, C. J. (2015). Autism occurrence by MMR vaccine status among U.S. children with older siblings with and without autism. *Journal of the American Medical Association, 313*, 1534–1540. doi:10.1001/jama.2015.3077

James, P. A., Oparil, S., Carter, B. L., Cushman, W. C., Dennison-Himmelfar, C., Handler, J.,... Ortiz, E. (2014). 2014 evidence-based guideline for the management of high blood pressure in adults: Report from the panel members appointed to the Eighth Joint National Committee. *Journal of the American Medical Association, 311*, 507–520. doi:10.1001/jama.2013.284427

Jamison, K. R. (1995). *An unquiet mind*. New York, NY: Knopf.

Janssen, E., & Bancroft, J. (2006). The dual-control model: The role of sexual inhibition & excitation in sexual arousal and behavior. In E. Janssen (Ed.), *The psychophysiology of sex* (pp. 197–222). Bloomington, IN: Indiana University Press.

Järnefelt, H., Sallinen, M., Luukkonen, R., Kajastec, S., Savolainen, A., & Hublina, C. (2014). Cognitive behavioral therapy for chronic insomnia in occupational health services: Analyses of outcomes up to 24 months post-treatment.

*Behaviour Research and Therapy, 56,* 16–21. doi.org/10.1016/j.brat.2014.02.007

Javier, R. (2010). Acculturation and changing roles. In J. S. Nevid & S. A. Rathus (Eds.), *Psychology and the challenges of life: Adjustment and growth* (p. 336). Hoboken, NJ: Wiley.

Jayasekara, H., MacInnis, R. J., Room, R., & English, D. R. (2015, September). Long-term alcohol consumption and breast, upper aero-digestive tract and colorectal cancer risk: A systematic review and meta-analysis. *Alcohol and Alcoholism.* doi:10.1093/alcalc/agv110

Jefferson, D. J. (2005, August 8). America's most dangerous drug. *Newsweek,* 41–48.

Jemmott, J. B., Borysenko, J. Z., Borysenko, M., McClelland, D. C., Chapman, R., Meyer, D., & Benson, H. (1983). Academic stress, power motivation, and decrease in secretion rate of salivary secretory immunoglobulin A. *The Lancet, 1,* 1400–1402.

Jenkins, C. D. (1988). Epidemiology of cardiovascular diseases. *Journal of Consulting and Clinical Psychology, 56,* 324–332.

Jenkins, P. E., Hoste, R. R., Meyer, C., & Blissett, M. M. (2011). Eating disorders and quality of life: A review of the literature. *Clinical Psychology Review, 31,* 113–121. doi:10.1016/j.cpr.2010.08.003

Jeon, H. J., Park, J.-I., Fava, M., Mischoulon, D., Sohn, J. H., Seong, S., . . . Choe, M. J. (2014). Feelings of worthlessness, traumatic experience, and their comorbidity in relation to lifetime suicide attempt in community adults with major depressive disorder. *Journal of Affective Disorders, 166,* 206–212.

Jha, P., & Peto, R. (2014). Global effects of smoking, of quitting, and of taxing tobacco. *New England Journal of Medicine, 370,* 60–68. doi:10.1056/NEJMra1308383

Jha, P., Ramasundarahettige, C., Landsman, V., Rostron, B., Thun, M., Anderson, R. N., McAfee, T., & Peto, R. (2013). 21st-century hazards of smoking and benefits of cessation in the United States. *New England Journal of Medicine, 368,* 341–350. doi:10.1056/NEJMsa1211128

Jian, X.-Q., Wang, K.-S., Wu, T.-J., Hillhouse, J. J., & Mullersman, J. E. (2011). Association of ADAM10 and CAMK2A polymorphisms with conduct disorder: Evidence from family-based studies. *Journal of Abnormal Child Psychology, 39,* 773–782. doi:10.1007/s10802-011-9524-4

Jiang, H., & Chess, L. (2006). Regulation of immune responses by T cells. *New England Journal of Medicine, 354,* 1166–1176.

Jobe, T. H., & Harrow, M. (2010). Schizophrenia course, long-term outcome, recovery, and prognosis. *Current Directions in Psychological Science, 19,* 220–225. doi:10.1177/0963721410378034

Joe, S., Baser, E., Breeden, G., Neighbors, H. W., & Jackson, J. S. (2006). Prevalence of and risk factors for lifetime suicide attempts among Blacks in the United States. *Journal of the American Medical Association, 296,* 2112–2123.

Joffe, A. (2014, February 10). Prognosis of adolescent mental disorders. *NEJM Journal Watch Psychiatry.* Retrieved from http://www.jwatch.org/na33485/2014/02/10/prognosis-adolescent-mental-disorders?query=etoc_jwpeds

Joffe, A. (2015, May 27). Preventing youth suicide. *NEJM Journal Watch Psychiatry.* Retrieved from http://www.jwatch.org/na37964/2015/05/27/preventing-youth-suicide?query=etoc_jwpeds

Johansson, A., Sundbom, E., Höjerback, T., & Bodlund, O. (2010). A five-year follow-up study of Swedish adults with gender identity disorder. *Archives of Sexual Behavior, 39,* 1429–1437. doi:10.1007/s10508-009-9551-1

Johnson, D. B., Oyama, N., LeMarchand, L., & Wilkens, L. (2004). Native Hawaiians mortality, morbidity, and lifestyle: Comparing data from 1982, 1990, and 2000. *Pacific Health Dialog, 11,* 120–130.

Johnson, D. C., Thom, N. J., Stanley, E. A., Haase, L., Simmons, A. N., Shih, P. B., . . . Paulus, M. P. (2014). Modifying resilience mechanisms in at-risk individuals: A controlled study of mindfulness training in marines preparing for deployment. *American Journal of Psychiatry, 171,* 844–853. doi:10.1176/appi.ajp.2014.13040502

Johnson, J. G., Cohen, P., Chen, H., Kasen, S., & Brook, J. S. (2006). Parenting behaviors associated with risk for offspring personality disorder during adulthood. *Archives of General Psychiatry, 63,* 579–587.

Johnson, S. L., Murray, G., Fredrickson, B., Youngstrom, E. A., Hinshaw, S., Bass, J. M., . . . Salloum, I. (2011). Creativity and bipolar disorder: Touched by fire or burning with questions? *Clinical Psychology Review, 32,* 1–12. doi:10.1016/j.cpr.2011.10.001

Johnston, B. C., Kanters, S., Bandayrel, K., Wu, P., Naji, F., Siemieniuk, R. A., . . . Mills, E. J. (2014). Comparison of weight loss among named diet programs in overweight and obese adults: A meta-analysis. *Journal of the American Medical Association, 312,* 923–933. doi:10.1001/jama.2014.10397

Johnston, C., Mash, E. J., Miller, N., & Ninowski, J. E. (2012). Parenting in adults with attention-deficit/hyperactivity disorder (ADHD). *Clinical Psychology Review, 32,* 215–228.

Joinson, C., Heron, J., Butler, U., von Gontard, A., & the Avon Longitudinal Study of Parents and Children Study Team. (2006). Psychological differences between children with and without soiling problems. *Pediatrics, 117,* 1575–1584.

Jokela, M., Keltikangas-Jarvinen, L., Kivimaki, M., Puttonen, S., Elovainio, M., Rontu R., & Lehtimaki, T. (2007). Serotonin receptor 2A gene and the influence of childhood maternal nurturance on adulthood depressive symptoms. *Archives of General Psychiatry, 64,* 356–360.

Jokela, M., Virtanen, M., Batty, G. D., & Kivimäki, M. (2016). Inflammation and specific symptoms of depression. *JAMA Psychiatry, 73,* 87–88. doi:10.1001/jamapsychiatry.2015.1977

Jones, C. (2003). Tightropes and tragedies: 25 years of Tarasoff. *Medicine, Science, and the Law, 43,* 13–22.

Jones, D. S. (2014). Still delirious after all these years. *New England Journal of Medicine, 370,* 399–401. doi:10.1056/NEJMp1400062

Jones, E. (1953). *The life and work of Sigmund Freud.* New York, NY: Basic Books.

Jones, K. E., & Hertlein, K. M. (2012). Four key dimensions for distinguishing Internet infidelity from Internet and sex addiction: Concepts and clinical application. *The American Journal of Family Therapy, 40,* 115–125.

Jones, M. P. (2006). The role of psychosocial factors in peptic ulcer disease: Beyond *Helicobacter pylori* and NSAIDs. *Journal of Psychosomatic Research, 60,* 407–412.

Jones, P. B., Rantakallio, P., Hartikainen, A. L., Isohanni, M., & Sipila, P. (1998). Schizophrenia as a long-term outcome of pregnancy, delivery, and perinatal complications: A 28-year follow-up of the 1966 North Finland general population birth cohort. *American Journal of Psychiatry, 155,* 355–364.

Joormann, J., Levens, S. M., & Gotlib, I. H. (2011). Depression and rumination are associated with difficulties manipulating emotional material in working memory. *Psychological Science, 22,* 979–983. doi:10.1177/0956797611415539

Jordan, K., Fromberger, P., Stolpmann, G., & Muller, J. L. (2011). The role of testosterone in sexuality and paraphilia: A neurobiological approach. *Sexual Medicine, 8*(11), 3008–3029.

Junco, R. (2015). Student class standing, Facebook use, and academic performance. *Journal of Applied Developmental Psychology, 36,* 18–29.

Jung, J., Forbes, G. B., & Lee, Y.-J. (2009). Body dissatisfaction and disordered eating among early adolescents from Korea and the U.S. *Sex Roles, 61,* 42–54. doi:10.1007/s11199-009-9609-5

Jurvelin, H., Takala, T., Nissilä., J., Timonen, M., Rüger, M., Jokelainen, J., . . . Räsänen, P. (2014). Transcranial bright light treatment via the ear canals in seasonal affective disorder: A randomized, double-blind dose-response study. *BMC Psychiatry, 14,* 288. doi:10.1186/s12888-014-0288-6

Just, N., Abramson, L. Y., & Alloy, L. B. (2001). Remitted depression studies as tests of the cognitive vulnerability hypotheses of depression onset: A critique and conceptual analysis. *Clinical Psychology Review, 21,* 63–83.

Jylhä, P., Rosenström, T., Mantere, O., Suominen, K., Melartin, T., Vuorilehto, M., . . . Isometsä, E. (2015). Personality disorders and suicide attempts in unipolar and bipolar mood disorders. *Journal of Affective Disorders, 190,* 632–639. doi:10.1016/j.jad.2015.11.006

Kafka, M. P. (2010). The DSM diagnostic criteria for fetishism. *Archives of Sexual Behavior, 39*(2), 357–362. doi:10.1007/s10508-009-9558-7

Kahn, M. W. (1982). Cultural clash and psychopathology in three aboriginal cultures. *Academic Psychology Bulletin, 4,* 553–561.

Kahn, R. S., & Keefe, R. S. E. (2013). Schizophrenia is a cognitive illness: Time for a change in focus. *JAMA Psychiatry, 70,* 1107–1112. doi:10.1001/jamapsychiatry.2013.155

Kaiser, R. H., Andrews-Hanna, J. R., Wager, T. D., & Pizzagalli, D. A. (2015). Large-scale network dysfunction in major depressive disorder: A meta-analysis of resting-state functional connectivity. *JAMA Psychiatry, 72,* 603–611. doi:10.1001/jamapsychiatry.2015.0071

Kaldo, V., Jernelöv, S., Blom, K., Ljótsson, B., Brodin, M., Jörgensen, M., Kraepelien, M., . . . Lindefors, N. (2015). Guided Internet cognitive behavioral therapy for insomnia compared to a control treatment: A randomized trial. *Behaviour Research and Therapy, 71,* 90–100. doi:10.1016/j.brat.2015.06.001

Kalibatseva, Z, & Leong, F. T. L. (2011). Depression among Asian Americans: Review and recommendations. *Depression Research and Treatment.* Retrieved from http://www.hindawi.com/journals/drt/2011/320902/

Kaller, C. P., Loosli, S. V., Rahm, B., Gössel, A., Schieting, S., Hornig, T., . . . Katzev, M. (2014). Working memory in schizophrenia: Behavioral and neural evidence for reduced susceptibility to item-specific proactive interference. *Biological Psychiatry, 76,* 486–494. doi:10.1016/j.biopsych.2014.03.012

Kam-Hansen, S., Jakubowski, M., Kelley, J. M., Kirsch, I., Hoaglin, D. C., Kaptchuk, T. J., . . . Burstein, R. (2014). Altered placebo and drug labeling changes the outcome of episodic migraine attacks. *Science Translational Medicine, 8,* 218ra5.

Kandel, D. B. (2003). Does marijuana use cause the use of other drugs? *Journal of the American Medical Association, 289,* 482–483.

Kane, J. M., Robinson, D. G., Schooler, N. R., Mueser, K. T., Penn, D. L., Rosenheck, R. A., . . . Heinssen, R. K. (2015). Comprehensive versus usual community care for first episode psychosis: Two-year outcomes from the NIMH RAISE Early Treatment Program. *American Journal of Psychiatry.* Retrieved from http://ajp.psychiatryonline.org/doi/10.1176/appi.ajp.2015.15050632

Kang, C., Riazuddin, S., Mundorff, J., Krasnewich, D., Friedman, P., Mullikin, J. C., & Drayna, D. (2010). Mutations in the lysosomal enzyme–targeting pathway and persistent stuttering. *New England Journal of Medicine, 362,* 677–685. doi:10.1056/NEJMoa0902630

Kangas, M., Henry, J. L., & Bryant, R. A. (2005). The relationship between acute stress disorder and posttraumatic stress disorder following cancer. *Journal of Consulting and Clinical Psychology, 73,* 360–364.

Kanner, L. (1943). Autistic disturbances of affective content. *Nervous Child, 2,* 217–240.

Kanter, J. W., Santiago-Rivera, A. L., Santos, M. M., Nagy, G., López, M., Diéguez Hurtado, G., & West, P. (2015). A randomized hybrid efficacy and effectiveness trial of behavioral activation for Latinos with depression. *Behavior Therapy, 46,* 177–192. doi:10.1016/j.beth.2014.09.011

Kaplan, B. J., Rucklidge, J. J., Romijn, A., & McLeod, K. (2015). The emerging field of nutritional mental health: Inflammation, the microbiome, oxidative stress, and mitochondrial function. *Clinical Psychological Science, 3,* 964–980. doi:10.1177/2167702614555413

Kaplan, M. S., & Krueger, R. B. (2012). Cognitive-behavioral treatment of the paraphilias. *The Israel Journal of Psychiatry and Related Sciences, 49,* 291–296.

Kaplan, R. M. (2000). Two pathways to prevention. *American Psychologist, 55,* 382–396.

Kaplan, S. J. (1986). *The private practice of behavior therapy: A guide for behavioral practitioners.* New York, NY: Plenum Press.

Kapur, V. K., & Weaver, E. M. (2012). Filling in the pieces of the sleep apnea–hypertension puzzle. [Editorial]. *Journal of the American Medical Association, 307,* 2197–2198. doi:10.1001/jama.2012.5039

Karatzias, T., Power, K., Brown, K., McGoldrick, T., Begum, M., Young, J., . . . Adams, S. (2011). A controlled comparison of the effectiveness and efficiency of two psychological therapies for posttraumatic stress disorder: Eye movement desensitization and reprocessing vs. emotional freedom techniques. *Journal of Nervous & Mental Disease, 199*, 372–378. doi:10.1097/NMD.0b013e31821cd262

Karel, M. J., Gatz, M., & Smyer, M. A. (2012). Aging and mental health in the decade ahead: What psychologists need to know. *American Psychologist, 67*, 184–198. doi:10.1037/a0025393

Karg, K., Burmeister, M., Shedden, K., & Sen, S. (2011). The serotonin transporter promoter variant (5-httlpr), stress, and depression meta-analysis revisited: Evidence of genetic moderation. *Archives of General Psychiatry, 68*, 444–454. doi:10.1001/archgenpsychiatry.2010.189

Karlson, C. W., Gallagher, M. W., Olson, C. A., & Hamilton, N A. (2013). Insomnia symptoms and well-being: Longitudinal follow-up. *Health Psychology, 32*, 311–319. doi:10.1037/a0028186

Karrass, J., Walden, T. A., Conturea, E. G., Graham, C. G., Arnold, H. S., Hartfield, K. N.,…Schwenk, K. A. (2006). Relation of emotional reactivity and regulation to childhood stuttering. *Journal of Communication Disorders, 39*, 402–423.

Karyotaki, E., Smit, Y., Henningsen, H., Huibers, M. J., Robays, J., de Beurs, D., & Cuijpers P. (2016). Combining pharmacotherapy and psychotherapy or monotherapy for major depression? A meta-analysis. *Journal of Affective Disorders, 20*, 144–152. doi:10.1016/j.jad.2016.01.036

Kaslow, N. J., Thompson, M. P., Okun, A., Price, A., Young, S., Bender, M.,…Parker, R. (2002). Risk and protective factors for suicidal behavior in abused African American women. *Journal of Consulting and Clinical Psychology, 70*, 311–319.

Kasper, L. J., Alderson, R. M., & Hudec, K. L. (2012). Moderators of working memory deficits in children with attention-deficit/hyperactivity disorder (ADHD): A meta-analytic review. *Clinical Psychology Review, 32*, 605–617. doi:10.1016/j.cpr.2012.07.001

Katon, W. J. (2006). Panic disorder. *New England Journal of Medicine, 354*, 2360–2367.

Katsiaficas, D., Suárez-Orozco, C., Sirin, S. R., & Gupta, T. (2013). Mediators of the relationship between acculturative stress and internalization symptoms for immigrant origin youth. *Cultural Diversity and Ethnic Minority Psychology, 19*, 27–37. doi:10.1037/a0031094

Kaufman, C. E., Beals, J., Croy, C., Jiang, L., Novins, D. K., & the AI-SUPERPFP Team. (2013). Multilevel context of depression in two American Indian tribes. *Journal of Consulting and Clinical Psychology, 81*, 1040–1051. doi:10.1037/a0034342

Kaunitz, A. M. (2011, November 3). Alcohol and breast cancer risk. *Journal Watch Women's Health.* Retrieved from http://womens-health.jwatch.org/cgi/content/full/2011/1103/1?q=etoc_jwwomen

Kaup, A. R., Byers, A. L., Falvey, C., Simonsick, E., Satterfield, S., Ayonayon, N. N.,…Yaffe, K. (2016). Trajectories of depressive symptoms in older adults and risk of dementia. *JAMA Psychiatry.* Retrieved from http://dx.doi.org/10.1001/jamapsychiatry.2016.0004

Kay, A. B. (2006). Natural killer T cells and asthma. *New England Journal of Medicine, 354*, 1186–1188.

Kaye, W., (2009). Eating disorders: Hope despite mortal risk. *American Journal of Psychiatry, 166*, 139–1311. doi:10.1176/appi.ajp.2009.09101424

Kazdin, A. E. (2003). *Research design in clinical psychology* (4th ed.). Boston, MA: Allyn & Bacon.

Kazdin, A. E., & Blasé, S. L. (2011). Rebooting psychotherapy research and practice to reduce the burden of mental illness. *Perspectives on Psychological Science, 6*, 21–37. doi:10.1177/1745691610393527

Keaney, J., Walsh, D. M., O'Malley, T., Hudson, N., Crosbie, D. E., Loftus, T.,…Campbell, M. (2015). Autoregulated paracellular clearance of amyloid-β across the blood-brain barrier. *Science Advances, 8*, e1500472. doi:10.1126/sciadv.1500472

Keefe, J. R., McCarthy, K. S., Dinger, U., Zilcha-Mano, S., & Barber, J. P. (2014). A meta-analytic review of psychodynamic therapies for anxiety disorders. *Clinical Psychology Review, 34*, 309–323. doi:10.1016/j.cpr.2014.03.004.

Keer, R., Ullrich, S., Destavola, B. L., & Coid, J. W. (2013). Association of violence with emergence of persecutory delusions in untreated schizophrenia. *American Journal of Psychiatry, 171*, 332–339. doi:10.1176/appi.ajp.2013.13010134.2013

Kellar, M. C., & Hignite, L. R. (2014). Chemical castration. *The encyclopedia of criminology and criminal justice*, 1–4. doi:10.1002/9781118517383.wbeccj025

Kellner, C. H., Fink, M., Knapp, R., Petrides, G., Husain, M., Rummans, T.,…Malur, C. (2005). Relief of expressed suicidal intent by ECT: A consortium for research in ECT study. *American Journal of Psychiatry, 162*, 977–982.

Kellner, C. H., Greenberg, R. M., Murrough, J. W., Bryson, E. O., Briggs, M. C., & Pasculli, R. M. (2012). ECT in treatment-resistant depression. *American Journal of Psychiatry, 169*, 1238–1244. doi:10.1176/appi.ajp.2012.12050648

Kemeny, M. E. (2003). The psychobiology of stress. *Current Directions in Psychological Science, 12*, 124–129.

Kempton, M. J., Stahl, D., Williams, S. C. R., & DeLisi, L. E. (2010). Progressive lateral ventricular enlargement in schizophrenia: A meta-analysis of longitudinal MRI studies. *Schizophrenia Research, 120*, 54–62.

Kendall, P. C., & Drabick, D. A. G. (2010). Problems for the book of problems? Diagnosing mental health disorders among youth. *Clinical Psychology: Science and Practice, 17*, 265–271. doi:10.1111/j.1468-2850.2010.01218.x

Kendall, P. C., & Treadwell, K. (2007). The role of self-statements as a mediator in treatment for anxiety-disordered youth. *Journal of Consulting and Clinical Psychology, 75*, 380–389.

Kendler, K. S. (2005). "A gene for…": The nature of gene action in psychiatric disorders. *American Journal of Psychiatry, 162*, 1243–1252.

Kendler, K. S., Aggen, S. H., Czajkowski, N., Røysamb, E., Tambs, K., Torgersen, S.,…Reichborn-Kjennerud, T. (2008). The structure of genetic and environmental risk factors for DSM-V personality disorders: A multivariate twin study. *Archives of General Psychiatry, 65*, 1438–1446.

Kendler, K. S., Aggen, S. H., Knudsen, G. P., Røysamb, E., Neale, M. C., & Reichborn-Kjennerud, T. (2011). The structure of genetic and environmental risk factors for syndromal and subsyndromal common DSM-IV axis I and all axis II disorders. *American Journal of Psychiatry, 168*, 29–34.

Kendler, K. S., Aggen, S. H., & Patrick, C. J. (2013). Familial influences on conduct disorder reflect 2 genetic factors and 1 shared environmental factor. *JAMA Psychiatry, 70*, 78–86. doi:10.1001/jamapsychiatry.2013.267

Kendler, K. S., & Gardner, C. O. (2010). Dependent stressful life events and prior depressive episodes in the prediction of major depression: The problem of causal inference in psychiatric epidemiology. *Archives of General Psychiatry, 67*, 1120–1127. doi:10.1001/archgenpsychiatry.2010.136

Kendler, K. S., Hettema, J. M., Butera, F., Gardner, C. O., & Prescott, C. A. (2003). Life event dimensions of loss, humiliation, entrapment, and danger in the prediction of onsets of major depression and generalized anxiety. *Archives of General Psychiatry, 60*, 789–796.

Kendler, K. S., Kuhn, J., & Prescott, C. A. (2004). The interrelationship of neuroticism, sex, and stressful life events in the prediction of episodes of major depression. *American Journal of Psychiatry, 161*, 631–636.

Kendler, K. S., MacLean, C., Neale, M., Kessler, R., Heath, A., & Eaves, L. (1991). The genetic epidemiology of bulimia nervosa. *American Journal of Psychiatry, 148*, 1627–1637.

Kendler, K. S., Myers, J., & Reichborn-Kjennerud, T. (2011). Borderline personality disorder traits and their relationship with dimensions of normative personality: A web-based cohort and twin study. *Acta Psychiatrica Scandinavica, 123*, 349–359.

Kendler, K. S., Neale, M. C., Kessler, R. C., Heath, A. C., & Eaves, L. J. (1993). The lifetime history of major depression in women: Reliability of diagnosis and heritability. *Archives of General Psychiatry, 50*, 863–870.

Kendler, K. S., Sundquist, K., Ohlsson, H., Palmér, K., Maes, H., Winkleby, M. A., & Sundquist, J. (2012). Genetic and familial environmental influences on the risk for drug abuse: A national Swedish adoption study. *Archives of General Psychiatry, 69*, 690–697. doi:10.1001/archgenpsychiatry.2011.2112

Kendrick, J. (2010, August 12). iPad may help communication for autistic children. Retrieved from http://gigaom.com/mobile/ipad-is-reaching-autistic-children/

Kendzerska, T., Gershon, A. S., Hawker, G., Tomlinson, G., & Leung. R. S. (2014). Obstructive sleep apnea and incident diabetes: A historical cohort study. *American Journal of Respiratory and Critical Care Medicine, 190*, 218–225. doi:10.1164/rccm.201312-2209OC

Kennedy, N., McDonough, M., Kelly, B., & Berrios, G. E. (2002). Erotomania revisited: Clinical course and treatment. *Comprehensive Psychiatry, 43*, 1–6.

Kennedy, S. H., Lam, R. W., Parikh, S. V., Patten, S. B., & Ravindran, A. V. (2009). Introduction: Canadian Network for Mood and Anxiety Treatments (CANMAT) clinical guidelines for the management of major depressive disorder in adults. *Journal of Affective Disorders, 117*(Suppl. 1), S1–S2. doi:10.1016/j.jad.2009.06.043

Kennedy, S. H., Milev, R., Giacobbe, P., Ramasubbu, R., Lam, R. W., Parikh, S. V.,…Ravindran, A. V. (2009). Canadian Network for Mood and Anxiety Treatments (CANMAT) clinical guidelines for the management of major depressive disorder in adults: IV. Neurostimulation therapies. *Journal of Affective Disorders, 117*(Suppl. 1), S44–S53. doi:10.1016/j.jad.2009.06.039

Kennedy, S. H., Young, A. H., & Blier, P. (2011). Strategies to achieve clinical effectiveness: Refining existing therapies and pursuing emerging targets. *Journal of Affective Disorders, 132*, S21–S28. doi:10.1016/j.jad.2011.03.048

Kent, A., & Waller, G. (2000). Childhood emotional abuse and eating psychopathology. *Clinical Psychology Review, 20*, 887–903.

Kéri, S., Beniczky, S., & Kelemen, O. (2010). Suppression of the P50 evoked response and neuregulin 1 induced AKT phosphorylation in first-episode schizophrenia. *American Journal of Psychiatry, 167*, 444–450. doi:10.1176/appi.ajp.2009.09050723

Kerling, A., Tegtbur, U., Gützlaff, E., Kück, M., Borchert, L., Ates, Z., von Bohlen, A.,…Kahl, K. G. (2015). Effects of adjunctive exercise on physiological and psychological parameters in depression: A randomized pilot trial. *Journal of Affective Disorders, 177*, 1–6.

Kernberg, O. F. (1975). *Borderline conditions and pathological narcissism.* New York, NY: Jason Aronson.

Kernberg, O. F., & Michels, R. (2009). Borderline personality disorder. *American Journal of Psychiatry, 166*, 505–508.

Kersting, K. (2003, November). Study shows two types of reading disability. *Monitor on Psychology.* Retrieved from http://www.apa.org/monitor/nov03/study.html

Kertesz, A. (2006). Progress in clinical neurosciences: Frontotemporal dementia-Pick's disease. *Canadian Journal of Neurological Sciences, 33*, 143–148.

Keshavan, M. S., Nasrallah, H. A., & Tandon, R. (2011). Schizophrenia, "just the facts" 6. Moving ahead with the schizophrenia concept: From the elephant to the mouse. *Schizophrenia Research, 127*, 3–13.

Keshavan, M. S., Tandon, R., Boutros, N. N., & Nasrallah, H. A. (2008). Schizophrenia, "just the facts": What we know in 2008 part 3: Neurobiology. *Schizophrenia Research, 106*(2–3), 89–107. doi:10.1016/j.schres.2008.07.020

Kessler, R. C., Adler, L., Barkley, R., Biederman, J., Conners, C. K.,…Zaslavsky, A. M. (2006). The prevalence and correlates of adult ADHD in the United States: Results from the National Comorbidity Survey Replication. *American Journal of Psychiatry, 163*, 716–723.

Kessler, R. C., Aguilar-Gaxiola, S., Alonso, J., Chatterji, S., Lee, S., Ormel, J.,…Wang, S. (2009). The global burden of mental disorders: An update from the WHO World Mental Health (WMH) surveys. *Epidemiologia e Psichiatria Sociale, 18*, 23–33.

Kessler, R. C., Avenevoli, S., Costello, E. J., Georgiades, K., Green, J. G., Gruber, M. J.,…Merikangas, K. R. (2012). Prevalence, persistence, and sociodemographic correlates of DSM-IV disorders in the National Comorbidity Survey Replication Adolescent Supplement. *Archives of General Psychiatry, 69*, 372–380. doi:10.1001/archgenpsychiatry.2011.160

Kessler, R. C., Berglund, P. A., Demler, O., Jin, R., & Walters, E. E. (2005). Lifetime prevalence and age-of-onset distributions of DSM-IV disorders in the

National Comorbidity Survey Replication (NCS-R). *Archives of General Psychiatry, 62,* 593–602.

Kessler, R. C., Chiu, W. T., Demler, O., & Walters, E. E. (2005). Prevalence, severity, and comorbidity of 12-month DSM-IV disorders in the National Comorbidity Survey Replication. *Archives of General Psychiatry, 62,* 617–627.

Kessler, R. C., Coccaro, E. F., Fava, M., & McLaughlin, K. A. (2012). The phenomenology and epidemiology of intermittent explosive disorder. In J. E. Grant & M. N. Potenza (Eds.), *The Oxford handbook of impulse control disorders* (pp. 149–164). New York, NY: Oxford University Press.

Kessler, R. C., Demler O., Frank, R. G., Olfson, M., Pincus, H. A., Walters, E. E.,... Zaslavsky, A. M. (2005). Prevalence and treatment of mental disorders, 1990 to 2003. *New England Journal of Medicine, 352,* 2515–2523.

Kessler, R. C., McGonagle, K. A., Zhao, S., & Nelson, C. B. (1994). Lifetime and 12-month prevalence of DSM-III-R psychiatric disorders in the United States: Results from the National Comorbidity Survey. *Archives of General Psychiatry, 51,* 8–19.

Kessler, R. C., Sonnega, A., Bromet, E., Hughes, M., & Nelson, C. B. (1995). Posttraumatic stress disorder in the National Comorbidity Survey. *Archives of General Psychiatry, 52,* 1048–1060.

Kessler, R. C., Warner, C. H., Ivany, C., Petukhova, M. V., Rose, S., Bromet, E. J.,... Army STARRS Collaborators. (2014). Predicting suicides after psychiatric hospitalization in U.S. Army soldiers: The Army study to assess risk and resilience in service members (Army STARRS). *JAMA Psychiatry, 72,* 49–57. doi:10.1001/jamapsychiatry.2014.1754

Kety, S. S., Rosenthal, D., Wender, P. H., Schulsinger, F., & Jacobsen, B. (1975). Mental illness in the biological and adoptive families of adoptive individuals who have become schizophrenic: A preliminary report based on psychiatric interviews. In R. R. Fieve, D. Rosenthal, & H. Brill (Eds.), *Genetic research in psychiatry* (pp. 147–165). Baltimore, MD: The Johns Hopkins University Press.

Kety, S. S., Rosenthal, D., Wender, P. H., Schulsinger, F., & Jacobsen, B. (1978). The biological and adoptive families of adopted individuals who become schizophrenic. In C. Wynne, R. L. Cromwell, & S. Mathysse (Eds.), *The nature of schizophrenia* (pp. 25–37). New York, NY: Wiley.

Keyes, D (1982). *The minds of Billy Milligan.* New York, NY: Bantam Books.

Keyes, K. M., Maslowsky, J., Hamilton, A., & Schulenberg, J. (2015). The great sleep recession: Changes in sleep duration among U.S. adolescents, 1991–2012. *Pediatrics, 135*(3), 460–468. doi:10.1542/peds.2014-2707

Khan, U. A., Liu, L., Provenzano, F. A., Berman, D. E., Profaci, C. P., Sloan, R.,... Small, S. A. (2013). Molecular drivers and cortical spread of lateral entorhinal cortex dysfunction in preclinical Alzheimer's disease. *Nature Neuroscience, 17,* 304–311. doi:10.1038/nn.3606

Khashan, A. S., Abel, K. M., McNamee, R., Pedersen, M. G., Webb, R. T., Baker, P. N.,... Mortensen, P. B. (2008). Higher risk of offspring schizophrenia following antenatal maternal exposure to severe adverse life events. *Archives of General Psychiatry, 65,* 146–152.

Khoo, J., Piantadosi, C., Duncan, R., Worthley, S. G., Jenkins, A., Noakes, M.,... Wittert, G. A. (2011). Comparing effects of a low-energy diet and a high-protein low-fat diet on sexual and endothelial function, urinary tract symptoms, and inflammation in obese diabetic men. *The Journal of Sexual Medicine, 8,* 2868–2875.

Khoury, B., Sharma, M., Rush, S. E., & Fournier, C. (2015). Mindfulness-based stress reduction for healthy individuals: A meta-analysis. *Journal of Psychosomatic Research, 78,* 519–528. doi:10.1016/j.jpsychores.2015.03.009

Kiecolt-Glaser, J. K. (2009). Psychoneuroimmunology: Psychology's gateway to the biomedical future. *Perspectives on Psychological Science, 4,* 367–369. doi:10.1111/j.1745-6924.2009.01139.x

Kiecolt-Glaser, J. K., Derry, H. M., & Fagundes, C. P. (2015). Inflammation: Depression fans the flames and feasts on the heat. *American Journal of Psychiatry, 172,* 1075–1091. http://dx.doi.org/10.1176/appi.ajp.2015.15020152

Kiecolt-Glaser, J. K., McGuire, L., Robles, T. F., & Glaser, R. (2002). Psychoneuroimmunology and psychosomatic medicine: Back to the future. *Psychosomatic Medicine, 64,* 15–28.

Kiecolt-Glaser, J. K., Speicher, C. E., Holliday, J. E., & Glaser, R. (1984). Stress and the transformation of lymphocytes in Epstein-Barr virus. *Journal of Behavioral Medicine, 7,* 1–12.

Kiehl, K. A. (2006). A cognitive neuroscience perspective on psychopathy: Evidence for paralimbic system dysfunction. *Psychiatry Research, 142,* 107–128.

Kieseppä, T., Partonen, T., Haukka, J., Kaprio, J., & Lönnqvist, J. (2004). High concordance of bipolar I disorder in a nationwide sample of twins. *American Journal of Psychiatry, 161,* 1814–1821.

Kiesner, J. (2009). Physical characteristics of the menstrual cycle and premenstrual depressive symptoms. *Psychological Science, 20,* 763–770.

Kilgore, K., Snyder, J., & Lentz, C. (2000). The contribution of parental discipline, parental monitoring, and school risk to early-onset conduct problems in African American boys and girls. *Developmental Psychology, 36,* 835–845.

Kilpatrick, D. G., Ruggiero, K. J., Acierno, R., Saunders, B. E., Resnick, H. S., & Best, C. L. (2003). Violence and risk of PTSD, major depression, substance abuse/dependence, and comorbidity: Results from the National Survey of Adolescents. *Journal of Consulting & Clinical Psychology, 71,* 692–700.

Kilts, C. D., Gross, R. E., Ely, T. D., & Drexler, K. P. G. (2004). The neural correlates of cue-induced craving in cocaine-dependent women. *American Journal of Psychiatry, 161,* 233–241.

Kim, J., Park, S., & Blake, R. (2011). Perception of biological motion in schizophrenia and healthy individuals: A behavioral and fMRI study. *PLOS ONE, 6,* e19971. doi:10.1371/journal.pone.0019971

Kim, J.-I., Ganesan, S., Luo, X., Wu, Y.-W., Park, E., Huang, E. J.,... Ding, B. (2015). Aldehyde dehydrogenase 1a1 mediates a GABA synthesis pathway in midbrain dopaminergic neurons. *Science, 350*(6256), 102. doi:10.1126/science.aac4690

Kim, J. M., & López, S. R. (2014). The expression of depression in Asian Americans and European Americans. *Journal of Abnormal Psychology, 123,* 754–763. http://dx.doi.org/10.1037/a0038114

Kim, J. Y., Liu, C. Y., Zhang, F., Duan, X., Wen, Z., Song, J.,... Ming, G.-L. (2012). Interplay between DISC1 and GABA signaling regulates neurogenesis in mice and risk for schizophrenia. *Cell, 148,* 1051. doi:10.1016/j.cell.2011.12.037

Kim, K.-H., Lee, S.-M., Paik, J.-W., & Kim, N.-S. (2011). The effects of continuous antidepressant treatment during the first 6 months on relapse or recurrence of depression. *Journal of Affective Disorders, 132,* 121–129.

Kim, Y.-K., Nab, K.-S., Myint, A.-M., & Leonard, B. E. (2015). The role of pro-inflammatory cytokines in neuroinflammation, neurogenesis and the neuroendocrine system in major depression. *Progress in Neuro-Psychopharmacology and Biological Psychiatry, 64,* 277–284. doi:10.1016/j.pnpbp.2015.06.008

Kindt, M., Soeter, M., & Vervliet, B. (2009). Beyond extinction: Erasing human fear responses and preventing the return of fear. *Nature Neuroscience, 12,* 256–258. doi:10.1038/nn.2271

Kinetz, E. (2006, September 26). Is hysteria real? Brain images say yes. *The New York Times,* pp. F1, F4.

King, B. H. (2015). Promising forecast for autism spectrum disorders. *Journal of the American Medical Association, 313,* 1518–1519. doi:10.1001/jama.2015.2628

King, D. L., Haagsma, M. C., Delfabbro, P. H., Gradisar, M., & Griffiths, M. D. (2013). Toward a consensus definition of pathological videogaming: A systematic review of psychometric assessment tools. *Clinical Psychology Review, 33,* 331–342.

King, I. F., Yandava, C. N., Mabb, A. M., Hsiao, J. S., Huang, H.-S., Pearson, B. L.,... Zylka, M. J. (2013). Topoisomerases facilitate transcription of long genes linked to autism. *Nature, 501,* 58–62. doi:10.1038/nature12504

King, M. (2008). A systematic review of mental disorder, suicide, and deliberate self harm in lesbian, gay and bisexual people. *BMC Psychiatry, 8,* 70. Retrieved from http://www.biomedcentral.com/1471-244X/8/70

King, S., & Dixon, M. J. (1999). Expressed emotion and relapse in young schizophrenia outpatients. *Schizophrenia Bulletin, 25,* 377–386.

King, S., St-Hilaire, A., & Heidkamp, D. (2010). Prenatal factors in schizophrenia. *Current Directions in Psychological Science, 19,* 209–213. doi:10.1177/0963721410378360

Kingsberg, S. (2010). Hypoactive sexual desire disorder: When is low sexual desire a disorder? *Journal of Sexual Medicine, 7,* 2907–2908.

Kinoshita, Y., Chen, J., Rapee, R. M., Bogels, S., Schneier, F. R., Choy, Y.,... Furukawa, T. A. (2008). Cross-cultural study of conviction subtype taijin kyofu: Proposal and reliability of Nagoya-Osaka diagnostic criteria for social anxiety disorder. *The Journal of Nervous and Mental Disease, 196,* 307–313.

Kirisci, L., Vanyukov, M., & Tarter, R. (2005). Detection of youth at high risk for substance use disorders: A longitudinal study. *Psychology of Addictive Behaviors, 19,* 243–252.

Kirkbride, J. B., Jones, P. B., Ullrich, S., & Coid, J. W. (2012). Social deprivation, inequality, and the neighborhood-level incidence of psychotic syndromes in East London. *Schizophrenia Bulletin.* doi:10.1093/schbul/sbs151

Kitayama, S., Park, J., Boylan, J. M., Miyamoto, Y., Levine, C. S., Markus, H. R.,... Ryff, C. D. (2015). Expression of anger and ill health in two cultures: An examination of inflammation and cardiovascular risk. *Psychological Science, 26,* 211–220. doi:10.1177/0956797614561268

Kivlighan III, D. M., Goldberg, S. B., Abbas, M., Pace, B. T., Yulish, N. E., Thomas, J. G.,... Wampold, B. E. (2015). The enduring effects of psychodynamic treatments vis-à-vis alternative treatments: A multilevel longitudinal meta-analysis. *Clinical Psychology Review, 40,* 1–14. doi:10.1016/j.cpr.2015.05.003

Klauser, P., Fornito, A., Lorenzetti, V., Davey, C. G., Dwyer, D. B., Allen, N. B.,... Yücel, M. (2014). Cortico-limbic network abnormalities in individuals with current and past major depressive disorder. *Journal of Affective Disorders, 173,* 45–52. doi:10.1016/j.jad.2014.10.041

Kleijweg, J. H. M., Verbraak, M. J. P. M., & Van Dijk, M. K. (2013). The clinical utility of the Maslach Burnout Inventory in a clinical population. *Psychological Assessment, 25,* 435–441. doi:10.1037/a0031334

Kleiman, E. M., & Liu, R. T. (2013). Social support as a protective factor in suicide: Findings from two nationally representative samples. *Journal of Affective Disorders, 150*(2), 540–545. doi:10.1016/j.jad.2013.01.033

Kleiman, M. A. R., Caulkins, J. P., & Hawken, A. (2012, April 21–22). Rethinking the war on drugs. *The Wall Street Journal,* p. C1.

Klein, D. N., Glenn, C. R., Kosty, D. B., Seeley, J. R., Rohde, P., & Lewinsohn, P. M. (2013). Predictors of first lifetime onset of major depressive disorder in young adulthood. *Journal of Abnormal Psychology, 122,* 16. doi:10.1037/a0029567

Klein, D. N., Schwartz, J. E., Rose, S., & Leader, J. B. (2000). Five-year course and outcome of dysthymic disorder: A prospective, naturalistic follow-up study. *American Journal of Psychiatry, 157,* 931–939.

Klein, R. G. (2011). Thinning of the cerebral cortex during development: A dimension of ADHD. *American Journal of Psychiatry, 168,* 111–113. doi:10.1176/appi.ajp.2010.10111679

Klein, R. G., Mannuzza, S., Olazagasti, M. A. R., Roizen, E., Hutchison, J. A., Lashua, E. C., & Castellanos, F. X. (2012). Clinical and functional outcome of childhood attention-deficit/hyperactivity disorder 33 years later. *Archives of General Psychiatry, 69,* 1295–1303. doi:10.1001/archgenpsychiatry.2012.271

Kleinman, A. (1987). Anthropology and psychiatry: The role of culture in cross-cultural research on illness. *British Journal of Psychiatry, 151,* 447–454.

Klerman, G. L., Weissman, M. M., Rounsaville, B. J., & Chevron, E. S. (1984). *Interpersonal psychotherapy of depression.* New York, NY: Basic Books.

Klingelhoefer, L., Samuel, M., Chaudhuri, K. R., & Ashkan, K. (2014). An update of the impact of deep brain stimulation on non motor symptoms in Parkinson's disease. *Journal of Parkinson's Disease, 4*(2), 289–300. doi:10.3233/JPD-130273

Kluger, J. (2001, June 18). How to manage teen drinking (the smart way). *Time*, 42–44.

Knapen, S. E., van de Werken, M., Gordijn, M. C. M., & Meesters, Y. (2014). The duration of light treatment and therapy outcome in seasonal affective disorder. *Journal of Affective Disorders, 166*, 343–346. doi:10.1016/j.jad.2014.05.034

Knapp, M., Romeo, R., Mogg, A., Eranti, S., Pluck, G., Purvis, R.,...McLoughlin, D. M. (2008). Cost-effectiveness of transcranial magnetic stimulation vs. electroconvulsive therapy for severe depression: A multi-centre randomized controlled trial. *Journal of Affective Disorders, 109*, 273–285.

Knight, R. G., Godfrey, H. P. D., & Shelton, E. J. (1988). The psychological deficits associated with Parkinson's disease. *Clinical Psychology Review, 8*, 391–410.

Knoblauch, S. (2009). From self psychology to selves in relationship: A radical process of micro and macro expansion in conceptual experience. *Self and Systems: Annals of the New York Academy of Sciences, 1159*, 262–278.

Knoll, J. L., & Hazelwood, R. R. (2009). Becoming the victim: Beyond sadism in serial sexual murderers. *Aggression and Violent Behavior, 14*, 106–114.

Know it's a placebo? New study shows the "medicine" could still work. (2015, July 24). *Medical Press*. Retrieved from http://medicalxpress.com/news/2015-07-placebo-medicine.html

Kobasa, S. C. (1979). Stressful life events, personality, and health: An inquiry into hardiness. *Journal of Personality and Social Psychology, 37*, 1–11.

Kobasa, S. C., Maddi, S. R., & Kahn, S. (1982). Hardiness and health: A prospective study. *Journal of Personality and Social Psychology, 42*, 168–177.

Koch, W. (2009, October 20). Abuse report: 10,440 kids died 2001–2007. *USA Today*, p. 3A.

Kocovskia, N. L., Fleming, I. E., Hawley, L. L., Huta, V., & Antony, M. M. (2013). Mindfulness and acceptance-based group therapy versus traditional cognitive behavioral group therapy for social anxiety disorder: A randomized controlled trial. *Behaviour Research and Therapy, 51*, 889–898. doi:10.1016/j.brat.2013.10.007

Koegelenberg, C. F. N., Noor, F., Bateman, E. D., van Zyl-Smit, R. N., Bruning, A., O'Brien, J. A.,...Irusen, E. M. (2014). Efficacy of varenicline combined with nicotine replacement therapy vs. varenicline alone for smoking cessation: A randomized clinical trial. *Journal of the American Medical Association, 312*, 155. http://dx.doi.org/10.1001/jama.2014.7195

Koehler, N., Holze, S., Gansera, L., Rebmann, U., Roth, S., Scholz, H. J.,...Braehler, E. (2012). Erectile dysfunction after radical prostatectomy: The impact of nerve-sparing status and surgical approach. *International Journal of Impotence Research, 24*(4), 155–160. doi:10.1038/ijir.2012.8

Koenders, M. A., Giltay, E. J., Spijker, A. T., Hoencamp, E., Spinhoven, P., & Elzinga, B. M. (2014). Stressful life events in bipolar I and II disorder: Cause or consequence of mood symptoms? *Journal of Affective Disorders, 161*, 55–64. doi:10.1016/j.jad.2014.02.036

Koenen, K. C., Stellman, J. M., & Stellman, S. D. (2003). Risk factors for course of posttraumatic stress disorder among Vietnam veterans: A 14-year follow-up of American Legionnaires. *Journal of Consulting and Clinical Psychology, 71*, 980–986.

Koh, H. K., & Sebelius, K. G. (2012). Ending the tobacco epidemic. *Journal of the American Medical Association, 308*, 767–768. doi:10.1001/jama.2012.9741

Köhling, J., Ehrenthal, J. C., Levy, K. N., Schauenburg, H., & Dinger, U. (2015). Quality and severity of depression in borderline personality disorder: A systematic review and meta-analysis. *Clinical Psychology Review, 37*, 13–25.

Kohut, H. (1966). Forms and transformations of narcissism. *Journal of the American Psychoanalytic Association, 14*, 243–272.

Kok, B. C., Herrell, R. K., Thomas, J. L., & Hoge, C. (2012). Posttraumatic stress disorder associated with combat service in Iraq or Afghanistan: Reconciling prevalence differences between studies. *Journal of Nervous & Mental Disease, 200*, 444–450. doi:10.1097/NMD.0b013e3182532312

Kolata, G. (2010, August 28). Years later, no magic bullet against Alzheimer's disease. *The New York Times*. Retrieved from http://www.nytimes.com/2010/08/29/health/research/29prevent.html?pagewanted=2&_r=

Kolata, G. (2012, November 16). For Alzheimer's patients, detection advances outpace treatment options. *The New York Times*, pp. A1, A24.

Kolata, G. (2013, March 1). 5 disorders share genetic risk factors, study finds. *The New York Times*, p. A11.

Kõlves, K., Ide, N., & De Leo, D. (2010). Suicidal ideation and behaviour in the aftermath of marital separation: Gender differences. *Journal of Affective Disorders, 120*, 48–53. doi:10.1016/j.jad.2009.04.019

Kong, A., Frigge, M. L., Masson, G., Besenbacher, S., Sulem, P., Magnusson, G.,...Stefansson, K. (2012). Rate of de novo mutations and the importance of father's age to disease risk. *Nature, 488*, 471–475. doi:10.1038/nature11396

Kong, L., Bachmann, S., Thomann, P. A., Essig, M., & Schröder, J. (2012). Neurological soft signs and gray matter changes: A longitudinal analysis in first-episode schizophrenia. *Schizophrenia Research, 134*, 27–32.

Kornfeld, B. D., Bair-Merritt, M. H., Frosch, E., & Solomon, B. S. (2012). Postpartum depression and intimate partner violence in urban mothers: Co-occurrence and child health care utilization. *The Journal of Pediatrics, 161*, 348–353. doi:10.1016/j.jpeds.2012.01.047

Koss, M. P., & Kilpatrick, D. G. (2001). Rape and sexual assault. In E. Gerrity, T. M. Keane, & F. Tuma (Eds.), *The mental health consequences of torture: Plenum series on stress and coping* (pp. 177–193). Dordrecht, the Netherlands: Kluwer Academic Publishers.

Kosson, D. S., Lorenz, A. R., & Newman, J. P. (2006). Effects of comorbid psychopathy on criminal offending and emotion processing in male offenders with antisocial personality disorder. *Journal of Abnormal Psychology, 115*, 798–780.

Kotov, R., Leong, S. H., Mojtabai, R., Erlanger, A. C. E., Fochtmann, L. J., Constantino, E.,...Bromet, E. J. (2013). Boundaries of schizoaffective disorder: Revisiting Kraepelin. *JAMA Psychiatry, 70*, 1276–1286. doi:10.1001/jamapsychiatry.2013.2350

Kraaimaat, F. W., Vanryckeghem, M., & Van Dam-Baggen, R. (2002). Stuttering and social anxiety. *Journal of Fluency Disorders, 27*, 319–330.

Kraemer, H. C. (2015). Research Domain Criteria (RDoC) and the DSM: Two methodological approaches to mental health diagnosis. *JAMA Psychiatry, 72*, 1163–1164. doi:10.1001/jamapsychiatry.2015.2134

Krahe, B., Waizenhofer, E., & Moller, I. (2003). Women's sexual aggression against men: Prevalence and predictors. *Sex Roles, 49*(5–6), 219–232.

Krakauer, S. Y. (2001). *Treating dissociative identity disorder: The power of the collective heart*. Philadelphia, PA: Brunner-Routledge.

Krantz, D. S., Contrada, R. J., Hills, D. R., & Friedler, E. (1988). Environmental stress and bio-behavioral antecedents of coronary heart disease. *Journal of Consulting and Clinical Psychology, 56*, 333–341.

Krantz, M. J., & Mehler, P. S. (2004). Treating opioid dependence: Growing implications for primary care. *Archives of Internal Medicine, 164*, 277–288.

Kranz, G. S., Hahn, A., Kaufmann, U., Küblböck, M., Hummer, A., Ganger, S.,...Lanzenberger, R. (2014). White matter microstructure in transsexuals and controls investigated by diffusion tensor imaging. *Journal of Neuroscience, 34*, 15466–15475.

Kranzler, H. R. (2006). Evidence-based treatments for alcohol dependence: New results and new questions. *Journal of the American Medical Association, 295*, 2075–2076.

Kratochvil, C. J. (2012). ADHD pharmacotherapy: Rates of stimulant use and cardiovascular risk. *American Journal of Psychiatry, 169*, 112–114. doi:10.1176/appi.ajp.2011.11111703

Krause-Utz, A., Sobanski, E., Alm, B., Valerius, G., Kleindienst, N., Bohus, M.,...Schmahl, D. (2013). Impulsivity in relation to stress in patients with borderline personality disorder with and without co-occurring attentiondeficit/hyperactivity disorder: An exploratory study. *Journal of Nervous & Mental Disease, 201*, 116–123. doi:10.1097/NMD.0b013e31827f6462

Krebs, G., & Heyman, I. (2014). Obsessive-compulsive disorder in children and adolescents. *Archives of Disease in Childhood, 100*(5), 495–499. doi:10.1136/archdischild-2014-306934

Kring, A. M., Gur, R. E., Blanchard, J. J., Horan, W. P., & Reise, S. P. (2013). The Clinical Assessment Interview for Negative Symptoms (CAINS): Final development and validation. *American Journal of Psychiatry, 170*, 165–172. doi:10.1176/appi.ajp.2012.12010109

Kroenke, K. (2009). Efficacy of treatment for somatoform disorders: A review of randomized controlled trials. *Psychosomatic Medicine, 69*, 881–888.

Kronmüller, K.-T., Backenstrass, M., Victor, D., Postelnicu, L., Schenkenbach, C., Joesta, K.,...Mundt, C. (2011). Quality of marital relationship and depression: Results of a 10-year prospective follow-up study. *Journal of Affective Disorders, 128*, 64–71. doi:10.1016/j.jad.2010.06.026

Kubota, M., Miyata, J., Sasamoto, A., Sugihara, G., Yoshida, H., Kawada, R.,...Murai, T. (2013). Thalamocortical disconnection in the orbitofrontal region associated with cortical thinning in schizophrenia. *JAMA Psychiatry, 70*, 12–21. doi:10.1001/archgenpsychiatry.2012.1023

Kuehn, B. M. (2011a). Antidepressant use increases. *Journal of the American Medical Association, 306*, 2207. doi:10.1001/jama.2011.1697

Kuehn, B. M. (2011b). Autism intervention. *Journal of the American Medical Association, 305*, 348. doi:10.1001/jama.2010.1963

Kuehn, B. M. (2011c). Cognitive therapy may aid patients with schizophrenia. *Journal of the American Medical Association, 306*, 1749. doi:10.1001/jama.2011.1553

Kuehn, B. M. (2011d). Mobile PTSD care. *Journal of the American Medical Association, 306*, 815. doi:10.1001/jama.2011.1198

Kuehn, B. M. (2012a). Challenge to Alzheimer drug. *Journal of the American Medical Association, 308*, 2557. doi:10.1001/jama.2012.156122.

Kuehn, B. M. (2012b). Evidence suggests complex links between violence and schizophrenia. *Journal of the American Medical Association, 308*, 658–659. doi:10.1001/jama.2012.9364

Kuester, A., Niemeyer, H., & Knaevelsrud, C. (2016). Internet-based interventions for posttraumatic stress: A meta-analysis of randomized controlled trials. *Clinical Psychology Review, 43*, 1–16. doi:10.1016/j.cpr.2015.11.004

Kulage, K. M., Smaldone, A. M., & Cohn, E. G. (2014). How will DSM-5 affect autism diagnosis? A systematic literature review and meta-analysis. *Journal of Autism and Developmental Disorders, 44*, 1918–1922. doi:10.1007/s10803-014-2065-2.

Kumra, S., Oberstar, J. V., Sikich, L., Findling, R. L., McClellan, J. M., & Schulz, S. C. (2008). Efficacy and tolerability of second-generation antipsychotics in children and adolescents with schizophrenia. *Schizophrenia Bulletin, 34*, 60–71.

Kuno, E., & Rothbard, A. B. (2002). Racial disparities in antipsychotic prescription patterns for patients with schizophrenia. *American Journal of Psychiatry, 159*, 567–572.

Kupfer, D. J. (2005). The increasing medical burden in bipolar disorder. *Journal of the American Medical Association, 293*, 2528–2530.

Kuriyan, A. B., Pelham Jr., W. E., Molina, B. S. G., Waschbusch, D. A., Gnagy, E. M., Sibley, M. H.,...Yu, J. (2013). Young adult educational and vocational outcomes of children diagnosed with ADHD. *Journal of Abnormal Child Psychology, 41*, 27–41.

Kuss, D. J., Griffiths, M. D., Karila, L., & Billieux, J. (2014). Internet addiction: A systematic review of epidemiological research for the last decade. *Current Pharmaceutical Design, 20*, 1–27.

Kutys, J., & Esterman, J. (2009, November). Guilty but Mentally Ill (GBMI) vs. Not Guilty by Reason of Insanity (NGRI): An annotated bibliography. *The Jury Expert, 21*(6). Retrieved from http://www.astcweb.org/public/publication/article.cfm/1/21/6/An-annotated-bibliography-of-theGBMI-&-NGRI-pleas

Kyaga, S. (2015). *Creativity and mental illness: The mad genius in question*. New York, NY: Palgrave Macmillan.

Labbe, C. (2011, March 7). Most teens with eating disorders go without treatment. *NIMH Science Update*. Retrieved from http://www.nimh.nih.gov/science-news/2011/mostteens-with-eating-disorders-go-without-treatment.shtml?WT.mc_id=rss

Labonté, B., Suderman, M., Maussion, G., Navaro, L., Yerko, V., Mahar, I.,... Turecki, G. (2012). Genomewide epigenetic regulation by early-life trauma. *Archives of General Psychiatry, 69*, 722–731. doi:10.1001/archgenpsychiatry.2011.2287

Ladabaum, Mannalithara, A., Parvathi, A., Myer, A., & Singh, G. (2014). Obesity, abdominal obesity, physical activity, and caloric intake in U.S. adults: 1988 to 2010. *The American Journal of Medicine, 127*, 717–727.

LaFromboise, T. D., Albright, K., & Harris, A. (2010). Patterns of hopelessness among American Indian adolescents: Relationships by levels of acculturation and residence. *Cultural Diversity and Ethnic Minority Psychology, 16*, 68–76. doi:10.1037/a0016181

LaGrange, B., Cole, D. A., Jacquez, F., Ciesla, J., Dallaire, D., Pineda, A.,... Felton, J. (2011). Disentangling the prospective relations between maladaptive cognitions and depressive symptoms. *Journal of Abnormal Psychology, 120*, 511–527. doi:10.1037/a0024685

Laguna, A., Schintu, N., Nobre, A., Alvarsson, A., Volakakis, N., Jacobsen, J. K.,... Perlmann, T. (2015). Dopaminergic control of autophagic-lysosomal function implicates Lmx1b in Parkinson's disease. *Nature Neuroscience, 18*, 826–835. doi:10.1038/nn.4004

Lahey, B. B., Rathouz, P. J., Lee, S. S., Chronis-Tuscano, A., Pelham, W. E., Waldman, I. D., Irwin D.,... Cook, E. H. (2011). Interactions between early parenting and a polymorphism of the child's dopamine transporter gene in predicting future child conduct disorder symptoms. *Journal of Abnormal Psychology, 120*, 33–45. doi:10.1037/a0021133

Lai, C.-H., & Wu, Y.-T. (2015). The gray matter alterations in major depressive disorder and panic disorder: Putative differences in the pathogenesis. *Journal of Affective Disorders, 186*, 1–6. doi:10.1016/j.jad.2015.07.022

Lalumière, M. L., Harris, G. T., Quinsey, V. L., & Rice, M. E. (2005). Introduction. In M. L. Lalumière, G. T. Harris, V. L. Quinsey, & M. E. Rice (Eds.), *The causes of rape: Understanding individual differences in male propensity for sexual aggression* (pp. 3–6). Washington, DC: American Psychological Association.

Lam, R. W., Levitt, A. J., Levitan, R. D., Enns, M. W., Morehouse, R., Michalak, E. E., & Tam, E. M. (2006). The Can-SAD Study: A randomized controlled trial of the effectiveness of light therapy and fluoxetine in patients with winter seasonal affective disorder. *American Journal of Psychiatry, 163*, 805–811.

Lamberg, L. (2003). Advances in eating disorders offer food for thought. *Journal of the American Medical Association, 290*, 1437–1442.

Lamberg, L. (2006). Rx for obesity: Eat less, exercise more, and–maybe–get more sleep. *Journal of the American Medical Association, 295*, 2341–2344.

Lanaj, K., Johnson, R. E., & Barnes, C. M. (2014). Beginning the workday yet already depleted? Consequences of late-night smartphone use and sleep. *Organizational Behavior and Human Decision Processes, 124*, 11–23.

Landa, R. J., Holman, K. C., O'Neill, A. H., & Stuart, E. A. (2011). Intervention targeting development of socially synchronous engagement in toddlers with autism spectrum disorder: A randomized controlled trial. *Journal of Child Psychology and Psychiatry, 52*, 13–21. doi:10.1111/j.1469-7610.2010.02288.x

Langstrom, N. (2010). The DSM diagnostic criteria for exhibitionism, voyeurism, and frotteurism. *Archives of Sexual Behavior, 39*, 317–324. doi:10.1007/s10508-009-9577-4

Långström, N., & Zucker, K. J. (2005). Transvestic fetishism in the general population: Prevalence and correlates. *Journal of Sex & Marital Therapy, 31*, 87–95.

Lanza, S. T., Vasilenko, S. A., Dziak, J. J., & Butera, N. M. (2015). Trends among U.S. high school seniors in recent marijuana use and associations with other substances: 1976–2013. *Journal of Adolescent Health, 57*, 198. doi:10.1016/j.jadohealth.2015.04.006

Larson, K., Russ, S. A., Kahn, R. S., & Halfon, N. (2011). Patterns of comorbidity, functioning, and service use for U.S. children with ADHD, 2007. *Pediatrics, 127*, 462–470.

Larsson, H., Andershed, H., & Lichtenstein, P. A. (2006). A genetic factor explains most of the variation in the psychopathic personality. *Journal of Abnormal Psychology, 115*, 221–230.

Laska, K. M., Gurman, A. S., & Wampold, B. E. (2014). Expanding the lens of evidence-based practice in psychotherapy: A common factors perspective. *Psychotherapy, 51*, 467–481. Retrieved from http://dx.doi.org/10.1037/a0034332

Lau, J. Y. F., & Eley, T. C. (2010). The genetics of mood disorders. *Annual Review of Clinical Psychology, 6*, 313–337. doi:10.1146/annurev.clinpsy.121208.131308

Lauzon, N. M., Bechard, M., Ahmad, T., & Laviolette, S. R. (2012). Supra-normal stimulation of dopamine D1 receptors in the prelimbic cortex blocks behavioral expression of both aversive and rewarding associative memories through a cyclic-AMP-dependent signaling pathway. *Neuropharmacology, 67*, 104. doi:10.1016/j.neuropharm.2012.10.029

Lavretsky, H., Reinlie, M., St. Cyr, N., Siddarth, M. A. P., Ercoli, L. M., & Senturk, D. (2015). Citalopram, methylphenidate, or their combination in geriatric depression: A randomized, double-blind, placebo-controlled trial. *American Journal of Psychiatry, 172*, 561–569. Retrieved from http://dx.doi.org/10.1176/appi.ajp.2014.14070889

Laws, D. R., & Marshall, W. L. (2003). A brief history of behavioral and cognitive behavioral approaches to sexual offenders: Part 1. Early developments. *Sexual Abuse: Journal of Research & Treatment, 15*(2), 75–92.

Laws, D. R., & O'Donohue, W. T. (2012). Introduction. In D. R. Laws & W. T. O'Donohue (Eds.), *Sexual deviance: Theory, assessment, and treatment* (2nd ed., pp. 1–20). New York, NY: Guilford Press.

Lazarus, R. S., & Folkman, S. (1984). *Stress, appraisal, and coping*. New York, NY: Springer.

Lazarus, S. A., Cheavens, J. S., Festa, F., & Rosenthal, M. Z. (2014). Interpersonal functioning in borderline personality disorder: A systematic review of behavioral and laboratory-based assessments. *Clinical Psychology Review, 34*, 193–205. Retrieved from http://dx.doi.org/10.1016/j.cpr.2014.01.007

Le Grange, D., Lock, J., Agras, W. S., Bryson, S. W., & Jo, B. (2015). Randomized clinical trial of family-based treatment and cognitive-behavioral therapy for adolescent bulimia nervosa. *Child & Adolescent Psychiatry, 54*, 886–894. Retrieved from http://dx.doi.org/10.1016/j.jaac.2015.08.008

Le Meyer, O., Zane, N., Cho, Y., II, & Takeuchi, D. T. (2009). Use of specialty mental health services by Asian Americans with psychiatric disorders. *Journal of Consulting and Clinical Psychology, 94*, 1000–1005. doi:10.1037/a0017065

Lear, M. S. (1988, July 3). Mad malady. *The New York Times*, pp. 21–22.

LeClerc, B., Beauregard, E., Forouzan, E., & Proulx, J. (2014). Offending pathways of intrafamilial child sexual offenders. In J. Proulx, E. Beauregard, P. Lussier, & B. Leclerc (Eds.), *Aggression* (pp. 156–178). New York, NY: Routledge.

Lecomte, T., Corbière, M., Simard, S., & Leclerc, C. (2014). Merging evidence-based psychosocial interventions in schizophrenia. *Behavioral Science, 4*(4), 437–447. doi:10.3390/bs4040437

Lee, D. T. S., Yip, A., Chiu, H., Leung, T., & Chung, T. (2001). A psychiatric epidemiological study of postpartum Chinese women. *American Journal of Psychiatry, 158*, 220–226.

Lee, E., Ahn, J., & Kim, Y. J. (2014). Personality traits and self-presentation at Facebook. *Personality and Individual Differences, 69*, 162–167. doi:10.1016/j.paid.2014.05.020

Lee, H.-J., Woo, H. G., Greenwood, T. A., Kripke, D. F., & Kelsoe, J. R. (2013). A genome-wide association study of seasonal pattern mania identifies NF1A as a possible susceptibility gene for bipolar disorder. *Journal of Affective Disorders, 145*, 200–207.

Lee, J., & Hahm, H. C. (2010). Acculturation and sexual risk behaviors among Latina adolescents transitioning to young adulthood. *Journal of Youth and Adolescence, 39*, 1573–6601.

Lee, R., Meyerhoff, J., & Coccaro, E. F. (2014). Intermittent explosive disorder and aversive parental care. *Psychiatry Research, 220*, 477–482. doi:10.1016/j.psychres.2014.05.059

Lee, S. S., Humphreys, K. L., Flory, K., Liu, R, & Glass, K. (2011). Prospective association of childhood attention-deficit/hyperactivity disorder (ADHD) and substance use and abuse/dependence: A meta-analytic review. *Clinical Psychology Review, 31*, 328–341. doi:10.1016/j.cpr.2011.01.006

Lee, S. Y., Xue, Q.-L., Spira, A. P., & Lee, H. B. (2014). Racial and ethnic differences in depressive subtypes and access to mental health care in the United States. *Journal of Affective Disorders, 155*, 130–137.

Leekam, S. R., Prior, M. R., & Uljarevic, M. (2011). Restricted and repetitive behaviors in autism spectrum disorders: A review of research in the last decade. *Psychological Bulletin, 137*, 562–593. doi:10.1037/a0023341

Lefley, H. P. (1990). Culture and chronic mental illness. *Hospital and Community Psychiatry, 41*, 277–286.

Lehne, G. K. (2009). Phenomenology of paraphilia: Lovemap theory. In F. M. Saleh, A. J. Grudzinskas, Jr., J. M. Bradford, & D. J. Brodsky (Eds.), *Sex offenders: Identification, risk assessment, treatment, and legal issues* (pp. 12–26). New York, NY: Oxford University Press.

Leiblum, S. R. (2010a). Introduction and overview: Clinical perspectives on and treatment for sexual desire disorders. In S. R. Leiblum (Ed.), *Treating sexual desire disorders: A clinical casebook* (pp. 1–22). New York, NY: Guilford Press.

Leiblum, S. R. (Ed.). (2010b). *Treating sexual desire disorders: A clinical casebook*. New York, NY: Guilford Press.

Leiblum, S. R., Koochaki, P. E., Rodenberg, C. A., Barton, I. P., & Rosen, R. C. (2006). Hypoactive sexual desire disorder in postmenopausal women: U.S. results from the Women's International Study of Health and Sexuality (WISHeS). *Menopause, 13*, 46–56.

Leiblum, S. R., & Rosen, R. C. (Eds.). (2000). *Principles and practice of sex therapy* (3rd ed.). New York, NY: Guilford Press.

Leichsenring, F., Leibling, E., Kruse, J., New, A. S., & Leweke, F. (2011). Borderline personality disorder. *The Lancet, 377*, 74–84.

Leichsenring, F., & Schauenburg, H. (2014). Empirically supported methods of short-term psychodynamic therapy in depression: Towards an evidence-based unified protocol. *Journal of Affective Disorders, 169*, 128–143. doi:10.1016/j.jad.2014.08.007

Leichsenring, F., Salzer, S., Beutel, M. E., Herpertz, S., Hiller, W., Hoyer, J.,... Leibing, E. (2013). Psychodynamic therapy and cognitive-behavioral therapy in social anxiety disorder: A multicenter randomized controlled trial. *American Journal of Psychiatry, 170*, 759–767. doi:10.1176/appi.ajp.2013.12081125

Leichsenring, F., Salzer, S., Beutel, M. E., Herpertz, S., Hiller, W., Hoyer, J.,... Leibing, E. (2014). Long-term outcome of psychodynamic therapy and cognitive-behavioral therapy in social anxiety disorder. *American Journal of Psychiatry, 171*, 1074–1082. doi:10.1176/appi.ajp.2014.13111514

Leigh, S., & Flatt, S. (2015). App-based psychological interventions: friend or foe? *Evidence Based Mental Health, 18*, 97–99. doi:10.1136/eb-2015-102203

Lejoyeux, M., & Germain, C. (2012). Pyromania: Phenomenology and epidemiology. In J. E. Grant & M. N. Potenza (Eds.), *The Oxford handbook of impulse control disorders* (pp. 135–148). New York, NY: Oxford University Press.

Lemay, R. A. (2009). Deinstitutionalization of people with developmental disabilities: A review of the literature. *Canadian Journal of Community Mental Health, 28*(1), 181–194.

Lentz, V., Robinson, J., & Bolton, J. M. (2010). Childhood adversity, mental disorder comorbidity, and suicidal behavior in schizotypal personality disorder. *Journal of Nervous and Mental Disease, 198*, 795–801. doi:10.1097/NMD.0b013e3181f9804c

Leocani, L., Locatelli, M., Bellodi, L., Fornara, C., Hénin, M., Magnani, G.,... Comi, G. (2001). Abnormal pattern of cortical activation associated with voluntary movement in obsessive-compulsive disorder: An EEG study. *American Journal of Psychiatry, 158*, 140–142.

Leue, A., Borchard, B., & Hoyer, J. (2004). Mental disorders in a forensic sample of sexual offenders. *European Psychiatry, 19*, 123–130.

Leung, P. W. L., & Poon, M. W. L. (2001). Dysfunctional schemas and cognitive distortions in psychopathology: A test of the specificity hypothesis. *Journal of Child Psychology & Psychiatry & Allied Disciplines, 42*, 755–765.

LeVine, E. S. (2012). Facilitating recovery for people with serious mental illness employing a psychobiosocial model of care. *Professional Psychology: Research and Practice, 43,* 58–64. doi:10.1037/a0026889

Levine, E. S., & Schmelkin, L. P. (2006). The move to prescribe: A change in paradigm? *Professional Psychology: Research and Practice, 37,* 205–209.

Levine, S. B. (2012). Problematic sexual excesses. *Neuropsychiatry,* 2(1), 69–79.

Levinson, D. F., Duan, J., Oh, S., Wang, K., Sanders, A. R., Shi, J., Zhang, N.,…Gejman, P. V. (2011). Copy number variants in schizophrenia: Confirmation of five previous findings and new evidence for 3q29 microdeletions and VIPR2 duplications. *American Journal of Psychiatry, 168,* 302–316. doi:10.1176/appi.ajp.2010.10060876

Levy, R. A., Ablon, J. S., & Kächele, H. (2013). *Psychodynamic psychotherapy research: Evidence-based practice and practice-based evidence.* Totowa, NJ: Humana Press.

Lewinsohn, P. M. (1974). A behavioral approach to depression. In R. J. Friedman & M. M. Katz (Eds.), *The psychology of depression: Contemporary theory and research* (pp. 54–77). Washington, DC: Winston-Wiley.

Lewis, R. W., Fugl-Meyer, K. S., Corona, G., Hayes, R. D., Laumann, E. O., Moreira, E. D., Jr.,…Segraves, T. (2010). Definitions/epidemiology/risk factors for sexual dysfunction. *Journal of Sexual Medicine, 7,* 1598–1607.

Lewis, S. J., Relton, C., Zammit, S., & Smith, G. D. (2013). Approaches for strengthening causal inference regarding prenatal risk factors for childhood behavioural and psychiatric disorders. *Journal of Child Psychology and Psychiatry, 54,* 1095–1108. doi:10.1111/jcpp.12127

Li, D., Morris, J. S., Liu, J., Hassan, M. M., Day, R. S., Bondy, M. L., & Abbruzzese, J. L. (2009). Body mass index and risk, age of onset, and survival in patients with pancreatic cancer. *Journal of the American Medical Association, 301,* 2553–2562.

Li, F., Liu, X., & Zhang, D. (2015). Fish consumption and risk of depression: A meta-analysis. *Journal of Epidemiology & Community Health.* doi:10.1136/jech-2015-206278

Li, J., Zhou, G., Ji, W., Feng, G., Zhao, Q., Liu, J.,…Shi, Y. (2011). Common variants in the BCL9 gene conferring risk of schizophrenia. *Archives of General Psychiatry, 68,* 232–240. doi:10.1001/archgenpsychiatry.2011.1

Liberman, R. P. (1994). Treatment and rehabilitation of the seriously mentally ill in China. *American Journal of Orthopsychiatry, 64,* 68–77.

Lichta, R. W. (2010). A new BALANCE in bipolar I disorder. *The Lancet, 375,* 350–352. doi:10.1016/S0140-6736(09)61970-X

Lichtman, J. H., Froelicher, E. S., Blumenthal, J. A., Carney, R. M., Doering, L. V., Frasure-Smith, N.,…Wulsin, L. (2014). Depression as a risk factoror poor prognosis among patients with acute coronary syndrome: Systematic review and recommendations: A scientific statement from the American Heart Association. *Circulation.* Retrieved from http://circ.ahajournals.org/content/early/2014/02/24/CIR.0000000000000019

Lieberman, J. S. A. (2010). Psychiatric care shortage: What the future holds. *Medscape Psychiatry and Mental Health.* Retrieved from www.medscape.com

Liebowitz, M. R., Gelenberg, A. J., & Munjack, D. (2005). Venlafaxine extended release vs. placebo and paroxetine in social anxiety disorder. *Archives of General Psychiatry, 62,* 190–198.

Liebowitz, M. R., Stein, M. B., Tancer, M., Carpenter, D., Oakes, R., & Pitts, C. D. (2002). A randomized, double-blind, fixed-dose comparison of paroxetine and placebo in treatment of generalized social anxiety disorder. *Journal of Clinical Psychiatry, 63,* 66–74.

Lim, J., & Dinges, D. F. (2010). A meta-analysis of the impact of short-term sleep deprivation on cognitive variables. *Psychological Bulletin, 136,* 375–389. doi:10.1037/a0018883

Lim, S. (2003, September 2). Beating the bed-wetting blues. Retrieved from http://www.msnbc.com/news/954846.asp

Lin, F., & Lei, H. (2015). Structural brain imaging and Internet addiction. In C. Montag & M. Reuter (Eds.), *Studies in neuroscience, psychology and behavioral economics* (pp. 21–42). New York, NY: Springer.

Lin, L. Y., Sidani, J. E., Shensa, A., Radovic, A., Miller, E., Colditz, J. B.,…Primack, B. A. (2016). *Depression and Anxiety,* in press. doi:10.1002/da.22466.

Lin, P.-Y., Mischoulon, D., Freeman, M. P., Matsuoka, Y., Hibbeln, J., Belmaker, R. H., & Su, K.-P. (2012). Are omega-3 fatty acids antidepressants or just mood-improving agents? The effect depends upon diagnosis, supplement preparation, and severity of depression. *Molecular Psychiatry, 17,* 1161.

Lincoln, A. (1841/1953). To John T. Stuart. In R. P. Basler, M. D. Pratt, & L. A. Dunlap (Eds.), *The collected works of Abraham Lincoln* (Vol. 1, p. 230). New Brunswick, NJ: Rutgers University Press.

Linder, D. (2004). The John Hinckley trial. [Hinckley's communications with Jodie Foster]. Retrieved from http://www.law.umkc.edu/faculty/projects/ftrials/hinckley/hinckleytrial.html

Lindwall, M., Gerber, M., Jonsdottir, I. H., Börjesson, M., & Ahlborg, G., Jr. (2014). The relationships of change in physical activity with change in depression, anxiety, and burnout: A longitudinal study of Swedish healthcare workers. *Health Psychology, 33,* 1309–1318. Retrieved from http://dx.doi.org/10.1037/a0034402

Linehan, M. M., Comtois, K. A., Murray, A. M., Brown, M. Z., Gallop, R. J., Heard, H. L.,…Lindenboim, M. S. (2006). Two-year randomized controlled trial and follow-up of dialectical behavior therapy vs. therapy by experts for suicidal behaviors and borderline personality disorder. *Archives of General Psychiatry, 63,* 757–766.

Linehan, M. M., Korslund, K. E., Harned, M. S., Gallop, R., Lungu, A., Neacsiu A.,…Murray-Gregory, A. M. (2015). Dialectical behavior therapy for high suicide risk in individuals with borderline personality disorder: A randomized clinical trial and component analysis. *JAMA Psychiatry, 72,* 475–482. doi:10.1001/jamapsychiatry.2014.3039

Ling, W., Casadonte, P., Bigelow, G., Kampman, K. M., Patkar, A., Bailey, G. L.,…Beebe, K. L. (2011). Buprenorphine implants for treatment of opioid dependence: A randomized controlled trial. *Journal of the American Medical Association, 304,* 1576–1583.

Lipsitz, J. D., & Markowitz, J. C. (2013). Mechanisms of change in interpersonal therapy (IPT). *Clinical Psychology Review, 33,* 1134–1147.

Lipton, E., Savage, C., & Shane, S. (2011, January 9). Arizona suspect's recent acts offer hints of alienation. *The New York Times.* Retrieved from http://www.nytimes.com/2011/01/09/us/politics/09shooter.html?pagewanted=all

Lister-Landman, K. M., Domoff, S. E., & Dubow, E. F. (2015). The role of compulsive texting in adolescents' academic functioning. *Psychology of Popular Media Culture.* Advance online publication. Retrieved from http://dx.doi.org/10.1037/ppm0000100

Littleton, H., & Henderson, C. E. (2009). If she is not a victim, does that mean she was not traumatized? Evaluation of predictors of PTSD symptomatology among college rape victims. *Violence Against Women, 15,* 148–167.

Liu B., Zhang, Y., Zhang, L., & Lingjiang, L. (2014). Repetitive transcranial magnetic stimulation as an augmentative strategy for treatment-resistant depression: A meta-analysis of randomized, double-blind and sham-controlled study. *BMC Psychiatry, 14,* 342. doi:10.1186/s12888-014-0342-4

Liu, H., Prause, N., Wyatt, G. E., Williams, J. K., Chin, D., Davis, T., Loeb, T.,…Myers, H. F. (2015). Development of a composite trauma exposure risk index. *Psychological Assessment, 27,* 965–974. doi:10.1037/pas000006

Liu, R. T., & Alloy, L B. (2010). Stress generation in depression: A systematic review of the empirical literature and recommendations for future study. *Clinical Psychology Review, 30,* 582–593.

Liu, R. T., & Miller, I. (2014). Life events and suicidal ideation and behavior: A systematic review. *Clinical Psychology Review, 34,* 181–192. Retrieved from http://dx.doi.org/10.1016/j.cpr.2014.01.006

Lobbestael, J., & Arntz, A. (2009). Emotional, cognitive and physiological correlates of abuse-related stress in borderline and antisocial personality disorder. *Behaviour Research and Therapy, 34,* 571–586. doi:10.1016/j.brat.2009.09.015

Locke, A. E., Kahali, B., Berndt, S. I., Justice, A. E., Pers, T. H., Day, F. R.,…Speliotes, E. K. (2015). Genetic studies of body mass index yield new insights for obesity biology. *Nature, 518*(7538), 197. doi:10.1038/nature14177

Lockwood, L. E., Su, S., & Youssef, N. A. (2015). The role of epigenetics in depression and suicide: A platform for gene–environment interactions. *Psychiatry Research, 228,* 235–242. doi:10.1016/j.psychres.2015.05.07

Loening-Baucke, V. (2002). Encopresis. *Current Opinions in Pediatrics, 14,* 570–575.

Loftus, E. F. (1996). The myth of repressed memory and the realities of science. *Clinical Psychology: Science and Practice, 3,* 356–365.

Logan, C. (2008). Sexual deviance in females. In D. R. Laws and W. T. O'Donohue (Eds.), *Sexual deviance: Theory, assessment, and treatment* (2nd ed., pp. 486–507). New York, NY: Guilford Press.

Logan, J., Hall, J., & Karch, D. (2011). Suicide categories by patterns of known risk factors: A latent class analysis. *Archives of General Psychiatry, 68,* 935–941. doi:10.1001/archgenpsychiatry.2011.85

Lohr, J. M., Lilienfeld, S. O., & Rosen, G. M. (2012). Anxiety and its treatment: Promoting science–based practice. *Journal of Anxiety Disorders, 26,* 719–727. doi:10.1016/j.janxdis.2012.06.007

Lohr, J. M. (2011). What is (and what is not) the meaning of evidence-based psychosocial intervention? *Clinical Psychology: Science and Practice, 18,* 100–104. doi:10.1111/j.1468-2850.2011.01240.x

Longmire, C. V. F., Drye, L. T., Frangakis, C. E., Martin, B. K., Meinert, C. L., Mintzer J. E., & DIADS-2 Research Group. (2013). Is sertraline treatment or depression remission in depressed Alzheimer patients associated with improved caregiver well-being? Depression in Alzheimer's disease study 2. *The American Journal of Geriatric Psychiatry, 22,* 14–24. doi:10.1016/j.jagp.2013.02.014

Lönnqvista, J. E., & Deters, F. G. (2016). Facebook friends, subjective well-being, social support, and personality. *Computers in Human Behavior, 55,* 113–120. doi:10.1016/j.chb.2015.09.002

Lonsdorf, T. B., Weike, A. I., Nikamo, P., Schalling, M., Hamm, A. O., & Ohman, A. (2009). Genetic gating of human fear learning and extinction: Possible implications for gene-environment interaction in anxiety disorder. *Psychological Science, 20,* 198–206. doi:10.1111/j.1467-9280.2009.02280.x

López, I., Rivera, R., Ramirez, R., Guarnaccia, P. J., Canino, G., & Bird, H. R. (2009). Ataques de nervios and their psychiatric correlates in Puerto Rican children from two different contexts. *The Journal of Nervous and Mental Disease, 297,* 923–929. doi:10.1097/NMD.0b013e3181c2997d

López, S. R., Barrio, C., Kopelowicz, A., & Vega, W. A. (2012). From documenting to eliminating disparities in mental health care for Latinos. *American Psychologist, 67,* 511–523. doi:10.1037/a0029737

Lopez, S. R., Nelson, H. K., Polo, A. J., Jenkins, J. H., Karno, M., Vaughn, C.,…Snyder, K. S. (2004). Ethnicity, expressed emotion, attributions, and course of schizophrenia: Family warmth matters. *Journal of Abnormal Psychology, 113,* 428–439.

LoPiccolo, J. (2011). Most difficult to treat: Sexual desire disorders. *PsycCRITIQUES, 56*(21).

Lopresti, A. L., Maes, M., Maker, G. L., Hood, S. D., & Drummond, P. D. (2014). Curcumin for the treatment of major depression: A randomised, double-blind, placebo controlled study. *Journal of Affective Disorders, 167,* 368–375. doi:10.1016/j.jad.2014.06.001

Lorenzo-Luaces, L., DeRubeis, R. J., & Webb, C. A. (2014). Client characteristics as moderators of the relation between the therapeutic alliance and outcome in cognitive therapy for depression. *Journal of Consulting and Clinical Psychology, 82,* 368–373. doi:10.1037/a0035994

Lorenzo-Luaces, L., German, R. E., & DeRubeis, R. J. (2015). It's complicated: The relation between cognitive change procedures, cognitive change, and symptom change in cognitive therapy for depression. *Clinical Psychology Review, 41,* 3–15. doi:10.1016/j.cpr.2014.12.003

Lothane, Z. (2006). Freud's legacy: Is it still with us? *Psychoanalytic Psychology, 23,* 285–301.

Lovaas, O. I. (1987). Behavioral treatment and normal educational and intellectual functioning in young autistic children. *Journal of Consulting and Clinical Psychology, 55,* 3–9.

Lovaas, O. I., Koegel, R. L., & Schreibman, L. (1979). Stimulus overselectivity in autism: A review of the research. *Psychological Bulletin, 86,* 1236–1254.

Love, S., & Spillantini, M. G. (2011). Unpicking frontotemporal lobar degeneration. *Brain, 134,* 2453–2455. doi:10.1093/brain/awr176

Lowe, J. K., Werling, D. M., Constantino, N. N., Cantor, R. M., & Geschwind, D. H. (2015). Social responsiveness, an autism endophenotype: Genomewide significant linkage to two regions on chromosome 8. *American Journal of Psychiatry, 172,* 266–275. Retrieved from http://dx.doi.org/10.1176/appi.ajp.2014.14050576

Lowe, J. R., & Widiger, T. A. (2008). Personality disorders. In J. E. Maddux & B. A. Winstead (Eds.), *Psychopathology: Foundations for a contemporary understanding* (2nd ed., pp. 223–250). New York, NY: Routledge.

Lowe, S. R., Chan, C. S., & Rhodes, J. E. (2010). Prehurricane perceived social support protects against psychological distress: A longitudinal analysis of low-income mothers. *Journal of Consulting and Clinical Psychology, 78,* 551–560. doi:10.1037/a0018317

Lu, H.-Y., & Hou, H.-Y. (2009). Testing a model of the predictors and consequences of body dissatisfaction. *Body Image, 6,* 19–23.

Lu, T., Aron, L., Zullo, J., Pan, Y., Kim, H., Chen, Y., & Yankner, B. A. (2014). REST and stress resistance in ageing and Alzheimer's disease. *Nature, 507,* 448–454. doi:10.1038/nature13163

Lubell, S. (2004, February 19). On therapist's couch, a jolt of virtual reality. *The New York Times,* p. G5.

Luczak, S. E., Glatt, S. J., & Wall, T. J. (2006). Meta-analyses of ALDH2 and ADH1B with alcohol dependence in Asians. *Psychological Bulletin, 132,* 607–621.

Lue, T. F., Giuliano, F., Montorsi, F., Rosen, R. C., Andersson, K. E., Althof, S., ... Wagner, G. (2010). Summary of the recommendations on sexual dysfunctions in men. *Journal of Sexual Medicine, 7,* 6–23.

Luijendijk, H. J., van den Berg, J. F., Marieke, J. H. J., Dekker, M. D., van Tuijl, H. R., Otte, W., ... Tiemeier, H. (2008). Incidence and recurrence of late-life depression. *Archives of General Psychiatry, 65,* 1394–1401.

Luo, M., & McIntire, M. (2013, December 21). When the right to bear arms includes the mentally ill. *The New York Times,* pp. A1, A30.

Luoma, J. B., Martin, C. E., & Pearson, J. L. (2002). Contact with mental health and primary care providers before suicide: A review of the evidence. *American Journal of Psychiatry, 159,* 909–916.

Lupski, J. R. (2007). Structural variation in the human genome. *New England Journal of Medicine, 356,* 1169–1171.

Lutz, W., Schiefele, A. K., Wucherpfennig, F., Rubel, J., & Stulz, N. (2015). Clinical effectiveness of cognitive behavioral therapy for depression in routine care: A propensity score based comparison between randomized controlled trials and clinical practice. *Journal of Affective Disorders, 25,* 150–158. doi:10.1016/j.jad.2015.08.072

Luxton, D. D., Pruitt, L. D., & Osenbach, J. E. (2014). Best practices for remote psychological assessment via telehealth technologies. *Professional Psychology: Research and Practice, 45,* 27–35. doi:10.1037/a0034547

Lv, K. H., Janni, E., Wrede, R., Sedem, M., Donker, T., Carlbring, P., ... Andersson, G. (2014). Experiences of a guided smartphone-based behavioral activation therapy for depression: A qualitative study. *Internet Interventions, 2,* 60–68. Retrieved from http://dx.doi.org/10.1016/j.invent.2014.12.002

Lymburner, J. A., & Roesch, R. (1999). The insanity defense: Five years of research (1993–1997). *International Journal of Law and Psychiatry, 22,* 213–240.

Lynch, F. L., Dickerson, J. F., Clarke, G., Vitiello, B., Porta, G., Wagner, K. D., ... Brent, D. (2011). Incremental cost-effectiveness of combined therapy vs. medication only for youth with selective serotonin reuptake inhibitor–resistant depression: Treatment of SSRI-l. *Archives of General Psychiatry, 68,* 253–262. doi:10.1001/archgenpsychiatry.2011.9

Lynn, S. J., Lilienfeld, S. O., Merckelbach, H., Giesbrecht, T., McNally, R. J., Loftus, E. F., ... Malaktaris, A. (2014). The trauma model of dissociation: Inconvenient truths and stubborn fictions. Comment on Dalenberg et al. (2012). *Psychological Bulletin, 40,* 896–910. doi:10.1037/a0035570

Ma, J., Ward, E. M., Siegel, R. L., & Jemal, A. (2015). Temporal trends in mortality in the United States, 1969–2013. *Journal of the American Medical Association, 314,* 1731–1739. doi:10.1001/jama.2015.12319.sciencedaily.com/releases/2015/10/151029111924.htm

Mabe, A. G., Forney, K. J., &. Keel, P. K. (2014). Do you "like" my photo? Facebook use maintains eating disorder risk. *International Journal of Eating Disorders, 47,* 516–523. doi:10.1002/eat.22254

MacDonald, R., Parry-Cruwys, D., Dupere, S., & Ahearn, W. (2014). Assessing progress and outcome of early intensive behavioral intervention for toddlers with autism. *Research in Developmental Disabilities, 35,* 3632–3644. doi:10.1016/j.ridd.2014.08.036

Macey, P. M., Kumar, R., Woo, M. A., Valladares, E. M., Yan-Go, F. L., & Harper, R. M. (2008). Brain structural changes in obstructive sleep apnea. *Sleep, 31,* 967.

Macey, P. M., Kumar, R., Woo, M. A., Yan-Go, F. L., & Harper, R. M. (2013). Heart rate responses to autonomic challenges in obstructive sleep apnea. *PLOS ONE, 8,* e76631. doi:10.1371/journal.pone.0076631

Mackenzie, C. S., El-Gabalawy, R., Chou, K. L., & Sareen, J. (2014). Prevalence and predictors of persistent versus remitting mood, anxiety, and substance disorders in a national sample of older adults. *American Journal of Geriatric Psychiatry, 22,* 854–865. doi:10.1016/j.jagp.2013.02.007

MacKillop, J., McGeary, J. E., & Ray, L. A. (2010). Genetic influences on addiction: Alcoholism as an exemplar. In D. Ross, P. Collins, & D. Spurrett (Eds.), *What is addiction?* (pp. 53–98). Cambridge, MA: MIT Press.

MacLaren, V. V., Best, L. A., Dixon, M. J., & Harrigan, K. A. (2011). Problem gambling and the five factor model in university students. *Personality and Individual Differences, 50,* 335–338. doi:10.1016/j.paid.2010.10.011

Maenner, M. J., Rice, C. E., Arneson, C. L., Cunniff, C., Schieve, L. A., Carpenter, L. A., ... Durkin, M. S. (2014). Potential impact of DSM-5 criteria on autism spectrum disorder prevalence estimates. *JAMA Psychiatry, 71,* 292–300. doi:10.1001/jamapsychiatry.2013.3893

Maggi, M. (2012). *Hormonal therapy for male sexual dysfunction.* Hoboken, NJ: Wiley.

Maher, B. (2007). Fragile X fixed in mice. *Nature News.* Retrieved from http://www.nature.com/news/2007/191207/full/news.2007.386.html

Maher, W. B., & Maher, B. A. (1985). Psychopathology. I. From ancient times to the eighteenth century. In G. A. Kimble & K. Schlesinger (Eds.), *Topics in the history of psychology* (Vol. 2, pp. 251–294). Hillsdale, NJ: Erlbaum.

Mahler, M., & Kaplan, L. (1977). Developmental aspects in the assessment of narcissistic and so-called borderline personalities. In P. Hartocollis (Ed.), *Borderline personality disorders: The concept, the syndrome, the patient* (pp. 71–85). New York, NY: International Universities Press.

Mahler, M. S., Pine, F., & Bergman, A. (1975). The borderline syndrome: The role of the mother in the genesis and psychic structure of the borderline personality. *International Journal of Psychoanalysis, 56,* 163–177.

Mahone, E. M., Crocetti, D., Ranta, M. E., Gaddis, A., Cataldo, M., Slifer, K. J., ... Mostofsky, H. (2011). A preliminary neuroimaging study of preschool children with ADHD. *The Clinical Neuropsychologist, 25,* 1009–1028. doi:10.1080/13854046.2011.580784

Mahoney, A. E. J., Mackenzie, A., Williams, A. D., Smith, J., & Andrews, G. (2014). Internet cognitive behavioural treatment for obsessive compulsive disorder: A randomised controlled trial. *Behaviour Research and Therapy, 63,* 99–106. doi:10.1016/j.brat.2014.09.012

Maia, T. V., & Cano-Colino, M. (2015). The role of serotonin in orbitofrontal function and obsessive-compulsive disorder. *Clinical Psychological Science, 3,* 460–482. doi:10.1177/2167702614566809

Maier, S. F., & Seligman, M. E. P. (1976). Learned helplessness: Theory and evidence. *Journal of Experimental Psychology (General), 105,* 3–46.

Maikovich-Fong, A. K., & Jaffee, S. R. (2010). Sex differences in childhood sexual abuse characteristics and victims' emotional and behavioral problems: Findings from a National Sample of Youth. *Child Abuse and Neglect, 34,* 429–437.

Maina, G., Rosso, G., & Bogetto, F. (2009). Brief dynamic therapy combined with pharmacotherapy in the treatment of major depressive disorder: Long-term results. *Journal of Affective Disorders, 114,* 200–207. doi:10.1016/j.jad.2008.07.010

Making sad sense of child abuse. (2013, December 27). *ScienceDaily.* Retrieved from http://www.sciencedaily.com/releases/2013/12/131223181821.htm

Malamuth, N. M., Huppin, M., & Paul, B. (2005). Sexual coercion. In D. M. Buss (Ed.), *The handbook of evolutionary psychology* (pp. 394–418). Hoboken, NJ: Wiley.

Maldonado, J. R., Butler, L. D., & Spiegel, D. (1998). Treatments for dissociative disorders. In P. E. Nathan & J. M. Gorman (Eds.), *A guide to treatments that work* (pp. 423–446). New York, NY: Oxford University Press.

Maletzky, B. M. (1980). Assisted covert sensitization in the treatment of exhibitionism. *Journal of Consulting and Clinical Psychology, 48,* 306–312.

Maletzky, B. M., & Steinhauser, C. (2002). A 25-year follow-up of cognitive/behavioral therapy with 7,275 sexual offenders. *Behavior Modification, 26*(2), 123–147.

Malhotra, D., McCarthy, S., Michaelson, J. J., Vacic, V., Burdick, K. E., Yoon, S., ... Sebat, J. (2011). High frequencies of de novo CNVs in bipolar disorder and schizophrenia. *Neuron, 72,* 951. doi:10.1016/j.neuron.2011.11.007

Malinauskas, B. M., Raedeke, T. D., Aeby, V. G., Smith, J. L., & Dallas, M. B. (2006). Dieting practices, weight perceptions, and body composition: A comparison of normal weight, overweight, and obese college females. *Nutrition Journal, 5,* 11.

Mammen, G., & Faulkner, G. (2013). Physical activity and the prevention of depression: A systematic review of prospective studies. *American Journal of Preventive Medicine, 45,* 649–657.

Manassis, K. (2013). Empirically supported psychosocial treatments. In C. A. Essau & T. H. Ollendick (Eds.), *The Wiley-Blackwell handbook of the treatment of childhood and adolescent anxiety* (pp. 207–228). Hoboken, NJ: John Wiley.

Mandell, D., Siegle, G. J., Shutt, L., Feldmiller, J., & Thase, M. E. (2014). Neural substrates of trait ruminations in depression. *Journal of Abnormal Psychology, 123,* 35–48. doi:10.1037/a0035834

Mann, D. (2013, December 4). More than 6 percent of U.S. teens take psychiatric meds: Survey. Retrieved from http://www.webmd.com/mental-health/news/20131204/more-than-6-percent-of-us-teens-take-psychiatric-meds-survey?src=RSS_PUBLIC

Mann, K., Vollstädt-Klein, S., Leménager, T., Fauth-Bühler, M. H. D., Hoffmann, S., Zimmermann, U. S., Kiefer, F., ... Smolka, M. N. (2014). Predicting naltrexone response in alcohol-dependent patients: The contribution of functional magnetic resonance imaging. *Alcoholism: Clinical and Experimental Research, 38,* 2754–2762. doi:10.1111/acer.12546.

Mapes, D. (2013, September 16). "Fat" comment report highlights beauty queen body issues. *Today.com.* Retrieved from http://www.today.com/health/fat-comment-report-highlights-beauty-queen-body-issues-8C11131587

Marcantonio, E. R., Ngo, L. H., O'Connor, M., Jones, R. N., Crane, P. K., Metzger, E. D., ... Inouye, S. K. (2014). Prospective validation of a brief diagnostic interview for delirium in geriatric, hospitalized patients. *Annals of Internal Medicine, 161,* 554. Retrieved from http://dx.doi.org/10.7326/M14-0865

March, J. S., & Vitiello, B. (2009). Clinical messages from the Treatment for Adolescents with Depression Study (TADS). *American Journal of Psychiatry, 166,* 1118–1123. doi:10.1176/appi.ajp.2009.08101606

Marchant, J. (2016, January 10). A placebo treatment for pain. *The New York Times Review,* p. 5.

Marcus, D. K., O'Connell, D., Norris, A. L., & Sawaqdeh, A. (2014). Is the Dodo bird endangered in the 21st century? A meta-analysis of treatment comparison studies. *Clinical Psychology Review, 34,* 519–530. doi:10.1016/j.cpr.2014.08.001

Marin, J. M., Agusti, A., Villar, I., Forner, M., Nieto, D., Carrizo, S. J.,... Jelic, S. (2012). Association between treated and untreated obstructive sleep apnea and risk of hypertension. *Journal of the American Medical Association, 307,* 2169–2176. doi:10.1001/jama.2012.

Marion, I. J. (2005, December). The neurobiology of cocaine addiction. *Science Practice Perspectives, National Institute on Drug Abuse, 3*(1), 25–31.

Mark, R. E., Muselaers, N., Scholten, H., van Boxtel, A., & Eerenberg, T. (2014). Short-term cognitive effects after recovery from a delirium in a hospitalized elderly sample. *Journal of Nervous & Mental Disease, 202,* 732–737. doi:10.1097/NMD.0000000000000182

Markowitz, J. C., Petkova, E., Neria, Y., Van Meter, P. E., Zhao, Y., Hembree, E.,... Marshall, R. D. (2015). Is exposure necessary? A randomized clinical trial of interpersonal psychotherapy for PTSD. *JAMA Psychiatry, 520,* E7–E8. doi:10.1038/nature14040

Marlatt, G. A. (1978). Craving for alcohol, loss of control, and relapse: A cognitive-behavioral analysis. In P. E. Nathan, G. A. Marlatt, & T. Loberg (Eds.), *Alcoholism: New directions in behavioral research and treatment* (pp. 271–314). New York, NY: Plenum Press.

Marlatt, G. A., & Gordon, J. R. (1985). *Relapse prevention: Maintenance strategies in the treatment of addictive behaviors.* New York, NY: Guilford Press.

Marmar, C. R., Schlenger, W., Henn-Haase, C., Qian, M., Purchia, E., Li, M.,... Kulka, R. A. (2015). Course of posttraumatic stress disorder 40 years after the Vietnam War: Findings from the National Vietnam Veterans Longitudinal Study. *JAMA Psychiatry, 72,* 875–881. doi:10.1001/jamapsychiatry.2015.0803

Marshal, M. P. (2003). For better or for worse? The effects of alcohol use on marital functioning. *Clinical Psychology Review, 23,* 959–997.

Marshall, W. L., & Marshall, L. E. (2015). Psychological treatment of the paraphilias: A review and appraisal of effectiveness. *Current Psychiatry Reports: Topical Collection on Sexual Disorders, 17,* 47.

Mart, E. G. (2003). Munchausen's syndrome by proxy reconsidered. *Child Maltreatment: Journal of the American Professional Society of the Abuse of Children, 8,* 72–73.

Mårtensson, B., Pettersson, A., Berglund, L., & Ekselius, L. (2015). Bright white light therapy in depression: A critical review of the evidence. *Journal of Affective Disorders, 182,* 1–7. doi:10.1016/j.jad.2015.04.013

Martin, E. K., Taft, C. T., & Resick, P. A. (2007). A review of marital rape. *Aggression and Violent Behavior, 12,* 329–347.

Martin, S. A., Atlantis, E., Lange, K., Taylor, A. W., O'Loughlin, P., & Wittert, G. A. (2014). Predictors of sexual dysfunction incidence and remission in men. *The Journal of Sexual Medicine, 11,* 1136–1147. doi:10.1111/jsm.12483

Martín-Blanco, A., Ferrer, M., Soler, J., Salazar, J., Vega, D., Andión, O.,... Pascual, J. C. (2014). Association between methylation of the glucocorticoid receptor gene, childhood maltreatment, and clinical severity in borderline personality disorder. *Journal of Psychiatric Research, 57,* 34–40. doi:10.1016/j.jpsychires.2014.06.011

Martinez, D., Greene, K., Broft, A., Kumar, D., Liu, F., Narendran, R.,... Kleber, H. D. (2009). Lower level of endogenous dopamine in patients with cocaine dependence: Findings from PET imaging of D2/D3 receptors following acute dopamine depletion export. *American Journal of Psychiatry, 166,* 1170–1177. doi:10.1176/appi.ajp.2009.08121801

Martinez, M. A., & Craighead, L. W. (2015). Toward person(ality)-centered treatment: How consideration of personality and individual differences in anorexia nervosa may improve treatment outcome. *Clinical Psychology: Science and Practice, 22,* 296–314. doi:10.1111/cpsp.12111

Martins, R. K., & McNeil, D. W. (2009). Review of motivational interviewing in promoting health behaviors. *Clinical Psychology Review, 29,* 283–293. doi:10.1016/j.cpr.2009.02.001

Martinsen, K. D., Kendall, P. C., Stark, K., & Neumer, S.-P. (2014). Prevention of anxiety and depression in children: Acceptability and feasibility of the transdiagnostic emotion program. *Cognitive and Behavioral Practice, 23,* 1–13. doi:10.1016/j.cbpra.2014.06.005

Marx, R. F., & Didziulis, V. (2009, March 1). A life, interrupted. *The New York Times,* pp. CY1, CY7.

Marzano, L., Bardill, A., Fields, B., Herd, K., Veale, D., Grey, N., & Moran, P. (2015). The application of mHealth to mental health: Opportunities and challenges. *The Lancet Psychiatry, 2,* 942–948. doi:10.1016/S2215-0366(15)00268-0

Masheb, R. M., Grilo, C. M., & Rolls, B. J. (2011). A randomized controlled trial for obesity and binge eating disorder: Low-energy-density dietary counseling and cognitive-behavioral therapy. *Behaviour Research and Therapy, 49,* 821–829. doi:10.1016/j.brat.2011.09.006

Masi, G., Mucci, M., & Millepiedi, S. (2001). Separation anxiety disorder in children and adolescents: Epidemiology, diagnosis, and management. *CNS Drugs, 15*(2), 93–104.

Mason, B. J., Crean, R., Goodell, V., Light, J. M., Quello, S., Shadan, F.,... Rao, S. (2012). A proof-of-concept randomized controlled study of gabapentin: Effects on cannabis use, withdrawal and executive function deficits in cannabis-dependent adults. *Neuropsychopharmacology, 37,* 1689–1698. doi:10.1038/npp.2012.37:1689

Mason, P. T., & Kreger, R. (1998). *Stop walking on eggshells.* Oakland, CA: New Harbinger Publications.

Mast, R. C., & Smith, A. B. (2012). Elimination disorders: Enuresis and encopresis. In W. M. Klykyo & J. Kay (Eds.), *Clinical child psychiatry* (pp. 305–328). New York, NY: Wiley Interscience.

Masters, M. C., Morris, J. C., & Roe, C. M. (2015). "Noncognitive" symptoms of early Alzheimer disease. *Neurology.* Advance online publication. Retrieved from http://dx.doi.org/10.1212/WNL.0000000000001238

Masters, W. H., & Johnson, V. E. (1970). *Human sexual inadequacy.* Boston, MA: Little, Brown.

Mataix-Cols, D., Frost, R. O., Pertusa, A., Clark, L. A., Saxena, S., Leckman, J. F.,... Wilhelm, S. (2010). Hoarding disorder: A new diagnosis for DSM-V? *Depression and Anxiety, 27,* 556–572. doi:10.1002/da.20693

Matson, J. J., & Shoemaker, M. (2009). Intellectual disability and its relationship to autism spectrum disorders. *Research in Developmental Disabilities, 30,* 1107–1114. doi:10.1016/j.ridd.2009.06.003

Matson, J. L., & Williams, L. W. (2013). The making of a field: The development of comorbid psychopathology research for persons with intellectual disabilities and autism. *Research in Developmental Disabilities, 35,* 234–238. doi:10.1016/j.ridd.2013.09.043

Mattheisen, M., Samuels, J. F., Wang, Y., Greenberg, B. D., Fyer, A. J., McCracken, J. T.,... Nestadt, G. (2014). Genome-wide association study in obsessive-compulsive disorder: Results from the OCGAS. *Molecular Psychiatry, 20,* 337–344. doi:10.1038/mp.2014.43

Matthews, B. R. (2014, January 1). Vitamin E outpaces memantine in mild-to-moderate Alzheimer disease. *NEJM Journal Watch.* Retrieved from http://www.jwatch.org/na33250/2014/01/07/vitamin-e-outpaces-memantine-mild-moderate-alzheimer?query=etoc_jwneuro

Matthews, K. A. (2013). Matters of the heart: Advancing psychological perspectives on cardiovascular diseases. *Perspectives on Psychological Science, 8,* 676–678. doi:10.1177/1745691613506908

Mauri, L. (2012). Why we still need randomized trials to compare effectiveness [Editorial]. *New England Journal of Medicine, 366,* 1538–1540.

Maxwell, L., & Scott, G. (2014). A review of the role of radical feminist theories in the understanding of rape myth acceptance. *Journal of Sexual Aggression, 20,* 40–54.

May, P. A., Baete, A., Russo, J., Elliott, A. J., Blankenship, J., Kalberg, W. O.,... Hoyme, H. E. (2014). Prevalence and characteristics of fetal alcohol spectrum disorders. *Pediatrics, 13,* 855. doi:10.1542/peds.2013-3319

Mazina, V., Gerdts, J., Trinh, S., Ankenman, K., Ward, T., Dennis, M. Y.,... Bernier R. (2015). Epigenetics of autism-related impairment: Copy number variation and maternal infection. *Journal of Developmental & Behavioral Pediatrics, 36,* 61. Retrieved from http://dx.doi.org/10.1097/DBP.0000000000000126

McCabe, M. P., & Connaughton, C. (2014). Psychosocial factors associated with male sexual difficulties. *Journal of Sex Research, 51,* 31–42.

McCain, N. L., Gray, D. P., Elswick, R. K., Jr., Robins, J. W., Tuck, I., Walter, J. M.,... Ketchum, J. M. (2008). A randomized clinical trial of alternative stress management interventions in persons with HIV infection. *Journal of Consulting and Clinical Psychology, 76,* 431–441.

McCall, C., & Winkelman, J W. (2015). Use of hypnotics to treat sleep problems in the elderly. *Psychiatric Annals, 45,* 342–347. doi:10.3928/00485713-20150626-05

McCarthy, B. W., Ginsberg, R. L., & Fucito, L. M. (2006). Resilient sexual desire in heterosexual couples. *Family Journal: Counseling and Therapy for Couples and Families, 14*(1), 59–64.

McCarthy-Jones, S., Trauer, T., Mackinnon, A., Sims, E., Thomas, N., & Copolov, D. L. (2014). A new phenomenological survey of auditory hallucinations: Evidence for subtypes and implications for theory and practice. *Schizophrenia Bulletin, 40,* S275–S284.

McClintock, S. M., Husain, M. M., Wisniewski, S. R., Nierenberg, A. A., Stewart, J. W., Trivedi, M. H.,... Rush, J. (2011). Residual symptoms in depressed outpatients who respond by 50% but do not remit to antidepressant medication. *Journal of Clinical Psychopharmacology, 31,* 180. doi:10.1097/JCP.0b013e31820ebd2c

McCord, C. E., Elliott, T. R., Wendel, M. L., Brossart, D. F., Cano, M. A., Gonzalez, G.,... Burdine, J. (2011). Community capacity and teleconference counseling in rural Texas. *Professional Psychology: Research and Practice, 42,* 521–527. doi:10.1037/a0025296

McCord, W., & McCord, J. (1964). *The psychopath: An essay on the criminal mind.* New York, NY: D. Van Nostrand.

McCrae, C. S., Bramoweth, A. D., Williams, J., Roth, A., & Mosti, C. (2014). Impact of brief cognitive behavioral treatment for insomnia on health care utilization and costs. *Journal of Clinical Sleep Medicine, 15,* 127–135. doi:10.5664/jcsm.3436.

McElroy, S. L., Hudson, J. J., Mitchell, J. E., Wilfley, D., Ferreira-Cornwell, M. C., Gao, J.,... Gasior, M. (2015). Efficacy and safety of lisdexamfetamine for treatment of adults with moderate to severe binge-eating disorder: A randomized clinical trial. *JAMA Psychiatry, 72,* 235–246. doi:10.1001/jamapsychiatry.2014.2162

McEvoy, J. P., Byerly, M., Hamer, R. M., Dominik, R., Swartz, M. S., Rosenheck, R. A.,... Stroup, T. S. (2014). Effectiveness of paliperidone palmitate vs. haloperidol decanoate for maintenance treatment of schizophrenia: A randomized clinical trial. *Journal of the American Medical Association, 311,* 1978–1987. doi:10.1001/jama.2014.4310

McEvoy, J. P., Citrome, L., Hernandez, D., Cucchiaro, J., Hsu, J., Pikalov, A.,... Loebel, A. (2013). Effectiveness of lurasidone in patients with schizophrenia or schizoaffective disorder switched from other antipsychotics: A randomized, 6-week, open-label study. *Journal of Clinical Psychiatry, 74,* 170–179. doi:10.4088/JCP.12m07992

McEvoy, P. M., (2008). Effectiveness of cognitive behavioural group therapy for social phobia in a community clinic: A benchmarking study. *Behaviour Research and Therapy, 45,* 3030–3040.

McEvoy, P. M., Nathan, P., Rapee, R. M., & Campbell, B. N. C. (2012). Cognitive behavioural group therapy for social phobia: Evidence of transportability to community clinics. *Behaviour Research and Therapy, 50,* 258–265.

McEwen, B. S. (2013). The brain on stress: Toward an integrative approach to brain, body, and behavior. *Perspectives on Psychological Science, 8,* 6673–6753. doi:10.1177/1745691613506907

McFeeters, D., Boyda, D., & O'Neill, S. (2015). Patterns of stressful life events: Distinguishing suicide ideators from suicide attempters. *Journal of Affective Disorders, 175,* 192–198. doi:10.1016/j.jad.2014.12.034

McGillivray, J. A., & Kershaw, M. M. (2013). The impact of staff initiated referral and intervention protocols on symptoms of depression in people with mild intellectual disability. *Research in Developmental Disabilities, 34,* 730–738.

McGinnis, J. M. (2015). Mortality trends and signs of health progress in the United States: Improving understanding and action. *Journal of the American Medical Association, 314,* 1699–1700. doi:10.1001/jama.2015.12391

McGowin, D. F. (1993). *Living in the labyrinth: A personal journey through the maze of Alzheimer's.* New York, NY: Dell.

McGrath, J. J., Saha, S., Al-Hamzawi, A., Alonso, J., Bromet, E. J., Bruffaerts, R.,... Kessler, R. C. (2015). Psychotic experiences in the general population: A cross-national analysis based on 31,261 respondents from 18 countries. *JAMA Psychiatry, 72,* 697–705. doi:10.1001/jamapsychiatry.2015.0575.

McIntyre, R. S., Liauw, S., & Taylor, V. H. (2011). Aripiprazole in the treatment of anxiety, major depressive disorder, and bipolar depression/disorder. *Journal of Affective Disorders, 128,* S29–S36.

McKay D., Sookman, D., Neziroglu, F., Wilhelm, S., Stein, D. J., Kyriosf, M.,... Vealeh, D. (2014). Efficacy of cognitive-behavioral therapy for obsessive-compulsive disorder. *Psychiatry Research, 225,* 236–246.

McKee, B. (2003, September 4). As suburbs grow, so do waistlines. *The New York Times,* pp. F1, F 13.

McKellar, J., Stewart, E., & Humphreys, K. (2003). Alcoholics Anonymous involvement and positive alcohol-related outcomes: Cause, consequence, or just a correlate? A prospective 2-year study of 2,319 alcohol-dependent men. *Journal of Consulting and Clinical Psychology, 71,* 302–308.

McKenzie, K. (2011). Providing services in the United Kingdom to people with an intellectual disability who present behaviour which challenges: A review of the literature. *Research in Developmental Disabilities, 32,* 395–403. doi:10.1016/j.ridd.2010.12.001

McLawsen, J. E., Scalora, M. J., & Darrow, C. (2012). Civilly committed sex offenders: A description and interstate comparison of populations. *Psychology, Public Policy, and Law, 18,* 453–476. doi:10.1037/a0026116

McLean, C. P., & Anderson, E. R. (2009). Brave men and timid women? A review of the gender differences in fear and anxiety. *Clinical Psychology Review, 29,* 496–505. doi:10.1016/j.cpr.2009.05.003

McMillan, J. R. (2003). Dangerousness, mental disorder, and responsibility. *Journal of Medical Ethics, 29,* 232–235.

McNally, M. R., & Fremouw, W. J. (2014). Examining risk of escalation: A critical review of the exhibitionistic behavior literature. *Aggression and Violent Behavior, 19,* 474–485.

McNally, R. J., & Geraerts, E. (2009). A new solution to the recovered memory debate. *Perspectives on Psychological Science, 4,* 126–134. doi:10.1111/j.1745-6924.2009.01112.x

McNiel, D. E., Gregory, A. L., Lam, J. N., Binder, R. L., & Sullivan, G. R. (2003). Utility of decision support tools for assessing acute risk of violence. *Journal of Consulting and Clinical Psychology, 71,* 945–953.

McNiel, D. E., Lam, J. N., & Binder, R. L. (2000). Relevance of interrater agreement to violence risk assessment. *Journal of Consulting and Clinical Psychology, 68,* 1111–1115.

McNulty, J. K., & Fincham, F. D. (2012). Beyond positive psychology? Toward a contextual view of psychological processes and well-being. *American Psychologist, 67,* 101–110.

McParland, J. L., & Eccleston, C. (2013). "It's not fair": Social justice appraisals in the context of chronic pain. *Current Directions in Psychological Science, 22,* 484–489. doi:10.1177/0963721413496811

Mead, M. (1935). *Sex and temperament in three primitive societies.* New York, NY: Dell.

Meadows, G. N., Shawyer, F., Enticott, J. C., Graham, A. L., Judd, F., Martin, P. R.,... Segal, Z. (2014). Mindfulness-based cognitive therapy for recurrent depression: A translational research study with 2-year follow-up. *Australian & New Zealand Journal of Psychiatry, 48,* 743–755.

Mechelli, A., Riecher-Rössler, A., Meisenzahl, E. M., Tognin, S., Wood, S. J., Borgwardt, S. J.,... McGuire, P. (2011). Neuroanatomical abnormalities that predate the onset of psychosis: A multicenter study. *Archives of General Psychiatry, 68,* 489–495. doi:10.1001/archgenpsychiatry.2011.42

Medda, P., Perugi, G., Zanello, S., Ciuffa, M., & Cassano, G. B. (2009). Response to ECT in bipolar I, bipolar II and unipolar depression. *Journal of Affective Disorders, 118,* 55–59. doi:10.1111/j.1399-5618.2009.00702.x

Mednick, S. A., Parnas, J., & Schulsinger, F. (1987). The Copenhagen High-Risk project, 1962–86. *Schizophrenia Bulletin, 13,* 485–495.

Mednick, S. A., & Schulsinger, F. (1968). Some premorbid characteristics related to breakdown in children with schizophrenic mothers. In D. Rosenthal & S. S. Kety (Eds.), *The transmission of schizophrenia* (pp. 267–291). New York, NY: Pergamon Press.

Meek, S. E., Lemery-Chalfant, K., Jahromi, L. B., & Valiente, C. (2013). A review of gene–environment correlations and their implications for autism: A conceptual model. *Psychological Review, 120,* 497–521. doi:10.1037/a0033139

Meeks, T. W., Vahia, I. V., Lavretsky, H., Kulkarni, G., & Jeste, D. V. (2011). A tune in "A minor" can "B major": A review of epidemiology, illness course, and public health implications of subthreshold depression in older adults. *Journal of Affective Disorders, 129,* 126.

Meehl, P. E. (1962). Schizotaxia, schizotypy, schizophrenia. *American Psychologist, 17,* 827–838.

Meehl, P. E. (1972). A critical afterword. In I. I. Gottesman & J. Shields (Eds.), *Schizophrenia and genetics: A twin study vantage point* (pp. 367–415). New York, NY: Academic Press.

Meeter, M., Murre, J. M. J., Janssen, S. M. J., Birkenhager, T., & van den Broek, W. W. (2011). Retrograde amnesia after electroconvulsive therapy: A temporary effect? *Journal of Affective Disorders, 132,* 216–222. doi:10.1016/j.jad.2011.02.026

Mefford, H. C., Batshaw, M. L., & Hoffman, E. P. (2012). Genomics, intellectual disability, and autism. *New England Journal of Medicine, 366,* 733–743.

Mehlum, L., Tørmoen, A., Ramberg, M., Haga, E., Diep, L. M., Laberg, S.,... Grøholt, B. (2014). Dialectical behavior therapy for adolescents with repeated suicidal and self-harming behavior: A randomized trial. *Journal of the American Academy of Child and Adolescent Psychiatry, 53,* 1082–1091. doi:10.1016/j.jaac.2014.07.003

Mehta, D., Gonik, M., Klengel, T., Rex-Haffner, M., Menke, A., Rubelt, J.,... Binder, E. B. (2011). Using polymorphisms in FKBP5 to define biologically distinct subtypes of posttraumatic stress disorder: Evidence from endocrine and gene expression studies. *Archives of General Psychiatry, 68,* 901.

Mehta, V., De, A., & Balachandran, C. (2009). Dhat syndrome: A reappraisal. *Indian Journal of Dermatology, 54,* 89–90.

Meier, M. H., Caspi, A., Ambler, A., Harrington, H., Houts, R., Keefe, R. S. E.,... Moffitt, T. E. (2012). Persistent cannabis users show neuropsychological decline from childhood to midlife. *Proceedings of the National Academy of Sciences, 109,* E2657–E2664.

Meier, M. H., Slutske, W. S., Heath, A. C., & Martin, N. G. (2011). Sex differences in the genetic and environmental influences on childhood conduct disorder and adult antisocial behavior. *Journal of Abnormal Psychology, 120,* 377–388. doi:10.1037/a0022303

Meinzer, M. C., Pettit, J. W., & Viswesvaran, C. (2014). The co-occurrence of attention-deficit/hyperactivity disorder and unipolar depression in children and adolescents: A meta-analytic review. *Clinical Psychology Review, 34,* 595–607. doi:10.1016/j.cpr.2014.10.002

Melas, P. A., Rogdaki, M., Osby, U., Schalling, M., Lavebratt, C., & Ekstrom, T. J. (2012). Epigenetic aberrations in leukocytes of patients with schizophrenia: Association of global DNA methylation with antipsychotic drug treatment and disease onset. *The FASEB Journal, 6,* 2712–2718. doi:10.1096/fj.11-202069

Mellor, C. S. (1970). First rank symptoms of schizophrenia. *The British Journal of Psychiatry, 117,* 15–23. doi:10.1192/bjp.117.536.15

Melville, C. A., Johnson, P. C. D., Smiley, E., Simpson, N., Purves, D., McConnachie, A.,... Cooper, S.-A. (2016). Problem behaviours and symptom dimensions of psychiatric disorders in adults with intellectual disabilities: An exploratory and confirmatory factor analysis. *Research in Developmental Disabilities, 55,* 1–13. doi:10.1016/j.ridd.2016.03.007

Melville, J. D., & Naimark, D. (2002). Punishing the insane: The verdict of guilty but mentally ill. *Journal of the American Academy of Psychiatry and the Law, 30,* 553–555.

Menatti, A. R., Weeks, J. W., Levinson, C. A., & McGowan, M. M. (2013). Exploring the relationship between social anxiety and bulimic symptoms: Mediational effects of perfectionism among females. *Cognitive Therapy and Research, 37,* 914–922. doi:10.1007/s10608-013-9521-8

Mendez, J. L. (2005). Conceptualizing sociocultural factors within clinical and research contexts. *Clinical Psychology: Science and Practice, 12,* 434–437.

Menon, C. V., & Harter, S. L. (2012). Examining the impact of acculturative stress on body image disturbance among Hispanic college students. *Cultural Diversity and Ethnic Minority Psychology, 18,* 239–246. doi:10.1037/a0028638

Mercer, K. B., Orcutt, H. K., Quinn, J. F., Fitzgerald, C. A., Conneely, K. N., Barfield, R. T.,... Ressler, K. J. (2012). Acute and posttraumatic stress symptoms in a prospective gene x environment study of a university campus shooting. *Archives of General Psychiatry, 69*(1), 89–97. Retrieved from http://dx.doi.org/10.1001/archgenpsychiatry.2011.109

Merckelbach, H., Arntz, A., & de Jong, P. (1991). Conditioning experiences in spider phobics. *Behaviour Research and Therapy, 29,* 301–304.

Merckelbach, H., de Jong, P. J., Muris, P., & van den Hout, M. A. (1996). The etiology of specific phobias: A review. *Clinical Psychology Review, 16,* 337–361.

Merikangas, K. R., Akiskal, H. S., Angst, J., Greenberg, P. E., Hirschfeld, R. M. A., Petukhova, M., &. Kessler, R. C. (2007). Lifetime and 12-month prevalence of bipolar spectrum disorder in the National Comorbidity Survey Replication. *Archives of General Psychiatry, 64,* 543–552. doi:10.1001/archpsyc.64.5.543

Merikangas, K. R., He, J.-P., Burstein, M., Swendsen, J., Avenevoli, S., Case, B.,... Olfson, M. (2011). Service utilization for lifetime mental disorders in U.S. adolescents: Results of the National Comorbidity Survey–Adolescent Supplement (NCS-A). *Journal of the American Academy of Child & Adolescent Psychiatry, 50,* 32–45. doi:10.1016/j.jaac.2010.10.006

Merikangas, K. R., & Pato, M. (2009). Recent developments in the epidemiology of bipolar disorder in adults and children: Magnitude, correlates, and future directions. *Clinical Psychology: Science and Practice, 16,* 121–133. doi:10.1111/j.1468-2850.2009.01152.x

Merluzzi, A. (2015, February). Cognitive shields. *APS Observer, 28*(2), 21–24.

Merwin, R. M. (2011). Anorexia nervosa as a disorder of emotion regulation: Theory, evidence, and treatment implications. *Clinical Psychology: Science and Practice, 18,* 208–214. doi:10.1111/j.1468-2850.2011.01252

Messer, S. B. (2001). Empirically supported treatments: What's a nonbehaviorist to do? In B. D. Slife & R. N. Williams (Eds.), *Critical issues in psychotherapy: Translating new ideas into practice* (pp. 3–19). Thousand Oaks, CA: Sage.

Messer, S. B. (2013). Three mechanisms of change in psychodynamic therapy: Insight, affect, and alliance. *Psychotherapy, 50,* 408–412. doi:10.1037/a0032414

Mestel, R. (2012, December 9). Changes to the psychiatrists' bible, DSM: Some reactions. Retrieved from latimes.com

Meuret, A. E., Rosenfield, D., Wilhelm, F. H., Zhou, E., Conrad, A., Ritza, T., & Roth, W. T. (2011). Do unexpected panic attacks occur spontaneously? *Biological Psychiatry, 70,* 985–991. doi:10.1016/j.biopsych.2011.05.027

Mewton, L., Smith, J., Rossouw, P., & Andrews, G. (2014). Current perspectives on Internet-delivered cognitive behavioral therapy for adults with anxiety and related disorders. *Psychology Research and Behavior Management, 7,* 37–46.

Meyer, B., Yuen, K. S., Ertl, M., Polomac, N., Mulert, C., Büchel, C.,... Kalisch, R. (2015). Neural mechanisms of placebo anxiolysis. *Journal of Neuroscience, 35,* 7365–7373. doi:10.1523/JNEUROSCI.4793-14.2015

Meyer, G. J., Finn, S. E., Eyde, L. D., Kay, G. F., Moreland, K. L., Dies, R. R.,... Reed, G. M. (2001). Psychological testing and psychological assessment:

A review of evidence and issues. *American Psychologist, 56,* 128–165.
Meyer, I. H. (2003). Prejudice, social stress, and mental health in lesbian, gay, and bisexual populations: Conceptual issues and research evidence. *Psychological Bulletin, 129,* 674–697.
Meyers, L. (2007, February). "A struggle for hope." *Monitor on Psychology, 38*(2), 30–31.
Meyler, A., Keller, T. A., Cherkassky, V. L., Gabrieli, J. D. E., & Just, M. A. (2008). Modifying the brain activation of poor readers during sentence comprehension with extended remedial instruction: A longitudinal study of neuroplasticity. *Neuropsychologia, 46,* 2580–2592.
Micco, J. A., Hirshfeld-Becker, D. R., Henin, A., & Ehrenreich-May, J. (2013). Content specificity of threat interpretation in anxious and non-clinical children. *Cognitive Therapy and Research, 37,* 78–88.
Michal, M., Wiltink, J., Subic-Wrana, C., Zwerenz, R., Tuin, I., Lichy, M.,... Beutel, M. E. (2009). Prevalence, correlates, and predictors of depersonalization experiences in the German general population. *The Journal of Nervous and Mental Disease, 197,* 499–506. doi:10.1097/NMD.0b013e3181aacd94
Michaud, J.-P., Hallé, M., Lampron, A., Thériault, P., Préfontaine, P., Filali, M.,... Rivest, S. (2013). Toll-like receptor 4 stimulation with the detoxified ligand monophosphoryl lipid A improves Alzheimer's disease-related pathology. *PNAS, 110*(5), 1941–1946. doi:10.1073/pnas.1215165110
Michikyan, M., Subrahmanyam, K., & Dennis, J. (2014). Can you tell who I am? Neuroticism, extraversion, and online self-presentation among young adults. *Computers in Human Behavior, 33,* 179–183. Retrieved from http://dx.doi.org/10.1016/j.chb.20
Mihura, J. L., Meyer, G. J., Bombel, G., & Dumitrascu, N. (2015). Standards, accuracy, and questions of bias in Rorschach meta-analyses: Reply to Wood, Garb, Nezworski, Lilienfeld, and Duke (2015). *Psychological Bulletin, 141,* 250–260.
Mihura, J. L., Meyer, G. J., Dumitrascu, N., & Bombel, G. (2013). The validity of individual Rorschach variables: Systematic reviews and meta-analyses of the comprehensive system. *Psychological Bulletin, 139,* 548–605. doi:10.1037/a0029406
Miklowitz, D. J., & Johnson, S. L. (2009). Social and familial factors in the course of bipolar disorder: Basic processes and relevant interventions. *Clinical Psychology: Science and Practice, 16,* 281–296. doi:10.1111/j.1468-2850.2009.01166.x
Milad, R. R., & Quirk, G. J. (2002). Neurons in medial prefrontal cortex signal memory for fear extinction. *Nature, 420,* 70–74.
Miller, E. (1987). Hysteria: Its nature and explanation. *British Journal of Clinical Psychology, 26,* 163–173.
Miller, G. (2011). Predicting the psychological risks of war. *Science, 333,* 520–521. doi:10.1126/science.333.6042.520
Miller, G. (2012). How to talk about Alzheimer's risk. *Science, 337*(6096), 792. Retrieved from http://www.sciencemag.org/content/337/6096/792.summary
Miller, M., Swanson, S. A., Azrael, D., Pate, V., & Stürmer, T. (2014). Antidepressant dose, age, and the risk of deliberate self-harm. *JAMA Internal Medicine, 174,* 899–909. doi:10.1001/jamainternmed.2014.1053
Miller, T. W., Nigg, J. T., & Miller, R. L (2009). Attention deficit hyperactivity disorder in African American children: What can be concluded from the past ten years? *Clinical Psychology Review, 29,* 77–86. doi:10.1016/j.cpr.2008.10.001
Miller, W. R., & Hester, R. K. (1986). Inpatient alcoholism treatment: Who benefits? *American Psychologist, 41,* 794–805.
Miller, W. R., & Rollnick, S. (2002). *Motivational interviewing: Preparing people to change.* New York, NY: Guilford Press.
Miller-Perrin, C. L., Perrin, R. D., & Kocur, K. L. (2009). Parental physical and psychological aggression: Psychological symptoms in young adults. *Child Abuse & Neglect, 33,* 1–11. doi:10.1016/S0145-2134(97)00009-4
Millon, T. (1981). *Disorders of personality DSM-III: Axis II.* New York, NY: Wiley.
Millon, T. (1982). *Millon Clinical Multiaxial Inventory manual* (3rd ed.). Minneapolis, MN: National Computer Systems.
Millon, T. (2011). *Disorders of personality: Introducing a DSM/ICD spectrum from normal to abnormal* (3rd ed.). Hoboken, NJ: Wiley.
Mills, J. F., Kroner, D. F., & Morgan, R. (2011). *Clinician's guide to violence risk assessment.* New York, NY: Guilford Press.
Mills, P. D., Watts, B. V., Huh, T. J. W., Boar, S., & Kemp, J. (2013). Helping elderly patients to avoid suicide: A review of case reports from a national veterans affairs database. *Journal of Nervous & Mental Disease, 201,* 12–16. doi:10.1097/NMD.0b013e31827ab29c
Milrod, B., Leon, A. C., Busch, F., Rudden, M., Schwalberg, M., Clarkin, J., Aronson, A.,... Shear, M. K. (2007). A randomized controlled clinical trial of psychoanalytic psychotherapy for panic disorder. *American Journal of Psychiatry, 164,* 265–272.
Minarik, M. L., & Ahrens, A. H. (1996). Relations of eating and symptoms of depression and anxiety to the dimensions of perfectionism among undergraduate women. *Cognitive Research & Therapy, 20,* 155–169.
Miner, M. M. (2011). Erectile dysfunction and cardiovascular disease: A harbinger for cardiovascular events. *Journal of Andrology, 32,* 125–134.
Minerd, J., & Jasmer, R. (2006, April). Forty winks or more to make a healthier America. Retrieved from http://www.medpagetoday.com/PrimaryCare/SleepDisorders/tb/3009
Ming, D. L., & Burmeister, M. (2009). New insights into the genetics of addiction. *Nature Reviews Genetics, 10,* 225–231. doi:10.1038/nrg2536
Miniati, M., Mauri, M., Ciberti, A., Mariani, M. G., Marazziti, D., & Dell'Osso L. (2015). Psychopharmacological options for adult patients with anorexia nervosa. *CNS Spectrum, 6,* 1–9.
Minuchin, S., Rosman, B. L., & Baker, L. (1978). *Psychosomatic families: Anorexia nervosa in context.* Cambridge, MA: Harvard University Press.
Minzenberg, M. J., Laird, A. R., Thelen, S., Carter, C. S., & Glahn, D. C. (2009). Meta-analysis of 41 functional neuroimaging studies of executive function in schizophrenia. *Archives of General Psychiatry, 66,* 811–822.
Mitchell, C. M., Beals, J., & The Pathways of Choice Team. (2006). The development of alcohol use and outcome expectancies among American Indian young adults: A growth mixture model. *Addictive Behaviors, 31,* 1–14.
Mitchell, J. E., Roerig, J., & Steffen, K. (2013). Biological therapies for eating disorders. *International Journal of Eating Disorders, 46,* 470–477. doi:10.1002/ eat.22104
Mitchell, J. M., O'Neil, J. P., Janabi, M., Marks, S. M., Jagust, W. J., & Fields, H. L. (2012). Alcohol consumption induces endogenous opioid release in the human orbitofrontal cortex and nucleus accumbens. *Science Translational Medicine, 4,* 116ra6. doi:10.1126/scitranslmed.3002902
Mitchison, D., & Hay, P. J. (2014). The epidemiology of eating disorders: Genetic, environmental, and societal factors. *Clinical Epidemiology, 6,* 89–97. doi:10.2147/CLEP.S40841
Mitka, M. (2011). Strategies sought for reducing cost, improving efficiency of clinical research. *Journal of the American Medical Association, 306,* 364–365. doi:10.1001/jama.2011.1018
Mitka, M. (2013). Groups release new, updated guidelines to reduce heart disease risk factors. *Journal of the American Medical Association, 310,* 2602–2604. doi:10.1001/jama.2013.284084
Mitte, K. (2005). Meta-analysis of cognitive-behavioral treatments for generalized anxiety disorder: A comparison with pharmacotherapy. *Psychological Bulletin, 131,* 785–795.
Mittelman, M. S., Roth, D. L., Coon, D. W., & Haley, W. E. (2004). Sustained benefit of supportive intervention for depressive symptoms in caregivers of patients with Alzheimer's disease. *American Journal of Psychiatry, 161,* 850–856.
Modestin, J. (1992). Multiple personality disorder in Switzerland. *American Journal of Psychiatry, 149,* 88–92.
Moffitt, T. E., Caspi, A., & Rutter, M. (2006). Measured gene-environment interactions in psychopathology concepts, research strategies, and implications for research, intervention, and public understanding of genetics. *Perspectives on Psychological Science, 1,* 5–27.
Mohatt, J., Bennett, S. M., & Walkup, J. T. (2014). Treatment of separation, generalized, and social anxiety disorders in youths. *American Journal of Psychiatry, 171,* 741–748. doi:10.1176/appi.ajp.2014.13101337
Mohee, A., & Eardley, I. (2011). Medical therapy for premature ejaculation. *Therapeutic Advances in Urology, 3,* 211–222.
Mohlman, J. (2012). A community based survey of older adults' preferences for treatment of anxiety. *Psychology and Aging, 27,* 1182–1190. doi:10.1037/a0023126
Mojtabai, R. (2014). Diagnosing depression in older adults in primary care. *New England Journal of Medicine, 370,* 1180–1182. doi:10.1056/NEJMp1311047
Mokros, A., Hare, R. D., Neumann, C. S., Santtila, P., Habermeyer, E., & Nitschke, J. (2015). Variants of psychopathy in adult male offenders: A latent profile analysis. *Journal of Abnormal Psychology, 124,* 372–386. Retrieved from http://dx.doi.org/10.1037/abn0000042
Moloo, J. (2014, August 14). Diagnosing obstructive sleep apnea. *Journal Watch.* Retrieved from http://www.jwatch.org/na35439/2014/08/14/diagnosing-obstructive-sleep-apnea?query=etoc_jwgenmed
Molyneaux, E., Trevillion, K., & Howard, L. M. (2015). Antidepressant treatment for postnatal depression. *Journal of the American Medical Association, 313,* 1965–1966. doi:10.1001/jama.2015.2276
Mondin, T. C., Cardoso, T. de A., Jansen, K., Silva G., Souza, L. D., & Silva, R. A. (2015). Long-term effects of cognitive therapy on biological rhythms and depressive symptoms: A randomized clinical trial. *Journal of Affective Disorders, 15,* 1–9. doi:10.1016/j.jad.2015.08.014
Money, J. (2000). Reflections of a gender biographer. *Men & Masculinities, 3,* 209–216.
Monk, C. S., Telzer, E. H., Mogg, K., Bradley, B. P., Mai, X., Louro, H. M. C., Chen, G.,... Pine, D. S. (2008). Amygdala and ventrolateral prefrontal cortex activation to masked angry faces in children and adolescents with generalized anxiety disorder. *Archives of General Psychiatry, 65,* 568–576.
Monroe, S. M., & Anderson, S. F. (2015). Depression: The shroud of heterogeneity. *Current Directions in Psychological Science, 10,* 226–228.
Monroe, S. M., & Reid, M. W. (2008). Gene-environment interactions in depression research: Genetic polymorphisms and life-stress polyprocedures. *Psychological Science, 19,* 947–956.
Monroe, S. M., & Reid, M. W. (2009). Life stress and major depression. *Current Directions in Psychological Science, 18,* 68–72. doi:10.1111/j.1467-8721.2009.01611.x
Monroe, S. M., Slavich, G. M., Torres, L. D., & Gotlib, I. H. (2007). Major life events and major chronic difficulties are differentially associated with history of major depressive episodes. *Journal of Abnormal Psychology, 116,* 116–124.
Monson, C. M., & Shnaider, P. (2014). *Treating PTSD with cognitive-behavioral therapies: Interventions that work: Concise guides on trauma care book series.* Washington, DC: American Psychological Association.
Monti, P. M., Binkoff, J. A., Abrams, D. B., Zwick, W. R., Nirenberg, T. D., & Liepman, M. R. (1987). Reactivity of alcoholics and nonalcoholics to drinking cues. *Journal of Abnormal Psychology, 96,* 122–126.
Montorsi, F., Adaikan, G., Becher, E., Giuliano, F., Khoury, S., Lue, T. F.,... Wasserman M. (2010). Summary of the recommendations on sexual dysfunctions in men. *Journal of Sexual Medicine, 7,* 572–588. doi:10.1111/j.1743-6109.2010.02062.x
Moore, A. S. (2014, November 2). This is your brain on drugs. *New York Times Education Life,* p. 17.
Moore, D. R., & Heiman, J. R. (2006). Women's sexuality in context: Relationship factors and female sexual functioning. In I. Goldstein, C. Meston, S. Davis, & A. Traish (Eds.), *Female sexual dysfunction* (pp. 63–84). New York, NY: Parthenon.
Moore, M. T., Fresco, D. M., Segal, Z. V., & Brown, T. A. (2014). An exploratory analysis of the factor structure of the Dysfunctional Attitude Scale–Form A (DAS). *Assessment, 21,* 570–579. doi:10.1177/1073191114524272
Moore, T. J., Furberg, C. D., Glenmullen, J., Maltsberger, J. T, & Singh, S. (2011). Suicidal behavior and depression in smoking cessation treatments. *PLOS ONE, 6,* e27016. doi:10.1371/journal.pone.0027016

Moos, R. H., & Moos, B. S. (2004). Long-term influence of duration and frequency of participation in Alcoholics Anonymous on individuals with alcohol use disorders. *Journal of Consulting and Clinical Psychology, 72,* 81–90.

Moos, R. H., & Moos, B. S. (2005). Paths of entry into Alcoholics Anonymous: Consequences for participation and remission. *Alcoholism: Clinical and Experimental Research, 29,* 1858–1868.

Mor, N., & Daches, S. (2015). Ruminative thinking: Lessons learned from cognitive training. *Clinical Psychological Science, 3,* 574–592. doi:10.1177/2167702615578130

Mor, N., & Winquist, J. (2002). Self-focused attention and negative affect: A meta-analysis. *Psychological Bulletin, 128,* 638–662.

Mora, L. E., Nevid, J., & Chaplin, W. T. (2008). Psychologist treatment recommendations for Internet-based therapeutic interventions. *Computers in Human Behavior, 24,* 3052–3062.

Morbidity and Mortality Weekly Report. (2015, October 22). Cigarette, cigar, and marijuana use among high school students: United States, 1997–2013. Retrieved from http://www.mdlinx.com/psychiatry/top-medical-news/article/2015/10/22/4

More than 3,000 survivors of the World Trade Center attacks experience long-term post-traumatic stress disorder. (2011, January 7). *ScienceDaily.* Retrieved from http://www.sciencedaily.com-/

Morehouse, R., MacQueen, G., & Kennedy, S. H. (2011). Barriers to achieving treatment goals: A focus on sleep disturbance and sexual dysfunction. *Journal of Affective Disorders, 132*(Suppl. 1), S14–S20. doi:10.1016/j.jad.2011.03.047

Moreno, C., Laje, G., Blanco, C., Jiang, H., Schmidt, A. B., & Olfson, M. (2007). National trends in the outpatient diagnosis and treatment of bipolar disorder in youth. *Archives of General Psychiatry, 64,* 1032–1039.

Moretz, M. W., & McKay, D. (2009). The role of perfectionism in obsessive–compulsive symptoms: "Not just right" experiences and checking compulsions. *Journal of Anxiety Disorders, 23,* 640–644. doi:10.1016/j.janxdis.2009.01.015

Morey, R. A., Gold, A. L., LaBar, K. S., Beall, S. K., Brown, V. M., Haswell, C. C., . . . for the Mid-Atlantic MIRECC Workgroup. (2012). Amygdala volume changes in posttraumatic stress disorder in a large case-controlled veterans group. *Archives of General Psychiatry, 69,* 1169–1178. doi:10.1001/archgenpsychiatry.2012.50

Morgenthaler, T. I., Kapur, V. K., Brown, T., Swick, T. J., Alessi, C., Aurora, N., . . . Standards of Practice Committee of the AASM. (2007). Practice parameters for the treatment of narcolepsy and other hypersomnias of central origin. *Sleep, 30,* 1705.

Mori, N., Lockwood, L., & McCall, W. V. (2015). Current antidepressant therapy: A critical examination. *Psychiatric Annals, 45,* 456–462. doi:10.3928/00485713-20150901-04

Morimoto, K., Miyatake, R., Nakamura, M., Watanabe, T., Hirao, T., & Suwaki, H. (2002). Delusional disorder: Molecular genetic evidence for dopamine psychosis. *Neuropsychopharmacology, 26,* 794–801.

Morin, C. M., Vallières, A., Guay, B., Ivers, H., Savard, J., Mérette, C., . . . Baillargeon, L. (2009). Cognitive behavioral therapy, singly and combined with medication, for persistent insomnia: A randomized controlled trial. *Journal of the American Medical Association, 301,* 2005–2015.

Morina, N., Ijntema, H., Meyerbröker, K., & Emmelkamp, P. M. G. (2015). Can virtual reality exposure therapy gains be generalized to real-life? A meta-analysis of studies applying behavioral assessments. *Behaviour Research and Therapy, 74,* 18–24. doi:10.1016/j.brat.2015.08.010

Morina, N., Wicherts, J. M., Lobbrecht, M., & Priebe, S. (2014). Remission from post-traumatic stress disorder in adults: A systematic review and meta-analysis of long term outcome studies. *Clinical Psychology Review, 34,* 249–255. doi:10.1016/j.cpr.2014.03.002

Moritz, S., Veckenstedt, R., Andreou, C., Bohn, F., Hottenrott, B., Leighton, L. Köther, U., Roesch-Ely, D. (2014). Sustained and "sleeper" effects of group metacognitive training for schizophrenia: A randomized clinical trial. *JAMA Psychiatry, 71,* 1103–1111. doi:10.1001/jamapsychiatry.2014.1038

Mørkved, N., Hartmann, K., Aarsheim, L. M., Holen, D., Milde, A. M., Bomyea, J., . . . Thorp, S. R. (2014). A comparison of narrative exposure therapy and prolonged exposure therapy for PTSD. *Clinical Psychology Review, 34,* 453–467. doi:10.1016/j.cpr.2014.06.005

Morley, T. E., & Moran, G. (2011). The origins of cognitive vulnerability in early childhood: Mechanisms linking early attachment to later depression. *Clinical Psychology Review, 31,* 1071–1082. doi:10.1016/j.cpr.2011.06.006

Morris, M. E., Kathawala, Q., Leen, T. K., Gorenstein, E. E., Guilak, F., Labhard, M., & Deleeuw, W. (2010). Mobile therapy: Case study evaluations of a cell phone application for emotional self-awareness. *Journal of Medical Internet Research, 12,* e10.

Morris, B. R. (2003, July 8). Two types of brain problems are found to cause dyslexia. *The New York Times,* p. F5.

Morris, G. H. (2002). Commentary: Punishing the unpunishable—the abuse of psychiatry to confine those we love to hate. *Journal of the American Academy of Psychiatry and the Law, 30,* 556–562.

Morris, J. K., Alberman, E., Scott, C., & Jacobs, P. (2008). Is the prevalence of Klinefelter syndrome increasing? *European Journal of Human Genetics, 16,* 163.

Morris, M. C., Ciesla, J. A., & Garber, J. (2008). A prospective study of the cognitive-stress model of depressive symptoms in adolescents. *Journal of Abnormal Psychology, 117,* 719–734.

Morris, R. W., Quail, S., Griffiths, K. R., Green, M. J., & Balleine, B. W. (2014). Corticostriatal control of goal-directed action is impaired in schizophrenia. *Biological Psychiatry, 77,* 187–195. doi:10.1016/j.biopsych.2014.06.005

Morrison, A. P., Turkington, D., Pyle, M., Spencer, H., Brabban, A., Dunn, G., & Hutton, P. (2014). Cognitive therapy for people with schizophrenia spectrum disorders not taking antipsychotic drugs: A single-blind randomised controlled trial. *The Lancet, 383,* 1395–1403. Retrieved from http://dx.doi.org/10.1016/S0140-6736(13)62246-1

Morrison, T., Waller, G., & Lawson, R. A. (2006). Attributional style in the eating disorders. *The Journal of Nervous and Mental Disease, 194,* 303–305.

Morrow, D. J. (1998, March 5). Stumble on the road to market. *The New York Times,* pp. D1, D4.

Mortiboys, H., Furmston, R., Bronstad, G., Aasly, J., Elliott, C., & Bandmann, O. (2015). UDCA exerts beneficial effect on mitochondrial dysfunction in LRRK2G2019S carriers and in vivo. *Neurology, 85,* 1–8. doi:10.1212/WNL.0000000000001905

Mossman, D. (1994). Assessing predictions of violence: Being accurate about accuracy. *Journal of Consulting and Clinical Psychology, 62,* 783–792.

Mote, J., Stuart, B. K., & Kring, A. M. (2014). Diminished emotion expressivity but not experience in men and women with schizophrenia. *Journal of Abnormal Psychology, 123,* 796–801. Retrieved from http://dx.doi.org/10.1037/abn0000006

Motzkin, J. C., Newman, J. P., Kiehl, K. A., & Koenigs, M. (2011). Reduced prefrontal connectivity in psychopathy. *Journal of Neuroscience, 31,* 17348–17357. doi:10.1523/JNEUROSCI.4215-11.2011

Moulds, M. L., & Nixon, R. D. (2006). In vivo flooding for anxiety disorders: Proposing its utility in the treatment of posttraumatic stress disorder. *Journal of Anxiety Disorder, 20,* 498–509.

Mowrer, O. H. (1960). *Learning theory and behavior.* New York, NY: Wiley.

Mukherjee, S. (2012, April 22). Post-Prozac nation. *The New York Times,* pp. 48–54.

Müller, C. A., Geisel, O., Banas, R., & Heinz, A. (2014). Current pharmacological treatment approaches for alcohol dependence. *Expert Opinion on Pharmacotherapy, 15,* 471–481. doi:10.1517/14656566.2014.876008

Müller, I., Çalışkan, G., & Stork, O. (2015). The GAD65 knock out mouse: A model for GABAergic processes in fear- and stress-induced psychopathology. *Genes, Brain and Behavior, 14,* 37–45. doi:10.1111/gbb.12188

Müller, K. W., Dreier, M., Beutel, M. E., Duven, E., Giralt, S., & Wölfling, K. (2016). A hidden type of Internet addiction? Intense and addictive use of social networking sites in adolescents. *Computers in Human Behavior, 55,* 172–177. doi:10.1016/j.chb.2015.09.007

Mullins-Sweatt, S. N., Glover, N. G., Derefinko, K. J., Miller, J. D., & Widiger, T. A. (2010). The search for the successful psychopath. *Journal of Research in Personality, 44,* 554–558. doi:10.1016/j.jrp.2010.05.010

Muran, J. C., Eubanks-Carter, C., & Safran, J. D. (2010). A relational approach the treatment of personality dysfunction. In J. J. Magnavita (Ed.), *Evidence-based treatment of personality dysfunction: Principles, methods, and processes* (pp. 167–192). Washington, DC: American Psychological Association.

Muraven, M. (2005). Self-focused attention and the self-regulation of attention: Implications for personality and pathology. *Journal of Social and Clinical Psychology, 24,* 382–400.

Muris, P., & Field, A. (2013). Information processing biases. In C. A. Essau & T. H. Ollendick (Eds.), *The Wiley-Blackwell handbook of the treatment of childhood and adolescent anxiety* (pp. 141–156). Hoboken, NJ: John Wiley.

Muroff, J., & Underwood, P. (2016). Treatment of an adult with hoarding disorder. In E. A. Storch & A. B. Lewin (Eds.), *Clinical handbook of obsessive-compulsive and related disorders: A case-based approach to treating pediatric and adult populations* (pp. 241–258). New York, NY: Springer.

Murphy, M. L. M., Slavich, G. M., Rohleder, N., & Miller, G. E. (2013). Targeted rejection triggers differential pro- and anti-inflammatory gene expression in adolescents as a function of social status. *Clinical Psychological Science, 1,* 30–40. doi:10.1177/2167702612455743

Murphy, W. D., & Page, I. J. (2008). Exhibitionism: Psychopathology and theory. In D. R. Laws and W. T. O'Donohue (Eds.), *Sexual deviance: Theory, assessment, and treatment* (2nd ed., pp. 61–75). New York, NY: Guilford Press.

Murray, H. A. (1943). *Thematic Apperception Test.* Cambridge, MA: Harvard University Press.

Murray, S. B., Rieger, E., Karlov, L., & Touyz, S. W. (2013). Masculinity and femininity in the divergence of male body image concerns. *Journal of Eating Disorders, 1,* 11. doi:10.1186/2050-2974-1-11

Must, A., Kõks, S., Vasar, E., Tasa, G., Lang, A., Maron, E., & Väli, M. (2009). Common variations in 4p locus are related to male completed suicide. *NeuroMolecular Medicine, 11,* 13–19. doi:10.1007/s12017-008-8056-8

Myers, H. F., Wyatt, G. E., Ullman, J. B., Loeb, T. B., Chin, D., Prause, N., . . . Liu, H. (2015). Cumulative burden of lifetime adversities: Trauma and mental health in low-SES African Americans and Latino/as. *Psychological Trauma: Theory, Research, Practice, and Policy, 7,* 243. doi:10.1037/a0039077

Myers, N.L. (2011). Update: Schizophrenia across cultures. *Current Psychiatry Reports, 13,* 305–311.

Myers, T. A., & Crowther, J. H. (2009). Social comparison as a predictor of body dissatisfaction: A meta-analytic review. *Journal of Abnormal Psychology, 118,* 683–698.

Myin-Germeys, I., Delespaul, P. A., & deVries, M.W. (2000). Schizophrenia patients are more emotionally active than is assumed based on their behavior. *Schizophrenia Bulletin, 26,* 847–854.

Myrick, H., Anton, R. F., Li, X., Henderson, S., Randall, P. K., & Voronin, K. (2008). Effect of naltrexone and ondansetron on alcohol cue–induced activation of the ventral striatum in alcohol-dependent people. *Archives of General Psychiatry, 65,* 466–475.

Naggiar, S. (2012, September 24). "Broken heart" syndrome can be triggered by stress, grief. Retrieved from http://vitals.nbcnews.com/_news/2012/09/24/14072649-broken-heartsyndrome-can-be-triggered-by-stress-grief?lite

Nakai, Y., Inoue, T., Toda, H., Toyomaki, A., Nakato, Y., Nakagawa, S., Kitaichi, Y., . . . Kusumi, I. (2014). The influence of childhood abuse, adult stressful life events and temperaments on depressive symptoms in the non-clinical general adult population. *Journal of Affective Disorders, 158,* 101–107. doi:10.1016/j.jad.2014.02.004

Nakao, T., Radua, J., Rubia, K., & Mataix-Cols, D. (2011). Gray matter volume abnormalities in ADHD: Voxel-based meta-analysis exploring the effects of age and stimulant medication. *American Journal of Psychiatry, 168,* 1154–1163. doi:10.1176/appi.ajp.2011.11020281

Narod, S. A. (2011). Alcohol and risk of breast cancer. *Journal of the American Medical Association, 306,* 1920–1921. doi:10.1001/jama.2011.1589

Nasrallah, H. A., Keshavan, M. S., Benes F. M., Braff, D. L., Green A. I., Gur, R.,... Correll, C. U. (2009). Proceedings and data from The Schizophrenia Summit: A critical appraisal to improve the management of schizophrenia. *The Journal of Clinical Psychiatry, 70*(Suppl 1), 4–46.

National Center for Health Statistics. (2012a). *Health, United States, 2012: In brief.* Hyattsville, MD: Author.

National Center for Health Statistics. (2012b). *Health, United States, 2011: With special feature on socioeconomic status and health.* Hyattsville, MD: Author.

National Down Syndrome Society. (2015). Down syndrome facts. Retrieved from http://www.ndss.org/Down-Syndrome/Down-Syndrome-Facts/

National Institute on Deafness and Other Communication Disorders. (2010). Stuttering. Retrieved from http://www.nidcd.nih.gov/health/voice/pages/stutter.aspx

National Institute of Mental Health. (2003, December 23). Suicide facts. Retrieved from http://www.nimh.nih.gov/research/suifact.cfm

National Institute of Mental Health. (2008a). *Bipolar disorder in children and teens: A parent's guide.* U.S. Department of Health and Human Services, NIH Publication 08-3679. Bethesda, MD: Author.

National Institute of Mental Health. (2008b, October 22). Social phobia patients have heightened reactions to negative comments. Retrieved from http://www.nimh.nih.gov/sciencenews/2008/social-phobiapatients-have-heightened-reactionsto-negative-comments.shtml

National Institute of Neurological Disorders and Stroke. (2012, May 16). NINDS dementia with lewy bodies information page. Retrieved from http://www.ninds.nih.gov/disorders/dementiawithlewybodies/dementiawithlewybodies.htm

National Institutes of Health. (2002). Mimicking brain's "all clear" quells fear in rats. *NIH News Release.* Retrieved from http://www.nimh.nih.gov/science-news/2002/mimicking-brains-all-clear-quells-fear-in-rats.shtml

National Strategy for Suicide Prevention. (2001, May). *National strategy for suicide prevention: Goals and objectives for action: Summary. A joint effort of SAMHS, CDC, NIH, and HRSA.* Washington, DC: Author.

Nauczyciel, C., Le Jeune, F., Naudet, F., Douabin, S., Esquevin, A., Vérin, M.,... Millet, B. (2014). Repetitive transcranial magnetic stimulation over the orbitofrontal cortex for obsessive-compulsive disorder: A double-blind, crossover study. *Translational Psychiatry, 9,* e436. doi:10.1038/tp.2014.62

NBC News. (2016, January 28). Iconic Barbie gets petite, tall, and curvy body makeovers. Retrieved from https://archives.nbclearn.com/portal/site/k-12/flatview?cuecard=105293

Ndetei, D. M., & Singh, A. (1983). Hallucination in Kenyan schizophrenic patients. *Acta Psychiatrica Scandinavica, 67,* 144–147.

Neacsiu, A. D., Lungu, A., Harned, M. S., Rizvi, S. L., & Linehan, M. M. (2014). Impact of dialectical behavior therapy versus community treatment by experts on emotional experience, expression, and acceptance in borderline personality disorder. *Behaviour Research and Therapy, 53,* 47–54.

Nearly one million children in U.S. potentially misdiagnosed with ADHD, study finds. (2010, August 17). *ScienceDaily.* Retrieved from www.sciencedaily.com

Negy, C., Hammons, M. E., Reig-Ferrer, A., & Carper, T. M. (2010). The importance of addressing acculturative stress in marital therapy with Hispanic immigrant women. *International Journal of Clinical and Health Psychology, 10,* 5–21.

Negy, C., Reig-Ferrer, A., Gaborit, M., & Ferguson, C. (2014). Psychological homelessness and enculturative stress among U.S.-deported Salvadorans: A novel approach. *Journal of Immigrant and Minority Health, 16,* 1278–1283.

Negy, C., Schwartz, S., & Reig-Ferrer, A. (2009). Violated expectations and acculturative stress among U.S. Hispanic immigrants. *Cultural Diversity and Ethnic Minority Psychology, 15,* 255–264. doi:10.1037/a0015109

Negy, C., & Snyder, D. K. (1997). Ethnicity and acculturation: Assessing Mexican American couples' relationships using the Marital Satisfaction Inventory—Revised. *Psychological Assessment, 9,* 414–421.

Negy, C., & Snyder, D. K. (2004). A research note on male chauvinism and Mexican Americans. *Psychology and Education, 41,* 22–27.

Negy, C., Snyder, D. K., & Diaz-Loving, R. (2004). A cross-national comparison of Mexican and Mexican American couples using the Marital Satisfaction Inventory-Revised (Spanish Version). *Assessment, 11,* 49–56.

Negy, C., & Woods, D. J. (1992a). Mexican Americans' performance on the Psychological Screening Inventory as a function of acculturation. *Journal of Clinical Psychology, 48,* 315–319.

Negy, C., & Woods, D. J. (1992b). A note on the relationship between acculturation and socioeconomic status. *Hispanic Journal of Behavioral Sciences, 14,* 248–251.

Negy, C., & Woods, D. J. (1993). Mexican and Anglo-American differences on the Psychological Screening Inventory. *Journal of Personality Assessment, 60,* 543–555.

Neighbors, C., Lee, C. M., Atkins, D. C., Lewis, M. A., Kaysen, D., Mittmann, A.,... Larimer, M. A. (2012). A randomized controlled trial of event-specific prevention strategies for reducing problematic drinking associated with 21st birthday celebrations. *Journal of Consulting and Clinical Psychology, 80,* 850–862. doi:10.1037/a0029480

Neighbors, H. W., Caldwell, C., Williams, D. R., Nesse, R., Taylor, R. J., Bullard, K. M.,... Jackson, J. S. (2007). Race, ethnicity, and the use of services for mental disorders: Results from the National Survey of American Life. *Archives of General Psychiatry, 64,* 485–494.

Nelson, J. C., Mankoski, R., Baker, R. A., Carlson, B. X., Eudicone, J. M., Pikalov, A., & Berman, R. M. (2010). Effects of aripiprazole adjunctive to standard antidepressant treatment on the core symptoms of depression: A post-hoc, pooled analysis of two large, placebo-controlled studies. *Journal of Affective Disorders, 120,* 133–140. doi:10.1016/j.jad.2009.06.026

Nenadic, I., Maitra, R., Dietzek, M., Langbein, K., Smesny, S., Sauer, H.,... Gaser, C. (2015). Prefrontal gyrification in psychotic bipolar I disorder vs. schizophrenia. *Journal of Affective Disorders, 185,* 104–107. doi:10.1016/j.jad.2015.06.014

Nes, R. B., Czajkowski, N. O., Røysamb, E., Ørstavik, R. E., Tambs, K., & Reichborn-Kjennerud, T. (2012). Major depression and life satisfaction: A population-based twin study. *Journal of Affective Disorders, 144*(1–2), 51–58. doi:10.1016/j.jad.2012.05.060

Nestler, E. J. (2011, December 1). Epigenetics offers new clues to mental illness. (2011, December 1). *Scientific American.* Retrieved from http://www.scientificamerican.com/article.cfm?id=hidden-switches-in-the-mind

Nestoriuc, Y., & Martin, A. (2007). Efficacy of biofeedback for migraine: A meta-analysis. *Radiology Source, 128,* 111–127.

Neugebauer, R. (1979). Medieval and early modern theories of mental illness. *Archives of General Psychiatry, 36,* 477–484.

Neumann, C. S., & Hare, R. D. (2008). Psychopathic traits in a large community sample: Links to violence, alcohol use, and intelligence. *Journal of Consulting and Clinical Psychology, 76,* 893–899.

Nevid, J. S. (2007). *Psychology: Concepts and applications* (2nd ed.). Boston, MA: Houghton Mifflin.

Nevid, J. S. (2009). *Psychology: Concepts and applications* (3rd ed.). Boston, MA: Houghton Mifflin.

Nevid, J. S. (2011, May/June). Teaching the millennials. *APS Observer, Teaching Tips, 24*(5), 53–56.

Nevid, J. S. (2013). *Psychology: Concepts and applications* (4th ed.). Belmont, CA: Cengage Learning.

Nevid, J. S., & Javier, R. A. (1997). Preliminary investigation of a culturally specific smoking cessation intervention for Hispanic smokers. *American Journal of Health Promotion, 11,* 198–207.

Nevid, J. S., Javier, R. A., & Moulton, J. (1996). Factors predicting participant attrition in a community-based culturally specific smoking cessation program for Hispanic smokers. *Health Psychology, 15,* 226–229.

Nevid, J. S., & Rathus, S. A. (2013). *Psychology and the challenges of life: Adjustment and growth* (12th ed.). New York, NY: Wiley.

Nevid, J. S., & Rathus, S. A. (2016). *Psychology and the challenges of life* (13th ed.). Hoboken, NJ: John Wiley & Sons, Inc.

Newby, J. M., Mewton, L., Williams, A. D., & Andrews, G. (2014). Effectiveness of transdiagnostic internet cognitive behavioural treatment for mixed anxiety and depression in primary care. *Journal of Affective Disorders, 165,* 45–52. Retrieved from http://www.sciencedirect.com/science/article/pii/S0165032714002316

Newcorn, J. H., Kratochvil, C. J., Allen, A. J., Casat, C. D., Ruff, D. D., Moore, R. J., Michelson, D.,... Atomoxetine/Methylphenidate Comparative Study Group. (2008). Atomoxetine and osmotically released methylphenidate for the treatment of attention deficit hyperactivity disorder: Acute comparison and differential response. *American Journal of Psychiatry, 165,* 721–730. doi:10.1176/appi.ajp.2007.05091676

Neylan, T. C. (2014). Pharmacologic augmentation of extinction learning during exposure therapy for PTSD. *American Journal of Psychiatry, 171,* 597–599. doi:10.1176/appi.ajp.2014.14030386

Ng, M., Freeman, M. K., Fleming, T. D., Robinson, M., Dwyer-Lindgren, L., Thomson, B.,... Gakidou, E. (2014). Smoking prevalence and cigarette consumption in 187 countries, 1980–2012. *Journal of the American Medical Association, 311,* 183–192. doi:10.1001/jama.2013.284692

Ng, M., Gakidou, E., Robinson, M., Thomson, B., Graetz, N., Margono, C.,... Gakidou, E. (2014). Global, regional, and national prevalence of overweight and obesity in children and adults during 1980–2013: A systematic analysis for the Global Burden of Disease Study 2013. *The Lancet, 384,* 766–781. doi:10.1016/S0140-6736(14)60460-8

Ngandu, T., Lehtisalo, J., Solomon, A., Levälahti, E., Ahtiluoto, S., Antikainen, R., Bäckman, L.,... Kivipelto, M. (2015). A 2 year multidomain intervention of diet, exercise, cognitive training, and vascular risk monitoring versus control to prevent cognitive decline in at-risk elderly people (FINGER): A randomised controlled trial. *The Lancet, 385,* 2255–2263. Retrieved from http://dx.doi.org/10.1016/S0140-6736(15)60461-5

Nicolson, R. I., & Fawcett, A. J. (2008). *Dyslexia, learning, and the brain.* Cambridge, MA: MIT Press.

Nielsen, S. F., Hjorthøj, C. R., Erlangsen, A., & Nordentoft, M. (2011). Psychiatric disorders and mortality among people in homeless shelters in Denmark: A nationwide register-based cohort study. *The Lancet, 377,* 2205–2214. doi:10.1016/S0140-6736(11)60747-2

Nierenberg, A. A., Friedman, E. S., Bowden, C. L., Sylvia, L. G., Thase, M. E.,... Calabrese, J. R. (2013). Lithium Treatment Moderate-Dose Use Study (LiTMUS) for bipolar disorder: A randomized comparative effectiveness trial of optimized personalized treatment with and without lithium. *American Journal of Psychiatry, 170,* 102–110. doi:10.1176/appi.ajp.2012.12060751

Nigg, J. T. (2013). Commentary: Gene by environment interplay and psychopathology—in search of a paradigm. *Journal of Child Psychology and Psychiatry, 54,* 1150–1152. doi:10.1111/jcpp.12134

Nigg, J. T., Lohr, N. E., Western, D., Gold, L. J., & Silk, K. R. (1992). Malevolent object representations in borderline personality disorder and major depression. *Journal of Abnormal Psychology, 101,* 61–67.

NIH Research Matters. (2015, August 24). Study details process involved in Parkinson's disease. Retrieved from http://www.nih.gov/researchmatters/august2015/08242015parkinsons.htm

Nisbett, R. E., Aronson, J., Blair, C., Dickens, W., Flynn, J., Halpern, D. E., & Turkheimer, E. (2012). Intelligence: New findings and theoretical developments. *American Psychologist, 67,* 130–159. doi:10.1037/a0026699

Nitschke, J. B., Sarinopoulos, I., Oathes, D. J., Johnstone, T., Whalen, P. J., Davidson, R. J., & Kalin, N. H. (2009). Anticipatory activation in the amygdala and anterior cingulate in generalized anxiety disorder and prediction of treatment response. *American Journal of Psychiatry, 166,* 302–310. doi:10.1176/appi.ajp.2008.0710168

Noaghiul, S., & Hibbeln, J. R. (2003). Cross-national comparisons of seafood consumption and rates of bipolar disorders. *American Journal of Psychiatry, 160,* 2222–2227.

Nock, M. K., Kazdin, A. E., Hiripi, E., & Kessler, R. C. (2006). Prevalence, subtypes, and correlates of DSM-IV conduct disorder in the National Comorbidity Survey Replication. *Psychological Medicine, 36,* 699–710.

Nolen-Hoeksema, S. (2006). The etiology of gender differences in depression. In C. M. Mazure & G. Puryear (Eds.), *Understanding depression in women: Applying empirical research to practice and policy* (pp. 9–43). Washington, DC: American Psychological Association.

Nolen-Hoeksema, S. (2008). It is not what you have; it is what you do with it: Support for Addis's gendered responding framework. *Clinical Psychology: Science and Practice, 15,* 178–181.

Nolen-Hoeksema, S. (2012). Emotion regulation and psychopathology: The role of gender. *Annual Review of Clinical Psychology, 8,* 161–187. doi:10.1146/annurevclinpsy-032511-143109

Nolen-Hoeksema, S., Morrow, J., & Fredrickson, B. L. (1993). Response styles and the duration of episodes of depressed mood. *Journal of Abnormal Psychology, 102,* 20–28.

Nolen-Hoeksema, S., Wisco, B. E., & Lyubomirsky, S. (2008). Rethinking rumination. *Perspectives on Psychological Science, 3,* 400–424.

Norbury, C. R., & Sparks, A. (2013). Difference or disorder? Cultural issues in understanding neurodevelopmental disorders. *Developmental Psychology, 49,* 45–58. doi:10.1037/a0027446

Norcross, J. C., & Beutler, L. (2011). Integrative psychotherapies. In R. J. Corsini & D. Wedding (Eds.), *Current psychotherapies* (9th ed., pp. 481–511). Belmont, CA: Brooks/Cole.

Norcross, J. C., & Karpiak, C. P. (2012). Clinical psychologists in the 2010s: 50 years of the APA Division of Clinical Psychology. *Clinical Psychology: Science and Practice, 19,* 1–12. doi:10.111 1/j.1468-2850.2012.01269

Norcross, J. C., & Lambert, M. J. (2014). Relationship science and practice in psychotherapy: Closing commentary. *Psychotherapy, 51,* 398–403. http://dx.doi.org/10.1037/a0037418

Nordsletten, A. E., Reichenberg, A., Hatch, S. L., Fernández de la Cruz, L., Pertusa, A., Hotopf, M.,... Mataix-Cols, D. (2013). Epidemiology of hoarding disorder. *British Journal of Psychiatry, 203,* 445–452. doi:10.1192/bjp.bp.113.130195

Norhayatia, M. N., Hazlina, N. H. N., Asrenee, A. R., & Emilind, W. M. A. W. (2015). Magnitude and risk factors for postpartum symptoms: A literature review. *Journal of Affective Disorders, 175,* 34–52. doi:10.1016/j.jad.2014.12.041

Normandi, E. E., & Roark, L. (1998). *It's not about food: Change your mind; change your life; end your obsession with food and weight.* New York, NY: Berkley.

Norris, F. N., Murphy, A. D., Baker, C. K., Perilla, J. L., Rodriguez, F. G., & Rodriguez, J. D. J. G. (2003). Epidemiology of trauma and posttraumatic stress disorder in Mexico. *Journal of Abnormal Psychology, 112,* 646–656.

North, C. S., Oliver, J., & Pandya, A. (2012). Examining a comprehensive model of disaster-related posttraumatic stress disorder in systematically studied survivors of 10 disasters. *American Journal of Public Health, 102,* e40.

Norton, E. (2012). Rewiring the autistic brain. *Science.* Retrieved from http://news.sciencemag.org/sciencenow/2012/09/rewiring-the-autistic-brain.html?ref=hp

Novotny, A. (2015, July/August). Are preschoolers being overmedicated? *Monitor on Psychology, 46*(7), 65–67.

Ntouros, E., Ntoumanis, A., Bozikas, V. P., Donias, S., Giouzepas, I., & Garyfalos, G. (2010). Koro-like symptoms in two Greek men. *BMJ Case Reports.* Retrieved from http://casereports.bmj.com/content/2010/bcr.08.2008.0679.abstract

Nurnberg, H. G., Hensley, P. L., Heiman, J. R., Croft, H. A., Debattista, C., & Paine, S. (2008). Sildenafil treatment of women with antidepressant-associated sexual dysfunction: A randomized controlled trial. *Journal of the American Medical Association, 300,* 395–404.

Nusslock, R., Harmon-Jones, E., Alloy, L. B., Urosevic, S., Goldstein, K., & Abramson, L. Y. (2012). Elevated left mid-frontal cortical activity prospectively predicts conversion to bipolar I disorder. *Journal of Abnormal Psychology, 121,* 592–601. doi:10.1037/a0028973

Nyklíček, I., Mommersteeg, P. M. C., Van Beugen, S., Ramakers, C., & Van Boxtel, G. J. (2013). Mindfulness-based stress reduction and physiological activity during acute stress: A randomized controlled trial. *Health Psychology, 32,* 1110–1113. doi:10.1037/a0032200

O'Connor, A. (2012). Sleep apnea is linked to a higher risk of cancer. *The New York Times,* pp. D5.

O'Keefe, V. M., Wingate, L. R., Tucker, R. P., Rhoades-Kerswill, S., Slish, M. L., & Davidson, C. L. (2014). Interpersonal suicide risk for American Indians: Investigating thwarted belongingness and perceived burdensomeness. *Cultural Diversity and Ethnic Minority Psychology, 20,* 61–67. doi:10.1037/a0033540

Odeh, M. S., Zeiss, R. A., & Huss, M. T. (2006). Cues they use: Clinicians' endorsement of risk cues in predictions of dangerousness. *Behavioral Sciences & the Law, 24,* 147–156.

Oestergaard, S., & Møldrup, C. (2011). Optimal duration of combined psychotherapy and pharmacotherapy for patients with moderate and severe depression: A meta-analysis. *Journal of Affective Disorders, 131,* 24–36. doi:10.1016/j.jad.2010.08.014

Ogawa, Y., Tajika, A., Takeshima, N., Hayasaka, Y., & Furukawa, T. A. (2014). Mood stabilizers and antipsychotics for acute mania: A systematic review and meta-analysis of combination/augmentation therapy versus monotherapy. *CNS Drugs, 28,* 989–1003. doi:10.1007/s40263-014-0197-8

Ohayon, M. M., Dauvilliers, Y., & Reynolds, C. F. (2012). Operational definitions and algorithms for excessive sleepiness in the general population: Implications for DSM-5 NOSOLOGY. *Archives of General Psychiatry, 69,* 71–79. doi:10.1001/archgenpsychiatry.2011.1240

Ohayon, M. M., Mahowald, M. W., Dauvilliers, Y., Krystal, A. D., & Leger, D. (2012). Prevalence and comorbidity of nocturnal wandering in the U.S. adult general population. *Neurology, 78,* 1583. doi:10.1212/WNL.0b013e3182563

Okie, S. (2010). A flood of opioids, a rising tide of deaths. *New England Journal of Medicine, 363,* 1981–1985.

Okuda, M., Balán, I., Petry, N. M., Oquendo, M., & Blanco, C. (2009). Cognitive-behavioral therapy for pathological gambling: Cultural considerations. *American Journal of Psychiatry, 166,* 1325–1330.

Okumura, Y., & Ichikura, K. (2014). Efficacy and acceptability of group cognitive behavioral therapy for depression: A systematic review and meta-analysis. *Journal of Affective Disorders, 164,* 155–164. Retrieved from http://dx.doi.org/10.1016/j.jad.2014.04.023

Okun, M. S. (2014). Deep-brain stimulation: Entering the era of human neural-network modulation. *New England Journal of Medicine, 371,* 1369–1373. doi:10.1056/NEJMp1408779

Olatunji, B. O. Kauffman, B. Y., Meltzer, S., Davis, M. L., Smits, J. A. J., & Powers, M. B. (2014). Cognitive-behavioral therapy for hypochondriasis/health anxiety: A meta-analysis of treatment outcome and moderators. *Behaviour Research and Therapy, 58,* 65–74. doi:10.1016/j.brat.2014.05.002

Oldenbeuving, A. W., de Kort, P. L., Jansen, B. P., Algra, A., Kappelle, L. J., & Roks G. (2011). Delirium in the acute phase after stroke: Incidence, risk factors, and outcome. *Neurology, 76,* 993–999.

Oldham, J. M. (1994). Personality disorders: Current perspectives. *Journal of the American Medical Association, 272,* 213–220.

O'Leary, S. T., Lee, M., Lockhart, S., Eisert, S., Furniss, A., Barnard, J.,... Kempe, A. (2015). Effectiveness and cost of bidirectional text messaging for adolescent vaccines and well care. *Pediatrics, 136*(5), e1220–e1227. doi:10.1542/peds.2015-1089

Olff, M., Langeland, W., Draijer, N., & Gersons, B. P. R. (2007). Gender differences in posttraumatic stress disorder. *Psychological Bulletin, 133,* 183–204.

Olfson, M., Druss, B. G., & Marcus, S. C. (2015). Trends in mental health care among children and adolescents. *New England Journal of Medicine, 372,* 2029–2038. doi:10.1056/NEJMsa1413512

Olfson, M., Gameroff, M. J., Marcus, S. C., Greenberg T., & Shaffer, D. (2005). Emergency treatment of young people following deliberate self-harm. *Archives of General Psychiatry, 62,* 1122–1128.

Olfson, M., King, M., & Schoenbaum, M. (2015). Treatment of young people with antipsychotic medications in the United States. *JAMA Psychiatry, 72,* 867–874. doi:10.1001/jamapsychiatry.2015.0500

Olino, T. M., Seeley, J. R., & Lewinsohn, P. M. (2010). Conduct disorder and psychosocial outcomes at age 30: Early adult psychopathology as a potential mediator. *Journal of Abnormal Child Psychology, 38,* 1139–1149. doi:10.1007/s10802-010-9427-9

Olivardia, R., Pope, H. G., Jr., Borowiecki, J. J., III, & Cohane, G. H. (2004). Biceps and body image: The relationship between muscularity and self-esteem, depression, and eating disorder symptoms. *Psychology of Men & Masculinity, 5,* 112–120.

Ollendick, T., Allen, B., Benoit, K., & Cowart, M. (2011). The tripartite model of fear in children with specific phobias: Assessing concordance and discordance using the behavioral approach test. *Behaviour Research and Therapy, 49,* 459–465. doi:10.1016/j.brat.2011.04.00

Olson, S. D., Kambal, A., Pollock, K., Mitchell, G.-M., Stewart, H., Kalomoiris, S., Cary, W.,... Nolta, J. A. (2011). Examination of mesenchymal stem cell-mediated RNAi transfer to Huntington's disease affected neuronal cells for reduction of huntingtin. *Molecular and Cellular Neuroscience, 49,* 271–281. doi:10.1016/j.mcn.2011.12.001

Olson, S. E. (1997). *Becoming one: A story of triumph over multiple personality disorder.* Pasadena, CA: Trilogy Books.

Oltedal, L., Kessler, U., Ersland, L., Grüner, R., Andreassen, O. A., Haavik, J.,... Oedegaard, K. J. (2015). Effects of ECT in treatment of depression: Study protocol for a prospective neuroradiological study of acute and longitudinal effects on brain structure and function. *BMC Psychiatry, 15,* 94. doi:10.1186/s12888-015-0477-y

Onken, L. S., Carroll, K. M., Shoham, V., Cuthbert, B. N., & Riddle, M. (2014). Reenvisioning clinical science: Unifying the discipline to improve the public health. *Clinical Psychological Science, 2,* 22–34. doi:10.1177/2167702613497932

Opendak, M., & Gould, E. (2015). Adult neurogenesis: A substrate for experience-dependent change. *Trends in Cognitive Sciences, 19,* 151–161. doi:10.1016/j.tics.2015.01.001

Oquendo, M. A., Hastings, R. S., Huang, Y., Simpson, N., Ogden, R. T., Hu, X.-Z.,... Parsey, R. V. (2007). Brain serotonin transporter binding in depressed patients with bipolar disorder using positron emission tomography. *Archives of General Psychiatry, 64,* 201–208.

Orchowski, L. M., Mastroleo, N. R., & Borsari, B. (2012). Correlates of alcohol-related sex among college students. *Psychology of Addictive Behaviors, 26,* 782–790. doi:10.1037/a0027840

Oren, D. A., Koziorowski, M., & Desan, P. H. (2013). SAD and the not-so-single photoreceptors. *American Journal of Psychiatry, 170,* 1403–1412. doi:10.1176/appi.ajp.2013.13010111View

Oren, E., & Solomon, R. (2012). EMDR therapy: An overview of its development and mechanisms of action. *European Review of Applied Psychology, 62,* 197–203.

Ortega, A. N., Rosenheck, R., Alegría, M., & Desai, R. A. (2000). Acculturation and the lifetime risk of psychiatric and substance use disorders among Hispanics. *Journal of Nervous & Mental Disease, 188,* 728–735.

Orth-Gomér, K., Wamala, S. P., Horsten, M., Schenck-Gustafsson, K., Schneiderman, N., & Mittleman, M. A. (2000). Marital stress worsens prognosis in women with coronary heart disease: The Stockholm Female Coronary Risk Study. *Journal of the American Medical Association, 284,* 3008–3014.

Osborn, I. (1998). *The hidden epidemic of obsessive-compulsive disorder.* New York, NY: Random House.

Osborne, L. (2002). *American normal: The hidden world of Asperger syndrome.* Katlenburg-Lindau, Germany: Copernicus Books.

Oslin, D. W., Leong, S. H., Lynch, K. G., Berrettini, W., O'Brien, C. P., Gordon, A. J.,... Rukstalis, M. (2015). Naltrexone vs. placebo for the treatment of alcohol dependence: A randomized clinical trial. *JAMA Psychiatry, 72,* 430–437. doi:10.1001/jamapsychiatry.2014.3053

Osman, S. L. (2003). Predicting men's rape perceptions based on the belief that "no" really means "yes." *Journal of Applied Social Psychology, 33*(4), 683–692.

Ossenkoppele, R., Jansen, W. J., Rabinovici, G. D., Knol, D. L., van der Flier, W. M., van Berckel, B. N. M.,... Amyloid PET Study Group. (2015). Prevalence of amyloid pet positivity in dementia syndromes: A meta-analysis. *Journal of the American Medical Association, 313*, 1939–1949. doi:10.1001/jama.2015.4669

Öst, L. (1987). Age of onset in different phobias. *Journal of Abnormal Psychology, 96*, 223–229.

Öst, L. (1992). Blood and injection phobia: Background and cognitive, physiological, and behavioral variables. *Journal of Abnormal Psychology, 101*, 68–74.

Öst, L.-G., Cederlund, R., & Reuterskiöld, L. (2015). Behavioral treatment of social phobia in youth: Does parent education training improve the outcome? *Behaviour Research and Therapy, 67*, 19–29. doi:10.1016/j.brat.2015.02.001

Öst, L.-G., Havnen, A., Hansen, B., & Kvale, G. (2015). Cognitive behavioral treatments of obsessive–compulsive disorder: A systematic review and meta-analysis of studies published 1993–2014. *Clinical Psychology Review, 40*, 156–169. doi:10.1016/j.cpr.2015.06.003

Otto, M. W. (2006, September 1). Three types of treatment for depression: A comparison. *Journal Watch Psychiatry*. Retrieved from http://psychiatry.jwatch.org/cgi/content/full/2006/901/2

Otto, M. W., & Deveney C. (2005). Cognitive-behavioral therapy and the treatment of panic disorder: Efficacy and strategies. *Journal of Clinical Psychiatry, 66*(Suppl. 4), 28–32.

Overmier, J. B. L., & Seligman, M. E. P. (1967). Effect of inescapable shock upon subsequent escape and avoidance learning. *Journal of Comparative and Physiological Psychology, 63*, 28–33.

Oyserman, D. (2008). Racial-ethnic self-schemas: Multidimensional identity-based motivation. *Journal of Research in Personality, 42*, 1186–1198.

Ozer, E. J., & Weiss, D. S. (2004). Who develops posttraumatic stress disorder? *Current Directions in Psychological Science, 13*, 169–172.

Ozer, E. J., Best, S. R., Lipsey, T. L., & Weiss, D. S. (2003). Predictors of posttraumatic stress disorder and symptoms in adults: A meta-analysis. *Psychological Bulletin, 129*, 52–73.

Pabian, Y. L., Welfel, E., & Beebe, R. S. (2009). Psychologists' knowledge of their states' laws pertaining to Tarasoff-type situations. *Professional Psychology, 40*, 8–14. doi:10.1037/a0014784

Pabst, A., Kraus, L., Piontek, D., Mueller, S., & Demmel, R. (2014). Direct and indirect effects of alcohol expectancies on alcohol-related problems. *Psychology of Addictive Behaviors, 28*, 20–30. doi:10.1037/a0031984

Pacchiarotti, I., Bond, D. J., Baldessarini, R. J., Nolen, W. A., Grunze, H., Licht, R. W.,... Vieta, E. (2013). The International Society for Bipolar Disorders (ISBD), Task Force Report on Antidepressant Use in Bipolar Disorders. *American Journal of Psychiatry, 170*, 1249–1262. doi:10.1176/appi.ajp.2013.13020185

Palfreman, J. (2015). Solving the mystery of Parkinson's. *Scientific American Mind, 26*(5). Retrieved from http://www.scientificamerican.com/article/solving-the-mystery-of-parkinson-s-book-excerpt/?WT.mc_id=SA_MND_20150813_Art_PPV

Pallanti, S., Grassi, G., Antonini, S., Quercioli, L., Salvadori, E., & Hollander, E. (2014). rTMS in resistant mixed states: An exploratory study. *Journal of Affective Disorders, 157*, 66–71. doi:10.1016/j.jad.2013.12.024

Palmer, C. A., & Hazelrigg, M. (2000). The guilty but mentally ill verdict: A review and conceptual analysis of intent and impact. *Journal of the American Academy of Psychiatry and the Law, 28*, 47–54.

Pan, D., Huey, S. J., Jr., & Hernandez, D. (2011). Culturally adapted versus standard exposure treatment for phobic Asian Americans: Treatment efficacy, moderators, and predictors. *Cultural Diversity and Ethnic Minority Psychology, 17*, 11–22. doi:10.1037/a0022534

Panek, R. (2002, November 24). Hmm, what did you mean by all that, Dr. Freud? *The New York Times*, p. AR36.

Pappas, S. (2013). Interested in sex? Hormones may have a little to say about that, ladies. Retrieved from msnbc.com

Paracchini, S., Steer, C. D., Buckingham, L.-L., Morris, A. P., Ring, S., Scerri, T.,... Monaco, A. P. (2008). Association of the KIAA0319 dyslexia susceptibility gene with reading skills in the general population. *American Journal of Psychiatry, 165*, 1576–1584.

Parikh, S. V., Hawke, L. D., Velyvis, V., Zaretsky, A., Beaulieu, S., Patelis-Siotis, I.,... Cervantes, P. (2014). Combined treatment: Impact of optimal psychotherapy and medication in bipolar disorder. *Bipolar Disorder, 17*, 86–96. doi:10.1111/bdi.12233

Paris, J. (2008). *Treatment of borderline personality disorder: A guide to evidence-based practice*. New York, NY: Guilford Press.

Paris, J. (2010). Estimating the prevalence of personality disorders in the community. *Journal of Personality Disorders, 24*, 405–411.

Paris, J. (2012). The outcome of borderline personality disorder: Good for most but not all patients. *American Journal of Psychiatry, 169*, 445–446. doi:10.1176/appi.ajp.2012.12010092

Park, S., & Thakkar, K. N. (2010). "Splitting of the mind" revisited: Recent neuroimaging evidence for functional dysconnection in schizophrenia and its relation to symptoms. *American Journal of Psychiatry, 167*, 366–368. doi:10.1176/appi.ajp.2010.10010089

Parker, G., Gibson, N. A., Brotchie, H., Heruc, G., Rees, A.-M., & Hadzi-Pavlovic, D. (2006). Omega-3 fatty acids and mood disorders. *American Journal of Psychiatry, 163*, 969–978.

Parloff, R. (2003, February 3). Is fat the next tobacco? *Fortune*, 51–54.

Parmet, S, Lynm, C., & Golub, R. M. (2011). Obsessive-compulsive disorder. *Journal of the American Medical Association, 305*, 1926. doi:10.1001/jama.305.18.1926

Parola, N., Bonierbale, M., Lemaire, A., Aghababian, V., Michel, A., & Lançon, C. (2010). Study of quality of life for transsexuals after hormonal and surgical reassignment. *Sexologies, 19*, 24–28. doi:10.1016/j.sexol.2009.05.004

Parto, J. A., Evans, M. K., & Zonderman, A. B. (2011). Symptoms of posttraumatic stress disorder among urban residents. *Journal of Nervous and Mental Disease, 199*, 436–439. doi:10.1097/NMD.0b013e3182214154

Pastor, P. N., Reuben, C. A., Duran, C. R., & Hawkins, L. D. (2015, May). Association between diagnosed ADHD and selected characteristics among children aged 4–17 years: United States, 2011–2013. Retrieved from http://www.cdc.gov/nchs/products/databriefs/db201.htm

Patel, R., Lloyd, T., Jackson, R., Ball, M., Shetty, H., Broadbent, M.,... Taylor, M. (2015). Mood instability is a common feature of mental health disorders and is associated with poor clinical outcomes. *BMJ Open*. Retrieved from https://kclpure.kcl.ac.uk/portal/en/publications/mood-instability-is-a-common-feature-of-mental-health-disorders-and-is-associated-with-poor-clinical-outcomes(86322d4a-1183-4d09-8cae-d8ff33c6fbc6).html

Patihis, L., Lilienfeld, S. O., Ho, L. Y., & Loftus, E. F. (2014). Unconscious repressed memory is scientifically questionable. *Psychological Science, 25*, 1967–1968. doi:10.1177/0956797614547365

Patrick, M. E., & Schulenberg, J. E. (2011). How trajectories of reasons for alcohol use relate to trajectories of binge drinking: National panel data spanning late adolescence to early adulthood. *Developmental Psychology, 47*, 311–317.

Patrick, R. P., & Ames, B. N. (2015). Vitamin D and the omega-3 fatty acids control serotonin synthesis and action, part 2: Relevance for ADHD, bipolar, schizophrenia, and impulsive behavior. *FASEB Journal, 29(6)*, 2207–2222. doi:10.1096/fj.14-268342

Patterson, F., Kerrin, K., Wileyto, P., & Lerman, C. (2008). Increase in anger symptoms after smoking cessation predicts relapse. *Drug and Alcohol Dependence, 95*, 173–176.

Patton, G. C., Coffey, C., Romaniuk, H., Mackinnon, A., Carlin, J. B., Degenhardt, L.,... Moran, P. (2014). The prognosis of common mental disorders in adolescents: A 14-year prospective cohort study. *The Lancet, 383*, 1404–1411. doi:10.1016/S0140-6736(13)62116-9

Patton, G. C., Romaniuk, H., Spry, E., Coffey, C., Olsson, C., Doyle, L. W.,... Brown, S. (2015). Prediction of perinatal depression from adolescence and before conception (VIHCS): 20-year prospective cohort study. *The Lancet, 386*, 875–883.

Paul, E., & Eckenrode, J. (2015). Childhood psychological maltreatment subtypes and adolescent depressive symptoms. *Child Abuse & Neglect, 47*, 38–47. doi:10.1016/j.chiabu.2015.05.018

Paulesu, E., Demonet, J. F., Fazio, F., McCrory, E., Chanoine, V., Brunswick, N.,... Frith, U. (2001). Dyslexia: Cultural diversity and biological unity. *Science, 291*, 2165–2167.

Payne, E., Ford, D., & Morris, J. (2015, February 25). Jury finds Eddie Ray Routh guilty in "American Sniper" case. *CNN.com*. Retrieved from http://www.cnn.com/2015/02/24/us/american-sniper-chris-kyle-trial/

Payne, J. L. (2007). Antidepressant use in the postpartum period: Practical considerations. *American Journal of Psychiatry, 164*, 1329–1332. doi:10.1176/appi.ajp.2007.07030390

Peciña, M., Bohnert, A. S., Sikora, M., Avery, E. T., Langenecker, S. A., Mickey, B. I.,... Zubieta, J. K. (2015). Association between placebo-activated neural systems and antidepressant responses: Neurochemistry of placebo effects in major depression. *JAMA Psychiatry, 30*, 1–8. doi:10.1001/jamapsychiatry.2015.1335

Pelham, W. E., Burrows-MacLean, L., Gnagy, E. M., Fabiano, G. A., Coles, E. K., Tresco, K. E.,... Hoffman, M. T. (2005). Transdermal methylphenidate, behavioral, and combined treatment for children with ADHD. *Experimental and Clinical Psychopharmacology, 13*, 111–126.

Pelkonen, M., & Marttunen, M. (2003). Child and adolescent suicide: Epidemiology, risk factors, and approaches to prevention. *Paediatric Drugs, 5*, 243–265.

Peltzer, K., & Machleidt, W. (1992). A traditional (African) approach towards Therapy of schizophrenia and its comparison with Western models. *Therapeutic Communities International Journal for Therapeutic and Supportive Organizations, 13*, 229–242.

Peng, Y., Hong, S., Qi, X., Xiao, C., Zhong, H., Ma, R. Z., & Su, B. (2010). The ADH1B Arg47His polymorphism in East Asian populations and expansion of rice domestication in history. *BMC Evolutionary Biology, 10*, 15. doi:10.1186/1471-2148-10-15

Pengilly, J. W., & Dowd, E. T. (2000). Hardiness and social support as moderators of stress. *Journal of Clinical Psychology, 56*, 813–820.

Pennant, M. E., Loucas, C. E., Whittington, C., Creswell, C., Fonagy, P., Fuggle, P.,... Kendall, T., on behalf of the Expert Advisory Group. (2015). Computerised therapies for anxiety and depression in children and young people: A systematic review and meta-analysis. *Behaviour Research and Therapy, 67*, 1–18. doi:10.1016/j.brat.2015.01.009

Pennesi, J. L., & Wade. T. D. (2016). A systematic review of the existing models of disordered eating: Do they inform the development of effective interventions? *Clinical Psychology Review, 43*, 175-192. doi:10.1016/j.cpr.2015.12.004

Penninx, B. W. J. H., Beekman, A. T. F., Honig, A., Deeg, D. J. H., Schoevers, R. A., van Eijk, J. T. M., & van Tilburg, W. (2000). Depression and cardiac mortality. *Archives of General Psychiatry, 58*, 221–227.

People with depression get stuck on bad thoughts, unable to turn their attention away, study suggests. (2011, June 3). *ScienceDaily*. Retrieved from http://www.sciencedaily.com/releases/2011/06/110602162828.htm

Peppard, P. E., Szklo-Coxe, M., Hla, K. M., & Young, T. (2006). Longitudinal association of sleep-related breathing disorder and depression. *Archives of Internal Medicine, 166*, 1709–1715.

Pereda, N., Guilera, G., Forns, M., & Gómez-Benito, J. (2009). The prevalence of child sexual abuse in community and student samples: A meta-analysis. *Clinical Psychology Review, 29*, 328–338. doi:10.1016/j.cpr.2009.02.007

Perlin, M. L. (2002–2003). Things have changed: Looking at non-institutional mental disability law through the sanism filter. *New York Law School Review, 46*, 3-4.

Perna, G., Alciati, A., Riva, A., Micieli, W., & Caldirola, D. (2016). Long-term pharmacological treatments of anxiety disorders: An updated

systematic review. *Current Psychiatry Reports, 18,* 23. doi:10.1007/s11920-016-0668-3
Perrin, S. (2013). Prolonged exposure therapy for PTSD in sexually abused adolescents. *Journal of the American Medical Association, 310,* 2619–2620. doi:10.1001/jama.2013.283944
Petersen, L., Sørensen, T. I. A., Andersen, P. K., Mortensen, P. B., & Hawton, K. (2014). Genetic and familial environmental effects on suicide attempts: A study of Danish adoptees and their biological and adoptive siblings. *Journal of Affective Disorders, 155,* 273–277.
Peterson, A. V., Jr., Leroux, B. G., Bricker, J., Kealey, K. A., Marek, P. M., Sarason, I. G., & Andersen, M. R. (2006). Nine-year prediction of adolescent smoking by number of smoking parents. *Addictive Behaviors, 31,* 788–801.
Peterson, B. S., Wang, Z., Horga, G., Warner, V., Rutherford, B., Klahr, K. W., . . . Weissman, M. M. (2014). Discriminating risk and resilience endophenotypes from lifetime illness effects in familial major depressive disorder. *JAMA Psychiatry, 71,* 136–148. doi:10.1001/jamapsychiatry.2013.4048
Peterson, E., & Yancy, C. W. (2009). Eliminating racial and ethnic disparities in cardiac care. *New England Journal of Medicine, 360,* 1172–1174. doi:10.1056/NEJMp0810121
Peterson, J. K., Skeem, J., Kennealy, P., Bray, B., & Zvonkovic, A. (2014). How often and how consistently do symptoms directly precede criminal behavior among offenders with mental illness? *Law and Human Behavior, 38,* 439–449. doi:10.1037/lhb0000075
Peterson, Z. D., Voller, E. K., Polusny, M. A., & Murdoch, M. (2010). Prevalence and consequences of adult sexual assault of men: Review of empirical findings and state of the literature. *Clinical Psychology Review, 31,* 1–24. doi:10.1016/j.cpr.2010.08
Petit, D., Pennestri, M. H., Paquet, J., Desautels, A., Zadra, A., Vitaro, F., Tremblay, R. E., . . . Montplaisir, J. (2015). Childhood sleepwalking and sleep terrors: A longitudinal study of prevalence and familial aggregation. *JAMA Pediatrics, 169*(7), 653–658. Retrieved from http://dx.doi.org/10.1001/jamapediatrics.2015.127
Petry, N. M., Alessi, S. M., Marx, J., Austin, M., & Tardif, M. (2005). Vouchers versus prizes: Contingency management treatment of substance abusers in community settings. *Journal of Consulting and Clinical Psychology, 73,* 1005–1014.
Petry, N. M., Ammerman, Y., Bohl, J., Doersch, A., Gay, H., Kadden, R., . . . Steinberg, K. (2006). Cognitive-behavioral therapy for pathological gamblers. *Journal of Consulting and Clinical Psychology, 74,* 555–567.
Petry, N. M., & Martin, B. (2002). Low-cost contingency management for treating cocaine- and opioid-abusing methadone patients. *Journal of Consulting and Clinical Psychology, 70,* 398–405.
Petry, N. M., Weinstock, J., Ledgerwood, D. M., & Morasco, B. (2008). A randomized trial of brief interventions for problem and pathological gamblers. *Journal of Consulting and Clinical Psychology, 76,* 318–328.
Pettinati, H. M., O'Brien, C. P., & Dundon, W. D. (2013). Current status of co-occurring mood and substance use disorders: A new therapeutic target. *American Journal of Psychiatry, 170,* 23–30. doi:10.1176/appi.ajp.2012.12010112
Philaretou, A. G. (2006). Female exotic dancers: Intrapersonal and interpersonal perspectives. *Sexual Addiction & Compulsivity, 13,* 41–52.
Philip, N. S., Carpenter, S. L., Ridout, S. J., Sanchez, G., Albright, S. E., Tyrka, A. R., Price, L. H., & Carpenter, L. L. (2015). 5 Hz repetitive transcranial magnetic stimulation to left prefrontal cortex for major depression. *Journal of Affective Disorders, 186,* 13–17.
Phillips, K. A., & Menard, W. (2006). Suicidality in body dysmorphic disorder: A prospective study. *American Journal of Psychiatry, 163,* 1280–1282.
Phillips, K. A., & Rogers, J. (2011). Cognitive-behavioral therapy for youth with body dysmorphic disorder: Current status and future directions. *Child and Adolescent Psychiatric Clinics of North America, 20,* 287–304.
Phillips, M. L., & Swartz, H. A. (2014). A critical appraisal of neuroimaging studies of bipolar disorder: Toward a new conceptualization of underlying neural circuitry and a road map for future research. *American Journal of Psychiatry, 171,* 829–843. doi:10.1176/appi.ajp.2014.13081008
Piasecki, T. M., Jorenby, D. E., Smith, S. S., Fiore, M. C., & Baker, T. B. (2003). Smoking withdrawal dynamics: I. Abstinence distress in lapsers and abstainers. *Journal of Consulting and Clinical Psychology, 112,* 3–13.
Pingault, J. B., Tremblay, R. E., Vitaro, F., Carbonneau, R., Genolini, C., Falissard, B., . . . Côté, S. M. (2011). Childhood trajectories of inattention and hyperactivity and prediction of educational attainment in early adulthood: A 16-year longitudinal population-based study. *American Journal of Psychiatry, 168,* 1164–1170.
Pingault, J.-B., Viding, E., Galéra, C., Greven, C. U., Zheng, Y., Plomin, R., . . . Rijsdijk, F. (2015). Genetic and environmental influences on the developmental course of attention-deficit/hyperactivity disorder symptoms from childhood to adolescence. *JAMA Psychiatry, 72*(7), 651–658. doi:10.1001/jamapsychiatry.2015.0469
Pinto, A. (2016). Treatment of obsessive-compulsive personality disorder. In E. A. Storch & A. B. Lewin (Eds.), *Clinical handbook of obsessive-compulsive and related disorders: A case-based approach to treating pediatric and adult populations* (pp. 415–429). New York, NY: Springer.
Pirelli, G., Gottdiener, W. H., & Zapf, P. (2011). A meta-analytic review of competency to stand trial research. *Psychology, Public Policy, & Law, 17,* 1–53. doi:10.1037/a0021713
Pistorello, J., Fruzzetti, A. E., & MacLane, C., Gallop, R., & Iverson, K. M. (2012). Dialectical behavior therapy (DBT) applied to college students: A randomized clinical trial. *Journal of Consulting and Clinical Psychology, 80,* 982–994. doi:10.1037/a0029096
Pitman, R. K. (2006). Combat effects on mental health: The more things change, the more they remain the same. *Archives of General Psychiatry, 63,* 127–128.
Pizzimenti, C. L., & Lattal, K. M. (2015). Epigenetics and memory: Causes, consequences and treatments for post-traumatic stress disorder and addiction. *Genes, Brain and Behavior, 14,* 73–84. doi:10.1111/gbb.12187
Plasschaert, R. N., & Bartolomei, M. S. (2013). Autism: A long genetic explanation. *Nature, 501,* 36–37. doi:10.1038/nature12553
Plewnia, C., Pasqualetti, P., Große, S., Schlipf, S., Wasserka, B., Zwissler, B., & Fallgatter, A. (2014). Treatment of major depression with bilateral theta burst stimulation: A randomized controlled pilot trial. *Journal of Affective Disorders, 156,* 219–223. doi:10.1016/j.jad.2013.12.025
Plunkett, A., O'Toole, B., Swanston, H., Oates, R. K., Shrimpton, S., & Parkinson, P. (2001). Suicide risk following child sexual abuse. *Ambulatory Pediatrics, 5,* 262–266.
PMDD proposed as new category in DSM-5. (2012, May 25). *Psychiatric News Alert.* Retrieved from www.psychiatricnews.org
Pocklington, A. J., Rees, E., Walters, J. T. R., Han, J., Kavanagh, D. H., Chambert, K. D., . . . Owen, M. J. (2015). Novel findings from CNVs implicate inhibitory and excitatory signaling complexes in schizophrenia. *Neuron, 86,* 1203. doi:10.1016/j.neuron.2015.04.022
Pogue-Geile, M. F., & Yokley, J. L. (2010). Current research on the genetic contributors to schizophrenia. *Current Directions in Psychological Science, 19,* 214–219. doi:10.1177/0963721410378490
Pokhrel, P., Herzog, T. A., Sun, P., Rohrbach, L. A., & Sussman, S. (2013). Acculturation, social self-control, and substance use among Hispanic adolescents. *Psychology of Addictive Behaviors, 27,* 674–686. doi:10.1037/a0032836
Polanczyk, G., Caspi, A., Williams, B., Price, T. S., Danese, A., Sugden, K., Uher, R., & Moffitt, T. E. (2009). Protective effect of CRHR1 gene variants on the development of adult depression following childhood maltreatment: Replication and extension. *Archives of General Psychiatry, 66,* 978–985. doi:10.1001/archgenpsychiatry.2009.114
Polderman, T. J. C., Benyamin, B., de Leeuw, C. A., Sullivan, P. F., van Bochoven, A., Visscher, P. M., & Posthuma, D. (2015). Meta-analysis of the heritability of human traits based on fifty years of twin studies. *Nature Genetics, 47,* 702–709. doi:10.1038/ng.3285
Poling, J., Oliveto, A., Petry, N., Sofuoglu, M., Gonsai, K., Gonzalez, G., . . . Kosten, T. R. (2006). Six-month trial of bupropion with contingency management for cocaine dependence in a methadone-maintained population. *Archives of General Psychiatry, 63,* 219–228.
Pollack, A. (2004a, January 13). Putting a price on a good night's sleep. *The New York Times,* pp. F1, F8.
Pollack, A. (2004b, January 13). Sleep experts debate root of insomnia: Body, mind or a little of each. *The New York Times,* p. F8.
Pollan, M. (2003, October 12). The (agri)cultural contradictions of obesity. *The New York Times Magazine,* 41, 48.
Polusny, M. A., Erbes, C. R., Thuras, P., Moran, A., Lamberty, G. J., Collins, R. C., . . . Lim, K. O. (2015). Mindfulness-based stress reduction for posttraumatic stress disorder among veterans. *Journal of the American Medical Association, 314,* 456. doi:10.1001/jama.2015.8361
Polusny, M. A., Kehle, S. M., Nelson, N. W., Erbes, C. R., Arbisi, P. A., & Thuras, P. (2011). Longitudinal effects of mild traumatic brain injury and posttraumatic stress disorder comorbidity on postdeployment outcomes in national guard soldiers deployed to Iraq. *Archives of General Psychiatry, 68,* 79–89. doi:10.1001/archgenpsychiatry.2010.172
Pompili, M., Sher, L., Serafini, G., Forte, A., Innamorati, M., Dominici, G., . . . Girardi, P. (2013). Posttaumatic stress disorder and suicide risk among veterans: A literature review. *Journal of Nervous & Mental Disease, 201,* 802–812. doi:10.1097/NMD.0b013e3182a21458
Ponseti, J., Granert, O., Jansen, O., Wolff, S., Beier, K., Neutze, J., . . . Bosinski, H. (2012). Assessment of pedophilia using hemodynamic brain response to sexual stimuli. *Archives of General Psychiatry, 69,* 187–194. doi:10.1001/archgenpsychiatry.2011.130
Postuma, R. B., Lang, A. E., Gagnon, J. F., Pelletier, A., & Montplaisir, J. Y. (2012). How does parkinsonism start? Prodromal parkinsonism motor changes in idiopathic REM sleep behaviour disorder. *Brain, 135,* 1860–1870.
Power, R. A., Steinberg, S., Bjornsdottir, G., Rietveld, C. A., Abdellaoui, A., Nivard, M. M., . . . Stefansson, K. (2015). Polygenic risk scores for schizophrenia and bipolar disorder predict creativity. *Nature Neuroscience, 8,* 953–955. doi:10.1038/nn.4040
Pramparo, T., Pierce, K., Lombardo, M. V., Barnes, C. C., Marinero, S., Ahrens-Barbeau, C., . . . Courchesne, E. (2015). Prediction of autism by translation and immune/inflammation coexpressed genes in toddlers from pediatric community practices. *JAMA Psychiatry, 72,* 386–394. doi:10.1001/jamapsychiatry.2014.3008
Pratt, L. A., & Brody, D. J. (2008, September). Depression in the United States household population, 2005–2006. *NCHS Data Brief,* Number 7. Retrieved from http://www.cdc.gov/nchs/data/databriefs/db07.htm
Price, M. (2009, December). More than shelter. *Monitor on Psychology, 40*(11), 59–62.
Prince, M., Prina, M., Guerchet, M., & Alzheimer's Disease International. (2013). *World Alzheimer report 2013: Journey of caring: An analysis of long-term care for dementia.* London, UK: Alzheimer's Disease Interational. Retrieved from http://www.alz.co.uk/research/WorldAlzheimerReport2013.pdf
Prins, H. (2013). *Psychopaths: An introduction.* Hampshire, UK: Waterside Press.
Prochaska, J. O., & Norcross, J. C. (2010). *Systems of psychotherapy* (7th ed.). Belmont, CA: Brooks/Cole.
Psychiatric GWAS Consortium Bipolar Disorder Working Group. (2011). Large-scale genome-wide association analysis of bipolar disorder identifies a new susceptibility locus near ODZ4. *Nature Genetics, 43,* 977–983. doi:10.1038/ng.943
Pulkki-Raback, L., Kivimaki, M., Ahola, K., Joutsenniemi, K., Elovainio, M., Rossi, H., . . . Virtanen, M. (2012). Living alone and antidepressant medication use: A prospective study in a working-age population. *BMC Public Health, 12,* 236. doi:10.1186/1471-2458-12-236
Pumariega, A. J. (1986). Acculturation and eating attitudes in adolescent girls. *Journal of the American Academy of Child Psychiatry, 25,* 276–279.
Purkis, H. M., Lester, K. J., & Field, A. P. (2011). But what about the Empress of Racnoss? The allocation

of attention to spiders and doctor who in a visual search task is predicted by fear and expertise. *Emotion, 11*, 1484–1488.

Pyszczynski, T., & Greenberg, J. (1987). Self-regulatory preservation and the depressive self-focusing style: A self-awareness theory of reactive depression. *Psychological Bulletin, 102*, 122–138.

Qaseem, A., Snow, V., Denberg, T. D., Casey, D. E., Jr., Forciea, M. A., Owens, D. K., & Shekelle, P. (2009). Testing and pharmacologic treatment of erectile dysfunction: A clinical practice guideline from the American College of Physicians. *Annals of Internal Medicine*. Retrieved from www.annals.org/content/early/2009/10/19/0000605-200911030-00151.abstract?sid=4f936910ee83-44d8-8f48-1f7f7124d93c

Qin, B., Zhang, Y., Zhou, X., Cheng, P., Liu, Y., Chen, J.,…Xie, P. (2014). Selective serotonin reuptake inhibitors versus tricyclic antidepressants in young patients: A meta-analysis of efficacy and acceptability. *Clinical Therapeutics, 36*, 1087–1095. doi:10.1016/j.clinthera.2014.06.001

Queen's man arraigned in therapist's slaying. (2008, February 17). *MSNBC.com*. Retrieved from http://www.msnbc.msn.com/id/23199458/ns/us_news-crime_and_courts/t/queensman-arraigned-therapists-killing/#.UPctQyeoOpU

Quenqua, D. (2012, May 22). Drugs help tailor alcoholism treatment. *The New York Times*, pp. D1, D6.

Querfurth, H. W., & LaFerla, F. M. (2010). Alzheimer's disease. *New England Journal of Medicine, 362*, 329–344.

Quinn, S. (1987). *A mind of her own: The life of Karen Horney*. New York, NY: Summit Books.

Rabasca, L. (2000, March). Listening instead of preaching. *Monitor on Psychology, 31*(3), 50–51.

Rabin, R. C. (2009, June 16). Alcohol's good for you? Some scientists doubt it. *The New York Times*, pp. D1, D6.

Rabin, R. C. (2011, December 14). Nearly 1 in 5 women in U.S. survey say they have been sexually assaulted. *The New York Times*, p. A32.

Rachman, S. (2000). Joseph Wolpe (1915–1997). *American Psychologist, 55*, 431.

Rachman, S. (2009). Psychological treatment of anxiety: The evolution of behavior therapy and cognitive behavior therapy. *Annual Review of Clinical Psychology, 5*, 97–119. doi:10.1146/annurev.clinpsy.032408.153635

Rachman, S. (2015). The evolution of behaviour therapy and cognitive behaviour therapy. *Behaviour Research and Therapy, 64*, 1–8.

Rachman, S., & DeSilva, P. (2009). *Obsessive-compulsive disorder* (4th ed.). Oxford, UK: Oxford University Press.

Racine, S. E., Burt, S. A., Iacono, W. G., McGue, M., & Klump, K. L. (2011). Dietary restraint moderates genetic risk for binge eating. *Journal of Abnormal Psychology, 120*, 119–128. doi:10.1037/a0020895

Radel, M., Vallejo, R. L., Iwata, N., Aragon, R., Long, J. C., Virkkunen, M., & Goldman, D. (2005). Haplotype based localization of an alcohol dependence gene to the 5q34{gamma} aminobutyric acid type A gene cluster. *Archives of General Psychiatry, 62*, 47–55.

Ragsdale, K., Porter, J. R., Zamboanga, B. L., St. Lawrence, J. S., Read-Wahidi, R., & White, A. (2012). High-risk drinking among female college drinkers at two reporting intervals: Comparing spring break to the 30 days prior. *Sexuality Research and Social Policy, 9*(1), 31–40.

Raine, A. (2008). From genes to brain to antisocial behavior. *Current Directions in Psychological Science, 17*, 323–328.

Rajkumar, R. P., & Kumaran, A. K. (2015). Depression and anxiety in men with sexual dysfunction: A retrospective study. *Comprehensive Psychiatry, 60*, 114–118. doi:10.1016/j.comppsych.2015.03.001

Rajwan, E., Chacko, A., & Moeller, M. (2012). Nonpharmacological interventions for preschool ADHD: State of the evidence and implications for practice. *Professional Psychology: Research and Practice, 43*, 520–526. doi:10.1037/a0028812

Rapee, R. M., Gaston, J. E., & Abbott, M. J. (2009). Testing the efficacy of theoretically derived improvements in the treatment of social phobia. *Journal of Consulting and Clinical Psychology, 77*, 317–327. doi:10.1037/a0014800

Raskin, N. J., Rogers, C. R., & Witty, M. C. (2011). Person-centered therapy. In R. J. Corsini & D. Wedding (Eds.), *Current psychotherapies* (9th ed., pp. 148–195). Belmont, CA: Brooks/Cole.

Rasmussen, H., Erritzoe, D., Andersen, R., Ebdrup, B., H., Aggernaes, B., Oranje, B.,…Glenthoj, B. (2010). Decreased frontal serotonin 2a receptor binding in antipsychotic-naive patients with first-episode schizophrenia. *Archives of General Psychiatry, 67*, 9–16.

Rasmussen, K. M., Negy, C., Carlson, R., & Burns, J. M. (1997). Suicide ideation and acculturation among low socioeconomic status Mexican American adolescents. *Journal of Early Adolescence, 17*, 390–407.

Rate of patients in psychiatric hospitals has fallen to level of 1850. (2012, December 8). Allgov.com. Retrieved from http://www.allgov.com/news/controversies/rate-ofpatients-in-psychiatric-hospitals-has-fallen-to-level-of-1850-121228?news=846605

Rathus, S. A., & Nevid, J. S. (1977). *BT/Behavior therapy*. New York, NY: Doubleday & Co.

Rathus, S. A., Nevid, J. S., & Fichner-Rathus, L. (2014). *Human sexuality in a world of diversity* (9th ed.). Upper Saddle River, NJ: Pearson Education.

Rawe, J., & Kingsbury, K. (2006, May 22). When colleges go on suicide watch. *Time*, 62–63.

Ray, R. A. (2012). Clinical neuroscience of addiction: Applications to psychological science and practice. *Clinical Psychology: Science and Practice, 19*, 154–166. doi:10.1111/j.1468-2850.2012.01280

Raykos, B. C., McEvoy, P. M., Erceg-Hurn, D., Byrne, S. M., Fursland, A., & Nathan, P. (2014). Therapeutic alliance in enhanced cognitive behavioural therapy for bulimia nervosa: Probably necessary but definitely insufficient. *Behavior Research and Therapy, 57*, 65–71. doi:10.1016/j.brat.2014.04.004

Reade, M. C., & Finfer, S. (2014). Sedation and delirium in the intensive care unit. *New England Journal of Medicine, 370*, 444–454. doi:10.1056/NEJMra1208705

Reas, D. L., & Grilo, C. M. (2007). Timing and sequence of the onset of overweight, dieting, and binge eating in overweight patients with binge eating disorder. *International Journal of Eating Disorders, 40*, 165–170.

Rechenberg, K. (2016). Nutritional interventions in clinical depression. *Clinical Psychological Science, 4*, 144–162. doi:10.1177/2167702614566815

Rees, C. S., & Pritchard, R. (2015). Brief cognitive therapy for avoidant personality disorder. *Psychotherapy, 52*, 45–55. Retrieved from http://dx.doi.org/10.1037/a0035158

Reeves, R. R., & Ladner, M. E. (2009). Antidepressant-induced suicidality: Implications for clinical practice. *Southern Medical Journal, 102*, 713–718. doi:10.1097/SMJ.0b013e3181a918bd

Rehm, L. P. (2010). *Depression: Advances in psychotherapy: Evidence-based practice*. Cambridge, MA: Hogrefe Publishing.

Rehman, U. S., Gollan, J., & Mortimer, A. R. (2008). The marital context of depression: Research, limitations, and new directions. *Clinical Psychology Review, 28*, 179–198.

Reichborn-Kjennerud, T., Ystrom, E., Neale, M. C., Aggen, S. H., Mazzeo, S. E., Knudsen, G. P.,…Kendler, K. S. (2013). Structure of genetic and environmental risk factors for symptoms of DSM-IV borderline personality disorder. *JAMA Psychiatry, 70*, 1206–1214. doi:10.1001/jamapsychiatry.2013.1944

Reid, B. V., & Whitehead, T. L. (1992). Introduction. In T. L. Whitehead & B. V. Reid (Eds.), *Gender constructs and social issues* (pp. 1–9). Chicago, IL: University of Illinois.

Reid, J. G., Gitlin, M. J., & Altshuler, L. L. (2013). Lamotrigine in psychiatric disorders. *The Journal of Clinical Psychiatry, 74*, 675–684. doi:10.4088/JCP.12r08046

Reifler, B. V. (2006). Play it again, Sam: Depression is recurring. *New England Journal of Medicine, 354*, 1189–1190.

Reinares, M., Sánchez-Moreno, J., & Fountoulakis, K. N. (2014). Psychosocial interventions in bipolar disorder: What, for whom, and when. *Journal of Affective Disorders, 156*, 46–55. doi:10.1016/j.jad.2013.12.017

Reinberg, S. (2009, January 12). Lack of sleep linked to common cold. *WashingtonPost.com*. Retrieved from http://www.washingtonpost.com/wp-dyn/content/article/2009/01/12/AR2009011202090.html

Reinisch, J. M. (1990). *The Kinsey Institute new report on sex: What you must know to be sexually literate*. New York, NY: St. Martin's Press.

Reisner, A. D. (1994). Multiple personality disorder diagnosis: A house of cards? *American Journal of Psychiatry, 151*, 629.

Reiss, D. (2005). The interplay between genotypes and family relationships: Reframing concepts of development and prevention. *Current Directions in Psychological Science, 14*, 139–143.

Reissing, E. D. (2012). Consultation and treatment history and causal attributions in an online sample of women with lifelong and acquired vaginismus. *Journal of Sexual Medicine, 9*(1), 251–258.

Reitan, R. M., & Wolfson, D. (2012). Detection of malingering and invalid test results using the Halstead–Reitan Battery. In C. R. Reynolds & A. M. Horton (Eds.), *Detection of malingering during head injury litigation* (pp. 241–272). New York, NY: Springer.

Remedial instruction rewires dyslexic brains, provides lasting results, study shows. (2008, August 7). *ScienceDaily*. Retrieved from http://www.sciencedaily.com/releases/2008/08/080805124056.htm

Ren, J., Li, H., Palaniyappan, L., Liu, H., Wang, J., Li, C., & Rossini, P. M. (2014). Repetitive transcranial magnetic stimulation versus electroconvulsive therapy for major depression: A systematic review and meta-analysis. *Progress in Neuro-Psychopharmacology and Biological Psychiatry, 3*, 181–189. doi:10.1016/j.pnpbp.2014.02.004

Renfrey, G. S. (1992). Cognitive-behavior therapy and the Native American client. *Behavior Therapy, 23*, 321–340.

Renner, M. J., & Mackin, R. S. (1998). A life stress instrument for classroom use. *Teaching of Psychology, 25*, 46–48.

Rennert, L., Denis, C., Peer, K., Lynch, K. G., Gelernter, J., & Kranzler, H. R. (2014). DSM-5 gambling disorder: Prevalence and characteristics in a substance use disorder sample. *Experimental and Clinical Psychopharmacology, 22*, 50–56. doi:10.1037/a0034518

Reppermund, S,. Brodaty, H., Crawford, J. D., Kochan, N. A., Slavin, M. J., Trollor, J. N., Draper, B., & Sachdev, P. S. (2011). The relationship of current depressive symptoms and past depression with cognitive impairment and instrumental activities of daily living in an elderly population: The Sydney Memory and Ageing Study. *Journal of Psychiatric Research, 45*, 1600–1607. doi:10.1016/j.jpsychires.2011.08.001

Resick, P. A., Williams, L. F., Suvak, M. K., Monson, C. M., & Gradus, J. L. (2012). Long-term outcomes of cognitive–behavioral treatments for posttraumatic stress disorder among female rape survivors. *Journal of Consulting and Clinical Psychology, 80*, 201–210. doi:10.1037/a0026602

Ressler, K. J., & Rothbaum, B. O. (2013). Augmenting obsessive-compulsive disorder treatment: From brain to mind. *JAMA Psychiatry, 70*, 1129–1131. doi:10.1001/jamapsychiatry.2013.2116

Rettner, R. (2011, April 10). Popular drug for mild Alzheimer's largely a flop. *MSNBC.com*. Retrieved from http://www.msnbc.msn.com/id/42540787/ns/health-alzheimers_disease/

Reuven-Magril, O., Dar, R., & Liberman, N. (2008). Illusion of control and behavioral control attempts in obsessive-compulsive disorder. *Journal of Abnormal Psychology, 117*, 334–341.

Rey, J. M. (1993). Oppositional defiant disorder. *American Journal of Psychiatry, 150*, 1769–1778.

Reynolds, C. F., III, & O'Hara, R. (2013). DSM-5 sleep-wake disorders classification: Overview for use in clinical practice. *American Journal of Psychiatry, 170*, 1099–1101. doi:10.1176/appi.ajp.2013.13010058

Reynolds, E. H. (2012). Hysteria, conversion and functional disorders: A neurological contribution to classification issues. *British Journal of Psychiatry, 201*, 253–254.

Rezai, A. R., Leehey, M. A., Ojemann, S. G., Flaherty, A. W., Eskandar, E. N., Kostyk, S. K.,…Feigin. A. (2011). AAV2-GAD gene therapy for advanced Parkinson's disease: A double-blind, sham-surgery controlled, randomized trial. *Lancet Neurology, 10*, 309–319. doi:10.1016/S1474-4422(11)70039-4

Ribisl, K. M., Cruz, T. B., Rohrbach, L. A., Ribisl, K. M., Baezconde-Garbanati, L., Chen, X.,…Johnson, C. A. (2000). English language use as a risk factor for smoking initiation among Hispanic and Asian American adolescents: Evidence for mediation by tobacco-related beliefs and social norms. *Health Psychology, 19*, 403–410.

Ricciardelli, L. A., & McCabe, M. P. (2004). A biopsychosocial model of disordered eating and the pursuit of muscularity in adolescent boys. *Psychological Bulletin, 130*, 179–205.

Richard, E., Reitz, C., Honig, L. H., Schupf, N., Tang, M. X., Manly, J. J.,... Luchsinger, J. A. (2012). Late-life depression, mild cognitive impairment, and dementia. *Archives of Neurology, 18*, 98–116. doi:10.1097/JGP.0b013e3181b0fa13

Richards, D. (2011). Prevalence and clinical course of depression: A review. *Clinical Psychology Review, 31*, 1117–11125. doi:10.1016/j.cpr.2011.07.004

Richards, D., Richardson, T., Timulak, L., & McElvaney, J. (2015). The efficacy of Internet-delivered treatment for generalized anxiety disorder: A systematic review and meta-analysis. *Internet Interventions, 2*, 272–282. http://dx.doi.org/10.1016/j.invent.2015.07.003

Richtel, M. (2015, April 26). Push, don't crush, the students. *The New York Times Sunday Review*, pp. 1, 7.

Rickards, H., & Silver, J. (2014). Don't know what they are, but treatable? Therapies for conversion disorder. *Journal of Neurology, Neurosurgery, and Psychiatry, 85*, 830–831.

Rief, W., & Sharpe, M. (2004). Somatoform disorders: New approaches to classification, conceptualization, and treatment. *Journal of Psychosomatic Research, 56*, 387–390.

Rief, W., Nestoriuc, Y., Weiss, S., Welzel, E., Barsky, A. J., & Hofmann, S. G. (2009). Meta-analysis of the placebo response in antidepressant trials. *Journal of Affective Disorders, 118*, 1–8. doi:10.1016/j.jad.2009.01.029

Rieger, E., Van Buren, D. J., Bishop, M., Tanofsky-Kraff, M., Welch, R., & Wilfley, D. E. (2010). An eating disorder-specific model of interpersonal psychotherapy (IPT-ED): Causal pathways and treatment implications. *Clinical Psychology Review, 30*(4), 400–410. doi:10.1016/j.cpr.2010.02.001

Riesel, A., Endrass, T., Auerbach, L. A., & Kathmann, N. (2015). Overactive performance monitoring as an endophenotype for obsessive-compulsive disorder: Evidence from a treatment study. *American Journal of Psychiatry, 172*, 665–673. Retrieved from http://dx.doi.org/10.1176/appi.ajp.2014.14070886

Rimm, E. (2000, May). Lifestyle may play role in potential for impotence. Paper presented to the annual meeting of the American Urological Association, Atlanta, GA.

Rink, L., Pagel, T., Franklin, J., & Baethge, C. (2016). Characteristics and heterogeneity of schizoaffective disorder compared with unipolar depression and schizophrenia: A systematic literature review and meta-analysis. *Journal of Affective Disorders, 191*, 8–14.

Ritz, T., Meuret, A. E., Trueba, A. F., Fritzsche, A., & von Leupoldt, A. (2013). Psychosocial factors and behavioral medicine interventions in asthma. *Journal of Consulting and Clinical Psychology, 81*, 231–250. doi:10.1037/a0030187

Riva-Posse, P., Choi, K. S., Holtzheimer, P. E., McIntyre, C. C., Gross, R. E., Chaturvedi, A.,... Mayberg, H. S. (2014). Defining critical white matter pathways mediating successful subcallosal cingulate deep brain stimulation for treatment-resistant depression. *Biological Psychiatry, 76*, 963–969. doi:10.1016/j.biopsych.2014.03.029

Roberts, J. A., Yaya, L. H. P., & Manolis, C. (2014). The invisible addiction: Cell-phone activities and addiction among male and female college students. *Journal of Behavioral Addictions, 3*(4), 254–265. doi:10.1556/JBA.3.2014.015

Roberts, R. E. (2008). Persistence and change in symptoms of insomnia among adolescents. *Sleep, 31*, 177.

Robin, R. W., Greene, R. L., Albaugh, B., Caldwell, A., & Goldman, D. (2003). Use of the MMPI-2 in American Indians: I. Comparability of the MMPI-2 between two tribes and with the MMPI-2 normative group. *Psychological Assessment, 15*, 351–359.

Robiner, W. N., Tumlin, T. R., & Tompkins, T. L. (2013). Psychologists and medications in the era of interprofessional care: Collaboration is less problematic and costly than prescribing. *Clinical Psychology: Science and Practice, 20*, 489–507. doi:10.1111/cpsp.12054

Robins, L. N., Locke, B. Z., & Reiger, D. A. (1991). An overview of psychiatric disorders in America. In L. N. Robins & D. A. Regier (Eds.), *Psychiatric disorders in America: The Epidemiologic Catchment Area Study* (pp. 328–366). New York, NY: Free Press.

Robinson, J. A., Sareen, J., Cox, B. J., & Bolton, J. M. (2009). Correlates of self-medication for anxiety disorders: Results from the National Epidemiologic Survey on Alcohol and Related Conditions. *The Journal of Nervous and Mental Disease, 297*, 873–878. doi:10.1097/NMD.0b013e3181c299c2

Robinson, L. J., & Freeston, M. H. (2014). Emotion and internal experience in obsessive compulsive disorder: Reviewing the role of alexithymia, anxiety sensitivity and distress tolerance. *Clinical Psychology Review, 34*, 256–272. doi:10.1016/j.cpr.2014.03.003

Rodgers, R. F., Salès, P., & Chabrol, H. (2010). Psychological functioning, media pressure and body dissatisfaction among college women. *European Review of Applied Psychology, 60*(2), 89–95. doi:10.1016/j.erap.2009.10.001

Rodriguez, C. I., Simpson, H. B., Liu, S.-M., Levinson, A., & Blanco, C. (2013). Prevalence and correlates of difficulty discarding: Results from a national sample of the U.S. population. *Journal of Nervous & Mental Disease, 201*, 795–801. doi:10.1097/NMD.0b013e3182a21471

Rodriguez, J., Umaña-Taylor, A., Smith, E. P., & Johnson, D. J. (2009). Cultural processes in parenting and youth outcomes: Examining a model of racial-ethnic socialization and identity in diverse populations. *Cultural Diversity and Ethnic Minority Psychology, 15*, 106–111. doi:10.1037/a0015510

Rodriguez-Seijas, C., Stohl, M., Hasin, D. S., & Eaton, N. R. (2015). Transdiagnostic factors and mediation of the relationship between perceived racial discrimination and mental disorders. *JAMA Psychiatry, 72*, 706–713. doi:10.1001/jamapsychiatry.2015.0148

Roesch, R., Zapf, P. A., & Hart, S. D. (2010). *Forensic psychology and law*. Hoboken, NJ: Wiley.

Rogan, A. (1986, Fall). Recovery from alcoholism: Issues for black and Native American alcoholics. *Alcohol Health and Research World, 10*, 42–44.

Roger, V. L. (2009). Lifestyle and cardiovascular health: Individual and societal choices. *Journal of the American Medical Association, 302*, 437–439.

Rogers, Carl. (1951). *Client-centered therapy: Its current practice, implications and theory*. London, UK: Constable.

Rogers, J. (2009, August 5). Alzheimer disease and inflammation: More epidemiology, more questions. *JournalWatch Neurology*. Retrieved from http://neurology.jwatch.org/cgi/content/full/2009/804/3?q=etoc_jwneuro

Rohan, K. J., Mahon, J. N., Evans, M., Ho, S.-Y., Meyerhoff, J., Postolache, T. T.,... Vacek, P. M. (2015). Randomized trial of cognitive-behavioral therapy versus light therapy for seasonal affective disorder: Acute outcomes. *American Journal of Psychiatry, 172*, 862–869. Received from http://dx.doi.org/10.1176/appi.ajp.2015.14101293

Rohan, K. J., Meyerhoff, J., Ho, S.-Y., Evans, M., Postolache, T. T., & Vacek, P. M. (2016). Outcomes one and two winters following cognitive-behavioral therapy or light therapy for seasonal affective disorder. *American Journal of Psychiatry, 173*, 244–251.

Rohan, K. J., Sigmon, S. T., & Dorhofer, D. M. (2003). Cognitive–behavioral factors in seasonal affective disorder. *Journal of Consulting and Clinical Psychology, 71*, 22–30.

Rohde, P., Lewinsohn, P. M., Klein, D. N., Seeley, J. R., & Gau, J. M. (2013). Key characteristics of major depressive disorder occurring in childhood, adolescence, emerging adulthood, and adulthood. *Clinical Psychological Science, 1*, 41–53. doi:10.1177/2167702612457599

Roisko, R., Wahlberg, K.-E., Miettunen, J., & Tienari, P. (2014). Association of parental communication deviance with offspring's psychiatric and thought disorders: A systematic review and meta-analysis. *European Psychiatry, 29*, 20–31. Received from http://dx.doi.org/10.1016/j.eurpsy.2013.05.002

Roll, J. M., Petry, N. M., Stitzer, M. L., Brecht, M. L., Peirce, J. M., McCann, M. J.,... Kellogg, S. (2006). Contingency management for the treatment of methamphetamine use disorders. *American Journal of Psychiatry, 163*, 1993–1999.

Rolle, L., Ceruti, C., Timpano, M., Falcone, M., & Frea, B. (2015). Quality of life after sexual reassignment surgery. In C. Trombetta, G. Liguori, & M. Bertolotto (Eds.), *Management of gender dysphoria* (pp. 193–203). Milan, Italy: Springer-Verlag Italia.

Rolon, Y. M., & Jones, J. C. W. (2008). Right to refuse treatment. *Journal of the American Academy of Psychiatry and the Law, 36*, 252–255.

Ronksley, P. E., Brien, S. E., Turner, B. J., Mukamal, K. J., & Ghali, W. A. (2011). Association of alcohol consumption with selected cardiovascular disease outcomes: A systematic review and meta-analysis. *British Medical Journal, 342*, 671. doi:10.1136/bmj.d671

Rooksby, M., Elouafkaoui, P., Humphris, G., Clarkson, J., & Freeman R. (2014). Internet-assisted delivery of cognitive behavioural therapy (CBT) for childhood anxiety: Systematic review and meta-analysis. *Journal of Anxiety Disorders, 29*, 83–92. doi:10.1016/j.janxdis.2014.11.006

Rosenberg, K. P., Carnes, P., & O'Connor, S. (2015). Evaluation and treatment of sex addiction. *Journal of Sex & Marital Therapy, 40*, 77–91. doi:10.1080/0092623X.2012.701268

Rosenfarb, I. S., Bellack, A. S., & Aziz, N. (2006). Family interactions and the course of schizophrenia in African American and white patients. *Journal of Abnormal Psychology, 115*, 112–120.

Rosenheck, R. (2012). Homelessness, housing, and mental illness. *American Journal of Psychiatry, 169*, 225–226. doi:10.1176/appi.ajp.2011.11081217

Rosenheck, R., & Lin, H. (2014). Noninferiority of perphenazine vs. three second-generation antipsychotics in chronic schizophrenia. *Journal of Nervous & Mental Disease, 202*, 18–24. doi:10.1097/NMD.0000000000000065

Rosenthal, E. (1993, April 9). Who will turn violent? Hospitals have to guess. *The New York Times*, pp. A1, C12.

Ross, C. A., & Ness, L. (2010). Symptom patterns in dissociative identity disorder patients and the general population. *Journal of Trauma & Dissociation, 11*, 458–468.

Ross, C. A., Miller, S. D., Reagor, P., Bjornson, L., Fraser, G. A., & Anderson, G. (1990). Structured interview data on 102 cases of multiple personality disorder from four centers. *American Journal of Psychiatry, 147*, 596–601.

Ross, C. A., Norton, G. R., & Wozney, K. (1989). Multiple personality disorder: An analysis of 236 cases. *Canadian Journal of Psychiatry, 34*, 413–418.

Ross, C. A., Schroeder, E., & Ness, L. (2013). Dissociation and symptoms of culture-bound syndromes in North America: A preliminary study. *Journal of Trauma & Dissociation, 14*(2), 224–235. doi:10.1080/15299732.2013.724338

Rosso, G., Martini, B., & Maina, G. (2012). Brief dynamic therapy and depression severity: A single-blind, randomized study. *Journal of Affective Disorders, 19*, S0165–S0327. doi:10.1016/j.jad.2012.10.017

Roth, T., Soubrane, C., & Titeux, L., & Walsh, J. K., on behalf of the Zoladult Study Group (2006). Efficacy and safety of zolpidem-MR: A double-blind, placebo-controlled study in adults with primary insomnia. *Sleep Medicine, 7*, 397–406.

Rothbaum, B. O., Price, M., Jovanovic, T., Norrholm, S. D., Gerardi, M., Dunlop, B.,... Ressler, K. J. (2014). A randomized, double-blind evaluation of d-cycloserine or alprazolam combined with virtual reality exposure therapy for posttraumatic stress disorder in Iraq and Afghanistan war veterans. *American Journal of Psychiatry, 171*, 640–648.

Rothbaum, B. O., Hodges, L., Anderson, P. L., Price, L., & Smith, S. (2002). Twelve-month follow-up of virtual reality and standard exposure therapies for the fear of flying. *Journal of Consulting and Clinical Psychology, 70*, 428–432.

Rotter, J. B. (1966). Generalized expectancies for internal vs. external control of reinforcement. *Psychological Monographs, 1*, 210–609.

Roudsari, M. J., Chun, J., & Manschreck, T. C. (2015). Current treatments for delusional disorder. *Current Treatment Options in Psychiatry, 2*, 151–167.

Rougeta, B. W., & Aubry, J.-M. (2007). Efficacy of psychoeducational approaches on bipolar disorders: A review of the literature. *Journal of Affective Disorders, 98*, 11–27.

Roussos, P., Giakoumaki, S. G., Zouraraki, C., Fullar, J. F., Karagiorga, V.-E., Tsapakis, E.-M., . . . Bitsios, P. (2015). The relationship of common risk variants and polygenic risk for schizophrenia to sensorimotor gating. *Biological Psychiatry, 27*, S0006–S3223. doi:10.1016/j.biopsych.2015.06.019

Rowland, D., McMahon, C. G., Abdo, C., Chen, J., Jannini, E., Waldinger, M. D., & Ahn, T. Y. (2010). Disorders of orgasm and ejaculation in men. *Journal of Sexual Medicine, 7*, 1668–1686.

Roy, A. K., Lopes, V., & Klein, R. G. (2014). Disruptive mood dysregulation disorder: A new diagnostic approach to chronic irritability in youth. *American Journal of Psychiatry, 71*, 918–924. Retrieved from http://dx.doi.org/10.1176/appi.ajp.2014.13101301

Roy-Byrne, P. (2013a). All psychotherapies equally effective for depression. *NEJM Journal Watch Psychiatry*. Retrieved from http://www.jwatch.org/na31260/2013/06/10/all-psychotherapies-equally-effective-depression

Roy-Byrne, P. (2013b). How common is hoarding disorder? *NEJM Journal Watch Psychiatry*. Retrieved from http://www.jwatch.org/na32776/2013/11/12/how-common-hoarding-disorder

Rozee, P. D., & Koss, M. P. (2001). Rape: A century of resistance. *Psychology of Women Quarterly, 25*, 295–311.

Rozin, P., Bauer, R., & Catanese, D. (2003). Food and life, pleasure and worry, among American college students: Gender differences and regional similarities. *Journal of Personality and Social Psychology, 85*, 132–141.

Rubinstein, S., & Caballero, B. (2000). Is Miss America an undernourished role model? *Journal of the American Medical Association, 283*, 1569.

Rudolph, K. D., Kurlakowsky, K. D., & Conley, C. S. (2001). Developmental and social-contextual origins of depressive control-related beliefs and behavior. *Cognitive Therapy & Research, 25*, 447–475.

Rumpf, H. J., Bischof, A., Wölfling, K., Leménager, T., Thon, N., Moggi, F., . . . Wurst, F. M. (2015). Non-substance-related disorders: Gambling disorder and Internet addiction. In G. Dom & F. Moggi (Eds.), *A practice-based handbook from a European perspective* (pp. 221–236). New York, NY: Springer.

Rutherford, B. R., & Roose, S. P. (2013). A model of placebo response in antidepressant clinical trials. *American Journal of Psychiatry, 170*, 723–733. doi:10.1176/appi.ajp.2012.12040474

Rutherford, B. R., Pott, E., Tandler, J. M., Wall, M. M., Roose, S. P., & Lieberman, J. A. (2014). Placebo response in antipsychotic clinical trials: A meta-analysis. *JAMA Psychiatry, 71*, 1409–1421. doi:10.1001/jamapsychiatry.2014.1319

Rutledge, P. C., Park, A., & Sher, K. J. (2008). 21st birthday drinking: Extremely extreme. *Journal of Consulting and Clinical Psychology, 76*, 517–523.

Rutter, M., Caspi, A., Fergusson, D., Horwood, L. J., Goodman, R., Maughan, B., . . . Meltzer, H. C. J. (2004). Sex differences in developmental reading disability: New findings from 4 epidemiological studies. *Journal of the American Medical Association, 291*, 2007–2012.

Ruzzo, E. K., & Geschwind, D. H. (2016). Schizophrenia genetics complements its mechanistic understanding. *Nature Neuroscience, 19*, 523–525. doi:10.1038/nn.4277

Ryder, A. G., Sun, J., Dere, J., & Fung, K. (2013). Personality disorders in Asians: Summary, and a call for cultural research. *Asian Journal of Psychiatry, 7*, 86–88. doi:10.1016/j.ajp.2013.11.009

Ryder, A. G., Yang, J., Zhu, X., Yao, S., Yi, J., Heine, S. J., & Bagby, R. M. (2008). The cultural shaping of depression: Somatic symptoms in China, psychological symptoms in North America? *Journal of Abnormal Psychology, 117*, 300–313.

Rye, D. B., Bliwise, D. L., Parker, K., Trotti, L. M., Saini, P., Fairley, J., . . . Jenkins, A. (2012). Modulation of vigilance in the primary hypersomnias by endogenous enhancement of GABAA receptors. *Science Translational Medicine, 4*, 161ra151. doi:10.1126/scitranslmed.3004685

Sackeim, H. A., Haskett, R. F., Mulsant, B. H., Thase, M. E., Mann, J. J., Pettinati, H. M., . . . Prudic, J. (2001). Continuation pharmacotherapy in the prevention of relapse following electroconvulsive therapy. *Journal of the American Medical Association, 285*, 1299–1307.

Sacks, O. (1985). *The man who mistook his wife for a hat and other clinical tales*. New York, NY: Summit.

Sacks, O. (2012). *Hallucinations*. New York, NY: Random House.

Sadoff, R. L. (2011). Expert psychiatric testimony. In R. L. Sadoff, J. A. Baird, S. M. Bertoglia, E. Valenti, & D. L. Vanderpool (Eds.), *Ethical issues in forensic psychiatry: Minimizing harm* (pp. 97–110). Hoboken, NJ: Wiley-Blackwell.

Safford, S. M. (2008). Gender and depression in men: Extending beyond depression and extending beyond gender. *Clinical Psychology: Science and Practice, 15*, 169–173.

Safren, S. A., Sprich, S., Mimiaga, M. J., Surman, C., Knouse, L., Groves, M., . . . Otto, M. W. (2010). Cognitive behavioral therapy vs. relaxation with educational support for medication-treated adults with ADHD and persistent symptoms: A randomized controlled trial. *Journal of the American Medical Association, 304*, 875–880. doi:10.1001/jama.2010.1192

Sagioglou, C., & Greitemeyer, T. (2014). Facebook's emotional consequences: Why Facebook causes a decrease in mood and why people still use it. *Computers in Human Behavior, 35*, 359–363. Retrieved from http://dx.doi.org/10.1016/j.chb.2014.03.003

Sahin, G., & Kirik, D. (2012). Efficacy of L-Dopa therapy in Parkinson's disease. In J. P. F. D'Mello (Ed.), *Amino acids in human nutrition and health* (pp. 454–463). Oxfordshire, UK: Cabi.

Saigal, C. S. (2004). Obesity and erectile dysfunction: common problems, common solution? *Journal of the American Medical Association, 291*, 3011–3012.

Sakai, Y., Shaw, C. A., Dawson, B. C., Dugas, D. V., Al-Mohtaseb, Z., Hill, D. E., . . . Zoghbi, H. Y. (2011). Protein interactome reveals converging molecular pathways among autism disorders. *Science Translational Medicine, 3*, 86. doi:10.1126/scitranslmed.3002166

Salas-Wright, C. P., Kagotho, N., & Vaughn, M. G. (2014). Mood, anxiety, and personality disorders among first- and second-generation immigrants to the United States. *Psychiatry Research, 220*, 1028–1036. doi:10.1016/j.psychres.2014.08.045

Salgado de Snyder, V. N. (1987). Factors associated with acculturative stress and depressive symptomatology among married Mexican immigrant women. *Psychology of Women Quarterly, 11*, 475–488.

Salgado de Snyder, V. N., Cervantes, R. C., & Padilla, A. M. (1990). Gender and ethnic differences in psychosocial stress and generalized distress among Hispanics. *Sex Roles, 22*, 441–453.

Salkovskis, P. M., & Clark, D. M. (1993). Panic disorder and hypochondriasis. *Advances in Behaviour Research and Therapy, 15*(Special issue: Panic, cognitions and sensations), 23–48.

Salkovskis, P. M., Thorpe, S. J., Wahl, K., Wroe, A. L., & Forrester, E. (2003). Neutralizing increases discomfort associated with obsessional thoughts: An experimental study with obsessional patients. *Journal of Abnormal Psychology, 112*, 709–715.

Salluh, J. I. J., Wang, H., Schneider, E. B., Nagaraja, N., Yenokyan, G., Damluji, A., Serafim, R. B., & Stevens, R. D. (2015). Outcome of delirium in critically ill patients: Systematic review and meta-analysis. *British Medical Journal, 350*, 2538.

Salvatore, J. E., Aliev, F., Bucholz, K., Agrawal, A., Hesselbrock, V., Hesselbrock, M., . . . Dick, D. M. (2015). Polygenic risk for externalizing disorders: Gene-by-development and gene-by-environment effects in adolescents and young adults. *Clinical Psychological Science, 3*, 189–201. doi:10.1177/2167702614534211

Sammons, M. T. (2005). Pharmacotherapy for delusional disorder and associated conditions. *Professional Psychology: Research and Practice, 36*, 476–479.

Samuels, J. (2011). Personality disorders: Epidemiology and public health issues. *International Journal of Psychiatry, 23*, 223–233. doi:10.3109/09540261.2011.588200

Sanchez, M. M., Heyn, S. N., Das, D., Moghadam, S., Martin, K. J., & Salehi, A. (2012). Neurobiological elements of cognitive dysfunction in Down Syndrome: Exploring the role of APP. *Biological Psychiatry, 71*, 403. doi:10.1016/j.biopsych.2011.08.016

Sanchez-Hucles, J. (2000). *The first session with African Americans: A step-by-step*. San Francisco, CA: Jossey Bass.

Sánchez-Morla, E. M., Santos, J. L., Aparicio, A., García-Jiménez, M. A, Soria, C., & Arango, C. (2013). Neuropsychological correlates of P50 sensory gating in patients with schizophrenia. *Schizophrenia Research, 143*, 102–106.

Sánchez-Ortuño, M. M., & Edinger, J. D. (2010). A penny for your thoughts: Patterns of sleep-related beliefs, insomnia symptoms and treatment outcome. *Behavior Research and Therapy, 48*, 125–133. doi:10.1016/j.brat.2009.10.003

Sanchez-Romera, J. F., Lopez, J., Bandin, C., Colodro-Conde, L., Madrid, J. A., Garaulet, M., . . . Ordoñana, J. R. (2014). Individual differences in chronobiology: Genetic and environmental factors. *Personality and Individual Differences, 60*(Suppl.), S31–S32. Retrieved from http://dx.doi.org/10.1016/j.paid.2013.07.061

Sanders, L. (2006, June 18). Heartache. *The New York Times*, pp. 27–28.

Sanders, S. J., Murtha, M. T., Gupta, A. R., Murdoch, J. D., Raubeson, M. J., Willsey, A. J., . . . State, M. W. (2012). De novo mutations revealed by whole-exome sequencing are strongly associated with autism. *Nature, 485*, 237–241. doi:10.1038/nature10945

Sanders Thompson, V. L., Bazile, A., & Akbar, M. (2004). African Americans' perceptions of psychotherapy and psychotherapists. *Professional Psychology: Research and Practice, 35*, 19–26.

Sandin, B., Sánchez-Arribas, C., Chorot, P., & Valiente, R. M. (2015). Anxiety sensitivity, catastrophic misinterpretations and panic self-efficacy in the prediction of panic disorder severity: Towards a tripartite cognitive model of panic disorder. *Behaviour Research and Therapy, 67*, 30–40.

Santangelo, P., Reinhard, I., Mussgay, L., Steil, R., Sawitzki, G., Klein, C., . . . Ebner-Priemer, U. W. (2014). Specificity of affective instability in patients with borderline personality disorder compared to posttraumatic stress disorder, bulimia nervosa, and healthy controls. *Journal of Abnormal Psychology, 123*, 258–272. doi:10.1037/a0035619

Sar, V., Yargic, L. I., & Tutkun, H. (1996). Structured interview data on 35 cases of dissociative identity disorder in Turkey. *American Journal of Psychiatry, 153*, 1329–1333.

Sareen, J., Afifi, T. O., McMillan, K. A., & Asmundson, G. J. G. (2011). Relationship between household income and mental disorders: Findings from a population-based longitudinal study. *Archives of General Psychiatry, 68*, 419. doi:10.1001/archgenpsychiatry.2011.15

Sass, L. (1982, August 22). The borderline personality. *The New York Times Magazine*, 12–15, 66–67.

Satcher, D. (2000). Mental health: A report of the Surgeon General—executive summary. *Professional Psychology: Research and Practice, 31*, 5–13.

Saulsmana, L. M. (2011). Depression, anxiety, and the MCMI–III: Construct validity and diagnostic efficiency. *Journal of Personality Assessment, 93*, 76–83. doi:10.1080/00223891.2010.528481

Saunders, E. F. H., Reider, A., Singh, G., Gelenberg, A. J., & Rapoport, S. I. (2015). Low unesterified esterified eicosapentaenoic acid (EPA) plasma concentration ratio is associated with bipolar disorder episodes, and omega-3 plasma concentrations are altered by treatment. *Bipolar Disorders, 17*, 729. doi:10.1111/bdi.12337

Savic, I., Garcia-Falgueras, A., & Swaab, D. F. (2010). Sexual differentiation of the human brain in relation to gender identity and sexual orientation. *Progress in Brain Research, 186*, 41–62. doi:10.1016/B978-0-444-53630-3.00004-X

Sayers, G. M. (2003). Psychiatry and the control of dangerousness: A comment. *Journal of Medical Ethics, 29*, 235–236.

Scahill, L., McDougle, C. J., Aman, M. G., Johnson, C., Handen, B., Bearss, K., . . . Vitiello, B. (2012). Effects of risperidone and parent training on adaptive functioning in children with pervasive developmental disorders and serious behavioral problems. *Journal of the American Academy of Child & Adolescent Psychiatry, 51*, 136. doi:10.1016/j.jaac.2011.11.010

Scammell, T. E. (2015). Narcolepsy. *New England Journal of Medicine, 373*, 2654–2662. doi:10.1056/NEJMra1500587

Schafer, S. M., Colloca, L., & Wager, T. D. (2015). Conditioned placebo analgesia persists when subjects know they are receiving a placebo. *Pain, 15*, 412–420. doi:10.1016/j.jpain.2014.12.008

Schaffer, A., Isometsä, E. T., Azorin, J. M., Cassidy, F., Goldstein, T., Rihmer, Z.,… Yatham L. (2015). A review of factors associated with greater likelihood of suicide attempts and suicide deaths in bipolar disorder: Part II of a report of the International Society for Bipolar Disorders Task Force on Suicide in Bipolar Disorder. *Australian and New Zealand Journal of Psychiatry, 49,* 1006–1020. doi:10.1177/0004867415594428

Schendel, D. E., Grønborg, T. K., & Parner, E. T. (2014). The genetic and environmental contributions to autism: Looking beyond twins. *Journal of the American Medical Association, 311,* 1738–1739. doi:10.1001/jama.2014.3554

Schiffer, B., Pawliczek, C., Müller, B., Forsting, M., Gizewski, E., Leygraf, N.,… Hodgins, S. (2014). Neural mechanisms underlying cognitive control of men with lifelong antisocial behavior. *Psychiatry Research: Neuroimaging, 222,* 43–51. doi:10.1016/j.pscychresns.2014.01.008

Schiller, L., & Bennett, A. (1994). *The quiet room: A journey out of the torment of madness.* New York, NY: Warner Books.

Schizophrenia Working Group of the Psychiatric Genomics Consortium. (2014). Biological insights from 108 schizophrenia-associated genetic loci. *Nature, 511,* 421–427. doi:10.1038/nature13595

Schmaal, L., Veltman, D. J., van Erp, T. G. M., Sämann, P. G., Frodl, T., Jahanshad, N.,… ENIGMA-Major Depressive Disorder Working Group. (2015). Subcortical brain alterations in major depressive disorder: Findings from the ENIGMA Major Depressive Disorder working group. *Molecular Psychiatry, 30,* 1–7. doi:10.1038/mp.2015.69

Schmahl, C., & Bremner, J. D. (2006). Neuroimaging in borderline personality disorder. *Journal of Psychiatric Research, 40,* 419–427.

Schmidt, A., Smieskova, R., Aston, J., Simon, A., Allen, P., Fusar-Poli, P.,… Borgwardt, S. (2013). Brain connectivity abnormalities predating the onset of psychosis correlation with the effect of medication. *JAMA Psychiatry, 70,* 903–912. doi:10.1001/jamapsychiatry.2013.117

Schmidt, N. B., & Keough, M. E. (2010). Treatment of panic. *Annual Review of Clinical Psychology, 6,* 241–256. doi:10.1146/annurev.clinpsy.121208.131317

Schmidt, N. B., Richey, J. A., Buckner, J. D., & Timpano, K. R. (2009). Attention training for generalized social anxiety disorder. *Journal of Abnormal Psychology, 118,* 5–14. doi:10.1037/a0013643

Schneck, C. D., Miklowitz, D. J., Calabrese, J. R., Allen, M. H., Thomas, M. R., Wisniewski, S. R.,… Sachs, G. S. (2004). Phenomenology of rapid-cycling bipolar disorder: Data from the first 500 participants in the systematic treatment enhancement program. *American Journal of Psychiatry, 161,* 1902–1908.

Schneck, C. D., Miklowitz, D. J., Miyahara, S., Araga, M., Wisniewski, S., Gyulai, L.,… Sachs, G. S. (2008). The prospective course of rapid-cycling bipolar disorder: Findings from the STEP-BD. *American Journal of Psychiatry, 165,* 370–377.

Schneider, J. P. (2003). The impact of compulsive cybersex behaviours on the family. *Sexual and Relationship Therapy, 18,* 329–354.

Schneider, J. P. (2004). Editorial: Sexual addiction & compulsivity: Twenty years of the field, ten years of the journal. *Sexual Addiction & Compulsivity, 11*(1–2), 3–5.

Schneider, J. P. (2005). Addiction is addiction is addiction. *Sexual Addiction & Compulsivity, 12*(2/3), 75–77.

Schneider, L. S., Dagerman, K. S., Higgins, J. P., & McShane, R. (2011). Lack of evidence for the efficacy of memantine in mild Alzheimer disease. *Archives of Neurology, 68,* 991–998.

Schneider, R. H., Grim, C. E., Rainforth, M. V., Kotchen, T., Nidich, S. I., Gaylord-King, C.,… Alexander, C. N. (2012). Stress reduction in the secondary prevention of cardiovascular disease: Randomized, controlled trial of transcendental meditation and health education in Blacks. *Circulation: Cardiovascular Quality and Outcomes, 5,* 750–758. doi:10.1161/CIRCOUTCOMES.112.967406

Schneier, F. R. (2006). Social anxiety disorder. *New England Journal of Medicine, 355,* 1029–1036.

Schneier, F. R., Neria, Y., Pavlicova, M., Hembree, E., Suh, E. J., Amsel, L.,… Marshall, R. D. (2012). Combined prolonged exposure therapy and paroxetine for PTSD related to the World Trade Center attack: A randomized controlled trial. *American Journal of Psychiatry, 169,* 80–88. doi:10.1176/appi.ajp.2011.11020321

Schniering, C. A., & Rapee, R. M. (2004). The relationship between automatic thoughts and negative emotions in children and adolescents: A test of the cognitive contentspecificity hypothesis. *Journal of Abnormal Psychology, 113,* 464–470.

Schoenman, T. J. (1984). The mentally ill witch in textbooks of abnormal psychology: Current status and implications of a fallacy. *Professional Psychiatry, 15,* 299–314.

Schönenberg, M., & Jusyte, A. (2014). Investigation of the hostile attribution bias toward ambiguous facial cues in antisocial violent offenders. *European Archives of Psychiatry and Clinical Neuroscience, 264,* 61–69.

Schönfeld, P., Brailovskaia, B., Bieda, A., Zhang, X. C., & Margraf, J. (2016). The effects of daily stress on positive and negative mental health: Mediation through self-efficacy. *International Journal of Clinical and Health Psychology, 16,* 1–10. doi:10.1016/j.ijchp.2015.08.005

Schreier, H., & Ricci, L. R. (2002). Follow-up of a case of Münchausen by proxy syndrome. *Journal of the American Academy of Child and Adolescent Psychiatry, 41,* 1395–1396.

Schreier, H. M. C., & Chen, E. (2008). Prospective associations between coping and health among youth with asthma. *Journal of Consulting and Clinical Psychology, 76,* 790–798.

Schroeder, S. A. (2013). New evidence that cigarette smoking remains the most important health hazard. *New England Journal of Medicine, 368,* 389–390. doi:10.1056/NEJMe1213751

Schroeder, S. A., & Koh, H. K. (2014). Tobacco control 50 years after the 1964 Surgeon General's Report. *Journal of the American Medical Association, 311,* 141–143. doi:10.1001/jama.2013.285243

Schuepbach, W. M. M., Rau, J., Knudsen, K., Volkmann, J., Krack, P., Timmermann, L., Hälbig, T. D.,… EARLYSTIM Study Group. (2013). Neurostimulation for Parkinson's disease with early motor complications. *New England Journal of Medicine, 368,* 610–622. doi:10.1056/NEJMoa1205158

Schultz, L. T., & Heimberg, R. G. (2008). Attentional focus in social anxiety disorder: Potential for interactive processes. *Clinical Psychology Review, 28,* 1206–1221.

Schulze, L., Schmahl, C., & Niedtfeld, I. (2015). Neural correlates of disturbed emotion processing in borderline personality disorder: A multimodal meta-analysis. *Biological Psychiatry, 79*(2), 97–106. doi:10.1016/j.biopsych.2015.03.027

Schulze, T. G., Ohlraun, S., Czerski, P. M., Schumacher, J., Kassem, L., Deschner, M.,… Rietschel, M. (2005). Genotype-phenotype studies in bipolar disorder showing association between the DAOA/G30 locus and persecutory delusions: A first step toward a molecular genetic classification of psychiatric phenotypes. *American Journal of Psychiatry, 162,* 2101–2108.

Schwartz, D., Gorman, A. H., Duong, M. T., & Nakamoto, J. (2008). Peer relationships and academic achievement as interacting predictors of depressive symptoms during middle childhood. *Journal of Abnormal Psychology, 117,* 289–299.

Schwartz, R. P., Highfield, D. A., Jaffe, J. H., Brady, J. V., Butler, C. B., Rouse, C. A.,… Battjes, R. J. (2006). A randomized controlled trial of interim methadone maintenance. *Archives of General Psychiatry, 63,* 102–109.

Schwarz, A. (2009, October 23). N.F.L. data reinforces dementia links. Retrieved from www.nytimes.com

Schwarz, A. (2013, December 15). The selling of attention deficit disorder. *The New York Times,* pp. A1, A22.

Schweitzer, I., Maguire, K., & Ng, C. (2009). Sexual side-effects of contemporary antidepressants: Review. *Australian and New Zealand Journal of Psychiatry, 43,* 795–808. doi:10.1080/00048670903107575

Schwitzgebel, R. L., & Schwitzgebel, R. K. (1980). *Law and psychological practice.* New York, NY: Wiley.

ScienceDaily. (2014a, January 19). Mechanism identified in Alzheimer's-related memory loss. *ScienceDaily.* Retrieved from http://www.sciencedaily.com/releases/2014/01/140119142456.htm

ScienceDaily. (2014b, November 25). Problem gambling, personality disorders often go hand in hand. *ScienceDaily.* Retrieved from http://www.sciencedaily.com/releases/2014/11/141125074751.htm

ScienceDaily. (2014c, July 7). Tremors, shuffling and confusion may not be Parkinson's but Lewy body dementia. *ScienceDaily.* Retrieved from http://www.sciencedaily.com/releases/2014/07/140707212539.htm

Scientists discover migraine gene. (2003, January 21). Retrieved from http://www.msnbc.com

Scogin, F., & Shah, A. (Eds.). (2012). *Making evidence-based psychological treatments work with older adults.* Washington, DC: American Psychological Association.

Scott, S., Briskman, J., & O'Connor, T. G. (2014). Early prevention of antisocial personality: Long-term follow-up of two randomized controlled trials comparing indicated and selective approaches. *American Journal of Psychiatry, 171,* 649–657. doi:10.1176/appi.ajp.2014.13050697

Scott-Sheldon, L. A. J., Carey, K. B., Elliott, J. C., Garey, L., & Carey, M. P. (2014). Efficacy of alcohol interventions for first-year college students: A meta-analytic review of randomized controlled trials. *Journal of Consulting and Clinical Psychology, 82,* 177–188. doi:10.1037/a0035192

Scott-Sheldon, L. A., Kalichman, S. C., Carey, M. P., & Fielder, R. L. (2008). Stress management interventions for HIV+ adults: A meta-analysis of randomized controlled trials, 1989 to 2006. *Health Psychology, 27,* 129–139.

Scroppo, J. C., Drob, S. L., Weinberger, J. L., & Eagle, P. (1998). Identifying dissociative identity disorder: A self-report and projective study. *Journal of Abnormal Psychology, 107,* 272–284.

Sederer, L. I., & Sharfstein, S. S. (2014). Fixing the troubled mental health system. *Journal of the American Medical Association, 312,* 1195–1196. doi:10.1001/jama.2014.10369

Seedat, S., Scott, K. M., Angermeyer, M. C., Berglund, P., Bromet, E. J., Brugha, T. S.,… Kessler, R. C. (2009). Cross-national associations between gender and mental disorders in the World Health Organization World Mental Health Surveys. *Archives of General Psychiatry, 66,* 785–795.

Segerstrom, S. C., & Miller, G. E. (2004). Psychological stress and the human immune system: A meta-analytic study of 30 years of inquiry. *Psychological Bulletin, 130,* 601–630.

Sekar, A., Bialas, A. R., de Rivera, H., Davis, A., Hammond, T. R., Kamitaki, N.,… McCarroll, S. A. (2016). Schizophrenia risk from complex variation of complement component. *Nature,* in press. doi:10.1038/nature16549

Selfe, L. (2011). *Nadia revisited: A longitudinal study of an autistic savant: Essays in developmental psychology series.* New York, NY: Psychology Press.

Seligman, M. E. P. (1973). Fall into helplessness. *Psychology Today, 7,* 43–48.

Seligman, M. E. P. (1975). *Helplessness: On depression, development, and death.* San Francisco, CA: Freeman.

Seligman, M. E. P. (1991). *Learned optimism.* New York, NY: Knopf.

Seligman, M. E. P., & Maier, S. F. (1967). Failure to escape traumatic shock. *Journal of Experimental Psychology, 74,* 1–9.

Seligman, M. E. P., Steen, T. A., Park, N., & Peterson, C. (2005). Positive psychology progress: Empirical validation of interventions. *American Psychologist, 60,* 410–421.

Selkoe, D. J. (2012). Preventing Alzheimer's disease. *Science, 337,* 1488–1492. doi:10.1126/science.1228541

Selye, H. (1976). *The stress of life* (Rev. ed.). New York, NY: McGraw-Hill.

Senn, C. Y., Eliasziw, M., Barata, P. C., Thurston, W. E., Newby-Clark, I. R., Radtke, H. L.,… Hobden, K. L. (2015). Efficacy of a sexual assault resistance program for university women. *New England Journal of Medicine, 372,* 2326–2335. doi:10.1056/NEJMsa1411131

Seo, D., Patrick, C. J., & Kennealy, P. J. (2008). Role of serotonin and dopamine system interactions in the neurobiology of impulsive aggression and its comorbidity with other clinical disorders. *Aggression and Violent Behavior, 13,* 383–395.

Serefoglu, E. C., McMahon, C. G., Waldinger, M. D., Althof, S. E., Shindel, A., Adaikan, G.,… Torres, L. O.

(2014). An evidence-based unified definition of lifelong and acquired premature ejaculation: Report of the Second International Society for Sexual Medicine Ad Hoc Committee for the Definition of Premature Ejaculation. *Sexual Medicine, 2,* 41–59. doi:10.1002/sm2.27

Serrano-Villar, M., & Calzada, E. J. (2016). Ethnic identity: Evidence of protective effects for young, Latino children. *Journal of Applied Developmental Psychology, 42,* 21–30.

Seto, M. C. (2008). Pedophilia: Psychopathology and theory. In D. R. Laws and W. T. O'Donohue (Eds.), *Sexual deviance: Theory, assessment, and treatment* (2nd ed., pp. 164–182). New York, NY: Guilford Press.

Seto, M. C., Lalumière, M. L., Harris, G. T., & Chivers, M. (2012). The sexual responses of sexual sadists. *Journal of Abnormal Psychology, 121,* 739–753. doi:10.1037/a0028714

Settles, I. H., Navarrete, C. D., Pagano, S. J., Abdou, C. M., & Sidanius, J. (2010). Racial identity and depression among African American women. *Cultural Diversity and Ethnic Minority Psychology, 16,* 248–255. doi:10.1037/a0016442

Shadish, W. R., Matt, G. E., Navarro, A. M., & Phillips, G. (2000). The effects of psychological therapies under clinically representative conditions: A meta-analysis. *Psychological Bulletin, 126,* 512–529.

Shaffer, H. J., & Martin, R. (2011). Disordered gambling: Etiology, trajectory, and clinical considerations. *Annual Review of Clinical Psychology, 7,* 483–510. doi:10.1146/annurev-clinpsy-040510-143928

Shafti, S. S. (2010). Olanzapine vs. lithium in management of acute mania. *Journal of Affective Disorders, 122,* 273–276. doi:10.1016/j.jad.2009.08.013

Shalev, A. Y., & Freedman, S. (2005). PTSD following terrorist attacks. *American Journal of Psychiatry, 162,* 1188–1191.

Shapiro, E. (1992, August 22). Fear returns to sidewalks of West 96th Street. *The New York Times,* pp. B3–B4.

Shapiro, F. (2001). *Eye movement desensitization and reprocessing: Basic principles, protocols and procedures* (2nd ed.). New York, NY: Guilford Press.

Sharma, T., Guski, L. S., Freund, N., & Gøtzsche, P. C. (2016). Suicidality and aggression during antidepressant treatment: Systematic review and meta-analyses based on clinical study reports. *British Medical Journal, 352,* i65. Retrieved from http://dx.doi.org/10.1136/bmj.i65

Sharp, T. A. (2006). New molecule to brighten the mood. *Science, 311,* 45–46.

Sharpe, K. (2012, June 30–July 1). The medication generation. *Wall Street Journal,* pp. C1, C2.

Shaw, H., Ramirez, L., Trost, A., Randall, P., & Stice, E. (2004). Body image and eating disturbances across ethnic groups: More similarities than differences. *Psychology of Addictive Behaviors, 18,* 12–18.

Shaw, P., Gilliam, M., Liverpool, M., Weddle, C., Malek, M., Sharp, W.,... Giedd, J. (2011). Cortical development in typically developing children with symptoms of hyperactivity and impulsivity: Support for a dimensional view of attention deficit hyperactivity disorder. *American Journal of Psychiatry, 168,* 143–151.

Shaw, R., Cohen, F., Doyle, B., & Pelesky, J. (1985). The impact of denial and repressive style on information gain and rehabilitation outcomes in myocardial infarction patients. *Psychosomatic Medicine, 47,* 262–275.

Shawyer, F., Mackinnon, A., Farhall, J., Sims, E., Blaney, S., Yardley, P.,... Copolov, D. (2008). Acting on harmful command hallucinations in psychotic disorders: An integrative approach. *The Journal of Nervous and Mental Disease, 196,* 390–398.

Shaywitz, S. E., Mody, M., & Shaywitz, B. (2006). Neural mechanisms in dyslexia. *Current Directions 15*(6), 278–281. doi:10.1111/j.1467-8721.2006.00452.x

Shaywitz, S. E., Shaywitz, B. A., Fulbright, R. K., Skudlarski, P., Mencl, W. E.,... Gore, J. C. (2003). Neural systems for compensation and persistence: Young adult outcome of childhood reading disability. *Biological Psychiatry, 54,* 25–33.

Shear, K., Jin, R., Ruscio, A. M., Walters, E. E., & Kessler, R. C. (2006). Prevalence and correlates of estimated DSM-IV child and adult separation anxiety disorder in the National Comorbidity Survey Replication. *American Journal of Psychiatry, 163,* 1074–1083.

Shedler, J. (2010). The efficacy of psychodynamic psychotherapy. *American Psychologist, 65,* 98–109. doi:10.1037/a0018378

Sheehan, D. V., & Mao, C. G. (2003). Paroxetine treatment of generalized anxiety disorder. *Psychopharmacology Bulletin, 37*(Suppl. 1), 64–75.

Sheline, Y. I., Disabato, B. M., Hranilovich, J., Morris, C., D'Angelo, G., Pieper, C.,... Doraiswamy, P. M. (2012). Treatment course with antidepressant therapy in late-life depression. *American Journal of Psychiatry, 169,* 1185–1193. doi:10.1176/appi.ajp.2012.12010122

Sher, L. (2005). Suicide and alcoholism. *Nordic Journal of Psychiatry, 59,* 152.

Sheridan, M. S. (2003). The deceit continues: An updated literature review of Münchausen syndrome by proxy. *Child Abuse and Neglect, 27,* 431–451.

Shields, A. E., Lerman, C., & Sullivan, P. (2005). The use of race variables in genetic studies of complex traits and the goal of reducing health disparities: A transdisciplinary perspective. *American Psychologist, 60,* 77–103.

Shields, D. C., Asaad, W., Eskandar, E. N., Jain, F. A., Cosgrove, G. R., Flaherty, A. W.,... Dougherty, D. D. (2008). Prospective assessment of stereotactic ablative surgery for intractable major depression. *Biological Psychiatry, 64,* 449.

Shinozaki, G., Romanowicz, M., Passov, V., Rundell, J., Mrazek, D., & Kung, S. (2013). State dependent gene–environment interaction: Serotonin transporter gene–child abuse interaction associated with suicide attempt history among depressed psychiatric inpatients. *Journal of Affective Disorders, 147,* 373–378.

Shiraishi, N., Watanabe, N., Kinoshita, Y., Kaneko, A., Yoshida, S., Furukawa, T.,... Akechi, T. (2014). Brief psychoeducation for schizophrenia primarily intended to change the cognition of auditory hallucinations: An exploratory study. *Journal of Nervous & Mental Disease, 202,* 35–39. doi:10.1097/NMD.0000000000000064

Shive, H. (2015, July 23). When it comes to depression, serotonin deficiency may not be to blame. Texas A&M Health Sciences Center Press Release. Retrieved from http://news.tamhsc.edu/?post=when-it-comes-to-depression-serotonin-deficiency-may-not-be-to-blame

Shneidman, E. (1985). *Definition of suicide.* New York, NY: Wiley.

Shneidman, E. (2005). Prediction of suicide revisited: A brief methodological note. *Suicide & Life-Threatening Behavior, 35,* 1–2.

Shoenfeld, N., & Dannon, P. N. (2012). Phenomenology and epidemiology of kleptomania. In J. E. Grant & M. N. Potenza (Eds.), *The Oxford handbook of impulse control disorders* (pp. 135–134). New York, NY: Oxford University Press.

Shore, J. H., Savin, D., Orton, H., Beals, J., & Manson, S. M. (2007). Diagnostic reliability of telepsychiatry in American Indian veterans. *American Journal of Psychiatry, 164,* 115–118.

Shorey, R., Cornelius, T. L., & Idema, C. (2011). Trait anger as a mediator of difficulties with emotion regulation and female-perpetrated psychological aggression. *Violence and Victims, 26,* 271–282.

Shukla, P. R., & Singh, R. H. (2000). Supportive psychotherapy in dhat syndrome patients. *Journal of Personality & Clinical Studies, 16*(1), 49–52.

Shulman, J. M. (2010, March 3). Incidence and risk for dementia in Parkinson disease. *Journal Watch Psychiatry.* Retrieved from http://neurology.jwatch.org/cgi/content/full/2010/302/2?q=etoc_jwneuro

Shungin, D., Winkler, T. W., Croteau-Chonka, D. C., Ferreira, T., Locke, A. E., Mägi, R.,... Mohlke, K. L. (2015). New genetic loci link adipose and insulin biology to body fat distribution. *Nature, 518*(7538), 187–196. doi:10.1038/nature14132

Sibley, M. H., Pelham, W. E., Molina, B. S. G., Gnagy, E. M., Waschbusch, D. A., Biswas, A., Karch, K. M. (2011). The delinquency outcomes of boys with ADHD with and without comorbidity. *Journal of Abnormal Child Psychology, 39,* 21–32. doi:10.1007/s10802-010-9443-9

Siddique, J., Chung, J. Y., Brown, C. H., & Miranda, J. (2012). Comparative effectiveness of medication versus cognitive-behavioral therapy in a randomized controlled trial of low-income young minority women with depression. *Journal of Consulting and Clinical Psychology, 80,* 995–1006. doi:10.1037/a0030452

Siegert, S., Seo, J., Kwon, E. J., Rudenko, A., Cho, S., Wang, W.,... Tsai, L.-H. (2015). The schizophrenia risk gene product miR-137 alters presynaptic plasticity. *Nature Neuroscience, 18,* 1008–1016. doi:10.1038/nn.4023

Sierra, M., Gomez, J., Molina, J. J., Luque, R., Munoz, J. F., & David, A. S. (2006). Depersonalization in psychiatric patients: A transcultural study. *The Journal of Nervous and Mental Disease, 194,* 356–361.

Sierra, M., Medford, N., Wyatt, G., & Davis, A. S. (2012). Depersonalization disorder and anxiety: A special relationship? *Psychiatry Research, 197,* 123–127.

Silbersweig, D., Clarkin, J. F., Goldstein, M., Kernberg, O. F., Tuescher, O., Levy, K. N.,... Stern, E. (2008). Failure of frontolimbic inhibitory function in the context of negative emotion in borderline personality disorder. *American Journal of Psychiatry, 164,* 1832.

Silfvernagel, K., Gren-Landell, M., Emanuelsson, M., Carlbring, P., & Andersson, G. (2015). Individually tailored Internet-based cognitive behavior therapy for adolescents with anxiety disorders: A pilot effectiveness study. *Internet Interventions, 2,* 297–302. Retrieved from http://dx.doi.org/10.1016/j.invent.2015.07.002

Silk, K. R. (2008). Augmenting psychotherapy for borderline personality disorder: The STEPPS Program. *American Journal of Psychiatry, 165,* 413–415.

Silove, D., Alonso, J., Bromet, E., Gruber, M., Sampson, N., Scott, K.,... Kessler, R. C. (2015). Pediatric-onset and adult-onset separation anxiety disorder across countries in the World Mental Health Survey. *American Journal of Psychiatry, 172,* 647–656. Retrieved from http://dx.doi.org/10.1176/appi.ajp.2015.14091185

Silver, E., Cirincione, C., & Steadman, H. J. (1994). Demythologizing inaccurate perceptions of the insanity defense. *Law and Human Behavior, 18,* 63–70.

Simeon, D., Guralnik, O., Hazlett, E. A., Spiegel-Cohen, J., Hollander, E., & Buchsbaum, M. S. (2000). Feeling unreal: A PET study of depersonalization disorder. *American Journal of Psychiatry, 157,* 1782–1788.

Simeon, D., Guralnik, O., Schmeidler, J., &, Knutelska, M. (2004). Fluoxetine therapy in depersonalisation disorder: Randomised controlled trial. *British Journal of Psychiatry, 185,* 31–36.

Simon, G. E., Fleck, M., Lucas, R., & Bushnell, D. M. (2004). Prevalence and predictors of depression treatment in an international primary care study. *American Journal of Psychiatry, 161,* 1626–1634.

Simons, D. J. (2014). The value of direct replication. *Perspectives on Psychological Science, 9,* 76–80. doi:10.1177/1745691613514755

Simpson, H. B. (2013). Cognitive-behavioral therapy vs. risperidone for augmenting serotonin reuptake inhibitors in obsessive-compulsive disorder: Randomized clinical trial serotonin reuptake inhibitor augmentation. *JAMA Psychiatry, 70,* 1190–1199. doi:10.1001/jamapsychiatry.2013.1932

Singh, G. (1985). Dhat syndrome revisited. *Indian Journal of Psychiatry, 27,* 119–122.

Singh, R., Meier, T. B., Kuplicki, R., Savitz, J., Mukai, I., Cavanagh, L.,... Bellgowan, P. S. F. (2014). Relationship of collegiate football experience and concussion with hippocampal volume and cognitive outcomes. *Journal of the American Medical Association, 311,* 1883. doi:10.1001/jama.2014.3313

Singh, R., Sandhu, J., Kaur, B., Juren, T., Steward, W. P., Segerbäck, D., & Farmer, P. B. (2009). Evaluation of the DNA damaging potential of cannabis cigarette smoke by the determination of acetaldehyde derived n2-ethyl-2-deoxyguanosine adducts. *Chemical Research in Toxicology, 22,* 1181–1188. doi:10.1021/tx900106y

Sitnikov, L., Rohan, K. J., Evans, M., Mahon, J. N., & Nillni, Y. I. (2013). Cognitive predictors and moderators of winter depression treatment outcomes in cognitive-behavioral therapy vs. light therapy. *Behaviour Research and Therapy, 51,* 872–881. doi:10.1016/j.brat.2013.09.010

Siu, A. L. (2015). Behavioral and pharmacotherapy interventions for tobacco smoking cessation in adults, including pregnant women: U.S. Preventive Services Task Force recommendation statement. *Annals of Internal Medicine, 163*, 622.

Sixel-Döring, F., Trautmann, E., Mollenhauer, B., & Trenkwalder, C. (2011). Associated factors for REM sleep behavior disorder in Parkinson disease. *Neurology, 77*, 1048–1054.

Skeldon, S. C., Detsky, A. S., Goldenberg, S. L., & Law, M. R. (2015). Erectile dysfunction and undiagnosed diabetes, hypertension, and hypercholesterolemia. *Annals of Family Medicine, 13*, 331–335. doi:10.1370/afm.1816

Skinner, B. F. (1938). *The behavior of organisms: An experimental analysis.* Cambridge, MA: B.F. Skinner Foundation.

Skodol, A. E. (2012). Personality disorders in DSM-5. *Annual Review of Clinical Psychology, 8*, 317–344. doi:10.1146/annurev-clinpsy-032511-143131

Skodol, A. E., & Bender, D. S. (2009). The future of personality disorders in DSM-V? *American Journal of Psychiatry, 166*, 388–391. doi:10.1176/appi.ajp.2009.09010090

Skoog, G., & Skoog, I. (1999). A 40-year follow-up of patients with obsessive-compulsive disorder. *Archives of General Psychiatry, 56*, 121–127.

Skritskaya, N. A., Carson-Woing, A. R., Moeller, J. R., Shen, S., Barsky, A. J., & Fallo, B. A. (2012). A clinician-administered severity rating scale for illness anxiety: Development, reliability and validity of the H-YBOCS-M. *Depression and Anxiety, 29*, 652–664.

Skudlarski, P., Schretlen, D. J., Thaker, G. K., Stevens, M. C., Keshavan, M. S., . . . Pearlson, G. D. (2013). Diffusion tensor imaging white matter endophenotypes in patients with schizophrenia or psychotic bipolar disorder and their relatives. *American Journal of Psychiatry, 170*, 886–898.

Sleep problems cost billions. (2012, November 1). *ScienceDaily.com.* Retrieved from http://www.sciencedaily.com/releases/2012/11/121101110514.htm

Slifstein, M., van de Giessen, E., Van Snellenberg, J., Thompson, J. L, Narendran, R., Gil, R., . . . Abi-Dargham, A. (2015). Deficits in prefrontal cortical and extrastriatal dopamine release in schizophrenia: A positron emission tomographic functional magnetic resonance imaging study. *JAMA Psychiatry, 72*, 316–324. doi:10.1001/jamapsychiatry.2014.2414

Slomski, A. (2013). Adding cognitive-behavioral therapy to SRIs may improve OCD symptoms. *Journal of the American Medical Association, 310*, 1665. doi:10.1001/jama.2013.281198

Slomski, A. (2014). Mindfulness-based intervention and substance abuse relapse. *Journal of the American Medical Association, 311*, 2472. doi:10.1001/jama.2014.7644

Slomski, A. (2015). ADHD drug decreased binge eating. *Journal of the American Medical Association, 313*, 1200. doi:10.1001/jama.2015.2209

Slovenko, R. (2009). *Psychiatry in law/Law in psychiatry* (2nd ed.). New York, NY: Routledge/Taylor & Francis Group.

Slutske, W. S. (2005). Alcohol use disorders among U.S. college students and their non-college-attending peers. *Archives of General Psychiatry, 62*, 321–327.

Slutske, W. S., Cho, S. B., Piasecki, T. M., & Martin, N. G. (2013). Genetic overlap between personality and risk for disordered gambling: Evidence from a national community-based Australian twin study. *Journal of Abnormal Psychology, 122*, 250–255. doi:10.1037/a0029999

Slutske, W. S., Zhu, G., Meier, M. H., & Martin, N. G. (2011). Disordered gambling as defined by the Diagnostic and Statistical Manual of Mental Disorders and the South Oaks Gambling Screen: Evidence for a common etiologic structure. *Journal of Abnormal Psychology, 120*, 743–751. doi:10.1037/a0022879

Slutske, W. S. (2006). Natural recovery and treatment-seeking in pathological gambling: Results of two U.S. national surveys. *American Journal of Psychiatry, 163*, 297–302.

Small, K. S., Hedman, A. K., Grundberg, E., Nica, A. C., Thorleifsson, G., Kong, A., . . . McCarthy, M. I. (2011). Identification of an imprinted master trans regulator at the KLF14 locus related to multiple metabolic phenotypes. *Nature Genetics, 43*, 561–564. doi:10.1038/ng.833

Smink, F. R. E., van Hoeken, D., & Hoek, H. W. (2012). Epidemiology of eating disorders: Incidence, prevalence and mortality rates. *Current Psychiatry Reports, 14*, 406–414. doi:10.1007/s11920-012-0282-y

Smith, A. R., Hames, J. L., &. Joiner, T. E., Jr. (2013). Status update: Maladaptive Facebook usage predicts increases in body dissatisfaction and bulimic symptoms. *Journal of Affective Disorders, 149*, 235–240. doi:10.1016/j.jad.2013.01.032

Smith, B. J. (2012, June). Inappropriate prescribing. *Monitor on Psychology, 43*, 36–40.

Smith, B. L. (2012, March). Bringing life into focus. *Monitor on Psychology, 43*, 62.

Smith, C. O., Levine, D. W., Smith, E. P., Dumas, J., & Prinz, R. J. (2009). A developmental perspective of the relationship of racial–ethnic identity to self-construct, achievement, and behavior in African American children. *Cultural Diversity and Ethnic Minority Psychology, 15*, 145–157. doi:10.1037/a0015538

Smith, D. B. (2009, Autumn). The doctor is in. *The American Scholar.* Retrieved from http://www.theamericanscholar.org/the-doctor-is-in

Smith, G. N., Ehmann, T. S., Flynn, S. W., MacEwan, G. W., Tee, K., Kopala, L. C., . . . Honer, W. G. (2011). The assessment of symptom severity and functional impairment with DSM-IV axis V. *Psychiatric Services, 62*(4), 411–417. doi:10.1176/appi.ps.62.4.411

Smith, G. T. (2005). On construct validity: Issues of method and measurement. *Psychological Assessment, 17*, 396–408.

Smith, I. C., Reichow, B., & Volkmar, F. R. (2015). The effects of DSM-5 criteria on number of individuals diagnosed with autism spectrum disorder: A systematic review. *Journal of Autism and Developmental Disorders, 45*, 2541–2552.

Smith, J. C., Nielson, K. A., Woodard, J. L., Seidenberg, M., Durgerian, S., Hazlett, K. E., . . . Rao, S. M. (2014). Physical activity reduces hippocampal atrophy in elders at genetic risk for Alzheimer's disease. *Frontiers in Aging Neuroscience, 6*, 61. doi:10.3389/fnagi.2014.00061

Smith, L. A., Cornelius, V. R., Azorin, J. M., Perugic, G., Vietad, E., Younge, A. H., & Bowden, C. L. (2010). Valproate for the treatment of acute bipolar depression: Systematic review and meta-analysis. *Journal of Affective Disorders, 122*, 1–9. doi:10.1016/j.jad.2009.10.033

Smith, M. L., & Glass, G. V. (1977). Meta-analysis of psychotherapy outcome studies. *American Psychologist, 32*, 752–760.

Smith, M. L., Glass, G. V., & Miller, T. I. (1980). *The benefits of psychotherapy.* Baltimore, MA: Johns Hopkins University Press.

Smith, M. T., & Perlis, M. L. (2006). Who is a candidate for cognitive-behavioral therapy for insomnia? *Health Psychology, 25*, 15–19.

Smith, T. K. (2003, February). We've got to stop eating like this. *Fortune*, 58–70.

Smith, Y. L. S., Van Goozen, S. H. M., Kuiper, A. J., & Cohen–Kettenis, P. T. (2005). Sex reassignment: Outcomes and predictors of treatment for adolescent and adult transsexuals. *Psychological Medicine, 35*, 89–99.

Smits, J. A., Hofmann, S. G., Rosenfield, D., DeBoer, L. B., Costa, P. T., Simon, N. M., . . . Pollack, M. H. (2013). D-cycloserine augmentation of cognitive behavioral group therapy of social anxiety disorder: Prognostic and prescriptive variables. *Journal of Consulting and Clinical Psychology, 81*, 1100–1112. doi:10.1037/a0034120

Smoller, J. W., Paulus, M. P., Fagerness, J. A., Purcell, S., Yamaki, L. H., Hirshfeld-Becker, D., . . . Stein, M. B. (2008). Influence of RGS2 on anxiety-related temperament, personality, and brain function. *Archives of General Psychiatry, 65*, 298–308.

Snowden, L. R. (2012, October). Health and mental health policies' role in better understanding and closing African American–White American disparities in treatment access and quality of care. *American Psychologist, 67*, 524–531. doi:10.1037/a0030054

Snyder, H. R., Kaiser, R. H., Warren, S. L., & Heller, W. (2015). Obsessive-compulsive disorder is associated with broad impairments in executive function: A meta-analysis. *Clinical Psychological Science, 3*, 301–330. doi:10.1177/2167702614534210

Sobell, M. B., & Sobell, L. C. (1973a). Alcoholics treated by individualized behavior therapy: One-year treatment outcome. *Behaviour Research and Therapy*, 11, 599–618.

Sobell, M. B., & Sobell, L. C. (1973b). Individualized behavior therapy for alcoholics. *Behavior Therapy, 4*, 49–72.

Sobell, M. B., & Sobell, L. C. (1984). The aftermath of heresy: A response to Pendery et al.'s (1982) critique of "Individualized behavior therapy for alcoholics." *Behaviour Research and Therapy, 22*, 413–440.

Sobot, V., Ivanovic-Kovacevic, S., Markovic, J., Misic-Pavkov, G., & Novovic, Z. (2012). Role of sexual abuse in development of conversion disorder: Case report. *European Review for Medical and Pharmacological Sciences, 16*, 276–279.

Sockol, L. E. (2015). A systematic review of the efficacy of cognitive behavioral therapy for treating and preventing perinatal depression. *Journal of Affective Disorders, 177*, 7–21.

Sockol, L. E., Epperson, C. N., & Barber, J. P. (2014). Preventing postpartum depression: A meta-analytic review. *Clinical Psychology Review, 33*, 1205–1217. doi:10.1016/j.cpr.2013.10.004

Sokolove, M. (2003, November 16). Should John Hinckley go free? *The New York Times Magazine*, 54–57.

Solanto, M. V., Marks, D. J., Wasserstein, J., Mitchell, K., Abikoff, H., Ma, J., . . . Kofman, M. D. (2010). Efficacy of meta-cognitive therapy for adult ADHD. *American Journal of Psychiatry, 167*, 958–968.

Solis, M., Ciullo, S., Vaughn, S., Pyle, N., Hassaram, B., & Leroux, A. (2012). Reading comprehension interventions for middle school students with learning disabilities: A synthesis of 30 years of research. *Journal of Learning Disabilities, 45*, 327–340. doi:10.1177/0022219411402691

Solomon, D. A., Keller, M. B., Leon, A. C., Mueller, T. I., Lavori, P. W., Shea, M. T., . . . Endicott, J. (2000). Multiple recurrences of major depressive disorder. *American Journal of Psychiatry, 157*, 229–233.

Song, W., Chen, J., Petrilli, A., Liot, G., Klinglmayr, E., Zhou, Y., . . . Bossy-Wetzel, E. (2011). Mutant huntingtin binds the mitochondrial fission GTPase dynamin-related protein-1 and increases its enzymatic activity. *Nature Medicine, 17*, 377–382. doi:10.1038/nm.231

Sookman, D., & Fineberg, N. A. (2015). Introduction: Psychological and pharmacological treatments for obsessive-compulsive disorder throughout the lifespan, a special series by the Accreditation Task Force (ATF) of the Canadian institute for obsessive-compulsive disorders. *Psychiatry Research, 30*, 74–77. doi:10.1016/j.psychres.2014.12.002

Sotiropoulos, I., Catania, C., Pinto, L. G., Silva, R., Pollerberg, G. E., Takashima, A., . . . Almeida, O. F. X. (2011). Stress acts cumulatively to precipitate Alzheimer's disease-like tau pathology and cognitive deficits. *Journal of Neuroscience, 31*, 7840–7847. doi:10.1523/JNEUROSCI.0730-11.2011

Spack, N. P. (2013). Management of transgenderism. *Journal of the American Medical Association, 309*, 478–484. doi:10.1001/jama.2012.165234

Spanos, N. P. (1978). Witchcraft in histories of psychiatry: A critical analysis and an alternative conceptualization. *Psychological Bulletin, 85*, 417–439.

Spanos, N. P. (1994). Multiple identity enactments and multiple personality disorder: A sociocognitive perspective. *Psychological Bulletin, 116*, 143–165.

Spatola, C. M. A., Scaini, S., Pesenti-Gritti, P., Medland, S. E., Moruzzi, S., Ogliari, A., . . . Battaglia, M. (2011). Gene–environment interactions in panic disorder and $CO_2$ sensitivity: Effects of events occurring early in life. *American Journal of Medical Genetics Part B: Neuropsychiatric Genetics, 156*, 79–88. doi:10.1002/ajmg.b.31144

Spear, S. E., Crevecoeur-MacPhail, D., Denering, L., Dickerson, D., & Brecht, M.-L. (2013). Determinants of successful treatment outcomes among a sample of urban American Indians/Alaska Natives: The role of social environments. *Journal of Behavioral Health Services & Research, 40*, 330–341. doi:10.1007/s11414-013-9324-4

Spector, P. (2011). The relationship of personality to counterproductive work behavior (CWB): An integration of perspectives. *Human Resource Management Review, 21*, 342–352.

Spence, J., Titov, N., Jones, M. P., Dear, B. F., & Solley, K. (2014). Internet-based trauma-focused cognitive behavioural therapy for PTSD with and without exposure components: A randomised controlled trial. *Journal of Affective Disorders, 162,* 73–80.

Spence, S. H., Donovan, C. L., March, S., Gamble, A., Anderson, R. E., Prosser, S.,…Kenardy, J. (2011). A randomized controlled trial of online versus clinic-based CBT for adolescent anxiety. *Journal of Consulting and Clinical Psychology, 79,* 629–642. doi:10.1037/a0024512

Spencer, D. J. (1983). Psychiatric dilemmas in Australian aborigines. *International Journal of Social Psychiatry, 29,* 208–214.

Spiegel, D. (2006). Recognizing traumatic dissociation. *American Journal of Psychiatry, 163,* 566–568.

Spiegel, D. (2009). Coming apart: Trauma and the fragmentation of the self. In D. Gordon (Ed.), *Cerebrum 2009: Emerging ideas in brain science* (p. 111). Washington, DC: Dana Press.

Spielmans, G. I., Berman, M. I., & Usitalo, A. N. (2011). Psychotherapy versus second-generation antidepressants in the treatment of depression: A meta-analysis. *Journal of Nervous and Mental Disease, 199,* 142–149. doi:10.1097/NMD.0b013e31820caefb

Spillane, N. S., & Smith, G. T. (2009). On the pursuit of sound science for the betterment of the American Indian community: Reply to Beals et al. (2009). *Psychological Bulletin, 135,* 344–346. doi:10.1037/a0014997

Spinazzola, J., Hodgdon, H., Liang, L. J., Ford, J. D., Layne, C. M., Pynoos, R.,…Kisiel, C. (2015, July/August). Unseen wounds. *Monitor on Psychology,* 69–73.

Spitzer, R. L., Gibbon, M., Skodol, A. E., Williams, J. B. W., & First, M. B. (1989). *DSM-III-R casebook.* Washington, DC: American Psychiatric Press.

Spitzer, R. L., Gibbon, M., Skodol, A. E., Williams, J. B. W., & First, M. B. (1994). *DSM-IV case book* (4th ed.). Washington, DC: American Psychiatric Press.

Sprenger, T. (2011, April 5). Weather and migraine. *Journal Watch Neurology.* Retrieved from http://neurology.jwatch.org/

Squeglia, L. M., Sorg, S. F., Schweinsburg, A. D., Wetherill, R. R., Pulido, C., & Tapert, S. F. (2012). Binge drinking differentially affects adolescent male and female brain morphometry. *Psychopharmacology, 220,* 529–539.

Sroufe, L. A. (2012, January 28). Ritalin gone wrong. *The New York Times Review.* Retrieved from www.nytimes.com

Staddon, J. E. R., & Cerutti, D. T. (2003). Operant conditioning. *Annual Review of Psychology, 4,* 115–144.

Staekenborg, S. S., Su, T., van Straaten, E. C. W., Lane, R., Scheltens, P., Barkhof, F., & van der Flier, W. M. (2009). Behavioural and psychological symptoms in vascular dementia: Differences between small and large vessel disease. *Journal of Neurology, Neurosurgery & Psychiatry.* Advance online publication. doi:10.1136/jnnp.2009.187500

Stambor, Z. (2006, October). Psychologist calls for more research on adolescents' brains. *Monitor on Psychology, 37*(9), 16.

Stanton, A. L., Luecken, L. J., MacKinnon, D. P., & Thompson, E. H. (2013). Mechanisms in psychosocial interventions for adults living with cancer: Opportunity for integration of theory, research, and practice. *Journal of Consulting and Clinical Psychology, 81,* 318–335. doi:10.1037/a0028833

Starkman, M. N. (2006). The terrorist attack of September 11, 2001 as psychological toxin: Increase in suicide attempts. *Journal of Nervous and Mental Disease, 194,* 547–550.

Starkstein, S. E., Jorge, R., Mizrahi, R., & Robinson, R. G. (2005). The construct of minor and major depression in Alzheimer's disease. *American Journal of Psychiatry, 62,* 2086–2093.

Starr, L. R., & Davila, J. (2008). Excessive reassurance seeking, depression, and interpersonal rejection: A meta-analytic review. *Journal of Abnormal Psychology, 117,* 762–775.

Statista Inc. (2015). Weekly time spent with media in the United States in fall 2013, by medium type and age (in hours). Retrieved from http://www.statista.com/statistics/348269/digital-traditional-media-consumption-age-usa/

Steele J. D., Christmas, D., Eljamel, M. S., & Matthews, K. (2008). Anterior cingulotomy for major depression: Clinical outcome and relationship to lesion characteristics. *Biological Psychiatry, 63,* 670.

Steenen, S. A., van Wijk, A. J., van der Heijden, G. J. M. C., van Westrhenen, R., de Lange, J., & de Jongh, A. (2016). Propranolol for the treatment of anxiety disorders: Systematic review and meta-analysis. *Journal of Psychopharmacology, 30,* 128–139. doi:10.1177/0269881115612236

Stefanopoulou, E., Hirsch, C. R., Hayes, S., Adlam, A., & Coker, S. (2014). Are attentional control resources reduced by worry in generalized anxiety disorder? *Journal of Abnormal Psychology, 123,* 330–335. doi:10.1037/a0036343

Stein, A. L., Trana, G. Q., Lund, L. M., Haji, U., Dashevsky, B. A., & Baker, D. G. (2005). Correlates for posttraumatic stress disorder in Gulf War veterans: A retrospective study of main and moderating effects. *Journal of Anxiety Disorders, 19,* 861–876.

Stein, D. J., Craske, M. A., Friedman, M. J., & Phillips, K. A. (2014). Anxiety disorders, obsessive-compulsive and related disorders, trauma- and stressor-related disorders, and dissociative disorders in DSM-5. *American Journal of Psychiatry, 171,* 611–613. doi:10.1176/appi.ajp.2014.14010003

Stein, M. B., & Sareen, J. (2015). Generalized anxiety disorder. *New England Journal of Medicine, 373,* 2059–2068. doi:10.1056/NEJMcp1502514

Stein, M. B., & Stein, D. J. (2008). Social anxiety disorder. *The Lancet, 371,* 1115–1125.

Stein, M. T. (2011, March 23). Most ADHD is complex. *Journal Watch Pediatrics and Adolescent Medicine.* Retrieved from http://pediatrics.jwatch.org/

Stein, M. T. (2012). No safe pattern of alcohol consumption during pregnancy. *Journal Watch Pediatrics and Adolescent Medicine.* Retrieved from http://pediatrics.jwatch.org/cgi/content/full/2012/229/2?q=etoc_jwpeds

Stein, M. T. (2013, December 23). A national and regional look at ADHD in children and adolescents. *Journal Watch.* Retrieved from http://www.jwatch.org/na33007/2013/12/23/national-and-regional-look-adhd-children-and-adolescents?query=etoc_jwpsych

Steinfeldt, M., & Steinfeldt, J. A. (2012). Athletic identity and conformity to masculine norms among college football players. *Journal of Applied Sport Psychology, 24,* 115–128.

A step toward controlling Huntington's disease? Potential new way of blocking activity of gene that causes HD. (2011, June 23). *ScienceDaily.* Retrieved from http://www.sciencedaily.com

Stephenson, J. (2008). Testosterone and depression. *Journal of the American Medical Association, 299,* 1764. doi:10.1001/jama.299.15.1764-d

Stergiakouli, E., Hamshere, M., Holmans, P., Langley, K., Zaharieva, I., Hawi, Z.,…Thapar, A. (2012). Investigating the contribution of common genetic variants to the risk and pathogenesis of ADHD. *American Journal of Psychiatry, 169,* 186–194. doi:10.1176/appi.ajp.2011.11040551

Stergiopoulos, V., Cusi, A., Bekele, T., Skosireva, A., Latimer, E., Schütz, C.,…Rourke, S. B. (2015). Neurocognitive impairment in a large sample of homeless adults with mental illness. *Acta Psychiatrica Scandinavica, 131,* 256–268. doi:10.1111/acps.12391

Stergiopoulos, V., Gozdzik, A., Misir, V., Skosireva, A., Connelly, J., Sarang, A.,…McKenzie, K. (2015). Effectiveness of housing first with intensive case management in an ethnically diverse sample of homeless adults with mental illness: A randomized controlled trial. *PLOS ONE, 10,* e0130281. doi:10.1371/journal.pone.0130281

Stevenson, J., Meares, R., & Comerford, A. (2003). Diminished impulsivity in older patients with borderline personality disorder. *American Journal of Psychiatry, 160,* 165–166.

Stevens-Watkins, D., Perry, B., Pullen, E., Jewell, J., & Oser, C. B. (2014). Examining the associations of racism, sexism, and stressful life events on psychological distress among African-American women. *Cultural Diversity and Ethnic Minority Psychology, 20,* 561–569. Retrieved from http://dx.doi.org/10.1037/a0036700

Stewart, A. L. (2014). The Men's Project: A sexual assault prevention program targeting college men. *Psychology of Men & Masculinity, 15,* 481–485.

Stewart, S. M., Kennard, B. D., Lee, P. W. H., Hughes, C. W., Mayes, T. L., Emslie, G. J.,…Lewinsohn, P. M. (2004). A cross-cultural investigation of cognitions and depressive symptoms in adolescents. *Journal of Abnormal Psychology, 113,* 248–257.

Stice, E., Hayward, C., Cameron, R. P., Killen, J. D., & Taylor, C. B. (2000). Body-image and eating disturbances predict onset of depression among female adolescents: A longitudinal study. *Journal of Abnormal Psychology, 109,* 438–444.

Stice, E., Marti, C. N., & Cheng, Z. H. (2014). Effectiveness of a dissonance-based eating disorder prevention program for ethnic groups in two randomized controlled trials. *Behaviour Research and Therapy, 55,* 54–64. doi:10.1016/j.brat.2014.02.002

Stoffers, J. M., & Lieb, K. (2015). Pharmacotherapy for borderline personality disorder: Current evidence and recent trends. *Current Psychiatry Reports, 17,* 534. doi:10.1007/s11920-014-0534-0

Stone, J., Smyth, R., Carson, A., Lewis, S., Prescott, R., Warlow, C., & Sharpe, M. (2005). Systematic review of misdiagnosis of conversion symptoms and "hysteria." *British Medical Journal, 331,* 989.

Stone, J., Smyth, R., Carson, A., Lewis, S., Prescott, R., Warlow, C., & Sharpe, M. (2006). La belle indifférence in conversion symptoms and hysteria: Systematic review. *British Journal of Psychiatry, 188,* 204–209.

Stone, M. H. (1980). *Borderline syndromes.* New York, NY: McGraw Hill.

Stone, M., Laughren, T., Jones, M. L., Levenson, M., Holland, P. C., Hughes, A.,…Temple, R. (2009). Risk of suicidality in clinical trials of antidepressants in adults: Analysis of proprietary data submitted to U.S. Food and Drug Administration. *British Medical Journal, 339,* 2880. doi:10.1136/bmj.b2880

Stoner, R., Chow, M. L., Boyle, M. P., Sunkin, S. M., Mouton, P. R., Roy, S.,…Courchesne, E. (2014). Patches of disorganization in the neocortex of children with autism. *New England Journal of Medicine, 370,* 1209–1219. doi:10.1056/NEJMoa1307491

Storch, E. A., & Lewin, A. B. (2016). Introduction. In E. A. Storch & A. B. Lewin (Eds.), *Clinical handbook of obsessive-compulsive and related disorders: A case-based approach to treating pediatric and adult populations* (pp. 3–4). New York, NY: Springer.

Stout-Shaffer, S., & Page, G. (2008). Effects of relaxation training on physiological and psychological measures of distress and quality of life in HIV-seropositive subjects. *Brain, Behavior, and Immunity, 22*(4, Suppl. 1), 8.

Strachen, E. (2008). Civil commitment evaluations. In R. Jackson (Ed.), *Learning forensic assessment* (pp. 509–535). New York, NY: Routledge/Taylor & Francis Group.

Strasser, A. A., Kaufmann, V., Jepson, C., Perkins, K. A., Pickworth, W. B., & Wileyto, E. P. (2005). Effects of different nicotine replacement therapies on postcessation psychological responses. *Addictive Behaviors, 30,* 9–17.

Strauss C., Cavanagh, K., Oliver, A., & Pettman, D. (2014). Mindfulness-based interventions for people diagnosed with a current episode of an anxiety or depressive disorder: A meta-analysis of randomised controlled trials. *PLOS ONE.* Published online. doi:10.1371/journal.pone.0096110

Strauss, G. P., Sandt, A. T., Catalano, L. T., & Allen, D. N. (2012). Negative symptoms and depression predict lower psychological well-being in individuals with schizophrenia. *Comprehensive Psychiatry, 53,* 1137–1144. doi:10.1016/j.comppsych.2012.05.009

Strauss, J. S. (2014). Psychological interventions for psychosis: Theme and variations. *American Journal of Psychiatry, 171,* 479–481. doi:10.1176/appi.ajp.2014.14020136

Stricker, G. (2003). Is this the right book at the wrong time? *Contemporary Psychology, 48,* 726–728.

Striegel-Moore, R. H., Dohm, F. A., Kraemer, H. C., Taylor, C. B., Daniels, S. D., Crawford, P. B., …Schreiber, G. B. (2003). Eating disorders in white and black women. *American Journal of Psychiatry, 160,* 1326–1331.

Striegel-Moore, R. H., Wilson, G. T., DeBar, L., Perrin, N., Lynch, F., Rosselli, F.,…Kraemer, H. (2010). Cognitive behavioral guided self-help for the treatment of recurrent binge eating. *Journal of Consulting and Clinical Psychology, 78,* 312–321.

Strike, P. C., Magid, K., Whitehead, D. L., Brydon, L., Bhattacharyya, M. R., & Steptoe, A. (2006). Pathophysiological processes underlying emotional triggering of acute cardiac events. *Proceedings of the*

*National Academy of Sciences.* Retrieved from http://www.pnas.org/cgi/content/abstract/103/11/4322

Strollo, P. J., Jr., Soose, R. J., Maurer, J. T., de Vries, N., Cornelius, J., Froymovich, O.,...the STAR Trial Group. (2014). Upper-airway stimulation for obstructive sleep apnea. *New England Journal of Medicine, 370,* 139–149. doi:10.1056/NEJMoa1308659

Stroud, C. B., Davila, J., & Moyer, A. (2008). The relationship between stress and depression in first onsets versus recurrences: A meta-analytic review. *Journal of Abnormal Psychology, 117,* 206–213.

Stroup, T. S., Gerhard, T., Crystal, S., Huang, C., & Olfson, M. (2016). Comparative effectiveness of clozapine and standard antipsychotic treatment in adults with schizophrenia. *American Journal of Psychiatry, 173,* 166–173. Retrieved from http://dx.doi.org/10.1176/appi.ajp.2015.15030332

Stroup, T. S., McEvoy, J. P., Ring, K. D., Hamer, R. H., LaVange, L. M., Swartz, M. S.,...Schizophrenia Trials Network. (2011). A randomized trial examining the effectiveness of switching from olanzapine, quetiapine, or risperidone to aripiprazole to reduce metabolic risk: Comparison of antipsychotics for metabolic problems (CAMP). *American Journal of Psychiatry, 168,* 947–956. doi:10.1176/Appi.Ajp.2011.10111609

Stuart, R. B. (2004). Twelve practical suggestions for achieving multicultural competence. *Professional Psychology: Research and Practice, 35,* 3–9.

Styron, W. (1990). *Darkness visible.* New York, NY: Vintage.

Subconscious signals can trigger brain's drug-craving centers. (2008, February 4). *NIH Research Matters.* Retrieved from http://www.nih.gov/news-events/nih-research-matters/subconscious-signals-can-trigger-brains-drug-craving-centers

Substance Abuse and Mental Health Services Administration. (2012). National Survey on Drug Use and Health, 2010 and 2011. Center for Behavioral Health Statistics and Quality. Retrieved from www.samhsa.gov

Sudak, D. M. (2011). *Combining CBT and medication: An evidence-based approach.* Hoboken, NJ: John Wiley & Sons Inc.

Sue, D. W. (2010). *Microaggressions in everyday life: Race, gender and sexual orientation.* New York, NY: John Wiley and Sons.

Sue, S., Yan Cheng, J. K., Saad, C. S., & Chu, J. P. (2012). Asian American mental health: A call to action. *American Psychologist, 67,* 532–544. doi:10.1037/a0028900

Suinn, R. M. (2001). The terrible twos—anger and anxiety: Hazardous to your health. *American Psychologist, 56,* 27–36.

Sukhodolsky, D. G., Golub, A., Stone, E. C., & Orban, L. (2005). Dismantling anger control training for children: A randomized pilot study of social problem-solving versus social skills training components. *Behavior Therapy, 36,* 15–23.

Sullivan, D., Pinsonneault, J. K., Papp, A. C., Zhu, H., Lemeshow, S., Mash, D.C., & Sadee, W. (2013). Dopamine transporter DAT and receptor DRD2 variants affect risk of lethal cocaine abuse: A gene–gene–environment interaction. *Translational Psychiatry, 3,* e222. doi:10.1038/tp.2012.146

Sullivan, G. M., Oquendo, M. A., Milak, M., Miller, J. M., Burke, A., Ogden, R. T.,...Mann, J. J. (2015). Positron emission tomography quantification of serotonin 1a receptor binding in suicide attempters with major depressive disorder. *JAMA Psychiatry, 72,* 169–178. doi:10.1001/jamapsychiatry.2014.240

Sullivan, H. S. (1962). *Schizophrenia as a human process.* New York, NY: Norton.

Sulloway, F. (1983). *Freud: Biologist of the mind.* New York, NY: Basic Books.

Sun, P., Cameron, A., Seftel, A., Shabsigh, R., Niederberger, C., & Guay, A. (2006). Erectile dysfunction: An observable marker of diabetes mellitus? A large national epidemiological study. *Journal of Urology, 176,* 1081–1085.

Sun, H., Lui, S., Yao, L., Deng, W., Xiao, Y., Zhang, W.,...Gong, Q. (2015). Two patterns of white matter abnormalities in medication-naive patients with first-episode schizophrenia revealed by diffusion tensor imaging and cluster analysis. *JAMA Psychiatry, 72,* 678–686. doi:10.1001/jamapsychiatry.2015.0505

Sundquist, J., Lilja, A., Palmér, K., Memon, A. A., Wang, X., Johansson, L. M.,...Sundquist K. (2014). Mindfulness group therapy in primary care patients with depression, anxiety and stress and adjustment disorders: Randomised controlled trial. *British Journal of Psychiatry, 206,* 128–135. doi:10.1192/bjp.bp.114.150243

Supekar, K., & Menon, V. (2015). Sex differences in structural organization of motor systems and their dissociable links with repetitive/restricted behaviors in children with autism. *Molecular Autism, 6.* doi:10.1186/s13229-015-0042-z

Supekar, K., Menon, V., Rubin, D., Musen, M., & Greicius, M. D. (2008). Network analysis of intrinsic functional brain connectivity in Alzheimer's disease. *PLOS Computational Biology,* 4(6), e1000100. doi:10.1371/journal.pcbi.1000100

Sutin, A. R., Stephan, Y., & Terracciano, A. (2016). Perceived discrimination and personality development in adulthood. *Developmental Psychology, 52,* 155–163. Retrieved from http://dx.doi.org/10.1037/dev0000069

Sutker, P. B., Davis, J. M., Uddo, M., & Ditta, S. R. (1995). War zone stress, personal resources, and PTSD in Persian Gulf War returnees. *Journal of Abnormal Psychology, 104,* 444–452.

Suzuki, T., Samuel, D. B., Pahlen, S., & Krueger, R. F. (2015). DSM-5 alternative personality disorder model traits as maladaptive extreme variants of the five-factor model: An item-response theory analysis. *Journal of Abnormal Psychology, 124,* 343–354. Retrieved from http://dx.doi.org/10.1037/abn0000035

Swann, A. C., Lafer, B., Perugi, G., Frye, M. A., Bauer, M., Bahk, W.-M.,...Suppes, T. (2013). Bipolar mixed states: An International Society for Bipolar Disorders Task Force Report of Symptom Structure, Course of Illness, and Diagnosis. *American Journal of Psychiatry, 170,* 31–42. doi:10.1176/appi.ajp.2012.12030301

Swann, A. C., Lijffijt, M., Lane, S. D., Steinberg, J. L., & Moeller, F. G. (2009). Trait impulsivity and response inhibition in antisocial personality disorder. *Journal of Psychiatric Research, 43,* 1057–1063. doi:10.1016/j.jpsychires.2009.03.003

Swanson, J. W., Swartz, M. S., Van Dorn, R. A., Elbogen, E. B., Wagner, R., Rosenheck, R. A.,...Lieberman, J. A. (2006). A national study of violent behavior in persons with schizophrenia. *Archives of General Psychiatry, 63,* 490–499.

Swanson, S. A., Crow, S. J., Le Grange, D., Swendsen, J., & Merikangas, K. R. (2011). Prevalence and correlates of eating disorders in adolescents: Results from the National Comorbidity Survey Replication Adolescent Supplement. *Archives of General Psychiatry, 68,* 714–723. doi:10.1001/archgenpsychiatry.2011.22

Szasz, T. (1970). *Ideology and insanity: Essays on the psychiatric dehumanization of man.* New York, NY: Doubleday Anchor.

Szasz, T. (2003a). Psychiatry and the control of dangerousness: On the apotropaic function of the term "mental illness." *Journal of Medical Ethics, 29,* 227–230.

Szasz, T. (2003b). Response to: "Comments on psychiatry and the control of dangerousness: On the apotropaic function of the term 'mental illness.'" *Journal of Medical Ethics, 29,* 237.

Szasz, T. (2007). *Coercion as cure: A critical history of psychiatry.* New Brunswick, NJ: Transaction.

Szasz, T. S. (1960). The myth of mental illness. *American Psychologist, 15,* 113–118.

Szasz, T. S. (2011). *The myth of mental illness: Foundations of a theory of personal conduct.* New York, NY: HarperCollins.

Tabak, B. A., Vrshek-Schallhorn, S., Zinbarg, R. E., Prenoveau, J. M., Mineka, S., Redei, E. E.,...Craske, M. G. (2016). Interaction of CD38 variant and chronic interpersonal stress prospectively predicts social anxiety and depression symptoms over 6 years. *Clinical Psychological Science, 4,* 17–27. doi:10.1177/2167702615577470

Tafoya, T. N. (1996). Native two-spirit people. In R. P. Cabaj & T. S. Stein (Eds.), *Textbook of homosexuality and mental health* (pp. 603–617). Washington, DC: American Psychiatric Press, Inc.

Taft, C. T., Watkins, L. E., Stafford, J., Street, A. E., & Monson, C. M. (2011). Posttraumatic stress disorder and intimate relationship problems: A meta-analysis. *Journal of Consulting and Clinical Psychology, 79,* 22–33. doi:10.1037/a0022196

Tamam, L., Eroğlu, M. Z., & Paltacı, O. (2011). Intermittent explosive disorder. *Current Approaches in Psychiatry, 3,* 387–425. doi:10.5455/cap.20110318

Tan, H. M., Tong, S. F., & Ho, C. C. K. (2012). Men's health: Sexual dysfunction, physical, and psychological health: Is there a link? *Journal of Sexual Medicine, 9,* 663–671.

Tandon, R., Keshavan, M. S., & Nasrallah, H. A. (2008). Schizophrenia, "just the facts": What we know in 2008: Part 1. Overview. *Schizophrenia Research, 100,* 4–19. doi:10.1016/j.schres.2008.01.022

Tandon, R., Nasrallah, H. A., & Keshavan, M. S. (2009). Schizophrenia, "just the facts": Part 4. Clinical features and conceptualization. *Schizophrenia Research, 110,* 1–23. doi:10.1016/j.schres.2009.03.005

Tandon, R., Nasrallah, H. A., & Keshavan, M. S. (2010). Schizophrenia, "just the facts": Part 5. Treatment and prevention, past, present, and future. *Schizophrenia Research, 122,* 1–23. doi:10.1016/j.schres.2010.05.025

Tanner, C. M. (2013). A second honeymoon for Parkinson's disease? *New England Journal of Medicine, 368,* 675–676. doi:10.1056/NEJMe121491313

Tanzi, R. E. (2015). TREM2 and risk of Alzheimer's disease: Friend or foe? *New England Journal of Medicine, 372,* 2564–2565. doi:10.1056/NEJMcibr1503954

Tapert, S. F., Brown, G. G., Baratta, M. V., & Brown, S. A. (2004). fMRI BOLD response to alcohol stimuli in alcohol dependent young women. *Addictive Behaviors, 29,* 33–50.

Tatarsky, A., & Kellogg, S. (2010). Integrative harm reduction psychotherapy: A case of substance use, multiple trauma, and suicidality. *Journal of Clinical Psychology, 66*(Special Issue: Harm Reduction in Psychotherapy), 123–135. doi:10.1002/jclp.20666

Taubes, G. (2012). Unraveling the obesity-cancer connection. *Science, 335,* 28–32. doi:10.1126/science.335.6064.28

Tavares, H. (2012). Assessment and treatment of pathological gambling. In J. E. Grant & M. N. Potenza (Eds.), *The Oxford handbook of impulse control disorders* (pp. 279–312). New York, NY: Oxford University Press.

Tavernise, S. (2012, December 11). Obesity in young is seen as falling in several cities. *The New York Times.* Retrieved from nytimes.com

Tavernisejan, S. (2014). List of smoking-related illnesses grows sgnificantly in U.S. report. *The New York Times,* p. A15.

Taylor, C. B., & Luce, K. H. (2003). Computer- and Internet-based psychotherapy interventions. *Current Directions in Psychological Science, 12,* 18–22.

Taylor, K. L., Lamdan, R. M., Siegel, J. E., Shelby, R., Moran-Klimi, K., & Hrywna, M. (2003). Psychological adjustment among African American breast cancer patients: One-year follow-up results of a randomized psychoeducational group intervention. *Health Psychology, 22,* 316–323.

Taylor, M. A., & Fink, M. (2003). Catatonia in psychiatric classification: A home of its own. *American Journal of Psychiatry, 160,* 1233–1241.

Taylor, S., & Jang, K. L. (2011). Biopsychosocial etiology of obsessions and compulsions: An integrated behavioral–genetic and cognitive–behavioral analysis. *Journal of Abnormal Psychology, 120,* 174–186. doi:10.1037/a0021403

Taylor, V., & Rupp, L. J. (2004). Chicks with dicks, men in dresses: What it means to be a drag queen. *Journal of Homosexuality, 46*(3–4), 113–133.

Taylor, W. D. (2014). Depression in the elderly. *New England Journal of Medicine, 371,* 1228–1236. doi:10.1056/NEJMcp1402180

Teachman, B. A., Marker, C. D., & Clerkin, E. M. (2010). Catastrophic misinterpretations as a predictor of symptom change during treatment for panic disorder. *Journal of Consulting and Clinical Psychology, 78,* 964–973. doi:10.1037/a0021067

Teplin, L. A., McClelland, G. M., Abram, K. M., & Weiner, D. A. (2005). Crime victimization in adults with severe mental illness: Comparison with the National Crime Victimization Survey. *Archives of General Psychiatry, 62,* 911–921.

ter Kuile, M. M., Melles, R., de Groot, H. E., Tuijnman-Raasveld, C. C., & van Lankveld, J. J. D. M. (2013). Therapist-aided exposure for women with lifelong vaginismus: A randomized waiting-list control trial of efficacy. *Journal of Consulting and Clinical Psychology, 81,* 1127–1136. doi:10.1037/a0034292

Tessier, A., Chemiakine, A., Inbar, B., Bagchi, S., Ray, R. S., Palmiter, R. D.,... Ansorge, M. S. (2015). Activity of raphe serotonergic neurons controls emotional behaviors. *Cell Reports, 13,* 1965–1976. Retrieved from http://dx.doi.org/10.1016/j.celrep.2015.10.061

Thase, M. E. (2014). Large-scale study suggests specific indicators for combined cognitive therapy and pharmacotherapy in major depressive disorder. *JAMA Psychiatry, 71,* 1101–1102. doi:10.1001/jamapsychiatry.2014.1524.

The BALANCE Investigators and Collaborators. (2010). Lithium plus valproate combination therapy versus monotherapy for relapse prevention in bipolar I disorder (BALANCE): A randomised open-label trial. *The Lancet, 375,* 385–395. doi:10.1016/S0140-6736(09)61828-6

The McKnight Investigators. (2003). Risk factors for the onset of eating disorders in adolescent girls: Results of the McKnight Longitudinal Risk Factor Study. *American Journal of Psychiatry, 160,* 248–254.

Therapy and hypochondriacs often make poor mix, study says. (2004, March 25). *The New York Times,* p. A19.

Thibaut, F. (2012). Pharmacological treatment of paraphilias. *Israel Journal of Psychiatry and Related Sciences, 49,* 297–305.

Thiedke, C. C. (2003). Nocturnal enuresis. *American Family Physician, 67,* 1509–1510.

Thioux, M., Stark, D. E., Klaiman, C., & Schultz, R. (2006). The day of the week when you were born in 700 ms: Calendar computation in an autistic savant. *Journal of Experimental Psychology: Human Perception and Performance, 32,* 1155–1168.

Thirlwall, K., Cooper, P. J., Karalus, J., Voysey, M., Willetts, L., & Creswell C. (2013). Treatment of child anxiety disorders via guided parent-delivered cognitive-behavioural therapy: Randomised controlled trial. *The British Journal of Psychiatry, 203,* 436–444. doi:10.1192/bjp.bp.113.126698

Thompson, M. A., Aberg, J. A., Hoy, J. E., Telenti, A., Benson, C., Cahn, P.,... Volberding, P. A. (2012). Antiretroviral treatment of adult HIV infection: 2012 recommendations of the International Antiviral Society–USA Panel. *Journal of the American Medical Association, 308,* 387–402. doi:10.1001/jama.2012.7961

Thompson, P. M., Hayashi, K. M., Simon, S. L., Geaga, J. A., Hong, M. S., Sui, Y.,... London, E. D. (2004). Structural abnormalities in the brains of human subjects who use methamphetamine. *Journal of Neuroscience, 30,* 6028–6036.

Thompson, P. M., Vidal, C., Gledd, J. N., Gochman, P., Blumenthal, J., Nicolson, R.,... Rapoport, J. L. (2001). Mapping adolescent brain change reveals dynamic wave of accelerated gray matter loss in very early-onset schizophrenia. *Proceedings of the National Academy of Science, 98,* 11650–11655.

Thompson, T. (1995). *The beast: A journey through depression.* New York, NY: Putnam.

Thompson-Brenner, H. (2013). Good news about psychotherapy for eating disorders: Comment on Warren, Schafer, Crowley, and Olivardia. *Psychotherapy, 50,* 565–567. doi:10.1037/a0031101

Thorlund, K., Druyts, E., Wu, P., Balijepalli, C., Keohane, D., & Mills, E. (2015). Comparative efficacy and safety of selective serotonin reuptake inhibitors and serotonin-norepinephrine reuptake inhibitors in older adults: A network meta-analysis. *Journal of the American Geriatrics Society, 63,* 1002. Retrieved from http://dx.doi.org/10.1111/jgs.13395

Thorpy, M. (2008). Brain structure in obstructive sleep apnea. *Journal Watch Neurology.* Retrieved from http://neurology.jwatch.org/cgi/content/full/2008/1007/4

Thun, M. J., Carter, B. D., Feskanich, D., Freedman, N. D., Prentice, R., Lopez, A. D.,... Gapstur, S. M. (2013). 50-year trends in smoking-related mortality in the United States. *New England Journal of Medicine, 368,* 351–364. doi:10.1056/NEJMsa1211127

Tienari, P., Wynne, L. C., Sorri, A., Lahti, I., Laksy, K., Moring, J.,... Wahlberg, K. (2004). Genotype-environment interaction in schizophrenia spectrum disorder. *British Journal of Psychiatry, 184,* 216–222.

Jenkins, J. H., & Karno, M. (1992). The meaning of expressed emotion: Theoretical issues raised by cross-cultural research. *American Journal of Psychiatry, 149,* 9–21.

Tiggemann, M., Martins, Y., & Kirkbride, A. (2007). Oh to be lean and muscular: Body image ideals in gay and heterosexual men. *Psychology of Men & Masculinity, 8,* 15–24.

Titov, N., Dear, B. F., Ali, S., Zou, J. B., Lorian, C. N., Johnston, L.,... Fogliati, V. J. (2015). Clinical and cost-effectiveness of therapist-guided Internet-delivered cognitive behavior therapy for older adults with symptoms of depression: A randomized controlled trial. *Behavior Therapy, 46,* 193–205. doi:10.1016/j.beth.2014.09.008

Tobacco use among middle and high school students: United States, 2013. (2014, November). *Morbidity and Mortality Weekly Report, 63*(45), 1021–1026.

Tohen, M., Zarate, C. A., Hennen, J., Khalsa, H.-M. K., Strakowski, S. M., Gebre-Medhin, P.,... Baldessarini, R. J. (2003). The McLean-Harvard First-Episode Mania Study: Prediction of recovery and first recurrence. *American Journal of Psychiatry, 160,* 2099–2107.

Tolin, D. F., & Foa, E. B. (2006). Sex differences in trauma and posttraumatic stress disorder: A quantitative review of 25 years of research. *Psychological Bulletin, 132,* 959–992.

Tolin, D. F., (2010). Is cognitive–behavioral therapy more effective than other therapies? A meta-analytic review. *Clinical Psychology Review, 30,* 710–720. doi:10.1016/j.cpr.2010.05.003

Tolin, D. F., Frost, R. O., Steketee, G., & Muroff, J. (2015). Cognitive behavioral therapy for hoarding disorder: A meta-analysis. *Depression and Anxiety, 32,* 158–166. doi:10.1002/da.22327

Tolin, D. F., Stevens, M. C., Nave, A., Villavicencio, A. L., & Morrison, S. (2012). Neural mechanisms of cognitive behavioral therapy response in hoarding disorder: A pilot study. *Journal of Obsessive-Compulsive and Related Disorders, 1,* 180–188.

Tomb, E., Rafanelli, C., Grandi, S., Guidi, J., & Fava. G. A. (2012). Clinical configuration of cyclothymic disturbances. *Journal of Affective Disorders, 139,* 244–249. Retrieved from http://dx.doi.org/10.1016/j.jad.2012.01.014

Tondo, L., Pompili, M., Forte, A., & Baldessarini R. J. (2015). Suicide attempts in bipolar disorders: Comprehensive review of 101 reports. *Acta Psychiatrica Scandinavica.* Retrieved from http://onlinelibrary.wiley.com/doi/10.1111/acps.12517/abstract

Toomey, R., Lyons, M. J., Eisen, S. A., Xian, H., Chantarujikapong, S., Seidman, L. J.,... Tsuang, M. T. (2003). A twin study of the neuropsychological consequences of stimulant abuse. *Archives of General Psychiatry, 60,* 303–310.

Toplak, M. E., Connors, L., Shuster, J., Knezevic, B., & Parks, S. (2008). Review of cognitive, cognitive-behavioral, and neural-based interventions for attention-deficit/hyperactivity disorder (ADHD). *Clinical Psychology Review, 28,* 801–820.

Torbey, E., Pachana, N. A., & Dissanayaka, N. N. W. (2015). Depression rating scales in Parkinson's disease: A critical review updating recent literature. *Journal of Affective Disorders, 184,* 216–224.

Torpy, J. M., Burke, A. E., & Golub, R. M. (2011). Generalized anxiety disorder. *Journal of the American Medical Association, 305,* 522. doi:10.1001/jama.305.5.522

Torres, L., & Vallejo, L.G. (2015). Ethnic discrimination and Latino depression: The mediating role of traumatic stress symptoms and alcohol use. *Cultural Diversity and Ethnic Minority Psychology, 21,* 517–526. Retrieved from http://dx.doi.org/10.1037/cdp0000020

Torrey, E. F. (2011). The association of stigma with violence [Letter]. *American Journal of Psychiatry, 168,* 325. doi:10.1176/appi.ajp.2011.10121710

Torrey, E. F., & Zdanowicz, M. (1999, May 28). A right to mental illness? *PsychLaws.Org.* Retrieved from http://www.psychlaws.org/GeneralResources/article14.htm

Torvik, F. A., Welander-Vatn, A., Ystrom, E., Knudsen, G. P., Czajkowski, N., Kendler, K. S., & Reichborn-Kjennerud, T. (2016). Longitudinal associations between social anxiety disorder and avoidant personality disorder: A twin study. *Journal of Abnormal Psychology, 125,* 114–124. Retrieved from http://dx.doi.org/10.1037/abn0000124

Town, J. M., Diener, M. J., Abbass, A., Leichsenring, F., Driessen, E., & Rabung, S. (2012). A meta-analysis of psychodynamic psychotherapy outcomes: Evaluating the effects of research-specific procedures. *Psychotherapy, 49,* 276–290. doi:10.1037/a0029564

Towner, B. (2009, March). 50 and still a doll. *AARP Bulletin, 50,* 35.

Trauer, J. M., Qian, M. Y., Doyle, J. S., Rajaratnam, S. M. W., & Cunningham, D. (2015). Cognitive behavioral therapy for chronic insomnia: A systematic review and meta-analysis. *Annals of Internal Medicine, 163,* 191–204. doi:10.7326/M14-2841

Travagin, G., Margola, D., & Revenson, T. A. (2015). How effective are expressive writing interventions for adolescents? A meta-analytic review. *Clinical Psychology Review, 36,* 42–55.

Treffert, D. A. (1988). The idiot savant: A review of the syndrome. *American Journal of Psychiatry, 145,* 563–572.

Trimble, J. E. (1991). The mental health service and training needs of American Indians. In H. F. Myers, P. Wohlford, L. P. Guzman, & R. J. Echemendia (Eds.), *Ethnic minority perspectives on clinical training and services in psychology* (pp. 43–48). Washington, DC: American Psychological Association.

Trockel, M., Karlin, B. E., Taylor, C. B., & Manber, R. (2014). Cognitive behavioral therapy for insomnia with veterans: Evaluation of effectiveness and correlates of treatment outcomes. *Behaviour Research and Therapy, 56,* 16–21. doi:10.1016/j.brat.2014.02.007

Trull, T., & Prinstein, M. (2013). *Clinical psychology* (8th edition). Belmont, CA: Cengage Learning.

Truman, J. T., & Langton, L. (2015). *Criminal victimization, 2014.* U.S. Department of Justice: Bureau of Justice Statistics. Retrieved from http://www.bjs.gov/content/pub/pdf/cv14.pdf

Tsai, L.-H., & Madabhushi, R. (2014). Alzheimer's disease: A protective factor for the ageing brain. *Nature, 507,* 439–440. doi:10.1038/nature13214

Tseng, M. C. M., Fang, D., Chang, C. H., & Lee, M. B. (2013). Identifying high-school dance students who will develop an eating disorder: A 1-year prospective study. *Psychiatry Research, 209,* 611–618. doi:10.1016/j.psychres.2013.04.008

Tseng, W., Mo, K. M., Li, L. S., Chen, G. Q., Ou, L. W., & Zheng, H. B. (1992). Koro epidemics in Guangdong, China: A questionnaire survey. *The Journal of Nervous and Mental Disease, 180,* 117–123.

Tsitsika, A. K., Tzavela, E. C., Janikian, M., Ólafsson, K., Iordache, A., Schoenmakers, T. M.,... Richardson, C. (2014). Online social networking in adolescence: Patterns of use in six European countries and links with psychosocial functioning. *Journal of Adolescent Health, 55,* 141–147. doi:10.1016/j.jadohealth.2013.11.010

Tsunemi, T., Ashe, T. D., Morrison, B. E., Soriano, K. R., Au, J., Vázquez Roque, R. A.,... La Spada, A. R. (2012). PGC-1a rescues Huntington's disease proteotoxicity by preventing oxidative stress and promoting TFEB function. *Science Translational Medicine, 4,* 142ra97. doi:10.1126/scitranslmed.3003799

Turetsky, B., Dress, E. M., Braff, D. L., Calkins, M. E., Green, M. F., Greenwood, T. A.,... Light, G. (2014). The utility of P300 as a schizophrenia endophenotype and predictive biomarker: Clinical and socio-demographic modulators in COGS-2. *Schizophrenia Research, 163,* 53–62. doi:10.1016/j.schres.2014.09.024

Turkington, D., & Morrison, A. P. (2012). Cognitive therapy for negative symptoms of schizophrenia. *Archives of General Psychiatry, 69,* 119–120. doi:10.1001/archgenpsychiatry.2011.141

Turkington, D., Munetz, M., Pelton, J., Montesano, V., Sivec, H., Nausheen, B.,... Kingdon, D. (2014). High-yield cognitive behavioral techniques for psychosis delivered by case managers to their clients with persistent psychotic symptoms: An exploratory trial. *Journal of Nervous & Mental Disease, 202,* 30–34. doi:10.1097/NMD.0000000000000070

Turner, D. T., van der Gaag, M., Karyotaki, E., & Cuijpers, P. (2014). Psychological interventions for psychosis: A meta-analysis of comparative outcome studies. *American Journal of Psychiatry, 171,* 523–538. doi:10.1176/appi.ajp.2013.13081159

Turner, S. M., & Beidel, D. C. (1989). Social phobia: Clinical syndrome, diagnosis, and comorbidity. *Clinical Psychology Review, 9,* 3–18.

Turner, W. A., & Casey, L. M. (2014). Outcomes associated with virtual reality in psychological interventions: Where are we now? *Clinical Psychology Review, 34,* 634–644. doi:10.1016/j.cpr.2014.10.003

U.S. Department of Health and Human Services, Substance Abuse and Mental Health Services Administration, Center for Mental Health Services, National Institutes of Health, National Institute of Mental Health. (1999). *Mental Health: A Report of the Surgeon General.* Rockville, MD: Author.

U.S. Department of Health and Human Services, Substance Abuse and Mental Health Services Administration, Center for Mental Health Services, National Institutes of Health, National Institute of Mental Health. (2001). *Mental health: Culture, race, and ethnicity: A supplement to mental health: A report of the Surgeon General—Executive summary.* Rockville, MD: Author.

Uhl, G. R., & Grow, R. W. (2004). The burden of complex genetics in brain disorders. *Archives of General Psychiatry, 61,* 223–229.

Uliaszek, A. A., Zinbarg, R. E., Mineka, S., Craske, M. G., Griffith, J. W., Sutton, J. M.,... Hammen, C. (2012). A longitudinal examination of stress generation in depressive and anxiety disorders. *Journal of Abnormal Psychology, 121,* 4–15. doi:10.1037/a0025835

Ullmann, L. P., & Krasner, L. (1975). *A psychological approach to abnormal behavior* (2nd ed.). Englewood Cliffs, NJ: Prentice Hall.

Underwood, E. (2013). Faulty brain connections in dyslexia? *Science, 342,* 1158. doi:10.1126/science.342.6163.1158

Underwood, E. (2015). Alzheimer's amyloid theory gets modest boost. *Science, 349,* 464. doi:10.1126/science.349.6247.464

Urbanoski, K. A., & Kelly, J. F. (2012). Understanding genetic risk for substance use and addiction: A guide for non-geneticists. *Clinical Psychology Review, 32,* 60–70. doi:10.1016/j.cpr.2011.11.002

Usami, M., Iwadare, Y., Watanabe, K., Ushijima, H., Kodaira, M, Okada, T.,... Saitob, K. (2015). A case-control study of the difficulties in daily functioning experienced by children with depressive disorder: Preliminary communication. *Journal of Affective Disorders, 179,* 167–174.

Utsey, S. O., Chae, M. H., Brown, C. F., & Kelly, D. (2002). Effect of ethnic group membership on ethnic identity, race-related stress, and quality of life. *Cultural Diversity and Ethnic Minority Psychology, 8,* 366–377.

Vachon, D. D., Krueger, R. F., Rogosch, F. A., & Cicchetti, D. (2015). Assessment of the harmful psychiatric and behavioral effects of different forms of child maltreatment. *JAMA Psychiatry, 72,* 1135–1142. doi:10.1001/jamapsychiatry.2015.1792

Vacic, V., McCarthy, S., Malhotra, D., Murray, F., Chou, H.-H., Peoples, A.,... Sebat, J. (2011). Duplications of the neuropeptide receptor gene VIPR2 confer significant risk for schizophrenia. *Nature, 471,* 499–503. doi:10.1038/nature0988

Valasquez-Manoff, M. (2012, August 26). An immune disorder at the root of autism. *The New York Times Sunday Review,* pp. 1, 12.

Valdivia-Salas, S., Blanchard, K. S., Lombas, A. S., & Wulfert, E. (2014). Treatment-seeking precipitators in problem gambling: Analysis of data from a gambling helpline. *Psychology of Addictive Behaviors, 28,* 300–306. doi:10.1037/a0035413

Valentí, M., Pacchiarotti, I., Undurraga, J., Bonnín, C. M., Popovic, D., Goikolea, J. M.,... Vieta, E. (2015). Risk factors for rapid cycling in bipolar disorder. *Bipolar Disorder, 17,* 549–559. doi:10.1111/bdi.12288

Valenti, O., Cifelli, P., Gill, K. M, & Grace, A. A. (2011). Antipsychotic drugs rapidly induce dopamine neuron depolarization block in a developmental rat model of schizophrenia. *Journal of Neuroscience, 31,* 12330–12338. doi:10.1523/JNEUROSCI.2808-11.2011

As Valentine's Day approaches. (2012, February 7). *ScienceDaily.* Retrieved from http://www.sciencedaily.com/releases/2012/02/120207121928.htm

Van Allen, J., & Roberts, M. C. (2011). Critical incidents in the marriage of psychology and technology: A discussion of potential ethical issues in practice, education, and policy. *Professional Psychology: Research and Practice, 42,* 433–439. doi:10.1037/a0025278

van den Berg, D. P. G., de Bont, P. A. J. M., van der Vleugel, B. M., de Roos, C., de Jongh, A., Van Minnen, A.,... van der Gaag, M. (2015). Prolonged exposure vs. eye movement desensitization and reprocessing vs. waiting list for posttraumatic stress disorder in patients with a psychotic disorder: A randomized clinical trial. *JAMA Psychiatry, 72,* 259–267. doi:10.1001/jamapsychiatry.2014.2637

van den Hout, M. A., Engelhard, I. M., Rijkeboer, M. M., Koekebakker, J., Hornsveld, H., Leer, A.,... Aksea, N. (2011). EMDR: Eye movements superior to beeps in taxing working memory and reducing vividness of recollections. *Behaviour Research and Therapy, 49,* 92–98. doi:10.1016/j.brat.2010.11.00

van der Kloet, D., Giesbrecht, T., Lynn, S. J., Merckelbach, H., & de Zutter, A. (2012). Sleep normalization and decrease in dissociative experiences: Evaluation in an inpatient sample. *Journal of Abnormal Psychology, 12,* 140–150. doi:10.1037/a0024781

van der Loos, M. L. M., Mulder, P. G., Hartong, E. G., Blom, M. B., Vergouwen, A. C., de Keyzer, H. J.,... Nolen, W. A. (2009). Efficacy and safety of lamotrigine as add-on treatment to lithium in bipolar depression: A multicenter, double-blind, placebo-controlled trial. *Clinical Psychiatry, 70,* 223–231.

van der Meer, D., Hoekstra, P. J., Zwiers, M., Mennes, M., Schweren, L. J., Franke, B.,... Hartman, C. A. (2015). Brain correlates of the interaction between 5-httlpr and psychosocial stress mediating attention deficit hyperactivity disorder severity. *American Journal of Psychiatry, 172,* 768–775. Retrieved from http://dx.doi.org/10.1176/appi.ajp.2015.14081035

Van der Oord, S., Prins, P. J. M., Oosterlaan, J., & Emmelkamp, P. M. G. (2008). Efficacy of methylphenidate, psychosocial treatments and their combination in schoolaged children with ADHD: A meta-analysis. *Clinical Psychology Review, 28,* 783–800.

van der Velden, A. M., Kuyken, W., Wattar, U., Crane, C., Pallesen, K. J., Dahlgaard, J., Fjorback, L. O.,... Piet, J. (2015). A systematic review of mechanisms of change in mindfulness-based cognitive therapy in the treatment of recurrent major depressive disorder. *Clinical Psychology Review, 37,* 26–39. doi:10.1016/j.cpr.2015.02.001

Van Horn, L. (2014). A diet by any other name is still about energy. *Journal of the American Medical Association, 312,* 900–901. doi:10.1001/jama.2014.10837

Van Hulle, C. A., Waldman, I. D., D'Onofrio, B. M., Rodgers, J. L., Rathouz, P. J., & Lahey, B. B. (2009). Developmental structure of genetic influences on antisocial behavior across childhood and adolescence. *Journal of Abnormal Psychology, 118,* 711–721.

van Lankveld, J. J., Granot, M., Weijmar Schultz, W. C., Binik, Y. M., Wesselmann, U., Pukall, C. F.,... Achtrari, C. (2010). Women's sexual pain disorders. *Journal of Sexual Medicine, 7,* 615–631. doi:10.1111/j.1743-6109.2009.01631.x

Van Meter, A. R., & Youngstrom, E. A. (2015). A tale of two diatheses: Temperament, BIS, and BAS as risk factors for mood disorder. *Journal of Affective Disorders, 180,* 170–178.

Van Meter, A. R., Youngstrom, E. A., & Findling, R. L. (2012). Cyclothymic disorder: A critical review. *Clinical Psychology Review, 32,* 229–243. doi:10.1016/j.cpr.2012.02.001

van Steensel, F. J. A., & Bögels, S. M. (2015). CBT for anxiety disorders in children with and without autism spectrum disorders. *Journal of Consulting and Clinical Psychology, 83,* 512–523. Retrieved from http://dx.doi.org/10.1037/a0039108

Van Susteren, L. (2002). The insanity defense, continued [Editorial]. *The Journal of the American Academy of Psychiatry and the Law, 30,* 474–475.

van Zessen, R., Phillips, J. L., Budygin, E. A., & Stuber, G. D. (2012). Activation of VTA GABA neurons disrupts reward consumption. *Neuron, 73,* 1184–1194. doi:10.1016/j.neuron.2012.02.016

VanderCreek, L., & Knapp, S. (2001). *Tarasoff and beyond: Legal and clinical considerations in the treatment of life-endangering patients.* Sarasota, FL: Professional Resource Press.

Vanderkam, L. (2003). Barbie and fat as a feminist issue. Retrieved from http://www.shethinks.org/articles/an00208.cfm

Varley, C. K., & McClellan, J. (2009). Implications of marked weight gain associated with atypical antipsychotic medications in children and adolescents. *Journal of the American Medical Association, 302,* 1811.

Vasey, M. W., Vilensky, M. R., Heath, J. H., Harbaugh, C. N., Buffington, A. G., & Fazio, R. H. (2012). It was as big as my head, I swear! *Journal of Anxiety Disorders, 26,* 20. doi:10.1016/j.janxdis.2011.08.009

Vaziri-Bozorg, S. M., Ghasemi-Esfe, A. R., Khalilzadeh, O., Sotoudeh, H., Rokni-Yazdi, H.,... Shakiba, M. (2012). Antidepressant effects of magnetic resonance imaging–based stimulation on major depressive disorder: A double-blind randomized clinical trial. *Brain Imaging and Behavior, 6,* 70–76. doi:10.1007/s11682-011-9143-2

Vega, W. A., Kolody, B., Aguilar-Gaxiola, S., Alderete, E., Catalano, R., & Caraveo-Anduaga, J. (1998). Lifetime prevalence of DSM-III-R psychiatric disorders among urban and rural Mexican Americans in California. *Archives of General Psychiatry, 55,* 771–778.

Vega, W. A., Rodriguez, M. A., & Ang, A. (2010). Addressing stigma of depression in Latino primary care patients. *General Hospital Psychiatry, 32(2),* 182–191. doi:10.1016/j.genhosppsych.2009.10.008

Veilleux, J. C., Colvin, P. J., Anderson, J., York, C., & Heinz, A. J. (2010). A review of opioid dependence treatment: Pharmacological and psychosocial interventions to treat opioid addiction. *Clinical Psychology Review, 30,* 155–166. doi:10.1016/j.cpr.2009.10.006

Venner, K. L., Greenfield, B. L., Vicuña, B., Muñoz, R., Bhatt, S., & O'Keefe, V. (2012). "I'm not one of them": Barriers to help-seeking among American Indians with alcohol dependence. *Cultural Diversity and Ethnic Minority Psychology, 18,* 352–362. doi:10.1037/a0029757

Vereenooghe, L., & Langdon, P. E. (2013). Psychological therapies for people with intellectual disabilities: A systematic review and meta-analysis. *Research in Developmental Disabilities, 34,* 4085–4102.

Vergink, V., & Kushner, S. A. (2014). Postpartum psychosis. In M. Galbally, M. Snellen, & A. Lewis (Eds.), *Psychopharmacology and pregnancy* (pp. 139–149). New York, NY: Springer-Verlag.

Verissimo, O., Denisse, A., Gee, G. C., Ford, C. L., & Iguchi, M. Y. (2014). Racial discrimination, gender discrimination, and substance abuse among Latina/os nationwide. *Cultural Diversity and Ethnic Minority Psychology, 20,* 43–51. doi:10.1037/a0034674

Vermetten E., Schmah, C., Lindner, S., Loewenstein, R. J., & Bremner, J. D. (2006). Hippocampal and amygdalar volumes in dissociative identity disorder. *American Journal of Psychiatry, 163,* 630–636.

Vickers, K., & McNallly, R. J. (2005). Respiratory symptoms and panic in the National Comorbidity Survey: A test of Klein's suffocation false alarm theory. *Behaviour Research and Therapy, 43,* 1011–1018.

Vidoni, E. D., Johnson, D. K., Morris, J. K., Van Sciver, A., Greer, C. S., Billinger, S. A.,... Burns, J. M. (2015). Dose-response of aerobic exercise on cognition: A community-based, pilot randomized controlled trial. *PLOS ONE, 10,* e0131647. doi:10.1371/journal.pone.0131647

Viguera, A. C., Tondo, L., Koukopoulos, A. E., Reginaldi, D., Lepri, B., & Baldessarini, R. J. (2011). Episodes of mood disorders in 2,252 pregnancies and postpartum periods. *American Journal of Psychiatry, 168,* 1179–1185. doi:10.1176/appi.ajp.2011.11010148

Virués-Ortega, J. (2010). Applied behavior analytic intervention for autism in early childhood: Meta-analysis, meta-regression and dose–response meta-analysis of multiple outcomes. *Clinical Psychology Review, 30,* 387–399. doi:10.1016/j.cpr.2010.01.008

Vismara, L. A., & Rogers, S. J. (2010). Behavioral treatments in autism spectrum disorder: What do we know? *Annual Review of Clinical Psychology, 6,* 447–468. doi:10.1146/annurev.clinpsy.121208.131151

Visser, S. N., Danielson, M. L., Bitsko, R. H., Holbrook, J. R., Kogan, M. D., Ghandour, R. M.,... Blumberg, S. G. (2014). Trends in the parent-report of health care provider-diagnosed and medicated attention-deficit/hyperactivity disorder: United States, 2003–2011. *Journal of the American Academy of Child and Adolescent Psychiatry, 53,*

34–46. Retrieved from http://dx.doi.org/10.1016/j.jaac.2013.09.001
Vitaliano, P. P., Zhang, J., & Scanlan, J. M. (2003). Is caregiving hazardous to one's physical health? A meta-analysis. *Psychological Bulletin, 129*, 946–972.
Vitiello, B., Elliott, G. R., Swanson, J. M., Arnold, L. E., Hechtman, L., Abikoff, H.,... Gibbons, R. (2012). Blood pressure and heart rate over 10 years in the multimodal treatment study of children with ADHD. *American Journal of Psychiatry, 169*, 167–177. doi:10.1176/appi.ajp.2011.10111705
Vliegen, N., Casalin, S., & Luyten, P. (2014). The course of postpartum depression. *Harvard Review of Psychiatry, 22*, 1. doi:10.1097/HRP.0000000000000013
Voelker, R. (2012). Asthma forecast: Why heat, humidity trigger symptoms. *Journal of the American Medical Association, 308*, 20–20. doi:10.1001/jama.2012.7533
Volavka, J., & Swanson, J. (2010). Violent behavior in mental illness: The role of substance abuse. *Journal of the American Medical Association, 304*, 563–564. doi:10.1001/jama.2010.1097
Volkow, N. D. (2006). Map of human genome opens new opportunities for drug abuse research. *NIDA Notes, 20*(4), 3.
von Polier, G. G., Meng, H., Lambert, M., Strauss, M., Zarotti, G., Karle, M.,... Schimmelmann, B. G. (2014). Patterns and correlates of expressed emotion, perceived criticism, and rearing style in first admitted early-onset schizophrenia spectrum disorders. *Journal of Nervous & Mental Disease, 202*, 783–787. doi:10.1097/NMD.0000000000000209
Vorspan, F., Mehtelli, W., Dupuy, G., Bloch, V., & Lépine, J. P. (2015). Anxiety and substance use disorders: Co-occurrence and clinical issues. *Current Psychiatry Reports, 17*, 4. doi:10.1007/s11920-014-0544-y
Vorstenbosch, V., Antony, M. M., Koerner, N., & Boivin, M. (2011). Assessing dog fear: Evaluating the psychometric properties of the Dog Phobia Questionnaire. *Journal of Behavior Therapy and Experimental Psychiatry, 43*, 780–786.
Vos, S. J., Verhey, F., Frölich, L., Kornhuber, J., Wiltfang, J., Maier, W.,... Visser, P. J. (2015). Prevalence and prognosis of Alzheimer's disease at the mild cognitive impairment stage. *Brain, 138*, 1327.
Vriends, N., Bolt, O. C., & Kunz, S. M. (2014). Social anxiety disorder, a lifelong disorder: A review of the spontaneous remission and its predictors. *Acta Psychiatrica Scandinavica, 130*, 109–122. doi:10.1111/acps.12249
Wadden, T. A., Butryn, M. L., Hong, P. S., & Tsai, A. G. (2014). Behavioral treatment of obesity in patients encountered in primary care settings: A systematic review. *Journal of the American Medical Association, 312*, 1779–1791. doi:10.1001/jama.2014.14173
Wade, T. D., Wilksch, S. M., Paxton, S. J., Byrne, S. M., & Austin, S. B. (2015). How perfectionism and ineffectiveness influence growth of eating disorder risk in young adolescent girls. *Behaviour Research and Therapy, 66*, 56–63. doi:10.1016/j.brat.2015.01.007
Wadsworth, M. E., & Achenbach, T. M. (2005). Explaining the link between low socioeconomic status and psychopathology: Testing two mechanisms of the social causation hypothesis. *Journal of Consulting and Clinical Psychology, 73*, 1146–1153.
Wagner, B., Schulz, W., & Knaevelsrud, C. (2011). Efficacy of an Internet-based intervention for posttraumatic stress disorder in Iraq: A pilot study. *Psychiatry Research, 195*, 85–88. doi:10.1016/j.psychres.2011.07.026
Wainwright, N. W. J., & Surtees, P. G. (2002). Childhood adversity, gender and depression over the life-course. *Journal of Affective Disorders, 72*, 33–44.
Waismann, R., Fenwick, P. B. C., Wilson, G. D., Hewett, T. D., & Lumsden, J. (2003). EEG responses to visual erotic stimuli in men with normal and paraphilic interests. *Archives of Sexual Behavior, 32*(2), 135–144.
Waldman, I. D., & Gizera, I. R. (2006). The genetics of attention deficit hyperactivity disorder. *Clinical Psychology Review, 26*, 396–432.
Walker, E., Shapiro, D., Esterberg, M., & Trotman, H. (2010). Neurodevelopment and schizophrenia: Broadening the focus. *Psychological Science, 19*, 204–208. doi:10.1177/0963721410377744
Walkup, J. T., Albano, A. M., Piacentini, J., Birmaher, B., Compton, S. N., Sherrill, J. T.,... Kendall, P. C. (2008). Cognitive behavioral therapy, sertraline, or a combination in childhood anxiety. *New England Journal of Medicine, 359*, 2753–2766.
Wallace, P. (2014). Internet addiction disorder and youth. *EMBO Reports, 15*(1), 12–16. doi:10.1002/embr.201338222
Waller, H., Garety, P. A., Jolley, S., Fornells-Ambrojo, M., Kuipers, E., Onwumere, J., Emsley, T. C.,... Craig, T. (2012). Low intensity cognitive behavioural therapy for psychosis: A pilot study. *Journal of Behavior Therapy and Experimental Psychiatry, 44*, 98–104. doi:10.1016/j.jbtep.2012.07.013
Waller, N. G., & Ross, C. A. (1997). The prevalence of biometric structure of pathological dissociation in the general population: Taxometric and behavior genetic findings. *Journal of Abnormal Psychology, 106*, 499–510.
Wallis, C. (2009, November 3). A powerful identity, a vanishing diagnosis. *The New York Times*, pp. D1, D4.
Walsh, B. T., Agras, W. S., Devlin, M. J., Fairburn, C. G., Wilson, G. T., Kahn, C., & Chally, M. K. (2000). Fluoxetine for bulimia nervosa following poor response to psychotherapy. *American Journal of Psychiatry, 157*, 1332–1334.
Walsh, B. T., Fairburn, C. G., Mickley, D., Sysko, R., & Parides, M. K. (2004). Treatment of bulimia nervosa in a primary care setting. *American Journal of Psychiatry, 161*, 556–561.
Walsh, R. (2011). Lifestyle and mental health. *American Psychologist, 66*, 579–592. doi:10.1037/a0021769
Wampold, B. E. (2001). *The great psychotherapy debate: Models, methods, and findings*. Mahwah, NJ: Erlbaum.
Wampold, B. E., Stephanie, L. B., Laska, K. M., Del Re, A. C., Baardseth, T. P., Flückiger, C., Minamic, T.,... Gunn, W. (2011). Evidence-based treatments for depression and anxiety versus treatment-as-usual: A meta-analysis of direct comparisons. *Clinical Psychology Review, 31*, 1304–1312. doi:10.1016/j.cpr.2011.07.012
Wang, C.-W., Ho, R. T. H., Chan, C. L. W., & Tse, S. (2015). Exploring personality characteristics of Chinese adolescents with Internet-related addictive behaviors: Trait differences for gaming addiction and social networking addiction. *Addictive Behaviors, 42*, 32–35. doi:10.1016/j.addbeh.2014.10.039
Wang, P. S., Lane, M., Olfson, M., Pincus, H. A., Wells, K. B., & Kessler, R. C. (2005). Twelve-month use of mental health services in the United States: Results from the National Comorbidity Survey Replication. *Archives of General Psychiatry, 62*, 590–592.
Wansink, B., & van Ittersum, K. (2013). Portion size me: Plate-size induced consumption norms and win-win solutions for reducing food intake and waste. *Journal of Experimental Psychology: Applied, 19*, 320–332. doi:10.1037/a0035053
Wartik, N. (2000, June 25). Depression comes out of hiding. *The New York Times*, pp. MH1, MH4.
Watson, J. B., & Rayner, R. (1920). Conditioned emotional reactions. *Journal of Experimental Psychology, 3*, 1–14.
Watts, S. E., Turnell, A., Kladnitski, N., Newby, J. M., & Andrews, G. (2015). Treatment-as-usual (TAU) is anything but usual: A meta-analysis of CBT versus TAU for anxiety and depression. *Journal of Affective Disorders, 175*, 152–167. doi:10.1016/j.jad.2014.12.025
Weaver, F. W., Follett, K., Stern, M., Hur, K., Harris, C., Marks, W. J., Jr.,... Huang, G. D. (2009). Bilateral deep brain stimulation vs. best medical therapy for patients with advanced Parkinson disease: A randomized controlled trial. *Journal of the American Medical Association, 301*, 63–73.
Weaver, J. (2012, March 1). Twitter reveals people are happiest in the morning. Retrieved from http://www.scientificamerican.com/article/happy-in-the-morning/
Weber, L. (2013, January 23). Go ahead, hit the snooze button. *Wall Street Journal*, pp. B1, B8.
Webster-Stratton, C., Reid, J., & Hammond, M. (2001). Social skills and problem-solving training for children with early-onset conduct problems: Who benefits? *Journal of Child Psychology & Psychiatry & Allied Disciplines*, 42, 943–952.
Wechsler, D. (1975). Intelligence defined and undefined: A relativistic appraisal. *American Psychologist, 30*, 135–139.
Wechsler, H., & Nelson, T. F. (2008). What we have learned from the Harvard School of Public Health College Alcohol Study: Focusing attention on college student alcohol consumption and the environmental conditions that promote it. *Journal of Studies on Alcohol and Drugs, 69*, 481.
Weck, F., & Neng, J. M. B. (2015). Response and remission after cognitive and exposure therapy for hypochondriasis. *Journal of Nervous & Mental Disease, 203*, 883–885. doi:10.1097/NMD.0000000000000385
Weck, F., Bleichhardt, G., Witthöft, M., & Hiller, W. (2011). Explicit and implicit anxiety: Differences between patients with hypochondriasis, patients with anxiety disorders, and healthy controls. *Cognitive Therapy and Research, 35*, 317–325. doi:10.1007/s10608-010-9303-5
Weck, F., Neng, J. M. B., Richtberg, S., Jakob, M., & Stangier, U. (2015). Cognitive therapy versus exposure therapy for hypochondriasis (health anxiety): A randomized controlled trial. *Journal of Consulting and Clinical Psychology, 83*, 665–676. Retrieved from http://dx.doi.org/10.1037/ccp0000013
Weed, W. S. (2003, December 14). Questions for Raymond Damadian: Scanscam? *The New York Times*. Retrieved from www.nytimes.com
Weems, C. F., Hayward, C., Killen, J., & Taylor, C. B. (2002). A longitudinal investigation of anxiety sensitivity in adolescence. *Journal of Abnormal Psychology, 111*, 471–477.
Weems, C. F., Pina, A. A., Costa, N. M., Watts, S. E., Taylor, L. K., & Cannon, M. F. (2007). Predisaster trait anxiety and negative affect predict posttraumatic stress in youths after Hurricane Katrina. *Journal of Consulting and Clinical Psychology, 75*, 154–159.
Wei, C.-C., Wan, L., Lin, W.-Y., & Tsai, F.-J. (2010). Rs 6313 polymorphism in 5-hydroxytryptamine receptor 2A gene association with polysymptomatic primary nocturnal enuresis. *Journal of Clinical Laboratory Analysis, 24*, 371–375. doi:10.1002/jcla.20386
Weiner, J. R. (2003). Tarasoff warnings resulting in criminal charges: Two case reports. *The Journal of the American Academy of Psychiatry and the Law, 31*, 239–241.
Weintraub, K. (2011). The prevalence puzzle: Autism counts. *Nature, 479*, 22–24. doi:10.1038/479022a
Weir, K. (2012a, December). Big kids. *Monitor on Psychology, 43*, 58–63.
Weir, K. (2012b, June). The roots of mental illness. *Monitor on Psychology, 43*, 30–33.
Weisman, A. G., Nuechterlein, K. H., Goldstein, M. J., & Snyder, K. S. (1998). Expressed emotion, attributions, and schizophrenia symptom dimensions. *Journal of Abnormal Psychology, 107*, 355–359.
Weisman, A. G., Rosales, G. A., Kymalainen, J. A., & Armesto, J. C. (2006). Ethnicity, expressed emotion, and schizophrenia patients' perceptions of their family members' criticism. *The Journal of Nervous and Mental Disease, 194*, 644–649.
Weiss, B., Han, S., Harris, V., Catron, T., Ngo, V. K., Caron, A.,... Guth, C. (2013). An independent randomized clinical trial of multisystemic therapy with non-court-referred adolescents with serious conduct problems. *Journal of Consulting and Clinical Psychology, 81*, 1027–1039. doi:10.1037/a0033928
Weiss, R. D., & Mirin, S. M. (1987). *Cocaine*. Washington, DC: American Psychiatric Press.
Weissman, A. N., & Beck, A. T. (1978). Development and validation of the Dysfunctional Attitudes Scale: A preliminary investigation. Paper Presented at the Annual Meeting of the American Educational Research Association, Toronto, Ontario, CA.
Weissman, J., Pratt, L. A., Miller, E. A., & Parker, J. D. (2015, May). Serious psychological distress among adults: United States, 2009–2013. Centers for Disease Control and Prevention, *NCHS Data Brief*, 203. Retrieved from http://www.cdc.gov/nchs/data/databriefs/db203.htm
Weissman, M. M. (2007). Cognitive therapy and interpersonal psychotherapy: 30 years later. *American Journal of Psychiatry, 164*, 693–696.
Weissman, M. M. (2014). Treatment of depression: Men and women are different? *American Journal of Psychiatry,171*, 384–387. doi:10.1176/appi.ajp.2013.13121668

Weissman, M. M., Bruce, M. L., Leaf, P. J., Florio, L. P., & Holzer, C. (1991). Affective disorders. In L. N. Robins & D. A. Regier (Eds.), *Psychiatric disorders in America: The Epidemiologic Catchment Area Study* (pp. 53–80). New York, NY: Free Press.

Weissman, M. M., Markowitz, J. C., & Klerman, G. L. (2000). *Comprehensive guide to interpersonal psychotherapy.* New York, NY: Basic Books.

Weissman, M. M., Pilowsky, D. J., Wickramaratne, P. J., Talati, A., Wisniewski, S. R., Fava, C. W., ... STAR*D-Child Team. (2006). Remissions in maternal depression and child psychopathology: A STAR*D-child report. *Journal of the American Medical Association, 295,* 1389–1398.

Weisstaub, N. V., Zhou, M., Lira, A., Lambe, E., Gonzalez-Maeso, J., Hornung, J. P., ... Gingrich, J. A. (2006). Cortical 5-HT2A receptor signaling modulates anxiety-like behaviors in mice. *Science, 313,* 536–540.

Weisz, J. R., Ng, M. Y., & Bearman, S. K. (2014). Odd couple? Reenvisioning the relation between science and practice in the dissemination-implementation era. *Clinical Psychological Science, 2,* 58-74. doi:10.1177/2167702613501307

Weisz, J. R., Southam-Gerow, M. A., Gordis, E. B., Connor-Smith, J. K., Chu, B. C., Langer, D. A., ... Weiss, B. (2009). Cognitive–behavioral therapy versus usual clinical care for youth depression: An initial test of transportability to community clinics and clinicians. *Journal of Consulting and Clinical Psychology, 77,* 383–396. doi:10.1037/a0013877

Weisz, J. R., Suwanlert, S., Chaiyasit, W., Weiss, B., Walter, B. R., & Anderson, W. W. (1988). Thai and American perspectives on over- and undercontrolled child behavior problems: Exploring the threshold model among parents, teachers, and psychologists. *Journal of Consulting and Clinical Psychology, 56,* 601–609.

Weitz, E. S., Hollon, S. D., Twisk, J., van Straten, A., Huibers, M. J. H., David, D., ... Cuijpers, P. (2015). Baseline depression severity as moderator of depression outcomes between cognitive behavioral therapy vs. pharmacotherapy: An individual patient data meta-analysis. *JAMA Psychiatry, 72,* 1102–1109. doi:10.1001/jamapsychiatry.2015.1516

Welch, M. R., & Kartub, P. (1978). Socio-cultural correlates of incidence of impotence: A cross-cultural study. *Journal of Sex Research, 14,* 218–230.

Wells, R. E., Burch, R., Paulsen, R. H., Wayne, P. M., Houle, T. T., & Loder, E. (2014). Meditation for migraines: A pilot randomized controlled trial. *Headache, 54,* 1484–1495. doi:10.1111/head.12420

Welte, G. M., Barnes, G. M., Tidwell, M. C. O., & Hoffman, J. H. (2008). The prevalence of problem gambling among U.S. adolescents and young adults: Results from a national survey. *Journal of Gambling Studies, 24,* 119–133.

Wender, P. H., Rosenthal, D., Kety, S. S., Schulsinger, F., & Welner, J. (1974). Cross-fostering: A research strategy for clarifying the role of genetic and experiential factors in the etiology of schizophrenia. *Archives of General Psychiatry, 30,* 121–128.

Wenzel, A., Finstroma, N., Jordan, J., & Brendle, J. R. (2005). Memory and interpretation of visual representations of threat in socially anxious and nonanxious individuals. *Behaviour Research and Therapy, 43,* 1029–1044.

Wessell, R., & Edwards, C. (2010). Biological and psychological interventions: Trends in substance use disorders intervention research. *Addictive Behaviors, 35,* 1083–1088. doi:10.1016/j.addbeh.2010.07.009

West, S. L., D'Aloisio, A. A., Agans, R. P., Kalsbeek W. D., Borisov, N. N., & Thorp, J. M. (2008). Prevalence of low sexual desire and hypoactive sexual desire disorder in a nationally representative sample of U.S. women. *Archives of Internal Medicine, 168*(13), 1441–1449.

Westen, D., & Gabbard, G. O. (2002). Developments in cognitive neuroscience: 1. Conflict, compromise, and connectionism. *Journal of the American Psychoanalytic Association, 50,* 53–98.

Wetherell, J. L., Petkus, A. J., White, K. S., Nguyen, H., Kornblith, S., Andreescu, C., ... Lenze, E. J. (2013). Antidepressant medication augmented with cognitive-behavioral therapy for generalized anxiety disorder in older adults. *American Journal of Psychiatry, 170,* 782–789. doi:10.1176/appi.ajp.2013.12081104

Wexler, B. E., Gottschalk, C. H., Fulbright, R. K., Prohovnik, I., Lacadie, C. M., Rounsaville, B. J., & Gore, J. C. (2001). Functional magnetic resonance imaging of cocaine craving. *American Journal of Psychiatry, 158,* 86–95.

Wheaton, M. G., Puliafico, A. C., Zuckoff, A., & Simpson, H. B. (2016). Treatment of an adult with obsessive-compulsive disorder with limited treatment motivation. In E. A. Storch & A. B. Lewin (Eds.), *Clinical handbook of obsessive-compulsive and related disorders: A case-based approach to treating pediatric and adult populations* (pp. 385–397). New York, NY: Springer.

Wheaton, S. (2001). Personal accounts: Memoirs of a compulsive firesetter. *Psychiatric Service, 62,* 1035–1036.

White, C. N., VanderDrifta, L. E., & Heffernan, K. S. (2015). Social isolation, cognitive decline, and cardiovascular disease risk. *Current Opinion in Psychology, 110,* 5797–5801. doi:10.1073/pnas.1219686110

Whitelock, C. F., Lamb, M. E., & Rentfrow, P. J. (2013). Overcoming trauma: Psychological and demographic characteristics of child sexual abuse survivors in adulthood. *Clinical Psychological Science, 1,* 351–362. doi:10.1177/2167702613480136

Whiteside, L. K., Walton, M. A., Bohnert, A. S. B., Blow, F. C., Bonar, E. E., Ehrlich, P., ... Cunningham, R. M. (2013). Nonmedical prescription opioid and sedative use among adolescents in the emergency department. *Pediatrics, 132,* 825. Retrieved from http://dx.doi.org/10.1542/peds.2013-0721

Whittal, M. L, Robichaud, M., Thordarson, D. S., & McLean, P. D. (2008). Group and individual treatment of obsessive-compulsive disorder using cognitive therapy and exposure plus response prevention: A 2-year follow-up of two randomized trials. *Journal of Consulting and Clinical Psychology, 76,* 1003–1014.

Whitten, L. (2009). Receptor complexes link dopamine to long-term neuronal effects. *NIDA Notes, 22*(4), 15–16.

Whooley, M. A., Kiefe, C. I., Chesney, M. A., Markovitz, J. H., Matthews, K., & Hulley, S. B. (2002). Depressive symptoms, unemployment, and loss of income: The CARDIA Study. *Archives of Internal Medicine, 162,* 2614–2620.

Wicks, S., Hjern, A., & Dalman, C. (2010). Social risk or genetic liability for psychosis? A study of children born in Sweden and reared by adoptive parents. *American Journal of Psychiatry, 167,* 1240–1246. http://dx.doi.org/10.1176/appi.ajp.2010.09010114

Widaman, K. F. (2009). Phenylketonuria in children and mothers: Genes, environments, behavior. *Current Directions in Psychological Science, 18,* 48–52. doi:10.1111/j.1467-8721.2009.01604.x

Widiger, T. A., Livesley, W. J., & Clark, L. A. (2009). An integrative dimensional classification of personality disorder. *Psychological Assessment, 21,* 243–255. doi:10.1037/a0016606

Widiger, T. A., & Mullins-Sweatt, S. N. (2009). Five-factor model of personality disorder: A proposal for DSM-V. *Annual Review of Clinical Psychology, 5,* 197–220. doi:10.1146/annurev.clinpsy.032408.153542

Widiger, T. A., & Simonsen, E. (2005). Alternative dimensional models of personality disorder: Finding a common ground. *Journal of Personality Disorders, 19,* 110–130.

Wierck, K., Van Caenegem, E., Elaut, E., Dedecker, D., Van de Peer, F., Toye, K., ... Sjoen, G. (2011). Quality of life and sexual health after sex reassignment surgery in transsexual men. *Journal of Sexual Medicine, 8,* 3379–3388.

Wierman, M. E., Rossella, E., Nappi, E., Avis, N., Davis, S. R., Labrie, F., Rosner, W., ... Shifren, J. L. (2010). Endocrine aspects of women's sexual function. *Journal of Sexual Medicine, 7,* 561–585. doi:10.1111/j.1743-6109.2009.01629.x

Wilbur, C. B. (1986). Psychoanalysis and multiple personality disorder. In B. G. Braun (Ed.), *Treatment of multiple personality disorder* (pp. 6–28). Washington, DC: American Psychiatric Press.

Wild Man brings back bad memories. (2009, June 4). *West Side Spirit,* p. 4.

Wildeman, C., Emanuel, N., Leventhal, J. M., Putnam-Hornstein, E., Waldfogel, J., & Lee, H. (2014). The prevalence of confirmed maltreatment among U.S. children, 2004 to 2011. *JAMA Pediatrics, 68,* 706–713. doi:10.1001/jamapediatrics.2014.410

Wilks, C. R., Korslund, K. E., Harned, M. S., & Linehan, M. M. (2016). Dialectical behavior therapy and domains of functioning over two years. *Behaviour Research and Therapy, 77,* 162–169. doi:10.1016/j.brat.2015.12.013

Williams, D. (1992). *Nobody nowhere: The extraordinary autobiography of an autistic.* New York, NY: Times Books.

Williams, J. F., Smith, V. C., & The Committee on Substance Abuse. (2015). Fetal alcohol spectrum disorders. *Pediatrics, 136*(5), e1395–e1406. doi:10.1542/peds.2015-3113

Williams, J. M. G., Crane, C., Barnhofer, T., Brennan, K., Duggan, D. S., Fennell, M. J. V., ... Russell, I. T. (2014). Mindfulness-based cognitive therapy for preventing relapse in recurrent depression: A randomized dismantling trial. *Journal of Consulting and Clinical Psychology, 82,* 275–286. doi:10.1037/a0035036

Williams, R. B., Marchuk, D. A., Gadde, K. M., Barefoot, J. C., Grichnik, K., Helms, M. J., ... Siegler, I. C. (2003). Serotonin-related gene polymorphisms and central nervous system serotonin function. *Neuropsychopharmacology, 28,* 533–541.

Willsey, A. J., Sanders, S. J., Li, M., Dong, S., Tebbenkamp, A. T., Muhle, R. A., ... State, M. W. (2013). Coexpression networks implicate human midfetal deep cortical projection neurons in the pathogenesis of autism. *Cell, 155,* 997. doi:10.1016/j.cell.2013.10.020

Wilson, D. (2011, April 13). As generics near, makers tweak erectile drugs. *The New York Times.* Retrieved from www.nytimes.com

Wilson, G. T., Grilo, C. M., & Vitousek, K. (2007). Psychological treatments for eating disorders. *American Psychologist, 62,* 199–216.

Wilson, K. A., & Hayward, C. (2006). Unique contributions of anxiety sensitivity to avoidance: A prospective study in adolescents. *Behaviour Research and Therapy, 44,* 601–609.

Wilson, R. E., Gosling, S. D., & Graham, L. T. (2012). A review of Facebook research in the social sciences. *Perspectives on Psychological Science, 7,* 203–220. doi:10.1177/1745691612442904

Windsor, L. C., Jemal, A., & Alessi, E. J. (2015). Cognitive behavioral therapy: A meta-analysis of race and substance use outcomes. *Cultural Diversity and Ethnic Minority Psychology, 21,* 300–313. Retrieved from http://dx.doi.org/10.1037/a0037929

Winerip, M. (1998, January 4). Binge nights. *The New York Times,* Education Section, pp. 28–31, 42.

Winerman, L. (2004, May). Panel stresses youth suicide prevention. *Monitor on Psychology, 35*(5), 18.

Wingert, P. (2000, December 4). No more "afternoon nasties." *Newsweek,* 59.

Winstanley, C. A., Eagle, D. M., & Robbins, T. W. (2006). Behavioral models of impulsivity in relation to ADHD: Translation between clinical and preclinical studies. *Clinical Psychology Review, 26,* 379–395.

Wisco, B. E., Sloan, D. M., & Marx, B. P. (2013). Cognitive emotion regulation and written exposure therapy for posttraumatic stress disorder. *Clinical Psychological Science, 1,* 435–442. doi:10.1177/2167702613486630

Witkiewicz, K., & Marlatt, G. A. (2004). Relapse prevention for alcohol and drug problems: That was Zen, this is Tao. *American Psychologist, 59,* 224–235.

Witte, T. K., Timmons, K. A., Fink, E., Smith, A. R., & Joiner, T. E. (2009). Do major depressive disorder and dysthymic disorder confer differential risk for suicide? *Journal of Affective Disorders, 115,* 69–78. doi:10.1016/j.jad.2008.09.003

Wittstein, I. S., Thiemann, D. R., Lima, J. A. C., Baughman, K. L., Schulman, S. P., Gerstenblith, G., ... Champion, H. C. (2006). Neurohumoral features of myocardial stunning due to sudden emotional stress. *New England Journal of Medicine, 352,* 539–548.

Witvliet, M., Brendgen, M., van Lier, P. A. C., Koot, H. M., & Vitaro, F. (2010). Early adolescent depressive symptoms: Prediction from clique isolation, loneliness, and perceived social acceptance. *Journal of Abnormal Child Psychology, 38,* 1045–1056. doi:10.1007/s10802-010-9426-x

Wolf, N. J., & Hopko, D. R. (2008). Psychosocial and pharmacological interventions for depressed adults in primary care: A critical review. *Clinical Psychology Review, 28,* 131–136.

Wolff, J. J., Gu, H., Gerig, G., Elison, J. T., Styner, M., Gouttard, S., ... The IBIS. (2012). Network differences in white matter fiber tract development present from 6 to 24 months in infants with autism. *American Journal of Psychiatry, 169,* 589–600. doi:10.1176/appi.ajp.2011.11091447

Wolpe, J., & Lazarus, A. A. (1966). *Behavior therapy techniques.* New York, NY: Pergamon Press.

Women more at risk of mental illness than men. (2012, January 20). *MSNBC.com.* Retrieved from http://www.msnbc.msn.com/id/46056751/ns/health-mental_health/#.TxiBj29Q6Ag

Wong, C. L., Holroyd-Leduc, J., Simel, D. L., & Straus, S. E. (2010). Does this patient have delirium? Value of bedside instruments. *Journal of the American Medical Association, 304,* 779–786. doi:10.1001/jama.2010.118

Wood, J. M., Garb, H. N., Nezworski, M. T., Lilienfeld, S. O., & Duke, M. C. A. (2015). A second look at the validity of widely used Rorschach indices: Comment on Mihura, Meyer, Dumitrascu, and Bombel (2013). *Psychological Bulletin, 141,* 236–249. Retrieved from http://dx.doi.org/10.1037/a0036005

Wood, J., M., Lilienfeld, S. O., Nezworski, M. T., Garb, H. N., Allen, K. H., & Wildermuth, J. L. (2010). Validity of Rorschach inkblot scores for discriminating psychopaths from nonpsychopaths in forensic populations: A meta-analysis. *Psychological Assessment, 22,* 336–349. doi:10.1037/a0018998

Wood, K. H., Ver Hoef, L. W., & Knight, D. C. (2014). The amygdala mediates the emotional modulation of threat-elicited skin conductance response. *Emotion, 14,* 693–700. doi:10.1037/a0036636

Woods, A., Jones, N., Alderson-Day, B., Callard, F., & Fernyhough, C. (2015). Experiences of hearing voices: Analysis of a novel phenomenological survey. *The Lancet Psychiatry, 2,* 323–331.

Woods, B., Spector, A. E., Prendergast, L., & Orrell, M. (2012). Cognitive stimulation to improve cognitive functioning in people with dementia. *The Cochrane Review.* Published online. doi:10.1002/14651858.CD005562

Woodworth, M., & Porter, S. (2002). In cold blood: Characteristics of criminal homicides as a function of psychopathy. *Journal of Abnormal Psychology, 111,* 436–445.

Woody, S. R., Kellman-McFarlane, K., & Welsted, A. (2014). Review of cognitive performance in hoarding disorder. *Clinical Psychology Review, 34,* 324–336. doi:10.1016/j.cpr.2014.04.002

Wootton, B. M., Dear, B. F., Johnston, L., Terides, M. D., & Titov, N. (2015). Self-guided Internet-delivered cognitive behavior therapy (iCBT) for obsessive-compulsive disorder: 12-month follow-up. *Internet Applications, 2,* 243–247. Retrieved from http://dx.doi.org/10.1016/j.invent.2015.05.003

World Health Organization. (2014). HIV/AIDS fact sheet. Retrieved from http://www.who.int/mediacentre/factsheets/fs360/en/

Wu, J. Q., Appleman, E. R., Salazar, R. D., & Ong J. C. (2015). Cognitive behavioral therapy for insomnia comorbid with psychiatric and medical conditions: A meta-analysis. *JAMA Internal Medicine, 175,* 1461–1472. doi:10.1001/jamainternmed.2015.3006

Wu, L.-T., Woody, G. E., Yang, C., Pan, J.-J., & Blazer, D. G. (2011). Racial/ethnic variations in substance-related disorders among adolescents in the United States. *Archives of General Psychiatry, 68,* 1176–1185. doi:10.1001/archgenpsychiatry.2011.120

Wu, M. S., Salloum, A., Lewin, A. B., Selles, R. R., McBride, N. M., Crawford, E. A., & Storch, E. A. (2015). Treatment concerns and functional impairment in pediatric anxiety. *Child Psychiatry and Human Development.* Advance online publication. doi:10.1007/s10587-015-0596-1

Wykes, T. (2014). Cognitive-behaviour therapy and schizophrenia. *Evidence-Based Mental Health, 17,* 67–68.

Xiang, A. H., Wang, X., Martinez, M. P., Walthall, J. C., Curry, E. S., Page, K., ... Getahun, D. (2015). Association of maternal diabetes with autism in offspring. *Journal of the American Medical Association, 313,* 1425–1434. doi:10.1001/jama.2015.2707

Xiao, L., Han, J., & Han, J. (2011). The adjustment of new recruits to military life in the Chinese Army: The longitudinal predictive power of MMPI-2. *Journal of Career Assessment, 19,* 392–404.

Xie, P., Kranzler, H. R., Poling, J., Stein, M. B., Anton, R. F., Brady, K., Weiss, R. D., & Gelernter, J. (2009). Interactive effect of stressful life events and the serotonin transporter 5-HTTLPR genotype on post-traumatic stress disorder diagnosis in 2 independent populations. *Archives of General Psychiatry, 66,* 1201–1209.

Xiong P., Zeng, Y., Zhu, Z., Tan, D., Xu, F., Lu, J., Wan, J., & Ma, M. (2010). Reduced NGF serum levels and abnormal P300 event-related potential in first episode schizophrenia. *Schizophrenia Research, 119,* 34–39.

Xue, C., Ge, Y., Tang, B., Liu, Y., Kang, P., Wang, M., & Zhang, L. (2015). A meta-analysis of risk factors for combat-related PTSD among military personnel and veterans. *PLOS ONE, 10*(3), e0120270. doi:10.1371/journal.pone.0120270

Yaccino, S. (2012, December 20). Arrests in a freshman's drinking death reflect a tougher approach. *The New York Times.* Retrieved from www.nytimes.com

Yager, J. (2008, May 23). Attempted suicides in anorexia nervosa. *Journal Watch Psychiatry.* Retrieved from http://psychiatry.jwatch.org/cgi/content/full/2008/523/2

Yager, J. (2011, August 29). Genetics of psychosocial stress–induced alcohol consumption. *Journal Watch Psychiatry.* Retrieved from http://psychiatry.jwatch.org

Yager, J. (2014, October 15). "The schizophrenias": Crossing genomics with "phenomics" produces a better understanding. *NEJM Journal Watch Psychiarty.* Retrieved from http://www.jwatch.org/na35881/2014/10/15/schizophrenias-crossing-genomics-with-phenomics-produces?query=etoc_jwpsych

Yager, J. (2015). Neurocognitive impairment in severely mentally ill homeless people. *NEJM Journal Watch Psychiatry.* Retrieved from http://www.jwatch.org/na36935/2015/02/09/neurocognitive-impairment-severely-mentally-ill-homeless

Yalcin–Siedentopf, N., Hoertnag, C. M., Biedermann, F., Baumgartner, S., Deisenhammer, E. A., Hausmann, A., ... Hofer, A. (2014). Facial affect recognition in symptomatically remitted patients with schizophrenia and bipolar disorder. *Schizophrenia Research, 152,* 440–445. doi:10.1016/j.schres.2013.11.024

Yang, L., & Colditz. G. A. (2015). Prevalence of overweight and obesity in the United States, 2007–2012. *JAMA Internal Medicine, 175,* 1412–1413. doi:10.1001/jamainternmed.2015.2405

Yang, M., Wong, S. C. P. W, & Coid, J. (2010). The efficacy of violence prediction: A meta-analytic comparison of nine risk assessment tools. *Psychological Bulletin, 136,* 740–746.

Yao, J. K., Dougherty, G. G., Jr., Gautier, C. H., Haas, G. L., Condray, R., Kasckow, J. W., ... Messamore, E. (2015). Prevalence and specificity of the abnormal niacin response: A potential endophenotype marker in schizophrenia. *Schizophrenia Bulletin.* Retrieved from http://schizophreniabulletin.oxfordjournals.org/content/early/2015/09/13/schbul.sbv130.full

Yates, P. M., Hucker, S. J., & Kingston, D. A. (2008). Sexual sadism: Psychopathology and theory. In D. R. Laws & W. T. O'Donohue (Eds.), *Sexual deviance: Theory, assessment, and treatment* (2nd ed., pp. 213–230). New York, NY: Guilford Press.

Yeargin-Allsopp, M., Rice, C., Karapurkan, T., Doernberg, N., Boyle, C., & Murphy, C. (2003). Prevalence of autism in a U.S. metropolitan area. *Journal of the American Medical Association, 289,* 49–55.

Yeh, C. J. (2003). Age, acculturation, cultural adjustment, and mental health symptoms of Chinese, Korean, and Japanese immigrant youths. *Cultural Diversity and Ethnic Minority Psychology, 9,* 34–48.

Yehuda, R., Daskalakis, N. P., Bierer, L. M., Bader, H. N., Klengel, T., Holsboer, F., ... Binder, E. B. (2015). Holocaust exposure induced intergenerational effects on FKBP5 methylation. *Biological Psychiatry.* Advance online publication. doi:10.1016/j.biopsych.2015.08.005

Yeung, A., Howarth, S., Chan, R., Sonawalla, S., Nierenberg, A. A., & Fava, M. (2002). Use of the Chinese version of the Beck Depression Inventory for screening depression in primary care. *Journal of Nervous & Mental Disease, 190,* 94–99.

Yi, J. J., Berrios, J., Newbern, J. M., Snider, W. D., Philpot, B. D., Hahn, K. M., & Zylka, M. J. (2015). An autism-linked mutation disables phosphorylation control of UBE3A. *Cell, 162,* 795–807. Retrieved from http://dx.doi.org/10.1016/j.cell.2015.06.045

Yoder, V. C., Virden, T. B., III, & Amin, K. (2005). Internet pornography and loneliness: An association? *Sexual Addiction & Compulsivity, 12*(1), 19–44.

Young, E. A., McFatter, R., & Clopton, J. R. (2001). Family functioning, peer influence, and media influence as predictors of bulimic behavior. *Eating Behaviors, 2,* 323–337.

Young, K. S. (2015). The evolution of Internet addiction. *Addictive Behaviors, 53,* 193–195. doi:10.1016/j.addbeh.2015.11.001

Youngstrom, E. A. (2009). Definitional issues in bipolar disorder across the life cycle. *Clinical Psychology: Science and Practice, 16,* 140–160. doi:10.1111/j.1468-2850.2009.01154.x

Young-Wolff, K. C., Enoch, M.-A., & Prescott, C. A. (2011). The influence of gene–environment interactions on alcohol consumption and alcohol use disorders: A comprehensive review. *Clinical Psychology Review, 31,* 800–816. doi:10.1016/j.cpr.2011.03.005

Yu, H. Y., Hsiao, C. Y., Chen, K. C., Lee, L. T., Chang, W. H., Chi, M. H., ... Yang, Y. K. (2015). A comparison of the effectiveness of risperidone, haloperidol and flupentixol long-acting injections in patients with schizophrenia: A nationwide study. *Schizophrenia Research, 169(1–3),* 400–405. doi:10.1016/j.schres.2015.09.006

Yuen, E. K., Goetter, E. M., Herbert, J. D., & Forman, E. M. (2012). Challenges and opportunities in Internet-mediated telemental health. *Professional Psychology: Research and Practice, 43,* 1–8. doi:10.1037/a0025524

Zahn, R., Lythe, K. E., Gethin, J. A., Green, S., Deakin, J. F. W., Young, A. H., ... Moll, J. (2015). The role of self-blame and worthlessness in the psychopathology of major depressive disorder. *Journal of Affective Disorders, 186,* 337–341. doi:10.1016/j.jad.2015.08.001

Zalesky, A., Pantelis, C., Cropley, V., Fornito, A., Cocchi, L., McAdams, H., ... Gogtay, N. (2015). Delayed development of brain connectivity in adolescents with schizophrenia and their unaffected siblings. *JAMA Psychiatry, 72,* 900–908. doi:10.1001/jamapsychiatry.2015.0226

Zamanian, K., Thackreyb, M., Starretta, R. A., Browna, L. G., Lassmanc, D. K., & Blanchard, A. (1992). Acculturation and depression in Mexican-American elderly. *Gerontologist, 11,* 109–121.

Zanarini, M. C., Skodol, A. E., Bender, D., Dolan, R., Sanislow, C., Schaefer, E., ... Gunderson, J. G. (2000). The Collaborative Longitudinal Personality Disorders Study: Reliability of axis I and II diagnoses. *Journal of Personality Disorders, 14,* 291–299.

Zane, N., & Sue, S. (1991). Culturally responsive mental health services for Asian Americans: Treatment and training issues. In H. F. Myers, P. Wohlford, L. P. Guzman, & R. J. Echemendia (Eds.), *Ethnic minority perspectives on clinical training and services in psychology* (pp. 49–58). Washington, DC: American Psychological Association.

Zapf, P. A., & Roesch, R. (2011). Future directions in the restoration of competency to stand trial. *Current Directions in Psychological Science, 20,* 43–47. doi:10.1177/0963721410396798

Zapolski, T. C. B., Pedersen, S. L., McCarthy, D. M., & Smith, G. T. (2014). Less drinking, yet more problems: Understanding African American drinking and related problems. *Psychological Bulletin, 140,* 188–223. doi:10.1037/a0032113

Zavos, H. M. S., Gregory, A. M., & Eley, T. C. (2012). Longitudinal genetic analysis of anxiety sensitivity. *Developmental Psychology, 48,* 204–212. doi:10.1037/a0024996

Zebenholzer, K., Rudel, E., Frantal, S., Brannath, W., Schmidt, K., Wöber-Bingöl, C., & Wöber, C. (2011). Migraine and weather: A prospective diary-based analysis. *Cephalalgia, 31,* 391.

Zhang, C., Wu, Z., Hong, W., Wang, Z., Peng, D., Chen, J., ... Fang, Y. (2014). Influence of BCL2 gene in major depression susceptibility and antidepressant treatment outcome. *Journal of Affective Disorders, 155,* 288–294.

Zhang, L. S., Hu, L., Li, X., & Zhang, J. (2014). The DRD2 rs1800497 polymorphism increase the risk of mood disorder: Evidence from an update meta-analysis. *Journal of Affective Disorders, 158,* 71–77. doi:10.1016/j.jad.2014.01.015

Zhang, T., Koutsouleris, N., Meisenzahl, E., & Davatzikos, C. (2014). Heterogeneity of structural brain changes in subtypes of schizophrenia revealed using magnetic resonance imaging pattern analysis. *Schizophrenia Bulletin.* Retrieved from http://schizophreniabulletin.oxfordjournals.org/content/early/2014/09/26/schbul.sbu136

Zhang, W., Deng, W., Yao, L., Xiao, Y., Li, F., Liu, J.,... Gong, M. Q. (2015). Brain structural abnormalities in a group of never-medicated patients with long-term schizophrenia. *American Journal of Psychiatry, 172,* 995–1003. Retrieved from http://dx.doi.org/10.1176/appi.ajp.2015.14091108

Zhang, X., Wang, L., Huang, F., Li, J., Xiong, L., Xue, H., & Zhang, Y. (2014). Gene-environment interaction in postpartum depression: A Chinese clinical study. *Journal of Affective Disorders, 208,* 212. doi:10.1016/j.jad.2014.04.049

Zhao, X., Sun, L., Sun, Y. H., Ren, C., Chen, J., Wu, Z.,... Lv, X. L. (2014). Association of HTR2A T102C and A-1438G polymorphisms with susceptibility to major depressive disorder: A meta-analysis. *Neurological Science, 35,* 1857–1866. doi:10.1007/s10072-014-1970-7

Zhao, Z., Sagare, A. P., Ma, Q., Halliday, M. R., Kong, P., Kisler, K.,... Zlokovic, B. V. (2015). Central role for PICALM in amyloid-β blood-brain barrier transcytosis and clearance. *Nature Neuroscience.* Retrieved from http://www.nature.com/neuro/journal/vaop/ncurrent/full/nn.4025.html

Zhou, X., Dere, J., Zhu, X., Yao, S., Chentsova-Dutton, Y. E., & Ryder, A. J. (2011). Anxiety symptom presentations in Han Chinese and Euro-Canadian outpatients: Is distress always somatized in China? *Journal of Affective Disorders, 135,* 111–114.

Zickler, P. (2006) Smoking decreases key enzyme throughout body: Research findings. *NIDA Notes.* Retrieved from www.drugabuse.gov

Zilcha-Mano, S., Dinger, U., McCarthy, K. S., & Barber, J. P. (2014). Does alliance predict symptoms throughout treatment, or is it the other way around? *Journal of Consulting and Clinical Psychology, 82,* 931–935. Retrieved from http://dx.doi.org/10.1037/a0035141

Zimak, E. H., Suhr, J., & Bolinger, E. M. (2014). Psychophysiological and neuropsychological characteristics of non-incarcerated adult males with higher levels of psychopathic personality traits. *Journal of Psychopathology and Behavioral Assessment, 36,* 542–554.

Zimmerman, M., & Morgan, T. A. (2014). Problematic boundaries in the diagnosis of bipolar disorder: The interface with borderline personality disorder. *Current Psychiatry Reports, 15,* 422. doi:10.1007/s11920-013-0422-z

Zipfel, S., Wild, B., Grob, G., Friederich, H.-C., Teufel, M., Schellberg, D.,... Herzog, W., on behalf of the ANTOP study group. (2013). Focal psychodynamic therapy, cognitive behaviour therapy, and optimised treatment as usual in outpatients with anorexia nervosa (ANTOP study): Randomised controlled trial. *The Lancet, 383,* 127–137. Retrieved from http://dx.doi.org/10.1016/S0140-6736(13)61746-8

Zivanovic, O., & Nedic, A. (2012). Kraepelin's concept of manic-depressive insanity: One hundred years. *Journal of Affective Disorders, 137,* 15–24.

Zlomuzica, A., Silva, M. D. S., Huston, J., & Dere, E. (2007). NMDA receptor modulation by D-cycloserine promotes episodic-like memory in mice. *Psychopharmacology.* Retrieved from http://lib.bioinfo.pl/pmid:17497136

Zou, J. B., Dear, B. F., Titov, N., Lorian, C. N., Johnston, L., Spence, J.,... Sachdev, P. (2012). Brief Internet-delivered cognitive behavioral therapy for anxiety in older adults: A feasibility trial. *Journal of Anxiety Disorders, 26,* 650–655.

Zubin, J., & Spring, B. (1977). Vulnerability: A new view of schizophrenia. *Journal of Abnormal Psychology, 86,* 103–126.

Zucker, K. J. (2005a). Gender identity disorder in children and adolescents. *Annual Review of Clinical Psychology, 1,* 467–492.

Zucker, K. J. (2005b). Gender identity disorder in girls. In D. J. Bell, S. L. Foster, & E. J. Mash (Eds.), *Handbook of behavioral and emotional problems in girls: Issues in clinical child psychology* (pp. 285–319). Norwell, MA: Kluwer Academic/Plenum Publishers.

Zucker, K. J. (2015). The DSM-5 diagnostic criteria for gender disorder. In C. Trombetta, L. Giovanni, & M. Bertolotto (Eds.), *Management of gender dysphoria* (pp. 33–37). Milan, Italy: Springer-Verlag Italia.

Zuckerman, K. E., Sinche, B., Cobian, M., Cervantes, M., Mejia, A., Becker, T.,... Nicolaidis, C. (2014). Conceptualization of autism in the Latino community and its relationship with early diagnosis. *Journal of Developmental & Behavioral Pediatrics, 35,* 522–532. doi:10.1097/DBP.0000000000000091

Zuckerman, M. (2007). *Sensation seeking and risky behavior.* Washington, DC: American Psychological Association.

Zvolensky, M. J., & Eifert, G. H. (2001). A review of psychological factors/processes affecting anxious responding during voluntary hyperventilation and inhalations of carbon dioxide-enriched air. *Clinical Psychology Review, 21,* 375–400.

Zvolensky, M. J., Kotov, R., Antipova, A. V., & Schmidt, N. B. (2005). Diathesis stress model for panic-related distress: A test in a Russian epidemiological sample. *Behaviour Research and Therapy, 43,* 521–532.

Zweig-Frank, H., & Paris, J. (1991). Parents' emotional neglect and overprotection according to the recollections of patients with borderline personality disorder. *American Journal of Psychiatry, 148,* 648–651.

# Credits

## Photo Credits

**p. 1**: Piotr Krzeslak/Shutterstock; **p. 5**: Monkey Business/Fotolia; **p. 6**: Shutterstock; **p. 9**: Arne Hodalic/Corbis; **p. 11**: Album/Prisma/Newscom; **p. 12**: Bassa, Ferrer/Bridgeman Images; **p. 12**: Ken Welsh/Newscom; **p. 13**: Lebrecht Music and Arts Photo Library/Alamy Stock Photo; **p. 14**: Charles Muller/AS400 DB/Corbis; **p. 14**: Amelie Benoist/BSIP SA/Alamy Stock Photo; **p. 16**: Janine Wiedel Photolibrary/Alamy Stock Photo; **p. 19**: AS400 DB/Corbis; **p. 19**: Sueddeutsche Zeitung Photo/Alamy Stock Photo; **p. 19**: INTERFOTO/Alamy Stock Photo; **p. 20**: pololia/Fotolia; **p. 24**: PhotoAlto/Alix Minde/PhotoAlto Agency RF Collections.Getty images; **p. 26**: Image Source/Ocean/Corbis; **p. 31**: LadyInBlack/Fotolia; **p. 38**: Westend61/Getty Images; **p. 42**: STEVE GSCHMEISSNER/Science Photo Library/Getty Images; **p. 47**: Andrew Brookes/Cultura/Getty Images; **p. 48**: Copyright Clearance Center; **p. 51**: Dulcie Wagstaff/Getty Images; **p. 52**: Aubord Dulac/Fotolia; **p. 52**: Darren Brode/Fotolia; **p. 53**: Digital Vision/Photodisc/Getty Images; **p. 53**: Warner Brothers Pictures/Topham/The Image Works; **p. 54**: AS400 DB/Bettmann/Corbis; **p. 54**: Bettmann/Corbis; **p. 54**: PhotoEdit; **p. 57**: Snark/Art Resource; **p. 59**: Nina Leen/The LIFE Picture Collection/Getty Images; **p. 60**: Steven Puetzer/DigitalVision/Getty Images; **p. 61**: Alexander Yakovlev/Fotolia; **p. 61**: Michael Rougier/The LIFE Picture Collection/Getty Images; **p. 61**: Corbis; **p. 62**: bst2012/Fotolia; **p. 63**: The Albert Ellis Institute; **p. 64**: Clem Murray/MCT/Newscom; **p. 65**: Rose-Marie Murray/Alamy Stock Photo; **p. 66**: Kryssia Campos/Getty Images; **p. 73**: nullplus/Getty Images; **p. 74**: rolffimages/Fotolia; **p. 75**: Lisa F. Young/Fotolia; **p. 77**: iakovenko. 123rf.com; **p. 80**: Fotolia; **p. 80**: nullplus/Getty Images; **p. 83**: Drugabuse.gov; **p. 84**: The National Institute on Drug Abuse (NIDA); **p. 85**: Pamela Moore/Getty Images; **p. 89**: TMS Reprints; **p. 92**: Will McIntyre/Science Source; **p. 97**: 68/Ocean/Corbis; **p. 100**: Marcel Jancovic/Shutterstock; **p. 101**: H.S. Photos/Alamy Stock Photo; **p. 104**: Tom Wang/Fotolia; **p. 109**: THOMAS A WIDIGER; **p. 111**: World History Archive/Alamy Stock Photo; **p. 112**: Iurii Sokolov/Fotolia; **p. 113**: Getty Images; **p. 119**: Pearson Education; **p. 119**: Lewis J. Merrim/Getty Images; **p. 125**: National Center for PTSD; **p. 126**: Matthew Cole/Fotolia; **p. 127**: Phanie/Alamy Stock Photo; **p. 128**: MIRIAM MASLO/Science Photo Library/Alamy Stock Photo; **p. 129**: Science Source; **p. 129**: Living Art Enterprises/Science Source; **p. 130**: Marcus Scholz/Fotolia; **p. 130**: American Medical Association; **p. 130**: WDCN / Univ. College London / Science Source; **p.131**: Marina Pousheva. Shutterstock; **p. 134** : Science Photo Library / Superstock; **p. 139**: Biology Pics/Science Source; **p. 140**: Corbis/Superstock; **p. 141**: Universal Press Syndicate; **p. 143**: Katrina Brown/Fotolia; **p. 143**: Fotolia; **p. 145**: DragonImages/Fotolia; **p. 145**: David Grossman/Alamy Stock Photo; **p. 147**: Charles Negy; **p. 149**: Jupiterimages/Stockbyte/Getty Images; **p. 151**: Kadmy/Fotolia; **p. 152**: Photographee.eu/Fotolia; **p. 155**: Dave Schwarz/AP Images; **p. 156**: epa european press photo agency b.v./Alamy Stock Photo; **p. 158**: Tom Uhlman/Alamy Stock Photo; **p. 160**: Pearson Education; **p. 163**: Shotshop GmbH/Alamy Stock Photo; **p. 168**: Spass/Fotolia; **p. 170**: ZUMA Press, Inc./Alamy Stock Photo; **p. 172**: Andrea Danti/Shutterstock; **p. 173**: Keystone Pictures USA/Alamy Stock Photo; **p. 177**: Denkou Images/Cultura/Getty Images; **p. 177**: Bill Aron/PhotoEdit; **p. 178**: Jeff Chiu/AP Images; **p. 181**: Photographee.eu/Fotolia; **p. 183**: National Institute of Mental Health; **p. 185**: Peter_Waters/Fotolia; **p. 187**: Jim Whitmer Photography; **p. 189**: Ric Feld/AP Images; **p. 192**: Erin Patrice O'Brien/Photodisc/Getty Images; **p. 193**: Jonathan Nourok/Getty Images; **p. 197**: Joshua Abbas/123RF; **p. 197**: Peter Armstrong/Fotolia; **p. 198**: David Papazian/Shutterstock; **p. 199**: auremar/Fotolia; **p. 199**: Luc Mallet, Research Director; **p. 201**: Jamie Feusner, M.D., UCLA Semel Institute for Neuroscience and Human Behavior; **p. 202**: WR Publishing/Alamy Stock Photo; **p. 205**: Holger Scheibe/Corbis; **p. 209**: 20th Century-Fox Film Corp/Everett Collection; **p. 210**: milkovasa/Fotolia; **p. 213**: Newscom; **p. 214**: Nicole Bengiveno/The New York Times/Redux; **p. 215**: Charlotte Observer Publishing Company; **p. 217**: Sergey Panychev/Fotolia; **p. 219**: Duplass/Shutterstock; **p. 223**: Custom Medical Stock Photo/Alamy Stock Photo; **p. 227**: Image Source/Getty Images; **p. 230**: Stock Montage/Getty Images; **p. 231**: Everett Historical/Shutterstock; **p. 234**: wavebreakmedia/Shutterstock; **p. 236**: EastWest Imaging/Fotolia; **p. 238**: littleny/Fotolia; **p. 246**: Bits and Splits/Fotolia; **p. 248**: Sean Gallup/Hulton Archive/Getty Images; **p. 248**: Voyagerix/Fotolia; **p. 251**: Corbis; **p. 255**: Image Point Fr/Shutterstock; **p. 256**: JGI/Tom Grill/Blend Images/Getty Images; **p. 259**: keith morris/Alamy Stock Photo; **p. 262**: PacificCoastNews/Newscom; **p. 262**: Loomis Dean/The LIFE Picture Collection/Getty Images; **p. 265**: elwynn/Shutterstock; **p. 266**: Fotolia; **p. 268**: shock/Fotolia; **p. 270**: Fotolia; **p. 274**: Noel Hendrickson/DigitalVision/Getty Images; **p. 275**: SCIEPRO/Getty Images; **p. 277**: lunamarina/Fotolia; **p. 278**: Photographee.eu/Fotolia; **p. 284**: Will McIntyre/Science Source; **p. 285**: Will & Deni Mcintyre/Getty Images; **p. 290**: Superstock; **p. 292**: Ken Howard/Alamy Stock Photo; **p. 296**: DCPhoto/Alamy Stock Photo; **p. 301**: Monkey Business Images/Shutterstock; **p. 301**: Africa Studio/Fotolia; **p. 303**: Lightpoet/Shutterstock; **p. 306**: VadimGuzhva/Fotolia; **p. 309**: Wallenrock/Shutterstock; **p. 310**: The SAM Spady Foundation; **p. 310**: DreamPictures/DigitalVision/Getty Images; **p. 311**: Redlink/Cardinal/Corbis; **p. 314**: Getty Images; **p. 319**: Jeffrey Rotman/Alamy Stock Photo; **p. 320**: gabe9000c/Fotolia; **p. 321**: Susan F. Tapert; **p. 325**: Littleny/Fotolia; **p. 328**: Public Library of Science; **p. 328**: Public Library of Science; **p. 329**: bikeriderlondon/Shutterstock; **p. 331**: David Grossman/Alamy Stock Photo; **p. 331**: Fotolia; **p. 338**: nazarovsergey/Fotolia; **p. 344**: Ted Foxx/Alamy Stock Photo; **p. 348**: Shutterstock; **p. 351**: Chamillew/Fotolia; **p. 353**: PressNet/TopFoto/The Image Works; **p. 353**: blackday/Fotolia; **p. 356**: Eugenio Savio/AP Images; **p. 357**: David J. Green/Alamy Stock Photo; **p. 360**: Getty Images; **p. 364**: Russell Curtis/Science Source; **p. 368**: Ljupco Smokovski/Fotolia; **p. 369**: BSIP SA/Alamy Stock Photo; **p. 373**: Joshua Resnick/123rf; **p. 377**: BraunS/Getty Images; **p. 380**: Tibrina Hobson/Getty Images; **p. 382**: wundervisuals/Getty Images; **p. 382**: paolodelpapa/Moment Open/Getty Images; **p. 385**: Getty Images; **p. 392**: NBC/NBCUniversal/Getty Images; **p. 393**: Superstock; **p. 395**: The Advertising Archives/Alamy Stock Photo; **p. 397**: Randy Matusow; **p. 400**: Digital Vision/Photodisc/Getty Images; **p. 403**: Radius/Superstock; **p. 404**: Juice Images/Alamy Stock Photo; **p. 410**: Image Source/Getty Images; **p. 414**: Elena Kulikova/Moment/Getty Images; **p. 416**: Ron Chapple/The Image Bank/Getty Images; **p. 420**: Bob Strong/AFP/Getty Images; **p. 421**: Bettmann/Corbis; **p. 422**: powerofforever/E+/Getty Images; **p. 423**: Rawpixel Ltd/E+/Getty Images; **p. 426**: Christos Georghiou/Shutterstock; **p. 426**: sdominick/Getty Images; **p. 427**: Arman Zhenikeyev/Shutterstock; **p. 427**: Grunnitus Studio/Science Source; **p. 432**: THOMPSON PAUL M. REED NEUROLOGICAL RESEARCH; **p. 433**: Nancy C. Andreasen, M.D.; **p. 437**: Martin Dimitrov/Getty Images; **p. 439**: isuaneye/Fotolia; **p. 444**: David Lees/Corbis; **p. 445**: Image Source/Superstock; **p. 455**: Corbis Premium RF/Alamy Stock Photo; **p. 457**: Mark Foley/AP Images; **p. 459**: Bettmann/Corbis; **p. 459**: Timothy A. Clary/Staff/Getty Images; **p. 463**: Olga Sapegina/Shutterstock; **p. 464**: Ira Berger/Alamy Stock Photo; **p. 465**: 123RF; **p. 467**: Kzenon/Fotolia; **p. 469**: Pearson Education; **p. 470**: Marlene Ford/Moment/Getty Images; **p. 472**: blackday/Fotolia; **p. 475**: DragonImages/Fotolia; **p. 476**: Newscom; **p. 477**: Diego Cervo/Fotolia; **p. 480**: CLIPAREA.com/Fotolia; **p. 488**: Jerry Deffenbacher; **p. 492**: Rafael Ben-Ari/Alamy Stock Photo; **p. 495**: The Cartoon Bank; **p. 496**: Mike Siluk/The Image Works; **p. 496**: Tatiana kostareva/123RF; **p. 500**: Yevgeny Kurskov/ITAR-TASS Photo Agency/Alamy Stock Photo; **p. 503**: ktaylorg/E+/Getty Images; **p. 504**: Michael Bergmann; **p. 507**: Moodboard_Images/Getty Images; **p. 508**: Bela Szandelszky/AP Images; **p. 511**: American Institute of Physics; **p. 511**: National Institute of Mental Health; **p. 512**: Marcel Just; **p. 515**: Westend61/Corbis; **p. 516**: National Institute of Mental Health; **p. 518**: Blend Images/SuperStock; **p. 521**: Cardinal/Corbis; **p. 524**: kmiragaya/Fotolia; **p. 526**: BSIP SA/Alamy Stock Photo; **p. 531**: PALCO LABS INC; **p. 559**: SuperStock; **p. 562**: SuperStock; **p. 567**: Paul Baldesare/Alamy Stock Photo; **p. 568**: NARA; **p. 569**: Science Source; **p. 570**: Creatista/YAY Media AS/Alamy Stock Photo; **p. 570**: Spike Walker/The Image Bank/Getty Images; **p. 571**: Robert Kneschke/Fotolia; **p. 572**: Monkey Business Images/Shutterstock; **p. 573**: George Gojkovich/Getty Images; **p. 575**: National Institutes of Health; **p. 575**: Jeff Frank/ZUMA Press, Inc./Alamy Stock Photo; **p. 576**: Mark Sagliocco/Getty Images; **p. 578**: Chris Schmidt/Getty Images; **p. 579**: Catherine Bauknight/ZUMA/Corbis; **p. 581**: Wissmann Design/Fotolia; **p. 582**: Diego Cervo/Fotolia; **p. 587**: WilleeCole Photography/Shutterstock; **p. 589**: Newscom; **p. 589**: U.S. Marshals Service/ZUMAPRESS/Newscom; **p. 592**: Andrew Savulich/AP Images; **p. 593**: PG/Splash News/Newscom; **p. 596**: AP Images; **p. 597**: Republic Pictures/Archive Photos/Getty Images; **p. 599**: Charles Bennett/AP Images; **p. 600**: Bettmann/Corbis; **p. 606**: Red Huber/AP Images;

## Text Credits

**p. 3**: From the Author's Files, Phil, 42, a police photographer; **p. 3**: Fieve, R. R. (1975). Moodswings: The third revolution in psychiatry, pp. 27–28. New York: Morrow.; **p. 4**: Republished with permission of Oxford University Press, from First person account: Falling on the pavement. Schizophrenia Bulletin, 26, 507–509, Campbell, T. (2000). Permission conveyed through Copyright Clearance Center, Inc.; **p. 8**: Based on Kessler, Chiu, Demler, & Walters, 2005; Kessler, Bergland, Demler, et al., 2005; **p. 40**: From the Author's Files, Jessica, a 20-year-old communications major; **p. 44**: From Nevid. Psychology, 4E. © 2013 South-Western, a part of Cengage Learning, Inc. Reproduced by permission. www.cengage.com/permissions; **p. 68**: Based on data from Nevid, J. S. (2013). Psychology: Concepts and applications (4th ed.). Belmont, CA: Cengage Learning.; **p. 71**: From Nevid. Psychology, 4E. © 2013 South-Western, a part of Cengage Learning, Inc. Reproduced by permission. www.cengage.com/permissions; **p. 75**: From Doing Psychotherapy by Michael Franz Basch, copyright © 1980. Reprinted by permission of Basic Books, an imprint of Perseus Books, a division of PBG Publishing, LLC, a subsidiary of Hachette Book Group, Inc.; **p. 79**: Data from Norcross, J. C., & Karpiak, C. P. (2012). Clinical psychologists in the 2010s: 50 years of the APA Division of Clinical Psychology. Clinical Psychology: Science and Practice, 19, 1–12. doi: 10.1111/j.1468-2850.2012.01269; **p. 90**: From Nevid. Psychology, 4E. © 2013 South-Western, a part of Cengage Learning, Inc. Reproduced by permission. www.cengage.com/permissions; **p. 99**: Excerpted from "Panic Disorder: The Case of Jerry," found on the Videos in Abnormal Psychology CD-ROM that accompanies this textbook; **p. 102**: Based on American Psychiatric Association (2013); **p. 103**: Reprinted with permission from the Diagnostic and Statistical Manual of Mental Disorders, Fifth Edition, (Copyright ©2013). American Psychiatric Association. All Rights Reserved.; **p. 105**: Adapted from the DSM-5 (American Psychiatric Association, 2013); Dzokoto & Adams (2005); and other sources; **p. 114**: From Nevid. Psychology, 4E. © 2013 South-Western, a part of Cengage Learning, Inc. Reproduced by permission. www.cengage.com/permissions; **p. 115**: Wechsler Adult Intelligence Scale (WAIS). Copyright © 1955 NCS Pearson, Inc. Reproduced with permission. All rights reserved. "Wechsler Adult Intelligence Scale" and WAIS are trademarks, in the US and/or other countries, of Pearson Education, Inc. or its affiliates(s).; **p. 122**: From the Author's Files; **p. 127**: Adapted from Hollon, S.D., Kendall, P.C. (1980), Cognitive self-statements in depression: Development of an automatic thoughts questionnaire. Cognitive Therapy and Research, 4, 383–395.; **p. 136**: Hagen, S., & Carouba, M.(2002). Women at Ground Zero: Stories of Courage and compassion. Indianapolis, IN: Alpha.; **p. 137**: Source of data: Adapted from American Psychological Association (2010). Stress in America 2011: Executive summary. Retrieved from http://www.apa.org/news/press/releases/stress-exec-summary.pdf; **p. 142**: "Managing traumatic stress: Tips for recovering from disasters and other traumatic events," Copyright © American Psychological Association, http://www.apa.org/helpcenter/recovering-disasters.aspx; **p. 152**: Based on the DSM-5 (American Psychological Association, 2013).; **p. 153**: Based on American Psychological Association, 2013; Conway, Compton, Stinson, & Grant, 2006; Kessler, Sonnega, Bromet, et al., 1995; Ozer & Weiss, 2004.; **p. 154**: From the Author's Files; **p. 156**: Based on Afifi et al., 2010; Elwood et al., 2009; Goenjian et al., 2008; Koenen, Stellman, & Stellman, 2003; North et al., 2012; Ozer, Best, Lipsey, Weiss, 2003; Xie et al., 2009.; **p. 165**: "The Case of Michael," from the Author's Files; **p. 167**: Prevalence rates derived from APA, 2013; Conway et al., 2006; Grant et al., 2005a; Grant et al., 2006b, 2006c; Kessler et al., 2005a; Stein & Sareen, 2015.; **p. 169**: Data from Grant, B. F., Hasin, D. S., Stinson, F. S., Dawson, D. A., Goldstein, R. B., Smith, S., ... Saha, T. D. (2006b). The epidemiology of DSM-IV panic disorder and agoraphobia in the United States: Results from the National Epidemiologic Survey on Alcohol and Related Conditions. Journal of Clinical Psychiatry, 67, 363–374.; **p. 169**: From the Author's Files; **p. 171**: Adapted from Clark, 1986, and other sources; **p. 174**: From the Author's Files; **p. 175**: Adapted from Grant et al., 2006c and Öst, 1987, 1992.; **p. 176**: From the Author's Files; **p. 177**: From the Author's Files; **p. 179**: Data from Turner, S. M., & Beidel, D. C. (1989). Social phobia: Clinical syndrome, diagnosis, and comorbidity. Clinical Psychology Review, 9, 3–18.; **p. 180**: From the Author's Files; **p. 183**: National Institute of Mental Health (NIMH). (2008). Bipolar disorder in children and teens: A parent's guide. U.S. Department of Health and Human Services. NIH Publication 08-3679.

Bethesda, MD: Author; **p. 183**: Milad & Quirk, 2002. Figure reprinted from "Mimicking brain's 'all clear' quells fear in rats," NIH News Release, Posted November 6, 2002.; **p. 185**: Essentials of Psychology (6th ed.) by S. A. Rathus, p. 537. Copyright © 2001. Reprinted with permission of Brooks/Cole, an imprint of Wadsworth Group, a division of Thomson Learning.; **p. 187**: From the Author's Files.; **p. 191**: From the Author's Files; **p. 194**: Based on APA, 2013; Grant, 2014; Mataix-Cols et al., 2010; Snyder et al., 2015; and other sources.; **p. 195**: Osborn, I. (1998). Tormenting Thoughts and Secret Rituals: The hidden epidemic of obsessive-compulsive disorder. New York: Random House.; **p. 196**: From the Author's Files; **p. 199**: From Pacemaker for brain may ease mental illness. (2008, November 12). Retrieved from http://www.msnbc.msn.com/id/27684083/ Used with permission of The Associated Press. Copyright© 2016. All rights reserved.; **p. 200**: From the Author's Files; **p. 202**: Adapted from Rachman & DeSilva, 2009; **p. 207**: Based on I Have Multiple Personality Disorder by Quiet Storm. Originally appeared in For Women First, late 1993. Retrieved from: http://www.astraeasweb.net/plural/quietstorm.html; **p. 208**: Prevalence rates derived from APA, 2013.; **p. 210**: Adapted from Keyes, D. (1982). The minds of Billy Milligan; **p. 213**: Adapted from Cameron, 1963, pp. 355–356. Personality development and psychopathology: A dynamic approach.; **p. 215**: Based on Spitzer, R. L., et al. (1994). DSM-IV case book (4th ed.), pp. 254–255. Washington, DC: American Psychiatric Association.; **p. 217**: From the Author's Files; **p. 218**: Based on Robert L Spitzer, et al. (1994). DSM-IV case book (4th ed.)., pp. 270–271. Washington, DC: American Psychiatric Association.; **p. 221**: Olson, S.E. (1997). Becoming one: A story of triumph over multiple personality disorder. Pasadena, CA: Trilogy Books.; **p. 221**: Based on Wilbur, C. B. (1986). Psychoanalysis and multiple personality disorder. In B. G. Braun (Ed.), Treatment of multiple personality disorder. Washington, DC: American Psychiatric Association.; **p. 223**: Prevalence rates derived from APA, 2013.; **p. 224**: Based on Spitzer, R. L., et al. (1994). DSM-IV case book (4th ed.). pp. 88–90. Washington, DC: American Psychiatric Association.; **p. 228**: Gregory, J. (2003). Sickened: The memoir of a Münchausen by proxy childhood. New York: Bantam.; **p. 236**: Brefczynski-Lewis, J. A., Lutz, A., Schaefer, H. S., Levinson, D. B., & Davidson, R. J. (2007). Neural correlates of attentional expertise in long-term meditation practitioners. Proceedings of the National Academy of Sciences, 104, 11483–11488. Copyright (2007) National Academy of Sciences, U.S.A.; **p. 236**: Wolpe, J., & Lazarus, A. A. (1966). Behavior therapy techniques: A guide to the treatment of neuroses, pp. 177–178. New York: Pergamon Press. Copyright © 1966. Reprinted by permission from Alan Wolpe and Clifford Lazarus.; **p. 237**: Wolpe, J., & Lazarus, A. A. (1966). Behavior therapy techniques: A guide to the treatment of neuroses, pp. 177–178. New York: Pergamon Press. Copyright © 1966. Reprinted by permission from Alan Wolpe and Clifford Lazarus.; **p. 240**: Based on National Center for Health Statistics. (2012b). Health, United States, 2011: With Special Feature on Socioeconomic Status and Health. Hyattsville, MD.; **p. 248**: Styron, W. (2010). Darkness Visible.; **p. 249**: From Nevid. Psychology, 4E. © 2013 South-Western, a part of Cengage Learning, Inc. Reproduced by permission. www.cengage.com/permissions.; **p. 250**: National Institute of Mental Health (NIMH). (2008, October 22). Social phobia patients have heightened reactions to negative comments. Retrieved from http://www.nimh.nih.gov/science-news/2008/social-phobiapatients-have-heightened-reactions-to-negative-comments.shtml; **p. 251**: Copyright © Tracy Thompson (1995). Originally published by G P Putnam. Permission granted by The Beth Vesel Literary Agency; **p. 252**: Reprinted with permission from the Diagnostic and Statistical Manual of Mental Disorders, Fifth Edition, (Copyright ©2013). American Psychiatric Association. All Rights Reserved.; **p. 253**: Conway, K. P., Compton, W., Stinson, F. S., & Grant, B. F. (2006). Lifetime comorbidity of DSM-IV mood and anxiety disorders and specific drug use disorders: Results from the National Epidemiologic Survey on Alcohol and Related Conditions. Journal of Clinical Psychiatry, 67, 247–257.; **p. 253**: Pratt, L. A., & Brody, D. J. (2008, September). Figure 3 in Depression in the United States household population, 2005–2006. NCHS Data Brief, Number 7. Retrieved from http://www.cdc.gov/nchs/data/databriefs/db07.htm; **p. 253**: Based on Spitzer, R. L., Gibbon, M., Skodol, A. E., Williams, J. B. W., & First, M. B. (1989). DSM-III-R casebook. Washington, DC: American Psychiatric Press.; **p. 257**: Source of data: Conway et al., 2006.; **p. 258**: Based on Spitzer, R. L., et al. (1994). DSM-IV case book (4th ed.)., pp. 110–112. Washington, DC: American Psychiatric Association.; **p. 258**: Used by permission of Mental Health America (Formerly known as the National Mental Health Association).; **p. 261**: Jamison, K. R. (1995). An unquiet mind. New York: Knopf.; **p. 263**: Electroboy by Andy Behrman; **p. 264**: Based on Spitzer, R. L., et al. (1994). DSM-IV case book (4th ed.)., pp. 155–157. Washington, DC: American Psychiatric Association.; **p. 269**: Adapted from Beck & Young, 1985; Beck et al., 1979.; **p. 271**: From the Author's Files; **p. 272**: Adapted from Beck & Young, 1985; Beck et al., 1979; **p. 278**: Adapted from Klerman et al., 1984, pp. 111–113.; **p. 279**: Republished with permission of Guilford Press, from Cognitive therapy of depression, Beck, A. T., Rush, A. J., Shaw, B. F., & Emery, G., pp. 68, (1979). Permission conveyed through Copyright Clearance Center, Inc.; **p. 280**: Adapted from Beck et al., (Aug. 1987). Differentiating anxiety and depression: A test of the cognitive content-specificity hypothesis. Journal of Abnormal Psychology, 96, 179–183.; **p. 287**: Center for Mental Health Services, 2001, updated in CDC, 2015a, 2015c, 2015d.; **p. 288**: Centers for Disease Control and Prevention. (2015a). Health, United States, 2014. Retrieved from http://www.cdc.gov/nchs/hus.htm; **p. 291**: Duke, P., & Hochman, G. (1992). A brilliant madness. New York: Bantam Dell.; **p. 292**: From Nevid. Psychology, 4E. © 2013 South-Western, a part of Cengage Learning, Inc. Reproduced by permission. www.cengage.com/permissions.; **p. 298**: Reprinted with permission from Cocaine, First Edition (Copyright ©1987). American Psychiatric Association. All Rights Reserved.; **p. 304**: Adapted from Wallace, 2014 and other sources; **p. 307**: Based on data from Grant, B. R., Goldstein, R. B., Saha, T. D., Chou, S. P., Jung, J., Zhang, H.,.. Hasin, D. S. (2015). Epidemiology of DSM-5 alcohol use disorder. JAMA Psychiatry, 72, 757–766.; **p. 317**: Centers for Disease Control. (2008). Smoking-attributable mortality, years of potential life lost, and productivity losses—United States, 2000–2004. Morbidity and Mortality Weekly Report, 57(45), 1226–1228.; **p. 317**: Centers for Disease Control. (2009). Obesity and overweight. FastStats. Retrieved from http://www.cdc.gov/nchs/fastats/overwt.htm; **p. 323**: Adapted from National Institute on Drug Abuse, U.S. Department of Health and Human Services, National Institutes of Health. Research Report Series: Cocaine Abuse and Addiction. NIH Publication Number 99-4342, revised November 2004. Reprinted from J. S. Nevid, Psychology: Concepts and Applications, 2009.; **p. 325**: From the Author's Files; **p. 325**: Reprinted with permission from Cocaine, First Edition (Copyright ©1987). American Psychiatric Association. All Rights Reserved.; **p. 336**: Adapted from a testimonial posted on an online support site, NYC Voices.; **p. 339**: Pearson Education, Speaking Out: Videos in Abnormal Psychology, Volume 2, 2nd Ed., © 2008. Reprinted and Electronically reproduced by permission of Pearson Education, Inc. Upper Saddle River, New Jersey.; **p. 339**: Pearson Education, Speaking Out: Videos in Abnormal Psychology, Volume 2, 2nd Ed., © 2008. Reprinted and Electronically reproduced by permission of Pearson Education, Inc. Upper Saddle River, New Jersey.; **p. 346**: Costin, C. (1997). Your dieting daughter: Is she dying for attention? New York: Brunner/Mazel.; **p. 347**: Prevalence rates derived from Hudson et al., 2006, 2007; Smink, van Hoeken, & Hoek, 2012.; **p. 347**: From the Author's Files; **p. 350**: Adapted from Boskind-White, M., & White, W. C. (1983). Bulimarexia: The binge–purge cycle. New York: W. W. Norton, p. 29.; **p. 354**: Normandi, E. E., & Roark, L. (1998). It's not about food: Change your mind; change your life; end your obsession with food and weight. New York: Berkley.; **p. 355**: Pearson Education, Speaking Out: Videos in Abnormal Psychology, Volume 2, 2nd Ed., © 2008. Reprinted and Electronically reproduced by permission of Pearson Education, Inc. Upper Saddle River, New Jersey.; **p. 360**: Physical Activity and Weight Control, National Institutes of Diabetes and Digestive and Kidney Diseases (NIDDK), http: //win.niddk.nih.gov/publications/physical.htm; **p. 362**: Health, United States, 2003, Centers for Disease Control and Prevention, National Center for Health Statistics, National Health and Nutrition Examination Survey; **p. 364**: Based on Prevalence rates drawn from APA, 2013; Bootzin & Epstein, 2011; Ohayon, 1999, Ohayon, Dauvilliers, & Reynolds, 2012; Scammell, 2015; Smith & Perlis, 2006.; **p. 367**: Pearson Education, Speaking Out: Videos in Abnormal Psychology, Volume 2, 2nd Ed., © 2008. Reprinted and Electronically reproduced by permission of Pearson Education, Inc. Upper Saddle River, New Jersey.; **p. 367**: Pearson Education, Speaking Out: Videos in Abnormal Psychology, Volume 2, 2nd Ed., © 2008. Reprinted and Electronically reproduced by permission of Pearson Education, Inc. Upper Saddle River, New Jersey.; **p. 370**: Hayes, B. (2001). Sleep demons: An insomniac's memoir. New York: Washington Square Press.; **p. 378**: From the Author's Files; **p. 378**: From the Author's Files; **p. 384**: Prevalence rates derived from Lewis et al., 2010, and based on most recent review of studies worldwide, and updated based on the DSM-5 (APA, 2013); **p. 389**: From the Author's Files; **p. 390**: Based on Spitzer, R. L., et al. (1994). DSM-IV case book (4th ed.). pp. 270–271. Washington, DC: American Psychiatric Association.; **p. 394**: From the Author's Files; **p. 398**: From the Author's Files; **p. 399**: From the Author's Files; **p. 400**: Based on Spitzer, R. L., et al. (1994). DSM-IV case book (4th ed.), pp. 164–165. Washington, DC: American Psychiatric Association.; **p. 409**: From the Author's Files; **p. 409**: From the Author's Files; **p. 416**: From The Quiet Room: A Journey Out of the Torment of Madness by Lori Schiller and Amanda Bennett. Copyright © 1994 by Lori Schiller and Amanda Bennett. Used by permission of Grand Central Publishing.; **p. 417**: From Chovil, I. (2000). First person account: I and I, dancing fool, challenge you the world to a duel. Schizophrenia Bulletin, 26, 745–747. National Institute of Mental Health.; **p. 418**: From Chovil, I. (2000). First person account: I and I, dancing fool, challenge you the world to a duel. Schizophrenia Bulletin, 26, 745–747. National Institute of Mental Health.; **p. 419**: From the Author's Files; **p. 420**: Reprinted with permission from the Diagnostic and Statistical Manual of Mental Disorders, Fifth Edition (Copyright ©2013). American Psychiatric Association. All Rights Reserved.; **p. 421**: From the Author's Files; **p. 424**: From the Author's Files; **p. 427**: Based on Arieti, S. (1974). Interpretation of schizophrenia. New York: Basic Books, p. 40.; **p. 430**: Based on Gottesman, I. I., McGuffin, P., & Farmer, A. E. (1987). Clinical genetics as clues to the real genetics of schizophrenia. Schizophrenia Bulletin,13, 2347.; **p. 435**: Based on Gottesman, I. I., & Gould, T. D. (2003). The endophenotype concept in psychiatry: Etymology and strategic intentions. American Journal of Psychiatry, 160, 636–645.; **p. 437**: Based on King & Dixon, 1999.; **p. 440**: From The Quiet Room: A Journey Out of the Torment of Madness by Lori Schiller and Amanda Bennett. Copyright © 1994 by Lori Schiller and Amanda Bennett. Used by permission of Grand Central Publishing.; **p. 446**: Based on Spitzer, R. L., et al. (1994). DSM-IV case book (4th ed.), pp. 177–179. Washington, DC: American Psychiatric Association.; **p. 447**: Based on Goldstein, 1986, p. 802; **p. 452**: Adapted from an anonymous posting on an online support site, New York City Voices; **p. 454**: Prevalence rates derived from APA, 2013; Cale & Lilienfeld, 2002; Kessler et al., 1994.; **p. 455**: Based on Spitzer, R. L., et al. (1994). DSM-IV case book (4th ed.), pp. 211–213. Washington, DC: American Psychiatric Association.; **p. 456**: From the Author's Files; **p. 457**: From the Author's Files; **p. 458**: Based on Kessler, R. C., Sonnega, A., Bromet, E., Hughes, M., & Nelson, C. B. (1995). Posttraumatic stress disorder in the National Comorbidity Survey. Archives of General Psychiatry, 52, 1048–1060.; **p. 460**: Based on Spitzer, R. L., et al. (1994). DSM-IV case book (4th ed.), pp. 81–83. Washington, DC: American Psychiatric Association.; **p. 464**: From the Author's Files; **p. 465**: Republished with permission of John Wiley & Sons, from Psychology and the Challenges of Life, Binder Ready Version: Adjustment and Growth. Nevid & Rathus, 2016. Permission conveyed though Copyright Clearance Center, Inc.; **p. 466**: Hotchkiss, S. (2002). Why is it always about you? The seven deadly sins of narcissism. Free Press. (Simon and Schuster); **p. 467**: From the Author's Files; **p. 468**: Based on Spitzer, R. L., et al. (1994). DSM-IV case book (4th ed.). pp. 179–180. Washington, DC: American Psychiatric Association.; **p. 469**: From the Author's Files; **p. 485**: Adapted from Glover, 1985; **p. 488**: Lejoyeux, M. & Germain, C. (2012). Pyromania: Phenomenology and epidemiology. In J. E. Grant & M. N. Potenza, The Oxford handbook of impulse control disorders (pp. 135–148). New York: Oxford University Press, p. 139; **p. 494**: Williams, D. (1992). Nobody nowhere: The extraordinary autobiography of an autistic. Reprinted by permission.; **p. 498**: Prevalence rates derived from APA, 2013; CDC, 2009, 2012; Frick & Silverthorn, 2001; Galanter, 2013; Kaper, Alderson, & Hude, 2012; Loeber et al., 2009; Masi, Mucci, & Millipiedi, 2001; Nock et al., 2006; Rhode et al., 2013; Shear et al., 2006; Wingert, 2000; Yeargin-Allsopp et al., 2003; **p. 499**: Adapted from Eberhardy, F. (1 967). The view from "the couch." Journal of Child Psychological Psychiatry,8, 257–263.; **p. 502**: From Judy Barron, Sean Barron (2002), There's a Boy in Here, published by Future Horizons, Inc.; **p. 509**: Based on Spitzer, R. L., et al. (1994). DSM-IV case book (4th ed.), pp. 338–340. Washington, DC: American Psychiatric Association.; **p. 517**: Based on Spitzer, R. L., et al. (1994). DSM-IV case book (4th ed.), pp. 315–317. Washington, DC: American Psychiatric Association.; **p. 520**: Based on Kaplan, S. J. (1986). The private practice of behavior therapy: A guide for behavioral practitioners. New York: Plenum Press.; **p. 522**: From the Author's Files; **p. 528**: From the Author's Files; **p. 537**: Excerpted from "Mary's Story," posted on the Alzheimer's Association website,www.alz.org; **p. 539**: Prevalence rates derived from APA, 2000, 2013; Hebert et al., 2003.; **p. 540**: Based on Freemon (1981) Organic mental disease. Jamaica, NY: Spectrum, p. 82.; **p. 543**: Based on Herbert, L. E., Scherr, P. A., Bienias, J. L., Bennett, D. A., & Evans, D. A., 2003. Alzheimer's disease in the U.S. population: Prevalence estimates using the 2000 census. Archives of Neurology, 60, 1119–1122.; **p. 544**: D. F. McGowin, 1993. Living in the labyrinth: A personal journey through the maze of Alzheimer's; **p. 550**: Freemon, F. R. (1981). Organic mental disease. Jamaica, NY: Spectrum.; **p. 552**: Adapted from Knight, R. G., Godfrey, H. P. D., & Shelton, E. J. (1988). The psychological deficits associated with Parkinson's disease. Clinical Psychology Review, 8, 391–410.; **p. 556**: Reprinted with permission of John Wiley & Sons from Psychology and the challenges of life: Adjustment and modern life (12th ed.), by Nevid & Rathus (2013), p. 484. Permission conveyed through Copyright Clearance Center.; **p. 565**: West Side Spirit and NYPress.com; **p. 575**: Linder, 2004, "The John Hinckley Trial." John Hinckley's letter to actress Jodie Foster, written on March 31, 1981, shortly before he attempted to assassinate President Ronald Reagan; **p. 576**: U.S. Supreme Court, *Durham* v. *United States of 1954*;

# Author Index

# Subject Index